The National cyclopedia of the colored race;

Clement Richardson

The
National Cyclopedia
of
The Colored Race

Editor-in-Chief
CLEMENT RICHARDSON
President of Lincoln Institute
Jefferson City, Mo.

ASSOCIATE EDITORS

Dr. C. V. ROMAN, Nashville, Tenn.
    Professor of Meharry Medical College.

W. T. B. WILLIAMS, Hampton Institute, Va.
    Field Agent of the Jeannes and Slater Funds.

H. M. MINTON, M. D., Philadelphia, Pa.
    Board of Directors Mercy Hospital.

SILAS X. FLOYD, Augusta, Ga.
    Principal of City Schools.

DR. R. E. JONES, New Orleans, La.
    Editor of South Western Christian Advocate.

DR. A. F. OWENS, Selma, Ala.
    Dean of Theological Dept. Selma University.

FRED MOORE, New York City.
    Editor New York Age.

ADVISORY BOARD

EMMETT J. SCOTT, Chairman,
    Secretary of Tuskegee Institute, Tuskegee
    Institute, Ala.

N. B. YOUNG, Tallahassee, Fla.
    President of A. and M. College.

DR. J. W. E. BOWEN, Atlanta, Ga.
    Dean of Gammon Theological Seminary.

J. R. E. LEE, Kansas City, Mo.
    Principal of Lincoln High School.

J. S. CLARK, Baton Route, La.
    President of Southern University.

DR. M. W. DOGAN, Marshall, Texas.
    President of Wiley University.

Volume One

NATIONAL PUBLISHING COMPANY, Inc.
PUBLISHERS
MONTGOMERY, ALABAMA
1 9 1 9

BOOKER TALIAFERRO WASHINGTON, M. A. LL. D.

Foreword

FOR the past 20 years Negroes have been coming to the front so rapidly that to list all whose names should appear in a work of this kind would, I know, be impossible. As it is true of names and biographies, so is it true of the general data concerning the Negro race. Almost daily something happens or some new development in the race records itself as monumental and historical. All of this, I know the Editors cannot record; yet I am thoroughly convinced, from what I have seen of the Cyclopedia of the Colored Race, that this book will be of inestimable good to both the white people and the black people of America.

It will be of service to the white people because it is the one work which gives a comprehensive knowledge of the Negro race, past and present.

It will be of great service to the Negro for two reasons. In the first place it will be an advocate pleading his cause by setting forth his achievements under the most trying circumstances. It will show to the world that the American Negro is worthy not only of what he has achieved, but of an open door to much greater achievements and much kindlier treatment.

In the second place it will teach the Negro more about himself. No Race, white or black, can get very far as a race or as individuals without a goodly amount of self-respect and race pride. Every biography, the story of every kind of property ownership, of a bank or store, owned and operated properly, will be a source of great inspiration to Negroes old and young. Were there no other reason, this one of valuable racial inspiration would more than justify the hard labor and careful thought that the publishers and editors have put into this work.

Finally the public can rely upon the honesty and integrity of the men whose names appear as editors of the Cyclopedia. Here and there these men may err in fact, but in principle I do not believe there is a man on the list who can be doubted. I know all of them personally, a good many of them intimately. The editor in chief, Mr. Clement Richardson, his chief advisor Mr. E. J. Scott, Mr. J. R. E. Lee, Mr. N. B. Young, are all men who have rendered years of most valuable services on the staff at Tuskegee Institute.

I commend this book highly to all Americans, with the hope that a perusal of it will bring a better understanding and a warmer spirit of friendship and inspiration, to both races.

[signature]

Principal Tuskegee Institute

PREFACE

Cyclopedia of the Negro race should, it seems to me, have two purposes—to inform and to inspire. The ordinary work of the kind has merely the task to inform. The inspiration story, the tale of struggle and achievement, is attended to by the daily paper, the magazine, the technical journal and the photographer. But the only sure hope that the black American can entertain for immediate notice comes through committing crime. The black man who assails a hen roost, one who perpetrates a blind tiger or commits even more revolting crimes is pretty certain of a big headline and several pages in the daily news, while he who pays his taxes, supports his family and lays away a few shekels or invests in land, houses or brain power, passes on unheralded.

Let the task of this work be to inform of the good deeds. Rapidly the Negro himself is casting out the discriminating hook, with the label, "Who is he?" written in pretty bold letters. Good deeds, a life of service, have come to be a passport required among groups of colored Americans as well as among groups of other people.

We have still also our weakness toward education. We like the diploma on the wall, the cap and gown, the enriching memories of college days. He, therefore, who would make his place in various groups must carry the stamp of merit in cultivation of intellect, in the acquisition of wealth, in deeds of good for the betterment of his people.

Therein does the Cyclopedia hope to fill what assuredly appears to be a crying need. Negroes over the country do not know one another, neither do the white Americans know what their darker countrymen are doing to make a stronger and nobler race and to make of all wholesome citizens.

As a rule, however, we cannot accomplish the end of this undertaking by cataloging a few dry, abstract facts. Thus to set down "John Smith, born 1884, proprietor of a drug store, candidate for Grand Secretary of K. P." and so on, would not, though thoroughly informing, give all that we want the Negro school boy and the Negro school girl to find

when they go to search for our names in the Cyclopedia. We want them to look there, both young and old, to find a brief succinct story,—one that while it informs, gives some measure of the man, some measure of the character he developed while becoming the proprietor of a drug store, or candidate for Grand Secretary. Here is the editor of a Negro paper. How did he get his education in general? How did he get his particular training for the craft? How many nights, as Horace Greely put it, did he "sleep on paper and eat ink"—or support his family on unpaid subscriptions? In other words, we want the Negro boy to feel inspired, to come away with a thrill; we want the older Negro to feel that he is among a great galaxy of black folk, great because of character, of education, of goodness.

Thanks to the breaking of a new day, we now have a great many friends who are genuinely interested in our progress. They want to see what the black folks have done; to see the fruit of their labor on the one hand and to uphold the black man's cause to those who still doubt, or who alas! simply do not know.

As we feel about the person so we feel about the organization, the institution. Here is a big Negro church whose night classes, rest rooms and the like owe their existence to the poor mothers who sweat over the wash tub: A Negro school whose first master likely as not taught in the rain, or waded through water and mud to reach his classes. Here again is a Negro bank, whose first president begged deposits from door to door: A big Negro farmer and land owner, who once grubbed his soil or chopped wood by the light of a pine torch: a Negro publisher who once was classed a little above a tramp: A Negro insurance man, who was once a cook: A big Negro physician who came from the farm or from the ranks of the hotel waiters. It is this we would chronicle, not of course that it may be known merely, but that there may be more and better banks, holier churches, finer schools, bigger farmers, a larger number forging forward from the ranks typifying the best in the race.

To have undertaken a task of this kind was, in the eyes of many, to pursue a course of rashness, if not madness The territory, it was thought, was far too wide. The task of selecting and rejecting was too nice and too hazardous To do even a reasonable amount of justice to all deserving persons was impossible And so why risk so much?

Now, the remarkable feature of all this is that those who made these objections were correct Indeed, each point in itself is sufficient to retard one from undertaking the task Yet, there was and is, at least an equal weight on the side that here is an opportunity to render good service, service of help on the one hand and of enlightenment on the other To sit by and let slip so fair an occasion merely because of fear per se, or because of fear of failure seemed as criminal as to try and even fail

The men whose lives are here sketched, the Institutions and Organizations here represented, by no means exhaust the list In fact, some of the most thrilling tales of struggle and conquest of both men and Organizations are, for one reason or another, not here at all It is doubtful, in many instances, if they can be secured Indifference to fame, a shrinking from publicity, intense engagement in one kind of work or another, all conspire to with-hold the desired information from the public

The Editor has drawn freely from the writings of others. Just what particular work he is most indebted to, he is at a loss to say He has consulted most printed matter on Negroes He is therefore grateful to Negro Magazine Editors, Negro News Paper Editors, and to all Authors of books bearing on Negro people If there has been any purloining, such has not been done through any wish to arrogate knowledge or talent, but with the full desire, bordering, it is hoped, upon enthusiasm, to send abroad the good news and glad tidings that the people for whom so many good tempers have

been spoiled, and for whom so much blood has been shed, are not being redeemed in vain.

One of the happiest phases of the endeavor, both to the publishers and to the Editor, has been the quick and hearty response accorded by the leading Negroes and those White people interested in Negroes throughout the country This was particularly true of professional and thinking men of the race, of the Ministers, of the Doctors, of the Editors, and of up-lift workers So numerous are these that to name them is impossible Again, the leading schools for Negroes, whether in the hands of Colored people or White have given an encouragement, without which the work could hardly have progressed Tuskegee, Fisk, Spelman, and scores of other such Institutions gave their backing in every sense unreservedly

Two men must be spoken of, else this Cyclopedia had not been—Dr R. R. Moton and Hon Emett J Scott The former was coming into the principalship of Tuskegee Institute at the inception of this work Without question, without hesitation, he not only gave his endorsement, but took the occasion whenever approached to commend the undertaking, an act wholly in keeping with the known generous traits of Dr Moton Upon the latter should have devolved the editing of this work While he occupies the place of Chairman of the Advisory Board, Mr Scott is, as a matter of fact, in many ways the Cyclopedia's sponsor His exceeding wide contact, his host of warm personal friends everywhere, made for the Editor and the Publishers a rose covered path, which might otherwise have been one strewn with gravel, if not with thorns.

CLEMENT RICHARDSON

Lincoln Institute,
Jefferson City, Mo, Nov 15th 1918

Booker Taliaferro Washington, M. A. LL. D.

BOOKER T. WASHINGTON, a model of efficiency, was born a slave—but he lived to absorb so much of the white man's civilization that he taught not only Negroes by a new method, but had his method adopted by white men as well. Dr. Washington attended Hampton Institute, earning his way as he went. Indeed all that Dr. Washington had as a start for his most remarkable career, was a determination to better himself and his people. He lived to found and serve till it was fully established with no possible chance of failure, the largest institution for Negroes in the world—Tuskegee Institute. This school has become a model for schools in all parts of the world. Dr. Washington also founded the National Negro Business League, The International Race Congress, and was instrumental in the founding of the Southern Education Board.

He was honored by Harvard University with the degree of Master of Arts and was given the degree of LL. D. by Dartmouth. In addition to these he was given honary degrees by a number of the leading Eastern and Southern Colleges. This was done as a recognition of his work. Dr. Washington never ceased to study, he studied at home, on the trains, on the long trips through the country. He was as close a student of books as he was of men. His judgments of men and things are brought out clearly in the many books and periodicals of which he is the author.

Booker T. Washington who died at his home early Sunday morning, Nov. 14, 1915, was a big man out in the world; he was a bigger man at home among his teachers. The world knew him for his eloquence, his homely wit, his tact, his shrewd diplomacy. We knew him at home for his broad sympathies, for his kindness, his attention to little things, his infinite power of planning and working. His two last acts, one abroad and one at home, are strikingly significant of his balanced life. His last act before the world was to make a journey to deliver an address. His last act at home was to repair an old board fence which he had unwittingly ordered torn down.

At home or abroad he was never too big for even the humblest man to approach. Indeed he had a sort of craze for bringing together the rude illiterate and the more cultivated members of his race. He liked to assemble the rude black farmer, the school teacher, the lawyer and the business man. He had a fondness for stopping the half illiterate preacher, for getting such in his office and looking into their minds. An oldtime mammy, or an old, old Negro farmer in his audiences seemed to inspire him more than the richest and most distinguished. He always rushed, as it were, into the arms of such at the closing of his big meetings. Probably no single organization with which he ever had connection gave him quite the genuine satisfaction he got from the Annual Farmers' Conference. He delighted to banter these old fellows, to listen to their rude speeches and homely sayings. Many of his own stories and anecdotes sprang out of these meetings.

But he was no mere stag acquaintance. He welcomed all such to his fireside, to his office, his precious time, his helping hand, the mother protesting that her child did not make a class high enough, the student smarting under some misunderstanding with a teacher, the white banker or white farmer wishing to transact business—all had free access to him. To be sure he kept a closed office, but this was to gain dispatch, not to exclude. It was no uncommon sight to find a vagrant Negro preacher, a distinguished visitor, a Negro farmer, a teacher or two, and a few students all waiting to see him.

Reports say that the doctors wondered how he lived so long. The more is the marvel when one thinks of the burdens he bore. Having to raise thousands of dollars to provide food, heat, comfortable lodgings for 1500 students, he nevertheless kept his finger on the smallest details. Now he was dictating a letter asking for funds, the next moment he would be summoning a workman or dictating a note about the weeds in a plot of ground, about a hedge, or a broken window pane. One moment he would be dictating a speech for some national occasion, the next he would be advising a means of disposing of "old Mollie," one of the cows of the dairy herd, or "old Phil," a lame mule. So it was with the eggs and chickens from the poultry yard, the sweet potatoes, the peaches, the corn, oats, pigs, the power plant, the lighting system, the way a new teacher was conducting a class in arithmetic or grammar. And this thing he kept up from day to day, whether he was in New York or Alabama. I myself have again and again, during the seven years in which I have had charge of the English work at Tuskegee Institute gotten notes making suggestions about a paragraph or a sentence in some student's talk or commencement address.

There was only one way under the sun he could do this. He regulated his life to the very second. He husbanded time most miserly, though he was prodigal with his energies. He had breakfasted and was out on horseback by 7:30 (he fancied the big iron gray pacer). His hour's ride was in a sense recreative, in another sense, it was work for he inspected the farm, the orchard, the shops, the school's supplies, taking notes and giving direction If he rode out into the country he usually returned with suggestions about a torn-off blind on a Negro church or the neglected garden of a Negro schoolhouse All the time he was stopping teachers and workmen by the way, giving them new tasks, requesting them to come to his office at a certain hour

By half past eight he was in his office For a certain time he read and dictated letters In the meantime the office boys were flying over the grounds and ringing the telephone bells summoning Council members, the heads of departments, to a committee meeting, a meeting on the budget, on Commencement, on a new building, on the actions of a student or a teacher Up to the last second he would keep his mind fixed on his reading or correspondence He then took up the business in hand, dispensed with it and went back to an article on teaching or on Negro homes or Negro business If he was slated to make a trip in a buggy or car he kept his work until the clock was on the second Then he stepped into the conveyance and was gone Woe unto him who brought a slow vehicle Even so he would be at work Between one stop and another on a speaking tour he would sketch a half dozen plans—for articles for grading a lawn, for remodeling a building, for rendering somebody a service Always and everywhere his plans inculcated this—to serve somebody to make somebody happier It might be by giving a body something, it was most often by giving one something to do

This having things to hand, which to some minds, might appear at times extravagant was the very essence of his efficiency, as it is of any man's efficiency The change of clothing was usually ready to hand He had push bells and telephones in his office, and push bells and telephones in his study at home Wherever and whenever he went about the grounds an office boy, sometimes a stenographer, followed at his elbow to summon a workman or to take down a note on some weak point in workmanship His pet diversion was hunting In the fall he would frequently steal an hour and run out to the woods To save time he kept a hunting outfit, gun cartridges, etc at his home and one at the work place of the young man who usually accompanied him, so that whenever the hunting time came he would not loose an hour in getting ready To some this would be extravagance To one whose time is precious it is the highest economy

With this practice of having things to hand he coupled the habit of doing the thing then His key word was "AT ONCE" Alas! how often Tuskegee teachers have seen that notice "Mr — will see the Principal "at once" The engagement

might not last one third the time it required you to walk to the office, but he attended to the thing there The errand boy gets the workman there The stenographer took down the note on the spot He went hunting then, he made his address then, he signed his letters then Each minute in the day seemed to have been for him an individual particle to be dealt with and settled by the time the next one ticked around For the last year or so he pushed this habit to the extreme, calling for teachers, workmen, council members, who were the advisory board, at midnight, at daybreak, at the meal hour Several times Mrs Washington protested, seeking to restrain him With the genius of premonition he would exclaim, "Let me alone Let me do it now I don't know where I'll be to-morrow"

Some local joker tells this story which, though likely enough untrue, illustrates this habit of attending to one thing at the moment One afternoon in the fall while stealing his hour's hunt he chanced to cross a part of the school's farm in order to reach the woods The name of the Director of the farming industries is Bridgeforth, that of the young man who went hunting with Dr Washington Foster Just as the Tuskegean and Foster entered the woods, a squirrel leaped from the ground and went scrambling up a tree Quick as a spark Dr Washington leveled his gun At the same moment some thought about improving the farm evidently flashed across his mind Relaxing his gun the slightest bit, he turned to the young man and said

"Foster get me Mr Bridgeforth at once"

Probably few Americans, white or black, have had a higher sense of duty than Booker T Washington It mattered little who imposed the task or whether it was great or small, the thing was promised and must be done Many of us here at Tuskegee feel that nothing but this sense of duty backed by a tremendous will, has kept him alive for the last few years A year or so ago we were holding our Annual Armstrong Memorial exercises Dr Washington had said that he would speak at this exercise, as he always did when he was at home Early in the afternoon of the appointed day he fell ill with a throbbing headache and his stomach in a turmoil The doctor put him to bed and ordered him to remain there At eight o'clock that night he appeared and made his address though he collapsed in the ante-room immediately afterwards

Finally, just as he willed to do, to hold on, he could will to let go

He was great in big things and in little things great in the world and at home, but he was greatest in the assertion of his tremendous will

FREDERICK DOUGLASS

REDERICK DOUGLASS, Orator
and Statesman, born a slave, rose
to be one of the great men of his
day, whose name will live in
American history. He was born
in Maryland, February 14, 1817.
His name at first was Frederick Augustus Washington Baily; he changed it, being hunted as a fugitive slave, to Douglass. He chose Douglass because of his facination for this character as portrayed by Sir Walter Scott, a character which the ex-slave in his grand manner much resembled.

In his childhood he saw little of his mother, nothing of his father. The mother worked on a plantation twelve miles from her son and could only see him by making the journey on foot and after work time. Whatever training the boy received up to the age of eight, he received it from his grandmother.

At the age of eight years he was put under Aunt Katy, who was cruel, often depriving the little fellow of food. On one occasion he went to bed so hungry that when all the household were asleep he rose and began to parch and eat corn. In the midst of the corn parching, his mother came in,

bringing a ginger cake, which made him feel that he was "somebody's child." This was the last time he saw his mother.

Douglass was sent to Baltimore, where after a time he learned to read, being taught by his new mistress, Mrs. Auld. When the master discovered what the mistress had done, he set a watch over Douglass lest he should escape. This he finally did, though he was long sought after and had one time to go to England to avoid capture. He was finally bought and set free.

He gave his life as a freedman to liberating his brethren and to improving the ex-slave condition after freedom came. He served during his life time as United States Marshall in the District of Columbia, as Recorder of Deeds in the District of Columbia, and as Consul General to the Republic of Hayti. He was the first Negro to hold these offices. He was much traveled and was admired as an orator and as a man wherever he went.

A few of the sayings of Douglass follow:

"Emancipation has liberated the land as well as the people."

"Neither the slave nor his master can abandon all at once the deeply entrenched errors and habits of centuries."

"There is no work that men are required to do, which they cannot better and more economically do with education than without it."

"Muscle is mighty but mind is mightier, and there is no field for the exercise of mind other than is found in the cultivation of the soul."

"As a race we have suffered from two very opposite causes, disparagement on the one hand and undue praise on the other."

"An important question to be answered by evidence of our progress is: Whether the black man will prove a better master to himself than the white man was to him."

"Accumulate property. This may sound to you like a new gospel. No people can ever make any social and mental improvement whose exertions are limited. Poverty is our greatest calamity—On the other hand, property, money, if you please, will produce for us the only condition upon which any people can rise to the dignity of genuine manhood."

"Without property there can be no leisure. Without leisure there can be no invention, without invention there can be no progress."

"We can work and by this means we can retrieve all our losses."

"Knowledge, wisdom, culture, refinement, manners, are all founded on work and the wealth which work brings."

"In nine cases out of ten a man's condition is worse by changing his location. You would better endeavor to remove the evil from your door than to move and leave it there."

9

Alexander Dumas, Novelist and Play-wright

HACKERY, the English Novelist, called Dumas "Alexander the Great." Like Alexander Pushkin of Russia, the great French romancer is the third descent from a Negro, only in this instance the line begins with the grandmother rather than the grandfather. Dumas' grandfather, who was a marquis, married a Creole of Haiti. The author's father was a dark giant of a man; one of the heroic generals of the army of Napoleon.

The general married the daughter of an innkeeper. From this union the novelist was born in 1802. The father died while the son was four years old. Having but small means, Alexander soon found himself in Paris seeking his fortune. For a time he attached himself to the Duke of Orleans as clerk. Like Voltaire, Hugo and many other French men of letters, Dumas sought to make his way as a play-wright. In this he succeeded modestly, having presented successfully, Henry III, Tower of Nelse and several other plays. But Dumas' claim to fame, a claim which he holds undisputably, rests upon his romances, "The three Musketeers," "The Count of Monte Cristo," "Twenty Years After," and scores of others. The critics call him, "Capriceius prolix, fertile puissant," as having a "rare mind, rare attention, subtle spirit, quick comprehension."

The following is taken from his writings:

FATALITY.

Scarcely had D'Artagnan uttered these words than a ringing and sudden noise was heard resounding through the felucca, which now became dim in the obscurity of the night.

"That, you may be sure," said the Gascon, "means something."

They then, at the same instant, perceived a large lantern carried on a pole appear on the deck, defining the forms of shadows behind it.

Suddenly a terrible cry, a cry of dispair, was wafted through the space, and as if the shrieks of anguish had driven away the clouds, the veil which hid the moon was cleared away, and the gray sails and dark shrouds of the felucca were plainly visible beneath the silvery light.

Shadows ran, as if bewildered, to and fro on the vessel, and mournful cries accompanied these delirious walkers. In the midst of these screams they saw Mordaunt upon the poop, with a torch in hand.

The agitated figures, apparently wild with terror, consisted of Groslow, who, at the hour fixed by Mordaunt, had collected his men, and the sailors. Groslow, after having listened at the door of the cabin to hear if the musketeers were still asleep, had gone down into the cellar, convinced by their silence that they were all in a deep slumber. Then Mordaunt had run to the train—impetuous as a man who is excited by revenge and full of confidence—as are those whom God blinds—he had set fire to the wick of niter.

All this while, Groslow and his men were assembled on the deck.

"Haul up the cable, and draw the boat to us," said Groslow.

One of the sailors got down the side of the ship, seized the cable, and drew it—it came without the least resistance.

"The cable is cut!" he cried, "no boat!"

"How! no boat!" exclaimed Groslow; "it is impossible."

"'Tis true, however," answered the sailor; "there's nothing in the wake of the ship, besides here's the end of the cable."

"What's the matter?" cried Mordaunt, who is coming up out of the hatchway, rushed to the stern, waving his torch.

"Only that our enemies have escaped—they have cut the cord, and gone off with the boat."

Mordaunt bounded with one step to the cabin, and kicked open the door.

"Empty!" he exclaimed; "the infernal demons!"

"We must pursue them," said Groslow; "they can't be gone far, and we will sink them, passing over them."

"Yes, but the fire," ejaculated Mordaunt; "I have lighted it."

"Ten thousand devils!" cried Groslow, rushing to the hatchway; "perhaps there is still time to save us."

Mordaunt answered only by a terrible laugh, threw his torch into the sea, and plunged in after it. The instant Groslow put his foot upon the hatchway steps, the ship opened like the crater of a volcano. A burst of flames rose toward the skies with an explosion like that of a hundred cannon; the air burned, ignited by flaming embers, then the frightful lightning disappeared, the brands sank, one after another, into the abyss, where they were extinguished, and, save for a slight vibration in the air, after a few minutes had lapsed, one would have thought that nothing had happened.

Only—the felucca had disappeared from the surface of the sea, and Groslow and his three sailors were consumed.

Alexander Pushkin, Father of Russian Poetry

ALEXANDER PUSHKIN is called the "Russian Byron," "demigod of Russian Verse," "father of Russian poetry," "the laureate of Czar Nicholas." The Pushkins had long been about the rulers of Russia as cited by Alexander in "My Pedigree." The first of the line the grandfather of the poet was an Abyssinian, who was stolen as a slave from Constantinople. The grandsire was not only adopted by Peter the Great, but given a title of nobility and rank of General.

The poet was proud of his African blood, which asserted itself unmistably in the curl of his hair

and the shape of his lips. He regarded himself as a drop of African blood on Arctic soil. He was born in 1799. During his childhood an old nurse beguiled him with many legends and fables of Russia. When he was twenty these legends brought forth fruit in his first great poem, "Ruslan and Liudmila." His democratic ideas, which encouched in an "Ode to Liberty," soon made him an exile from home and from Czar Nicholas I. However, the Czar loved the poet and speedily pardoned him. He died quite young, having written not only poetry that survives, but many prose tales. It is said that every youth in Russia knows his poetry by heart.

MY PEDEGREE.

IV. 66.

With scorning laughter at a fellow writer,
In a chorus the Russian scribes
With name of aristocrat me chide:
Just look, if please you... nonsense what!
Court Coachman not I, nor assessor,
Nor am I nobleman by cross;
No academician, nor proffer,
I'm simply of Russiana citizen.

Well I know the times' corruption,
And surely, not gain say it shall I:
Our nobility but recent is:
The more recent it, the more noble 'tis.
But of humble races a chip,
And, God be thanked, not alone
Of ancient Lords am scion I;
Citizen I am, a citizen!

Not in cakes my grandsire traded,
Not a prince was newly-baked he;
Not at church sang he in choir,
Nor polished he the boots of Tsar;
Was not escaped a soldier he
From the German powdered ranks;
How then aristocrat am I to be?
God be thanked, I am but a citizen.

My grandsire Radshaa in warlike service
To Alexander Nefsky was attached,
The Crowned Wrathful, Fourth Ivan,
His descendents in his ire had spared.
About the Tsars the Pushkins moved;
And more than one acquired renoun,
When against the poles battling was
Of Nizhny Novgorod the citizen plain.

When treason conquered was and falsehood,
And the rage of storms of war,
When the Romanoffs upon the throne
The nation called by its Chart—
We upon it laid our hands;
The martyr's son then favored us;
Time was, our race was prized,
But I .. am but a citizen obscure.

Our stubborn spirit us tricks has played;
Most irrepressible of his race,
With Peter my sire could not get on;
And for this was hung by him.
Let his example a lesson be;
Not contradiction loves a ruler,
Not all can be Prince Dolgorukys,
Happy only is the simple citizen.

My grandfather, when the rebels rose
In the palace of Peterhof,
Like Munich, faithful he remained
To the fallen Peter Third;
To honor came then the Orloffs,
But my sire into fortress, prison,—
Quiet now was our stern race,
And i was born merely—citizen.

Beneath my crested seal
The roll of family charts I've kept;
Not running after magnates new,
My pride of blood I have subdued;
I'm but an unknown singer
Simply Pushkin, not Moussin,
My strength is mine, not from court;
I am a writer, a citizen.

PAUL LAWRENCE DUNBAR

AUL LAWRENCE DUNBAR, Poet, is well known, as ought to be, to all Negroes. His songs in dialect and in plain English are known and quoted by all English speaking people. Many of the pieces have been set to music and are sung with remarkable pathos. "Poor Li'l Lamb," and "Seen Mah Lady Home Las' Night," to quote two of the well known songs, are applauded by all grades of audiences throughout the land.

Paul Lawrence Dunbar was born in Dayton, Ohio, in 1872. He was named Paul after the famous apostle in the scripture and Lawrence after a friend of his parents. The poet is said to have written his first verse when he was seven years old. Paul was a very bashful boy, but he had courage enough to take his poems to his teacher, who encouraged him. His favorite studies were, grammar, spelling and literature. He edited the High School Times, a monthly school paper in the Steel High School of Dayton, where Dunbar was a pupil and from which he was graduated with honors in 1891.

Dunbar went out from school to earn his bread as best he may. His father had died, the support of home therefore fell on the boy, who was none too sound in health. He had aided his mother with the washing and had done such odd jobs as he could find. All he could find as a graduate from the High School was the part as elevator boy in the Callahan Building of Dayton. But he made the best of it, using every spare moment to study or to write.

He soon triumphed over his hardships, publishing his poems in the best magazines of the country, appearing before the most select audiences both in this country and in England and numbering among his friends such persons as James Whitcomb Riley, William Dean Howell, John Hay, William McKinley, Theodore Roosevelt, R. R. Moton, and Booker T. Washington.

The following are favorite lines:

LITTLE BROWN BABY

Little brown baby wif spa'klin' eyes,
  Come to yo' pappy an' set on his knee
What you been doin' suh—makin' san' pies?
  Look at dat bib—you's ez du'ty ez me.
Look at dat mouf—dat's merlasses, I bet;
  Come hyeah, Maria, an' wipe off his han's.
Bees gwine to ketch you an' eat you up yit,
  Bein' so sticky an' sweet—goodness lan's!

Little brown baby wif sparkin' eyes,
  Who's papyy's darlin' an' who's pappy's chile?
Who is it all de day nevah once tries
  Fu' to be cross, er once looses dat smile?
Whah did you git dem teef? My you's a scamp!
  Wah did dat dimple come f'om in yo' chin?
Pappy do'n know yo'—I b'lieves you's a tramp;
  Mammy, dis hyeah's some ol' straggler got in!

Let's th'ow him outen de do' in de san',
  We don' want stragglers a-layin' 'round hyeah;
Let's gin him 'way to de big buggah-man;
  I know he's hidin' erroun' hyeah right neah.
Buggah-man, buggah-man, come in de do',
  Hyeah's a bad boy you kin have fu' to eat.
Mammy an' pappy don' want him no mo',
  Swaller him down f'om his haid to his feet!

Dah, now, I t'ought dat you'd hug me up close,
  Go back, buggah, you shan't have dis boy.
He ain't no tramp ner no straggler, of co'se;
  He's pappy's pa'dner an' playmate an' joy.
Come to yo' pallet now—go to yo' res';
  Wisht you could allus know ease and cleah skies;
Wisht you could stay jes' a chile on my breas'—
  Little brown baby wif' spa'klin eyes!
            —Paul Lawrence Dunbar.

Sojouner Truth, Emancipation Lecturer

THE NEGRO RACE has developed some unique characters who stand out conspicuous in their line of endeavor. Not the least among these is Sojourner Truth a woman of considerable native ability though an illiterate.

She was born a slave in Ulser County, N. Y., about the year 1775 and died in Battle Creek, Michigan, Nov. 26th, 1883. She was held in slavery even after its abolition in the same State. In 1827 she escaped from her owner and went to New York City and from thence to Northampton, Mass., and then to Rochester, N. Y.

Like Joan of Arc, she claimed that she was called to her work through a vision.

Her mother was brought from Africa, but her father was a mixture of Negro and Indian blood.

The early training of her mother influenced her entire after life. She taught her the value of honesty and truth and directed her mind to contemplate God as a Father and friend to whom she could go in confidence and trust.

Naturally Isabella (her slave name) developed a very religious trait.

She learned the true meaning of prayer and approached it in the spirit of a confident telling her troubles to God and invoking his aid.

One day she thought that she met God face to face and it so startled her that she exclaimed: "O God, I did not know you as you was so big!"

She changed her name from Isabella, the one given her by her master, to Sojourner, claiming that the Lord had bestowed it upon her in a vision and added the appellation "Truth" because that was the substance of the message she felt impelled to declare to men.

From the issue of her marriage Sojourner became the mother of five children, the father dying when they were quite young, left their care and support to her.

The following incident tends to show that the mother instinct was strong in her.

One of her sons was sold into slavery in Alabama and she was anxious to find him so she sought council of God. Now simple and childlike her plea, "Now, God, help me get my son. If you were in trouble as I am, and I could help you, as you can help me, think I wouldn't do it? Yes, God, you know I would do it. I will never give you peace 'till you do, God!" and then taking it for granted that she would receive the required help, she continued, "Lord, what would thou have me do?" the answer coming, "Go out of the city." Not knowing the direction she should take, she made further inquiry and received instruction to "Go East."

Accordingly on the morning of the first day of June, 1845, with a few clothes in her bag, a few shillings and a basket of food, she left the city and turned her face towards the rising sun.

It was on this morning that she gave herself, feeling divinely directed, her new name, saying that since she was to be a traveler, a sojourner, her name should be Sojourner. Being asked her surname she exclaimed that she had not thought of that, but immediately went to God about it and in her characterictic way exclaimed, "Oh, God, give me a name with a handle to it," and then came the thought that God's name was truth and she at once adopted that as her sur-name, which so pleased her that she lifted up her eyes to God in thanks, saying, "Why, thank you God, that is a very good name."

Sojourner was a woman of great shrewdness, wit and impressive voice which together with force of character made her an effective speaker.

The great theme of her lectures and the object of her effort was the emancipation of her people, though she touched upon woman's rights, temperance and political reforms.

She traveled widely in the northern part of the United States, but during the Civil War she spent much of her time in Washington.

Her power to electrify audiences was compared with that of the great French actress, Rachel.

On one occasion Frederick Douglass was speaking to a large audience and was painting a gloomy picture of the conditions of slavery and was upbraiding the church and State. Just as he had got the audience under his sway, Sojourner suddenly arose in the rear of the room and cried:

"Frederick! Frederick! is God dead?" It broke the spell of pessimism and for a time left the audience and the speaker dumbfounded.

She composed a battle hymn for a Negro regiment of Michigan and sang it herself both at Detroit and Washington:

"We hear the proclamation Massa, hush it as you will;
The birds will sing it to us, hopping on the cotton hill;
The possum up the gum tree couldn't keep it still;
As we went climbing on,"

Her's was a life of service and though of humble origin and of meager ability other than that conferred upon her by nature, she died in her home in Battle Creek, Michigan, with the satisfaction that she had contributed her mite in the service of her people.

Benjamin Banneker, Mathematician--Astronomer

THE first Banneker known of among Negroes in American history was an African Prince. This son of an African king was captured, brought to this country and sold to Molly Welsh of Maryland. Set free some years after his arrival, Banneker, who was a man of fine bearing and contemplative habits, married his former owner. The African Prince died early leaving his wife four children. One of these, a daughter by the name of Mary, married a native African, who became converted, joined the church and took his wife's sur-name of Banneker. This couple in turn had four children of whom Benjamin was the oldest and only son.

Benjamin Banneker was born Sept. 9th, 1731. The boy had a brilliant mind, was popular at school and a great favorite with his grand-mother who used to give him of her small share of knowledge and have him read much from the Bible.

His study under teachers was not at all extensive but he gained an early love for books and continued to "dive into books", as was said of him, all his life. Benjamin was twenty years old when his father died. The latter had bought one hundred acres of land when Benjamin was six years old, for which he paid 1700 pounds of tobacco. To the son and the widow the father left seventy-two acres of land and the home, dividing the remaining twenty-eight acres among his daughters. Though very studious, Benjamin was an excellent farmer, having a good garden and a fine assortment of fruit trees. He kept two horses, several cows and was very skillful in handling bees. Thus situated, life was very busy for him, but he made all things a school.

When he was twenty years old having no tools but a jack knife and having seen nothing but a sundial and a watch, Benjamin made himself a time piece which struck the hours and which kept the time for more than twenty years. When he was fifty-eight years of age, Banneker, who all these years had made the study of Astronomy a passion, transferred his land to Ellicott and Company for an annuity of twelve pounds. He was now free to give his whole time to his favorite study. Night after night he lay upon the ground, wrapped in his great coat, watching the heavens. In the morning he retired to rest, but appeared to acquire but little sleep. He still hoed in the garden and trimmed fruit trees for exercise and played on the flute or the violin for diversion.

He ventured from home but little. The only occasion on which he spent much time from his farm was in the year 1790 and thereabout when he aided in laying off or surveying the Federal Territory for the District of Columbia. He also aided in locating the spot for the capitol, the Presidents' House, Treasury and other public buildings.

On his return from Washington, he published his first Almanac, 1792, a copy of which he sent Thomas Jefferson. The latter forwarded the manuscript to Condercet, Secretary of the Academy of Sciences at Paris. The publishers advertised it as "an extraordinary effort of genius, calculated by a sable descendent of Africa." From this he became widely known as a writer and thinker and famous people frequently sought him out. He died October 9th, 1806 at the age of seventy-five.

Maryland, Baltimore County, Near Ellicott's Lower Mills, August 19, 1791.

To Thomas Jefferson, Secretary of State,
    Philadelphia.

Sir:

I have taken up my pen in order to direct to you, as a present, a copy of an Almanac which I have calculated for the ensuing year.

This calculation, Sir, is the production of my arduous study, in this my advanced stage of life; for having long had unbounded desires to become acquainted with the secrets of nature, I have had to gratify my curiosity herein, thro' my own assiduous application to astronomical study, in which I need not recount to you the many difficulties and disadvantages I have had to encounter.

And, altho' I had almost declined to make my calculation for the ensuing year, in consequence of the time which I had allotted therefor being taken up at the Federal Territory, by the request of Mr. Andrew Ellicott; yet finding myself under several engagements to printers of this State, to whom I had communicated my design, on my return to my place of residence, I industriously applied myself thereto, which I hope I have accomplished with correctness and accuracy, a copy of which I have taken the liberty to direct to you, and which I humbly request you will favorably receive; and, altho' you may have the opportunity of perusing it after its publication, yet I chose to send it to you in manuscript previous thereto, that thereby you might not only have an earlier inspection, but that you might also view it in my own handwriting.

And, now, Sir, I shall conclude, and subscribe myself with the most profound respect,
    Your most obedient, humble servant,
        B. BANNEKER.

Mr. Thomas Jefferson, Secretary of State,
    Philadelphia.

N. B.—Any communication to me may be had by a direction to Mr. Elias Ellicott, Baltimore Town.

Phillis Wheatley, Poetess

PHILLIS WHEATLEY was one of the first literary women of America; the first woman poet of the United States; the first Negro author, the first, as far as has thus far been discovered, to speak of George Washington as the "first in peace."

The first Negro poet was a slave brought over in a cargo of captives in 1781. The ship of human cargo landed at Boston. There among other slave buyers, were Mr. and Mrs. John Wheatley who came to select and purchase a girl for their home. Phillis came forth a frail creature of seven or eight years of age. The Bostonians bought her and christened her Phillis Wheatley. Of course the slave child was unable to read or write. But the Wheatleys taught her. In less than sixteen months she had acquired a fair knowledge of English and was able to read the most difficult parts of the "Sacred Writings." From the Bible she began to read Latin, the Latin poets and mythology. Soon she began to write verses, which to the people of Boston were very good, indeed excellent for one with so little training.

She was frail in health. To aid her in gaining strength her friends advised taking a trip to England which she duly made. In England she was the guest of the Countess of Huntington, to whom she, later dedicated her book of poems published in 1773, and was entertained by Lord Dartmouth and other leading men and women of the Empire. She wrote so well that people doubted her authorship. Such men as Governor Thomas Hutchinson of Massachusetts, Andrew Oliver, and John Hancock, the first signers of the Declaration of Independence, declared that they verily believed that the poems were her own composition.

On her return to America, she found Mrs. Wheatley poor in health. Later the Mistress died, the Wheatley home was broken up and the poet left quite unprotected. Shortly after this she received an offer of marriage from one Samuel Peters who was a Negro grocer and a writer and speaker of high repute. The marriage turned out unhappily and the poet died deserted, December 5th, 1794.

Benson J. Lossing, the Historian says of her, "Piety was the ruling sentiment in her character."

The following are taken from Phillis Wheatley's:

ON BEING BROUGHT FROM AFRICA TO AMERICA.

'Twas mercy brought me from my Pagan land,
Taught my benighted soul to understand
That there's a God, that there's a Savior, too;
Once I redemption neither sought nor knew.
Some view our sable race with scornful eye,
"Their color is a diabolic die."
Remember, Christians, Negroes, black as Cain,
May be refined, and join th' angelic train.

A FAREWELL TO AMERICA (1773)
To Mrs. Susannah W. Wheatley.

Adieu, New England's smiling meads,
Adieu, the flow'ry plain:
I leave thine op'ning charms, O spring,
And tempt the roaring main.

In vain for me the flow'rets rise,
And boast their gaudy pride,
While here beneath the Northern skies
I mourn for health deny'd.

Celestial maid of rosy hue,
O let me feel thy reign!
I languish till thy face I view
Thy van sh'd joys regain.

Susanna mourns, nor can I bear,
To see the crystal shower,
Or mark the tender falling tear
At sad departure's hour;

Not unregarding can I see
Her soul with grief opprest
But let no sigh, nor groans for me
Steal from her pensive breast.

In vain the feather'd warblers sing,
In vain the garden blooms,
And on the bosom of the spring
Breathes out her sweet perfumes.

While for Britannia's distant shore
We sweep the liquid plain,

And with astonish'd eyes explore
The wide-extended main.

Lo! Health appears! celestial dame!
Complacent and serene,
With Hebe's mantle o'er her Frame,
With soul-delighted mien.

To mark the vale where London lies
With misty vapors crown'd
Which cloud Aurora's thousand dyes,
And veil her charms around.

Why, Phoebus, moves thy car so slow?
So slow thy rising ray?
Give us the famous town to view,
Thou glorious king of day!

For thee, Britannia, I resign
New England's smiling fields;
To view again her charms devine,
What joy the prospect yields.

But thou! Temptation hence away,
With all thy fatal train
Nor once seduce my soul away,
By thine enchanting strain.

Thrice happy they, whose heav'nly shield
Secures their souls from harms
And fell Temptation on the field
Of all its pow'r disarm—!

Harriet Tubman, "The Moses of Her People"

HARRIET TUBMAN was called the Moses of her people because during the years of the Fugitive Law, she rescued some three or four hundred slaves and led them to freedom. She was born about 1820 in Dorchester County, Maryland. She worked as a nurse, as a trapper; field hand and wood chopper while she was a slave. She is said to have begun her labors about 1845 and to have continued until 1860. She made 19 trips into slave States at exceedingly great risks. She went into her own native town more than once, bringing away her brothers and her old parents as well as many neighbors.

John Brown nick-named her. General Tubman because of her shrewd management and great endurance. In her trips to and from the North she spent days and nights out of doors, in caves and often without food. She spent a whole night out of doors at one time in the beating snow with only a tree for protection. She waded creeks and rivers, neck high, forcing those whom she was piloting to follow her. The babies she managed by drugging them with opium. No wonder a price of $40,000 was once put upon her head.

She was an eloquent speaker, though she could neither read nor write. Her words are always forceful, her descriptions vivid.

She was once sent with an exposition during the Civil War to bring away slaves. This is her description of the slaves as they flocked to the boats:

"I nebber see such a sight." "Here you'd see a woman wid a pail on her head, rice a smokin' in it jus' as she'd taken it from de fire, young one hangin' on behind, one han roun' her forehead to hold on, 'tother han' diggin' into de rice-pot, eatin' wid all its might; hold of her dress two or three more; down her back a bag wid a pig in it. One woman brought two pigs, a white one an' a black one; we took 'em all on board; named de white pig Beauregard, and de black pig Jeff Davis. Sometimes de women would come wid twins hangin' roun' der necks; 'pears like I nebber see so many twins in my life; bags on der shoulders, baskets on der heads, and young ones taggin' behin', all loaded; pigs squealin', chickens screamin', young ones squallin'."

Her story of an incident of her childhood days is told as only Harriet Tubman could relate experiences.

"I was only seven years old when I was sent away to take car' of a baby. I was so little dat I had to sit down on de flo' and hab de baby put in my lap. An' dat baby was allus in my lap 'cept when it was asleep, or its mother was feedin' it.

"One mornin' after breakfast she had de baby, and I stood by de table waitin' till I was to take it; just by me was a bowl of lumps of white sugar. My Missus got into a great quarrel wid her husband; she had an awful temper, an' she would scole an' storm, an' call him all sorts of names. Now, you know I never had nothing good; no sweet, no sugar, an' dat sugar, right by me, did look so nice, an' my Missus's back turned to me while she was fightin' wid her husband, so I jes' put my fingers in de sugar bowl to take one lump, an' maybe she heard me, an' she turned an' saw me. De nex' minute she had de raw hide down; I give one jump out of de do', an' I saw dey came after me, but I jes' flew, an' dey didn't catch me. I run, an' I run, I passed many a house, but I didn't dare to stop, for dey all knew my Missus an' dey would send me back. By an' by, when I was clar tuckered out, I come to a great big pig-pen. Dar was an' ole sow dar, an' perhaps eight or ten pigs. I was too little to climb into it, but I tumbled ober de high board, an' fell in on de ground; I was so beat out I couldn't stir.

"An' dere, I stays from Friday till de next Chuesday, fightin' wid dose little pigs for de potato peelin's an' oder scraps dat come down in de trough. Do ole sow would push me away when I tried to git her chillen's food, an' I was awful afeard of her. By Chuesday I was so starved I knowed I'd got to go back to my Missus, I hadn't got no whar else to go, but I knowed what was comin'. So I went back."

Frederick Douglas wrote her in 1868: "The difference between us is very marked. Most that I have done and suffered in the service of our cause has been in public, and I have received much encouragement at every step of the way. You, on the other hand, have labored in a private way. I have wrought in the day—you in the night. I have had the applause of the crowd and the satisfaction that comes of being approved by the multitudes, while the most that you have done has been witnessed by a few trembling, scarred, and foot-sore bondmen and women, whom you have led out of the house of bondage, and whose heartfelt "God bless you" has been your only reward. The midnight sky and the silent stars have been the witnesses of your devotion to freedom and of your heroism."

Harriet Tubman lived to a ripe old age and was always, even after freedom, the friend of the downtrodden. Her house was always full of dependents, who were supported solely by Harriet's "Faith."

OSCAR WILLIAM ADAMS

MONG the enterprising young men who threw their weight into making the Negro Birmingham a success, none has fought harder or more creditably than Oscar W Adams. On graduating from Normal A. and M. College, Normal, Ala., Mr. Adams cast his lot with "The Birmingham Reporter," now without question the leading Negro Newspaper of Alabama. For a number of years he lived out pretty faithfully the advice of Horace Greeley to the young aspirants to Journalism—"to sleep on paper and eat ink." But in time the paper came into Mr. Adams' possession, and the struggle was even more bitter, if possible. Business did not hum in Birmingham then as now and so his subscribers were few and his advertisers small, and uncertain, and payment for both subscriptions and advertisements very slow in coming in.

To keep the paper alive, Mr. Adams gave up his lodgings and slept in the office on a lounge. He ate a full meal whenever he could afford to do so.

"But, " says he, "I always paid my helpers. I didn't think it right to keep them waiting. It was none of their affair if the paper failed." However, the Reporter is on its feet today. It has passed

through the day of test for twelve years, and a Negro paper that survives the test that length of time can be said to be fully established.

Of course, Mr. Adams had been thoroughly schooled for the struggle with The Reporter, and from this schooling one would expect nothing but victory to the end. Mr. Adams was born in Gulf Crest, one time known as Beaver Meadow, a community about 25 miles out of Mobile. He attended the district school to the 8th grade and then made his way to Normal, Alabama, to the A. and M. College. To make his way through school, both in public school and for the first year in College, Mr. Adams worked as a laborer on a turpentine farm. During his life in College he served now as agent in the Commissary, now as the assistant bookkeeper and finally as the Editor of the Normal Index, the official paper of the Normal College. Going through so many experiences and coming out of each successful, Mr. Adams built the character which has stood him in such good stead as editor of The Reporter, as a business man, and a leader in the fraternal orders.

Mr. Adams is most loyal, even enthusiastic fraternity man. As has already been stated, his paper is the official organ of the Knights of Pythias, Odd Fellows, and Masonic Order of Alabama. He holds membership also in the Masonic Lodge, in the Elks, in the K. L. of H., and in the Mosaic Templars. He is Secretary of the United Brothers of Friendship, as well as its spokesman in his journal.

Second only to his interest in his journal is Mr. Adams' interest in education. He is present at all educational gatherings he can reach and gives freely space in his paper to the reports upon all schools and school work, both in the city and in the state. He is very loyal to Normal, not only because this is his Alma Mater, but because he really knows what it means for most of our boys and girls to secure even a fair education, an education rising but little above the three R's.

Oscar W. Adams, though a young man, has filled some of the most important speaking engagements of any member of his race. He is a man of rare quality in this special line of work. He is a student of history and his delivery is easy and pleasant. At present he is Chairman of the Four Minute Men Speakers of the State of Alabama, directed by the United States Government, and is a member of the State Committee on War Savings Certificates. He has, no doubt, appeared before more audiences in the past five years than any man in the race of his age.

Mr. Adams was married to Miss Mamie Tuggle in 1910. The happy union, happy in sympathy and co-operation as well as in affection, for both were very hard workers, lasted but five years, Mrs. Adams dying in 1915. He lives now for his paper, for his school, for his lodge and for Negro enterprise in every direction.

BISHOP JOHN WESLEY ALSTORK, D. D., LL. D.

ISHOP John Wesley Alstork was born in Talladega, Alabama, September 1st, 1852. From the date of his birth we gather that he was born early enough to see a little of Negro Slavery. But the Bishop was fortunate in the place of birth and in his parentage. Talladega is a conservative college town. It was one of the first places to be given colleges for the higher education of the Negro after the Civil War. Here in his own home town he had advantages of education that were denied to many men born in the same period. The advantage in parentage is seen from the fact that his father was a minister and was willing and anxious to see his son have better educational advantages than he himself had been able to enjoy. Bishop Alstork is the son of Rev. and Mrs. Frank Alstork, who were greatly loved and honored.

Bishop Alstork did not confine his studying to the courses laid down at Talladega. Livingston College, Salisbury, North Carolina, conferred D. D. upon him in 1892. The Degree of LL. D. was conferred upon him by the Princeton College in Indiana in 1908. Though born a slave, Bishop Al-

stork persevered in acquiring an education till he had thoroughly prepared himself for the work he had to do in life.

Bishop Alstork was married to Miss Mamie Lawson in 1872 when only twenty years of age. Mrs. Alstork has been a true helpmate to the Bishop and has helped in his development. Ten years after his marriage he was ordained in the A. M. E. Zion ministry. In 1884 he was elected Financial Secretary of the Alabama Conference This position he held till 1892. In 1892 he was elected Financial Secretary for the A. M. E. Zion Connection. In this position he served till 1900. His excellent management keeping the finances of the church in good condition.

Bishop Alstork had the usual gradual rise from the ministry to the position of Bishop. He served as a regular pastor from the time of his ordination to 1889. In that year he was made Presiding Elder and he served in this capacity till 1900 when he was elected Bishop. Many of the honors within the gift of his church have come to Bishop Alstork. He was Delegate to the Ecumenial Conference, which met in London, England, in 1901. He was sent as a delegate to the Conference in Toronto, Canada, in 1911.

Although Bishop Alstork is thoroughly interested in the church and in all the work of the church, he has still had time to show a great deal of interest in all the phases of education. He is a trustee of the Livingston College, of the Lomax-Hannon Industrial College. Indeed Bishop Alstork was the founder of the last named institution which is located at Greenville, Alabama. He is Trustee of Langridge Academy at Montgomery, Alabama and a Trustee of the Hale Infirmary also of Montgomery. Bishop Alstork is a member of the Federation of Churches, a member of the Southern Sociological Congress, Director of Loan and Investment Company, Montgomery, Alabama, member of the Board of Control of the Good Shepherd Society, Inspector of the General G. G. A. Order of Love and Charity, National Grand Master of F. A. A. York Masons Colored of the United States, Lieutenant Commander of the Supreme Council 33rd degree Masonry. In fact Bishop Alstork lives a very full and a very useful life.

Bishop Alstork has traveled over the whole of this country and extensively in foreign lands. He is a loyal citizen of his country. During this war he has been a faithful worker in all the war activities. His patriotism has been manifested in every war work campaign. He is a heavy purchaser of bonds, and a large contributor to Red Cross and Y. M. C. A. work. He owns a great deal of real estate and lives in his own beautiful home at 231 Cleveland Avenue, Montgomery, Alabama.

BENJAMIN H. BARNES

OR fully a score of years Booker T. Washington thundered from the Tuskegee Institute platform the doctrine of service. "Go back to your homes, put a hinge on the gate, a latch on the door. Don't stand around and whine. Get into the church, into the school, into the shop and help. Own your own homes and become a tax-paying, respectable citizen."

Benjamin H. Barnes after graduating under his father's teaching, sat beneath the voice of the Tuskegean and caught the vision that the great leader sought to impart. He did not pick out any one of of these suggestions but seemed to absorb them all. While at Tuskegee Mr. Barnes excelled not only in his studies both in trade and in books but also in music. He played the violin, the piano and sang. For part of three years he traveled as a Tuskegee singer. Returning to Tuscaloosa his native town, he accepted work as a teacher in the city public school and began to live to the full the life that Booker T. Washington had so ardently preached. Mr. Barnes immediately connected himself with the work of the town church, the First African Baptist Church. He had been in attendance here

but a short time when he was elected superintendent of the Sunday School, a post at which he served for twenty-five years. Not long after this Mr. Barnes was made church organist: and for twenty years the Baptists of Tuscaloosa have sung to his playing in the church.

Some years ago this church set out to erect a new building. The cost of the house was to be $25,000.00. Mr. Barnes along with his church and Sunday School work had demonstrated that he was a business man. The church members placed him at the head of the Committee, rallied to his support and put up a splendid brick structure. The ministers came and went, Barnes stayed by his post till the last brick was laid. He is now financial secretary of the church, secretary of the board of trustees and one of the strong active deacons.

However, his biggest service as a Christian worker is being rendered among the young people of the state. Alabama is peppered with Negro Baptists. Blow your Baptist trumpet in the remotest hamlet and a regiment of loyal followers will come forward to bear up the standard. Among their organization is a Baptist Young People's Union. Mr. Barnes has been the president of this organization for sixteen years. In recognition of his religious services and of his exemplary scholarship, Selma University some years ago conferred upon him the honorary degree of Master of Arts.

All through his life Mr. Barnes has been a very intense student, both in books and in affairs. He spends many hours in home study, in a very exceptional home library. From time to time he has taken home correspondence courses from the University of Chicago. In addition to this he keeps thoroughly abreast with all educational movements in the state. No convention or gathering of educators in the state is likely to assemble without finding Benjamin H. Barnes on hand ready to give advice, time or money to make things go.

The home of Benjamin H. Barnes, all paid for, is one of the most handsome of the half dozen excellent Negro homes of Tuscaloosa. As one purchase whets the appetite for another Mr. Barnes after paying for his home, bought other buildings and now owns property to rent.

This is not the full business story of Prof. Barnes. The Union Central Life Relief company of Birmingham is one of the comparatively few Negro firms of the kind to stem the tide of business adversity. Casting about for a manager of a branch office in Tuscaloosa, the Union Central Relief found the man they wanted in Prof. Barnes. In this office and in visiting patrons Mr. Barnes spends his summer and spare hours when not on duty in the school.

One dominant trait is unmistakable in the Barnes family, that of holding fast to the duties in hand — a father, school teacher in one place forty-two years: a son, school teacher for nearly twenty years. Sunday School superintendent twenty-five years, president of Young People's Baptist Union sixteen years.

Mr. Barnes is married; his wife is his partner. She has rendered valuable service in all of his endeavors. They have celebrated their crystal wedding with much pomp.

JEREMIAH BARNES

HEN you go to Tuscaloosa, Alabama, on school matters, the County Superintendent, the bankers and other people will tell you to "see Jeremiah Barnes". Mr. Barnes is principal of the Negro Public Schools of Tuscaloosa, and is most likely the oldest Negro School man today engaged in active service. He began his career as a school teacher back in 1874, when a Negro school master was indeed a rare person. From that date scarcely a day has passed during the school session without finding the veteran at his post. Indeed, he goes to school whether he teaches or not; for he keeps the keys of the Tuscaloosa High School and almost daily, even in summer, you will find him about the school going over the grounds, attending the school garden, inspecting the rooms inside.

The veteran school master of Tuscaloosa was reared a slave, on the farm of Judge Washington Wood, eight miles west of Tuscaloosa. Here he learned to read and write and found some opportunity to improve himself generally. He was a brick mason back in the 60's. Ten years later he was running a variety store, at which time he became alderman of Tuscaloosa, grand juror of the county

and a teacher in the public schools. In 1874 the same year that he began his school work, Mr. Barnes became a Master Mason and later was made Worshipful Grandmaster for three terms. Since that time he has been made Secretary of foreign correspondence for his Grand Lodge, a position which he held for fourteen years. He was one time grand patron of the Alabama Order Eastern Star and is a charter member of the Oak City Lodge No. 1785, Grand United Order of Odd Fellows. He twice served his own district rgand lodge as deputy grand master.

All this wealth of life experience along with constant study of books Mr. Barnes brought to the school room. For years he was a teacher, being promoted step by step until he reached the highest post in the Negro schools of his native city. In his work as teacher he has taken rightful pride in the graduates he has turned out. Some have gone to college, some to industrial schools, some settled to trades, some to school teaching after leaving him. Wherever they have gone they have made their mark as very useful hightoned citizens.

In his school curriculum Prof. Barnes balances his courses pretty well between class room work and industrial work. His courses run into studies in Algebra, Geometry and Latin; out under the window you will see a flourishing school garden, and a place for cooking in the basement. He teaches the children by deed as well as by word, that work is honorable and intellectual, just as solving a problem in Algebra or constructing a verb in English or Latin.

To this, too, he adds a most needed phase of education, that of beautifying one's surroundings. The Negro High School building of Tuscaloosa happens to be in a rather unhappy section of the city. A railroad yard is nearby, so also is the city refuse pile and the city stables. Yet by setting out trees, constructing fences and laying out walks, the veteran educator has managed to shut out pretty nearly these obnoxious features of his school environment, thus showing the pupils that their own lives within need not be disturbed by the lives without.

Along with helping the students of his school, Prof. Barnes has reared and educated several children of his own. His son, Benjamin, is the strong assistant of his father in the Tuscaloosa school work, is the great Negro Baptist Young People's Union leader of Alabama, church organist, and business man. The other son is the treasurer of the Snow Hill Normal and Industrial School of Snow Hill, Alabama.

How long Prof. Barnes will remain in the school work none but a higher power can tell. So far he shows no signs of retreat. He is vigorous, active, both in body and in mind. Best of all as a school teacher he is very cheerful and very optimistic for himself and his people.

EDWARD AUSTIN BROWN

 THERE are about 800 Negro lawyers in the United States. Some of them have occupied positions of trust and prominence, political, judicial and diplomatic. Yet whenever a colored man thinks of entering the legal profession he is instructed to have well in mind Socrates' definition of courage. Said the sage, "He who rushes into battle without knowing all the consequences does not represent genuine courage but rashness." Thus it is with the law for the Negro. Of all the professions it is very probably the least hospitable to the black man. As a rule, he is not accorded a square deal in the courts of the South, while in the North he finds himself, for the most part, up against the most lively competition. He, then, who enters here must weigh between courage and rashness; and he who succeeds in compelling a fair measure of success is either a giant in intellect or a wizard in tact and diplomacy.

That Edward A. Brown did not enter the law through rashness, through not knowing the attendant dangers, can be fairly inferred from the fact that he was born in the South, where the situation is quite patent. Mr. Brown was born in Raleigh, N. C., forty odd years ago. After completing the public school course in his native town he had private tuition in order to prepare himself for college, and soon thereafter entered Lincoln University, in Pennsylvania, where four years later he finished the collegiate course, graduating with honors. Just as Mr. Brown was about to enter a New England Law school he was offered an opportunity to study law in the office of Judge Henry McKinney, who was at the time one of the ablest lawyers at the Cleveland, Ohio, bar. This offer was accepted and in due time the young law student was admitted to the bar by the Supreme Court of Ohio. Incidentally, it may be mentioned that of the 108 applicants for admission at the time, Mr. Brown offered the best examination.

After practicing his profession for a while in Cleveland Mr. Brown came to Alabama, where again he made a record in his examination for admission, winning from the presiding judge the statement that this was the best examination he had ever witnessed. Ever since his admission to the Alabama bar Mr. Brown has pursued the active practice of his profession in Birmingham, where he resides, except for the period of eight months during which he was an army officer at the time of the Spanish-American War, serving under a commission of First Lieutenant in the 10th U. S. Volunteer Infantry.

Mr. Brown enjoys a lucrative practice and, like thousands of the best lawyers of the country, is what is known as a "civil" lawyer, giving no attention to criminal practice. He is regarded by the judges and members of the bar generally as an able lawyer and as a man of the highest personal character. His clients and friends believe in him, in his knowledge of the law, his integrity and his unfailing sane judgment. To illustrate the unselfish public spirit of the man a single incident may be related: The commissioners of the city of Birmingham, following the example of certain other municipalities, undertook to enact a law providing segregation of residences based upon race. Mr. Brown, without being employed or even requested, went before the commissioners with a strong protest against the adoption of the proposed ordinance and made such a forceful argument against its constitutionality as to defeat it then and there. Here was an example of his unselfish spirit, for although this was legal service of the highest order and dealing with a matter of far-reaching importance to his race, not a dollar was charged by him or accepted.

Mr. Brown has succeeded in accumulating a competency, owning a residence valued at $5,000 and other real estate; and besides, he has some money. For several years he has served as general attorney for the Knights of Pythias of Alabama, of which fraternal order he is a leading and influential member. He is active in all movements touching the welfare of his people and is one of the really strong and substantial men of his community and state.

The Brown family is small, consisting of Mrs. Brown and one son, Edward, Jr. Mrs. Brown, who was Miss Nettie Jones of Cleveland, Ohio, is active in club work and various charities. Edward, Jr., is a quiet, studious lad, having made first year high school at the age of thirteen.

MISS CORNELIA BOWEN

N a certain day in May if you are anywhere in Montgomery County, Alabama, you will see wagons from the country, cars and carriages from the city, crowding and jamming along the road, all going in one direction. On inquiry you will learn that they are making their way toward the Mt. Meigs Institute, to attend the commencement exercises. When you reach the school, there will break on you a sort of vision of a new city, suddenly peopled. This is the work of Miss Cornelia Bowen of Mt. Meigs.

Miss Bowen went to Mt. Meigs in 1888 to plant a school in the wilderness, as it were. To reach the rural man and woman as well as the small boy and small girl was a demand which both Miss Bowen and the late Dr. Washington felt it a sacred duty to answer. To use Miss Bowen's own words in "Tuskegee and Its People"—"a call reached Dr. Washington in 1888 for a teacher to begin work in the vicinity of Mt. Meigs, Alabama, similar to the work done at Tuskegee, but of course on a smaller scale. Mr. E. N. Pierce of Plainville, Connecticutt, had resolved to do something in the way of providing better school facilities for the colored people living on a large plantation, into the possession of

which he had come. Mr. Washington answered the call while in Boston, and telegraphed me that he thought me the proper person to take charge of and carry on the settlement work Mr. Pierce and his friend had in mind."

The place itself is far away, out of contact. The people were weighted down with debt, mild peonage, morals were at a low ebb. Miss Bowen set out to improve the lives of the old people while building a school for the young. She taught Bible classes in the leaky country church and held meetings and conferences for the mothers and fathers. In a little while the people began to know that there were ideals of health, of family, of property ownership. Thus it is that today they troop on horseback, in buggy, in wagon to Mt. Meigs Commencement. Here along with the diversion offered they come upon the first impulse to do good.

It has become quite common nowadays to speak of the pioneer, but the Mt. Meigs school was in a very real sense a pioneer in its own kind of work. To set up in the country a school which was a community center: a school which called in the country women to teach them cooking, sewing, and house-keeping, to teach them how to rear and treat their children; to instruct them in finer manners towards their husbands and towards their neighbors; to persuade them to eliminate certain habits, like dipping snuff and smoking and chewing tobacco, as unfeminine and un-womanly; to have done all this in those early days of any kind of Negro school in Alabama was genuinely pioneer work.

The same constructive program was adopted with the men and boys. Men were better farmers, better husbands, fathers, cleaner in their habits, more ambitious in their ideals because of Mt. Meigs. They formed more definite ideals of home, of family, of church, from this teaching and from their contact in the school. Where there was no farm ownership, they began to buy farms. Where there were no flowers, flowers began to grow: an air of refinement and of taste began to assert itself.

There is nothing so new about this now, for we begin to see the very definite results of this training. Mt. Meigs opened a boarding department and rooms for the children and taught them new lessons of life. It fired them with zeal to go back to their village and teach what they themselves had learned. This situation now so prevalent was at first a most startling innovation when Mt. Meigs began. It was the first trumpet call to the man in the fields that somebody really cared for him, for the life he lived, whether or not he was really happy.

While thus laboring among the elders, Miss Bowen was founding a school. She bought her land, forty-odd acres, and began to put up buildings. She put on the curriculum, not only grammar, arithmetic and the like, but the study of practical industries, such trades as the boys and girls could use immediately in their homes. Thus she teaches her own school gardening, farming, poultry-raising, the care of live stock and bee culture.

VIEW MT. MEIGS INSTITUTE

In the meantime she was not forgetting her own education. She had attended school at Tuskegee Institute, where Dr. Washington was examiner, school teacher, principal, lecturer and a good many other things. Under him she sat, got her Tuskegee diploma, then spent some time as principal of the "Children's House", of Tuskegee Institute. To the education of experience, which her principal and friend, Dr. Washington, so ardently believed in, Miss Bowen added study in New York City and further study in Queen Margaret's College, Glasgow, Scotland.

Miss Bowen is through and through a product of Tuskegee Institute. She was born on what is now the Institute Campus. The little cottage in which she was born was the first building of Tuskegee Institute to be used for teaching girls' industries. "And never do I go to Tuskegee," says Miss Bowen, "that I do not search it out among the more imposing and pretentious buildings, which have come during the later years of the school's history."

The cottage in which she was born stood on the plantation of Colonel William Bowen, to whom Miss Bowen's mother was a slave. Unlike most slave mothers, Miss Bowen's mother could read, having been taught by a former mistress in Baltimore. She was therefore able to superintend her daughter's education to greater degree than most mothers of the time, hence arises, no doubt, the daughter's very strong grasp on people and affairs.

Miss Bowen was first taught by a southern white woman of the town of Tuskegee.: She then attended the public school of Tuskegee until Booker T. Washington came and founded the Institute. Her school on "Zion Hill" was then closed and the children all flocked to the new school. Booker T. Washington was then an active teacher. He gave her the examination and placed her in the Junior class. He taught many of the subjects. Miss Bowen looks back with no end of pleasure to those days when Dr. Washington taught grammar, history and spelling.

She was a member of the first class to graduate from Tuskegee Institute. This was in 1885, before the school had even conceived of the great industrial idea. Miss Bowen was an honor student, receiving a first grade diploma and winning one of the three Peabody medals; medals which were awarded for excellence in scholarship.

With this foundation she went out to establish the Mt. Meigs Institute, full of confidence. Her work in the school has made a name for Miss Bowen. She has several times held various offices in the National Association of Colored Women's Clubs, State Teachers' Association of Alabama, and in the Colored Women's Federation of the State, and its president for fourteen years.

While a very excellent administrator, and a rare student of both men and books, Miss Bowen excels in the mind of many, through her gift of eloquent speech. Few persons on the platform today can bring so much power to bear, go so directly to the point and so eloquently as can Miss Bowen.

RICHARD ANDERSON BLOUNT

T was Robert Browning, who expressing his fondness for Italy, said, "If you open my heart you will find the word 'Italy' written therein." If you made an incison in the heart of Richard Anderson Blount of Birmingham, Alabama, you would find "Knights of Pythias." For nearly twenty years now Mr. Blount has thought Knights of Pythias, talked Knights of Pythias, traveled for Knights of Pythias, and what the order of the Knights of Pythias in Alabama is today, is traceable very largely to Richard Anderson Blount.

Back in 1887 Mr. Blount came into Birmingham to seek his fortune, attracted by the prospects of the town. He found employment with the Laweson Carpet Company and spent some time in their service. He worked also for sixteen years for Ben M. Jacobs & Brothers. It was during his employ with the Jacobs Brothers that Mr. Blount became engrossed in the work of the Knights of Pythias. His zeal for the order and his business acumen soon attracted attention, with the result that in 1898 he was elected Grand Keeper of Records and Seal. In three years he had given such good service and had established the records on such a sound business basis that the body of the state made him Grand Chancellor, a post at which he has served now for fifteen years.

The records show that when Mr. Blount assumed office there were in the state some sixty-five lodges, with a total membership of 16000 people. In fifteen years through the efforts of Mr. Blount the Knights of Pythias of Alabama have three hundred and forty-five lodges with a total membership of ten thousand. The order of Knights of Pythias is much better known, more popular, enjoys a wider confidence of the people, both of those who are members and those who are not.

Of course the Knights of Pythias of Alabama must have a building of their own. It just chances that the Alabama Penny Savings Bank is available. Mr. Blount and his helpers are pressing home plans to secure this building. To secure a splendid four story brick structure like the Alabama Penny Savings Bank Building, which has an office rent of several hundred, requires money, backing, appreciation of values, and confidence. All this the Knights of Pythias have and they have it very largely through Richard Anderson Blount.

Mr. Blount is not a native of Birmingham. He came from Montgomery where he was born in the early seventies. He attended the Swayne school in his native town. While he was going to school, Mr. Blount had to work. He somehow got into carpet laying; a trade which did him great service in the early years of his manhood.

His affiliation with and leadership of the Knights of Pythias do not blind him to the merits of other fraternities and organizations. He is an active member of the Sixteenth Street Baptist Church, a staunch member of the Masonic Lodge of the Shriners, of the Odd Fellows and of the Elks.

One of the most conspicuous things about Richard Anderson Blount is the beautiful home he has erected and paid for. In going up Seventh Avenue the passer-by turns round to look again and again as he passes this residence. This house is by no means the extent of Mr. Blount's ownership of property. He owns several rent houses and lots in and about town.

But the home and the home life were a vision of long ago. He saw big and handsome homes and happy families about. Into his own spirit crept the vision of such a home with a happy family. Both he now has. He has been married for more than twenty years. His first wife who was Miss Lucy Massey, died some eight years ago. The daughter of this union is now a student at Spelman Seminary in Atlanta, Ga. He recently married Miss Mary Lue Crawford. Mr. Blount has traveled much in the South and in the East and has to do so in the interest of and for the development of his lodge.

CLINTON J. CALLOWAY. A. B.

RAVELING through the rural districts of Alabama, especially through Macon County, everywhere one sees new up-to-date school houses. These schools have three and four rooms or more. Some are used as Model schools in which the teacher lives and has around her all the animals and other things to be had on a farm. These model schools are to train the country boys and girls how to live happily amid their native surroundings. In some places the old half-decayed school buildings are still standing making a marked contrast with the new and up-to-date structures. The one man who is more largely responsible for this condition than any other is Clinton J. Calloway of Tuskegee Institute.

Mr. Calloway was born April 18, 1869, in Cleveland, Tennessee. Here in his native town he attended the public school, remaining to finish the Grammar grades. For his High School work he went to Chattanooga, Tennessee. As a young man he had the trait of sticking to a thing and so he remained in the school till he completed the course in 1889. He then matriculated at Fisk University. All through his school career he was in earnest,

careful student, deserving and receiving the praise of his teachers. In 1895 he completed the classical course of Fisk and graduated with the degree of A. B. All through his years of study he gave close attention to practical ideas and ideals.

After graduation Mr. Calloway accepted work in the Extension Department at Tuskegee Institute and here he has remained ever since. During the years spent in the Extension Department of Tuskegee, Mr. Calloway has done much to develop and make of service his department. In 1895 when Mr. Calloway took charge, the work was restricted to dealing with the farm and country folk in general. It was then in its rudimentary stage. Mr. Calloway saw the great need of better schools. It has been largely through the demonstrations of Mr. Calloway that Miss Jeannes of the Jeannes Fund was convinced of the value of outside aid in rural school work among Negroes. To this end there are now all through Alabama and other Southern States workers among the rural teachers who travel back and forth supervising the work of the country schools. These are the Jeannes supervisors.

Another great advance in the Rural Schools of Alabama and now of other Southern states is due to the vision and thought of Mr. Calloway. It was he who suggested to Dr. Washington that Mr. Julius Rosenwald of Chicago would help in the erection of new and up-to-date schools for the rural districts of Alabama. Acting on this suggestion Mr. Rosenwald has invested the largest sum of money set aside for educational purposes. The schools built from the fund are known as the Rosenwald schools. The suggestion came from Mr. Calloway and he is the man who has had to work out the detail of the investment and he has also had to help the rural people raise their share of the money. All of them turn to Mr. Calloway when discouraged and expect to be shown the way out of difficulties. Never has he failed them. Mr. Calloway is now the head of the Extension Department with a number of workers under him, instead of being the whole of the Department as he was when he first took the work.

Mr. Calloway was married to Miss Josie Elizabeth Schooler March 12th, 1901 at Kowaliga, Alabama. To Mrs. Calloway her husband gives credit for his success in acquiring property. They own their own beautiful home and 1,000 acres of land and the implements, stock, etc., that are required for this sort of farming. Mr. Calloway is a Congregationalist in Religious belief. He is a practical Christian and commands the respect of all who know him.

Mr. Calloway is through and through a man of business. Whatever he undertakes to do is seen through the amount of good done for the amount of money spent. He is President of Homeseekers Land Company, Capital Stock $10,000.00 and manager of the Tuskegee Farm and Improvement Company with a capitalization of $25,000.00.

There are many better schools, better homes and better farms in Macon County and in fact all through Alabama because of the work of Mr. Calloway in the Extension Department of Tuskegee.

T. M. CAMPBELL

ATCHING the spirit of his illustrious teacher, Booker T. Washington, Mr. Campbell, the pioneer Negro Farm Demonstrator is bringing to a realization the dreams of the late Dr. Seaman A. Knapp, the father of farm demonstration work—1 am thinking, said Dr. Knapp, "of the people of rose covered cottages in the country, of the strong glad father and his con-tented, cheerful wife, of the whistling boy an dthe dancing girl with school books under her arms so that knowledge may soak into them as they go; I am thinking of the orchards and the vineyards, of the flocks and the herds, of the waving woodlands, of the hills carpeted with luxuriant verdure, and the valleys inviting to the golden harvest." Mr. Campbell and his large corps of workers are doing all this for the colored people of Alabama and the South.

Born February 11, 1883, just outside the corporate limits of the little town of Bowman, Elbert County, Ga., Mr. Campbell's life was typical of the average boy of that section, and at the age of fifteen, he found that he had attended school less than twelve months. Hearing of Tuskegee from an old

er brother who had gone there, the lad determined to attend. His father failing to keep a promise to let him use the money earned working on a neighboring plantation, the boy walked and worked his way to Tuskegee from which he was graduated eight years later in 1906. He speaks as follows of his Tuskegee experience: "My training was such that I was unable to make the lowest class when I came to Tuskegee, and I sometimes think that my only salvation was that I was large and strong and my services were needed on the farm. By constant study, both day and night, I was able to make a class the next year and every year after until my graduation. During my eight years stay here as a student, I received only $2.00 cash and one suit of clothes as assistance."

When Dr. Knapp came to Tuskegee in 1906 seeking his first Negro demonstrator, he found his man in the field following a two-horse plow. This man was T. M. Campbell, who had recently been graduated and was specializing in agriculture.

"Young man", said Dr. Knapp, "I want you to travel over a given territory and show the Negroes how to prepare land just as you are doing now." This Mr. Campbell did, traveling in the Jesup Agricultural Wagon, an idea of the far seeing Dr. Washington who conceived the idea of taking education to the farmer. This work was later merged into the United States Farm Demonstration work and has taken Mr. Campbell into every part of Alabama and other portions of the South.

For the past twelve years, early and late, in sunshine and in rain, he has been going about Alabama and other Southern States making the waste places blossom. Mr. Campbell defining the term demonstrator says: "A Demonstrator is a farmer chosen by the government Agent because of his ability to attract the people of his community to himself, he is commonly called a community leader." Mr. Campbell, who is now officially known as District Agent for Farm Demonstraton Work for the colored people of Alabama, possesses these qualifications in a high degree. He has a very winning personality, and a rich musical voice which wins friends wherever he goes.

Unlike most public men of the race, Mr. Campbell is not a lodge man, due perhaps to the fact that he is so seldom at home; for his duties keep him ever on the road. He is a Methodist and zealous church worker.

On June 1st, 1911, Mr. Campbell was married to Miss Annie M. Ayers of Virginia, who is also a Tuskegee graduate. Four children, Thomas Jr., Carver, Virginia and William help to make the home a happy, cheery place. The two older boys are in school and promise to follow in years to come the footsteps of their father.

JAMES HENRY EASON, D. D.

R. James Henry Eason, the pastor of the very select congregation of the Jackson Street Baptist Church, Birmingham, Ala., is an ideal product of his state. He was born October 24, 1866 to Channie Bingham Eason and Jesse Bigham. Born, reared and for the most part educated in Alabama, he has turned all his time and his talent—has brought his vision to pass in the state of his birth. He was born in Sumpterville, Sumpter County. Gaining all he could in the Sumpterville public school he entered Selma University and after graduation from Selma Dr. Eason took his course in theological training at Virginia Union University, Richmond, Va., receiving the degree of D. D. On finishing his studies he immediately returned to Alabama to give account of his education. Although he earned his way, he felt that he owed a great debt to the people of his state. In 1884 he began teaching school in Gadsden. He taught one year in Garfield Academy at Auburn, Ala., and seven years in Selma University. In the meantime he had been appointed state Missionary for Alabama by the Home Missionary Society of New York. In this office, he served several years.

The year 1891 saw the formal beginning of Dr. Eason's career as a pastor. In this year he accepted the pastorate of the Union Baptist Church at Marion, Ala. Here he became moderator of the new Cahaba Association. From Marion Mr. Eason went to Anniston. Here he really began to assert himself as a minister and as a community builder. When he accepted the pastorate of the Eleventh Street Baptist Church in Anniston, there were eighty-five members of the congregation. This body was then known as the Galilee Church. Dr. Eason held his post here for fifteen years. In that time he increased the membership from eighty-five to seven hundred and put up a new building which cost $25,000.00. While building this church in Anniston, he noticed that comparatively few colored people owned homes. To aid the people in securing homes, he organized the Mercantile Investment Company, whose efforts have resulted in hundreds of colored people owning their homes in this city.

His name now spreads abroad as a worker and a man of exceptional gifts and rare industry. He was for ten years Editor of the Baptist Leader; the official organ of 280,000 Alabama Baptists. He edited and published the Union Leader of Anniston Alabama for five years; meanwhile he had written and published a book entitled, "Sanctification versus Fanaticism," which was the first book published by the National Baptist Board, and had written articles and historical sketches for the magazines.

Thus asserting himself, he became a candidate for many honors. Guadaloupe College, Texas, and Benedict College, S. C., each honored him with the degree of Doctor of Divinity. He was given the presidency of the Colored Baptist State Convention which he held ten years, resigning in 1916. For seven years he was vice president of the National Baptist Convention. Selma University elected him a member of the Board of Trustees and for one year he carried the presidency of the Anniston Industrial College. June 11th, 1917, Dr. Eason was elected president of Birmingham Baptist College, Birmingham, Alabama. He was a delegate to the World's Missionary Conference, which met a few years ago in Edinburgh, Scotland. He preached in Scotland and traveled extensively in Scotland, in England, in Belgium and in France. For several years now Dr. Eason has been pastor of the Jackson Street Baptist church in Birmingham, where he has put in many improvements. He takes great interest in the business life of the Negro in Birmingham just as he did in Anniston. He was a director of the Alabama Penny Savings Bank in its early days and a depositor in it to the last. He is himself a property owner, owning his home and other real estate which are valued at $5,000.

Dr. Eason was married in 1894 to Miss Phoebe A. Kigh of Selma, Ala. Of three children born into the Eason home, only one, Miss Gladys is living. She is married to Mr. Edward A. Trammell. Little Phoebe Mae Trammell is Dr. Eason's only grandchild.

SCENE IN GROVE

ALHOUN Colored School is located at Calhoun, in the agricultural County of Lowndes, southern Alabama, 27 miles south of Montgomery, on the main line of the Louisville and Nashville Railroad. Eighty-five per cent of the people of the County are Colored, 95 per cent of the precinct.

The School was founded in 1892 by Miss Mabel W. Dillingham and Miss Charlotte R. Thorn, Northern white workers at Hampton Institute. Shortly before nearly forty Negroes of the vicinity had lost their lives in a race conflict. After this catastrophe the people held religious services for two weeks, praying for a school from the North.

Among the original trustees were Booker T. Washington, who continued in that office until his death, John Bigelow, and Thomas Wentworth Higginson, who was succeeded by Richard P. Hallowell. General Armstrong, though in failing health, gave invaluable endorsement and counsel.

Lowndes and the adjacent Counties south and west were of the most neglected regions of the South. There was almost no Negro ownership of land. The crop lien tenancy conditions were unusually repressive. The cabins lacked even the crudest sanitary equipment. The meager public school funds of Lowndes County were divided between White and Colored in the ratio of thirteen to one per child.

Conditions at once shaped the work into the following departments: First, the school centre for a limited number of boarding pupils, with farm and industries; second, instruction of pupils from the cabins; third, community work; fourth extension work into the County and gradually beyond.

Miss Dillingham survived only two years of Calhoun's early toils and hardships. Miss Thorn is still principal.

In 1896, 3,283 acres adjoining the school were purchased for resale to Negroes for $21,565.00. The resale was virtually at cost price, with the legal rate of 8 per cent interest on notes. Lots averaged 40 acres. Notwithstanding the purchasers' lack of capital, tools, and stock, and against a series of unfavorable seasons, all payments were completed within seven years.

In 1907, 600 additional acres in the vicinity were brought under Negro ownership. There are now 83 proprietors on a tract of about 4000 acres, of whom two-fifths have built cottages of from three to seven rooms. Nearly all these homes are paid for.

The result of this land movement is a community which is described by standard books on the South as exceptionally moral, intelligent, and progressive, with far-reaching influence, and intimately co-operative with all the work of the school. The enlargement of this Negro land ownership under Calhoun's direction is earnestly desired by the people and urged by educational authorities South and North.

Calhoun had in the year 1916-17, 35 salaried workers, White and Colored, in nearly equal numbers. 405 pupils were enrolled, 32 in excess of any previous year. There are 92 boarding students, boys and girls. Over 150 additional applications were refused for lack of room. The graduating class numbered 18

The endowment May 31, 1917, was $107,039.25. The value of land, 21 buildings, and equipment was $95,307.36. This includes a water system with complete fire protection. The library numbers 3,853 volumes, and is well supplied with daily papers and periodicals. The following buildings have been contracted for: new barn, silo, grist and saw mill with tractor engine, and a three-room school. The rapid and permanent increase of pupils demands an addition of three large buildings for assembly hall, class rooms, shops, and dormitory space for 200 boarding pupils.

28

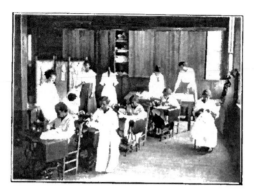

SEWING ROOM

The property is vested in an independent board of trustees: H. B. Frissell, president, Hampton Institute; Paul Revere Frothingham, vice-president, Boston; Charlotte R. Thorn, Treasurer, Calhoun; Pitt Dillingham, Secretary, Boston; Henry W. Farnaw, chairman Investment Committee, New Haven; N. Penrose Hallowell, member Investment Committee, Boston; William Jay Schieffelin, member Investment Committee, New York; Henry Ware Sprague, Buffalo; Joseph O. Thompson, Birmingham.

The support is mainly from contributions. There is no State aid. The total income of the last fiscal year was $73,236.26. Of this sum $31,803.07 was for endowment, buildings, permanent improvement, and equipment.

The purpose of Calhoun is the progress of the agricultural region of southern Alabama. The first obligation is to its own neighborhood, then to the County, then to further sections as its work extends and develops. It is in intimate and uncompetitive co-operation with the larger institutions which serve the Colored population of the South generally, and with schools of higher education.

The academic course, originally limited to the six lowest grades, has gradually increased to ten with the progressive needs of the people. Thorough drill is united with inspirational teaching, with training is given as far as the limits of the course outlooks into the world's life and thought. Normal will permit, as graduates are in great demand for

MILKING TIME

public school teaching. Calhoun graduates teach more than 1400 public school children in Lowndes County alone. Teachers of Calhoun's higher academic grades have all been trained in Northern colleges and universities. Those in charge of the lower grades are graduates of colleges or standard normal schools. Moral and religious training is prominent, in which the school's undenominational character is an advantage under the conditions of the field.

Agricultural training is of chief importance. The school farm has 388 acres under intensive cultivation; 300 acres of this are rented, from necessity. There are three expert farmers and teachers. A fourth directs the people's farming and business. The Colored farm demonstrator of the County is paid in part by the school. This department held last year a County Fair and eight farmers' conferences. Its counsel is sought continually by farmers of the region. Public conferences and extension lectures on farming are increasing through an enlarging number of communities. The response to President Wilson's appeal for more food production to meet the needs of the world war was answered by Calhoun with a doubling of farm acre-

BLACKSMITH SHOP

age, large increase in buildings, equipment, stock and summer force of working students.

The trades taught are carpentry, house building, repairing and painting, blacksmithing, cobbling, with harness repairing, cooking, sewing, laundry, and domestic crafts. Certificates are given in blacksmithing, cobbling and domestic arts, also in agriculture. The addition of a year to the course ensures the equivalent of two years' trade school instruction in carpentry and building.

Community and extension work is no less prominent than the school work proper. Community clubs and classes are held. Medical assistance is given by the school nurses at a low cost. Community sales held weekly through the term provide second-hand clothing from the North. The school's community and extension workers and others of the force are continually among the people, whose visits to the school are frequent for meetings, entertainments, and private counsel. The life of home, farm, church, public school, and lodge is open to the school's directive influence through an ever widening area, in a way to develop initiative. The County and extension work is largely done through approved persons, graduates and others, who render enthusiastic and unintrusive service.

GEORGE W. CHANDLER

EORGE W. CHANDLER is a produce of Talladega College, though a farm lad by birth. He is a member of the Masonic, Mosaic Templars, Rising Sons and Daughters of Protection, and United Order of Good Shepherds. To these connections add that he is Notary Public of Montgomery County, a trustee and steward of the C. M. E. Church of Montgomery, Trustee of Miles Memorial College of Birmingham, and founder and trustee of the Good Shepherd's Home of Dallas County, Alabama, Editor Good Shepherd's Magazine, and you have the list of services a man in quiet life can perform.

Mr. Chandler was born on a farm some six miles from the town of Talladega. He attended the country school until he was twelve years old, after which he entered the preparatory department in Talladega College. Five years here fitted him in a measure to begin to earn a livelihood.

At the age of nineteen he left Talladega and found employment in a grocery store. On spending three years at this he became inspector for an insurance company. This position he held for four years. From this date he began his life work,

that in connection with the United Order of Good Shepherds. He is now Supreme President of this organization, which operates pretty generally in the South and which owns some 3100 acres of land in Dallas County, Alabama, owns a Shepherd Home and does a great deal of useful work among its members.

His great achievement is the establishment of this order. Mr. Chandler founded this order in the town of Eufaula, Alabama, the third Wednesday in July, 1904. Those who stood by Mr. Chandler and were joint founders with him were Clark Richardson, Thomas Williams, Mary A. Jackson, Ellen Turner, J. A. Ward, P. H. Harmon, and John L. Thomas. The body at that time had one little book of eight pages and a financial card. Its largest membership was one hundred and fifty.

Very clearly re-organization was urgent, if the order really hoped to take its place among the substantial orders of the race. With some misgiving but with ardent persistence Mr. Chandler set to work. Exactly one year later he called a meeting in Montgomery, offered fifty-six resolutions, one of which let the organization be incorporated, the membership had increased, confidence had been gained. All that he asked was done.

Year by year the order began now to gain more members and a wider usefulness. It established an endowment system one year; another year it raised its policy; a third year it established several additional Fountains, another year it passed resolutions to buy and build a home for old and decrepit members, widows and orphans. With seven hundred dollars in his pocket Mr. Chandler set forth to buy land for this home. Two thousand acres were bargained for in Dallas County, for which a first payment of $2000 was made. The order was now extending its arm into other States. It had Fountains in Georgia, in Florida, in Mississippi, in Oklahoma, as well as in Alabama. In 1910 the trustees added 1000 acres of land to that already purchased, making a tract of 3000 acres.

Thus has the Order grown and fought its way to its feet. Its two farms have cost $36,000 with interest at 8%. The home for the aged and decrepit has been under continual improvement and care. During the last five years more than $6,000 has been raised and expended on the Home. All this goes to show that the trustees and George W. Chandler have not been idle to the opportunities of the man on the land. About one thousand acres of the land is improved, the remainder is good timber land, land on which flourish white oak, pine, poplar, cedars, ash and red oak. Taken for all and all, this land which cost the Good Shepherds $34,000 with interest, is now valued at $150,000.

The Order has gained the confidence and good wishes of many of the leading citizens of Mont-

NATIONAL HEADQUARTERS OF THE UNITED ORDER OF GOOD SHEPHERDS

gomery, its headquarters, both white and black. Everywhere, it has kept its obligations and made friends, and employed reliable people as its representatives. A letter from Bishop J. W. Alstork will illustrate the good standing the Order of Good Shepherds has gained through the hard work of C. W. Chandler.

Bishop J. W. Alstork of the A. M. E. Zion Church says in part:

If men are to be commended and rewarded for what they have done, you deserve a place in the first rank of those who have done something for the advancement and general uplift of the people. I regard the project of purchasing the Good Shepherd Home as one of the most advanced steps ever taken for the race in this Country. When it comes to Agriculture and economics it stands far above any Negro Society for broadness in scope and comprehension in arrangements.

Mr. Chandler believes in real estate as one of the best investments for anyone, especially for the colored people. He believes that such investments tend to raise a man in the esteem of his fellows

in a community, and to make him feel on the other hand responsibility. Through very close economy which he learned to practice early in his career, Mr. Chandler has been able to make many very happy investments in the business of real estate. His investments and property holdings are rated at $20,000.

For both business and pleasure he has been able to travel much, having covered practically all the Southern States and a few Northern States in his journeys. Mainly his trips have been in the interest of the Order of the Good Shepherds which owes to him much credit for its success as an organization.

Mr. Chandler's family is small, consisting of three, himself, Mrs. Chandler and daughter. He was married in 1904. Mrs. Chandler was Miss Lizzie Redding of Macon, Georgia. The daughter, Nettie Lena Chandler, is a pupil in school.

Mr. Chandler has the confidence and the good wishes of the leading citizens of the State of Alabama.

S. N. DICKERSON

PTIMISM and pessimism are to be found in all the walks of life and are not confined to any race, class or profession. While this is true to find a business enthusiast among the colored race is a rarity.

Such a one is Samuel Newton Dickerson of Talladega, Ala. A business rather than a professional life appealed to him and he has put into his business that energy, zeal and intelligence which wins success.

Mr. Dickerson was born in Talladega, the city where he began his business career and which has been the field of his business activities.

He was born at the close of the civil war and received his education at the Talladega College. He first entered the public school where he was prepared for the college course. Like most young colored men his way to an education was not a rosy path.

The educational facilities of the town were ample for his purposes but the question of a livelihood made it difficult for him to avail himself of them.

In addition to his own support he had the care of his mother and sister to whose comforts he devot-

ed his life. One of his outstanding traits is his devotion and loyalty to his family.

Difficulties are not fatal to a strong man but act as a tonic to spur him on so it is not surprising that Mr. Dickerson succeeded in the face of difficulties in securing an education.

Mr. Dickerson's first business venture was that of a painter which he followed for fifteen years from 1890. He then entered the Drug business which he continued for ten years with marked success.

From this line of business he entered the general mercantile business which now occupies his time and attention.

While push is his watchword in business conservatism steadies his place and it is to these two characteristics that he has scored so great a success.

Concerning life as a poor man through thrift and good management he has accumulated a good property. Besides his home he owns a store, six rental houses, several city lots and one hundred and ten suburban lots. He also owns a share of stock in the Chinabar Cotton Mill.

He is a great advocate of the Negro entering the marts of trade and encourages the establishment of individual firms but his ideals of business take a wider range than the individual and reaches out to the community life. He believes in co-operation and takes the position that the colored citizen has a part to play in the development of the civic life of the community and should take part in all enterprises of a public nature which has for its end the upbuilding of the community life.

He sees in this way the best method to win recognition and respect for the worthy colored citizens.

Mr. Dickerson's talent as a business man and promoter is recognized by his friends who constantly come to him for advice, and they always find in him a friendly and sound adviser.

Aside from his personal business connections he has headed a number of business associations.

He has served as President of the Talladega Business League, President of the Farmers Investment and Benevolent Association, President of the Negro Merchant's Association, and Vice-President of the Alabama Negro Business League. He has given much time and thought to these organizations and they have profited through his wise counsel.

In business matters he is a leader, but in the domain of religion he prefers to follow. He is a member of the Baptist Church and does his part in keeping up the church enterprises. He is also a Mason and has served as Worshipful Master of the Mariah division.

Mr. Dickerson's home life is happy though deprived of children. In 1890 he married Miss Alice Camp of his home city. Although they have no children of their own, childhood makes a strong appeal to them and they spend much time and money in helping the children of others. They are the children's friends.

He gave his sister, Mrs. T. B. Barnett, the best of educational advantages and fitted her for teaching. She is now a teacher in the Swayne College, Montgomery and ranks high in the profession.

JOHN WILLIAM BEVERLY.

EFORE SLAVERY was abolished there was born in Hale County, Alabama, not far from Greensboro, a baby boy who was destined to play a large part in the educational advancement of the colored race of Alabama. That babe was John William Beverly.

Nature endowed him with a bright mind which was largely developed through the agency of the Lincoln Normal College, then located at Greensboro, where he received his education.

After reaching that period of life when he must decide upon a calling he chose the profession of teaching and his first work in the school room after his graduation was at a school near Demopolis, Alabama. Here he served during the years 1886 and 1887.

From 1887 to 1890 he taught in the Lincoln Normal College and from there he went to Brown University, Providence, R. I.

He returned to Alabama in 1894 and became the Assistant Principal of the State Normal School.

This school was established as Lincoln Normal University at Marion, Perry County, by act of the Alabama Legislature in 1873. It was moved to Montgomery in 1889 and the name changed to its present title.

When Professor William B. Patterson, a white man, who for forty years had presided over the school and contributed much to its development,

died in the year 1915, Prof. Beverly was called to take his place and since that time he has devoted his time, energy and talents to its welfare. Under his leadership the school has not only maintained the high standard to which his predecessor had brought it but has advanced beyond it.

Having a good foundation to build upon he has proved himself a master builder.

While his main thought is concentrated upon the school room his interest in the welfare of his people does not end there. His vision carries him beyond the domain of the college and he finds opportunities to serve his people on the outside through the medium of his pen.

He possesses exceptional talent as a writer and it has served him well in the preparation of pamphlets for distribution among those who are denied educational advantages. In this way many who are denied privileges are kept in touch with the educational progress of the day and are influenced to make sacrifice in the interest of the education of the children.

He is the editor of "Practical Ethics for Children" and "Guide to the English Oration."

His writings have taken a broad range but possibly the work which has brought him into greater prominence as a writer is his History of Alabama. This work has been adopted by the State Board as a supplementary study of Alabama History. Professor Beverly is a man of deep thought and considers well his plans before executing them.

He is a farmer and owns and cultivates farms in Elmore and Montgomery Counties. He has studied closely the advanced theories of farming and has watched their practical test and has adopted those which appealed to his judgment. In this way he has brought his farming operations to a higher standard of success.

He owns his home which is located at 105 Tatum Street, Montgomery, the refined elegance of which is the reflection of the refined taste of the occupant.

Associated with Professor Beverly in the operation of the State Normal Institute are a corps of teachers, gifted in their particular branches and who render valuable assistance to the Principle in promoting the welfare of the college.

Through the splendid system of operation put into effect by the Principle and forcibly carried out by the faculty, the pupils are thoroughly equipped to fill their places in life in their chosen fields of endeavor.

The faculty of the State Normal College is as follows: J. W. Beverly, Principal; Annie W. Doak, Secretary; Mary L. Strong, Literature; Rev. E. E. Scott, History; Miss Mary F. Monroe, Mathematics; J. L. Kilpatrick, Science; Venus H. Lewis, Supervisor Study room; Albert H. Beverly, English; Christine L. Graves, English; Rosa L. Shaw, Drawing; Gertrude L. Watkins, Domestic Science; Josie Murray, Domestic Art; F. M. Lewis, Carpentry; Annie L. Brown, Music; Bertha L. Smith, Supervisor of Model School and Pedagogics; H. S. Murphy, Agriculture; Camille Hightower, Sewing and Physical Culture; Minnie J. Lewis, first grade; Josie Govan, second grade; Bertha West, third grade; Merille T. Garner, fourth grade; Dora D. Beverly, fifth grade; Bessie L. Nelms, sixth grade; Mary F. Terrell seventh grade; M. J. Moore, eighth grade

LINCOLN LACONIA BURWELL, M. D.

INCOLN LACONIA BURWELL, of Selma, Alabama, is, like the other professional men in these pages, an answer to the query: "We give money to educate Negroes, but what becomes of them afterwards?"

As a boy in Marengo County, Alabama, where he was born, he was all but destitute. He was given away to rear when eight years old, to his brother, Charles A. Burwell. While working on the farm in the usual way of a country boy, he showed ability to grasp more than the rural school had to offer.

Accordingly, in 1883, he went to the Alabama Baptist Normal and Theological School, now Selma University. By 1886 he finished the college preparatory course as valedictorian of the class. In the same year he entered the Leonard Medical College, Shaw University, Raleigh, North Carolina, completed in three years the course in medicine which usually covers four years. Here, again, he was valedictorian.

With no money and no backing Dr. Burwell returned to Selma. At first he worked as a pharmacist. Having an opportunity to buy a business, he entered into a partnership to purchase a drug store equipment and stock. He borrowed one hundred dollars, which each partner was to pay in cash, from his brother-in-law, and gave notes for the balance. In a little while, however, he sold his share, and devoted all his attention to the practice of medicine. Four months after this step, the business failed. But Dr. Burwell felt that the colored people ought to have a place to have their prescriptions filled and to get soda water without embarrassment, and therefore set up a business for himself. The store was a room, twelve feet by fourteen, which he built near his home. Perfume bottles took the place of regular stock bottles, and the tinctures were made in spare hours.

As the business grew Dr. Burwell moved, always getting larger quarters and nearer the center of town. On April 20, 1895, when steady development had brought much increased volume, the drug store was destroyed by fire. In two months, however, the store was open again, notwithstanding the small insurance. In 1904 he put up a splendid brick structure opposite the City Buildings in the business section of Selma. Here are all the attractions and accommodations that the best drug stores anywhere offer, with four persons regularly employed. There is a large soda fountain, chairs and tables in the center of the room, telephone booth, offices for medical consultation and treatment. Everything is so well arranged and kept that it makes a Negro a little proud of himself just to enter here.

Dr. Burwell has constantly kept in view his duty of service to his fellows. Educated under Christian auspices, he felt, indeed he knew, that accomplishment, talent, knowledge, and wealth were but loans to be repaid in helping others. So, he taught pharmacy to Drs. G. W. Clark, T. L. A. Tomlinson and C. W. Reid. These young men were thus able to pass the Alabama Pharmacy Board without the expense of attending the schools. Several others, now doctors, were able to shorten their course in college because of help from him.

In the late nineties, yellow fever invaded the lower South, and, of course struck Selma. The rich and well-to-do fled northward, leaving their homes and property to the mercy of those who remained. The white citizens organized a protective league to see that no vandalism was practised in the city. Dr. Burwell organized a similar league among the colored people, which detailed seven men to patrol the colored sections and any other district assigned to them. No vandalism was practiced, and both races to this day point to the incident with pride. Another evidence of the public spirit of our subject is the fact that he raised a group of thirty three men who enlisted in Company C, Third Alabama Volunteers, for service in the Spanish-American War.

BURWELL'S INFIRMARY

Notwithstanding the heavy burden of business activities, Dr. Burwell does not neglect his religious duties. He is a devout Christian worker. During the twenty-seven years of his life in Selma his interest has constantly followed both church and school. For thirteen years he was Secretary of the Board of Trustees of Selma University, of which he is still a member, giving to his Alma Mater time and service and often carrying financial responsibilities with no thought of return.

The city of Selma is one of the few in which Negroes have an infirmary. The average colored patient must stay at home, however inconvenient it may be for him, and expose his family. Dr. Burwell it was who founded the infirmary in Selma in 1907, providing competent trained nurses to give the colored people the same chance at health and recovery that others may have. At present, besides the founder, nine white physicians take their colored patients here for operation and treatment. Incidentally, this is no inconsiderable haven for the Negro nurses.

When Dr. Burwell announced the opening of the Infirmary, an announcement which gave him no little pleasure, as it voiced the consummation of a noble achievement, he took occasion to speak

DR. BURWELL'S RESIDENCE

of another of his enterprises in the following significant words:

"With a big store erected and paid for, where the Negro can come and does come, without any timidity or fear, with such business as gives employment to four Negroes daily, and with six young men inspired and prepared to do life's work as they may choose, the fondest hope of what I wanted to do for my race is realized."

These words evince a commendable pride for achievements in the interest of his race.

Dr. Burwell possessed of a zeal in the interest of his people and devoting much of his time and talent to their advancement was not unmindful of his life calling and the steady development of his practice bears testimony to his popularity as a physician.

With all these big things, Dr. Burwell is a rather intense family man. You will not talk with him long before you are informed that to Mrs. Burwell, who was Miss Lavinia Richardson, is due the greatest credit for his success. His two daughters were educated in Oberlin, Ohio. Miss Almedia L. Burwell was graduated from the College, having taken also extensive work in the Conservatory of Music of the same institution. She is now teacher of music in the Florida Agricultural and Mechanical College, Tallahassee, Florida. The other daughter, Miss Flezora L. Burwell, is interested in business.

DR. BURWELL'S LIBRARY

She was graduated from the Oberlin Business College in 1915, and is now Secretary to the President of Selma Univeristy.

Thus it appears that this man, starting rather destitute in Marengo County, has given a good account of his stewardship. Being a member of the Baptist State Convention of the Order of Ancient Free and Accepted Masons, trustee of Selma University, builder of a big drug store business, helper of the poor student and the poor people, founder and promoter of a Negro infirmary, he has certainly earned the title of big and public-spirited citizen. Add to this the splendid education of his children and his erection of one of the finest homes in Selma, and you will see why Dr. Burwell is pointed to with pride by members of the race, and you will also read the answer to the query with which we began.

WILLIAM HENRY COLEMAN. M. D.

R. WILLIAM HENRY COLEMAN of Bessemer, Alabama, followed in the wake of many of our leading men in getting his education, only he used a greater variety of occupations perhaps than most of those who have made their way from the bottom. Born in Montgomery, Alabama, January 9th 1877 he attended school for a while in his native city.

Finishing such training as he could get here at that time he became a student in Payne University, Selma, Alabama. From Payne he finally made his way into Meharry Medical College at Nashville, where he was graduated in 1900.

His ambition to fit himself for the medical profession did not lead him along a smooth path but he won the victory when he formed the purpose to succeed and his subsequent efforts were more incidents in his plan.

In order to complete the courses both in college and medicine he found it necessary to put his hand to a variety of tasks. One session he taught school but the revenue from this source was inadequate to meet his expenses so he gave up this employment and sought another. His next employment was that of Bell boy in a hotel and while not so dignified a position as teaching school it added to his income and served his purposes better.

From Hotel bellman he became a Pullman porter, covering in his journeys the greater part of the United States and going into Canada and into Mexico.

From this latter work he was enabled to save sufficient money to pursue and finish his medical studies, though he had to practice the greatest economy and added to his fund by working as janitor of the college and filling other posts that would yield him a penny to carry forward his education. Having to work hard for an education he learned to appreciate its value more and the very sacrifices he made to secure it added to its impelling forces in his after life. Graduating from Meharry in 1900, he first began practice in Crawfordsville, Arkansas. While the life of a country physician brought a rich reward in health and strength he felt the call of a larger field and so after one years residence in Crawfordsville he removed to Bessemer, Alabama, where he opened an office in 1901 and where he has continued to reside until now.

His practice has grown wonderfully during his eighteen years residence in Bessemer as has his popularity as a man and physician. He is inured to hard work and notwithstanding his large practice he finds time to devote to his social, civic and religious duties.

He is an active churchman and makes his personality felt in the religious body to which he belongs, Allen Temple A. M. E. Church.

He is also actively identified with a number of secret orders, the Masons, Knights of Pythias, Mosaic Templers and others.

While giving close attention to his patients and not neglecting the manifold duties crowding into the life of busy men he still continues his studies and often the product of his pen finds its way to the medical journals.

He made it a rule to consider the problems of life with calmness and wisdom and never to yield to the suggestions of worry. He realized that all action is followed by equal reaction and so he fortified himself against all depressive influences.

The reason why he is enabled to accomplish so much is that he carefully plans his work and works to a definite point.

One of his theories is, that the margin between success and failure is very small and that success is not so much due to great ability as the use you make of the ability you have, whether it be great or small.

He loves his profession and has given to it the best that is in him.

The domestic life of Dr. Coleman is very happy and it is an abiding joy to care for his aged mother, who makes her home with him.

He was married in 1914 to Miss Mattie Kirkpatrick of Nashville, Tennessee, who is a help meet in every sense of the word.

They live in a modern home worth about $5000.00 and have investments in both residence and business property

The atmosphere of hospitality and good will pervades their home.

ARTHUR WILLIS DAVIS, B. S., M. D.

N the year 1875, in Marion Alabama, Dr. Arthur Willis Davis was born. At that time for a black man to aspire to the study of medicine was to approach a field shrouded in awe and mystery. But notwithstanding the veil of mystery covering the profession, Dr. Davis decided to enter its domain.

The facilities offered to the colored youth in this line of endeavor in his section of the country was much beclouded, the teachers few and not especially competent, which made the road that young Davis had to travel to reach his aspiration full of difficulties.

Difficulties discourage the weak but brace the strong so Dr. Davis made his way through them to a gratifying success.

Marion, the birth place of Dr. Davis and where he received a public school education, was an educational center, the very atmosphere of the place breathing the spirit of education, which no doubt contributed to his aspirations. He had seen many young men and women leave the educational institutions located there achieve success in life and naturally he attributed their success to the preparation they had received in college. He formed the determination to secure a good education himself and having come to that decision he left home in search of his goal.

He first attended the Talladega College at Talladega, Alabama, where he received his B. S. degree.

He specialized in the sciences for the good it would serve him in his life work.

After completing his course at Talladega College he next entered Meharry Medical College and completed his course of study there in 1903.

He was now ready to hang out his shingle and in casting about for a place to begin his life work his eyes turned towards his native State, ambitious alike to serve his own people as well as himself.

Tuscumbia won his favor and it was in this town that he began the practice of his profession which extended to the near-by City of Sheffield.

It proved to be a wise choice. In the section he had selected as a field of labor the colored man lived in great numbers and stood together in all efforts towards advancement. It is hardly necessary to add that he soon had a number of patients.

When he opened his office in Tuscumbia his sole wealth was $25. This nest egg has multiplied many times.

After fourteen years of practice his list of assets show that he owns a comfortable home, a drug store and stock, two farms and a residence in Sheffield which he rents. To have accumulated such a property in so short a time shows business ability as well as professional skill. He had learned the art of saving which is the first lesson in permanent success.

His term at the Talladega College left a religious impress upon his life which remained with him. In his religious belief he is a Congregationalist though in sympathy with all religious bodies.

In Fraternal matters Dr. Davis is a Mason and a member of the Mosaic Templars.

He is the State medical examiner for the Mosaic Templars and is also the medical examiner for the Conservative Life Insurance Company of West Virginia, the Standard Life Insurance Company of Atlanta, Georgia, and for the Lincoln Reserve Company of Birmingham, Alabama.

Dr. Davis was married December 26th, 1905, to Miss Hattie Lee Jackson of Nashville, Tennessee, a Christmas gift, which has always appealed to his heart. They have one child, a daughter, who makes sunshine in their home.

Miss Sadie May Davis is still a young Miss in school, seeking like her father to fit herself for a life of service. No doubt under his guiding hand she will find her place and fill it with the same credit that he has filled his.

JAMES OLIVER DIFFAY.

NE of the quietest, most courteous and most humble men of Birmingham, Alabama is J. O. Diffay. Mr. Diffay has the habit, more common in the country than in town, of seeing strangers. In a quiet, easy way he soon manages to get them by the hand to find out what they are looking for and to help them secure the object of their search, whether this be a lodging house, a good meal, a business proposition or a railway station.

Of course there is more or less reason for this on the part of Mr. Diffay. He is one of the oldest citizens of the giant Southern city. He knew Birmingham when the town was near rural, when there were few if any street lights, no cars or taxicabs, and no street signs to guide the stranger.

How rural it was is brought out by a few facts of Mr. Diffay's early childhood. Mr. Diffay was born back in the early sixties in what is now Birmingham. He attended the county school up to the fifth grade, attending about 4 months in the year. While going to school Mr. Diffay worked on the farm. Thus the setting hereabout was closely akin to rural in Mr. Diffay's early days.

At the age of twenty-four Mr. Diffay entered the business of selling produce. Finding this not so much to his liking he next set up a barber shop for colored people and set out to grow with the town. Mr. Diffay always felt that the colored people should have just as attractive shop, just as competent and polite service as any other people. Thus as Birmingham grew he improved his shop. Here is a $10,000 emporium with some twelve odd revolving chairs, large mirrors, hot and cold water, baths, electric fans, pool room parlors, social club, indeed all that makes a barber shop pleasant to look upon and a refreshing place to visit. Twelve barbers, neat and alert, are employed steadily here to wait on the colored customers. Probably taken all in all there is nowhere a better shop for colored people than this of Mr. Diffay's in Birmingham.

For years Mr. Diffay labored here, working behind the chair himself superintending his helpers, acting as cashier and watching for and putting in improvements. His big shop in recent years has become well known, his business secure. He has therefore for a good while been free to look about the city, to watch the progress of the people and to play a formidable part in the growth of Negro business. Finding himself comparatively free, Mr. Diffay turned much attention to real estate, with the result that before the hard times came on his business in real estate almost rivaled that in the barber shop.

When the late Dr. Pettiford, sometimes spoken of as the "Nestor of Negro Bankers," started the Penny Savings Bank, Mr. Diffay was among the first whose good will and cooperation were sought. He seconded Dr. Pettiford in all his actions, was for years the vice-president of the bank. When Dr. Pettiford died, Mr. Diffay succeeded him, becoming president of the Alabama Penny Savings Bank and the Prudential Bank which had combined their interests.

Though his education was not far advanced during his youth, Mr. Diffay, besides the advantages of very good local contact, has embraced every chance of self-improvement. He is especially zealous of race education, of knowing what colored people are really doing. Then, you will find him in a teachers convention, a farmers' conference, a Y. M. C. A. cabinet meeting, a doctor's gathering, listening and quietly questioning. In this way he keeps himself young, well informed and surrounded by a host of warm friends.

These meetings are not on Mr. Diffay's required list. His Grand Lodge meetings, his church meetings are. Few men are seen oftener in their pews of the famous 16th Street Baptist Church than Mr. Diffay. Few are more liberal towards it with support, time and counsel than he.

Mr. Diffay owns and lives in a beautiful new home near the rush of the city, yet removed from the noise of traffic and cars. Here Mrs. Diffay, formerly Miss Soselle Bradford, makes stranger or friend feel perfectly at ease. Indeed, the Diffays have a cordial way of turning you loose, to go when you please and where you please and to come back when you please. Very likely there is no colored man in Birmingham who has made as many friends for the city as has J. O. Diffay.

DARIUS H. HENRY, D. D.

R. Darius H. Henry is a type of that Emersonian American who does a great many things pretty well. He has taught school, been a farm demonstrator, an editor and a pastor. Of these he still holds one or two pastorates and he still farms.

Dr. Henry was born in 1866 in Coy, Alabama. At a tender age he was given to his grandparents who spared no pains in trying to train him up in the fear of God and educate him to become a useful citizen. To them he owes all his education and all the inspiration that he received in his youth. The lad was first sent to the public school of Coy, Alabama where he remained till he needed more advanced work and he was then sent to the public school at Camden, Alabama. From Camden he entered Tuskegee Normal and Industrial Institute and was graduated from the Normal department in 1890.

On leaving Tuskegee, Dr. Henry returned to his native town, Coy, and for two years taught the public school there. Thinking to enlarge his usefulness and better himself at the same time, he left Coy and went to Avenger, Texas. Here for five years he taught the public school and, with Mr. J. W. Friday edited a school Medical Journal. He was later editor-in-chief of the Watchman, a paper published in Texarkana.

Giving up his work as editor and teacher in Texas, Dr. Henry returned to Alabama, to Coy, and began to farm. Dr. Henry owns his own farm of 1240 acres, and valued at $25.00 per acre and runs it himself. His average cotton yield is seventy-five bales a year. He runs on his plantation a saw mill, a ginnery and a grist mill. In the ginnery alone he does a great business, for there passes through his mill from 250 to 300 bales of cotton a year. Mr. Henry has not neglected to put around himself and family all the comforts of country life. The family lives in their own home which is valued at $1800 and they have around them all those comforts of fruit trees, vines, garden and stock that make life in the rural districts content. Indeed so successful has Dr. Henry been as a farmer that the late Dr. Washington once sent him to a Governor of Alabama as an example of Negro progress in agriculture. For two years he served the Government of his country as United States Demonstration Agent in Wilcox County.

Dr. Henry's work as pastor is not eclipsed by his labors as a farmer. He was introduced to the Baptist State Convention by the Rev. L. S. Steinbach. And he has proven worthy of the trust put in him. He is a member of and pastor of the Little Zion Baptist Church, at Coy, Alabama, his native home. Dr. Henry divides his time as pastor with the Magnolia Baptist Church at Camden, where as a boy he attended school. Nor is the labor of Dr. Henry confined solely to his locality. He is Moderator of the Star Hope Association of his section and he was for eighteen years clerk of this association. He has served on boards for the association and for the convention as well. Indeed so freely has Dr. Henry given himself to the cause of the Baptists of the state and so great has been his development along these lines that Selma University conferred upon him the degree of Doctor of Divinity in recognition of his growth and of his service.

In fraternal membership Dr. Henry belongs to the Masonic Lodge 195 of Coy, Alabama, and to the Eastern Star 75. He is Master of the former and Worthy Patron of the latter. Dr. Henry was married in 1897 to Miss Julia A. Brewer. There are no children in the Henry family.

When it was known that I. T. Vernon was to resign his post as Register of the United States Treasury, Dr. Henry's friends highly recommended him for the vacancy. This application was endorsed by both Democrats and Republicans as well as the leading colored men of Alabama. His credentials arrived too late but the effort served to show him the high esteem in which he was held by his fellow citizens.

WILLIAM J. EDWARDS

MONG the men who sat under Booker T. Washington and caught his vision of service in the uplift of the unfortunate in out-of-the-way places, William J. Edwards is a brilliant example. Born in Snow Hill, Wilcox County, Alabama, in the year 1870, his career has been marked with privation and difficulties almost impassable. Difficulties either make or break a man and in the case of Professor Edwards they proved his making.

His mother died when he was only twelve months old and his father left Snow Hill when he was about six years of age and in a short while the message came that he too was dead. Left an orphan at the early age of six he was placed in the care of his old grand-mother who did her best to meet the responsibility and provide for the development of his mind as well as his body.

She sent him to the neighboring school but often with only bread for his lunch. The lack of food, however, did not quench the thirst for knowledge and he applied himself to his books with great energy and determination.

When he reached the age of twelve this friend and protector was also taken from him and he was left to shift for himself. Perplexed and almost bewildered he consulted a minister in the community and through him learned of the Tuskegee Institute. He at once determined to attend this school and in order to provide the means for his tuition he rented two acres of land, cultivated it and in the fall when his crop was gathered he entered the Institution. He not only entered the school but finished his course and finally stood outside of its walls to face the problem which confronts most young men who graduate and are ready to take up the active duties of life. "What next?" Law and the Ministry both made a strong appeal to him and he gave them the closest consideration but the vision of service to the unfortunate which Booker T. Washington had placed before his mind had gotten too strong a hold upon him to be easily cast off so it decided his life work. The outcome of this plan was the founding of the Snow Hill Normal and Industrial Institute.

When his purpose was formed his mind instinctively turned towards Snow Hill, the place of his boyhood struggles. He moved cautiously, however, not wishing to make a mistake at the inception of his plans. He wanted to be sure of his ground. To this end he canvassed several of the Black belt centers, noting the condition of the people, the relation of the races and the educational advantages enjoyed by them.

When he first went to the Tuskegee Institute he made most of the journey on foot and the initial journey through the counties of the black belt in the interest of his proposed enterprise was made in a like manner. It was best to travel in this way from two standpoints. It was cheaper, and money was a consideration with him at that time, and by this method of travel it gave him an opportunity to meet more of the people among whom he hoped to labor.

The result of this journey decided him where to locate his school and also determined its character.

He found that there was a colored population in the Snow Hill district of more than 200,000 and a school population of 85,499. The people he found to be ignorant and superstitious and that strictly speaking there were no public schools and but one private one. That they were being taught by ministers and teachers not far above them in intelligence.

Visions are given us to inspire to noble effort so Professor Edwards immediately set to work to translate his vision into reality and the Snow Hill Normal and Industrial Institute is the monument to his labors. To this institution he has given his life. He has expanded it, developed its courses, added many buildings and best of all has realized his dream of a school for the people.

The founder of this school must have kept before his mind the line "Tall oaks from little acorns grow" and had learned well the lesson "not to despise the day of small things." When his school started in the year 1894 its housing was an old log cabin, its teaching force one and the number of

40

SNOW HILL NORMAL AND INDUSTRIAL INSTITUTE

pupils three. This equipment backed by a capital of fifty cents marked its modest beginning.

By the way of contrast we quote from the Government Bulletin No. 39 issued in 1916:

"Total attendance 293; male 145 and female 148. Total teaching forces 29; all colored; male 15, and female 14; academic 14, boys' industries 5, girls industries 2, matron 1, executive and office workers 6, agriculture 1.

The acorn has become a tree and proudly stands as a monument to faith, energy and an abiding purpose to serve the people among whom the founder was born and reared.

As stated above the school was founded in the year 1894 and is the outgrowth of a vision which came to the principal, Professor William J. Edwards, while a student at the Tuskegee Institute. The school is owned and controlled by a board of capable Northern and Southern men.

Its material growth has been very rapid and while it has contributed to the pride of the institute its chief glory lies in the educational advantages it has given the community and the preparation it has given its pupils for their life work.

It has given them especial training in the literary branches but in addition has given them the choice of thirteen trades.

Being located near the center of a rich agricultural belt it has laid emphasis upon the Agricultural Department.

Farming is the chief industry of the people and it was realized that a very large per cent of the graduates would turn to the soil, so it was determined to teach them the science of farming so that they would make better farmers and win from the land larger and more diversified crops. It has been slow work to teach the pupils the advantage of scientific farming over the old methods but the leaven is beginning to work and ere long the whole community will see the advantage of the Scientific method.

The school has a large acreage of land (about 2000 acres and considerable industrial equipment. It hs twenty-one buildings and a property valuation of about $90,000. Its organization comprises Elementary, Industrial and Agriculture. The elementary work covers eight years, divided into primary school of six years, and the preparatory and junior classes of one year each. There are four upper classes which include some elementary subjects, called "B middle," "A middle," "Senior preparatory" and "Senior."

The secondary subjects are english, chemistry, physics, biology, agriculture, geometry, algebra, civil government, moral philosophy, school management and psychology.

In the Industrial department is taught carpentry, blacksmithing, printing, leather work, masonry, tailoring and commercial.

In the agricultural department the chief thing taught is agriculture.

To this school its founder and principal has given his entire time, his best thought and his physical strength. In its development he has not spared himself. He has traveled far and wide in its interest and has often been heard on the platform in its behalf. Possessing oratorical powers he has been much in demand as a speaker which has given him many opportunities to keep his school before the public. His theory is that a teacher should ever be a student and acting upon this theory he attends the summer school at Chicago, Harvard and other places.

Snow Hill Institute has been conducted in such a manner as to win the confidence and respect of the entire community, white and black alike.

RICHARD BYRON HUDSON, A. B.

OR a score or more of years few activities in any kind of up-lift work have existed either in Alabama or elsewhere among colored people without the enthusiastic support of R. B. Hudson, of Selma, Alabama. He has been prominent in Sunday School work, in Baptist Church work, in Masonic Lodge, and in the State and National Association for Colored Teachers, holding at one time or another prominent and responsible offices in all of these bodies.

In working in Alabama, Mr. Hudson is on his native heath. He was born in Uniontown, Alabama, Feb. 7, 1866. He received his first education in the Uniontown District Academy. From here he entered Selma University, whence he received the Degree of Bachelor of Arts. He has taken Post Graduate courses in the College of Liberal Arts in Chatauqua, N. Y.

Like most men of the earlier days, Mr. Hudson had to work his way through school. In Selma University he paid for a great deal of his education by working at the printer's trade, and by tutoring mathematics. This tutoring led him to choose a life career. From tutoring he went to teaching in Selma University, where he taught mathematics from 1889 to 1890.

Of course Prof. Hudson is best known in the State of Alabama and in the educational world through the Clark School of Selma. This is known throughout the State as one of the best kept buildings and one in which some of the most thorough teaching is done anywhere in the South. Inspectors, State Supervisors, and State Superintendents all point to Clark School as a model public school.

As has been already stated, Prof. Hudson has been a leader in many Secret Orders, in the Church and Sunday School throughout his career. He is a member of the Knights of Pythias, a Woodman, a Mason, and an Odd Fellow. He has been both President and Secretary of the Alabama State Teachers Association and County Chairman of the Alabama Colored Teachers' Association. He is Secretary of the State Baptist Convention and of the National Baptist Convention. He is President of the District Sunday School Convention, and a member of the Executive Board of the Federal Council of Churches of America. He was delegate to the World's Missionary Conference which met in Edinburgh, Scotland, in 1910. He is Endowment Treasurer of the Endowment Department of the Masonic Grand Lodge of Alabama.

During the recent war troubles Mr. Hudson has been Chairman of the Food Conservation Committee of Dallas County, and Chairman of the Red Cross for Colored people of Dallas County.

For many years he was the close personal friend of the late great leader of the race, Dr. Booker T. Washington. It seemed a great pleasure to Dr. Washington for him to speak of the high esteem in which he held Prof. Hudson. On one occasion Dr. Washington writing the "Colored Alabamian," a paper then published at Montgomery, said: "I want to thank you most earnestly and heartily for your publishing the picture and sketch of the life of Prof. R. B. Hudson, of Selma, Ala. I am afraid that the people of Alabama do not appreciate the real worth and ability of Prof. Hudson in the way they should. He has shown himself to be a leader of rare ability and especially a clear-headed systematic thinker and worker.

The main purpose of this letter is to impress upon the people of our State the fact that we have a man in our midst, a man of such rare ability, and I repeat that you are to be congratulated for presenting him before the public through the medium of your paper."

Prof. Hudson was married in 1890 to Miss Lula C. Richardson who died in 1898. He was married in 1900 to Miss Irene M. Thompson. Mr. Hudson has two children, Misses E. Leola and Bernice Hudson, the former is a graduate of Spellman Seminary, Atlanta, Ga., and Pratt Institute, Brooklyn, N. Y. She is at present a teacher in the Florida A. & M. College at Tallahassee, Fla. The latter is still a student.

REV. JOHN WASHINGTON GOODGAME.

N Birmingham, Alabama, out on Avenue F, stands a monumental Baptist Church. The engravings on the corner stones outside record the names of laborers, business and professional men who joined hands to make this building the splendid edifice that it is. It has its big pipe organ, its animated well trained choir, its pastor's study, its spacious galleries as well as its big audience room. It cost $50,000 when it was built, now valued at $80,000. Its organization, its distribution of workers, is exceptional. It has of course its auxiliary clubs among the women, its young people's societies, its deacons' board and the like. But above all it has a regular man, in addition to the pastor, whose business it is to visit the sick and the needy and to collect funds and minister to their relief. The man behind all this work, who raised the funds, very largely from working people; who in person superintended the construction of the building is Rev. John Washington Goodgame.

Rev. Goodgame was born in the country, some years after the civil war, and while performing his farm duties he had time for calm meditation. He was a poor lad with no very inspiring environments; he was without money, and to boys without grit and ambition, his situation could have appeared hopeless. Not so with Rev. Goodgame.

He was ambitious to learn and he determined to secure an education and he turned difficulties in to propellers to bring him to his goal.

God had raised him up for leadership and whom God calls to service He prepares for the work to be done.

Without money but with a consciousness that he would succeed, he entered Talladega College in 1885 and spent his first year in college in the work department. He finally completed his Grammar and Normal courses and entered the Theological department. While pursuing the theological course he served the country churches in and around Talladega as pastor, later accepting a call to his home church in Talladega.

He was next called to pastor the leading Baptist church of Anniston for a few years and then came to Birmingham, his present home.

Members of the Baptist church felt that a school should be started around Birmingham, Who was there so fit to blaze the way as J. W. Goodgame, the man who never failed in business as well as in religion. Thus Birmingham Baptist College was launched with Rev. Goodgame at the head of the board of trustees, as the real sponsor for the institution.

The Alabama Baptist State Convention elected him treasurer, and the Mosaic Templars placed upon him the task of carrying the money for its organization. This then is the load he carries —the personal interest of two Baptist institutions the exchequer of the Mosaic Templars and of the Alabama State Baptist Convention and the charge of a big city church. To this have been added many other responsibilities. He was stock holder and one of the directors of the Alabama Penny Savings Bank and one time secretary of the Atlanta, Birmingham Mutual Aid Association, the latter an insurance company which flourished under his administration and which was recently merged with another company.

Unlike many ministers, Rev. Goodgame has changed pastorates but seldom, preferring to build substantially in one place. Growing as Birmingham grew he has had opportunity to judge property and to invest wisely. He owns, thanks to his business acumen, nine rent houses, and eight vacant lots in this city of high priced property.

All this time Rev. Goodgame has been rearing and educating a large family. He was married to Miss Mollie Bledsoe in 1890. Five children, now all practically grown and well educated form the Goodgame family. Miss Fannie B. is a graduate of the Talladega Normal course and of Selma University; Miss Minnie of the Barber Seminary, Anniston, Alabama; Miss Jennie of Cheney Institute, Penn.; Miss Lucile, a senior, 1917, at Normal, Alabama, Mr. John Washington, Jr., a student at the State Normal School in Montgomery, Alabama. Miss Fannie B. who is now Fannie B. Eastland was teacher for several years, having taught in the Birmingham City Schools a number of terms.

To protect himself and his family, as well as to further good causes, Rev. Goodgame is a Mason, a Knight of Pythias, and a Mosaic Templar. Few men are harder workers and more optimistic in both religion and race progress than is Rev. John W. Goodgame of Birmingham, Alabama.

REV. PRICE S. LENTON HUTCHINS.

HE REV. PRICE S. LENTON HUTCHINS, of Mobile, Alabama, is the seventh child of Reuben and Sylvia Hutchins. He was born in Cowikee, Barbour County, Alabama, October 13th, 1862.. At an early age he was given to his grandparents who sent him to school and did everything to encourage his intellectual growth. But his grandparents died and he was returned to his parents. They were poor and unable to send him to school. Accordingly he was put on the farm where he worked with his body but his mind was in the school room he had left. His thirst for knowledge was satisfied to a small extent by a white playmate and co-laborer, Mr. Walter T. Harwell, but he soon passed beyond the information that his teacher could impart and he was again facing the problem of where to turn for an education. This young man's development was not one sided for along with the development of the mind and body he was not neglectful of the spirit. At an early age he was converted and was baptized into the fellowship of the Pleasant Grove Baptist church, Eufaula, Alabama, by the Rev. Jerry Short. Religion became the dominant factor in his life which finally led him into the ministry.

June 12th, 1882 he was licensed by his church to preach, but dissatisfied with his preparation for his work he entered the Selma University February

3rd, 1884 where he finished a two years English course and received his certificate for same from Rev. E. M. Brawley D. D., President.

Four years later, 1890, he graduated with honors from the Collegiate Course under C. L. Purce, D. D. having taken at the same time a partial course in Theology under C. S. Dinkins, D. D., and C. L. Fisher, receiving the equivalent of a year's Seminary work in Church History, Theology, New Testament, Greek and Old Testament Hebrew. He continued his study of Hebrew under Rabbi E. M. B. Brown, Columbus, Ga., who speaks of his work in the highest terms. Among his pastorates was the Bethlehem Church, Gallion and the First Baptist Church of Newberne, Alabama. He served both churches seven years and built a house of worship for each costing more than $2000.00.

The recorded number of his baptisms during these pastorates was over five hundred. September 28th, 1891, he baptized into the fellowship of the First Baptist Church, Newberne, one hundred and twenty-eight persons in one hour and thirty minutes.

June 3rd, 1897 he became Pastor of one of the largest churches in Columbus, Ga., and during his period of service he added to its membership 185 members and reduced a debt upon the church several thousand dollars. He also served the Tabernacle Baptist Church of Eufaula and the First Baptist Church of Hurtsboro, Alabama, as pastor and was serving these churches when called to Franklin Street Baptist Church, Mobile, which church he is now serving. His call to the Franklin Street Baptist Church was extended August 2nd, 1917, and was unanimous. This church is one of the leading Baptist Churches in the State and he enters upon his work under the most favorable conditions. He has already endeared himself to the members of the church and is held in high esteem by the entire community.

It has been his good fortune to retain the confidence and love of the people he served, an evidence of work well done. In addition to his Pastorates, Rev. Hutchins, has held a number of official positions in his denomination. He is a life member of the National Baptist Convention and a strong supporter of all its interests; a Trustee of the Selma University, Selma, Alabama, and of Central City College, Macon, Ga.

He served as Sunday School State Missionary under joint appointment of the National Baptist Publication Board and the State Sunday School Board, and as State Organizer for Georgia under joint appointment of National B. Y. P. U., and State B. Y. P. U. Boards.

Rev. Hutchins is a man of family and is blessed with a wife devoted to his interests and the proud mother of eight children. These bring joy and sunshine to his home and has inspired that economy in the conduct of his affairs that has enabled him to accumulate a nice property.

His possessions are scattered from Alabama to New York and consist of improved and vacant city lots and farm property. Rev. Hutchins is yet comparatively young. His zenith may not be reached for years; many more such startling strides as he has made in the past thirteen years, will lift him easily to the rank of ministerial wonders.

JOHN A. KENNEY, M. D.

OHN A. KENNEY, M. D., was born June 11, 1874, in Albemarle County, Virginia. Here he lived on the farm and did the work of a farm lad, enjoying at the same time the pleasures that come to those who live in the country, till he was sixteen years of age. During the last two years of that time he was practically the head of the family, running the farm which his father left to his care and also the grocery store which his father had kept during his life time. Although born on the farm and although he remained for such a number of years in the country, his mother had other plans for him. She inspired him with the ambition to live his life away from the narrowing effect of the farm life, away out in the world where he could make himself felt.

After spending a great deal of time in the public schools of Albemarle County and Charlottesville he went to Hampton Institute, Virginia and later to Shaw University, North Carolina. In order to attend school he had also to work. Nothing that would turn an honest penny was turned down by this ambitious young man. He worked as a waiter, he worked in the family of one of the professors of the University of Virginia, and he kept grocery store. After leaving Shaw University Dr. Kenney went to Leonard Medical College from which he was graduated with the degree M. D. in 1901.

This was the beginning of Dr. Kenney's real career. He served the first year as interne at Freedmen's Hospital, Washington, District of Columbia and then came to Tuskegee Institute. At Tuskegee he is Medical Director of the Tuskegee Institute Hospital and Nurse Training School. For the past sixteen years Dr. Kenney has labored in this field and the work has grown steadily under his management. When he took the work there was a frame hospital, not very well equipped and not large enough to accommodate the number of patients that come to Tuskegee. During his stay the John A. Andrew Memorial Hospital has been built, and the Nurse Training Course strengthened. The hospital is well equipped and the nurses turned out are efficient.

While developing the material side of the work at Tuskegee, Dr. Kenney has himself developed in skill. He is now looked upon as one of the leading surgeons of the race and people from all over the south come to Tuskegee to John A. Andrew Memorial Hospital in order to have Dr. Kenney operate on them. This is true fame—that speads from one patient to another and brings more work, which in turn means added skill.

The profession will probably know Dr. Kenney best as Secretary of the National Medical Association. In this position he served for eight years in succession. He then gave up the work because he was over worked. Contrary to his expressed wishes he was unanimously elected in 1912 as president of the National Medical Association.

Dr. Kenney with Dr. C. V. Roman of Nashville Tennessee founded the Journal of the National Medical Association. This is today one of the most important publications among the Colored People and it takes high rank as a professional journal. What this periodical is today and in fact very largely what the National Medical Association is today is due to the energies and unbounded faith of Dr. Kenney. At the last meeting of the N. M. A. in Richmond, Va., 1918, Dr. Kenney by action of the Executive Board was made editor-in-chief and manager of the Journal.

Since entering the medical profession he has done constructive work.

Dr. Kenney had direct charge of the health of Dr. Booker T. Washington during all the years he was in Tuskegee. During the last years of Dr. Washington's life Dr. Kenney spent a great deal of time with him, accompanying him on the various trips made over the South. It is a source of great pride to Dr. Kenney that when Dr. Washington, ill in the hospital in New York was examined by famous specialists they said that Dr. Kenney had done all that any one could have done for the great educator.

Dr. Kenney was married to Miss Alice Talbot of Bedford County, Virginia in Dec. 27, 1902. Dr. Kenney was married a second time to Miss Frieda F. Armstrong of Boston, Massachusetts, in 1913. There are three small sons, John A Kenney, Jr., Oscar Armstrong Kenney and Howard Washington Kenney

GEORGE W. LEWIS, A. M., D. D.

E who is inclined to grow doubtful of rare strength, scholarship, force, personality should look upon a company of Methodist Ministers and Bishops. Gathered in convention they make a grand substitute for an assembly of statesmen. They are grave and scholarly, stalwarth of physique, pictures of health and prosperity. They are analysts and orators and logicians with splendid touches of the visionary. Dr. George W. Lewis A. M., D. D. is one of these Methodist Episcopal peers. There are few riper scholars, fewer better orators than he.

Dr. Lewis is a thorough going Georgian. He was born in Burke County shortly after slavery. He was born during the reconstruction period after the war when the efforts of the South were directed mainly in caring for the body and but little attention was given to the development of the mind. It was a day of poor schools, unprepared teachers and short school terms. The opportunities for the negroes to obtain an education were but meager but the very difficulties in their way acted as a spur to the ambitions and developed a number of strong men intellectually.

Dr. Lewis was among this number. When a mere boy Dr. Lewis started life as a farm laborer which he followed for sixteen years but during this period he attended school two or three months each year.

The activity of the mind would not permit him to remain on the farm so he left the farm and attended the Haven Normal School at Waynesborough, Ga. Here his real development began. Here the leading of his mind and heart decided his future. Here he was converted and here he responded to the call to the ministry.

From Haven Norman school at Waynesborough he went to Clark University at Atlanta and after finishing his course of study there he turned to the study of theology in Gammon Seminary in the same University.

After completing his theological course he took up the active duties of Pastor and served a number of churches in his active native State. He joined the Savannah Conference at Augusta, Ga., and was sent to Mt. Vernon church. From Mt. Vernon he went to Readsville, from Readsville to Valdosta, thence to Atlanta and from Atlanta to Rome.

In 1895 Dr. Lewis was transferred to the Alabama Conference and served churches in Montgomery, Mobile and in Pensacola, Fla.

It was during his residence in Florida that Dr. Lewis branched out in educational work.

Seeing a grave need for a school in Pensacola he set his mind to work to supply it and in 1901 he founded the Pensacola Normal, Industrial and Agricultural school. For nine years he was the Principal of this school, shaping its policies and giving it the benefit of his rare gifts as an orator. He possessed in a remarkable degree the powers of oratory which greatly aided him in raising money for his enterprises, a work in which he succeeded to a most satisfactory degree.

His talent as an orator and writer brought him into great prominence and his services were sought from all over the country. For stirring and searching addresses, such as are required on memorial and emancipation occasions, he probably has no equal on the platform of today. He has delivered addresses of this character at Montgomery, at Mobile, at Evergreen, at Tampa and at Pensacola, many of which at the request of his hearers were printed and distributed.

Dr. Lewis was frequently elected to represent the M. E. Conference at the General Conference. He was a delegate to the Omaha General Conference in 1894 and to the conference at Saratoga in 1916. For years he has been the Secretary of his Annual Conference and chairman of the Old Ministers fund. His brethren were not slow to recognize in him a wise leader a man of sound judgment and one whose devotion to religion and education and unexcelled oratory gave him unbounded influence among them. He won their confidence early in his ministerial life and still holds it in a most flattering degree.

Dr. Lewis family consists of a wife and one child, a daughter who has inherited his mental vigor.

He married in 1889 Miss Lucy Griffin, of Tuscaloosa, Ala. Their daughter, Miss Emma C. Lewis, received her B. A. degree from Clark University, Atlanta, Ga., and wears it with as much ease and grace as the average man. At present she is teaching in New Orleans University.

While the church is his chief consideration Dr. Lewis is also interested in the benevolent orders of his people and has membership in the Masons and Knights of Pythias.

HENRY ALLEN LOVELESS.

MONG the foremost colored citizens of Alabama is Henry Allen Loveless of Montgomery who has proved to his people that they can make a marked success in their business ventures and still preserve the respect and esteem of the entire community, both white and black.

Mr. Loveless was born in Bullock County, Alabama in the year 1854 near the town of Union Springs.

He had no educational advantages until he reached his eighteenth year. Spending the day in manual labor he attended a night school which gave him the foundation upon which he built to a limited extent.

Some years after his first marraige he attended the Selma University but for only two terms. At the end of the second term he returned home to arrange his business matters so that he could complete his course but found that the requirements of his business were such that he had to forego his plans for a finished education.

His first business was that of a butcher which he plied for several years but gave up to enter the Undertaking business. Here he had to meet strong competition from a long established business

controlled by a member of his race who had much influence with the colored people.

He saw the difficulties in his way but instead of deterring him they nerved him to push forward.

Meeting competition upon fair grounds he forged to the front and not only built up the large business over which he now presides but finally purchased the business of his competitor.

He has been in this business for twenty-five years which together with its adjuncts is easily valued at $25,000.00. In connection with his undertaking business he runs a transfer and hack line and has among his patrons a number of white citizens.

His business has brought him a comfortable living and enabled him to secure a home worth ten thousand dollars. In addition it has enabled him to give employment to a great many of his people.

Mr. Loveless is a deeply religious man and takes an active part in his church life.

He has been connected with the Dexter Avenue Baptist church from its organization and is its leading deacon. He is also the Church Treasurer and a member of the Board of Trustees. The ministers who have served the church have always found in him a friend and helper.

Mr. Loveless' activities do not end with his church and his business. He has countless affiliations with various other bodies and is interested in the educational interests of his people.

He is a King Solomon Mason, Knights of Pythias, member of Wm. J. Simmons Lodge, No. 34, the Eastern Star, Knights of Tabor, Eureka Lodge of the Mosaic Templars, Sisters and Brothers of Tabor, Daughters and Sons of Zera, and the United Order of Good Shepherds. He has held office in a number of these orders.

He is a member of the Negro business men's league, Treasurer of the Alabama Realty Company and a Trustee of the Swayne school of Montgomery.

Mr. Loveless has been married three times. He married his first wife, Miss Lucy Arrington of Montgomery, in 1885. She died after bearing him five children, three of whom are living. His son John H. Loveless and daughters, Miss Mary G. and Bertha L. Loveless, are associated with him in his business and have contributed no little to his success.

In 1913 he married Mrs. Emma A. Anderson, who lived but a short while with him when death claimed her.

His present wife, formerly Mrs. Dora Evelyn, was married to him in 1916. She was a resident of Eufaula, Ala.

Mr. Loveless is a successful man and in summing up his traits of character which contributed to his success we would mention first his quiet, courteous but positive demeanor. He never gets unduly excited but is not slow to take in a situation and to face it with a calm determination which impresses others that he means business. He is a just man and honest which gives him a good standing in the business world. Then he is sympathetic, helpful and dependable and above all is recognized as an humble Christian.

REVEREND WILLIAM MADISON.

HEN asked for matter for a biographical sketch, Rev. Wm. Madison sent in such scant material that the required length for a page was not to be gotten. When asked for matter for his church, the matter came in so freely that it had to be condensed. Such is the modesty of the man that he takes to himself very little of the credit for the very splendid church which he built and which under his administration has grown by leaps and bounds. But the church is a reflection of his boundless energy and great business ability.

Rev. Madison was born in Marion, Dallas County, Alabama, in 1873. As a small boy and as a young man, he toiled in the cotton and corn fields on a Dallas County plantation. Here he received his early training in the public schools. Whatever the schools of the country may have failed to give him in accurate book knowledge was more than made up by the ambition which filled him because of this contact with books and thoughts. He felt most keenly the preparation that he needed to make himself happy, and at the same time render those about him glad. He entered Selma University in 1905,

and was graduated in the class of 1910 at the head of the class in the Theological Department. This gave him the place of valedictorian. This and other honors bestowed upon him by his Alma Mater bespeak his life and conduct as a school boy and his efficiency as a student.

Rev. Wm. Madison has climbed all the way from the bottom to the top of his profession. He is at present and has been for some time pastor of the Day Street Baptist Church, Montgomery, Alabama. This church represents the capstone in his career as the builder of splendid houses of worship. Beginning his ministry back in his home village of Marion, Alabama, he has raised and put into churches $45,000.00. He has built churches at Uniontown, Sawyerville, Grove Hill and Montgomery.

In the meantime he has pastored, held evangelistic services, baptized thousands, held conspicuous offices in his church and denominational bodies, been orator and Commencement speaker at many important school celebrations and gatherings and traveled extensively over the country as preacher and worker.

Rev. Madison did not get his fame as a speaker and able builder without a struggle. Leaving Selma University, he followed the profession of school teaching in both Dallas and Hale counties. Later he studied bookkeeping and was a bookkeeper for five years. In filling these two posts he got for himself experiences that were destined to be of untold good to him in his pastoral work later. His five years spent in bookkeeping cannot be underestimated as to the good effect they have had on the building and organizing of churches. At the age of twenty-two, Rev. Madison was ordained and he has held a most constructive career in his church ever since. He has followed the circuit of his native state, having occupied pulpits at Marion, Uniontown, Sawyerville, Lanesville, Newberne, Jackson, Grove Hill, Birmingham and his present post in Montgomery.

The great work that Rev. Madison is doing in Montgomery is recorded elsewhere under the sketch of Day Street Baptist Church. He is well known as a leader, for his executive skill and also for his ability to follow details. Rev. Madison has for years occupied high places in his church and in secular and fraternal bodies. He is a member of the Allen Temple Lodge, of the Knights of Pythians and of the Good Shepherds. In his church, which is missionary Baptist he has served as Treasurer of the Publishing Board; chairman of the State Mission Board; Treasurer of the Selma Alumni Association; President of the Baptist Ministers Conference of Montgomery and Member of the National Baptist Convention.

Rev. Madison was married in 1899 to Miss Mary Soloman of Saffold, Alabama. There are six children in the Madison family all of whom are attending school.

DAY STREET BAPTIST CHURCH.

EEING what they considered a great need of another church in the City of Montgomery, in 1884, Mr. T. H. Garner and Mr. Edward Patterson secured the services of Rev. J. C. Casby, organized a church and erected a frame building in which to serve God. Thus we have Day Street Baptist Church, one of the best managed institutions of its kind in the South. Among the ministers who administered to the needs of the people from the pulpit of Day Street Baptist Church, who deserve special mention in these pages is Rev. T. C. Croom, who took charge of the church in 1894 and pastored it till his death in 1906. During his administration the membership was greatly increased and the church building remodled and enlarged. Succeeding Rev. Croom, Rev. T. J. Flood gave the rest of his life to the development of the Day Street Baptist Church. His pastorate was a short one, lasting but one year and four months. During this short time he raised $1200 for the new church. At the death of Rev. Flood, Rev. Wm. Madison was chosen leader of this flock..

The church business is administered by the Pastor and Board of Trustees, composed of T. H. Garner, M. D. Easterly, C. Posey, J. J. Neal, C. Lewis, Morris Smith, F. S. Starks, Mathew Wallace and J. S. Gregory.

The present structure was completed in 1910. The Pastor supervised the building of it and raised the money for its erection. It cost $80,000, but with the lot is valued at $50,000. The church also owns a parsonage valued at $3,000.

Rev. Madison has changed the entire system of running the affairs of the church. This was done in 1909. It has been put on a business basis. He incorporated the church holdings on a capitalization of $25,000.

While directing the finances of the church the Rev. Madison has not eebn unmindful of its activities. He believes in a division of work and responsibilities and has divided up the work so as to get the highest results. The Sunday School with an excellent teaching force is placed in the hands of J. J. Neal, the superintendent. The Baptist Young People's Union is in charge of Miss Lula Mattox, the President. The Woman's Missionary Society is presided over by Mrs. A. Easterly, while the Junior Missionary Society is committed to Miss Almetta Goldsmith.

In addition to these there is a Dorcas Sewing Circle for girls from four to twelve years of age. This circle makes garments for poor children. Then there is a Cadet Department for boys from four to sixteen years of age.

The Sun Beam Band is under the direction of Mrs. Mary Taylor and is composed of children from four to eight years of age. Finally there is the Cooks, Washerwomen and Porters Club, under direction of Mrs. Laura Hollis, President, the object of which is to promote efficiency along these lines. In connection therewith an employment bureau is operated with great success.

Robert Lee Mabry

ROBERT LEE MABRY was born in Tuscaloosa, Alabama October 1st 1874, and at an early age moved with his parents to Birmingham, Alabama. Here in Birmingham, he received the foundation for his education through the excellent school system of the city. After finishing his course in the city public schools of Birmingham he entered the Tuskegee Institute for the final touches. While taking the Academic work he specialized in the Tailoring division of the Institute. Having to depend upon his own efforts for paying his tuition he learned to take advantage of his opportunity and applied himself diligently to his studies and consequently left the Institute thoroughly equipped for his life work.

He spent his first year after graduating at the Tuskegee Institute in teaching but his inclination and gift did not lead him into that profession so he seized upon the first opening to enter a business of his liking.

He was offered a position with the People's Tailoring Company which he promptly accepted and which was the beginning of a career which has brought him reputation and financial success.

While in College he took orders for clothing from his fellow students and in his new position the experience he thus gained stood him well in hand and made his work comparatively easy.

While the connection with the People's Tailoring Company was pleasant he decided to sever his connection for purposes of his own. He aspired to head a business himself so in 1898 he formed a partnership with four other salesmen and opened a cleaning and pressing shop at No. 103 North 19th Street. This partnership continued for only a short time when Mr. J. W. Taylor and Mr. Mabry purchased the other's interest and became the sole proprietors of the business. Even this arrangement was unsatisfactory to Mr. Mabry who was ambitious to have absolute control of the business which he finally acquired, and associated with him his brother. Since that time the business has been known as the "Mabry Brothers."

In the conduct of his business Mr. Mabry has proved a most excellent executive and by close attention and honest service has built up a trade which enables him to live and lay up in store against the day of adversity.

His investments are mostly in real estate and real estate mortgages and here as in the conduct of his business his good judgment directed him unerringly. Mr. Mabry is fortunate in having a help meet who is in sympathy with his purposes and plans and whose wise economy has aided in his effort to accumulate an independence.

His wife was Miss Nettie Faith of Mobile and they were married in Birmingham August 23rd, 1899.

The issue of this marriage is an only son who is now attending the Public Schools of Birmingham. It is the ambition of Mr. Mabry to give this boy a fine education and fit him for some useful occupation in life. Like most men who have struggled for an education he knows its value and has learned that it is necessary to any marked degree of success along any endeavor.

Mr. Mabry is something of a traveler and his travels have carried him over a large portion of the United States. He has visited practically all of the Southern States, the Middle Atlantic States and in New England and has lived in Alabama, Tennessee and New Jersey.

Mr. Mabry is a religious man and in affiliation a Baptist. He became a member of the church in 1906 and in his church life as in his business life he was not content to be a passive member.

His membership is in the 16th Street Baptist church where he is actively engaged in religious work.

Mr. Mabry is greatly interested in the welfare of his people as is evidenced by the fact that he is connected with a number of orders which seek their uplift.

He is a member of the Knights of Pythias, Ancient Free and Accepted Masons, Knights and Ladies of Honor of America, the Eastern Star, United Order of Odd Fellows and of the I. B. P. O. E.

His worth as an executive has been recognized by these different orders in which he has advanced, to official distinction from time to time.

At this time he is Most Worshipful Master of the Free and Accepted Masons, Past Exalted Ruler of the I. B. P. O. E. and Past Grand Director of the Knights and Ladies of Honor of America. He is also the Grand Master of the Exchequer of the Knights of Pythias.

Possibly Mr. Mabry's chief characteristic is his love of his fellow man and he never tires in his endeavors in their behalf. He gives of himself and his means to their service and it is this which accounts for his great influence and popularity.

"Forget thyself; console the sadness near thee,
    Thine own shall then depart,
And songs of joy, like heavenly birds, shall
    cheer thee,
    And dwell within thy heart."

GEORGE E. NEWSTELL.

HE only Negro dry goods merchant in Montgomery, Ala. worthy of the name is George E. Newstell. Mr. Newstell keeps his store on Monroe Street, in the Newstell building, meaning that the building is owned by the merchant. Here one sees clothing for men and women as attractively displayed as they are in the big store- up town.

Mr. Newstell is out and out a product of the city in which he does business. He was born here, attended the Swayne school here, and has made all his ventures in business here. Graduating from the Swayne school in 1886, Mr. Newstell began his career as a porter in a store working for $2.50 per week. On completing three years as a porter he was promoted to manager at a salary of $15 per week. From this post he went to another at a larger salary. By this time he had accumulated money and bought property. As he rose in the business world and gained insight into the workings of business he decided to launch out for himself. This he finally did, buying out his former employers.

He continued in this business for some years and by giving it his personal and close attention he not only added to his wealth but gained additional business knowledge which enabled him to score a marked success in his last and present business venture.

Mr. Newstell has very decided convictions regarding business ventures. He holds that one should engage in a business which appeals first to his inclination and for which he has an aptitude, and even then he should give the matter close consideration before he comes to a decision.

Following this rule he considered various branches of trade and decided in favor of the dry goods business. It had been his rule to study from the ground up every business into which he entered but in the selection of the dry goods business he entered a field entirely new to him, but to which he brought his general knowledge of business and ripe experience in other lines.

The rapid development of the Newstell Dry Goods Store is a tribute to his business sagacity no less than to his great popularity.

In addition to his dry goods business, Mr. Newstell carries on a Real Estate business under the firm name of Newstell and Beverly. Here again he showed his business sense. Before venturing this field of operations he studied the business for two and a half years under two competent and practical teachers and even then he moved slowly until he had mastered it.

Few men have been wiser and more fortunate in their investment. Thirty years in business have yielded him, besides a comfortable living for himself and family, and besides his dry goods and furnishing store, ownership of property valued at approximately $40,000. His income from rents is about $250 per month. This he attributes to two main sources; first, a loyal and very helpful wife; second, the careful study of a business before making investments.

Success in business has brought to Mr. Newstell honors in many other walks of life. For fifteen years he has been an Executive officer in the order of the Knights and Daughters of Tabor. He is a Mason, Odd Fellow, a Knight of Pythias. He has been a member of Endowment Board of the Knights of Pythias, and is at present treasurer of the Odd Fellows of Alabama. He is chairman of the Board of Trustees of Mt. Zion A. M. E. Church, a trustee of the Lomax-Hannon Industrial School of Greenville, Ala., a trustee of the Swayne school of Montgomery, and chairman of the Republican county Executive committee of Montgomery County.

Mr. Newstell was married in 1894 to Miss Belle Saunders of Montgomery County. It is worth repeating, as Mr. Newstell never tires of repeating, that much of this man's success is due to her.

ALBERT FRANKLIN OWENS, D. D.

EASURED from the depths whence he came and the heights he has attained Dr. A. F. Owens is one of the most remarkable men of the race. Born a slave fifty-six years ago in Wilcox county, Alabama, and left an orphan at six years of age, he has steadily climbed from the position of a boy porter in a book store in New Orleans, Louisiana, to the post of Dean of the Theological Department of Selma University, Selma, Alabama.

Dr. Owens early education was picked up in night schools while he worked for a living during the day. Soon he began to teach and preach in St. Landry Parish, Lousiana. Realizing the need of better preparation for the work of the ministry, he entered Leland University, New Orleans, in 1873, and finished in 1877.

From the first of his career Dr. Owens has been interested in newspaper work. While attending the University, he edited the "Baptist Messenger," the organ of the State Convention in Missionary work in Louisiana. In 1885 he was editor of the "Baptist Pioneer," the official organ of the Alabama Baptist State Convention. Because of his experience as a journalist he is now a special correspondent for the great white dailies published in Mobile, Montgomery, and Birmingham.

Dr. Owens has pastored in such cities as Mobile, and Montgomery. He is no less an educator, hav-

ing served as a Trustee and teacher of Selma University. After resigning his pastorate in Mobile in 1906, he accepted the position of Dean of the Theological Department of Selma University where he remained until 1908, when he accepted a similar post in the Phelps Hall Bible Training School, of Tuskegee Institute. In 1913 Dr. Owens returned to his former work at Selma University where he is now located.

During the year 1911, Dr. Owens representing the State Federation of Colored Women's clubs, went before the Alabama Legislature and secured an appropriation of $8,000 for the Mt. Meigs Reformatory for colored boys and induced the legislature to incorporate that reform school as a state institution. Up to this time it had been supported wholly by the colored women of the state by whom it was organized. The following letter will show something of the labors and the esteem in which Dr. Owens is held by the white people of Mobile, – The Mobile Register.

GOVERNOR O'NEAL'S TRIBUTE TO DR. A. F. OWENS.

Birmingham, Ala., June, 1918.

During my administration as Governor I became acquainted with Dr. A. F. Owens. He rendered me very active and efficient service in securing the passage of the bill establishing the Mount Meigs School for the Reformatory of Juvenile Negro Delinquents. After the establishment of this institution, I appointed Dr. Owens as one of the trustees, and came in contact with him very frequently in many matters affecting the interest of both races. I was deeply impressed with his broad and liberal culture, his high ideals and his sincere devotion to the cause of education and the betterment of both races.

I soon learned to rank him with the lamented Booker T. Washington and W. H. Council, as a man who had a clear and comprehensive conception of those measures which would best promote the most amicable and friendly relation between the races. I early learned to recognize him as a man whose councils and teachings if followed, would create the very cordial and friendly relation between the races so essential to the interest of both.

As a public speaker, Dr. Owens has rare gifts of oratory, is polished and forceful and by his clear and intelligent conception of public questions never fails to make an impress upon his auditors. He is unquestionably a worthy successor of Washington and Council, and I earnestly believe his influence will only redound to the benefit of his own race and to the creation of that cordial relation and the removal of that friction between the races which is too often the result of ignorance and prejudice.

Very respectfully,
EMMET O'NEAL.

When the Spanish-American War broke out, Dr. Owen rendered valuable service in organizing the Third Alabama Colored Regiment in Mobile.

Dr. Owens has been twice married. His first wife, Mrs. Mary Mims Taylor of Mobile, Alabama, died in 1900. His present wife is Miss Sallie Mae Pruitt of Leighton, Alabama.

LAWRENCE L. POWELL

L. POWELL, State Grand Master Mosaic Templars of America, was born near Conyers, Ga., Oct. 1876 and educated in the city of Atlanta. After spending his boyhood days in Atlanta, he decided to travel. His first stop was in the State of Alabama. After some interesting investigation of many places as to their future worth, Mr. Powell decided to locate in the Northern part of the state in the little city of Sheffield, which at this time seemed the most prominent industrial city. There he entered the mercantile business and was a success from the start. He was successful in making a number of friends not only in Sheffield but in all the adjacent towns, many of whom he remembers with gratitude, and many of whom to this day are his strongest indorsers and supporters in his work as Grand Master.

He owns some very valuable property in Montgomery and Birmingham and is regarded as one among the Negroes who have made good in Alabama in the face of many disappointments and difficulties.

Mr. Powell is identified with many leading Lodges, the one in which he is most prominent being the National Order of the Mosaic Templars. He has been identified with it now for twenty years and has filled many places of honor and trust. Slowly he has climbed to the top of this organization in his state, and today is State Grand Master of the Alabama Jurisdiction, master over 600 Lodges with a membership of quite 15000.

As to honorary positions few men of his race have received so many pleasant returns. For eight years he has represented his state as a delegate at large in the National Assembly of his order, and for eight years has been a fraternal delegate to visit all the Grand Lodges in the National Jurisdiction.

In the fall of 1911 he was married to Mrs. Willie R. Lee, a widow of many splendid qualities, and a mother of two children, a boy and a girl, both of whom are making a place for themselves. The young man Clarence W. Lee has reached his majority and is filling a very important position in the Mosaic Templars of Alabama. The young woman, Miss Annie Helen Lee is a student at the State Normal.

L. L. Powell, State Grand Master of the National Order of Mosaic Templare of Alabama has in eight years built from 45 lodges and 900 members, quite 600 Lodges and 1500 members. This organization has added many features for the betterment of the members: Namely the burial department. When Powell was made State Grand Master Wm. Alexander (deceased) was the National Grand Master. Having Wm. Alexander's friendship and confidence he was able to get Alexander's co-operation in many ways. It was predicted by no few that this department would never be able to sustain itself, but its success the past several years has proven by careful management a "Great Boon" to unfortunate members, and today this department alone receives between nine and ten thousand dollars annually and is self-sustaining. This burial department is exclusive of endowment. It is said that the Mosaics is the only lodge of its kind that makes the last resting place of its dead.

The Mosaic Lodge was organized in Little Rock in 1882 by the Hon. J. E. Bush and Hon. C. W. Keatts. Since date of organization it has entered thirty-one states and has grand Lodge in South Africa, Central America and Panama Zone. It has a total membership of between 80,000 and 100,000. It has stood every crisis and is said to have more cash money in hand than any colored organization of its kind in the world, with no outstanding indebtedness, having to its credit over a quarter of a million dollars.

L. T. SIMPSON, B. D., D. D.

R. L. T. SIMPSON is present pastor of the African Baptist Church at Tuscaloosa, Alabama. Dr Simpson was born in troublous times, troublous historically and troublous for Dr. Simpson personally. He was born in the late 50's in Conecuh County, Alabama.

Even in this enlightened day Conecuh County is not wholly peppered with school houses. In the 50's, 60's and 70's chances for a black boy to learn the mere rudiments were exceedingly rare. They were worse for the Tuscaloosa pastor. Dr. Simpson was an orphan. Very early in his childhood he was "bound out", as the phrase used to run. He was given a sort of stint; namely he had to milk twelves cows a day and chop an acre of cotton. When this was done he could go to school as the case might be. When going to school was not possible he prevailed upon the sons of the man he was "bound to" to teach him.

Arriving at young manhood, Dr. Simpson set out for himself. His first real training was received at the State Normal School in Montgomery. Alabama. From Montgomery he entered Selma University, finishing from each department in the school, the last being the Department of Theology and was later made a trustee of Selma University.

Equipped now for life work, he set out to find a field. His first charge, as the clergymen speak of it, was found at Evergreen, the First Baptist Church near the town. This, while it was the beginning of his life work as pastor marked also the beginning of a round of charges, some very long, some of comparative short duration. From Evergreen he went to Mt. Arrirat, thence to Selma, thence to Friendship at Marion. Leaving that section of the country, he next accepted the pastorate of the First Baptist Church of Opelika and of the Ebenezer Baptist Church, of Auburn, Alabama. Over both of these churches he presided at the same time, holding Opelika fourteen years and Auburn ten years.

During the four years of his pastorate at Tuscaloosa, Alabama, where he now presides, Dr. Simpson has been engaged mainly in raising funds to complete a handsome brick church. He has been able to assemble the aid of the white people and colored people to the extent of raising $17,000 in four years.

During his pastorate and career, Dr. Simpson has held many important offices in his denomination in the state. As has been stated he is a trustee of Selma University, a place he has held for twenty years. He was at one time a state missionary, and was the state treasurer of the Missionary Baptist Convention for twelve years. He lifted a debt of $2,800 from the Chattanooga Baptist church in a short pastorate of fifteen months. At present he is treasurer of the N. W. Baptist state convention. In his life as a preacher he has baptized 6000 souls.

The Tuscaloosa pastor has tried to make himself secure for the day when he will no longer be vigorous and full of health. He owns a lot in Birmingham, three lots in Tuscaloosa, where he is now pastoring and one lot in Steel City, St. Clair County.

Dr. Simpson has been married more than a quarter of a century. His wife was Miss Julia A. Cunningham of Bellville, Conecuh County. The family group is happiest when Dr. F. R. Simpson of Ensley, the son, runs down to Tuscaloosa for a short stay with his parents.

To quote Dr. C. O. Boothe in his Alabama Baptists, "He (Dr. Simpson) is peculiarly himself and not another—clear headed, comprehensive, reasonable, self-reliant, genial in his home as well as in the public harness."

54

ELIJAH STRONG SMITH.

EGRO insurance is still in its infancy. Though the first company is said to have been established in 1810, the genuine Negro insurance business could not have taken form until after 1865. Even then, there were vascilations, timidity, mistrust. The Negro had to be converted to his own. Moreover, he had to be educated to the point to be insured and he had to develop earning power to pay the premium. Finally, the aspirant to insurance business had to be educated to conduct and manage such an undertaking—an education which one is inclined to admit the black man came, by clandestinely, peeping out of the corner of one eye while dusting the counters or adjusting the elevator.

Elijah Strong Smith of Tuscaloosa, Alabama, seems, however, to have been to the manor born, in insurance as well as in other forms of business. While yet a boy in his home town, Henderson, Kentucky, Mr. Smith was paying his expenses in school by selling books, and he who can sell books has already made his business career secure. Finishing the public school in Henderson, he entered the State University in Louisville. Again the selling

of books and merchandise furnished the money to defray the expenses of his education.

Finishing College, Mr. Smith went to Alabama and joined the Mutual Aid Association of Mobile, the company over which C. F. Johnson presides. Finding Mr. Smith already seasoned in business, much unlike the average school graduate who had entered the service of the company, Mr. Johnson sent Mr. Smith to Pratt City to be district agent. In one year's time the young man had risen from district agent to district manager. Seven years later he was made district auditor. In 1911, the company having developed a large business in Tuscaloosa, appointed Mr. Smith manager of the district.

Though a stranger in Tuscaloosa, a town in which Negroes are keenly alert in business, Mr. Smith took immediately a leading place among the business men. He had been in the city but one year when he was chosen President of the Negro Business Men's League of the city. From this time on he has represented Tuscaloosa in all the Negro business gatherings of Alabama. He was delegate to the National Negro Business League in 1912 and was chosen Secretary of his State League in 1916.

Useful in business circles, Mr. Smith is also a vital force in the church and in the big organizations of Alabama. He is an active member and worker of the First Baptist Church. For four years he has been President of the Tuscaloosa Baptist Young People's Union, and for two years Assistant Superintendent of the Sunday School. In 1914 and 1915 he was President of the District Baptist Young People's Union. He is a member of the Advisory Board of the Federation of Colored Women of Alabama.

To be sure Mr. Smith came to business and to every day life well equipped. He had enjoyed exceptional advantages of travel and contact, having traveled all over the United States as an advance representative for the Eckstein Norton University of Cane Springs, Kentucky. The officials of the government striving to select leading men in different localities to lead in war activities, eagerly sought for and selected Mr. Smith to assume the office of Chairman of the Food Conservation campaign in Tuscaloosa County, Alabama.

The whole county of Tuscaloosa fell in behind his leadership and the result was that the war department realized that it had made no mistake in selecting him and the result of his activities along this line will always be a bright spot in his work for his country.

He was also selected as one of the four minute speakers for his county and he was everywhere in the city of Tuscaloosa and Tuscaloosa County where any gathering was being held to impress upon the people their full duty in whatever momentous work was being pushed by the government at that time. In fact he was always a leading factor in all war work activities.

In all his endeavors, Mr. Smith relies much on Mrs. Smith, his wife, to whom he was married in 1896, before taking residence in Alabama. Mrs. Smith was Miss Nellie Montgomery, of Starksville, Mississippi.

Soloman Sharp Sykes

F course I don't look at the books every day, but I keep pretty good track of things both outside and in the court house here. As far as I know, Sykes owns all this property without one cent of mortgage."

These were the words of an officer of the court of Decatur, Alabama, in speaking of Soloman Sharp Sykes, self-made, self-educated.

Even these details are not germain. The essential question is what this exslave, almost illiterate man, accomplished during these 50 years of his freedom. Of course Mr. Sykes is the most modest of men. You have to wrest facts from him about himself. Even then he gives only fragments. To know about him you have to go to his neighbors. These neighbors tell you that Sharp Sykes is always doing something for his people, helping somebody through school ,contributing to buy a church, to help a school, to give somebody a start. They tell you further, white or black, that Mr. Sykes carries a thousand or two of dollars in each of the several banks of the town. Then you go to the records and along the streets and find his property holdings about as follows: His neighbors and the books all confirm this. He owns his home, a real residence. He owns his undertaking establishment. He owns his seven stores, eighteen rent houses, one farm and a seven acre cemetery. This is the property of which the officer of the court said, "As far as I know there is not one cent of mortgage on it."

He gives without ceasing. Moreover, he has reared and has educated an unusually large family. And Mr. Sykes lives for, and in a sense, in, these children. The man does not grow old. He has been able to grow with his children, to get much of their education, to absorb from contact with them an abundance of the culture which he in his youth and later struggle had to miss.

Mrs. Sykes has had more education to start with, having had a pretty good common school education. They are both religious people, being members of the First Baptist Church, where Mr. Sykes is a deacon. Mr. Sykes is a lodge member, holding membership in the Masonic Lodge and in the Eastern Star. His real life interest, however, is centered in the church, in his family and in making people about him happy and content.

Mr. Sykes was born in Lawrence County, Alabama, about ten years before emancipation and lived at a time when it was hard to get an education. He made the best of his opportunities, however, and managed to secure one or two months of schooling each year. The balance of his time was devoted to manual labor.

In 1878, while still a young man in his early twenties, he saw an opportunity to enter business, which he was quick to seize, and started upon his business career with only a strong body, a quick mind and a large endowment of common sense. This trio of gifts was sure to win success and the sequence of his life shows that in his case they did make a successful score. It is unnecessary to follow his rise step by step. Sufficient to say that he won out and that today, after twenty years of business life, he is the proprietor of a number of business enterprises. Among his business ventures is that of Undertaker and Embalmer, a large business in which his son is associated.

Mr. Sykes is not only a money getter, but a liberal spender. He does not spend his money foolishly, but in a way to help others. He has learned the joy of service and to him money has opened up a wider avenue to this blessed state. Money is a good servant but a hard master and Mr. Sykes has relegated money to its proper place of servant. Mr. Sykes also appreciates the uncertainty of riches and instead of hoarding them to leave to his children when he is gone he employs his money in giving his children the best advantages of education and to fit them for useful lives, knowing that what he gives them in this respect cannot be taken from them.

Mr. Sykes was married to Miss Ada Garth of Morgan County, Alabama, in 1880, and for forty years they have labored side by side for the good of their community and the welfare of their children. God has blessed them with a large family of children, eight in number, who constitute their pride of life and in whose interest their lives are devoted. They have grown with their children and the reflex influence of the educational advantages they have given their children are seen in their own mental advancement.

Several of his children have entered the professions and the others are being fitted to fill well any position in life that they may elect.

Miss Rebecca is a graduate of Fisk University; Miss Mamie Estelle is a graduate of Spellman Seminary, Atlanta, Georgia; his son, Newman M., is a graduate of Fisk University and is now pursuing graduate studies for a medical degree in the University of Illinois. Another son, Leo M. Sykes, is now a student at Howard University and is taking a course in Dentistry. Carl M. is a student at Moorehouse College, Atlanta, Georgia, while Melvin and Eunice are pursuing their studies in the public schools of their home city. When their foundation is laid they will no doubt receive a college training also. Children with such advantages and springing from such a sire are sure to make their impress upon the world, and will be pointed to as a monument to the wisdom of the parents who trained them for service.

JOHN LEVY THOMAS.

N Union Springs, Alabama, the county seat of Bullock County, lives a colored man who for a quarter of a century has been judge, jury and court regarding all matters pertaining to the public good of the Negro. Step by step from a poor and unlettered farmer, he has made his way to the post. At every stage he has had to stop and demonstrate. It was doubted in that section if a colored man could own and operate a farm successfully. J. L. Thomas bought a farm and demonstrated. It was thought that a Negro could not own and operate a city business successfully, the prophecy being that business equipment, Negro and all would in a short time be back in the hands of the white people. Thomas bought a block and set up a grocery and provision store and proved the fallacy of this notion.

Some years ago advanced thought and democracy poked their heads far enough in some sections of the South to declare that a Negro County Fair would be a very helpful, indeed an inspiring thing. In and around the home of Mr. Thomas timidity and inexperience asserted that such a notion was little short of preposterous. Taking his

own hard earned money from the bank, Mr. Thomas financed the Negro Fair, showing that the thing could be done. Last year the white citizens of Union Springs gave one hundred dollars for prizes for fairs between two small Negro communities. Today Mr. Thomas is preaching vegetable, poultry and stock raising. Once more he demonstrates with his own products, and once more his doctrine is being heeded by the masses around him.

Mr. Thomas was born in Pike County, Alabama, March 5th, 1863. A farm lad, he had but a slight chance to gain even the rudiments of education. What education he got was gained by night study after plowing all day. The following is told by Dr. Washington regarding Mr. Thomas' getting a foothold:

"Thompson contracted to pay Thomas five dollars per month, with the privilege of coming to town very other Saturday afternoon to see his mother. He was allowed to stay over Sunday, but was obliged to be on hand at sunrise Monday morning to catch his mules and go to plowing. He was always on time early Monday morning.

"The colored farmer took such a liking to the boy that the gave him a little patch of land to cultivate himself. This land was planted in peanuts and yielded between ten and fifteen bushels, which were carefully dried and housed.

"At that time it was the custom among the colored people to give corn shuckings and suppers were attended by people from ten miles around. Whenever Mr. Thomas heard of one of these events he would parch about one-half bushel of his peanuts and carry them to the gathering to sell. By offering them at five cents a pint he was able to make as much as three dollars per bushel. He often walked as far as eight miles with his peanuts to a big supper or dance, after plowing hard all day, and with another hard day before him. He parched them during dinner hour, when other hands were resting, and was often up as late as three o'clock in the morning to sell them, although he had to go to work at daybreak."

Although his education was small in book learning he had a fund of practical knowledge which backed by a wealth of common sense has enabled him to do things of great worth and to be a help and blessing to his race. After all this is the secret of a successful life and measured by this standard he has not lived in vain.

Mr. Thomas is a large real estate owner; his possessions comprise about two hundred city lots and several farms. While interested in the city the farm is his first love. He lives on his farm and takes great delight in his cattle, poultry and garden and from the waving corn and snowy cotton field he finds his chief joy.

Mr. Thomas is ambitious to see his people advance along all right lines and he never tires in giving them the word of encouragement and in extending the helping hand.

"A friend in need is a friend indeed," and Mr. Thomas tries to be that friend and has learned as so many have that a life of service is the only life worth living.

MISS GEORGIA WASHINGTON.

ISS Georgia Washington, the
founder and Principal of the
Peoples' Village School, Mt.
Meigs, Alabama, was born a Virginia slave, and with her mother
and brother, was sold away from
her father when she was a mere child.

After their emancipation the problem of a livelihood confronted her mother, for the new conditions imposed new and untried responsibilities.
Following the course pursued by many ex-slaves,
the mother worked out with her old master and
left her daughter to care for the other children in
the family and look after the household duties.
This was a grave responsibility to place upon
young shoulders but the struggle for existence left
no other alternative. Who can say that the hand
of Providence was not in this early direction of
her life. The discipline she received through duties thus early placed upon her no doubt played an
important part in her selection of a life work.
Home cares stood as a barrier to school privileges
and often she stood at the window of her home and
watched the children pass too and fro from school
and longed to be with them. The thirst for knowledge was born in her and would not be quenched
because of difficulties. She felt that the time
would come when she, too, could attend school and

she made the most of the little instruction that
her mother gave her.

Her mother had somewhere learned the alphabet and some few words, mostly from the Bible,
and these she taught her daughter.

It was a proud day for Miss Georgia when she
could read the Bible and this daily companion not
only served to in part satisfy the cravings of an
active mind but its principles became so instilled
into her being that her after life was moulded by
them.

Miss Georgia's ambition to learn could not be
satisfied with what she had attained. The knowledge she possessed gave her a keen appetite for
more. She applied to a white lady to further her
instructions who gladly complied with her request
and who took pride in her eager and successful
pupil.

The expense of city life became too great for
the meager income of the family and it was necessary to make a change in order to reduce the expense of living. With this end in view her mother
moved to the country.

This move brightened the hope of Miss Georgia
for an education, for there was a good school in
the vicinity of their new home.

However, disappointment again met her. Grim
necessity of earning bread thrust her back to all
of those myriad duties attendant upon keeping
house.

Her mother noting her daughter's disappointment and recognizing the activity of her mind, was
as eager as she for her to have a chance for its development, and determined at the first opportunity
to give her this chance. The opportunity came before her mother felt herself in a position to act.

It chanced that the school teacher here was a
Hampton graduate. By hard persuasion the mother was prevailed upon to let the daughter go to
school for a few months. Thus in October, 1876,
she entered the country school. By Christmas
time, necessity in the home caused the mother to
declare against further attendance. Again the
mother was prevailed upon and allowed the
daughter to go on until Spring. However, Miss
Washington had scored another triumph in her
career. She had learned to write with pen and
ink, a feat of magic to her, one which she had de-
spaired of accomplishing.

Then came other scenes of persuasion and of
triumph in the Washington cabin. The teacher
wished Miss Washington to go to Hampton. Once
more necessity stood in the way. She went, notwithstanding, but it was agreed that she would
have to return in a little while, as funds would soon
run out. But she did no such thing. She entered in
1877; saw the Indians come to the school in 1878;
saw new buildings go up and old ones torn down;
was graduated in 1882; joined the teachers' staff
and taught and helped the Indian girls in what is
known as "Winona Lodge" for ten years after
graduation.

Proud as Miss Washington was of her detention
at Hampton, yet such an engagement did not
square with her ideals. She had dreamed of forming a school in some out-of-the-way place. This
she found finally in Alabama. At the end of her
ten years service at Hampton, she was asked to go
to Calhoun, Alabama, to aid Miss Mabel Dilling-

CAMPUS SCENE PEOPLE'S VILLAGE SCHOOL

ham and Miss Charlotte Thorn, two Hampton teachers, to found a school. Remaining here a year Miss Washington set out to realize her own vision, to establish a school.

Dr. Washington knowing her desire chose her a spot near the village of Mt. Meigs, Alabama a spot forty miles from the Calhoun Institute, and twenty-five miles from Tuskegee Institute. Hither in 1893 Miss Washington went. Miss Washington came to the village in cotton picking time, thus she found that no place had been provided for either herself or the school and that very few people were interested in either her or the school. The pastor of the colored church gave her lodging for the first month. By October, 1893, she had been able to rent a cabin, 12 by 13, and to open the public village school at Mt. Meigs. Four small boys completed the enrollment for the first month. Shortly after this they were crowded out of the cabin and went into the Negro church.

A quarter of a mile from the school cabin, she rented another cabin for herself. Here during the first year she lived alone, cooking and keeping house for herself and paying four dollars a month for rent and laundry. On Saturdays, her holidays, she taught sewing classes and wrote to the North seeking to interest friends in the school. She had mothers' meetings Sunday afternoons.

By February the people had bought and partly paid for two acres of land and built a small school house, 18 by 36. The enrollment the first year was one hundred, representing thirty-five families. As the children had to pay 50c or 75c according to age, a great many failed to enroll. Indeed, the one hundred represented scarcely a third. After the first year, however, the school grew rapidly. Out-

side aid came, new buildings were added. Two Hampton teachers joined Miss Washington, who was now able to distribute the work and to teach more industries. A Board of trustees was incorporated, two white men of the community being on the board.

Miss Washington has fully realized the vision of her school days at Hampton. She has planted a school in the wilderness. From an enrollment of 4 small boys and one teacher in 1893, the school enrolled in 1916, 225 students and had five teachers. From no place at all in which to assemble the pupils, Miss Washington has put up a two-story school house with three recitation rooms, an assembly hall, and rooms for teaching industries to both boys and girls. Twenty-seven acres of land are now owned and cultivated by the school, furnishing a means of teaching the boys and girls how to farm and live a farm life and at the same time supply food for students and teachers. All and all the school has a property valuation of $9,000.00. It has touched and lifted old and young in many ways during these twenty-four years of its existence. It has taught mothers better house keeping and fathers to buy land and to put their farms on a business basis. Among the young people, it has turned out 85 graduates, many of whom have gone to Hampton, Tuskegee, Normal, Meharry Medical College, Talladega College, Spelman Seminary, Howard University and many other schools. These are now filling places of leadership where they are living. Those who did not elect to study further have gone back home and are applying their knowledge gained at the Village School in living clean, useful lives.

VICTOR HUGO TULANE.

RAVELLING around on the south side of Montgomery, Ala., you come all at once upon a two-story brick building which you feel ought to be down town. It is clean, wholesome, spacious, up-to-date in all appointments. This is the Tulane Grocery on the corner of South Ripley and High Sts. The building and business alike are owned by Victor H. Tulane, who in many ways is the foremost colored citizen of Montgomery.

Mr. Tulane is a farm lad by birth, coming from Wetumpka, Ala. When a lad of fifteen having amassed the sum of $13.60 from picking cotton, he left his native heath and walked into Montgomery in his bare feet. It took but a little while to find employment. In a year's time he with the assistance of a hard working mother, had saved $100.00. With this sum he resolved to enter business for himself.

Now this was back in the late eighties—1888, to be explicit, when a Negro grocer, indeed a Negro anything worth while in business was a very rare creature. However, investing his savings in a rust-eaten set of scales, a broken meat knife, a lamp, a peck measure, and a few grocery remnants, he set forth on his business career.

Being a pioneer he proceeded upon anything but a pretentious basis. His first purchase of new stock consisted of one five pound bucket of lard and ten cents worth of salt. As can be readily seen his fifteen feet by twenty feet store was far

too large for his merchandise. To meet a local demand he turned one side of the store into a charcoal bin and sold charcoal along with, or perhaps in excess of his groceries.

There were other embarrassments for the pioneer. Mr. Tulane had not been in business long before he decided that plowing and picking cotton taught one very little about dealing in weights and measures. Nor were there skilled Negroes in business as there are now who could give instructions. Mr. Tulane found out, however, a lad who had worked around a grocery store. This boy taught his employer the use of scales and many other points about the grocery business. It was in this early business that he went from house to house to solicit trade that crediting people well nigh closed out his then petty business, that he closed his store to deliver orders, carrying on his back bags of meal, half barrels of flour, and the like.

In four years the light began to break. He had gotten some education in grocery keeping; his business had grown. A Texas pony hauled around the goods. A fifteen by twenty feet building was growing too small, but the store now leaked painfully. The young grocer had by this time saved three hundred dollars. He resolved since the landlord would not repair to buy a place of his own. Thus began the spacious business quarters on the corner of South Ripley and High Sts. Here, after twenty odd years he keeps stock worth several thousand dollars, employs regularly seven assistants, not counting himself and wife, both of whom give their time to the store, runs several grocery wagons—in a word, does from twenty-five thousand to forty thousand dollars worth of business a year. Besides this, Mr. Tulane has branched out into other businesses and in public service work. He is the owner of many pieces of real estate in Montgomery. For some years he was the Cashier of the Montgomery Penny Savings Bank, which of course had to close when the parent bank failed in Birmingham. That Mr. Tulane's books were above question is shown by the fact that both the leading white banks and the big stores of Montgomery came forward immediately to proffer their assistance. Throughout his career he has been interested in uplift work of his community. He is Chairman of the Board of Trustees of Old Ship A. M. E. Church, the oldest colored church in Montgomery. For years he has been a member of the Swayne School Board and is one of the chief promoters of a new building and better surroundings for this school. He is an honorary member of the Montgomery Chamber of Commerce, the only Negro enjoying such an honor, a member of the Executive Committee of the National Negro Business League, and a member of the Board of Trustees of Tuskegee Institute, as well as of other smaller schools.

Mr. Tulane bases his business success around which all other distinctions hover upon straightforward dealings, giving full measure for value received, meeting all obligations promptly, avoiding cheap goods, studying needs of customers, keeping his surroundings clean, in letting his business advertise itself. Far above all this are, two Mrs. Tulanes to whom this business man expresses lasting gratitude for all that he has achieved, his own mother and also his wife, Mrs. V. H. Tulane.

CHARLES WINTER WOOD, A. B., B. D., M. A.

E is a reader, an orator, an educator and a Gentleman." It is with these words that the Chicago Defender characterizes Charles Winter Wood. So far as they go they do well enough. But the man whom all call "Charlie," who is known for his generosity to friend and foe, whose unselfishness runs to the point of abnegation, who works without regard to hours and with indifference to remuneration, who speaks no ill and thinks no ill, who never abuses even those who abuse him, can stand a good deal heavier coat of felicitation than is laid on him in these few words from his good friend the Defender.

Professionally Mr. Wood could fill several posts with distinction. So long as all these posts run to one tenor; namely the tenor of oratory, Charles Winter Wood could come away with great eclat. He commenced his course as an actor; but a Negro actor of the days when Mr. Wood made his debut, was as positive of starvation as was the early founder of a new religion. Stranded on the road and smitten with hunger the young Shakespearean, and Shakespearean he was and is, shook the sack and biskin and began in dead earnest for some hum-

bler calling where applause was perhaps not so vociferous but, bread and broth much more regular. Wood's greatest Dramatic achievement was Aldepus Rex of Sophocles which was produced by Beloit College at Auditorium of Chicago. This was in Greek.

Then, too, even if the stage had been more luring, Mr. Wood had in him a virile streak of the missionary. Somebody had put him on his feet, had shown him the way, Charlie Wood burned with the desire to do some sort of thing for another. Booker Washington was looking for a man with just Mr. Wood's zeal and ability. Thither to Tuskegee, in those early days when men got water by allowance and had to get credit for a postage stamp Mr. Wood went and began to teach English and Public Speaking. Much of the dramatic industrial work, which later made Tuskegee Institute famous was begun and developed under Mr. Wood.

But Mr. Washington was too shrewd an observer and interpreter of men to keep Mr. Wood chained very long to the class room. His talent as an orator and as an entertainer was far too marked to allow his remaining in the school room. And so Mr. Wood went on the road. He trained students to speak, he drilled quartets; he took the interests of Tuskegee Institute to bankers and millionaires, making friends for the institution and for Dr. Washington everywhere.

This man who has done so much to help make Tuskegee Institute of today possible was born in Tennessee December 17, 1870. He got what he could from the public schools of his native town, went to Chicago a poor boy and blacked boots to buy his bread and learned and recited Shakespeare for extras. One day Gaumsarlens, a preacher of great renown, was having his boots blacked, Shakespeare was as usual thrown in. The great divine saw the worth of the boy at once. Charles Winter Wood was soon in school. He was graduated from the Grammar Schools of Chicago, matriculated in Beloit and came forth a Bachelor of Arts. He was also graduated from the Saper School of Oratory, was graduated from Chicago University Divinity School as B. D., as Master of Arts from Columbia University in New York. All these degrees he earned by hard work of body and brain for he had to pay his own way.

Today he is a preacher who could fill any pulpit with much credit to himself and great delight to the congregation. He is one of the best entertainers on the road. He is an orator of great talent. Secretary of War Baker and his assistant Emmett Jay Scott saw in Wood a power as a special war speaker and Wood was called on to do his bit during the great war.

All these he has subordinated to serving Tuskegee Institute. All these he uses to be sure, but he uses them to win friends and money for the school Booker T. Washington gave his life to build. On the faculty list he is manager of the Publicity Campaign, and Field Work, but at the school and elsewhere in the country he is one of the big men whom Tuskegee has made and who has made Tuskegee.

MRS. MARGARET WASHINGTON.

Mrs. Margaret Washington

TO have been the wife of Booker T. Washington, to have stood by him in those trying years of starvation at Tuskegee, to have been of tremendous aid in making Tuskegee Institute and making in a very literal way its founder would, it appears, be distinction—enough for any lady of the land. Yet apart from anything that Tuskegee Institute could have meant to her save a place giving opportunity to expand, Mrs. Washington will go down in Negro history as one of the greatest women of her century.

Further, her distinction, though marked, will not be a distinction of press clippings and applause. Hers will be a personal one, handed on from neighbor to neighbor, from father and mother to child. Her real service in the world will be estimated, not upon the fact that she was once President of the Alabama State Federation of Colored Women's Clubs or of the National Federation of Colored Women's Clubs, not that she spoke to crowded audiences or dined with distinguished men and women. Rather it will be reckoned upon the lost and half-wayward girls whom she shielded, encouraged and brought to paths of rectitude, upon the kind sympathetic training she gave to young girls who knew no wrong and who because of her teaching remained always the pure, clean minded persons they were in childhood, upon the comfort and sustenance she has taken into the destitute country homes around Tuskegee; upon the country schools she has founded; upon the rest room which she founded and keeps open for the Negro country women in the town of Tuskegee; upon the actual teaching she has given these women on how to live and attend to their homes; upon the disease eaten men and women whom she has had clothed, housed, fed and doctored; upon the out-cast children she has reared and educated and placed in good positions. These are the people who will forever place her name along side of her lamented husband, not because she was partner in all his struggles, but because she was also a servant to the poor and the neglected.

Mrs. Washington is, like Dr. Washington, bone and fibre a Southerner. She loves the South, knows Southern people, white and black and prefers to live and work in the South. She was born in Macon Mississippi, March 9, 1865. She was one of a large family, there being in the Murray home ten children. A frail girl from her youth, she set out early to master her physical weakness and secure a thorough education. On completing such courses as she could get in the town in which she was living

she matriculated at Fisk University. Entering here in 1889 she spent nine years preparing for and completing her college course. Though poor in health during her school career, she nevertheless made an enviable record as a student, took leading parts in debates and in all forms of school activities and was the student most relied upon to see that good order and good behavior prevailed everywhere. On finishing her work at Fisk she became teacher of English at Tuskegee Institute. She had not been at Tuskegee long before she became lady principal. It was in this position even in early days at Tuskegee that Mrs. Washington began to show her real worth as a leader and helper. She soon took over all the problems of the girls and women, not only in the school but in a radius of at least five miles around the school. When therefore she became Mrs. Booker T. Washington, which was in 1892, she had grasped the whole range of problems which would confront the wife of the principal of Tuskegee Institute. From that day she has been one of the greatest forces at Tuskegee Institute, and among the Negro leaders and thinkers of the country. Practically nothing pertaining to Negro home life is undertaken without a conference with Mrs. Washington.

Mrs. Washington is a prodigious worker. She reads much, both popular matter and classic literature. She sees people by hundreds. From the time she goes to her office in Dorothy Hall in the morning until she literally makes herself leave, she is seeing people and helping solve their problems. Here is a score of student girls, a dozen country women, a half dozen teachers, all in line to confer with her about some matter vital to themselves.

For all this she finds time for the cultivation of all those delicate family and friendly relations, personal touches, a thing which has endeared the Washingtons to thousands of people. Dr. Washington's two sons, Booker Jr. and E. Davidson and his daughter Portia, she has always cared for as if they were her own. Though they are now all married and have families of their own she still cares for them with that deftness of family touch peculiar to a few master mothers. Day after day you will see her leave her office and go after Booker T. III, who is the image of his grandfather, and take him walking or driving. She is as interested in health and manners and education of child and grandchild as if they were all but one young family just starting in life. Tuskegee owes her more than it can ever pay, more perhaps than it will ever even know; for she has wrought directly much that will never die; and indirectly she performed wonders by the side of him who blazed legions of new tracks in education, in labor, in economics and in society for the American Negro.

JOHN WESLEY WILLIAMS.

OHN Wesley Williams was born July 10, 1881, in Quitman, Ga. He received his early education in the public schools of Quitman and other points in the state of Georgia. His father being a Methodist Minister he changed his home frequently and of course changed schools at the same time. He went to Dorchester Academy, McIntosh, Georgia, after getting what he could from the public schools and later did some work in Oberlin College, Oberlin, Ohio.

When Mr. Williams went to Dorchester Academy he had twelve dollars in his pocket and two suits of clothes. He remained seven years at this institution of learning and during that time did not receive one cent in help. He worked his way with an idea of making the most of his time and of himself. After the first year he was put in charge of the buildings and grounds. In this way he earned his way through the institution. Although a great portion of his time was taken up with his work he never neglected his lessons. He is in fact a proof of the old saying that "Those who labor hardest, appreciate most what they get." He appreciated every opportunity that came his way that

was for his betterment. He came out of that institution at the head of the class, graduating with highest honors.

From the age of twelve Mr. Williams had looked out for himself. In this early start he learned the value of the dollar, and once he had the money, he knew how to take care of it. His first business venture was in Oberlin, Ohio. Here he opened his establishment with forty dollars as capital. He built up a business worth $20,000.00 in five years. He did this through attending strictly to the matter in hand and letting no opportunity pass him by.

In 1912 he left Oberlin and went to Birmingham. Here he opened a Cleaning and Dyeing Business with a capital of $500.00. His business here is now worth $15,000.00. Besides what he has put back into his business he has invested in real estate and personal property. In all his property holdings are valued at $35,000.00. The business of Mr. Williams is reputed to be the largest cleaning and dyeing plant of any colored man in the world. This is very gratifying to him when he remembers that he has done it all unaided, that even in his childhood he had to be self supporting.

Mr. Williams is an active member of the A. M. E. Church. Here he gives his money freely to the support of the gospel and lends his aid in every way possible for the advancement of the cause. In fraternal matters he is a member of the Knights of Pythias.

Mr. Williams is President and Treasurer of the O. K. French Dye and Cleaning Company, incorporated, Chairman of the Industrial Committee of the United States Four Minute men of Birmingham, Alabama, Manager of a Land Improvement Company, in Cleveland, Ohio. In fact most of the time and energy of Mr. John Wesley Williams is spent in business. And in this field he is a success.

On business and for pleasure Mr. Williams has traveled through most of the middle western States and through all of the Southern. He has also spent some time in various cities of Canada. In his travels from one place to another, and from one section of the country to another section, he has been able to compare his business with that of others following his line. In every instance he has found that he was doing the greater amount of work and running the larger establishment. There is nothing of the braggart in this estimation he has made of his work. Merely a stating of facts. Indeed, wherever Mr. Williams has found a new suggestion he has accepted it gladly, eagerly. This is in fact one of the reasons for his success.

Mr. Williams was married to Miss Alice L. Neely of Bolivar, Tennessee, October 19, 1915. Two beautiful babies have come to share the home of Mr. and Mrs. Williams. Frances is two years of age and Baby Alice only six months old.

ARTHUR McKIMMON BROWN, A. B., M. D.

RTHUR McKimmon Brown, physician, surgeon, was born in Raleigh, North Carolina, November 9, 1867. He came from an educated family. He was the son of Winfield Scott, and Jane M. Brown. His grandmother was one of the first public school teachers in Raleigh, North Carolina. Both of his parents being educated and moderately prosperous they saw that their son got the best preparation that the schools of his day could offer. His first school days were spent in the public schools, at Raleigh. From the public schools he entered Shaw University, taking preparatory work. He was but twelve years of age, when he first registered at Shaw. After spending two years he returned to the city and pursued advanced study in the public schools. It was during the second course in the public schools that he began to show himself as a brilliant and promising student. By competition he won the four years scholarship at Lincoln University in Pennsylvania. Entering Lincoln University in 1884 he soon became conspicuous as a student and talented singer. His exceptional ability as a musician gained for him membership in the Silver Leaf Glee Club.

In 1888 he was graduated from the Lincoln University with the degree of Bachelor of Arts. In the same year he matriculated in the University of Michigan for the study of medicine. At Michigan University he applied himself even harder than he had done at Lincoln, and became before the close of his career there assistant in the office of one of the professors. Dr. Brown was graduated as doctor of medicine from Michigan University, in 1891. Of all the men who came out that year he was the only one who dared face the rigid examination of the medical board of Alabama. As is well known among the physicians that the examinations of this board are exceedingly rigid, Dr. Brown, however, took the examination and passed. For two years he practiced in the mining town of Bessemer. Subsequently he practiced in Chicago, and in Cleveland but returned to Birmingham in 1894. Here he remained until the beginning of the Spanish-American War. Wishing to serve his country and his people he enlisted in the United States Army, as a surgeon. He was the first Negro surgeon to secure a commission in the regular army of the United States. In 1899 he received an honorable dismissal and returned to Birmingham. Here he has since pursued a successful practice and has become one of the leading citizens in many activities.

While serving in the army he accumulated enough material to join in writing a very fascinating and informing book, entitled "Under Fire with the Tenth United States Cavalry." This is one of the most authentic documents, as well as fascinating reading on the service of the famous Tenth.

Dr. Brown enjoys an enviable reputation as a surgeon and stands high among the Negro physicians.

Throughout his career, Dr. Brown has taken intensive interest in his profession and in many enterprises, both social and business, about the city of Birmingham. He was interested in the Peoples' Drug Store, of Birmingham, in 1895. He was at one time also chairman of the Prison Improvement Board; director of the Alabama Penny Saving Bank; at another time he served as surgeon in the Provident and John C. Hall hospitals, in Birmingham. He is at present surgeon to the Home Hospital, Birmingham, and is a member of the Surgical Staff of M. O. A., Andrew Memorial Hospital, Tuskegee, Alabama. He is one of the leading Baptists of the city. He is a member of the Masonic Lodge, Odd Fellows, Elks, and Knights of Honor. In his profession, he has been president of the National Medical Association; president Tri-state Medical, Dental and Pharmaceutical Association; the Tri-States being Alabama, Georgia, and Florida. Socially he holds active membership in the Owl, Whist and Advance clubs. He is a frequent contributor to the National Medical Journal.

Dr. Brown has been married twice. His first wife was Miss Mamie Lou Coleman, of Atlanta, Georgia. They were married June 5, 1895. The present Mrs. Brown was Miss Mamie Nellie Adams, of Birmingham. He married her September 27th, 1905. They have four children, Arthur, Herald, Walter and Majorie. Dr. and Mrs. Brown live in their beautiful home on Fifth Avenue, where their generous hospitality is dispensed to friends.

NATHANIEL JOSEPH BROUGHTON, M. D.

F all the sections in Alabama to produce Negro leaders and men and women who have given ample account of their stewardship, the locality in and around Marion and Selma would no doubt carry the palm. These sections are probably just fertile enough to produce men physically strong and fit for life's wagers and yet barren enough to make them rise and go forth. Dr. Nathaniel Joseph Broughton was born in Selma. He came along in a better day than most men who have made their mark. He was born in the latter seventies, when Selma University, Payne University as well as a great many Negro institutions both in and out of the State were no longer a question, but schools fairly well established with courses and policies rather definitely shaped.

Dr. Broughton was first a student at Payne Institute when his educational foundation was laid. From this institute he entered the Selma University, a few blocks away. Here he received additional training which prepared him for his next move. He next enrolled in Walden University, Nashville, Tennessee.

Up to this time Dr. Broughton had but one

though—to secure a good education and to this end he bent all of his energies and applied himself with untiring effort.

As he approached the goal of his ambition the question of a career forced itself upon his mind. After considering the various vocations he finally chose that of medicine, seeing in this profession not only honorable calling, but a field of great usefulness.

This decision was no doubt influenced by his work in and around a drug store and where he had an opportunity to study pharmacy. He labored in this store as a means to help pay his way through college. Thus it often happens that Providence interposes to lead us to our life work.

However, there is much distinction between decision and action. It is much easier to plan than to execute. To determine upon a course is the first and important step and then follows the hours, days and often months of patient toil and effort to carry out your plans. This was the case with Dr. Broughton. He had for years driven himself, as he thought, to his limit in securing his college training.

In the summer he was working hard in Pullman service and during the school year was putting in spare hours in the drug store or anywhere else he could find employment. He had elected to be a physician and in order to fit himself for his profession he must assume additional burden and he went to his task with a zeal and determination which won him the fight.

In Meharry Medical College, not far from Walden, indeed the two schools are run under the same auspices, though with different executives and teachers, Mr. Daniel Williams, the celebrated Negro Surgeon of Chicago, was delivering lectures. Dr. Williams often wished to show how plaster of Paris was put on and how plaster of Paris and the patient behaved. Thus they needed what the artist might call a model, somebody who would allow himself in part or in toto to be shut up in Plaster of Paris. Dr. Broughton secured this rather undesirable post, undesirable for some but most desirable for him. The job served him most lucratively in two ways. It increased his fund considerably to pay his college bills. Far more valuable still it gave the doctor his first real lasting incentive for medicine. He learned to love the profession; he saw its opportunities; he got very helpful instruction both from the experience and from the lectures. He is one of the comparatively few doctors in the profession who "know how it feels" to be cased up in plaster of Paris, a sympathy well worth while and one which brings more business than can be readily appreciated.

Though Dr. Broughton is still young, and younger yet in his profession, he is well established in all that the world terms prosperous. He began practice in Woodlawn, Alabama, one of the suburbs of Birmingham, in 1906. In ten years he has thoroughly equipped himself and his office to render the best of service in the profession. He owns his home and three vacant lots in this town of his adoption.

A happy head, the family surrounds him. He was married in 1906 to Miss Beatrice L. Statton of Chattanooga, Tenn. They have two daughters, Misses Genevieve and Mary George, both of whom are students in Normal School.

ORION LAWRENCE CAMPBELL.

R. Orion Lawrence Campbell was born in Montgomery County, Alabama, December 13th, 1875. When quite a small boy it was his delight to visit a barber shop and watch the barbers at their work. Then and there he formed the ambition to be a barber, but he reached the goal of his ambition in later life, and after he had given several other lines of business his attention.

He received his preparatory education at the County School, but finished at Tuskegee Institute. An incident at the Tuskegee Institute revived his ambition to be a barber and no doubt contributed largely in the final determination to follow this line of work. He had a difficulty with another student in which he proved an expert in the use of a razor. His room mate joked him about his ability to use a razor and suggested that he open a tonsorial shop. Acting upon the suggestion of the joker he began business and while at the Institute he not only shaved the students but numbered among his customers, many of the Professors and as he expressed it, felt himself a full fledged barber, when Dr. Booker T. Washington sat in the chair.

After leaving the Tuskegee Institute he engaged in the Upholstering business, but soon gave that up for the Printer's trade. Like a great number of young men, he was posessed with the false notion that one business was more honorable that another, and lost sight of the fact that all legitimate businesses are honorable, and that the honor lies in doing well what you undertake. Under the spell of this idea he took advantage of an opening to take charge of the type stand, and press at the State Normal School, Montgomery, at a salary of $12.00 per week. He essayed to be a printer but the call of the barber shop had become too strongly intrenched in his mind to be effaced, and so his good common sense came to his rescue, and he gave up the press and type for the barber's tools. He entered a barber shop on the per centage basis, and his earnings the first week only amounted to $1.55, but he was not to be discouraged. Other barbers were earning from $15. to $20. per week, and of they could earn it he could. He more than doubled his earnings the second week and at the end of six weeks he was earning as much as any barber in the shop. By his courteous manner and fidelity to his business he soon won the confidence of the Proprietor of the shop, who left him in charge when absent. After twelve years service in this shop he acquired a half interest in the business, but only continued partnership one year. After disposing of his interest he opened up a shop of his own. He opened his shop in 1908, and still operates it. It is well equipped with all the modern conveniences and is well patronized. His motto is, "Courteous and Efficient Service," and living up to his motto has secured for him the best of trade.

His gross receipts for the year 1918, amounted to $14,000.00 Mr. Campbell has made a success of his business by following the bent of his inclination and giving his talent fullplay, and by strict and honest attention to his affairs.

It is a matter of honest pride with him that his barber shop ranks with the first class colored shops throughout the country, both in management and equipment.

He has accumulated quite a nice property. He owns a home of about $4000 value and six additional houses worth about $800 each, which brings him in a good income.

While giving close attention to his business, Mr. Campbell finds time to interest himself in all enterprises which have for their object the betterment of his race. He belongs to the A. M. E. Church, and is a member of the Board of Trustees; he is a member of the Board of Trustees of Swayne College; He is a member of the K. of P. Lodge and was a member of the Masons and Odd Fellows. As a Pythian he ranks as Past Chancellor.

Mr. Campbell has been quite a traveler and has visited the leading cities of America.

January 4th, 1911 he was married to Beatrice Gorham, of Montgomery, who is still his beloved companion. They have no children. He occupies a high position of respect both among the white and colored citizens.

ROBERT RUSSA MOTON.

Robert Russa Moton LL. D.

DR. Robert Russa Moton, who is now the distinguished Principal of the Tuskegee Institute in Alabama, takes pride in tracing his ancestry to pure African lineage. He is a direct descendant of a young African Prince, who was brought over to this country and was purchased by a Virginia planter.

Born on August 26, on a Virginia plantation ,and inheriting some of the taste for knowledge from his mother, who had under difficulty learned to read and write, Robert Moton early developed a desire to broaden and obtain more of the world's knowledge. Accordingly, he set out for Hampton Institute with a definite goal in view and reached the Institute a few years after Booker T. Washington had graduated.

Dr. Moton was early endowed with a generous supply of common sense and wise judgment. His fellow comrades often sought his advice and were wisely and sanely directed. He graduated from Hampton Institute in 1890 and soon after was employed by his Alma Mater as Commandant of Cadets, which position he filled creditably for over twenty years.

In 1905 he was married to Elizabeth Hunt Harris, of Williamsburg, Virginia, who died the following year, 1906. In 1908, he married Jennie Dee Booth, of Glocester County, Virginia. As a result of this marriage, four children are living; Catherine, Charlotte, Robert and Allen.

During his term of service at Hampton Institute he became closely allied with Dr. Booker T. Washington, in their dual efforts to secure funds for the maintenance of the Institutions which each represented. In one of his books, Dr. Washington said of him, "Major Moton knows by intuition Northern white people and Southern white people. I have often heard the remark made that the Southern white man knows more about the Negro in the South than anybody else. I will not stop here to debate that question, but I will add that colored men like Major Moton, know more about the Southern White man than anybody else on earth.

"At the Hampton Institute, for example, they have white teachers and colored teachers; they have Southern white people and Northern white people; besides, they have colored students and Indian students. Major Moton knows how to keep his hands on all of these different elements, to see to it that friction is kept down and that each works in harmony with the other. It is a difficult job, but Major Moton knows how to negotiate it."

"This thorough understanding of both races which Major Moton possesses has enabled him to give his students just the sort of practical and helpful advice and counsel that no White man who has not himself faced peculiar conditions of the Negro could be able to give."

Because of their intimate relationship and the mutual ideas of education and human development which they entertained, when Dr. Washington passed away, the name of this friend of his,

about whom he had expressed himself so beautifully, came into the minds of hundreds of people, and almost unanimously, he was chosen to be the successor of this illustrious Colored American. The following extract taken from Major Moton's inaugural address at Tuskegee, shows in what spirit he assumed the "mantle" of his illustrious predecessor.

"No greater or more serious responsibility was ever placed upon the Negro than is left us here at Tuskegee. The importance of the work and the gravity of the duties that have been assigned the principal, the officers and the teachers in the forwarding of this work cannot be over-estimated. But along with the responsibility and difficulties we have a rare opportunity; one almost to be envied, —an opportunity to help in the solution of a great problem——The Human Race problem, not merely changing the modes of life and the ideals of a race, but of almost equal importance, the changing of ideas of other races regarding that race."

Going beyond his regular duties, at Hampton, Dr. Moton formed what is known as the Negro Organization Society, in Virginia. Through its influence, 350,000 Negroes are being helped in the fundamentals of life, health, education, agriculture, home making. Dr. Moton is the founder and present honorary president. He is also the chairman of the Executive Committee of the National Negro Business League and the Chairman of the Executive Committee of the Anna T. Jeanes Foundation.

During the period of the war, Dr. Moton was instrumental in negotiating a loan of five million dollars from the United States government for use in Liberia. He also was very active in speaking to the people on many tours in the interest of War Savings Stamps, Liberty Loan Drives and the conservation of food. He has recently been appointed the Negro representatives on the Permanent Roosevelt Memorial National Committee.

Early in December, 1918, at the sacrifice of a great many matters of his own which needed immediate attention, Dr. Moton left his own important work to go to France at the special request of President Wilson and Secretary Baker, to do special morale work among the colored soldiers, who had made such a fine record for valor and courage. He spoke to thousands of these soldiers, black and white, urging them to return to their homes in a spirit of service and firm in their efforts to help uplift humanity and establish a real democracy in America.

The degree of L. L. D. has been conferred upon him by Oberlin College and Virginia Union University in Richmond, Virginia.

To show in what degree Dr. Moton is keeping alive the spirit of Tuskegee Institute, and of Dr. Washington, the following quotation is taken from one of the leading Southern White papers, in Charlotte, North Carolina:

"So long as the Booker T. Washington ideals prevail at Tuskegee, that institution will continue to perform a valuable service to the Negroes of the South, and under the management of Dr. Moton, these ideals have been lived up to in an admirable manner.'

CADETS ON PARADE AT TUSKEGEE INSTITUTE.

THE school was established by an an act of Alabama Legislature——session of 1880, as the Tuskegee State Normal School. Two thousand dolars was appropriated to pay salaries. The first session, July 4, 1881, opened in a rented shanty church, with 30 pupils, and one teacher. The first prncipal of the institution, Booker T. Washington, brought to the work his own creative ability and the educational ideals of his friend and teacher, Samuel Chapman Armstrong, the founder of Hampton Institute. He continued as principal until his death, in November, 1915. Through his tact and energy the plant and endowment have been increased to an aggregate value of almost 4,000,000. In 1893 the institution was incorporated under its present name. In 1899 the United States Congress gave the school 25,000 acres of mineral land. Of this, 5,100 acres have been sold and the proceeds applied to the endowment fund. The remaining 19,900 acres are valued at $250,000. The ownership and control of the institution are vested in a board of trustees composed of influential white and colored men from the North and from the South.

Since the foundation of the school over ten thousand men and women have finished a full or partial course. They have gone out and are doing good work, mainly as industrial workers.

The total enrollment in the normal and industrial departments in 1918-1919 was 1,620. This included representatives from thirty-five states and eighteen foreign countries. This did not, however, include 242 pupils in the training school or Children's House; and 572 in the Summer School. The total number of those who had the benefit of the schools training was 2,432.

There are forty trades or professions taught. The industries are grouped under three departments:

The school of agriculture, the department of mechanical industries and the industries for girls. There is also a hospital and nurse training school. Each of these departments has a separate building or group of buildings in which its work is carried on. The agricultural school, in addition to its laboratories, has the farm and experiment station where practical and experimental work is done. The farm includes over 2,000 acres. The work of the farm is carried on by 200 students and 14 instructors.

The mechanical industries include auto-mechanics, carpentry, brickmasonry, wood working, printing, tailoring, blacksmithing, shoemaking, founding, wheelwrighting, harness making, carriage trimming, plumbing, steam fitting, electrical engineering, architectual and mechanical drawing, tin-smithing, painting and brick making.

The girls' industries include laundering, domestic science, plain sewing, dressmaking, millinery, and home crafts, under which are included bead work, broom making, rug making, chair seating and home decorations basketry.

There is a systematic effort to correlate the academic studies with the industrial training and practical interests of the pupils. By this means, the industrial work of the students is lifted above the level of mere drudgery and becomes a demonstration. On the other hand, the principals acquired in the academic studies gain in definiteness, precision and interest by application to actual situations and real objects. The academic department is divided into a night and a day school. The night school is designed for those who are too poor to pay the small charges made to the day school. The night school pupils spend five evenings each week in academic work; the day school pupils, three days each week. Teaching in the academic department is carried on by a faculty of forty-four teachers. They are expected to visit every week

WHITE HALL, ONE OF THE DORMITORIES FOR YOUNG WOMEN AT TUSKEGEE INSTITUTE.

some one division of the shops or farm and report upon it in order to find the illustrative material for their class room work. Pupils in their rhetoricals, read papers on and give demonstrations of the work they have done in the shops.

The Phelps Hall Bible Training School was established in 1892 to assist in improving the Negro ministry. It aims to give its students a comprehensive knowledge of the English Bible and such training as will fit them to work as preachers and missionaries under the conditions existing among their people.

The hospital and nurse training school was started in 1892. Over one hundred nurses have graduated and are doing good work in different parts of the country.

EXTENSION: The extension department provides a large number of activities for the improvement of educational, agricultural, business, home health and religious life of the colored people of the United States. These activities vary from those limited to the needs of the institute community to those of national significance. The local organizations include the building and loan associations, home building society, women's clubs, health and religious organizations. Country-wide movements include the supervision and building of rural schools, farm demonstration work, and health campaigns. The State-wide and national activities are largely the result of Dr. Washington's influence over the colored people and the esteem with which he was regarded by white people, North and South. The most important of these are the National Business League, with its State and local organizations, and the State educational tours which Dr. Washington conducted in almost every Southern State.

Probably the most influential of the extension efforts is the Negro Farmers' Conference, held annually at the institute. The conference brings together thousands of colored farmers from neighboring counties and hundreds from other parts of the State and neighboring States. In addition, many influential white and colored people from every part of the country have gone to Tuskegee to see the assembly guided by Dr. Washington. On the day following the large meeting a "Workers' conference" is held. This is composed of persons who are directing all forms of endeavor for the improvement of the Negro race. Closely connected with the farmers' conference is the short course in agriculture consisting of two weeks of study and observation at the institute. It is widely attended by farmers of surrounding countries.

The experiment farm established at Tuskegee in 1896 by the State legislature is conducting experiments in soil cultivation for the benefit of the colored farmers of the State.

The school publications include two regular papers and many valuable pamphlets. The Tuskegee Student is a bimonthly devoted to the interests of the pupils, teachers and graduates. The Southern Letter, a record of the graduates and former students is issued monthly and sent to persons interested in Tuskegee. The Negro Year Book is a compendium of valuable facts concerning the Negro in the United States.

TEACHER TRAINING: The teacher-training course includes psychology, history of education, methods, management, school administration, reviews, and methods in elementary subjects, drawing, physical training, nature study, and 10 weeks of practice teaching at the Children's House. The Children's House is a large seven-grade school maintained co-operatively by Tuskegee and the county. It has facilities for manual work, household arts, and school garden. It is an excellent laboratory for observation and practice teaching. Arrangements have also been made with the county superintendents whereby a limited number of seniors in the course teach six weeks in the country schools. Some pay is received for this teaching. The work outlined covers two years for graduate students. If, however, the teacher-training hamama last two undergraduate years are elected the course may be completed in one year of graduate work.

GIRLS OF THE SENIOR CLASS AT TUSKEGEE INSTITUTE LEARNING MANUAL TRAINING.

MUSIC: All pupils receive some training in vocal music. Special attention is given to the plantation melodies, which are taught not only for their musical value, but as an expression of the spiritual life and moral struggles of the Negroes in America. Instruction on the piano is provided for those who are able to pay the special fee.

DISCIPLINE AND PHYSICAL TRAINING: The military system is maintained among the young men to cultivate habits or order, neatness and obedience. The rooms are inspected and the grounds are policed through the military system. Physical training is provided for the young women under the direction of a woman trained in gymnastics. The

young women's rooms are inspected by the matrons in charge of the dormitories.

Religious training: Considerable provision is made for religious services. The activities include Sunday school classes and daily chapel services, which are attended by all pupils. The voluntary religious organizations are the Young Men's Christian Association, the Young Women's Christian Association, Christian Endeavor Society, Temperance Union, and Missionary Society.

LIBRARY: The Carnegie Library contains a stock room, reading room, librarian's office, and two rooms for magazines and newspapers. Three workers have charge of the library department

THE SUMMER SCHOOL AT TUSKEGEE INSTITUTE.

TOMPKINS DINING HALL, TUSKEGEE INSTITUTE.

HON EMMETT JAY SCOTT

Emmett Jay Scott

FROM "Who's Who in America," we learn that Mr. Scott was born February 13th, 1873, at Houston, Texas, the son of Mr. and Mrs. Horace L. Scott. At an early age, after he completed the course of instruction in the Colored High School.

He was influenced by Bishop J. B. Scott and Rev. W. H. Logan, D. D., to enter Wiley University. In order to help provide funds for his education young "Emmett" carried the mail from the post-office at Marshall, to the school, a distance of a mile and a half.

For his services he received Five Dollars per month. This was during the years of 1887-1888.

Having to divide his summer earnings with the younger children of the family, he did not return to Wiley, during the 1889 term until late, for the lack of funds, and in consequence lost his position of mail carrier. Nothing daunted, he chopped wood and fed the school's hogs; later on, however during the same year, he became bookkeeper in the President's office, which "job" he held until the end of the school year. The following summer young Scott was employed as janitor in the Pillot Building, and it was here that he first had a real opportunity to demonstrate his natural aptitude for office work. He attracted the attention of a good-hearted Yankee, who was President of the Warren Lumber Company and publisher of the "Texas Trade Journal." During odd hours of the day when he was around in the building he was given an opportunity to make a little extra money addressing wrappers and envelopes for this company and a little later on, through the kindness of a Southern White man, he was permitted to do similar work for the Houston Commercial Club, and finally became one of their regular workers until the club was disbanded. For several months after this he was unable to find any work to do until a colored man, Mr. Gibbs McDonald, who was generally known in Houston as "Old Man Gibbs," secured for him a position as assistant janitor and messenger in the office of the "Houston Daily Post."

Mr. J. L. Watson, Secretary and Treasurer of the Post Publishing Company, very soon noticed his good penmanship, and on one occasion, on a very busy day, put him to addressing envelopes. Later, as they found his willing and ambitious, other responsibilities were given him, to all of which he measured up with surprising satisfaction.

Even at that time the "Houston Post" was the leading paper of the Southwest and under Mr. Watson's management became a strong and powerful influence in the political and business development of the South, a place which it still holds.

Mr. Scott himself did not know how well-developed were his powers of observation and expression until on one occasion, when the commencement exercises at Prairie View Normal School were being held and "The Post" could not spare a reporter to go to attend. Mr. Johnson suggest-

ed that he go to Prairie View and secure the story for "The Post." The story which he brought back from Prairieview, and which was published in "The Post" was prepared with all the detail and finesse of a veteran reporter. When he left the employ of the "Houston Post" he had reached that stage of his growth where he needed a further outlet for his natural talents. About that time the "Texas Freeman" was launched at Houston with J. S. Tibbitt as Editor; Emmett J. Scott, Associate Editor, and Charles N. Love as Business Manager. Later Mr. Scott and Mr. Love acquired Mr. Tibbitt's interest and for three years "The Freeman," under their management, was the most powerful and influential organ of the colored people of Texas. Mr. Love continues the publication.

It was one of the most significant occurances in Mr. Scott's career as Editor of "The Freeman" that he was one of the first colored men with sufficient vision and interpretation of the signs of times to see that Booker T. Washington was destined to be the leader of thought among his race. This is best told in the recent book, entitled "Booker T. Washington—Builder of a Civilization," of which Mr. Scott and Mr. Lyman Beecher Stowe, grandson of the late Harriet Beecher Stowe, are co-authors. Concerning Dr. Washington's famous Atlanta address in 1895 the book says:

"One of the first colored men so to acclaim him was Emmett J. Scott, who was then editing a Negro newspaper in Houston, Texas, and little realized that he was to become the most intimate associate of the new leader. In an editorial Mr. Scott said of this, the famous Atlanta address: 'Without resort to exaggeration, it is but simple justice to call the address great. Great in the absolute modesty, self-respect and dignity with which the speaker presented a platform upon which, as Clark Howell, of the "Atlanta Constitution" says, "both races, blacks and whites, can stand with full justice to each."

Since he went to Tuskegee in 1897 as Mr. Washington's secretary, the part which he has played in the development of Tuskegee Institute and its varied activities is well known to those of our race who are conversant with current activities. In 1901, he was elected Secretary of the National Negro Business League, which position he has held regularly ever since, and no one in touch with the work of the Business League can think of this splendid organization without associating with it the name of Emmett J. Scott. In 1909, Mr. Scott was a member of the American Commission to Liberia, appointed by President William H. Taft. His study of Liberian conditions has been put in pamphlet form, under the title "Is Liberia Worth Saving?" and is recognized as an authoritative treatise on Liberia and its possibilities. In 1912 he was Secretary of the International Conference on the Negro, which met at Tuskegee Institute.

Mr. Scott's larger activities, other than these here outlined, have been his co-authorship with Dr. Washington in writing the book "Tuskegee and Its

People," published in 1910, and with Lyman Beecher Stowe in writing the book "Booker T Washington," published in 1916

When America entered the war in 1917, there was considerable uneasiness as to what would be the status of the Negro in the war and quite naturally Tuskegee Institute was one of the centers which helped in adjusting these conditions Dr Moton, Principal, and Mr Scott made frequent visits to New York and Washington, and were constantly in consultation with the authorities at Washington Out of these discussions and together with the activities of other agencies working towards the same end, the Officer's Training Camp for Negro Officers was established at Des Moines, Iowa, and later following a conversation between Dr Moton and Mr Scott, Dr Moton interviewed President Wilson and suggested that a colored man be designated as an Assistant or Advisor in the War Department to pass upon various matters affecting the Negro soldiers who were then being inducted into the service and as the result, Mr Scott went to Washington on October 1st, 1917, and from then until July 1st, 1919, served as Special Assistant to the Secretary of War

Among the things that the record of Mr Scott's work in the War Department will show are the following

1   The formation of a Speakers' Bureau, or "Committee of One Hundred," to enlighten the Colored Americans on the war aims of the government

2   Aiding in the breaking up of discrimination based on color, in the great ship-building plant at Hog Island

3   Establishing morale officers and agents at the Industrial plants, North and South where large numbers of colored workmen were employed

4   He was largely instrumental in the enrollment of Colored Red Cross Nurses and securing authorization for the utilization of their services in base hospitals at six army camps, in which colored soldiers were located—Funston, Dix, Taylor, Sherman, Grant and Dodge

5   The continuance of the training camps for colored officers and the increase in their number and an enlargement of their scope of training

6   Betterment of the general conditions in the camps where Negroes are stationed in large numbers, and positive steps taken to reduce race friction to a minimum wherever soldiers or opposite races are brought into contact

7   The extension to young colored men the opportunity for special training in technical, mechanical, and military science in the various schools and colleges of the country, provision having been made for the training of twenty thousand through the Students' Army Training Corps, and other practical agencies of instruction

8   An increase from four to sixty in the number of colored chaplains for the army service

9   The recall of Colonel Charles Young to active service in the United States Army

10   The establishment of a Woman's Branch under the Council of National Defense, with a colored field agent, Mrs Alice Dunbar Nelson, to organize the colored women of the country for systematic war work

11   The appointment of the first colored regularly-commissioned war correspondent, to report military operations on the western front in France

12   The opening of every branch of the military service to colored men, on equal terms with all others, and the commissioning of many colored men as officers in the Medical Corps

13   Large increase in the number of colored line officers—the total increasing from less than a dozen at the beginning of the war to more than 1,200

14   Direct aid and material encouragement in the "drives" for the Liberty Loans, the Red Cross, the Y M C A, Y W C A, and United War Work Relief Agencies in general

15   The calling and successful direction of a Conference of Colored Editors and Leaders, which went far to promote the morale of the 12 000,000 colored Americans, and led to a declaration of the Government's sympathetic attitude toward the desires and aspirations of its colored citizenry No conference held for the consideration of Negro problems has been so fruitful of big results as this

Dr Moton, in making his annual report to the Trustees of Tuskegee Institute in 1918, said of Mr Scott

"Our Secretary Mr Emmett J Scott, who labored so faithfully with Dr Washington during his lifetime, and who is standing by the present Principal with equal loyalty, was loaned to the Government to become Special Assistant to the Secretary of War Mr Scott is fitted, as perhaps no other man in the country, to do this work with rare tact and good judgment Added to his splendid native ability, he has had a peculiar experience here at Tuskegee which has given him as broad a conception of and insight into the problems of race relationship as any man I know

"I wish I could put into this report some of his real accomplishments which are having a far-reaching effect in making lighter the burdens of our wise, patient and courageous President and the Secretary of War, in meeting many of the problems which have grown out of the enlistment of thousands of colored soldiers, and at the same time making it easier for approximately 400 000 colored soldiers now in the service to adjust themselves to the many trying and difficult situations which must necessarily arise in the new life into which they have been so suddenly entered "

Late in June, 1919, it was announced through the press that Mr Scott had been elected Secretary-Treasurer of Howard University, thus bringing to a close twenty-two years of successful, faithful service to Tuskegee Institute, and upon July first he entered upon his new duties

Perhaps the most beautiful estimate of Mr Scott is the following comment from Dr Booker T Washington, which appeared in his book entitled, "Tuskegee and Its People"

"For many years now, Mr Scott has served the school with rare fidelity and zeal and has been to the Principal not only a loyal assistant in every phase of his manifold, and frequently trying duties, but has proved a valuable personal friend and counselor in matters of the most delicate nature exhibiting in emergencies a quality of judgment and diplomatic calmness seldom found in men of even riper maturity and more extended experience "

ULYSSES GRANT MASON, M. D.

HE good book tells us that men have varying talents and that man is not limited to one talent. It is often noted in men of renown that they possess a number of talents with one or more very conspicuous.

This is illustrated in the case of Dr. Mason. He is prominent in his profession as a physician and no less prominent as a business man and withal he is a man of marked initiative ability.

Dr. Mason is the son of Isaac and Mary Mason, and was born in Birmingham, Alabama, November 20th, 1872.

He received his preparatory education at Huntsville College (now A. & M. College, Normal, Alabama.) Having chosen the medical profession he next entered the Meharry Medical College, (Walden University,) at Nashville, Tennessee. Graduating from this college he sought additional preparation in Europe and took a special course in surgery, at the University of Edinburgh, Scotland. Returning to this country, he entered upon his medical career in Birmingham, Alabama, the city of his birth. He at once won recognition as a physician and soon had an extended practice.

His ability as a physician was recognized by the City authorities, who appointed him assistant city physician, which position he held for about eight years.

Dr. Mason was sympathetic with all movements which looked to the elevation and advancement of his people and himself initiated several institutions which sought their good.

He was the organizer and founder of the Home and George, C. M. Hall Hospital; Founder and Surgeon to the Northside Infirmary, located at 1508 Seventh Avenue, Birmingham, Alabama. In 1910 he organized the Prudential Savings Bank, and has been its President since the organization.

These organizations indicate the trend of his mind—to ameliorate the sufferings of his people, and encourage them in habits of thrift.

From 1897 to 1908, he had been the Vice President of the Alabama Penny Saving Bank.

He is regarded as a man of remarkable business ability and his reputation is well sustained in the creditable manner in which he handles all matters confided to him. He has filled many honorable positions, both as a citizen and in a professional way.

He was Delegate at large to the Republican National Conventions, 1908-1912. Member Clinical Congress of Surgeons of North America; member of the Medical Society of the United States of America; member John A. Andrew Clinical Society; member National Medical Association; member of the State Medical, Dental and Pharmaceutical Association, and of the Birmingham District Medical, Dental and Pharmacy Association. He is the Endowment Treasurer of Knights of Pythias; Trustee of the Central Alabama Institute, and Trustee of the 16th. Street Baptist Church, of Birmingham. He has always taken a prominent part in public affairs. Secretary Baker appointed him on a committee of one hundred to represent the Government on War Aims; he was chairman of the War Saving Stamps Committee; Member of the State National Council Defense and member of Volunteer Medical Service Corps, Council of National Defense.

Dr. Mason has been twice married. His first wife, Miss Alice Nelson, of Greensboro, Alabama, died September 19th, 1910, leaving him four children, Vivian, Ellariz, Ulysses G. Jr., and Alice F. June 17th, 1916 he married Mrs. Elsie Downs Baker, of Columbus Ohio, who has borne him one child, Dorothy Downs. Dr. Mason finds great pleasure and pride in his family and home life.

Dr. Mason has accumulated considerable property and is among the wealthiest negroes of the South.

Regarded from every standpoint he is a success.

DAVID HENRY CLAY SCOTT, M. D.

ICKNESS and disease is to be found in all races of men and in all stations of life and the marvelous advance made by science in combating its ravages has attracted to the profession of medicine a great many young men. Aside from its remunerative attraction they see in the medical profession a field of unlimited usefulness. A doctor's life is not one of ease but the faithful physician who spends himself in the interest of humanity feels that he has given his life to a good cause. Among the young men who were attracted to this profession was Dr. David Henry Clay Scott.

Dr. Scott was born in Hollywood, Alabama, November 21st, 1871. Like quite a large number of colored youths he aspired to rise above the lot of a day laborer and realized that in order to do so he must have an education and fit himself for some useful and remunerative occupations. His choice of a life work was that of medicine so he set that profesion as his goal and bent all of his energies to attain a doctor's certificate.

He received his first educational training at the Huntsville State Normal School where he acquir-

ed a good foundation upon which he continued to build until his education was complete.

He entered the Meharry Medical College, to prepare for his life work, from which institution he received his M. D. Finishing his course he was ready for business and selected Selma as the city in which to hang out his shingle. However, he remained in this city only from March to November, when he moved to Montgomery. His career in Montgomery is the best testimony as to the wisdom of this change. His practice continued to grow from the beginning which is evidence of his ability as a physician.

While Dr. Scott's large practice keeps him busy he manages to find time to devote to civic matters and is interested in all matters which look to city developement.

He was appointed chairman for the colored citizens in the 4th. Liberty Loan Drive, the success of which demonstrated his ability as a leader.

The following extracts from a statement issued by him in one of the local papers tells the spirit in which he entered upon this work.

"As chairman of the colored people's Fourth Liberty Loan drive, I am extremely anxious that we do not falter in the last hours of this all important effort to put Montgomery 'over the top," and again "There is no special honor coming to any one because of this effort. Selfish be he who buys bonds for the sake of any honor that may come to him in so doing." Dr. Scott has marked executive ability as well a liberal endowment of business sagacity which he has used to great advantage.

Recognizing the need for a better class of buildings for the colored business man, he purchased a lot at the corner of Monroe and Lawrence Streets, and erected thereon a handsome three-story structure. The first floor is occupied as a drug store, which is run in first class style, having a fine sodafount and other modern attractions. The second and third floors are used for offices and are all occupied by live, wide-awake business men. When you enter this biulding you are at once impressed with its business atmosphere. Dr. Scott also owns and occupies his residence and owns several other pieces of property.

Dr. Scott was married December 28th, 1897, to Miss Viola Watkins, daughter of a prominent Contractor of the city of Montgomery, who erected his store building. They have no living children.

While Dr. Scott is interested in all enterprises which seek the good of his people he is especially interested in that institution, which in addition to its humanitarian appeal, interests him from the standpoint of his profession as a physician and surgeon—The Hale Infirmary. He is officially connected with this institution and gives to it his best thought and skill and much of his time.

KAWALIGA ACADEMIC AND INDUSTRIAL INSTITUTE

HE Kowaliga School was founded in 1898, by William E. Benson, a native of the community in which it is located. It is located in Tallapoosa County, Alabama, in the center of a community of colored people comprising about one thousand inhabitants. It was a part of a general enterprise which includes besides the school, the Dixie Industrial Company. It is owned by a board of trustees of prominent Northern men and women and local colored men.

Represented upon the board is John J. Benson, father of the founder, a man known far and wide for his marvelous success as a farmer and a man who commands the highest respect from both the white and black citizens.

The need for better educational facilities for the colored youth of the community had long been felt and it was to meet this need that suggested the enterprise which resulted in the building of the school.

Primarily it was not the aim of the school to train teachers, but to give to the boys and girls of the community an elementary education. While thorough instruction is given to the grammar grades, the scholars are also given instruction in manual, domestic and agricultural training. Manual training in wood and iron is taught the boys, along with training in agriculture, while the girls are taught cooking, sewing, millinery and basketry. The school is non-sectarian but kept under a strong religious influence. Although the Bible is not taught in the day school, devotional exercises are held each morning before the school work begins.

The teachers and students visit all the churches in the community and quite often the ministers of the churches visit the school. The first Saturday afternoon of each month is known as Mother's day, when the mothers meet and receive instruction in bread making, house cleaning, laundering, care of children, etc. They are given samples of yeast and baking-powder with instructions how to use them. In addition to their school duties, the teachers give as much time as is possible in doing extensive work. They make a house to house canvass in order to ascertain just the needs

of the patrons and show them the advantage of sending their children to school. This extension work is making the school many friends. The school has a boy's brass band, which arouses much interest, both in the school and community. The school has a library of 900 volumes which are used by the students. The Library needs replenishing and a better selection of books to stimulate a new interest in it. Mr. Benson, the founder, died October 14th, 1915, and was succeeded by James Andrew Dingus, who took charge of the school December 2nd, 1915.

Professor Dingus was born in Jiles County, Virginia, March 3rd, 1877, and received his education in Marietta, Ohio, where he graduated from the High School and received the finishing touches at the Hampton Institute, in Virginia. He was especially fitted for agricultural instruction and for three years was placed in charge of the Dairy and Poultry departments at Hampton Institute, and for three years had charge of the Agricultural department at Langston, Oklahoma.

When he took charge of Kawaliga school he found evidence of excellent construction work along the line of buildings, but the patrons somewhat disorganized owing to the death of Mr. Benson. His first work was to meet the local members of the Board of Trustees and learn the needs and condition of the school. He realized that three things were necessary to guarantee success in his efforts—children to instruct, teachers to teach them and money to pay the teachers. Having satisfied himself upon these points he put his life and energy into the work with the most gratifying results. The enrollment 1917-18 was 196, with an average attendance of 115.

The land upon which the school is located comprises 240 acres, about fifty of which is under cultivation. It is the purpose of Professor Dingus to make this farm not only self-sustaining but a source of profit to the school. Thus it will serve the double purpose of a model farm for instruction and a source of income. Kowaliga is an Indian name, the name of a little river in the uplands of Alabama, along whose borders was once an Indian Reservation. Here is now to be found a thickly settled farming community, inhabited by a comparatively thrifty and industrious class of colored people. In the center of this community is the Kowaliga school, exerting an influence over the inhabitants elevating, refining, and inspiring to a nobler life.

REVEREND JOHN BONHAM McDUFFEE

EV. John Bonham McDuffee was born in Montgomery County, Alabama, May 1st, 1868, and has resided in the county of his birth almost his entire life. The call of the farm had a fascination for him, and a tan early age he began his farming operations. At the age of sixteen he began work on his own account. His farm was located in Beat 10, Montgomery County, where he has almost continuously since tilled the soil.

Like a great many colored men, his thirst for knowledge kept pace with his manual efforts so he gave a fourth of his time to the cultivation of his mind. He gave three-fourths of his time to the farm and attended the district school in the winter.

In 1895 he joined the Baptist church at Hope Alabama and was by that church ordained to the ministry and called to be the Pastor of the church at Letohatchie. He served his church for twelve years before accepting work elsewhere. The result of his ministerial work has been the serving of seven churches, two of which he founded and built from the ground up.

In 1897 he was elected President of the Alabama Middle district Sunday School Convention, and held the office continuously for nine years.

In the year 1915 he was elected Secretary of the same convention, which position he now fills.

Rev. McDuffee believes in taking time by the foreclock, so when he read that the Boll Weevil was headed for Alabama, he immediately began to plan to give him a warm reception, not in the sense of a cordial reception but such a welcome as would prompt him to seek a more congenial clime. The outcome of his tests and experiments was the "McDuffee Boll Weevil Remedy," a remedy that has brought him into notice throughout the cotton producing states.

His name has become a by-word in the homes of many farmers in the cotton belts.

The cotton production has had to face many difficulties and has met and overcome many formidable enemies, the great enemy it now faces being the boll weevil. In finding a remedy for this pest the Rev. McDuffee will save to the cotton producing states much wealth.

No other remedy has accomplished the good in the destruction of the boll weevil that McDuffee's preparation has done and hundreds of farmers have voiced their praise of the remedy in letters of commendation. It came at a time when the farmers were blue and it seemed that the death knell to cotton culture had been sounded and like the morning sun it dispelled the mists of doubt and uncertainty which hung over the farmer and gave him a new hope.

Thus it often happens that our brightest visions come in the midst of our hardest trials. For every evil there is a remedy and it fell to the lot of Reverend McDuffee to find the remedy for the Boll Weevil.

Before giving his remedy to the public, Rev. McDuffee partook freely of his own medicine. He reasoned that if it did not keep his own fields free of the pest it would be of no practical use to others. His experiments were so successful that he immediately told others of the blessing he had found. Others have tried it, much to the discomfort of the Boll Weevil, and the reputation of the McDuffee Boll Weevil Remedy was assured.

The home life of Rev. McDuffee has been a mingling of joy and sorrow. He has been married three times and twice has he stood at the open grave and watched the bodies of his companions lowered into mother earth.

His first wife was Miss Elizia Normon, who he married in 1886. She died leaving him four children. He next married Miss Susia Woodley, who gave him nine children. She died August 11th, 1913. His present wife was Miss Arlean Johnson, and from this union has been born two children.

GEORGE AUGUSTUS WEAVER, M .D.

R. George Augustus Weaver, the subject of this sketch was born in Tuscaloosa, Alabama, November 1st, 1870, where the very atmosphere breathed the spirit of education. Here the Alabama State University is located, and it is quite natural that a colored youth who was born and raised in such a community should have aspirations for learning and position.

With the fires of ambition kindled he formed the purpose to secure an education and the fact that the way seemed hard did not deter him nor change his purpose. He persevered until his course was completed and he was enabled to hang out his shingle as an M. D. With the exception of five dollars a month given him by his father he paid his own way through school and college. He served as porter with the Wagner Palace Car Company and the Pullman Company, and spent such time as not engaged in the school, upon the road.

This work while it gave him the funds to continue his studies also added to the developement of his mind. His travels carried him all over the United States and to many of the cities of Canada, thus broadening his outlook and giving him a greater knowledge of men. He commenced his studies in the city school, of Tuscaloos, his native city, where a good foundation was laid and prepared him for the advanced course in other institutions. After finishing the Tuscaloosa schools he entered the Talladega College where he graduated in 1892. From Talladega College he went to Howard University, at Washington, D. C., and took the medical course, graduating in 1897. The Howard University was founded in 1867 by an act of Congress and in variety and quality of profesional training stands first among educational institutions for colored people.

Thus by his indomitable spirit, energy, patience and perseverence he secured an education, and completed his medical course in one of the strongest institutions in the land. When he left the University he was well equipped for his profession so far as knowledge goes, but without the means to rent and furnish an office, so he turned again to the road, and for several months, from May to January, donned the uniform of a pullman porter. He opened his office and began the practice of medicine and surgery, in March, 1898, in the city of Tuscaloosa, where he has continuously practiced since.

Dr. Weaver is a member of the First African Baptist Church and takes an active part in church life. In recognition of his ability and consecrated life the church made him Chairman of the Board of Trustees. He is a member of the Masonic Lodge and has served as Senior Grand Warden. He is a Knight of Pythias, and an Odd Fellow, being Grand Medical Director of the latter. He is also a member of the volunteer Medical Service Corp. Ex-President of Alabama Dental and Pharmaceutical Association.

Dr. Weaver was selected as Chairman of the Fourth Loan drive, and under his management it went far "over the top." He was one of the "Four minute-Speakers," in the speaking force to push the War Saving Stamp campaign, and organized a class of Red Cross First Aid.

In this time of his country's need his soul burned with the firts of patriotism, and in this way he gave expression to his loyalty and relieved the pent up fires of patriotism which urged him to action.

In 1900 Dr. Weaver was united in marriage to Miss Mattie A. Wallace, of Wilsonville, Ala., who together, with two children born of this union, constitutes his family. One, a boy eight years of age, bears his father's name, and the other a daughter, two and a half years of age, they named Marie Elizabeth, and an adopted boy, Everard Weaver, now a student at Tuskegee Institute.

Dr. Weaver owns his home, which is a pretty structure, worth $4000, and in addition he owns real estate to the value of approximately $13,500.

STONE HALL, SELMA UNIVERSITY

R. Robert Thomas Pollard, A. B., D. D., was born in Gainesville, Alabama, October 4th, 1860. He received his early education in the common schools after which he entered the Selma University, an institution to which he gave many of his active and useful years. After graduating from the collegiate course he began his work as a minister. His first labors were that of a missionary in the state of Alabama. In this work, he traveled for a number of years all over the state. He next became an agent of the American Baptist Publication Society, of Philadelphia, in advancing the Sunday School work. He gave up this work to enter the service of the American Baptist Home Mission Society. Again he became a missionary for the Southern Baptist Convention and for the Society of Alabama Baptists. In this service he traveled from church to church, and from convention to convention, of the colored people of Alabama.

Having served for a long period as a missionary he gave up his field of labor for the pastorate and in this capacity he served a number of the leading churches in Alabama. He was pastor of the churches in Montgomery, Marion, Selma, Union Springs and Eufaula. The next step in his career was that of an educator, being called to the Presidency of his alma mater, the Selma University. He continued in this position for nine years, from 1902 to 1911. While holding this office he found frequent opportunities to preach, presenting the claims of the University and raising funds to finance the institution. His arduous duties in connection with this institution impaired his health and caused him to resign his office as president. He re-entered the pastorate for a short period, when he was elected President of Florida Memorial College, Live Oak, Florida.

In 1916, his successor, as president of the Selma University, Dr. M. W. Gilbert resigned on account of failing health, and Dr. Pollard was again called to fill the post. Although he had just been re-elected to the presidency of the Florida Memorial College, he felt it his duty to respond to the call to again head the Selma University, which position he now holds.

The Selma University was born of deep seated conviction that the great need of the colored race was an educated ministry. This conviction deepened from year to year and was earnestly discussed at the Alabama Colored Baptist State conventions. It finally took shape at the convention held in Tuscaloosa in 1873, by adopting the following resolution offered by Rev. W. H. McAlpine:

"Resolved: That we plant in the State of Alabama, a Theological school to educate our young men." This gave to the movement a definite aim and purpose and inspired it with great activity. The fight was on and although the battle for success was hard and long, it was finally won and the institution is now the pride of the Colored Baptists of the state.

Starting the enterprise forty-five years ago without funds and only a resolution to incite enthusiasm and energy, the founders persevered in their work until their dream of a great university became a reality.

The University is located at Selma, Alabama, upon a thirty-two acre tract. It has three brick dormitories and a home for the President. Its property is valued at $175,000.00, and is free of debt.

Both Montgomery and Marion wanted the University, but Selma won over them and secured the prize.

The first president of the institution was the Rev. Harris Woodsmall, who was elected December 20th, 1877, and directed to open the school the following January which he did, with only four pupils. He had an assistant, the Rev. W. R. Pettiford. The session was held in the St. Phillips

SUSIE FOSTER HALL, SELMA UNIVERSITY

Street Baptist church, now the First Baptist church.

May 30th, 1878, five months after the opening of the school, the Trustees held a meeting in Selma, and authorized the Executive Committee to negotiate for the purchase of the "Old Fair Grounds," which is its present location. The large amphitheatre upon the grounds was repaired at a cost of about $700.00, and used for school purposes. In 1880 the school was adopted by the American Baptist Home Mission Society, which has since contributed to its support.

March 1st, 1881, the school was incorporated as the Alabama Baptist Normal and Theological School, and in 1885 the name was changed to Selma University.

In 1895 the name was again changed to Alabama Baptist Colored University, but in 1908, its former name, Selma University, was restored.

Overcoming difficulties, facing many vicissitudes, and through great sacrifice, the founders of the institution, like all great men, these pioneers of Alabama Colored Baptist, built better than they knew. The two towering figures among the Colored Baptist of Alabama in those days of struggle and pioneer work were W. H. Alpine, and C. C. Boothe. They were both self-made men but men of great natural ability and force and their influence was great among the colored Baptists of Alabama, and they held the confidence and respect of their white brethren. It was under their leadership that the school had its inception and through their effort it was brought to a successful issue, aided of course by their brethren, who put their souls, their strength and their means into the enterprise. Dr. McAlpine has gone to his reward, but Dr. Boothe is still using his great powers for the uplift of his people.

The following officers of the Board of Trustees are men of culture and rare gifts:

P. S., L. Lutchins, D. D., is chairman, R. B. Hudson, A. M., is Secretary and L. German, A. B., is Treasurer.

It is a divine principle that "By their fruits ye shall know them." Measured by this standard the Selma University occupies a high place in the estimation of those who have watched its course from the beginning. Beginning with two teachers and four pupils, the school now has twenty-three instructors in charge of about five hundred pupils. It enrolled one year 782 pupils. It opened with Normal and Theological courses, but now has a college course, Bachelor of Theology, Bachelor of Divinity Course, a Pastor's course, a Missionary course, manual art, Agriculture, Domestic Science, Sewing and Dress making, Stenography, Typewriting, etc. It has turned out more than six hundred graduates, who have taken high places in the various avocations of life. The Institution has been careful in the selection of its teaching force, who have come from the noted colleges of the country, Brown University, Chicago University, Leland University, Virginia Union University, Harvard, Yale, Johns Hopkins, Vassar, Columbia College, Cornell University, Meharry Medical College, Tuskegee Institute, Oberlin Business College, etc., have all made their contributoin. The University has had eight presidents; Rev. Harrison Woodsmall, Dr. W. H. McAlpine, Dr. E. M. Brawley, Dr. Charles L. Purse, Dr. Charles S. Dinkins, Dr. C. O. Boothe, Dr. M. W. Gilbert and the present president, Dr. Robert Thomas Pollard.

Dr. Pollard was married in 1887 to Miss Elizabeth J. Washington, also a graduate of Selma University, who has been a great help to him in his educational work. They have one son who is a prosperous dentist at Florence, Alabama. Mrs. Pollard was for ten years President of the Woman's State Convention, Editress of the "Woman's Era," author of "Guide," one to four and matron of the Florida Memorial College.

Dr. Pollard has devoted most of his life to the cause of Baptist education, both in the churches and the schools, and the greater part of his activities have been confined to the State of Alabama.

MANUAL TRAINING SHOP, SELMA UNIVERSITY

ANDREW JACKSON STOKES, D. D.

OST of those who fill the sacred office are called to the ministry after reaching man's estate, but occasionally one is born to the cloth. Among these is the Rev. Andrew Jackson Stokes, who commenced his pulpit work when a boy only ten years of age.

Dr. Stokes was born in Orangeburg County, S. C., July 25th, 1859, and began his ministerial work in Orangeburg County in the year 1870. From the first he showed an aptitude for church building and during his ministry he has built and remodeled a number of church edifices. His first work was to build the Mt. Zion and Pisgah churches in Orangeburg County, and Black Jack Church, in Winnsboro County. From 1884 to 1886 his field of labor was Clarksville, Tenn., and here again his talent for church building was called into play. Before he completed his labors in this city he had erected a church building costing twenty thousand dollars. From Clarksville he went to Fernandina, Florida, where he added largely to the numerical strength of the church and remodeled its building.

It was in Montgomery, Alabama, however, where he reached the zenith of his active and useful life. Upon the death of the Rev. James Foster, Pastor of the Columbus Street Baptist Church, Dr. Stokes was called to succeed him. Coming to Montgomery in 1891, he has continuously served the church and is today its beloved Pastor. When he took charge of the church its membership numbered 500, which has increased to over 5000. The church, during his administration has had many seasons of revival and he bears the distinction of having baptised 1001 candidates in one day. The growing membership required greater housing, and the old frame building in which the church worshipped, was enlarged and remodeled. The requirements of the congregation soon called for a more modern structure and the Pastor with his natural gift for church building proved to be the successful leader in the enterprise. Like a wise leader he first perfected his plans and then made his people see the vision which had come to him and enthused them with the spirit of the enterprise.

After months of patient waiting, unbounding sacrifices, unquenchable zeal and determined effort, the new edifice was completed and dedicated. And today is pointed to with commendable pride, not alone by the congregation but by the colored citizens of the Capital City.

While his main thought and effort was the development of the church life of his people, Dr. Stokes was not unmindful of their educational needs, and to meet these, he established in 1891, the Montgomery Academy, the success of which, has met his fondest expectations. Starting in a small way, with two teachers and fifty pupils, it has steadily grown until today it has six teachers and two hundred pupils and is housed in a well apportioned school building. From its birth, Dr. Stokes has been the President of the Academy. The object of the founder was to give to the children a Normal school education and to fit them for some useful occupaion in life. The range of Dr. Stokes' active life extends for beyond his home field. He is a Trustee of the Selma University; Treasurer of the National Baptist Convention, an office he has held for the past twenty years, and Moderator of the Spring Hill Association. By acclamation he was elected by the Congress for the advancement of Colored People, as one of a committee to go to France and study conditions of enlisted men of the United States Army.

Dr. Stokes has been a great traveler, his travels covering the United States and Mexico, the countries of Europe, Egypt and the Holy Land.

He has accumulated quite a nice property, owning about 2000 acres of land, besides an elegant home, which adjoins the handsome church building of which mention has been made. His family consists of a wife and two children, Lou Rosa Stokes, and Hugo Benton Stokes. His son is an M. D. graduate of Meharry and served as First Lieutenin the U. S. Army. Dr. Stokes received his degree from Princeton in 1914. He is author of a book called "Select Sermons."

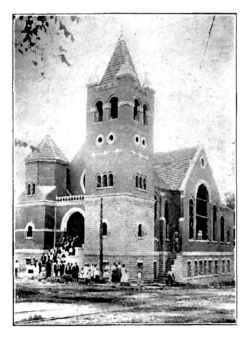

FIRST BAPTIST CHURCH, COLORED,
MONTGOMERY, ALA.

RIOR to the Civil War and for
several years after its close, the
Colored Baptists of Montgomery
worshipped with the white Baptists, in their brick church building, situated at the intersection of
Court, Coosa and Bibb Streets. For their accommodation a gallery was built on both the east and
west side of the auditorium and their spiritual interests were looked after by the Pastor of the
church and the white members. They received
baptism at the hands of the Pastor and in the bap-
tistry of the church.

Several years after the war the colored members decided that it would be best to withdraw
their membership from the white church and form
a church of their own, to be ministered to by a
member of their own race. Accordingly in 1867
letters were granted to about forty of the colored
members who organized the Columbus Street Baptist church, and called the Reverend Nathan Ashby
to be their Pastor. He served them until the year
1877 when he resigned and the Reverend James
Foster was elected as his successor. During his
pastorate the membership of the church was increased to five hundred, like the illustrious William
Carey, the Rev. Foster was a shoe-maker before
he entered the ministry. He served the church
until 1891, when he entered into his long rest. He

was greatly beloved by his people and was highly
respected and esteemed by the citizens of Montgomery in general, both white and black. Succeeding him as Pastor of the church, was the Reverend
Andrew Jackson Stokes, who came to Montgomery
from Fernandena, Florida. It was under his administration that the church began that marvelous
growth which has placed it near, if not at the head
of the list of churches in point of membership.
From five hundred members it has grown to five
thousand members, requiring the enlarging of the
old frame building, in which the church worshipped
to accomodate the congregation.

The church saw the need for better equipment,
and were planning, under the leadership of their
Pastor, for a new building and while assembling
material for the new structure, the frame building
was destroyed by fire. This hastened their plans
and gave them new zeal for their work. After
months of untiring effort, generous giving and
willing sacrifices, the building was completed, and
the congregation is now worshipping in one of the
handsomest church edifices to be found among the
colored citizens of the South. The building has a
large auditorium, a commodious Sunday school
room, and the necessary smaller rooms for the accomodation of the church societies, class rooms,
etc. It is well located on a corner lot facing the
Cemetary Park, with nothing to obstruct its front
view for a long distance.

After serving so large a congregation for twenty-eight years, the Pastor, Dr. Stokes, is still a man
of great energy, and vigor, and full of zeal for the
welfare of his people. His people stand by him and
it is only necessary for him to lay before them his
plans of work to inlist their cooperation and support. They have found in him a wise and active
leader and they gladly follow him when he points
out the way.

The church will soon have a pipe organ to aid
its splendid choir, which will add no little to the
Sunday services.

The pastor is ably assisted by the following of-
ficers: Deacons Wm. Clayton, Chairman, Russell
Johnson, Treas; Kiltis Singleton, Henry Spear,
Wallace Johnson, Robert Carlton, Wm. Bruher,
Ned Casby, Professor, Henry Ray, Levy Coates,
Sol Wallace, Champ Williams, and Isaac Croom.

The Sunday School is divided into two divisions
—A and B. Prof Henry Ray is head of Division A.
and Division B. is presided over by Willie Beasley
and Pat Johnson. Fred Thomas is at the head
of the Board of Ushers.

Missionary Board: Mrs. Fannie Gable is President, assisted by Eliza Jones, Mary Miles, Hardy
Martin, Lucy Prichard, Mary Ward, Willie Hall,
and Jeanette McAlpin

MONROE N. WORK, PH. B., M. A.

ONROE N. Work, Sociologist and Writer, Head of the Division of Records and Research of the Tuskegee Normal and Industrial Institute, Editor of the Negro Year Book. The subject of his sketch was born in Iredell County, North Carolina. He was reared in Illinois and Kansas. His education has been as follows:

Graduated from high school, Arkansas City, Kansas, 1892; in 1895, he entered the Chicago Theological Seminary, graduating in 1898. While here he became interested in the subject of sociology, and decided to enter the University of Chicago, and prepare himself for work in this field. He remained in this institution five years. In 1902 received the degree of Bachelor of Philosophy, in 1903 the degree of Master of Arts, with sociology as a major subject and experimental psychology as a minor. His thesis for the masters degree was "Negro Real Estate Holding in Chicago." This attracted widespread attention and brought forth many comments from the press throughout the country. He showed that the first owner of property on the site of what is now Chicago was a San Domingo Negro, Baptist Point De Saible, who settled here as an Indian trader, about 1790.

The first position, Mr. Work held after graduation from the University of Chicago was with the Georgia State Industrial College, as professor of History and Education. This position he held for five years. In 1908 he came to Tuskegee Institute and established the Department of Records and Research. The results of the work of this department are embodied in the Negro Year Book, the first edition of which appeared in 1912. This publication has become a standard authority on matters pertaining to the race. It circulates widely, not only in this country, but throughout the world. Wherever there are persons interested in the Negro and wish to secure reliable comprehensive facts concerning him, they consult the Negro Year Book. The following are examples of the comments of the press concerning this publication:

"Interesting and important is the array of facts relating to the Negro contained in the Negro Year Book. The book is a perfect encyclopedia of achievements by Negroes in all ranks of life, of the history of the race in the United States, of legislative enactments relating to them, of activity in all branches, particularly education. The book is indispensable to all who have to deal with any phase of the Negro question."—New York Sun.

"No better prepared or more comprehensive annual comes to hand than the Negro Year Book. It covers every phase of Negro activity in the United States, reviews progress in all lines, discusses grievances, outlines the economic condition of the race, presents religious and social problems, educational statistics and political questions as they relate to the race. The book is a valuable and authoritative book of reference."—Indianapolis Star.

Mr. Work is a member of the following learned societies: The American Negro Academy, The Association for the Study of Negro Life, and History, The American Sociological Society, The American Economic Association, The National Economic League, The National Geographical Society, and the Southern Sociological Congress.

Mr. Work is also the compiler of statistics on lynching. His annual reports of lynchings are the recognized authority on this subject.

The subjects of important articles which Mr. Work has published in magizines and periodicals, are: "Geechee Folklore," Southern Workman, November and December, 1905; "Some Parallelism in the Development of Africans and other Races," Southern Workman, November, 1906 and January, February, March, 1907; "The African Family as an Institution," Southern Workman, June, July, August, 1909; "The African Medicine Man," Southern Workman, October, 1907; "African Agriculture," Southern Workman, November, December, 1910, and January, February, 1911; "An African System of Writing," Southern Workman, October, 1908; "The Negro and Crime in Chicago," American Journal of Sociology, September, 1900; "Negro Criminality in the South," Annals of American Academy of Political and Social Science, September, 1913; "The Negro Church and the Community," Southern Workman, August, 1908; "How to Fit the School to the Needs of the Community," Southern Workman, September, 1908; and many other articles of like nature and importance. "The Negroes Industrial Problem," Southern Workman, August, 1914; "Self Help Among Negroes," Survey, August 7, 1909.

REVEREND ALFRED C. WILLIAMS, A. B., A. M.

EV. Alfred C. Williams, the son of Hampton A. and Chanly Williams, was born at Monticello, Florida, May 28th, 1883. He developed great mental vigor in his youth and graduated from the Howard Academy, of his own town at fourteen years of age.

He was converted and joined the church at the age of fifteen. During the fall of the same year he entered the Florida Memorial College, at Live Oak, Florida, from which he was graduated at the age of nineteen. In his nineteenth year he was ordained to the ministry and elected as supply pastor of his home church. In June of his twentieth year he was called to the pastorate of the First Baptist Church, of Green Cove Springs, Florida, which pastorate he filled until he was twenty-two, at which time he resigned to enter Morehouse College, Atlanta, Georgia. During the first year of his student life, at Morehouse, he was called to the pastorate of the Antioch Baptist Church, of Atlanta, Georgia, which pastorate he filled until June 1912. In May 1912, he received the Bachelor of Arts degree from Morehouse College. In June he was married to Miss Laura N. Maxwell, the

oldest daughter of the late Dr. L. B. Maxwell. Having received a call to the Mt. Tabor Baptist Church, of Pulaska, Florida, he resigned the pastorate of the Antioch Baptist Church, Atlanta, to accept this the second largest church in his home state. In one year and three months he led this church from under debt of more than Five Thousand Dollars, ($5000,) and the membership was increased more than three hundred. On account of the illness of his wife, he accepted a call to the Mt. Zion Baptist Church, of Los Angeles, California, where he remained for three years and at which time he studied at the University of Southern California, at which school he completed work for the degree of Master of Arts. In May, 1916, he was called to the pastorate of Sixteenth Street Baptist Church, Birmingham, Alabama, which he now fills. The Sixteenth Street Baptist Church was organized in 1873, by Reverend James Readen and Reverend Warner Reed. Succeeding pastors were Reverend J. S. Jackson, Dr. W. R. Pettiford, Reverend T. L. Jordan, Dr. C. L. Fisher, Dr. J. A. Whitted, and its present Pastor, Reverend A. C. Williams. All of these men wrought well and are credited with having done a great work. The church has always stood as a monument to the Negro race, especially the Negro Baptists, of Alabama who have felt a commendable pride in its work and achievements. It has had much to do with the shaping of the religious thought, and molding sentiment for the race. The Church clings to the "Old time" religious principles of its faith, but employs modern methods of bringing the Gospel message to the hearts and minds of the people. It recognized the power and uplifting influence of music and organized a choir whose famous high class musicals attract hundreds of white people of all classes throughout the city and district who come to listen to the old plantation melodies, and jubilees as well as their high class solos, quartettes and anthems. All races and creeds in Birmingham have high regard for this church's attitude in matters affecting the social and moral uplift of the community. The church has a membership of more than one thousand. It worships in a most beautiful structure, an edifice built of brick and stone, which together with the Interior furnishings cost about Eighty thousand Dollars, ($80,000.) It also owns the Pastor's home which is a good substantial building. The entire church property is valued at more than $125,000.00. The interior is beautifully adorned by expensive art glass, windows and other architectural designs calculated to give tone, grace and beauty and is highly attractive and pleasing to the most discriminating eye. A church of this character with a choir holding an enviable place in the estimation of music loving people of course has a pipe organ in keeping with it. The organ is large and expensive and an ornament as well as an instrument of use.

Since becoming its Pastor, Reverend Williams has received into its membership more than 700 accessions, and has raised over $23,000 for current expenses and debts.

JOHN G. WRIGHT.

EW Negroes there are in the South who can conduct their business in the largest building of the city in which they live. Mr. Wright's barber shop has a first floor location in the largest business building in Tuscaloosa, adjoining the leading city drug store and under the rooms of the city Board of Trade. His shop is patronized by the leading white men of the city and is looked upon as the most up-to-date business of the kind in Tuscaloosa.

Mr. Wright was a self-made man, who had no very great early advantages, either of school, of parentage, money or environment. He was born in Hanover, Hale County, in the late sixties. A white lady taught him the fundamentals of education. Of general education, such as our children get, he appears to have had very little.

In 1892 Mr. Wright made his way into Birmingham, a town at he time, and began his apprenticeship as a barber. For eight years he served in the shops of others in the city of Birmingham, first as an apprentice and then as a regular workman.

His ambitions led him to establish a business of his own. In casting about for a location he decided in favor of Tuscaloosa. Here was located the State University, which offered a good field for patronage aside from the local trade.

Tuscaloosa has since been the scene of his active life. Here he established a barber's business, which is today one of the best in the State.

Courteous in demeanor, attentive to his business and maintaining a strict integrity, he has won the confidence and respect of the entire community and occupies the proud position of being one of the leading colored citizens of the city.

In thinking of Mr. Wright you do not regard him simply as a barber but as a business men with an unusual aptitude for large business enterprises. He is the proprietor of two shops and they occupy the best locations in Tuscaloosa, one in the leading hotel of the city and one in its largest business building.

He does not confine himself exclusively to his barber shops. He is a dealer in real estate which has brought him much profit and in a sense is a promoter of Negro enterprises.

He owns his home—a residence to which his neighbors point with pride. It is beautifully located and is built on a quarter of a block. Since the building for himself he has bought and now rents thirteen other houses.

From being strictly in business for himself he has become a promoter and backer of Negro undertakings generally. He is president of the Alabama Protection and Aid Association, Stockholder and promoter of the People's Drug Company of Tuscaloosa, Trustee and Treasurer of the A. M. E. Zion Church of his town and was Grand Master of the Grand United Order of Odd Fellows of Alabama for four years, and resigned this office in August, 1917, on account of his business requiring all of his time.

Tuscaloosa is one of the best towns of the South. One does not here feel the stricture of race prejudice or opposition. In few if any other towns in the South can a colored man find such happy accommodations, handsome homes, educated people, good restaurants, clean surroundings and the best of cooking. It needed only the up-to-date Drug store to round out the comforts of the colored people. This was provided mainly by Mr. Wright, who is both president and treasurer of the company.

Mr. Wright is a Mason, Knight of Pythias and Odd Fellow. In his work as Grand Master of the Odd Fellows of Alabama he has traveled over the whole country.

Mr. Wright has no children, but he will tell you that much of his success in business and in life is due to Mrs. Wright, who was Miss Ophelia Edmonds of Tuscaloosa.

ARKANSAS BAPTIST COLLEGE.

THE college is a creature of the Arkansas Negro Baptist State Convention and came into existence at the Convention held at Hot Springs, in August, 1884. After an experiment of one year it was incorporated under the name of the Arkansas Baptist College. For the first several year of its existence it had no permanent abiding place, but moved from church to church. It finally located upon its own property, some distance beyond the city limits of Little Rock where it has continued until the present time. Its equipment is not in keeping with the growth and importance of the institution. The Administration building is its only structure of real and permanent value. While the college has grown the City of Little Rock has far outstripped it and while encroaching upon it has added greatly to the value of the real estate holdings. The Trustees have already considered the question of a new location and have secured and paid for one hundred acres of land, some four miles distant. The land purchased has a good elevation, is dry and well drained and excellent for farming operations.

When the present location is sold it should supply sufficient funds to erect a number of modern structures to meet its requirements. Even with this advantage it will require outside aid to make the move and place the institution upon a sure foundation.

The President, Dr. Joseph A. Booker, who has been the President since 1887, is now maturing a plan to secure help from the wealthy friends of the college.

Its original purpose was to train preachers and teachers, but the scope has been enlarged to reach all clases of the Negro race, and prepare them for some useful occupation in life.

Special training is given to the developement of the mind while industrial and farming is a marked feature of the institution. The training is thoroughly practical, the students being required to put to a practical test the theories they are taught.

The attendance of pupils has gone beyond the three hundred mark, while the teachers number eighteen. All of the teachers are colored; male, eight, and female, ten; divided as follows: grades, four; academic, seven; girls' industries, two; theology, one; music, one; and Matron, one. It is organized as follows: Elementary—The elementary work covers the usual eight grades. Secondary: The secondary, or preparatory course, includes Latin, four years; English, four; Mathematics, four; Greek or German, two; Elementary Scinece two and one half; History, one; Psychology, one; Bible, three and one half. Emphasis is placed on ancient languages. Industrial: The girls are instructed in cooking and sewing.

The industrial instruction for boys is chiefly manual training; good work in making brackets, tie racks, and chairs is done. A few pupils work on the farm, which is located seven miles from the school. Gardening has recently been added to the course of study, with practice on the school grounds. While it is yet in the nature of an experiment, it is hoped and expected to be a valuable addition to the course.

JOSEPH HERCULES BARABIN, A. B., M. D.

HE prince of good fellows, the king of diagnosticians, this is what they tell you out in Arkansas about Dr. Joseph Hercules Barabin of Mariana. And then you are regaled with all the honors that colored Arkansas has been only too pleased to bestow upon its leading physician; a distinguished Mason, a leading Odd Fellow, a prominent Knight of Pythias, a substantial Mosiac Templar, a foremost member of the Royal Circle of Friends and of the Supreme Council of Good Shepherds, the local examiner for all the secret orders in the State, a former athlete, the patron of all athletics.

Moreover, he is a big business man, being president of the Colored Commercial Club of Mariana, and owning in addition to his residence, a brick store, seven rent houses, 286 acres of farm land, all improved, all free from debt.

Dr. Barabin's rise to a prominent place makes one of those romantic biographical tales so interesting in all democracies, so dear to the heart of all Americans. Dr. Barabin was born in Jeanerette, Louisiana, March 19th, 1874. An ex-union soldier, left over from the war, and none too advanced in education, gave the young lad his first lessons in

books. When he was sixteen years of age, he made his way into Gilbert Academy, at Baldwin, Louisiana. Five years of study and work, of work and study, for he was in and out of his classes, having to pay his own way, completed his studies at Gilbert Academy. The adage of the ancients, that a little learning is a dangerous thing impressed him; and so the young man sought a higher institution in which to pursue his studies.

Fisk University was then, as it still is, the star of hope for a great many Negroes with college aspirations. Here in 1895, Dr. Barabin matriculated. In a while he was a leader in all the big things of college life. He was a brilliant man in the college and city societies (and who knows how much this social success has counted in his professional career?) he was a formidable adversary in the debates and in the oratory of the college, and he was a ferocious plunger on the football field.

Graduating as a Bachelor of Arts in 1900, Dr. Barabin resolved that he would study medicine. Business careers for young Negroes were not common then. The young college graduate had essayed school teaching at odd times, and decided that he did not especially care for life in the school room.

Casting about for a medical college of high standing, moderate expense and congenial to colored people, he finally selected the Illinois Medical College of Chicago. Moreover, he felt that Chicago would offer the best opportunity for clinical practice and also work in odd times for a student who was earning his own way. All happily came out as he had planned, or even better. He was able along with working in the Pullman service during summer, to pay two years expenses by playing foot ball, and to pay the other two years by embalming the bodies in the medical school. Indeed it was not long before the embalming department was put in his charge. Despite his having to work, the young doctor was one of the two men in his class to receive a special honor diploma for excellence in scholarship, and up to that time, the only colored man to receive this honorary diploma.

In 1905, having finished his medical course, Dr. Barabin, after casting about for a while, hung out his sign in Mariana, where it has hung these thirteen years, and where instead of being forty dollars in debt, the sum borrowed to start business on, he is worth thirty thousand dollars. He is a physician and surgeon, practicing within a radius of fifty miles, going into the country as well as in the town. He is frequently called in consultation in Little Rock, in Memphis, Oklahoma and in many smaller places.

Dr. Barabin was married on December 28th, 1905, to Miss Lulu Margaret Benson of Kowaliga, Alabama. Their four children, Jennie Maudeline; Joseph Benson; William Strickland and Harold Crockett are all little folks getting their first days in school.

WALLACE LEON PURIFOY.

 AVE you ever heard of the United Order of Jugamos? It is one of those secret and useful bodies, whose secrets are no secrets at all. It has head and several subheads in various capacities.

The head and subordinate officers make up the Imperial Council of the Jugamos. These are responsible for insurance relief funds, burial and the like, of members of the Jugamos. Its present habitat is Arkansas, the head quarters being in Forest City. However, it is to have state headquarters in Tennessee, in Illinois, in Mississippi, in Louisiana, in Oklahoma. It has a membership of 7,500 and an annual income of $35,000. The organization has grown at the rate of more than a thousand members per year, being founded in 1910 and having now a membership of 7,500.

The founder of this order is Mr. Wallace Leon Purifoy. Mr. Purifoy was born near Perry, Georgia, in Houston County, February, ninth, 1869. Born on the farm, he put in much time with the plow and hoe.

While still young, Mr. Purifoy left Georgia, and took up residence in Arkansas, in Forest City.

Here he began his education, attending the public schools of that city, and Philander Smith College, in Little Rock. All this seeking and studying to complete his training was accompanied by hard work and privation, on his own part and on the part of a sacrificing mother. The mother did washing and ironing to aid him through school. He helped here, however, in the actual work of bundling the clothes. Mr. Purifoy did many other jobs to gain his education. For a while he worked as a laborer on big buildings; then he drove drays; then he taught school.

When he reached the point in his career where he could command a school, the burden on both his shoulders and his mother's began to lighten. Beginning to teach school at the age of sixteen, he devoted many years to the class room both for pupils and for teachers before he founded the Jugamos.

During his early years at the work, he taught many schools in St. Francis County. He was for twenty-five years Deputy County Examiner. He conducted a summer Normal School for teachers, taught for two years in Texas, and for a while as principal in Pine Bluff, Arkansas. His real substantial school work, however, was done in Forest City, his home. Here, for twenty-three years he has been principal of the Colored High School, regulating the courses until the students from the Forest City High School are admitted without examinations to any college in the state.

As regular and as steady as has been Mr. Purifoy's courses in education, it has been just as steady and persistent in business. Looking about him, he saw the city growing and his people needing homes. Investing his earnings wisely, he soon became the owner of several pieces of valuable property. He built homes to rent and bought lots. He also built a beautiful residence for himself. His property holdings, in rent houses, vacant lots, and his own residence now amounts to $20,000.

Mr. Purifoy has also been Grand Keeper of the Record and Seals of the Knights of Pythias, of the state of Arkansas. He is a member and Deacon of the First Baptist Church of Forest City. He has traveled extensively in the eastern and Western parts of the United States.

Mr. Purifoy was married to Miss Fannie J. Waterford, of Edmonston, Arkansas, in 1895. They were married at Forest City, where they now reside. There are several children in the Purifoy family, all of whom, except Harold, a deceased son, are pursuing their work in school. Wallace Leon, Jr., is studying pharmacy at North Western University; Mayme Marie is attending Knoxville College, in Tennessee; Minnie Edna Roosevelt, and Middlebrook are students in the Forest City High School.

SCOTT BOND.

Scott Bond

IN the Southwest they call him "Unc Scott" and number him among the sages. They quote Socrates, Cicero, and Benj. Franklin: And then they will quote "Unc Scott" Bond of Madison Arkansas.

Born a slave in Mississippi in 1852. Mr. Bond migrated as chattel to Tennessee, thence to Arkansas. In grapic language such as few others can employ Mr. Bond told of his coming into the village of Madison, with all his personal belongings done up in a red bandana handkerchief thrust on the end of a stick and swung over his shoulder.

During slavery days and in migrating from State to State Mr. Bond had learned to judge the soil. When his eyes fell on the rich loam land of Madison, which is really in the valley of the Mississippi, he flung down his load and exclaimed, "Lord, this is the place for me."

Like most ex-slaves, who struck out for themselves, Mr. Bond rented land on which to farm. You should hear him tell the story of those rentals. The rent ran up into the hundreds. He used to sell his cotton to a local merchant who was a sort of banker, the merchant would credit Bond with the cotton and then pay the farm rents and other bills, balancing from time to time. But the banker and the landlord got at logger-heads. Thus it turned out that Mr. Bond had to get the money and take it to the landlord. The sum demanded was $500 which he counted out to "Unc Scott" in crisp bills. Mr. Bond says he looked at the money, then looked again and again before he would touch it. Finally he put it away down in his inside pocket and "sort a hugged it." On his way to the landlord's he was beseiged with a desire to look at the money. Fearing robbery he rode into the deep wood, tied his horse and spread the money out on a log and went around the log gazing. Then he said:

"Lord, if I live, I'm goin' to have somebody pay me rents just this way."

From this hour his struggle began. He married poor, having little else but a bed and a broken skillet. He began to work from "Can't to can't"—can't see in the morning until can't see at night.

He worked in season and out of season, bright days and rainy days, the weather never stopping him in the accomplishment of his set purpose. On cold, rainy days he chopped or hauled or sold wood. He had caught his vision and had formed his purpose and no work was too hard for him nor no obstacles could stand in his way until he had accumulated a large rent roll.

The way to his goal was extremely hard until by chance he invested in a small tract of land. Part of it was a wash out in a creek bottom and offered but little prospect for farm purposes. His neighbors thought he was a fool and told him so for they use plain language out in Arkansas.

Mr. Bond's eye keen for judging the soil no doubt failed to see in the tract he purchased much encouragement for growing a crop, but he saw value in the gravel and sand found in the creek bottom. The sequel to his purchase showed the wisdom of his venture.

The Rock Island Railroad was greatly in need of sand and gravel and just such a deposit as was found on Mr. Bond's land.

They investigated his gravel pit and immediately saw they had found what they had been looking for for many months. They entered into negotiations with him which resulted in the signing of a contract which brought about the development of one if not the best gravel pit in the state. With the signing of this contract with the Rock Island Railroad the stream of money began to flow his way and it was not long before he realized his dream and made good his vow. Money was no longer a marvel to him.

Mr. Bond saw the possibilities of his contract with the Rock Island Railroad and to meet it would call for large and modern facilities for handling the output of his pit. With his characteristic energy and push he addressed himself to this task and now has an equipment which meets all demands and enables him to meet his part of the contract.

As fast as money came in he began to buy more land to rent out. Today he owns more than four thousand acres of rich fertile land and has these acres peopled with tenants. He owns and operates one of the largest cotton gins of that section. Along with farm land Bond bought timber land. Finding a big demand for timber Mr. Bond established a saw mill, now he ships lumber to Chicago, Pittsburg, and other large cities.

The spot on which he chopped wood for 30 cents a day when he first came to Madison now holds his large co-operative store. He owns and lives in the house of the man who first hired him to plow. In all, the property and holdings of this ex-slave are valued at $280,000.

Finer than all this is the fact that this "black Rockefeller," as some call him, has given his children college education.

He was married in 1877, and his wife has borne him eleven children, four of which are living. She has been not only a great help in his affairs but an inspiration to his life.

J. H. BLOUNT.

CHOOLMASTER and a business man, Professor J. H. Blount, of Forest City, Arkansas, has been fortunate enough to attain and hold distinction in both his vocation and avocation for more than a quarter of a century. He was born in Clinton, Jones County, Georgia, September 17, 1860. Madison Blount, the father was a slave belonging to the Blount family of Jones County; the mother belonged to another family by the name of Anderson. During the refugeeing of the two white owners of the parents, the mother and father were separated.

The parents were thus so widely separated that they lost track of each other for many years, and when they learned of each other's whereabouts, both had married again. The son remained with his mother all the time, except when he went to live with his father for the purpose of going to school in Macon, Georgia.

During the great exodus from Georgia, which took place in 1873, Rev. I. H. Anderson took many immigrants to Arkansas as tenants. Among this number was William Clark, the stepfather of Mr. J. H. Blount. After spending a few years in the public schools in Arkansas, Mr. Blount yearned for more and better learning than he could get at that time in Arkansas. At this time Dr. R. F. Boyd came to his home town lecturing and soliciting students for Central Tennessee College and Meharry Medical College. He induced the young Georgian to go to Nashville, Tennessee, instead of attending Atlanta University, Atlanta, Georgia, as he and his parents had planned. He entered Central Tennessee College in 1884 and continued in school there until 1890. During his vacation he taught summer school in the town of Forest City, Arkansas. As the summer school of this town gradually grew under his tutorship, from a summer school to an eight months graded school, he finally concluded to satisfy his thirst for an education by spending his vacation in the University of Chicago, where he worked very hard for four summers.

He is still a diligent student, and thinks more of his library than anything, except his children. For the past twenty-eight years, he has served as principal of the following named schools: Forest City Public School, Langston High School, Hot Springs Arkansas; Orr High School, Texarkana, Arkansas and Peabody High School, Helena, Arkansas.

He was deputy County Examiner of St. Francis County for ten years, and his prominence in educational affairs, made him without his seeking, take a leading part in politics. His people soon required that he should take an active part in the affairs of his county and state. His education and abundance of general information, coupled with his skill to manage public affairs, made him a favorite in his community and county. From state politics, he became active in national affairs. He was an alternate delegate at large, to the Republican National Convention, that gave the Nation Roosevelt and Fairbanks for president and vice-president respectively.

Being a teacher in education and in politics, did not cause Mr. Blount to neglect his church and the fraternal orders of which he was a member. He is one of the few thirty-third degree masons of the state of Arkansas, and has served in nearly every official position in the Masonic Grand Lodge of Arkansas. He has held the position of Secretary-Treasurer for four terms and that of Deputy Grand Master for five terms; he is chairman of the committee on Foreign Correspondence at the present time.

Mr. Blount is an active member of other fraternal orders such as the Odd Fellows, Knights of Pythias, Royal Circle of Friends of the World, Knights and Daughters of Tabor, and the United Brothers of Friendship. He is also a leading member of the Missionary Baptist Church and a Sunday School worker.

Professor Blount owns hundreds of acres of land, both farm and forest; and city property in three Arkansas towns. His property will readily bring $50,000.00, which is a conservative valuation. He also carries $20,000.00 in life insurance, not including his fraternal insurance.

He was married in August 1906 to Miss Almira Justina E. Payne of Holly Springs, Mississippi, who was to him a real helpmate till her death in January 1917. In the Blount home there are three children J. H. Blount, Jr., Scott Bond, and E. Louise, all of whom are pupils in their father's school.

94

BISHOP JAMES M. CONNER, S. T. B., B. D.,
D. D., LL. D., PH. D.

ORN in Winston County, in Mississippi, in 1863, Bishop James M. Conner fought hard for even a rudimentary education. Against all kinds of poor school facilities, which facilities include the teacher, he managed to secure his foundation in Mississippi and Alabama. While still a young man and but mid-way his education he had thought and planned out for himself his career.

He felt called to the ministry and like Paul, yielding to the divine call, he immediately set to work to prepare himself for his heavenly mission.

Without waiting to complete his education he took up his life work and went forth holding aloft the banner of the cross, to an unselfish and devoted service which he has steadily pursued during his long and useful career.

Converted in 1881 he at once joined the A. M. E. Church and was licensed to preach one year later.

He was given his first appointment in 1883 and placed in charge of the Aberdeen Mission, Aberdeen, Mississippi. He entered upon his work with enthusiasm and soon converted his mission into a live church, erecting a new building for them and building up a fine congregation. Recognizing his ability and special endowment for such work Bishop T. W. D. Ward, the following year, 1884, made him a Deacon and an Elder.

From this time on his reputation was established and his co-operation eagerly sought. He was recognized as a man who did things and it was generally accepted that when he undertook a service it would be satisfactorily rendered.

Thenceforth for a number of years he became known as a church builder and a champion "Dollar" money raiser. He built a church at Forrest City, Arkansas, in 1885. Then a new church at Osceola and a church at Newport, Arkansas. To quote Mr. R. R. Wright, Jr.: "At all these places he gave the connection good churches and added many new members to the church and carried excellent conference reports, excelling all previous records."

However vigorously he waged campaigns for money, erected churches, and converted souls, Bishop Conner never forgot personal growth. Like the dying German poet he was always crying "More Light." To satisfy his longing he went from time to time to some large institution to pursue such courses as he needed for his work. In 1891 he received from the National University of Chicago the degree of Bachelor of Sacred Theology. He later finished courses gaining the degree of B. D. from the American Institute in the University of Chicago, in 1897, and from Shorter College in 1905. Campbell College conferred upon him the degree of LL. D. He became President of the Board of Trustees of Shorter College and chancellor of Campbell College and Lampton College at Alexandria, Louisiana. Morris Brown University conferred upon him the degree of Doctor of Divinity, and Paul Quinn College at Waco, Texas, made him Doctor of Philosophy.

That he has richly earned these honors is made clear from his advancements. He is the author of several books. Among these being his "Outlines of Christian Theology," "Doctrines of Christ" and "The Elements of Success." He has been a delegate to every General Conference since 1896. He was a member of the financial board for eight years.

Bishop Conner was married to Miss Glovenia L. Stewart, of Kentucky, in 1886. They had three children, two of which died. Zola X, their only living child was a student of Shorter College. James and Qu'ntella died young.

Bishop Conner is an extensive property holder, owning his home and other valuable pieces of real estate. At present he is Bishop of Arkansas and Oklahoma.

S. W. HARRISON, M. D.

 HAT no man is a hero to his valet, or to his neighbor, is somtimes disapproved. This is true in the case of Dr. S. W. Harrison of Fort Smith, Arkansas. He was born in Fort Smith; was educated as far as possible there and returned there to practice his profession. Yet, so useful has been his career that his neighbors speak of him in their papers as follows:

"Dr. S. W. Harrison, President of the Negro Business League and Colored Fair Association, is one of the best known leading Negroes of this section.

"He is one of the greatest exponents of the progressive side of his race, and delights to furnish others with examples of race progress. He ranks with the foremost physicians of the state; is one the most astute of business men and wields an influence in the city among both races that is equaled by few."

As his life story will show, not always has Dr. Harrison's name been a symbol of progress and emulation. Born in Fort Smith, September 22nd, 1879, he began at a very early age to taste the fruits of combat sometimes bitter, but nevertheless stimulating. He attended Lincoln High School of his native city and was graduated in 1895. He was graduated from Meharry Medical College in 1900.

Both in medical school and in high school his education cost him dearly. In his early school days he made himself a sort of grocery delivery wagon, carrying goods to so many customers for a stipulated sum. However, this latter proved a most profitable investment; for the people he once served with groceries are now among his best patrons.

Dr. Harrison's choice of a life work was medicine and surgery, but how to secure the necessary preparation for his work was a problem which required great nerve and determination on his part to solve. Nothing daunted he left for Nashville and arrived there with only ten cents in his pocket. He did not have the money to purchase his necessary books but overcame this difficulty by borrowing books until he had earned sufficient money to buy his own.

During the summer he taught school but at one time this post failed him, and he was again confronted with the problem of how to continue his course. However, he was determined to do so and while brightening his wits to find a way to secure his end, he gave up the school master's rod and books for the boot black's brush and box and went forth to shine shoes.

Graduating in 1900 Dr. Harrison first opened office in Smithville, Texas. After remaining here four years he decided to return to his native city. Here he has worked, as a physician, a business man, a man of public service. He is a member of the A. M. E. Church, a Mason, an Odd Fellow, a Knight of Pythias, a Mosaic, a member of the U. B. F. of Tabor and of all local societes. As has been quoted he is president of the Negro Business League; he is ex-president of the state Medical Association; he is a trustee of Shorter College; Grand Trustee of the Knights of Pythias, medical inspector of the Negro Public Schools of Fort Smith and a high ranking candidate for the Grand Chancellorship of the Knights of Pythias.

His business ventures have been as successful as his practice in medicine and his public service. He owns his home, an elegant two story residence on Ninth Street in Fort Smith. He owns eight rent houses and six unimproved lots. He is a stockholder in the Standard Life Insurance Company of Atlanta, Georgia. He has traveled extensively in this country on business and for pleasure.

Dr. Harrison was married to Miss Margie Katona Gordon, December 31, 1902. Their two children, Margie Edith, who is fourteen, and Gordon Henry, who is twelve, are in school.

FERDINAND HAVIS.

HERE are few men of any race who carry so much of the bone and fibre of American history in their personal experience as does Ferdinand Havis, of Pine Bluff, Arkansas. He is one of those typical Americans, almost impossible in other countries, who from the bottom of the scale, succeeds by hard work in reaching the top.

Mr. Havis was born in Shay County, Arkansas, November 15th, 1847. He attended for a little while the public school. But at an early age he had to leave school to work. A very novel plan was then hit upon as a means of getting an education for the young man. His mother went to the school each day, mastered the lessons and then at night taught them to the ambitious boy who was so eagerly waiting for them. A boy with the ambition makes a man of mark.

By the time Mr. Havis was twenty-one he had run the gauntlet as a laborer. He had learned the barber's trade and opened a ship in Pine Bluff. Three years later he was elected alderman from the third ward. Year after year for the space of twenty-four years, Mr. Havis was elected and served in this capacity. In 1873 he was elected to the state

Legislature, but he resigned this post to serve as assessor. This post of assessor was offered him by Governor Baxter, and he served in it for two years. In 1882 he was elected Circuit Clerk, a post which he held for ten years. He was Republican Nominee for United States Senator from Arkansas, in 1886. Mr. Havis has served his party as a delegate to the National Republican Convention every year since 1880 with the exception of two years. These exceptions were in 1912 and 1916, when Taft and Hughes were nominated. He was a colonel on the staff of General H. King in the Brooks and Baxter War, and was one of the 306 who stood by General Grant in his endeavor to become president of the United States. He is on record as having voted for General Grant thirty-six times. He was chairman of the Republican County Control Committee of Arkansas for twelve years. This shows in brief the political life of Mr. Ferdinand Havis.

Having made good in his political career by applying himself to the task in hand, Mr. Havis, when he decided to retire to private life, used the same method of self application in the work he began. The same acumen which kept him in office and on boards of importance soon asserted itself in dealing in real estate and in farming. Mr. Havis has invested heavily in farm lands. He owns about 3000 acres. Of this amount, 1000 acres are under cultivation. The rest is in pasture land and timber. In addition to this country property, Mr. Havis has large interests in the city. One of the buildings which he owns, a building on Main Street, rents for $200 per month. He also has half interest in four stores which bring in rent. Then to private families he is able to rent twenty-five homes.

Mr. Havis owns his own home. This is a beautiful place on one of the principal residence streets of Pine Bluff. Here he lives with his family. Mr. Havis has been married three times.

There are two sons and one daughter.

In his church and loge affiliations, Mr. Havis is a member of the A. M. E. church, of the Masons, a member of the United Brothers of Friendship, of the Odd Fellows and of the Knights of Pythias. He is the Grand Master of the United Brotherhood of Friendship of America and of the world. He is president of the Board of Trustees, of the Lucy Memorial Hospital. Mr. Havis is referred to by all Pine Bluff as their Colored Millionaire.

———————

Since the above was written, Mr. Ferdinand Havis has passed away. After about a month's illness he died at his home on Baraque Street, August 25, 1918. Pine Bluff feels that it has lost a very substantial citizen.

NAPOLEON BONAPARTE HOUSER, M. D.

OMING from a family of workers, Dr. N. B. Houser, M. D., of Helena, Arkansas, has found it second nature to make work his diversion as well as his occupation When he was nine years old he began working with his father. It was not an easy trade that he put his hands to, being that of making brick. However he acquired and worked with a diligence and patience that astonished and pleased his parents. From the age of nine to the age of sixteen during spare hours and school holidays and vacations, he labored away, making brick, learning the ins and outs of the trade.

At the age of sixteen, the father's business having greatly multiplied, the son became private secretary and bookkeeper. This post he held for sixteen years, estimating contracts, and figuring out margins, pertaining to his father's interest as if he were really joint partner of the firm. It was really through him that the father was able to gain fair profits and to maintain his contracting business on a systematic scale. Though engrossed in keeping accounts, the young man did not forget, however, that he had a duty to himself and to his people, the duty of educating himself and of

serving. Born near Castoria, in Gaston County, North Carolina, February 14, 1869, he attended the schools round about, until he was sufficiently advanced in years and books to enroll at Biddle University at Charlotte, N. C. Completing this work at Biddle and becoming convinced that his calling in life was that of a doctor, though a good position was awaiting him back there with his father, he became a student in Leonard College of Medicine at Shaw University in 1887, won the prize "for superior knowledge in Obstetrics", did the four year's work in a little less than three years, graduating in 1891.

Returning to Charlotte, the seat of his alma mater, Biddle University, he hung out his sign and began life's business. He soon became what is known as a "successful practicing physician." With his general practice he became the consulting physician for Biddle University. Paying a visit to his brother in Arkansas in 1900, Dr. Houser was so favorably impressed with the possibility for a good doctor and drug business that though having well established himself in his ten year's practice at Charlotte, he decided to go west and build anew his practice and to contribute his mite in building up the country; and so he left North Carolina, where he was most popular with the men of his profession, having served as president and secretary of the North Carolina Colored Medical Association, and having been physician in charge of the Samaritan Hospital at Charlotte for three years.

In Helena, Arkansas, where he began his new career, progress in his profession surpassed even that of North Carolina. Beginning practice here in 1901, he had by 1908 gained sufficient footing and confidence to open the Black Diamond Drug Store, a business which prospered from the outset, which, because of expanse, he had to move three times, until now he has it on one of the main streets and in one of the most desirable spots in Helena.

Had Dr. Houser not been a brilliant success as a physician and a man of business, he would still no doubt have been a very popular man; for he is a musician of rare talent, playing on many different instruments, an engaging companion, a fervent church worker, being a Baptist in his religious choice, and a member of nearly every lodge extant in the state of Arkansas—a Mason, an Odd Fellow, a Knight of Pythias and a Mosaic Templar.

In all of these orders he made his personality felt and contributed no little to their work and development. He was not content to be a member only but brought to their aid his great fund of intelligent executive ability.

Dr. Houser was married to Miss Amie A. Alston of Louisburg, North Carolina, January 18th, 1902. One daughter, Weillie Henry, graces their home.

MRS. MAME STEWART JOSENBERGER, A. B.

RS. Mame Stewart Josenberger, one of the really remarkable women of the age, was born in Oswega, New York. In her youth she attended the grammar schools, the high school and the Free Academy of Oswega. From the Free Academy of Oswega she went to the Fisk University, Tennessee, where she graduated with the degree of Bachelor of Arts.

After her graduation at Fisk she entered the profession of school teaching and began a long career as a school teacher. This covered a period from 1888 to 1903.

During her first year as teacher she gave instruction at the State Normal School, at Holly Springs, Mississippi. This was in 1888 and 1889. In 1890 she taught in the graded schools of Fort Smith, Arkansas, and from 1891 to 1901 she was a teacher in the Fort Smith High School.

While in the school room Mrs. Josenberger was the model teacher, her whole thought and attention given to her work, but after school hours her mind had time to take in other interests and she was soon identified with those institutions seeking the uplift of the Negro race. It was contrary to her disposition to be a passive member in the orders to which she belonged and her activity and thorough equipment for service was soon recognized by them and led to her rapid promotion among them.

These duties finally took so much of her time that it became necessary for her to choose between them and her profession of teacher. Believing that she could serve her people best along the lines of public service she yielded to the pointing of Providence and gave up the school room for a larger sphere of usefulness.

Thus in 1903 she left the school room to take the position of Grand Register of Deeds in the Order of Calanthe, a position she has held continuously for fifteen years.

Mrs. Josenberger lost her husband in 1909. From then until she became Register of Deeds for Calanthe she conducted the undertaking business left by him. Her public duties and engagments now became so pressing that she gave up altogether the business of her husband and devoted her energies to work for the public good. She had joined the Episcopal Church in 1909, being confirmed by Rev. Father McClure, who was at that time archdeacon of Arkansas. She joined also the Royal Circle, the Eastern Star, the American Woodmen, and several other fraternal orders. In all these bodies she became an adviser and a leading worker.

It would seem that these were enough memberships for any one person to hold, especially where one is a worker as is Mrs. Josenberger. But Mrs. Josenberger was soon enlisted outside the state. She became a member of the Standard Life Insurance Company and was forthwith put on the Advisory Board. She joined the National Negro Business League, soon becoming a life member. She is a member of the N. A. A. C. P., Past Supreme Conductress of the Order of Calanthe; President of the Phyllis Wheatley Club, which is the first local Federation Club of Fort Smith, is vice president of the State Federation and chairman of the peace committee among the N. A. colored women.

Serving in so many positions Mrs. Josenberger has traveled extensively and has had wide and helpful contact.

Mrs. Josenberger was married in 1892 to Mr. William Ernest Josenberger, who was a postman in Fort Smith, then an undertaker. She is as successful in business affairs as she is in doing uplift work. She is worth about $30,000 which includes a two-story cement store building and a two-story brick building, which has five stores on the first floor and a large auditorium on the second.

Mrs. Josenberger has one daughter, William Ernest Josenberger now Mrs. Joseph L. Stevens, a musician.

Scipio Africanus Jordan

CIPIO Africanus Jordan, is one of the old and leading citizens of Little Rock, Arkansas. He has grown with the city and each is a sort of mutual contributor to the growth of the year. He was born in Montgomery County, Arkansas, January 1st, 1860. Mr. Jordan, when a lad, attended the public schools of Little Rock and later the colored High School. He was a member of the first graduating class of the Little Rock Colored High School which awarded its first diploma in 1880.

After graduating from the Little Rock Colored High School, Mr. Jordan cast about for work and entered the service of the United States Government, becoming a janitor of the post office building. This position he held for twelve months when he received the appointment of letter carrier. As letter carrier he went his daily rounds over the streets of Little Rock for more than thirty-six years delivering mail. By his courteous and obliging manner he made many friends among all classes. He was possibly the best known man in Little Rock—men, women and children knowing him by name and watching for his daily visits.

In 1896 he was appointed chairman of the Board of Civil Service Examiners for the Post Office of Little Rock.

While Mr. Jordan gave his first thought and attention to his business and won favor with the Government, as his promotions give evidence, he always found time to serve his people and became interested in all agencies looking to their good. In all matters pertaining to the betterment of the colored race he gave the benefit of his wise counsel and help and his fellow citizens found in him a willing helper.

He joined most of the secret orders of his state and became very active in their work and soon was a recognized leader among them, taking a prominent part in all their gatherings and in the working out of their plans.

His fine executive ability advanced him to posts of honor and responsibility. In 1889 he was elected Chief Grand Mentor for the Knights of Tabor and then ten years later in 1899 he succeeded Father Moses Dickson as International Chief Grand Mentor. Both of these positions he is still holding which is a glowing tribute to his worth and popularity.

However, these posts did not tend to lighten his responsibilities, but rather to increase them. He has long been a member of the Bethel A. M. E. Church of his city, for twenty years he has been a trustee. He is a Mason, and an Odd Fellow as well as a Knight of Tabor. He became a member of the Lincoln Farm Association in 1907. He has been colonel, acting on the staff of the major of the Grand United Order of Odd Fellows for a number of years. Working in so many positions Mr. Jordan has traveled in all of the United States combining business and pleasure.

Mr. Jordan has accumulated a goodly amount of real estate and personal property in Little Rock. He owns his home, one of the best residences of Colored Little Rock. He owns eleven vacant lots and eleven rent houses.

Mr. Jordan was married in 1884 to Miss Pinkie E. Venable of Little Rock. Mr. and Mrs. Jordan have a large family, there being born to them 9 children, seven of whom are living. Toney C. Jordon, who is deceased, was a graduate of Howard University; Miss Mabel E., who is now married, is a graduate of the public schools of Little Rock; Dr. J. V. Jordan is a dentist, being a graduate from the school of denistry, of Howard University, and of Northwestern; Miss Scipio is a graduate of the public schools of Little Rocok and of Philander Smith Commercial department; Yancy B. is a graduate of the pupils schools, mechanical course, and is now in the Virginia shipyards; Miss Myrtle is pursuing a commercial and high school course at the Arkansas Baptist College; Valmer H. is a school boy and Olga is still enjoying the freedom of childhood.

Had Mr. Jordan done nothing but rear and educate this large family he would still have deserved a place of honor among those of his race or any race for contributing so largely to the welfare of the race and state. His children stand as monuments to the earnest endeavors of this man. Not one of the large family, but was sent through at least one school and most of them secured two diplomas. Mr. Jordan himself, though born at a time when it was easy for the colored lad to miss getting an education, was a graduate. Having educated himself at a sacrifice, he was willing to do all in his power for the development of his children. But as is the law of things, while doing for his children, he continued to advance himself. We find Mr. Jordan developed into one of the leading citizens of his city and state. He is a real asset to the community of which he is a member. His work in the various organizations of which he has been for a great number of years one of the leaders has been one of the things that has made of Little Rock a good community for our people. Mr. Scipio A. Jordan can well be pointed out to the young as one worthy of emulation.

ELIAS CAMP MORRIS, D. D., PH. D.

EAR Spring Place in Georgia, born a slave, May 7, 1855, Dr. E. C. Morris of Helena, Arkansas, was fortunate enough to have a father who could read and write. The father, a tradesman from North Carolina, was permitted to visit his children on the plantation twice a week. At such times he taught his children to read and write.

In 1864-65 Dr. E. C. Morris attended school at Dalton. He also studied in the public schools of Chattanooga, Tennessee and at the Stevenson Institute in Alabama. In 1874-75, he was a student at the Nashville Institute, now Roger Williams University.

Going into life Dr. Morris essayed many things. For a time he taught school in North Alabama. While serving as a minister in Alabama, he worked at his trade as a shoemaker. In 1877 he set his face westward, intending to go to Kansas. Stopping over in Arkansas he decided to remain in Helena. Here in 1879, he was ordained; here he was given his first church, the only church over which he has presided and he is the only pastor the church has had for nearly forty years. This church, the Centennial Baptist, over which he became pastor, was at that time composed of a group of twenty-two members, homeless and without property of any kind. Today it has a membership of seven hundred, a stately edifice, which is valued

at $40,000, an active Sunday School of 399 children.

While toiling for the growth of his church, Dr. Morris launched forth every kind of movement to promote the religious growth of the whole state. In 1879, the same year he became pastor of Centennial Church, he organized the Phillips Lee and Monroe County District Association, and was secretary for two years. In 1880 he was elected secretary of the Arkansas Baptist State Convention and served in this capacity for two years. In 1882 he was chosen president of the Arkansas Baptist State Convention, a position he has held for thirty six years. He founded the Baptist Vanguard, a Baptist weekly newspaper, and was its editor for two years. He helped to found Arkansas Baptist College in 1884, and was chairman of the board of trustees for twenty-four years. For eighteen years he has been chairman of the Arkansas State Mission Board, an organization which works in conjunction with the National Baptist Convention and with the Southern White Baptist Convention. In 1891 he was made vice president of the National Baptist Convention, and president in 1894.

Under his administration many plans for expansion have been effected. At his recommendation, the National Publishing Board of Nashville, the Baptist Young People's Union of Nashville, the National Baptist Woman's Auxiliary of Washington, D. C., the National Benefit Association, and the Baptist Home Mission Board of Little Rock, have all been organized and advanced until they are now among the perfect bodies of their kind.

Outside of his special sphere Dr. Morris began to win many honors both in the church and in public affairs. He aided in organizing the General Convention of North America, which is made up of all Baptists of both races, and is the only Negro member of the executive committee of this body. He aided in organizing the American executive committee of this body. In public life he represented the First Arkansas Congressional District at the Republican National Convention three times—at the nomination of James G. Blaine in 1884, of Benj. Harrison in 1892; of Theodore Roosevelt in 1904. He was alternate delegate at large in 1908 to nominate William H. Taft. He has been a delegate to every Arkansas State Republican Convention for nearly forty years.

Active in the church and in the state Dr. Morris has not forgotten the business interest of colored people. He organized the State Business League; he took great interest in the Mound Bayou Oil Mill project, becoming one of the directors; he is director of the Phillips County Land and Investment Company. He himself owns mining stock, has a seventy-five acre farm, owns unimproved property, has a home and four pieces of improved property, valued at $10,000.

Dr. Morris was married in 1884 to Miss Fannie E. Austin of Fackler, Alabama. Their five children, Elias Austin, Frederick Douglass, Mattie M. Marquess, Sarah Hope and John Spurgeon, are all giving good account of themselves. Mr. Elias Austin is First Lieutenant in Company M. 366 Infantry U. S. A.; Frederick Douglass is Grand Keeper of Records and Seal of Knights of Pythias Grand Lodge, of the Arkansas jurisdiction. Mrs. Marquess and Miss Morris are teaching school. John Spurgeon is a student in the Arkansas Baptist College.

JOHN EDWARD BUSH.

John Edward Bush

EVER since J. E. Bush departed this life he has been the subject of eulogy. And yet it is very doubtful if any assembling of words, no matter how frought with poetic figures, will prove so eloquent, as the plain simple recitation of the facts of that heroic struggle of his from poverty and neglect to a place of the highest esteem in the hearts of all American Negroes. Mr. Bush was born a slave. He was born in Moscow, Tennessee, in 1858. Shortly after slavery he was brought to Little Rock, Arkansas, by his mother. In a little while the mother died, and the ex-slave lad was left in the streets of Little Rock an orphan.

Merely to live now became to him a very serious problem. He slept in houses when he could find a man or woman so kind as to extend to him that privilege, a privilege which was some times accorded for such small services as the little boy could render. Most commonly however he slept under bridges, in the livery stables and in deserted houses. He earned his bread by doing chores, running errands, watering stock, and washing dishes. Moreover, J. E. Bush was classed as a bad boy, which did not help him to get a night's lodging or an extra crust of bread. However, some good soul forced him off the streets into a school house. In a little while the boy of mischief was lost in the study of books. Though he could not afford regular attendance, yet he tasted enough to pronounce the food of the right kind and wholesome. Henceforth John E. Bush was a student.

He made such good out of his spare time in the midnight hours that he soon became a school teacher. This post he held in Little Rock for a number of years. However, it appears that he overstepped the bounds circumscribed for one of his station, by marrying out of his class. He lost his position immediately. He secured the principalship of a school in Hot Springs and taught here for two years. In 1875 he entered the railway mail service. For seventeen years he followed this calling, but finally resigned to start a newspaper.

All the time Mr. Bush was an active Republican. In 1884 he ran for the county clerkship of Rosalie County, Arkansas, on the Greenback Ticket. In 1898 he was appointed United States Land Office Receiver by President McKinley. He was reappointed by Theodore Roosevelt and again by President Taft. He even survived the Republican Black Broom, which swept Negroes so very clean from Federal Offices, under the kind Mr. Taft. This appointment had come and was the result of a long series of hard fights and small victories in the politics of Arkansas.

In 1882 Mr. Bush founded the Mosaic Templars of America. How he came to found this order, and what the order means to the Negroes of America has been briefly told elsewhere—for the few who may not know the whole history already. Suffice it to say here that the need of a poor woman, begging for help to bury her husband, the contempt of a white man and the chagrin of Mr. Bush at the whole situation started this organization. The body grew rapidly, and with it grew also J. E. Bush. He learned not only more about the intricacies of business but he learned a great deal about men. Most important of all, the organization brought J. E. Bush the deserved place he had won by hard work.

In a few years he became known the country over as a strong business man and a public benefactor. He was introduced to Booker T. Washington, and almost immediately these two giants, both with the experience of sleeping under bridges, behind them, became fast friends. When Booker T. Washington, who was himself a great political adviser, sought political advice, it was to J. E. Bush he turned. When the wizard of Tuskegee was touring the states of the south and bewitching the great crowds with his anecdotes and shrewd common sense, he frequently called into service the founder of the Mosaic Templars of America, and when Dr. Washington saw the need of laying the task of carrying forward the work of the Negro National Business League upon the shoulders of a group of strong men, J. E. Bush was one of the first looked to . He was for years one of the Vice-presidents and a member of the executive committee of this body.

Though an extremely busy man J. E. Bush found time to do many deeds of uplift in schools, churches and the like. He was a strong supporter of the Arkansas Baptist College and a trustee of the First Baptist Church of Little Rock. In secret orders, he was a Mason, an Odd Fellow, and of course the founder and promoter of The Mosaic Templars of America.

Mr. Bush was married in 1879, to Miss Winfry of Little Rock. Mr. and Mrs. Bush had three children, all three of whom survive their father: Miss Stella E. Bush, Mr. Chester E. Bush, who succeeds his father as the National Grand Secretary and Treasurer of the Mosaic Templars and Alridge E. Bush, who is the Secretary and Treasurer of the Monument Department of the Mosaic Templars.

John E. Bush left a fair name, a business in perfect order, and worldly possessions amounting to $500,000.

MOSAIC TEMPLARS' OFFICE BUILDING, LITTLE ROCK, ARKANSAS.

 ENTION the Mosaic Templars of America and you think of John E. Bush. Mention John E. Bush and you think of the Mosaic Templars. The Mosaic Templars of America was founded by J. E. Bush in 1883. Its two sponsors were John E. Bush and C. W. Keats. As stated by Hamilton McConico, the organization had its beginning from a three-fold source: The scorn of a white man, "a Negro woman's poverty and a Negro man's shame." All this arose out of J. E. Bush standing on the street talking to a white man when a colored woman came by begging for alms to bury her dead husband. The white man like Mr. Bush, gave, but he afterwards cast aspersions on the Negro people for their improvidence. From this John E. Bush resolved to found an order which should protect the poor of his race.

The organization was started as a benevolent society, with no intention of operation outside of Little Rock. But in a few years the demands for its services drew it into other states. It began with one lodge and fifteen members. It now has 2,000 lodges and a membership of more than 80,000. It began in one city. It now operates in twenty-six

states, in Central America, Panama and the West Indies. It opened without sufficient funds to incorporate. It now has assets exceeding $300,000. It started without shelter, the two founders working out their plans on the door-steps of an old building. Today upon the site of the old building it has one of the finest brick, steel and stone structures of any Negro lodge in America, a building which has offices, stores, and all kinds of rooms to accommodate the business and professional men of Little Rock. Thus has it brought pride and self-respect to all the Negroes of Little Rock and indeed to the Negro everywhere.

When the two founders of the Mosaic Templars sat on the steps of that old building in Little Rock, their only thought was to provide a means of safeguarding the pennies of the poor and needy. They had no dream of departments, sections and various ramifications of a great order. As the body grew and gained the unlimited confidence of the people everywhere, however, they with the helpers it was necessary to call in, found that many departments and divisions had to be formed to meet the more complex needs of the public. Thus one after another departments were organized, until now there are in the body six main divisions or departments, each with its head, yet all working under the central head of the Mosaic Templars These are the Endowment Department, The Juvenile Department the Temple Department, the Uniform Rank Department, the Monument Department, the Arkansas Charity Fund, Recapitulation, Analysis, Recommendations Each Department is a unit in itself yet each is a part of the great whole For example, though each Department is a member of the whole, yet each must be responsible for all the business coming under its head If the given Department runs behind in its accounts, or gets entangled in its bookkeeping that Department and not the whole organization, becomes sponsor Thus, while all move under a general head, yet there is ample departmental responsibility to keep the whole body on the qui vive Each head of a Department and each worker in the department feels a personal responsibility and a personal and departmental pride in keeping his work to the fore For in every instance, if the department fails the head and all his co-workers also fail

It therefore turns out that while J E Bush founded a most helpful organization he also established a body which is a splendid object lesson of what the Negro can do when working together, a body which is helpful in promoting the respect of the white for the black man and in inspiring self-respect in the black man

Of equal service perhaps is this order, in that it furnishes dignified employment to hundreds of our educated men and women

When we consider that all these people would be living on half pay from the school room, or whole pay from the Pullman or steam boat services, some adequate notion can be formed as to the real service of this organization, outside of its direct purpose Every such organization is a great milestone in a race's progress, and he who establishes such is building a school and a business at the same time For in no other way could our men and women become accustomed to handling the intricacies of bookkeeping and the question of high finance

Finally The Mosaic Templars have found men In its own state it began very early to teach the people of Arkansas who their great thinkers and leaders were Then it reached out its hand into this, then into that, until in every state of the south and in many in the north there are scores more of solid leaders than would otherwise have been known The organization has been left in the hands largely of the sons of the founder, C F Bush, National Grand Secretary and A E Bush, Secretary-Treasurer This again follows the line of a great service affording a big lesson for the men of the race Young Morgan is running his father's bank young Hill is carrying forward the great railroad interests of James J Hill And the

sons of J E Bush are holding and increasing the heritage left to them and to the Negro people of America

The following is an extract from report to the National Grand Lodge,, meeting at Little Rock, Ark, July 10-13 1917, by the National Grand Scribe, "From comparative insignificance we have now forged to the front and have attracted nationwide attention We have set a pace in the Fraternal World that up to this writing has not been out-distanced Our growth being steady having increased membership about 25 per cent since our Tuskegee meeting and our assets have increased approximately more than one hundred thousand dollars above what they were at Tuskegee

"The same plan of economy inaugurated at the birth of the organization has been steadfastly adhered to The main object in view is to properly safeguard and handle the money that the people intrust to our keeping If we have achieved any success it is due more to this principle than any other element Examiners from various insurance departments have marveled at the low expense budget maintained to operate our organization

"That our Organization is well organized is evidenced by the minimum amount of friction in the management All of our officials and leaders with few exceptions, are men and women of level heads and well balanced minds The discordant element is so little encouraged in our Organization that it soon seeks other quarters of its own volition A big business like the Mosaic Templars of America can only have successful management by having harmony in all of its working departments Many people in dealing with the Mosaic Templars are very much surprised when they learn that the National Grand Master's office, the National Grand Scribe's office, the Attorney General's office, the Auditor's office, the Monument office all operate without one interfering with the other Each department head is held responsible for success in his or her department If he fails then no blame can be placed upon any other department and the report must be made to you, the final judges"

The Mosaic Templars stand for the unification of one common brotherhood of every man or woman with Negro blood coursing through his or her veins of good moral character, into a common brotherhood of helpfulness and usefulness It believes that whatever agencies or forces that are conducive to the uplift of the white race will have a corresponding effect on the Negro

It stands for a symmetrical development of the Negro on moral religious educational and industrial lines It believes that whatever safeguards that are thrown around one race to ennoble it, and prepare it for better citizenship the same ought to be extended the Negro

RICHARD ARNETT WILLIAMS, M. D

HE unthinking world is too apt to discredit men of visions, and yet, without the visionary men this world would be poor indeed, and would still be in a chaotic state. Men must see things before they can be accomplished and to the credit of the men of visions, be it said, that they paved the way for all great achievements. Such a man is Dr. R. A. Williams.

Dr. Williams was born September 13th, 1879, in Forest City, Arkansas. Although his parents were not rich, they possessed sufficient means to enable them to aid their son to secure an education. They saw the advantages of a good education and determined that they could do no better part for their children than to do what they could in the development of their minds. They early placed the Doctor in the public schools of his native city, where he graduated at the tender age of twelve. His appetite for knowledge was whetted by his course in the public school, and he determined to pursue his studies further. This he did at the Danville Industrial High school, of Danville Virginia. After a course at this school he continued his literary studies in the Arkansas Baptist College,

Little Rock, Arkansas, and graduated from the Academic Department of this institution, in 1896. He bears the distinction and honor of being the first graduate of this department which has since sent out so many well prepared young men and women. At an early age, Dr. Williams gave much thought to the question of his life work, and decided upon the medical profession. This decision remained with him through all of his college life, and all of his preparation looked to this end. It was in 1898, that he began to see the fruition of his hope and the consummation of his dream. It was this year that he matriculated at Meharry Medical College. He finished his course of study in this well known school and not only won honors but also the confidence and esteem of his fellow students. His career as a student was not without its trials and difficulties and he found it necessary to engage in business ventures from time to time in order to raise the money necessary to pay his way.

At the early age of fourteen he assumed the duties of the school master and governed himself, even, at this early age, with the dignity befitting one in that profession. His next venture was that of a merchant and under the firm name of Williams and Brown he conducted for two years a grocery business. This venture was successful but could not tempt him to give up the purpose to become a physician. It enabled him, however, to carry out his well-formed plan for a medical education.

After graduating at the Meharry College, he went to Knoxville, Tenn., and commenced his professional career. Here he remained for three years and won the confidence of the people, and established a good practice. He could not remain satisfied at Knoxville, for the lure of his native state was upon him. He could not turn a deaf ear to its call, so in 1905, he left Knoxville, and turned his face toward Arkansas. Helena was the city of his choice and here he located and here he has remained, building up for himself a good practice and an enviable reputation. Being a man of sympathetic nature, he was not slow to put himself in touch with the needs of his people, and to interest himself in their behalf. His work as a physician enabled him to see the great need of money in times of sickness and when the death angel spread its wings over the home and it was this that gave him this vision of a society that would supply this need. He put his mind to work and as a result of his thinking he brought into existence the "Royal Circle of Friends of the World." To this organization he has given his time and executive skill and in its interest he has had to travel extensively. Seeing in it such great possibilities, he has given it so much of his time that he has had to curtail his general practice and confine himself to an office practice and to a specialty.

The Royal Circle of Friends is one of the most modern organizations calling upon the public for its support It bases its claims for support alone upon merit It has found favor from the start, and continues to hold its friends Its growth is phenomenal and has exceeded the hopes of its founder Its first lodge was organized in 1909 and the number has increased to about three hundred lodges, and about nine thousand members The lodges are scattered over five states, Arkansas, Mississippi, Alabama, Kentucky and Oklahoma The order has several main features It has an endowment feature by which the beneficiary of a deceased member gets Three Hundred Dollars at his or her death This endowment is paid promptly within a week after the death of a member and if the family is in great need it is paid immediately Another feature rewards the member for a ten year connection therewith It is a one hundred dollar endowment It also provides for a sick and accident benefit This feature alone, has done incalculable good The order is noted for its promptness in settlement of its claims and is multiplying its strength in the accumulation of a surplus The founder recognizes the importance of keeping in touch with its members and to this end he has established a paper, known as the Royal Messenger

Much of the success of the Royal Circle of Friends is due to the popularity of its founder and his rare business judgment

The aim of the founder of the Royal Circle of Friends was to give to his people the largest benefits at the least cost and to insure the prompt payment of all claims To make it possible for all to share in its benefits the initiation fee was placed at Two Dollars and Fifty Cents, and a quarterly endowment fee of One Dollar When the substantial benefits derived from this organization are considered its fee's are more reasonable than any other order

The great majority of the men and women who come into the organization are young This gave the order an advantage To meet conditions which will naturally arise as the members grow older a surplus has been created which is being added to annually

Dr Williams, the founder and President, has the handling of funds of the order and has already demonstrated his ability to handle them with consumate business skill His integrity is above question and the members feel safe, so long as the affairs of the order remain in his hands An order of this character has to get out much printed matter and in keeping with its economical management a printing press was purchased and by means of this outfit much money has been saved the Order in the item of printing alone Dr Williams is constantly in receipt of letters commending the order and acknowledging the good it has done for the colored race It has been especially gratifying to him to receive so many letters of personal commendation and to know that he is held in such high personal esteem by his friends To feel that you have done something worth while always brings pleasing reflections but to know that you have started a movement which will continue long after you have passed away, to bless the people whom you love and wish to serve is thrilling in its contemplation Such is the joy that has come to Dr Williams in establishing the order of the Royal Circle of Friends He has lived to see it a success and to see the great good it has already accomplished If he should cease from his labors now he has done enough to hand down his name to posterity and in a way to bring only pleasant memories of him

He has built his monument which will be more enduring than granite, or stone, and as long as the Royal Circle of Friends exists, Dr Williams will be held in fond remembrance

"Fading away like the stars of the morning,
Losing their light in the glorious sun—
Thus would we pass from earth and its toiling,
Only remembered by what we have done"

August 25th, 1903 Dr Williams was married to Miss Cora E Morgan of Memphis, Tennessee She is a daughter of one of the wealthiest planters of Shelby County, Tennessee, and is a woman of culture, refinement and great ability

Mrs Williams was graduated from the LeMoyne Institute of Memphis and for several years was one of the leading teachers in her native county

A daughter, Vera Louise Williams, makes the Williams' home one of happiness

She is a very bright young person and makes life interesting for the father and mother

At the time of his marriage Dr Williams was a man of small means and only attained to his present standing in the financial world by the practice of the strictest economy He is now housed in his own home and lives in a style that is befitting a high class professional man

Dr Williams gives much of the credit for their financial success to his wife She it was who helped him to rise in life and who was an inspiration to him in the dark hours that come to all who struggle upward

It is not often that a man accomplishes so much in so short a period of his life and it must be a matter of supreme satisfaction to Dr Williams to see the seed of his planting blossom into so fragrant and beautiful a flower, whose aroma of friendship will bless the coming generations The man who confers a benefit upon his race is blessed in his work for others and the reflex influence upon his own life brings to him a personal blessing

A life of service is a successful life and brings its own sure and blessed reward

E. O. TRENT.

OR a man to hold the same position for considerably over a quarter of a century, and still keep thoroughly abreast with the times, shows a great strength of character. One of the easiest things for a man who serves the public to do, is to get in a rut. Then his days of usefulness are numbered. But when a man can serve the public year in and year out, giving something new to each set of people who come directly under his care, when a man can do this, he is a success.

For thirty-three years E. O. Trent has served as principal of the High and Industrial School, at Fort Smith, Arkansas. During all these years he has kept his school up to the standard in every particular. His teachers have caught something of his spirit of service and give freely of their time and energies during off hours.

Professor Trent was born in Columbus, Ohio, February 24, 1859. Fortunate for him he was in a section, where even in those days a boy of color could have some chance at an education. So from the age of six to twenty-three he attended school in his native state. He graduated from the Gar-

man High School of Columbus and then entered the Ohio State University. From this institution he was graduated in 1882. In seeking for a place where he could best serve his people in the capacity of school master, he left his native state and went to Missouri. Here for one year he taught and then having received the opening at Fort Smith, Arkansas, he gave up his work in Missouri and went to Arkansas. Here he has remained, teaching in the school room and out of it both young and old, some of the lessons from books and many of the fundamental lessons of life.

Professor Trent did not confine his work to the town of Fort Smith. He saw the need of a State Teachers Association for the colored teachers of Arkansas, and became one of the prime movers in organizing this body. That through this act alone Professor Trent has served the entire State of Arkansas, can not well be disputed. All the teachers through this organization have been brought up to a higher standard of teaching. All of them know more fully just what they are trying to do for the boys and girls, who come directly under their care. In this way has the influence of Professor Trent been broadened.

In religious affiliation the subject of this sketch is a stanch Baptist. He is an active member of the Missionary Baptist Church in Fort Smith. In this church he has held many responsible positions. He has served as deacon, as clerk, as a leader of the young people's organization and as Superintendent of the Sunday School. Through the Sunday School, Professor Trent has been able to touch the lives of his pupils from the standpoint of religion, and because of this he has been able to help develop well rounded young men and women.

In fraternal Orders he is also a man of prominence. He was for seventeen years Secretary of the Odd Fellows Benefit Association. He is C. C. of the Knights of Pythias, he is a member of the Masonic Order, he is H. H. R., of the Eastern Star, a member of the Mosiac Templars and of the Royal Arch Masons. Through these organizations, Professor Trent has come more directly in contact with the men and women of his adopted town. And so we see that his life has touched the lives of the people of Fort Smith, from many different points. In return for all the things he has done for the people of Fort Smith, they have given him honor in many particulars. He has held positions of honor and trust in the churches, fraternal orders and in the Sociological Congress.

Professor Trent was married to Miss Hattie S. Smith, August 25, 1886, in Columbus, Ohio. There are two children in the Trent family. E. E. Trent is in business for himself in Fort Smith. He is a very successful merchant. Alphonso Trent is still a student. He is in the Lincoln High School at Fort Smith.

During all the years that he has been out working for himself, Professor Trent has managed to accumulate considerable of this worlds goods. He owns thirty-two rent houses and a truck farm. A conservative estimate of the value of his holdings is placed at $50,000.00.

BIRD'S EYE VIEW OF ATLANTA UNIVERSITY

ATLANTA University is one of the pioneer institutions for the Christian education of Negro youth. It possesses excellent equipment for the work of high school, normal school and college classes, and has accommodations for one hundred and sixty boarding students. It is the first institution in the State of Georgia to undertake work of college grade for Negroes, and steadily emphasizes the importance of genuine scholarship. It enjoys the cumulative advantage which results from forty-nine years of continuous effective work. It has been unusually fortunate in the continuity of its administration. It was founded in 1865 under the auspices of the American Missionary Association, by Edmund Asa Ware. It was presided over by him until his death, in 1885. President Ware was a graduate of Yale University of the class of 1863. In 1875 his Yale classmate Horace Bumstead, succeeded to the presidency and held the position until 1907, when he resigned, and became the recipient of a Carnegie pension. His successor is Edward Twichell Ware, son of the founder and first president, a graduate of Yale University of the class of 1897. On the teaching force, there have always been, as there are now, men and women who have received the best education that this country affords. Among the colleges represented by the teachers are Harvard, Dartmouth, Chicago, Smith, and Wellesley.

The University is beautifully situated upon the summit of a hill in the Western part of the City of Atlanta, and is surrounded by a campus of sixty acres. There are seven substantial brick buildings, three of them covered with Boston Ivy. The value of the property, all told, is $300,000. The invested funds amount to about $125,000. For the proper maintenance of the work, about $39,000 is required each year in addition to the amount reasonably to be expected from payments of students and income from funds. For this extra amount the Institution depends upon the endowment of friends who give from year to year.

Instruction in domestic science and manual training is required of all the high school students and there are opportunities for pursuing this work further in the college course of mechanic arts and

in the Furber Cottage for the normal students. The normal course comprises two years following the high school course.

During the Senior year the girls live in the Furber Cottage in groups of fifteen and under the supervision of the matron, do all the work of the home.

The Institution also possesses a well equipped printing office, from which is issued the catalogue, the school and alumni papers. Here, there is an opportunity to learn the art of printing. It is the purpose of Atlanta University to make the home life in the school strong and wholesome.

There is probably no school for the Negroes in the South better equipped with facilities for home training, for library work, or for the preparation of teachers. This institution has also been long prominent for the excellence of its work in sociology. Its annual publications on the Negro problem have received wide recognition from scholars and may be found in the best libraries in this country and abroad.

Opportunities for Post Graduate Study leading to the degree of A. M. are offered to a limited extent.

There are enrolled over five hundred students. About two-thirds of them come up the hill every day from the City of Atlanta. The rest are in the boarding department and represent sixteen states, and thirty-nine counties in the State of Georgia. These young people are many of them children of the graduates of Atlanta University and most of them have received their training in schools over which the graduates preside.

This Institution is an outgrowth of the Christian spirit which brought so many earnest and devoted teachers South, in the educational crusade of the sixties and seventies. The work is essentially Christian. It is undenominational and strong in religious motive. Students attend church and Sunday school. They also have their voluntary religious organizations, the Y. M. C. A. and Y. W. C. A. Participation in the religious exercises and in the home life of the school has often been instrumental in molding the character of the student for the most efficient service among their people.

The chief source of encouragement for the work rests in the almost uniform success of the graduates of Atlanta University.

MRS. ROSA LULA BARNES.

N recent years the Negro woman has begun to find herself. Time was when both by herself and in the minds of the general public it was decided, yea determined, that her place was in the home, in the school room and in the Sunday School. Gradually she got into founding institutions, schools, social settlements and the like. She went on the lecture platform. She traveled in America and in Europe as a singer. In all these places she found herself a complete success.

Then a few ventured into unheard of fields—into politics and in business. Again success is crowning their endeavors. Why should they not enter any and all branches of work?

One of the leading Negro women in business, in lodge, and general social work is Mrs. Lula Barnes of Savannah, Georgia. Though an Alabamian by birth and education Mrs. Barnes is a Georgian by adoption and achievement. She was born in Huntsville, Alabama, near the scene of the labors of the late Dr. Council. Born August 22nd, 1868, she had many difficulties in getting an early education. However, Huntsville Normal and Industrial Insti-

tute was near at hand; and so after several years she entered here and gained her life training.

Soon after her school days she was married and set about to make a happy home and to aid her husband in every possible way. Providence deemed it otherwise. Spurred by adversity, she now began to cast about for a livelihood. Living in Savannah, she thought she saw an opening for a Negro grocery. She thought also that a Negro woman should just as well conduct this business as could a man. Hence she launched forth into the business. She opened a store on Price Street, and by courtesy, fair dealing and shrewd business tact made her store one to be reckoned with in the business world. For ten years she was a grocer, and gave up, or sold out, only to enter other fields.

The grocery business proving very confining, and an opportunity opening for her services in lodge work, she closed her grocery books in 1893, and accepted work with the Court of Calanthe. She became Grand Worthy Counsellor of the Court of Calanthe and of the Knights of Pythias. The post with the latter she still holds.

During her ten years in business Mrs. Barnes had practiced economy. She now made several paying investments. She bought a handsome residence, which is her home, on East Henry Street. She bought twelve rent houses, which in themselves provide her with a pretty comfortable income. She owns five vacant lots in Savannah.

Having made these investments, which were safe and which would protect her in case of inability, she felt safe in placing money in several worthy enterprises. She owns stock and is a director in the Wage Earner's Bank of Savannah, in the Standard Life Insurance Company, in the Afro-American Company and in the Union Development Company.

Mrs. Barnes now gives her life very largely to service in lodges and in the church. She is a member of the A. M. E. Church, of the Court of Calanthe, of the Household of Ruth, of the Eastern Star, of the Good Samaritan. She has been honored with the post of Grand Worthy Chancellor of the Court of Calanthe of Georgia; Supreme Worthy Inspector of the National Court of Calanthe; Past District Most Noble Governor of Georgia; Past Grand Worthy Superior of the Household of Ruth; and Past Grand Matron of the Eastern Star.

With these honorary positions, with the duties and responsibilities entailed, Mrs. Barnes has traveled in all parts of the United States. There are few people and places in the country, about which she cannot give a very intimate account.

Mrs. Barnes was married to Mr. Richard Barnes at Savannah, Aug. 16th, 1884. Mr. Barnes died in Sept. 2nd, 1911. Left alone Mrs. Barnes has devoted her life to making bright the every day lives of others.

HENRY RUTHERFORD BUTLER, M. D.

 NE of the conspicuous figures in colored Georgia during this last quarter century has been Dr. H. R. Butler. He has been the exponent in business enterprises and in uplift work and has been a sort of sponsor for the good name of Atlanta to the world. To him, being a physician is but an item in his career. He is a strong church man, being a member of the African Methodist Episcopal Church and a steward in the Bethel Church of Atlanta.

In membership and activity in secret orders as well as in national bodies, few men anywhere are his peers. He is a thirty-third degree Mason. More than this he is the Grand Master of the Masons of Georgia, a post he has held for fifteen years. He is also a Royal Arch Mason and Past Eminent Grand Commander of Georgia. He is an Odd Fellow, a Knight of Pythias, being a Brigadier General of the Uniform Department and Supreme representative of this body. He is a member of the Eastern Star and Court of Calanthe. He belongs to the Red Cross Society and to the National Geographical Society. He was surgeon, with rank of first lieutenant in the Second Battalion of Georgia Vol-

unteers until that battalion was mustered out in 1896.

He organized the colored Medical Association of Georgia in 1891 and was its first president. He was for four years, physician to Spelman Seminary, the largest school in the world for Negro girls. He was one of the organizers of the Atlanta State Savings Bank and is now one of its directors. He was the first regular Negro contributor to the Atlanta Constitution. He is manager of the Fair Haven Infirmary of the M. B. U.

Amazing as all this work may appear, it becomes more so when it is known that Dr. Butler gained his education by the hardest of struggle. He was born in the country in a log cabin, in Cumberland County, North Carolina, April 11, 1861. The spot of his birth place is some four miles from Fayetteville, on the Willington Road. The first few years of his life, he worked on the farm as a laborer. Then he moved to Wilmington and became a wharf hand, then a stevedore. From here he went into the lumber yard as a workman, thence to the Wilmington Compress Company, for whom he finally became a cotton buyer.

All this time he was carrying a burning desire to be educated, to become a man and hold positions of trust and responsibility. To be sure he had but little to book on or build on. Back there in Cumberland he had enjoyed three months schooling in a log cabin school house. His parents could give him no more. To pay his way he worked as bell boy, waiter, side waiter and finally head waiter in the Northern Hotels. His mother sent him one green back dollar, while he was in school. The rest, for both his elementary, college and professional education, he raised himself.

Completing his course in the study of medicine, Dr. Butler went to Atlanta in 1890 and began to practice medicine and to become a part of the life in Atlanta and in Georgia. In his profession he ranks foremost and enjoys a very wide practice in Atlanta and surroundings. In company with Dr. T. H. Slater, he was owner of the flourishing Drug Store under the name of Butler, Slater and Company. Dr. Butler is one of the leading property owners in Atlanta. He owns a very handsome home, owns other property in Atlanta, in Southern Georgia, and in Lincoln, property and buildings which amount in value to twenty-five thousand dollars.

Dr. Butler was married May 2nd, 1893, to Miss Selana May Sloan. They have one son, Henry Rutherford, Junior, who is at present a student in Atlanta University, but who is to attend and be graduated from the Harvard Divinity School in Cambridge, Massachusetts.

The Butler family of three has traveled much. Dr. Butler himself has crossed the American Continent, indeed is a registered physician in California, and in Los Angeles. He and his family have traveled through Canada and Europe, where he spent much time in study in the hospitals of London and Paris.

BISHOP RANDALL ALBERT CARTER
A. B., A. M., D. D.

ISHOP Randall A. Carter of the C.
M. E. Church, in his early years,
planned to enter the law, but
thanks to an early conversion and
a deep interest in religious matters growing out of this, he
changed his plans, and became a minister instead.

Bishop Carter was born in Fort Valley, Georgia,
January 1, 1867; but while still a small child he
moved with his parents to Columbia, South Carolina. Here in Columbia he attended the public
schools, applying himself to all the tasks that were
set for him. He completed the common schools of
his home and was ready for higher training, at the
time of the founding of the Allen University, in
Columbia, S. C. So, instead of going away to college he was fortunate enough to have the college
come to him. Bishop Carter was among the first
students to matriculate in the University. He remained in Allen University long enough to complete the Freshman Class.

While studying in this school he was converted
during a great revival. It was not long after this
that he felt a call to the ministry and so he joined
the South Carolina Conference of the C. M. E.

Church. Bishop Wm. H. Willis, of Louisville, Kentucky, was the presiding officer at the Conference
at the time Bishop Carter joined.

Bishop Carter, as a minister, served many important charges both in South Carolina, and in
Georgia. While working in Georgia, Bishop Carter completed his full college course at Payne College. He graduated with the degree of A. B., with
the highest honors. For a number of years the
subject of this sketch served as presiding Elder in
the Georgia Conference. He was the confidential
advisor of Bishop Holsey for many years and was
the recognized leader of the Georgia Conference,
of the C. M. E. Church. He was elected chairman
of the delegation from his conference to the general conference for twenty years in succession. He
was the first Epworth League Secretary of that
department of his church. He was the fraternal
delegate from his church to the general conference
of the M. E. Church, held in Chicago, Illinois. He
was a member of the delegation from his church
to the Ecumenical Conference of Methodism, held
in London, England. While abroad, Bishop Carter
took advantage of the opportunity and visited
many of the countries of Europe.

In 1914 in St. Louis, Mo., he was elected a Bishop
of his church. At this time Bishop Carter received
the highest vote ever given any aspirant for that
position. Thus Bishop Carter has come from the
ranks to the highest position in the gift of his
church. Starting as a school teacher, who wanted
to be a preacher, joining the conference and serving first small and then larger charges, he has
developed wonderfully in this time. In recognition
of his growth and development he was given the
degree of A. M. in 1900 and of D. D. in 1901. Both
of these came from his Alma Mater.

Bishop Carter is recognized as one of the foremost orators and most scholarly preachers in his
church. He is a member of the National Geographic Society, the National Association for the Advancement of the Colored People. A member of
the committee on Church and Country Life of the
Federal Council of Churches, and a member of the
Association for the Study of Negro Life and History. Bishop Carter has held and served in many
other positions which are honorary and which work
for the public good. Among those in which he
is still actively engaged we might mention that he
is President of the Board of Missions of the C. M.
E. Church. President of the Board of Trustees, of
the Texas College of Hagood, Arkansas, and of the
Indiana College, of Pine Bluff, Arkansas.

Bishop Carter has traveled extensively in this
country and abroad. He has covered this country
from the Atlantic to the Pacific. He owns property, in the District of Columbia, in Columbia,
South Carolina, and in Atlanta, Georgia.

In 1891, on the 22nd of April, Bishop Carter was
married to Miss Janie S. Hooks, of Macon, Georgia.
There is one child in the family, Miss Carrie Carter, who is a freshman in Atlanta University.

Born of poor parents, we might say born in real
poverty, Randall Albert Carter has made a good
record for himself during his half century. His
is a life that will lend inspiration.

SILAS X. FLOYD, A. M. D. D.

ILAS X. Floyd was born October 2nd, 1869, in the City of Augusta, Georgia, and here he has lived for the greater part of his life. During his childhood period it was hard for a colored youth to secure a thorough education, but Dr. Floyd was an exception. He secured a good education but through close application to his studies and a determination to succeed. When a lad he attended the schools of his native city and then entered Atlanta University. He graduated at this institution in 1891, and in 1894 received his M. A. degree from his Alma Mater. Finishing his course he returned to Augusta, Georgia, where he immediately began and has continued a marvelously active life. An enumeration of his activities seems almost incredible that one man could accomplish so much and retain his health and strength. But Dr. Floyd is an unusual man. Dr. Floyd is first a preacher and from 1899 to 1900 he was the Pastor of the Augusta Tabernacle Baptist Church. Prior to this, from 1891 to 1896, he was principal of the Public School and editor of the Augusta Sentinel. From 1896 to 1899 he was field representative of the International Sunday School Association, and

from 1900 to February, 1903, he was field worker for Georgia and Alabama for the American Baptist Publication Society. Since that time he has served continuously as Principal of the Public School of his native city.

Dr. Floyd has many gifts but the two which are preeminent are those of teacher and author. By means of these he has left an impress upon the colored citizens of Augusta, and in fact the entire country, which will tell for the good of the race for ages to come.

For many years he has conducted every Sunday morning a colored people's page in each of the two white daily newspapers published in Augusta. He has also held the unique position of being a paid reporter on two Southern white papers in the same city. This has given him a great local power to help his people. But Dr. Floyd has not confined his work to the school room, nor to the pen. His great heart embraces the whole colored race and he is interested in all efforts for their uplift. To this end he has served as Secretary of the National Association of Teachers in Colored schools; he was the President of the first Negro State Press Association, in the United States, for Colored Newspapers; he was the originator of a system of syndicating the news among colored newspapers; he is a member of the Walker Baptist Institute, Augusta; he is a member of the American Historical Association, and a member of the American Social Science Association. In these various organizations he has come face to face with many of the problems of the race and has done his share towards the adjustment of them.

Dr. Floyd's writings have been voluminous and have been extensively read. He has made contributions to such well known periodicals as the New York Independent, Youth's Companion, Lippincotts, Judge, and Leslie's Weekly. He is the author of "Floyd's Flowers," a book of stories for colored children, the first book of its kind ever published in the history of the race in the United States. He has also written the "Life of C. T. Walker," the "Gospel of Service and other Sermons," and a number of stories and verses which have appeared from time to time in the leading papers and magazines of the country.

Dr. Floyd has made his contribution to the civic life of Augusta, and has rendered valuable service to the commonwealth on many occasions. In recognition of his invaluable aid in relief work, following the great fire which swept Augusta, the Chairman of the White Relief Committee publicly presented him with a beautiful gold watch and fob. During the war which has happily come to a close, Dr. Floyd was conspicuous for his patriotic service and was placed at the head of many of the committees which this service called into existence.

Space alone prevents further record of his achievements. A fitting end is to speak of his happy home life. His family consists of a wife, (formerly Mrs. Ella James,) and a daughter, Miss Marietta James, who are in perfect accord and sympathy with him and in their own home they present the ideal family circle.

BENJAMIN JEFFERSON DAVIS.

Benjamin Jefferson Davis

MR. Benjamin Jefferson Davis, the subject of this sketch, was born in Dawson, Georgia, in 1870. He passed his childhood under the usual disadvantages of the Negro child in those days. He was born with an insatiable thirst for knowledge, and with an ambition and will to do whatever his hands found to do better than anybody else could do it. His longing to render service for his race and mankind ripened, and accordingly he resolved to acquire an education that would fit him for life's work; and he entered Atlanta University and availed himself of every opportunity to better his condition. As a student he was brilliant and showed unmistakably the elements of leadership, which has made him a leader of men. As success marked his efforts, he never forgot to appreciate the friends who encouraged and helped him to prepare himself for the task which he had mapped out.

After spending several terms in Atlanta University, he decided to teach school to aid him in his preparation and to secure the amount of money necessary to carry out what he had undertaken and planned for the future. Meanwhile, he was tendered a government position which he accepted; but it was not long before he felt that he could better serve his race and generation by giving up the government service and taking up work more in keeping with his Life's ambition. But he had the foresight to see that there were great possibilities for racial development in the G. U. O. O. F., in America. He joined the Order at seventeen. His mother, Mrs. Katherine Davis, who was very much devoted to her boy, partly kept up his dues during the time he was attending school. He rose rapidly in the Order and became a Past officer in 1891, and a member of the District Grand Lodge in 1892; he was elected District Grand Treasurer in 1900; was elected Grand Director of the National Branch of the Order, in Columbus, Ohio, in 1904, and served two years. He was elected Grand Treasurer of the National Branch in 1906 at Richmond, Va., which position he filled four years. He was elected Chief Justice of the Supreme Court of the Order in Baltimore in 1910, and served four year. In 1917, at the Macon District Grand Lodge, he was again re-elected District Grand Secretary for the Eighth Biennial term, making sixteen years; and he was elected General Manager of the Corporation of the G. U. O. O. F. of America, Jurisdiction of Georgia. In 1916, when the Order was placed in the hands of a Receiver by the courts, he, on account of his signal ability, and intricate knowledge of the affairs of the Order was appointed by the court as Assistant Receiver.

He is a member of the K. of P., Supreme Circle, Knights of Tabor, a Director of the Standard Life Insurance Company, Stockholder of the Atlanta State Savings Bank and President of the Atlanta Independent Publishing Company—publishers of the Atlanta Independent.

In politics, he is a Republican, and is usually one of the Big Four Delegates from the State-at-large to the Republican National Convention every four years. At the 19th Republican National Convention he was a member of the Committee on Platform and Resolutions of which Senator Henry Cabot Lodge of Massachusetts, was the Chairman.

The strongest institution in which Mr. Davis is interested, and the one which wields a world of good for both races, is the Atlanta Independent. As owner and editor of this widely read and circulated journal, he shapes its policy and is considered one of the ablest journalists and writers of his day.

It is impossible to discuss the Negro progress in America without mentioning "Ben Davis" and the Odd Fellows Block in Atlanta, which stands as a monument to his vision, perseverance and organizing genius. He is essentially an organizer and leader of men. Twenty years ago when he became officially identified with the G. U. O. O. F. in Georgia, it represented a membership of less than 10,000 and as a state organization, it was struggling and gasping for breath, so to speak. Today the membership is more than fifty thousand, including the Household of Ruth, Juveniles, Division Meeting and Deputy and Supervisor's Institute.

When Mr. Davis took charge of the office of District Grand Secretary, he addressed himself to the task of re-constructing the Order and placing it upon a substantial basis. His first efforts were to systematize the business of the office and build up confidence in the Order in the minds of the people. This having been accomplished, he felt that the time was propitious to have a strong organ in the State of Georgia with which to give publicity to the work and the benefit of the Order, and widen the circle of the Race's influence. Out of this idea sprang the Atlanta Independent, which, from the beginning, was a popular and fearless sheet and exerted a powerful influence for good not only in Georgia, but throughout the country—and today the Independent is the most widely read Negro paper in America and is read by white and black people alike.

In his struggles for the erection of the present Odd Fellow Block on Auburn Avenue in the City of Atlanta in the year 1912, the story will never be known in its entirety, for only God and Mr Davis alone know in the broadest sense the fiery ordeals through which he passed Even those who were most intimately associated with him do not know as he did, for in many respects "He trod the wine-press alone" Mr Davis conceived the idea in the erection of the Odd Fellow Block that every member of the Order in Georgia give $1.00 as a Free-Will offering on Thanksgiving Day, May 14, 1911 As a result of this idea over $50,000 was raised in one day The Block was completed at a cost of more than $300,000 without a dollar of incumbrance upon it

When you think of Benjamin Jefferson Davis, you think of three things—The Atlanta Independent, The growth of the Odd Fellows and the Odd Fellows' Block in Atlanta, Ga The paper speaks for itself—it is the most aggressive and influential paper published in the country for Negro people No paper is more eagerly sought-for and more widely read than the Atlanta Independent Of his work among the Odd Fellows, his chief distinction arises from putting the organization on a business basis and extending the membership in a little more than ten years in the State of Georgia, from 10,000 to 50,000, from a depleted treasury to an accumulated wealth of $600,000, carrying a cash balance of $50,000

But, perhaps, his crowning achievement in connection with his great work with the G U O O F, is the establishment of the Bureau of Endowment for widows and orphans, who, until this time had been left destitute at the death of their husbands and fathers He, therefore, put through an amendment whereby every member must carry a death benefit of not less than $200.00 and not more than $500.00 The effect of this act has been far-reaching and has laid a broad foundation upon which the Race can build for all time to come It has been the forerunner for many other institutions of the Race—such as banks, insurance companies, first-class professional offices and hundreds of business places for young men and women of the Race

He was happily married August, 1898, to Miss Jimmie W Porter of Dawson, Ga, and their home has been blessed with two children—a boy B J Davis, Jr, and a girl, Johnnie Katherine

Mr Davis is less than fifty years old and is in the very prime of his intellectual and physical powers He is ambitious, gifted and determined He knows no such thing as "can't" and never ceases until the thing undertaken is put "Over the top" It is not too much to say that he is one of the Race's greatest leaders He is today the greatest exponent of the principles of Odd Fellowship in America He is a National character and a born leader

The race's greatest constructive and economic contribution to the national growth is Odd Fellow Block, 200 Auburn Ave, between Bell and Butler Streets, Atlanta, Georgia

Odd Fellow Block, which consists of two large buildings, is the largest and the most up-to-date office building owned by the Race in America These vast properties were erected in 1912 and 1913 by District Grand Lodge No 18 G U O O F of America Jurisdiction of Georgia a corporation The corporation consists of fifty thousand male and female members of G U O O F, of America, Jurisdiction of Georgia The main building is known as Odd Fellow Building and is located on the northeast corner of Auburn Avenue and Bell Street, and is seven stories high above the ground The building consists of six stores fifty-six offices three lodge rooms and the roof garden The roof garden will seat and accommodate one thousand people It is the largest and the most modern roof garden in the country, adapted to use all seasons of the year—sanitary, ventilated and heated by the most modern systems The lodge rooms are occupied by many of the different secret Orders in the city The offices are used by such substantial concerns as the Standard Life Insurance Company, Atlanta Mutual Insurance Company, Chatham Mutual Insurance Company Atlanta State Savings Bank, District Grand Lodge No 18, G U O O F, of America, Jurisdiction of Georgia The N C Mutual & Provident Association and the Masonic Relief Association The main building fronts Auburn Avenue 60 feet, and runs north on Bell Street one hundred feet

The Odd Fellow Auditorium and Office Building is situated on the corner of Auburn Avenue and Butler Street, facing Auburn Avenue 138 feet front, and consists of eight stores, eighteen offices and the Odd Fellow Auditorium Theatre The building is two stories high, and the offices on the second floor are occupied almost entirely by the leading colored physicians of the city The stores are always rented, the Gate City Drug Store occupies the corner This great property of the Order was erected at a cost to the Corporation, including the land, quite $400,000 and is today valued at a half million dollars The Order contributes to the State of Georgia and the City of Atlanta $5,000 in taxes each year on its holdings

More than two hundred and fifty young men and women are engaged in the various enterprises, doing business in the Odd Fellow Block This investment is a paying proposition, netting to the Order—above operating expenses—each year $10,000 which is credited to the Endowment Fund guaranteeing the payment of the Death Benefit Certificates held by the members of the Order throughout the Jurisdiction This the greatest contribution of the Race to the National growth argues most largely its possibilities and is due entirely to the leadership of the District Grand Secretary Benjamin Jefferson Davis, and stands as a monument to his energy, push and pluck

ODD FELLOWS BLOCK, MAIN BUILDING, ATLANTA, GA.

CHARLES HENRY DOUGLASS.

N Macon, Georgia, there is an up-to-date negro theatre, one of the few negro theatres of any kind to be owned and managed by a Negro. It was built in 1911, with modern appliances. It has a seating capacity of 330 and is sanitary throughout. It has both oscilating and exhaust fans to keep the air within pure and the building sanitary. This enterprise is the work of Charles Henry Douglass, who in this way has made provision for the recreation and pleasure of his people. Here every afternoon and evening the tired housewife, servant or laborer can drop in and enjoy a pleasant hour without embarrassment or discrimination. Seeing an opportunity for a Negro amusement house in Macon, he leased in 1904, the Ocmulgee Park Theatre, which he operated for two years, when he sold his lease and purchased a lot on Broadway and erected the Colonial Hotel, a three story brick building, which stands on this business thoroughfare in the midst of the big business of the city. The building cost eighteen thousand dollars ($18,000), and is the only piece of property on Broadway to be owned by a Ne-

gro. While operating his hotel, Mr. Douglass organized a theatrical company of about thirty-five of forty colored people and traveled with his company through fourteen states, giving performances in many cities, winning favorable patronage which established his reputation and earned him much money. Selling out his interest in the Theatrical Company he added the proceeds to other funds and erected the "Douglas Theatre." This theatre he operates entirely with Negro help. He has the only Negro picture operator permitted to operate a machine in the State of Georgia. In contemplating a successful man it is interesting to note the steps by which he climbed the ladder of success. We will go back now and trace the history of Mr. Douglass from his childhood days.

Mr. Douglass was born in Macon, Georgia, in 1870 and reared in comparative poverty, his parents being very poor. Necessity laid upon him the burden of money making from early life, in fact from the time that he could earn a penny. His first job was to peddle light wood and vegetables. To this work he devoted his mornings but attended the public school in the afternoon. He chopped cotton when he was so small that he had to saw off the hoe handle so that he might wield the hoe. When fourteen years of age he left the cotton patch and went to the city. Here he secured a position as buggy boy for a physician, and received as wages, Six Dollars, ($6.00) per month.

This position he held until the death of his father. When his father died the support of his mother and two sisters fell upon his shoulders. Without flinching he assumed the responsibility and set himself to the task.

He realized that he could not meet the demands of the family upon the small wages that he was receiving, so he gave up his position of buggy boy and sought employment in other lines. He secured work as a day laborer, finding employment in a saw mill, where he received seventy-seven (77) cents per day. Here he labored until he found an opening where the wages were larger. From the saw mill he returned to Macon, where he entered a box factory, earning wages of from $1.75 to $2.00 per day. It cost him five dollars to get this job.

While working as a laborer with his hands his mind was working upon a plan to start a business of his own, and to this end he began to save his money. When he had saved twenty-four dollars ($24), he was ready for his venture. With this small capital he opened a bicycle repair shop, which continued to grow until the auto made its appearance. This was the beginning of his business career, but very far from being its end.

When the automobile bid for popular favor the

COLONIAL HOTEL AND DOUGLASS THEATRE

bicycle had to take a back seat so he took time by the forelock and disposed of his repair shop and entered another line of endeavor.

He next entered the Real Estate business which he conducted with marked success.

Ne never shirked the responsibility which his father's death placed upon him, but cared for his mother and sisters with devotion and loyalty which made their paths smooth and pleasant.

When his mother died he remained the devoted brother and supported and looked after the interests of his two sisters until they married and made homes for themselves. He not only supported them but gave them the advantages of education which contributed to their pleasure and usefulness in life.

When he worked at the saw mill he often saw the porters and waiters in the Pullman car service and was deeply impressed at the smug and satisfied air they exhibited, and the spirit of contentment that seemed to possess them. He also noted that they were well dressed. Thus unconsciously they inspired in him the desire to have good clothes and to enjoy their seemingly spirit of contentment.

This desire he has realized far beyond his fondest hopes and aspirations. With him to desire is the determination to attain and determination and energy usually brought him the coveted reward.

His personal appearance while not gaudy was always attractive and he is what may be termed a well dressed man. Mr. Douglass has always depended upon himself and all his moves originated with himself and he paid for any and all assistance he received. He never put himself in the attitude of a beggar. When he secured the position in the box factory he paid one of the laborers therein to recommend him and he has followed that policy

through all his business career. He attributes his success in a large measure to this principle.

Another element in his character which helped in his successful career was his power to discern a need and the grit to venture. If he saw a need it was to him an opportunity and opportunity found in him a willing follower.

Mr. Douglass has acquired considerable property. In addition to his hotel and theatre he owns thirty tenement houses, which contain from three to eight rooms, two pressed brick stores with flats in second story; these are in the Broadway block and the flats rent for $140 per month. He has a thirty acre farm just outside of Macon where he raises Duroc and Berkshire hogs, truck, fruit and game chickens.

Mr. Douglass was married in 1902 to Miss Fannie Appling of Macon, Georgia. Six children make up the Douglass family, Winna, Marsenia, Charles Henry, Jr., Peter, Carro and Lilly. His close attention to business matters did not lessen his interest in his family life and he endeavored to make his home attractive and comfortable. Recently he built an attractive bungalow for his family. Here he finds his greatest relaxation from business cares. It is not surprising that a man who was such a good son and brother should make an ideal husband and father. The importance he felt for the education of his sisters, which he accomplished, under the stress of poverty, he now feels for his children and being in a financial condition to give them a good education he plans to fit them for useful and honorable positions in life. He is a living illustration of what a man with a vision and a strong will can do in brushing aside difficulties to reach his goal.

RESIDENCE OF C. H. DOUGLASS.

BISHOP JOSEPH SIMEON FLIPPER, D. D., LL. D.

Bishop Joseph Simeon Flipper

FOR nearly forty years Bishop Joseph Simeon Flipper, of the A. M. E. Church, has been a leader in the South; a leader in education, in religion, and in organizations of uplift for the American Negro. Born Feb. 22, 1859, in the days of slavery, and educated amidst the confusion of reconstruction, he has risen from school teacher to pastor, from pastor to dean, then college president, and finally to Bishop.

In 1867, when the Northern Missionaries came South, he attended school in Bethel A. M. E. Church. From here he went to the Storrs School on Houston street. In October, 1869, he enrolled among the first students to enter the Atlanta University, where he remained until 1876. In the summer of this year he began teaching school at Thomaston, Georgia. He was converted in March 1877, and joined St. Thomas, A. M. E. Church. In 1877 and 1878 he taught school in Thomas County. In 1879 he was commissioned by his Excellency, Governor Alford H. Colquitt, Captain of the Thomasville Independants, a colored company forming a part of the State Militia. In the same year he taught school at Groverville, now Key, Brooks County, Georgia. Here he was licensed both as an exhorter and local preacher, and recommended by the local church for admission into the Georgia Annual Conference of the African Methodist Episcopal Church. In January, 1880, he was received into the itinerant ministry of the Georgia Conference at Americus, Georgia, by Bishop J. P. Campbell, and assigned to the Groverville Circuit. He was ordained Deacon in January, 1882, in St. Thomas A. M. E. Church, Thomasville, the same church in which he was converted and which he joined in 1877. Here he was elected Secretary of the Georgia Conference, and a Trustee of Morris Brown College. He was appointed to Darien, Georgia, in 1882. The next year he taught school at Cairo and Whigham, Georgia. In 1884, he was ordained Elder at Valdosta, and appointed to Quitman. Remaining here until January, 1886, he was transferred from the Georgia Conference to the North Georgia Conference, and appointed to Bethel A. M. E. Church, on Wheat Street, Atlanta. This was the largest church in the State and he was the youngest man that had ever been appointed to such an important charge in the State. His mother had been a member of this church, he had attended its Sunday School when a boy, and had first learned his alphabet here. He remained here four years, the full limit of the law, and raised more Dollar Money than had ever been raised, not only in the history of this church, but of the entire State. It was here in 1886, he became one of the Dollar Money Kings of the entire connection, for which he was honored with a gold badge, making a record which stood for a quarter of a century before any other pastor exceeded it. From Bethel he was appointed pastor of Pierce Chapel A. M. E. Church, Athens.

In 1891, he was elected delegate to the General Conference which met in Philadelphia, Pa., in May, 1892. It was in this same year that he was appointed by Bishop A. Grant, Presiding Elder of the Athens district. Two years later Allen University, Columbia, S. C. conferred upon him the title of Doctor of Divinity. Remaining in the Athens District three years, he was appointed pastor of Allen Temple, Atlanta. This was in 1895, the same year he was elected delegate to the General Conference, which met in Wilmington, N. C., May 1896. In 1899 he was elected leader of the delegation of the North Georgia Conference, to the General Conference which met in Columbus, Ohio, May 1900. It was at this conference that he was elected Chairman of the Episcopal Committee, the most important committee of the General Conference. At this General Conference, also, he was appointed a member of the Financial Board, which has the oversight of all money raised by the church. In 1899 he was appointed pastor of St. Paul, A. M. E. Church, Atlanta, serving four years. In 1903 he was elected by the Trustee Board of Morris Brown College, Dean of the Theological Department, where he served one year. The year, 1903, saw him elected leader of the delegation of the Atlanta, Georgia Conference to the General Conference, which met at Chicago, Ill., May 1904. Here again he was elected Chairman of the Episcopal Committee, which committee for his faithful service, presented him with a large silver loving cup. He was again appointed a member of the Financial Board. Upon his return home he was elected by the Trustee Board, President of Morris Brown College, and enrolled the largest number of students in the school's history. This position he held for four years. In 1906, Wilberforce University, Ohio, conferred on him the title of Doctor of Laws.

In 1908, at the General Conference held in Norfolk, Virginia, he was elected one of the Bishops of the African Methodist Episcopal Church and assigned to the Ninth Episcopal District, consisting of Arkansas and Oklahoma. In 1912, when the General Conference met in Kansas City, Missouri, the delegation from Georgia, his native state, requested that he be sent to preside over Georgia, which request was granted. On coming to Georgia, he erected the Flipper Hall, the boys dormitory at Morris Brown College, the Central Normal and Industrial Institute, at Savannah, bought ten acres of land for Payne College, at Cuthbert, Georgia, and united all the schools into one system, known as Morris Brown University.

Bishop Flipper owns his home and three rent houses, in Atlanta, two vacant lots in Waycross, five in Savannah, and one in Lincoln, Md. He is a stockholder of the Standard Life Insurance Company. He is a stockholder and Director of the Atlanta State Savings Bank, and a stockholder in the Independant, of New York City. He is a member of the Southern Sociological Congress; of the National Geographic Society, Washington, D. C., a Trustee of the World's Christian Endeavor—president of the Sunday School Union Board of the A. M. E. Church.

Bishop Flipper was married in Thomasville, Georgia, in 1880, to Miss Amanda Isabella Slater. There are three children in the Flipper family: Josephine G., Nathan and Carl.

WILLIAM ALFRED FOUNTAIN, A. B., M. A.,
S. T. B., B. D., Ph. D.

R. William A. Fountain, now President of Morris Brown University, is the son of Reverend Richard and Virginia Fountain, both of whom were devoted members of the African Methodist Episcopal Church.

He was born October 29, 1870, at Elberton, Georgia, and was one of seventeen children. He entered school at the age of six and attended about sixteen years. Passing through the public school at Elberton, he graduated successively from Morris Brown University, Allen University, Turner Theological Seminary, and took a post-graduate course at Chicago University, and non-resident courses in Central University. He has the following degrees: Bachelor of Arts, from Morris Brown University, in 1901; Master of Arts from Allen University; S. T. B., from Turner Seminary; B. D. and Ph. D., from Central University. He was also a student at Garrett Biblical Institute, Evanston, Ill., in 1916.

He was converted April 1888, at the age of eighteen and joined Allen Temple A. M. E. Church, Atlanta, Georgia, the same year. He became very active in the church work and has held almost every office in the body.

He was licensed to preach at Elberton, Georgia, in 1893, by Rev. (now Bishop,) J. S. Flipper. He joined the annual conference at Marietta, Georgia, under Bishop Grant; was ordained deacon at Athens, Georgia, by Bishop A. Grant; ordained elder at Cedartown, Georgia, by Bishop Turner. He has held the following appointments: Pendergrass Mission; Athens-Bethel; Washington-Jackson Chapel and Pope's Chapel, Marietta, Georgia; Turner Chapel, Atlanta, Georgia; Allen Temple, Wilmington, North Carolina; St. Stephens, Macon Georgia; Steward Chapel; Presiding Elder of Athens district. Each change carried him to an enlarged field of work.

His accomplishment's as a church builder and debt liquidator show a decided ability in those lines. He built Pope's Chapel, at Washington, Georgia, at a cost of $20,000; repaired the Parsonage at Marietta, Georgia, at a cost of $2,000; bought lot and beautified church, paid church out of debt, at Atlanta, at cost of $5,000; left $500 to build a Sunday School room for St. Stephens at Wilmington, N. C.; established an Old Folk's Home and built a Parsonage at a cost of $4,000, for Steward Chapel, Macon, Georgia. He has lifted mortgages at Athens, Marietta, Allen Temple and Steward Chapel.

Dr. Fountain has been a delegate to the following General Conferences: Columbus, Ohio, in 1900; Chicago, in 1904; Norfolk, in 1908; Kansas City, in 1912, and the Centennial General Conference at Philadelphia, in 1916.

Before becoming active as a minister, Dr. Fountain gave part of his time to the school room, so when he was called to succeed the lamented Dr. E. W. Lee, as president of Morris Brown University he was not without experience as a teacher.

Dr. Fountain holds membership in many organizations and has an active interest in them. He is an Odd Fellow, a Mason, and a Knight of Pythias. He has been twice married. He was first married to Miss Jessie M. Williams, of Sumter, S. C., in 1893. She died in 1898. In 1899 he married Miss Julia T. Allen. His first wife gave him two children, W. A. Fountain, Jr., and Jessie Mamie and his second wife gave him four children, Louise Virginia, Sue Jette, Julia Bell and Allen McNeal, deceased. Dr. Fountain has a high ambition for his children which he is trying to realize by training their heart and mind as he was himself trained. He finds great satisfaction and pleasure in his home life. He has another great ambition also—to make the Morris Brown University a great Institution, taking high rank among the Negro schools of the land. He is fast advancing it towards his goal and has received much encouragement to persevere in his efforts.

JOHN WESLEY GILBERT, Ph. D.

OME years ago the public was startled to know that Brown University had sent a Negro scholar to Athens, Greece. There were many causes for this surprise. In the first place it had been widely exploited that the Negro could not learn Greek. In the second place the Negro had been chosen as a representative of a New England college. This was how it all came about. Brown University, at Providence, Rhode Island, holds what is known as an Athens scholarship. This scholarship is awarded to the best Greek scholar in the University. John Wesley Gilbert won this scholarship over the sons of Anne Hutchinson, of Roger Williams, and over many other lads of distinguished ancestry. Thus it came about that the American Negro in a quarter of a century after slavery had sent a scholar abroad.

John Wesley Gilbert was born in Hepsibah, Georgia, July 6, 1865. His first years of training were spent in the public schools of Augusta, Georgia. From the public schools of Augusta, he registered in the Atlanta Baptist Seminary, now the theological department of Morehouse College, Atlanta, Georgia. Going up from the South, Mr.

Gilbert made his way into Brown University, and soon made his mark as a scholar of the classics. He especially excelled in Greek; so that when the award was made for the representative from Brown University, the Negro scholar was chosen to go to the American school of classics in the city of Socrates and Plato, of Pericles and Demosthenes. It was here he won his Master's degree.

However, one must live in Athens, and scholarships do not always defray all expenses. To pay his way the Greek scholar served as a guide to American tourists, who came to visit this ancient citadel of culture and war. In those days excavations in Greece were exceedingly popular. Before long, Mr. Gilbert was numbered among those who sought to exhume the old walls, pillars and gates, made famous in ancient Greek stories. He conducted excavations not only in Greece, but on the Mediterranean Islands. Few men have been thus favored to use their classical scholarship.

Mr. Gilbert has been an extensive traveler. He has traveled practically over the whole of the United States and visited most places of note and interest and has visited many countries in Europe.

The trip to Athens only whetted the young scholar's taste for more travel. He made two more trips abroad, when he visited many countries in Africa and most of the countries in Europe. He was not only traveling, he was working. While in the Belgian Congo, he, with Bishop W. R. Lambuth, founded the mission at Wimbo, Miami, a mission which is still in full operation. His work of investigation and research won him a membership in the Archaeological Institute and in the Philological Association of America.

Mr. Gilbert has been engaged for years in teaching and preaching. He began his course as a teacher in Paine College, Augusta, Georgia, in 1889. He was Dean of Theology in Paine for three years. Mr. Gilbert entered the ministry in 1895, in the C. M. E. Church. In 1901 he was a member of the Ecumenical Congress, which assembled in London, England. He is at present commissioner for and professor of Greek, in Paine College.

He has kept his membership alive in many of the organizations at home. His membership in the A. M. E. Church has been one of much activity. He has held the office of superintendent of African missions for many years. He is a Mason, a Knight of Pythias and an Odd Fellow. In the Knight of Pythias he is Grand Auditor.

He was married in 1889 to Miss Oceola Pleasant, a native of Augusta, Georgia. Four children have been born to them, of whom three are living.

His real estate holdings are valued at $15,000 and he is a holder of several shares in a realty company of Augusta.

KEMPER HARRELD.

EMPER Harreld, known the country over as a concert violinist, popular also as a teacher of violin and as a chorus director, was born and reared in Muncie, Indiana. From his youth he was a musical prodigy. His special talent first manifested itself in song; so much so that under the tutelage of Miss Nannie C. Love, who was in charge of the public school music, he soon became known as the boy singer. However, the violin had early fallen into his hands, and while singing, he was also after his boy fashion making rich tones on the violin, becoming in a short time, at least a fiddler.

Following his bent Mr. Harreld took special studies in his home town and then in Indianapolis. From Indianapolis he entered the Chicago Musical College and studied violin under Chiheiser, theory under Maryott and Falk, and composition under Borowski. Mr. Harreld's next studies were pursued under Frederick Frederiksen, a celebrated violinist from the Royal College of Music in London. Three years of hard work with Frederiksen gave Mr. Harreld a much finer touch, higher technique and greater confidence in himself.

Meantime he had become well known in America as one of the leading violinists. To the laity he was already perfect in technique, harmony, and those points of excellence for which musicians so eagerly and so sedulously strive.

Morehouse College in Atlanta, Georgia, was among the institutions to invite Mr. Harreld to become a member of their teaching staff. Atlanta being a field of rare possibility, due to the high intellectual standard, Mr. Harreld became a teacher of music at Morehouse, and established a studio on Chestnut Street in the city.

Here in Atlanta Mr. Harreld lives an exceedingly busy life. As a teacher of private pupils he takes every minute of his spare time. As a chorus director he with his chorus is constantly in demand. He has developed an orchestra for Morehouse, an orchestra of from eighteen to twenty-three members, picked from a student body of not more than four hundred and fifty students. Biggest of all, Mr. Harreld has a choir chorus of three hundred voices, a chorus which is made up of choirs from twenty-eight churches. When Billy Sunday preached in Atlanta his chorus was increased to fifteen hundred voices, who sang to an audience of seventeen thousand.

Dear as these honors are, Mr. Harreld has not decided to rest on what he already knows and can do. Busy as he is with his regular music at Morehouse, with private pupils, chorus work and violin recital, he nevertheless steals time here and there for intense study and observation. The year 1914, for example, found him stealing away to spend his vacation to study in Berlin. Unhappily, the war broke forth during his stay in Berlin, and he and Mrs. Harreld were held by the German Government for twenty-five days, before they were allowed to leave for America.

Since that time owing to disturbances everywhere Mr. Harreld has not returned to Europe to study. He has traveled, however, in England, Holland and Germany in recital engagements, and in nearly every part of the United States. His studies have during his work at Morehouse taken a practical turn, going into Negro music and its possibilities.

It is difficult to determine what branch of music Mr. Harreld excels in, as a music master, a chorus director, or as a concert violinist. In the first two—Atlanta gives him the leading place. In the last named the papers of various cities in which he has appeared vie with one another in singing his praise. This from the College Bulletin of Birmingham is typical, and at the same time expresses the great esteem in which he is held.

"Plays in most finished and artistic style with brilliancy and very beautiful tone. Has no equal in temperament and expression."

What Mr. Harreld himself considers his best effort was a benefit concert given in the Auditorium-Armory in Atlanta. For this he organized the choral and orchestral forces of the six higher institutions for Negro education in Atlanta—Atlanta University, Morris Brown University, Clark University, Morehouse College, Spelman Seminary and Gammon Theological Seminary. There were five hundred in the chorus and a large orchestra. This program was rendered before 5000 persons.

Mr. Harreld was married on June 11, 1913, to Miss Claudia White, daughter of the famous Dr. W. J. White, of Augusta. They have one child, a daughter, Josephine Eleanor, who is three years of age.

JOHN HOPE, A. B., A. M.

OHN Hope, President of Morehouse College, was born in Augusta, Georgia, June, 1868, the son of James and Mary Francis Hope. After some years of elementary education, secured largely by his own efforts, he entered Worcester Academy, (Mass.,) in the fall of 1886. He was prominent in the activities of the school, becoming editor-in-chief of the Academy, the Student Monthly; and at graduation he was class historian and a commencement speaker. Entering Brown University in 1890, he received the A. B. Degree in 1894, with the distinction of being class orator. In 1907 his Alma Mater conferred on him the A. M. degree. In October 1894, Mr. Hope entered the service of the American Baptist Home Mission Society as a teacher in Roger Williams University, Nashville, Tenn. In 1898 he was transferred to Atlanta Baptist College. On the resignation of president Sale he was promoted to the presidency, serving for the first year as Acting President. In 1897 he was married to Miss Lugenia D. Burns, of Chicago, Ill., He is the father of two boys, Edward Swain and John, Jr. President Hope is one of the leading figures in the education of the negro in the South, and his time is largely drawn upon by many activities for social or educational service. In 1915-16 he was President of the National Association of Teachers in Colored Schools; he is a member of the Board of Managers of the Y. M. C. A., of Atlanta, of the Advisory Board of the National Association for the advancement of the Colored People, of the Executive Committee of the Urban League of New York, of the committees on the Spingarn Medal, of the Anti-Tuberculosis Association, of Atlanta, and of various boards of the State Baptist Convention. President Hope's chief interest, however, remains, the education of men and boys; and the fact that he has given himself to his work in such wholehearted fashion largely accounts for the rapid advancement that Morehouse College has made within the last ten years.

In the summer of 1918, President Hope was given a leave of absence by the American Baptist Home Mission Society and was appointed by the Young Men's Christian Association as a Special Secretary for the oversight of the Negro soldiers of America in France. In this capacity he has rendered such distinguished service for the improvement of the morale of the army that he has been requested to continue in this work until the summer of 1919. He has complied with this request, and is still at his work that covers over fifty cities.

The following estimate of the administration of President Hope has been taken from the "History of Morehouse College," written by the Dean. "One of the outstanding features of the administration of President Hope has been the excellent understanding between the head of the college and the student body. In the era of "Atlanta Baptist College" the aggressive spirit that caused the institution to be widely known first received real impetus. In more recent years it has developed into a devotion with which the youngest student becomes acquainted as soon as he is enrolled. Whatever question may arise, the students know that presiding over the college is one looking out for their best interests, in vacation as well as term time, and one with whom there may be the frankest conference. The response comes in a loyalty that has never failed when anything involving the highest welfare of the college was at stake."

President Hope lived the life he endeavored to impress upon the young men coming under his influence and stands out before them as an example worthy of their imitation.

To impress oneself upon the rising generation in such a way as to incite them to a high ideal of life is worthy the effort of any man. This pleasure and satisfaction is President Hope's.

GRAVES HALL, MOREHOUSE COLLEGE, ATLANTA, GA.

THE Morehouse College in the city of Atlanta, Georgia, is operated by the American Baptist Home Mission Society, of New York, for the education of Negro young men, with special reference to the preparation of ministers and teachers.

HISTORY

The College was organized in the year 1867, in the city of Augusta, Georgia, under the name of "The Augusta Institute." In 1879, under the presidency of Rev. Joseph T. Robert, LL. D. (1871-1884), it was removed to Atlanta and incorporated under the name "Atlanta Baptist Seminary." At this stage of its growth the institution owned only one building, that a comparatively small three-story structure, located near what is now the Terminal Station. President Robert was succeeded by President Samuel Graves, D. D., in 1885. Dr. Graves served as president until 1890, continuing as Professor of Theology for four years longer. In 1889, as the surroundings of the old location in Atlanta had become unfavorable, a new site was secured, and in the spring of 1890 the school was removed to its present location. In the autumn of this year President George Sale, (1890-1906- entered upon his duties. In 1897 amendments to the charter were secured, granting full college powers and changing the name of the institution to "Atlanta Baptist College." In 1906 President Sale resigned to become Superintendent of Education of the American Baptist Home Mis-

sion Society, and was succeeded by President John Hope, who had been a professor on the faculty since 1898. By a vote in 1912 of the Board of Trustees, concurred in by the American Baptist Home Mission Society, and by a change in 1913, of the charter granted by the State of Georgia, the name of the institution became "Morehouse College," in honor of Rev. Henry L. Morehouse, D. D., Corresponding Secretary of the American Baptist Home Mission Society and the constant friend and benefactor of the Negro race.

CAMPUS

The campus is thirteen acres in extent. It occupies one of the highest points of land in the city, 1,100 feet above sea-level, and commands a fine view of the city and surrounding country. For beauty and healthfulness, the situation could not be surpassed. The property is on West Fair Street, at the junction of Chestnut Street, within half an hour's walk from the post-office and railroad stations.

The following is taken from the Department of Interior bureau of education Bulletin, 1916, No. 39:

"It is a young men's school of secondary and college grade with classes in theology and an elementary department. It is the leading Baptist school of Georgia, and holds high rank among the schools of the South.

The institution is owned by the American Baptist Home Mission Society. A self-perpetuating board of trustees acts in an advisory capacity.

MOREHOUSE REPRESENTATIVES AT CAMP DODGE, DES MOINES, IOWA.

It has an attendance of 277, of which number 150 are boarders; the teaching force consists of 14 males and five females, two of which are white and the remainder colored. The teachers are devoted to the welfare of their pupils and command the confidence of the student body. Besides the elementary and secondary grades, there is a short course in music, Bible and manual training. This preparatory course is required of all students. There are no elective courses. All pupils entering the college are required to complete the foreign languages of the secondary course.

The simple theological courses offered serve a useful end, in training ministerial students.

Graves Hall, erected in 1889, at a cost of twenty eight thousand dollars, and named in honor of President Graves is the chief college dormitory. Quarles Hall, erected in 1898, at a cost of Fourteen thousand dollars, and named in honor of Reverend Frank Quarles, for many years pastor of Friendship Baptist Church, Atlanta, Georgia, and president of the Georgia State Baptist Convention, contains the class rooms in which the work of the English Preparatory Department is done with a floor for science work in Chemistry and Physics. Sale Hall, erected at a cost of forty thousand dollars, in 1910, and named in honor of President Sale, has recitation rooms and a chapel with seating capacity of seven hundred. Robert Hall, erected in 1917, at a total cost of thirty thousand dollars, has a basement that is used as a dining room and three floors devoted to dormitory purposes.

This is emphatically a Christian school. The faculty keeps constantly in mind the fact that it was founded by a missionary organization, and is sustained by the contributions of Christian people for the Christian education of young men. The Bible has a place in the regular course of study. Generally, Morehouse College encourages all activities—religious, literary, athletic—which make for the development of Christian Ideals and for the culture of a sound mind, in a sound body.

The College has taken a prominent part in the war. Already recently from the student body two hundred men have been furnished for active service. As many as fourteen were commissioned at the Officers' Training Camp, at Camp Dodge, Iowa. Twenty-four volunteered for service in the Signal Corps at Camp Sherman, Ohio. In the fall of known to be either preaching or teaching, while Government for the formation of a unit of the Student Army Training Corps, and a broad plan was launched whereby the total resources of the institution were made available for war uses.

In the summer of 1918 President Hope, was summoned to France for special Y. M. C. A. work among Negro soldiers.

The large idea of the alumni of the college is that of service. No less than three fifths of the living graduates of Morehouse College are definitely known to be either preaching or teaching, while at least another fifth are engaged in the work of the medical profession, the Y .M. C. A. or other lines of definite service.

ALEXANDER D. HAMILTON.

R. Alexander D. Hamilton of Atlanta, Georgia, is the father of a large family, the owner of a substantial business, and of considerable property and has investments in many Negro enterprises in and around Atlanta.

Mr. Hamilton was born in Eufaula, Alabama, in the year 1870. When but six years of age, his father moved to Atlanta, Georgia, where he was immediately enrolled as a pupil in the public school, thus beginning his preparation for life at an early age. His parents were not only concerned about his mental development, but had regard for his spiritual training and saw that he was placed under the uplifting influence of the church. These two agencies, the church and the school, developed him rapidly. He completed his course in the public school when only thirteen years old and was received into the membership of the church at the age of eleven.

After passing through the public schools Mr. Hamilton entered the Atlanta University, where he remained until he had completed the preparatory course.

Atlanta University has long been noted for its thorough course in manual training. It was at Atlanta University in this course that Mr. Hamilton learned the further use of the carpenters' tools, for which he cultivated so great a liking.

This disposition to the carpenter trade was instilled in him from childhood. His father pursued this trade and had become a contractor of some note. The youthful Hamilton, quick to learn and of an observant tendency, soon learned the use of the tools, which greatly aided him in his studies in the industrial department of the Atlanta University. Now ready for his life work he entered the employment of his father and applied himself energetically to his task. Fidelity to the interest of his fathers' business brought its reward and after five years of service he was admitted to the membership of the firm. From that date until the death of his father the name of the firm was A. Hamilton and Son. His father died in 1911, since which time the son has continued the business alone. His conduct of the business keeps it up to the high standard for which the firm is noted.

As a young man, Mr. Hamilton worked hard to gain a footing. The fact that he was in the employ of his father seemed to spur him on rather than to make him take his ease. Struggling hard to make his place as a carpenter, he wished also to establish a certain financial competence. To this end he saved as regularly and as systematically as he worked. Thirty years of working and saving have brought encouraging returns. He owns a $7,000 home, has pieces of rent property valued at $5,500, carries $17,000 Life insurance, the payment of whose policies requires a pretty large income, and has some $3,000 invested in various Negro enterprises.

He appraised money, however, not as a means of luxury, and show, but as a means of usefulness, an avenue to larger service. This too, has come to him. He is a member of the board of directors of the Standard Life Insurance Company, of Atlanta, and secretary and treasurer of Georgia Real Estate and Loan Company. He is a member of the First Congregational Church, of St. James Masonic Lodge, and of the Century Odd Fellows. He has been able to travel and to make friends in the East, in the West and in the South.

With his savings and investments and with his other responsibilities, Mr. Hamilton has been rearing a big family. He was married in 1892, to Miss Nellie M. Cooke, of Atlanta. Seven children grace the Hamilton home. The oldest, Alexander D. Jr., is 23 years of age, is associated with his father in the business of contracting and building. The second oldest child, Miss Eunice Evlyn, is a teacher in the Atlanta Public Schools. T. Bertram, Henry Cooke, Marion Murphy, Nellie Marie, and Joseph Thomas, who is only seven are all students in the school.

THE HALE INFIRMARY, MONTGOMERY, ALA.

THIS Institution was born in the mind of one of Montgomery's most respected colored citizens, the late James Hale, who for many years was one of the city's leading contractors. He was known for the high character of his work and his reliability as a man. As he drew near the sun-set of life his mind centered upon his people and upon his two children who had passed into the great beyond.

The Hale Infirmary is the outcome of his meditations and is an expression of his deep interest in the welfare of his people and at the same time a memorial to his children. It was incorporated as the James Hale Infirmary Society, Montgomery, Alabama, in 1889.

The original plant cost about seven thousand, ($7,000). It consisted of a two story frame structure with capacity to care for sixty patients.

It is modern in its equipment, having sanitary plumbing throughout and with bath rooms for both male and females. It is supplied with hot and cold water, and has modern operating room with the necessary modern equipments. In addition to the main building there is a laundry, and small buildings for isolating patients who could not be admitted to the main building. The maintenance of the Institution is dependant upon a nominal charge for services and revenue derived from the nurses. It has no endowment. The nurses are trained in a three year course and during their training are frequently called upon to render service outside of the infirmary and the revenue derived from their services is a valuable asset to the Institution. The experience gained by the nurses in the operating room becomes invaluable to them in their course of training. The head nurse of the Infirmary is the superintendent of the training school and she has the assistance of two graduate nurses who teach them the theory of nursing with practical illustrations. Lectures are also given before the class by the large corps of physicians who daily visit the infirmary and contribute to its upbuild. Dr. David Henry Scott is the head of the Institution and is keenly alive to its interests and never tires in his efforts in its behalf.

The control and government of the infirmary is vested in a Board of Trustees, composed of nine members.

The Board of Trustees is as follows:

Bishop J. W. Alstork, Chairman; J. M. C. Logan, Geo. W. Doak, H. A. Loveless, Belton Murphree, Dr. D. H. C. Scott, V. H. Tulane, Jas. H. Fagain, and Jas. Alexander.

BISHOP LUCIUS H. HOLSEY.

ISHOP L. H. Holsey was born near Columbus, Georgia, in 1845, and therefore saw more slavery than most men now living. He was even traded in, having had three masters before the Emancipation Proclamation set him free.

Educational facilities for the colored race at the date of his birth were very meager in the place where he was born, so he had but little opporunity to learn but he was a man to make the most of his opportunities and ride them to a successful career.

When but seven years of age he was deprived of a mother's loving and tender care, which added to the struggle of his early days.

Bishop Holsey is a man of strong initiative ability and when emancipation gave him the opportunity to exercise his gift he immediately brought it into active play.

Coming in a period when men of initiative were in crying need he helped meet the demands of the day and the wonderful manner in which he filled his place is shown in the many honors and distinctions carried by him in his old age.

He is the oldest ordained Bishop of his church,

and one of the oldest men to be in active service of any kind. He is the first Negro to petition for a C. M. E. Church, and first to establish a church after the civil war. He was delegate to the first general conference of his church and first delegate to the Ecumenical church Conference and the first delegate to the conference of the Methodist Episcopal Church South.

His initiative first manifesting itself in church work has by no means been confined to that branch of activities, but has been almost eclipsed by his labors for education. He is an ardent avocate of education and was quick to realize that next to religion education would be the great uplifting power to help elevate his people.

He founded the Paine College, in Augusta, Georgia, took steps for the founding of Lane College, in Jackson, Tenn.; founded Holsey Industrial Institute at Cordell, Georgia; Helen B. Cobb Institute for girls at Barnesville, Georgia. He still is a trustee and patron of all of these institutions. He was agent of the Paine College for 25 years.

With these honors from his labors and many other good judgment, he served as the Secretary for the College of Bishops for quarter of a century, and was for many years, General Corresponding Secretary for the connection. He has compiled for his church, a Hymnal and a Manual for discipline. He once edited a church paper, the "Gospel Trumpet," and held the post as church Commissioner of education. Surely if one were bedecked for uplift deeds of this sort Bishop Holsey would be literally covered.

All through his youth and early manhood, Bishop Holsey felt the call for a larger service. Picking up knowledge when and where he could he secured his first church as pastor in 1868, on the Hancock Circuit in Georgia. Five years later at the close of a two years pastorate in Savannah, he was ordained Bishop of his church. This makes him push close to a half century of service as Bishop of his church.

Bishop Holsey was married at Sunshine, near Sparta, Georgia., in 1862, to Miss Harriet Turner. Nine children have been born to the Holsey family; of these, three are deceased—among those deceased was Miss Ruth M. Holsey, whose talent as a musician was already becoming widely known. She had won distinction in this country and had studied two years in Paris. Of the children living; James Henry is a graduate of Howard University and a Dentist in Atlanta. Georgia.; Miss Katie M., a graduate of Paine College, lives with her father; Miss Ella B. and Claud Lucia are living in Boston. The former is a matron, the latter married and resides there. Sumner L., who is a printer, also lives in Boston. Rev. C. Wesley is a Presiding Elder and Missionary in and around Atlanta.

MISS CLARA A. HOWARD.

ISS Clara A. Howard was born in Greenville, Merriwether County, Georgia. It has been in Georgia that she has spent the greatest number of years in service. She was one of the first students to enter Spelman Seminary, when it was founded in 1881. Miss Howard says of this fact that she feels almost as though she was one of the founders. From Spelman she was graduated in 1887. After her graduation, Miss Howard taught in the public schools of Atlanta. But she did not feel that this was her place for life work. Always before her were the needs of the people of Africa; and so May 3, 1890, she sailed for Africa. For five years Miss Howard remained in Africa. She was stationed at Lukungu, Congo, South West Africa. Here she tried in her very effective manner to reach the people and to teach them how to live, as well as how to be Christians. At the same time, Miss Howard had to fight the African fever. After five years of work she had to come back to America to rest. Her health was very slow in returning, and after a time she had to give up all hope of ever returning to Africa.

In 1899, Miss Howard became a member of the faculty of Spelman Seminary. At first she served as assistant matron in the Student Boarding Department, but in 1909 she became the only matron in that department. Of her work here, Miss Howard says, "As Matron in the Student Boarding Department, I come to know every boarding student each year, and I assure you the field for usefulness is about as wide as the one in Africa." Any one hearing a group of Spelman girls discussing their teachers either before or after graduation will soon hear them come to Miss Howard. By her quiet, kindly treatment, she has won all of them and, in winning them as friends, she has helped each one to a higher plane of thinking and living.

Of the work that Miss Howard is doing in Spelman, Miss Tapley, the president of the Institution says. "She is invaluable to us. She fills a large place and fills it as well as any person we ever had or can ever expect to have. Very few women could carry her work so well as she does. No matter what our difficulties, we can count on Miss Howard being brave, co-operative and helpful."

Besides the oversight in a general way of all the girls and in particular in the Dining room. Miss Howard has had direct charge of a number of small children, who have entered Spelman. Among these was one little African girl, Flora Zeto, whom she brought with her from Africa. To Flora, Miss Howard was everything that a mother could be. No one talking with Flora after a few years under the direct influence of this good woman, would have imagined her origin. Her voice and manner took on the culture of her friend. Miss Howard has played the part of mother to a number of other small girls. During all the years she has been working in this Institution she has been able to keep up the habit of treating girls as individuals. She never thinks of them in mass. All over the South there are girls and women who remember the times when Miss Howard stood for them as a guardian angel. As a part of her work in the school, Miss Howard has monthly meeting with the girls in which various subjects of a very personal nature are discussed. Miss Howard handles these as only a few persons know how to handle delicate subjects. From her the girls will take any suggestions for their betterment. Surely her's has been a life of usefulness. Her five years in Africa, in Lukungu, alone, represents great good done, but back in her native country, her native state and her Alma Mata, she has done a work that few are permitted to accomplish in a lifetime.

The influence of her useful and consecrated life will make itself felt throughout the land, as the girls go forth from this institution, and will remain to bless her people long after she has gone to her reward.

David Tobias Howard

MR. David Howard of Atlanta, Georgia, is one of the pioneers among Negro undertakers. Born in Crawford County, Ga., in 1849, he saw much of slavery, of the Civil War and of the reconstruction period. A lad of 15 years when the Civil War came, he was placed in charge of a train load of colored people, who were being shipped from Atlanta to Barnesville. Like most of the ex-slaves he found himself poor, uneducated, deserted when freedom was declared.

His first steady job was that of a porter in a railroad office. Here in 1869, he began work for $5.00 per month, boarding and lodging himself out of this sum. Here he worked for fourteen years. During this period, his salary, rather his wages, had risen from $5.00 to $45.00 per month. By this time he had managed to save a pretty snug sum of money and had made up his mind to venture into business for himself.

He was led to his business venture through observing the business of a firm to whom he had loaned money from time to time. It was an undertaking firm and he observed that they could afford to pay interest on money borrowed and make a good profit out of it.

He had no knowledge of the business further than his visit to the establishment in collecting his interest, but he had the good sense to see the possibilities in it, so when he decided to enter a business career for himself he had also decided the character of business he would pursue. In those days very few of the colored race, whether teachers, preachers or even physicians had specialized very highly in their chosen occupations.

Mr. Howard saw an opening for the business and an inviting field and he trusted to his own energy and business ability to win success.

Like many a man who started out with bright hopes he soon learned that the path to success is not a rosy path but rather a rugged way.

He invested his earnings in the Undertaking business after he had married and had begun to raise a family, hoping and expecting large profits, but the profits fell below his expectation and he realized that the business must be of slow and gradual growth.

This made it necessary for him to supplement the business with some other line of work in order to support his family while his business grew. He drove a hack which was really in line with the undertaking business so that he could give attention to both without neglecting either.

Mr. Howard is not easily discouraged and is a man of great determination so the difficulties in his way did not deter him but rather acted as a spur to awaken his energy. He went forward and in the course of time won his fight and established the large undertaking establishment over which he now presides.

He not only established a large business, but also a reputation as a business man who commands the respect of the citizens of Atlanta, Georgia, and of the entire state.

Mr. Howard has not confined his business operations to the city. As his undertaking business developed and he made a surplus money for investment he turned his attention to the country and invested in farm lands and the raising of cattle. He has several farms outside of Atlanta where he cultivated gardens, planted orchards and raised cattle. His country places serve to rest his mind from the exactions of his undertaking business and the stress of city life. The country air and diversions of the farm no doubt account for his own fine health and that of his family and contributes to the optimistic spirit which characterizes him.

Incidentally this ex-slave who started working for $5.00 a month nearly half a century ago is now worth $175,000. Most of this he has invested in real estate and farms, the way he thinks most colored people should invest their money, especially in farm lands. Though he has amassed so large a sum Mr. Howard is by no means a stingy man. Indeed, he is quite the opposite, having an open purse for any uplift work of his city. A recent instance of this kind is his being the first among the few to subscribe $1000 for the Negro Y. M. C. A. building of Atlanta.

Much of his income, too, he has spent in educating his children. Mr. Howard was married in 1870 to Miss Ella Buanner of Summerville, Georgia. Nine children have been born into the Howard family. These Mr. Howard has given the best education available. Some have been graduated from Atlanta University, some from the Oberlin Conservatory of Music, some have attended Morehouse and other colleges. The children are Frank David, Willie Gladstone, Paul, Thomas Edward, Misses Eleanor B., Lottie Lee, Julia and Henry Gladstone. His son, Henry Gladstone is associated with his father in business.

Mr. Howard is a member of the A. M. E. Church. He is also a member of fraternal organizations, belonging to the St. John's Masonic Lodge, to the Good Samaritan, to the Knights of Pythias, and to the Knights of Tabor.

GEORGE RUBIN HUTTO.

LL who read the history of the steady advance that has been made by the colored Knights of Pythias of Georgia will know that back of the organization is a strong man. A man who is fearless in his endeavor to do the right things for his people, a man who has the courage of his convictions, a man who is a born leader of men is the only sort of man who could get in behind an order and see it develop so steadily. The Colored Knights of Pythias of Georgia are fortunate indeed to have at its head such a man in the person of George R. Hutto.

Mr. Hutto was born n Barnelwell, South Carolina in 1870. His training in the school room began at an early age and so at the age of twenty we find him graduating from Claflin University, Orangeburg, South Carolina. He was a member of the class of 1890. The following year he was married to Miss Addie E. Dillard. Miss Dillard was a graduate of Benedict College which is located at Columbia, South Carolina. To the Hutto's, two children were born. One, Marcus Hutto, is a senior in the Meharry Medical school. The other is a daughter, Miss Callie Hutto.

In church affiliation, Mr. Hutto is a Baptist. This is another point on which Mr. Hutto, early made his decision. In fact Mr. Hutto is a man of prompt action. He was early at school, early out of school, early married and early settled down

to the development of his life along the line he had chosen. In the year 1895 Mr. Hutto was elected Principal of the Public School, at Bainbridge, Georgia. The same year he joined the Masonic order. Thus at an early age we find Mr. Hutto starting out in fraternal orders. In 1897 there was organized in Bainbridge, Georgia, a court of the Order of the Knights of Pythias, known as the Lucullus Lodge, No 45. Mr. Hutto joined the order at the organization of this new lodge. From the first, his great interest and ability as a leader, won for Mr. Hutto distinction in the ranks of Pythians. In 1900 in the City of Valdosta, he was elected Grand Lecturer of the Knights of Pythias of Georgia. For four consecutive times he was re-elected to this position. In 1905 he was elected Vice-Chancellor of the organization for his State. At that time serving as Chancellor was Mr. C. D. Creswell. At the death of the Chancellor in 1910, Mr. Hutto filled out the unexpired term and at the next session, which was held in the city of Macon, he was elected to the position of Grand Chancellor. To this position he has been re-elected each year since. The figures of the order show the marvelous growth of the organization, Mr. Hutto's influence in the development of the body did not begin with his election to the position of Grand Chancellor. It began rather with his admission as a member when the court was formed in Bainbridge. Through all the following years his influence for the development of the Knights of the State of Georgia was secured. As a lecturer he served and served well. In this position he had ample opportunity to bring before the people the merits of the order and the benefits to be derived therefrom. His next step upward in this body was that position of Vice-Chancellor. Here he learned all the workings and rulings of the order and when the death of Mr. Creswell put upon Mr. Hutto the work of head man for the State of Georgia, he was ready. The order has developed steadily under his leadership. Of the State of Georgia has been said, "This is our Banner State." For the truth of this statement much of the credit is due Mr. Hutto.

The first Court organized in this State was the Opal Court, No. 41, by Sir J. C. Ross, at Savannah, 1889, with Sir J. C. Ross, W. C.

The Grand Court was organized at Atlanta, Ga., July, 1892, by Rev Israel Derricks, Supreme Worthy Counsellor, with the following Grand Officers: Mrs. W. L. Catledge (Hill,) G. W. C.; Mrs. R. L. Barnes, G. W. Ix.; Sir C. A. Catledge, G. R., of Deeds; Sir F. M. Cohen, G. R., of Deps.; with Sir J. C. Ross and Dr. T. James Davis, P. G. W. C., Mrs. Catledge (Hill,) served one year, 1902-3, as G. W. C. Mrs. R. L. Barnes was elected 1893, and has served continuously until 1917.

In 1900 there were 21 Courts, 450 members, with $92.75 Endowment on hand.

1910. 218 Courts, 8,000 members, 94 deaths, $11,-318.60 collected for Endowment, $10,140.00 paid on claims, $20,353.73 balance on hand, 36 Juvenile Courts, 1150 members.

1915. 350 Courts, 12,500 members, 268 deaths, $26,408.10 Endowment collected, $24,380.00 paid on claims, $29,450.80 balance on hand. Grand Court fund balance on hand, $2,250. Georgia is the Banner Grand Court of the order.

REVEREND EDWIN POSEY JOHNSON, A. B.

HE subject of this sketch was born Feb. 22, 1849, in Columbus, Georgia. His father, William Warren Johnson, was brought to Georgia from Maryland, where he received considerable education and was taught the Stage-building trade. His mother, Caroline Posey came from Virginia to Georgia, with her owners, in whose family her people had been reared for generations. Her master, Major Nelson, believed that colored people, as well as white should be taught to read so as to study the Bible for themselves. Hence his mother was a constant reader of the Bible and other good books.

Freedom came to him when at the age of sixteen. The first opportunity for learning to read and write was in a little dirt-floor school house in an alley. Here with many others he tackled a Blue Back Spelling Book. The next year he hired himself to work on a farm and walked a mile and a half to a night school, taught by Mrs. Lucy E. Case and others. When Mrs. Case became matron at Atlanta University, she persuaded him to attend school there. In the fall of 1873, having saved up $150, he matriculated at Atlanta University. By working as an engineer at school and teaching during the summers, he was enabled to remain in school. In 1874 he was converted under the ministry of Rev. Geo. W. Walker, one of the instruc-

tors.. With an unfailing courage he continued his studies until he graduated in 1879, with the degree of A. B. On July of that year he was ordained as a minister of the Gospel by his pastor, Rev. Frank Quarles, and others in Friendship Baptist Church, Atlanta, Georgia. He served his denomination one year as a missionary, then taught six years in Hawkinsville, during which time he built the two-story school house at the cost of $1,600.00. From his arduous labors at Hawkinsville, he has had the pleasure of seeing many of his pupils occupying places of usefulness. Leaving Hawkinsville, he served as principal of the Mitchell Street School, Atlanta, Georgia, for two terms.

On December 26, 1882, he was married by Rev. Henry Way, to Miss E. S. Key. In 1888 he was called to the pastorate of Calvary Baptist Church, Madison, Georgia. During the eleven years of his stay there, he made many improvements on the church property and added to the church more than five hundred precious souls. While at Madison, he was elected by the board of Education as the first principal of the city school for colored people, which he organized and directed till a suitable man could be found.

In 1899 he was elected as general manager of the New Era Institute Work, under the joint auspices of the Home Mission Society of New York, The Southern Baptist Convention and the General Missionary and Educational Convention of Georgia. This position, for three years took him to all parts of the state.

For several years he was instructor at Phelps Hall Bible Training School, Tuskegee Institute, Alabama. Here he filled the position with satisfaction to all concerned.

In 1901 Rev. Johnson was called to pastor the Reed Street Baptist Church, Atlanta, Georgia. Here he has been, laboring for sixteen years, organizing, building, giving to the church the ripe fruits of all his experiences in the school room and country and town churches. As a result, the church is now organized into practical and useful committees and auxiliaries. Also a new stone church edifice, situated on the corner of Frasier and Crumley Streets, which when finished will cost $25,000, is now almost completed and more than 400 members have been added. When the new building was begun, the pastor reduced his own salary $15 per month, thereby setting an example of economy. He sets a further example by living in his own home, keeping his credit up to such a high standard that he and the church of which he is pastor can secure money and commodities on his name.

Rev. Johnson is treasurer of the Atlanta Baptist Minister's Union; Secretary of the Board of Trustees of Spelman Seminary; Secretary of the Reformatory Board; Treasurer of the General Missionary Educational Board; Treasurer of the State B. Y. P. U. Convention; Chairman of the Reid Orphan Home, at Covington, Georgia; Member of the Executive Board of the Madison Association; Georgia's Foreign representative of the National Baptist Convention and Instructor in the Divinity Department of Morehouse College.

ROBERT EDWARD PHARROW.

LTHOUGH there are a great number of Negro carpenters and builders there are comparatively few who might be termed contractors, taking that term in its larger sense of erecting large buildings, dormitories, school houses, temples for the fraternities, hotels and office buildings. This is due in a large measure to the fact that such contracts call for a large outlay of money and very few Negroes have the capital to back up such contracts nor the influence and ability to secure it.

Another reason why so few Negroes undertake the erection of large buildings is that it requires a special training and equipment for such work. It involves confidence, bookkeeping, managing big squads of men, time-keeping, dealing in large freight orders, running engines and so marshalling it all that the structure will be reliable and satisfactory and the profits ample.

Mr. Pharrow is among the few Negro contractors who have risen to prominence in the contracting business. He did not rise to this distinction at a bound, but reached it after years of patient toil and strict application to his work.

He began his career as a brick mason, when a lad of only sixteen years of age, working under the old system of apprenticeship. He was quick to learn and made the best of the opportunity offered him while serving his apprenticeship and in seventeen years' time had not only learned the trade of Masonry, but all that one could learn of the intricacies of the business without being in it.

At the age of thirty-three he began the contracting business upon his own account.

Mr. Pharrow exhibited the virtue of patience during his long apprenticeship and was so well fitted for his work when he started business on his own account that he rose rapidly in the confidence of the public and received a goodly share of its patronage.

His reputation as a builder was not confined to his home town of Macon, Georgia, but he entered and won, in competing for contracts throughout the States of Georgia and Alabama. He erected the new Recitation Hall at Morehouse College, Atlanta, and has built structures in most of the large cities of Alabama and Georgia.

Mr. Pharrow figures close and does good work and consequently has made money out of his contracts.

Besides the capital invested in a well established business he owns a good home and twelve additional houses which brings him in a monthly rental of pleasing amount.

Mr. Pharrow has sought health and pleasure in travel, his travels having carried him over the greater part of United States, Canada and Cuba.

Mr. Pharrow was born in Washington, Georgia, in 1868. As he went to work at his trade when very young the amount of his schooling was really very small. But he has always made haste slowly and has thereby atoned for much that he might possibly have gained from further schooling.

He has, further, kept himself intellectually and socially fit by membership in the church and in many of the leading organizations of his State. Mr. Pharrow is a member of the A. M. E. Church —of the Masons, of the Odd Fellows, of the Elks, of the Knights of Pythias. He is Past Grand Master of the Patriarchs, Past Chancellor of the Pythians and Senior Warden of the Masons, Ancient Free and Accepted Masons.

Mr. Pharrow bases much of his success upon the sympathy, advice and cooperation of his helpmates at home. He has been twice married. He was married to Miss Martha L. Harris, of Atlanta, in 1892. She it was who stood by him so faithfully in his first ventures as a contractor. Mrs. Pharrow died in 1911. The present Mrs. Pharrow was Miss R. V. Gariy, of Savannah, Georgia. Mr. Pharrow has one child, Miss Estelle, who is a graduate of Atlanta University, and who teaches in the Atlanta public schools.

HENRY HUGH PROCTOR, A. B., D. D.

NE of the best known Congregational ministers of the Colored Race is Dr. Henry Hugh Proctor born in Fayetteville, Tennessee, December 8, 1868, and it was a very fortunate date, because he was among the first to enjoy the fruits of freedom.

As a boy he attended the public school of his town. This school was not among the best, judged even by the standard of that time, but the young man applied himself most diligently and acquired at least the habit of organized studying aside from some real knowledge. He worked hard here and when he had gotten all that he could from his town school, he entered Fisk University. Here, where the standard was high and the method of instruction good, the young student developed very rapidly, distinguishing himself both by conduct and scholarship. Before finishing his college course one ideal so took possession of him as to dominate his being—service through the Christian Ministry. Thus when he graduated from the College Department of Fisk, he went to New England, the cradle of American culture, and entered Yale Divinity School in New Haven, Connecticut. Here he lived and worked, studying hard while he laid the foundation for his great life work. His scholarship rewarded his efforts and when he completed the prescribed course, his was truly a commencement—a commencement of work in a field toward which he had so eagerly looked.

His first regular charge was Pastor of the First Congregational Church at Atlanta, Georgia. Of this church Dr. Proctor is still the beloved pastor. To the year of his taking charge of the work, 1894, Dr. Proctor looks back as the beginning of his vital career. One would be justified in saying that the church was really established by Rev. Proctor.

Here in Atlanta, for twenty-four years Dr. Proctor has labored, developing his church and of necessity growing himself. With wonderful foresight as to the needs of our people—not necessarily the needs of the people of his congregation, but the needs of the Colored people of Atlanta—Dr. Proctor developed his church, adding to it one line of work after another until today it is one of our foremost institutional churches.

Aside from the regular church with its Services, Bible School, Y. P. S. C. E. and Prayer Meetings, there are the Employment Bureau, Free Public Library, consisting of 3000 volumes and the only Public Library accessible to Negroes in Atlanta; a gymnasium open afternoons and evenings; the Avery Congregational Home for Working Girls; the Conally Water Fountain, whereby through a unique device ice water is furnished the passerby in summer; the Prison Mission, whose object is to help those held in prison through religious services, literature distribution, and visits giving pastoral comfort; a Trouble Department whose object is to render any service possible to those in trouble; an Auditorium with a seating capacity of 1000, provided with grand pipe organ, heated by steam, lighted by electricity and opened for any beneficial gathering for the community; and the Georgia Music Association, which gives the city an opportunity to hear the best musical talent of the race. The Annual Musical Festival held by the colored people in the Auditorium Armory is due largely to the Musical Association.

For all this Dr. Proctor is directly responsible. He has been able to obtain aid for his work from both the white and the colored people of Atlanta because they could see the benefit of the organization.

Though the Institution and his church demand a large share of his time, Dr. Proctor has still found time to serve in other ways. He is President of the Carrie Steel Orphanage in Atlanta; Assistant Moderator of the National Council of the Congregational Church; Vice-President of the American Missionary Association of New York; and Secretary of the Congregational Workers among Colored People.

One year before he came to Atlanta, Rev. Proctor married Miss Adeline Davis of Nashville, Tennessee. Their home has been blessed by the coming of six children, Henry Hugh, Jr., a graduate of Fisk University, and at present serving as a First Lieutenant in France; Richard Davis, deceased; Muriel Morgan and Lillian Steele, students at Atlanta University; Roy and Vashti, public school children.

Dr. Proctor is beloved by all. He is acknowledged a Reformer and an Educator. He is doing much good in bringing about a better understanding between the races.

Thomas Heath Slater, A. B., M. D.

IN the South there are at least two cities in which there is a splendid galaxy of educated, prosperous, refined Negroes. These are Nashville, Tennessee, and Atlanta, Georgia, which could claim superiority is a grave question. Both have a Negro College or University on nearly every hill in the city. Both are full of business men, professional men and tradesmen. Competition among the colored men in nearly all pursuits is close. Therefore, he who gains his place and holds it, does so largely by dint of excellence.

In Atlanta one could count on all the fingers of his hands physicians with conspicious careers, with reputations and practices well established. Very prominent among these is Dr. Thomas H. Slater. Dr. Slater is a North Carolinian by birth, having been born in Salisbury, December 25, 1865. He attended the schools of Salisbury, his birthplace, and then went to college at Lincoln University, Pennslyvania, where he received his Bachelor's Degree in 1887, and was graduated with first honors. He then entered Meharry Medical College in Nashville, Tennessee, completing his course early in 1890, here he also won first honors.

In March of the same year, Dr. Slater went to Atlanta, Georgia and began the practice of his profession. Here in the same city in nearly the same spot, he has continued for this quarter of a century. Dr. Slater, (with Dr. H. R. Butler) was the real pioneer of the Negro Medical profession in Atlanta.

Up to this period the Negroes were attended almost exclusively by the white physicians, in whom they had the utmost confidence, and it was not an easy matter to turn them to the colored physicians who were then beginning to establish themselves in the South.

It was Dr. Slaters mission to win the confidence of his people and turn them to the physicians of their own race, and it was largely due to the fact that Dr. Slater's unusual ability and qualifications as a diagnostician and practitioner were recognized by Dr. J. S. Todd, at that time Atlanta's leading practitioner of internal medicine, enabled him to so rapidly gain this confidence. Dr. Slater has always been grateful to Dr. J. S. Todd for his recommendations and kind assistance in those early days.

In the midst of sharp competition, the constant injection of new blood and the rapid advancement of the profession, he has held his place both in Atlanta and in the state of Georgia as one of the leading and best equipped physicians.

This has not been done through idleness or a satisfied state of mind. He has studied continually, both in theory and in practice. His eye is ever alert for the latest and best in medicine and in the equipment of service. His office equipment is among the best and most modern in the city. It has every modern convenience and appliance, including an equipment for Chemical and Blood tests. There is possibly no physician who realized more forcibly the importance of hard, continuous study in keeping up with the latest and most successful methods of diagnosis and treatment of all internal diseases. He has viewed with keen interest the rapid yet positive changes in the therapy of his profession. From the excessive use of drugs in the general treatment of diseases he has watched and followed the successful advancement of the practice to specific treatment through the use of specific agents, vaccines, bacterins, phylacogens and organic extracts. His work as a physician early won for him distinction, both among the men of his profession and in other bodies. He is President of the Atlanta Meharry Alumni Association and has served among the doctors of the state as President and as Secretary of the Georgia State Medical Association of Negro Physicians, Dentists and Pharmacists.

Dr. Slater was reared and educated a Presbyterian, and has always found time to faithfully discharge has religious duties toward his church. He has learned that the opportunities for service comes to the Christian physician in a larger measure than from any other line of endeavor outside of the Christian ministry. He believes that a strong moral and religious character is the best asset that any physician can have, and at this period of racial development and progress he deems it absolutely essential.

Dr. Slater is interested in the various orders of the Colored race, and takes an active part in them. He is a member of the Masonic Fraternity, the Odd Fellows and is a Knight of Pythias. He is a Master of the Local Lodge of Masons.

Dr. Slater has been twice married. His first wife, Mrs. Marie A. Taylor, of Austin, Texas, and a graduate of Wilberforce University, he married in June, 1903, but lost her by death in February, 1905. In July, 1907 he married Mrs. Celestine Bass Phillips, of Michigan, a graduate of Bay City High School. He had only one child, a son, Thomas Heathe, Jr., who was born February 21st, 1905, and died November 5th, 1906.

Dr. Slater's home on Piedmont Avenue is among the colored residences that Atlantans point to for proofs of their prosperity and good taste. His home life is a source of pride, pleasure and comfort, and he attributes his success to domestic peace and happiness.

PANORAMIC VIEW OF SPELMAN SEMINARY.

PELMAN Seminary, of Atlanta, Georgia, the largest school in the world for Negro girls, carries in the story of its growth many a thrilling romance—the romance of faith, of prayer, of struggle, of successful rendering of service. For fifteen years Father Quarles, ex-slave and pastor of the Friendship Baptist Church, laid the Spelman foundation in prayer, beseeching that God would send some means of elevating the Negro women of Georgia. In the fifteenth year while he tarried in supplication, the answer came. Two ladies, Miss Sophie Packard and Miss Harriet E. Giles, of Massachusetts, were the evangels. They came to seek out Faather Quarles and actually knocked on his study door while the good man still lingered in prayer.

With the coming of the two ladies began the romance of struggle. Here were the workers, the pupils were legion; but there was no school room. Combining faith and work as best he could, Father Quarles surrendered to the workers the basement of his church. This was the setting for the struggle. To begin with the school was sneered at by white and black, being stigmatized as the "Out Hill." The basement was cold and damp, admitting water when it would rain. There were no desks, no seats. The flooring was rotting away. A rickety, smoking flue, held up by wire; darkness, approaching gloom! the increase of enrollment causing them even to hold a class in the coal bin; no salary, no definite assurance of support—all this confronted two women far from home, on soil still hostile; women who had taught in buildings comfortably heated and properly ventilated, who had drawn their salary regularly and lived amidst happy relatives and cordial friends. However, prayer

again entered the struggle. The school had formally opened its doors, April 11, 1881. It had eleven pupils, some old and some young; some were single, some married. Among the older students was a grown woman, who day by day looked up the hill which was then occupied by the Barracks, and prayed that one day Spelman, (then Atlanta Baptist Female Seminary,) might occupy this spot. Each day they gathered, prayed, toiled in the basement. The enrollment increased from eleven to eighty in three months and to one hundred seventy five by the end of the year. The next year, 1882, saw the prayers answered. The American Baptist Home Missionary Society bought a part of the Barracks, nine acres, which had on the grounds, five frame buildings. Here Spelman has remained expanding in territory, in number of buildings and in useful service to the people.

Grappling every day with want of buildings, of equipment, of food, clothes and comforts for their students, the founders nevertheless began early to shape the courses of study to suit the need of the people among whom their students had to labor. To this end they started the Spelman Nurse Training Course in 1886, the Missionary Department in 1891, the Teachers' Professional Department in 1892, the College Department in 1897. In doing this Spelman was not only serving its graduates and those among whom they would work, but was serving as pioneer to a host of Negro schools in the South, which only in recent years have adopted similar courses in their curriculums. Later, Spelman further expanded its courses. To Nurse Training, Teaching, Missionary Courses, have been added courses in music, in Domestic Science, in Laundering, Sewing, Dressmaking, Millinery, Basketry, Gardening, Printing. There are, too, courses in High School and College Departments, which comprehend the study of Latin and German, Higher Mathematics and the Sciences, looking to careers of thought and scholarship.

PANORAMIC VIEW OF SPELMAN SEMINARY.

The school is under the direct control of a strong board of trustees and affiliated with the American Baptist Home Mission Society. It has had three presidents, its two founders, Miss Sophia Packard and Miss Harriet E. Giles, Miss Giles succeeding Miss Packard in 1891. The present encumbent is Miss Lucy Hale Tapley, who came all the way from the ranks of the teachers and who has grown with the school. Spelman has a faculty of fifty teachers. Each teacher receives her commission direct from the Women's Baptist Home Mission Board. It registers an average attendance of 750 students a year. In all the departments the school is thoroughly and intensely religious. Whatever courses a student may pursue, prayer and Bible study, required and volunteer, and the doctrine of service play a major part in shaping the lives of those who come within her walls.

The usefulness of an institution is judged by the amount of good work done by the graduates and former students turned out. Judged from this point of view, Spelman ranks among the highest institutions in the country. Teaching has been and continues to be the leading occupation of Spelman graduates. They are found to be in nearly every State of the South—in city graded schools, in industrial schools and in ungraded schools in rural districts, and a number have served on the faculty of their Alma Mater, Morehouse College, Selma University, and similar schools. One tribute to the ability of these Spelman girls as teachers came from a former State School Commissioner of Georgia. He said that if he had fifty teachers from Spelman's Normal department, he would revolutionize teaching in Georgia.

A large and important class of the graduates are bright examples of Christian wives and mothers. Of these many are helpful wives of ministers; others are assisting their husbands in their work as teachers; all are exerting a helpful influence on the lives of the next generation. Then there are graduates in a number of other callings—there is an editor, bookkeepers, stenographers, several doctors. There are workers in Orphan Homes—

kindergartens, charity work, Y. W. C. A. work, home and foreign mission work. All of these young women go out as representatives of the school that has done so much for them and they are proud to hold up her banner.

Spelman graduates do not confine their teaching to books. They undertake to teach their pupils both old and young, how to live. One encouraging thing about the work of these young women is the fact that, as a rule, women and girls, living in communities where Spelman students have labored, have a higher ideal of life, which manifests itself in the care and the training of the children.

The grounds of Spelman are an expression of well-organized orderly life within. The campus itself has a good effect on the pupils who attend the school. Going out from Spelman, each girl is opposed to dirt and trash. Each girl feels that she must make her surroundings attractive. Then there is about Spelman an air of having time to think, to feel, to commune with one's self and with one's God. The value of this time cannot be overestimated.

Another feature of the life of the students at Spelman Seminary is the manner in which they are cared for while students there. The system is unique. The boarders are divided into groups of about fifty, and placed in the care—not of a matron, not in the care of a preceptress, but in the care of a "Hall Mother." Each girl is at home with the "Hall Mother," and a "Hall Mother" feels just as responsible for the girls in her care as though they were really her own. Here in the privacy of their own halls the girls of any given group, have their prayers, their study hours, their little concerts and Christmas entertainments, etc.; and then go out and enjoy the more public ones which take in the whole school. In this manner, the atmosphere of home is thrown around the girls and they have the feeling of being really loved and protected.

Spelman Seminary is one of the best, if not the best, organized institution among our people. Its training is thorough.

GEORGE WASHINGTON HILL, PRESIDENT
WALKER BAPTIST INSTITUTE.

HE Walker Baptist Institute is located in Augusta, Georgia, where it was moved eleven years after it was founded, from Waynesboro, Ga. It was founded in the year 1881 by Father Nathan Walker. Since its removal it has grown in popularity and efficiency until it has become known as one of the most substantial secondary schools in the State of Georgia.

It is owned and partly supported by a board of seventy-eight trustees selected by the Walker Baptist Association.

While the property of the Institute belongs to the Walker Baptist Association it has been fostered by the Negro Baptists of the entire state of Georgia, and in a considerable measure of late years, by the General Education Board of New York.

In recent years the general public has also contributed to its support. In addition to this it has had many srong Baptists as sponsors.

The founder, Nathan Walker, was followed by T. J. Hornsby who in turn was succeeded by the Reverand C. T. Walker.

Under the care of C. T. Walker, popularly known as the "Black Spurgeon", Walker Baptist Institute has gained its widest publicity, expanded most, and done its best service.

The Walker Baptist Institute is a secondary school with large elementary enrollment. It has three departments: Grammar School, a College Course, and a Department of Theology.

The Grammar School covers a course of eight years. This department is under the direction of Professor G. W. Hill, who is the principle and who is assisted by Dr. James M. Mabritt, Dr. L. C. Walker, Mrs. Rubena Newson, Mrs. U. L. Golden, Misses Labara Kech, Naomi Wright, and Mrs. Annie E. Wheelston.

This organization under the management of Professor Hill, has done much for the young Baptist pupils for whom it was especially organized.

While it is a denominational school no student is kept from receiving its instruction because of his religious beliefs.

After passing through this department the scholars are prepared for their college course and for the study of Theology.

The aim of the school is to prepare its students for entrance into life where they must further advance through the school of experience.

The foundation laid for them here will enable them to gain from the school of experience additional knowledge and strength to ensure a noble and useful life.

The courses in the college and theological departments cover Latin, Greek, Mathematics, Theology, Psychology, English, Pedagogy, Domestic Science, and where there are young lady students, music and studies relating to the Bible as well as the Bible itself.

The Institution is now nearly forty years old. It has grown slowly but steadily, both in size and efficiency. It has rendered a large service to the students coming under its influence and to the denomination which brought it into existence.

Its property valuation is thirty-five thousand dollars and includes three large buildings, one of which is a four story brick building containing thirty-two rooms, used for a girl's dormitory, chapel and dining room.

The Institution has never been satisfied with its attainment, though pleasing, but is continuously striving to advance. Its president has caught a vision of a great and influential school and he is bending his energies to translate his vision into an accomplished fact. The Institution has a bright outlook for an enlarged and more efficient service.

In this effort he is ably assisted by the Baptists of the Walker Baptist Association, and especially by the Reverend C. T. Walker and the members of his congregation.

CHARLES T. WALKER, D. D., LL. D.

R. Charles T. Walker is among the leading colored men of the world today. Few are better known. By common consent, he is the ablest Negro preacher in the world without regard to denomination. He is pastor of the Tabernacle Baptist Institutional Church of Augusta, Georgia, where he has been laboring for nearly thirty-five years continuously, excepting two or three years when he was pastor of the Mount Olivet Baptist Church, in New York City.

His church in Augusta is frequented on each Sunday morning during the winter or tourist season by scores and scores of the wealthiest and most influential American people, both men and women. John D. Rockfellow was for years among his regular attendants. The same is true of former President, William Howard Taft, who declares that Dr. Walker is the most eloquent man he ever heard. The late Booker T. Washington said: "I do not know of any man, white or black, who is a more fascinating speaker either in private conversation or on the public platform."

Dr. Walker was born in the little town of Hepzibah, Georgia, a few miles South of Augusta, in the county of Richmond, on February 5, 1858. His father was a deacon of the Baptist church and was also the coachman of the family that owned him. Dr. Walker comes of a race of preachers. One of his uncles was pastor of the little church which was organized in 1848, and of which Dr. Walker's father was a deacon. The freedom of this uncle—Rev. Joseph T. Walker, was purchased by the slaves in order that he might devote his entire time to preaching the gospel. It is after this same uncle that the Walker Baptist Association is named. This association founded and maintains the Walker Baptist Institute at Augusta.

The Johnson's the Hornsby's the Youngs, the Whitehead's and, of course, the Walker's are all related to the family of the older Walker's. These men are the foremost ministers, and have been for many years the leading ministers and pastors in Eastern Georgia. Quite recently the Walker Baptist Association, of which Dr. Walker has been the moderator for the past eighteen years, raised for educational purposes, $22,000 in cash—the largest amount ever raised by any Baptist Association or State or national convention in the history of the United States.

Dr. Walker's work has not been confined to the pastorate. He has been interested in the publication of two weekly newspapers—the "Augusta Sentinel," of which he was business manager for several years, and the "Georgia Baptist," founded at Augusta, by Dr. W. J. White, and at whose death Dr. C. T. Walker became editor-in-chief of the paper in which position he served for many successful years. His accounts of travel in the Holy Land, originally published in the Sentinel, were afterwards published in book form and received a very wide circulation. He was founder and for many years president of the Negro Fair Association, at Augusta. He founded the colored men's branch Y. M. C. A., on 53rd Street, in New York City, and also founded the colored Y. M. C. A., at Augusta.

As an evangelist, Dr. Walker has no superior among the colored preachers and pastors of this country. He has been holding meetings in all parts of this country from Maine to California, for the past thirty years, and always with success. No colored preacher in this country draws larger crowds anywhere .

He has also taken a prominent and active part in the business and political developement of his race. He is a director in the Penny Bank, Augusta's only colored savings bank; he is director in the Pilgrim Health and Life Insurance Company, the biggest corporation of any kind in the city of Augusta, owned and operated by colored people; he is a member of the Augusta Realty Corporation—a band of seven men owning and controlling some of the best city property; and he has long been a member of the Republican State Central Committee and he has twice been elected by the people of his district to represent them in Republican National Conventions.

In all this work, and in all his many activities, Dr. Walker has not been an agitator. He has done more than any other colored citizen of his home town to bring about pleasant relations between the two races, and Booker T. Washington says that he did more than any man he knew to bring about peace and good will between the two sections of our country and the white and colored races.

It is a benediction to have lived in the same age and in the same country with Dr. C. T. Walker.

JAMES RUFUS WEBB.

 OR some years the city of Macon, Georgia, has been making bids to have the state headquarters removed from Atlanta to her soil. Macon's arguments have not always been convincing, but somehow they have more than worried the thinkers and writers of Atlanta. If wide awake progress of the Negro means anything Macon certainly cannot be dismissed with a wave of the hand. Atlanta has her Odd Fellows building, but Macon has her Pythian Temple, not so pretentious, but very useful nevertheless. Her Negroes have not the complicated interests, due to the multiplicity of big schools and strong religious denominations, that Atlanta has. Her black people move more in unison.

Conspicuous among the big Negro business men who would aid in weighing down the scales for Macon, is James Rufus Webb, grocer, real estate dealer, farmer, barber shop proprietor, holder of big shares in and promoter of undertaking and broom manufacturing establishments. Indeed they look upon him in Macon, as a sort of Cotton Avenue King.

Mr. Webb was born in 1863, in Crawford county, Ga. He got his education in Bibb County, in the city schools and in Ballard High School. Much of his way he earned, the other his father paid. Finishing his school career, Mr. Webb was none too certain just what he was to do to earn a livelihood and to make his place in the world. However he thought he saw an opening.

The Negro business man was making his way, but feebly, with a rare exception, in Macon in those days. There was no Douglass Hotel on Broad Street, no Pythian building, little Negro real estate. However, in 1889 Mr. Webb courageously set forth as a grocer on Cotton Avenue. Prosperity came quicker and more abundantly than he had dared hope. His business flourished without a failure for thirteen years, when he thought he would change.

Selling out the grocery business he took up that of dealing in Realty. He had some money and had learned some of the tricks of business and of investments. Situated in his office in the Pythian building where he could think and plan, he not only made profitable investments for himself but became a thinker, a planner, and a promoter for Negro business in general. He saw that there was a big opportunity as well as a chance to render improved service in the business of undertaking. Hence two undertaking establishments were soon under way, backed by his name, influence and capital. The Central City Undertaking Company of Macon is his own business and he carries a controlling interest in the Webb and Hartley Undertaking establishment.

Just as he saw the chance for the Negro undertaker to render bigger and better service, so he saw it in several other callings. He thought there was much room for the improved barber shop in his town, and he started the Union Barber shop. He thought there was a chance for the Negro to succeed as a broom maker and he established the O. R. Broom factory.

Planning and working incessantly, working not only to succeed himself, but also to give the colored people employment, it is no wonder that Mr. Webb has prospered. He does not hoard money, rather he keeps money moving, investing it, making it increase itself. He owns thirty houses, three stores, and a 165 acre farm in addition to his other business interests. The farm which has its houses, barns and the like, he takes pride in looking after himself.

Thus engrossed in business Mr. Webb has devoted but little time to organizations of any other kind. He and his wife, Mrs. Clara B. Webb, are members of the A. M. E. Church. He is a Mason, a St. Lukes Knight of Pythias. He has been treasurer of the Macon Lodge of Masons and past Chancellor of the Knights of Pythias.

All his business career, running over a quarter of a century, Mr. Webb has spent on Cotton Avenue. Here are the scenes of most of his investments. Here are all the business establishments of the King of Cotton Avenue. Thus it is that through Webb, through Douglass and others, that if Macon were bidding for the capital on the basis of Negro business, she could not be dismissed with a mere gesture.

MADAM MARTHA BROADUS ANDERSON B. M.

HICHEVER city of America may claim to be the Negro money center, social and intellectual center and the like, it is certain that Chicago alone carries the palm as the center of Negro music. There are but a few of our best musicians before the public today, whatever be their specialty, but have come by the way of Chicago. Their talent may have been discovered elsewhere, but the finish and the courage to mount stages of the country and sometimes of the entire globe, come from Chicago. Such among the many are the Williams', Singers, Kemper Harreld, Morehouse and Madame Martha Broadus—Anderson. Mrs. Anderson is among those whose talent was discovered and in goodly measure developed elsewhere. Born in Richmond, Virginia, she gained her early literary education in the public schools of Washington, D. C. It was in the public schools of the District of Columbia that she first discovered her talent on the one hand, and learned the elementary technique on the other, under the tutelage of the late Professor John T. Layton. She soon became the leading singer in all public school singing.

At the age of fifteen she was chosen official chorus director of the Second Baptist Lyceum, a lyceum which at that time was regarded as one of the best literary societies in the country.

On finishing her studies in the public schools of

Washington, Mrs. Anderson took the civil service examination and was appointed to a position in the Government Printing service, where she worked for many years. In the meantime, however, she did not wholly neglect her talent. She studied and practiced regularly, and appeared in public whenever time and opportunity permitted.

In 1898 Mrs. Anderson was married to Mr. Henry S. Anderson and took up residence in Chicago. Here she made her home, launched out into musical studies and into the musical life of Chicago. To quote George L. Williams of the Williams Jubilee Singers—"Madam Anderson is in the first division of the men and women of the race who are doing things musical. For ten years she has been active in the musical life of Chicago, having built up and directed a great choir at Quinn Chapel, A. M. E. Church, which, during the time of her direction, was acknowledged to be the best organization of its kind in the great city of Chicago. She is now a director of an excellent choir at Bethesda Baptist Church and maintains a beautiful and well appointed studio at 3518-22 South State Street, Chicago, to which a large number of students go to study vocal and instrumental music."

She was graduated from the Chicago Musical College in 1908, with the degree of Bachelor of Music. This is one of the oldest colleges of music in the West, and Mrs. Anderson is one of the few colored people to have studied there and the only Negro to obtain a degree there. Her voice is described as lyric soprano, very flexible, capable of wonderful range. She numbers among teachers, in addition to those at the Chicago Musical College, Herbert Miller, Pedro T. Tinsley, both well known in the musical world. Herbert Miller says of her:

"She has had a protracted course of study with me, covering a period of years and understands the principles which underly and govern the art of singing. I also know her to be an accomplished musician, her studies of composition, history, sight-reading and piano giving her education a breadth unusual among vocalists."

Mrs. Anderson spends her time teaching private pupils, directing choruses and appearing in recitals. She appears before the public not only in lighter solo singing but in prolonged and heroic roles. For example, some of the best work on the stage, that by which audiences best remember her are the "Rose Maidens," "Esther the Beautiful Queen," and "The Messiah." In these she is a great favorite before the general public and before audiences of college students. She has sung, among many institutions, at Howard and at Fisk. At Fisk, where music is in the foundation stones of the University and throbs in everybody's pulse, she won words like this from the Nashville Globe:

"The entirely new feature on the program was the appearance of the soprano soloist, Mrs. Martha Broadus—Anderson, of Chicago, Illinois. To say that she won a place in the hearts of her audience is to state it mildly. Her stage manners were simply perfect, and her perfection lay in her simplicity. To be received as she was by such a gathering as greeted her was an enviable compliment. She was to sing four solos, but the audience compelled her to sing seven, and clamored for more, but the length of the program forbade her singing longer."

GEORGE WASHINGTON ELLIS.

George Washington Ellis, K. C., F. R. G. S., LL. D.

THOSE who marvel at the versatility of Mr. George W. Ellis, of Chicago, will be even more amazed to know of the wide range of his education. Mr. Ellis was born in Platte County, at Weston, Missouri, May 4th, 1876. His parents were also Missourians, his father being of Lexington, Missouri. His mother was Miss Amanda Drace of Clinton, County, Missouri. Mr. Ellis began his education in his native city, of Weston, where he attended public schools. From Weston he entered Atchison High School, Atchison, Kansas. Graduating from here, he spent the next two years in the Law Department of the University of Kansas. Then he began the practice of law to assist in paying his way for four years in the College of Arts in the University of Kansas. Next he spent two years in the Gunton's Institute of Economics and Sociology, in New York. From New York he enrolled in the Department of Philosophy, and Psychology, in Howard University, Washington. D. C. He has a diploma from Gunton's Institute (of Economics and Sociology), a diploma from Gray's School of Stenography and Typewriting, and the degree of LL. B., from the University of Kansas. In 1918 Wilberforce conferred upon him the degree of LL. D., in appreciation of his extensive work.

Set over against this long list of achievements in education are his many successes in life. Mr. Ellis began the practice of law in Lawrence, Kansas, in 1893. In 1899 he passed the Census Board of Examiners, and was appointed a clerk in the Interior Department at Washington. Transferred in 1902, he was appointed by President Roosevelt and confirmed by the Senate as Secretary of the Legation to the Republic of Liberia. The next eight years, Mr. Ellis spent in Africa. He made no end of excursions into the hinterland, studying the lives and manners of the African people. Retiring in 1910 Mr. Ellis began the practice of law in Chicago, under the firm name of Ellis and Ward. This name was changed in 1912 to Ellis and Westbrooks, as it now stands. In addition to a large general practice, Mr. Ellis was elected in 1917 as assistant Corporation Counsel, a position which he still holds.

Throughout his career, Mr. Ellis has been a strong and active Republican. He has been much in demand as a campaign speaker and advisor. He is very active in all political movements in Chicago, taking a conspicious part in their direction and giving voice to their outcome in various magazine and newspapers. Active and useful as he is in National and city politics, Mr. Ellis will no doubt be the longest remembered, as he is probably best known by his writings. A mere list of his writings will illustrate how very prolific he has been with his pen and what service he has been able to render all black peoples through the press. His three books are "Negro Culture in West Africa." "The Leopard's Claw," and "Negro Achievements in Social Progress." Among his contributions to various publications are "Education in Liberia," (National Bureau of Education;) "Justice in the West African Jungle," (New York Independent;) "Liberia in the Political Psycology of West Africa," (African Journal;) "The Mission of Dunbar," (The Champion;) "Negro Morality in West Africa," (The Light;) "Negro Morality in the African Black Belt," (The Light;) "The Outlook of the Negro in Literature," (The Champion;) "The Chicago Negro in Law and Politics," (The Champion;) "Dynamic Factors in the Liberian Situation;" "Islam as a Factor in West African Culture;"

To enter into the merits of these publications is far beyond the limits of space alloted here. Suffice it to say that most of the leading daily papers of the country along with many of the best magazines have given most wholesome praise to both his books and articles. Fully as substantial, if not more so, is the endorsement given him by many of the leading intellectual societies of the world. In recognition of his contributions in ethnological studies, Mr. Ellis upon the recommendation of Sir Harry Johnston, and Dr. J. Scott Keltie, has been elected Fellow of the Royal Geographical Society of Great Britian. Upon the merits of the same writings he has been made a member of the African Society, London, of the American Sociological Society, of the American Political Association, of the American Society of International Law. He has been decorated a Knight Commander of the Order of African Redemption, and has been chosen an honorary member of the Luther Burbank Society.

Mr. Ellis was married to Miss Clavender Sherman, in 1906. Mrs. Ellis died in 1916.

He is as has been indicated a strong Republican, a Methodist in his religious belief, and was last delegate to the General Conference, 1912-1916. He was given a place in Who's Who in America, in 1912, and in The Book of Chicagoans, in 1917. He has just been selected for a place in the National Encyclopedia, of American Biography, volume XVIII, now in the press.

July 1, 1918, at the Coliseum, in a convention of 15,000 people, Mr. Ellis was nominated for judge of the Municipal Court, of Chicago, for the Republican primaries, September 11, 1918.

RICHARD EDWARD MOORE.

EBRUARY 7, 1850, Richard Edward Moore was born in Brownsville, Pennsylvania. He moved with his parents to Chicago in 1858

In 1871 when he was thirty-one years old ,he joined Bethel A. M. E. Church, where he has labored for the past forty-six years, filling almost every position a layman can fill in a church.

He is Superintendent of the Sunday School which is now a splendid working force. Having all the advanced ideas of Sunday School work, taught. At the present time the membership is 740 pupils.

In 1868, at the age of eighteen, Mr. Moore organized a military company of boys, ranging from fourteen to twenty years. They were called the "Hannibal Zouaves," fashioned in dress after the famous French Zouaves, of France. The company adopted the lightning quick Zouave tactcis and soon became the pride of Chicago, and whenever they appeared in public parades, they were given rousing applause by the citizens, white and colored, who saw them.

And a few years later this company entered the State Militia of Illinois and was enrolled in company "A," 16th Battalion, Illinois State Guards under Governor Tanner. Mr. Moore received the first Captain's commission ever issued to a colored man in the State of Illinois. It was the military spirit of Captain Moore and good service rendered by the "Hannibal Guards," in the railroad riots and the 16th Battalion in the services of the State, that paved the way for the admission into the State of the now famous 8th. regiment, Illinois Infantry, now doing service in the regular army of the United States. This company is now in France, known as the 370 Regt., U. S. Infantry, and which

is the only regiment of Colored men in military service in the world that is commanded by Negro officers from corporal to colonel.

When a boy sixteen years of age, Mr. Moore's mother had Richard to join, with his mother, the Good Samaritans. With the coming years he became a member of the Odd Fellows, Masons, Knights of Pythias, True Reformers, and several Social and Business organizations. Finding it impossible to render his full duty to all of these fraternal organizations, he confined his efforts to the Masonic Order. From October 1878, to October, 1913, he served as R. W. Grand Secretary of the Most Worshipful Grand Lodge of the State of Illinois, for 35 years. During the same time for 5 years he filled with credit to himself and the Masonic Order, the offices of Secretary of the Grand Chapter of the Royal Arch Masons, Grand Recorder of the Grand Commandery Knights Templar, and later on, the Supreme Council Scottish Rite Masons 33, of the Northwestern jurisdiction; and Imperial Recorder of the Imperial Council of Nobles of the Mystic Shrine of the United States.

In 1890 he organized the Grand Chapter of the Eastern Star, and served as Grand Patron for four years. In 1892, he began a three year's term in the office of Grand Joshua Heroines of Jericho. In 1913, he organized the Arabic Court, Daughters of Isis, auxiliary to the Nobles of the Mystic Shrine. In 1916 he organized the Chicago Assembly Loyal Ladies of the Golden Circle, auxiliary to the Supreme Council Scottish Rite Masons. At the present time he is serving in the office of Lieutenant Commander of the Supreme Council Scottish Rite, of the Northern jurisdiction and Chief Rabban of the Imperial Council A. E. A. O. Nobles of the Mystic Shrine of the United States and Canada.

On April 1, 1871, Mr. Moore was employed as porter in the office of the American Express Company. He gradually worked his way up to private messenger to Mr. Charles Fargo, Vice-President and General Manager of the Company. He remained in this position until the death of Mr. Fargo, in 1902. He was then transferred as filing clerk to the new Foreign Department of the company, and had charge of more than fifty thousand files which covered the transactions of that very important branch of the company's business from the date of its introduction, 1909 to April 30, 1913.

The world's war caused a general reduction in the employee's rank of all express companies and the company generously placed Mr. Moore on the Pension Roll, after having served for forty-six years and six months without ever losing a day's pay or causing a demerit to be placed against his record.

At the present time Mr. Moore is actively engaged in Y. M. C. A., Church, Sunday School, and Social uplift work .

On December 5, 1874, Mr. Moore was united in marriage to Miss Rosa E. Hawkins, who was a charming young Chicago belle, of that period. They lived happily together until the time of her death, April 15, 1912. Mr. Moore is now pleasantly located with his daughters, Mrs. Alberta Moore-Smith, and Mrs. Etta M. Shecraft, and their husbands, and his son, Richard Moore, Jr., all forming one happy household group.

High Degree Masonry in Illinois

HE three high branches of the Masonic Order of the State of Illinois, are the M. E. Grand Chapter of Royal Arch Masons, the Occidental Consistory, A. A. Scottish Rite Masons, Valley of Chicago, and Arabic Temple No. 44, Nobles of the Mystic Shrine, of Chicago.

The Grand Chapter of the Royal Arch Masons was organized in the city of Chicago, October 9, 1879, with four chapters, Saint Mark's, Chicago; Saint John's, Springfield; Eureka, Chicago, and Mount Moriah, Cairo. These chapters were charted by the most excellent Grand Chapter Royal Arch Masons, of the State of Pennsylvania, which was organized about twenty-two years, prior to the organization of the Grand Chapter of Illinois, by Royal Masons, who were regularly made Masons in lodges established by Prince Hall, Grand Lodge F. and A. M., and successors, in the State of Pennsylvania and Massachusetts, the members of which afterwards received the Royal Arch degrees in regular constituted chapters in Philadelphia, Pennsylvania, and Boston, Massachusetts, said chapters organized the Grand Chapter of Pennsylvania. The four chapters, composing the Grand Chapter of Illinois, at the time of organization, numbered only one hundred and sixty companions Royal Arch Masons. At this time there were thirty subordinate lodges of Master Masons with a membership of eight hundred and thirty. The higher one goes into the higher degrees of the Masonic fraternity, the number of eligibles to draw from in order to increase the membership decreases; this accounts for the small membership composing the four Chapters which formed the Grand Chapter.

Joseph Washington Moore, was elected the first M. E. Grand High Priest. He was a Mason of exceptional executive ability and integrity. Companion, William D. Berry, was elected the first M. E. Grand Secretary. At the present time, there are fifty-four subordinate Chapters in the State, with the membership of 2370. The present M. E. Grand High Priest Companion, Albert R. Lee, of Champaign, a man of extraordinary ability, is the youngest Companion who has occupied the exalted position of Grand High Priest.

Occidental Consistory, No. 28, Valley of Chicago, was organized in the year 1889, by the consolidation of Prince Hall Consistory, holding a chapter issued by the Supreme Council of Illustrious Inspectors Generals of the thirty-third and last degree of the Southern jurisdiction; whose Grand East is at the city of Washington, D. C.. Illustrious Thornton A. Jackson, is Sov-Grand Commender, and Excelsior Consistory, holding a charter issued by the Supreme Council of Illustrious Inspectors General of the thirty-third and last degree of the United States, whose Grand East is at the City of New York, N. Y., Illustrious Brother, Peter W. Ray, Sov-Grand Commander. The illustrious brethren of the thirty-third degree of the two Consistories were consolidated under the name of Occidental Consistory, which was granted a patent issued by the Supreme Council of Inspectors Generals of the Northern jurisdiction in the year of 1913. Their Grand East is at the city of Philadelphia, Pennsylvania. Illustrious Brother J. Francis Rickards is Sov-Grand Commander. The two Consistories held concurrent jurisdiction in the Valley of Chicago, for a period of eighteen years, before a consolidation was effected, owing to the long dispute, as to the legality of the five existing Supreme Councils, which was finally settled by recognizing one for the Southern jurisdiction and one for the Northern jurisdiction, which by the two Supreme Councils was consummated during the administration of Illustrious Brother James E. Bish, Commander-in-Chief of Occidental Consistory.

Occidental is the largest consistory among Colored men in the United States, having a membership of three hundred and five Sublime Princes. The present commander of Occidental Consitory, Illustrious Brother, Charles T. Scott, is considered to be one of the best ritualists and thorough Masonic workers in the Northern Jurisdiction, and to him, is due the credit of having brought the Consistory up to its present high standard among Scottish Rite Masons in America.

Arabic Temple, No. 44, of the Oasis of Chicago, Nobles of the Mystic Shrine, was organized in the month of June, 1893, by Noble Milton F. Fields, a duly accredited representative of the Imperial Council Nobles of the Mystic Shriners of the United States of North America. There existed at the time of organization, another Imperial Council, called "The Ancient Arabic Order Nobles of the Mystic Shrine of the United States and Canada." The right to the supreme control of work of the Order was a serious contention between the two Imperial Councils for twenty years, but was finally settled by all the Temples of the two factions in 1913, by agreeing to amalgamate. In order to prevent future trouble and to obtain incorporation papers, the title of the order was changed to be known in the future as the "Ancient Egyptian Arabic Order of Nobles of the Mystic Shrine."

When Arabic Temple was organized in 1913, Noble Henry Graham was elected the first illustrious potentate and Noble R. E. Moore, the first illustrious Recorder, with an enrollment membership of twenty-six Nobles. By careful management, by these two officers, with the undivided support of the charter members, the Temple was built upon a strong foundation and succeeded in increasing the membership until 1913, when the Temple took out a charter under the amalgamated Imperial Council, Noble Robert I. Hodge being the Illustrious Protentate, and Noble Richard E. Moore, Illustrious Recorder. The present Illustrious Potentate Noble Marcellus F. Coley has no equal in the country as a live, wide-awake, soul-stirring, potenate, always presenting something new for the edification of the members. The Temple now has a membership of 345, which makes it the largest temple of Colored Shriners in the United States.

WILLIAMS FAMOUS SINGERS.

Williams Famous Singers

CHICAGO is their post office address: the world is their home. From Canada to Mexico, from Maine to California, from London to Berlin, they journey with all the ease of the cosmopolite. The impassable snow banks of Montana, the washouts in Florida, the heatless theatres in Alabama, none of these can suppress the rich melody, the good cheer, the masterly rendition of these singers gathered and blended from many parts of America.

For fifteen years this troup of William Colored Singers has had an unparalleled vogue before the international public. It had its origin back in 1904, being organized by Mr. Charles P. Williams, from whom the company takes its name. The personnel of the troup has been practically the same from the beginning; no wonder they can blend their voices with equal fascination in "Who Built de Ark?" and in the sextet by Lucia

These are no picked-up 'harmonizers," but educated, refined people, to begin with; and intense students of music besides. Mr. Charles P. Williams, the organizer, was formerly a student in Rust University, Holly Springs, Mississippi. His father, D. A. Williams, Presiding Elder of the Methodist Episcopal Church, of Mississippi, was one of the leading men of his race, but died when Charles was eighteen years of age. When his father died Charles was left with the care of a mother and five sisters. Prior to this time he had been a student of Rust University, and had known no responsibility greater than that of study and college athletics. However, he went to Chicago, and working in various capacities managed to take care of the family and home. He was not contented with the nature of his occupation, and finally secured a position with a traveling Male Quartette, which in time was abandoned by its leader and which was ultimately taken over by Mr. Williams. With the remaining members of that quartette, he, with the assistance of Dr. Frank L. Loveland, of the M. E. Church, of Iowa, organized the Dixie Singers. In the Spring of 1904, Mr. and Mrs. Williams, and J. H. Johnson resigned from the last named company to organize what is at present the famous "Williams' Singers."

Mr. J. H. Johnson, who is Mr. Williams business partner and Musical Director of the company, was born in Coal Creek, Tennessee. He and his brother, G. L. Johnson, the first tenor singer of the company, are sons of a Methodist minister, but they were in early life sent to Knoxville College, a United Presbyterian School, Knoxville, Tennessee, where they each received their literary and musical education. Each of them afterwards traveled with the Knoxville College Glee Club, until J. H. Johnson located in Chicago, and G. L. Johnson accepted a call to one of the mission schools of the United Presbyterian Church. Mr. Williams was attracted to J. H. Johnson when he was directing a choir in one of the large Chicago churches and induced him to fill a vacancy with the Dixies, and to ultimately join Mr. Williams in organizing the present "Williams' Singers," G. L. Johnson was then called to this new company. Mr. J. S. Crabbe, the basso, was formerly manager for the Mutual Lyceum Bureau. Mrs. Chas. P. Williams was formerly Miss Clara Kindle of Oberlin College and of the Maggie Porter-Cole Fisk Singers. The prima donna, Mrs. Virginia Greene, studied under Professors Perkins and Tinsley of Chicago. Mrs. Hattie Franklin Johnson was trained at Fisk University, at Walden and in Chicago under Professor Tinsley. Mrs. Marie Peeke Johnson was born in Madison, Wis., and reared in the city of Chicago. She was sent at early age to Fisk University at Nashville, Tennessee, where she had eight years in literary branches combined with piano and vocal music under Miss Grass and Miss Robinson, respectively. Later Mrs. Johnson studied under Mr. Kurt Donath and Mr. A. Ray Carpenter, Chicago, and in the meantime filled professional engagements with Fisk Jubilee Singers.

Miss Inez L. McAllister was born at Pueblo, Colo., and is a graduate from the High School of that city, is a contralto singer and is Mr. Williams' private secretary. She substitutes for Mrs. Williams as contralto singer of the company.

To years of constant devotion to their life's work in the United States and Canada, they have added a year of travel and study in England, Scotland, Wales, Holland, Belgium, Germany and France. They were eighteen weeks in London, where they gave 130 performances, singing in many of its best known theatres, among which was the World-famous Coliseum. While in London the entire company was under the instruction of one of the world's greatest vocal teachers—Miss Ira Aldridge, who is a scholar of the London Royal Conservatory of Music, and whose early teacher was the famous Jennie Lind. This experience added to natural talent and former years of faithful application enhances the ability of each individual singer, and has produced in their case a remarkable musical combination.

The World war has brought changes among these singers, as it has among all kinds of groups the world over. But their popularity is unchanged; their enthusiasm is unabated their talent seems to grow richer and richer as the days pass by.

A. WILBERFORCE WILLIAMS, M. D.

 ANUARY, 1864, Dr. A. Wilberforce was born to Baptice and Flora Williams. For thirteen years young Williams lived on the plantation, toiling happily without the knowledge of his A. B. C's. Then, in 1876, he came to Springfield, Missouri, and for the first time had a chance to attend school. In 1881, he obtained a license to teach common school in Mount Vernon County, Mo.

He alternated teaching and studying until he was graduated from the Normal Department at Lincoln Institute, Jefferson City, Mo. He then taught in the summer school, Kansas City, Mo., and at the same time continued to study. He pursued private studies, took a course at the Y. M. C. A., attended evening school and the Summer Normal.

Young Williams had some difficulty in choosing his life work. He was a most excellent teacher, but he felt that he would not like to make it his life work. He was advised to become a minister. The young man decided that he was not fitted for such a calling. Then for a time he felt that his future happiness depended upon his becoming a lawyer and a member of the bar. There had been a cyclone and young Williams had watched the skill of Dr. Taft, an ex-army surgeon care for the wounded. He admired that skill as a boy, and he could not forget it as a young man. And so in the choice of his profession, Dr. Williams, one of our foremost surgeons, went back to his childhood for the inspiration that made him choose the profession for which he was best fitted. And having definitely decided on his profession, Dr. A. Wilberforce Williams set his heart on becoming one of the best, with the ability to saw bones and bind up wounds as he had seen Dr. Taft do.

Thus it was that in 1890, he left Kansas City, Mo., and went to New York to attend Bellevue College—but, they refused him admittance and he returned to his school room for another year. When next he started out to get admittance in a medical school, he applied for the place before leaving his home. And so, we find him a student of medicine in Northwestern University, Chicago, Ill., where he received the same credit as that of any other student. He was graduated in 1894, and then served for two years as resident physician in Provident Hospital in Chicago.

Dr. A. Wilberforce Williams is Professor of Internal Medicine; head of the Medical Department of the Post Graduate School of Provident Hospital; Secretary of the Medical Staff and Attending Physician of Provident Hospital and lecturer on Hygiene, Sanitation and Medicine in its Training School for Nurses. Attending Physician for six years at the South Side Municipal Tuberculosis Dispensary, Supervisor of the Municipal Tuberculosis Sanitation Survey; he is an authority on all forms of tuberculous diseases, a well recognized Heart and Lung Specialist and Health Editor of the Chicago Defender. He is an active member of the A. M. A., Illinois State and Chicago Medical Societies, Mississippi Valley Tuberculosis Conference, Robert Koch Society for the Prevention and Study of Tuberculosis, the National Society for the Study and Prevention of Tuberculosis and a member of the Executive Board of the National Medical Association and also a member of a committee of that Association, to wait on Secretary Baker for the purpose of having colored professional men (physicians and dentists) commissioned in the U. S. Army or to give them deferred classification and not be forced to enlist as privates on account of racial relations. He is President of the Physicians, Dentists and Pharmacists Association of Chicago.

The U .S. Government selected him to act as a member of the Advisory Board in the supervision of the work of Local Exemption Boards in the examinations of registrants. He was Chairman of the Second Ward Committee of the Fourth Liberty Loan, Chairman of the Committee of Physicians of the Red Cross Home Service Medical Section in the medical care of dependents of relatives now fighting at the front; and aside from these purely medical organizations, he is a member of the Knights of Pythias, Odd Fellows, Y. M. C. A., Court General Robt. Elliott, A .O. F., Urban League and Social Service Club.

In connection with his profession he has traveled extensively over the United States, Mexico and Canada.

He was married June 1902, to Miss Marry Elizabeth Tibbs, of Danville, Ky., who enjoys with him the comforts of their attractive modern home.

Forty years ago he stood before his cabin door an unlettered boy of thirteen. Now he has found his place in life and fills it with credit and honor.

WILLIAM H. ANDERSON, D. D.

ORN in Vigo County, Indiana, May 8th, 1843, the Reverend William H. Anderson has seen innumerable changes in the history of the country, has been party to many of them, and has enjoyed with delight approaching ecstasy the strides forward by his own people.

From his youth until the outbreak of the Civil War, his life was much like that of the ordinary boy of the northwest. The school being four miles from his home, he got his first teaching from an older sister. As soon as he was large enough to walk the distance to school in Vigo County, he began to attend the public schools. As a pupil he became very brilliant, usually standing at the head of his class.

He was just coming into young manhood when the Civil War broke forth. His first appearance as a speaker before the public was due to conditions surrounding the enlistment of Negroes. As is common knowledge now Massachusetts was forming two Negro regiments, the Fifty Fourth and the Fifty Fifth. The recruiting officers were seeking to draft the Negroes of Indiana into the Massachusetts regiments. This Mr. Anderson opposed, taking the position that the Indiana Negroes should be enlisted for Indiana and not for another state.

That he was sincere in his protest and not seeking to evade, was made clear by later action. When the time came for the Indiana Negro to take up arms and bear his share of the burden of war, all four of the Anderson sons, he and three others, shouldered arms and went to the front in the United States Army and served until the close of the war.

The war over, he began immediately on his life as a public servant, and later as a minister. In 1865 he was sent by his regiment as a delegate to the Negro Convention, which met in Nashville in August, 1865. In 1870 he began his pastorate. His first pastorial work was in Rockville, Indiana, which church he served one year. From Rockville he went to Terre Haute, Indiana, where he was pastor of the Baptist church there for ten years. From Terre Haute he went to the McFarland Chapel, in Evansville, Indiana, where for thirty-five years he has served this church with untiring zeal and fidelity. This long pastorate places Dr. Anderson at the head of the Indiana Colored pastors in point of continuous service to one church, and but very few if any can claim a like distinction in the United States. Another mark of distinction in his long life of service as a pastor, (forty seven years) is that he has only served three churches—the one at Rockville, one at Terre Haute and the McFarland Chapel at Evansville. The fact of a preacher serving a church as pastor for thirty five years is itself evidence of wise leadership but to cover this period with only two unpleasant meetings of the church, is a remarkable showing. Such has been the record of Dr. Anderson.

Dr. Anderson has not been an extensive traveler, but his mind has visited almost the entire globe. He spends much of his time in his library where he has access to books of travel and history. He can converse intelligently with those who have visited this and other countries.

He has held many posts of honor in the Indiana Baptist Association and in secret orders. He has been a Mason for forty years, and is at present Grand Chaplain of the Masons of Indiana, a position which he has held continuously for twenty-seven years. He is said to be the first preacher of his denomination in Indiana to receive the degree of Doctor of Divinity, this was conferred upon him by the State University of Kentucky, in 1889. The Kentucky Colored people chose him to fight the Jim Crow Coach Law in the Blue Grass State. This law was declared unconstitutional by Judge Barr of Louisville.

He owns his home in Evansville and has interest in other property. He is the author of a booklet, "Negro Criminality", which is pronounced one of the best publications on that subject. Indiana knows him as the young preacher's friend.

Reverend Anderson has been twice married: He was married to Miss Sarah Jane Stewart of Terre Haute, May 31st, 1866. He was married to Mrs. Mattie D. Griggsby of Indianapolis, November 8th, 1917.

MOSES A. DAVIS.

IRECTOR of Manual Training and of Vocational Education, in the colored schools of Evansville, Indiana. Moses A. Davis was born in Savannah, Georgia, February 3rd, 1870. In his early years he attended the public schools and then Knox Institute of Athens, Georgia. His study in Athens brought to the surface an almost insatiable desire for learning of all kinds, but especially of the mechanical and technical branches.

These he sought as the old scholars pursued learning in the various centers of Europe. He entered Hampton Institute, was graduated there in 1891, then did post graduate work there. During summer sessions he went to the Stout Institute at Menomine, Wisconsin; then to the Massachusetts Institute of Technology at Boston; then to Chicago University; and Greer's Automobile College of Chicago. He has also in his spare time pursued technical courses in the International Correspondence School of Scranton, Pennsylvania.

Mr. Davis was among the last to receive a commission from General Armstrong. One of his first positions as a teacher was given him through General Armstrong, who sent Mr. Davis to Frankfort,

Kentucky, to take charge of the technical course and manual training work in the Kentucky State Normal School at Frankfort. Here, being among the first colored men to teach these subjects successfully, and knowing his work from a practical as well as from a theoretical angle, Mr. Davis became very popular both as a teacher and as a practical builder. Many of the buildings of Frankfort were both designed and constructed by him during his thirteen years as a teacher in the State Normal School. From Frankfort he went to the State College in Savannah, his native city, where he taught for one year.

From 1905 to 1918 he has held his present position as director of Manual and Vocational training in Evansville. All along the line Mr. Davis has been a pioneer in his work, as a manual training teacher, directing knowledge into useful channels and converting prejudice and information into enthusiasm and devotion.

Great indeed has been his joy in his work. During the twenty-seven years of his teaching he has seen his favorite subjects shake off the ashes of rejection and become a main feature in nearly every curriculum in the country. He has put up many buildings along with giving class instruction. He is at present erecting with the students of the Clark High School of Evansville an Industrial Art Building, which is to be the largest of its kind north of the Ohio River. Most agreeable to him however, of all his constructive endeavors, is the fact that while he was a post graduate at Hampton, he designed the school residence of Dr. Booker T. Washington.

As busy as he is professionally, Mr. Davis finds time to do many useful things as a citizen and as an organization worker. Though a Christian Scientist in his beliefs, he has affiliated himself with the A. M. E. Church as a Sunday School teacher and worker in this body. He is a Mason and a Knight Templar, and is a Past Deputy Grand Master of Masons of Kentucky. He organized the present Colored Y. M. C. A., of Evansville, and was for many years chairman of the committee of management.

Mr. Davis is very fond of one kind of travel, he likes to attend the National Exposition. He numbers on his list the Atlanta Exposition, 1895; the St. Louis Exposition, 1904; Jamestown Exposition, 1907; and the Panama Exposition, 1915.

Mr. Davis was married in 1895 in Atlanta, Ga., to Miss Beulah Thompson, Mrs. Davis is a graduate of Hampton Institute, of the class of 1889. She was trained in the famous Whittier School at Hampton, and was later a teacher at Tuskegee Institute. Mrs. Davis is, like her husband, devoted to practical arts. She is director of the Domestic Science work of Evansville.

Mr. and Mrs. Davis live in their own home, a very well equipped and modern residence in Evansville. They own property valued at about $10,000.

On March 13th, 1918, Mr. Davis gave up his work in Evansville with an indefinite leave of absence from the Board of Education, to go to New York City, from whence he sailed March 30th, for Y. M. C. A. War work with the men in France under General Pershing.

JOHN WALTER HODGE.

N the establishment of the National Negro Men's Business League, the founder, Booker T. Washington, had as one of the objects the lending of inspiration and incentive to men of color to venture for themselves, out in the realm of business. This it has done. It has been the cause of doing more and better business among those who were already out for themselves, and it has caused many who were timid to cut loose from the jobs that held them, and take the final plunge for themselves. Mr. John Walter Hodge belongs to this latter class. When this organization met in Boston, at its first meeting he was present. He was at that time a Pullman Porter. He had served in this work for six years, and like many another young man was content with the easy money to be made in this work. But when Mr. Hodge heard of the work in the business world, done by other men in his race, when he heard them tell of how they had built up their business from very meager beginnings, he became inspired with the idea of venturing out for himself.

Mr. Hodge was born in Chattanooga, Tennessee, September 29th, 1878. Here he spent his childhood and young manhood. He entered the Public Schools of his native city and remained to get all that was offered in that line. As a boy he worked at odd jobs, in and around places of business in Chattanooga. In 1899 he obtained a place in the Pullman service and remained in this until 1905. In 1905 he left the service of the Pullman Company and went to Indianapolis, Indiana, where he opened a Real Estate office. His office does General Sales business, rental and Commission business. Among the big deals that have been made by Mr. Hodge might be mentioned the sale of the present site for the Y. M. C. A. Building, and the site for the Knights of Pythias Building.

After adopting Indianapolis for his home town, Mr. Hodge decided to indentify himself with all the worthy institutions there. So we find him a very active member of the Y. M. C. A., of this city. This branch is one of the most prosperous and most beautiful among colored people. Mr. Hodge serves the organization in the capacity of Secretary of the Board of Managers. He is Past Chancellor of the Knights of Pythias and Secretary of the Local Negro Business League. He is a Mason and a member of the Baptist church. In fact, wherever we find colored men gathered together working for the betterment of the race there we will find J. Walter Hodge. He is interested in all movements for the advancement of the race, and is one of the most popular leaders out in Indianapolis.

In the interest of his business and for pleasure the subject of this sketch has traveled all over the United States. This has served to broaden him and to make him easy of approach to all men. August 15, 1910, Mr. Hodge was married to Miss Janie Parrish, of Boston, Massachusetts. Mrs. Hodge has as great an interest in the uplift of the race as has her husband. In fact they are one in their efforts to improve the people around them. Mrs. Hodge is an active worker in the Y. W. C. A., of Indianapolis and stood by the organization through all the struggles when it was getting its footing. All of the city love and respect this very unselfish couple. They live in their own home at 924 Fayette Street.

This is a record of a man who, when he heard the call of a bigger chance, even though he could not see his way to the end of it, did not hesitate to accept the challenge. And having accepted the chance offered him, he has used every opportunity to better others while he was helping himself. For this unselfishness, he has gotten a reward in the esteem in which he is held. All of Indianapolis look upon him as one of her most useful and most prosperous business men.

F. B. RANSOM, LL. D.

R. F. B. Ransom of Indianapolis,
Indiana, is a southerner by birth,
having been born in Grenada,
Mississippi, July 13, 1882. He
spent his early days in Grenada,
working on the farm and attending the public schools.

Completing his course in the public schools he
went to Walden University, Nashville, Tennessee,
where he finished his literary training, and where
he also gained the degree of L. L. D. His L. L. D.
he won in 1908. He studied Theology in the same
university. Later he read law in Columbia University in New York. In 1910 he began to practice
law in Indianapolis.

In Indianapolis he began not only his career as a
lawyer, but a career of usefulness. Walden had
taught him that no matter what his chosen career,
a man counted in a community or state only in so
far as he made himself a genuine asset to his community. This general teaching had been very largely supplemented by his study and application of
Theology.

Going into Indianapolis he immediately allied
himself with the Bethel A. M. E. Church and began

to take hold and give practical help in all deliberations and undertakings of the church. Here again
both his training in Theology and his education and
practice in law made him a most decided asset to
the Indianapolis Church.

He joined the Masons and Knights of Pyhthias
and, once more put his shoulder to the wheel to
make those organizations greater lights to their
members and to the world.

It was not long before both the church and the
city saw his worth. When therefore there was an
honor to bestow or a responsibility to be assumed
Mr. Ransom was forthwith thought of. Bethel
Church soon elected him to the Board of Trustees.
The Good Citizens' League made him president of
their organization. He had been in the city but a
few years when Mr. Julius Rosenwald, the Chicago
philanthropist, sent abroad his offer to give twenty
five thousand dollars towards building Negro
Young Men's Christian Associations. Indianapolis
had a great many young men. She had been struggling to keep their feet in good and circumspect
paths, especially during evening hours of leisure.
The colored citizens saw here the opportunity of a
life time, to build an attractive building, to equip
it with such appointments as the young men would
find in the pool rooms and in the parks without
the liability of vice. A committee was formed to
devise plans for raising funds to put up and equip
such a building. Who but F. B. Ransom, skilled
in law, in theology, in the affairs of life, should constitute the bone and sinew of such committee? The
Y. M. C. A. was built and equipped. It was one
of the first to embrace Mr. Rosenwald's offer and
one of the best Negro Y. M. C. A. buildings of the
country, of the world. Much of the credit of all
this is due to F. B. Ransom, to his skill, to his willingness to serve.

One by one other honors came to him. If the
church and Y. M. C. A. relied upon him, why not
the world? The Advisory Committee of the Colored Alpha Home for the aged colored people needed an attending attorney, who was concerned not
so much with fees, but with the general welfare of
the Home and of the people. Mr. Ransom was
called upon to fill this post. The Knights of Pythias chose him to serve for a number of years as
its Grand Lecturer. Thus today in church, in
civic work as well as in the courts of law, Mr.
Ransom is numbered among the best citizens of
Indianapolis. For the last seven years he has been
acting attorney for the Mme. C. J. Walker Manufacturing Company and for the last year he has
acted solely in that capacity, having had to give up
all other clients, and perhaps Mr. Ransom receives
the highest annual retainer of any colored attorney practicing law.

Mr. Ransom has traveled much both on business
and for pleasure, his trips having taken him over
the whole country. He was married on July 31,
1912, to Miss Nettie L. Cox, of Jackson, Mississippi.
Three little lads brighten the home of the Ransom
family; Frank, Frederick, and Willard, aged four,
three and two, respectively.

REVEREND DIXIE CICERO CARTER

NVIABLE indeed is the attainment of Reverend D. C. Carter of Frankfort, Kentucky. He is both a minister and a physician. Standing on the vantage point of these two professions, he commands the secrets of the body and of the spirit. His approach must be one of large sympathy; for looking into the Mechanism of men's bodies he can understand wherein the spirit has free play in some and is debarred or suppressed in others. In him science and religion unite and clasp hands instead of crossing swords as they often do in other instances.

Reverend Carter, who follows the ministerial career, was born in Giles County, Tennessee, Nov. 25, 1866. A poor lad, he garnered bits of learning wherever he could, laboring in the meantime for bread. Having accumulated sufficient knowledge he finally entered Walden University in Nashville, Tenn. He later studied medicine in the Louisville National College, in Louisville, Kentucky. Coming in a time when education for his people was unpopular and when the few who wished well had only wishes to offer, he had to labor at all kinds of tasks to pay his way. Now he toiled in the bristling August sun, picking cotton, now on the railroad, in the hotels, wherever he could turn an honest and honorable penny, here he was found.

He entered the ministry under the impulse of an inner suggestion or as it is often called, a divine call to service, but the inspiration to study medicine came from quite another source—it was the suggestion of the son of his employer. The young man had just graduated in medicine and was at home on a visit before beginning his practice. While at home he urged the young colored lad to study for the career of doctor of medicine. So deeply was he impressed with the suggestion that he decided to act upon his advice and in due time entered the Louisville National College to prepare for this line of work.

However, the call to preach took a much stronger hold upon him than the desire to enter the medical profession and to the service of the ministry he has in the main devoted his life. His knowledge of medicine gives added strength to his work and influence as a minister.

Reverend Carter is blessed with a good, vigorous mind which he is using to the best advantage and being a man of unusual energy it is not surprising that he was soon equipped mentally for his profession of a minister. His first charge as a minister was at Elkton Tennessee which he assumed in 1885 at the age of nineteen years. In accordance with the policy of the A. M. E. church, he was moved from place to place at stated intervals but always gave up a charge with the best of feeling between him and his people. He never left a community without leaving some imprint of his work for the betterment of both the church and community, which caused him to be held in grateful remembrance by his people and won the gratitude of his successor.

When he was pastor in Brandenburg, Ky. he built a church there. He bought a parsonage during his sojourn at Elizabethtown, Kentucky; another during his stay at Shelbyville and built still another church at Pleasureville, Kentucky. He was the pastor of the A. M. E. Church in Frankfort for five years, but is now pastor of the A. M. E. Church at Ashland, Kentucky.

Reverend Carter has four times been representative to the General Conference of his church; is a life Trustee of Wilberforce University and a Trustee of Wayman Institute of Kentucky.

He is a member of the National Medical Association and a member of the Mosaic Templars of America.

He was married in Jefferson, Indiana, in December, 1902, to Miss Jennie Williams, and they have one child, Geneva Ossin, six years of age.

JAMES NEWTON SHELTON.

HEN you go to Indianapolis, Indiana, on business, and wish to talk business with the colored men who not only know business, but do business, it will not be long before some one will introduce you to James Newton Shelton. Mr. Shelton is working in his native state. He was born in Charlestown, Indiana, June 12, 1872. He had from his earliest youth, good educational advantages. His mother and father moved to Indianapolis when he was one year of age. He attended the public schools of Indianapolis, Marion county, till he was ready for the High school and then he entered The Indiana High School. Here he made a record for himself not only in scholarship, but in deportment. While still in High school, Mr. Shelton decided to be a business man. No other business to his mind offered the opportunities to the colored man that are offered in the undertaking business. Colored people die at a rapid rate, if not at a greater rate than do the people of other races, and of course they require a burial. This, to the mind of Mr. Shelton, was work for a colored man.

So on leaving high school he entered Chicago University. Here, along with other subjects taken up he took up the embalming. In this sub-

ject he did all the work offered by the University and on leaving received a diploma in Embalming. Mr. Shelton had as much foresight in choosing the place to establish his business, as he had in choosing the kind of business. And so instead of returning to his native town to open his shop, he stayed in Indianapolis. Here colored people live in large numbers and here he felt sure that he could get a great deal of the colored undertaking business. Starting out on a small scale, Mr. Shelton has steadily developed his business, putting back into the business the profits received from it, till today his is one of the choice business houses operated by colored people in the city of Indianapolis. For his work he now uses Auto Hearses entirely. And because of the good equipment of his establishment and because of the courtesy with which all persons are received he gets a very large share of the work in this line.

Mr. Shelton, while he has in no way neglected his business, has, nevertheless taken time to serve his people and his city in other capacities. He has served as delegate to the last three Republican National Conventions. This shows the esteem in which he is held by his people in the matters of political issue, not only is he a good organizer, but an orator of ability also. He has for the past twelve years served as Deputy of the Department of Assessor of Center Township, Indianapolis. Mr. Shelton is the Past Grand Chancellor of the Knights of Pythias for the state of Indiana, and has served the order as supreme delegate for the past ten years. He is equally as active, though not in so prominent a post, in other orders. He is a Mason, Shriner, an Odd Fellow, a member of the United Brothers of Friendship, and a prominent member of the Negro Men's Business League. In all of these organizations, Mr. Shelton lends his weight for the betterment of the majority. Not only has this man loaned his business ability to the development of secular orders that look for the betterment of the race, but he gives freely of his means and of his advice to the church of which he is an active member. Although a member of the Baptist church, he helps all the Colored churches.

November 25, 1894, Mr. Shelton was married to Miss Mamie E. Pettiford, of Franklin, Indiana. Mrs. Shelton has been of great help in the business of her husband, helping not only with her advice, but with actual work, whenever the occasion demanded this. There is one daughter born to them, and who is the joy of their life. This is Miss Zeralda Marion Shelton. She attended Fisk University, Nashville, Tennessee, and for a time was a student of music in the Chicago School of Music. She is now Mrs. Scott, her husband being a soldier in Company A, '2 Brigade, now stationed in France.

LOGAN H. STEWART, LL. B.

HE son of Wesley and Victoria Stewart, Logan H. Stewart, newsboy, reporter, real estate dealer, was born in Union Town, Kentucky, July 22, 1879. Shortly after his birth he was taken to Indiana. When Mr. Stewart was three years old his father died, leaving the mother and three small children. When he was ten years old his mother took him with the other children to Evansville, where they lived for a time in want, but at least one son achieved victory over want, and success in life.

Mr. Stewart began his career in Evansville by selling papers. He sold the Evansville News, now the Evansville Journal-News. Here the young man of fourteen proved his worth. In a short time he had built up one of the best routes of the city. In return the Evansville News made him manager of a district. He was also given the post of reporter for the colored people, being responsible for all local news about Negroes.

However, the young man with all this success was not merely working for the newspaper. He was also going to school. In 1899 he was graduated from the Latin course in Evansville High School.

Having decided to enter business he took a commercial course in the High School in 1900.

Mr. Stewart thanks all newspapers for his business career. He gained his first experience in business by handling newspapers. Moreover, while he was attending school, he was able to save three hundred dollars. In the year of his graduation he invested a part of this sum in real estate. The venture proved so profitable that he immediately resolved to enter the business of buying and selling land and lots.

In this business, Mr. Stewart has been both a pioneer and a benefactor in Evansville. Before he entered the business of real estate, the 10,000 Negro population of Evansville was thought of merely as workers and church goers, not as dealers in finance. Their realty holdings were less than $10,000. They had no bank credit, and woefully little business recognition. Thus matters stood when Mr. Stewart opened his office in 1900. By January 1, 1917, the Negroes of Evansville had $500,000 invested in real estate, substantial bank credit, and a wider general credit and recognition throughout the city. Mr. Stewart himself, beginning in poverty back in 1889, now owns his home, which is valued at $7,000; one quarter block of stores and shops in a business section, valued at $15,000; a factory for the manufacture of concrete stone and building material, worth $3,500; and other real estate values amounting to $15,000.

Absorbed in business Mr. Stewart has, however, missed no opportunity to grow and to serve. While joining no special church he has worked with the Methodist in his town and with any denomination that set out to serve the people. He was one of the early members of the National Negro Business League, joining that body in 1905. He was charter member of the Negro Y. M. C. A. of Evansville and very instrumental in securing funds for the Negro Association when it was in its infancy. In 1915 he organized Health and Clean-Up Week in Evansville causing five thousand colored people to clean up and beautify their homes and surroundings, and two hundred and thirty-five gardens to be planted. He was president of the Evansville Negro Business League for more than ten years and a member of the Executive Committee of the National Negro Business League. He is on the Board of Management of the Negro Y. M. C. A. of Evansville. He is a member of the Evansville Chamber of Commerce, the only colored man to have this honor. He has traveled extensively in the East, in the West, and in the South. He has spent much time and energy in putting on their feet struggling Negro business men, who needed recognition at the banks and instruction in handling business matters. In honor of his good services to his fellow men and in appreciation of his continued education, Lincoln-Jefferson University of Hammond, Ind., conferred upon him the degree of Bachelor of Laws, in 1913.

Mr. Stewart was married on November 30, 1911, to Miss Sallie L. Wyatt of Evansville. Mrs. Stewart was formerly a teacher of Domestic Science in the Evansville High School.

GEORGE WILLIAM WARD, D. D.

R. George William Ward, pastor of the Mount Zion Baptist Church of Indianapolis, Indiana, was born in Port Gibson, Mississippi, July 2, 1869. His early days were spent on the farm, where he found his first inspiration to labor and wait; where he learned to dream in big terms and to execute patiently and persistently. This by the way, this quiet country life, in a warm and fertile country, was his first school.

He had two more early schools. He attended the district schools of Clayborne County, learning from books what knowledge he and his teacher could dig out. Neither of them at that time was over adept at this task, the times being considerably out of joint, by reason of Reconstruction and general restlessness, and by reason of the scarcity and very limited preparation of the Negro teachers. However, a third means of learning supplemented the efforts of the struggling young lad and his district teacher. He was fortunate enough to be thrown into a private white family, and was given five years schooling by a white teacher. Here he got environment, which did in actuality what he had been taught in books. Hence Dr. Ward learned to speak, to think, to act, by example as well as by precept.

These three were his preparatory schools, nature, the district school, the private white family, in the last named speaking and acting education were a habit and not a theory. These prepared him for college. He chose Roger Williams University, of Nashville, entered Corresponding department Theology, under Dr. Geurnsey, having already become a thorough going Baptist. Theology and a higher literary training completed his studies and he went forth ready to preach and to work among his people.

In his pastorates he has been unusually fortunate, as Baptist pastorates go. He has been pastoring now for a quarter of a century, and yet he has had but four charges in all this time. His first two charges were in Mississippi, at Duncan, Mississippi and at Gumunion, Mississippi; at the latter named he worked for five years, developing here the habit of staying at one post long enough to make his work count. In 1899 he was called to Chattanooga, Tennessee. In Chattanooga he built the Monumental Baptist Church, and so made for himself a name in this section of the country, and also got in the habit of church building.

From Chattanooga he was called to his present charge in Indianapolis, Indiana, 1907. Here he again applied his old practice of getting congregations into new and spacious church homes. In 1908 he built the Mount Zion Baptist Church on Twelfth and Fayette Streets, a handsome brick structure, modern in all of its appointments and conveniences.

From building churches and giving his services in other directions, honors have come to him. He is a Past Master Mason and a moderator of the Union Baptist Association of Indiana. State University at Louisville, Kentucky, has conferred upon him the honorary degree of Doctor of Divinity.

Dr. Ward has evidently made up his mind to settle down in the West, or at any rate he is remaining true to the old habit formed back there in Gumunion, Mississippi, of becoming part and parcel of the place and section he works in. Moreover, as a minister he feels that he must teach by example as well as by precept. Therefore he has invested his savings and his influence in homes and enterprises in and around Indianapolis. He owns his home on West Street in Indianapolis and one rent house, and he is stockholder in the Studebaker Auto Tire Corporation of South Bend and in the Irvington Sick and Accident Insurance Company of Indiana.

Dr. Ward was married at Cartersville, Georgia, in 1904. Mrs. Ward was formerly Miss Emma Robinson. What Dr. Ward is by example to the men of his congregation, Mrs. Ward has in great measure been to the women. She has been a great helper in church organization and in church building.

William Henry Ballard

REARED in Kentucky where he seems to have found the Elixir of youth as well as business success, Dr. William H. Ballard, though approaching close upon three scole years, carries upon him no mark of age, either in his actions or in his mind. To be sure, his profession may be responsible for this as he is a pharmacist. Or it may be the full life of achievement for himself and of helpfulness to others which he has led.

Among the picturesqe scenes of Franklin County, Kentucky, with its rugged cliffs overhanging the placid waters of the Kentucky River, was born to Down and Matilda Ballard, October 31, 1862, a son, whom they named William Henry. His parents being industrious and energetic people, and seeing that a liberal education was essential to success, moved to Louisville in 1870. Here their son was placed under a private tutor and remained under his instruction until the opening of the public schools in 1873, when he entered the public schools and continued his course of studies in them. His progress was rapid; he took advantage of every opportunity to improve himself. After seven years of faithful application to his studies he was graduated from the Louisville High School. His thirst for knowledge was far from being quenched when he completed his course in the high school. What he had attained only whetted his appetite for greater knowledge, and made him dissatisfied with the preparation he had received, which was far above that of many youths. Dr. Ballard entered Roger Williams University, where he pursued a special course in science and languages, completing it in 1884. While at Roger Williams University, Dr. Ballard began the work of teaching. He, like many others who were striving to be a credit to their race and ancestry, taught in the common school districts of Tennessee and Kentucky during the summer and pursued his studies at the University during the winter.

The next step in the upward progress of Dr. Ballard was his election to the principalship of the Mayfield, Graves County, Kentucky, where he served with satisfaction for some time. His success as a teacher is shown by the great number of ambitious young men and women now employed in the schools of Southwestern Kentucky, many of whom were under his immediate charge. This also shows that the fourteen years spent in the school room were characterized by conscientious and painstaking study.

In 1890 he entered Northwestern University at Chicago, Ill., for the purpose of studying pharmacy. He was graduated from this course in 1892 receiving honorable mention. Shortly after graduating from Northwestern University, Dr. Ballard was married to Miss Bessie H. Brady, one of the most estimable young women of Nashville, Tennessee, a teacher in Meig's High School, a woman respected and beloved by all who knew her.

He has an interesting family, consisting of a wife and four children—three sons and a daughter. Upon these he bestows his most devoted care and affection and seeks their highest good. The children have listened to the counsel of their father, and like him are making something of their lives. William Henry Ballard, Jr., is studying Pharmacy at Howard University, Washington, D. C.; Orville L. Ballard is studying medicine at the same Institution; Edward H. Ballard is a student in the Lexington High School, and Miss Vivian Elizabeth Ballard is studying in the Chandler Normal School.

Dr. Ballard began business in Lexington, Kentucky, February, 1893, opening the first Pharmacy owned and controlled by Negroes in the State. He has the confidence of all his acquaintances and has been highly honored by many fraternal orders to which he belongs. He is Past Chancellor of the Knights of Pythias; ex-State Grand Master of the United Brothers of Friendship; Commander in Chief of Blue Consistory Scottish Rite Masons; and has the distinction of being a polished, capable and conservative business man.

Dr. Ballard is a Methodist in church affiliation, and is a member of St. Paul African Methodist Episcopal Church. He is also a Trustee of the St. Paul A. M. E. Church. His interest in the welfare of the colored race enlists him in all enterprises looking to their development. The Colored Agricultural and Mechanical Fair Association was organized to encourage the colored citizen to take more active interest in agriculture and mechanical pursuits. Dr. Ballard not only connected himself with this enterprise but served as Assistant Secretary, thus giving it the benefit of his organizing ability.

While he has not visited foreign countries, Dr. Ballard has seen much of the United States.

Dr. Ballard exemplifies what a man of strong character and indomitable courage may do. He is worthy of emulation, not only for what he has achieved for himself, but for the service he has rendered in putting others on their feet. The clerks who worked in his store have been inspired to launch out for themselves. Four of the drug stores of the state are run by men who were one time clerks in the Ballard Pharmacy. One doctor, Doctor White of Owensboro, also served time as clerk in this same store. Indeed so high is the business in the esteem of both races that Dr. Ballard has been for years a member of the State Pharmaceutical Association. Thus Dr. Ballard has lived a long life of usefulness, helping to better all whom he touched.

The man who makes the most of his opportunities both for fitting himself for a useful life and in serving others gets the most out of life, and learns from experience that a life of service is a life of joy.

"What we are is God's gift to us.
What we make ourselves is our gift to God."

THOMAS L. BROOKS.

R. T. L. Brooks, the subject of this sketch, was born in Charlottesville, Albemarle County, Virginia, in 1862, being the fourth child of Thomas and Mildred Brooks. His father was a carpenter by trade and was employed at the University of Virginia to help in keeping up the repairs around the College and it was here that young Brooks learned the trade of his father.

Commencing at the early age of ten he continued to work with his father until 1883 when he came to Frankfort, Ky., secured employment with Rodman and Sneed, Contractors, and later with Wakefield & Choate. He remained with the latter firm eight years serving the last half as Foreman.

On October 18, 1892, he was married to Miss Mary L. Hocker of Frankfort, Ky., one of the Public School teachers of Franklin County. From this union one child was born, which died in infancy. Both being very fond of children the home has never been without a child, having adopted one daughter who remained with them until her marriage and at present they are rearing two of his Sister's children.

In the same year Mr. Brooks decided to go into the contracting business for himself. Although he has contracted and built throughout Eastern Kentucky, it has been in Frankfort that he has made his chief mark. Some of the most beautiful and costly edifices erected all over the Capitol City and wth values ranging in the thousands are the product of his brain and skill. It can be truthfully stated that fully ninety percent of his work has been for white people and against the sharp opposition of white competitors. Over one-half of the residences of the celebrated "Watson Court"—the most exclusive and handsome section (white) of Frankfort was built by him. The Columbia Theatre, a $15,000 structure and the leading and most attractive moving picture theatre of the city is also his work.

The Auditorium and the Trades Buildings of the Kentucky Normal & Industrial Institute which were erected at a cost of thirty thousand dollars were also contracted for and built by him and it is an object of pride that both these handsome stone buildings were built exclusively by Negro labor. The ten thousand-dollar Colored Odd Fellows building and the twenty-five thousand-dollar Colored Baptist Church were also erected under his immediate supervision.

Mr. Brooks has a high standing among the banks and business men of Frankfort and has accumulated much valuable property, and his word is accepted as readily as most men's bond. He is held in the very highest esteem by both races, and is one of the most popular men in the Capitol City. He also takes high rank as a Churchman, being one of the most widely known Baptist laymen in Kentucky. He has been a Sunday School Superintendent for twenty years, a Trustee for sixteen years, Deacon for six years and was Church Clerk for over four years.

He is also a prominent Secret Society man, having been Secretary of the Capitol City Lodge of Odd Fellows for twenty-seven years, frequently a delegate to the B. M. C. and has served his state as Secretary-Treasurer of the Insurance Bureau and State Grand Master, at present being State Grand Treasurer. He was the pioneer of the Negro Fraternal Insurance in Kentucky Grand Lodge of Odd Fellows over twenty-six years ago. He also holds high official positions in the Masons, Knights of Pythias and the United Brothers of Frendship. At this time he holds position as Secretary of Meridian Sun Lodge which he has held for sixteen years. He is Past Grand Chancellor and Treasurer of the Knights of Pythias which office he has held for twelve years and has held the office of Secretary of Charity Lodge, United Brothers of Friendship for five years and is also a member of the Union Benevolent Society and of the Mosaic Templars of America.

Mr. Brooks is of an affable temperament, upright life and a high Christian character with an intense interest in the welfare and advancement of his people.

JOHN BENJAMIN COOPER.

JOHN Benjamin Cooper, Funeral Director, Embalmer, a business man of many interests, and a member of all the secret orders of his state, was born in Mobile, Alabama, in April, 1872. He is the son of Benjamin and Elizabeth Aga Cooper. In early childhood he was possessed of an ambition to make something of his life and following his career from childhood to man's estate it will be seen that he kept his eye upon his goal and followed his course unwaveringly. He received his early education in the public schools of Mobile and in the Emerson Institute, and A. M. E. School, also of Mobile.

With this foundation, Mr. Cooper left Mobile and continued his education in Cincinnati, Ohio, where he entered the City High School. Finishing his course here he felt himself sufficiently equipped for a business career, but like numerous other young men he found it necessary to earn some money before branching out for himself.

With this aim in view he entered the service of the Pullman Company and was soon rated among their best employees. While in the employ of the Pullman Company he came to a decision as to the character of business he would embark in and entered the Barnes School of Embalming in Chicago to study the Undertaking business. Completing his studies here he went to Louisville in 1907 and took charge of the Watson and Est which he now owns and controls, conducting a very successful business.

However, the business of funeral director appears to be but a convenient peg upon which Mr. Cooper hangs an excuse for being in business. From this, to change the figure, he radiates into every sort of Negro enterprise national or local, that one finds on the calendar. One wonders where he finds time and thought for it all. He is a member of the National Negro Business League, a member of the Kentucky Funeral Directors' Association, and of the Falls-Cities Undertaking Association. In each of these he is a live member, keeping track of the workings of the organizations and keeping abreast of and bringing before these bodies all the latest inventions and devices in handling and embalming the dead.

In business he is director of the Falls City Realty Company of Louisville, a director of the Louisville Cemetery Association and Treasurer of the Colored Funeral Directors' Association of Louisville.

These obligations together with the demands of a large business would seem to be more than the average mortal could bear, but Mr. Cooper is equal to the task and does his work well. But Mr. Cooper is especially more than the average mortal. He has united himself with fully a score or more other organizations, all of which require time, thought, and in many instances, a good deal of study and travel. He is a member of the Methodist Church and is a Republican in politics. He is a Mason, having reached the thirty-second degree. He is a member of the Odd Fellows, of the Pythians, of the United Brothers of Friendship, of the Sons and Daughters of Moses, of Cooper's Union, of the Son's and Daughters of Morning, of the Brilliant Comet Tabernacle, Sisters and Brothers of Friendship, Maces Lodge, Union Star Lodge, Lampton Street Aid Society, Grand Star Court, and active member of Y. M. C. A. In none of these is he merely a member but is active in all the matters of business transactions and in all that pertains to disposing of and handling the dead members of these orders.

Mr. Cooper was married to Mrs. Lavinia Brady Watson of Louisville, August 19th, 1907. Mr. and Mrs. Cooper live in their own home on West Chestnut Street, and are both looked upon as leaders in social uplift work, as well as in business and in secret orders

THOMAS MADISON DORAM, M. D. V.

HE Negro has yet in any considerable numbers to make his way into the field of Veterinary practice. For this there appears to be several causes. In many cases the calling appears not to have been attractive. Again to practice it, has been rather expensive; and finally many of the Veterinary schools have been hard for the black man to enter and still harder for him to leave—with a diploma.

Thus it is that Dr. T. M. Doram, M. D. V., of Danville, Kentucky, will have an added attraction for the average reader beyond that of mere personal achievement. Dr. Doram is on record as the first and only Negro in the state of Kentucky to receive a diploma from a Veterinary College and one of the first two colored men in the United States to win such a diploma at all.

Dr. Doram was born in Danville, Ky., in 1871. He comes of a hardy stock of farmers and tradesmen, who loved to handle animals and wield tools. Dr. Doram's father, though a Carpenter by trade, owned valuable land and kept good horses. It was here that the young man discovered and cultivated further his love for the horse. It is a Kentucky instinct to love a good horse and from this state has come some of the best blooded stock of the world. Young Doram was born and bread in the Kentucky atmosphere and it only needed that he should be brought into a personal contact with the horse to develop a strong attachment for this noble animal.

While attending public school at Danville, and during vacation, the young man worked with his father at the trade of carpentry. Finishing the public school, Dr. Doram entered the Eckstein Norton University at Cane Springs, Ky., the institution referred to in the story of Dr. C. H. Parrish in this volume. It was here, that the young man had his skill acquired at carpentry under his father stand him in good stead. During his course here, one of the University buildings burned. Young Doram now turned to and lent great aid in rebuilding the University.

In 1896 he matriculated in the McKillip Veterinary College at Chicago, Ill. As a matter of course the rest of the students were white, but to show what one can do with an opportunity, at the close of the first year, Doram led his class in Materia Medica; the second year he was at the head of his class in Pharmacy, and during his last or senior year he was appointed senior assistant instructor in Pharmacology of his class, an honor of which he may be justly proud.

After graduating, in 1899, he opened an office in Evanston, Illinois, a beautiful suburb of Chicago, with a population of thirty thousand, where he commenced the practice of his profession.

While his practice here was successful and growing, numbering among his patrons many of the wealthy people of that aristocratic community, he gave it up after three years residence there and moved to his old home in Danville, Kentucky. His practice has continuously grown and Dr. Doram is now fully satisfied that he made no mistake when he entered the Veterinary profession.

In October of same year, at Danville, Kentucky, he was married to Miss Bertha James Hancock, a native of Austin, Texas. She received her education at Mary Allen Seminary, Crockett, Tex. They are now the parents of eight children, three girls and five boys. Dr. Doram very much hopes that at least one or more of his boys may be inspired to take up the profession of Veterinary Medicine and Surgery, as well as many other young men of his race; for he is confident that many could succeed in many parts of the country. Notwithstanding that we are in the day of the Automobile, and that so many of them are in use, Dr. Doram is thoroughly convinced that the horse is not a back issue and that this noble animal will always be in demand, which will call for expert men of his profession.

S. H. GEORGE. M. D.

HE story of the small boy left
alone, either by desertion of his
relatives, by robbery or by the
death of his parents used to be a
favorite subject of the writers of
fiction. The subject was one that
always elicited eager perusal and often sobs. Then,
however, the matter was very remote. No one
thought of such a thing as happening in real life.
The rise of modern biography and autobiography,
the willingness of our great men to talk about
themselves in magazine articles and to be interviewed by the reporters, have turned the light on
quite a different aspect of the growth of our youths
into manhood. No longer is this matter of privation, of sleeping out in the open, of tattered clothes
and blistered feet a fiction. It is all a very every
day reality. Booker T. Washington, Jacob Riis,
Henry W. Grady, with the numberless capitalists
who have risen from hunger to opulence, have
made early hardships a sort of premium in the life
of the American. So much is this so that it is
counted a sort of blessing to start off handicapped
with hunger, lack of antecedents and with nobody
to appeal to but your own strong arms.

Such was the early beginning of Dr. S. H. George

of Paducah, Kentucky. Dr. George lays no particular claim to distinction, is rather stingy with the
data of his boyhood and early life, indeed is rather
inclined to withdraw within his shell when he is
pressed for the story of his career. Yet the distinction of his career lies in a most desirable direction.
It is this: It is all normal. It is just what the
average boy with pluck and hard work could do.
The story of Douglass or Washington might be dis-
heartening to some; because those men seemed
to accomplish so very much out of so little. That
of Dr. George comes quite within the reach of us
all.

Dr. George was born in Kentucky. His mother
having died when he was three years old, the lad
soon found it necessary to go forth and earn a penny wherever he could. He attended the public
schools of his native state, whenever he could afford to do so. The farm, the restaurant, the railroad all held out chances for him to earn his way.
Many of these opportunities he embraced, now
dropping out of school, now returning, when he
had earned enough to sustain him for a whole or
part of a term. When he had been sufficiently
trained to do school work, he became a teacher, and
for seven years labored in the school room. With
school teaching and other work he finally became
able to push his education to the desired end. He
entered Walden University in Nashville, Tennessee,
and after a good long struggle was graduated.
Daunting nothing because of the cost of the college course he next registered in the Meharry Medical College. Again he had to fight a lone battle,
having few to whom he could look in the time of
need. Expenses here were higher, the hours of
work were much longer, because of experiments,
lectures and outside reading. Yet Dr. George was
not to be halted. A doctor he wanted to be and a
doctor he became; and he used only those means
which any aspiring youth with good strong arms
and lusty will can use to attain the goal.

Completing his course in Meharry Medical College, he returned to his native state and began to
practice. In a few years he felt more than rewarded
for all the hardships he had suffered; for he had
hung out his sign at Paducah, had made many
friends and had built up a very successful practice.
He joined forces with all the progressive organizations of his state and community. He allied himself
with the church and with many of the secret societies of Kentucky. He is a Mason, an Odd Fellow, a Pythian, and a member of the Court of
Calanthe. As a professional man and a leader Dr.
George felt that he must both teach and show the
people of his section the ideal way to live. He,
therefore, joined the several business organizations. He joined the Pythian Mutual Industrial
Association of the State and soon became its Vice-
President. In a little while the leading Negroes of
Kentucky saw a wider need for reliable insurance
for colored people. They founded the Mamouth
Life and Accident Insurance Company. Dr. George
was one of these founders and promoters, and has
been one of the staunch supporters of the company.

Dr. George was married to Miss Nettie N. Mc-
Claine. Dr. George owns his home in Paducah.

JAMES H. HATHAWAY.

ENTUCKY has long taken a leading place as a prosperous state. She has made a happy adjustment of the so-called race question, by giving all her citizens a fair measure of privileges, yet holding to the social restriction. Apparently this is all her darker sons have wanted, indeed all that black folk want any where. The Kentucky men of color have gone far beyond their brothers in farming, in business and in many instances in education. Thus her sons, like the one here mentioned, have an open road to essay their talents.

Among the big business men in Louisville, Kentucky, James H. Hathaway looms large and important. He is not only a business success in one direction, but in several. Indeed Mr. Hathaway appears to have acquired the Midas' touch; only unlike the king of old, Mr. Hathaway worked for his touch instead of gaining it through any special favor of the Gods.

Of the business he has developed, Mr. Hathaway can hardly tell which, had he to make a choice, he would select above all the rest. He tried his hand at running a grocery. He succeeded at that. He tried Undertaking, and again he was a success. He

essayed farming, both tilling the soil and raising stock; again he received abundant yield. He put his hands to the transfer business and once more the gods of fortune smiled upon him.

Born in Montgomery, Kentucky, Mr. Hathaway did not spend much time in gaining an education. He is educated, but his is an education of things; an education from intimate contact and combat, rather than the brand gained from schools and books. He began his business experiences in Mount Stirling, Kentucky, where he set up and ran for a good many years a grocery store.

Selling out his grocery, he made his way to Louisville, Kentucky, and secured a wagon or two and started in the transfer business. Thus for fourteen years he plied his trade and continually increased and multiplied. When Mr. Hathaway entered business, there was a transfer firm in Louisville, known as Smith and Nixon. Seeing the business acumen and dispatch of their colored rival, they sold him their wagons and horses for a mere song and got him to handle their business by contract.

In 1902, Mr. Hathaway saw an opportunity to buy an Undertaking business. He secured this and is now one of Louisville's most successful colored Undertakers.

As he increased his income from transfer work and from Undertaking, Mr. Hathaway looked out upon the farmers and saw what a happy investment could be made in farms and in stock raising, especially in Kentucky, where the grass is luxuriant and the temperature is congenial to raising nearly every breed of useful animals. Thus he has annexed to his holdings a 118 acre farm, which is now well stocked with thorough-bred horses, sheep, hogs, and cattle. After entering the transfer business it was an easy glide into the other branches of business he took on. As a transfer men his vehicles was called into constant demand for funeral occasions and this brought to his attention the undertaker's business. It did not take him long to see that this business and the transfer business could be worked together and with the large stock of horses such a business demanded it was easy for him to determine that farming would be a valuable adjunct to his business. So the three worked together to his profit. Mr. Hathaway's other property holdings are his own house and the building in which he runs his undertaking business.

He divides his energies between his family and his business. Other than his membership in the Christian church, he has few affiliations. He was married in 1892 to Miss Columbia Gray of Louisville, Ky. There are six children in the Hathaway family: Miss Ethel Louise, a graduate of the Louisville High School, is her father's secretary. James Harris, Warner Mason, Columbia S. and Ruth are still of school age.

ROBERT HORACE HOGAN.

HE words of the song, "Inch by Inch" find apt significance in the life of Mr. Robert H. Hogan, contractor and builder, of Lexington, Kentucky. Mr. Hogan was born on a farm near Macon, Ga., Feb. 12, 1881. The Hogans were a very large family who lived the earlier years of their history in the country, but who later moved into Macon. Mr. Hogan was born on the farm near Macon before the family had migrated to the city.

Born of a large family the young man had no time for school, but had to earn money to aid in supporting the family. One of his first jobs was that of elevator boy in the Wesleyan Female College at Macon, Georgia. As good fortune would have it, the president's wife, Mrs. John D. Hammond, passed up and down on that elevator. She saw that young Hogan had no learning and set out to teach him. Mrs. Hammond not only taught him herself but made arrangement for several of the teachers to give him help. She went further. She wrote Dr. Washington about the boy and later had him enter Tuskegee Institute.

While Mr. Hogan liked Tuskegee well enough, the call of the large family once more threw him out into the world. He worked a while in Macon, Ga., then in Jacksonville, Florida, as a Government brick-layer. In the meantime he was doing private studying with the International Correspondence school. For five years he worked about in Florida, Georgia, Alabama and Tennessee as a brick-layer, studying and working at the same time. In 1905, leaving Alabama, where he had been assisting in the building of a steel mill, he went to Lexington, Kentucky, and accepted work as foreman for H. A. Tandy, an old and successful contractor of that city. By this time his studies began to bear fruit. On completing his studies with the International Correspondence School, he was offered a position with the Combs Lumber Company, as superintendent of their brick construction work. This was one of the largest firms of the kind in the state and gave Mr. Hogan opportunity to apply his theories, to learn new ones, and to practice on big undertakings. For the past seven years he has superintended the construction of all the largest buildings of Lexington. Continuing to study in private, and now having completed a course in Building Superintendence, Contracting and Estimating, with the American School of Correspondence, Mr. Hogan thought it was time for him to launch into business for himself. This step he took, Jan. 1, 1916. Since that time he has built a mansion for C. B. Shafer, which cost $40,000; constructed the brick work in the Physicians' Office Building at a cost of $20,000; put up the Bamby Flat for $10,000 and erected and superintended many residences and smaller buildings and including his own two-story brick residence. At present he is doing the brick work on the new Senior High School Building, a $60,000 building.

One feature in connection with Mr. Hogan's new line of work is that upon the guarantee to Combs Lumber Co. that he would take care of a certain amount of their work as well as the fact that he has an excellent standing with them, he has been able to secure financial backing from that strong company.

Mr. Hogan in all his rush of study and work has maintained his connection with the church and many other bodies. He is a member of the First Baptist Church of his city, chairman of the Board of Deacons and Superintendent of the Sunday School. In Lodge affiliation he is a Mason of the 32nd degree.

Mr. Hogan was married in 1903 to Miss Letetia Hunter Jones of Macon, Ga. Of the three children born in the household, two are living. Robert H., Jr., died in infancy. Horace Wesley, 10 years of age, is in the sixth grade of the public school; Marion Letetia is five years old.

MARSHALL BELL LANIER, A. B., B. D.

EVEREND Lanier was born in North Carolina, at Mocksville, in 1869. He first attended the public schools of Salem, North Carolina, but did not remain there a great while, but went to Washington, D. C., where he enrolled in Wayland Seminary. Here he studied for two years, when he made another change. He had become deeply impressed that he was called to preach and with a view of preparing himself for his ministerial work he left Wayland and entered the Lincoln University, located near Philadelphia. He was then a young man, barely eighteen years of age, but very ambitious.

He graduated from the Lincoln University in 1892, and received from that Institution his degree of Bachelor of Arts. Wishing to specialize further in Theological studies he took a course in Western Theological Seminary, in Pittsburg, Penn., and was graduated as Bachelor of Divinity in 1896. This was the eventful year in the life of Reverend Lanier, for he not only completed his studies and received his degree, but it was the year in which he was ordained to the ministry and installed in his first pastorate. His first pastorate was that of Grace church, Pittsburg, Penn. He was soon regarded as an eloquent preacher and a sound theologian and his progress in his new field of labor was rapid.

His reputation as a preacher soon spread and before he had served his church very long he received a call to be the Dean of the Theological Department of the State University. At the same time he was called to be Dean of the University at Louisville, Kentucky. He accepted the latter call and for eight years has served the institution. The holding of this office has not prevented him from continuing his work as a minister. He has not neglected his duties in connection with the University, but has at the same time acceptably served the following churches as Pastor: First Baptist Church of Irvington, Kentucky, and the Corinthian Baptist Church, of Frankfort, Kentucky. He is still the Pastor of the latter church.

Reverend Lanier is especially interested in young men and boys and never tires in working in their interest. He sees in them great possibilities for the advancement of the race, and is exceedingly ambitious to place before them high ideas of life.

Along with his duties as Pastor and Dean, he is trustee of the Home for Colored boys. This office gives him a fine opportunity to get in close touch with the boys and lead them to improve their minds and hearts.

While a minister, he does not forget his duties to his country and State, and in politics he very naturally sides with the Republicans. He is also a member of the Masonic fraternity and makes his personality felt in that order.

He was married in 1901, to Miss Maud E. Bryce, of Pittsburg, Penn., in whose companionship he finds great delight. They live in their own home on West Chestnut Street, in Louisville, Kentucky.

Reviewing the life and work of Reverend Lanier it is probable that in no other way could he have served his people better than in the manner chosen by him. First his years of preparation gave him a fund of information which not only fitted him for his work, but enabled him to scatter with a lavish hand to the youth growing up about him.

As Dean of the Theological Department of the State University at Louisville, Kentucky, he has had the privilege of touching with his life a large number of young men who are preparing to enter the ministry. He has impressed them with his high ideals and has sent them forth to influence other lives in like manner.

All over the State of Kentucky, you will find men, young and old, who have been helped to a better life because at some point, the life of Reverend Lanier touched their's.

JOHN A. C. LATTIMORE, M. D.

O man is a hero to his valet, someone has said. This was not the
case with Dr. John A. C. Lattimore, of Louisville, Kentucky.
Dr. Lattimore was not a valet, but
he fulfilled the real spirit of the
saying in that he was very close to the man who
influenced him to enter the medical profession.

Dr. Lattimore when a lad was a buggy boy for
a physician, Dr. Bullock of Greensboro, North
Carolina. He was a very observant boy and was
quick to note, as he went with the Doctor in
making his daily calls, the cordial greeting he received and the high esteem in which he was held.
He also made a note of the handsome income
which came from a large practice. Thus unconsciously, Dr. Bullock influenced his buggy boy to
become a physician. Seeing the interest magni-
fied by his buggy boy in his work the good Doctor
suggested to him that he study medicine, a suggestion which he was quick to adopt. Having
formed the purpose he held to his course until
he received his diploma and hung out his shingle.

Dr. Lattimore was born in Lawndale, North Carolina, where he received his early training in the
Lawndale Public Schools. After passing through
the public schools he entered Bennett College,
Greensboro, North Carolina, and was graduated
from this Institution in the fall of 1897. His next
enrollment was in Meharry Medical College in
Nashville, Tennessee, from which institution he
received his doctors degree and the same year,
1901, he began practicing in Louisville, Kentucky.

The goal was a magnet to draw him through
meshes of difficulties before the end was obtained.

However, his way through school was not one
fraction so easy as it is to relate. The young medical student was far from rich and had to toil at
many things to defray his expenses. In vacation
time, like many other students, he worked in the
hotels of Atlantic City, N. J., and New York as bell
boy and waiter. Throughout Dr. Lattimore's life
of hardship as a student he remembers with great
tenderness the kindness of the president of Bennett College, who took the young man into his
home and cared for him as a father would do for
his son. This side of his training brought into the
life of the young man a new phase, that side which
neither the text-books nor the laboratory can dis-
cover; that is, the spirit of helpfulness. This, Dr.
Lattimore exercises in his relation to the individual,
but more so in his public spirited attitude toward
life and needs in his community. He is always
willing and eager to lend a hand to any progressive
enterprise of his city or state. With money, with
counsel or with time, he has helped all movements
for the betterment of his race in his city, state, or
country. He is found holding many responsible positions of his city: A member of the executive board
of National Association for the Advancement of
Colored People, an ex-member of the board of managers of the Y. M. C. A., a trustee of his church.
He is a member of the K. of P., of the Masons, of
the U. B. F. and of the Court of Calanthe. He is
ex-Grand Medical Register of the Knights of Pythias of the state, a postion which he held until he
resigned to become Treasurer of the Pythian Mutual Industrial Association of Grand Lodge of the
State, a position he holds until today. In all these
bodies he is looked upon as a wise leader, a generous helper, and a man with initiative. He also
belongs to all the leading Natonal organizations
of his race: the National Medical Association, and
National Negro Business League, etc. Dr. Lattimore is a member of the African Methodist Episcopal Church.

Dr. Lattimore has been fairly successful financially. He owns a beautiful home and other property to the value of ten thousand dollars. He is
also interested in several business enterprises in
Louisville

ALBERT ERNEST MEYZEEK, A. M.

ROFESSOR Albert E. Meyzeek, Principal of the Normal and Eastern School of Louisville, Kentucky, is the proverbial human dynamo in the school teaching world of Louisville. He was once pictured as one who is first to fight for the rights of his fellow countrymen. Serious to the point of severity, business like to a fault, a friend to be sought after, a foe to be feared, a champion for the rights of the black man, but with all a jolly good fellow. In business life a mighty factor in the struggle to mould the characters of our future men and women in the private life, a model husband, a property owner and a Christian gentleman.

The original of the above drawn picture was born in Toledo, Ohio. Completing the course in the public schools of his native city, he pursued further study in Terre Haute, Indiana. Finishing in Terre Haute, having planned definitely to make school teaching his life work, he entered Indiana State Normal College and later studied at the state University. Ready now for the business of life, he went to Louisville, Kentucky, and began to work in his chosen field.

Inch by inch he rose in the scale as a school teacher, becoming principal of the Grammar, then of the Normal and Eastern Schools of Louisville and then of the Kentucky State Normal and Industrial School.

In his school work, Prof. Meyzeek always leaned towards the practical, the useful. He put discipline and order into the Eastern schools of Louisville, because he looked upon discipline as a fundamental item in education. He established courses in domestic science even when the city could not provide funds for it, because he felt that such was needed in the every day lives of his pupils. He organized clubs for parents because he saw a means of bringnig parent and child to a better understanding with each other and both in a relation to the school. He established the Normal training school on a business basis, employing teachers specially trained to teach teachers, and he organized his courses so that those who studied the theory could later secure the practice.

To him was intrusted the establishment of the Normal courses and the organization and equipment of same was left entirely to his discretion and supervision. Students are appointed to positions in the public schools according to a list furnished by him and alone upon merit and no influence can change the plan adopted by him.

Thoroughly alive in all the details of school work, Professor Meyzeek nevertheless connected his school life with the life of a citizen. Noticing that the advertisements in the papers stated "white preferred" in asking for cooks, he opened courses for domestic science that he might improve the efficiency of the colored cooks already in service. He entered the campaign for a new Y. M. C. A., was the means of securing a pledge of $6,500 from the white citizens. He entered in the fight against the separate street car law in Louisville and broke the back of that measure. He fought the Louisville Segregation ordinance tooth and nail, pointing out that the white people drove the best colored people out of colored sections of the city by planting there the white "palaces of sin."

It is no wonder that the Kentucky people loved Prof. Meyzeek and that various organizations honor him. For more than seventeen years he has been a member of the Y. M. C. A. board of directors and for ten years, president. The state University recently honored him with the degree of Master of Arts. He is a pioneer Juvenile Court worker, a promoter of libraries and an all round citizen of whom Louisville is exceedingly proud.

Prof. Meyzeek owns his own home and three rent houses in Terre Haute. In 1896 Prof. Meyzeek was married to Miss Pearl Hill, who was a teacher in the Louisville Public School.

ROBERT MITCHELL, A. M., D. D.

EW big undertakings have occurred among the Negroes of Kentucky, or indeed among the colored people of the Nation during the
past quarter of a century without
enlisting the services of Reverend
Robert Mitchell, A. M. D. D. of Lexington, Kentucky. He has been in constant demand on the lecture platform, at Chautauquas, at temperance gatherings and at revivals. In his denomination and
out he has worked incessantly. For two years he
was president of the Kentucky State Teachers Association. For four years he was moderator of the
General Association of Kentucky Baptists. He was
for fourteen years Auditor of the National Baptist
Convention and is now its vice president. For
twenty-five years he has been a Trustee of State
University at Louisville and still holds his place
there. He was a member of the committee which
appeared before the state legislature in 1891 against
the separate car law. Reverend Mitchell was chos-
en by his committee to address the legislature of
Kentucky on that occasion. Two years later in
1893, he was a member of the committee from the
National Baptist Convention to appear before

President Cleveland on matters pertaining to the
Negro race.

In spite of all these extra duties, Dr. Mitchell has
been a constant and hard worker at a special post.
He was born in Fulton County, Kentucky, March
1, 1864. When a mere infant he was taken to Mississippi where he attended the public schools and
studied also in private schools. From Mississippi he
attended the State University in Kentucky, where
he gained the degree of Master of Arts. From
Louisville he entered Gaudaloupe, Seguin, Texas,
where he won the degree of D. D. He is one of
the many to get his education by waiting on the
tables mornings and evenings. He preached in odd
times when he could get a hearing.

Finishing his course he immediately entered the
ministry. His first charge was at Paducah, Ky.,
over the Seventh Street Baptist Church. Here he
was pastor four years. From Paducah he went to
Bowling Green, where he served eighteen years,
two periods of nine years each. He was pastor of
the Main Street Baptist Church, Lexington, for two
years; of the First Baptist church of Frankfort five
and a half years; of the First Baptist church of
Kansas City, Kansas, three years and of the First
Baptist Church of Lexington, his present charge,
two years. He was president of Simmons Memorial College at Bowling Green for eight years. He
has built one church, completed and paid for the
State Street Baptist Church of Bowling Green at a
cost of $7,500, purchased and paid for the present
site of the First Baptist Church of Frankfort at a
cost of more than five thousand dollars.

While he has given himself untiringly to the development of his work among his churches, he has
not been altogether unmindful of his obligations
to his family and has accumulated a property, personal and real, valued at eight or ten thousand dollars.

Dr. Mitchell was married in 1885 to Miss Virginia
Leech of Paducah. One daughter, Miss Emma B.
Mitchell has been their only child. She died in
1911. She was a young woman of rare attainments,
having been graduated from the Frankfort High
School and from the Kansas City High School and
having done special work in both Chicago University and Miami University.

Dr. Mitchell was appointed also by the National
Baptist Convention as a member of the delegation
to the World's Baptist Alliance, that convened in
London, England, July 1905, but owing to pressing
home obligations it was not possible for him to attend.

He is a splendid specimen of what honesty,
sturdy pluck, and persistency will do for one, although born and reared under unfavorable circumstances.

REVEREND JAMES JODY McCUTCHEN.

N November 9th, 1868, in Logan County, Kentucky, was born Reverend James J. McCutchen, of Lexington, Kentucky, who began his career in public by winning honors, and throughout his long and serviceable career he has continued to carry laurels won on fields of labor. Attending the public schools of his native county he was awarded the gold medal for excellence in scholarship and was Valedictorian of his class, in 1891, at Simmons Memorial College, Bowling Green, Kentucky.

His habit of study acquired in Logan County led him into several institutions and into courses, of study in various ways.——He took a post graduate correspondence course in the scientific studies from Danville, New York; gained an honorary degree from Eckstein Norton Institute at Cane Spring, Kentucky, finished a teacher's training course with the American Baptist Publication Society, and completed a course of study in stenography.

The early age at which he finished his educational courses gives evidence of an ususually vigorous mind, which his after career enlarged and developed. These courses he finished at the early age of

sixteen and for some years thereafter he taught school. He taught nine years in Logan County, where he was born, and two years in Bowling Green Kentucky. From Bowling Green he entered the Theological College of Glasgow, Kentucky, where he served as Principal for one year.

Rev. McCutchen is a Missionary Baptist and was ordained to the ministry of that church in the year 1893. He took up his work as a minister at once after his ordination and found his first field of labor in the pastorate of the Bristow Baptist Church, of Bristow, Kentucky. Here he labored for one year, but gave up the work for a larger field, to which he was called. From 1905 to 1913, he served as State Missionary for the Western district of Kentucky, in which capacity he rendered his denomination a great service. The National Baptist Home Mission Board and the Southern Baptist Board co-operated with the State Board in this work.

He built the church at Daniel Boone, Kentucky; remodeled the church at Adairville, Ky., remodeled the church at Townsends Grove, Ky., built the church at Auburn, Ky., and two school houses in Logan County. He also assisted in establishing the "Baptist Voice," a Baptist paper which is published at Princeton, Ky., and is at present the official organ of the Baptists of Western Kentucky.

His good work was of a character to stand, for he built upon a good foundation

When he accepted the Main Street Baptist Church, Lexington, Kentucky., that body was heavily in debt and much discouraged, and there was a great falling off in membership.

Reverend McCutchen in less than two years raised over nine thousand dollars ($9,000), re-united the forces of the church, lifted the mortgage, put in a two thousand dollar ($2,000) pipe organ, put in modern equipment and appliances, and added 275 members, which gave the church a total membership of 1200. In his career as minister, he has baptized some 1400 souls.

The great denomination to which he belongs recognized his ability as a leader and has placed him in many positions of honor and responsibility. He is First Assistant Moderator for the State, and holds the position of Secretary of the Minister's and Deacons' meeting of Lexington and vicinity.

Reverend McCutchen has been twice married; the first time to Miss Katy Morrow, of Mortimer, Kentucky, in 1892. She died in 1897, leaving a son, Walter L., who died at the age of sixteen, having graduated from the preparatory department of M. and F. College, Hopkinsville, Ky. The second Mrs. McCutchen was Mrs. Lucy Morse, of Mayfield, Kentucky. They were married at Mayfield in 1900.

REVEREND ELMORE THEVALL OFFUTT.

MONG the Baptist of Kentucky, Reverend Elmore Thevall Offutt, Lexington, Kentucky, is one of the peers. His preparation has been ample and thorough; his knowledge or education from contact and experience has been fully as broad and intimate as his studies in books.

He is out and out a Kentuckian. He was born in Logan County March 17th, 1871. For several years he attended common school but because of a lack of finance he was forced to stop school and to remain on the farm where he worked in the tobacco fields to aid in the support of the family. At the age of eighteen by the consent of his father he went to Louisville to find work with the idea of finishing his education. It was there he learned the tanner's trade, working during the day and studying at night. At noon hours or whenever opportunity permitted he used the blacked side of a tanned cow hide as a substitute for a black board upon which he solved problems in mathematics and diagramed sentences which he had not been able to solve the preceding night.

He was married in Louisville in 1893 to Miss Jo

anna Kemble, whose faithful cooperation and Christian life has made his success possible. There are nine children in the Offutt family: Miss Elnora B. who is teaching in the public school, Elmore T. Jr., Barnett, James Arthur, Olivia, Queenie, Garland and William, who are students and pupils in school and Joanna Kimbie Offutt who is yet a baby.

He was converted and baptized into the fellowship of the Portland Baptist Church in 1894 and was ordained to the gospel ministry in 1896. In connection with his school work he has sucessfully pastored the following churches each of which protested his resignation: Harrods Creek, Jefferson County; Elk Creek, Spencer County; Indiana Ave. Baptist Church, Jeffersonville, Ind.; La Grange, Oldham County, Ky.; Eminence, Henry County; Portland Baptist Church, Louisville, which he resigned to accept his present charge, the Pleasant Green Baptist Church, Lexington, Ky. He has recently written a short history of this church which is of great value to those who are interested in the early history of Baptists in this country. This is the oldest Colored Baptist church west of the Alleghanies and one of the oldest in the United States. It was organized in 1790, has a membership of twelve hundred and a property valuation of thirty thousand dollars. The prosperity of the church was never greater than at present.

In 1901, he entered State University, Louisville, an opportunity he recognized as answer to prayer. Here, he was not long in making his presence felt, becoming a brilliant student in most of the branches he pursued. After his graduation from the Collegiate and Theological departments, he became a teacher in the University, a position he filled with credit for several years. While teaching at the University he continued his pastoral duties and studied medicine in the Louisville National Medical College. He has also taken a course in law from the American Correspondence School of Law, Chicago.

Rev. Offutt is active in both the state and national work of his denomination. For several years he served as moderator of Central District Association of Kentucky Baptist. Because of his modesty and Christian piety combined with his general knowledge, especially of the Bible, he is held in high esteem by the ministry and has been honored for the past three years by the minister's meeting of his city as lecturer on the Sunday School lesson, one of which is delivered each Monday morning. In his church he conducts a class twice a week for the benefit of all ministers who have not had the advantage of theological training. He is interested in the Sunday School work of the State and conducts institutes in his own district convention. He is a contributor to the Sunday School Teacher publisher by the National Baptist Publishing Board, Nashville, Tenn. From time to time he has served on the various boards of the National Baptist Convention and is now a member and treasurer of the Educational Board of that body

CHARLES HENRY PARRISH, A. B., A. M.,
D. D., LL. D., F. R. G. S.

T was the late Mark Twain who insisted that mere facts contained by far more mystery and more thrills than fiction. Such certainly are the facts of the life of Dr. C. H. Parrish, D. D., F. R. G. S., President of the Eckstein Norton University, Cane Springs, Ky., and thirty years pastor of the Calvary Baptist Church, Louisville, Ky. Dr. Parrish was born a slave on the Beverly A. Hicks plantation in Lexington, Ky. At ten years of age he was converted and baptized, by Reverend James Monroe, Pastor First Baptist Church, Lexington, Ky. Shortly after this he began a life that has been crowned with rare distinctions, unusual and out-of-the-way honors and happenings.

Dr. Parrish began to win laurels in school. One of the early students in the State University, he was the first valedictorian from the college department of that insitution. This was in 1886. The University thought so well of its first valedictorian that it afterwards engaged him as a Professor of Greek and secretary and treasurer of Eckstein University.

Jointly with the Reverend Wm. J. Simmons, he founded the Eckstein Institute, in 1890, where he remained as its President for twenty two years, at which time Eckstein Institute was connected with Lincoln Institute. Dr Parrish is Secretary of the Board of Trustees of Lincoln Institute.

During this period, so full of responsible labors, he remained the Pastor of the Calvary Baptist Church, of Louisville Kentucky, never once halting in his active duties in connection therewith. His time was fully occupied in teaching, preaching, visiting and the other multiform duties of a city pastorate. He won the degree of A. B. and A. M. and D. D. from the Kentucky State University, LL. D. from the Central Law School and Fellow of the Royal Geographical Society from London.

He went to the world's Baptist Congress, which met in Jerusalem in 1894; was messenger to the World's Sunday School Convention the same year; under the direction of Karl Maschar inspector of German Baptist Missions, he traveled through Germany and preached in seventeen German towns, winning six hundred converts; he was a messenger to the Baptists of Jamaica in 1915; he has traveled through the Holy Land and has stood waist deep in the waters of the river Jordan; he has baptised believers in the Carribean Sea, and in the Gulf of Mexico.

Traveling thus abroad and extensively in this country, Dr. Parrish has nevertheless held no end of important posts at home. As has been stated, he has been the pastor of the Calvary Baptist Church of Louisville for thirty years. He is Superintendent of the Kentucky Home for Colored Children; president of the citizens National Hospital and Vice President of the Mammoth Life and Accident Insurance Company; Ex-Moderator of the General Association of Kentucky Baptists. Yet these side duties appear only to have multiplied Dr. Parrish's offices in the church. He has baptised 1500 persons, united 160 couples in marriage, preached 548 funerals, preached 3000 sermons and delivered even more lectures. Probably his greatest effort as a pulpit orator came at the Nashville Convention a few years ago, known as the fiftieth Jubilee sermon. Dr. J. M. Frost of Nashville, said of the sermon: "It was a most fitting crown of the fifty years of remarkable progress of the colored people."

Many of his sermons and tracts have appeared in print. Aside from these he has published several books entitled: "What Baptists Believe," "God and His People," "The Gospel in the Adjustment of Race Differences," "Orient Light or Travels in the Holy Land," "The Golden Jubilee of Kentucky Baptists."

Dr. Parrish was married in 1898 to Miss Mary V. Cook, of Bowling Green, Kentucky. One son, Charles Henry, Jr., has been born into the Parrish Home. The young man is now in school in Howard University, Washington, D. C.

OTHO DANDRITH PORTER, A. B., M. D.

R. O. D. Porter, A. B. and M. D. is one of those to contradict the saying that the prophet is without honor in his own country. Born in Bowling Green, Kentucky, he has spent most of his life there. As a boy he attended the public schools there. As a young man struggling to find the light he worked in and around his native city.

On finishing the public schools of Bowling Green, Dr. Porter went out as a school teacher and for years gave instruction in the country schools. Two factors contributed to his stay in the school room: one was that he was not yet fully persuaded of his calling: the other, persuasion or not, he had to earn a livelihood and also pay his way if he decided to study further.

His experience with the people in the country soon pointed to a decision. The people's ways of eating, of sleeping, of wearing clothes convinced him that no need was so crying as that for a physician and a social worker, one who not only administered drugs, but spread everywhere and at all times common knowledge of health and sanitation.

So persuaded, he entered Fisk University preparatory department in 1884. He was not seeking short cuts but thorough preparaton. From the preparatory department, he entered the college from which he obtained his Bachelor of Arts degree in 1891. During this time he taught school in Kentucky, Tennessee, Texas, and many other places to earn money to make his way. However, though he had to work his way, he stood as one of the best scholars of his class and one of the institution's strongest men.

From Fisk, Mr. Porter enrolled as a medical student in Meharry Medical College. From here he received his doctor's degree in three years. Back to his native home he went, passed the state examination and set out to right the wrongs of health such as he had seen during his boyhood days and during his school teaching in the country. Knowing his community and state, Dr. Porter was able to go to the heart of his work at once. He has been practicing a little more than 20 years. During this period, though he came out of school all but penniless, he has equipped himself with the best books and tools his profession affords, has his automobile, owns some of the choicest real estate in Bowling Green and owns and lives in a two-story brick residence. His two-story office building faces main street and joins the costly lot on which is built the $150,000.00 Custom House.

During the few years of his practice, Dr. Porter has been president of the National Medical Association of Colored Physicians and Surgeons, a post to which he was elected in 1899. One of the best facts about his election to this post is the fact that it came unsought. He is one of the founders of the State Medical Association and is a member of the State Association of both white and colored doctors.

Doctor Porter was married in April, 1895, to Miss Carry Bridges of Macon, Miss. Mrs. Porter was educated at Fisk University. To her Dr. Porter gives most of the praise for his success.

From his own town comes this tribute:

"The public takes keen interest in Dr. Porter's work. The white physicians have no hesitancy in sitting in consultation with him because they know his worth and ability as a physician, and therefore value highly his opinion in cases which require rare skill and experience. He is thoroughly interested in all business, social or benevolent movements for the advancement of the race in this city and vicinity, and never refuses to give encouragement to the struggling young men and women of the race. As busy as Dr. Porter is with matters as above indicated, he devotes time to religious work in his church in an official capacity.

Dr. Porter believes in race co-operation along all lines, and his willingness to help his people by serving at the head of many organized bodies for uplift in this city is an evidence of his sincerity."

WILLIAM HENRY STEWARD.

William Henry Steward

BY virtue of devoted services as well as by dint of years, William H. Steward of Louisville, Kentucky, is known throughout the country as the "Dean of Colored Editors." He began the publication of the American Baptist in 1879. For thirty eight years therefore he has molded the sentiments of his people both in his state and wherever Baptists are found. But the American Baptist has merely served as a sort of peg for him to hang on while he labored here and advised there. For fourteen years he was secretary of the National Baptist Convention. For forty years he has been secretary of the Kentucky Baptist Association, and for forty years chairman of the Board of Trustees of the Kentucky State University.

Mr. Steward was born on July 26, 1847, at a time when neither the advantages of education nor opportunities knocked very energetically on the black boy's cabin door, but his ear was keen to hear even the slight knocking of opportunity and to seize it by the forelocks while it was passing.

He received the ground work of his education through private instruction and when he had advanced to a certain point he was sent to Louisville where he entered private schools. He proved an apt pupil and became very proficient as a scholar so that when emancipation came he was ready to take his place as an efficient worker and leader among his people.

His preparation during the period of slavery was a God send to both himself and his people for his services came at a time when the demand for educated leadership among the Negroes was great and the supply exceedingly small.

Mr. Steward was quick to recognize the situation and quick to respond to the cry of help and to devote his life to the uplift of his race.

Like most persons who at that time chanced to have an education, Mr. Steward entered the profession of school teaching. He began at Frankfort, Kentucky, where he taught for three years. From Frankfort, he returned to his native heath, Louisville, continuing in the same profession.

The teaching profession did not offer the moderate income and fair opportunities for service and advancement as it does now. Mr. Steward therefore left the schoolrooms. He entered the employ of the railroad and for a number of years served as messenger for the Louisville and Nashville Railroad Company. From Railroad messenger he became letter carrier, being the first colored mail carrier ever appointed in the city of Louisville. This post he held for sixteen years. By this time he had established himself as a thinker and writer. His paper had become known along with him. He could now give his time to the publishing of the American Baptist and to the uplift work with which he had aligned himself from the beginning of his career.

He had begun his career by joining the church. In 1867, when he launched out as a school teacher, he became a member of the Fifth Street Baptist Church in Louisville. Subsequently he taught a Sunday School class, the largest in his church, became secretary of the choir and Sunday School Superintendent. He was elected secretary of the Board of Directors of the Louisville Colored Public Schools from which place he was later advanced to chairman of the board. He joined the Masonic Lodge and was soon made Grand Master. In 1905 he was chosen one of the lay delegates to the World's Congress which was held in London, England.

Mr. Steward has traveled much, mainly as a newspaper man and as an active servant of his people. Few Negro organizations assemble without him. The late Dr. Washington was won't to say, speaking at the annual Farmers Conference, "This conference would be very incomplete without the presence of Mr. W. H. Steward, he has come here regularly with his sympathy and words of cheer for years."

Mr. Steward lives in his own home, a brick residence in Louisville, surrounded by a happy and well educated family. He was married to Miss Mamie E. Lee, in Lexington, in 1878. Mrs. Steward is well known herself as an educator and a woman of talent. She was for years a teacher of music at the State University, a native Baptist worker among women and a lecturer in continual demand. There are three daughters and one son in the Steward family Misses Lucy B. and Jennette L. are graduates of the Louisville High School; Miss Carolyna is not only a graduate from the High School, but from the State University. All three have been successful school teachers. Willim H. Jr., is a Mechanical Engineer, being a graduate of the Armour School of Technology of Chicago. He was for two years a teacher in Tuskegee Institute, having charge of the school's heating plant and lending great aid in the construction of the larger Tuskegee heating and lighting plant. He is drafting engineer.

The veteran editor and worker, though seventy years of age, is still in the heyday of service, active in mind and in body, editing, lending aid, giving advice, attending organizations just as if he were never to grow old.

EDWARD E. UNDERWOOD, M. D.

HE black man of the North and of the West is rapidly coming into his own. Time was when the man of the South boasted that the "Doers" all came from their ranks. Not so in these days. Dr. E. E. Underwood is a conspicuous example of the plucky boy born and reared in the West. Dr. Underwood was born in Mt. Pleasant, Ohio, in 1864. As a lad he attended the Mt. Pleasant High School, where he was graduated in 1881. Ten years later he was graduated from the medical department of the Western Reserve College of Cleveland, Ohio. For a time he studied theology under the direction of a private tutor.

On graduating from the Medical College, Dr. Underwood began to practice medicine, hanging out his sign in Frankfort, Kentucky. For twenty-five years, now he has practiced medicine in Frankfort. In that time he has carried honors and responsibilities enough to stagger the average man. He was for seven years a school teacher, teaching in the Emerson Colored School, of Ohio. In 1891 he began the editorship of the "Blue Grass Bugle," the colored weekly of Frankfort, which was edited by him for ten years. He was for four years assistant city physician of Frankfort; for fourteen years secretary of the U. S. Board of Pension Examining Surgeons. In 1910 he established the People's Pharmacy and was its

first president. He has been its secretary since 1911. He is Educational Editor of the Lexington News; is author of the "History of Colored Churches of Frankfort," and of several poems.

Besides all of these duties and honors, Dr. Underwood has been a "Daniel Boone" among and for the Negroes of his section. The numbers of first times for a colored man to do things in his section seems to fall upon him. He was the first colored student to enter and graduate from the Mt. Pleasant, (Ohio) High School; first colored member of the Jefferson County (Ohio) Republican Committee; first Negro member of the Mt. Pleasant, City Council, being elected over four white aspirants for the office. He is the first colored member of the Board of Regents of Kentucky Normal and Industrial Institute, having been appointed by Governor Bradley in 1898, and appointed again by Governor Wilson, in 1907.

Large as the number of first things that Dr. Underwood has done, they utterly pale before the number of organizations with which he is actively affiliated.

Dr. Underwood is a Mason, a Knight Templar, a Knight of Pythias, an Odd Fellow, United Brother of Friendship, member of the Union Benevolent Society, and of the Mosaic Templars. He is not merely a member of good standing in these bodies, but has held offices in all of them. He is at present Supreme Keeper of Records and Seals, of the Knights of Pythias, N. A. S. A. E. A. and A., and member of the Kentucky State Board of Managers of the United Brothers of Friendship.

Having so wide and intimate contact with his people, Dr. Underwood became extremely sensitive to their needs and to the wrongs they have suffered. Thus he is found undertaking many services in their defense and for their uplift. From 1891 to 1893, he was Executive Secretary of the Anti-Separate Coach State Executive Committee, which tested the constitutionality of the "Jim Crow" law. In 1895, he was the Kentucky Commissioner to the Cotton States Exposition, which was held in Atlanta, and at which Booker T. Washington leaped into fame as an orator. Two years later he was commissioner from his State to the Tennessee Centennial Exposition, held in Nashville. In 1898, he organized and was first president of the State League of Colored Republican Clubs of Kentucky. He is a member of the Franklin County Republican Committee in his State and has been a delegate to every Republican State Convention since 1892. He was delegate at large to the Republican National Convention of 1904 and was strongly endorsed in his State for Register of the United States Treasury in 1909. He is president of the Franklin County Colored Agricultural and Industrial Association, member of the National Medical Association, of the National Association of Pension Examining Surgeons, of the National Negro Business League, of the National Association for the Advancement of Thrift among Colored people and of the Kentucky State Medical Association.

Dr. Underwood married Miss Sarah J. Walker. There are two sons: Ellsworth W. and Robert M., the former is a student in the Dept. of Pharmacy, Western Reserve University of Cleveland, the latter a Senior in the Frankfort Colored High School.

DR. RANDOLPH FRANKLIN WHITE.

HILE he is really filling the place of a modest business and professional man, Dr. Randolph Franklin White, the Negro Pharmacist, of Owensboro, Kentucky, has so so happily mixed business, education, work and travel, that he may be almost called a globe trotter. His travels, which all the time had in them the purpose of business, have taken him into the leading cities of America, into Canada, into Hawaii, into Japan, and into the Philippine Islands. Few men have made the profession of pharmacy serve them such triple service—provide travel, gain experience and supply a livelihood.

Dr. White was born in Warrentown, Florida, June 25th., 1870. He spent his early school days in his native State, and early made up his mind to become a pharmacist. To this end he entered Howard University, from which he graduated in 1897. But Dr. White cannot be said to have begun or to have completed his course at any one time. As he mixed travel with business, so he mixed school education and practical education. Thus while he was attending Howard University, pursuing a course in Pharmacy, he was at the same time gain-ing practical experience in Pharmacy, working for the Plumnur Pharmacy, in Washington, D. C.

His graduation in 1897 was therefore more attaining freedom and license for he was already ripe in his calling, ready to take charge and manage rather than serve the usual apprenticeship. He found no trouble under the circumstances with securing good responsible posts at the very outset. His first position was in Louisville, Kentucky. Here he took charge of the Peoples' Drug Store, and ran it, giving satisfaction to its stockholders. From Louisville he went to Lexington and for a time joined forces with Dr. Ballard. He was already well known as a pharmacist. The United States Government, needing a Hospital Steward, Dr. White was appointed to the post, and commissioned to serve in the Philippines. Here he worked for two years, from 1899 to 1901. Hence it was that he got his trip to the Orient, and other countries while he was away from the United States.

Having completed his travels and finished his services with the Government, he returned to Kentucky, to begin business for himself. In 1901 he opened a drug store in Owensboro. Dr. White had some difficulty in securing a place to begin business. He therefore bought the store which he was to use and which he still uses. His business prospered from the outset, as he had had wide experience in handling drugs and in handling people. He owns his home and his store in Owensboro and owns three rent houses in Lexington.

Dr. White is a good churchman and a member of several fraternal bodies. He is an Episcopalian, a Mason, an Odd Fellow, U. B. F., and a Knight of Pythias. In the Masonic order he is Deputy Grand Master of the State.

Dr. White was married in Lexington, July 23, 1901, to Miss Fannie Hathaway.

Almost every city has some one individual or business which holds a unique position because of some marked and distinctive feature or characteristic.

Thus in Owensboro, Kentucky, Dr. Randolph Franklin White is known as the Pharmacist.

He has won this distinction from his remarkable success in business, which is universally recognized, but not from this alone, his valued services to the Government during his travels abroad make their contribution to the enviable reputation he enjoys.

His thorough knowledge of his business is evidenced in the great success he has achieved in it and this with his courteous manner and elevated bearing commands the respect of all who deal with him.

WILLIAM HILLIARD WRIGHT.

HERE was a time when the Negro lawyer was the jest of his own and of the white race. He was not allowed to practice in the courts; or if accorded the technical privilege, he was denied the genuine right. He was a lawyer in name and often well prepared for his work, but prejudice stepped between him and the practice of his profession and embarrassed him in his efforts to win recognition. His earnings were therefore next to nothing. His clothes were thread-bare; his home depleted; he and his family, were he so rash as to marry, went hungry.

Yet with the true spirit of the pioneer, the black lawyer has endured the whips and scorns of the courts and of the public until he is no longer the mark of open rebuke. Patiently winning his way he has faced and overcome opposition, met ridicule with intellectual force, and dignity, and with a kind though determined spirit, has finally won recognition from both the Court and the Bar.

He now even boasts a home of his own; good clothes, and a happy family. He enters the courts, especially in the West and handles his cases on his merit.

Slowly the men of his profession have developed sufficient esprit d'corps to accord him at least common courtesy. To win this recognition he has had to study hard, endure and persevere. All the time, he like all men of professional careers among black folk, has had to serve as missionary to his people on the one hand and batter down by every sort of means their prejudices on the other. Surely no men deserve more gratitude from their people, for whatever has been their endeavor, the first impulse of the public was that the lawyer was really "something out for a suit" and not really seeking the public good.

While Mr. Wright's large and ever-growing law practice requires most of his time, and attention, he is not unmindful of civic matters and the development of his people. He is always on the alert to seize upon every suggestion that will conduce to their uplift and is foremost in all plans looking to that end.

In Louisville, for example, the white citizens have what is known as the "Million Dollar Foundation Fund." Mr. Wright was much impressed with the idea resulting in the organization and reasoned that a like organization would be helpful to the colored race. Co-operating with the colored business and professional men of the city, a club similar in purpose is in process of forming. The Negro Club is to be a $100,000 Mercantile Foundation Fund.

The prime mover in this endeavor among the colored people is William H. Wright of Louisville. Mr. Wright has been before the public of his state for many years, both as a professional man and as a man of business. As a student, a professional and business man, Mr. Wright is amply equipped for the great undertaking. Born in Livingston, Alabama, he was educated in Selma University, Selma, Alabama, in the State University, Louisville, Kentucky, and in the department of law, Howard University, Washington, D C. For the most part he worked his way through all these schools. He began the practice of law in Louisville, in 1904. He organized the first Negro Insurance Company of Kentucky and thus educated many colored people up to the idea of insurance and to entrusting their money to Negro enterprises. Since 1904 he has been able to amass considerable property holdings, as he owns his office building on Sixth Street in Louisville, and several rent houses.

Mr. Wright is a Baptist in religious affiliation, and is a member of the Fifth Street Baptist Church, a Mason, Odd Fellow, K. of P. and Mosaic Templar.

He has traveled extensively both in the United States and Canada, his travels giving him an enlarged view of life. He has not yet traveled upon the sea of matrimony, and so the pleasure of that voyage still awaits him.

HOMER MILTON CHARLES.

HIS successful business man, of Chalmette, Louisiana St. Bernard Parish, has one of the most prosperous businesses in Louisiana. His reputation is not only statewide, but generally national. He is a life member of the National Negro Business Men's League, is an attendant at all meetings of this body, and an enthusiastic supporter of the Negro Business ideas. Mr. Charles has not always moved with men of larger finance among Negroes. He has know the pinch of need and has vivid recollections of hard struggles to gain a footing.

Mr. Charles was born in St. Martin Parish, La., July 4, 1861. Two years later his parents moved to St. Bernard Parish. His schooling consisted of what he gained in the public school of said Parish and of a private tutor, at home. However, he was one of the family of thirteen children, which usually means that as soon as the boys are able to earn a penny they must be up and away to their post. Being very industrious, he was employed on a sugar farm, where he filled many positions. Later on he began truck farming with his father. In 1887, feeling that he must still make the de-

termined start, he launched forth in business. His undertaking was modest enough; consisting of a fruit stand on the river bank in a store nine by nine feet. There were three conspicious features to the whole setting; first, that he was determined to sell as cheap as his competitors; second, that with the assistance of his wife, he was satisfied to be as economical as any one else; third, that as he had that ambition to push forward, was determined to be as polite to his customers as his competitors. This spot was near Chalmette National Cemetary, on the historic spot where the "Battle of New Orleans" was fought. It was one of the rather few instances in which a Negro dared to become a fruit dealer. Inch by inch, as the song goes, he developed his business. Taking his basket on his shoulder, he peddled his fruits from house to house, until he had built up confidence, gained patronage and the respect of the entire community. Then he purchased a one-horse wagon; then followed two horses and wagon to meet the demand for deliveries.

He was already married to Miss Hester Anderson of St. Bernard in the year 1885. She was the silent but effective partner during these stages of uncertainty. She did work in private families, helping to provide food for the family and sometimes capital for the business. Four daughters sprang from this union, three of whom are living. Miss Sadie died while preparing for graduation at New Orleans University. The others are: Misses Augusta, Mary and Clara. Miss Clara, the youngest, is still in school.

Today Mr. and Mrs. Charles are among the leading property owners of Louisiana. Besides owning their home, they have stock in the Friscoville Realty Company, of St. Bernard and have several houses for rent.

Mr. Charles is what is often called an organization man, believing as he does in organization of men into bodies as means of promoting race welfare. He is Catholic in his religion; a member of Felicity Lodge K. P. No. 199, Daughters of Crescent Tab. No. 27, Progressive Aid Mutual Benefit Association. In the business and educational world, he is a life member of the National Negro Business Men's League, an honorary member of the Bergemont Educational Association, a member of the Fazendville Educational Association, a stock holder in the Bank of St. Bernard, a stock holder in the World Bottling Company, New Orleans. He has traveled over the United States on business, and for pleasure and relaxation.

During his residence in St. Bernard Parish, Mr. Charles has built up such a reputation of integrity and honesty as to be considered the most responsible Negro Citizen in his community by both his people and the White authorities.

179

Walter L. Cohen

IN New Orleans, Louisiana, January 22, 1860, was born Walter L. Cohen; and the place of his birth has been the scene of most of his active life. Here he has lived and made a place for himself in the business world, in the fraternal world, and in the political world, as well as one of prominence in the social world. As a young lad, he attended the public schools of New Orleans, and then spent two years in Straight University, of New Orleans, and one year in the St. Louis Catholic School. While his opportunity for attending school lasted we find the young man applying himself diligently to the work in hand. Indeed this has been the keynote of his whole life—applying himself to the work then in hand.

While still a boy he started out to learn to be a cigar maker, but because he was not a smoker, he was made ill by this work and had to give it up. His next work was in a saloon. Here he remained for about four years. In 1889 he gave up his work in the saloon to take up the work of United States Inspector. Later he was promoted to the position of Lieutenant of the United States Inspectors. In this capacity he served until the democrats took charge, when he resigned the position. In 1899 he was appointed Register of the United States Land Office at New Orleans. This appointment came from President McKinley and he was re-appointed by President Roosevelt. He served in this office until 1911. We find that Mr. Cohen has been very active in politics for a great number of years. He was a delegate to the National Republican Convention, in 1892, 1898, 1900, 1904, 1908, 1912 and in 1916. He is the recognized leader of the fight against the "Lily White Republicans of Louisiana." So active has Mr. Cohen been in the interest of his people in his native city that the Mayor of the city appointed him as a chairman of the colored citizens committee. This committee has charge of all matters concerning the education and general welfare of the colored people of New Orleans. In this capacity Mr. Cohen has had a great opportunity to help his race, an opportunity which he was quick to seize and which he used to their best advantage.

In another line of work, he has done equally as much for the betterment of his people. He is President of the People's Industrial Life Insurance Company.. Mr. Cohen owns three-fifths of the stock of this company. To do the work of the company there are employed nearly one hundred colored agents. In all they collect over $100,000.00 in premiums yearly. The organization of this company furnishes work—work where our young people can earn a livelihood and still keep their self respect. Mr. Cohen has also one third interest in two drug stores. In addition to the money invested in these concerns he owns his beautiful residence in the city and a summer home in Bay St. Louis, Mississippi.

Mr. Cohen leads a full, active life and it would seem that his private interests would command his entire time, nevertheless, he is found upon the membership roll of a number of organizations.

He is a member of Mt. Olive Lodge, No 21, Masons; Zenith Lodge No. 175, Knights of Pythias; Pride of Louisiana, No. 1324, Grand United Order of Odd Fellows. He has been president of the Economy Benefit Association for twenty-four years. This last named organization is composed of the old creole citizens in New Orleans, they first organized themselves in 1836. Mr. Cohen is also President of the Iroquois Social Club, and Vice-President of Providence Hospital Board of Administrators.

In these times of war our country has not failed to recognize the need of strong men to help back her in all her efforts to conquer Germany. It is not surprising that Mr. Cohen was early called upon to take a part and he did his share of the work well. He was a member of the Speakers Bureau, whose duty was to speak in the interest of Liberty Bonds, Red Cross and other war measures. He was also the representative of the colored people on the Executive Committee for War Saving Stamps for New Orleans.

In religious belief, Mr. Cohen is a Catholic. He is active in the affairs of his church. He serves as a member of the board of Directors of the St. Louis Catholic School. In the St Joseph Catholic Church, New Orleans, Louisiana, Mr. Cohen was married, to Miss Wilhelmina M. Seldon, March 19, 1882. There is a family of four children, two boys and two girls. Walter L. Cohen, Jr., and Benjamin B. Cohen, work with their father in the Insurance Company and are following in his footsteps, and are being trained to carry on this business, when their father retires. Miss Margret R. Cohen is a school teacher and Miss Camille is now Mrs. Bell and is a cashier in one of her father's drug stores. As is seen from this, Mr. Cohen has provided paying positions for his own children in developing his business ability, as well as providing places for the children of others. What he is doing for his children in a material way will not compare with what he has done to fit them for life.

PAUL H. V. DEJOIE, M. D.

ORN and educated in New Orleans, La., Dr. Paul H. V. Dejoie entered upon and successfully pursued his practice in his native city. Born July 2nd, 1872, he was the first child of Artistide Dejoie and Ellen Chambers. Because of the fact that his father held many responsible positions during his life time, the young lad did not have all the struggle for an education that some of our prominent men have had. So we find that Mr. Dejoie as a boy was a constant pupil in the New Orleans Public Schools. Having gotten from the public course of instruction all that they had to offer, Dr. Dejoie entered Southern University. Here he was one of the best known and most popular students of his day. He won the Peabody Scholarship Medal. After graduation from Southern he decided to take up the study of medicine. To this end he matriculated at the New Orleans University, and completed the course in 1895. He went before the Louisiana State Board of Medical Examiners and passed. This fact is striking because he was the first colored man to pass that board.

Having secured his privilege to practice medicine he settled down to that work in his own native city, New Orleans. Here he remained for the past twenty-three years. During this time he has been successful as a practitioner, having built up quite a practice. Seeing the need of the colored people for a Drug Store, he busied himself in opening one. In this drug store he owns half interest. It was from the first a very successful undertaking. The store bears his name—Dejoie Cut Rate Pharmacy, being the name of the Drug Store.

In the work as a physician, he had an abundant chance to see the needs of the colored people when they were sick, and the needs of the bereaved families. To in a measure alleviate the suffering from these two sources, he has interested himself in the Unity Industrial Life Insurance and Sick Benefit Association. For two years he served the organization in the capacity of Secretary, and since that time he has been president of the organization. Under his management he has seen the association grow rapidly. It has gone to the front and now is ahead of all companies doing similar insurance in the State. This company is conducted on broad and liberal principles by conservative and well-qualified persons. The company paid over $350,000.00 to members in Louisiana for sickness, accident and death. It gives profitable employment to over two hundred colored people. In this way, Dr. Dejoie has been able to serve his race from two entirely different points. He has made work for a number, and he has made it possible for many sick to have some of the comforts of life.

Dr. Dejoie has made it a point to come in contact with the better men of the race. In order to do this he had connected himself with several fraternal orders. He is a thirty-second degree Mason, an Odd Fellow, and a Knight of Pythias. To these organizations he has brought his good business judgment, his strong sense of right and wrong and his pleasing personality.

During the twenty-three years, Dr. Dejoie has been out in the world for himself, he has formed the habit of saving. So among his worldly possessions we might note his beautiful home, a double cottage and his stock in various banks, oil wells and gold mines.

Although born, partly educated and established in business in the same city, Dr. Dejoie has, never-the-less taken time to travel about a great deal in his own country. He has traveled extensively in the East, and through most of the Southern States. He also spent some time in Jaures, Mexico. Dr. Dejoie has served his Alma Mater as president of the Alumni Association.

On June 16th, 1900, he was married to Miss Ella Brown, of New Orleans. There are two sons in the Dejoie family, P. H. V. Jr., and Pradhomme, who are now attending school in New Orleans.

SMITH WENDELL GREEN.

W. GREEN became a member of the order of K. of P. on July 17, 1883 when the Order was in its infancy, being a charter member of Pride of Tensas Lodge No. 21, St. Joseph, La. He was elected to the station of V. C. of the lodge, but served as C. C. from the time of the organization of the lodge until June 30, 1886. He was the Grand Representative from this lodge, and immediately upon entering the Grand Lodge, his ability to handle finances commenced to show itself, and in May, 1884, he was elected to the position of G. M. of F., and served for one year; the office has since been abolished.

In April, 1886, he was elected to the position of G. K. of R. and S. and served in that station until 1891. He was elected to the position of G. C. in May, 1892, served until 1897, and declined re-election. In April, 1899, he was again elected to the position of G. C. Upon assuming that station he found the finances of the Grand Lodge in an insolvent condition. The general fund had no assets, while its liabilities amounted to $105.62. The Endowment Fund showed the small amount of assets as $196.40, while its liabilities showed death claims

due and unpaid, aggregating $3,424.25. The membership at that time was only 897.

He found that it was necessary to increase the endowment dues if the Grand Lodge of the State of Louisiana was to be resurrected. The recommendation he made was adopted and became a part of the laws of the Grand Lodge with the result that a sufficient sum was soon accumulated to pay off all outstanding claims for endowment. When the Grand Lodge met in April, 1902, they found themselves entirely out of debt, with a small surplus on hand to the credit of the endowment department. The Grand Lodge was then paying an endowment of $300.00, ninety days after filing the claim.

In April, 1905, he recommended that the endowment policies be raised to $500, and the claims be paid within thirty days after they were filed. In the year of 1906, the surplus in the Endowment Fund had reached such a large sum, and was growing all the time, that the question arose, "What shall we do with this money?" It was then necessary for S. W. Green to study out a way of investing it. Accordingly, in 1906, at the Grand Lodge Session in Alexandria, La., he recommended that the Grand Lodge State of Louisiana erect a Pythian Temple, and accordingly an appropriation of $12,000 was made by the Grand Lodge for the purchase of a site.

This appropriation was found to be insufficient to purchase a site in the desired locality, and an additional $3,000 was therefore appropriated to pay for same. This appropriation resulted in the purchase of a desirable site in the city of New Orleans, La., to be used at later date for a Pythian Temple. The original appropriation for the temple was only $60,000 but realizing that a $60,000 building in a city like New Orleans would not serve the purpose for which it was intended, he allied his forces, and carried them to the Grand Lodge, which convened in the city of New Orleans in 1908. Here the Grand Lodge approved his action in reference to building a magnificent structure, which is now completed and cost in the neighborhood of $200,000. Today we see that from the crippled conditions of affairs when Mr. Green assumed control of the office, the Grand Lodge of the State of Louisiana has 180 lodges in the state, with a membership of 9,000 and with the total resources of $123,354.07, endowment claims being paid within thirty days after filing.

Mr. Green attended the first Supreme Lodge session in August, 1893 as Supreme Representative for the State of Louisiana, in August, 1895, at St. Louis, Mo., and has attended every Supreme Lodge session as a representative since that date.

At the Supreme Lodge session at Pittsburg, Pa., in 1905, he was elected to the position of Supreme Vice Chancellor and ex-officio, Supreme Worthy Counsellor. At the Supreme Lodge session in Louisville, Ky., in 1907, he was re-elected to the position and held that position until April 3, 1908, when he assumed the duties of Supreme Chancellor the place made vacant by the death of the late S. W. Starks.

HENRY CLAUDE HUDSON, D. D. S.

LL those doubting the efficacy of a young man's acquiring a trade in his early years should know the story of Dr. Henry Claude Hudson, D. D. S. of Shreveport, Louisiana. A trade not only provided him his daily bread, even when he was very young, but it was the agency whereby he gained funds to pursue his education and whereby he was able on at least one occasion to render almost priceless service to himself and to his people.

Born in Marksville, Avoyles Parish, Louisiana, April 19th, 1886, his parents moved to Alexandria, La., when he was a five-year-old where he passed his early school days. Having aspiration for higher education he entered the eighth District Academy at Alexandria, where he prepared to enter college.

However there was no means in sight to defray his expenses through school and so dropping out of school he went forth and became apprentice at brickmasonry. Having mastered this trade he re-entered school and once more pursued his studies. From the academy in Alexandria, he went to Wiley University in Marshall, Texas. It was here that his trade served him in such good stead and did such excellent service for his people. When Dr. Hudson entered Wiley, in 1910, that institution was about to erect a Carnegie Library. All was ready except the labor. This was under the control of the

unions. A dead lock insued. In this situation the young man came forward, stated that he was a brickmason and that he would take charge of the work and complete it, if the University would provide students to help. This was agreed to, and the library was built, much to the satisfaction of the university and the glory and profit of the young man.

Finding him a thoroughly reliable builder and that it saved money by his taking the contract, Wiley University soon had him on other buildings. Several dormitories for boys were to be erected. It engaged his services as superintendent, and thus erected its buildings with a considerable saving to itself and with no further trouble from the labor unions.

Having now decided to become a dentist, and having solved pretty well the difficulty of financing himself, Dr. Hudson entered Howard University in Washington, D. C. Several times, however, he found during his course in dentistry that he could not turn his trade to immediate account. Competition was a good deal sharper in the North, he found, than it was in the South. Thus in his short vacations when time was exceedingly precious he turned his energies to whatever task his hands could find. He found the Pennsylvania Dining Car service the most immediate employment and the largest remuneration for a short space of time. Engaging in this service he was able to continue his education. Incidently he traveled all over the eastern states while he was in this work.

Graduating from the Howard University Dental course in June, 1913, he immediately returned to his home land and prepared for the state examinations. To make assurance doubly sure he took the examinations in two states, Louisiana and Arkansas. In both states he passed. Louisiana was his home, and in his home he preferred to try first. Hanging out his sign in Shreveport, he began his career as a dentist. His success has far exceeded even his ambition. In a short time he found that one chair was not sufficient to accommodate his patrons. He found also that he could not meet all the demands made upon him. He therefore set up a second chair and employed an assistant, a young lady who is giving most efficient service.

That he has been unusually successful as a professional man is shown from the amount he has been able to accumulate during the few years of his practice. Dr. Hudson owns his home, a very attractive residence on Jordan Street in Alexandria. He has equipped his office with the most up-to-date dental appliances available. All these he owns, having paid for them $3000.

Though genuinely interested in the life of Shreveport, Dr. Hudson has but little time to give to lodge or social engagements. Only his Sabbaths are free, and frequently only a part of these. He is a member of the St. James Methodist Episcopal Church of Shreveport, where he attends services, and takes such active part in church work as his time will allow. He was elected a member of the Board of trustees of Wiley University in May, 1918.

Dr. Hudson was married to Miss Thomey B. Thomas of Shreveport, September 14, 1914. Dr. and Mrs. Hudson have two children, Henry Claude, Jr., who was born January 5th, 1916; and Gloria T., who was born April 11, 1917.

MASON ALBERT HAWKINS, A. B., A. M.

ASON Albert Hawkins, of Baltimore, Maryland, is a Virginian by birth. On October 21, 1874, he was born in Charlottsville, Albermarle County. At an early age he went from Virginia to Maryland where he attended the Elementary schools, of Baltimore. Completing the work of the graded schools he prepared for college at Morgan College, also in Baltimore. From Morgan College Mr. Hawkins went to Harvard University. Here he spent four years in the classical course of this great institution, graduating in 1901, with the degree A. B. He received the degree of A. M., from Columbia University in 1910.

Upon finishing the course at Harvard, Mr. Hawkins became a teacher of Latin, German, and Economics, in the Colored High School, of Baltimore. In this position he worked for five years, when he became head of Department of Foreign Languages in 1906. In 1909 he was made Vice-Principal of this school and Principal the latter part of the same year. Here Mr. Hawkins still labors. Most of his life has been spent in the school rooms of Baltimore.

Since Mr. Hawkins took charge of the Colored High School it has had a great growth. He has modified the course of study to meet in a large degree the needs of the community which it serves. He emphasizes the obligations of the teacher to the parents. He also lays great stress upon the need of broad vision and sympathy and the requirement of high professional skill. With these views it is but natural that Mr. Hawkins himself should go out of the school room to touch the lives of all in the community. So we find him an active member of the Union Baptist Church, a member of the American Academy of Political and Social Sciences, and a Fellow of American Geographical Society. But his interests in the people of his immediate community is shown more in the fact that he serves as a member of the Board of Provident Hospital; President of the Maryland Colored Public Health Association; Treasurer of the Maryland Colored Blind Association; Member of the Commission on Preparedness and Defense for the Colored People of Maryland.

He was appointed to the Commission on Preparedness by Governor Harrington. This alone goes to show that his efforts in the behalf of the Race has attracted the attention of the whole State. So numerous and so varied are these bodies which he serves, that it is readily seen that it is no one phase of the development of the Race which Mr. Hawkins has at heart, but the advancement of the entire people.

Along with all the interests which are ever before Principal Hawkins, he has an interest in certain inventions. On this he spends considerable time. It to him is a recreation from the other kind of work which is ever with him. He has been awarded patents on a cabinet for player music rolls and he has patents pending on a number of various devices.

On October 14, 1905, Mr. Hawkins was married to Miss Margaret B. Gregory. Mrs. Hawkins is the daughter of the late Professor James M. Gregory, of Bordentown Industrial School, Bordentown, New Jersey. Mr. Hawkins has two sons, Gregory Hawkins, and Mason A. Hawkins. These two lads are in the schools of Baltimore and give promise of great intellectual development. Mr. Hawkins ambition is to prepare them for an honorable and useful life.

Mr. Hawkins has set the example of thrift for those who take him as a pattern. He pays taxes on both real-estate and personal property. In this man we see one well rounded. He is a sound scholar, a progressive educator, and an excellent administrator. At the same time he touches the lives of all the people about him, even the most lowly in a helpful manner.

WILLIAM PICKENS, A. B., A M., LIT. D., LL. D.

S a very young man in school, William Pickens won for himself honors and the name of a close student and a good speaker. What the young man gave promise of being William Pickens, the man, is. He was born in South Carolina, Jan. 15, 1881. His public school training was received in Arkansas. In 1899 he graduated from the High School in Little Rock, as Valedictorian of the class. Not only had young Pickens led his particular class, but he had higher marks than any student had ever made in the school. After leaving High School, Mr. Pickens entered Talledega College, Talledega, Alabama, and graduated with the degree of A .B., again valedictorian of his class. Not yet satisfied with his training the subject of this sketch next entered Yale University. After two years stay he graduated in the highest grade, "Philosophical Oration Grade" in class of over three hundred. One of the rewards of his high scholarship was receiving Phi Beta Kappa. During his first year at Yale Mr. Pickens won the highest of ten different prizes for Oratory in the James Teneyck Oratorical Contest. Thousands of people complimented him on this achievement among them being ex-President Cleveland. President Roosevelt's family.

Having completed the work at Yale, Professor Pickens first worked in his old school, Talladega College. Here for ten years he was Professor of Language. While in Talladega, he took a very special interest in the students. At all times he was willing and ready to see their side of any question and to see that they were given their rights. While teaching in Talladega, Fisk University, Nashville, Tennessee gave him the degree of Master of Arts, for a Latin thesis. After ten years of work at Talladega, Professor Pickens gave up the work there and accepted the position as Professor of Greek and Sociology in Wiley University, Marshall, Texas, 1914-15, and then the post of Dean of Morgan College, Baltimore, Md. This position he held till 1917, when the Trustees of Morgan made him Vice-President. Selma University honored him with the degree Lit. D., in 1915, and Wiley with L. L. D., in 1918.

Mr.. Pickens did not leap suddenly into fame as a speaker. From his earliest young manhood he led his mates in this particular line. While in the Sophomore year at Talladega, he began lecturing in the North. At this time he was only nineteen years of age. And so well were his hearers pleased with the words of wisdom uttered by one so young, that they requested the publication of these addresses.

Since this beginning as a public speaker, Mr. Pickens has made for himself a great name in this particular line. He appeared on the American Missionary Association program at Springfield, Massachusetts, in 1900, in the Court Square Theatre. At the same time Booker T. Washington, the great race leader, and Newell Dwight Hillis, famous New York preacher, were speakers. Many times since that day Mr. Pickens has appeared in similar meetings. He is in constant demand in both the North and the South for the lecture platform.

At the same time that he was making a name for himself in this line of speaking, he was making known his powers as a writer. He has written many articles for magizines and many phamplets. He has out now a book, "The New Negro." It is a book of merit and one that has met with ready appreciation.

That Mr. Pickens is no dreamer but can handle practical problems very well is evidenced by the manner in which he is serving his country during this war. He, with Mr. Spingarn are reputed to be the first to make a move for an officers' Training Camp for Negroes. At the time many were hostile to the idea, especially is this true of the attitude of the Negro press. But today we are proud of that camp and its results. Mr. Pickens has taken his time to busy himself with the different cantonments, visiting and speaking to the men. As a member of the Maryland Council of Defense, he is doing many sorts of war work.

Mr. Pickens was married in 1905, to Miss Minnie McAlpine of Meridian Mississippi. To them have been born three children, William, Jr., Harriet Ida, Ruby Annie. They are all pupils in school and are showing that they have inherited from their father some of his ability.

Mr. Pickens has traveled extensively. He has covered the greater part of this country and has traveled in Europe. He is a fine example of "The New Negro" himself.

WILLIAM STANLEY BRAITHWAITE.

N Boston, Massachusetts, in the year 1868, there was born a child who was destined to take a leading place as an authority on American Verse. This child was William Stanley Braithwaite. At the age of twelve years he had to leave school in order that he might help provide for his mother. This was due to the fact that he had lost his father. Up to the time he left school the lad had been a close student and had mastered all the tasks that were set for him. And even though he was out of school, young Braithwaite did not cease to study but continued to be thoughtful and to absorb all the culture that surrounded him.

Mr. Braithwaite says of himself: "At the age of fifteen like a revelation, there broke out in me a great passion for poetry, an intense love for literature, and a yearning for the ideal life which fosters the creation of things that come out of dreams and visions and symbols. I dedicated my future to literature, though the altar upon which I was to lay my sacrificial life seemed beyond all likelihood of opportunity and strength and equipment to reach. I set about it, however, with fortitude, hope and patience."

What the exercise of these three virtues brought about in the life of this young man may be readily seen from the results that he has been able to achieve. In America and abroad as well he is recognized as the leading authority on American Poetry. This high place did not come to him because of his love for this work, but because of the time and effort he put into the study of the subject. For the past twelve years he has devoted most of his time to the study of American poetry. Each year he has published in the Boston Transcript a review of poetry for the year and each year he has published an Anthology of American Poems. In this work Mr. Braithwaite includes all of the poems written during the year that are, in his opinion worth while. In such high regard is the opinion of this man held that not to be in his book for the year, is not to be known as a poet. In fact in the opinion of literary folk in England Mr. Braithwaite is not only an authority on American Poetry, but The Authority on the subject.

Mr. Braithwaite stands to the colored boy and the colored girl as an example of the man who has gone to the top in spite of his color. So many hold that the best place is never given to a person of color. Mr. Braithwaite is a positive denial of this saying. In fact with him, and with a few others who have dared to go ahead, starts the saying— a man can be just what he wants to be in spite of his color.

The works of Braithwaite include "Lyrics of Life and Love," "The Book of Elizabethian Verse," "The House of Falling Leaves," "The Book of Georgian Verse," "The Book of Restoration Verse," and "The Book of Victorian Verse." The publishers for the works of Braithwaite say of his Poetic Year for 1916: "Here is a book that is actually 'Something new under the sun,' and furthermore, 'fills a long felt want.'" Any lover of poetry, any student of contemporary literature, who desires to form an intelligent estimate of recent poetry, or to make an acquaintance with any individual poet of our time sufficiently definite to give him the requisite knowledge for an intelligent discussion, will find the book indispensable.

"The method of the book is not the least of its virtues. A friendly discussion takes place among a group of four friends, including Mr. Braithwaite himself, who provides the guiding hand."

"By this lively treatment, so surprisingly different from the usual method of critical writing, the reader forms a personal impression, as human as it is well founded of the poetry" of all contemporary poets who are really deserving of that title.

William Stanley Braithwaite has made a place for himself at the top in his chosen work. He is held up here as an ideal along his line to all young persons of color. He is an example of what concentrated endeavor will do for a person of determination.

WILLIAM NELSON DeBERRY, D. D.

HEN Fisk University wishes to point to her useful and scholarly graduates, she usually comes very soon to the name of William N DeBerry. As it is with Fisk, so it is with the whole of Nashville. He is especially a source of pride to Nashville, not because she is lacking in conspicious men among her colored citizens, but because of the theory that the men living nearest institutions of learning frequently make the least use of them. This saying is far from true in the case of the subject of this sketch.

Mr. DeBerry was born in Nashville, Tennessee, August 29, 1870. He was fortunate enough to be able to attend school from early childhood. So we find him as a lad attending the public schools of his native city. Here he applied himself very diligently to the work in hand. Always he had before him the chance of attending the University which was open for him at his very door. So we find him while still a young man entering Fisk. Here he remained to complete the course of study and graduate. He finished with the class of 1896. While in Fisk University young DeBerry was always

ready to receive with an open mind the instruction of his teachers. Hence we have him as a shining example of the good scholars that are turned out by Fisk University.

Leaving Fisk, Mr. DeBerry matriculated at Oberlin College in Ohio. Here he was a student in the theological Department. From the full course of that department he was graduated in 1899. Mr. DeBerry is a Congregationalist in church affiliation. Leaving Oberlin he went to Springfield, Massachusetts to pastor the St. John's Congregational Church there. Here he has remained since that time, having had but the one charge in all these years. This is remarkable for a pastor of any denomination.

Working hard and steadily at his post, studying to keep abreast of the times, Dr. DeBerry is much in demand as a public speaker and lecturer and freely welcomed into many organizations for his usefulness. His has been a life spent in developing the younger people with whom he came in contact. He has endeavored to make them better men and women—better mentally, morally and spiritually.

The St. John's Congregational Church has what is perhaps the most modern and best equipped plant of all the colored churches in New England. The present edifice which was erected in 1911 is valued, together with its equipment, at $30,000. It is free from debt.

The Church is unique in its plan of organization and in the method of its varied activities. It seeks to adapt its work in all its phases to the religious and social needs of the people whom it serves. It is known throughout the country for the well organized and very efficient institutional work which it carries on. The institutional activities include a parish home for working girls, a night school of Domestic Science, a social center for women and girls, a club house for young men and boys, a free employment bureau and a department of family housing. The institutional staff includes six paid workers in addition to the pastor. The real estate and equipment of the institutional department are valued conservatively at $50,000 making the total valuation of the property owned by the church at about $80,000.

Among the many organizations which are proud to claim Dr. DeBerry a member are the American Missionary Association, and the American Board of Commissioners for Foreign Missions. Of both these organizations he is a life member.

In 1914 Fisk University elected him a member of her board of trustees. In this capacity he still serves the school that gave him his inspiration for his life of usefulness.

Recognizing the excellent work of this man, Lincoln University conferred upon him the degree of Doctor of Divinity, in 1915. In 1917 he was elected to honorary membership in the fraternity of Alpha Phi Alpha. In this way some of the honor due Dr. DeBerry is being received by him now.

Dr. DeBerry was married in 1899 to Miss Amanda McKissack, of Pulaski, Tennessee. Mrs. DeBerry is a graduate of Fisk University. Two children have been born to brighten and gladden the home of the DeBerry's. Charlotte Pearl and Anna Mae. They are both young misses in school.

DAVID EUGENE CRAWFORD.

ROM a date somewhere near the days of Plymouth Rock and the first Pilgrims, Boston, Massachusetts, has had its famous Negroes. Phillis Wheatley was the first famous Negro of Massachusetts, as she was the first woman poet of the state and the first, and perhaps the only Negro woman poet of the ages. Crispus Attucks and Peter Salem were the famous black men of the Revolutionary times, then came the Ruffins, the Trotters, but history becomes confused. She cannot distinguish between the real Bostonian and the man and woman who went to Boston to become famous, or who became famous because they went to Boston.

However, from Phillis Wheatley to this day Boston has never lacked for genuinely strong and useful colored people. Among the modern leaders of the practical, modest yet very powerful and useful type is numbered David Eugene Crawford.

Mr. Crawford was born in Lynchburg, Virginia, December 26th, 1869. He attended the public schools of Lynchburg, and then attended Hampton Institute. Getting the Hampton stamp upon him he went to Boston and began work. All along he has linked work and education; because he could not pursue his studies without working and he would not work without studying. When he was sixteen he began dealing in produce in the Virginia markets. In Boston, at the age of twenty, he became a caterer, pursuing his studies in the meantime in the Boston Y. M. C. A.. This business of caterer and student he followed until 1907 when he was admitted to the Bar to practice law. Thus he became after a struggle of a quarter of a century to realize his dream of a professional life.

But Mr. Crawford found entrance into the profession of law by no means marked his entrance into public life. It rather marked a public recognition of what he had done and been in Massachusetts for more than a score of years. He has been closely allied with the New England Suffrage League, with civic movements, with meetings and petitions for justice to the black man throughout the country. Indeed there has scarcely been a step taken among the colored people of Boston during these years but Mr. Crawford has been a conspicuous figure.

What the leading citizens of Massachusetts think of him is shown by the many prominent offices he holds and by the cooperation he has been able to gain in his undertakings. He is treasurer of the Ebenezer Baptist Church, of which he has for years been a member. He has been a Mason for twenty-five years. He is a thirty-third degree Mason and Past Master of the Eureka Lodge, a member of all masonic branches and Deputy of the Valley of Massachusetts. In 1915 the Governor of Massachusetts appointed him master in Chancery, and in 1916 the citizens of Boston elected him as a delegate to the National Republican Convention, which met at Chicago. The crowning mark of public confidence, however, came to Mr. Crawford, in 1910, when he opened the Eureka Co-Operative Bank, the only Negro Bank in the Bay State. That it has run successfully ever since in a city and in a state where banks are common and competition for money very sharp, is highly expressive of the public in Mr. Crawford.

Through studying and serving Mr. Crawford managed all along to accumulate property and to educate a growing family. He has traveled in the North, Middle West, and in some parts of the South and in Canada. His property holdings of apartments, stores and commercial properties are valued in all at $150,000.

Mr. Crawford was married to Miss Almira G. Lewis of Boston in 1894. Their four children are all making careers worthy of their father, who has set such a high standard of attainment. J. William Crawford, who is twenty-two years of age is a senior in the Boston University Law School; Miss Mildred L., age twenty-one, is a bookkeeper and stenographer, Miss Helen F is a sophomore in Radcliff College, and Miss M. Virginia is a senior in the Girl's High School of Boston.

ROLAND WILTSE HAYES.

OLAND W. Hayes, easily the leading tenor of the Colored Race was born June 5, 1887, at Curryville, Georgia. Here in Georgia he lived on the farm, working, attending school when it was in session, till he was fourteen years of age. His father died, leaving seven children, and Roland was among the older ones. On him therefore fell some of the responsibility. His mother moved, when he was fourteen, to Chattanooga, Tennessee. The problem of educating the children was a serious one. Mrs. Hayes finally hit upon the plan of letting the two older boys, Robert and Roland, take turns at attending school. One went to school one year, while the other worked to help in the support of the family and the next year this turned it about. In this manner Roland W. Hayes had a chance to attend school. He made the most of his opportunity during the four years they were thus taking their turns at school.

Arthur W. Calhoun, (Colored), a graduate of the Oberlin Conservatory of Music, heard young Hayes sing one day and persuaded him to take lessons and urged him to adopt singing as a profession. His first public appearance aroused enthusiastic comment and a sum of money was raised to permit the boy to continue his studies at the musical college. With this help and by his own labors he

spent four years in Fisk University. Here his voice was under the care of the Vocal teacher, Miss Jennie A. Robinson, head of the music department.

In the summer of 1910 Mr. Hayes went to Louisville, Kentucky, where he worked for eight months. His object in working in Louisville was to save money enough to go North for further training. Combining work and education, Mr. Hayes took a job as a waiter in Pendennis club. Some of the members learned that he could sing, through the head waiter, Mr. Henry T. Bain. Through them he had many opportunities to fill engagements as a singer. It was through this club that he met a theatrical manager, who hired him at five dollars a day for a month. At the conclusion of this engagement, through one of the members of the Pendennis club, in which he was a waiter, made arrangements for him to sing in Louisville at the National Fire Insurance Agent's Banquet. A few weeks after this engagement he was asked to sing in the missionary meeting "The World in Boston." Here he appeared with the Fisk Jubilee Singers, where the engagement lasted for six weeks.

In the Fall of 1911, Mr. Henry H. Putman, of Boston, arranged for Mr. Hayes to begin his musical training in Boston, under Maestro Arthur J. Hubbard, where he has continued his studies until the present. Under the teaching of the great Maestro Hubbard, for the last seven years, the naturally sweet voice of Mr. Hayes has been developed and strengthened until now, he as an artist, ranks among the best artists of the land. In November of 1917, he made his first appearance in the great Symphony Hall, of Boston.

He is the first Colored Artist to have a recital in this Hall. To quote from the Guardian we can see how Mr. Hayes was received.

"Doff the hat to Roland W. Hayes, the singer! He essayed the difficult and succeeded. He made the fight and won. In size of audience, in financial profit, in auditorium and in his own musical performance Hayes scored a triumph.

"The great Symphony Hall was packed, even the platform was filled with seats and persons stood thick along both hall aisles. It was a mixed audience with no segregation and thoroughly representative of both rates, as big an audience as world-famous white artists have there. No Colored Artist ever had a recital in Symphony Hall.

"In this respect and in the talent displayed by Mr. Hayes, as well as in the size and character of the audience the recital made musical history for Colored Bostonians. Mr. Hayes rendered a wide variety of songs. After Mr. Hayes' singing Thursday night, Colored Boston can claim to have the leading tenor of the day. His voice was full and robust with a long range. It was resonant and flexible.

Mr. Hayes has traveled over the United States as a Concert Artist. His time has been given wholly to the development of his voice and in earning means for that purpose. He is a member of the Baptist Church, of Boston, but has connected himself with no other organizations. His is the life of the true artist, one of continual application of self for continued artistic development, for the sake of art and for the inspiration of the members (musical), of his race.

ALEXANDER HUGHES.

ORN a slave in Richmond, Virginia January 17, 1857, growing to manhood without even the rudiments of an education, Alexander Hughes of Springfield, Massachusetts, has won his way into the hearts of his fellow townsmen, until he is one of the most respected and best loved men of his section of Massachusetts. The respect of his fellow citizens he gained through careful attention to his work and to his business relation, paying his debts and meeting obligations promptly, a thing that pleases a New Englander. Their affections he won through flowers; through growing flowers and giving away flowers. For three successive years he has won a prize offered by the Springfield Republican for the prettiest flowers in back and front yards. He even went further. He rented, or borrowed, vacant lots and planted flowers in these. Then, when the flowers grew, he would give them in handsome bouqets to the sick, to invalids, to the members of old people's homes.

Mr. Hughes was nine years old when his master returned from the war. The master gave Mr. Hughes' father five days to leave the plantation.

The father departed, but left Mr. Hughes with one brother and two sisters to aid the master. From nine to twelve Mr. Hughes tended cows and did chores about the plantation. From twelve to eighteen he worked in a tobacco factory of Richmond; from eighteen to twenty he drove a grocery wagon from twenty to twenty-four he carried brick and mortar. From twenty-four to twenty-seven, he drove a wholesale grocery wagon in Springfield. Then he cared for furnaces for two years, and was a janitor for two years. In October, 1888, he became shipping clerk for the Massachusetts Mutual Life Insurance Company.

Here he has remained, winning distinction in many directions. In 1889 he added night catering to his list, his patrons being of social exclusiveness; and won distinction and made money. He became a member of the Springfield Chamber of Commerce; of the St. John's Congregational Church, also deacon, church treasurer, Sunday School teacher and member of the Standing Committee, member of the Y. M. C. A., member of the Golden Chain Lodge of Odd Fellows; treasurer of the Household of Ruth; member of the Negro Civic League of the Springfield Improvement Association; of the Union Relief Association; of the Home Guards, a war defense organization. He is treasurer and trustee of the Mutual Housing Company, a company which keeps homes for colored people.

All these posts he fills with honor. Yet Mr. Hughes began life a slave and rose to maturity illiterate. Indeed his education in books is very limited. Back in 1881, when he was twenty-four years old, he attended for a while the Springfield Night Schools, where he learned some reading, writing and arithmetic.

Mr. Hughes has been twice married. In 1882 he was married to Miss Bettie A. White; she died in 1892. The second Mrs. Hughes was Miss Pauline Simms. Both came from Virginia, his native home.

Mr. Hughes' story has been a source of much inspiration even in Massachusetts. The following from New England Character, edited by Thomas Dreier, will show how highly Mr. Hughes is esteemed and how widely he is written of in the Old Bay State.

"Recently I wrote for a magazine a little squib, about Alexander Hughes of Springfield, Massachusetts. I told how this negro, born in slavery, has for two years won the prize offered by this city for the best-kept lawn and garden, how it is his habit to appropriate the vacant ground belonging to his neighbors and plant flowers on it, how he carries flowers to the hospitals to make brighter the days of those forced to lie in their beds—taking especial care to provide flowers for strangers and those who have no friends at hand, how he works all day in the shipping department of the Massachusetts Mutual, and at nights serves as a caterer where rich folks want service plus, how he stands as a leader in religious work among his people, and how each year he sends part of his salary to southern educational institutions. All these things and more I told, and what I wrote was reprinted with editorial backing in the Springfield "Republican.""

WILLIAM H. LEWIS, A. B., LL. B., LL. D.

N November 28, in Berkley, Virginia, William H. Lewis was born. Berkley is now a part of Norfolk. At an early age he went to Portsmouth, Virginia, where he was a student in the public schools of that city. Leaving the schools of Portsmouth he next entered the State Normal School at Petersburg. He next matriculated at Amherst, from whence he was graduated in 1892. Having decided upon the practice of law as a profession he then entered the Harvard Law School and was graduated in 1895. In 1918 Hon. Lewis once more received a degree. This time is was the degree of Doctor of Law and it came from Wilberforce University.

During his school days Mr. Lewis was noted for his foot ball. He was one of the best centers that they have ever had in Harvard. He was Captain of the foot ball team of Amherst and was also the Class Orator of his class. When he entered Harvard he once more had a place with the foot ball team. For two years he played on the team and then for ten years he served as the coach for the foot ball eleven. His knowledge of college men and his interest in them has extended over a greater period of years than is given most men in his profession.

Having finished law at the Harvard School of Law in 1895, Mr. Lewis was promptly admitted to the practice of law in Boston. Since that time many positions of honor have been filled by him. He was member of the City Council, Cambridge, Massachusetts, in 1899, 1900, 1901. He was member of Massachusetts Legislature, 1902. President Roosevelt appointed him Assistant United States District Attorney in 1903. He was made a member of the Public Library Trustees of the City of Cambridge. From 1908 to 1909 he was the Attorney in charge of Naturalization for the New England States. President Taft appointed him Assistant Attorney General of the United States in 1911.

Mr. Lewis has been fearless in standing for the rights of the colored people of the United States. He was invited to join the American Bar Association. Later he had an invitation to resign, but in his characteristic manner he refused to comply with the invitation. Mr. Lewis has had many honors from the government. He has done good for the entire race by the manner in which he has filled the various posts that have been given him.

In religious belief Mr. Lewis is a Congregationalist. He has traveled extensively through the United States and in 1912 he visited England and France. September 26, 1896, Mr. Lewis was married to Miss Elizabeth Baker of Cambridge, Massachusetts. Three children have been born to brighten this home. Miss Dorothy Lewis is a student of Wellesley. Here Miss Lewis gives a good account of herself among her fellows. Miss Elizabeth Lewis is a student at High School, Cambridge, Massachusetts, and Mr. William H. Lewis, Jr., is also a High School student. In the point of education the young people of this family bid fair to follow in the footsteps of their father.

Mr. Lewis has made a success of his life. In school besides being a good student he was a good orator and a first class athlete. Out in life he has carried the same idea of success in everything undertaken. The many duties that have been showered upon him have been filled to his credit. In his profession he is a good lawyer. If the case involves some things in the medical world, Mr. Lewis is not satisfied till he has mastered all the knowledge on the subject. If it is a matter of boundaries he studies equally as hard. To him the thing desired is a complete knowledge of all the things that touch the case even remotely. He has been quoted on some of his famous cases throughout the United States. Of course the fact that he was colored was not known. But the color of his skin could not change the facts that were gathered in his brain. Nothing short of perfect understanding of the matter in hand satisfied Mr. Lewis. Because of this he is one of our most prominent men.

HORACE G. McKERROW, M. D., C. M.

R. Horace G. Mackerrow, of Worcester, Massachusetts, invested many years in education, in attending various institutions of learning. He appears to have set over against each year and each institution, all itemized, some definite service to men and to the state. He was born in Halifax, Nova Scotia, October thirteenth, 1879. As a lad he attended the public schools of Halifax. From 1893 to 1897 he was a student in Halifax Academy. The next year 1898, he spent in the Teachers' Training Class of Dollwise College. From this institution he enrolled in the Montreal Business College. Still forging to the front he taught school in Halifax for two years. Finding this none too much to his liking he came to the "states." For a while he oscilated between the Montreal postal service and hotel work at Atlantic City. He spent some time also in Pullman service. Running on the Grand Trunk Rail Road in dining car service.

By this time he had fully made up his mind as to the career he wished to follow. In October 1900 he enrolled in the Leonard Medical College at Shaw University, Raleigh, North Carolina. Completing his medical course in 1904, he entered Bishop's University. Here he was graduated with the degree of M. D. C. M. in 1905. Returing to Canada, he was for six months resident house surgeon for the Wo-

man's Hospital. In September, 1905, he took the medical examination in Massachusetts. Passing, he opened office in Worcester of the same year.

It is in Worcester that he has translated all his former experiences, all his years of study into useful action. Here he is a member of the John Street Baptist Church, and superintendent of the Sunday School. He is Past Master of Masonic Lodge of King David. He is a member of the St. John Chapter of R. A. M. and Zion Commandery, K. T. C. P., of the Holy Shepherds Consistory, Lizra Temple A. E. O. N. M. S., and Past Examiner of this body; he is Grand Commander of the Knight Templars of Rhode Island and Massachusetts; he is Past Grand Master of the Council of the Odd Fellows, North Star Lodge, G. U. O. O. and P. N. F. To his activities in the various lodges, Dr. Mackerrow add many activities in civil and social life. He is a member of the Executive Board of the Citizens League of Worcester, of the Massachusetts State Guards, 19th regiment of Worcester, of the Worcester Military Training School, of the Pistol and Rife Club, of Worcester, of the Anglo-Saxon Club, of Worcester, of the Gun and Rod Club of Cambridge and Boston. Not forgetting his profession Dr. Mackerrow has allied himself to all medical associations of his section of the country. He is a member of the Worcester District Medical Association, of the Massachusetts Medical Association, of the American Medical Association and of the National Association of Physicians, Doctors and Pharmacists. He has traveled extensively in the United States and Canada.

Dr. Mackerrow comes from a substantial line of Europeans. His father was a Canadian fur dealer, having dealt in furs for forty three years. The paternal grandfather was a Scotchman, coming from Aberdeen, Scotland. The maternal grandfather was of Welch origin. Both ancestors had landed in Canada and had made themselves substantial and loyal subjects of their Government. Their offspring was true to their example; for Dr. Mackerrow not only set forth to make for himself a most enviable career, but even in his early years in Canada, he joined the battalion of the Halifax Academy and became before he left that institution a major in his company. In his early years as well as later Dr. Mackerrow has also shown himself a substantial citizen, by owning and paying taxes on property, both in his native country and in his adopted land. He is a property owner in his native city, Halifax, in the state of New York, and in Worcester. More than this, by his conversation with his patients as he goes about, he has encouraged many to buy property, to pay taxes, to clean up to join with all the forces of civic improvement in making Worcester one of the best cities in the land for colored people. To him, and this is often his text, thorough participation with all the myrid activities of the city and of the state is the very bone and fibre of citizenship. This explains his almost countless membership in lodges, in civic clubs, in recreation clubs and in various military organizations.

Dr. Mackerrow was married in 1916, to Miss Effie S. Wolf of Allston, Massachusetts. Mrs. Mackerrow is the daughter of the famous James H. Wolf G. A. R. Commander. Mr. and Mrs. Mackerrow are parents of one child, a son, Horace Gilford Mackerrow, Jr., who is now two years old.

GEORGE BUNDY, M. D.

R. George Bundy, M. D. was born May 4th, 1868, at Mt. Pleasant, Jefferson County, Ohio. Like so many people, born in Ohio, he made his way to Michigan to work, but this was not done until after he had spent a number of years in the schools and colleges of his native State. He spent the usual years in the common schools and then went to Wilberforce University, to Wittenberg College, Springfield, Ohio and to Payne Divinity School, Petersburg, Virginia, and later to Detroit College of Medicine and Surgery.

When but fifteen years of age, Dr. Bundy had his first lesson in the Medical science under a noted, wealthy, white physician in Ohio. Under this kind of physician, Dr. J. E. Finley, he got a taste of the healing art that he could never quite get out of his system. So we find Dr. Bundy at the age of forty-four, graduating from the full medical course in the Detroit College of Medicine and Surgery. He graduated with honors in a class of fifty and he had the distinction of being the only colored man in his class. Since graduating from the medical college, he has enjoyed a very lucrative practice in the city of Detroit.

During the years, between college days and the taking up of medicine, Dr. Bundy spent in church work. He was first ordained for the ministry in the A. M. E. Church. He afterwards studied for the Priesthood of the Protestant Episcopal Church. He was made priest in St. Paul's Cathedral, Cincinnati, Ohio, in 1900. He was recommended by the Episcopal Church for chaplaincy in the United States Army, and was received by President Roosevelt at Washington concerning the appointment. He was offered the Arch deaconry of Colored Work in Diocease of Lexington, Kentucky, but the study of medicine that he had done when a lad could never be really forgotten, and so although rather late for one to change professions, Dr. Bundy entered the medical college, and gave up the ministry.

In the residence district of Detroit, Dr. Bundy has a home worth $5,500.00 this as a showing for the savings during the years of his practice of medicine. Presiding over this beautiful home is Mrs. Bundy, who was Miss Evelyn Tardif, of Columbia, South Carolina. They were married April 26th, 1905, in Springfield, Ohio. Mrs. Bundy has been to Dr. Bundy a great help in carrying out his ambition to become a physician. In it all and through it all, she has been an inspiration. Now she helps make life pleasant for their many friends at their home.

It is difficult to estimate the value of a good wife who enters sympathetically and actively into the plans of her husband and helps him bear the burdens when heavy and rejoice with him when success crowns his efforts.

Dr. Bundy has, along with all other whole hearted Americans, done his part in helping win this world war. Besides contributing freely of his means in the cause of the various charities, the Red Cross, Y. M. C. A., and other relief funds, he served for six months on the Draft Board for the United States Army.

Dr. Bundy has become a part of the community life there in Detroit. He is still active in the church of his profession and through the church he is able to reach many. He is a member of the Paul Lawrence Dunbar Memorial and Scholarship Fund, as he was a personal friend of Mr. Dunbar. Through this organization he has helped not only in honoring the most noted of our Negro poets, but in aiding many students.

Dr. Bundy should be a source of inspiration to the many men who are now engaged in work that is not altogether to their liking. Reading of his success when he had the courage to give up a work in which he had made good, but which could never have his whole heart, one should take courage and try, even if late in life, for the one thing that is his heart's ambition.

KENTUCKY PYTHIAN TEMPLE BUILDING—LOUIS-
VILLE, KENTUCKY—AND THE MEN LARGELY
RESPONSIBLE FOR ITS ERECTION.

Kentucky Pythian Temple

THE Kentucky Pythian Temple is the outgrowth and an outward expression of a deep seated idea which had taken a strong hold of the Pythians of Kentucky and which was born of the conviction that fraternal organizations could and should make wider use of their strength and authority. Once the idea had been presented to the Pythian Grand lodge, jurisdiction of Kentucky, it would not down but session after session it was kept to the front until the idea took concrete form. A number of prominent knights championed it and fought for it until the temple was built. Sir Knight, J. L. V. Washington raised his voice in its behalf and Sir Knight, J. H. Garvin, at Mt. Sterling, fanned the coals into a blazing fire by a beautiful, eloquent and practical speech which he delivered. The movement took form in the appointment of a commission whose duty was to formulate and submit a plan for securing the building. It was styled the "Kentucky Pythian Temple Commission. Sir Knight, H. Francis Jones, was made President of the commission. He was a man of fine parts, of propelling energy and unselfishly devoted to the task assigned him. Under the leadership of Sir Knight Jones, the commission set to work and after a season of patient toil they worked out a plan which made their dream of a temple a living led the "Kentucky Pythian Temple Commission." was presented to the Grand Lodge at its meeting at Winchester. It so happened that the Supreme Chancellor, Sir Knight S. W. Starks, visited the Kentucky jurisdiction at this session of the Grand Lodge and was present when the plan was submitted. He was first impressed with the enthusiasm with which the plan was received, but after a careful consideration of it he caught the fever himself, and returned to his home in Charleston. West Virginia, a strong convert to the plan and fired by the Kentucky spirit. He procured a copy of the plans and immediately started a similar movement in his home jurisdiction and within a year had organized his forces and erected the first Pythian Temple of the colored race. The temple idea carried with it not accommodations for the lodge alone, but suitable quarters for the colored men to carry on their business enterprises. Fraternity is the spirit of the order and its policy is to encourage the negro to make the best of his talents and opportunities and in the erection of their temple this idea was kept in mind. So much for the spirit which gave vision to the enterprise and inspired the erection of the temple. Now for a description of it:

It is a beautiful seven-story structure, built of reinforced concrete and brick crowned with a roof garden. It is situated in the heart of a Negro settlement—the gateway of the Metropolis of the South. The building contains five business rooms; a theatre, operated by a colored man; twelve offices; fifty-two sleeping apartments, and a commodious amusement hall, 40x97 feet—which cares for the needs of a pleasure-seeking public. Besides these it has a kitchen, dining room, pool room, barber shop, buffet and cabaret. It is lighted with electricity and is steam heated, has elevator service, and has bath arrangements for the use of tenants. The building cost approximately $150,000.00. This sketch could not be properly closed without mentioning a few of the men who have brought the enterprise to a successful issue.

Sir Knight Jones and Grand Chancellor Garvin and their assistants have been the moving spirits but they have been ably assisted by the following Knights: J. H. Garvin, J. L. V. Washington, W. W. Wilson, Rev. J. M. Mundy, B. E. Smith, S. H. George, M D., F. C. Dillon, W. H. Wright, Attorney, J. A. C. Lattimore, M. D. French Thompson, Directors and Van J. Davis, M. D., G. G. Young, T. T. Wendell, M. D., Owen Robinson, Dr. E. E. Underwood, M. D., William and John B. Caulder, Grand Lodge Officers.

The vision inspired these men and held them to their task was not, as has been stated, simply a Pythian Temple, although that in itself was a strong incentive, but a wider outlook which took in the interests of their race in all departments of their life. In addition to the accommodations provided for the business enterprises of their people and for their social pleasures, they kept in mind possibilities not yet developed. Among the things they hope for at an early date is a Negro bank, to stimulate their people to lives of thrift and to encourage them to buy their homes. Another, being the establishment of a Negro newspaper, whose aim and purpose will be to influence their people to higher ideals of living and to inform the world of the progress being made by the Negro race. When this portion of their dream is realized the mission of the Pythian Temple will very nearly have filled its place.

Thus a building has been erected in which the Colored Pythians take a commendable pride, and which forms a center of influence for the colored race which will work for their good for many years to come.

ALBERT H. JOHNSON, M. D.

LBERT H. Johnson, is a Canadian by birth. He was born in Windsor, Ontario, June 23, 1870. His early schooling was had in the public school system of Canada. After leaving Canada, the young man attended school in Detroit, Michigan. From the Detroit High School he was graduated in 1889. From the Detroit High School he entered the Detroit College of medicine and surgery, and was graduated with the degree of M. D. in 1893.

This recital of the school training gotten by Dr. Johnson seems simple enough, and so it is for the young man with ample means for support. But this was not the fact in the case of Dr. Johnson. In order to get his education he had to work his way. He started his career as a newsboy. In this he had the usual life of the newsboy. He learned to give and take, he learned human nature as only a newsboy or one in a similar line can learn it. From newsboy he next became a news agent. In this occupation he continued throughout his High School career. Dr. Johnson made the sale of news items purchase for him, in a large measure his life work.

After receiving his M. D. from the Detroit College of Medicine and Surgery Dr. Johnson hung out his shingle in the City of Detroit. At first he took up the general practice of medicine; but in 1909 he was appointed Medical Inspector for schools. This caused the interest of Dr. Johnson to center on children and their ailments. For the past ten years he has given most of his time to the study and practice of this branch of his work. This is a field that is wide and is not as yet overcrowded. In this line Dr. Johnson has made a marked success.

The subject of this sketch is also a member of the firm of W. E. & A. H. Johnson, Pharmacists. This firm is doing a very good retail drug business. They own the building in which the business is housed and get a good trade. To this business venture as to his practice, Dr. Johnson has applied himself and made good. The wealth of experience that falls to the lot of the physician doing a good practice is enjoyed by the subject of this sketch.

Dr. Johnson has taken a part in the life of the city of his choice. He is a member of the St. Matthews Protestant Episcopal Church. Of this Church he is vestryman and Senior Warden. He is a member of the Grand United Order of Odd Fellows and of the Masonic Order. Dr. Johnson also serves as trustee and physician to the Phillis Wheatley Home for Aged Women of Detroit, Michigan. The positions held by him show the breadth of the interest of Dr. Johnson. He is very active in the National Association for the Advancement of Colored People. Of this organization he is the treasurer of the Detroit Branch. He is a member of the Executive Committee of the Detroit League on Urban Conditions among Negroes. Dr. Johnson also has the honor of having served as the first president of the Allied Medical Association, an organization consisting of doctors, dentists, pharmacists of the city of Detroit.

During the years he has been out of school, Dr. Johnson has saved his money and invested it wisely. He owns besides half interest in the drug business and its business block mentioned earlier in this sketch, a six family apartment house and a two family apartment house. The home in which his own family lives is also his property.

For business and for pleasure Dr. Johnson has traveled extensively in the United States and in Canada. He was married to Miss Lucile Russell, of Oberlin, Ohio, September 26th, 1900. Dr. and Mrs. Johnson are the proud parents of one beautiful young daughter, Phyllis Mary Johnson. Little Miss Johnson is ten years of age and is devoting her time time to the duties and pleasures of childhood.

EDWARD WATSON   GABRIEL DAVIS

EDWARD Watson, was born July 31, 1890, in Detroit, Michigan. He was educated in the public schools of his native city. Mr. Watson's father died before he had an opportunity for college work and he had to leave school in order to help his mother with the business. At the time of his death his step-father was engaged in the undertaking business, which his mother decided to continue and undertook its management. This she found difficult to do without the aid of her son, but with his assistance the business was continued with great success. He managed the business jointly with his mother until he reached the age of twenty-four, when he took sole charge of it and ran it successfully for one year. At the end of that period, Mr. Watson joined Mr. Gabriel Davis, as a partner in the undertaking business. The firm is known as Davis and Watson. Together they have done a prosperous business and have very good prospects for the future.

Mr. Watson is an active member of the St. Matthews Episcopal Church. For seven years he served as Altar and Cross Bearer. He is a member of the Masonic Hiram, Lodge No. 1. He has been a member of the lodge for eight years.

Mr. Watson is not married and has only twenty-eight years behind him. For one so young he is doing an enviable business.

Gabriel Davis was born in Uniontown, Kentucky, May 22, 1872. He lived on a farm till thirteen years of age when his parents moved to Detroit, Michigan. He worked for his father till 1887, and then he entered the employ of the Detroit Street Railway. He worked with this company till 1897, and then took up the duties of motorman, till 1912.

It was in the year 1912, that Mr. Davis decided to start in business for himself. He chose for this the Undertaking Business and has remained true to the business of his choice. From the time he established his business he has made it earn for him a good living. By combining with the Undertaking business of Edward Watson a joint interest of decided proportions and lucrative nature was established. He owns his place of business and three other pieces of property.

In religious belief, Mr. Davis is a Baptist. He is liberal when it comes to the support of his denomination and he also gives freely of his time in the interest of the work of the church. He is a member of the Masonic Lodge, and the Elks. Mr. Davis has lived in Kentucky, the State of his birth, in Ontario, the State in which he got his education, and in Michigan, the State in which he has become a successful business man.

It is his success in business that earns for Mr. Davis mention in these pages. In education he was able to go only through the Grammar school. But he is one of the many who demonstrate the fact that business ability is not dependent wholly on education, in the regular school courses.

WILLIAM PAUL KEMP

 ATE in life some men find their talent, some in middle age, and a few glide into their life work, almost unconsciously, in their youth. Thus its was with William Paul Kemp. He was a born editor, and he commenced his career as a writer at the early age of seventeen years.

Mr. Kemp was born in Plattsmouth, Nebraska, March 13th., 1881, but moved to Lincoln, Nebraska when a child and there received his early educational training. He attended the Public schools of Lincoln, and for two years studied in the High school. He also attended the University of Nebraska School of Music, and the night school of the Young Men's Christian Association.

At the age of seventeen, he left school to take a position on Omaha Bee (White) as assistant Capital correspondent. This was in 1898. From the money saved during his connection with this paper he purchased and established, April 29th, 1899, The Lincoln Leader. He gave up this enterprise for a time to become assistant correspondent for the Nebraska State Journal (White) at Washington, D. C., but returned to Lincoln the latter part of 1900, where he resumed the publication of the Lincoln Leader. While engaged in this work he became active in politics, affiliating with the Republican party. For six campaigns he was connected with the Nebraska Republican State Central Committee, rising from messenger to manager of the Literature Department.

October 8th., 1907, he moved to Detroit, Michigan, and December 7th, of the same year, he started the Detroit Leader. It had a short life and passed out February 13th., 1908. He entered the Mayor's office as clerk after the failure of his paper, and while still holding his position as clerk, he started in January, 1909, the present Detroit Leader. November 1st., 1909, he resigned his position in the Mayor's office and devoted his entire time to his business venture.

He purchased the Owl Printing Co. plant August 13th., 1912, which he consolidated with the Howitt Printing Co., September 26th, 1913, conducting all under the name of The Detroit Leader, of which he is the sole owner.

In addition to his literary attainments Mr. Kemp is an accomplished musician and vocalist, he is also an athlete. For the season of 1902 he coached the Lincoln Business College Football team. He is a member of St. Mathew's Episcopal church, Detroit, and five times has been a delegate to the Diocesan Convention. He is Past Master in Masonic Lodge and Ex-Officer of Masonic Grand Lodge, which position he held from 1905 to 1907; Past Grand Master Council of G. U. O. O. F., Grand Director of Michigan D. G. L., Delegate to 1918 B. M. C; Elk; Deputy Supreme Chancellor of Knights of Pythias of Michigan and Western Canada 1917-1918; Major in Uniform Rank Knights of Pythias At the age of nineteen years he was President of Abraham Lincoln Political Club. He was First Vice-President of the Republican League Clubs (White) of Nebraska; only Colored member of Delegation from Michigan to First Good Road Convention of United States. He was a Director of Kemp Military Band of Lincoln Nebraska, and Palestine Commandry Band, of Windsor, Ontario. He polled the largest vote of any colored man ever received in Detroit, when a candidate for Board of Estimators. He was President of the District Business League; President Soldier's Welfare League of Detroit; Chairman of Publicity, N. A. A. C. P., of Detroit; First Chairman of Detroit Urban League; Chairman of Negro Committee to cooperate with National League of Women's service. These are but a few of the honors conferred upon him. To mention all would make this sketch too lengthy for the space alloted to it.

Mr. Kemp was married December 24th, 1900, to Miss Mary Della Elder. They have no children.

REVEREND AUGER AUGUSTUS COSEY

EV. A. A. Cosey, born in Newellton County, Louisiana, July 2nd, 1874 has spent a long and useful career as pastor on the one hand and as builder and promoter on the other. His early days were spent on the farm engaged in performing such tasks as one of his age was capable of performing and attending school, when such was possible.

When he was sixteen years of age, Rev. Cosey leaving both the farm and his native state, enrolled in Natchez College, Natchez, Mississippi. Following the example of the vast majority who sought education in the nineties Rev. Cosey, as the phrase goes, had to work his way. Happily he had so well mastered his subjects that he could teach. Thus he spent his summer vacations in the school room earning money to return to his college. Finishing the Natchez College Academic course in 1896 he again went out to teach, teaching for six years in the State of Mississippi before engaging exclusively in his chosen profession. While attending Natchez College, Rev. Cosey devoted much time to the study of Theology, having decided long before to enter the Baptist ministry. In 1896, the year of his graduation, he was ordained and united his

work as school teacher and minister. One year after ordination, he was chosen pastor of the Metropolitan Baptist Church, Clarksdale, Mississippi, a post he filled until 1905. He held pastorates also at Greenville and at Shelby. For the last ten years, Rev. Cosey has been pastor of the Green Grove Baptist Church, at Mound Bayou, the famous Negro town, where he has not only been performing duties as pastor, but has been lending a hand in many ways to the growth and development of the town.

From the beginnig of his career Rev. Cosey proved to be an organizer and a builder as well as a pastor. He was really the organizer of the Metropolitan Church at Clarksdale, the Church in which he first preached as pastor. His pastorate of the First Baptist Church of Mound Bayou over which he still presides took on again the form of builder. This church he also started, giving it all the modern equipment, for Sunday School, social uplift and communty work. Twelve thousand dollars have already been put into this building, having four thousand more to be raised.

As a church man and as a man of affairs, Rev. Cosey has been a leader not only in Mound Bayou but in Mississippi for many years. He has been Corresponding Secretary of the General Misionary Baptist Convention of the state, has been for many years one of the leaders of the National Baptist Convention and served for a number of years as the Corresponding Secretary of the National Baptist Association.

Powerful as well as useful in the church, Rev. Cosey is also a conspicuous leader in fraternal orders. He is a Mason, a Knight of Pythias and a Knight of Tabor. He is International Chief Grand Orator of the Knights of Tabor and special enlistment Master for Mississippi.

When the people of Mound Bayou organized a bank, he became vice-president and stock holder. He took an active part in organizing and promoting the Mound Bayou Oil Mill Enterprise and lent his influence to the establishment of schools and small businesses throughout the town.

He owns a splendid two-story residence in Mound Bayou and seven rent houses, six lots and forty acres of delta farm land.

Rev. Cosey was married in 1901 to Miss Ida Hope Carter, of Helena, Arkansas. Mrs. Cosey is a graduate of A. & M. College, Normal, Ala. She was for years a teacher both in Alabama and in Arkansas. Throughout Rev. Cosey's work, she has been the power behind the throne. Both in company with Mrs. Cosey and on behalf of his church and fraternities, Rev. Cosey has traveled over the whole of the United States.

CHARLES PRICE JONES, D. D.

ORN in Rome, Georgia, educated in the public schools of his native state and in Arkansas Baptist College, Dr. Charles Price Jones is celebrated as a writer of hymns and as a founder of a religion. But he disclaims the latter title. He claims only to give emphasis to an old neglected doctrine. He was converted in 1884, and baptized in 1885 by Rev. J. D. Petty. Two years later he was licensed to preach, and in 1888 was ordained by Rev. Chas. L. Fisher However, he felt that a higher literary training was essential to one who has visions of a useful career in the church. It was with this in view that he entered Arkansas Baptist College, and was graduated from the academic Department in 1891.

Dr. Jones began to ponder more deeply the words of the scripture. To him all things seemed possible in Christ. He began to take the Bible literally. Hence arose his belief in holiness. He says, "I pastored in Arkansas until 1892. During this time I was corresponding secretary of the convention, a trustee of the Arkansas Baptist College and editor of the Baptist Vanguard.

In 1892 I accepted a call from Bethlehem Church,

Searcy, Arkansas, where I had pastored 18 months, to the Tabernacle Baptist Church, Selma, Alabama. Here I was called after a time, to the life and ministry of holiness, but had no idea that it would result in a disruption with the Baptists; for I believed that the more faithful a man was to Christ in his daily living the more he would and ought to be prized by the people of God. But I was mistaken. Yet I, myself was partly to blame. Like all who get an important vision, I was extreme in my views and endeavors. I understood it to mean, the standing of every believer in Christ in the presence of God. 2nd, the condition of heart that the Holy Ghost imparts to make us delight in God's will, the daily effort of the believer's faith to conform to that will; the inevitable result of living in Christ by faith. Indeed, I merely conceived it to be a trust in God that obtained grace to walk before Him in all pleasing, trusting the blood of Christ to deal with the sin of our nature. I do not teach the impossibility of our sinning, but the necessity of having grace to live Godly, that "the wages of sin is death,"—(Romans).

"In February, 1895, I accepted a call to Mount Helm Baptist Church, Jackson, Miss. In 1897 I called the first Holiness Convention to meet at Jackson, June 6th and study the Bible two weeks. There were present at this convention such men as Dr. J. A. Jeter of Little Rock, Arkansas, Pastor W. S. Pleasant, of Hazelhurst, Miss., and many others.

"In 1898 the convention was more largely attended and the opposition had gathered power; and in 1898 at the convention at Winona steps were taken to fight our extreme attitude, then we built the present commodious building. We have a school at Jackson incorporated as Christ's Missionary and Industrial College. Through the efforts of Elders W. S. Pleasant, J. A. Jeter, L. W. Lee, Thomas Sanders, F. S. Sheriff, G. H. Funches, Deacon Henry Moore, Clarke Kendricks and others, this work was established. It has carried in prosperous years 200 students and 12 instructors. It has turned a number of graduates from the 12th grade who are making good. The value of the property (encumbered) is $15,000."

He was for twenty-one years editor of the "Truth." He is author of several hymn books, which are used widely by ministers and members of both races. In 1915 Arkansas Baptist College conferred upon him the degree of Doctor of Divinity. However, in his own words, "I attended strictly to my own business, no time for worldly honors."

He was married in 1892 to Miss Fannie A. Brown of Little Rock, Arkansas. Mrs. Jones died in 1916. Their one child is also deceased.

He is now pastor of Christ Tabernacle, a new church at Los Angeles, Calif., and is General Overseer of the Holiness work. Jan. 4, 1918, he was married to Miss Pearl Reed of that city.

The school at Jackson is now under the Presidency of Dr. J. L. Conic.

EPHRIAM H. McKISSACK, A. B., A. M.

OR many years Ephriam H. Mc-
Kissack has been a leader in the
state of Mississippi. This leadership has radiated in many directions. It first asserted itself in his
work as a school man. Well edu-
cated and possessing an easy adaptation he soon
became a leader in business, in politics, in church
and secret orders.

Professor McKissack was born in Memphis, Tennessee, November 22, 1860. His parents were
William and Katie Mitchell, both of whom died
when he was four years old. The young lad was
adopted and reared by his aunt, Fannie McKissack,
from whom he took his name.

As an adopted son he fared well in the home of
his aunt. He had ample care, was provided generously with clothing, books, indeed everything to
encourage him to achieve. To all this he readily
responded. After attending the public schools he
entered Rust University. From this institution he
gained the degrees of Bachelor of Arts and Master
of Arts; the former in 1895, the latter in 1898.

Long before he completed his course Professor
McKissack had become active in the affairs of his

state. He had joined the Methodist Church and
had become one of its leading directors and workers. He was a trustee, a steward and a Sunday
School teacher in Asbury Church; was a member
of the upper Mississippi Conference and president
of the Conference Board of Church Extensions. In
1896 he was a member of the Church General Conference, then again in 1900-1904, 1908-1912-1916.
He served one year, the year following his attainment of Master of Arts, as principal of the
Holly Springs City Schools. Then his alma mater
called him to a chair within her walls. From 1890
to 1911 he was a member of the Rust University
faculty. In 1911 he resigned his post in Rust and
became manager of the Union Guaranty and Insurance Company of Holly Springs.

His departure from the schoolroom did not sever
his connections with the school, it did signal however, a wider activity in his business and in other
practical matters. He entered politics and became
an active and aggressive Republican; so effective
was his work that he was made chairman of the
seventh Congressional District of his State, and in
1908-1912, he was made delegate to the Republican
National Convention. For twenty years Professor
McKissack has been secretary and treasurer of the
Odd Fellows Benefit Association. He has so carefully handled his accounts and adjusted claims, that
little friction has ever arisen, a thing rare indeed
in any sort of benefit or insurance organization.

Prominent in the Odd Fellows Association he is a
conspicuous worker in practically all Negro lodges
in the state of Mississippi, a state thoroughly in-
fested with secret orders. He is a Mason, a Knight
of Pythias, a member of the United Sons and
Daughters of Jacob, of the Eastern Star, of the Im-
maculates, of the Reformers. He is still, as in former days, a pillar in the church and in the school. He
keeps up his connection with conferences and with
the Sunday School and has added to those his membership in the Federated Commission of Colored
Churches. Although he has long since left the
school room he still keeps in close touch with the
schools of the State, with the schools in the city,
and of course with every twist and turn of the af-
Rust University. In Rust he has reached a most
honored post, he has not only been elected a mem-
be of the Board of Trustees, he is vice-president of
the Board of Trustees. Professor McKissack has
done what to some seems the incredible thing. He
has the refusal of the presidency of the institution.
He had served Rust as head of the Commercial department, as professor of mathematics, professor
of natural science and as secretary of the faculty.
when, therefore, Rust needed a president in 1909,
the office was tendered Professor McKissack but
he declined, preferring business and a more general
public career.

Professor McKissack was married to Miss Mary
A. Exum of Yazoo City. Mr. and Mrs. McKissack
have one son, Dr. Autrey C. McKissack, M. D. who
is a successful physician of Memphis, Tennessee.
Professor and Mrs. McKissack live in their own
home in Holly Springs, a residence second to but
few in the town.

WILLIAM CLAUD GORDON

OMETIME ago, a business census of St. Louis, Missouri, revealed the fact that Mr. W. C. Gordon, a colored undertaker of that city, had handled the largest number of bodies of any undertaker, regardless of color, in the city of St. Louis. For this remarkable fact, those who knew him well accounted in several ways; first, they say that he is a good man, and they give great stress to this first point; then they say he is fair in his business dealings, especially in his dealings with the widows and orphans; and the third point on which they lay stress in that his equipment and his headquarters are such as to make any customer proud to employ his services.

Risen from poverty to that envious stage of competence, if not wealth, Mr. Gordon has kept an open hand for aspiring young men and women, and has maintained a ready sheckle for church, orphanage, school—indeed he has been ready and willing to help all worthy undertakings for the advancement of the colored people.

Unlike many who have climbed successfully, he did not kick the ladder down, once he gained the ascent but remembering his own early struggles he has been always ready to help another over the first rough stretch. Mr. Gordon was born in Columbia, Tennessee, March 15, 1862. From this date, we can gather that Mr. Gordon as a very small lad saw a little of the last bitter days of slavery and all of the struggles for freedom and readjustment. There is therefore nothing surprising in the fact that the young man had no opportunity to develop his mind in the school room. While still a young man, Mr. Gordon went to St. Louis. Here he found himself in a very unfortunate position—he was without means, without education and without friends. To earn a living for himself he first entered the employ of the Pullman service, where for several years he served as a porter. But Mr. Gordon was an ambitions man, and so was not satisfied with being a porter for life. When he had saved a small sum of money, he quit the service and went into the undertaking business for himself. His first business was on a very small scale, and as a venture it was feeble, very feeble. But putting all his mind and thought on his work, it began to develop and Mr. Gordon himself, was among those who was surprised at the very great rapidity of the growth of the venture. From his very feeble beginning his business has developed until today his is among the best equipped and largest firms of Negro undertakers. Indeed west of the Mississippi, he is one of the leading men in the undertaking business, regardless of race. He gives regular employment to eight persons.

His natural habit of saving did not leave him, when he began to make money in larger sums, and so after a time, Mr. Gordon had enough money saved to invest in some other line of work. Casting about for a profitable investment for this surplus, and investment which would be yielded fair interest and at the same time give employment to a large number of colored people Mr. Gordon opened a steam laundry. This he has been running for the last seven years. The laundry is equipped with all modern appliances, washers, mangles, driers, and the like. In St. Louis it is well known and is liberally patronized for its prompt and efficient work. In the operation of this laundry with its great number of patrons, Mr. Gordon employs thirty-five persons. This entails a payroll of $335.00 per week.

A conservative valuation of the two businesses is placed at $30,000.00. Besides this, Mr. Gordon owns his home, much real estate and has interest in motor hacks and vehicles. In all Mr. Gordon is worth about $70,000.00 Mr. Gordon is a member of the National Negro Business Men's League, an organization in which he has taken a great deal of interest. In his religious belief he is African Methodist Episcopal. He is an active member of the St. Paul Church, of St. Louis.

In 1908, Mr. Gordon was married to Miss Mary Hunton, of Detroit, Michigan. Two little children have come to help make the home of the Gordon's a happy one. They are Charity, age six years, and Claud, age eight. The two little pupils are in the public school of St. Louis.

JOHN EDWARD PERRY, M. D.

R. J. Edward Perry, of Kansas City, Missouri, born in Clarksville, Texas, Red River- County, April 2nd, 1870. His parents were ex-slaves and refugeed from Missouri and Arkansas. They were remarkable characters, noted for their integrity, industry, courtesy, generosity and honesty. Their ambition was to provide a home for their children and educate them. Johnny had no opportunity to go to school until he was nine years of age. He was then sent to a log cabin, which was on a small plot of ground given by his father.

His early days were spent in the cotton fields of Texas, going to school about three months in a year until he was over thirteen years of age. When he entered Bishop College he earned a greater portion of his expenses by doing daily services for the teachers of the schools. This service consisted of duties such as—milking the cows, scrubbing floors, cutting wood, and building fires. He then taught a country school from 1891 until 1894, making and saving sufficient funds to graduate from Meharry Medical College, in 1895, and began his practice February 15, 1895, and made a competency from the first week of his practice. This was begun in Mexico, Missouri, where he remained six months, then moved to Columbia, Missouri where the great University of the State of Missouri is located. Giving up practice in 1898, he served his Country as 1st Lieutenant in 7th. U. S. Vol. Infantry. After the close of the war he returned to Columbia, resuming his practice.

By his suave nature, genial disposition and effective work, he pushed his way into the State Hospital at Columbia, Missouri, where he enjoyed the professional association of the best talent that money of this State would employ. There is as much prejudice in Missouri, as in any other Southern State, and when those in authority were brought to task about the consideration given Dr. Perry they denied the fact that he was a Negro though he is extremely dark and no one would ever think of calling him even a mulatto.

He has spent considerable time working for professional uplift, built a private Hospital in 1910, loaned the hospital to the community three years later, and through that medium created sentiment sufficient to raise quite an ample sum for the erection of an Institution for the people. He has worked in the Y. M. C. A., was its first president of this city and he works in every avenue for racial uplift. He has been interested in a number of business enterprises, always trying to provide a place for young men and women. He is Secretary and Treasurer of the S. P. L. Mercantile and Investment Company, a firm growing out of the People's Drug Store, a very successful enterprise.

He married Miss Fredericka D. Sprague, July 3, 1912. Mrs. Perry is the granddaughter of Frederick Douglass.

Dr. Perry is considered the leading colored physician in Kansas City, both as a practititioneer and as a surgeon. In these later years he has given most of his time to surgery, both in connection with the General Hospital and his private Sanitarium. As evidence of his skill in surgery, he is frequently called to operate, as far south as Texas and to various points in Missouri, including St. Louis. He is regarded the leading Negro surgeon west of Chicago. After Dr. Perry had practiced a few years, he sought further preparation specializing in surgery by attending the Post Graduate Hospital of Chicago, Illinois.

As a physician, Dr. Perry is progressive. In all matters he is conservative and especially frank. He can be depended upon at all times to be fair in dealings with his patients, both in information and treatment and in his business dealings with them. The new hospital which has just been acquired by the colored people of Kansas City is largely the result of Dr. Perry's untiring labors and is indeed a fitting reward for his unselfish devotion to the people of Kansas City.

ANDERSON RUSSELL

R. Anderson Russell was born in Smith County, Mississippi, April 1st., 1864, and died in St. Louis Missouri, September 2nd., 1917, after spending a useful and successful life. His education was confined to the Rural Schools of his neighborhood, which were greatly inferior to such schools of the present day, which even now are far from being what they should be.

If the schools failed to give him a high standard of learning they still served him a good turn for his contact with books set his active mind to work and caused him to form the habit of thinking clearly.

When he was twenty years of age his parents left Mississippi, and moved to Alton, Illinois.

In his new home he entered the service of a number of private families. Here he labored until 1890, when he left Alton, and went to St. Louis, to enter the service of the Pullman Palace Car Co. His connection with this company continued for four years. At the end of this term he had saved sufficient funds from his wages to enter a business of his own.

He formed a co-partnership under the firm name of Russell and Gordon, and conducted an undertaking business. They remained together and did business under the original firm name until in 1902, when they separated and each opened a business of his own.

Mr. Russell's business continued to prosper and he soon was enabled to take from the business funds to purchase real estate. His investments were wisely chosen and became a source of revenue to him. He purchased the building in which his business was located and adjusted it to meet his wants. He also purchased a double flat and four rent houses.

Mr. Russell was a religious man, and took an active part in the work of the church. He was a member of the Union Memorial Church, which he joined in 1908.

At the time of his death he was serving as a member of the Board of Trustees of the church.

Mr. Russell's business brought him into intimate contact with the home life of many families and he soon formed the habit of thinking and planning for their betterment. He saw the value of many of the societies organized for their benefit and became actively identified with them. He might be termed a Society man for his name was on the roster of most of them.

He was a member of the Masons, Knights of Pythias, Odd Fellows, and United Brothers of Friendship.

His service in the Pullman Palace Car Company gave him the opportunity for travel and enabled him to visit all parts of the United States and parts of Mexico.

He met his life companion, Miss Priscilla Pringle, in St. Louis, where he was married to her June 28, 1906. Although their married life was without issue it was thoroughly congenial and happy.

Mr. Russell's health began to fail him in 1916, and he soon got too ill to give attention to his business. He grew weaker continuously and was never again able to look after his affairs. He lingered until September 2nd, 1917, when he passed into the other State.

The business which he had so carefully built up and to which he had given so much of his time and thought did not die with him. It was incorporated into a company, known as the "A. Russell Undertaking Company, Incorporated." His sister, Annie K. Russell, was elected President of the Company, and carries on the business along the same business principles employed by her brother, working out the plans outlined by him.

Under the new management the business still continues to prosper.

HOME OF A. RUSSELL UNDERTAKING CO.

CHARLES HYMEN TURPIN

HARLES Hymen Turpin, is a successful business man of St. Louis, Missouri. Mr. Turpin belongs to the class of men who do things. He is a man who will meet an opportunity squarely and use it advantageously. He has a natural ability, is industrious and persistent. He is practical and never enters a project without first weighing that keen competition which always besets every venture worth while. He is not the type of man who will shrink from the arrows of opposition, but is spurred on by them to the accomplishment of his aims. Once started, his resolute determination and indomitable courage, backed by explicit confidence in himself, usually carries him through all difficulties to the goal of his ambitions.

That these qualities are natural, is best illustrated by a few incidents in his boyhood life. At the age of ten, when he was a boot-black, he attempted to organize a union, in order to raise the price of "shines". Failing to interest the other boys, he aggressively declared the "Union" in effect with himself as the only member, and elected himself president, secretary and treasurer, raised the price of "shines" and proceeded to monopolize the industry to the detriment of his faint-hearted competitors. One day at the old St. Louis Fairgrounds, he noticed that the paddock was not being used. He immediately appointed himself, "Paddock manager", hired a few boys and earned $18.00 f himself that day. His first real salary was $1.00 per week as a house servant and since drawing his first week's pay he declares he has never been "broke."

Mr. Turpin was born in Columbus, Georgia and came to St. Louis, with his parents, when a small boy. He was educated in the public schools and holds two diplomas from business colleges. At the age of 21 he was appointed to a position in the Assessor's office and later in the office of Recorder of Deeds. At one time he accepted an appointment as clerk in the St. Louis Post Office, having been second on a list of 89 eligibles. His progressive ambition, however, would not permit him to remain long, being always haunted with the feeling the service meant, "Abandon hope all ye who enter here."

In the year 1910 Mr. Turpin was elected Constable of the Fourth District, by the Republican Party, St. Louis. His election was an agreeable surprise to even his dearest friends and when he took the office he had the distinction of being the only Negro ever elected to a State office in Missouri. He served a four year term with efficiency and credit, raised the dignity of the office, increased the revenue and was instrumental in establishing new rules more favorable to the poorer classes. Mixed juries, of white and colored, were also established during this time.

He was again re-nominated and re-elected in 1914, was counted out, and although, after a contest in which the ballot boxes were opened, the Supreme Court sustained the decision of the Circuit Court, that he was duly elected and was entitled to the office, that tribunal, failed to hand down the final mandamus that would permit him to take his seat. He has announced that he will be a candidate again in 1918.

Mr. Turpin is owner and manager of the Booker Washington Theatre, in St. Louis. This modern fire-proof vaudeville and picture house, with a seating capacity of a thousand, is the first in the country, to be built by a Negro and operated by and for Negroes. Mr. Turpin is also interested in the motion picture business. His "Salambo," now showing throughout the country, is one of the most magnificent spectacles ever filmed. He has also personally supervised the filming of many notable events of the race, the latest being complete reproduction of the Pythian Parade and Encampment in St. Louis, in Aug., 1917. Also he shows the colored drafted men at Camp Funston, Kan., part of the 92nd Division. This is the only moving picture of colored troops made up to this time since war has been declared between the U. S. and Germany. This industrious business man also finds time and is energetic in helping to stimulate and develop interest in race pride, co-operation and loyalty; and is always conspicuously identified with every movement for the advancement of colored people.

FORTUNE J. WEAVER

HE business instinct seems born in some men and it only needs a favorable opportunity to bring it into the light. The fire may burn low for a while, but the instinct will show itself when only a very small breeze of prosperity fans the embers into a flame. It was so with Fortune J. Weaver, the subject of this sketch. He was the son of Fortune and Millie Weaver, and was born in Council Grove, Morris County, Kansas, May the eighth, 1874. When a child only eight years of age his father died and left a widow and eight children. The burden of their support made it necessary to send Fortune to a neighboring farm to live. He found a home with Alfred and Emma Smith, who owned a small farm near Council Grove. This proved a great blessing to Fortune, for his foster parents treated him with every consideration and gave him every advantage of education that their means would admit. Speaking of his foster parents, he gives them the credit for his life inspiration and success in attaining his goal. He lived with his foster parents on the farm until he was seventeen years of age, when he went out in the world to hustle for himself. The common school education he had received while working on the farm and a determined spirit was his full equipment. This may appear to many a small asset with which to begin life but in the case of Mr. Weaver it proved an ample start. With it he went forth to work out his destiny, and with it he carved his way to success.

Kansas City, Missouri was the city of his choice, and to reach it he had to ride on a freight train. When he arrived in Kansas City it was with an empty pocket book, but nothing daunted he sought employment which partially supplied his needs. For two weeks he worked without a daily square meals, frequently feeling the pangs of hunger and consequently the lowering of his vitality for lack of sufficient and nourishing food. While it was hard at the time he now regards the experience as a blessing for it taught him the value of a dollar and inculcated the principle of economy, a principle which has stood him well throughout his business career. While it was hard at the time he now retbrougout his business career, causing him to save the dimes and accumulate a nice fortune.

Passing over the period of his development as a business man and the steps by which he has reached his present high position, it is only necessary to point out the value of his possessions, which amount to $50,000.00, and which consist of residences and apartment buildings in Kansas City, and turn to the institutions which he heads and to which he has given his best thought and business talents. He is the President and founder of the Afro-American Investment and Employment Company, Inc. Through this Company, he has made a connecting link between the White property owners and business firms, and the Negro citizens of greater Kansas City. He has made it possible for them to buy modern homes, in desirable sections of the city, on the easy payment plan, and employment furnished them while they were paying their installments.

He is the President and Founder of the Kansas City branch of the National Negro Business League, which position he has held for nine years. This institution has encouraged hundreds of Negro men and women to embark in business enterprises of various kinds.

Seeking the co-operation of the late Booker T. Washington, he succeeded in having the National Negro Business League hold its annual session in Kansas City in 1916. At this meeting he was elected as a member of the Executive Committee.

Mr. Weaver has been married three times—first to Miss Lizzie Stewart in 1890, then to Miss Stranella Hoyl, in 1895, and to Miss Bessie Henderson, in 1901. He has but two children, a boy and a girl, Fortune Weaver, Jr., and Cornaleta Odessa Weaver.

LEE S. WILLIAMS

HEN asked to write of his life so that the facts of his rise to a place of importance in the world of Negro business in St. Louis might be an inspiration to Negro youth everywhere. Mr. Williams, after some hesitation, sent this report of his life work. In this report he goes into detail about the steps that marked his steady growth. Even the very young lad who reads this will be led to aspire to a place in the business world.

"I was born at Jonesburg, Montgomery Co., Missouri, on May 11, 1868. My mother brought me to St. Louis, Mo., in December, 1873, and I entered the public school in 1875; at the age of eight years I was errand boy for the neighborhood, and did chores for the neighbors such as cutting kindling and carrying coal before and after school. During vacation I helped my mother do laundry work and continued doing chores for the neighbors.

At the age of ten years, during my vacation, I secured a job at a brick-yard brushing brick at a salary of forty cents per day; worked at that one month and then was promoted to driving a cart at a salary of fifty cents per day, and worked at that until school opened again. I again started at my old job of doing chores for the neighbors before and after school hours.

The next vacation, I secured a position in a rope-walk and made rope at a salary of two dollars and fifty cents per week, but being the only Negro boy there, and not getting the same salary for the same work as done by the white boys, I left there and secured a position in a Nursery at a salary of three dollars per week, and held this position until the fall term of school, when I again started doing chores as before.

The following summer I began driving a one-horse coal wagon at a salary of three dollars and fifty cents per week, and stayed at that work until school opened again when I secured a position in a repair shop and learned to repair shoes and cane chairs by working before and after school hours, and I sold papers on Sunday mornings. I stayed at this place about eighteen months, then secured a place in a tobacco factory, at a salary of four dollars per week and after being there six months was promoted to foreman over eight boys, who had been there about two or three years.

On account of a strike the factory closed and I was forced to find other employment so I started as a delivery boy in a butcher-shop, and continued at this work for two years, attending school at night. I then started working as a Pullman porter, and worked at that for three years, then started teaming for myself; business became dull, so I returned to the Pullman service and stayed there another year. I then started as a huckster in business for myself and controlled the first huckster business owned by a Negro in St. Louis. I continued working for the Pullman Company during the winter season, and followed my huckster business during the summer months. I leased twenty-one acres of land and worked it for three years, to keep up the huckster business, and still worked for the R. R. Company. From that I went to work at the undertaking establishment of A. Russel, and stayed at this position four years, and then started the undertaking business for myself, at 2317 Market Street. I stayed at that location about six years and then bought the property and built the establishment that is my present location 3232-34, Pine Street. The first to peddle coal in St. Louis; the first Negro Huckster in St. Louis; the first Negro to own and operate the Monument business in St. Louis; The first Negro to hold the position of City Undertaker; the first Negro to run an automobile funeral in St Louis; 'First in Everything."

In this story of his life, showing its ups and downs, Mr. Williams reveals a wonderful wealth of energy, patience and perseverance, traits which almost invariably lead to success and prosperity, and accounts for his being listed as a successful man.

CLEMENT RICHARDSON

HE Editor of this Volume, Clement Richardson, is a Virginian by birth. He was born in Halifax County, in 1878, where for a number of years he tilled tobacco and attended the White Oak Grove country school. While still a lad he went to Massachusetts to seek work, and to further his education. After spending some years in Winchester, Mass., where he worked as a tanner and a farmer, Mr. Richardson entered Mt. Hermon, the Boy's school of Dwight L. Moody. "I was prep of Preps" says Professor Richardson, "for what little book knowledge I had picked up back there in Virginia had been lost or supplanted by the rapid change of surroundings."

From Mt. Hermon Mr. Richardson entered Brown University, Providence, Rhode Island, but changed to Harvard after three years. He was graduated from Harvard in 1907.

Throughout his career Professor Richardson leaned toward English studies. He recalls for you with a genial smile, one or two thrilling debates he took part in back there in the boyhood days in Halifax, where he argued that women should not vote and that the wheelbarrow was more essential to the farmer than the ox. He was one of the ed-

itors of his preparatory school paper, the reader for the Mt. Hermon Glee Club, president of the Pierien Literary Society of that institution and frequent winner of prizes in both oratory and declamation throughout his school course. The same kind of work was kept up at college, where he preferred to pursue extra courses in literature to taking extensive part in college activities.

On finishing college Mr. Richardson did some work for the Boston Daily Globe and corresponded for several colored papers. In the fall of 1907 he filled the temporary vacancy made in Morehouse college, Atlanta, Ga. by the absence of Prof. Brawley. In 1908 Professor Richardson accepted work as teacher of English in Tuskegee Institute, where for the last nine years he has been head of the English Department.

At Tuskegee Institute, Professor Richardson was kept in close touch with all the students and teachers. He is a man of action, as well as one who likes to dally with his pen. He was responsible for all the public speaking at the famous Booker T. Washington school. During the year he staged in dramatic form a Halloween exercise and a Thanksgiving exercise for the senior class, a drama for the teachers and one for the senior class. One year he put on the Merchant of Venice for the teachers as actors and Mid-Summer Night Dream for the students. He staged once a year an exercise by the African students to raise funds to support a Tuskegee chapel in Liberia. Christmas 1916, Mr. Richardson established at Tuskegee the Community Christmas tree, bringing joy to some three or four hundred students who otherwise would have had no pleasant reminder of the season.

For the last few years Mr. Richardson has taken enthusiastic interest in rural education. He makes many trips into the country with the agent of the Tuskegee Extension Department, making addresses to the people and writing about them for the papers and magazines on his return.

During all these years, Mr. Richardson has been a frequent contributor to magazines and daily papers, having written the Country Gentleman, American magazine, Independant, Survey, Southern Workman and in daily and weekly papers. He was often with Dr. Booker T. Washington on the latter's tours, as a writer for papers and magazines. He is the author of several booklets and phamplets.

In June, 1918, Mr. Richardson was chosen by the Board of Regents of Missouri as President of Lincoln Institute, and he assumed office at once. If there is anything in the expression "First impresson the lasting one," Mr. Richardson will hold the good will of his new teachers and the citizens of the town, for they have given him a hearty welcome during his few months of Presidency.

Prof. Richardson was married Sept. 1st, 1908, to Miss Ida J. Rivers of Meridian, Mississippi. There are four daughters in the Richardson home: Louise Elizabeth, Ida Mae, Clementine and Evelyn Adele. All except the last named are in school.

WALTER G. ALEXANDER, A. B. M. D.

ALTER G. Alexander, M. D., of Orange, New Jersey, prominent in civil and business progress of Orange and a conspicuous leader in politics and in his profession, was born in Lynchburg, Virginia, December 3, 1880. His father, Royal Alexander, had seven children and a regular income of $15 a month, and so could do little to help his son through school. Young Alexander attended the public schools of Lynchburg until he was 14 years of age.

From the public schools he entered Lincoln University, Pennsylvania, at the rare age of fourteen. At Lincoln he became distinguished for excellence in scholarship from the outset, and remained so throughout his four years stay there. From Lincoln where he gained the degree of Bachelor of Arts he enrolled in the Boston College of Physicians and Surgeons. Against even a keener competition than he had met at Lincoln, he once more carried away honors in scholarship. He had been first honor man throughout his course at Lincoln; had won the Bradley Medal in Natural Science and had been made Latin Salutatorian. At the Boston College of Physicians and Surgeons, he carried off first prize for his thesis on "Cerebral Localization" and second prize on an essay entitled, "The Social Aspects of Tuberculosis."

Obtaining his doctor's degree in 1903, he served time as an interne in the Boston North End Hospital and Dispensary. Completing his work here he began his career in West Virginia. After spending a year in West Virginia, he located in Orange.

However, the doctor has by no means ceased to win honors. Almost from the day he began, he took the leading part as a citizen as well as a physician in this New Jersey City. He joined the Elks, the Odd Fellows, the Knights of Pythias, the Samaritans and Court of Calanthe. He allied himself as an active member of the Essex County, Jersey State and American Medical Associations; with the William Pierson Medical Library Association, of Orange; with the North Jersey Medical Society; with the National Medical Association; for 6 years Secretary of National Medical Association; with the Orange Civic Society; with the Orange Board of Trade; with the Orange Colored Citizens Union; with the Federation of Colored Organizations of New Jersey. He soon became director of the Progressive Building and Loan Association, director of the Douglass Film Company, President of the Home Benefit Association and a member of the Essex County Republican Committee.

In all these organizations, marvelous to relate, he became the dominating factor, an unquestioned leader. He became Past Noble Father of the Independent Order of Odd Fellows, past chancellor of the Knights of Pythias, past exalted ruler of the Elks. In the affairs of State he has been just as conspicuous, just as formidable. In 1912 he ran for the state legislature on the Progressive Ticket, receiving more than 22,000 votes, running fourth in a group of twelve. In 1913, he was "high man" in the Progressive Primary for the state Legislature, receiving three hundred more votes than the candidate for governor.

He is the Alumni member of the Lincoln University Athlete Association and spends and gives much enthusiasm to Lincoln sports.

He was married in 1914, to Miss Elizabeth Hemmings of Boston. Dr. and Mrs. Alexander live in their own residence in Webster Place, a residence which is among the best in the city and from which pulsates much of the social and civic life of Orange.

In a word, Dr. Alexander's marvelous mind, which he has continuously developed, his social disposition which has enabled him to influence men for their good, and a noble ambition for his race, causing him to persistently seek their uplift, has made him a great and useful man.

GEORGE E. CANNON. M. D., LL. D.

ULY 7, 1869 Dr. George E. Cannon son of Barnett G. and Mary Cannon, was born in Carlisle, South Carolina. He received his early education in the public schools of Carlisle and in the Brainard Institute at Chester, South Carolina. On completing his work in the Brainard Institute, he returned to his native town and taught schools for two years. The revenue derived from this source enabled him to take up his studies again, which he did in Lincoln University, in Pennsylvania. Here he applied himself with great diligence and graduated with honors in 1893. Again he was forced to give up his studies because the care of his family called for his aid and support, but it was only for a time. The fires of ambition having once been kindled would not go out and the thirst for knowledge intensified rather than diminished by his forced absence from school. In 1896 the way opened again for him to continue his studies and as he had determined upon the profession he would adopt he entered a college which would prepare him for his work. He enrolled in the New York Homeopathic College, from which Institution he graduated in 1900, with the degree of M. D.

After graduating from the New York Homeopathic College he moved to Jersey City, New Jersey where he immediately took up the practice of medicine. Here he has since remained and pursued his practice and has built up a large and lucrative business. His reputation as a physician is not confined to the community in which he lives, but he also stands high in the professional circles of the State. He has achieved much distinction as a physician, and is widely known throughout the country. He is ex-President of the North Jersey Medical Association; a member of the Academy of Medicine of Northern New Jersey; President of the Northeastern Medical Association; and for eight years, chairman of the Executive Board of the National Medical Association.

During the past five years, he has been president of the Lincoln University Alumni Association. Under his administraton, a handsome bronze tablet has been erected to the memory of the beloved President, Isaac N. Randall; a scholarship has been endowed ($2500) the first to be endowed by colored men; and funds have been raised to erect a magnificent archway over the main entrance to the University.

He is an extensive writer on medical and civic subjects; and is much in demand as a public speaker. His best known medical article, is the "Health Problems of the New Jersey Negro."

He takes a strong and controlling part in public affairs as well as in medical matters. He stands for the highest type of leadership in all that pertains to a good citizen. As president of the famous Committee of One Hundred of Houston County, he has been successful in advancing the civic interest of his race throughout the state of New Jersey. He is recognized as one of the foremost, if not the foremost, man of his race in the State of New Jersey.

He is president of the John Brown Building and Loan Association; treasurer of the Fredrick Douglass Film Company (which produces high class Negro motion pictures); treasurer of the Home Benefit Association; and of the Negro Welfare League of New Jersey. He is a devout church member and elder in the Lafayette Presbyterian Church. In 1914, Lincoln University, his alma mater, conferred on him the honorary degree of LL. D. On October 2, 1917, Governor Walter E. Edge commissioned him a captain in the New Jersey State Militia.

In 1901, Dr. Cannon was married to Miss Genevive Wilkinson, of Washington, D. C. Unto them two children have been born, George and Gladys.

Dr. Cannon is one of the few men of the race to enjoy a wide patronage from both races. His income from his practice is far above the average. His investments are large and varied.

Norman Therkield Cotton, A. B., M. D.

THERE are those who hold that the Negro should be educated in his own schools located in the South, and there only. They further contend that having received his education in the South that he should give the benefit of his training to his people located in that section. If such people would read the story of Dr. Norman Therkield Cotton, of Patterson, New Jersey, they would no doubt change their minds upon this subject.

His is an instance of what hundreds of colored men have done all over the country, and what they can do by finishing their training in the Northern schools. These Northern schools are well equipped and give facilities for education along certain lines not possessed by those located in the South though many of the Southern schools deservedly stand high.

Dr. Cotton won his degrees of Bachelor of Arts and Doctor of Medicine.

He was born in Greensboro, North Carolina, August 25th, 1885. His first schooling was in the public schools of his native city. After passing through the different grades and completing his course in the public schools he next became a student in the A. and M. College, which is also located at Greensboro. Completing his work in the A. and M. College, he decided to finish his education in the North and accordingly began his pilgrimage to the Northern clime. He first went to the Lincoln University, in Pennsylvania, completing his course and received his degree of Bachelor of Arts. Up to this time he had not definitely decided upon his life work, but his mind was now made up and he chose medicine and surgery. After giving the matter due thought, he was convinced that Boston offered the best schools and environment for the training he desired, so he enrolled at the Boston College of Physicians and Surgeons. Here he applied himself with diligence and completed his course. After the completion of his course he served an internship and extended training in the City Hospital of Boston, and the North End Dispensary and Hospital, Boston, Mass. It was while he was attending the medical school in Boston that his ambition was fired and he began to taste the fruits of place and honor. Because of his excellent and enviable record in scholarship and good standing with his fellows he was chosen orator of his class. He acquitted himself well and the well deserved praise showered upon him gave him a keen relish for such distinctions and since then he has captured one post of honor after another. While sojourning in the Hub he was chosen a member of the Boston Gamma Psi Zeta Society of Boston.

Beginning his work in Patterson, he soon established himself as a physician and surgeon, and started immediately to add many other honors to his list. He is President of the North Jersey Medical Society, of New Jersey; member of the Society of the State; of the Passaic County Medical Society; of the National Association, and of the American Medical Association. Dr. Cotton's unusual skill as a physician and surgeon soon put him in the front ranks along with the leading physicians of New Jersey. Though still a very young man, he has built up a splendid practice, and a reputation to be envied. Dr. Cotton enjoys as large, if not the largest practice of any physician in North Jersey. White patients constitute the bulk of his practice..

Along with his professional work, he has joined hands with the church and with secret orders. He is a member of the Saint Augustine Presbyterian Church of Patterson; he is Past Master of the Entegrity No. 51, F. A. M. of Patterson; of Oceanic 4559 G. U. O. O. F. of Atlantic City, and of the Good Samaritans.

Though intensely engaged in social and professional life, and having traveled very extensively, Dr. Cotton has nevertheless accumulated property and made himself comfortable surroundings. He owns two houses on Graham Avenue in Patterson, the one his own home; the other, a rent house. His home is valued at $9,000; his rent house at $2,900. He has much other property both in Patterson and in Greensboro, North Carolina, his native home.

Dr. Cotton was married to Miss Bertha May Doyle Lee of Boston in 1911. Their home is a sort of proud citadel among the colored people of Patterson, being the spot from which radiates good service, genial fellowship and prosperity.

Dr. J. WILLIAM FORD

EXT to the Negro doctor, or rather along with the Negro physician, the dentist is doing some of the most helpful service to the Negro race. He himself and his office with its equipment are sources of courage, ease and freedom; for here one enters without misgiving, without fear of slight or discrimination; realizing that all the equipment, the dentist's best skill and courtesy are all his. To this very valuable service the dentist adds that of a teacher. He gives lessons to the patient sitting in the chair; lessons on the care of the teeth, on when to fill instead of pulling, on the use of the teeth; all of which are most essential and none, or very few, of which the average Negro patient would get under other circumstances.

Perhaps this cold business method of handling the patient is no where more common than in the North, where competition is sharp, sympathy none too common. Happily our dentists are taking their places here and are rendering the Negro people good service.

Dr. J. William Ford, of Newark, New Jersey, is one of the dentists of the North to fill just such a post as has been outlined. His high grade prompt service, his office equipment, which after a time the public described as "ideal," soon drew to him an exceedingly large practice. So much so that though he left college in 1907 in debt to the instructors and to his friends, he was able to invest $500 in the First Liberty Loan and $500 in the Second Liberty Loan, also $2,000 in the Third Liberty Loan in addition to having accumulated valuable property holdings.

Dr. Ford was born in Williamsport, Pennsylvania, September, 1877. On finishing the public schools of Williamsport, he entered Howard University, and was graduated from the preparatory department. He spent two years in the College Department of Howard and then made dentistry a specialty. He completed his course in Dentistry in 1907. His life through college, however had been one of struggle and of want and hard work. He left the University in debt, for which his diploma was withheld. He owed his friends, he had a mother to support. There was therefore no money to buy this "ideal" equipment and furnish this ideal office, of which his patrons now boast. The proverbial starvation period of the professional man was not to be gone through, it was already upon him. And so for six years he worked on the railroads to pay off his debts and work had its happy side. Working on the railroads both in the East and in California, gave him extensive travel, and contact, two invaluable assets for a professional man; for often his success hangs as much on his good conversation as it does on his excellent work.

It was only in 1913 that Dr. Ford was able to leave the railroads and begin to try his fortune at his profession. In spite of the fact he had been out of school six years, he succeeded in passing the State examinations, and at one trial, something unusual for New Jersey, and was able to enter on his professional career.

Two years after beginning his practice Dr. Ford was married to Miss Edith Anna Braxton, of New York City. They were married in their own church, St. Phillips Episcopal Church, of New York. Mrs. Ford was formerly a public school teacher of New York. Dr. and Mrs. Ford live in Newark, but they own a very handsome Brown stone front residence in Brooklyn.

DR. FORD'S OPERATING ROOM.

George A. Kyle, D. D. S.

GEORGE A. Kyle, D. D. S., of Patterson, New Jersey, was a born athlete and early began to develop his powers as such. His career as a college athlete brought him into prominent notice and gave him a wonderful influence with the students. His reputation was not confined to his college but went beyond the bounds of the campus and made him known throughout the country. He became very popular, especially in the athletic world. He was both popular for his personal excellence and for the variety of athletics in which he excelled. He was a track man and through unquestioned merit rose to be captain of the track team. He brought his team up to a state of marked excellence. Football and basket ball were games in which he also excelled and in which he took an active interest. He was elected manager of the football squad.

In Howard University, where he was educated, there were few activities in which he did not play a conspicious part.

But his prowess was not limited to the gridiron, to the track and to the gymnasium, it was recognized in other fields of endeavor. As a rule athletes are not given to literature and the cultivation of the mind, for in the development of the physical the mind is neglected and it is hard for them to concentrate the mind upon literary matters. Dr. Kyle is a notable exception to the rule and was regarded at college as much for his literary attainments as for his athletic renown. His counsel and aid was sought in staging college plays and exercises of that character, and his interest in them was active and not of a passive nature. In a number of the college plays he took leading parts throughout his career at Howard.

Dr. Kyle was born and lived and worked wholly above the Mason and Dixon Line. None of his success can be check up to the hardships of oppression which sometimes rush in to claim the glory of achievement of those southern Negroes who have conquered in spite of oppression. He was born in Mainesville, Ohio, July 20, 1881. Much of his early education was gained in the public schools of Cincinnati, Ohio, which is not a southern city, geographically speaking at any rate. However, Dr. Kyle may be very truly set down as educated at Howard University. Leaving the public schools of Cincinnati, he entered the Howard College Preparatory Department. Being graduated from this Department he entered the college. Completing the college course, he enrolled in the Dental School. Thus completing his years in school and in school activities, Dr. Kyle will go down in a literal sense as being educated at Howard.

On graduating from the Howard Dental School, Dr. Kyle gave himself to serious thought as to where he would locate. It was not an easy question to settle, and not wishing to make a mistake he did not act in the matter hastily. Not wishing to remain idle while determining a question of so great importance to him he entered the service of a dental firm in Buffalo, New York. He remained with this firm several years, but the time was not lost for he gained from them a practical experience, confidence in his own ability and money to open an office when he ventured for himself.

He had selected Patterson, New Jersey, as a desirable post, and here he began. He had already many friends in various parts of the country, many of them Howard graduates, many friends whom he gained in his travels as an athlete. His activities at Howard had made him so popular that he became a welcome member of Patterson circles, and the circles round about Patterson, reaching New York.

He is a member of many medical organizations and of those bodies which keep alive the fraternal spirit and connection which meant so much in his college days. He is a member of the Alpha Phi Alpha Fraternity and of the College Men's Round Table of New York City. He belongs to the North Jersey Medical Association, and to the National Medical Association. He is secretary of the North Jersey Medical Association.

Dr. Kyle was married July 16, 1916, to Miss Charlotte McCracken of New York City. Between his profession on the one hand and his many social and fraternal connections on the other, Dr. Kyle, with Mrs. Kyle leads an exceedingly busy life.

PETER F. GHEE, M. D.

 R. Ghee belongs to the younger generation of Negro physicians, or rather to the physicians of the transition period. In the olden days the idea was to get to practice and gain a competence. The modern school, with its glaring exceptions, says rather, "Get Education." This takes time and patience. It goes to one school for one kind of training and to another for another, so that when the medical student comes forth with his diploma, he comes not only a technically educated doctor, but as an educated and cultivated man, fit to practice medicine, to teach his patience, to write readable articles on various topics of his profession, to take his place as a citizen as well as a physician.

Dr. Ghee was born in Luxenburg County, Virginia, May 5, 1871, and is the son of Peter Ghee, a farmer. He had as a lad the training on the farm that makes in so many instances for strong manhood. He knew the use of the axe, the hoe and the plow. He also learned to appreciate the great out-of-doors—the trees, birds, flowers and above all the great distances in the wide open country. His preliminary education was obtained in the public schools of his native country, where he laid the foundation for his later success in the literary line. He was a graduate from Boyaton Institute in the class of 1891. He thence matriculated at Shaw University, from which having taken an elective

course instead of the regular one, he could not obtain his Bachelor of Arts Degree when he graduated in 1894. Dr. Ghee next entered Leonard Medical College, from which he was graduated in 1898 with the degree of Doctor of Medicine. During his senior year at this institution he was engaged in practical work in the hospital, and after graduation he served an internship. Upon the conclusion of this period he established himself in active practice in Jersey City, New Jersey, which has since that time been the seat of his professional activity. His practice is a large and widely extended one, and he has the affection as well as the confidence of his patients. This is true because of the warm hearted sympathy always apparent in his ministrations, and his unselfish manner of serving.

Although Dr. Ghee has a very wide practice he has still taken time to associate with and work for various organizations in Jersey City and the state. He is a member of the North New Jersey Medical Association; the National Medical Association; Hudson Lodge, Independent Order of Odd Fellows, Progressive Lodge, Benevolent and Protective Order of Elks of Jersey City. In all of these he is held in high esteem for his wise counsel.

Dr. Ghee was married to Miss Lucy Boyd of Washington, D. C. Two children have come to bless their home; Euclid and Irven Ghee. The father is fond of all out-door sports and finds his chief recreation in automobiling. He is a member of the New Jersey Automobile and Motor Club.

In political matters he is affiliated with the Progressive Party of Hudson County and keeps well in touch with the trend of public events.

The greater part of his spare time is devoted to study and research work along the lines of his profession, which appears to be of ever increasing interest to him as the years advance.

Dr. Ghee is a tireless worker. His office hours seem to know no limit. Although Dr. Ghee is a very busy man, he is extremely modest and it was only with the greatest persuasion he could be prevailed upon to give even a meagre account of his life and career.

RESIDENCE OF DR. PETER F. GHEE

REVEREND FLORENCE RANDOLPH

O full of experience, service, and promotion has been the life of Rev. Florence Randolph that nothing more than a catalogue of her career can be offered here. She was born in Charleston, South Carolina, and was educated at Avery Normal Institute, after completing the course in the public schools of Charleston. Rev. Randolph was converted when she was about thirteen years of age. She joined the Methodist Episcopal church, and engaged immediately in active service.

On finishing her studies in the South she went to Jersey City, where she allied herself with the A. M. E. Zion Church of that city. Though she was following dress making as an occupation, she early began to exhort and do very active church work.

In 1897 she was granted license to preach. She began immediately to preach, addressing crowded houses, supplying pulpits, and doing evangelistical work wherever she received a call. For fourteen years she served Jersey City as a voluntary and un-salaried missionary, and for two years was the superintendent of the Negro work for the Christian Endeavor Society of the State.

On the recommendation of the late Bishop Alexander Walters, she was admitted to the Conference and became Conference Evangelist. In the meantime she was chosen pastor of several churches – the A. M. E. Zion Church, of Newark, N. J., Little

Zion A. M. E. Church, of New York City, and the A. M. E. Zion Church, of Poughkeepsie, N. Y. Bishop Walters ordained her a Deacon in 1901, and an Elder in 1903. In 1901 Rev. Randolph was chosen to attend the Ecumenical Conference, which met in London.

While in London, Rev. Randolph preached in the Primitive Methodist Church, of Mattison ,Road, where she won the highest praise from the congregation and from the public press. Completing her Conference duties in London, Rev. Randolph made several visits on the continent. She traveled through the remainder of England, through Scotland, Belgium and France.

In America Rev. Randolph's work falls into several groups. She is a well known social and club worker, a Christian Endeavor Worker, a Temperance Lecturer. She is president of the New Jersey State Federation of Women's Clubs, and is a member of the Executive Board of the New Jersey State Suffrage Association. She is chaplain of the North Eastern Federation of Colored Women's Clubs, and is head of the Religious Department of the National Association of Colored Women's Clubs. She works almost constantly in the prisons of her city, as well as in the prisons of New York and in other cities and towns where she chances to have a moment to spare. Rev. Randolph is one of the official lecturers of the Women's Christian Temperance Union of New Jersey. In this capacity she has won great distinction for herself and for the cause of Temperance. Indeed the papers in and around New Jersey, where she is best known vie with one another in singing her praise both as a worker and a speaker.

Of equal weight with Rev. Randolph in the cause of foreign missions. All through her course as a church and social worker she has kept the cause of Africa steadily before herself and before the public. Her church and the Conference were not slow in recognizing her as a most valuable asset in this branch of service. Seventeen years the Women's Foreign Society of the state of New Jersey has kept her as its president, and in 1916 the general Conference, which assembled at Louisville, Ky., made her president of the Woman's Home and Foreign Missionary Society of the A. M. E. Zion Connection.

Rev. Randolph comes from an old Charleston family, her father being John Spearing of that city. She was married to Hugh Randolph, of Richmond, Va., May 5, 1886. Mr. and Mrs. Randolph had one daughter, Miss Leah Viola. She is now Mrs. J. Francis Johnson, wife of Dr. J. F. Johnson of Jersey City. Mr. Randolph died February 13, 1913.

In Jersey City Rev. Randolph still makes her home. She is one of the few prophets to reap honor in her own country. White and black alike seek her presence whenever she is in the city. A welcome speaker and advisor, she is nevertheless sought for her conversation, experience and her personal charm. On many occasions she has been feasted, tendered gifts and testimonials by her fellow citizens of both races.

To quote the Zion Star, "Truly Rev. Randolph by her life, character and work gives substantial proof against the pessimistic views of those who hold the Negro race incapable of higher development.

215

Isaac Henry Nutter, LL. B., LL. D.

ONE of Atlantic City's busiest and most successful lawyers is Isaac Henry Nutter. Although New Jersey proudly proclaims him her own, he was born August 20, 1878, at Princess Anne, Maryland.

His parents were William and Emma Nutter, ex-slaves, who were highly respected for their strength of character and industry. While uneducated themselves, they were great lovers of education and made many sacrifices in order to give their children an education.

Their sacrifices in behalf of their children have been amply rewarded. Two of their boys, the subject of this sketch, and his brother, T. Gillis Nutter, have risen to high places at the bar and are occupying honored positions in other spheres of life. Other children have also reached places of honor and trust.

While his father was a great believer in education he did not believe in bringing up his children in idleness. He had a monopoly of the saw wood business of his community and the boys were required to help him in his work.

As a youth Isaac H. Nutter made remarkable progress in both his Preparatory and College Courses. While he was attending the Law Department of Howard University, he convinced all who had dealings with him of the fact that he had chosen the right profession.

He was even at this early age both a student and a scholar, showing a remarkable knowledge and appreciation of History, Civil Government and Economics. He was naturally endowed with a most powerful faculty of logical reasoning and he used every opportunity to develop this power. Since then many a legal battle has been won by his exercising this power. June, 1901 he was graduated with the degree of LL. B., later in the year, 1913, Wilberforce University conferred upon him the honorary degree of LL. D.

Three years after his graduation, that is in 1905, Mr. Nutter went before the Board of Examiners of New Jersey, and passed a very successful examination. Since that time he has practiced in Atlantic City. For some time he was associated in his practice with ex-Judge John J. Crandall. This helped to establish his place in the legal circle but his own power has held him there.

His court practice averages about twenty civil and criminal cases a month. Thus far Lawyer Nutter has defended in all thirty murder cases, one of which was convicted in the second degree, four sentenced for manslaughter, and twenty five acquitted. In the County Court of Mays Landing, New Jersey, in less than four days he secured acquittal in two cases and in the middle of the trial of a third client, had a "Not-Guilty" of murder plea changed to "guilty" of manslaughter with imprisonment for one year.

Mr. Nutter handles all cases with a great deal of earnest enthusiasm. His is not a play on words nor perplexing ambiguity, but it is the ultimate truth, clean cut justice and overwhelming logic clothed in a most fascinating and attractive rhetorical eloquence.

Aside from his legal business, Mr. Nutter finds time to devote himself to other worthy causes. He is solicitor and General Advisor of the New Jersey State Republican League; Solicitor of Atlantic County Republican League, and President of Nutter's Real Estate Company, which is one of the most active companies of the State.

His fraternal spirit is also felt in the State of New Jersey. He is a member of the Masons, the Odd Fellows, the Knights of Pythias, and of the Elks. Then Mr. Nutter was one of the first to catch the real spirit of the migration of the Negro to the North, and with a keen understanding of the situation he became Director of the Bureau for Welfare and Employment of Negroes migrating from the South. This Bureau was organized in 1917, and has done a most commendable work.

Lawyer Nutter is a member of the Governor's Cabinet, which is a most worthy post. Through his influence he has secured the following appointments for Negroes; one assistant Supreme Court Clerk, one Medical examiner, six Inspectors in Labor Department, one Secretary of Bureau, and one chief clerk and stenographer.

One year before beginning his legal practice, April 26, 1901, Isaac Henry Nutter was married to Miss Mary Alice E. Reed, of Coatville, Pa., who died June 18th., 1915. In a most beautiful home on Washington Avenue, Douglass Park, Pleasantville, New Jersey, he lives free from many of the petty cares of this world, secure in the respect and esteem of his neighbors and friends. Mr. Nutter attends the Methodist church and takes an active part in its activities.

Lawyer Nutter's office is 200-209, Sheen Building, Atlantic City, New Jersey. Here he works late and early, thinking, pondering, weighing his words. On these thoughts often the life of a man hangs. He is cool, deliberate and when a client enters his office, he is made to feel that on the walls of Lawyer Nutter's office is written in big letters one word justice.

WILLIAM H. SUTHERLAND, D. D. S.

R. William H. Sutherland, one of the leading and most prominent dentists in the State of New Jersey, was born August 9th, 1880, in Camden, South Carolina. As a lad he attended the Public School of Camden and later the Presbyterian Parochial School. He had small means to pay for an education, but a great ambition to learn. So he learned the barber's trade while still in his native town. In this new field of work he earned only twenty-five cents per week at first. But nothing daunted, he kept at this trade till he was able to do better work and therefore earn more money. With his trade for his bank account, he entered the Avery Normal Institute in Charleston, South Carolina and worked at off hours at his trade. In this way he earned enough money to complete the course there. With the same trade as his banker he entered Howard University, Washington, D. C., and earned his way there. Dr. Sutherland had by that time fully made up his mind what he wished to do in life and so he entered the Dental Department. From Howard he was graduated with the degree of Doctor of Dental Surgery, in 1905.

Since that time Dr. Sutherland has practiced his profession in Providence, R. I., Newark, and Orange, New Jersey. He makes his home in Orange, where he owns his home at 75 Oakwood Avenue.

In his home he has offices with operating room equipped with the largest modern electrical Dental appliances. Dr. Sutherland also maintains an office at 301, Glenwood Avenue, Bloomfield, New Jersey. He enjoys a lucrative practice which is not confined wholly to his own people, but he numbers among his patrons many prominent business people of the white race in the Oranges and adjoining towns. To keep both his offices open and to fill all his engagements with his patrons causes Dr. Sutherland to lead a very busy life.

But in spite of the very strenuous life which he leads during office hours, Dr. Sutherland still has time to devote to the social and religious life of the community. He is a member of the 13th. Avenue Presbyterian Church, of Newark. In this church he is Elder and also President of the Brotherhood. He is chairman of the board of management of the Orange Branch of the Y. M. C. A., a member of the National Medical Association and of the North Jersey Medical Association. Of the last named he is a chairman of the Dental Section.

And still Dr. Sutherland finds time to really enjoy his home. He was married to Miss Reiter L. Thomas, of Washington, D. C., December 27, 1906. Their home life is most ideal. Mrs. Sutherland presides over the home in a truly charming manner. She is a graduate of the Armstrong Manual Training School of Washington and is a lady of an optimistic and amiable character. To her Dr. Sutherland attributes much of his success. The family is blessed with two beautiful children. Reiter L. Sutherland is ten years old and is in the public school. Muriel S. Sutherland is still a baby only twenty-two months old. The two little ones add grace and charm to the wedded life of Dr. and Mrs. Sutherland.

Every summer for about four weeks this ideal family leaves home for their vacation. With his own car, Dr. Sutherland can go where he wills and when he pleases. Indeed this is one of the chief delights in the life of this very busy servant of the people. On one of these trips he took his family to Atlantic City, Baltimore, Philadelphia and Washington, D. C., and parts of Virginia.

To quote Dr. Sutherland's own words—"My pleasure is touring with my car, accompanied with my family. In this way we get much needed rest."

In no profession can a thoroughly consecrated man better his people than in dentistry. Many of the ills of the body come from the lack of proper care of the teeth. Of course only one thing lies at the root of this lack of care; and that one thing is ignorance. The Negro dentist has a wide field before him. He not only has to correct the faults already caused through this lack of knowledge, but he has the still greater field, teaching the proper care of the mouth and in this way doing preventive dentistry. This Dr. Sutherland does. As chairman of the Dental Section of the Medical Association of New Jersey, he has an opportunity to reach, indirectly, a great number of people. Add his work as a dentist to the great number of things done for the public in the capacity of Elder and President of the Brotherhood in his church and chairman of Y. M. C. A., we are compelled to number Dr. Sutherland among those who are shining examples of the best type of public men.

WILLIAM ROBERT VALENTINE, A. B.,
PRESIDENT OF THE MANUAL TRAINING INDUS-
TRIAL SCHOOL FOR COLORED YOUTHS—
BORDENTOWN, N. J.

ORTUNATE indeed was the subject of this sketch in the state of
his birth and his station as well.
Mr. Valentine was born in New
Jersey, where the colored youth
are given equal advantages with
the youth of any race. This, however, was not the
sole reason for his acquiring his thorough training.
Indeed many young people who have every advantage take no thought of them. But Mr. Valentine
came of stock that saw clearly just what standing
a good classical education would give to him. His
later record in the educational world has fully
shown that they were not wrong in their estimation. When the State of New Jersey wanted a
head for the school at Bordentown, it was decided
that they would like to use a native of the State if
possible. Immediately Mr. W. R. Valentine was
mentioned for the place. "In Valentine, who is
working in Indianapolis we have just the man we
want."

Mr. Valentine finished the High School of Mont-
clair, New Jersey, in June, 1900, and entered Harvard University the following September, graduating with A. B. degree in 1904. The following September he went to Indianapolis, where he was
made principal of a three-room Public school building; two years later of a five-room building, and
the following year appointed Supervising Principal of a group of buildings having about fifty
teachers under his supervision. His office building
or main building was Public School No. 26. It was
there that the experiment was tried of making the
school the educational, social, and economic center of all the people in the community. The extensive community work was made possible by reason
of the fact that the School Board upon the advice
of Superintendent C. N. Kendall, bought the frame
tenement buildings surrounding the main brick
structure, which were remodelled by the students
as a part of their industrial training, the money
furnished largely by the community itself. The
men of the community also donated labor. It was,
therefore the flexibility of the plant which gave
the school its opportunity and advantage over the
usual stereotype elaborate brick city Public School
building. One tenement building on the grounds
was converted into a boys' club house, which was
remodeled and equipped by the contributions of
money and labor by the people of the community
itself. The club house was directed and supervised
by teachers after school hours. Another large tenement was converted into an industrial building,
and included all of the industries such as wood
work, sewing, tailoring, printing, and shoe-making. Another building was used wholly for Domestic Science and included dining room, sitting
room and bed rooms for demonstration purposes
and use. This house was helpful in carrying on
the social activities of the school. The play ground,
covering about one-half acre of land, was part of
the equipment of this school. About three-fourths
of an acre of land, consisting of vacant lots within
easy reach of the buildings, were available for gar-

den purposes The school was as active at night as it was in the day time, for the teaching of the adults in the community, of all the branches of industry taught in the day The school aimed to reach out into all phases of the life of the community as an intensive dynamic force for its uplift and improvement Dr John Dewey of Columbia has devoted a whole chapter to the work of this school No 26 in his "Schools of Tomorrow"

He came to the Manual Training and Industrial School in the summer of 1915 This school was started as a private school by its founder, the Rev W A Rice, in the town of Bordentown New Jersey in the year 1886 It was supported entirely by such voluntary subscriptions as he could collect But in 1894 the school passed under the control of the State and later in 1900 was placed under the supervision of the State Board of Education forming a part of the State educational system This was the year that Professor James M Gregory, of Washington D C, took charge of the school and gave it its first impetus forward after its founding This was the year also that the State purchased the Old Parnell estate which constitutes its present site It is one of the most beautiful sites in the country, on a high bluff overlooking the bend of the Delaware River, consisting of about 250 acres of land Professor Gregory resigned in May 1915, the date on which Mr Valentine took charge

The property at Bordentown is valued at about $250 000 00 The main buildings are of brick with hot and cold water, gas and electric lights One hundred fifteen (115) acres of land are now in a high state of actual cultivation The gross receipts from the farm for the year 1917-1918 were $14 000 00 We are able to produce sufficient stable products to sell to other State institutions These cash sales amounted during this same year to about $1200 00 There is a herd of about twenty-five (25) Holstein cows, nine (9) horses, one hundred (100) head of hogs and seven hundred (700) chickens Much labor has been placed on the grounds and buildings by way of permanent improvements within the last four years For ex-

ample, the fertility of the soil has been greatly increased, land has been cleared and fenced off roads repaired, and hedges removed in order that the plant may present a well kept appearance New buildings have been constructed, including four teachers' residences, costing altogether about $25,000 00 The new trade building was added last year, costing $28,000 00, including equipment The addition to the girls' dormitory costing $39,000 00, is about completed A new sewage disposal system has been installed, a domestic water supply system is under way The Legislature has appropriated for permanent improvements alone within the last three years $110,000 00 Whereas four years ago there were about 100 students in attendance there are now about 170 The demand is for twice that number if the housing facilities were adequate Whereas the State appropriated four years ago only $28,000 00 for maintenance, it now appropriates $60 000 00

The industrial work has been able to meet the requirements of the Federal Board of Vocational Trade and as a result benefits from the Smith-Hughes bill It is hoped to enlarge the extension work of the school as fast as possible that it may reach out into the State Farmers conferences are now held in certain communities of the State, monthly. Teachers in the public schools in the neighboring cities and towns hold a Study Center meeting at the school once a month and the State organization meets once a year It is hoped finally to make the Bordentown School do for the people of the North what Hampton and Tuskegee have done for the people of the South Hand in hand with the improvement and extension of the industrial work will also follow the improvements and extension of the academic work Such colleges as Radcliff, Columbia, Harvard and Oberlin are represented on the faculty

The encouraging feature of the work is the growing interest which the State officials are manifesting towards the school and the confidence in the future of the school as shown by the colored people themselves

William Henry Washington, A. B., M. D.

THE Negro race, in its march upward, has developed, as has the other races, different types of men. That race has even developed that rare type of men, known throughout the world as "college men."

Dr. William Henry Washington, of Newark New Jersey, is one of the finest of the type of the young colored college man, out in life's busy world that one can meet. He has the bearing, the attitude, the appearance, the culture, the stature of a modern college man. And what is more, Dr. Washington is, in the truest sense of the word, a college man, and just such a college man as to reflect credit on any college from which he might have graduated.

Dr. Washington was born in Portsmouth, Virginia, August 23, 1878. He began his education in the County School, Virginia, and attended two years the Normal and Collegiate Institute, at Petersburg, Virginia. From there he went to Washington, and entered the preparatory school of Howard University, from which he graduated in 1900. He next took a four year Collegiate Course in Howard University, and followed that with a four year Medical course in the same institution. There he received his degree of Bachelor of Arts and his M. D. degree.

He has the same interest in Howard University, his Alma Mater, that he had while attending that famous institution. Ten years after his graduation from the Medical School of Howard University, in 1908, he is found President of the Alumni of that school, for the State of New Jersey. He keeps as closely in touch with the interests and activities of that school today as he did in those days when, as captain of the Howard football eleven, he led the team to victory after victory and became the most popular foot-ball captain that Howard has ever had.

A leader in school life, he has, without apparent effort, gained a fine place of vantage in the Medical world. This young man who was for three years captain of Howard's foot-ball team, (the most highly conveted athletic honor in a college,) who was manager of the varsity baseball nine, who was business manager of the college newspaper, and president of the exclusive organization known as the Council of Upper Classmen, is, as if those college activities prepared him for larger activities, now actively identified with professional and civic organizations of city, state and nation. The New Jersey State Medical Society

—the Essex County Medical Association, the American Medical Association, the North Jersey Medical Society, the last of which organizations he served as secretary and treasurer for several years, are among the many professional organizations in which he holds membership.

Coming to Newark, New Jersey nine years ago, Dr. Washington, who is a native of Virginia, has built up a splendid practice. His medical ability is recognized and appreciated not only by his many patients, but also is conceded by his professional brethren.

While Dr. Washington is now well advanced on the road of prosperity, yet it has not always been thus with him. He, like most men who have amounted to anything, has also encountered the vicissitudes of life. He worked his way through college, through the medical school, and, at the same time, and even yet, gave financial assistance to dependent relatives who aided him when aid was most needed. His mother and father died while he was yet in infancy, but loving relatives carefully looked after him. These relatives have, since he came to manhood, been the object of his solicitude and beneficence.

The home life of Dr. Washington is sweetened and made happy by his cultured and attractive helpmeet, who was, before their marriage, Miss Ardele Smith. Mrs. Washington was principal of a public school in Roanoke, Virginia, at the time of her marriage. She too is a Virginian by birth and is also a graduate of Howard University. In their home they have collected a beautiful and expensive library, the doctor being a connoiseur of the best literature and a lover of fine editions in magnificent bindings. One perusing the volumes in Dr. Washington's library will see some of the rarest and most expensively bound books that have come from the binders.

Dr. Washington is said by some to be the most widely known Alumnus of Howard University, among the former students of that school. He is the same congenial fellow that he was when he was known on "Howard Hill," as "Cap," (football captain). And his rise should be an inspiration to the aspiring youth.

When quite a small boy his aspiration was to be a soldier; while watching the drills of sailors at Portsmouth, it almost decided him to be a sailor; and then attracted by the work of the exponents of the law he thought he would be a lawyer, but no doubt chose wisely in entering the Medical profession.

HARRY RICHARDSON

NOWN as the friend of all colored
people who seek pleasant lodging
and wholesome food at Cape May,
New Jersey, Harry Richardson,
proprietor of the New Cape May
Hotel, and one of the leading
Cape May Opera houses has served many an apprenticeship in life's great factory. Mr. Richardson
was born in Philadelphia, November 3, 1867. Although born in a locality where the black boy had a
great chance to educate himself, young Richardson
was able to attend school but a limited time. This
was due to the fact that very early in life he had to
support himself. So we find the young lad after
a few years spent in Birds Public School, leaving
the school room and working for his maintanence.

The first work that was tried by Mr. Richardson
was really very hard labor. This was in a brick
yard. He was still but a boy, and the work was
so hard that when an opportunity came for a different work, he was very glad to make the change.
Thus at the early age of thirteen he left the brick
yard and began an apprenticeship at electroplating
and stereotyping. For thirteen and a half years he
worked at this trade and from the position of an

apprentice he rose step by step to the position of
foreman of the shop of Hanson Brothers, Philadelphia. He changed his place of work but not
the kind of work in his next move. He went to
Boston and served as foreman in the electroplate
room of the Boston Globe.

Leaving Boston, Mr. Richardson returned to his
native city, and went in business for himself. In
this his first venture he chose tobacco as the com-
modity to handle. Mr. Richardson succeeded with
his tobacco business and was soon able to venture in a larger business concern. He then opened
a hotel for the colored traveling public. And for
the past seventeen years he has been the owner and
manager of a hotel in Cape May, New Jersey. In
this line of work, Mr. Richardson has been very
farseeing. He saw that the best class of colored
people had no place of amusement, and so he added
an Opera House to his list of business ventures.
He saw the crying need of a good hotel for the Colored Man, he attempted to supply that need in his
locality. In doing this he has served his race while
helping himself. Again he saw the need of a place
where the best people could go to get clean amusement and again he attempted to supply that need.
In this he has succeeded. Both his places of business are very heartily supported by his patrons.
His hotel is celebrated in the east for comfortable rooms, prompt and polite service, the best class
of guests, and the most congenial surroundings.
What Mr. Richardson has not in his hotel, he makes it a point to get even though he sustains a loss
in doing so.

While Mr. Richardson was living in Philadelphia
he became interested in politics. He was president of the seventh ward, Executive Committee,
for several years, was appointed delegate to many
conventions, and was one of the State commissioners to the St. Louis World's Fair. Mr. Richardson served also as an employee at the State Senate
House in Harrisburg for several terms.

All through his life the proprietor of the Cape
May Hotel has allied himself with the leading or-
ganizations of his community. While in Phila-
delphia he was President of the Philadelphia Turf
Club, and was nine years a member of the Mathew
Stanley Quay Club. Mr. Richardson is a member
of the Friday Night Banquet Association, of Phil-
adelphia, a member of the Citizen's Republican
Club, of Philadelphia, and a member of the Masonic
Olive No. 8.

In religious belief, Mr. Richardson is a Baptist.
In connection with his business and for pleasure
Mr. Richardson has traveled all over the eastern
part of the United States. Mrs. Richardson, like
Mr. Richardson himself is a native of Philadelphia.
They both show their love of their native city by
the number of times they return to its hospitable
gates. But Cape May, and the traveling public
that passes through Cape May, know Mr. Richardson, and think of him and talk of him as the proprietor of the Cape May Hotel and Opera House.

INTERIOR VIEW OF ST. PHILLIPS CHURCH

N 1818, St. Phillips Church was organized under the leadership of Mr. Peter A. Williams, who after being admitted to the order of Deacons and advanced to the Priesthood was made its first rector. From its very beginning the parish has endeavored to do two things:

(a) To demonstrate the capacity of the Colored man for leadership and group action, and:

(b) To foster his sense of manly independence. The first of these endeavors has been abundantly justified in the marvelous work which has been accomplished during these one hundred years. From a very modest beginning in an upper room on Cliff Street seeking recognition from the ecclesiastical authorities, the parish has developed into one whose position commands the approval of the diocesan authorities. The upper room in Cliff Street is today the magnificent Gothic structure in West One Hundred and Thirty Fourth Street, with a seating capacity of over nine hundred; a well planned Parish House of four floors and basement, which houses all the parochial activities—administrative, clerical, recreational and communal; a Home for Aged Women and a Rectory. To this must be added the endowment painfully accumulated but wisely managed, which consists of a block of ten apartment houses in West One Hundred and Thirty-Fifth Street, which shelters upward of two hundred families. This achievement in some measure demonstrates the capacity of the colored man, for leadership and harmonious group action, for it has all been wrought under the management

of Colored men.

(b) In the working out of the second endeavor the Parish has been equally successful. Bishop Hobart in his Convention address of 1819, says, "I consecrated the new church of St. Phillip's in Collect Street, designed for the use of the Colored people of our Church in that city. To its creation they contributed largely in proportion to their means and the trustees were unwearied in their exertions to obtain the contributions of others, and in their attention to the building while it was erecting, in which their own mechanics principally were employed and which they finished with judgement and taste."

The present church of the perpendicular Gothic type was designed by a firm of Colored architects, Tandy and Foster. It is cruciform in shape and is built of artificial stone, closely resembling limestone and yellow pressed brick. To the west of the chancel and sanctuary are the vestry room and sacristy; while on the east are two choir rooms, with lockers for men and boys—an ambulatory connects these east and west rooms.

In the basement is a large and well appointed room used for the Sunday School, a neat attractively equipped chapel, choir, rehearsal room, work rooms and lavatories. The church consists in part of an exquisite altar of marble, with chastely carved grape vines and panels of four of the apostles, and in the centre the Paschal Lamb; surmounting the altar is a reredos of caen stone, and a background of blue mosiacs tinted with gold in the midst of which and looking down upon the altar are figures of adoring cherubim and seraphim; a three manual pipe-organ and eagle lectern and pulpit of brass.

To meet the needs of a changed environment there are many institutional activities connected with the church, but all the club and guild work which is done has for its sole purpose the building of permanent Christian character. For the boys and young men there are the following organizations: The Knights of King Arthur; St. Christopher, Juniors; St. Christopher, Intermediates; St. Christopher, Seniors; St. Phillip's Men's Guild; Brotherhood of St. Andrew; Men's Bible Class.

The activities among the girls and women are: St. Mary's Guild; St. Agnes, Juniors; St. Agnes, Intermediates; St. Agnes, Seniors; Alter Guild; Woman's Auxiliary to Board of Missions; Dorcas Society; Woman's Auxiliary to the Parish Home; Women's Bible Class.

Reverend Hutchens Chew Bishop, D. D., went to St. Phillips Church January 1st, 1886, where he has rendered great and effective work and for thirty-two years has been the directing genius of the Parish. He graduated from General Theological Seminary, N. Y. City in 1881. At that time there were divisions in the church in America and the parties constituting the division were at times hostile to each other. Mr. Bishop, as he then was, belonged to the High Church party, then hopelessly in the minority. Mt. Calvary Church, of which he was a member, was of the same party. Owing to an unusual ill-feeling on the part of the diocesan authorities towards Mt. Cavalry, Mr. Bishop was denied the grace of orders in the Diocese of Maryland. He was afterwards made Deacon and Priest by the Diocese of Albany.

WILLIAM HENRY BROOKS, D. D.

ILLIAM Henry Brooks, was born in Calvert County, Maryland, September 6, 1859. Although this date was just before the Emancipation Proclamation, for the Negro with ambitious parents or guardians or an inborn ambition for himself, no better date could have been decided upon for his entrance upon the stage of life. The pendulum swung a long way in favor of the education of the blacks, and in some sections where the prejudice was not quite so great, their educational advantages were equal or nearly equal to those offered the white boys. Thus we see Rev. Brooks with a chance to educate himself.

To begin his training he entered the Public schools of the county. From the Public Schools he entered Morgan College, Baltimore. Here he applied himself to his books in a most scholarly manner and when an opportunity came to him he entered Howard University, at Washington, D. C. Leaving Howard he studied in turn in Union Seminary, New York, and in New York University and later in University-Dijon, France. Had not Rev. Brooks been a close student of books, he would still have been benefitted by his sojourn in these institutions of learning. But being of a scholarly turn of mind, and at the same time a student of men and events, he saw a great opportunity for educating himself.

At the age of twenty-one he joined the Washington Annual Conference. Then he began his round of charges. His first three charges were all in West Virginia; Spring Creek, Summers Circuit, and Harpers Ferry. He then served two charges in Maryland; Hartford Circuit, and Frederick, in Maryland. He then served Central Church in Washington D. C., and Wheeling, West Va. Having served all these minor charges and served them well he was next made a Presiding Elder in the Washington District. He was transferred to St. Marks, New York. In the last named, he has been actively engaged since 1897.

Because of the length and kind of the work done by Rev. Brooks, he has been shown many honors by the Denomination. In 1896 he was a Delegate to the General Conference. He was Fraternal Delegate to the General Conference of C. M. E. Church at Nashville, Tennessee, in 1902. Again he was honored by his church in 1910 when he was sent as a Delegate to the World's Conference at Endinburg, Scotland. He is a member of the Methodist Episcopal Church. Here the competition for the Bishopric is keener because of the many men with generations of training and culture behind them.

Not all the honors which have come to him have come from his church. This is due no doubt to the fact, that he has not confined all his efforts to the workings of the church. So we find him on the Board of Control of the White Rose Mission, Friendly Shelter, and of the National Urban League. In this last named he has been able with his associates to do considerable good. He is on the Board of Managers of the Y. M. C. A., he is an active worker in the Musical Settlement and is Chaplain in the 15th Regiment. This represents a very active life and a life of great usefulness.

In connection with his church work, while getting his education and for pleasure it has been the privilege of Rev. Brooks to travel quite extensively in this country. In fact he has traveled throughout the United States, in England, in Scotland, France, Belgium, Canada, Switzerland, Germany, and Mexico. This has helped to develope the man almost as much as did his years spent in the various institutions of learning.

The degree of Doctor of Divinity was conferred on him by Wiley University, Marshall Texas, in 1897, and also by Morgan College, Baltimore, Md., in 1917.

He was married to Miss Sarah Catherine Carroll, Nov. 2, 1882. Mrs. Brooks is the daughter of Rev. N. M. Carroll, D. D. Rev. and Mrs. Brooks were married in Asbuy Church, Washington, D. C., where her father was at that time pastoring. Five children have been born to them to share their home and help make it a bright, happy one. Mamie V., is married to Rev. A. A. Brown, of Philadelphia; Arthur E. is a physician in New York; A. Cnuton is a clerk in Philadelphia; Estelle Beartrice is a nurse in New York; and N. Cannon is a sergeant in the 15th Regiment. All of these children have been to their parents a great blessing

Rev. Brooks has accumulated some of this world's goods while pastoring. He has real estate valued at about $5,000.00. In all that he has undertaken, Rev. Brooks has been a success. His life should be an inspiration to any young man who intends to be a preacher of the Gospel.

Rev. James Walter Brown---Mother A. M. E. Zion Church

THE Reverend Mr. James Walter Brown, pastor of the famous Mother Zion Church of New York City, was born in Elizabeth City, North Carolina, July 19, 1872. He numbers among his Alma Maters both Shaw University of his native state and Lincoln University in Chester County, Pennsylvania. However, he did not go from one to the other so rapidly or quickly as it takes to tell. Having finished his public school, he entered Shaw University. On completing his career here he became a school teacher, or schoolman for several years. From 1893 to 1899 he was the assistant principal of the State Normal School of Elizabeth City. In September of 1900 he became a student at Lincoln in the theological Seminary.

He graduated from this department in 1903 and began immediately his career as a pastor. His first charge was the African Methodist Episcopal Zion Church of Bethlehem, Pennsylvania. He served this church as pastor from 1903 to 1905. From Bethlehem he went to Rochester, New York, and became the Pastor of the African Methodist Episcopal Zion Church of that city, and served them from 1903 to 1913. His two years experience at Bethlehem not only gave him practical training he needed for pastoral work, but also kindled his enthusiasm as a worker and won for him considerable reputation as a pulpit orator. He first surveyed the field and made a note of its needs and possibilities, then began his work with zeal and soon imparted to his congregation much of his enthusiasm.

He pointed out to them the need of a new and more commodious house of worship and influenced them to undertake the enterprise. Under his direction they commenced the work and soon had a building of which they were proud. They did not stop with the erection of the church building, but while the spirit of enterprise was upon them they built a parsonage also. The value of their church property now amounts to thirty-five thousand dollars, ($35,000.00).

Reverend Brown learned from experience that the divinely taught principle of fidelity in small things leads to larger service is a true principle.

The fact that he had a comparatively small field did not deter him from doing his best and his success in Rochester brought him into prominent notice and into a larger field of work. The large churches began to take note of him and he was soon occupying their pulpits. Among the churches which was attracted to him was the old Mother African Methodist Episcopal Zion church of New York City. This church called him in 1913, and since that period he has been its pastor. This church, which has a fame co-extensive with Methodism in this country made no mistake in its estimate of the young preacher. He has not only sustained the reputation of the church, but has raised it to a higher plane of usefulness and honor.

He has introduced modern ideas into the church life and has inspired them with a new vision of endeavor. The old Gospel message is the same in all ages but the method of presenting and disseminating the truth changes with each generation.

The Reverend Brown recognized this fact, and organized in his church committees and clubs which would bring the members into closer relations and cooperation with each other. Already the effect of his innovations have been felt in the church life, and it is advancing to larger achievements.

With him the church comes first and even the outside enterprises which engage his interest fall largely within religious and uplift channels. He is President of the Board of Control of the Varick Christian Endeavor Society of the African Methodist Episcopal Zion Church, a member of the Board of Management of the Young Men's Christian Association of New York; District Superintendent of the Sunday Schools of New York City for the African Methodist Episcopal Zion Conference.

To these and to activities of his church he devotes the major part of his time and thought. When he has given attention to his duties connected with these he has but little time left to devote to other interests, yet he is a man among men and finds pleasure in mingling with them outside of his church life, when he can do so without neglecting his work.

This social proclivity has carried him into a number of fraternal orders. He is a member of the Masonic fraternity, an Odd Fellow, and a member of the Southern Beneficial League.

Reverend Brown has not been unmindful of his material interests, believing that it is a man's duty to make provision for his family. His savings he has invested in property in Elizabeth City, North Carolina, in Rochester and in New York City.

Mr. Brown was married in 1903 to Miss Martha Hill, of Philadelphia. In all his endeavors Mrs. Brown takes a helpful and leading part, relieving him whenever possible, sharing the burden and responsibility when it is not possible wholly to relieve him.

EUGENE P. ROBERTS, A. B., M. A., M. D.

UGENE P. Roberts, of New York City was born in Louisburg, North Carolina, October 5, 1868. He got his elementary and preparatory training in Louisburg, and then entered Lincoln University, Pennsylvania. From this institution he received the degree of A. B. in 1891, and later the degree of M. A. Leaving Lincoln he matriculated at the New York Homeopathic Medical Association, and Flower Hospital. Here he received the Degree of M. D., in 1894.

Dr. Roberts began his career as a physician when but twenty-four years of age, and he has enjoyed a long and very useful career in his profession. He is a member of the National Medical Association, New York County Medical Society, New York Materia Medical Society, Medico-Chirugical Society, Academy Pathological Science, Durham Medical Club, Medical Society of Inspectors of greater New York. He is inspector of the Department of Health, lecturer on Care of Babies in Public Schools of New York City, physician in charge of St. Cyprian's Babies Clinic, chairman of Colored Men's Branch of Y. M. C. A., member of the Executive Board of National League on Urban Conditions Among Colored People, committee for Improving the Industrial Condition of Negroes in New York, and the National League for the protecion of Colered Women.

To meet all the demands made on his time by these various duties and to attend to his practice, Dr. Roberts leads a very busy life. Yet he takes time to meet his fellows from another angle. He is an active member of the St. James Presbyterian Church, a member of the Southern Beneficial and Hotel Bellmen's Beneficial Association. Dr. Roberts served one term on the Board of Education for New York City. This was an honor well deserved because of the many things done by this very busy physician for his people in the city of New York.

Dr. Roberts has made a special study of the diseases of children. New York furnishes a good field for extensive study along this line. Because of the special skill and knowledge along this line, Dr. Roberts has been frequently asked to address the National Medical Association on this subject.

Dr. Roberts has traveled very extensively. He has covered the greater part of his own country in his journeyings and has been three times abroad. He visited Spain, Germany, Austria, France, Italy, Switzerland and England. The time spent in these travels was well spent. In fact, Dr. Roberts has made all the events of his life help him along in his profession.

Dr. Roberts has been twice married. He was married to Miss Mollie Beatty, New York City, June 6, 1900. He was married a second time to Miss Ruth M. Logan, of Tuskegee Institute, Alabama, December 4th, 1917. The present Mrs. Roberts is the daughter of Warren Logan, Treasurer of Tuskegee Institute, and for a number of years advisor and friend of Dr. Booker T. Washington. Dr. and Mrs. Roberts live in their beautiful brown stone dwelling in one of the best sections of New York City. Here they make life pleasant for their many friends. Besides owning the home in which he lives, Dr. Roberts has other valuable property in the city of New York.

Dr. Roberts is a man worthy of emulation. He is a competent physician, an untiring worker for the good of his people and his country, a conservative Christian gentleman.

In every department of life he seeks the highest good of those he serves, and is a glowing example of what a man can accomplish who has before him a high ideal of life. When God called Moses out of Ur of Chaldee he called him to be a blessing to his race, and when God led Dr. Roberts to be a Christian physician, he made him a channel of blessing.

Fred R. Moore

FRED R. MOORE, publisher and editor of the New York Age, is generally conceded to be the most fearless as well as the most influential newspaper man in America. "Fred Moore," as everybody speaks of him, never hesitates to take a strong stand either pro or con on any public question, and there is never any doubt as to his position; for he either is for or against you. He may be found at any time on the firing line, and nothing seems to please him better than to be in what he terms "a fight for principle."

Owing to the high literary value of The Age editorials and the independence of thought at all times expressed on questions involving the rights and progress of the Negro, be it in America, Haiti, the West Indies or in Africa. The New York Age is quoted by more white and colored papers than any other publication. The recognition paid so widely-known a journal naturally helps to keep its editor in the limelight, and the public quite often reads in the daily press of what the editor of the Age has to say on this or that subject.

Fred R. Moore is a self-made man, one who has made his way to the top and become a national figure mainly through dogged determination and an unfailing spirit of optimism. One's success in life largely depends on himself-upon the amount of effort put forth in spite of obtacles, he believes and on this theory Mr. Moore has reached his present important status among his people.

Receiving only a common school education in the District of Columbia, where he spent his childhood days, as well as the most romantic period of his life-courtship-Fred R. Moore began to take advantage of close contact with men of high character and prominence when in his teens. While living in Washington, D. C., he spent many years in the Treasury Department, serving as confidential messenger to five Secretaries of the Treasury during the Grant, Hayes, Arthur and Cleveland administrations. Secretary Daniel Manning, who was a member of Grover Cleveland's Cabinet during the first administration, was very much attached to Mr. Moore and had the latter accompany him to England, treating the colored man as a companion and friend in every particular.

In 1887, Fred R. Moore accepted a position with the Western National Bank, where he worked in all of the various departments and had charge of the vault. He also served as delivery clerk in the Clearing House. The Western National Bank afterwards merged with the National Bank of Commerce. While with the bank, Mr. Moore purchased the Colored American Magazine, and in 1905, left the banking institution to become deputy collector of the Internal Revenue for the Second District of New York. A few months later he resigned to become National organizer of the National Negro Business League.

Fred R. Moore acquired the controlling interest in The New York Age, of T. Thomas Fortune, and Jerome B. Peterson, in 1907, and under his management the paper has steadily grown in influence and circulation. Mr. Moore was known as a staunch and devoted friend of Booker T. Washington, and the renowned Tuskegean placed implicit confidence in his New York friend, who showed a disposition to go to the front for the Negro leader at any and all times. No one was more profoundly touched by Booker T. Washington's death than Fred R. Moore.

Just at the close of the Taft administration Fred R. Moore, was confirmed by the Senate as United States Minister to Liberia, the appointment having been made some months before, but the Democratic Senators had shown a disposition to hold up many of President Taft's last appointments. Although given the proper credentials by the State Department, and the duly accredited representative of the United States Government to the black republic, Mr. Moore never went to Africa. His resignation was accepted by William Jennings Bryan about three months later. Minister Moore received the emoluments due this country's diplomatic representative to Liberia for the three months.

Mr. Moore has been active in politics and in 1902 was nominated by his district in Brooklyn for the State Legislature, receiving 2,156 votes. There were 150 colored voters in the district. He was an alternate delegate to the Republican National Convention in 1908, and a member of the Advisory Committee of the National Republican Committee in 1912 and 1916. Mr. Moore is deeply interested in civic affairs and is a member of the National Negro Business League; Member of the Executive Committee National League on Urban Conditions Among Negroes; Empire Friendly Shelter; Auxiliary Member Committee of Fourteen, and other organizations for the betterment of race conditions. In his church affiliation, Mr. Moore is an Episcopalian.

In 1879, Fred R. Moore and Ida Lawrence were married in Washington, D. C., and eighteen children have been born of the marriage. Mr. Moore was born Jun 16, 1857.

REVEREND A. CLAYTON POWELL, D .D.

LAYTON Powell, son of Anthony and Sallie Dunning Powell, was born in a one-room log cabin in Franklin County, Va., May 5, 1865, near the spot where Booker T. Washington first saw the light. In his tenth year he moved with his father and mother to Knawha County, West Virginia, and later to Ohio. He received his early training in the public schools of West Virginia and Ohio. On March 8, 1885, he was converted and baptised into the fellowship of the First Baptist Church, of Rendville, Ohio. A year later he went to Washington, D. C. with the intention of studying law, but because of a deep religious experience his mind was turned to theology. He holds two diplomas from Virginia Union University, Richmond Virginia, and spent two years, 1895-96, at Yale University, New Haven, Conn.

His first call was to the First Baptist Church, San Diego, California, but he finally accepted the Ebenezer Baptist Church, of Philadelphia, where he served for one year and was then called to the pastorate of the Emanuel Baptist Church, New Haven, Connetticutt. Here he had one of the most successful pastorates of the country for fifteen and a half years. The membership was increased from 135 to 625; the church building was remodeled at a cost of $10,000 and every cent paid within two years, and a splendid piece of property adjoining the church purchased. In 1908 he resigned this charge to accept a call to the Abyssinian Baptist Church, New York City, where he still serves. During his nine years pastorate, 2200 persons have been added to the membership. This is considered the wealthiest Negro Baptist church in America, having under its control about $350,000 worth of property, with a membership of 3300.

Rev. Powell uses his pulpit every Sunday, not only to preach the gospel but to secure good positions for the members of his congregation and to urge them to support Negro business enterprises. He is especially interested in educational and social service work. He is a trustee of Virginia Seminary and College, the National Training School for Women and Girls, Downingtown Industrial and Agricultural College, a member of the Board of Directors of the White Rose Industrial Home, the Young Men's Christian Association, the National League on Urban Conditions Among Negroes, member of the National Association for the Advancement of Colored People, P .N. F., of the Grand United Order of Odd Fellows, 32nd degree Mason, and Knights of Pythias. He received the title of Doctor of Divinity from Virginia Union University, May 1904, and from Virginia Seminary and College ,the same month. In 1900 he was delegate to the World's Christian Endeavor Convention, in London, and spent two months abroad visiting many places in Great Britian, France and Ireland. He has also travelled through Canada, Bermuda, and Mexico. Very few public speakers are in greater demand than Rev. Powell. He has crossed the American continent four times in answer to invitations to lecture and preach in California and other western states. He has spoken on the platform with such men as Ex-President Taft and Governor Charles S. Whitman, of New York. He has been invited to lecture and deliver commencement addresses at several of the leading universities and schools. He is an honorary member of the Garnett Society of Lincoln University. Extracts from his sermons and addresses often appear in papers like the New York Times, Sun, Brooklyn Eagle, and the leading dailies of New England.

He is author of the following pamphlets: Emanuel Baptist Church, Pastor and Members; Some Rights Not Denied the Negro Race; A Plea for Strong Manhood; A Three Fold Cord; Valley of Dry Bones; Power of the Spirit the Need of the Church; Significance of the Hour; Broken, But Not Off; Watch Your Step. The pamphlets are widely read. Some of them have run into the seven thousandth edition. Proceeds of these are used to educate young men to the ministry.

He was Chairman of the Booker T. Washington Memorial Committee of New York State.

Rev. Powell was married to Miss Mattie F. Schafer, of Pratt, West Virginia. Two children, Blanche F. and Adam Clayton, Jr., were born to bless the home of this couple.

Lester A. Walton

ESTER A. Walton, journalist and theatrical promoter, was born at St. Louis, Mo., April 20, 1881, and is the son of Benjamin A. Walton and Ollie May Walton; old and highly respected residents of St. Louis, Mo. Mr. Walton is a product of the public schools of his native city and is a graduate of Summer High School.

After completing a business course in a local business college, Mr. Walton decided to take up journalism as a profession and his first work was on the St. Louis Globe-Democrat. At the time R. A. Hudlin, a boyhood friend of Mr. Walton's parents, was postmaster of Clayton, Mo., and had for years been the St. Louis County reporter for the Globe-Democrat with headquarters at the county seat, Clayton. Taking notice that young Walton possessed the earmarks of a newspaper man, Mr. Hudlin made him his assistant as reporter on the St. Louis Globe Democrat, which position Lester A. Walton filled until he become "county man" for the St. Louis Post-Despatch. The city editor of that paper and the young reporter did not get along very well and Mr. Walton resigned after a short time and became "county man" for the St. Louis Star Sayings, another evening paper, now known as the St. Louis Star. The "county men" from the St. Louis evening papers used to write their articles and then dictate their articles over the long distance telephone to stenographers in the local room. It was not until the young colored reporter was summoned one Saturday afternoon to report at the Star Sayings' office and write a detailed account of a big elopement to Clayton of prominent St. Louisians that his racial identity was made known. Clayton was known as the "rural Gretna Green." That Saturday evening Lester A. Walton walked into the local room of the Star Sayings, going up to John W. Kearney, the city editor, exclaimed: "I am Walton." "You are Walton?" asked Mr. Kearney in surprise. "Well," continued the city editor, "if you are game enough to report for us and continue to make good I am game enough to keep you on the staff." From that day the two became fast friends.

After serving for nearly a year as "county man" Lester A. Walton was brought into St. Louis and made a member of the local Staff. He was assigned to the courthouse as Court Reporter. Together with the eight divisions of the Circuit Court, the Circuit Clerk's Office, Sheriff's Office, Court of Appeals, Probate Court, Probate Clerk's Office, he for five years "covered" the Second District

Police Court in the morning where he was a familiar figure. No matter whether the judge or city attorney was Republican or Democrat, Lester A. Walton was known to be on the most friendly terms with them. The spectacle of a police court judge, known to many in the neighborhood, leaving the Walton home on Sunday afternoon, was a mild sensation in the immediate vicinity.

After six years on the St. Louis Star Sayings, serving both as court reporter and general assignment man, Lester A. Walton went to New York during the theatrical season of 1906-7, to write the lyrics for the Rufus Rastus Company, of which Ernest Hogan was the star. In St. Louis the comedian and newspaper man had formed an acquaintanceship and the former delegated his St. Louis friend to write the lyrics for his show. When the company went on the road, Mr. Walton served as personal representative for Mr. Hogan, looking after his business interests.

The following season, Lester A. Walton put out a big act of ten people with Thomas Johnson, of Klaw and Erlanger, and in February, 1908, became dramatic editor of the New York Age, which had been taken over by Fred R. Moore, some months previous. The dramatic department was an instantaneous hit with both public and performer, and was regarded by many as a feature of the paper. A few months later, Mr. Walton was also made managing editor, and has filled the respective position ever since. He is regarded as an authority on colored theatricals.

On June 29th, 1912, Lester A. Walton and Miss Gladys F. Moore, daughter of Fred R. Moore, were joined in wedlock and two fine children help to make the Walton household a happy one.

For nearly two years Mr. Walton and associate was lessee and manager of the Lafayette Theatre, located in Harlem. The undertaking was a large one, as the original rent asked for the house was $25,000 yearly. Although the theatre originally planned primarily for white people, had been a rank failure; it was a success under the Walton management.

In December, 1917, Mr. Walton was appointed a member of the Military Entertainment Service by Mr. Marc Klaw, of the big theatrical firm of Klaw and Erlanger, to supervise theatricals among the colored draftees at all cantonments, working under the direction of the War Department Commission on Training Camp Activities. He is also connected with the Walton Publishing Company, organized to publish songs and instrumental numbers of talented and ambitious colored writers, encountering difficulty in getting their compositions published and put on the market.

WILLIAM P. HAYES, JR., D. D.

NE thing that is being pressed home to us in this the crisis of the world, is that so many men have had no chance for educating themselves. Or worse still, having had the chance neglected it. This fact is brought out by the government records in all the different phases of life's activities. They want men trained in every branch and in every walk of life. The greater portion of the ministry would be turned down if examined by Uncle Sam for work in his department. This is a sad state of affairs, and yet, not such a surprising one. For the life of the race as a free people is not yet the length of the life of a man who considers himself middleaged. Maybe the greater surprise should be shown because of the great number of men, who in spite of hardships, poverty, back sets of all kinds still persevered and are today thinkers—educators—persons of note and of weight. Then there is the class of young men, born to parents who had gotten just a taste of slavery, just enough slavery to make them appreciate the privilege of educating their children and themselves at the same time. Of such parents, Rev. William P. Hayes, D. D., was born.

January 18, 1881, in Bullocks, North Carolina, there was born in the family of Rev. Hayes, a prominent Methodist minister, a young son. From the first the father determined that the young lad should have every advantage which he had enjoyed and more. So at an early age we find young William in school, where he made for himself an enviable record. The first school of his own choosing was Bennett College, Greensboro, North Carolina. Leaving Bennett he went to Richmond, Virginia, where he matriculated in the Virginia Union University.

As he studied and worked to prepare himself for life out in the world, Rev. Hayes spent much time planning and deciding just what work to follow. Medicine was alluring as was also the remuneration that usually goes with one thoroughly prepared in this profession. So he definitely decided to become a physician. But while he was still very young the call of the ministry was so strong that he had to give up his idea of medicine and take up the study of theology instead. To the mind of Rev. Hayes this is the principal episode of his life.

After leaving school, Rev. Hayes taught in Boydton Institute, Boydton, Virginia. Leaving Boydton he went to the Keysville Industrial School, and taught there for a short while. Still using teaching as his point of contract with people and their development, he went back to his Alma Mater and taught for a while in Virginia Union University. He then branched out into his real life work—that of preaching. For six years he served as pastor of churches in Virginia. He then accepted the call from the Mount Olivet Baptist Church, New York City. Here he has remained for the past seven years, preaching and leading his people to a higher plane of thinking and of living.

He has not confined his work to the church. He is a member of the Odd Fellows, of the Banquet Beneficial League, of New York, and of the Southern Beneficial League, of New York, and the Independent Order of St. Luke. He serves on the committee of Management of the Y. M. C .A., of New York City; Music School Settlement for Colored People; Howard Orphanage and Industrial Institute; Liberty Loan Committee, New York, Secretary of the Trustee Board, Northern Baptist University. In all these organizations he is not just a member but is active in the development of each.

On November 16, 1910, Rev. Hayes was married to Miss Carolyne Amee, of New York City. There are no children in the family. Mrs. Hayes is active in all the affairs of her husband's church. She has his interest at heart and lends her aid in every place where she can. She, with her husband work together for the social uplift of all who are around them.

ANDREW N. JOHNSON

NDREW N. Johnson, of Nashville, is a business man from tip to toe. As such he has his own notions as to the way of conducting business enterprises and one's personal affairs. He believes and asserts very emphatically that no customer should be asked to spend his money from a motive of sympathy or race loyalty, but that rather the Negro merchant should bring his wares up to the standard of competition with the best in the market. Another set policy of Mr. Johnson's is that he never goes in debt, does not believe in credit, refuses to sign notes and enter into any of that form of pay-to-morrow, so common in all practices of business. He pays cash or refuses to buy.

Mr. Johnson was born in Marion, Alabama, in 1866. He attended the public schools in Marion and then the Marion State Normal School. From the State Normal Institution, Mr. Johnson entered Talladega College. On leaving Talladega, he took Civil Service Examination and served as Postal Clerk for three years, being retired for political activity, then he went to Mobile, Alabama and began the business of Undertaking, and publishing

"The Mobile Press." After fourteen years of remarkable success here he moved to Nashville, Tenn., and established there once more his Undertaking house.

Mr. Johnson's is not a shop, but a house with its waiting rooms, offices, its departments containing all classes of caskets and funeral equipment; with its gallant span of horses and some half score of limousines backed by Winton, McFarlan, Hudson, and other high grade makes of cars, lined before the door—all owned, paid for in cash. The establishment rises, yes, soars far above the level even of the better class of Undertaking businesses. Indeed, Mr. Johnson is reported by reliable authorities to own the finest Undertaking equipment in the South; white or colored.

The late Dr. Booker T. Washington was exceedingly fond of preaching from the text, "To him that hath,.' etc., which appears to be both a natural and spiritual law. Mr. Johnson is a conspicuous instance of the truth of this law. With all of this establishment on his hands he does not cry, "hold, enough", but rather reaches out for more kinds of business to master. He was a member of the Republican National Convention, which nominated McKinley, Roosevelt and Hughes. He was also the last Negro nominated for Congress by the Republican party of Alabama. He is President of the Nashville Board of Trade, which organization was instrumental in building a Negro Library, creating blocks and playgrounds and civic improvements in Nashville—especially caring for the thousands made homeless in the conflagration in Nashville in the spring of 1918.

Mr. Johnson is the owner of the Johnson Block, consisting of the Lincoln Theatre and a half dozen business houses in the centre of the business district of Nashville, one block from the State Capitol Building and on the same street. He is also chairman of the Board of Trustees of the Grand Lodge Knights of Pythias, and a member of the Y. M. C. A. managing committee. He is president of the Johnson-Allen Undertaking Co., of Mobile, Ala.

With all this responsibility on his shoulders, and he attends to most of it personally, Mr. Johnson finds time and money to join in most local and national enterprises for progress, such as entertaining visitors, giving banquets, aiding in handling conventions, attending sessions of business leagues, and of Undertakers, holding and playing a strong hand in local political and projecting quite into national politics. In all situations, he is ready to be energetic, patient, pugnacious, hospitable and generous as the situation may demand.

Mr. Johnson was married in 1886 to Miss Lillie A. Jones, of Marion. Mrs. Johnson is a graduate of Talladega college. The two sons of the family are already grown and in business. Mr. L. E. Johnson is Secretary of the Johnson-Allen Undertaking Company of Mobile, and Dr. A. N. Johnson, Jr., is a practicing physician of Nashville, Tenn.

LEO FRITZ NEARON, M. D.

N recent years Colored men of foreign birth have taken on many of the traits and ambitions of the American. This is especially true in regard to gaining an education and making a career. Time was when people of any caste whatsoever in the foreign countries regarded work as a calamity. They were satisfied with their training, with their own environment, preferring to stay at home and husband out their fortunes, small or large, to getting out in the open and combating for a place in the sun.

Among those to come forth and out-American, the Yankee himself for education and career is Dr. Leo Fitz Nearon, of New York City. Dr. Nearon was born at St. George, Bermuda, July 17, 1881. His early days were spent at home, where he attended the public schools and St. George Academy.

His academy days over, he began his struggle for education and for a livelihood. For a time he worked in the Bermuda shipyards, serving an apprenticeship. From shipyard apprentice he became a school teacher, teaching in the Bermuda public schools 6 months, when he was but seven-

teen years of age. School teaching failing to prove the "Open Seasame" to him, as it has to many others on their way forward, he took up work with the St. George Bicycle Company, of Bermuda. Again wages were too small.

Working here and there he finally made his way to America. Here he set out to complete his education and to become master of a profession. Working summers and odd times during his school days, he managed to enter, and to complete the college course of Lincoln University in Pennsylvania, from which he was graduated in 1903.

What he had done to defray his expenses in college he must now repeat for his course in the study of medicine. Only, he had to redouble his efforts, as his expenses were much heavier. Going into New York, he registered in the New York Medical College. He completed his course here in 1898. His internship was the next step forward. He was fortunate enough to become an interne in New York, where he had been graduated. He did his time in the Flower Hospital, and then did post graduate work in the Lying-in Hospital, in the Flower and Metropolitan Hospitals.

New York, though rife with competition, appealed to him as a desirable place in whch to begin practice. He hung out his sign as a physician and surgeon and began his work. In ten years he has built up a very extensive practice and made many friends in Gotham. He owns a three-story residence, a residence with a brown stone front, and one which cost $12,500.

While Dr. Nearon has not yet taken on the responsibilities of domestic life, he has allied himself with many available organizations for personal uplift and professional service. He is a member of the Protestant Episcopal Church. He holds membership in many lodges and medical organizations. He is Past Deputy Grand Master of the I. O. U. of M. A., a member of the B. K. Bruce 8171, G. U. O. of O. F., of the Juanita Household of Ruth 4091; of the Lincoln Tabernacle 6024, G. U. O. of F. G., and Past Grand Master of Council 403, of New York Patriarchs Number 2; Past Exalted Ruler of Elks. Professionally he is a physician to the Day Nursery, to the B. K. Bruce Lodge, to the Imperial Lodge of Elks, to the St. Mannal Lodge, to Eureka Temple, Invincible Temple, and to Excelsior Lodge.

In addition to his affiliation in these bodies he carries membership in seven medical bodies. He belongs to the County Medical Socety of New York, to the State Medical Society, to the Aescolopian Medical Society, the National Medical Society, to the Manhattan Medical Society, to the Medical Clinical Society. In all these organizations he takes an active part, bringing in his experiences, throwing light upon many of the vexing problems in the practice of both medicine and surgery.

THE CLEF CLUB GRAND ORCHESTRA, N. Y. CITY

ROBABLY the most written of
and deservedly popular Negro organization of New York City today is the Clef Club. Its name
is a synonoym for all that is excellent, original, and aristocratic in music and in musical and
lighter drama. Whether its sig-
nature stands back of an individual, a quartet, a
troup, or an orchestra of one hundred pieces, it
means finished eclat.

This talented body was incorporated in the City
of New York, in May, 1910. Considering the material out of which it was formed, it stands as a
modern miracle. About the date named, a number
of aspirants to musical honors met with James
Reese Europe, to learn and practice note reading.
They made their debut at the Manhattan Casino,
under the direction of the founder and president,
James Reese Europe, who now, by the way is
leading a band "Somewhere in France," was assisted by William H. Tyler. In a few years they were
in Carnegie Hall and in about any other Hall, private or public, they wanted in New York.

To original song and music, meaning thereby
that a great many instrumental and vocal selection numbers were the work of the members of the
company, were interspersed with very entertaining and original dramatic parts. Confidence and
ambition growing, they ventured out of New York.
They went down to Philadelphia, Washington, and
Richmond, were banqueted and applauded to their
heart's content, and returned to New York in a
halo of glory and inspiration, the organization in-
tact; the railroad fares and other expenses more
than generously cared for. Perhaps no other
summary can be made of their success than is giv-
en in the "Richmond Times Dispatch."

"In many respects the most remarkable concert
ever given in Richmond was offered at the City
Auditorium last night by the Clef Club, an organization of Negro singers and instrumentalists, under the direction of the well known James Reese
Europe, assisted by William H. Tyler."

"An orchestra of sixty men, playing and singing fortissimo—remarkable indeed; and theirs are
not the rusty, unused voices of musicians who are
instrumentalists alone, but those of strong, vigorous
young Negro men, to whom singing comes as naturally as breathing. Nor did they attempt to sing
difficult, elaborate music, though, for a matter,
Europe is abundantly able to teach them anything
he might select, but confined their choral singing
to rousing, melodious, full-voiced pieces that lent
themselves admirably to their natural style.

"Practically every number on the program was
the composition of a Negro, from Coleridge-Taylor, who was an international figure in the world
of music, to lesser but competent men. Several
of the pieces were written by Europe himself, and
excellently written, while the work of the assistant conductor, Tyler, was also represented."

To the roles of leaders in music the Clef Club
has added another feature that is varying with its
musical reputation; that is the social feature. New
York society makes it as a gala day when the Clef
Club entertains. Then one can gain a glimpse
of the elite en masse, among the colored people.
Their balls at the Manhattan Casino have become
famous throughout the country. Mr. Daniel Kil-
gore succeeded Mr. Europe as President of the
Club and was in turn succeeded by Deacon Johnson, its present head.

Its policies, though undergoing refinements, remains the same to produce original Negro music
and to place deserving talent before the public.

BERRY O'KELLY

O see a man of prominence and of comparative wealth who has climbed from the bottom of the ladder unaided—a man who does not even know the date of his birth is one of the anomalies of the Negro race. No where else in the world in this privilege given so freely to the common man. Mr. Berry O'Kelly, of Method, North Carolina, is one of the many Negroes in America who has seized upon this opportunity and made the most of it.

Mr. O'Kelly was born in Chapel Hill, Orange County, North Carolina. The date of his birth he does not know. He never saw his mother or his father to know them, his mother having died when he was still an infant. As a lad he attended the public schools of Orange and Wake Counties, getting from his meager chances for schooling all that he could, in fact getting more from this chance than many young boy of his day got from much better opportunities. So we find Mr. O'Kelly as a man with a foundation laid in childhood and in young manhood upon which he has builded a superstructure of culture and refinement. This has been done through the medium of contact and travel.

At the early age of sixteen, Mr. O'Kelly started out in the mercantile business. He has never changed his business. He has only added to it. So today we find Mr. O'Kelly in the mercantile business and dealing in Real Estate. When we look at all that this man stands for, all that he owns in his own name, it is hard for us to look back and see the start he had. He worked for $5.00 to $12.00 a month until he had saved $100.00. He never had but two employers. This took time and the very strictest economy. To Mr. O'Kelly this was no real hardship for he had his goal before him. Having gotten the $100.00 he went into business with Mr. C. H. Woods. The business was known as Wood and O'Kelly. After a short time Mr. Wood wished to go west and sold out. So Mr. O'Kelly came into the possession of the whole business. Starting with the small capital of $100.00, the business has grown to the the extent that two railroad warehouses are used constantly for the accomodation of it.

In addition to owning his business and business interests, the subject of this sketch has accumulated considerable real estate. He owns over 1,000 acres of farm land, and a lot of city property, bank stock and other stock of value. Mr. O'Kelly has continued with the habit formed while he was still very young, the habit of saving and investing wisely.

In religious belief, Mr. O'Kelly is a member of the African Episcopal Church, and a helper in all denominations. He is a Mason and an Odd Fellow. For more than twenty-five years he served his town in the capacity of Post-Master. He is now the Chairman of the School Committee of the Berry O'Kelly County Teachers Training School. This is an institution which because of the very liberal way in which Mr. O'Kelly gave to its support bears his name. The Governors of North Carolina have given him many appointments. In all the duties thus thrust upon him he has measured up to the expectations of the people. On several occasions he has been elected a delegate to National Bodies, and he is a life member of the National Negro Business League.

One of the things that has made the culture of this man is the travels it has been his opportunity to enjoy. He has traveled all over this country and over Europe, Asia, and over parts of Africa. The effect of these days spent in travel are apparent in the talks and actions of Mr. O'Kelly. It is this that has made the superstructure of culture and refinement upon the foundation laid in the little country school back in Orange and Wake County, North Carolina.

About twenty years ago, Mr. O'Kelly was married to Miss Chanie Ligon. For twelve years she was to him a helpmate in the truest sense of the word. About eight years ago she died. There were no children and so once more Berry O'Kelly was left alone in the world. But the conditions are so different from the other time when both his father and mother left him to the mercies of the world. The man himself, has been the sole cause of the change in these conditions—then there was nothing. Today he is a man of means, of business ability, of social prominence, of culture and refinement.

Isaac A. Lawrence, M. D.

ARCH 3rd, 1870, there was born at Morg Neck, Maryland, a baby boy, whose destiny carried him along a rocky path in his early life, but which led him finally to a goal which any one might envy. This boy was Dr. I. A. Lawrence of Elizabeth, New Jersey. His father died when he, an only child, was only two years of age, leaving his mother in abject poverty. This entailed upon young Isaac the extreme hardships which follow in the wake of poverty. His early days were marked with great privations and suffering. Frequently during severe winters he went without an overcoat and with but meager garments of any kind to protect him from the cold. The dump heap became his friend, and he often resorted to it to fish out the old and discarded shoes of other boys, for his mother was unable to buy him covering for his feet. His feet would present an odd appearance for it was not often that he could secure mates of the same kind of shoes. Frequently he would be seen with a lace shoe on one foot and a button shoe on the other. Necessity knew no fashion as well as no law with him, and so long as his feet were fairly well protected he did not mind the smiles of the passers by.

Adversity did another thing for him—it early developed in him those qualities which go to make up the man. He began doing his part in sustaining the family at the early age of six years. His first work was to turn bricks, which earned him five cents per thousand. He was an industrious boy, and very frugal, habits which aided him in all of his life struggles.

It is not surprising that a boy exhibiting such grit and determination should elect to educate himself and he worked and saved to this end. His progress through school was marked by the same hardships that characterized his early boyhood. To add to his difficulties him money was frequently stolen from him at the most inopportune times. At one time after working all summer and saving his money earned as waiter at a seashore resort, the whole sum was stolen the day before the hotel closed for the season.

He was the first colored pupil admitted to the South Chester High School, from which he graduated in 1888. To do this he was compelled to work in a mill, from six in the evening, until six in the morning, attending school during the day, the session being from 9 A. M. to 2 P. M. In this way —working at night and studying during the day, he not only graduated from the South Chester High School, but saved enough money to enter the Lin-

coln University. He entered the University in 1888, and graduated therefrom in 1892. His first idea was to practice law and on leaving college he took up the study of law, but owing to the death of his preceptor, and his change of mind regarding the profession, he gave up this study and turned his mind towards medicine. In order to take a medical course the money question again came to the front so he was compelled to teach for a while before entering college.

He matriculated at Howard University in 1893, and remained there one year, when he went to Shaw University and finshed the medical course.

Pluck, energy, integrity and patience are sure to bring a rich reward, not only in the development of character, but in material blessings, and so it was with Dr. Lawrence. The day of his prosperity dawned when he completed his medical course at Shaw University. From that day his star of hope and prosperity began to rise.

On completing his medical course at Shaw he began the practice of his profession in Elizabeth, N. J. From this time fortune began to smile upon him and has ever since.

He was married to Miss Ardelia Matthews, of Hawkinsville, Georgia, in 1902. They have one daughter, who is nine years old, Hattie Christine, a musical prodigy.

Aside from the practice of his profession, Dr. Lawrence has been very active along all lines that tend to uplift his people. He was for several years the Superintendent of Mt. Teman A. M. E. Sunday School, which prospered greatly under his administration. He was the first president of the North Jersey Medical Association. This is perhaps the best and most widely known local colored medical society in the United States. He helped to organize and was first and the only president of the Alpha Ben Association which for thirteen years has been the leading insurance company among the colored people of the North. He was organizer of the Alpha Investment Company and its only president. This is the leading investment company among colored people in the United States, and has been in existence since 1905.

In fraternal organizations he has taken a prominent part, being Past Chancellor Commander of Knights of Pyhias, a member of the Elks, and Odd Fellows, and at present Grand Master of Masons of New Jersey. His real estate holdings are extensive. Indeed, whenever Dr. Lawrence casts up his accounts and estimates his holdings he smiles and says that they are worth far more than all the boys whose cast off shoes he wore back there in his day of want and poverty.

SAMUEL H. VICK

CHOOL man and public servant, Samuel H. Vick of Wilson, North Carolina worked his way from the ground, as it were, to a place of eminence in both school work and in the service of his government. Mr. Vick was born in Castalia, North Carolina, April 1st, 1863. As a boy he attended the public schools of Wilson, the town to which he was to return and in which he was to make for himself an enviable career. Completing his work in the public schools of Wilson, he matriculated in Lincoln University, in Pennsylvana. He was graduated from Lincoln in 1884.

His course through school and college was by no means one of ease or opulence. Even when he was very young he must needs work, not only to go to school, but for his own sustenance. When he was but thirteen years of age he found employment in a grocery store. Here he worked in spare hours and went to school during school session. His vacations were also spent in working in this grocery store. Thus as a grocery clerk he made his way through the public schools and through Lincoln University.

Graduating from Lincoln in 1884 he returned to Wilson and secured a post as an assistant teacher in the city graded schools. This position he held for one year. At the end of the school year he was promoted to a principalship in Wilson. For the next five years he was principal of the Negro public school of his native town. It was at that time common to appoint respectable and deserving colored men to political office especially when the Republican Party was in power. When Benjamin Harrison came into office several of these more deserving positions were given to leading Negroes. Among those to fall heir to one of these posts was Mr. Vick, who was made postmaster of Wilson. In many sections of the south the loud complaints were made about putting Negroes in public office at all, and especially in office where they would be over white people, and would be brought more or less in social contact with white people. But Mr. Vick managed to escape most of this protest, and to conduct the post office with such efficiency that whatever complaint might have come forth at first was soon stifled. Indeed, so thoroughly had he administered his office that when the administration changed there were not a few of the leading citizens of Wilson who eagerly desired his retention.

However, he went out of office, and sought other fields for his talents. The Presbyterian church, which had given Lincoln University, and which was working among the churches as well as among the schools soon enlisted his services. This body put Mr. Vick in the field to labor among the Sunday Schools, working as a Sunday School Missionary. His own home town had not however forgot his services either as a school man or as a postmaster. He had not therefore been out of the post office many years before they appointed him to another post of public service. He was made a member of the County Board of Education of Wilson County, and served his county with the same credit to himself that he had served in the Wilson Post Office.

Then came further evidence that the people of Wilson, white as well as black, were well pleased with the service he had given them as postmaster. When McKinley was elected Mr. Vick was once more made post master of his native city. Here he served a second time for a period of five years. He was now ready to retire from active service which he did, devoting his time to public service and to looking after his personal interests.

During his early days in Wilson he had made some investments in real estate and in land improvement. This work with his various secret order obligations he now retired to superintend. Mr. Vick is a member of the Presbyterian church, a Mason, an Odd Fellow and a Pythian. In the first named secret body he is First Colonel of the North Carolina Patriarchy, and has been twice Grand Master of the Odd Fellows of North Carolina. He has traveled very extensively in America, having toured the east, and much of the west and south.

Mr. Vick was married to Miss Annie M. Washington of Wilson, in May 1892. Mr. and Mrs. Vick have seven children.

WILLIAM GASTON PEARSON, B. S., A. M., PH. D.

ILLIAM G. Pearson, school teacher, business man and educator, is one of those stalwart men of Durham, North Carolina. He was born in the days of slavery, in 1859, in the place which is now known as Durham, but unknown then as anything save a semi-rural settlement. Of course early education with him was out of the question, except that severe brand which many of the young slaves tasted on the plantations.

When public schools for Negroes were established in Durham, Mr. Pearson enrolled and began his education in books. However, these schools ran but six months in the year and had teachers with only meagre preparation. The young exslave needed merely to get a start. After this he taught himself until after the age of twenty-one when he entered Shaw University.

Graduating from Shaw in 1886, with the degree of Bachelor of Science, Mr. Pearson began his career as a teacher in public schools. From that time on he was a teacher, principal, worker in the graded school of Durham for twenty years. However, he did not cease to study. He did not only continue to labor with his books during spare hours at home but pursued courses in Cornell University and in other institutions in the summer. In recognition of his continuous growth and of service to education, Shaw University conferred upon him the degree of Master of Arts, in 1890, and in 1915, Kittrel College made him Doctor of Philosophy.

Professor Pearson as he came to be known, has widened his influence and his activities, from year to year, both in school work and in business. He soon became a trustee of Kittrell College, Secretary of the Board of Trustees of the National Training School, of Durham, and a director of the Mechanics and Farmers' Bank of Durham, trustee of Lincoln Hospital, and one of the prime movers in practically every uplift undertaking of Durham, indeed of North Carolina. In this respect he became not only a worker, but a giver as well. The most celebrated donation he has made, though he has an open hand for all good causes, was the giving to Kittrell College, a model school building.

Distinguished as are Mr. Pearson's services as teacher and Educator, probably his most lasting and most helpful contribution is the organization known as the Royal Knights of King David. This body, which is, strictly speaking, an insurance order, operates in several states, and has deposits with insurance Commissioners in these states to protect its patrons. Its fees are small; it insures men, women and children; but its dividends and benefits are sure and prompt. It ranks as one of the best Negro Insurance companies in America. In his office of six clerks, graduates from the best institutions, Mr. Pearson keeps in intimate touch with all the branch houses and orders both in North Carolina and in other states.

Mr. Pearson was married in 1893 to Mrs. Minnie S. Summer of Charlotte, North Carolina. Mrs. Pearson is a graduate of Livingston College, at Salisbury, and a woman of rare talent. She has done, much as Dr. Pearson will very frequently tell you, in shaping the career of her distinguished husband.

Mr. Pearson is an ardent church worker, being one of the pillars of the A. M. E. Church. His high standing in the church, coupled with his clean reputation in business and in school work make his word his bond and a guide to all who know him. The records show that Mr. Pearson's wealth is valued at $75,000.

William G. Pearson is a many sided man and every aspect of his attainments and service shine forth with a resplendance so great that it has attracted attention to him near and far. He is a schools teacher, an educator of marked ability and a business man and in all of these lines he is recognized as a man of great intelligence and power. He is a most influencial citizen of North Carolina.

ALBERT WITHERSPOON PEGUES. A. B., B. D.

ORN Nov. 25, 1859, Albert W. Pegues, had a little taste of slavery, but not enough to effect in any way his ambitions as a young man. He was born in Raleigh, North Carolina, and he set for himself the attainment of learning and a distinct position in the world as an educator. To this end he sat under many men of learning and made intimate acquaintance with a very large number of American Colleges and Universities.

Mr. Pegues is a Baptist in his faith, and so it was that in choosing his first school he made one of the Baptist schools his choice. Thus we find him first as student at Benedict College, Columbia, S. C., where he stayed for a time and then changed to Richmond Institute—now Union University. We next find the young student enrolled in Bucknell University, in Lewisburg, Pennsylvania, where he remained till he received his Bachelor Degree. Mr. Pegues, when he had opportunity to pursue his studies further, went to Chicago and attended lecture courses at the University of Chicago, Illinois.

By the time he was twenty-seven years of age,

Dr. Pegues was ready to undertake his career as an educator. His first post of responsibility in school was that of Principal of the Summer High School, of Parkersburg, West Virginia. This position he accepted in 1886 and held for one year. Then he got an appointment to a larger institution, left Parkersburg, and took up the work in the new field which was in Shaw University, in Raleigh, North Carolina. Thus we have the young man in a very responsible position in his native town, a sight which is altogether too rare. In Shaw he labored for sixteen years. Owing to his very thorough preparation he was able to serve in the capacity of Dean of the College Department and in that of Dean of the Theological Department. For six years he held the former and for ten years he held the latter position.

At the end of sixteen years of service for Shaw University, Dr. Pegues resigned to accept the Principalship of the Colored Department of the North Carolina State School for the Blind and Deaf, the position which he now holds.

Along with his duties as an educator, Dr. Pegues has found time to do considerable writing. About twenty-five years ago he published a book "Our Ministers and Schools." This book was very widely read and it did a great deal toward making a name for Dr. Pegues. He has also been a very liberal contributor to papers. Then Dr. Pegues has spent much time and thought in the preparation of speeches, for in connection with his school work he has been in constant demand as a speaker. For some years he was statistical Secretary of the National Baptist Convention. In North Carolina he has had the honor of serving his denomination in every capacity. He is Secretary of the Lott Carey Baptist Foreign Mission Convention, a position he had held since its organization. For eighteen years he has been Corresponding Secretary of the Baptist State Sunday School Convention, a position of trust and one in which Dr. Pegues has had opportunity to do great good.

Severing his connection with Shaw University as Dean did not really sever his connections with the school, for Dr. Pegues still serves this institution, where for so many years he labored, in the capacity of Trustee. He is also a Trustee of Girl's Training School, of Franklinton, North Carolina.

Dr. Pegues has given of his energy and strength in still one other direction. He has taken considerable interest in business. During the years he has been out of school and at work for himself he has been able to accumulate considerable property.

Dr. Pegues is an Odd Fellow and Mason. In 1890, Dr. Pegues was married to Miss Ella Christian, of Richmond, Virginia. They have two children.

BISHOP ALEXANDER P. CAMPHOR, A. B., B. D.

ISHOP Alexander P. Camphor, Bishop of the African Methodist Episcopal Church, was born in a cabin that comprised one of a group of shacks known as "Negro Quarters," in Jefferson Parish, Louisiana, on a large sugar plantation twelve miles east of New Orleans. The Bishop has told his own story so well that we shall read as he has written:

"Both my parents," says he, "had been slaves, the Emancipation Proclamation having gone into effect two years previous to my birth. My mother is still living but my father died when I was an infant. My father had secured knowledge enough to read the Bible and to write his mother's name.

"Mother made a solemn pledge to father before he died, that she would spare no pains in giving me an education. Being unlearned and without means she decided that the only way to do this was to give me away to one whom she believed could more easily educate me than herself. Accordingly when eight years of age I left the plantation to live in the city of New Orleans, with Stephen Priestley.

"It seems providential that I should have fallen into such hands as those of Stephen Priestley, for in my foster father I had both rigid school-master and a rugged old fashioned Methodist preacher to direct my feet aright.

I attended public school in Carrolton, and after completing the work there entered New Orleans

University, where I graduated in 1889, receiving the Bachelor of Arts Degree. During the greatest revival in the history of the University, conducted by the Rev. Wm. R. Webster, D. D., of Massachusetts ,I was converted and later licensed to preach. I was then 16 years of age. After graduation I taught four years as Professor of Mathematics in my Alma Mater. Completing the full course there and securing the Bachelor of Divinity degree, I entered the ministry and was appointed pastor of James M. E. Church, Germantown, Pa. My next appointment was to Orange, N. J., while there I received an invitation from Bishop Hartzell to go as missionary to Africa, and I was ready to go.

"My wife and I were the first regularly appointed colored missionaries under the Prent Board to the "Dark Continent." As president of the college of West Africa and superintendent of the Methodist Schools in Liberia from 1896 to 1907, I had the pleasure of contributing to the advancement of the work.

"While in Liberia I gathered original material for two volumes "Missionary Story Sketches and Folklore from Africa" and "Liberia, the Afro-American Republic." Returning to America in 1907 I was persuaded that I could better serve Africa by helping to educate the youth of my race in America. For this reason I accepted the presidency of the Central Alabama Institute located at Birmingham, Ala., where I have labored for the past eight years.

"I was three times elected delegate to the General Conference and once a delegate to the World's Missionary Conference at Edinburgh, Scotland. At the General Conference of the Methodist Episcopal Church that met at Saratoga Springs, N. Y., by an almost unanimous vote of that body I was elected Bishop of Africa. In this office I succeeded Bishop I. B. Scott and will be associated with Bishop E. S. Johnson. These evidences of confidence on the part of the church have only served to intensify and inflame my zeal for unselfish service, that the cause of education and Religion might be all the more speedily advanced."

Bishop Camphor is an illustration of the law of service as laid down by the master whom he serves —the Lord Jesus Christ—who said that the road to greatness is through service. "When God wants a worker He calls a worker. When He has work to be done, he goes to those who are already at work. When God wants a great servant, He calls a busy man."

Bishop Camphor is not only a busy man but a very busy man, just such a man as God can use, and his remarkable accomplishments attest to the divine guidance and help. The secret of his success lies in his great love of humanity and his love of service. It is this spirit that makes him a man beloved by all who come in personal contact with him and who fall under the spell of his influence.

Bishop Camphor could say with Thomas H. Gill:

"The more I triumph in thy gifts,
The more I wait on thee;
The grace that mightily uplifts
Most sweetly humbleth me."

Bishop Camphor was married to Miss Mamie Anna Rebecca Weathers in 1893, at Atlanta, Ga. They have no children.

LEWIS GARNETT JORDAN, D. D.

R. Lewis Garnett Jordan in one of those who has climbed all the way from the abject ignorance of slavery to a manhood of travel and culture, from being the property of his master to owning property in his own name and acquiring great property for his church. He was born a slave in 1853, near Meridian, Mississippi. His father was Jack Gaddis, and his mother Mariah Carey, but when he became a free man he chose a name for himself and so we have Dr. Jordan. Although born when it was impossible to get an education and hard to get one even after he was freed, we find Dr. Jordan as a lad getting all that he could in the way of book knowledge in the public schools of both Meridian and Natchez, Mississippi. He also spent some time as a student in Roger Williams University, at Nashville, Tennessee. Here in Roger Williams, one of the largest and oldest institutions of the Baptist Church, Dr. Jordan got an insight into things and an inspiration that has never left him. His degree of Doctor of Divinity was received from Natchez College in 1880, and from Gaudaloupe in 1903.

Merely the bare facts of the very active life lead by Dr. Jordan can be recorded here. He was ordained to the Baptist Ministry in 1875. He built churches while pastoring at Yazoo City, Mississippi, in 1878; in San Antonio, Texas, in 1885; in Waco, Texas, in 1886, in Hearne, Texas, in 1888; in Philadelphia, Pennsylvania, in 1893. This is a great service for any man to render to his church. Since 1896, Dr. Jordan has served his denomination in the capacity of Corresponding Secretary of the Foreign Mission Board, of the National Baptist Convention, and he still holds this position. He is the Senior Secretary of the National Baptist Convention and is regarded as one of its most influential members.

During his incumbency in office more than forty missionaries have been sent into its field in South America, the West Indies, the western, southern and central parts of Africa. During this time they have received several bequests, the latest of importance exceeding $30,000.00. Under his administration of the affairs of this branch of the work the board has acquired property in its fields valued at about $47,000.00. This includes the land, churches, stations, schools and homes. Dr. Jordan has had other honors showered upon him by his denomination. He was delegate to the World's Baptist Alliance, England, in 1904, and to the World's Missionary Conference, Edinburgh.

Dr. Jordan has not confined his work to the church. He is an active member of the Y. M. C. A., and active in the Equal Rights of League Society for the Advancement of Colored People. He is President of the Douglass Improvement Company and trustee of the National Baptist Training School for Women and Girls in Washington, D. C. He has also taken an active interest in the political life of his country. He is a Prohibitionist and has had the honor of being delegate to nearly every National Convention of his party since 1888. At one time he was candidate for Congressman-at-large for Pennsylvania. He is a life member of the National Negro Business Men's League, a Mason, a member of the Independent Order of St. Luke and a member of the American Woodmen of the world.

Dr. Jordan has traveled all over this country and has visited England and Scotland, has been to the West Indies twice, to Africa three times, to South America once. During his trip to Africa, in 1917 the President of Liberia conferred upon him the Knighthood of the Republic "Knight Commander of the Liberian Humane Order of African Redemption." The effect of this extensive travel is seen in the writings and the lectures of this public spirited man. He is the founder and Editor of the Mission Herald, author of "Up the Ladder in Missions," 1908; "Prince of Africa," 1911; "In Our Stead," 1913; "Pebbles from an African Beach," 1917. This represents a great deal of work on the part of Dr. Jordan and has added immeasurably to his usefulness in the denomination.

Dr. Jordan, while not a man of means, the bulk of his earnings having been contributed to further Religious and Civil enterprises for national and racial uplift, may, however, easily be rated at $10,000.00 realty holdings, besides several thousand dollars interest in a number of undeveloped enterprises.

Dr. Jordan has been twice married. His first wife was Mrs. Fannie Armstrong. They were married in 1880, and they lived together till her death, thirty years later. He was married, May 29, 1913, to Mrs. M. J. Marquess, of Helena, Ark.

BISHOP WILLIAM HENRY HEARD

HAT the life of Bishop William Henry Heard, Bishop for Louisiana and Mississippi has been one of steady climbing is seen by a simple recital of the main facts in his life. He was born in Elbert County, Georgia, June 25, 1850. From the date we may gather the facts of his early life. Although too young to know many of the horrors of slavery, he still knew enough of that period to appreciate his personal freedom.

One of the blessings that came to him was that he lived with people who had ambition for his betterment. So the young man had plenty of opportunities to attend school. He was a student in the South Carolina University, Atlanta University, Clark University, Atlanta, Georgia, and in the Reform Divinity School, in West Philadelphia, Pennsylvania. In all of these institutions he distinguished himself both by his good scholarship and by his manly conduct.

It was not a sudden jump to the Bishopric for Bishop Heard. He traveled the long road that has to be taken by all who achieve success. He has served in political offices of various kinds. He was at one time a Railway Postal Clerk, he was a member of the South Carolina Legislature from Abbeville County, he was United States Minister Resident and Council General to the Court of Liberia, Africa. In this manner he has been able to serve his government.

At the age of thirty, in 1880 Bishop Heard joined the A. M. E. Conference of North Georgia. Thus began the round of charges that fall to the lot of the minister of any denomination and especially to the lot of the Methodist Minister. He served Johnston Mission, Athens, Georgia; Markham Street Mission, Atlanta, Georgia; Aiken Station, Aiken, South Carolina; Mt. Zion Station, Charleston, South Carolina; and Allen Chapel, Philadelphia, Pennsylvania. At this time, having served his charges so very well, Bishop Heard was promoted to the position of Presiding Elder. He was at this time working in the Philadelphia Conference. His first district was the Lancaster District. He pastored the Bethel Church at Philadelphia, Pennsylvania, and the Mother Church of the Connection. He then had the two charges of Wilmington Station and Harrisburg. At this time he gave up the work in this country and served as superintendent of Missions in West Africa, but returned to the work of his own land to take the Zion Chapel, at Philadelphia, and Presiding Elder of Long Island District, New York Conference. He next served Phoenixville, Pennsylvania and Allen Temple, Atlanta, Georgia. This represents working with a great number of people. A great many souls were by this time saved through the ministration of this man.

While still serving in the capacity of pastor, Bishop Heard realized the need of the Preachers' Aid Society. To help this organization along he served as its Secretary for four years. This service was given freely without any remuneration whatever. As a culmination of the long years of service in the various places he was elected Bishop of his church. No more worthy man could have been found to fill the place. May 20, 1908, at Norfolk, Virginia, he was ordained. This was not the end of his very active career, but merely a broadening of his field of labor. So well had he served in the small fields given him that his denomination had the confidence in him to believe that he would do the work of the greater fields.

His first charge in the capacity of Bishop was in Africa. Here he remained for eight years. The Church there grew under his ministration. He added materially to the cause while serving in this post. At the same time he served his government in an official capacity. So we see that the name of Heard is well known in West Africa. Returning to this country, Bishop Heard was made Bishop of Mississippi and Louisiana. In this position he is still serving.

The life of this man should be an inspiration to any young man who has for his aim in life the preaching of the Gospel. In Bishop Heard we have an excellent example of a man who has done what he set out to do. Helping him all along the way in every step of the journey we find Mrs. Heard. She was Miss Josephine D. Henderson, daughter of Lafayette and Anna Henderson. The Heard's were married in 1882, in their Georgia home. Both Bishop and Mrs. Heard have the love and the esteem of all who know them.

BIRDS-EYE VIEW OF LINCOLN UNIVERSITY, PENNSYLVANIA

INCOLN University is the oldest Institution for the Higher Education of the Negro. It was pledged to God in an ordination service in 1849. The General Assembly of the Presbyterian Church gave its sanction in 1853. The Legislature of Pennsylvania granted a Charter to Ashmun Institute in 1854. A modest building was erected and the doors were opened to four students in 1857. The Legislature changed the name to Lincoln University in 1866. The Reverend Mr. John Pym Carter, and Reverend Mr. John Wynn Martin. D D., were the two successive Presidents and the whole Faculty in themselves from 1857 to 1865. The Reverend Mr. Isaac Norton Rendall, D. D., was President from 1865 to 1906 and the Reverend Mr. John B. Rendall, D. D., has been President since 1906.

The University owns equipment, buildings and grounds, costing $350,000, and productive endowment to the amount of $650,000. Its annual current expenditures approximate $50,000. It has two Departments, a College, and a Theological Seminary. In its 60 years of history, Lincoln University has had 1638 students in its College, and 628 in its Seminary.

The Alumni statistics show 656 ministers of all denominations; 263 doctors including dentists and druggists; 255 teachers; 227 in business; and 86 lawyers. The students have come from almost every state of the Union, and the Alumni have gone to virtually every state of the Union, as well as to Africa, South America, and the Isles of the Sea.

At the close of the Civil War most of the students had been soldiers in the United States Army; and in the world war, the student body in large number again wore the American uniform The University is proud to give its choicest sons in this holiest of all wars. A full proportion of them were commissioned officers, some serving in France.

The general control is vested in a Board of 21 Trustees. The College has full recognition and membership in the Association of the Colleges of the State of Pennsylvania, and the Theological Seminary is under the full control of the Presbyterian General Assembly.

White Institutions have since taken the name of Lincoln, but this Institute for the Higher Christian Education of the Negro was the first to bear the name of the Immortal President. This Christian school was also the first to establish a chair of the English Bible and make it a required course for every student in every class.

Mrs. Susan Dod Brown endowed this chair and also gave the chapel in which each day the work is opened with 15 minutes of Devotional Exercises, and in which regular preaching services are held each Sabbath.

Lincoln University is not a rival of other schools in this field. She never advertises for students, and cannot receive a fourth of those who apply. She has nothing but a good will and a God speed to all.

Edwin J. Turner, M. D.

HE following tribute to Dr. Turner, taken from the Columbus, (Georgia) Ledger, is a most appropriate introduction to the sketch of his life prepared for the Negro Cyclopedia:

"What Daniel Boone and other pioneers, who labored, toiled and endured hardships which would have chilled the hearts and swerved the purpose of less earnest and able men, did toward peopling the West, and toward opening up a hitherto unknown country, Dr. Edwin J. Turner, who is well and favorably known by all but a very few of the people of Columbus, both White and Colored, has done for the colored race in this section of the State, and the United States. And the influence of his life, and possibly the measure of success which he has wrought has inspired, who knows how many of his countrymen and members of his race, to go and do likewise. For Dr. Turner has the heart and the ability of a pioneer, and such, literally he was in the field of education, and in the line of progress to the people of his race in Columbus, and the surrounding country—who can say how far his influence has spread abroad throughout the land."

Dr. Turner was born in Meridian, Mississippi, in 1876, and until he reached the age of fifteen he attended the public schools of his native city.

After his course in the public schools he entered the Clark University, of Atlanta, Georgia, where he took up the study of Pharmacy. He graduated from this Institution and then entered the New Orleans University, where he graduated in the school of medicine in 1912.

Having prepared himself for his life work he chose Columbus, Georgia, as the field of his endeavors. Here he soon built up a large practice and has the distinction of being the first colored physician to locate in Muscogee County. He soon established himself high in the esteem of his community among all classes, white and black, and holds an enviable position in the ranks of his colleagues in other counties and other states.

Without neglecting his practice, which always commands his closest attention, he has actively identified himself with the public interest, keeping always in mind the good of his community and especially the elevation of his race.

When the Young Men's Christian Association was tottering and almost ready to fall under the burden of debt and in-ability to keep up its current expenses, he was called to the rescue. He promptly accepted the Presidency, went thoroughly into the investigation of its condition and intelligently addressed himself to relieving its distressing situation. The Association under his direction has weathered the financial storms, been raised to a paying basis and is now in a flourishing condition. His ambition is to have his people so live as to command the respect and esteem of all citizens and by his own exemplary life he has set them the example. He has possibly done more to raise them to this high place in the public estimation than any other man in the State.

A mere list of accomplishments of Dr. Turner would be indeed a bare record without taking into consideration the conditions under which they were accomplished. When convinced that a course was right no difficulties could prevent him from going forward in the accomplishments of the object set before him. He was not reckless in meeting difficulties, but faced them patiently and firmly with a courage born of a deep conviction.

The honors which have been conferred upon him are insufficient to show how they were earned, and how worthy he is to bear them.

Dr. Turner's interest in his people has led him into the field of politics and there as elsewhere he is an active factor. He is not constituted to be passive in any field of endeavor he enters.

He is a member of the Republican party and a member of the State Republican Executive Committee, representing Muscogee County. He was a National Delegate to the Republican Convention which nominated Mr. Taft for President, and his influence and vote went for Mr. Taft at that time. He was the first colored man that was ever appointed Notary Public in Muscogee County, and throughout his term of office he has demonstrated his reliability and worth in that capacity, and has fulfilled his duties to the entire satisfaction of those whom he serves.

Dr. Turner is a member of the Presbyterian Church where his disposition for work is also manifested and where his counsel and help is in constant demand.

He is also a member of the Masonic Fraternity, a Knight of Pythias and a member of the Knights of Tabor. He is the Grand Medical Director of the Colored Knights of Pythias of Georgia, and Grand Chief Mentor of the Knights and Daughters of Tabor of Georgia.

He is proprietor of the 10th Street Drug Store, which carries a stock valued at $5000.

In 1904 he married Miss Lela Benner, of Macon, Georgia, and they have but one child, a son, ten years of age, Benner C. Turner.

NORVAL COBB VAUGHAN, A. B., M. D.

MONG the Negro physicians who have won laurels in the West and who has risen to a high place in the profession, Dr. Norval Cobb Vaughan, of Cincinnatti, Ohio, stands as a brilliant instance. He exemplifies the very spirit of loyalty and is true to his fraternity throughout the country and especially so to the Negro fraternity. Although engaged in active practice he remains the hard and close student. He realizes that there is always something to learn in his profession and he keeps abreast of the times and for this reason gives all the time that he can spare from his work as a physician to reading and studying.

Hacing the interest of his race at heart his life has been given in unselfish service to them in every way where he could lend a helping hand. It is the exhibition of these traits and spirit that has won him distinction and praise.

Dr. Vaughn is a native of Virginia. He was born in Farmvile, Virginia, August, 1867. He received his early school training in another State but returned to "Old Virginia" for finishing touches. He secured his elementary training in East Orange, New Jersey, attending and passing through the public schools there. After his course in the public schools of Orange, he returned to his native State, Virgina, and entered the Richmond Institute, taking the Academic course. Completing his course at the Richmond Institute, he enrolled at the Virginia Normal and Collegiate Institute, at Petersburg, Virginia, where he was graduated as a Bachelor of Arts.

He was now ready to give thought to a career and after due consideration of the various calls held out to men he decided upon medicine, and having determined to be a physician he entered the Medical Department of Howard University, to get the necessary preparation for his work. He graduated from this Institution in 1897.

Dr. Vaughan is a man of cool calculation, rather than one given to impulse so in deciding the question of a location he surveyed the field before coming to a decision. He made note of the fact that Cincinnati, Ohio was not only a large and growing city, but that it had a large Negro population and that this class of its population was constantly growing. He decided that this was a most promising field so in this city he pitched his tent, and hung out his shingle, and here he has labored for twenty-two years. He has demonstrated the wisdom of his choice for with patience, energy and loyalty to his profession he has built up a large and lucrative practice.

Without neglecting his special work he his interested himself in welfare work.

His spare moments have been devoted to uplift work and study in many directions. He is holder of many valuable pieces of real estate, to which he gives some thought and study. He is also greatly interested in inventions and patents. He has invented and had patented a bullet proof breast shield. He is a member of the Academy of Medicine of Cincinnati, wherein much time and study are devoted to modern and local problems in medicine. He is also a member of the Medical Council of Pensylvania; member of the Council of Social Agencies of Cincinnati; and Staff Physician of the Evangeline Home and Hospital of Cincinnati. Besides this he is a member of and in close contact with every local organization which has for its purpose Negro uplift or advance in any direction.

On entering his professional career, Dr. Vaughan took the advice of those modern philosophers, who say that the first step in a successful career of a young man is marriage. In 1899, the same year he opened office in Cincinnati, he was married to Miss Victoria Powell of Richmond, Virginia. Two children have been born to Dr. and Mrs. Vaughan but both are deceased. One died when it was a month old; the other at the age of five and a half years.

248

HON. JOHN P. GREEN

R. John P. Green was born in Newbern, North Carolina, April 2nd, 1845. His parents John R. Green and Temperance Green were both free and honorable. Mr. Green was educated in Common, High and Law Schools, of Cleveland, Ohio. But this education came to him through his own efforts. Between the ages of fourteen and twenty two, Mr. Green worked in all sorts of menial employments, buying a home for his widowed mother. After that, he followed the same pursuits in striving for an education for himself.

He began his professional career in 1870, when he was admitted to the South Carolina Bar, and, in 1872, he returned to Ohio and began the practice of law, in Cleveland. His has been a very active life, since being admitted to the bar. He was elected justice of the peace of the city of Cleveland, in 1873, and served for three terms, (nine years). During this time, he disposed of about twelve thousand cases. In 1882 he was elected to the lower branch of the Ohio General Assembly, and re-elected in 1890. In 1892, he was elected to the Senate of Ohio. He is the first and only colored man, as yet, elected to the Senate. When he was in the Senate, he presided over that body, and was for that space of time, defacto Lieutenant-Governor of Ohio. When he was in the Lower House of the Ohio General Assembly, Mr. Green wrote and secured the passage of the bill creating Labor Day in Ohio. This was subsequently, made a national Holiday, by Congress. In 1897, President McKinley appointed him United States Postage Stamp agent. For nine years, he manufactured and distributed all the postage stamps for the government. For eighteen months, he was defacto Superintendent of Finance, of Post Office Department; during which time he signed many thousand warrants for money due to mail contractors.

Mr. Green has traveled extensively. He has been to Europe four times. In 1809 he was received, with his wife, by Pope Leo; he was also received by the Lord Bishop, of London, and the Dean of West Minister Abbey. He sat with his family in the Choir of the Abbey, and also of Saint Pauls during divine services. Mr. Green visited France, Italy, Austria, also the Midera Islands, Gibralter and Scotland. While in Scotland he lectured eleven times to large audiences. Another pleasant memory of Mr. Green if the fact that, while in Ireland, he visited Blarney Castle, and, by the courtesy of fellow tourists, was enabled to kiss the Blarney Stone.

Mr. Green has been active in the affairs of the nation as well as in those of the State of Ohio. He has been Alternate Delegate at large to National Republican Conventions. He has also associated with a number of the most prominent Republican statesmen.

Mr. Green is Junior Warden and Lay-reader in St. Andrews Episcopal Church, and, in eighteen years, he has not missed attendance at church in the morning or been late, when in town..

At the age of seventy-four he is still engaged in practice of law. In thirty-one murder cases, he has lost but one client. All the others have been either acquitted or let off with reduced sentences. From the practice of his profession, Mr. Green has been enabled to earn not only a very good living for himself, and family, but to invest in real estate.

Mr. Green was married to Miss Annie Walker, in Cleveland, in 1869. He was married a second time to Mrs. Lottie Mitchell Richardson, in 1912, with whom he is now happily living. Four children were born to Mr. Green to help brighten his home. Captain William R. Green, lawyer; Mr. Theodore B. Green, lawyer; Mr. Jesse B. Green, Chef; and Mrs. C. C. Johnson, who was Miss Clara Annie Green.

Mr. Green has for his hobbies the reading and reviewing of his classical school studies, with the addition of French, which he reads almost without effort. During the two years just passed, he has read the four Gospels in Greek twice. In this way he, at his ripe age, keeps his mind in good working condition, and is enabled to transact the large amount of business which confronts him.

JACOB E. REED

ACOB E. Reed, of Cleveland, Ohio, was born in Harrisburg, Pennsylvania, Dauphin County, November 30th, 1852. His education was limited to that of the Grammar School. For the first twenty one years of his life he lived on a farm, where he acquired a strong body that has been one of his chief assets during his long business life.

Because of his mother's interests, Mr. Reed moved into the town of Harrisburg, when he was twenty-one years of age. Here he worked first in the Harrisburg Car Works. Then for a number of years he worked at Wheatland, Pennsylvania, in the Weeds Brothers Iron Works. He was maimed while engaged with the firm and had to give up his work. He went to Youngstown, Ohio, and went into the Barber business with his brother-in-law. At this trade he worked for four years, when he moved once more, this time to Cleveland. Here he has remained building up for himself a business that is very creditable.

When he first went to Cleveland, Mr. Reed took a position as a waiter for a year. This was merely used as a stepping stone. His next step was to the position of conductor and motorman for the East Cleveland Street Railway Company. Colonel Louis Block, one of the regular passengers on the car on which Mr. Reed was conductor, opened a new market and gave to Mr. Reed the position as special police and janitor. The new undertaking was not a success, and so Mr. Block, who felt himself responsible for getting Mr. Reed out of a job, offered him the chance to install a fish market in the building, rent free for the first six months. Mr. Reed recognized the fact that he was ignorant of the fish business and so took a partner in the business with him. The partner was a Mr. Reitz, a white man. Together they in nineteen years built up a very successful business.

At the death of Mr. Reitz the interest which was his was purchased from his widow by Mr. Reed. So after a number of years in various callings, Mr. Reed found himself in one in which he was very successful. Among his customers, he numbers a number of the best families in the city of Cleveland. Besides he sells to some of the leading hotels and restaurants. The Hollenden Hotel alone runs a monthly account of about $700.00 with Mr. Reed. His annual business is from $15,000.00 to $18,000.00. This is no small achievement for one who started with almost no capital. One of the secrets of Mr. Reed's success is the fact that he never lets his bills run any time. He makes it a habit to pay all his bills weekly.

Mr. Reed has saved considerable from his business. He owns his own home which represents an investment of $10,000.00 and two pieces of rental property that represents the investment of $10,000.00.

Mr. Reed has been twice married. His first wife was Miss Rebecca Jackson, of Foxburg, Pennysylvania. They were married June, 1874. She died October 20th, 1915. He was married a second time to Mrs. Emma Clayge, of Chattanooga, Tennessee, on June 25th, 1918. Mr. Reed had one son, Addison D. Reed, who died at the age of seven years. There is one adopted daughter in the family, Miss Byrdie L. Reed. Miss Byrdie is now eighteen years of age and she was adopted at the age of nine years.

The fish business does not take up all of Mr. Reed's time. He is an active member of the Episcopal Church, of the Odd Fellows, Masons, Elks, 33 degree Mason and Shriner. For eight years he served as treasurer of the Odd Fellows. He has been appointed delegate to both national State conventions of the Elks, Odd Fellows and Masons.

It took Mr. Reed more than thirty years to find the business of which he was to make such a success, but having found it, he has not changed, but has continued 26 years, in the same line and built up for himself a very lucrative enterprise.

JOHN WILLIS HUGHES

R. J. W. Hughes, of Tulsa, is one of the comparatively few colored men of this country, who has left his native State and gone to seek his fortune at a distance without doing it of his own free will. This in the mind of Mr. Hughes is the principal episode in his life. And well may all consider it, as we shall see.

Mr. Hughes was born in Rutherford County, Tennessee, April 30, 1865. Here he spent his early childhood on the farms of his native county, working hard during the greater part of the year and attending school during the short winter session. In this way he lived till he was eighteen years of age. At that time he left the farm for the more lucrative employment of the railroad. While working on the road he managed to save enough money to enter school at Fisk University. At Fisk he was one of the steady, studious boys, and when he went out, he left the class room as a student to enter it as a teacher. He entered the public schools of his State and served as principal of the city school at Springfield, and later at Orlinda for thirteen years. During this time, Mr. Hughes had been careful of the money he earned and had quite

a bit invested in farm, stock and all the things that go to make up country property.

His farming operations proved unusually productive and brought to him much prosperity, so much so, that it caused his neighbors to be envious of him. The enmity between him and his neighbors, finally reached such a stage that he decided to sell his farm and change his location. This he did, leaving his native town and State and went out to begin all over once more.

Having made up his mind to sell his farm and equipment, he acted with his usual promptness, and disposed of same at a loss to him of between three and four thousand dollars.

Leaving Tennessee with its "Night Riders" Mr. Hughes went to Oklahoma. For two years he had a partnership in a store and then he accepted the principalship of the Dunbar School. This was in 1911. This position he still holds, working for the education of the young people in that part of the country and helping uplift all about him. In his endeavor to help in this work of uplift, Mr. Hughes has not confined himself to work in the class room. He is a deacon of the First Baptist Church, and a teacher in the Sunday School. Here every Sunday we will find him teaching the advanced Bible Class in the Sunday School.

In fraternal matters, Mr. Hughes is also a prominent man in his section of the country. He is Worthy Master of Coal Creek Lodge No. 88, of the Free Masons, he is Grand High Priest in the Royal Arch Chapter, and in the Consistory he is Grand Master of Ceremonies. So again we find Mr. Hughes taking a leading part in matters that certainly work for the betterment of the people.

Although Mr. Hughes had to make a new start when he was forty-three years of age, and make this start at a disadvantage, he has been able to accumulate a goodly share of the choice property in and around Tulsa. He owns four different pieces of property in the business district of the town, his own home and three rent houses, all of which is in a good section of the town.

Mr. Hughes has traveled extensively in this country and in the southern part of Canada. This has served to broaden him. While still in Tennessee, in 1886, he was married to Miss Sarah Elizabeth Owens, at Eglesville. They lived very happily together till the time of her death, Nov. 24, 1907. Three children were born of this union Miss Annie C. Hughes has gone back to her father's old state of Tennessee, where she is an excellent teacher. Talmage Cravath Hughes is with the United States Army in France, and Johnnie Vista Hughes died while still very young. Mr. Hughes was married a second time, May 30, 1914, to Miss Nettie A. Ledsinger of Dyersburg, Tennessee. A graduate of Fisk University, Mrs. Hughes was at the time of her marriage, principal of the Primary Department of the City school of Okmulgee, Oklahoma. In his community Mr. Hughes is an example in all matters to the younger people. His work in the school room, in the church, in the lodges and in all points where his life touches the lives of others, is all for the uplift of mankind. He is an example in thrift as well as in religious matters. He and his family like to help make the social life in Tulsa pleasant.

FRENCH WILSON BRUNER

NCE the Seminole Nation of Indians occupied the beautiful land of Florida. Many years ago, they moved to Oklahoma, the land of the Fair Gods. The Seminoles held slaves in Florida before the Civil war. It is an interesting bit of history to know that the Bruners not only were free men and women all of their lives, but are descendants of a Seminole chief. Today they can trace their ancestors seven generations to the good old days when Seminoles lived happily on the extreme peninsular of the southland.

Yesterday in the old Indian Territory, were large ranches, and cornfields, and meadows where Natives and Indian-wards of the Federal Government stood together like free men. Nor were they one whit behind civilization in lodges and other fraternal organizations for free Masonary was known and practiced by all upright free inhabitants. And where the Federal Government failed to establish any institution for the betterment of society, the Baptist Missionaries and the Presbyterian Missionaries, and the representatives of other churches established churches, school houses and academies.

French Wilson Bruner, was born January 13, 1883. He cast his first vote in Seminole County, Oklahoma. In his early days he attended the Me-

kusukey Academy, an institution which belonged to the Seminole Nation, Indian territory, now Seminole County, Oklahoma.

And later, finishing his course at Hampton, he did work in the Summer Schools of Chicago University. In 1908, he taught a common school on the Bruner estate in Oklahoma. The next year he took charge of the Manual Training Department of Douglas High School, Oklahoma City, Okla. For ten years Mr. F. W. Bruner has been in charge of this work with great success and marvelous advancement from a small uncouth manual training room in 1909, to a $10,000.00 structure, in 1915, where he has prepared students for Pratt University, New York, and other institutions of learning.

Mr. Bruner is more of a business man than otherwise. In Oklahoma City, in 1909, he invested with a partner in the drug business. Later, he interested himself in the oil industry, and later still he sold his drug interest to his partner and turned all of his attention to the development of oils. He joined the Springvale Oil and Gas Company, and is now the company's Secretary. Inheriting some money, he become very well off. He owns lands in Seminole County, land in Garvin County, a residence in Oklahoma City, a stock farm in Oklahoma, and carries investments in various oil companies.

Again, true, to the Bruner instinct, French Wilson Bruner takes an interest in all form of life work about him. He is an active member of the Baptist Church, a member of Knights of Pythias, CC and past CC of star Chamber No. 23, Past Master of Keystone Lodge No. 2, A. F. & A. M., and a Shriner, and a member of the Great Western Consistory, Oklahoma Jurisdiction. Too, he is a chairman of the teachers divisional and High School faculty, of the Oklahoma Negro Teachers Association. Moreover he has been Vice President and secretary of the said association.

The number and diversity of such connections, all of them highly honorable and useful, indicates the regard that has fixed for this prominent man so high a measure of Civic service, and he has nobly responded to the call in every phaze of the duty that this draft on his fidelity and capacities has imposed. In no relation has the worth of Mr. Bruner been more strikingly demonstrated than in the manner in which he has responded to these high demands which lie so completely out of the narrow realms of self.

Mr. Bruner was married to Miss Bloosie Bell of Muskogee, Oklahoma, Sept. 1914. They live in their beautiful residence in Oklahoma City; a residence which is valued at ten thousand dollars. The one thing lacking to make their home life ideal is the absence of children.

WILLIAM HARRISON

EW men at the bar have attained the distinction of Mr. William Harrison of Oklahoma City, Oklahoma. A southern man by birth, rearing and education, he has so conducted himself on the one hand, and has been so thorough a master in his profession on the other, that many a door that has been shut to others has freely opened to him. This does not mean that others do not deserve all the courtesies of the courts, without any special consideration, save the stamp of merit, but we are discussing things as they are rather than things as they ought to be.

Mr. Harrison's prestige in the courts has been truly remarkable, not only for a Negro of the South, but for a man of any section. Admitted to the bar in 1902, he was first permitted step by step to practice in all the State courts of Oklahoma. Gaining a footing here he steadily made his way to the front until today he practices in all the Federal courts, and in the Supreme Court of the United States .

As has already been pointed out, Mr. Harrison is out and out a southern man. He was born in Mississippi, in Clay County, in 1874. His father, devoting most of his energies to the raising of cotton, raising starch and grain as supplement. For a number of years the son served an apprenticeship with the father. But somehow the quiet humdrum of the farmers' life did not appeal to him. A life of sharp competition, of give and take, began very early to lure him from behind the plow, from the hoe and the wagon, and attract him to the city.

In spare months, that is in months when the crops were "laid by," and in winter when there was no farm labor to be performed the future lawyer attended the public schools. When he grew older he saw that he would never reach his goal by attending school one fourth or one third of the year. And so the day came when he took leave of the farm and the old folks and sped away Northward, from Mississippi to Nashville. He entered Roger Williams and completed the elementary education. From Roger Wiliams, he went to Chicago University where he pursued a college course. Returning to Nashville, he matriculated at Walden, where he completed his course in law. In 1902, he was admitted to the bar in Oklahoma.

He was not long in becoming known, once he had gotten before the courts. Sound reasoning, thorough scholarship and common sense soon gave him extraordinary prestige. On one occasion he was chosen special judge of the Superior Court in Oklahoma County, to sit in judgment on a case in which all the litigants were white.

Mr. Harrison keeps in touch with practically all the activities of his State, and indeed of the whole country. He is an extensive traveller, having covered the whole country on business and pleasure trips. He is wide awake to business chances as well as to planning out a suit. He owns heavy interests in zinc, lead and oil companies, as well as a home and several pieces of real estate. He is a good Baptist, a Mason, a loyal Knight of Pythias. In these latter organizations, as well as in others, not named, he has taken a leading part in many councils. He is Past Grand Chancellor of the Oklahoma Knights of Pythias, former attorney of the National Baptist Convention, President of the Negro Civic League, President of the People's Protective Circle, member of the Chamber of Commerce of Oklahoma City, being the only colored man to hold membership in this body.

Mr. Harrison was married in Clanton, Mississippi, June, 1898, to Miss Idella B. Carmichael. Mr. and Mrs. Harrison have two children; Wilhelmina, who is fifteen years of age, and who is in school; and William Alfred, who is twelve years old, and a school boy.

R. W. WESTBERRY

OME day, R. W. Westberry of Sumter, South Carolina, should go apart and set down in some sort of form a few of his experiences and describe the types of men he has known in given occupations. Was the account a mere catalogue, it would prove an instructive document, in that it would not only afford an engaging panorama, but would demonstrate how wide a variety of tasks one man can perform passably well.

Mr. Westberry was born in Sumter, South Carolina, near Horatio Post Office, July 11, 1871. A member of the younger generation, he managed to eke out a good education. He attended the public schools in Sumter County, then went to Benedict College at Columbia, S. C. and finished his school career at Wilberforce University, Ohio.

Mr. Westberry began his life on the farm, where as a lad he worked for his father. His life experience widened Summer by Summer during his school life and year by year after his graduation. For a time he was a waiter in a Chicago Hotel. From this he took up the task of odd jobs. In a little time he became a Chicago letter carrier,

working at this post twelve years. For two years he was a member of the letter carrier's Council, one year of which he was the only Negro member of the body.

Although the West, especially Chicago had many attractions for a live, wide-awake man like Mr. Westberry, he could not resist the call of the South and hither he turned his steps and again found himself in his native state of South Carolina.

The first five years after his return South he worked as a United States Demonstration Agent. He gave up this work to accept the Secretaryship of the South Carolina State Fair, which position he held for three years, when he was elected Superintendent of the same organization and served the Company three years more in that capacity.

At the end of his six year's service for the fair organization he decided that the time had come to strike out for himself so he organized the Westberry Realty Company, and became its President.

To this variety of experiences in occupations, he adds a career fuller still in honorary pursuits. In 1909 he was one of the leading members in the Booker T. Washington party that toured South Carolina. He was a volunteer soldier in the Spanish American War. When the Negroes of South Carolina were waging a campaign for a boy's reformatory, Mr. Westberry was one of the committee to appear before the Governor in the interest of the cause. Again when the Negroes of the State were laboring for a Colored People's Fair, Mr. Westberry advocated their cause before the State legislature.

His membership in Church and Lodge and on various boards shows how wide are his interests and activities. He is a member of the Baptist Church, and a Deacon and Trustee. He is a Mason, Odd Fellow; a Knight of Pythias; a member of the Gospel Aid Society. He was a member of the finance committee of the Masonic Lodge of his state three years; a state officer of the Odd Fellows two years, a Master of Finance for the Knights of Pythias one year; Grand Deputy Archon of the Wise Men one year; local secretary of the Gospel Aid Society one year. He is a trustee of the Maysville Institute and of Morris College; a life member of the National Negro Business Men's League; President of the South Carolina Farmer's Conference and of the National Farmer's Association and an honorary member of the Sumter Chamber of Commerce, the only Negro member of that body.

Mr. Westberry is an extensive property holder in South Carolina, and in other places. He owns two lots on Oyster Bay, Long Island; three lots and two two-story buildings in Chicago, and his property in Sumter, among which is included his two-story house valued at $30,000.

He was married in 1902, to Miss Iva Anderson, of Chatham, Canada.

JACOB JAVAN DURHAM, A. B., M. D.

ACOB Javan Durham, famous as
an orator and debater was born
near Spartanburg, South Carolina,
April 13th, 1849. He attended the
public school, at Greenville, South
Carolina. From the public school
he entered the State University of South Carolina, remaining in that institution until 1877,
when it was closed against Colored students.
He then entered Fisk University, Nashville, Tennessee, where he was graduated two years later
with the degree A. B.

He graduated from Meharry Medical College,
Nashville, Tenn., in 1880, and received his M. D.
degree. At his graduation he won the honor of
being the class valedictorian, having made 98½ on
his final examination. Recognizing his great ability he was offered a professorship in the college
but declined the honor as he wished to enter at
once upon his chosen fields of labor—that of medicine and the ministry.

His first charge was the Bethesda Baptist church
at Society Hill, which was one of the largest
churches in the State of South Carolina, receiving
and accepting a call to this church immediately up-

on his leaving Meharry Medical College. He entered upon his work both as a preacher and a physician with energy and zeal, and did the work of
both with marked success.

He gave up his work in Society Hill to enter a
larger field. He was elected Educational Missionary of the Baptist State Convention of South Carolina, which office he filled so ably that he was advanced a step higher and made the Financial Secretary of the Baptist State Convention. Here he
had a wider scope for the exercise of his gifts and
for ten years he applied himself to his work with
such skill and tact that he won the cooperation of
his brethren and raised large sums of money and
paid off large debts.

He was especially gifted in this line, an illustration of which is seen in his accomplishment when
pastor of the Second Baptist Church, of Savannah,
Georgia. In one rally he raised for this church
$3059.33.

Dr. Durham was then recalled to South Carolina
to become educational secretary. At the close of
his first year's work as Educational Secretary he
recommended among other things the establishment of an institution of learning to be owned and
operated by the Negro Baptists of the State. The
report was followed by an eloquent and powerful
speech on the subject by the Secretary, and in a few
minutes. more than $12,000 was subscribed, and
Morris College, at Sumter, South Carolina, is the
result. The presidency of this institution was
offered him but he declined it. Dr. Durham has
been often referred to as "the Daniel Webster of
his race," because of his unusual ability and eloquence as a debater.

He has been called upon to introduce some of the
great public men of the Nation. Frederick Douglas
on being introduced once by Dr. Durham, said:
"That was the most eloquent introduction I ever
had. That man ought to be in Congress pleading
the cause of the people."

After introducing President McKinley on one
occasion, the President remarked, "That was the
most beautiful and eloquent speech I ever heard."

Dr. Durham is a great scholar and has been a
hard student. He reads the Bible in five different
languages—English, German, Latin, Greek, and
Hebrew.

Dr. Durham has been twice married, first to Miss
Ella Simpkins, and from this union there was one
son. His second wife was Miss Emma Ramey of
Edgefield, South Carolina, daughter of Judge W.
D. and Katie Ramey.

Dr. Durham is a man of considerable wealth. He
is public spirited; has made many great public and
patriotic speeches; written much on great public
questions. He stands high as a man and citizen and
has received many honorary degrees from repu-
table institutions.

ROBERT E. L. HOLLAND, M. D.

DOCTOR Robert E. L. Holland, the eldest of eight living children of Benjamin and Margaret Holland, was born in Montgomery County, Texas, November eleventh, 1864. The father was a farmer; and as such set a glowing example of hard work and thrift for his son. All day the parent would labor in the field and then at night time split rails or chop wood. For a while the eldest son followed this example. He, too, labored on the farm, and at night split rails, chopped wood and built char-coal kilns until midnight. He attended school when time permitted and when the two or three months country school was in session. As he was ambitious, however, he studied in and out of season.

Such close application to his studies soon began to bear fruit and note was made of his mental development, and at the age of seventeen years he was advised to stand for a teacher's certificate, and was offered the position of assistant teacher if he should successfully pass the teacher's examination. He passed the examination, got his certificate for second grade and secured the teacher's position. Thus he began his career as a teacher. He had

started up the ladder and the following year had advanced so far as to be made principal of one of the largest schools of his county. While he was teaching he continued his studies and in two years he stood his examination for first grade license and got his certificate. After receiving this certificate he continued to teach and applied himself more vigorously to his studies. Continuing this course for seven years he entered a competitive contest for a scholarship in Prairie View State Normal School which he won after standing a most rigid examination. He entered the Prairie View State Normal School with his ambition whetted by his success in the scholarship competition and finished his course with honor, in 1888.

He returned home and taught one year in the school in which he taught before he went away to Prairie View. In 1890, on passing a rigid examination he was made principal of one of the Ward Schools, of Austin. However, though he was continually climbing as a teacher, he had long felt called to another profession—that of medicine. And so, after three years teaching in Austin, he resigned his post and went away to Meharry Medical College, Nashville, and then to the University of Vermont, to study medicine, obtaining his degree from the latter school.

Finishing his course in medicine in 1895, he returned to his native state and began practice in Temple. Here he rapidly gained the confidence of all the people and soon had a lucrative practice. For twenty-one years he followed his profession in Temple, equipping his office with the best implements, widening his services and usefulness in many directions.

On returning to Texas, Doctor Holland decided to affiliate himself with all local organizations that stood for the good of his race. He allied himself with the Eighth Street Baptist Church at Temple, became a Knights of Pythias, an Odd Fellow, a United Brother of Friendship, and a member of the Court of Calauthe. At one time he was a past Grand officer in the Knights of Pythias. He joined the Lone Star State Medical Association, was Secretary for eight years, and President for one year.

Dr. Holland was married in 1898 to Miss Mary B. Pittman of Taybora, North Carolina. Dr. and Mrs. Holland have one son, Robert E. L. Jr., who is a student at Tillotson College, Austin, Texas.

The crowning recognition came to Dr. Holland in 1916, when the Governor of the State of Texas appointed him Superintendent of the Texas Deaf, Dumb and Blind Institute for Colored youths, at Austin, Texas. Within a year marked signs of improvement had already become manifested under him. The attendance has increased 35 per cent, the teaching force has been enlarged, new industries added and larger appropriations gained for the maintenance of the institution.

JOHN MARION FRIERSON

OMMENCING at the bottom in business, John M. Frierson, Undertaker and Embalmer, of Houston, Texas, has climed steadily and persistently until he is the leader in his kind of business in the State of Texas. With no special training for his task and no very large bulk of capital, he enter a city where competition was sharp and rent high; yet he has never moved, never failed. He has only expanded. The room which once held the business of his whole plant is now the store room for his caskets.

Mr. Frierson was born in Columbia, Tennessee, June 10th, 1865. He was born in a period which was fraught with great difficulties for the colored race, for it was passing through the transition from slavery to freedom and had to encounter the many problems which opened up in meeting this crucial test. Trials met him when a small lad and he had his turn at hard labor, scant food, scant clothing, and very meager facilities for education. He soon learned that the way of success in life was not a path of ease, but a way of thorns. He aspired to make something of hi life and had an ambition to be an educated man. This he deter

mined to be and he never took his eye from the goal until he had reached it. In order to earn the money to pursue his studies he toiled as a laborer, as a carpenter's helper to his father, as a teacher in country schools. Sometimes his earnings amounted to two dollars per week, but frequently fell below that amount and occasionally went above it. Frugality and perseverance won their reward and he was enabled to enter college.

Finally he was able to enter Roger Williams University, Nashville, Tenn. Graduating here in the spring of 1891, he went out and became principal of the colored school in Galletin, Tenn. in the fall of the same year. Texas at that time, as it is now, was a more attractive field in education than most of the Southern States. It paid better salaries, held longer school terms, had better schools and proved more respectable for a teacher. Hither in 1892, Mr. Frierson went to take charge of a school near Waxahatchie, in Ellis County. The next year he became associate principal of Hearne Academy in Roberson County. For the next five years he taught in Hearne Academy and in the County schools.

Feeling that teaching was too itinerant and in many ways too restrictive in the opportunities for advancement, Mr. Frierson left the school room and began his present business of Undertaking in Houston, Texas. He opened a shop at 203 San Felipe Street, where his shop still stands, though much expanded. His was the first Negro Undertaking business to open in the State of Texas. Hence for a number of years he had to overcome the obstacles common to all pioneers, to overcome prejudice and to establish confidence. This he had to do while buying his horses and equipment, learning those detals of business which only experience can give The obstacles overcome, he rose rapidly, as a business man. Today his stock room which as has been said, was his original establishment, is full of the best caskets available. He is accredited with having the finest outfit of horses of any Negro in Texas. These, however, he is now converting into automobile hearses. In addition to this business in Houston, he owns interests in businesses in Texarkana and in Brenham.

Mr. Frierson stands high in many of the leading organizations of his state. He is a member of the Baptist Church, of the the Masonic Lodge, of the Knights of Pythias, of the Odd Fellows, of the Knights and Daughters of Tabor and of the American Woodman. He is one of the leading members of the National Undertakers' Association and of the National Negro Business Men's League. He has attended every meeting of the two latter since their founding. He has traveled over practically the whole United States, on business and on pleasure.

Mr. Frierson was married to Miss Hattie Eskridge of Atlanta, Ga., December 23, 1906. They live in their own home on San Felipe Street in Houston.

REVEREND CHARLES AUGUSTUS BELL.

EV. Charles Augustus Bell was born in Knoxville, Tennessee. He was of poor parentage and so had to work at an early age to help support himself. His earliest school days were spent in the public schools of Knox County, where he applied himself diligently and secured all that he could. Finishing the course offered in the public school, the young man entered Knoxville College and by working at odd jobs he was able to remain in school till he had completed the course prescribed. During this period of study Rev. Bell spent his summers in teaching in the rural districts of his state. In this way he kept himself in funds sufficient to keep up with his needs.

Rev. Bell at an early age decided to take up the ministry as his life work. To this end he spent a great deal of time in study with correspondence schools. He took a course of study with the Extension Department of the University of Chicago, and later took a course with the Oskaloosa College, of Iowa. In this way he fitted himself very thoroughly for the work he had before him, as a minister of the Gospel and a servant of the people.

Feeling himself to be fairly well equipped now for his life work he entered the ministry in 1890. His first charge was the Rogers Memorial Church

of Knoxville, Tenn. For six years Rev. Bell served his home congregation, endearing himself to them by his kind ministrations to their many needs and his ready help in time of great trouble. Rev. Bell from the first decided that he could best serve by remaining long enough in one place to really accomplish some good in the community. To bear this out, he has during his nearly twenty years of pastoring, served only two churches.

After leaving Knoxville, he accepted work in Chattanooga, Tennessee. Here he has remained, pastoring the First Baptist Church. Rev. Bell is well beloved by all of his congregation. He has won the interest and co-operation of the children, young men, and women as well as that of the older members of his congregation. To do this has meant work on the part of the pastor. In this work he has shown great executive ability. He has reorganized his church, putting it on a working basis. Rev. Bell has his own ideas about a church and its functions. He believes that a church is not merely a place for Sunday meetings or rather he believes that this is not the purpose at all. He believes that a church is a center for thought, for culture, for activities of all kinds for the people. He believes that the church should train the young, and spur up the old in things temporal and intellectual as well as in things which are purely spiritual.

Thus the first Baptist Church at Chattanooga is one of those modern churches. It is organized upon thoroughly business method, and it seeks to render the highest possible efficiency in the church and religious work. This church, under the direction and inspiration of Rev. Bell has developed a mission and Educational Society. This organization is an auxiliary to the Church proper. There are several other organizations that are auxiliaries to the church. Among these are the Teachers' training Class; the Christian Culture Class; the Dunbar Literary Society; the Young Men's auxiliary; a corps of Boy Cadets. Rev. Bell has taken pleasure and pride in adding these branches to his church. They have added much to the life of his congregation and to the community in general. In these organizations Rev. Bell has sought to promote and sustain the efficiency of the church.

One direct result of the establishing of all these auxiliaries to the First Baptist church, is the directing of the thoughts and actions of the young and the adult toward the good, the useful and the beautiful. Through them the people are kept bouyed up, enthusiastic, the church is freely supported and the pastor encouraged. By reorganizing his church Rev. Bell has been able to use all the members of his congregation. In this way, every member is given a chance for growth and every member feels that he is of use to the church.

Rev. Bell is a member of the executive board of the State Convention and a Trustee of the Nelson Mary Academy of Jefferson City, Tenn. He is also a Mason and a great traveler, having toured the whole of this country and Canada.

Rev. Bell was married in 1901 to Miss Mary A. Bell, of Knoxville, Tennessee.

BISHOP CHARLES HENRY PHILLIPS, A. B., A. M.,
M. D., D. D., LL. D.

ISHOP Charles Henry Phillips,
Bishop of the 4th Episcopal District, Colored Methodist Episcopal Church, is easily one of the
leading churchmen of his generation. He was born in Milledge-
ville, Ga., January 17, 1858. His
parents the Rev. and Mrs. George
Washington Phillips, were devout Christians.

As a boy young Phillips worked on his father's
farm and attended the common schools. Converted at the age of sixteen, four years later he was licensed to preach by Rev. R. T. White, D. D., one
of the leaders of Georgia Methodism.

Seeking a higher education he attended first Atlanta University, Atlanta, Ga., and in 1880 graduated from Walden University, Nashville, Tenn., with
the degree of A. B., and "Cum Laude." Bishop I.
B. Scott of the M. E. Church and the late Dr. Robert Fulton Boyd were classmates, and both declare
Bishop Phillips to be an expert Linguist, especially
in Hebrew, Latin and Greek. Studying Theology
at Walden he also graduated from Meharry Medical College, with the M. D. degree, in 1882. Since
his graduation he is universally recognized a brilliant scholar. Wiley University, of Marshall, Texas,
and Philander Smith College, of Little Rock, Ark.,
conferred on him D. D.; Walden University, M.
A., and Wilberforce University of Ohio, LL. D.

ferred D. D.; Walden University, M. A., and Wilberforce University, of Ohio, LL. D.

Bishop Phillips taught school a few years and
served as President of Lane College, of Jackson,
Tenn. From the latter position he was called to
the pastorate. He served a "circuit," a "station"
and as Presiding Elder. His rise was rapid, for
soon the young minister was pastor in charge of
Collins Chapel, of Memphis, Tenn., one of the largest and most aristocratic congregations in the
South. From here he was sent to Israel Metropolitan C. M. E. Church, of Washington, D. C., where
for four years he was one of the leading and most
popular ministers of the Nation's capital. He was
in constant demand, both as speaker and preacher,
and the daily press often reported his sermons and
addresses. The citizens of Washington, in 1890,
regardless of color and denomination, sent him a
delegate to the First World's Sunday School Convention, which convened in London, England.

At the farewell reception given him by Israel
and citizens when transferred to Kentucky, the
Hon. Frederick Douglass, John Mercer Langston,
the Rev. J. C. Price and other notables were on the
program. It was pronounced one of the most
brilliant affairs of its kind ever given. From
Washington he was sent to old historic Center
Street C. M. E. Church, of Louisville, Ky., and
serving out his time there, he was made presiding
elder of the Mt. Sterling District. He visited Europe a second time in 1901, when his church sent
him a delegate to the Third Ecumenical Conference. While abroad Bishop Phillips traveled and
lectured in England, Scotland, France, Belgium,
and other countries. He was elected editor of
the Christian Index in 1894, after coming within
three votes of the Bishopric.

In 1902, after serving The Index two terms he
was elevated to the high office of Bishop, with the
largest majority ever given a Negro for that office.
At the Toronto Ecumenical Conference in 1911
Bishop Phillips served as assistant-secretary, the
first time a Negro ever filled so distinguished a
position. He has attended every General Conference since 1886 as a delegate; is at present an official member of the Federal Council of Churches,
the Ecumenical Methodist Conference, the Church
Council and various other inter-racial organizations, and was recently appointed by the United
State Government, one of its spokesmen. He is
called the scholar of the bench of bishops and pioneer bishop of the church, having established the
C. M. E. Church in Western, Texas, Arizona, New
Mexico, California and sections of Ohio and Indiana. He is author of the History of the C. M. E.
Church and a writer of great force and power.

Bishop Phillips married Miss Lucy Ellis Tappan
in 1880, who was a graduate of Fisk University.
She died in Nashville, Tenn., in 1913, survived
by five children: Dr. Chas. Phillips, Jr., Dr. Jasper Tappan Phillips; Miss Lady Emma; Mrs. Lucy
Phillips-Stewart, and Mrs. Lottie Phillips-James.

Bishop Phillips was married a second time in
1918, to Miss Ella Cheeks, of Cleveland, Ohio. She
is a very charming woman, and one of culture. She
graduated from Hampton Institute and did post
graduate work in Columbia University and Cheney
Institute. Bishop and Mrs. Phillips reside at
"Sunshine," their Nashville home.

O. W. JAMES, M. D.

HEN the people of Chattanooga want a man to head a list of donors to a good cause, someone whose name will inspire friends for the cause, they very frequently seek out the office of Dr. O. W. James. This is particularly the case if the cause for which they are working is that of education. Dr. James very seldom turns a deaf ear to appeals of help for schools. This he does because he likes to and because of what the schools have done for him. For in point of education, Dr. James is not very unlike a great many persons whose struggle for book-learning is recorded in these pages. The great majority had to work with the hands in order that they might have the oportunity to study.

Dr. James was born in Missouri, Warren County, in 1868. Because he was born in 1868, he had the privilege of studying and becoming a great man in any profession he might choose. But because he was born in 1868, he had to work his way, for very few Negroes had gotten together means enough to educate their children at that early date. But in so many of our colored families the lack of means was made up by the great desire to study, and the willingness to do any kind of work in order to satisfy that desire. So we find Dr. James as a lad attending the public schools of his home town, studying, applying himself, and getting more ambitious each day to become a man of culture, helpfulness, and wealth.

When he had gotten all from the public schools that he could, he made up his mind to attend college. He had heard of Tougaloo University, an A. M. A. school about seven miles out of Jackson, Mississippi, and made up his mind to enter there. And so he matriculated at Tougaloo and remained there to finish his literary training. On leaving Tougaloo he entered Meharry Medical College, at Nashville, Tennessee, and remained to complete his course. He was graduated with the degree of M. D., in 1890.

After graduating and giving thought to the question of a location, Chattanooga became the City of his choice, and he moved there the year he graduated. He has never regretted his choice, for he has built up a good practice, and has become very much attached to its citizens. In fact, so well pleased is he with Chattanooga, that during his long period of residence in that city he has never been tempted to make a change. He feels that he is located there for life, and is giving his best service to this city in which he has made his home.

All over the city of Chattanooga, Dr. James is well known, both as a physician and as a man. All Chattanooga knows and speaks of the James Building. This is a three-story double brick building which stands near the heart of the city. In this building is one of the big drug stores of the city, spacious ice cream parlors, carrying a most elaborate bill of sodas, creams and ices. It is the center of the colored population of the city and headquarters of most of the colored physicians. It is also a sort of bureau of information and sponsor for all things pertaining to the Chattanooga Negro. Seeking for a colored man's residence or his standing in the community, you are instructed to "ask at the James Building, they can tell you if anybody can."

This building stands as a monument to the man who began life almost penniless and in this short time has acquired so choice a bit of property. The building is used for offices and stores. In addition to this Dr. James owns his own home and six rent houses, which net him a good monthly income.

The home of Dr. James is without a mother, Mrs. James having passed away in June of 1916. Mrs. James was a native of Chattanooga, and was beloved by the many friends of the good Doctor. There is one child, a little four-year-old daughter, Charlotte. She is a bit of sunshine in the home.

Dr. James is considered the leading colored physician of Chattanooga, and numbers many of the best people among his patrons.

BISHOP EVANS TYREE, D. D., M. D., LL. D.

ISHOP Evans Tyree of the A. M.
E. Church is one of those church
fathers, who spends all of their
days about the altar and wax old
slowly in the service for men and
for their Maker. Putting aside
the finer distinction of denominatons and proceed-
ing rather upon the basis of men, Bishop Tyree belongs in that galaxy of giants with the late Bishop
Grant, Turner, and Gaines, with the fine veteran,
—still active—Bishop Holsey.

Bishop Tyree, the twenty-sixth bishop of the A.
M. E. Church, the son of Harry and Winifree Tyree
—both African Methodists, was born a slave, in
DeKalb County Tennessee, in 1854. He was one
of the twelve children. He began attending school
in 1876, and received about ten years schooling in
all, attending principally Central Tennessee College, Walden University, and graduated from the
theological department without a degree. He received D. D. degree from Livingston; M. D. from
Louisville Medical School; LL. D. from Paul
Quinn, and also from Wilberforce. Most of his
educational struggle was outside of school, by private instructors. He was converted in 1866, at

Carthage, and joined the Methodist Episcopal
Church the same year, as there was no A. M. E.
Church then. He was always active in the church,
and has held almost every office in the body. He
was licensed to preach in 1869, at Hartselle, Tenn.,
by Rev. Jordon W. Earley.

In 1872, he began his career as minister ,start-
ing in the Alexandria Mission, DeKalb County, the
place of his birth. For 28 years he followed the
humble career of minister; filling posts, raising
collections, moving from place to place, organizing
Sunday Schools, Conventions, and other bodies
necessary for the uplift of the people .

In May 1900 came his promotion. While at Columbus, Ohio, he was consecrated bishop. Once
more, however, he began to go from place to place.
On election to the bishopric he was assigned to the
8th Episcopal District, comprised of Mississippi
and Arkansas.

Four years later he was transferred to the District covered by Texas and Oklahoma; over which
section he remained until 1912.

January 1912 Bishop Gaines having died, Bishop
Tyree was called to fill out his unexpired term in
the East and immediately was given charge of the
First Episcopal District which covers one half of
Pennsylvania, all of Delaware, New Jersey, New
York and the New England States.

This he held until the General Conference, which
met at Kansas City, Mo., May, 1912, when he was
given permanent charge of the First Episcopal District and remained in that district until the General
Conference of 1916, when he was returned to the
First District for a second full term.

Bishop Tyree holds membership of a fraternal
nature and of honor in several bodies. He is a member of the Masons and of the Knights of Pythias
in the fraternal bodies. He is a member of the
Board of Trustees of Wilberforce University, Ohio;
chairman of the Executive Board of Payne Theological Seminary, of the same University, a member
of the Board of Directors of the One Cent Savings
Bank and of the People's Saving Bank and Trust
Co. of Nashville, Tenn.

Bishop Tyree makes his home in Nashville, Tenn.
Here he owns his home, a two and one-half story
brick structure on North Hill St.

He was married to Miss Ellen Thompkins in
Smith County, Tenn., in 1871. Seven children were
born of this union. Of these two are deceased,
namely: Mattie and Wayman Tyree. Misses Eu-
genia and Carrie are married, Miss Alberta is employed by the Sunday School Union of the African
Methodist Church; Evans, Jr., is a printer in Chicago, and Herman is a minister in Texas; all showing their splendid home training.

JAMES WELDON JOHNSON, A. B., A. M., LITT. D.

AMES Weldon Johnson, writer and poet, was born in Jacksonville, Florida, where he attended the Public Schools. In 1894 he graduated from Atlanta University, with the degree of A. B., and he received the degree of A. M. from the same University in 1904. Mr. Johnson also spent three years in post graduate work at Columbia University, in the City of New York. In 1917, the honorary degree of Litt. D., was conferred upon him by the Talladega College, Talladega, Alabama.

For several years, Mr. Johnson was principal of the Colored high school at Jacksonville. He was admitted to the Florida Bar in 1897, and practiced law in Jacksonville until 1901, when he removed to New York to collaborate with his brother, J. Rosamond Johnson, in writing for the light opera stage.

In 1906, he was appointed United States Consul at Puerto Cabello, Venezuela, being transferred as Consul to Corinto, Nicaragua, in 1909, and to the Azores in 1912. While in Corinto, he looked after the interests of his country during the stormy days of revolution which resulted in the downfall of Zelaya, and through the abortive revolution against Diaz.

His knowledge of Spanish has been put to use in the translation of a number of Spanish plays. He was the translator for the English libretto of "Goy-escas," the Spanish grand opera produced by the Metropolitan Opera Company in 1915. Mr. Johnson also has several French translations to his credit.

Mr. Johnson is well known throughout the country as the Contributing Editor of the New York Age. He added to his distinction as a newspaper writer by winning in an editorial contest, one of three prizes offered by the Philadelphia Public Ledger, in 1916.

During the fall of 1916 Mr. Johnson went on a six weeks mission throughout the South, when he interviewed the editors of the leading white newspapers and talked with them regarding the attitude they should take on the exodus of Negro labor, which was then reaching its height, and upon the whole Negro question.

Mr. Johnson contributes to various magazines and periodicals. His poems have appeared in the Century, the Independent, the Crisis and other publications. He is the author of a novel, "The Autobiography of an Ex-Colored Man," and a volume of poems, "Fifty Years and Other Poems." He is a member of the American Society of Authors and Composers, the American Sociological Society, and of the Civic Club of New York, and is the Field Secretary of the National Association for the Advancement of Colored People.

It is as a writer that Mr. Johnson is best known. His novel, "The Autobiography of an Ex-Colored Man" aroused considerable comment, and his recent volume of poems, "Fifty Years and Other Poems" has been favorably reviewed by a number of the best critics of the country. Professor Branden Matthews, of Columbia University, in his introduction which he wrote for the book, says of Mr. Johnson and his work, "But where he shows himself a pioneer is in the half-dozen larger and bolder poems, of a loftier strain, in which he has been nobly successful in expressing amply the higher aspirations of his own people. It is in uttering this cry for recognition, for sympathy, for understanding, and, above all, for justice, that Mr. Johnson is most original and most powerful."

Mr. Elias Lieberman, in the American Hebrew, says of him, "James Weldon Johnson is not only versatile but more than that—sincere. He has continued to do for the Negro race what Paul Lawrence Dunbar began so inimitably. He has thrown the illuminating light of interpretation upon lives which for so many of us are puzzles."

The following was taken from a tribute to him in the Boston Evening Transcript:

"And in other verse that strike a universal note there is more often both felicity of conception and expression. Particular reference should be made to Mr. Johnson's poem, "The Young Warrior," which, set to music by Mr. Harry T. Burleigh, has been sung throughout Italy as a martial song inspiring the Italian soldier on his way to the front. The pieces in Negro dialect are characteristic of work of this kind and Mr. Johnson's possesses the usual intensity of pathos and the usual humorous abandon. One notes particularly, however, in the dialect verses in this volume, the absence of coarseness, of crudity, in the humor which has more or less pervaded the racial writers of dialect since Dunbar. Mr. Johnson, if he has done nothing else to enhance the value of this kind of speech in verse, has given it a quality of refinement."

PHILLIP A. PAYTON

HE late Phillip A. Payton, of New York City, was without doubt the greatest Negro real estate dealer that ever lived. Measured by the competition he met, by the contracts he executed and considering the city in which he operated, going right into the lair of the tiger, he has up to this time not even a second.

Mr. Payton was born in Westfield, Massachusetts, February 27th, 1876. Finishing the public and high schools of his native town, he went down to Livingston College, Salisbury, North Carolina, for his college course. Completing his college course, Mr. Payton went to New York and began a career of want and penury which none but a stout heart like his could endure. Others would have succumbed to the easy living in the hotel or Pullman Service. Going to New York in 1899, he found a job as penny-in-the-slot-man, at the wage of six dollars per week—scarcely board money. On losing this post, he took up barbering, a trade he had learned from his father. Again his earnings amounted to five or six dollars a week. In 1900 he secured a job as porter in a real estate office. His wages here were eight dollars a week, but his time proved an investment, for here he conceived the idea of going into the real estate business for himself.

Opening his real estate business with a partner he soon found that his former job had been a luxury. The business began in October, 1900. By spring the partner had grown weary and quit. A little later, Mr. Payton was himself dispossessed because he could not pay his rent. In all these seven months the gross receipts had amounted to one hundred and twenty dollars.

Ousted in one place he opened another office. In a few months he was again put out for his inability to pay his rent. Three times he suffered this fate. Then a grim sort of fortune held out her hand. A murder had been committed in a certain tenement. Nobody would live there. Mr. Payton agreed to take charge of the house. He soon filled it with tenants. This gained the respect and gratitude of the owner, who gave him more houses to rent.

Mr. Payton, feeling that the colored people should be better housed, set about getting them more decent homes in Harlem.

The "Outlook" of December 14, 1914 says of him, "It was Payton's theory that equal housing conditions for colored people as for white would make for healthier and more self-respecting Negro Citizens."

Working day and night at this idea he moved to Harlem, which he opened up for the colored people. He became known as the "Father of Harlem" because he was the pioneer in securing for the colored people the best houses in this district.

His last and greatest effort in this direction was the securing of six elevator houses in 141st and 142nd Street, which were valued at more than $1,500,000.00 and which are now known as the Payton Apartments Corporation. These houses are among the most modern and up-to-date to be found anywhere, and are the largest group of elevator houses owned by Negroes in the United States.

Mr. Payton's fearless aggressiveness and thorough knowledge of his business earned him the respect of the greatest real estate dealers of the country. Ninety-nine per cent of his clients were white, and he necessarily had to be well grounded in his business to retain them.

He has a country home in Allenhurst, New Jersey, which is valued at $25,000.00. Of his last deal which secured him the 141st and 142nd Street houses, the Press of the city had the following to say:

Evening Mail. (N. Y.: "The most notable transaction in which Negroes have ever figured in this City."

New York Sun: "Reflects progress of Negro Race in this city. Largest deal associated with housing of colored families that has ever been consummated in this city."

HENRY PARKER   JOHN E. NAIL

THE time was when good self-respecting, well-to-do colored people could not find a decent home in which to dwell and rear their children. For the last quarter of a century New York has been undergoing a very wholesome change in Negro housing. This change has asserted itself for the most part in Harlem, and happy to relate has been brought about by the enterprising colored men themselves. Philip A. Payton, Jr., was the pioneer in this field. Following close upon his trail, and indeed associated with him for a time were the two real estate dealers, Nail and Parker.

The firm of John E. Nail and Henry Parker opened its doors for business December 10th, 1907. They began in a one-room apartment on West 133rd Street. Harlem then had a Negro population of about fifteen thousand people. These inhabitants dwelt for the most part between 133th and 135th Streets. In 1900 the white population began to move out of Harlem. The property owners were on the verge of realizing a panic. But the colored people, led by their business men, saved the dealers and at the same time gained the option on good comfortable homes. Nail and Parker were among the few astute dealers to see the opportunity for housing respectable colored people. They combined as a firm and from that move won their place in the real estate world. Today, thanks to their enterprise the Negro population of Harlem numbers more than 100,000 people. These inhabitants have

spread themselves in two directions. From 133rd Street they have pushed their way all the way up to 144th Street, and back to 131st Street, all of this turned on one heroic move, the opening of one or two houses on West 134th Street.

The effecting of this wholesale change was a service indeed, but it wholly pales before the other impetus which it gave the colored people. Though they were realizing fair and satisfactory returns as renters, Nail and Parker began to inspire by their dealings the desire to buy. Thus began the Negro home owner in Harlem. Before the change in 1900 the colored householder was very rare in New York perhaps a half million dollars would cover all their holdings. It would take twenty millions to cover it today.

Among the big realty owners in this section is the St. Philip P. E. Church. This church controlled about $1,500,000 worth of realty, which property is controlled wholly by Negroes. In 1911 Nail and Parker made an exchange of properties with this church. This involved the sum of $1,700,000. The firm then moved into its present spacious office apartments on 135th Street, where they have ever since been established, and where their business has steadily developed. They manage more than fifty buildings and do a monthly business amounting to One Hundred Thousand Dollars. They handle property and serve in advisory capacity for some of the largest mortgage institutions in New York, and are prime movers in all civic and uplift work of the city.

Photo By C. M. Battey

WILLIAM EDWARD BURGHARDT DUBOIS, A. B., A. M., PH. D.

William Edward Burghardt Dubois, A. B., A. M., Ph. D.

NO history of the Negro race is complete without a sketch of the life of William Edward Burghardt Dubois. His place in the literature of the race is a most prominent one. The book that won for him fame, was the first he published, "The Soul of Black Folk." Of this book Professor Brawley, who is a writer of no mean note himself, says: "The remarkable style of this book has made it unquestionably the most important work in Classic English yet written by a Negro. It is marked by all the arts of Rhetoric, especially by liquid and alliterative effects, strong antithesis, frequent allusion, and poetic suggestiveness." Had Dr. Dubois done nothing more than produce this master piece of English he would have a place in any history of the Race."

W. E. B. Dubois was born February 23, 1868, at Great Barrington, Massachusetts. Here, where most of his associates were of the white race, the young lad was slow in realizing that he was not one of them. When this realization came he says that he always felt himself "the superior, not the inferior, and any advantages which they had were quite accidental." At the age of sixteen years he graduated from the school in his home town and upon the advice of friends turned his face Southward. Here he entered Fisk University, and for the first time came to know his own people.

From Fisk University he received the degree of Bachelor of Arts, in 1888, the same degree from Harvard in 1890, and the degree of Master of Arts from Harvard in 1891. Thoroughly a student and not satisfied with his attainments, Mr. Dubois next spent a season of study in Berlin. From Harvard he received the degree of Doctor of Philsophy in 1895.

Dr. Dubois taught for a short time in Wilberforce University, and also for a time as assistant and fellow in Sociology at the University of Pennsylvania. One direct result of the work in Pennsylvania was his study "The Philadelphia Negro," which he produced in 1899. His next work was in Atlanta, Georgia. While in Atlanta, Dr. Dubois was Professor of History and Economics at Atlanta University. Of this work during this period Dr. Dubois says:

"My real life work was done in Atlanta," for thirteen years, from my twenty-ninth to my forty-second birthday. They were years of great spiritual upturning, of the making and unmaking of ideals, of hard work and hard play. Here I found myself. I lost most of my mannerisms. I became more broadly human, made my closest and most holy friendships, and studied human beings.

I became widely acquainted with the real condition of my people. I realized the terrific odds which faced them. From captious criticisms I changed to cold science; then to hot, indignant defense.

At last, forbear and waver as I would I faced the great Decision. Against all my natural reticence and hatred of forwardness, contrary to my dream of racial unity and my deep desire to serve and follow and think, rather than to lead and inspire and decide, I found myself suddenly the leader of a great wing of my people, fighting against another and greater wing. I hated the role. For the first time I faced criticism and cared. Every ideal and habit of my life was cruelly misjudged. I, who had always over-striven to give credit for good work, who had never consciously stooped to envy, was accused by honest colored people of every sort of small and petty jealousy; and white people said I was ashamed of my race and wanted to be white! I realized the real tragedy of life. We simply had doggedly to insist, explain, fight and fight again, until, at last, slowly, grudgingly, we saw the world turn slightly to listen. My Age of Miracles returned again.

My cause grew, and with it I was pushed into a larger field. I was invited to come to New York and take charge of one part of a new organization. I came in 1910. It was an experiment. My salary even for a year was not assured, and I gave up a life position. I insisted on starting The Crisis as the main part of my work, and this, after hesitation was approved. In this position Dr. Dubois has been able to make many investigations, many of them for the United States Government. He still has this work.

Dr. Dubois is recognized as one of the great Sociologists of the day. His articles on this subject have been published in the leading magazines of the country. He more than any one else has given to the world accurate knowledge concerning conditions surounding the Negro. He is also one of the great Negro writers. His books, "John Brown," "The Quest of the Silver Fleece," and "Soul of Black Folk" give him a place of prominence among the writers of today.

Dr. Dubois was married in 1896. From the union two children were born. The oldest passed away at an early age. The writing "The passing of the First-Born" shows plainly the soul of the parents over this. The other child is a beautiful young daughter, Miss Yoland Dubois. The Dubois family are at present residing in New York, where Dr. Dubois makes his headquarters.

Dr. Dubois is a clear thinker, a matchless writer and a fearless advocate for Negro rights.

MADAM C. J. WALKER

Madam C. J. Walker,

FOREMOST among the few women who have membership in the National Negro Business Men's League is Madam Walker. This is the place for her by dint of her achievements. The work that she has done in building up a business, the manner in which she has made use of the deep insight that she had in the minds of her fellows, the way in which she has handled the business once it was started, and the use to which she has put her funds, all claim for her, a place among the noted business characters of the Negro Race.

A few years ago she was poor and unknown, save to her neighbors, and those for whom she toiled, and because of her close application to her work, which her necessities required, she had but little time and opportunity to cultivate these and consequently had but few friends. Because of this the wonderful change that has taken place in her life and surroundings within twelve years is indeed most remarkable. From obscurity she has jumped into great prominence, and we find the large newspapers of the country devoting space to her accomplishments.

Madam Walker is one of the few persons who having a vision made use of it. The vision came to her thrice repeated and left no doubt upon her mind that she had been commissioned to confer a benefit upon her race. She realized that men and women, as a rule, were concerned about their personal appearance and that one of the objects of special care was the head, both in preserving and beautifying the hair. She felt sure that sooner or later all men and women who were interested in their personal appearance would come to her or to some one else for help for their dry scalps, and she had not a doubt that the remedy she would place upon the market would win its way to popular favor because of its great merit.

The remarkable thing about Madam Walker was that she persisted in trying to establish a business and a large lucrative one. She thought in terms of thousands of boxes of her preparations and to go to the Indianapolis Factory and see those thousands of boxes being loaded daily into her private mail truck or to go into her office and see four or five office girls—each opening letters from the same mail, and see the large baskets being piled high with postal money orders, makes one feel that she has created that for which she has striven.

To some there might be the tendency to look down upon a business based wholly on the sale of hair goods, but as John D. Rockefeller gained his fortune by the sale of oil, Madam Walker has a right to gain her fortune by the sale of (a hair) oil. When we think of Mr. Rockefeller, we do not get a mental picture of him as a man with a kerosene can in one hand and a jar of petroleum in the other. Thus it is when we think of Madam Walker, we do not get a picture of her with a box of her "grower" in one hand and a "Pressing comb" in the other. In both cases we think of their individual fortune, their philanthropy and their ingenuity as Business Magnates.

How many a poor mortal has spent his whole life in the vain hopes of the acquisition of a fortune, and after having arrived at the desired end lost it in one mad play. How different with Madam Walker. In a space of fourteen years, she by her dexterity and business foresight, has acquired a fortune and serves as an inspiration for others to feel that truly, "All service ranks the same with God." A few years ago she was poor and unknown, save to her neighbors and those for whom she toiled. Yet, on September 2, 1917, The New York Times Magazine gave her space with cuts of the exterior and interior of her beautiful New York home. She is easily the wealthiest Negro woman in the country.

Although the formula for the "grower" came, as she tells it, to her in a dream, her fortune has not been acquired by any chance, nor did she have any inherited wealth, with which to start in business.

Her only asset was her unbounding faith in her formula, that it would do what she claimed for it, and her determination to make the public regard it in the same light.

She began in a small way, the wash tub furnishing the means to commence her enterprise.

She has labored, thought, and carried out her plans with such business tact that today she gives employment to a thousand Negro women and to a lawyer, who finds all his time taken with her affairs.

As has been said, Madam Walker began with no inherited wealth for her capital. Her birth and early life, were amid the most humble surroundings. She was born in Delta, Louisiana. Her parents, Owen and Minerva Breedlove, were honest farmers. At the age of seven, Madam Walker found herself an orphan. She was then taken to Vicksburg, Mississippi, to live with her sister, and a none-too-kind Brother-in-law. Her life was so miserable that at the age of fourteen she married in order to get a more comfortable home. The marriage proved a happy one and though the home was humble it was brightened by love and the merry laughter of their only child, Lelia. The family

RESIDENCE OF MADAM C. J. WALKER—IRVINGTON, ON HUDSON, N. Y.—(FRONT VIEW)

circle was broken by the death of the husband, leaving Madam Walker a widow at the age of twenty. She moved from Vicksburg to St. Louis, Missouri, where she lived for eighteen years. Here she reared and educated her daughter and succeeded in sending her to Fisk University. In order to do this Madam Walker endured many hardships and much toil.

In 1905 came the turning point in her life; she discovered a remedy for growing hair. After having tried it successfully on herself and family, she decided to make a business of it. Thus July 19, 1905, she left St. Louis, Missouri, for Denver, Colorado, to enter upon her business. She was called upon to face many obstacles and much discouragement, but these she over came, and like a shrewd business clerk, she succeeded in convincing the people that she was offering them just what they wanted. After they had bought once they continued to buy. This grew into a fair business in Denver in the space of a year.

While the people in Denver were convinced the outside public was prone to be a little skeptical regarding this new wonder. Here again her clear, calm mind responded to the situation. She started to travel in the interest fo her work. Many of her friends told her that she would not make fare from one town to the other. But this very strong willed woman saw only success ahead of her, and she went out to claim it. She started out on this mission September 15, 1906. For a year and a half she traveled and at the end of that time the mail order business had become so large that she had to settle somewhere temporarily. Pittsburg, Pennsylvania was selected and she established her business there and left it in charge of her daughter and again started out to travel. Her travels led her all over the United States, Cuba, Panama, and the West Indies. This gave her an excellent opportunity to decide on a permanent place for a factory. It so happened that Indianapolis, Indiana, through its cordial welcome impressed her as a most favorable place for home and factory. Here she has since purchased and paid for a beautiful home, valued at ten thousand dollars, adjoining which is a factory, and laboratory, said to be the most complete of its kind in the United States.

For a number of years, Madam Walker lived here, managing the home and the factory. Throughout the city were many agents and wherever she traveled there were other agents. In fact, Madam Walker had to employ a lawyer, now her business combined with her investments and real estate demands the entire attention of her lawyer.

RESIDENCE OF MADAM C. J. WALKER—IRVINGTON ON HUDSON, N. Y.—(REAR VIEW)

Mr. F. B. Ransom. The business is incorporated with a capital stock of $10,000, with an income of $1000.00 per week.

Since coming to Indianapolis she is regarded as one of the most active in its commercial life and her business methods are unquestionable. But that which has endeared her even more to the people is her philanthropy. Her donations to Charity are many and varied and one perhaps better depicts the real soul of this woman from her annual donations of fifty Christmas baskets to poor families of Indianapolis. Many of these people Madam Walker has never seen and even though she no longer lives in the city, she has arranged that this annual affair be continued.

Aside from the annual donations to the Old Folk's Home and Orphans' Home in Indianapolis, St. Louis, and other cities, Madam Walker donates largely to temperance cause and gives fifty dollars annually for the current expenses of the Y. M. C. A. and Y. W. C. A., as well as contributes one hundred dollars a year to the International Y. M. C. A. Much has been said of Madam Walker being the first to donate $1000.00 to the Y. M. C. A. when she made this contribution to the Colored Branch of Indianapolis, but the true greatness of her gift

was the Christian spirit which prompted her and the inspiration that it gave to others of her race to do likewise.

Madam Walker's philanthrophy is not restricted to Home, but extends even to Africa. She has established an industrial school in Africa and she has set aside a certain percentage of her annual income for its upkeep. She also maintains many scholarships at Tuskegee and other institutions.

In her travels, Madam Walker meets many who afterwards seek her aid and after she has carefully investigated their condition she lends them a helping hand in one way or another. Surely an unbiased historian will record her as a shrewd business manager, a broad philanthropist and a devoted Christian worker.

Since writing this sketch, Madam Walker has passed to the "Great beyond." She died Sunday morning, May 25th, 1919, leaving an estate valued at $1,000,000.00. The estimated value of her real estate was about $800,000.00 and the other was in personal property, stocks, bonds, etc.

GEORGE HENRY SIMS, D. D.

R. George Henry Sims, D. D., was born in a double log cabin in Cumland County, Virginia, April 8th, 1871. His parents had been slaves. Set free, they moved into Cumberland County, and reared their children there. Born on the farm, the future pastor of popular Union Baptist Church of New York, spent his early days with the mule and the plow and the hoe. He was converted at the age of eleven and was baptized one year later.

Coming into young manhood, Dr. Sims left the farm and began to work on the railroads. Here he labored for seven years. On going to New York he sought and obtained employment as an elevator runner. Eager to push ahead, however, he carried his books with him and studied during his spare moments in the day and at night. He had from his experience on the railroad become interested in stationary engineering. This subject he now pursued, and in a little while obtained a license as a mechanical engineer, a license which he held in the city of New York for ten years. This again, however, was but the stepping stone to a higher calling. He had long yearned to preach. His opportunity to study theology now arrived. While working as a stationary engineer he took studies in theology.

By 1898 he felt himself ready to follow the real life mission he believed he was called to perform. On August 23rd, 1898, he was ordained at Nyack, New York. Here for a time he was pastor of a small church, but in 1898 he went to New York City to organize the present Union Baptist Church, 204-06 West 63rd Street, a church in the district much neglected by church workers; a church, which, as an organization, had nailed up its doors for want of a congregation and for need of support for a pastor.

Opening first a mission here, then the old church, then building a new one, Dr. Sims became famous as a preacher and a worker in New York, and in the country round about. Honors now began to come to him from nearly every section of the country. He was made a Doctor of Divinity by Guadalupe College of Seguin, Texas, in 1905. He was chosen a member of the board of trustees of Virginia Theological Seminary, a member of the board of Managers of the New England Baptist Missionary Convention, President of the New York Colored Baptist State Convention, Vice-President of the National Baptist Convention, a member of the Board of Trustees of the Northern University, a member of the Board of Managers of the Walton Kindergarden, and President of the West End Workers Association of New York.

To honors in service and uplift work have been added many appointments from the various governors of New York. The governor's party politics seems to make but little difference in his case. In 1913 he was appointed by Governor Sulzer as a member of the Emancipation Proclamation Commission; in the fall of the same year he was appointed by Governor Glynn a delegate to the Emancipation Proclamation Commission which convened at Atlantic City, New Jersey; he was also appointed by Governor Glynn, as a delegate to the fifth annual convention of National Educational Congress, of Oklahoma, in 1914; and was appointed by Governor Whitman, as a delegate to attend the Negro National Educational Congress, which was held at Washington, D. C., 1916. Thus has he stood with the rulers of the state regardless of party or creed.

Prominent in sacred and religious work, Dr. Sims does not neglect his membership and standing in secret bodies. He was made a 33rd degree Mason in 1911. He is a member of the Independent Order of St. Luke and of the Ancient Daughters of the Sphinx. He has traveled extensively in the United States and in Canada.

Dr. Sims has been twice married. He was first married to Miss Mary E. Davis, September 25th, 1895. Their one child, Ethel, lived but two years. The mother died in August 1908. The second Mrs. Sims was Miss Louise D. Russell, to whom Dr. Sims was married in 1909. Five children have been born from this union, of whom three are living: Edith Thelma, aged seven; George H., Jr., aged five; and Arial Louise, aged two years.

FRANK S. HARGRAVE, M. D.

F the professions open to men, the two which seem to appeal to the colored man more than others is the ministry and medicine. Both of these look to the betterment of the human family. One has the spiritual interest of man at heart and the other seeks his physical well-being. Both are high callings and both occupy important places in the affairs of men.

Dr. Hargrave is an honored member of the latter profession, and has reached a high place in it.

Dr. Hargrave was born in Lexington, North Carolina, and was a member of a large family, which made it difficult for him to secure help in obtaining his education.

In his early days he attended the public schools of Lexington, North Carolina, and the State Normal School, of Salisbury, North Carolina.

At the age of sixteen he assumed the responsibility of his further education and in order to meet the expense of his tuition he worked in tobacco factories in Western North Carolina. The money earned in this way carried him through Shaw University, at Raleigh, North Carolina. At this famous institution he took both the Literary and Medical courses, winning his degrees. After completing his work at the University he immediately took up the practice of medicine.

He first located in Winston-Salem North Carolina, where he remained from 1901 to 1903, but was convinced that he had made a mistake in the location selected and so decided upon a change. In 1903 he removed from Winston-Salem to Wilson, North Carolina, where he has since lived. Here he has built up a large and lucrative practice and is held in high esteem by all classes.

Very few men have greater opportunities for doing good than the Christian physician, and Dr. Hargrave is not only a Christian, but a very active one. He is a member and deacon of the First Baptist Church of Wilson, North Carolina, and the Superintendent of the Sunday school. With him the offices held in the church are not merely places of honor, but of work, and he is giving his best efforts to the cause. He is a member of the Executive Committee of the North Carolina Baptist Sunday School Convention, and is thus brought into close and sympathetic touch with the religious sentiment of the State.

In 1912 he was elected President of the North Carolina Medical, Dental, and Pharmaceutical Association. The same year he was elected a member of the Executive Board of the National Medical Association.

In 1914, at Raleigh, North Carolina Dr. Hargrave had the honor of being elected President of the National Medical Association, an unusual honor as he was elected practically without opposition. This election gave the Doctor much pleasure and was a matter of commendable pride to him. Dr. Hargrave does not confine his activities to his profession, and the interests of his denomination, though these are his first love, but ardently labors with a number of secret orders fostered by his people. He is a member of the Masonic fraternity, Knights of Pythias, and is the President of the Lincoln Benefit Society, of Wilson, North Carolina. He is actively identified with all of these orders. While serving the public, Dr. Hargrave has not neglected his personal affairs and by close economy and wise use of his money he has accumulated quite a nice property and is one of the large property owners of his race in the town of Wilson. He is loyal to the town in which he located and believes that he helps himself when he invests his means in property in his home city. He thus sets a worthy example to others.

Possibly the pride of his heart, as the inspiration came from his heart, is the "Verona Cottage," the beautiful home he erected for his wife in Eastern North Carolina. Here they find great joy and pleasure in a sweet companion-hip the only dreg in their cup of bliss being the absence of children.

JAMES EDWARD SHEPHERD, PH. G., D. D., A. M.
PRESIDENT NATIONAL TRAINING SCHOOL
—DURHAM, N. C.

 HAT the good work being done in the many institutions in the South is not confined to the schools established right after Emancipation of the Negro or soon after, but is shared by the younger institutions, is brought out in the history of the National Training School, at Durham, North Carolina. This institution of learning was established in 1910. At that time it was known as The National Religious Training School. For five years it worked under this name and with the Religious Training as its chief aim. In 1916 it was completely reorganized and rechartered under the laws of North Carolina, as the National Training School.

The National Training School stands for efficiency; this is abundantly proven by the high scholarship maintained by its students in Northern and Southern Colleges, as well as by the work done by pupils who have gone out into the active affairs of the world. In 1918 the Institution sent out from its Theological Department three thoroughly prepared ministers; from the Academic department, eleven, and from the commercial, nine; Domestic

Art, two; Domestic Science, two.

The school is still young and is still forming its courses. In the near future it hopes to number along with the courses already mentioned the following:

1. A thorough teacher-Training Course, especially adapted to the needs of the rural teacher.

2. A bureau of investigation to study the social, moral, physical and economic conditions of the Negro, so as to be able to co-operate in an intelligent manner with organized bodies and civic authorities so as to really better the condition of the Negro.

3. Conferences along the various lines as suggested above.

4. Group studies in various sections of the country.

5. Extension courses, so as to carry the idea of this school into every section of the country.

One of the prime aims of the school is to lift the race into racial consciousness thus helping it to come into its own. In this way it hopes that by lifting and serving its own to serve and aid the State and the nation. One of the particular beliefs of those in authority at the National Training School is that the large schools cannot reach its students in the close, intimate way for real constructive work in the same manner as the smaller institutions. Hence one of the aims of this school has been to gather together a particular group of well-selected persons, train them and send them out in turn to train others.

In order to put the school within the means of all the people, the charges are very small indeed. There is a charge of only ten dollars for board, room rent, lights, heat and tuition. This means that the school must be supported by the public. This is the real reason why this institution has to keep ever before the public its many needs. But the aim of the institution and the amount of good already being done justifies the appeal for help.

Look at the Religious Education as Set Forth by the National Training School:

1. Awakens the dormant energies of an individual and directs these aroused forces into channels of usefulness and service.

2. Causes a man to see himself as he really is; no man is worth while who has not seen himself, his powers, his possibilities.

3. Reduces crime, stops idleness, prevents violence, thus adds to the peace and prosperity of a community.

4. Alleviates race prejudice.

5. Brings about at all times a peaceful adjustment between capital and labor.

6. Promotes steadfastness and reliability, because it is a character builder.

7. Teaches absolute self-control.

8 Makes religion a practical every-day reality, not simply an emotional noise

9 Will promote race consciousness

10 It is founded on the Bible

The National Training School has a high standard for its students Students are received from high schools and academies approved by the faculty and placed in corresponding classes without examination This is done only on the presentation of certificates showing their rank in the school which they are leaving Others are admitted to the school through examination In order that the full stamp of the spirit of the school may be made upon each person leaving her doors, there is a rule requiring students to spend their senior year as residents of the dormitory Frequently students make application for special courses To supply this demand the National Training School has rulings and regulations that permit such persons to become students there But before they are taken on this ground they have to satisfy a committee that they are fitted for the type of work that they are preparing to do

These special courses in the trade religious and academic line are open especially to persons of mature years and judgement

One of the theories and it is working out well of this school is this "Change the man and the man will change the environment" Therefore above all else the school stands for a sound Christian character a sound body a trained mind and well directed industrial training To fully effect this change and to get the greatest benefit from the change, the National Training School uses a system of self-government To this end each student is allowed as far as possible, to regulate his conduct by his or her sense of honor justice and propriety The school looks to the self-control of each individual student in the end Their regulations are such as have been tested and proven of value in the development of well-rounded character and students who think that they cannot abide by these regulations are advised not to seek entrance in the school at all In all things the student of the National Training School is looked upon and treated as a gentleman or lady The only thing that can change this attitude of the teachers' and officers toward a student is the misbehavior of the individual himself

The students maintain numerous organizations religious, athletic, literary musical and social Then there are numerous class and inter-class organizations All these make for the personal acquaintance of the teachers and pupils The socials of the Y M C A and the Y W C A are especially attractive to the new students and to the old students as well The officers of the various student organizations can be held only by students who are doing their work in a satisfactory manner

This applies to the athletic teams and the publishing board In fact in order to get any of the honor that comes from representing the school in the athletic world or the literary world good work in the regular class room regime must be done In addition to this ruling there is another which is equally as good No student will be eligible to active participation in conduct and management of more than two such organizations during the same semester Any time that a student begins to fail in his studies he is noticed that he must give up some of his outside duties

Backing this institution and helping shape its courses and destinies we find some very strong men On the Board of Trustees are Mr Howard J Chidley, D D of Winchester Mass Judge Jeter C Pritchard Asheville North Carolina, James E Shepard Durham, North Carolina General Julian S Carr, Durham North Carolina James B Mason Durham North Carolina, W Y Chapman Newark New Jersey William G Pearson Durham North Carolina, J Elmer Dellinger M D, Greensboro, North Carolina and J Stanley Durkee Ph D C, Mr Gordan Parker Winchester Mass and F J West, N Y With these men back of him the president Mr James E Shepard, in his characteristic fearless manner is establishing this school and shaping its courses Somewhere President Shepard is on record as saying "The Negro begs little for himself as an individual but he does beg for his schools and his churches so that the masses may be lifted up"

"The home field cannot be neglected and the foundations of the Government remain secure In a Republic next to the homes the schools are the Nation's bulwark and strength They must teach lessons of patriotism and lessons of self-control Hence they must be fostered and supported"

Before taking up the work in Durham President Shepard spent years in active service that fully prepared him for the many different tasks that devolve upon the President of an institution of learning Indeed President Shepard has had all the experience necessary to make him a real guiding star to the National Training School

President James Edward Shepard was born at Raleigh N C Nov 3 1875, and educated at Shaw University, 1883-90, and received the degree of Ph G Department of Pharmacy, same college In 1894 he took private course in theology and in 1912 he received the degree of Doctor of Divinity Musgingum's College, Ohio and has A M degree from Selma University (Ala) in 1913

He has been honored with many positions of trust and honor, Companer of deeds recorder's office Washington D C 1898 deputy collector U S Internal Revenue Raleigh, N C 1899-05 Field Superintendent International Sunday School Association (work among Negroes) 1905-09 President National Training School for Colored Race, Durham April 1910 Director Mechanics and Farmers Bank State Industrial Association President Interdenominational Sunday School Convention (Exec Com 1909-14) Trustee Lincoln School for Nurses, Durham, Member North Carolina Medical Association, Delegate and only Negro speaker World's S S Convention Rome, Italy 1907 a Mason Clubs Civic National Arts Aerial League He has traveled extensively in Europe Africa and Asia, a lecturer

HENRY LAWRENCE McCROREY, D. D.

EV. H. L. McCrorey, D. D., is one of those quiet presidents in the smaller Southern College, one who is doing his work quietly, conscientiously, effectively. He was born in Fairfield County, South Carolina, March 2nd, 1863. As a boy he worked on the farm and attended the Richardson school at Winnsboro, S. C. Finally, in 1886, he enrolled as a student in Biddle University, North Carolina. This marked the turning point in his career. Here was to be laid the scene of all his achievements, as a student, as a teacher, as an executive. He was graduated from the High School and Collegiate and Theological departments. Later he specialized in the Semitic languages in the University of Chicago. He was appointed teacher in the High School department of his alma mater after this special preparation. Having gained a reputation here as a teacher, he was promoted to the position of Principal. From here he was moved to the position of head Latin teacher in the Collegiate department, where he made a good record as a teacher of the classics. He was again promoted, this time to the chair of Hebrew and Greek in the department of Theology. This position has in itself an interesting and helpful phase. As is well known, in some instances, in the denominational schools where there are white teachers, colored teachers will be and are substituted whenever available. Biddle, which is under the Presbyterian Church, has followed this policy,

as has Morehouse in Atlanta and Jackson College in Jackson, Mississippi, the two latter being Baptist schools. Dr. McCrorey enjoys the distinction of succeeding the last white man who taught in Biddle. In 1907 he was again promoted to the presidency of Biddle University, succeeding the late Dr. Sanders.

Dr. McCrorey has taken an active part in the work of uplift in the church and among the people. He was delegate in 1909 to the Pan-Presbyterian Alliance in New York City; a delegate in 1915, appointed by the State, to the Southern Sociological Congress, which met in Houston, Texas. He is a member of the American Academy of Political and Social Science, and of a committee of the Federal Council of the Churches of Christ in America, and a member of the Social Service Commission of the Northern Presbyterian Church. He is closely identified with the local uplift work in Charlotte, being the president of the colored Chamber of Commerce in that city.

Dr. McCrorey has been twice married. His first wife was Miss Karie N. Hughes, of Mebane, N. C., who died in 1911. His present wife was Miss Mary C. Jackson of Athens, Ga., who was for several years a close co-laborer with Miss Lucy Laney as Associate Principal of Haynes Institute, Augusta, Ga. To the first wife were born four children, one boy and three girls. The boy is now a college student in Biddle University. The oldest girl is a student in Fisk University, the next a student in Scotia College for Women, and the third is attending public school in Charlotte.

As president of Biddle University, Dr. McCrorey is of course best known.

Biddle University is located in Charlotte, North Carolina. It owns seventy acres of land and fourteen buildings, the whole being valued at $225,000. It has four departments: High School, Arts and Sciences, Theological and Industrial. It is conservative, thorough, clean and straight-forward in its policy. Many leading Negroes, especially in the professions, owe all they have become to Biddle.

Biddle's position in North Carolina, as well as that of Dr. Crorey, is seen happily in the following clipping from a column editorial appearing in the Charlotte Observer, November 16, 1911, the day following the laying of the corner-stone of the splendid new Carnegie Library which cost $15,000.00.

"Biddle University is now in its forty-fourth year. It has been pursuing its mission quietly and without any blowing of trumpets, preferring to make its way on merit rather than by the circus methods adopted by some schools, and encouraged by the success it has attained. Mr. D. A. Tompkins, who was present at the corner-stone laying yesterday and who was highly praised by Dr. McCrorey for the unselfish interest he has always taken in the school, thinks that Biddle is a model school and that it would well repay those who are interested in the solution of race questions everywhere throughout the world to visit this place and study the methods that have made this institution one of the most conservative influences in the land. In his address, Mr. Clarkson, who for seven years was solicitor for the 12th Judicial District, said yesterday that during his term of office he had never been called upon to prosecute any man who had ever attended this school."

ADMINISTRATION BUILDING, BIDDLE UNIVERSITY—CHARLOTTE, N. C.

 N the first years of the work of the Presbyterian Church for the Freed-Men of the South, a special necessity developed the need of a training school which, with God's blessing, might prepare, for the work of the church and a trained ministry.

Through the generous gift, in memory of Maj. Henry J. Biddle of Philadelphia, from his widow the necessary buildings were built on a beautiful tract of eight acres, the gift of Col. W. R. Myers, a citizen of Charlotte. Biddle Institute, located at Charlotte, North Carolina, was opened for students September 16th, 1867. When the first session opened there were present forty-three students, twenty of these candidates for the ministry, and the others seeking preparation for the work of teaching.

"Biddle Institute" has grown into "Biddle University." It is a chartered institution with property vested in a Board of Trustees, for the Presbyterian Church. U. S. A., under the care of the Presbyterian Board of Missions for Freedmen, and the salaries of the professors and other expenses of this institution are paid out of the board's funds.

Biddle University now consists of about 80 acres of land, 14 buildings, 18 professors and other teachers, and combines all the advantages of academic seclusion and easy access to a business center. There are four main departments in the University. The Preparatory trains for teaching and for business and for college. The College department offers two courses, classical and scientific, covering the usual four years, and affording the advantages of a liberal education.

The Theological department is organized on the usual plan of the Seminaries of the Presbyterian church with a full three year's course. The Industrial department includes training in carpentry, printing, plastering, tailoring, bricklaying, shoemaking, blacksmithing, and to some extent agriculture.

Biddle has sent out from its various departments 1433 graduates, 169 of these being ministers of the gospel. There have been enrolled over 10,000 students, of whom about nine-tenths became professing Christians, mostly Presbyterians.

At first a white president and professors presided over and conducted the affairs of Biddle, but in 1891, the entire faculty was colored, with Rev. D. J. Sanders, D. D., as president. At his death Dr. H. L. McCrorey was called to the presidency.

271

VIEW OF CAMPUS, HENDERSON NORMAL AND INDUSTRIAL INSTITUTE—HENDERSON, N. C.

N 1865, in Manchester, Kentucky, was born Rev. John Adams Cotton, A. B., of Henderson, North Carolina. Having spent some time in the public schools of his native town, he left Manchester, and entered Berea College, Berea, Ky., where he studied for four years doing preparatory work, later entering Knoxville College, Tennessee. Here he received his Bachelor's degree. Long before this he had decided to enter the ministry. Having now finished his college course, he turned his attention to prepartion for his chosen life work, that of the Christian Ministry. He enrolled as a student of Divinity in the Pittsburg Theological Seminary, Pittsburg, Pennsylvania, where he remained until he had finished his course.

Finishing his course in Theology, Mr. Cotton decided that though he would preach, he would put decided emphasis on education and that if Providence so directed, he would invest his energies in school work. He took his first charge at Cleveland, Tennessee. The charge was significant in that it represented at the outset the very dual situation he had preferred—preaching and teaching. In 1899 he took charge of a church and became principal of the Cleveland Academy in Cleveland, Tennessee. From Cleveland he was called to the head of the Henderson Normal and Industrial Institute, Henderson, North Carolina, where he is still laboring.

The Henderson Institute is one of those strong conservative Presbyterian schools under the control of the United Presbyterian Church. It is an example of the kind of work this church is trying to do. It provides buildings and grounds as comfortable as possible, offers courses for the training of the hand and head, and seeks to mould at the bottom sound Christian character. Assuming and planning that every teacher shall be a Christian worker, the school has regular training classes for student teachers in Sunday teaching and Bible study.

While planning definitely for the career of service for the teacher, the school does not forget the character and development of the every day student. It maintains a flourishing Y. M. C. A., and a flourishing Y. W. C. A. It has three literary societies, which give the members opportunity for debate and for general training in public speaking. Its "Things Required" show how persistent is the endeavor to provide men and women of clean character and lofty ideals. These things show how close and careful a watch is kept over the actions and health of the students.

Of equal significance is the school's "Things Forbidden."

THINGS FORBIDDEN.

1. Unpermitted association of ladies and gentlemen, communication in writing between them or visiting to the halls or rooms of the other.

2. Boisterousness, dancing, running in the buildings, etc.

3. Games of chance, profane or indecent language, the use or possession of tobacco, snuff, intoxicating liquor or of weapons of any kind.

4. Calling, conversing or throwing from the windows.

5. No light literature is allowed among the students.

6. Visitors cannot be received during school or study hours, and gentlemen, unknown to the Matron or Principal are not permitted to see lady students at any time, unless they bring letters of introduction from parents or guardians to the Matron or Principal, and then subject to the discretion of the Principal."

Such in brief is the school over which Reverend

MAIN BUILDING—HENDERSON NORMAL &
INDUSTRIAL INSTITUTE.

Cotton presides and to which he gives character.
It has an enrollment of 461 students, most of whom
are boarders, but all of whom are subject to the
regulations. Principal Cotton has been in charge
here 15 years. Under him many new courses have
been introduced and many reforms made.

Reverend Cotton was married in 1900 to Miss
Maud R. Brooks, of Oberlin, Ohio. They have
one daughter, Carol Blanche, who is 12 years old.

The following from the 1916 U. S. Bulletin No.
39, gives a more complete account of its plans and
equipment:

The school was founded in 1891, by the Board of
Freedmen's Missions of the United Presbyterian
Church, and is owned and supported by that board.

ATTENDANCE: Total, 375; elementary 334;
secondary 41; male 152, female 223. Of those reporting, 26 were from Henderson, 42 from other
places in North Carolina, and eight from other
States. There were 43 pupils above the seventh
grade boarding at the school.

TEACHERS AND WORKERS: Total 18; all colored; male 5, female, 13; academic 9, music 1;
girls' industries 3, boys' industries 1, matrons 2,
superintendent of broom factory and superintendent of hospital.

INDUSTRIAL: The industrial course for boys
are limited to instruction in printing, broommak-
ing, and simple manual training. The girls above
the seventh grade receive good instruction in cooking and sewing under the direction of three teachers.

NURSE TRAINING: Nurse training is provided
in a well-equipped hospital built by the women's
board, with a training nurse in charge. Students
needing medical attention and patients from the
community or surrounding counties are admitted
The number of patients is comparatively small.

The Financial department is well cared for. The
accounts are carefully kept and the financial management appears to be economical.

SOURCES OF INCOME: United Presbyterian
Board, $8,000; tuition and fees $500. The non educational receipts amounted to $4,100, or which
$4,000 was from boarding department and $100
from the trade school.

PLANT: Land: Estimated value, $2,000. The
land comprises 13 acres just outside the corporate
limits of the town. About half of the land is used
for campus and recreation purposes. The remainder is used for orchard, pasture, and a small farm.

BUILDINGS: Estimated value, $41,500. The
main building is a frame structure, two stories high
and contains class-rooms and a chapel seating 500.
Fulton Home is the girl's dormitory, accommodating 75. It contains the dining room, domestic
science department, laundry, and matron's office.
The boys' dormitory, a two-story frame building,
accommodates 75, also houses the printing office.
The teachers' home is a neat two story building.
Jubilee Hospital is a two-story brick building, with
wards for men, women, and children, an operating
room and several private rooms. There are also
several small buildings, including the janitor's cottage. The buildings are simple in construction, in
good repair and neat in appearance.

MOVABLE EQUIPMENT: Estimated value $6,900.
$6,900. Of this $5,700 was in furniture and hospital
equipment, $500 in farm implements, and live
stock, $450 in library books, and $250 in shop tools.

HOSPITAL BUILDING HENDERSON NORMAL
& INDUSTRIAL INSTITUTE.

273

JAMES B. DUDLEY, A. M., LL. D.

HERE are those who drift into the work of education; those who are pressed in by necessity, and those who enlist in the cause by choice. Dr. James B. Dudley, of Greensboro, North Carolina, is one of those to enter and to remain by choice. Educated when learning was rare among American Negroes; he looked upon school teaching as a calling, a mission. The idea of the Quaker and of the Puritan, that being taught you should go teach others, took possession of Dr. Dudley, long before his school career ended. Further there was inculcated into his education, that one should not go to Africa, South America, but back home, to lift those of your own kith and kin.

Born in Wilmington, North Carolina, in 1859, Dr. Dudley received his first training through private instruction, public education for the colored youth being out of the question in North Carolina at that time. From Wilmington Dr. Dudley made his way to Philadelphia, Pennsylvania, where he studied at the Philadelphia Institute for Colored Youths. He later gained the degree of Master of Arts at Livingston College, Salisbury, North Carolina, and LL. D., from Wilberforce University.

His early education completed, Dr. Dudley returned to his State and began his labor as a school teacher. He began in the rural school, where his help was most needed and where he gained the experience which was to serve him most valuably in his work as college president. From the rural schools he was called to the principalship of the Peabody Graded School, of Wilmington. Here for sixteen years he labored, doing much toward putting the Negro public schools here on a solid footing. Sixteen years principalship at Wilmington, with experience in the rural schools and among rural folks had seasoned him for larger service. Thus when the Agricultural and Technical College, formerly known as the A. & M. College, began to take form, choice quite readily settled upon Dr. Dudley; he who had been an educator all his career; who had labored in city and in country; who was a native of the soil came very rightfully to the best his native State had to offer for one of his race.

The Negro Agricultural and Technical College was founded in 1891. It is one of the several colleges established under the Morrill Act. To the funds authorized by the Morrill Act were added fourteen acres of land and eleven thousand dollars by the citizens of Greensboro. To this sum again was added ten thousand dollars by the General Assembly of North Carolina. Five years after the founding of this institution, Dr. Dudley was called to its presidency. This was in 1896. Thus for twenty-three years he has administered its work. Under him new buildings have been erected, old ones renovated, farms cultivated, courses added and adjusted to suit the demands of the day. True to its title the institution has courses leading to degrees in Agriculture in many branches, in Mechanical Arts and Technical subjects. Yet has never lost sight of the fact that the head is master of the hand, indeed of the whole body. To this end it has maintained very high standards in literary branches.

In deportment, as well as in scholarship, A. & T. College has set for its students unusually high and rigid standards. Many of its rules are worth quoting and worthy of emulation. Thus it requires:

1. Regular students must take a minimum of fifteen hours of credit work per week at least six of which shall be industrial work.

2. Examinations for the removal of conditions will be held at no time than the regular term examination periods. A minimum credit of 85 per cent must be made to remove conditions.

3. Students making an average of 70 per cent or more will be passed; over 85 per cent passed honorably.

4. Student candidates for graduation will be required to pass a satisfactory examination in all the subjects in their respective courses.

5. Any student failing to secure 50 per cent of the total marks obtainable during any term, will be required to take a lower class or sever his connection with the college and be allowed to return the following session.

It is the aim of this institution to send forth men who are fit representatives. To this end, the faculty reserves the right to refuse to admit any student to the senior class or to graduate any one who though qualified by class record, may otherwise be unfit.

Again to influence and to restrict, the institution rules that each student upon applying for admission will be required to sign a pledge, binding obedience to the rules of the college. Parents and guard-

MAIN BUILDING STATE AGRICULTURAL & TECHNICAL COLLEGE—GREENSBORO, N. C.

ians are particularly requested to examine our rules and regulations, to be found on another page of this catalogue.

It will be the purpose of the college to maintain a high moral tone and to develope a broad, tolerant religious spirit among the students. In this connection there is a well-organized Y. M. C. A., which meets twice a week for song and praise. A special service will be conducted in the chapel each Sunday by pastors representing the different denominations of the city. Sunday School is conducted every Sunday during school year. All religious services will be free from sectarianism. A flourishing Temperance Society is now in operation.

All this system has taken shape under the hand of Dr. Dudley, backed by the State Board of Trustees and by a sympathetic public.

While putting his school on an up-to-date basis, Dr. Dudley did not forget the demands upon the present day college. He was one of the first Negro educators to see that an institution must go without its walls, must seek to educate the old as well as the young. He founded the Metropolitan Trust Company, of Wilmington, to stimulate and to combine Negro business and established the Pioneer Building and Loan Association, of Greensboro, the oldest organization of its kind in Greensboro.

Beyond local services he has taken active part in many educational and uplift undertakings in other States and before the nation and in so doing has been recipient of many honors. For nearly thirty years he was foreign correspondent for the Masonic Grand Lodge, of North Carolina. He was delegate to the Republican National Convention in St. Louis, in 1896. He is president of the North Carolina Teachers' Association; trustee of the Annual A. M. E. Conference; honorary member of the Board of Trustees of Palmer Institute of Se-

dalia, North Carolina; president of the North Carolina Anti-Tuberculosis League; chairman of the Negro Railroad Commission; founder of the Rural Extension work and was the successful champion against lawful segregation in North Carolina.

Dr. Dudley is a Mason, and a Pythian, and an active member of the National Association for Teachers in Colored Schools. He has traveled extensively in America and to some extent in Canada. He owns property in Wilmington and in Greensboro.

The Dudley family consists of three members, Dr. and Mrs. Dudley and Miss Annie Vivian. Mrs. Dudley was Miss Sampson, of Wilmington. They were married in 1884. Miss Dudley has finished her education and was her father's bookkeeper, until her marriage in 1917 to Dr. S. B. Jones, Vice-President and physician, of the A. and T. College.

GREEN HOUSE, STATE A. & T. COLLEGE.

JOHN WAKEFIELD WALKER, A. B., M. D.

F humble parentage, John Wakefield Walker was born December 26, 1872. His mother, Mrs. Amanda Walker, was refugeed from eastern North Carolina, to Salisbury, during the Civil War. There were six children in the Walker family, of whom the subject of this sketch was the youngest. Mrs. Walker was a woman of ambition and she succeeded in firing her young son with a zeal to render Christian service when he was still but a lad. She died September 23, 1897.

From his early childhood, Dr. Walker had the privilege of attending school. His first schooling was received in the city schools of Asheville. Having gotten from them all that he could he went to Livingston College. His sister, Mrs. Hester Lee, was largely responsible for his being able to attend Livingston College. From Livingston he was graduated in 1898, with the degree of A. B. Dr. Walker lost no time but matriculated at the Leonard Medical College, Shaw University, Raleigh, North Carolina. From Shaw he was graduated with the degree of M. D., in 1902. Not yet satisfied with his preparation for his life work, the young doctor served an internship in the Freedman's Hospital at Washington, D. C., before he settled down to his work.

The path of Dr. Walker from his humble home to his present practice was not wholly strewn with roses. In fact he had to work a great deal and in many kinds of jobs in order to get the training he now enjoys. He served as footman, butler, bellboy, waiter, office boy, sleeping-car porter. But his ambition had been fired by his mother and he used these jobs merely as means to an end and was never satisfied with them, and the easy money they brought in.

Dr. Walker today is located in Asheville, North Carolina. Asheville is a resort for patinets suffering with pulmonary troubles. Here from all parts of the south and the east persons suffering from this disease gather. Dr. Walker owns and runs his own sanatarium here for the treatment of such cases. In fact, Dr. Walker has made a specialty of this type of tuberculosis. Because of the climatic conditions of the city and the gathering of patients from other parts of the United States, Dr. Walker has a large field. He does not, however, confine himself solely to this work. He serves as City Inspector of the Colored Schools of Asheville. In this work he has the chance of preventing many a case of this sort by recognizing early symptoms and rendering aid before the real disease sets in.

Dr. Walker finds time to take part in all the varied activities for the uplife of his people. He is a member of the A. M. E. Zion Church, serving as the Superintendent of the Sunday School. He is a member of the Free and Accepted Masons, "The Beauty of the West Lodge," and of the Grand United Order of Odd Fellows. He served as President of the North Carolina Medical Association, as President of the Y. M. C. A., of Asheville, trustee of the Livingston College, delegate to the General Conference at Charlotte in 1912, and at Louisville in 1916, and he is a member of the National Medical Association. In all the lines of endeavor that are for the advancement of the Colored people there you will find Dr. J. W. Walker taking an active part.

Dr. Walker was married to Miss Eleanor Curtis Mitchell, in Raleigh, North Carolina, on June 22, 1904. From this union three children have been born. The oldest, John Wakefield Walker, Jr., is a lad of twelve years. Miss Amanda Lee Walker is in her tenth year and little Miss Anna Belle Walker is still a baby, being but four years of age. This happy family lives in their own home on College Street.

Dr. Walker is an inspiration to the young men of his acquaintance. He has risen to a point of prominence through his own efforts.

Besides owning his own home and his sanitarium he owns several tenement houses.

JOSEPH LAWRENCE JONES

OUNDER and President of the Central Regalia Company, Joseph Lawrence Jones, was born June 12, 1868, at Mt. Healthy, Ohio, near Cincinnati. He attended the public schools of Cincinnati, and graduated from Gaines High School, in 1886, after which he taught school in Kentucky, Texas and Ohio. He is also a graduate of the Sheldon Business College.

In 1902, Mr. Jones established the business which has made his name well known wherever colored lodges exist. The Central Regalia Company is strictly a Negro enterprise, giving employment to our own men and women. We find Mr. Jones active in other fields. He is Vice Supreme Chancellor of the Knights of Pythias, Supreme Worthy Counsellor of the Order of Calanthe, Vice-President of the Civic Welfare Committee of the Council of Social Agencies of Cincinnati, Chairman of the Executive Committee of the National Negro Press Association, a Director of the Fireside Mutual Aid Insurance Co., Secretary of the African Union Co., Trustee of Colored Industrial School of Cincinnati, Secretary of the Trustee Board of the New Orphan Asylum, for Colored Youth and President of the National Congress of Negro Fraternities. In all these the business ability of Mr. Jones is very apparent. The African Union Company imports mahogany direct from Africa. Mr. Jones is also editor in chief of the Fraternal Monitor, a monthly fraternal paper. Mr. Jones executes his varied duties with singular grace and ease, which is an evidence of his business acumen and rare poise. He is a member of the A. M. E. Church, and belongs to the leading fraternities of the county. In the interest of business or for pleasure, Mr. Jones has traveled all over the United States and consequently is well known nationally.

Mr. Jones is happily married. Mrs. Jos. L. Jones, (nee Helena Caffrey,) is the proud mother of five children, four girls and one boy. Myra, the eldest daughter, being the wife of Dr. Henry C. Bryant, of Birmingham, Ala. Joseph Lawrence Jr., is the active Manager of the Central Regalia Co., Helen, is a teacher of Music in the Colored Industrial School; Ida and Martha are attending High School. Mr. Jones lives in a well appointed home in one of the best sections of the city and has entertained there many of the leading men and women of the race. For a man of good advice and sound business ability, we would have to go a long way to find a more successful man than Mr. Jones. He is worthy of emulation by any young man who is looking forward to business as his career. For many years Mr. Jones was very active in local Republican politics and served several years as Deputy County Recorder and Deputy County Clerk. He has served also as a member of the National Negro Advisory Committee of the National Republican Campaign Committee.

WORK ROOM OF THE CENTRAL REGALIA COMPANY CINCINNATI, OHIO

GEORGE A. MYERS

George A. Myers

IN 1859, on March 5th, George A. Myers was born in Baltimore, Maryland, being the eldest of the three children of Isaac and Emma V. Myers. In May, 1868, he had the misfortune to lose his mother and consequently never had the full advantage of a loving mother's care. He was sent to Providence, R. I., and entered the public schools; from there to Washington, D. C. where he also attended the public schools and then to Preparatory Department of Lincoln University, Chester County, Pa. His father, in the meantime married Miss Sarah E. Deaver, and he returned to Baltimore that he might be near his father, and entered the First Grammar School for Colored Children, graduating therefrom; he attempted to gain admission to the Baltimore City College, but was refused by reason of his color.

In 1875 he was apprenticed to the Veteran Painter of Washington, S. C., Mr. Thomas James but the trade not being to his liking, he returned to Baltimore and took up the barber trade with Messrs. George S. Ridgeway and Thomas Gamble.

In 1879, he settled in Cleveland and was for nine years foreman for Mr. James E. Benson, at the Weddell House. Being of an affable nature, he made many friends and in 1888 opened the now famous Hollenden Hotel Barber Shop, which was styled by his friend, Elbert Hubbard, as "the best barber shop in America," and at present numbers 27 employees.

Growing up as he did with the City of Cleveland and having the benefit of a large acquaintance he became very active in politics and matters of race advancement. In 1892, he was elected as an alternate delegate from the 21st District of Ohio, to the Republican National Convention, at Minneapolis. His vote in the delegation elected William M. Hahn, national committeeman from Ohio, and it was largely instrumental in assisting the McKinley-Hanna organization into being, and made M. A. Hanna and William McKinley his life-long friends.

During the McKinley pre-convention campaign of 1896 he materially assisted Mr. Hanna and his home was always open to those of our people who came to Cleveland to consult with Mr. Hanna.

At St. Louis he had charge of the Ohio delegation that so ably looked after and cared for those of our people who were delegates. After the convention Mr. McKinley personally thanked him for his efforts in assisting Mr. Hanna, and tendered him whatever place within reason he desired. He declined to accept any office. Through his instigation and recommendation, the now Major W. T. Anderson, was appointed Chaplain of the 10th U. S. Cavalry, Hon. John R. Lynch, Paymaster in the U. S. Army, and Hon. B. K. Bruce, Registrar of the U. S. Treasury. In later years he secured the appointment of Hon. Chas. A. Cottrell as Collector of Internal Revenues at Honolulu. He was Senator M. A. Hanna's personal representative on the Republican State Executive Committee, (of seven), for 1897-1898, which eventually proved to be the most important State Committee in the history of the Republican Party, of Ohio. In the bitter Senatorial campaign that followed, Mr. Myers was in the thickest of the fray. It was he who settled the doubt when anxiety had settled on every countenance by bringing in the 72nd vote and thereby assured Senator Hanna's return to the U. S. Senate.

In 1900 he was elected by the Republican State Convention as an Alternate-Delegate-at-Large to the Republican National Convention at Philadelphia, and through his instrumentality the resolution of Senator Quay reducing southern representation was defeated. After serving three terms as a member of the Republican State Executive Committee, and following the death of President McKinley and Senator M. A. Hanna, Mr. Myers voluntarily retired from active politics and is now devoting his whole time to business.

In 1912, through the instigation of Dr. Booker T. Washington, Mr. Myers was tendered the management of the entire organization among the Negro voters of the country, by Mr. Charles D. Hilles, Chairman of the Republican National Committee, having in charge President Taft's campaign. For business reasons only he declined. This was the first and only time that the full conduct of this work among the Negroes for a national campaign was ever tendered to a single individual. A fitting recognition of his political worth and ability.

It was Mr. Myers, at St. Louis, who referred to Mr. Hanna, as "Uncle Mark." This was taken up by the Cleveland Plain Dealer, and Columbus Dispatch and stuck to Mr. Hanna so long as he lived.

Mr. Myers, though not identified with the active management, is a member of St. John A. M. E. Church, and has done much to promote its interest. He is a Past Master of Masons and Past Exalted Ruler, Cuyahoga Lodge No. 95, of the I. B. P. O., of Elks of the World. At present he is actively identified with The Caterers' Association, the leading and best Club of its kind among our people in this country. He is also a member of the City Club of Cleveland, and actively identified with every civic movement of importance to his people. He has a beautiful and well-furnished home on one of the best avenues and a wife and two children.

In 1896 he married Miss Maude E. Stewart. His son, Herbert D. Myers, is a mechanic with The White Automobile and Truck Company, and his daughter, Dorothy Virginia Myers, is a teacher in the public schools of Cleveland.

Mr. Myers attributes much of his success to the tireless teachings of his stepmother and the friends acquired through the same. There is no man of his race that can boast of more intimate and personal friendships among both races and no man who more unselfishly loves to serve his people.

WILLIAM R. GREEN

ILLIAM R. Green, is a man who was born educated and made good in his profession in the same place. He was born in Cleveland, Ohio, on November 10th, 1872. Here in Cleveland he attended the Public Schools, the High School and later the Law School. In all of these distinct steps in his training he applied himself most diligently to his tasks. He was always ambitious and it was this that carried him on through the law school in spite of the fact that the colored man as a usual thing has a hard time in this profession.

June 8, 1895, Mr. Green was admitted to the Practice of Law and since that time he has practiced continually in Cleveland, Ohio. That he has made a good living from his practice and been able to save something out of it for the proverbial rainy day is seen from the fact that he owns his own home and two other houses and lots, all of which are in the city of Cleveland. There is a tendency on the part of some to try to starve out the colored lawyer. The sense of justice makes them admit one to the practice of law but then the prejudice steps in. It is all this that Mr. Green has succeeded in overcoming. To him and to oth-

er young colored men of his time who have had the courage to face the situation as it was and still is in some places, great credit is due, for they are in the true meaning of the word "pioneers."

Mr. Green is a member of the Republican Party, and on two different occasions he was nominated by the Republicans of Cuyahoga County, Ohio. On both of these occasions the entire Republican ticket was defeated by the Democratic Party. Mr. Green was not defeated by another man on the same ticket, but because the whole party was unable to swing things. Mr. Green has long interested in military affairs, and is regarded as a well equipped military man. He has also been a Captain in the United States Army. For twelve years he was Captain in the Ohio National Guard, and was highly regarded by the men of his command, as is shown by his long services as their Captain. On July 15th, 1917 he was mustered into the Federal Service. He served as Captain of 372 Infantry in the United States National Guard until January 12, 1918. At this time he was honorably discharged for physical disibility.

In Religious belief, Mr. Green is a Catholic. Like all men of this faith he is an earnest and faithful worker in the interest of his church. He is a member of the Catholic Mutual Benefit Association, and also of the Knights of St. John. In all the things pertaining to the members of his race, Mr. Green is deeply interested, showing his interest in the welfare of his people by giving to them his best and continuous service. He is willing to spend and be spent in their behalf, if thereby, he can raise them to a higher standard of living. There is in the City of Cleveland an Association of Colored men. Of this organization, Mr. Green is an interesting member, always doing all that is in his power for the organization and the people for whose help it was organized. For two terms he served this organization in the capacity of President.

Mr. Green has been an extensive traveler, his travels covering the greater part of America and Europe. He has been abroad three times. His first trip to Europe was in 1893, when he visited England and Scotland. He next crossed the ocean in 1907, when he again traveled in England and visited Ireland. His last trip was made in 1908, and this time he revisited England and extended his travels to France, visited Paris and other points of interest. His travels have not only been to him excursions of pleasure, but have broadened his mind, and have given him a larger view of life.

Mr. Green was married to Miss Agnes C. Bolden, September 19, 1900, at Niagra Falls, New York. Mrs. Green presides over the home with charm, and with her husband helps make life pleasant for their many friends.

GEORGE W. CRAWFORD, A. B., LL. B.

R. George W. Crawford is a good example of the man born in the South, reared there, and become thoroughly acquainted with its views, who has gone North and made a place for himself. Born in Tuscaloosa, Alabama, October 21, 1877, he spent his earliest years in the public schools of this place. Tuscaloosa is one of the best of the Southern towns as regards the harmonious relations of the races. Many of the young sons of Tuscaloosa go out to prominence. In 1886 Mr. Crawford moved to Birmingham. Here he had another influence enter his life. It was almost the reverse of that of Tuscaloosa. Birmingham is a city of bustle and progress. To keep abreast of things in Birmingham one has to think and move quickly. This had its influence on the growing young lad.

When he first left home for study in boarding school, the school of his choice was Tuskegee Institute. From this school he was graduated in the class of 1896. The learning received here but whetted the appetite of Mr. Crawford for more. And so we find him at school in Talladega College, Talladega, Alabama shortly after finishing at Tuskegee. From Talladega he was graduated in the class of 1900. Talladega is one of the oldest of the A. M. A. Schools and is one of the most thorough in its preparation of students. Mr. Crawford was a good student while at Talladega, where he made a good record. He was elected to the Board of Trustees of this Institution, in 1905, and is at present Chairman of its Executive Committee.

After graduating at the Talladega College, in 1900, Mr. Crawford decided to enter the profession of law, and in order to secure as good a preparation for his work as possible, he entered the Yale Law School. Here he applied himself with great diligence, and won distinction. From this course he was graduated with high honors, in the class of 1903. The same year he was appointed clerk of the Probate Court for the District of New Haven Connecticut, and formed many warm friendships and strong connections among the people of that city. In this position he served until 1907. During the time he served as clerk, he had the opportunity to get the confidence of the New Haven public. When he gave up the work of clerk he had already acquired a substantial clientele, which has been greatly extended under demonstrated proofs of his eminent abilities to serve it. Since that time Mr. Crawford has been engaged in the successful practice of the law in New Haven, where he has been a conspicious figure in the public life, serving on many of its important commissions, and active generally in the affairs of the City.

Mr. Crawford has found leisure from his many and varied activities, to indulge his taste for literature and in its pursuit has achieved distinction, having one excellent book to his credit. He is the author of "Prince Hall and his Followers." His interest in altruistic and benevolent work is evidenced in his connection with numerous organic bodies of that nature and the prominent part he takes in their affairs. He is a Thirty-third degree Mason, an active member of the Odd Fellows, and of the Ancient Order of Forresters. He is also a member of Sigma Psi Phi.

The interest of Mr. Crawford in his people is genuine. He serves as a director of the National Association for the Advancement of the Colored People. This organization has done a great deal for the Negro by taking up the various questions that come before them. The subject of lynch Law, employment of colored people in cities, etc.

Mr. Crawford was married to Miss Sedella M. Donalson, of Aberdeen, Mississippi, in 1911. Mrs. Crawford, like her husband, has a prideful record in educational training, being a graduate of Teacher's College of Columbia University, and before her marriage was a teacher of English at Tuskegee Institute. The Crawford's have one child, Charlotte Elizabeth, a beautiful little girl of six.

HENRY M. MINTON, PH. G., M. D.

R. Henry M. Minton, one of Philadelphia's most prominent physician, was born in Columbia, South Carolina, December 25, 1871. His father, Thophiluy J. Minton, and his mother, Mrs. Martha McKee Minton, were both natives of Philadelphia. It has been in the native city of his parents that Dr. Minton has lived and made his success. He was educated in the Grammar schools of Washington. Here he laid a foundation and formed habits of study that have helped him in all his later life. Leaving school Dr. Minton entered the Preparatory Department of Howard University, and later the Phillips Exeter Academy, in New Hampshire. From the latter institution he was graduated in 1891. The record for good scholarship which had been his in the schools of Washington was kept up throughout his career in Exeter. He was the Orator of the class at graduation, managing editor of the Literary Monthly, and Assistant Managing Editor of the Exonian. The Exonian was the semi-weekly paper of the school. Even with all these outside duties, his scholarship never was in any way lowered.

Dr. Minton's first venture in the world of medicine was in the capacity of Pharmacist. He studied at the Philadelphia College of Pharmacy, finishing the prescribed course in 1895, with the degree of Graduate in Pharmacy, (Ph G.). Having obtained his degree Dr. Minton opened a drug store. This was the first venture of the young man in the business world and his venture was the first of any colored man in the state of Pennsylvania in drugs. In this respect Dr. Minton was a pioneer. He made a success of his undertaking and continued therein till 1903.

Dr. Minton gave up the drug business to enter the medical profession as a practicing physician. In 1906 he was graduated from the Jefferson Medical College, Philadelphia. He began the practice of medicine in Philadelphia the same year and has continued there. To him have come many opportunities for service. And through service has come honor. He is physician to Mercy Hospital, and at the present time he is acting Superintendent; he is also a member of the Board of Directors of this institution.

Dr. Minton has given a great deal of his time to the study of Tuberculosis. He is an authority on the subject and is Dispensary Physician to Henry Phipps Institute for study and treatment of Tuberculosis, (University of Pennsylvania.) He is author of Causes and Prevention of Tuberculosis, having published the volume in 1915.

Dr. Minton does not confine his interests to purely medical matters, but is interested in all things that look toward the uplift of the colored man. He is Treasurer of Downington Industrial School; a member of the Board of Directors of Whittier Center. He is a member of the Sigma Pi Phi; of the Grand United Order of Odd Fellows; and of the Free and Accepted Masons. He has made an exhaustive study of the conditions surrounding the Negroes in Philadelphia and is author of "Early History of Negroes in Business in Philadelphia."

Dr. Minton is still studying the subject of Tuberculosis as it pertains to the Negro in Philadelphia. He is chairman of a committee of representative colored persons who are working under the auspices of the Pennsylvania Society for the Prevention of Tuberculosis. This Society has for its aim an extensive survey of this problem in Philadelphia.

Dr. Minton was married in 1902, to Miss Edith G. Wormley, of Washington, D. C. They live at 1130 S. 18 St., Philadelphia.

Dr. Minton has accumulated several pieces of valuable real estate in Philadelphia.

BISHOP GEORGE LINCOLN BLACKWELL, A. B.,
S. T. B., A. M., D. D., LL. D.

 EORGE Lincoln Blackwell was born at Henderson, N. C., July 3, 1861. His father was Hailey and his mother was Catherine (Wyche) Blackwell. Young Blackwell was reared on Tar river, in Granville County, and about the plantation known as "Squire William Blackwell's." School facilities were very poor, the terms were three and four months in the year and the quality of teachers was mediocre, hence young Blackwell's opportunities for an elementary education was very meagre. When he was seventeen he became a night pupil of Joseph Blackwell, who would have been his young master had slavery held on, and thus prepared himself to acquire a third grade teacher's certificate. The examiner frankly told him that it was not his literary qualifications that caused him to grant the certificate but the recommendation of good character by Squire William Blackwell. Obtaining the certificate, young Blackwell taught four months, and studying hard himself during the same time he returned and made a good second grade. Deeply impressed of his call to preach (having professed faith in God and joined the church at the age of

fifteen) he connected himself with the North Carolina Conference of the A. M. E. Zion Church in 1881 at Beaufort, N. C. After one year's successful service he realized the need of further preparation, so he was relieved of regular pastoral duty and entered Livingston College, from which after six years, he graduated (1888) with the degree of Bachelor of Arts. After one year's intermission, he entered Boston University School of Theology, from which he graduated in 1892 with the degree of Bachelor of Sacred Theology in class with Edwin H. Hughes and E. F. Hamilton, both of whom are now bishops in the Methodist Episcopal Church.

Young Blackwell (who had already married Miss Annie E. Walker, daughter of the late D. I. Walker, Chester, S. C.) was called to Livingston College, his alma mater, to teach theology, and entered upon that duty Oct. 1893, just three weeks after the lamented president Dr. J. C. Price, passed away, so that Rev. W. H. Goler, D. D., succeeded to the presidency and young Blackwell was made dean of the Theological Department which position he held for three years. His church called him in 1896 to become manager of the publication house, Charlotte, N. C., and the editor of the Sunday School literature. This dual office he held for four years. He then became the pastor of the foremost church of the connection, Wesley, Philadelphia, for four years following which he was made the Secretary of Missions and Editor of the Missionary Seer, a monthly magazine. After four years service, satisfactory to the whole church, George Lincoln Blackwell, was elected and consecrated bishop of the African Methodist Episcopal Zion Church in 1908 in his own home town. Since being elevated to this high and important post of duty, the Bishop has given good account of himself. In the west where he served for eight years, he and his men erected forty seven churches and he organized two new annual conferences and three new presiding elder districts. His district now takes in a part of the State of New York, Michigan and a part of Illinois including Chicago; it also includes Virginia and two conferences in North Carolina.

Bishop Blackwell is known in his church both as the Editor of the Book of Discipline and as authority on ecclesiastical law. He is an aggressive and tireless worker and wherever he presides the men quicken their pace and do a third more work and yet he never scolds nor quarrels with his men; his stock in trade is to make each man feel that he is a man and that he can do a man's part.

Bishop Blackwell has received the following literary degrees: A. M., Livingston College 1894; D. D., Kansas Wesleyan University 1896; LL. D., Campbell College 1913.

He and his estimable wife live happily in their own well appointed home 624 South Sixteenth Street, Philadelphia.

JOHN MILLER MARQUESS, A. B., F. A. G. S.

OHN Miller Marquess— President of the Colored Agricultural and Normal University, at Langston, Oklahoma, has had a very thorough preparation for his work. In his life as a student and in his first years out of school, while he served as teacher in various institutions, he was unconsciously getting just the training that he needed to make him an all-round man for the Presidency of some institution.

He was born in Helena, Arkansas, February 23, 1882, and here he received his early school training, and enjoyed the privilege of attending school regularly, a privilege denied many. So well did young Marquess apply himself while in Helena, that we find him at the tender age of thirteen leaving home and entering the preparatory department of Fisk University, Nashville, Tennessee. Here he remained from 1895 till 1902, when he was graduated from the college department of Fisk, with the degree of A. B. At this time President Marquess was only twenty years of age.

While in Fisk, although he spent a great deal of his time on his books and kept himself up with his class in every respect, he still found time to take a very active part in all the life of the institution. He won his letters in football and was captain of the team for two years. He was also one of the star players on the base ball team. He was a member of the Glee Club, Jubilee Club, and Bass soloist for four years. In 1902, he traveled with the Fisk Quartett during the summer.

Still not satisfied with his preparation and being just a young man, we find President Marquess leaving Fisk and matriculating at Dartsmouth. Here he remained for two years, receiving the degree of Bachelor of Arts, from the University when he left. In Dartmouth we find him as active as he was in Fisk. He was a member of the track team, football squad and of the Glee Club. He won his letters on the track team. Again we find him a soloist, this time in the Dartmouth Choral Club.

On leaving school President Marquess served first as Instructor in Mathematics and Languages in Shorter College, Argenta, Arkansas, for two years; then he held the same work in Kittrell College, North Carolina, for two years. The next change gave him a chance to develop his executive ability. This opportunity came to him—as principal of the Summer High School, Kansas City, Kansas. Here for eight years, Mr. Marquess worked, training the young people who came under his care directly and so directing the teachers in his school that each child in the school was benefitted by the presence of the principal. In 1916, he was placed at the head of the State University for Colored People, in Oklahoma. Mr. Marquess served one year as President of the Citizen's Forum, of Kansas City. He is a member of the Knights and Daughters of Tabor, of the Knights of Pythias—in this last named he is the present Chancellor Commander, of the Ancient Free and Accepted Masons, of which organization he is serving as Past Grand Secretary for the State of Kansas, of the United Brothers of Friendship and of the Royal Circle of Friends of the World. He is also Past Potentate in Shrine, a member of Royal Arch Chapter Commandery, (Knight Templar), and Scottish Rite consistory, with 32nd degree. In religious belief and church affiliation, Mr. Marquess is African Methodist Episcopal. At present Mr. Marquess is Vice-President, a director and member of the executive committee of the Oklahoma Negro State Fair Association. This is a chartered organization. He is also a Fellow in American Geographical Society. He has traveled extensively in the United States and has been also in Canada and Mexico.

August 28, 1908, President Marquess was married to Miss Anna Edna Dickson, of Springfield, O. Three children have come to bless their home.

MAIN BUILDING, COLORED AGRICULTURAL AND NORMAL UNIVERSITY, LANGSTON, OKLA.

THE Colored A. & N. University, of Oklahoma, is situated in the town of Langston. No better site could have been chosen for the establishment of this institution, — for here in Langston, the Negroes have the whole town to themselves and get all the lessons in self-government that come with the management of a town. The University has in all thirteen buildings. There is the Main Building, which is the largest and most important of the group. The other buildings are dormitories, trades buildings, etc. All the buildings are heated and lighted from a central plant. To make the Colored Agricultural and Normal University even more sustaining they have their own water and sewerage system.

The University was established at Langston by an act of the Territorial Legislature in 1897. The purpose of the University is to give the colored people of Oklahoma an opportunity to get within the State a very thorough training for life's work. Here they may receive Collegiate, Mechanical and Agricultural training without the expense of traveling to distant States for the purpose, and at a minimum cost per month for board, lodging, etc. Forty acres of land were donated by the Negroes of Langston and its immediate vicinity. As the school grew, they became pressed for space for farm demonstration, actual farm land, etc, and so the acreage was increased. Today they have three hundred and twenty acres of land.

The support of the University is derived from three distinct sources. Yearly they have appropriated for their support a sum from the State Treasury. Then they receive one third of one tenth of the proceeds from the rental of Section Thirteen which was reserved by Congress for the benefit of institutions of higher learning. They also get one tenth of the Morrill Fund, a fund appropriated by the United States government for the teaching of trades to its citizens. This one tenth received by the Colored Agricultural and Normal University represents the amount due the Colored people in the State of Oklahoma; the division being made according to the population.

The plant of the University is now valued at about $225,000.00.

The Faculty of A. & N. University is composed of thirty-two individuals. All of these teachers have had very thorough preparation for their tasks. All are graduates of some standard College or Normal and several have their masters degrees from institutions like Yale and Columbia University of New York City. Among the schools represented on the faculty of the University are Fisk, Howard, Tuskegee, Hampton, Oberlin, Pratt, Tougaloo, Bennett, Wilberforce, Walden, University of California, Spelman Seminary, Wiley, and Tillotson.

In addition to the College work leading the degree of Bachelor of Arts, the Teacher Training Course and Agricultural Course, the school offers training in all the mechanical trades. The equipment for the work is complete. The school has not forgotten to develop the asthetical side of its students. There is a musical department that includes instrumental and vocal music. It has its Glee Club, Jubilee Clubs, Band and Orchestra. Special emphasis is laid on the training of Sunday School workers. The development of the physical side of the students is looked after in the athletics which are endorsed and encouraged.

No tuition is charged students who reside in the the State of Oklahoma. Eleven dollars mental music lessons there is placed an extra charge of one dollar per month.

The graduates, for the most part, are engaged in teaching. The demand for them is much larger than the supply.

JAMES ROYAL JOHNSON

R. Johnson, Superintendent of Oklahoma State Institute for Deaf, Blind and Orphan Colored Children, was born in Washington, Wilkes County, Georgia, September, 1870. He is the son of Johanna and Amos Johnson, who were slaves of Senator Robert Toombs, Secretary of State in Jeff Davis' Cabinet.

His early life as a boy was like that of other Negro boys of his time and section, only distinguished by his intense, longing for an education. H. H. Williams, prosperous business man, of Atlanta, Georgia, and R. R. Wright, President of the Georgia State Industrial College, Savannah, were among his teachers. Completing his education, Mr. Johnson taught school in Georgia for a number of years and then went west. After teaching in Mississippi Arkansas and Texas, he landed in Oklahoma City, April, 1905. His first and only public school work was near Edmond, a town then and now without a single Colored inhabitant. Here Mr. Johnson lived for two years. During his sojourn here the citizens united in a monster petition to the Regents of Langston University, that he be given a place on the faculty of that Institution. Whereupon he was elected Assistant Professor of Mathematics, and two years later Vice-President of the University. In this capacity he was in absolute control of the Langston Literary activities. Langston University reached its highest place as a useful factor in race life while Mr. Johnson was its Vice-President.

Thus it was that when Oklahoma came into Statehood, and founded an Institute for the deaf, blind and orphan, her officials elected Mr. Johnson to preside over the institute. What he is doing at this post can be seen from two excerpts from the Muskogee Times-Democrat, a white daily paper.

MANAGEMENT OF TAFT INSTITUTION

"It is very gratifying to learn that the State Board of Education and the Legislative Committee on Appropriations, after having gone over the reports of the various educational and eleemosynary institutions of the State, unite in saying that the Institution that makes the best showing, as to business management, is the institution for colored, at Taft, of which J. R. Johnson is Superintendent. Johnson's management of this Institution deserves the highest commendation and his record ought to be a matter of very great pride to the members of his race."

INVITE BAPTISTS TO TAFT SCHOOL ON A BUSINESS BASIS

"President Johnson has the unique distinction of conducting his institution on what is admitted by all to be the best business basis of any institution in the State. Johnson not only looks after the educational features of the school, but keeps the school absolutely free from criticism and scandal; but he teaches the students to work, and produce on the farm owned by the State and on land which he personally rents, crops which go far toward paying the living expenses of 200 pupils."

"President Johnson is a most remarkable man. It is not generally known that early in this year, feeling the positive necessity of having a large sanitary barn, he undertook to build the barn out of savings from his appropriation for maintenance. The cost exceeded the estimate and in order not to have a deficit. Johnson waived three months salary. This does not mean that he passed it up for future payment, but it means that he just gave the State three months of his salary in order to have the barn.

PAYS FROM OWN POCKET

"Appropriation has been made for more land but the land has not been purchased. Johnson rented 160 acres, paid the rent, bought the seed and fertilizer out of his own pocket and has 141 acres of as fine cotton as is in the State. The State will realize after reimbursing Johnson for the rent, a net profit of twice the value of the land. Not many State officials would do this. If the crop had been a failure Johnson would have lost what he put into it. The State stood to win but not to lose. Many people believe that President Johnson of the Taft Institute, measured by results of his work, is the biggest Afro-American in Oklahoma."

The size of the institute and what it is doing can be best judged by two reports, one from the State Superintendent of Education, the other from Superintendent Johnson:

STATE INSTITUTE FOR DEAF, BLIND AND ORPHAN COLORED CHILDREN—TAFT, OKLAHOMA.

INDUSTRIAL INSTITUTE FOR DEAF, BLIND AND
ORPHANS—S. DOUGLASS RUSSELL PRES-
IDENT—TAFT, OKLAOHMA.

Land _____$ 5,000.00
One frame building _____$ 1,000.00
One brick building _____$35,000.00
One power house and boiler _____$ 3,000.00
Furniture and equipment in two buildings $ 3,000.00

STATE INSTITUTE FOR DEAF, BLIND AND COLO-
RED ORPHANS—TAFT, OKLAHOMA—J. R.
JOHNSON, SUPERINTENDENT.

1. Property:
1. Total acreage belonging to Institution 101,
valued at _____$ 5,000.00

Buildings:

Girl's dormitory, brick _____$35,000.00
Boy's dormitory, frame _____ 1,000.00
Superintendent's residence, frame _____ 1,800.00
Light and heating plant _____ 3,000.00
Modern barn, valued at _____ 3,100.00
                                      _____
Total _____$43,900.00

As shown above, the farm consists of 101 acres
and is entirely too small to give proper employment to the large number of boys living at this institution. The Superintendent, with the advice and
consent of the State Board of Public Affairs and
Dr. E. B. Fite, resident member of the State Board

of Education, rented 180 acres of land which he
planted in wheat and oats. We have harvested
from this land 2,467 bushels of oats and 809 bushels
of wheat, a plentiful supply for all our wants.

In addition to wheat and oats we have raised 300
bushels of Irish potatoes, 400 bushels of sweet potatoes, 380 gallons of syrup, canned 452 gallons of
tomatoes, and 10 barrels of kraut. We have 62
hogs, and will kill 5000 pounds of meat this winter.

Because of the abundance of our farm and garden produce, we have been able to furnish food for
an average of 186 children at an average cost of
three and six mills per day.

While we are able to furnish healthful and profitable employment for our boys, the same condition does not obtain with regard to the girls. We
are doing something toward training them to become bread winners, but not enough. We need an
Industrial building wherein our girls will receive
practical training in every day house work; cleaning, cooking, sewing, etc. This is not possible as
we are now situated.

To have invested his own money to make the
farm feed his school, to have built up sources and
increased the general usefulness of this Institute
would seem a good life work for any one man.
But to this Superintendent Johnson adds the responsibility of caring for the State Reformatory of
Negro Boys and the Home for incorrigible Girls.
These he is shaping and giving character just as he
is doing for the institute for the Deaf, Blind and
the Orphans.

SAMUEL I. MOONE, A. B., M. D.

F we stop to note the list of great men who have been born on the farm and who spent their early life in tilling the soil, we are forced to conclude that there is something in such a life which lays a strong foundation for a successful career. It may be due to the discipline of early rising and hard physical labor which develops the body, or the opportunity for quiet contemplation which helps to develop the mind, but whatever the cause it is a fact that many of our great men come from the country.

Dr. Samuel I. Moone was born on a farm and passed his early days working as a farm laborer. He was born in Spartanburg County, South Carolina, January 6th., 1874. He attended the County schools, when they were in session.

School terms in the County were short; the hours of labor on the farm, even for a lad, were long. Tiring of this life, seeing that he made but little headway in gaining an education, the young man sought to try his fortune elsewhere.

Leaving his native home at the age of fifteen, he went to Chattanooga, Tennessee, and found em-

ployment as a day laborer in the rolling mills. The work was hard, too hard for one so young, but he kept in mind his goal, that of getting an education, of being a man of service and distinction among his fellowmen.

Finally he was able to pursue his course. Leaving the rolling mills, he entered Biddle University, Charlotte, North Carolina, in 1890. Working at any task he could find both in vacations and at odd times, he completed the Normal and Collegiate Courses in 1898.

After teaching through the winter of 1898 and the spring of 1899, he left the school room and sought harder but surer means of pursuing his course. Once more he resorted to the rolling mills, going to Pittsburg, Pennsylvania, for the purpose. This hard and arduous labor provided him with sufficient money to take up the study of medicine. In 1899 he entered the Leonard Medical School, completing his course in 1904. He had worked hard, had suffered privations, but he could now see the horizon, and he went out to begin life as a professional man.

Fixing upon Norfolk, Virginia, as a desirable place, he opened an office and put up his shingle. As is true of most doctors and professional men, he waited a short while before patronage became sufficiently large to insure a living. However, he had courage and the confidence to labor and wait. In due time the public found him out, and his success as a physician was assured. A practice of fourteen years has yielded him a comfortable living for himself and for his family, has enabled him to provide himself with a home and several valuable pieces of property in the city of Norfolk.

Dr. Moone was wise enough at the beginning not to keep to himself. Experience in life had taught him how to mingle quite at ease with his fellows and his success was due largely to the fact that he had the welfare of his people at heart and being willing to lift while rising. He joined the Presbyterian Church of Norfolk and became an elder. He joined the Masonic Lodge and became one of the leading members of the body. He soon came to be sought out for all big undertakings among the colored people of Norfolk. He is a director and a stockholder in Brown Savings and Banking Company, of Norfolk. He is a director and a stockholder in the Seaside Building Association of Norfolk, and a stockholder in the Bayshore Summer Resort, at Hampton.

Dr. Moone has been twice married. The first Mrs. Moone was Miss Susie Fox, of Charlotte, North Carolina. She died in 1907. The present Mrs. Moone was Miss Jessie E. Stoney, who for several years was a teacher in Claflin University, Orangeburg, South Carolina.

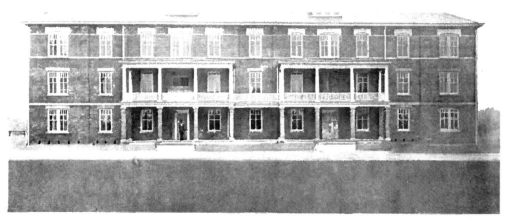

GIRLS' DORMITORY, STATE COLLEGE—ELIZABETH CITY, N. C.—PETER W. MOORE. PRESIDENT.

PETER W. Moore, of Elizabeth City, North Carolina, was born near Clinton, Sampson County, North Carolina. June 1859. His early education was received in the rural school of this county. Here he applied himself, getting from his books all that the teacher could explain to him, and reading into them a great deal from his own mind.

While in the rural schools he led the life of a farm boy. Here he had all the toil of the farmer, and he had also the joys that come to the farm lad. So although he had to hoe and plow and milk cows and catch the horses and feed them, the young lad also had time off here and there to enjoy a fishing trip and to go hunting, and look after his traps. It is this diversion that comes with the farm life that keeps it from breaking the ambition of those who are born to become leaders, although born in out-of-the-way places.

Leaving the farm in 1879, Mr. Moore entered Shaw University. Here for eight years he remained, making for himself a record as a student and as a man at the same time. In order to remain in school, each summer he returned to the farm and worked at all the odd jobs and hard labor as well, to which he had become so accustomed and which he had not as yet out-grown. Mr. Moore went to the North Carolina State Normal school, located at New Bern. Here he trained for the definite work of teaching.

After his graduation in 1887, he was elected Vice Principal of the State Normal school, at Plymouth, North Carolina. Here he remained for four years, serving in this capacity. During these years he got the practical experience of an executive in the school world. These four years only helped fit him for the more responsible position which await-

ed him. In 1892 Mr. Moore was elected principal of the State Normal and Industrial School, at Elizabeth City, North Carolina. Here he has remained. When he took the work, January, 1892, he had an enrollment of 64 pupils and one assistant. In 1918 he had an enrollment of 473 and a faculty of thirteen. This growth has been due not only to the untiring efforts of Mr. Moore, in advertising his school, but to the good work done there. The fact of this good work has been told by the many pupils going out, and so the work has grown.

Mr. Moore has not confined his efforts to the running of his school alone. In fact, he has had a conspicious place in the educational world in his State. He served as Teachers' Institute Conductor and as Assistant Superintendent of Public Schools. He has served as President of the North Carolina Teachers' Association, and is at present serving that organization in the capacity of Secretary. Because of the prominent place he held in the educational circles of his state, when the Governor wanted a representative in the National Educational Congress on two occasions he chose Mr. Moore for the job.

In 1889 Mr. Peter W. Moore was married to Miss S. T. Rayner, at Windsor, North Carolina. To them have been born two daughters. Miss Ruth S. Moore is married to Mr. Henry Garnes. Although married, she still teaches. Miss Bessie V. Moore is still a student.

No better prepared man could be found to serve at the head of the institution over which Mr. Moore is now President. His training in early youth fits him to sympathize with the students from the rural districts of North Carolina. He knows their problems and can help solve them. And then, going out from his school, his pupils carry with them the enthusiasm and high ideals of service which they have imbibed under the influence of Mr. Moore.

CAPTAIN J. E. HAMLIN

 MONG the few men who passed through the schools and secured a thorough education and chose a business career instead of entering the professions, is James Edward Hamlin, of Raleigh, North Carolina. He not only chose a business career, but made a conspicious success of the business, which finally claimed his attention. He did not find the line of endeavor which gripped his interest and awakened his business talent and energies until after he had tried several different ventures.

He turned instinctively from tailoring, and the pressing club, and all the other easier, self-running enterprises failed to attract him. The business instinct in him was strong and he sought an occupation which would give free play to his gifts. For a time, on leaving school he worked in the Raleigh Post Office. This gave him time to cast about for a business of his own. He soon noticed that there was a good opening for a Negro fish market, a business in which but few Negroes are engaged in even today. The business did not suit him altogether so he yielded to the lure of travel, disposed of his stand, and went to New York, where he secured a position in the dining car service. Again his mind turned towards Raleigh, and a business career. This time he opened a restaurant which he conducted with marked success, but the call of his Government, just when his restaurant had reached a high point of prosperity, caused him to give it up and lay himself upon the altar of his country. The war with Spain was announced and Mr. Hamlin was quick to volunteer for service. He was made Captain of Company B., of the North Carolina Thirty-Second volunteers.

He served through the Spanish-American war and won the respect of his commanding officers and love and confidence of the men of his company, and merited the gratitude of his country to which he gave his loyal support. After returning from the Spanish-American War, Captain Hamlin decided to remain in the army and enlisted for service in the Phillipines, and served in those islands as Captain of the Forty-eighth Infantry Volunteers for two years.

After remaining in the Phillipines for the term of his enlistment he received his honorable discharge from the army, and returned to the United States. For the time that he was in the army all thoughts of business were dismissed from his mind, but immediately after his retirement his mind again reverted to it, and his face was turned again towards Raleigh. This time he ventured into the drug business, and in that he found a business to his liking, although he still had a leaning to the restaurant. He opened his first drug store in 1904.

Today he owns two drug stores, and a lunch room in Raleigh, a large farm not far from the city, and has interest in a drug store in Bluefield, North Carolina. All of these business ventures have proved successful and very remunerative, the earnings from same he very wisely invested in real estate, which in turn has added to his income.

He is a member of the African Methodist Episcopal Church.

Though he has moved several times, Mr. Hamlin has been a very useful citizen. He was Secretary of the Negro State Fair of North Carolina for twelve years, during which period he lifted the organization out of confusion and loss to one of the best Negro Fairs in the country. He is a notary public, the only Negro Notary in Raleigh. He is connected with the North Carolina Mutual Industrial Association. He is a thirty-second degree Mason, an Odd Fellow, a Knight of Pythias, Knight of Gideon, and a Good Samaritan.

Mr. Hamlin has traveled very extensively, having gone all over the United States, in the Phillipines and in Europe. For all his travel he has accumulated a comfortable sum of money and large property holdings. He owns his home, a store building in the heart of the city, and fourteen rent houses, and a farm valued at $6,800. His wealth is estimated at from $65,000 to $78,000.

Mr. Hamlin was married in 1885 to Miss Annie W. Foushee, of Raleigh. There are two children, Miss Annie Ethel, now Mrs. Rogers, and Dr. V. C. Hamlin, of Raleigh.

JONAH EMANUEL.

ANY a man has gone from the farm to carve his way to high positions of honor and proficiency in his chosen profession. We find such an instance in the career of Dr. Jonah Emanuel. Dr. Emanuel was born in Bible County, Georgia, September 9th, 1858. He removed from Georgia with his parents at the age of seven years and located in the State of Arkansas. He attended the public schools of Arkansas for three years.

His father, Benjamin Emanuel, was a farmer, for some years, and in fact until he was twenty one years of age, Dr. Emanuel worked with his father on the farm. When he reached his majority he decided to shift for himself, and his eyes turned towards the city.

He left the farm and came to the city of New York. When he reached Jersey City, he had exhausted his funds and found that he did not have sufficient money to pay his way from that city to the point of his destination. Nothing daunted he continued his way on foot and reached Bedford, New York, where he obtained work at one dollar and a half a day.

Remaining a few months in Bedford he saved enough money to continue his way to New York City where he obtained employment at four dollars per week. For two years he labored hard during the day and attended school at night. He applied himself diligently to his studies and built largely upon the foundation he had received at the public schools.

He chose Chiropody as his profession and set about preparing himself for his work. He served three years under a most proficient Chiropodist, and when he acquired sufficient skill he opened an office for himself in the Windsor Hotel, and then located at 46th Street and 5th Avenue.

For the first two or three years he averaged about one hundred and fifty dollars per month; this was much below the amount he hoped to realize but his disappointment did not discourage him, it only made him more determined to succeed. He applied himself more diligently and worked hard day and night to improve his knowledge of his profession, and to give perfect satisfaction to his patients; and in the course of time increased his income to more than five thousand dollars per annum.

Some of the richest and best families of New York and many other cities are to be found among his large and ever-increasing number of patients, about ninety-nine per cent of which are white He has the reputation of having no superior in his profession, the character of his patients bearing testimony to the correctness of this estimate placed upon his ability. He has the distinction of being the one Colored charter member of the New York State Pedic Society.

Dr. Emanuel has been thrice married; the first time to Miss Susie Johnson, of Virginia, in 1888; in 1890 he married Miss Louise Dyer, of Virginia, by whom three children—Gussie, Blanch, and Viola were born. In 1909 he married Miss Bertha B. Harper, of South Carolina.

Dr. Emanuel is a member of the St. Marks Methodist Episcopal Church, and is actively and officially identified with its work. He is also a member of the Young Men's Christian Association. He is connected with the Masonic fraternity, being a Master Mason.

Dr. Emanuel is deeply interested in the development of his race, and in every way possible, according to his ability, contributes to their uplift, both in time, talent and money.

Notwithstanding his most generous contributions to the various enterprises of his people, and the making of investments to his own disadvantage in order to encourage them along business lines, he has succeeded in accumulating considerable wealth and is now well fixed financially.

GEORGE WASHINGTON GOODE, B. D., D. D.

O day, no month, no year is long enough" to accomplish the tasks that devolve upon Dr. George Washington Goode, B. D., D. D., of Danville, Virginia, so he states it himself, and so it is. Born in Patrick County, Virginia, March 14th, 1865, Dr. Goode spent the larger part of the first seventeen years of his life on the farm.

Completing the High School Course in Marion, Virginia, at the age of eighteen, he taught school in his home County, in Smyth, in Bedford and Montgomery for seven years. Converted about the age of twenty one, he felt his call to the ministry. His first charge was at Red Hill, Pulaski County, Va., a mining town. Here he organized a church and was the means of forty souls being converted. From Red Hill, where he gathered his strength and established his fame as a coming preacher, he entered the Richmond Theological Seminary. Here he spent six years; three in completing the institute course and three in the theological, graduating from the full Greek and Hebrew course in 1895.

For three years he was student teacher of arithmetic and beginnner's Greek. Dr. Goode pastored the Salem Baptist Church, West Point, and the Mt.

Zion Baptist Church, Churchview, Va. Four years labor in these churches, which he pastored jointly, gained him the call to the Calvary Baptist Church, Danville, Va. Here he has labored for twenty-two years, making the Calvary Baptist Church a power in the state, making it also the center from which he radiated into other kinds of needed services.

To pastor a big church as Dr. Goode has done is ample work for the average minister. To Dr. Goode, so thoroughly prepared, so rich in the common man's experience, it was an item in a big career. He founded the P. I. N. and C. Institute, and has been its president for fifteen years. He was president of the General Baptist Association of Virginia for seven years; secretary of the Cherry Stone Baptist Association for eighteen years, member of the Executve Board of the State Sunday School Convention; treasurer and Board member of the B. Y. P. U.; member of the Lott Carey Foreign Missionary Convention; member of the Negro Organization Society and of the State Teachers' Association; chairman of the Executive Board of the United Charity and Welfare League, an organization which supports a sick nurse in the city of Danville. No wonder he bewails the days, months and years as being too short to do all the tasks before him.

Dr. Goode was married to Miss Mary L. Gaines, who was formerly a school teacher of Richmond, Virginia, in 1896. To her he cheerfully owns that he is indebted for much of his success. There have been no children born to Dr. and Mrs. Goode, but they have turned this seeming misfortune into a blessing. They have taken into their home and educated five children: Miss Rosa B. Gaines they have educated in the public schools of Richmond, then at Hartshorn College; Caleb S. Mahlemgara, an African, they have had for ten years, taking him directly from Africa. He has been graduated from the P. I. N. and C. Institute, from the Virginia Union University Academic Department, and is now studying agriculture in the State Agricultural College at Columbus, Ohio. Warner H. Gaines is the third child to receive parental care from Dr. and Mrs. Goode. This young man is now a finished carpenter in Richmond, Virginia. George W. Goode, Jr., is now in their care. Margaret Smith, the fifth adopted child, is also with them.

Along with all these responsibilities at home and abroad Dr. Goode has kept upon his heart one great task for mankind, that of bringing about Temperance. For twenty years he has labored in and out of season at this, taking active part in all meetings and campaigns in its behalf. He is an aggressive and fearless fighter, yet much loved for his genuineness and for his services throughout Virginia. He wears one of the finest gold medals available, given by the Baptist Association of his state.

He owns a beautiful ten room residence in the residential section of Danville, a farm of one hundred acres, with other city and country property. He is, as has been said of him, "a busy man with a willing spirit, with hands and heart open to help everybody that he can."

John P. Morris, A. B., B. D.

AN educator of no mean attainment and a church-man of deep consecration and abiding faith, Reverend John P. Morris, of Greensboro, North Carolina, has devoted a full quarter of a century in active service to his people, giving especial attention to the advancement of the Negro along lines of education and religion. His work has carried him into the remote districts of his native state, and he is tireless in his efforts to help uplift the Negro race.

While he is more concerned about their religious and educational advance he is not unmindful of their physical welfare.

Rev. Morris was born in Caswell County, North Carolina, January 23rd, 1861. His early school days were far from pleasant and were fraught with many discouragements, and indeed, he met with so many rebuffs and deep privations that a spirit less courageous than his would have lost his ambition. He would not have been human had he not felt the pressure of these trials, which at times almost suppressed his ambition to be a scholar, but grit and determination won out, and the flame while it flickered at times, continued to burn and never went out.

Overcoming all obstacles and pressing forward towards his goal, perseverance at last rewarded him and he was enabled to attend Bennett College. It was at this college that he secured his preparatory work which enabled him to move with greater freedom in the accomplishment of his fixed purpose to obtain an education. It may be said that here the shackles fell from him and he progressed rapidly in completing his education.

He remained at Bennett College until he had finished his preparatory course, when he left that institution and entered Clark University, Atlanta, Ga. He continued at Clark University until he received his degree of Bachelor of Arts, and then enrolled in Gammon Theological Seminary, an instituton with a large endowment devoted entirely to the training of ministers, and with an equipment and teaching force capable of standard theological work. He remained in this institution for three years, where he applied himself diligently to his duties and where he gained some practical experience as a preacher. This Institution bestowed upon him the degree of Bachelor of Divinity. During his preparation in other schools, the Bennett College had never lost trace of him, for his personality had been deeply impressed upon this school, and it was not long after his graduation before he was

called to a post on the faculty. He accepted the call and for twenty-three years served the college with distinction. His teaching and executive ability was recognized by the college and he was promoted to the office of Vice-President.

Mr. Morris felt that the finger of Providence pointed him to educational work and impressed upon his mind this as a great field of endeavor for the development of his people, at the same time keeping before him their spiritual needs, so while he devoted the best of his life to the college work, he never neglected his church work, but made them work together for the one purpose of his life to help his people. His labors in the interest of his denomination have been marked by long and efficient service. For four years he served as Secretary for the North Carolina Conference and for sixteen years he was the Conference statistican. While he is an earnest believer in Methodism, and adheres strictly to its principals, he is big enough to work for the good of all people regardless of creed. As the years went by the church began to lay heavier duties upon him which finally claimed all of his time. It was not an easy thing for him to give up the school room and especially the college which had sheltered his struggling youth and fostered his maturer dreams, and to which he had devoted so many years of his life, but the call of duty was stronger with him than personal desires, so he gave up the school and devoted his entire time to the work of the church. Rev. Morris was married to Miss Mary E. Waugh, of Salem, North Carolina, September fifteenth, 1889. They have seven children of which they are very proud. There is Robert Gammon, who is a graduate of Bennett College, of Gammon Theological Seminary, and of the North Western College; Miss Lucy L. Tillman, who holds a diploma from Bennett College, and from the Musical department of Fisk University; Mrs. Agnes P. Whiteman, who graduated at the Bennett College and then finished a course in the Pharmaceutical Department of Meharry Medical College, of Nashville, Tennessee, and then the younger children, John P. Jr., Elsie Gladys, Mary Esther and Frank Bristol, are still doing college preparatory work.

It is too often the case where men are so much engaged in work outside of the family that they neglect the training of their children, but not so with Mr. Morris, he wishes his children, like himself, to find some useful occupation in life, and he wishes them well equipped for their work, and to this end he has wisely directed and prepared them for their life work.

JOHN THOMAS WILSON, M. D.

T is no mean satisfaction to the Black Race that it has men in the medical profession who can be classed with Verchow, Pasteur, or the Mayo Brothers. Such a man is Dr. J. T. Wilson, of Nashville, Tennessee.

Dr. Wilson was born in Atlanta, Georgia. His mother died when he was but a year old and his father survived but a few years, leaving young Wilson an orphan.

The first fourteen years of his life were spent on a farm ten miles outside of Atlanta. Here he knew no luxury. The bare necessities of life were all he coveted. Out in this hard life the young lad learned three lessons: industry, obedience, and punctuality. On this farm he toiled early and late, yet he found time to attend the short term summer school. This was his only opportunity to learn to read and write. Coupled with this he found time to attend the rude log church. Here he listened most attentively to the preacher expound the gospel, and having given himself to God he lifted up his heart in hymns of praise. Here he laid the firm foundation for the kind, sympathetic doctor he was to become.

After having eked out a common school education, he entered Atlanta University, where he studied not only books, but also his teachers and his fellow students. He learned that his life affected theirs and and their lives affected his. This made him sure that there was a real place in the universe for him.

From Atlanta University he went to Roger Williams University, in Nashville, Tennessee, and it was here that he decided to study medicine. In 1889 he went to Meharry Medical College. He kept up his expenses by running a grocery and huckster. He put as much effort in his work as in his study. In 1895 he was graduated and after having practiced three years he was elected a member of Meharry's staff.

He realized his own deficiencies when he began to teach. So to broaden his store of knowledge he entered the Post Course in the Chicago Medical College. Here he remained two years and finished two courses. He was then elected Head of the Hospital of Hydrotherapy at Nashville, Tennessee, which is a branch of the Battle Creek Hospital. This position he resigned after a year to go to Philadelphia. In this city he made a study of the work of three hospitals, Poly-Clinic, Jefferson Hospital and Medicochirugical. From Philadelphia he went to Canada to study, and he then spent eleven years at St. Mary's Hospital, under the supervision of the Mayo Brothers. Dr. Wilson next went to Clyde at Cleveland, Ohio, to do research work and to make an exhaustive study of the nerves.

The next five years Dr. Wilson served as Chief Surgeon at Collins Chapel, Home and Hospital, Memphis, Tennessee. He left this in March of 1917, to establish a hospital of his own. This is known as the Wilson Surgical Hospital and Nurse Training School. The hospital is a large, well equipped one, sanitary throughout and located in a quiet, healthful district.

Many and varied are the operations that have established the reputation of Dr. Wilson. One is truly remarkable. A man was dead from a shot near the heart. Dr. Wilson cut a window through the man's fourth rib, cleansed the heart of the clot of blood, started the heart to moving, and this man now moves among his fellow men.

Dr. Wilson was naturally endowed with the tendencies to heal the ills of the body. Not content with this gift of nature he has spent years and years in study as we have already pointed out. And his mind is still open and ready to receive information about the human body. Then his unbounded faith in God has played a great part in the work of this great and good man.

W. Curtis Reid

CURTIS Reid, of Muskogee, Oklahoma, is by birth a Texan. Some of the sterling qualities that are the birthright of most of the sons of this broad, liberal state are to be found in Mr. Reid. The ability to go ahead and get for himself the things desired is not the least developed of these traits in the character of this young man. Mr. Reid is from one of the best families in the State of Texas. In his native state he received his education in the common schools, and later at the Prairie View State Normal School. Throughout his school career he was looked upon as one of the brightest students. This was particularly true of his work in the State Normal School.

He went to Muskogee, Oklahoma in 1909, for the purpose of attending school and completing his education. Here he met Miss Sallie Hodges, whom he later made his wife. They were married in July 1912, Mr. Reid thereby securing a companion for his home and a helper in his business. In both spheres she has proved a help-meet indeed and her husband praises her. Mrs. Reid was born in Taft, Oklahoma, and received her education in her native state. She has received a thorough training and because of this she has been enabled to render her husband great assistance in his business affairs. Mr. and Mrs. Reid are very congenial in their ideas of life and consequently have made their home an ideal one. They have two little girls who add sunshine to their home, and cement more strongly the bond which binds their parents to each other. The names of these little girls are Velma, five years of age, and baby Jack.

While attending school at Muskogee, Mr. Reid noticed that the city was growing at a rate which made real estate investments very profitable and this suggested to him the idea of establishing a real estate business. He had already formed a great liking for the place, so it was not hard for him to make up his mind to locate here. He matured his plans so there was no delay in starting his business after he had finished his school course. He opened his real estate and loan office immediately and went to work.

With a good mental equipment, and energy born of a fine physical condition he set out to win his way which he did by giving close and faithful attention to his business. It was not long before his business began to grow and it continued to develop until it soon was a large and lucrative affair. His clientile grew with his business for his fidelity to their interest made them his friends and through them added others to his list. In selecting an office he chose one in the heart of the city, where he would be in the midst of business activities, at 115 Court Square. Here he delights to receive friends but they know his rule not to neglect his business interests, so they are not offended when he excuses himself from time to time to look after his affairs.

Mr. Reid, so ably assisted by his good wife, has succeeded far beyond his most sanguine expectations, and is now classed among the wealthy citizens of his community, and is one of the wealthiest colored men in his State. He and his wife hold their possessions jointly and are pleased to point to them as theirs rather than his. Their realty and other holdings are valued at about three hundred and fifty thousand dollars. In the list of their assets may be found eleven hundred acres of farm lands, oil lands and city property.

They own a beautiful home containing all the modern conveniences, with surroundings conducive to a pleasant home life. The home is only valued at $5600.00, their plan being to make it home-like rather than expensive.

His personal interests do not claim all of the time and energy of Mr. Reid; he is one of those men who recognizes the right of a community to require tribute from its citizens, not alone in taxes, but in the support of all its interests; and though he is yet a young man, he is conspicious for his public spirited activities. His activities are especially notable when the enterprises look to the advancement of his race. He is deeply interested in the Negro State Fair Corporation and is among its most ardent supporters. The Automobile display at the Fair is under his control and direction.

Mr. Reid, like so many men has become an auto enthusiast, and is the owner of three of these fast moving vehicles. He owns a Ford runabout, a Hudson Super-Six, and a 1917 model Morman.

In their religious belief, Mr. and Mrs. Reid are united as they are in every department of their lives, and are ardent supporters of the First Baptist Church, of which they are members. They not only contribute their money to its support, but give to it their time and talent, and are numbered among its most active members.

Mr. Reid is a Mason (thirty-second degree), Odd Fellow, U. B. F. and K. of P.

With a growing real estate business, income bearing property and oil wells spouting thousands of dollars in the much-sought-for liquid gold, Mr. Reid has the prospect of becoming a very rich man, but he considers that the greatest blessing that Fortune has bestowed upon him is his wife and children.

JOHN HARRIS HENDERSON, B. D.

 HE life of John Harris Henderson has been one of action and of decision. He has been able to accomplish things and to accomplish them with dispatch. Born on a plantation near Bayou, S a r a, Louisiana, December 23rd, 1872, he had the start of the average boy with his environment. When nine years old he entered the public school and remained there for ten years getting what he could from the poor teaching which was to be had at that time in that section. In 1891 he entered Howe Institute, New Iberia, Louisiana, and remained in this institution for three years.

After leaving Howe Institute he entered Leland University, and spent four years in study there. Rev. Henderson was still not satisfied with his preparation for his life work, and so we find him once more entering a new school. The one of his choice was this time Virginia Union University, at Richmond. Here he remained for three years and received the degree of B. D.

To read about the school life of Rev. Henderson one would suppose that he had nothing to do but attend the various schools of his choice. This however was not the case. During his early school days, in fact all through his school career, he was a young man who worked with his hands in order that he might have the privilege of studying. The one form of work that Rev. Henderson remembers most distinctly is that of rail splitter. At this task he became quite accomplished. In fact he could split as many as 410 rails per day.

Having received his degree in 1902 and having been ordained the year previous, Rev. Henderson went out into life well equipped, able to hold his position and make good at any place. Thus we find him in 1902 teaching theology in Coleman College, Gibsland, La., from 1903 to 1906 President of the Thirteenth District Normal and Collegiate Institute, Shreveport, La. Here in this institution he did such effective work that for the first time the school became self supporting. He bought and paid for 120 acres of farm land for the school while serving at its head.

At the same time that Rev. Henderson was serving as President of the Institute in Shreveport, he was pastoring the Trinity Baptist Church of that city. Here he added $8000 to its property and 200 members to its roll. In 1908 Rev. Henderson Founded the Henderson Chapel Baptist Church, to which he was elected Pastor for life, and the same year organized the Baptist Ministers Union in Shreveport. In 1910 he was called to pastor the First Baptist Church, Minden, Louisiana, where he erected a new house of worship at a cost of $4000. In the year 1911 the state of Louisiana honored him by electing him Vice-President of the Baptist Convention of that State. In 1913 Rev. Henderson answered a call which came to him from Hot Springs, Arkansas. He resigned his important posts in the State of Louisiana and went to Arkansas where he pastored the Roanoke Baptist Church. While pastoring this charge he erected a new edifice at a cost of $35,000.00. Of this amount in a single effort he raised with the strong support of all his people, the sum of $4,619.11.

In the year 1917 Rev. Henderson was appointed General Field Secretary by the Educational Board of the National Baptist Convention of the United States; he is also a member of the Federal Alliance of the Church as of Christ in America. This organization had honored him before by giving him very responsible work to do. The same year he was made field Secretary; he was called to the pastorate of Mt. Zion Baptist Church of Knoxville, Tennessee. Already he has canceled the debt on the church, and the Baptists of the State have made him Vice-President of the State Convention.

December 30, 1902, Rev. Henderson was married to Miss Rainey F. Butler, of Arnandville, Louisiana. There are four children who have come to bless the home—Leona B., Joseph L., Harvey A. and John H. Jr.

JOSEPH SAMUEL CLARK, A. B.

OSEPH Samuel Clark, President of Southern University, and Agricultural and Mechanical College, was born on a cotton farm in Bienville Parish, near Sparta, La., in 1871. His early education consisted of three months in a private school and from two to three months during the year in the little public schools of that time. Fortunately his parents were of that sterling stock from which have sprung so many of our best men. They taught him many good lessons of thrift and industry during the day, and many lessons in character before the fire at night.

At the age of twenty-one he entered Coleman College, at Gibsland, Louisiana, where he remained three years. During this time he filled every position from janitor to student teacher. The industrious habits he had acquired in his home training never forsook him and stood him well when he entered the Coleman College. These coupled with grace of manners and sterling character made college life easy and pleasant for him. He won the confidence, respect and admiration of schoolmates and teachers and added them to his long list of friends.

In the fall of 1896 his ambition was gratified by entering Leland University. In the first session there he graduated from the normal and prepara-

tory courses. Immediately he entered the four-year college course, taking his A. B. degree in 1901.

Closely following his graduation he was elected President of Baton Rouge College, where his reputation as an educator and an administrator was soon established. For thirteen years he presided over this college and gave to it the service of a wise and intelligent head. His administration was such as to win the approval of his people who were quick to realize that they had made no mistake in calling him to the presidential chair. It was his service in this institution that led to his election to the position he now occupies. He did not rest upon his laurels when called to preside over this college, but took advantage of every opportunity to improve his mind and add to his fund of information. He studied in summer at Harvard and other great Universities, and especially made a close study of human nature.

So, when there was to be a colored man chosen for Southern University, there was but one man in the minds of all concerned—and that was Dr. Clark. His election was appreciated by both races, and while he has been at the head of the school but four years, the wisdom of the selection is amply shown by the wonderful progress the institution is making.

Dr. Clark is a big-hearted, big-brained man. Both as a speaker and writer he has done much in the State to encourage his people in making for themselves names worthy of consideration.

In addition to being the leading educator in his State he may be considered among the leading property holders among the pedagogues. He owns valuable property in Baton Rouge and New Orleans —Outside of a small heritage through his grandmother he has accumulated most of this property since being out of school. He is a stockholder in one of the leading banks of Baton Rouge. Besides, he has shares in the Building Loan Association and other firms of financial standing.

For eight years he was president of the Louisiana Colored State Teachers Association. He led the movement for the establishment of a State school; served six years as registrar of the National Association of Teachers in Colored Schools and is at present president of that organization.

While he is a staunch member of the Baptist Church, he is broad enough to worship freely with all denominations. He is loved and admired by all of the denominations in the State.

He has been initiated as a Pythian and a Mason.

At present he is a member of the Council of the American Geographical Society. He is an honorary member of the State Medical Association, and enjoys the distinction of being chairman of the Louisiana Council of Defense for Colored People. No man in the State is asked to serve in more capacities than the subject of this sketch.

Dr. Clark has traveled extensively, though his travels have been confined to the United States. He is following the injunction to 'see your own country before going abroad.'

He married Miss Octavia Head, December 29, 1901, West Monroe, La. Miss Head is the daughter of Rev. W. G. Head, a prominent Baptist minister of Louisiana. He has a son of fifteen, a very promising young man. He is a devoted father and an ideal companion.

WILLIAM THOMAS FULLER, M. D.

R. William Thomas Fuller was born in Caswell County, North Carolina, on January the twenty-fourth, 1886. Although a native of North Carolina, at an early age he went to Virginia. Here in the city of Danville he got his early training. He was a pupil in the public schools of the city for a number of years. He applied himself diligently to his tasks, and even as a boy gave promise of becoming a man of power. When he had completed the work of the public schools of Danville young Fuller went to Hampton Institute. Here he studied long enough to get the real spirit of the school. In all his after life the real spirit of service, of helpfulness to others, of making the most of opportunities, of improving ones self and ones surroundings, has been with him to spur him on to good deeds.

Having completed the work of Hampton Institute, Mr. Fuller returned to his native State and matriculated in the Leonard Medical College, at Raleigh, North Carolina. Here he remained to complete the work of his profession. In 1895 Dr. Fuller opened office for practice in Reedville, North Carolina. Finding the place not altogether to his liking he moved the next year to Winston-Salem, North Carolina. Here he remained for five years. Still Dr. Fuller was not satisfied with his location, and the opportunity offered him for service and progress. So for a third time we find him removing his sign and journeying to another town. This time he left his native State altogether and returned to the State of his early adoption. Here in Suffolk, Virginia, Dr. Fuller started out anew, and here he has remained.

For the past seventeen years the practice and business of the subject of the sketch has grown steadily. In 1903 he opened a Drug Store. This he has maintained since that date with the help of his wife. Mrs. Fuller is a woman of unusual ability and she has done her part toward making the life of Dr. Fuller in Suffolk a success. Although Dr. Fuller is not affiliated with any church in particular he is a thorough believer in Christianty and gives of his means to the support of all denominations. He also gives liberally to all the movements for the uplift of his people. He is a public spirited man, according to the testimony of the local white bankers and is a credit to any community.

Dr. Fuller was among the men who made it possible for the late Dr. Booker T. Washington to go to Suffolk. This Dr. Fuller did in the interests of his own race, and in the interest of the people of Suffolk in general. The visit left a lasting feeling of good will and better understanding between the white and the colored people of that section. While Dr. Fuller will not take the credit of this to himself, he is in a large measure responsible for it.

Dr. Fuller has been twice married. His first wife was Miss Alberta F. Boyd, of Asheville, North Carolina. They were married May 25, 1895. She died September 13, 1896. Eleven years later he was again married; this time to Miss Lavonia A. Carter, of Petersburg, Virginia. It is she who so ably administers the business of the drug store when Dr. Fuller is out making calls. There are two daughters in the family, Cory L. and Goler Mae. Both are young misses in school.

Dr. Fuller, with his family lives in one of the most beautiful homes in the country. Nor does the beauty of this home stop with the beauty of the structure. The home life is also beautiful. Mrs. Fuller makes a very charming hostess on all occasions and manages the home, along with the Drug Store and at the same time in no way neglects the young girls.

During the years Dr. Fuller has spent in Suffolk he has managed to save from his practice and from the business conducted in his Drug Store, enough money to invest in and around the city. He is rated as one of the very substantial citizens of the place. A conservative estimate of the value of his holdings is placed at $50,000,00.

REVEREND JOHN EDMUND WOOD

ORN in Kentucky shortly after slavery, Reverend John Edmund Wood has clung tenaciously to his native soil, attending school there, working there, and becoming a power there. He was born in Baren County, May 21, 1867. He was educated in the common schools and in the state schools. Finishing at the State Normal and Industrial Institute, he decided at first upon a life work in the class room. As the harvest was ripe in the rural communities he went out into the country schools and began his labors. Here for sixteen years he put his life into instructing the country youth of his state; teaching in Baren, his native County; in Metcalf and in Hardin Counties. Meantime he began to find himself as a speaker, leader and organizer. More and more also he began to realize that his place was in the pulpit alone, directing the spirits and minds of old and young rather than in the class room instructing only the young. Sometimes he preached and taught but he soon found that each task was likely to be half performed, owing to the energy expended on the other. He was called to Bardstown, Kentucky, in 1891. Leaving here he

went in response to a call to Elizabeth Town, where he spent seven years and where he established his reputation state-wide as a speaker, thinker and presiding officer.

His last charge is Danville. Here he has spent the last eighteen years of his life, pastoring, organizing, and for the last year, being elected in 1916, serving as state moderator of the Baptist denomination of his state.

Reverend Wood is allied with many strong organizations outside the church. He is a Mason; an Odd Fellow; a Knight of Pythias, and a Good Samaritan. He is National Chief Good Samaritan in the last named body. He has traveled all over the eastern part of the United States; over the middle west and south, mainly on business in connection with Lodge and Church duties.

He owns his residence and several pieces of rent property in Danville, his home. Married in 1891 to Miss Ella B. Reid, he is the father of a large family. Miss Iola is a teacher in the public schools of Berryville; John Franklin is a student at Lincoln Institute of Simpsonville; Miss Frances Ophelia is attending the National Training school for women at Washington, D. C.; Simon Elsworth, Margaret and Virginia are pupils in the public schools of Danville.

Next perhaps to the Pullman service the Negro school room has been one of the strongest agencies in the advancement of our able men. Some might argue, "Yes, much to the detriment of the public." Such, however, is most likely not the case. Our young men have come out of college and preparatory school full of enthusiasm, full of zeal to do. They were to our people like pilgrims from a far country, bringing fresh cargoes of rich lore. Moreover, had they not taught our children and our parents in the early days, there would very likely have been but little teaching. Thus while these young teachers gained a few sheckles to advance their education they left behind them a precious heritage of enthusiasm and scholarship which more than paid for the mere pittance of a salary which they received.

Moreover, such time and energy were a splendid investment for the race; for whereas these men afterwards went to advanced schools, completed their courses and took their places in community life, they carried with them experiences that have tided many over its roughest seas. These Doctors and ministers were able from experience thus gained to direct school activities, to build new schools, to advise in business, to save the community from no end of fatal disasters, in health, in business, in social and racial affairs.

Such was the help gained by John F. Wood, and such returns he has been able to give to his community, church, and lodge wherever he has made his home.

SOLOMON HENRY THOMPSON, M. D.

HEN a boy wishes an education
and wants it bad enough to work
for it he is certain to get that for
which he seeks. Education does
not come easy, even under the
most favorable conditions, and is
intensely hard when the student has to add to the
mental labor necessary to pay his own way. This
was the lot of Solomon Henry Thompson, M. D.

He worked his way through school from the time
he was thirteen years of age until he graduated in
medicine. He first passed through the schools of
his native town and then Storer College, Harpers
Ferry. From Storer he went to Howard University, D. C., and graduated in medicine in 1892.

In all this time and in all the years it took to
obtain this education, for with the Doctor it was
a case of work a while and study a while, he
never once faltered or gave up hope of one day
ranking with the best physicians and surgeons in
the land. He, however, determined that if ever
he was so fortunate as to be blessed with a family, his children should never have to suffer the
hardships endured by their father. It was this
spirit of pluck and perseverance of the men of
a generation back in overcoming difficulties of a
hundred fold greater than encountered at the pres-

ent day, that should serve as an inspiration to future generations, and spur them on to greater
achievements.

Realizing that the greatest need of his people
was highly skilled physicians with practical experience, that would be qualified, not only to aid
in sickness and distress, but to act as instructors
and leaders in matters of home hygiene, and civic
sanitation. Feeling the technical knowledge gleaned
from the medical department of Howard, while unsurpassed an so far as it went was not all that was
needed, he served a full internship in the Freedman's Hospital at Washinyton, D. C. Then taking Horace Greely's advice he "went West," and
settled in Kansas City, Kansas.

So highly had his sense of Racial and Civic
Pride been developed that he attracted the attention of his fellow citizens from the start. Soon,
no movement for social or public uplift was started without Dr. S. H. Thompson being consulted.
He was elected chief surgeon of Douglass Hospital; The Masons, Odd Fellows, K. of P's and
Knights of Tabor, vied with each other in electing him to honorary positions Today he ranks
Pre-Eminently as one of the strongest characters as well as the most brilliant Negro Sur-
geans and Physicians in Kansas.

He has held the position of Grand Commander of
the Grand Commandery of Kansas, and Grand
Chancellor of the K. of P.'s. Dr. Thompson has not
been an extensive tralever, these having been confined to this country and from Colorado to the extreme East. He is following the advice to see the
United States before visiting Europe. Dr. Thompson married June 1st, 1898, Miss Belle J. Armstrong, og St. Louis, Missouri. Four children
have been born to them, making their home
life bright and happy beyond the companionship
of their own congenial spirits. Always bearing in
mind the difficulties he struggled under in obtaining his own education, the Doctor is determined to
aid his children in fitting themselves to meet life's
battle by giving them the best education obtainable. One, a girl of seventeen, is a student of Kansas University, two boys are in High School, and
the baby, a girl of ten, is in the graded schools.
Parents cannot do a better part for their children
than to give them a good education. What they
leave them in material wealth may be swept away
but what they put into their minds is there forever. This is especially true when the religious
training of children keeps pace with their mental
development. In this home the value of both are
recognized and encouraged.

In Church affiliation, Dr. Thompson is a member
of the African Methodist Episcopal. He and his
family occupy a handsome residence in Kansas
City, Kansas, where one is impressed that they are
in a home of culture and refinement, where hospitality is a gift rather than a study.

Isaac Napoleon Porter, M. D.

DR. I. N. Porter, of New Haven, Connecticut, is a striking example of a man who has made good in his profession, regardless of color. The fact that he is a man of the Negro race has not militated against his success and in fact is not to be considered in connection with his achievement in his chosen line of work. In spite of his color he has risen to his high place because of merit alone, which is recognized by the white as well as the colored citizens of New Haven, the former constituting the vastly larger number of his patrons.

Dr. Porter was born October 15th, 1865, in Summit Bridge, Delaware. He was born at a time when the attention of Negroes everywhere was directed to the subject of education. The Negro, having had but little or no opportunities to secure an education had learned considerable from observation, and he was quick to see what education had done for the white race, and reasoned that it would also help to elevate the colored race so that the subject of mind development became one of the utmost thoughts of his mind. Even in the extreme South men of color at this time were thinking in terms of books for their children. Dr. Porter had the advantage over many in the place of birth. Here the question of his color was not one of such great importance after all. He had the opportunity to attend school with all the other boys and girls of the town. This he did, getting from the public school system of Delaware all that he could. Having finished the public schools at his home, he matriculated at Lincoln University. This was in the year 1886 and four years later he was graduated from this institution. Lincoln University leaves its stamp of good scholarship and true manhood on all who go from her doors. Dr. Porter went from her with this stamp and also with the ambition to increase his store of learning. He went the fall of the same year to Yale, where he entered the medical department. From Yale he was graduated in 1903.

Feeling that his student days were at last behind him, Dr. Porter immediately settled down to the practice of his profession in New Haven. Here he has made a place for himself. He enjoys a large and remunerative practice. The number of colored families in New Haven is not great when compared to the number of white families. But in spite of this fact, Dr. Porter has built up for himself a large practice, 90% of which is white. He stands as a proof of the fact that a well trained colored physician can get and hold the trade of the white

people by competence. The position of this young physician was very similar to that of a number of young colored men who found it necessary to look to the white race for support. Great merit in their line of endeavor overcame race prejudice and won their favor. But he has had the experience that has come to many others. When the white man finds out that the colored man can do what he wants and needs done, the question of his color is entirely forgotten and the quality of his work takes precedence over all other facts. Because of this fact, Dr. Porter has been enabled to build for himself a fine practice.

As evidence of his large and remunerative practice no less than his thrifty habits, Dr. Porter has met all the demands of his various interests and has been able to invest in property to the amount of twenty thousand dollars. He has made all of his investments in the city of New Haven, where he could give them his personal attention.

Dr. Porter while giving strict attention to his business has not been unmindful of the general interests of his people and works untiringly in their behalf. All organizations which have for their aim the uplift of the colored race receive his earnest cooperation. He is actively identified with the cause of religion and has found his place as a church worker in the Baptist Church of which he is a member. He is also a member of the Masonic Order, of the Grand United Order of Odd Fellows, and of the Elks. Through these organizations he has had ample opportunity to touch the lives of men along lines other than those strictly held to by physicians.

His home city has not been slow to recognize Dr. Porter's ability and sterling worth and on a number of occasions has called him to positions of honor and trust, in the various city organizations. He is a member of the Historical Society. He is a member of the Chamber of Commerce. He is a member of the New Haven Medical Society, and he is also a member of the American Medical Society. Membership in these organizations indicate the interest he takes in civic matters and his desire to contribute to his city's advance in its higher ideals of service, and is also a tribute to his thorough training for service and recognition of his obligations as a citizen.

In 1908 Dr. Porter was married to Miss Gertrude C. Ward, of St. Joseph, Michigan. There are no children in the Porter family. Dr. Porter has traveled through Canada and in some parts of the United States. The record of this man's life since leaving school speaks for itself.

ALBERT BRYSON SINGFIELD

OR all the scoffs hurled at her, Georgia, as far as the Negro is concerned, is making her mark in some praiseworthy things. Georgia is distinguished for a large number of very good Negro schools, there being a cluster of colleges in Atlanta, and good colleges and secondary schools in every city and town of any considerable size. If she excels in good schools, she goes a step further in Negro Insurance. The Standard Life weathered the storm and kept its mooring in Atlanta. The North Carolina Mutual has in Atlanta a branch office that competes for distinction with the home office in Durham.

If Atlanta surpasses in the old line companies, Savannah takes the lead in Benefit Insurance. Of these the Pilgrim Health and Life Insurance Company is one of the best and most substantial. To use its own wording is, "The oldest, ablest and safest of all."

Mr. Albert B. Singfield is General Superintendent of this company for the State, and is manager of the Savannah District. Mr. Singfield was born in Harlem, Georgia, March 15, 1876. Mr. Singfield went to school in Columbia County, at a very early age, and received a Normal education. After taking a Normal course he entered the insurance business.

Augusta is twenty-five miles from Mr. Singfield's birthplace. There was difficulty in getting in touch with the city life and city opportunities from Mr. Singfield's native home. In 1903 he began business in Augusta for the Pilgrim Health and Life Insurance Company. For six years he was the Augusta local agent. From the first Mr. Singfield and the company grew hand in hand, as it were. Taking over the business in Savannah he found but few agents and few members. He studied the field and how to handle soliciters, becoming himself an active worker.

He began in 1903; and traveled for years thru the State; in 1909 he was called to Savannah to become Manager of that District. Immediately the business took on new life. Its reputation spread its force rapidly increased. He knew the field back there in Augusta; and though he had left it himself, he worked it over harder than when he was there. The result was that wheareas Savannah was supporting but five agents in 1909, when Mr. Singfield took the Superintendency of the Pilgrim, as it is called, it now supports twenty-one agents. Again, in 1909, one person constituted the office force of Savannah, today five persons are necessary to do all the office work entailed in the employment of twenty one agents.

There are several reasons for the wonderful strides of the Pilgrim Health and Life, under Superintendency of Mr. Singfield. In the first place Mr. Singfield knew the game of soliciting at first hand. His own knowledge gained in the field taught him how to handle agents; but more important still it gave him an intimate knowledge of the situations which would confront the agents. He knew the weakness of the agents demands. He knew their inspirations. He knew the weak points and the strong points in a prospective member's argument. When therefore he talked with his men he did not have to read theory; he knew, and his men knew that he knew all the highways and byways of the territory. It is this that enabled him to add so quickly four to an office force of one, and eighteen agents to an agent's force of five.

Mr. Singfield made Savannah his home. He united with the First Baptist Church, and he and Mrs. Singfield began immediately to take an active part in church work. He bought a home for his family in Savannah, and then he became a tax payer and a promoter of civil life; he is a Deacon of his church, and he joined all worthy local lodges. He is a Mason, Odd Fellow and Knight of Pythias.

Mr. Singfield was married in 1894 to Miss Anna Wilson, of Harlem Georgia. They have two daughters, Misses Mary Bertha and Nellie Louise.

Reverend Archibald James Carey

EV. Archibald James Carey, was the son of the Rev. Jefferson and Anna B. Carey, both members of the African Methodist Episcopal Church. He was born in Atlanta, Georgia, August 25th, 1868, and was one of three children.

His educational training began when he was quite young, having entered school at the early age of four years. From the beginning and ending of his school days he made continuous progress and upon the completion of his course of training he was thoroughly equipped for his life work. In the course of his educational career he has attended Atlanta University, Chicago Theological Seminary, and the University of Chicago, and is a graduate of Chicago Theological Seminary and has received the honorary degrees of A. M., D. D., and Ph. D.

Like his school days, his religious life began when he was a mere child. He was converted when nine years of age and joined the African Methodist Episcopal Church, and at once became incorporated in its activities. He has held nearly every office in the local church to which he belongs, and made his influence felt in its work and life.

He received his license to preach in Atlanta, Georgia in 1888, when he was twenty years of age, and the following year was ordained a deacon at Washington, Georgia. In 1890, he was made an Elder at Monticello, Georgia. Bishop Gaines officiated at all of these services.

In 1888 he joined the North Georgia Annual Conference, under Bishop Gaines, and has held the following appointments: Bethel, Athens, Georgia, 1891-1895; Mt. Zion, Jacksonville, 1895-1898; Quinn Chapel, Chicago, 1898-1904; Bethel, Chicago, 1904-1909; Institutional, Chicago, 1909 to 1918, when he was appointed Presiding Elder of the Chicago district.

He built Bethel, Athens, Georgia, at a cost of twenty-five hundred dollars ($2500), in 1892; lifted a mortgage on Quinn Chapel, to the amount of twenty-three thousand dollars ($23,000.), in 1898-1904; on Bethel, Chicago, to the amount of twelve thousand five hundred dollars ($12.500), in 1904-1909, and has taken about five thousand people into the church.

He was a delegate to the General Conference of 1904, 1908, 1912, and 1916. He was a member of the Financial Board from 1904 to 1912; member of the Commission on Federation of Methodist churches, 1915; and was voted for for Financial Secretary in 1912, and for Bishop in 1916.

Dr. Carey is as gifted with his pen as he is on the platform, which he uses for the good of his people; he is a frequent contributor to newspapers and his articles command attention and are read with much interest; as a platform speaker his ability is recognized by all who have enjoyed his appealing eloquence and he is in great demand for public addresses.

Being a man of friendly disposition and a sympathetic spirit he found pleasure in mingling with his fellows not only in their church life, but in their social activities.

He is a member of the Odd Fellows, Knights of Pythias, Foresters, Elks, and Tabor, and is prominently connected with these orders. In politics he is a Republican and stands high in the councils of his party in his city.

In 1890 he married Miss Elizabeth Davis, of Athens, Georgia, who has borne him five children—Eloise, 22 years; Annabell, 21; Madison, 19; Dorothy, 10; and Archibald, Jr., 7 years. Eloise and Anabel are graduates of Chicago University, and received degrees of A. B. and Ph. B. respectively.

This sketch would be incomplete without recording additional honors conferred upon Dr. Carey, which show that his rare gifts were known and appreciated outside of his church and local community.

On the occasion of the centennial celebration of Perry's victory on the Lakes, he was chosen by the International Commission to deliver the oration for the Negroes, which he did with great credit to himself and the race he represented.

All states participating in the War of 1812, made appropriations and were represented on the program. Other speakers were: President Wilson, Ex-President Taft, Dr. McDonald, of Montreal, and Governor Cox, of Ohio. To sit on the platform with such distinguished characters is an honor which any man might covet and which comes to but few.

Dr. Carey was appointed by Governor Dunn as Commissioner of Half-Century Negro Freedom Celebration held in Chicago; he was appointed by Mayor Harrison, member of the Chicago Board of Moving Picture Censors, and appointed by Mayor Thompson, Chief Examiner of Law Claims.

Besides his rich mental endowment and magnetic manner, Dr. Carey possesses a good physique which added to the impressiveness of his pulpit work has made him conspicious among men.

A life consecrated to religion and elevation of his people, his influence is felt in every circle in which he moves.

ISAIAH MONTGOMERY

R. Montgomery was born a slave. His name will ever inspire a certain degree of romance because of his close association with Jefferson Davis, the President of the Confederacy. He was the property of Joseph E. Davis, Jefferson Davis' elder brother, being born on the Hurricane Plantation, in 1847. His father came from Virginia, where through his young master he picked up a knowledge of the alphabet and the rudiments of spelling and writing; his fondness for education was encouraged by Mr. Davis until he obtained a good knowledge of English, and became a fair accountant, mechanical engineer, and architect. The son, Isaiah, and an elder brother, William Thornton, and two sisters were carefully instructed by their father during his spare time.

At the age of nine years the slave lad became the master's office boy, carried the mails for New Orleans and Vicksburg steamers.

Shortly after Admiral Porter ran part of his Fleet past the Vicksburg batteries, he came into contact with Isaiah through making inquiries in regard to the Gunboat Indianola, which had been sunk at the Hurricane landing. The Admiral persuaded Isaiah's parents to let him go as his cabin boy, and also advised them to leave the south for a time, predicting that times would be very rough for a period. The Admiral supplied transportation to Cincinnati.

Isaiah participated in the battle of Grand Gulf, went with the Gunboat expedition up Red River as far as Fort De-Russey, and took part in the bombardment of Vicksburg on several occasions, and was at the capitulation of that famous city in July, 1863.

After the war, Isaiah, and his brother with their father, agreed to purchase the plantation of Joseph Davis and that of his Brother Jefferson Davis, altogether some four thousand acres, for $300,000 in gold. Mr. Montgomery signed the purchase notes before he had reached his majority. Gen. Grant had been using the places for headquarters of refugees. The Government accounted for the rents amounting to $26,000.00. Ben Montgomery acted as Mr. Davis' auditor and approved the settlement. The Montgomerys occupied the Davis properties for thirteen years, part of the time ranking third among the largest cotton raisers of the south.

It was the dream of Joseph that the Negroes of his plantation be kept together making the old plantation their permanent home. Catching the vision of the Master the young ex-save book-keeper went into the wilderness of the great Yazoo, Miss., Delta in Bolivar County, and began a Negro Colony. On reaching the chosen spot, Isaiah Montgomery said to the few men who followed him: "You see this is a pretty wild place. But this whole country was like this once. You have seen it change. You and your fathers for the most part performed the work that has made it what it is. You and your fathers did this for some one else. Can't you do the same for yourselves?"

This was the way he went forth to found a town. Here Mr. Montgomery has worked ever since. In 1872 he had married Miss Martha Robb, whose mother was a favorite servant in the family of Mrs. Sallie Bridges. Mrs. Bridges was very much attached to Miss Robb and gave her careful training. Mr. Montgomery brought his young wife and growing family to Mound Bayou in the early spring of 1888. Out of a number of children born to them, only four are now living, Mrs. Mary C. Booze, Misses Estella and Lillie Belle and Mrs. Eva Pearl Canton, the latter is her father's private secretary.

Mr. Montgomery was the only colored member of the Mississippi Constitutional Convention of 1890 and delivered a noted speech on the adoption of the new Constitution. The same year he headed a committee of Negroes, who called on President Harrison and Speaker Reed; also appeared before the Senate Committee on Rivers and Harbors, where he summed up the evidence and quoted authorities in behalf of levee building to withstand the floods of the Mississippi River. And during the early fall he was called to New York to appear before the U. S. River Commission to assist in securing the largest possible allotment for levees in the Yazoo-Mississippi Delta. He assisted in founding the National Negro Business League at Boston, and became one of its earliest life members. He is considerably interested in planting, operates a Gin and Saw Mill, is President of the Farmers Co-operative Mercantile Co., the largest business house in Mound Bayou, is one of the leading Directors in the Mound Bayou State Bank, and gives much time to Church and School work.

William J. Tompkins, M. D. and Old City Hospital

WHEN a magnificent new building was erected in Kansas City, Mo., in 1906, for a general Hospital, and the white patients transferred there, the old building was thrown open to Negro patients, where they had formerly only been allowed in the basement. But the institution remained under white management with white doctors, nurses and employees.

Some of the Negro physicians saw how, since this segregation could not be avoided, it might be used to the advantage of their race. They saw that not only would the Negroes receive more considerate treatment at the hands of their own people, but also vast opportunities would be open to the Negro physicians in the forum of hospital experience and the direct association with white surgeons who had had greater advantages, and also that great facilities would be afforded Negro girls for becoming proficient nurses. They worked perserveringly toward the accomplishment of this hope, but it was not until 1911, that the first tangible results of these efforts became evident. In October of that year Negro nurses and internes entered the Old City Hospital (as it was now called) to care for their own people, and four Negro physicians and surgeons were appointed as assistants to the various chiefs on the visiting staff.

Dr. Thompkins succeeded in convincing a broad-minded President of the Hospital and Health Board, and a sympathetic Mayor of the city that it would be best for all concerned to place the institution entirely in the hands of the Negroes.

Consequently, in November, 1914, whites were removed, and all positions filled by Negroes. So that now the Institution affords thirty-five (35) pupil nurses, a Superintendent of Nurses, and five assistants, a Superintendent, Matron, Pathologist and assistant, three clerks, eight internes and twenty-five employees.

This hospital is in A Class, and is the largest Negro hospital in the country. It consists of four buildings, including a main brick building that accomodates two hundred and twenty-five (225) patients, a tuberculosis pavilion of forty (40) beds, an isolation cottage of forty (40) beds, and a two-story Nurses House. To this was added this year (1918), a beautiful stone building, accomodating one hundred and eighty-five (185) patients, that is used for United State Government detention patients, which department has three nurses, a visiting physician, clinic, and clinician, a Matron and twelve employees, all under the same administration.

The training school of this hospital offers a three year course of instruction, graduates from which are eligible to State registration and enrollment in the National Red Cross organization. In recognition of the needs of the government for more nurses in time of war, the hospital instituted an auxiliary school for nurses assistants which gives an eight week course in Elementary Hygiene and Home Care of the sick.

Dr. Wm. Thompkins was born in Jefferson City, Missouri, July 6, 1878. He finished the course given in the public school; and then completed the Academic and Normal course at Lincoln Institute, in 1901. After spending two years of study in the College of Medicine at the University of Colorado, he went to Howard University, in Washington, D. C., where he received the degree of M. D., in 1905. After a year's internship at the Freedmen's Hospital, in Washington, he located in Kansas City, Missouri, in 1906, where he is still engaged in the practice of medicine.

Dr. Thompkins was the first Negro Medical Inspector of schools in the State of Missouri, at that time being city physician for Negroes, all of which work was later divided among three men, he retaining one-third of the work at the same salary for which he had done it all.

Through his efforts the St. Simon Nursery was established, an institution which cared for between four and five hundred children annually. There he established the first Child Hygiene Department among Negroes in Kansas City, a work that was later taken over and maintained by the city. He was also for seven years physician to the Old Folks and Orphans Home.

He was President of the Kansas City Medical Society, is Secretary of the Pan-Missouri State Medical Association, a charter member of the Tri-State Medical Society, of Missouri, Kansas and Oklahoma and an honorary member of the Oklahoma State Medical Asociation. So, when a City Hospital was given to the Negroes of Kansas City, for their own, Dr. Thompkins was naturally the logical one decided upon to manage the institution, which he took charge of in November, 1914.

He is a member of the Allen Chapel A. M. E. Church, a thirty-third degree Mason, a U. B. F., an Odd Fellow, and a Knight of Pythias. In the last named organization he was for seven consecutive years Grand Medical Registrar of Missouri. He is a member of the Educational and Industrial Commission of Missouri, and was recently appointed by the Governor of Missouri, a delegate to the National Educational Congress, to meet in New York City. He has been a member of all State delegations appearing before the Governor or Legislature of his State for the past ten years in the interest of his people. He has also been interested in all civic movements for his people, being instrumental in securing for them the Garrison Square Field House and Play Ground.

At one time he was endorsed for the position of Surgeon-in-chief at the Freedmen's Hospital by the State Medical Association of Missouri, Speaker Champ Clark, of the House of Representatives, and both United States Senators from the State of Missouri, and the Missouri State Legislature for the first time in its history gave him unanimous endorsement.

He owns a beautiful residence, valuable property in Spring Valley Park of Kansas City and oil land in Oklahoma and land in Mexico.

In 1913 Dr. Thompkins was married to Miss Jessie Embry, of Columbus, Ohio. They have one daughter, three years old.

CLINTON METROPOLITAN A. M. E. ZION CHURCH, CHARLOTTE, N. C.

This church has had a long and glorious history. It was organized fifty one years ago, and has numbered among its pastors some of the most prominent ministers of the denomination. Several of them have advanced to the office of Bishop, Bishop James Walker Hood; Bishop Andrew Jackson Warner; Bishop Lomax. This beautiful church edifice was erected during the pastorate of Dr. Warner, (now Bishop). It has a large membership; pays a salary of $1800, and has a splendid parsonage. The present Board of Trustees are: W. P. Robinson, President; Col. C. S. L. A. Taylor, Secretary-Treasurer; W. R. Moore, J. R. Funderburk, John Gray, Thomas Davis, James Taylor, W. M. Peoples, and Walter Fronabarger. M. D. Smith, D. D., is Pastor.

306

Dinwiddie Normal and Industrial Institute

IN 1898 the Dinwiddie Agricultural and Industrial School was organized. It was incorporated in March, 1899, as the John A. Dix Industrial School. Under this name the school continued to grow and develop till 1907, when the name was changed to the Dinwiddie Agricultural and Industrial School. The first purchase of land for the school was a tract of 114 acres. On this land they erected a building 40x50 with six large rooms in which school was opened in 1900. Later the Board purchased and increased the farm tract to 250 acres.

One man who played a large part in the development of the school was Mr. Alexander Van Ranssellaer, a philanthropist of Philadelphia, Pennsylvania. He was a staunch friend of the colored people and assisted in the development of the Dinwiddie School till he brought it up to a high degree of efficiency. When the school was fully established and running smoothly, Mr. Ranssallaer decided to place the school in the custody of the colored people. With this in view he conveyed it to the Board of Education of the African Methodist Episcopal Zion Church, in 1908.

PROPERTY AND LOCATION

The property of the school consists of two hundred and fifty acres of land, the Southern part of which borders on a creek. There is also a stream running through the farm from which, with the use of a reservoir, the grounds and buildings are supplied with water. There is a large two-story dormitory with an airy basement. This is in reality the Boys' Building, but the girls are using it at present, their own building having been destroyed by fire. The boys are using a two-story cottage for dormitory. There is a cottage used as the home for the farm manager, and the Principals' Home. Aside from these buildings there are several wagon sheds, barns, two industrial shops and the poultry houses. The property is valued at $18,750. The school owns a number of hogs, chickens, cattle, two mules, and a horse.

The property is situated on the Seaboard Air Line Railway, fifteen miles South of Petersburg, in a most healthful and appropriate locality, and is accessible to a large Negro population.

GENERAL AIM

The general aim of the school is to develop men and women. It offers Negro youth an opportunity to build a foundation for useful life. This is done through moral, literary and manual training. The Normal Training is given to all who are preparing to teach. The Preparatory Training is given those who expect to go to college and the Comprehensive High School Course is designed especially for those who plan to leave school early for business careers.

With Agriculture as a central thought such industries are taught as are closely related to agriculture. Carpentry and blacksmithing are given, not only for their training values, but also because they are closely related to the work of the farmer. Gardening, dairying, poultry raising, cooking, sewing and laundrying. The school seeks to teach boys and girls, not only books and trades, but how to live and become a vital part of the community life.

ADVANTAGES

Some of the advantages of the school are the healthfulness of the location and the wholesome rural surroundings, the literary and industrial courses offered; the personal attention given each student; and the earnest, conscientious, Christian teachers. The pupils while in the school live in the dormitories and take up the regular life of the well regulated Christian home. Another homelike feature of the school plan is that every student bears a portion of the burden of the household.

In the development of Christian character the schools puts great emphasis. There are distinctive religious services, attendance upon which is required. There is the Sunday School, preaching services and the Sunday evening services as well as the regular student's Prayer Meeting. In this way the students are trained to do active work in the religious life of their communities when they leave school.

The Present Principal of the Dinwiddie Normal School is Mr. W. E. Woodyard. Under his efficient management the school has developed greatly.

ORGANIZATION

Elementary—The elementary work covers the three upper elementary grades, with liberal time for physiology and hygiene.

Secondary — The preparatory course of three years includes the usual secondary subjects with three years of Latin and two years of Greek or German. The teachers' course differs from the preparatory course in the omission of languages and the institution of science, animal husbandry, and principles of teaching.

Industrial—Four hours a week of industrial work is required of all pupils. A little training in carpentry and blacksmithing is provided for the boys and cooking and sewing for the girls. The farm is maintained on a commercial basis.

HENRY FLOYD GAMBLE, M. D.

 HOUGH born in 1862, when education was almost impossible for the Negro, Dr. Henry F. Gamble, of Charleston, West Virginia, managed to gain the best of both literary and professional training. He was born on the farm at North Garden, Albermarle County, Virginia, January 16th, 1862. For a good while the road to learning and attainment seemed as dark and impossible as it was to the millions of other colored people.

Working and hoping and trying, working on the farm in the day and making what headway he could at night, he at length found someone to teach him at night. He now began to master his books and was soon able to enter Lincoln University in Pennsylvania. His drawbacks of early days appeared now to have been a spur rather than a hindrance; for though his early education had been irregular, he was able to graduate with honors in 1888, and this, even though he had to earn his way. From Lincoln University he entered the Medical Department of Yale University, where, in 1891, he gained his doctors' degree.

He began to practice at Charlottsville, Virginia.

Here he remained but one year, moving at the close of the year, 1892 to Charleston, West Virginia, where for a little more than a quarter of a century he has been practicing, to use his own modest words, "with a reasonable amount of success."

Dr. Gamble has been according to professional men who know and honor him, an intensely hard worker and a close student in his profession, studying not only books and treatises, but everyday cases that come under his observation.

His work engages almost his exclusive time and attention and has kept him from entering the mystic doors of the secret orders. His ear is ever attuned to the cry of distress and the call of the suffering and he holds himself in readiness to quickly respond when the summons comes.

When Dr. Gamble in 1911-12 was elected President of the National Medical Association, the daily papers of his home city showed how very much the laity agreed with the medical profession. The Charleston Gazette said: "The Gazette desires to extend to Dr. Gamble its heartiest congratulations upon his election to the presidency of the National Medical Association.

"Dr. Gamble, alone, however, should not be congratulated. The Medical Association should come in for its share of felicitations. To the people of Charleston the choice seems to have been a fitting and a splendid one. Dr. Gamble is a man who has reflected credit upon his race and profession. He is an educated man, who, by his ability and personality has earned many friends and much admiration here. It is in men of the stamp and character of Dr. Gamble that the Negro race will find its real salvation. Charleston is glad that Dr. Gamble has been honored."

To win such an endorsement from his home people is an honor that any man may covet and is a reward worth striving for. The Doctor accepts the honor with commendable pride but with a modesty which itself is an evidence of greatness coming from such a source.

Dr. Gamble was married in 1894, to Miss Gilmer of Charleston, West Virginia. Miss Gilmer was a graduate of Storer College. She died in 1901. Dr. Gamble was again married in 1917, to Miss Nina H. Clinton of Zanesville, Ohio. Mrs. Gamble is a graduate of Wilberforce University. Dr. Gamble's two children, Catherine Lee and Henry Floyd, Jr., are both in school. The former is a Freshman in Oberlin College; the latter attending school in Charleston.

Dr. Gamble owns his home, office and office equipment. He is a Baptist in his religious beliefs, being a faithful member of the First Baptist Church of Charleston.

John C. Asbury, LL. B., LL. M.

IT is worthy of note that the educated Negro, as a rule, has aspirations looking to the betterment and elevation of his race, and wherever the interests of the race are concerned you will find him at work.

His operations are not confined to the church, the school and the medical profession, but reach out and touch the home life of their people, and has regard to their social comforts and recreational diversions.

They have learned in their own experience that education not only enlightens the mind but broadens the concept of life, and excites the ambition to rise to higher attainments in the higher ideals of life. Feeling these impulses in their own souls they wish the same for their people and almost as a natural instinct they are led to work for race elevation.

John C. Asbury is among this class, and his intensive habits of mind have caused him to consider the interests of the Colored citizens of his community from every aspect of their lives. This was carried beyond the bounds of the living to contemplate the resting place of the dead. The outcome of this investigation is told elsewhere in this sketch.

Mr. Asbury is a native of Washington County, Pennsylvania, in which State he received in large part his education. He got the ground work of his education from the public schools of Washington County, and after finishing at these schools he entered the Washington and Jefferson College, located at Washington, Pennsylvania.

Choosing Law as his profession, he next enrolled at Howard University, Washington, D. C. and took the law course. Here he won the degrees of LL. B. and LL. M. In June, 1885, he was admitted to the Bar of the district of Columbia, but began his practice in the State of Virginia. He opened his office in Norfolk, Virginia, in 1885, and soon won recognition which brought him into prominent notice.

In May, 1887, he was elected Commonwealth (District) Attorney, of Norfolk County, in which office he served four years. During his term of office he had no assistant but conducted the business of the Court alone.

Among the many cases prosecuted by him there were eleven murder cases which he handled with consummate skill. Mr. Asbury takes a deep interest in the political questions which stir the country and true to his nature he lets his interest take

active form. In politics he is a staunch Republican, and he gives to his party the best that is in him.

In January, 1892 he was a delegate to the National Republican Convention, at Minneapolis, representing the Second Congressional District of Virginia.

In January, 1897, Mr. Asbury left Virginia, and located in Philadelphia, since which time he has been an active practitioner at the Philadelphia Bar.

While investigating the conditions of his people Mr. Asbury made a note of the very inadequate provision made for their burial, and set about to work a change to give them pleasanter surroundings for their dead.

It is one thing to see a need but quite another thing to undertake the task of supplying it. Mr. Asbury did both and succeeded beyond his expectation in the effort. He organized the Eden Cemetery Company, of which he is the President and directing head, and it has the reputation of being the most beautiful and best managed Negro cemetery in America. It comprises fifty-three acres (53), and it is estimated that it will furnish graves for the colored population of Philadelphia for the next hundred years. While the enterprise was born of a desire to help the colored race to find an attractive place to bury their dead, it has proved a fine investment for the stockholders. They have already received a dividend upon their stock exceeding the cost of the shares and the great bulk of the property yet remains to be disposed of.

The cemetery was established in 1902. This Company is not the extent of his activities for his people. He is connected with other institutions which seek their good. He is President of the Keystone Beneficial Society, the largest institution of its kind among colored people in the North. He is Chairman of the Board of Trustees of the Union Baptist Church, among the largest of Baptist Churches, having a membership of thirty-five hundred (3500).

He is a member of the Masonic Fraternity, the Odd Fellows, and the Elks.

Notwithstanding the demands upon his time which his connection with these various institutions call for, he never neglects his business as an Attorney. His large and lucrative practice attest it. He has made a good record in the trial of the cases assigned him, being many times complimented by the trial judge in open Court.

In February 1916, he was appointed Court assistant in the Municipal Court by City Solicitor Connelly.

VIRGINIA NORMAL AND INDUSTRIAL INSTITUTE. UPPER VIEW — TEACHERS' COTTAGES, MAIN
BUILDING, VAWTER BUILDING, PRESIDENT'S RESIDENCE, AND THE JAMES HUGO JOHN-
STON BUILDING. LOWER VIEW—SECTION OF FARM AND BARN YARD

The Virginia Normal and Industrial Institute

HE Virginia Normal and Industrial Institute owns seventy-two acres of land, forty-two are under cultivation and twenty-six make up the Campus and Athletic Field. There are twelve permanent buildings — five cottages for married teachers, a residence for the President, the main building, three smaller buildings, a boiler house, and a laundry. The Institution is beautifully located on the top of a high hill over-looking the surrounding country. The land has a natural drainage and the health conditions are excellent.

The Institute is primarily a Normal School, preparing teachers for the Colored public schools of Virginia. It has graduated 1477 men and women. These graduates are engaged in practically all the pursuits of life. Some of them are physicians, lawyers, preachers, farmers, business men, home-keepers and the like. Most of them however are engaged as teachers in the public schools of the State and as social workers in various centers.

The program of studies of the Institute comprises a High School, a Normal School, a Normal Industrial School, and departments in Agriculture, Domestic Science, Manual Training, business, and music. The high school comprises four years of high school work above the eighth grade. The Normal School, two years of professional work above the four year high school, and the Normal Industrial, two years of industrial work and teacher training above the first two years of the high school. This last course is to train teachers for the rural public schools. The High school and Normal School are accredited by the State in their respective classes.

Industrial work in conducted with a view to the training of young people to teach the subject in the schools of the State. Particularly strong courses in household arts and agriculture are given. The agricultural department has the distinction of being run on a "paying basis." The Manual Training Work leads to practical skill in handling situations around the home and on the farm. The domestic science is correlated with the student's and teachers' kitchen and dining rooms.

Physical training receives special attention. There is a coach for the athletic interest of the boys and a physical director for the girls. Military drill is given the boys under the direction of a competent drill master.

The religious life receives emphasis in the activities of the Christian Associations, Bible Classes, weekly prayer meetings, daily devotional exercises, and annual week of prayer and Sunday afternoon preaching services.

The faculty is composed of thirty seven officers, teachers and workers. Of this number twelve are

men and twenty-five are women. Most of these men and women were trained in the best Negro Colleges of the South; some of them come from the larger institutions of the North. Practically all of them have studied in the Summer Schools of the large institutions of the North.

For the session 1916-1917 nine hundred and nineteen students were enrolled in the regular session and three hundred and fifty in the summer session, making a total of one thousand two hundred and sixty-nine instructed in the Institute during the year. Of the nine hundred and nineteen in the regular session two hundred and twenty-six were boys and six hundred and ninety-three were girls. The enrollment was distributed as follows; professional department 146; Senior High School 388; Junior High School 198; and training school 117.

JOHN MANUEL GANDY, A. B.

John Manuel Gandy, President of the Virginia State Normal School, was born near Starkesville, Mississippi. He began his educational career early in life in the rural public schools of Oktibba County, Mississippi, where the strong intellect which characterized his later life, thus early began to unfold.

In 1889 he left his rural home and went to the Capitol of the State, where he entered Jackson College, remained there two years, graduating from the Normal Department in 1892. Due to the shortage of money, he left Oberlin and entered Fisk University in 1894, and was graduated with the degree of A. B. in 1898. Before graduation he was offered a position as instructor of Latin and Greek in the Virginia Normal and Collegiate Institute, and also the secretaryship of the Y. M. C. A., in New Haven, Conn. He accepted the latter. After serving for a couple of months he discovered that it was hardly possible to develop a work in New Haven. He then accepted the first position offered him as it was at that time open.

President Gandy went to Virginia and put his life into his work. He allied himself with the social uplift movements of the State, attending most of the State meetings. His value became gradually known and when the Negro Organization Society looked around for an Executive Secretary the mantle fell on him. This position took him into practically every County of the State. He gave himself freely in helping the people into new ideas and practices of health, education, and farming. He introduced the Negro Organization Society to the people.

When the President of the State Normal School died Mr. Gandy was elected his successor. He has had phenomenal success as an administrator and educator. Practically every feature of the school has been reorganized. The courses of study have been raised; the equipment and plant greatly improved; the student body and teaching force nearly doubled.

MISS EMMA J. WILSON

AYESVILLE Educational and Industrial Institute is Miss Emma Wilson's monument, her life story. Born in the days bordering on slavery, Miss Wilson early grew eager for an education. In making known her desire to her slave mother, the latter replied, "Why you are crazy child, you can't go to school. Only white children go to school." Since this was so the child did the next best thing. She got three little white children to teach her. Having learned her alphabet, she got hold of a speller and began to master the big words. Later she attended a Mission School taught by Northern women. From here she enrolled at Scotia Seminary, at Concord, North Carolina.

When she was planning and praying that she might go to Scotia, she promised the Lord that she would go to Africa as a Missionary, if that was his will. Finishing her course at Scotia, she returned to Mayesville, her birth place, and found her Africa at her own door." That is she found her home village without a Negro school building or any one to teach. Securing the use of an old abandoned cotton gin house, she opened school with ten pupils. Books were donated, children paid tuition in eggs, chickens and provisions. However, Miss Wilson did not accept these as her pay. She had her mother cook these and sell them. The proceeds she turned in to the work of her cotton gin school house.

In a short time the school outgrew the gin house. Believing in her work, Dr. Mayes, for whom the little town was named influenced the County Board of Education to grant her forty-five dollars a year to aid in her work. This she invested in an Assistant Teacher, and then used for a school house any building she could secure free of rent charges. Pupils now began to pour in from the surrounding country. To meet the increasing demand, Dr. Mayes advised her to go north and solicit funds.

She started her journey North by asking the minister in her church for the Sunday night col-

lection. This he granted. The sum amounted to fifty cents. With this she rode to the next town where she found a camp meeting. Given the collection here, she raised seventy-five cents. In this way she made her way North, where she often suffered rebuffs and extreme hunger. Sometimes she washed and ironed by the day to earn her food. Finally, however, she got the ear of Lloyd Garrison and Richard H. Dana, who investigated her work and pronounced it sound and deserving. She remained in the North three years, sending back funds to keep the school going. When she returned she had money enough to put up a new school building.

This marked the formal beginning of the Mayesville Institute. From this point it grew in number, in standing, in building, in land, in friends, in money. In 1896 it obtained a charter from the State of South Carolina. Its trustee Board is composed of Northern white men, Southern white men and Southern colored men. Mr. Richard H. Dana subsequently became the school's Treasurer, other representative people of the North, Reverend Howard Brown, Mrs. Quincy Shaw, Mrs. Paul Revere Frothington, Mrs. R. R. Booker, joined the Board of Trustees.

The school is now well equipped and has substantial courses for teachers, and for industrial students. It has an enrollment of 500 students, 150 of whom are boarders; 40 are orphans. It teaches Agriculture in all its forms, giving theory and practice on the school's farm, in the Truck Garden, Orchard, and in Diary. Among the Mechanical and Domestic Arts are taught Carpentry, Shoe-making, Brick-making, Tailoring, Sewing, Cooking, Nursing and House Work. Miss Wilson herself is the founder of the course in brick-making. Having found clay on her farm, she went to Pittsburg and learned brick-making first hand. The institution's running expenses are $9000, $200 of which is given by the State of South Carolina. The rest, save the proceeds from the truck garden and from a few rented cottages, is raised by Miss Wilson. She has an annual Farmers' Conference, of which she is President. The United States Government has established an Experiment Station here.

IOSLYN HALL AND HARRIET IOSLYN HALL

312

Will Henry Bennett Vodery

AS a musical prodigy, Will Henry Bennett Vodery, the subject of this sketch, may be properly classed, for he wrote music and played upon musical instruments at a very early age. He played the piano in the Sunday School when only nine years of age, and at the age of thirteen he was the church organist. He wrote the song, "My Country I Love Thee," when he was twelve years old.

His musical talent showing itself thus early in life, being developed by Master instructors, has brought him much fame in his later years and has made him a notable character.

Mr. Vodery is a native of Pensylvania. He was born in Philadelphia, October 8, 1885, and received his education in the public schools of that city, graduating from the Central High School in 1902.

Unlike a great many men, he was quick to discern his talent and to determine upon his life career. He was a born musician and with a soul fully attuned to music's melody, it was natural that he should surrender to the compelling call of the Divine Muse.

After graduating from the Central High School, he immediately entered upon the study of music at the Hugh A. Clark University, Pennsylvania, and was under the instruction of Louis Koemunenick, Grand Director of the University of Leipsic.

He commenced his professional career in 1904, in the City of New York, arranged for M. Whitmark & Sons their play, "A Trip To Africa," and accompanied the show on its tour through the middle West and the South. He wrote the music for the plays, "South Africa," and "Time, Place and Girl." The music was inspiring and fun-provoking.

Leaving New York in 1905, he went to Chicago, and was made custodian for the Theodore Thomas Orchestra. While serving in this capacity he studied symphony under the concert manager.

In addition to his duties in connection with the Theodore Thomas Orchestra, he managed the Professional Department of Charles K. Harris.

While in Chicago he wrote the song, "After The Ball Was Over," which made a decided 'hit' with the public and became very popular. It was sung in every part of the country, in the theatres, in the homes and upon the streets. The street urchins whistled it and young men and maidens danced to its catchy music.

He left Chicago in 1907, and returned to New York City, where he wrote "Oyster Man," and many other popular songs. He also arranged the music for Williams and Walker's "Bandanna

Land," and traveled with the show as musical director, going with it to Europe. It gave an exhibition in Shaftes Bury Theatre, London.

In 1908 he managed a show in which the famous comedian, Hogan, featured and scored so great a success that the next season he secured control of the show for himself, making an eighteen weeks tour which added to its popularity.

After this he wrote a number of songs, among which were "Too Much Isaacs," "Girls From Happy Land," "Saucy Maid," and "Me Hun And I."

From New York he went to Washington, D. C., to take charge of the Vaudeville show of Rosenthald & Benedict, which was afterwards changed to a stock company. The first play of the new company was "My Friend From Dixie." The play was well received and proved a great financial success. His satisfactory management of this venture added to his reputation and brought about a business connection between him and J. Lubrie Hull, who formed a partnership and traveled together during the season 1910-1911. Their itinerary covered the entire country—their show was highly pleasing, as was its financial outcome. Mr. Vodery was in constant demand and his talent as a song writer generally recognized. He wrote the music for "Dr. Beans From Boston," a show in which S. H. Dudley was the comedian.

For the season of 1912-1913, he took charge of the Overton & Walker enterprise, a Vaudeville show, and wrote the music for "Porto Rico Girls," and "Happy Girls." The show proved a drawing card and was so well received on the coast that a second trip was made there. He also did special work in 1913 for Florence Ziegfield, writing several successes for Bert A. Williams, among them, "Can't Get Away From It," "Dark Town Poker Club," and "Land Lady."

Mr. Vodery's ability as a song writer is recognized by all of the big Broadway producers, such as Klaw & Erlanger, Schubert, Ziegfield and others, and he is often engaged by them to arrange and construct the music of their plays. He is a prolific writer of songs and music, some of his most popular pieces being—"Dearest Memories," "West Virginia Dance," and "Carolina Fox Trot," this latter being a musical innovation, being the first fox trot ever written. It was published by Joseph Stern & Co.

Mr. Vodery has traveled extensively, both in this country and in Europe.

Mr. Vodery is a member of the Presbyterian Church, a member of the Masons, the Odd Fellows, the Knights of Pythias and of the Elks.

RT. REV. WILLIAM DAVID CHAPPELLE, A. B.,
A. M., D. D., LL. D.

ILLIAM David Chappelle was born
a slave in or about the year 1857,
November 16th, and began school
in the Fairfield Normal school in
1869. His parents Henry and Pat-
sey Chappelle, were slaves and
belonged to one Henry McCrorey.
They had thirteen children, Wil-
liam being the sixth child and as a child was feeble;
but was keen in intellect and always eager to go
to school.

He finished his Normal or English course under
the Rev. Willard Richardson and began teaching in
a country school near Winnsboro. To secure his
first book, he dug up a stump of kindling wood
from his father's field and carried, in turns of ten
cent bunches to town a mile away at night and
sold it, this was done for four nights to secure
forty cents with which to buy a book that he might
have something to study from to get his lessons.

After this struggle he secured a certificate, second grade, but it was the highest marked second
grade in the county white or black, so said the
school supervisor. His school was five miles in
the country to which he walked daily that he might
save his money and enter college.

In 1875 he was converted and finding that he was
not prepared to preach he joined the Columbia Annual Conference and was sent to the Pine Grove
Mission, at the same time he entered Allen University and kept up his studies while preaching at this
Mission; but it was not long before his money gave
out and he had to stop and go to teaching that he
might better support his wife and child, having
married in December 1875 and had at this time one
child.

After three months he re-entered school and
made his classes and continued until 1887, at which
time he graduated from the college Department,
with the degree of A. B. He led his class. He was
ordained Deacon in 1883, Bethel A. M. E. Church,

Columbia, S. C., by Bishop W. F. Dickerson. Ordained Elder by Bishop James A. Shorter, Greenville, S. C., in 1885. He served in the Pastorate
eight years, pastoring the following places: Pine
Grove Mission, two years, 1882-83; Lexington Circuit, 1884; Rockhill Circuit, 1885-87; Pendleton
Station, 1889-1900. He served as P. E. eleven
years; Manning District, 1889-93; Orangeburg District, 1893-98; Sumter District, 1899-1900.

At the General Conference which met in Columbus, Ohio, in 1900, he was elected Secretary and
Treasurer of the Sunday School Union with Headquarters at Nashville, Tenn., where he prepared
and Edited the Sunday School literature for eight
years. When he took charge of the S. S. Union of
the A. M. E. Church, the Methodist Episcopal
Church South, was doing the printing. Dr. Chappelle after figuring out the cost of printing the literature himself and also the income of the circulation of his periodicals, ventured to do the work
himself, which was a successful venture. Thus,
he built for the A. M. E. Church, one of the best
Negro Printing Houses in the country. Leaving there, when he left, about fifty thousand dollars worth of assets consisting of a complete outfit,
machinery, type and fixtures and the plant out of
debt.

In June 1908 he was re-elected President of Allen University, a position which he occupied for
two years, 1898-99, before he was elected General
Officer. He served Allen University as President
for four years, 1908-12. At the General Conference
in 1912 he was elected Bishop with 406 votes, the
largest amount of ballots ever cast for a bishop in
the A. M. E. Church. As Bishop he was assigned to
Arkansas and Oklahoma, the twelfth Episcopal
District of the A. M. E. Church. In 1916 at the General Conference which met in Philadelphia, he was
assigned by that body to his home State, South
Carolina, the seventh Episcopal District of the A.
M. E. Church. He received the degrees of A. M., D.
D., from Allen University and the degree LL. D.
from Campbell College, Miss. He was elected
President of Allen University twice, elected Trustee of A. U. 1887, and elected to the General Conference the same year, to which position he has
been elected for thirty consecutive years. He is
now President of the Educational Board of the A.
M. E. Church, and President of the Trustee Board
of Allen University.

ALLEN UNIVERSITY

Allen University, a Co-educational Institution,
under the auspices of the African Methodist Episcopal Church, was founded in 1881.

Departments: College, Normal Grammar School,
Music, Sewing, Theological, and Printing.

During the thirty seven years existence of this
institution over two thousand graduates have gone
forth into public service from the various departments, reflecting credit, upon themselves, the race,
and the institution.

The yearly enrollment is approximately six hundred and fifty.

The denomination, in this State, raises, yearly,
between twenty-five and thirty thousand dollars
for the maintenance of the school.

ROBERT WESTON MANSE. A. B., A. M. D. D.

 EV. Robert Weston Manse was born at Coksbury, S. C., September 27th, 1876, in the Old Paine Institute, an institution operated under the auspices of the African Methodist Episcopal Church, in South Carolina.

His father was the station pastor of the A. M. E. Church at Coksbury during the operation of the Paine Institute and was a charter member of Allen University that grew out of the Paine Institute.

The mother of this subject was Charity Ann Nash, the youngest daughter of the historic Nash family of Coksbury, Abbeville County, who, alone, struggled, after the death of her husband to secure funds with which to educate Robert, her eldest son.

His early training was had in the Public School at Newberry, S. C., subsequently entering Claflin University, Orangeburg, S. C., and graduating from the Collegiate Department, with the degree of Bachelor of Arts, in the year 1899.

Shortly after his graduation, he was elected Principal of the Newberry High School, which position he held for eight consecutive years.

He was converted in 1889, joined Miller Chapel A. M. E. Church, Newberry, S. C., joined the ministry at Greenville, S. C., December 1902 and served the following charges:

New Miller Mission, Sulada Old Town, S. C., 1904; Jalapa Mission, Jalapa, S. C., 1904, six months; Enoree Mission, 1905; St. Paul Circuit, Chapin, S. C., 1906; South Carolina Conference; Georgetown Station, Georgetown, S. C., 1907-9; Presiding Elder, Beaufort District, 1910-15; Pastor Mt. Zion Station, Charleston, S. C., 1915-16; President Allen University, S. C., 1916-18.

Dr. Manse was elected Chairman of the South Carolina Conference delegation to the General Conference at Kansas City, Mo., 1912, a delegation to the Centennial General Conference at Philadelphia, Pa., 1912, and Chairman of the State delegation.

He is now President of the A. M. E. Connectional Council, which position he has held for the past two years.

He married Miss Elizabeth Clara Grimes, of Newberry, S. C., April 12th, 1902, and to them have been born five children; Evelyn Frederica, Robert Weston, Jr., Charity Marguerite, Nerissa Terrell, and Mercer Montgomery, the first four of them being under fifteen years of age and now in school.

Other positions which he has held are Past Chancellor Meridian Lodge Masonry, Grand Prelate K. of P., Jurisdiction of South Carolina.

COPPIN HALL ADMINISTRATION BUILDING ALLEN UNIVERSITY COLUMBIA, S. C.

315

J. W. WILLIAMS

 ULY third, 1884, in Pittsburg, Pennsylvania, there was born a little boy who was destined to use all three sections of this great country in getting his training for life. This lad was J. W. Williams. While he was born as far North as Pittsburg, Pennsylvania, it was in the extreme south, Holly Springs, Mississippi, that he received his education. Here in Mississippi he took his chances at education with the other colored boys of Holly Springs. While the school lasted he received pretty good instruction, but it was soon closed and the boy was thrown upon his own resources, and received a great portion of his education in the school of experience.

At an early age he developed an aptness with mechanical tools. But he was unable to enter a trade for his training. This did not restrain him from following the bent of his inclination and developing the talent he felt that he possessed. Being denied the privilege of obtaining it in the industrial schools, he sought it in the various work shops where he served as a laborer. He made the best of his opportunities and in time received a pretty thorough education in mechanism.

He lost his parents while quite young. His father died when he was only two years of age, and his mother followed his father to the grave when he reached his thirteenth year. Thus early in life he was left to shift for himself, so his training in the practical school of the every day work shop was rather an advantage than otherwise as it provided for his sustenance while he learned his trade. His mother had trained him to stick to his task until he had mastered it, and the memory of this training together with his natural ability caused him to hold to his work with great tenacity until he became proficient in the line in which he was engaged. The exhibition of these qualities in either man or boy usually bring a sure reward and it was so with

young Williams for today he is highly regarded as a very thorough and reliable mechanic.

Having in mind the desire to learn the art of mechanism rather than earning a livelihood, Mr. Williams did not confine himself to one city or to any section of the country, but went from place to place as his judgement and opportunity dictated, finally locating in the far West, not as a laborer, but as the owner of a large Auto shop, where he is putting into practical use the information he learned in the various shops where he had worked. It is now his turn to employ labor and to direct it which he does with a master hand, but with a consideration he did not always enjoy. He keeps in his employ six men as master mechanics. But remembering his own boyhood and young manhood, he gives employment to the unskilled and allows them to gather from watching the others as much as possible. In this manner, Mr. Williams endeavors to help others along, as his own experience had taught him that a kind and encouraging word is a help to any man who is trying to rise.

This auto shop of which Mr. Williams is the owner and manager is fifty feet by ninety feet. Here he has sufficient space to do a great deal of work. Besides being interested in his work at the shop and the work of the men under him, Mr. Williams has taken time to do some real estate work. In 1914, he was appointed by the Town Site Company to sell the Skidmore addition at Tulsa, Oklahoma. This he did at a great profit to himself.

Mr. Williams is a member of the A. M. E. church. Here he gives of his time and of his means to the support of the Gospel. In all the undertakings of the denomination he is ever ready with his support. In fraternal orders he is a Mason. This as elsewhere is in itself a recommendation for the worth of the man in the community.

Ably assisted by Mrs. Williams, Mr. Williams has been successful in starting other business concerns that come more directly under the control of Mrs. Williams. There is the Dreamland Theatre and the Williams Confectionery. These are told of more fully in the sketch of Mrs. Williams.

Mr. Williams was married to Miss Lula Cotton, March 10, 1901, at Tulsa, Oklahoma. There is one son who is now a high school student. He helps to make life happy for his parents and lends incentive to their working so hard in their various lines of business.

WILLIAMS AUTO REPAIR SHOP

MRS. J. W. WILLIAMS

HAT back of every man who is succeeding, either in the business world, the literary world, or political world, there is an efficient woman, is one of the sayings that we hear a great deal. Whether this be true or not it is not for us to decide. But it does hold good in the case of Mr. and Mrs. J. W. Williams, of Tulsa, Oklahoma. Mrs. Williams was born February 12, 1878, at Jackson, Tennessee, Madison County. Here, as Lola Thomas Cotton, she spent her childhood and young womanhood. In Madison County she attended the public school till she had gotten from them all that they could give her. She then entered Lane College, where she remained to complete the course of study offered there. June 2nd, 1898, she was graduated from this institution.

Not entirely satisfied with her training, Mrs. Williams went to the Agricultural and Mechanical College, at Normal, Alabama. Here she took her industrial training. She entered the classes offered in dressmaking and in millinery. From these she received her certificate in 1903.

For a number of years Mrs. William taught school in the rural districts of her native State. She had an abundant chance to develop her powers as an executive. Not only as an executive was she developed in the rural work, but as a close business woman as well. For the teacher in the rural district has to be all things to the people with whom she makes her home. After a number of years she left Tennessee and went out to Oklahoma. Here she taught for some time. But after working for a time in the school rooms of Oklahoma, she decided that she could do more with her life in the millinery and dressmaking trade. To this end she worked in this line for three years. In the meantime she had married Mr. Williams, and they were anxious to go in business. From the proceeds of the millinery and dressmaking establishment she

managed to save enough to open a large moving picture house. This they have run ever since. At present they own and operate the Dreamland Theatre. This is in a large two-story brick structure, at 127 N. Greenwood Avenue, Tulsa, Oklahoma.

But the running of the Dreamland has not taken all the time of Mrs. Williams, nor all of their money and so she, with the aid of her husband have opened the Williams Confectionery Store, on one of the prominent streets of Tulsa. This store is housed in a three-story brick building, which is owned by the Willams'. In addition to the two businesses mentioned here in which Mrs. Williams is interested, there is the Auto business that belongs strictly to her husband and seven lots in the city which have not as yet been improved.

To the church of her choice, Mrs. Williams brings her business ability and her strong personality. She is a member of the C. M. E. Church, and is ever ready to do for it. She gives her time, her money and her influence to the betterment of this church. She is Captain of the Lane College Club. In this organization she is able to render aid, both directly and indirectly to the College, which is in a large measure responsible for her training. Not to cut herself off from her people, in any line of endeavor, we find Mrs. Williams working as a member of the Eastern Star Lodge. She is also a member of the S. M. T. Lodge. In both of these lodges she has held positions of honor and trust. And in them she has proven herself worthy of the trust put in her.

For her health and on business trips, Mrs. Williams has traveled over the greater portion of the United States. This travel has served to broaden her and render her of greater service to her people wherever she has worked.

She was married to Mr. J. W. Williams, in Tulsa, Oklahoma, March 10, 1909. To them has been born one son. He is now a young man in the High School. To her husband, Mrs. Williams has always been a very great help. In all matters of business she has been able to give advice.

Though still a young woman, Mrs. Williams has spent a great number of years serving in the interest of her race. She, through her teaching has been able to reach hundreds of young people, who are better off for having come in contact with one of so positive a character.

WILLIAMS' DREAMLAND THEATRE

WILLIAM H. CROGMAN, A. M., LITT. D.

R. Crogman was graduated from Atlanta University in 1876, having made an enviable record for industry and thorough scholarship. He has since been honored by the degree of Doctor of Letters, the only degree of the kind ever bestowed by Atlanta University. About the time of his graduation there was established in South Atlanta Clark University, which was destined to become one of the strongest and most influential of the schools of the Methodist Church for the Negro race. He was immediately called to a position on the faculty of this institution, where he has remained working quietly and faithfully until this day. For seven years, 1903-10, he was President of Clark University, and under his wise and careful administration the work grew continually in numbers and strength.

Affiliated with Clark University and located nearby is Gammon Theological Seminary of the Methodist Church. Dr. Crogman is a charter member and the Secretary of the Boards of Trustees of both these institutions, the only Secretary they have ever had. The records have been kept with great accuracy and in a marvelously regular and beautiful hand. For twenty-nine years he was also Superintendent of the Sunday School of Clark University and during all that time was not once tardy. His work brought him into relationship with the larger field of the Methodist Church. He was

three times a member of the General Conference. He was also for eight years a member of the University Senate of this church, and afterwards a member of the commission for the Unification of the Book Concern.

In 1878 he married Lavinia C. Mott, a graduate of the Normal School of Atlanta University of the class of 1877. They have a family of eight children, for all of whom their parents have provided a good education. Their family life has had a beautiful influence upon the institution in which their life work has centered.

As a teacher Dr. Crogman has been remarkably successful. He is a born teacher, loving his work, and his power rests not only in his thorough familiarity with the subjects but in his strong personality. During the past thirty-five years thousands of students have come under his influence, and many lives have been strengthened for useful service.

As a public speaker, Dr. Crogman's power rests in his quiet dignity, the beauty of his diction and the clear and forceful treatment of his subject. He has a deep and musical voice and an irresistible sense of quiet humor. His addresses have been collected into book form under the title of "Talks for the Times." When a new edition was brought out in 1897, many favorable book notices appeared in the press. The Atlanta Journal for February 13, 1897, comments as follows:

"All the subjects of these talks relate to the Negro race. They show marked ability, research, excellent literary finish and have the ring of sincerity from end to end."

Perhaps no stronger evidence of the force of Dr. Crogman's character can be found than the high esteem in which the citizens of Atlanta of both races hold him. There is absolutely nothing undignified or servile in his speech or bearing. He is fearless in his denunciation of all unfairness to the Negro race and yet seems never to have aroused the antagonism of the white South.

Who can measure the good which a man of this stamp accomplishes? In him are combined the qualities of courage and of faith. In the preface of his volume of addresses as well as its dedication to his children, he has given utterance to the principles which have characterized his life work and which make him so powerful an influence for good. In the preface he says: "All the subjects treated are such as relate to the race with which I am identified. In the discussion of these subjects I have endeavored, whatever may have been my success, to use candor and moderation, to condemn the wrong where I have seen the wrong, and commend the right where I have seen the right, regardless of the section of country in which the one or the other has appeared."

T. GILLIS NUTTER

Gillis Nutter was born at Princess Anne, Md., June 15, 1876. His parents were William and Emma Nutter, ex-slaves, who were highly respected for their strength of character and industry. While uneducated themselves they were great lovers of education and made many sacrifices in order to give their children an education.

T. Gillis Nutter attended the public schools of Princess Anne and graduated from the high school thereof, in 1892. Being one of eight children, he was put to work at the early age of nine years, splitting wood with his father, who had a monopoly on sawing fire-wood in his native town. Young Nutter soon became the champion wood-sawyer in his town, sawing a cord of wood a day and attending school. He would go to work at five in the morning and saw until 8:35, run all the way to school, about a mile from his home, eating breakfast as he ran, and return to his saw-horse, immediately after school was out. He decided to give up "Old Pomp," as he called his old saw-horse, and left for Philadelphia, June 4, 1896, and worked at Old Gerard Hotel until the fall of 1897, when he entered Howard University Law School, having been inspired to take up the study of law by the eloquent appeals of Judge Walter L. Dixon and Joshua W. Miles, to hear whom argue a case, he would steal away from school. He was graduated from

Howard in the class of 1899, being one of the big four of his class.

His father having died a few months after his graduation, he was forced to return to Princess Anne to look after his mother, to whom he was greatly devoted. He was principal of one of the graded schools of Fairmont, Md., for two years, declining the third appointment in order to enter upon his profession. He was admitted to the Marion County (Ind.) Bar Nov. 13, 1901, but being without sufficient means to carry him through the starvation period, he was forced to return to the hotels for a short time. On March 12, 1903, he received a telegram from his boyhood friend and classmate, R. S. King, to come to Charleston, W. Va., to assist in the trial of the famous Guice murder case. Guice's friends felt confident that he would go to the gallows, but the brilliant defense of his young attorneys, reduced his offense to voluntary man-slaughter. The eloquent and forceful plea of Nutter attracted wide attention and brought him quite a clientele. His rise dates from the Guice case and today he enjoys a lucrative practice.

His greatest criminal triumph was the skillful handling of the Campbell Clark rape case. For four days he faced a seething-blood-thirsty mob, but with unfailing courtesy and a fearlessness that challenged admiration, he calmed the mob and got his client off with conviction of attempted assault.

Only one poor white man in the entire town dared face the mob, aside from Nutter.

It is generally believed that Gov. Samuel W. McCall, of Massachusetts was greatly influenced in reaching his decision in the Johnny Johnson extradition case by the State of public mind in the Clark case.

He has appeared as Chief Counsel in the three most noted murder cases tried in Kanawha County in the last fourteen years.

His work has not been confined to the criminal side of the court as he has appeared as advocate in numbers of chancery and land cases involving thousands of dollars and has been generally successful. He is Grand Attorney of the Knights of Pythias and numbers of other corporations, including the Peoples Exchange Bank, white, for which institution he has made a number of investments.

He is a Mason, Knight of Pythias and an Elk. For three years he was Grand Exalted Ruler of the Elks of the World, and the Order witnessed a wonderful growth under his administration. He is quite active in civic matters, having led the fight against the Birth of a Nation, taking the case to the Supreme Court of Appeals, which court, by an evenly divided vote, over-ruled his motion to dissolve the injunction granted by the Circuit Court, prohibiting the Mayor and Chief of Police of Charleston from interferring with the exhibition of the photo-play.

He edited the Mountain Leader, of Charleston, W. Va., for several years and gave the paper a standing in the journalistic field.

He is a Methodist and founded the first colored Y. M. C. A. in the city of Charleston and was its president for several years.

Mr. Nutter owns a beautiful home on one of the aristocratic streets of his home city, as well as other valuable property in Kanawha County.

Payne University, Selma, Alabama

PAYNE University, Selma, Alabama, is owned by the six Alabama Conferences of the African Methodist Church. It is a State Institution to the extent that it is supported wholly by the Colored Methodists of the State in which it is situated. Governing this school there is a Board of Trustees that numbers 125 members. Each Trustee is expected to contribute at least ten dollars a year toward the support of this institution. This yearly donation from the Trustees, the support of the A. M. M. Conference and Sunday Schools and the tuition fees represent the total income of the school. This amounts to about $6,500.00 yearly.

The school was founded in 1888, and has grown to be such a large and notable institution that it stands today as a monument to the Self-Help of the Colored people. It originated with them—they built it and they have maintained it, and they may be excused for pointing to it with a commendable pride at what they have achieved.

The courses offered to the people are elementary and secondary. The elementary work is done in the sixth grades and in two additional years. Of the attendance the greater portion of the pupils are in the elementary classes. These students are for the most part children of public school age who live in Selma. In the Higher classes are about sixty pupils. There are seventy-five boarding pupils in the dormitories of the school. The pupils above the eighth year are designated as "Normal" or "College" students. The course includes: Latin, 4 years; Greek, 1 year; German, 1 year; English, 4 years; Mathematics, 7 years; History, 2 years; Economics, 1 year; Psychology, 1 year; Education, 1 year; Physiology, 1 year; Elementar Science, 3 years.

The land owned by the school comprises a city block conveniently located for school purposes. There are two large buildings and several small cottages on the grounds. They have a total valuation of $24,000.00. The academic building is a two-story brick structure and contains classrooms, chapel and offices. The girls' dormitory is a three-story frame building. The smaller cottages are used for teachers' homes and for dormitories for the boys. The school is managed by the President and seven teachers. This represents a great deal of work on the part of all the people connected with the institution. Each person is called upon to do more than one distinct thing in the running of this organization.

Being a church school, Payne is also a school in which young men aspiring to the ministry can go for training. The course offered to the young minister is such that while getting the theological training needed, he can at the same time get a more thorough preparation in the other branches of study that go to make up the well-rounded minister. Because of this fact, a man is not barred from the theological course because of lack of book knowledge, but is taken in and trained in all the subjects at one and the same time. This makes the course of study more or less complicated, but even in spite of this the teaching in this branch of the school is effective.

At the head of this institution and responsible for its development to his church and for its finances to the trustees is Professor H. E. Archer. President Archer is a man well fitted to the duties that have been his since he took charge of this school. He is a graduate of Olivet College, Olivet, Michigan. From this College he took the degree of B. S. He later took a post graduate course and received the degree of M. S. Not satisfied with his preparation he then took special work in the University of Chicago. After leaving school he went to the Agricultural and Mechanical College, at Normal, Alabama. Here for a number of years he served as head of the Department of Science, and at the same time was special assistant to Dr. Council, the founder of that Institution. Under Dr. Council he got the training that fitted him for the duties of an Executive. At the death of Dr. Council, Professor Archer was considered for the Presidency of that school, but went instead to take the Presidency of Payne University, in Selma, Alabama.

Mrs. Archer is a very capable woman. She has been of great service to her husband in his work in the Payne University. She is also connected with the National Colored Woman's Association. To the school she brings the experience of years of teaching in the Agricultural and Normal College at Normal, Alabama.

Payne University stands as a monument to the Colored people of Alabama, especially to the A. M. E. Church. They do a very effective work that is felt all over the State.

RESIDENCE OF JOHN BROWN BELL

OHN Brown Bell, business man and public servant, was born in Tombabaro County, Georgia, December 25, 1858. In his early youth he migrated to Houston, Texas, and attended the public school for a while in that city. In 1881, after spending a few months in Tennison College, of Austin, Texas, he withdrew and entered business.

His apprenticeship in business was spent behind the counters of the grocery store of Rubin and Thorton, in Houston. At the end of one year, Mr. Thornton, having died and his wife wishing to sell, Mr. Bell bought the business for $315.00. Now when Mr. Bell came to Houston he had worked for a man for $5.00 per month. From this employer, Mr. Bell borrowed $250.00 to invest in the business. In three years and four months he had made enough from this undertaking to purchase property, which brought him $200.00 a month, not counting a number of vacant lots. This opened his eyes to the possibilities of real estate. Hence he sold his grocery business, geting $500.00 for it, and staked his future on dealing in real estate and in building and selling houses and stores. Today he owns forty nine rent houses, which include the store in which he made his first business venture as a grocery clerk. These buildings are valued at $125,000, and yield him an income of $500.00 per month.

Looming far above this is John B. Bell, the public servant. He appears to have taken a sort of an inspired view of his talents in business and of his wealth, looking upon it all as merely a fee in trust. This contact in business and the position gained by his wealth soon set him apart in Houston, giving him a hearing and an entre, not according to the common run of men of either race. In this he was as quick to see the opportunity to serve his people as he had been to detect a good sale in real estate.

Probably in no one part of his career does this appear clearer than in his dealing with the Emancipation Park, a Negro City Park, of Houston. For fourteen years he was member of the Board of Trustees of this park. In 1915 Mr. Bell and others entered suit against the park Board, alleging that the ground was insolvent and would be sold for debt, thus being lost to the colored people. In the meantime, the Mayor of Houston, Ben Campbell, who is a close friend of Dr. Bell, appointed him manager of the park for two years. As soon as this appointment became effective, things at the colored park took on new life. At the solicitation of Mr. Bell, the Mayor authorized the building of a park house with cement floors and drop curtains all around to shield the people in case of bad weather, also the building of three restaurants, the establishment of public sanitary toilets and the construction of gravel walks. Plans for all this have been drawn up awaiting the approval of the City before the work is begun.

In 1910, E. J. Scott, of Tuskegee Institute informed certain citizens of Houston that Mr. Carnegie would give the city a $15,000 Colored Library if the city would guarantee $1500 a year for up-keep. Once more Bell was called into service and delegated to see the Mayor of the City, then Mayor Rice. The Mayor agreed if the Negroes of Houston would buy the ground, the city would vote the up-keep fund. Mr. Bell was appointed chairman of the committee to raise the money to purchase the site. The colored people appointed him chairman of the committee to raise the money to buy the ground. In six months, Mr. Bell had received $500.00. He loaned the $1000 necessary to hold the property. In six months he had raised the $1000 to repay the loan. On April fourth, 1913, the library was dedicated. J. B. Bell was made treasurer of the Library Association.

Houston now discovered another demand for this public servant. In 1915 the Mayor of the city appealed to the colored people at the Carnegie Library to aid the city in doing charity work. Immediately Bell was made chairman of the Negro branch of this undertaking. He leased the former home of Emmett J. Scott, fitting it up as a modern hospital and established there a clinic for the colored people. In this way he divided his time and his energies, giving about one third to his own personal affairs and two-thirds to the public service. No wonder when Booker T. Washington was to tour Texas, J. B. Bell was chosen from among the able Negroes of the "lone star state" to manage the trip.

Mr. Bell was married in 1900 to Miss V. Nora Allen, the daughter of Hon. Richard Allen. Since the above was written, Mr. Bell has passed away.

JOHN T. GIBSON

LOBBY ENTRANCE & TIKET SELLER'S BOOTH

TWO cities of America will always be historic for the Negro; they were among the earliest places of refuge, they have fostered his welfare even to this day. One of these is Boston, the other Philadelphia. The "Hub" early had Negroes within her precincts, and though the Puritan was a stickler for the letter as well as for the spirit of the law, he almost invariably gave in a bit when the Negro was involved. So true did this become in Boston that at times it appeared to one's advantage to be colored.

Philadelphia, however, proved a happier home for the Negroes. There they had a wider range of intellectual and social freedom. A great many remained there and established themselves as leading citizens, notwithstanding the fact that they were persons of color.

Coming thus to the front they put up stores, established businesses, took an active part in city government, built handsome churches, hospitals and schools; with this result, the Negroes of the Quaker City usually get a representative not only in the city, but in the State government. Here in Philadelphia he stands upon his merit alone.

A product of this environment, one who stands as an example of the type of business men possible to the race we have John T. Gibson, who is one of the remarkable men of modern times, who within a very short time and with a small capital has made for himself a fortune that is rated at $600,-000.00. This is indeed a very great achievement. Born in Maryland in 1878, he received his education in Baltimore. He finished the courses offered by the public schools of that city after which he entered Morgan College. While there he applied himself diligently to his studies, and even then was a young man of great promise. Well may Morgan be proud of this son who received his inspiration within her walls.

After leaving Morgan College, Mr. Gibson engaged in a number of business enterprises before he decided upon his present career. He was always successful in whatever he undertook, and when one day it came his chance to purchase a small theatre he grasped the opportunity, for he saw far in the future, and right from the first, began to lay plans that meant the development of the finest theatre in the country owned and managed by a colored man.

Mr. Gibson has one trait of character which served him well in the development of his scheme. He is a patient man. So step by step he developed his idea, never hurrying things but always directing the course they took, so to-day, after his first venture he has invested in the Gibson New Standard Theatre half a million dollars! The building in which this sagacious man invested his money and is making 100 per cent on the investment has helped make a world-wide reputation for him. It is located on South street at twelfth, the third greatest business street in the city, and this great big structure can be seen glowing with its myriad of lights, throwing into bold relief the

EAST PROMENADE

WEST PROMENADE

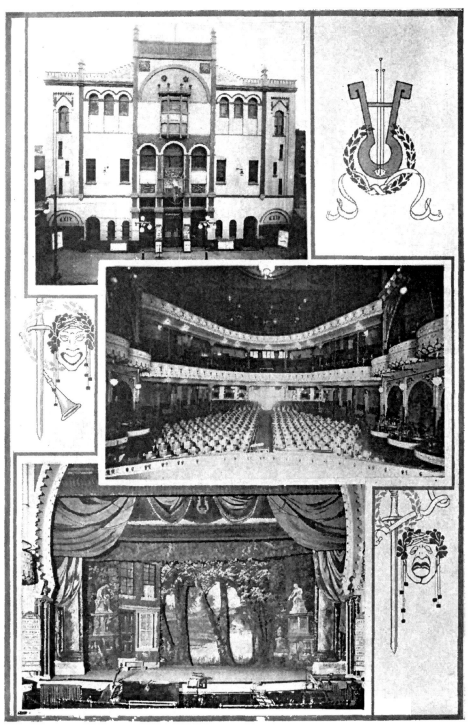

GIBSON'S NEW STANDARD THEATRE—EXTERIOR FRONT VIEW—INTERIOR VIEW FROM STAGE—
INTERIOR VIEW FROM ORCHESTRA

JOHN T. GIBSON'S PRIVATE OFFICE

TREASURER'S OFFICE

beautiful design of the exterior while the interior with its beauty of gold, purple, marble, and tints of rose, looks like fairy land. Out of all the theatres in the city, of which there are 59, Gibson's New Standard Theatre is the only one owned and run by a single person, and he is also the first colored business man in the history of the city to make so great an investment in property. The theatre has an ideal location as it is accessible to all lines of cars which radiate in every direction.

Mr. Gibson in his social hours is a good companion and a humorous one. He is very clever in applying his jests to illustrate a point. His shrewdness, sagacity and promptness have won for him an enviable reputation and many seek his counsel.

Mr. Gibson married Miss Ella Lewis, of Chester County, Pennsylvania, a highly cultured woman, coming from one of the oldest families in the state, and with her tender, lovable disposition and business acumen she makes an ideal help-mate; she surrounds her husband with ties that are the truest and most tender that a noble woman can create about a home. Indeed the home of the

Gibsons is one of the most beautiful in the northern part of the city. Its beauty of architecture is not surpassed by the beautiful home life within.

Mr. Gibson is a public spirited citizen. Everything for the betterment of his people always interest him. As his means grow so he continues to grow and shares his fortune with others. His hand is open and his heart is warm.

What a difference a few years makes in the career of an ambitious and energetic man. A few short years ago John T. Gibson was practically unknown, to-day he is known all over the world having reached the top round of his managerial career. It is not often it can be said with genuine verity that an event marks an epoch. The people of Philadelphia bow at the shrine of the man who has made it possible for them to have the finest play-house in the country to witness the best that the amusement world affords and out of which he has made a name and a fortune. Mr. Gibson is a member of the Masonic order and a true Mason at heart.

STENOGRAPHER'S OFFICE

LADIES' ROOM SECOND FLOOR

THOMAS H. PINCKNEY

HOMAS H. Pinckney was born in Columbia, in 1863, on the campus of the old South Carolina College. As early as age would permit, he entered the Howard Public School, of Columbia, and continued his course until he was ready to enter South Carolina College, where he remained until the law of separating the races in school compelled him to leave.

Somehow, he grasped the principle that any work was honorable, that only idleness was a curse. For a while he shined shoes; then he sold newspapers; then he bought and sold rags and bones, an occupation sneered at by the masses of men. From this he took to peddling. He would go hunting and catch rabbits, squirrels and birds. Immediately he dressed these, put them in a basket and peddled them out. He went fishing. Once more he filled his basket and became a walking fish wagon. Then his ingenuity discovered a way to coin extra pennies while an apprentice in a white barber shop. Mr. Pinckey found himself getting theory on the front and practice out back in the wood shed. Working for the white people in the front he would every little while step out in the back and cut the hair of, and shave his Negro friends at half price. In a little while his clientele in the wood shed yielded him not only a larger income than that he received in the shop, but larger than that of any man working in the shop.

He then opened a shop for Negro customers. A few years proved that his first shop was too small. He sought larger quarters. Again his shop became too small and again he changed. This was repeated several times before he could accommodate the hosts of customers who poured into his parlors.

The shop made another contribution to the life of Thomas H. Pinckney. In the old shop lay a fiddle. It was stroked by musicians and no musicians. Mr. Pinckney took his turn at this violin. In a little while he discovered that he had musical talent of the first order. He cultivated his talent in music and soon he was not only training young Negro barbers, but also Negro musicians. He organized choruses, he conducted orchestras, both of which brought snug sums to his coffers and more business to his establishment.

Known widely as a man of business and of talent he began to receive suggestions for local improvements in business and in accomodation. One day a young man noticed at a funeral that the White undertaker was none too considerate. This was the basis of an argument for a Negro undertaking firm, with Mr. Pinckney as the senior member. Forthwith the young man was dispatched to New York to learn the business. He returned, passed the required State examination, and organized the firm of Harly, Pinckney and Briggs, whose capital was $1,500. The firm was soon able to buy its own building and established a branch at Greenville, S. C., and already plans other branch houses.

Finding this buisiness very attractive, Mr. Pinckney has made a special study of embalming, and in 1915 passed the State examination as an embalmer.

From his business he has accumulated some ready money and much real estate in his native city. He owns his home, several vacant lots and rent houses. With his business and real estate he finds time for membership in several organizations and for some volunteer services. He is a Mason, an Odd Fellow, and a Good Samaritan. He is an active member of the Zion Baptist church and a clarinet player in the choir.

Mr. Pinckney was married in 1885 to Miss Lottie M. Howell, of Conguill, South Carolina. Two daughters have been born and reared in the Pinckney family. Miss Beatrice Pinckney is now Mrs. Alonzo Hardy and Miss Theosina is now Mrs. Louis Gaten. Fifty odd years lie upon Mr. Pinckney as he keeps in close contact with all the Negro life in Columbia.

ALEXANDER ARTHUR GALVIN, D. D.

LEXANDER A. Galvin, was born May 12th., 1869, on a farm near New Glasgow, Amherst County. Virginia. Prior to his birth his father followed the carpenter trade, but having a large family, most of whom were boys he decided that he could sustain and rear them better in the country than he could in town, so he gave up the hammer and saw for the plow. Thus it was that Alexander Galvin was country bred and got his early training on the farm. Here he learned to follow the plow, swing the axe, and form an intimate acquaintance with animals, plants, streams and mountains and here he formed those habits of thought which finally led to his conversion and entrance into the ministry. He was converted at the age of seventeen, and early felt the call to preach, but his father needed him on the farm, so he had to be satisfied for a while with such preparation as he could get from the public school at New Glasgow. He made the most of this and laid a good foundation upon which he built until better educational advantages were within his reach.

He remained on the farm with his father until he reached his majority, and then decided to yield to the divine call to preach, and left home, in order to earn the money to pay his way through college. He realized that he could not do his best work without a course of preparation and he determined to use every exertion to secure it.

That he succeeded is not surprising, and in the course of time he was enabled to enter the Virginia Theological Seminary and College, at Lynchburg, Virginia, where he graduated with honors from the Academic and Theological courses in May 1897.

Shortly after graduation, Dr. Galvin was called to the pastorate of the Ebenezer Baptist Church Staunton, Va. In this field he labored until June 1902 when he accepted a call to the Loyal Street Baptist Church, Danville, Virginia, where he still pastors. Thus Dr. Galvin has spent twenty years in two pastorates, which puts him on the exceptional list from the viewpoint of long pastorates. He has worked intensively rather than extensively, becoming one of the people, and not a sojourner, where he has preached.

He and his wife are property owners in Danville, having a city lot there on which is built a two story tenement house. As he worked in the city so has he worked in his state. He was Moderator of the Berean Valley Baptist Association four years and has been the President of the Virginia Baptist State Convention four years. The latter position he still holds.

President Galvin presided at the golden jubilee meeting of the Virginia Baptist State Convention. July 10th-15th, 1917, on Seminary Hill, Lynchburg, when the Woman's State Educational, the Sunday School and Baptist Young People's Union State Conventions all met in joint sessions and $13,698.31 was raised, in cash, for education and missions.

While Doctor Galvin has not been an extensive traveler, other than much travel in his native state upon business incident to his interest, office and calling, short trips into the middle west, the far south, and the eastern states constitute his record in this direction.

In Clifton Forge, Virginia in 1897, Doctor Galvin was married to Miss Janie Penn Toles of Lexington, Va. They have three children, in the persons of Misses Susie C. and Elizabeth and Master G. Alexander. In May 1917 Miss Susie, at the age of 18 years, graduated from the Normal Department of the Virginia Theological Seminary and College, while G. Alexander a lad of thirteen and Elizabeth a child of seven are attending the High School and graded school respectively in the city of Danville.

In 1906, Rev. Galvin was honored by his Alma Mater with the title of Doctor of Divinity. And he is generally regarded as one of the leading preachers of his race and denomination.

WILLIAM VIVIAN CHAMBLISS

William Vivian Chambliss

SOONER or later most people visit Tuskegee. That this is true is due to the fact that from its founding it has stood for things of an advanced nature for the colored people of this country. It is the greatest institution operated by Negroes in the world and has from the first used a system of education that is now being copied by schools in all parts of this country and other countries. And so daily there are men and women who seek the school. Some seek inspiration, some knowledge, that they may run a school on similar plan; some seek information on how to handle colored men in mass and some seek to know how the much advertised agricultural department is run, and how well the men who have gone out from this department have been able to fit into rural life. Whenever the question of rural life comes up and a concrete example is wanted of a Tuskegee man who has made a success of his life in the country—those in authority point, and they point with pride, to W. V. Chambliss, who lives only a few miles from the school.

Mr. Chambliss is an example of the man who made a success of his life on his native soil. He was born in Macon County, Alabama, Dec. 4th, 1866. He received his early training in the rural schools of his country and then entered Tuskegee Institute. From this school he was graduated in 1890. As a lad, Mr. Chambliss was poor. He not only did odd chores, but during the summer he mined coal at the tender age of seventeen, and worked in the steel plants as well. In this way Mr. Chambliss got his first lessons in handling money.

The summer after his graduation, he taught school in Macon County. The school term was short and the pay small. He was then employed by Tuskegee Institute as an instructor in the brick masonry division. This work was not to the liking of Mr. Chambliss either. When the school stood in need of a trained man to take charge of the live stock that they were gradually acquiring, Mr. Chambliss was chosen as the man who had natural ability along this line. He was sent to Hampton Institute where he received a special training in the subject. He then returned to Tuskegee and took charge of the live stock of the school. In this capacity he served the school for ten years. During this time he so conducted his division, and so handled his duties that he had the implicit confidence of Dr. Booker T. Washington, the Founder of the school. Because of this confidence, which he won by marked ability and faithfulness to duty, Mr. Chambliss stands today an example of the successful planter and a successful business man as well. Mr. Robert C. Ogden and Mr. Alexander Purvis, two Northern philanthropists, organized a stock company under the laws of New York and purchased several thousand acres of land in Macon County. This land was to be sold on easy terms, long time payments, to colored people. They opened a general store where these farmers could trade and they bought up the necessary stock to work

the land. Five thousand acres of land represent a big tract and $75,000.00 represents a big investment. These men, Mr. Ogden and Mr. Purvis, sought the advice of Dr. Washington when they wanted a man to take entire charge of this undertaking. Dr. Washington recommended Mr. William Vivian Chambliss, the subject of this sketch. That he made a success of the undertaking the records of the company will show.

The plan was to sell off the land in forty acre lots to colored farmers. Not only did Mr. Chambliss seek the purchasers and sell the land, but he served in the capacity of general guardian and advisor. He supplied them with live stock, tools, farm implements, fertilizer, groceries and other supplies. He built their homes, marketed their produce for them and helped them settle their accounts. As Superintendent of the Southern Improvement Company, the name of the organization, he became responsible for the people living on the land. The unsold land was cultivated by him and by renters. In his management of the enterprise he evinced great executive ability. Although the Company was of philanthropic nature, he paid the stockholders 6% annual dividends, and received himself a salary and 5% of the net earnings of the company. He bought and operated with a partner, A. J. Wilborn, a colored man of Tuskegee, 1700 acres of land. From time to time he invested in other tracts of land. In 1913 he bought from the company 1000 acres of the land owned by the Southern Improvement Co.

After eighteen years the company dissolved. At that time Mr. Chambliss bought all the unsold land that remained of the original tract. He bought the store, the gin, all the live stock, implements, equipment, etc., and assumed all the company's liabilities. Thus after eighteen years of service for the Company we find him sole owner of the Company's holdings.

In all his business dealings Mr. Chambliss never once gave a mortgage and only once in his life borrowed money from a bank. In the Liberty Loan Drive Mr. Chambliss bought $30,000 in Bonds and $1000.00 in War Savings Stamps. He was the largest purchaser of bonds in Macon County regardless of color. He owns 3000 acres of land, 2000 acres of which he cultivates and advances to 120 plows; operates a general store that does between $20,000 and $24,000 business annually; owns and operates a cotton gin that handles as high as 11,000 bales of cotton annually.

Mr. Chambliss is a member and a trustee of the A. M. E. Zion Church, of Tuskegee, and served for a long time as steward of the church. He is a Mason, he was several times State delegate to the National Republican Convention; he was speaker for the graduates of Tuskegee Institute at the First Memorial Exercise held in honor of Dr. B. T. Washington. He subscribed $800.00 to the Booker T. Washington Memorial Fund, which was one of the largest donations made by colored people. He has traveled in all parts of the U. S., and to some places in Canada. He is unmarried; he lives in his own home with his sister.

JOHN J. STARKS. D. D.

 T falls to the good fortune of but few to found and establish on a sound business basis one institution, administer its affairs for a long time, then take over the presidency of another. Such, however, has been the fortune of President John J. Starks, President of the Morris College, at Sumter, South Carolina. Leaving his Alma Mater on graduating in 1898, he went into South Carolina, and one year later, 1899, founded the Seneca Institute, at Seneca, South Carolina.

The founding of Seneca Institute was no easy task. There was no money, no building, no land on which he could begin to build. The school was opened in a frame building which measured thirty-six feet by forty feet. It had but a handful of students and exceedingly meagre equipment. For thirteen years the young founder worked away, now begging for land, now for money, for a building, now for equipment, now for students, now for salary for teachers. At the end of this period he had accumulated property and buildings for the Seneca Institute, worth thirty thousand dollars. He had an enrollment of two hundred and thirty-

five students, one hundred of whom were in the boarding department. He left the institute at the close of a thirteen years administration, free of debt. In 1912, he was elected President of Morris College, in Sumter, the position which he still holds.

President Starks was born in South Carolina, in Greenwood, April fifteenth, 1872. He attended school in his native state until he was ready to go away to further his education. Choosing Morehouse, in Atlanta, he was graduated there in 1898. Ten years after graduation, in view of his service of education, Benedict College conferred upon him the honorary degree of Doctor of Divinity. He is a member of the Executive Board of the Baptist State Convention, and is one of the leading denominational educators and thinkers of South Carolina. President Starks was married in 1897, to Miss Julia A. Sherard, of Anderson, South Carolina. She has been a strong second in all the uplift works of her husband.

MORRIS COLLEGE

This Institution was founded in 1905, by the Baptist Missionary and Educational Convention, of South Carolina. It is controlled by a Board of Trustees elected by the Convention. It is a school of elementary and secondary grade. The elementary work covers the usual elementary grades. In the secondary work emphasis is placed on the ancient languages and mathematics. One teacher gives all his time to languages, teaching Latin, Greek and German. The other subjects offered in the four-year "preparatory" course and the two-year "college" course, are English, History, Bible, and Chemistry. A few of the girls take sewing.

The school has twelve teachers, all colored; three male and nine female, the teachers are well trained. It has an enrollment of about sixty. In addition a few ministers attend irregularly. Its sources of income are from Baptist Churches, tuition and fees and from the boarding department.

The plant consists of eight acres of land on the outskirts of Sumter, valued at $5,000, part of which is used for truck gardening; buildings valued at $18,500, consisting of three large frame buildings, one comparatively new and the others in fairly good condition, and the movable equipment, which consists of furniture for class rooms and dormitories and a few farm implements. The movable equipment is valued at $1,500.

President Starks is giving to the college the benefit of his fine executive ability and profound mental training, and under his management the school is showing marked signs of development. It is his purpose and plan to make it one of the best schools in the land.

REVEREND EPHRIAM MELMUM SEYMOUR

EVEREND Ephriam M. Seymour,
pastor of the Rogers Memorial
Baptist Church, Knoxville, Tennessee, was born in Fayette County, Tenn., in 1873. When yet a
small boy he was possessed of the
desire to do something for his people that would
be worth while. For a desire of this character to
enter the heart and brain of a mere lad bespoke a
career of great usefulness and was prophecy of a
life of note. This desire became intensified with
his growing years, and after a careful survey of the
field which offered to the colored youth avenues
of service, he was led to concentrate his mind upon
the Gospel ministry. He realized that Christian
religion was the foundation stone upon which to
build character and that if built upon any other it
could not stand the test of temptation and adversity. He wished the best for his people and felt
that if he could help them lay a good foundation
for their life work, he would make a contribution
for their development which would be worth while
and meet the dream of his early childhood. It was
this line of reasoning together with the influence
of the church which led him to his life work.

He had seen the evil effects of ignorant preachers presiding over the churches of his people and
was fully persuaded that the time had come when
the men who offered themselves for that sacred
office should be prepared for their work. He knew
that he was not prepared educationally for the
work of a minister and he decided that his first
step was to secure an education.

The fact that his parents were not in a position
to give him financial aid and the knowledge of the
hardships which faced those who had to educate
themselves, did not deter him from his purpose,
but rather served to strengthen his determination
and nerve him to his task, encouraged and sustained, no doubt, by the noble end he had in view.

He began his school life in the public schools
of Sommersville. From here he made his way
in the Baptist College, at Memphis, Tenn., from
which he was graduated in 1900. On finishing from
the college, he entered Roger Williams in Nashville, for a course in theology. None of these
courses came to him without struggle. All through
his school life he worked early in the morning and
late in the evenings and at spare times to earn
money for his board and lodging.

Completing his college work and his studies in
theology he began pastoral duties at Franklin,
Tenn., occupying the pulpit here in the First Baptist Church. Spending two years in Franklin, he
was called to Shelbyville, Tenn., where he remained one year. From Shelbyville, Rev. Seymour
went to Mt. Olive, Clarksville, Tenn., where he
was pastor for five years. Thence he accepted the
pastorate of Holly Grove Baptist Church, Ripley,
Tenn. From Ripley, he came to Knoxville to the
Rogers Memorial Church, where he is now pastor.

The bulk of his work has been done at the Roger
Memorial Church, of Knoxville. He accepted the
call here when every thing about the church was
ebbing rather low. The old church had gone, the
new was started, merely started. Enthusiasm and
money were rapidly diminishing. Rev Seymour
took hold, rallied the forces, organized communities to secure more funds, and completed the Memorial Church. This task he looks upon as coming
nearer to fulfilling his early visions of service than
anything else he has thus far undertaken.

Mr. Seymour was married in 1906. Mrs. Seymour was formerly Miss Lizzie Saunders, of Memphis, Tenn. Sadie B. is the only child in the Seymour household. She is eight years of age.

Mr. Seymour has translated his vision which
came to him in early life, into an effective and loving service for his people.

GASTON ALONZO EDWARDS, M. S.

E hear of Negro physicians, Negro school teachers, Negro dentists, Negro merchants etc., but seldom find one who has made his mark as an architect.

Professor Edwards is a notable exception, his gifts as an architect being recognized by both white and black. While occupying a high place in architecture he also stands high as a scholar.

Professor Edwards was born in Belvoir, North Carolina, April 12th, 1875. Passing through the common schools he entered the Agricultural and Mechanical College at Greensboro, North Carolina, and completed his education at Cornell University, Ithaca, New York.

In 1901-1902, he established the Mechanical Department of the N. C. D. D., and B. Institute, at Raleigh, North Carolina. In October of 1902, he accepted the position as teacher of Natural Science and Superintendent of Men's Industrial Department of Shaw University, which position he held for fifteen years.

While at Shaw University his fame as an architect spread throughout the country and brought him into conspicious note as a designer of buildings. He was the first Negro to design and construct buildings for the American Baptist Home Mission Society.

His work as an architect is not confined to his own race, but because of his strict adherence to the three F's in architectture, fit, firm and fair, he enjoys a liberal patronage of the white race as well.

On March 9th, 1915, by an act of the General Assembly of North Carolina, all architects were required to be examined, licensed and registered in order to practice Architecture in the State of North Carolina.

He successfully passed the Board and has the distinction of being the only licensed colored architect in the State.

On June 12th, 1912 he was commissioned by Hon. W. W. Kitchen, Governor of North Carolina, as a delegate to the third annual session of the Negro National Educational Congress held in St. Paul, Minn., July 1st., 1912.

He received the degree of Master of Science from his Alma Mater, May 27th, 1909, being the first graduate of that school to be so honored.

In the spring of 1917, by unanimous vote of the Board of Trustees of Kittrell College, he was elected President, which position he now holds.

Under his administration the school has taken on new life and is destined to become one of the greatest schools for higher education of the Negro.

Kittrell College is located on the historic place known as "Kittrell Springs," in Vance County, North Carolina, on the main line of the Seaboard Air Line Railway, eight miles south of Henderson, and thirty-six miles north of Raleigh, the Capital, on one of the most beautiful sites in the country. It is 480 feet above sea level on a hill that slopes gently to the north and west, affording perfect drainage. The site contains 240 acres, with two streams flowing through it. Upon the school premises are two mineral springs, which prior to its purchase for a school site was known as a health resort attracting hither hundreds of tourists in search of health and rest.

Touching the history of Kittrell College, it is related that several years previous to the purchase of the property, Miss Louise Dorr, a faithful teacher from the North, conducted a Bible Training Class in connection with her school work in the city of Raleigh.

Several of the young men became enthusiastic over the studies and started to talk of better facilities. The matter was taken to the North Carolina Conference of the A. M. E. Church, and at once assumed definite shape, resulting in the proposition to establish a school at Kittrell, N. C. In 1885 the North Carolina Conference passed a resolution au-

DUKE MEMORIAL HALL—GIRLS' DORMITORY—KITTRELL COLLEGE, KITTRELL, N. C.

thorizing the establishment of a Normal and In-dustrial School, and appointed a Committee to se-lect a suitable site. In the selection of Kittrell the Committee secured one of the most desirable lo-calities in North Carolina. The leading spirit in the organization of the school was Rev. R. N. W. Leak, D. D., and associated with him were such men as Rev. George D. Jimmerson, Rev. J. W. Telfair, Rev. J. E. C. Barham, Rev. George Hunter, Rev. W. D. Cook, Rev. W. H. Giles, Rev. Henry Epps, Rev. Cornelius Sampson, Rev. W. H. Bishop, Rev. R. Lucas and Rev. J. C. Fry, who were under the Es-piscopal supervision of Bishop W. F. Dickerson. The first session began February 7th., 1886, with three teachers, Prof. B. B. Goins, Principal; Mrs. M. A. Goins, Matron, and Prof. J. R. Hawkins. Business Manager. The charter was granted by the Legislature of North Carolina March 7th, 1887.

The first Commencement exercises were held in 1890. In 1888, the Virginia Conference agreed to support this school and transferred its school in-terest from Portsmouth, Va., to Kittrell, said Con-ference being given equal representation on the Trustee Board.

In 1892, the General Conference in session in Philadelphia, Pa., changed the Educational Dis-tricts so as to add the State of Maryland and the District of Columbia to the territory supporting Kittrell Institute, and it now receives liberal pat-ronage and support from the entire Second Episco-pal District, viz: North Carolina, West North Car-olina, Virginia and Baltimore Conferences.

The school had a steady growth and its present status ranks it along with Wilberforce, Morris

Brown, Allen University and Paul Quinn; these five forming the first group of connectional schools. Its students come from several States.

The outlook is that Kittrell is destined to be-come a great educational centre, attracting hither not only hundreds of boys and girls, but families who wish to locate where the best educational ad-vantages may be enjoyed.

BUILDINGS

At present it has seven buildings: Shady Side Cottage, Northside Cottage, Orient Cottage, Fair-view Cottage.

DUKE-MEMORIAL HALL is a large four story brick structure with ample accommodations for two hundred girls, has modern conveniences and the very best arrangements for home and school life. It contains the college chapel, dining room, music room, parlor and offices.

THE PEARSON O'KELLY MODEL SCHOOL is a beautiful structure made of native stone.

THE MARTHA MERRICK LIBRARY is a modern building erected by the banker-philanthropist, John Merrick, President of the North Carolina Mutual Provident Association.

THE BOYS' DORMITORY AND CHAPEL BUILD-ING. The plans for these buildings to be con-structed of brick and stone at a cost of $50,000.00 has been raised already. When completed the dor-mitory will accommodate two hundred and fifty young men.

The Institution has its own water and sewerage systems extending through all the buildings.

LIBRARY—The Library contains many import-ant works of reference and is open daily.

ORGANIZATIONN—Elementary, normal, com-mercial, industrial, college, music and theological departments.

The elementary department comprises eight grades. The secondary work is done in the "Nor-mal" department.

REVEREND PRESTON TAYLOR

E often hear of self-made men and sometimes wonder what the expression really means. In essence it means that a man who in spite of adverse circumstances and meagre advantages has made a success of life and left an impress upon the world. Such a man is Rev. Preston Taylor, an eloquent preacher and a marvelous successful business man.

Rev. Taylor was born in Shreveport, La., November 7th, 1849, of humble parentage, in fact he was born into slavery. Little did his parents think when their baby came that they had given birth to a child who was destined to occupy a high place in the church and influence the business world. When one year of age he was moved from Louisiana to Lexington, Ky., the resting place of Henry Clay.

At the early age of four he sat in the First Baptist Church, Lexington, Ky., under the sound of the pious and impressive voice of Rev. Ferrell, which deeply impressed his youthful mind. He gave expression to this impression in a remark made to his mother, "Some day I'll be a preacher." His wise and good mother used every influence to deepen the impression. Under the fostering care of parents and religious friends he grew in the knowledge of the scriptures and was filled with the spirit of Christ. At the age of twenty-one he entered the ministry of the Christian Church, and ranks high in that denomination.

For fifteen years he was Pastor of a church in Sterling, Ky. When he took charge of the church it was in its infancy, and when he left it the membership had reached about eight hundred. Under his ministry the church erected one of the finest church edifices of the colored race in Kentucky.

His ability was so marked that his denomination felt that he should fill a larger field and so elected him as General Evangelist, a position he held for many years. About eight years ago he gave up his office as Evangelist to take charge of the Gay Street Church, in Nashville, and now in his declining years, he is the beloved and zealous leader of Lee Avenue Christian Church.

Like a number of great men his educational facilities were small, much of his information and knowledge having been acquired from observation and experience, and such helps as he could master himself. In a large degree his education is practical and his knowledge experimental.

In preparation for his ministerial work he received a few month's training in the Bible School in Louisville. Even this training was marked with great hardships which, however, were propellers rather than a hindrance to his development and advance.

We turn now to his business career, throughout which you can trace the pride of race and a desire to help his people. When the "Big Sandy" railroad, now operated by the Chespeake & Ohio Railroad, was being built the contractors refused to hire colored men, preferring white labor. Mr. Taylor, being a man of nerve and iron-will determined to pave the way for his people. He made a bid and fortune crowned his effort. He received the contract and then the difficult task was begun. It was one of the most hazardous undertakings ever attempted by a man of color. As is his usual custom he invoked the help of his Maker, and then with determination and energy he completed the job. He erected a large commissary and quarters for his men; bought 75 head of mules and horses, carts, wagons, cars and all the necessary implements and tools and with 150 men he went to work. He completed his contract in less time than the contract called for, receiving the contract price of $75,000.00, and the following words of praise from Mr. C. P. Huntington, President of the road: "I have built thousands of miles of road but I never before saw a contractor who finished his contract in advance.

This removed the prejudice of Negro labor and from that time it was sought instead of being rejected. He won his fight and enshrined himself in the affection and memory of the 150 men who he had succored by his resolute action.

Another evidence of his great business ability is the large undertaking business he has established. In the face of great opposition and acting under an impulse to see that his people were amply provided for in this line of their need he opened his undertaking establishment. He now has the largest establishment of its kind and does the largest business of any man of his race in the county. He has purchased for his business a large two-story brick building 42x180 feet, which he has converted into a model undertaking establishment.

Dr. Taylor married Miss Georgia Gordon one of the original Fisk Jubilee Singers, who presides with grace and dignity over his home.

In 1866, Dr. Taylor started without a dollar. He is now said to be worth not less than $350,000.

It seems that Dr. Taylor never tires of working, and planning for the comfort and welfare of his people. This sketch would be incomplete if reference was made to another enterprise of his which has done much to elevate the ideals of his race. No people can rise to a high state of refinement who neglect the resting place of their dead. Dr. Taylor recognized this fact and determined to provide a resting place for the colored people which would be keeping with the high ideals which he was trying to bring them up to.

He secured a plot of ground close by Greenwood Park, which he had provided for their recreation, and laid out a cemetery which will compare in arrangements, and beautiful surroundings with any in the land. It is sodded with grass and subdivided into lots and shaded with beautiful trees, and is conceded to be one of the most beautiful cemeteries in the whole country. An attractive arch way spans the entrance to the cemetery which makes a fitting entrance to this beautiful though silent city.

GREENWOOD PARK NASHVILLE, TENNESSEE

All men need recreation which applies with equal force to women and children, for the well-known aphorism "All work and no play makes Jack a dull boy," is a well recognized truth. There must be moments in the life of every one when work and the many cares of life can be set aside for a while and the mind given over to ease and diversion.

Possibly no better source of recreation can be found than a well regulated park with its attendant amusement auxiliaries. Such a pleasure resort is Greenwood Park. It is situated in one of the most beautiful suburban portions of Nashville, Tennessee, at a distance of only three miles from the city

on the Lebanon Pike. Electric cars run to it on regular scheduled time with privileges of transferring to all parts of the city for five cents fare. The situation of Greenwood Park is ideal for such an enterprise. It comprises forty acres of hills and dales, surrounded by clusters of ever-green that adorn the hills, for which Nashville is so famously noted, and is well shaded with numerous forest trees. A number of limpid streams flow through it, giving coolness to the atmosphere and adding to its beauty. These streams also afford abundance of refreshing drinking water thus combining pleasure with utility. Besides the many inviting walks and shady nooks provided by nature provision has been made for those who desire other forms of recreation. A club house, with restaurant and refreshment stand, a theatre skating rink roller coaster shooting gallery, box ball, knife cane and baby rack merry-go-round a zoo, and a base-ball park. A grand stand has been erected at the ball park which will seat several thousand persons.

This park is the home of the "Greenwood Giants" one of the "crack" baseball teams of the South. This team has crossed bats with some of the best teams of the country. The park is open day and night and is made unusually attractive at night by the glare and glimmer of hundreds of electric lights. The park is regarded with much pride by the colored population of Nashville, who give it cordial support visiting it in large numbers. The park is highly appreciated by the colored people generally and many important functions of the colored race are held there.

The "Tennessee Colored Fair Association" holds its annual meeting at Greenwood Park. For its accomodation a splendid track has been built for exhibiting stock and sufficient stable room, erected for the accomodation and housing of stock in large numbers.

The design of the Park is not alone for pleasure but also has an educational feature. A Chatauqua for teachers is planned for the summer season which will bring together a great crowd of the best educators and workers of the race. It is expected that this feature will attract teachers from near and far as well as others interested in educational matters. Then the 'Good Old-Fashioned Camp Meeting" has not been overlooked. Provisions have been made for that which lends additional attractions for this pleasure and educational resort.

Nashville has a Negro population of about forty thousand who will compare favorably with any community for industry and wealth, and who appreciate the value of such a Park as has been outlined. Their support of the enterprise has been so genuine and hearty that it has greatly pleased the management.

THOMAS PRYOR TURNER

HOMAS Pryor Turner, Principal of the High School, at Pulaski, Tennessee, was born near Selma, Alabama, in August, 1867. His parents were very poor. After his father died in South Alabama, his mother, with her five children, moved to Giles County, Tennessee. Thus at a tender age we find Thomas P. Turner with his mother, sister and brothers trying to earn a living from the soil. Young Turner remained on the farm till he was sixteen years of age, working at all the jobs of a farm boy when school was not in session, and getting a chance to attend the county schools whenever they were being taught.

Having gotten all in the way of book learning from the County Schools that he could, the young man entered Roger Williams University, at Nashville, Tennessee. While in Roger Williams he earned his way by teaching country school in the summer. In this way he managed to get his education. He was still in his teens when he began earning his living by teaching. So when he came out of Roger Williams he was already a teacher of experience. He secured work in the Pulaski High School. Here he served first as Assistant Principal, and was later given the Principalship. Here for twenty-seven consecutive years Prof. Turner has labored with the young people of Pulaski, and surrounding country, and here he still works.

That Professor Turner was bound to make a success of his life was evident from his early boyhood. He was willing to do any sort of work that would turn an honest penny, and having taken hold of any given work, he kept at it till success was his. He was at one period a book agent. This is one of the most difficult of all the known kinds of work and yet he made a success at it. He never let himself get out of touch with public affairs. To this end he spent his money for daily papers, and took the time to read them in order that he might know all that was happening in the world. Even after he took up the work of teaching, Professor Turner did other kinds of work. He deals largely in real estate and is the owner of property valued at more than $20,000.00.

He is an ardent supporter of the Fraternal Orders of his section of the country. He is Worthy Master of the St. John Lodge No. 19, of the Ancient Free and Accepted Masons, Member and C. C. of the Masonic Lodge, of the Knights of Pythias. Member and P. S., of the Giles County Union Lodge, Member and C. S. of the Zephoniah Lodge of Pulaski. Not only has he served these fraternal orders in their local meetings, but he has been for eighteen years Grand Secretary of the Grand United Order of Odd Fellows, and for four years Grand Auditor of this same order in America at Philadelphia, Pennsylvania. He is also Grand Auditor of the Masonic Order for Tennessee.

Professor Turner is an active member of the Bulah Baptist Church. Here he serves as a deacon and as the clerk. In the Sunday School he is the Superintendent. All the people of Pulaski know, love and respect Professor Turner. His influence, however, is not confined to the limits of his adopted town. He is known throughout the State of Tennessee, and in many parts of the country. He has traveled extensively in the United States and Canada.

Professor Turner was married to Miss Mary Agnes Bramlett, of Pulaski, Tennessee, on November 24th, 1892. Four children have been born to them. Three of whom are living, and the second one, Willis James Turner, died when only three years old. Miss Mamie A. Turner is a graduate from Fisk University. She finished the classical course and received the degree of A. B. At the same time she specialized in Education and so fitted herself very definitely for the task of school teaching. At present she is teaching in the Topeka Industrial and Educational Institute, Tokepa, Kansas. Thomas Pryor, Jr., is a Junior College student in Union University, at Richmond, Virginia. Edward Roosevelt is still a High School student.

BURRELL HAEMAN MORRELL

T is no disadvantage but rather the reverse for a man to be born in the country and spend his early days upon the farm. Cultivating the soil and breathing the fresh country air develops him physically and brings him into closer touch with nature and nature's God. It is a fact often noted that many of our great men came from the farm.

Mr. Burrell Haeman Morrell was born on a farm and spent his early life in the country and the love of the soil has clung to him through all his years. He was born near Elkton, in the Southern part of Giles County, Tennessee, December the 2nd, 1863, and this county has always been his home. His father died, when he was quite young, at a Federal prison in Mobile, Alabama, during the Civil War, and left him and his brother Albert a soldier's bounty of eleven hundred and forty dollars and a Government pension for their support. This bounty was a monthly payment from the Federal Government to the guardian of the heirs of the deceased soldier. The guardian paid out this money for the education and support of these children until they were sixteen and when they reached the age of

twenty-one the balance was paid to them in full. The portion coming to Burrell Haeman was four hundred dollars.

While working upon the farm he took advantage of the opportunity the rural schools offered for an education. While these did not carry him very far in mental development the training created in him a greater thirst for knowledge which took him temporarily from the farm to Fisk Unversity. He entered this Institution when he was sixteen years of age. He completed the College course, with the exception of Greek, at the age of twenty-seven, having attended the college about eight years. Three years of his time after first entering Fisk Unversity was lost from school on account of poor health. He adopted teaching as his life work, though the lure of the farm was still upon him and claimed a portion of his time.

After graduating from the Fisk University he was for five years the Principal of the McMinnville City school and for twenty years he has been and is now an assistant in the Pulaski High School.

When he was twenty years old he purchased a farm of eighty-five acres, which he operated for twenty-one years and sold for twice its cost. While actively working this farm he taught in the country school.

He is still a land owner and has two farms of considerable value. One of 101 acres he values at $8000.00 and the other of 178 acres at $6000.00. In addition to these he owns three houses and two vacant lots in the town of Pulaski, and one vacant lot in Washington, D. C. The value of his town property is about $2000.00.

With the exception of a homestead inherited by his wife from her parents, their property was acquired by the practice of the closest economy and self denial.

Mr. Morrell points with much pride to the part his wife has taken in aiding him to acquire property. They worked together with a unanimity of purpose and have sacrificed the comforts of youth that they might provide for the necessities of old age. Their aims and hopes were realized while still in their prime and they now enjoy not only the comforts of life, but many of its luxuries and are able to gratify a desire to make contributions for the uplift of their people.

Mr. Morrell was married to Miss Addie Florine Taylor, of Giles County, Tennessee, September 24th, 1896, which has proved a most happy marriage, the only cloud upon their union being the death of two of their children. One child, a boy, E. M. Morrell, has been spared to them, and they are giving to him the best of educational advantages.

JAMES DELBRIDGE RYAN

AMES Delbridge Ryan was born October 25, 1872, in Navasota, Grimes County, Texas, being the second of four children born to Huldah and James Ryan. He attended the Public Schools of Navasota, then administered by very excellent teachers, and entered the Prairie View Normal and Industrial College in September, 1889. From this institution he was graduated in June 1890. In October of the same year he was elected a grade-teacher in the Public Schools of the City of Houston, where he has been continuously employed since that time.

When the Colored High School was reorganized on the Departmental basis in September, 1900, he was selected as the teacher of Mathematics, and having thoroughly qualified himself by close application to study under private tutors and in Summer Schools, when a vacancy occurred in 1912, he was elected to the Principalship, with the distinction of having taught in every grade in the system through the four-year High School Course, excepting the first Primary Grade only.

During his administration the enrollment of the school has increased from 212 to 446, the number of teachers doing High School work only from 7 to 11, and the graduates of the school make the Freshman Year in some of the best Colleges and Universities in the Country. In a system that prides itself on being one of the best in the South, Mr. Ryan easily ranks among the first, and because of his ability as a school man he was elected President of the Colored Teachers' State Association in November, 1916.

His property holdings, excluding exemptions, consists of improved and unimproved city property, and securities, which are conservatively estimated at Ten Thousand Dollars. He is a member of the Board of Park Commissioners for Colored people through appointment by the Mayor, and is a member of Trinity Methodist Episcopal Church, now serving his fourteenth year as Superintendent of the Sunday School.

He is a member of the Ancient Free and Accepted Masons, the Colored Knights of Pythias, the United Brothers of Friendship and the Sisters of the Mysterious Ten, and of the Ancient Order of Pilgrims.

During the past 21 years Mr. Ryan has been the guiding genius in the development of the Ancient Order of Pilgrims, a Fraternal Beneficiary Association founded by Henry Cohen Hardy, who was joined in the incorporation thereof by Reuben Thornton and Joseph I. Rogers, October 23, 1882. The purpose of this organization is thus stated in the articles of incorporation:

"To promote industry, temperance and economy; to enable us to assist ourselves and each other and every member of said corporation while living; to provide for the increased expenses of life, the destitution of old age, sickness, misfortune, calamity and death; to leave our widows, mothers sisters, and children adequate support; to promote charity and benevolence, and to build and furnish halls for the use of this Order for these purposes."

The principal officers are B. H. Grimes, Principal of Dunbar School, President; James D. Ryan, Secretary; Jesse Washington, President of Guadalupe College, Treasurer; Dr. W. F. Warren, Tyler, R. G. Lockett and W. C. Conway, Houston, Trustees; L. D. Lyons of Austin, B. J. Mathis of Marlin, Texas, T. D. Mitchell, E. P. Harrison, and Van H. McKinley, members of the Supreme Council.

The Order has a membership of 5,600; Assets, $24,804.81; Surplus of $4,068.51, and has paid to beneficiaries of deceased members $297,000.60 within the past 21 years. A cash benefit is paid to members during illness, and at death a mortuary benefit of $480.00.

The last Actual Valuation of its Certificates in force December 31, 1916, indicates that the future net premiums to be collected, together with the invested assets, are sufficient to meet all certificates as they mature, by their terms, with a margin of safety of $90,486.14 (or 16 per cent.) over the statutory requirements.

Mr. Ryan was married to Miss Ella Sims in June, 1896. Mrs. Ryan is a native of Houston. She is a strong support to her husband in all his arduous undertakings.

338

WILLIAM LEONARD DAVIS

RACE advances only as far as its individuals. The colored people have been held down by the masses, because of their ignorance and their indifference to all the detail that make for a higher civilization. Very rapidly now this condition of affairs is being changed. This is being done through the schools, the churches and the fraternal organizations as well as through the influence of the better homes. One man who has done his share of this work in all of these lines is William Leonard Davis, of Houston, Texas.

William L. Davis, prominent in Texas as an educator and as a leader in secret orders, conspicuous in a state of conspicuous leaders, was born in Lavaca County, Texas, January 6th., 1873. Receiving his early education in the public schools of LaGrange, Texas, he entered Paul Quinn College, at Waco, Texas. To finish his training for the profession of school teaching, he enrolled in the Prairie View Normal and Industrial Institute, at Prairie View, Texas.

Completing his studies while still young, Mr. Davis went out as a teacher in the rural schools. Rural school teaching in Texas in those days yielded very good salaries, better by far than are paid today for the same work in other states. Out there among the country folk Mr. Davis soon became interested and active in the business undertakings of farmers and of all people who were working to invest in land. Soon he was promoted from teacher of rural schools to principal of the Hempstead City School. It was then he became Grand Secretary of the Farmers Improvement Society of Texas. This post he held for twelve years. This post, like the teaching in rural schools, served to place him in more important places. Resigning his position in the Hempstead City School and the Secretaryship of the Farmers Improvement Society, he became Grand Secretary of the Grand Lodge of the United Brothers of Friendship of Texas, and Assistant Principal of the Emancipation School at Houston.

School work now appears to give way to the thing the man seemed born to; namely ,the job of Secretary. For twelve years he served as Secretary of the F. I. S., at Waco. Then in 1915, he left Waco, and became Secretary of the State Grand Lodge United Brothers of Friendship, at Houston, a post which means the keeping track of ten thousand state members. He also accepted the port folio as secretary of the Baptist Sunday School State Convention

In order to be given the post of Secretary of the State Baptist Sunday School Convention, Mr. Davis had to be a very active member of the church. This he is beyond doubt. He is a member of the Baptist Church and an active member of the local Sunday School. Here he takes a great interest in the religious development of the younger generation, and all the young people love and respect him. To him they go with their questions and doubts and Mr. Davis never fails to give them the aid they seek.

His is a labor for humanity, a labor for the betterment of all his people. As secretary of the United Brothers of Friendship he has many an opportunity to lend aid to the bereaved and to give sympathy and good cheer to the sick. In fact all the activities of Mr. Davis have been of a nature to endear him to people; for years in the school room, in the lodges and in the Sunday School work.

In changing from place to place, Secretary Davis accumulated some valuable holdings in both towns and country. He owns his residence in Houston, one of the best colored homes in the city. Back in Hempstead, the scene of his earlier activities, he owns city property and a farm, consisting of seventy-five acres of land. He is also a stock holder in an overall factory in Waco, Texas.

In addition to his membership in the F. I. S., and U. B. F., Mr. Davis is a Mason, Odd Fellow and a Knight of Pythias.

Secretary Davis was married to Miss Emma R Sampson, of Carmine, Texas, in 1906. Mr. and Mrs. Davis live in their own home in the city of Houston. Here they help make life pleasant for their many friends. Although there are no children in the Davis family, they take great interest in other people's children and have the pleasure of seeing their young friends in large numbers at least on Sunday.

REVEREND S. A. BROWN

 HOSE who jest at the perennial "split" going on in the Baptist Church must pause when they come face to face with the Gillfield Baptist Church at Petersburg, Virginia. Organized in 1803, it has had but six pastors, having never had a division, and maintains to this day the practice of receiving, disciplining and expelling its members. It has a membership of 1500, among which are many of the most substantial Negro citizens of Petersburg. It carries a Sunday School of six hundred, under twenty-four teachers. It has a library of eight hundred volumes. Recently the church bought a parsonage for which it paid four thousand dollars. Its remodeling now under way will cost fifteen thousand dollars. It has no indebtedness and is valued at seventy-seven thousand dollars.

The history of the pastorates in the Gillfield Church is short, there having been but three pastors from 1803 up to the close of the civil war and but three since the close of the civil war. The first pastor, Dr. Henry Williams, after the civil war served for thirty-four years. He was followed by Reverend G. B. Howard, who served eleven years.

In 1913 the present pastor, Reverend S. A. Brown accepted the call to this venerable pulpit. He came of Baptist preachers, his father having been the first Negro minister in Virginia to be ordained. Unlike his predecessors, Reverend Brown is on his native heath. He was born in Ruthsville, Charles City County, February twenty-seventh, 1876. Reared on the farm, he attended the public schools, until he was nineteen when he left to seek funds to further his education. However, from his early youth he has had to earn a livlihood, for his father had died, leaving the mother with eight children, Mr. Brown being at the time but five years old. Reaching the Petersburg Normal and Collegiate Institute, he took both preparatory and college courses. Meantime he read theology under a private tutor. He commenced his ministerial work in 1902. For ten years he was principal of a school in Fredericksburg, Va., serving three country churches at the same time.

When he came to the Gillfield Church in 1913, he was ripe for the kind of work that lay before him. He had built one church, remodeled two, and had been in the habit of dealing with people who called a spade a spade. Thus when it became necessary to remodel the Petersburg building he knew what to ask for and how to go about the work of getting the money and plans.

During his career Reverend Brown has been able, though working against heavy odds, to purchase some property and join many helpful organizations.

He is a Mason, an Odd Fellow and District Moderator of the Baptist Association.

Reverend Brown was married in 1903 to Miss Clementine Poole, of Hampton. Six children have been born to Mr. and Mrs. Brown: Mildred O. Brown, age 13; Anna E. Brown, 10 years; Samuel H. Brown, 9 years; Lucile Brown, 7 years; Wilbur Hughes Brown, 5 years; Abraham L. Brown, 2 years. They are all in school, except the last named.

GILLFIELD BAPTIST CHURCH

BISHOP ELIAS COTTRELL, D. D.

Bishop Elias Cottrell, D. D.

OT to many men is it given to have the wonderful experience of Bishop Elias Cottrell, of the Colored Methodist Episcopal Church. When a lad of only four years of age he was placed on the block in Holly Springs, Mississippi, and sold at auction. He with all the other members of his family, was taken to the auction block. The father, mother, and seven children were all sold at the same time, and as was so often the case, they were sold to five different masters, and separated. Thus the lad was brought face to face with one of the direful effects of slavery. Some of these members of his family Bishop Cottrell has never since seen. Young as he was this scene was never effaced from his memory and had its influence upon his after life. In fact it was the most vivid memory which clung to him, and later in life when he came to do a noble work for his people in the establishment of a college, the site selected was within four blocks of the spot where he was sold at auction. The presence of this institution so near the spot, which marked the separation of his family, has no doubt mitigated the intense feeling of resentment which has rankled in his brain against an institution which caused his people so many heart aches.

Standing over against the block is the college, and the close proximity of the two, is a constant reminder to his people of the great change that has taken place in their condition. It is a contrast to the surroundings of his own youth and the opportunities to the colored children of today. He has no doubt pointed out to the students attending the college, the spot where he was sold, and urged them to take advantage of their improved conditions and make the most of their lives.

This one fact shows that during his lifetime he has used every opportunity that has come his way for his personal development and for the development of his people.

Bishop Elias Cottrell was born a slave in Marshall County, Mississippi, January 31, 1867. His father came from the State of North Carolina, and while living in that State, he had been given an opportunity to gain some knowledge of reading, writing and arithmetic. Being of a bright mind he had made the most of his opportunity and was thus providently prepared to instruct his young son, who inherited his wonderful mental endowment. His father taught him habits of studiousness that have served him well in his future development. It

was fortunate for Bishop Cottrell that in the separation of the family he remained with his father, and received his early training under his eye and guidance. As stated his father had secured some learning and this he imparted to his son, and when he had carried him as far as he was able, he aided him to obtain additional knowledge from other sources. For two years he attended a night school that was taught by a white man of German extraction. Little progress, however, could be made in this school for the facilities were very poor indeed. In the early seventies a number of well prepared teachers came into that section of Mississippi and Bishop Cottrell took advantage of this to get a thorough knowledge of the common branches. Under their instruction he made such rapid progress that his thirst for knowledge was greatly stimulated and he determined to seek wisdom from other and higher sources. To decide with him was to act, so he entered the Central Tennessee College, now Walden University, and took a two years course in English Theology. After finishing this course he did not consider himself an educated man but only beginning. He had acquired sufficient equipment to start upon his life work, but his career as a student would never end until his mind ceased to act. As a matter of fact, most of his hardest work along educational lines has been done since he left the class room. He has worked incessantly under private instructors until he has a good knowledge of Latin, Greek, Hebrew, and German, as well as ability along other lines.

In the year 1876 Bishop Cottrell began his career as a minister of the Gospel. From this year to 1894, when he was made Bishop, the subject of this sketch worked with a good will in all the capacities that are offered in his branch of the church. He was elected delegate to the first, second and third Ecumenical Conferences, and he has been elected to every General Conference of his church since he was eligible for membership in the year of 1878

He was for four years the one to collect all moneys that were used for schools under the jurisdiction of his church. This brought him very closely in touch with all the educational interests of his denomination. One direct result of this great interest in the uplift of his people through education is Mississippi Industrial College, which stands as a monument to Bishop Cottrell.

The school is located at Holly Springs, Mississippi, and has three very beautiful and substantial

buildings in which to work. These three buildings were erected at a cost of about $85,000.00. In addition to these three main buildings there are several smaller houses on the campus. In land the school owns two hundred ten acres which are valued at $30,000.00. The college has courses leading to the degree of Bachelor of Arts, Bachelor of Science, Thelogical course, business course, and industrial courses. In this school Bishop Cottrell has been able to gather many men and women of great worth, to associate with him in this work.

Throughout his life, Bishop Cottrell has been a good business man. He has managed his own affairs and now is worth several thousands of dollars. He is a good farmer as well as a great educator and a great Bishop. To him many honors have come. The degree of D. D. was given him by Rust University, Holly Springs, because of his great worth to the community, to the church and to the country at large. He is recognized as one of the great leaders of the race and in this capacity has done a wonderful work for the down-trodden race.

Bishop Cottrell was married June 6th, 1880, to Miss Catherine Davis, of Columbia, Tennessee. To him she has been a wonderful helpmate. Through all the steps that led to the present exalted position now held by him she has been a great source of inspiration and to her he gives credit for much of his success. One daughter, Mrs. C. Gillis, Jr., has been to the Cottrells a constant source of delight. She was educated in Holly Springs, and at Walden University, Nashville, Tennessee. She is now the teacher of music in the Mississippi Industrial College.

At this writing Bishop Cottrell is in the early sixties. In this time he has been able to accomplish a great deal for the uplift of colored people. He can be pointed out as an example to men in many walks in life. To the farmer he is a good farmer, to the business man, a successful example of business management, to preachers a good preacher, and to all his people, a great Bishop.

He has put his best into every undertaking and has conducted his work with characteristic energy and uprightness and has won the respect and love of all whose lives he touches.

CHARLES C. SPAULDING—JOHN MERRICK—AARON McDUFFIE MOORE, M. D., LL. D.

O find a better locality than Durham, North Carolina, for the beginning of a Negro business concern of any high standard, would be a difficult task. Here the colored people work together and help build up all worthy causes among this people; here the relation between the races is exceedingly good, with the result that a number of good business men and women too, have been encouraged to establish themselves in Durham.

The North Carolina Mutual and Provident Association with its home office at 112-122 West Parrish Street, was founded by John Merrick, in 1898. When they opened their office for business it was without capital and in a rented office furnished at a cost of $15.00, and paying a rental of $2.00 per month. This was in 1899. Six years later they erected the present home office at a cost of $35,000.-00. When the company began business it was as a Mutual assessment life insurance company, but in 1909 the charter was amended and the assessment feature eliminated and the business placed on the regular old line legal reserve basis.

In 1899, the company had a weekly debit of $29.00. Today it collects on industrial business alone over $12,000.00 per week and on ordinary premiums over $100,000.00 per year. For the year 1917, the company collected over $625,000.00, paid out in sick and death claims, $231,283.83, and closed the year with assets amounting to $372,000.-00, and with liabilities amounting to $270,000.00. This figure includes the net reserve according to the American Experience Table, and 3 1-2 per cent interest, $258,918.00. This leaves in unassigned funds or surplus, $87,562.46, and Insurance in force, $11,157,472.00.

The company has not confined its operations to Durham nor to North Carolina. But as the business grew it sought larger territory. So we find the North Carolina Mutual now operating in both North and South Carolina, Georgia, Virginia, the District of Columbia, Maryland, and Tennessee.

The company issues policies from $5.00 to $5,000.00 and in a few years will be able to get up a table of Mortality, of purely Negro risks.

The Company is officered by John Merrick,

VICE PRESIDENT AND GENERAL MANAGER,
C. C. SPAULDING'S OFFICE

CASHIER'S OFFICE.

Founder and President; A. M. Moore, Secretary-Treasurer and Medical Examiner; C. C. Spaulding, Vice-President and General Manager; E. R. Merrick, Assistant Secretary; J. M. Avery, Assistant Manager.

The company has prospered because is was founded upon correct business principles and because it was managed by men of great business and executive ability who have given their best thought and effort to its development. They have made no move without wise consideration and when a policy was decided upon they have given their time, and energy to its presecution. While the officers are busy men and it would seem had enough in their business life to engage their whole time and thought, they are also Christian men and prominent in church work, uplift work, and civic affairs, and recognize that they owe an obligation to the church, and the community in which they live.

JOHN MERRICK

John Merrick, the man whose brain conceived and whose energies made possible the North Carolina Mutual and Provident Association, was born in Clinton, Sampson County, North Carolina, in 1859. He did not have the advantages of much training in the school room, but got his training in the school of experience. He began his career as a brick mason, but moved to Durham at the age of 22, and started in the barber business. Of this work he made a great success. In fact success seems to be the keynote of Mr. Merrick's character. He was considered one of the most successful barbers in the South, having amassed quite a fortune from this trade.

In 1898, he founded the North Carolina Mutual and Provident Association, at Durham, and he still serves as the chief executive of this company. In addition to looking after the affairs of the Mutual, he is also president of the Mechanics and Farmers Bank, Supreme Grand Treasurer of the Royal Knights of King David, and President and Director of the Lincoln Hospital Board.

Mr. Merrick does not give all his time to business. He is an active member of the St. Joseph A. M. E. Church. In this church he serves as president of the Allen Christian Endeavor, and as a Trustee. In fraternal matters, Mr. Merrick is a Mason. He has traveled to all points of importance in the United States and in Cuba. In 1879 he was married to Miss Martha Hunter, at Raleigh, North Carolina. Five children were born to them to give them an incentive for better living—Mrs. Dr. P. H. Williams, Raleigh, North Carolina; Mrs. Dr. Wm. H. Bruce, Winston Salem, North Carolina; Mr. E. R. Merrick, Assistant Secretary of the North Carolina Mutual and Provident Association; Mr. John T. Merrick, Jr., Real Estate Agent, Durham, North Carolina; and Miss Martha C. Merrick, Durham.

In establishing the widely known company of which he is president, Mr. Merrick became a great benefactor to the race. Not only does he make it possible for men of color to obtain insurance with ease, but he has furnished good employment to many of our young men and women.

AARON McDUFFIE MOORE, M. D., LL. D.

Dr. A. M. Moore, Secretary-Treasurer and Medical Examiner of the North Carolina Mutual and

GENERAL OFFICE.

Provident Association, was born near Whiteville, Columbus County, North Carolina, September 6, 1863. As a lad he attended the Public Schools of Columbus County, the State Normal, Fayetteville, North Carolina., and later entered the Leonard Medical School, of Shaw University, Raleigh, North Carolina. From this school he was graduated with the degree M. D., in 1887, having completed the four years course of study in three years. That he was thoroughly prepared for the profession of his choice was shown when he went before the board of examiners. He stood second in a class of forty-two. He is a very successful physician.

Dr. Moore was in the organization of the North Carolina Mutual and Provident Association and has been one of its officers ever since. He is the founder and Superintendent of the Lincoln Hospital, of Durham, Director of the Mechanics and Farmers Bank, Durham; Director of the Oxford Orphan Asylum, Oxford; Secretary of the Extension Department of the State Teachers' Association; member of the Executive Board of Shaw University; Founder and Superintendent of the Durham Colored Library.

Dr. Moore is an active member of the White Rock Baptist Church, one of the most successful churches of the denomination. He is chairman of the Deacon Board, and Superintendent of the Sunday School. Through the medium of the Sunday School he is able to come in contact with many of the young people of Durham, and so to impress them with his excellent example. Dr. Moore is a Mason. He has traveled extensively in the United States, Cuba and Haiti.

In 1889, Dr. Moore was married to Miss Cottie S. Dancy, at Tarboro, North Carolina. There are two beautiful daughters in the family, Miss Mattie Louise Moore, Durham, and Mrs. E. R. Merrick, also of Durham.

CHARLES C. SPAULDING

Mr. C. C. Spaulding, Vice President and General Manager of the North Carolina Mutual and Provident Association, was born near Whiteville, Columbus County, North Carolina, in 1874. He attended the Public Schools of Columbus County and the Whitted High School, at Durham. After graduating from the high school course, Mr. Spaulding was for years a merchant, doing at the same time, agency work for the North Carolina Mutual and Provident Association. In 1900 he was elected Director and General Manager of this Association. In this capacity he served for five years, when he was elected Vice-President. Mr. Spaulding serves also as a member of the Finance committee and a Director and Cashier of the Mechanics and Farmer's Bank and he is a director of the Lincoln Hospital Board.

Mr. Spaulding is a Deacon and Treasurer of the White Rock Baptist Church and Assistant Superintendent of the Sunday School. In 1900 Mr. Spaulding was married to Miss Fannie Jones of Washington, D. C. There are four children in the Spaulding home. Miss Margaret Louise Spaulding, age 16, is a student at Scotia Seminary, Concord, North Carolina; Charles Spaulding, Jr., age 11, and John Aaron Spaulding, age 8, are pupils in the Durham public schools. Booker B. Spaulding is still a baby at home, being but three years of age.

His wife is not only a congenial companion but has been a great help to him. She is in full sympathy with his efforts to rear their children so that they will fill positions of honor and usefulness.

It can be said without fear of contradiction that the foregoing triumvirate not only set a splendid example for members of their race, but have proved to be a powerful force for the elimination of racial prejudice and gaining the respect and co-operation of the white citizens. And it is by selecting such men as leaders, that the Merchant Princes of Durham have been induced to contribute so liberally to colored hospitals and educational institutions.

CHARLES WADDELL CHESTNUT

HARLES Waddell Chestnut, author, was born at Cleveland, Ohio, June 20th, 1858, son of Andrew J. and Maria (Sampson) Chestnutt. Both his parents were natives of North Carolina. He attended the public schools of Cleveland until his father, after serving four years in the Union Army, returned to the South. In North Carolina, Charles attended the Public schools, and began to teach at a very early age, first as a pupil teacher, then, successively, in primary and grammar schools at various points in North and South Carolina. At the age of nineteen he was appointed a teacher in the State Colored Normal School at Fayetteville, N. C., and upon the death of the principal several years later was chosen to fill his place, in which he served acceptably for three years. At the age of twenty-five he removed to New York City, where he found employment in a Wall Street News Agency, contributing at the same time a daily column of Wall Street gossip to the "Mail and Express."

After a brief sojourn in New York he resigned and went to Cleveland, Ohio, where he became a stenographer and bookkeeper in the accounting department of the New York, Chicago & St. Louis Railroad Co. A year and a half later he was transferred to the legal department, where he remained two years, during which time he studied law and was admitted to the Ohio bar in 1887. He has never practiced his profession of the law very ac-

tively, his principal occupation having been that of a court and convention shorthand reporter, for which business he has for many years conducted an office with a staff of assistants.

Mr. Chestnutt's first story was written at fourteen, and was published in a North Carolina newspaper. It was intended to show the evil effects upon the youthful mind of reading dime novels. Beginning in 1884 he contributed many stories and articles to the periodical press. His best short story, "The Wife of His Youth," appeared in the Atlantic Monthly, in 1898, since which he has published "The Conjure Woman," (1899), a volume of dialect stories of plantation life in North Carolina, most of which had appeared in the Atlantic; "The Wife of His Youth," and "Other Stories of the Color Line" (1899); "The House Behind the Cedars" (1900); "The Marrow of Tradition" (1901); and "The Colonel's Dream" (1905). All of these books deal with race problem motives. Mr. Chestnutt is also the author of "The Life of Frederick Douglass," which forms one of the volumes of the Beacon Series of Biographies of Eminent Americans.

He was married at Fayetteville, North Carolina, in 1897, to Susan, daughter of Edwin and Catherine Perry, who has borne him four children. Two of his daughters are graduates of Smith College, another of the College for Women of Western Reserve University.

His only son is a graduate of Harvard University, studied dentistry in Northwestern University, Chicago, and is practicing his profession in Chicago. One of his daughters, Mrs. Ethel C. Williams, is the wife of Professor Edward C. Williams, of Howard University; another, Miss Helen Chestnut is a teacher in Central High School, Cleveland, and the third, Miss Dorothy Chestnut, is a teacher in the Cleveland public schools.

Mr. Chestnut is a member of the Rowfant Club, The Chamber of Commerce, The City Club, The Western Reserve Club, The Cleveland Bar Association, The Church Club, and the Council of Sociology, of which latter body he served one year as President. He and his family are connected with Emanuel Episcopal Church, on Euclid Avenue.

Mr. Chestnut has appeared upon the platform as a reader of his own writings and has charmed large audiences with the rare skill with which he handles the dialect of the North Carolina Negro.

The Washington Times says: "There was not a dull moment in the two hours spent with Mr. Chestnut last evening, and at the conclusion of the program he received the hearty applause and individual congratulations of his auditors."

From The Augusta Ga., Chronicle: "There have arisen many interpreters of the Negro character, but none have made him more humorous than Charles W. Chestnut in the various stories brought together in 'The Conjure Woman.' The 'Uncle Julius' who relates these stories of Negro superstition bids fair to become as popular as 'Uncle Remus' because of his rich, lazy dialect, his characteristic dark garrulousness, and his cunning consciousness of effect his yarns have upon his hearers."

The Christian Register, Boston, says: "They are like none of the other Negro stories with which we are familiar, and take an exceptionally high place both as a study of race characteristics and for genuine dramatic interest.

MACK MATTHEW RODGERS

OME men fall far behind the times; while there are others ahead of the times; then, too, there are many right along with the times. It is to this latter class belongs the subject now claiming our attention. His mind is ever opened to light and old-time dogmas are feasible to him only as they apply to the greater enlightenment of the present.

Mack Matthew Rodgers first saw the light of day July 13th, 1859, in Wharton County, Texas, where he grew to manhood. He is the only surviving child of Stephen and Lucinda Rodgers.

In 1878 he married Miss Caroline Jackson, and of the union were born six daughters and one son.

In the fall of 1878 Mr. Rodgers removed to Fayette County, graduating in 1881, with honors, from the Prairie View State Normal School. In 1887, having located at LaGrange, he was elected principal of the city school. His career as a teacher commenced at the age of sixteen.

Mr. Rodgers became interested in politics, and

for three successive terms—twice from his ward and once from the city at large—he was elected alderman of the city of LaGrange.

His political service and reputation soon extended over the state, and he was elected in 1888, 1892, 1900, 1904, and 1912, to the National Republican Convention. In 1897 he resigned the position of Principal of the LaGrange City School to accept the appointment, under Collector Webster Flanagan, of deputy collector of Internal Revenue for the Third District of Texas. He was the first Negro in Texas to hold such an office.

Mr. Rodgers is regarded as a good business man, a deep thinker, a close writer, a fearless but conservative debater, a sane and safe leader and a smooth but reliable politician. It is because of his manly qualities that he is recognized and respected by the people of his state.

He accepted Christ in 1879 and was baptized by Elder James Davenport. In religion, as in politics, he became active and manifested a lively interest in the work of the Church and in the development of denominational principles. In 1883 he was made secretary of the LaGrange Baptist Association—a position which he still holds—and in 1889 he became secretary of the Baptist Missionary and Educational Convention of Texas. To both organizations he has given his best thought and energies. For the last eighteen years he has striven to systematize the business and improve the financial status of the Convention and of its institutions of learning. To him, more than to any other person, credit should be given for incorporating the Convention. Its present healthy condition and splendid school regulations are also due to his efforts.

Mr. Rodgers is Auditor of the National Baptist Convention of the United States of America and is giving much attention to the affairs of the National Baptist Convention, and his opinions are attracting the attention not only of that body, but of Baptists throughout the country.

TEXAS PYTHIAN TEMPLE

About 1912 a peculiar current shot through nearly all big organizations of Negroes, especially in the fraternal bodies. This current asserted itself in the form of big buildings. In Atlanta, it was the Odd Fellows Building; in Macon, Georgia, the Masonic Temple; in Little Rock, the Mosiac; in Dallas, Texas, the Knights of Pythias. It was a capital instance of Negro readiness, of the Negro acting when he was equipped. The Archi-

PYTHIAN TEMPLE BUILDING,
DALLAS, TEXAS.

tects and Contractors were Negroes, Negro money paid the bills, Negro bookkeepers and business men managed the business, Negro business men, merchants and professional men occupy the rooms in these temples. Very clearly these structures represent a mile stone in Negro progress.

The Pythian Temple, at Dallas, is one of the brilliant mile stones. W. Sydney Pittman, son-in-law of Booker T. Washington, designed the sructure. S. A. Harper was the contractor, Dr. A. N. Prince, the Grand Chancellor, M. M. Rodgers, Secretary and Grand Keeper of Records and Seals, Grand Worthy Councellor, Mrs. A. M. Key, Dr. J. W. Anderson, J. M. Frierson, G. M. Guest, J. H. Hinds, Commissioners.

The entire building rising 76 feet in the air above sidewalk level, is constructed from the foundation to the roof with a complete non-vibratory steel frame and brick walls securely laid in cement mortar. The stairway and elevator hall is entirely fire-proof from top to bottom. In this hall way are two sets of iron stairs, each five feet wide all the way up, and a twelve passenger standard Otis Electric Elevator installed in a fire-proof enclosure. In addition to these stairway and elevator services there are also two sets of approved fire (stairway) escapes, located at two separate and distinct places of escape in case of panics or other emergencies.

Properly speaking, the building is five stories high; the first floor containing two large stories, three small "shops" and a large spacious cafe in the rear. On this floor is also a large well-lighted corridor and lobby leading from the beautiful stone and marble vestibule entrance.

On the second floor are seventeen suites of offices, each containing a private office and a re-

ception office. Ninety percent of the partition wall space on this floor is taken up with Florentine glass sash and transom. Spacious Corridors and Lobby provide ample means of exit and inter communication.

On the third floor are three large rooms and Anterooms, four robin rooms, ten sets of lockers, and corridors, and Lobby similar to those on second floor. One of these Lodge rooms is devoted mainly to the Dallas Knights of Pythias Lodge. Another (the largest), is set aside for the use of the Grand Court of Calanthe, and the third to be rented to lodges of other Orders. The Lodge rooms are equipped wih individual locker rooms for each tenant Lodge.

On the fourth floor is located the Grand Lodge (K. of P.) Auditorium, with its Committee Rooms, Ante-rooms, stairs, hall, lobby, rostrum and Mezzanine, toilet and dressing room. The Auditorium extends through the fourth and fifth floors—the clear height of the ceiling from main floor being twenty-five feet.

On all floors are provided separate toilets for men and women, conveniently arranged in plain view on all corridors. On the second and third floors in the lobbies is installed a drinking fountain for the benefit of the patrons. All offices, all stores, shops, lodge rooms, Ante-rooms, cafe, etc., are equipped with a lavatory and running water.

The building throughout, is lighted with the "Reflecto-lite" system fixtures, the very latest electric light fixtures on the market. All electric wires are laid in conduits arranged so as to produce the least friction possible to tenants. Electric fans are provided in all lodge rooms, exit lights at all exterior doors and two handsome bracket lamps on either side of the Main Entrance on Elm Street. All offices are also provided with a wall socket for buzz fan attachment.

Other special interior features include the beautiful color scheme on all floors and especially in the Grand Lodge Auditorium, also the great stage and its procenium,, and the seventeen large 8x15 feet windows in this Auditorium. This stage is typical of all theatre stages in essentials, including foot lights, border lights, scenery, dressing rooms, fly gallerys, electric switch board, etc.

A special feature on this floor is the separate Department (a suite of rooms) set apart for the Grand Lodge officers. It includes a private lobby, or reception hall, a private entrance and other appurtenances necessary in creating a distinct and separate grouping of rooms for its State Headquarters, particularly requested in the original conditions submitted to the architect.

COLONEL JAMES HUNTER YOUNG

Colonel James Hunter Young

ORN in Henderson, North Carolina, in 1860, Colonel James Hunter Young has served in and witnessed the deeds of well nigh two generations of American History. The young man got all he could in the way of book-learning in his home town and then entered Shaw University. Here he remained for five years. During this time he gave good account of himself, and although he left the institution before he finished his course of study, he now serves as President of the Alumni Association. This is indeed a great tribute to the time spent in the school and to the life of the man after leaving.

Young left Shaw in 1877, and immediately accepted employment as a federal officer. He became deputy Collector of Internal Revenue, holding the position for eight years. In 1886 he resigned the post and was made Registrar of Deeds at Wake County, North Carolina, which position he held for three years. The next four years saw him Special Inspector of Customs in the districts of North Carolina, South Carolina, and Georgia. In 1895, he became a member of the State Legislature from Wake County, North Carolina. Two years later he was State Inspector of Agriculture. This position he held till the Spanish-American War caused him to go to the front and here he was Colonel of the Thirty-second North Carolina Volunteers.

After giving his country such long service in the army, Colonel Young once more returned to private life, but he was not destined to give up the service of "Uncle-Sam," for he was immediately called into another branch of work by the United States Government. The excellent record he made in the Internal Revenue Department in 1877 had not been forgotten and he was again called to enter the revenue service as a Deputy Collector of Internal Revenue, a position he held from 1899 to 1913.

Although he has far passed the half century mark, he is ever ready to respond to his country's call. He rendered valuable aid in the Selective Draft, and did his "Bit" to win the World War for Democracy.

Thus we have recorded the work of a public man in a very brief form. Indeed from the entrance of the United States in the World War, this public spirited man gave freely of his time.

He was one of the Advisors and Workers in the Selective Draft, and he made one of the best speeches delivered in his section in the interest of the war. On this occasion he addressed a Mass Meeting of both white and colored citizens and he had for his theme "Co-operation in the War." Thus the veteran of the Spanish-American War served in the World War in a different way, but never-the less he served.

In religious belief, Colonel Young is a Baptist. He is very active in Sunday School work. For over thirty years he has served his denomination in an official capacity. He is the Clerk of the Baptist church and Superintendent of the Sunday School. His interest in Sunday School work has caused him to go beyond the limits of his home and take up the broader work of the State. Thus we find him Treasurer of the State Sunday School Convention of North Carolina.

Colonel Young has had time to devote to other organizations that work for the betterment of the colored race also. He is an Odd Fellow and serves this organization as District Grand Master. He is a Mason and serves the Masons of his town and State as Endowment Secretary and as Past Grand Master. He is a member of the order of the Knights of Pythias and in this body he served as Chairman of the Finance Committee. Colonel Young is also a member of the Eastern Star and of the Household of Ruth. Thus he gives his time to many organizations which work for the betterment of his people.

In business matters, Colonel Young is as wide awake and as active for the good of his people as he is in Church and Fraternal matters. So we find him serving as President of the Raleigh Undertaking Company, acting as a director of the Mallette Drug Company, President of the Masonic Benevolent Company and Director of the North Carolina Industrial Association. To carry on all these responsible positions, Colonel Young has to husband his strength and his energies. But he is always ready to serve when he is needed.

Colonel Young has been three times married. His first and second wives were natives of Raleigh. Miss Bettie Ellison and Mrs. Mary Christmas. Both are dead. The present Mrs. Young was Miss Lula Evans, also of Raleigh. The third marriage took place July 27, 1913. Colonel Young has one child a daughter, Miss Maud Electa Young. She is now married and is Mrs. Carter, of Winston-Salem, North Carolina.

Colonel and Mrs. Young live in their handsome two-story residence. Here they receive their many friends and help make life pleasant for Colored Raleigh. Colonel Young, a soldier, a Federal officer, in many positions; a leading church worker, a distinguished Mason and Odd Fellow, a member of the State legislature, a man of great business ability and a natural leader of men, is a man worthy of our praise and emulation.

Bert Williams

WHO in America has not heard of the "Follies?" Who, having heard of the "Follies" does not lean back and chuckle or laugh outright at the drollery, the wit, the surprising turn of humor, both in phrase and incident? The leading spirit of this company is Bert Williams. Now it is a song talked or chanted, now a dialogue, now an anecdote, now mere humorous manner. Address a letter to him in care of the Follies, or to the Follies in the care of him. Each would reach its proper destination. Each has contributed to the making of the other. It is a sort of compact—the "Follies" is one member of the firm, Bert Williams is the other.

The critics say that one evidence of the immortality of author's comes when the latter are quoted. If this be so the comedian of the Follies and of the famous Williams and Walker troupe can already lay claim to living beyond his generation. The Scotchman counts it a special mark of patriotism to preface his remarks with a quotation from "Bobbie Burns." The American Negro is no less proud, when wishing to embellish a jest to introduce or conclude with a saying or a situation from Bert Williams.

One has to speak of situation in discussing Bert Williams; for many, many times the whole success of the piece hangs upon the comical picture that he is able to conjure before the mind. Thus the parody on "Woodman spare that tree" hangs upon the vision of the rude male of the home rapidly ascending the tree to escape the dire punishment of an irate spouse. So with the goat story, "Wait Till Martin Comes and you aint Gwine Play 'dis game 'cording to Hoyle, but Cordin' to ME."

Harlenguin was comical on the stage, but a poor melancholy creature when left to himself. Not so is it with this man of the "Follies." In the street, in the office, everywhere, Mr. Williams bounteously gifted with good health, is always brim full of fun and good humor. And then that accent, who can immitate it? It is original with Mr. Williams.

He is one of the hardest workers on the stage. To see him toss off his jest one would think that the whole thing was easy and had come to him in a moment. As a matter of fact, he travels about with his note book constantly jotting down whatever chance remark he hears from passers by, and also the scraps of stories or plot suggestions that are brought to him as he goes about the city in the day.

Moreover, Mr. Williams has gone abroad to study under the world's best artists and keeps in close touch with these and with all the modern changes on the stage. It is thus, and not by dint of good health and ready and fertile wit, that he has been able to hold thus securely his enviable post with the world famous "Follies".

Mr. Williams came upon his vocation by chance. He had shaped for himself a wholly different career. He was born a British subject, being a native of New Providence, Nassau, in the British Bahama Islands. When he was two years old his family moved to New York. His father was a maker of Papier mache. This, of course, brought the father, and through him the son, into contact with the stage. In this way the young lad came to know at least some of the mechanics of the stage. The family later moved to California, where the son was graduated from High School. At this time young Williams decided that he wanted to be a civil engineer, and he left home and went to San Francisco, to study.

However, falling in with some youths who wished to do some local stage work, he became a member of a mountebank minstrel show, who toured the lumber camps and the mining camps, making fun for themselves and for the rough workmen on the frontiers years ago. It was in this rude work that Mr. Williams discovered his talent, and was drawn upon the stage. Next, he discovered George Walker. These two later formed the celebrated company of Williams and Walker, which with the fine dancing, melodious singing, and clever jokes, held them in vogue on the stage till Walker died.

After the death of his partner Williams struck out alone. For a long time he fought an uphill conflict. The play houses and managers who welcomed a whole company of Negro stars, because they would do their play and pass on, were at a loss to use a lone Negro star. Of course the color question frequently bobbed up. White stars and near stars, too, did not wish to appear on the same bill with a black man. However his own good nature, his splendid candor and above all, his genuine worth, gradually wore down the timidity of the manager as well as the resentment of fellow players, so that today few players are more popular in New York or elsewhere, on the stage or with the public, than Bert Williams. He has been with the Follies for about ten years.

The Negro of America owes Mr. Williams much. He has portrayed Negro humor without burlesquing it and without teaching the public to despise the black man. He has made it easier for any talented Negro actor to gain the hearing of managers, and he has by his clean living, demonstrated to both the Negro and the White public, that a colored actor can be sane, decent, and straight forward in every day civilian life.

COLLEGE CHAPEL—BRANCH NORMAL COLLEGE

THE Branch Normal College, located at Pine Bluff, Jefferson County, Arkansas, is a branch of the University of Arkansas. It was established pursuant to an act of the General Assembly of Arkansas, approved April 27, 1873, and has been in operation since April, 1875. Its primary object is to provide practical instruction in agriculture, mechanical arts, home economics, and such branches of learning as relate thereto and to train teachers for efficient service in public school work.

The school property consists of a beautiful tract of twenty acres of ground in the western suburbs of the city of Pine Bluff, Arkansas, on which are located the main building, the dormitory for young women and the mechanical arts building. The school building, completed in 1881, and occupied in January, 1882, is a two-story edifice, containing an assembly hall on the second floor with a seating capacity for four hundred students.

GOVERNMENT

The government of the school is vested primarily in the Board of Trustees of the Unversity of Arkansas. The administration of the school is vested in the Superintendent and the Prudential Committee. The Superintendent is the administrative head of the school. The directors of the departments are responsible to the Superintendent for carrying out the policies and rules of the college in their departments and for the development and efficiency of the work.

By the laws of the state the appointment of students to the Branch Normal College in numbers from each county in the State, is the same as to the University of Arkansas at Fayetteville. The power to make appointments is vested in the county judge of each county. Students so appointed are entitled to four years' free tuition, upon the payment of ($5.00) five dollars matriculation fee, in advance.

The departments maintained in the School are Preparatory, High School,, Normal, Mechanical Home Economics. Agricultural and Music. In all the departments of the school, the aim is to prepare the student for life. To that end the teaching in one department is, as far as possible correlated with that of another. The religious life of the student, the general health and all points in which young people need supervision are looked out for by the authorities.

The Superintendent of Branch Normal College, and the man directly responsible for all the affairs of the institution is Jefferson G. Ish, Jr., B. S., A. B. Mr. Ish is a native of the city of Little Rock. Both his father and his mother are teachers and they gave him a very early start in school. He is a graduate of the High School of Little Rock, of Talladega College, (Alabama), and of Yale University. His preparation for the post he now fills has been very thorough indeed. Mrs. Ish was Miss Florence Ross, of Oklahoma. She is a graduate of Fisk University, from both the College and Musical departments. One little daughter, Marietta, aged six years, completes the Ish family.

Ably seconding Superintendent Ish in all affairs pertaining to the school, we find Professor Frederick T. Venegar. He is Director of the Normal Department. He is a graduate of Wilberforce University, and has for the past fifteen years been connected with Branch Normal College. He teaches the Pedagogy, Geometry and Physical Science.

During the world war, Branch Normal was used as one of the schools in which soldiers were trained in the mechanical arts. In this way she served her government. At present the school is greatly overcrowded and could easily get many more students if they had the room to accommodate them. But full use is made of all the facilities at hand. Branch Normal is considered one of the best of the Land Grant Schools.

MECHANICS ARTS BUILDING, BRANCH NORMAL COLLEGE

MAIN BUILDING—CLARK UNIVERSITY, ATLANTA, GA.

LARK University is a Christian school, founded in the year 1870, by the Freedmen's Aid Society of the Methodist Episcopal Church. From the beginning it has been open to all classes, regardless of sex, color or creed. The sole conditions of admission being a desire to learn, good moral character, and obedience to lawfully constituted authority.

The prime object in the founding of this institution was to furnish to the newly emancipated people an open door into the higher and broader realms of learning, where they might have an opportunity to develop whatever in them is potentially best mentally and spiritually.

The institution, though at present largely dependent upon the Freedmen's Aid Society for financial support, has, nevertheless, a large prospective endowment in the four hundred acres of land it possesses on the outskirts of the growing city of Atlanta. In fact, more than one hundred acres of this land is already within the corporate limits. This property, it should be said, was largely se-

cured through the persistent and untiring efforts of Bishop Gilbert Haven, of the Methodist Episcopal Church. With prophetic insight he saw Atlanta then as Atlanta is today—a large, thriving, progressive city, spreading out in every direction, and by its salubrious climate attracting people to it from all sections of the country. This was the place for a large school. When most of the trustees, the writer included, expressed fears lest by locating the school so far beyond the city limits, few students would come to it, the good Bishop replied, "The city will come to you," and with his hand pointing down what was then called McDonnough Street, said: "Georgia is on the eve of building a new capitol. It will be built at the end of this street, and this street will then be called Capitol Avenue, leading straight to the front entrance of this campus." It is interesting to note how these predictions have been fulfilled.

Few schools have been favored with a more desirable location for the ends to be reached. Of all the states Georgia has one of the largest Negro populations, and by its central position places the other states within easy reach of the institution, while the numerous railroads radiating from Atlanta render it easy of access to students

The campus beautiful for situation, consisting of fifty acres, heavily wooded with oak and pine and hickory and other trees native to the South occupies one of the highest points around Atlanta and because of its elevation, has a perfect natural drainage on all sides. A more healthful location it would be difficult to find. At first, more than a mile outside the corporate limits today the electric cars communicating with all parts of the city, pass by the campus gates

There are three substantial brick buildings—Chrisman Hall Warren Hall, and Ballard Hall. Chrisman Hall was named for Mrs Eliza Chrisman of Topeka Kansas who furnished the larger part of the twenty-five thousand dollars for its construction. Burnt down in 1892 it was immediately rebuilt and somewhat enlarged. Used for administration purposes it also furnishes dormitory accommodations for boys. In it are the offices, class room reading room library, and a chapel with seating capacity of six hundred

Warren Hall a girls' dormitory, accommodating approximately one hundred girls' contains also a dining room for the whole student body. This hall was named for Bishop Henry W. Warren, who spent the first four years of his Bishopric on the University campus, and whose presence was a constant benediction to both students and teachers. Noticing the crowded condition of things consequent upon the growth of the school, he undertook to raise half the amount for the erection of another building. This he did. The other half was given by Mr F H Gammon the generous founder of the Gammon Theological Seminary. The building cost twenty-seven thousand dollars

As a matter of history, and to the credit of Bishop Warren, it ought also to be said that with Bishop Warren originated the idea of the "Model Home" the institution that today under the management of the Woman's Home Missionary Society, is found in every State of the union, where womanhood needs to be helped and elevated. The original conception of Bishop Warren was to have a cottage connected with the school in which under the direction of a matron, a few girls at a time might live and be instructed in all matters pertaining to a well ordered home. Timber was cut

a small cottage erected and a good Christian woman in the person of Miss Flora Mitchell, took upon herself the responsibility of this new venture. Her success may be seen in the fact, that she is still in charge but not of that little cottage. Indeed it is a far cry from that humble beginning to the now imposing and spacious Thayer Home with its modern appointments giving instruction in domestic Science to hundreds of young women. No young woman is allowed to graduate from Clark University, from any course without knowledge of Domestic Science, and no young woman is allowed to graduate without spending her senior year in residence in the Thayer Home. A number of young women thus trained have gone to Africa as Missionaries, and the wives of Missionaries

Credit should also be given to Bishop Warren for the emphasis placed on the necessity of industrial training for the youth. It was under his direction that a little carpenter's shop and blacksmith shop were called into existence. From this as a nucleus was envolved that trades department which attracted the attention of Dr Atticus G Haygood at that time agent of the Slater Board. This man generous sympathetic with a heart large enough to include all mankind and with an ardent desire for the prosperity of the "New South" wished to see in Atlanta a large industrial school that would be an object lesson to the whole South but such a school he wished to see connected with a large literary institution as a part of it for Dr Haygood believed in the education of the whole man. Hence it was through the influence of Dr Haygood that the Slater Board was led to give to Clark University for several years for its industrial department an annual appropriation of five thousand dollars. With the withdrawal of this appropriation the interest in the department waned. The building in which the industries were conducted is now the home of the Science department. This building was the gift of Mr Stephen Ballard of Brooklyn, N Y for whom it was named. The University was named for Bishop D W Clark who shortly after the close of the War visited this section and organized the work of the church

Clark University has had many Presidents. Any information needed now with a reference to the school may be had by addressing President Harry Andrew King

THOMAS W. FLEMING, LL. B.

HOMAS W. Fleming was born on May 13th, 1874, in Mercer, Mercer County, Pennsylvania. He commenced earning money in early life. First he worked on the farm where he labored for a while and then went to the city. He located in Meadville, Pennsylvania, where he became a newsboy, and a shoeblack. While pursuing his work he attended the Common school and High School and received a fairly good education. In 1892 he left Meadville and went to Cleveland, Ohio. Here he entered a barber shop and followed his trade as a barber for twelve years. His aspirations rose higher than the barber shop, and he decided to enter the profession of law.

At the age of twenty-five he entered the Cleveland Law School and took up the study of law. Having put his hand to the plow he did not turn back until he had accomplished his purpose. He was graduated from Baldwin, Wallace College, with the degree of LL. B., in 1906, passed the Ohio Bar examination the same year and started to practice law in Cleveland, Ohio. His interest in civic matters led him into politics and he became active in municipal political affairs. In 1907 he was nominated by the Republicans of Cleveland, as Councilman at Large, being defeated with his ticket. In 1909 he was again nominated for Councilman at Large and was elected, being the first Colored man to ever occupy a seat in the City Council of Cleveland. In 1911 he was again nominated for Councilman at Large, but was defeated with the balance of the Republican ticket. In 1914 he was appointed as Deputy State Oil Inspector, by Governor Frank B. Willis. In 1915, Mr. Fleming was nominated over five white opponents for Councilman of Ward Eleven (11),) and was elected, being the first Colored man to ever represent a Ward in the City Council of Cleveland. In 1917, he was again nominated and elected to the City Council from his Ward and is now serving his third term as member of that body. He is a member of several of its most important committees. This action of the citizens of Cleveland in placing Mr. Fleming in the Council and of that body in placing him upon its most important committees is stronger testimony than mere words of his ability and worth as a leader in municipal affairs.

Mr. Fleming is Congregational in his church affiliation, and is connected with one of the leading Congregational churches of Cleveland. He is social in his disposition and is connected with several of the Clubs. He is a member of the Tippecanoe Club, The Western Reserve Club, and is President of the Attucks Club. He is a member of and ex-President of The Cleveland Association of Colored Men, a member of the local branch of the National Association for the Advancement of Colored People, and a director in several business concerns.

Mr. Fleming is a man of family and lives in a beautiful home at 2342 East 40th Street with his wife and three sons. Here he finds sweet comfort and rest from the heavy burdens of professional and civic duties. While devoting his energy of brain to his work he has not been unmindful of the future, when advanced age will weaken his efforts, and is making provision for that period of his life. He has already accumulated a nice property, which he hopes to add to as the days go by.

VIEW OF LINCOLN INSTITUTE—JEFFERSON CITY, MO.

INCOLN Institute is one of the few State schools, if not the only one, to owe its origin to the contribution of Negroes. Shortly after the Civil War, the soldiers of the Sixty-second and Sixty-fifth Regiments of the United States Colored Infantry contributed a fund of $6,379.00 to establish a Negro school in the State of Missouri.

The Board of Trustees was organized on June eighth, and incorporated on the twenty-fifth of the same month, 1866. In the same year on the seventeenth of September school opened.

The first President of Lincoln Institute was Richard Baxter Foster, of Hanover, N. H. He was born October 25, 1826, and died April 26, 1901. He was the first and only white president of Lincoln Institute.

"The Legislature of 1879 appropriated $15,000 for the support of the Institute, provided $5,000 should be applied to the payment of its indebtedness. This appropriation was contained in the general appropriation bill, and was a grant to a corporation managing a charity.

The school could not accept the money, however, till the board met and transferred the entire school property to the State. Since that time the school has been the State School for the Colored people of Missouri.

The main building was destroyed by fire on the first of August, 1894, but was soon replaced by a far more commodious structure, for the erection of which the Legislature appropriated the sum of $40,000.

Since then the Legislature has appropriated at different times money to erect a dormitory for young men, one for the young women and a central heating plant.

Lincoln Institute has a high school department, a normal department, a college department, a preparatory department, departments of mechanical industries, a musical department, a model school, and a farm.

Dr. Inman Page was for eighteen years at the head of this School. Under him sat some of the men who are now men of importance in the State of Missouri, and of other States. Among those who have gone out from Lincoln might be mentioned Dr. A. Wilberforce Williams of Chicago. He is a physician of note, and has made a place for himself in the medical world. Dr. I. T. Vernon is another man who received training in Lincoln Institute. Dr. Vernon was at one time Registrar of the Treasury of the United States. He is one of the most brilliant of the sons who have gone forth from Lincoln.

Following Dr. Page, Dr. B. F. Allen was at the head of the school for a period of sixteen years. Dr. Allen resigned his post in 1918, and accepted the Presidency of Turner College, in Tennessee.

Clement Richardson, the editor of this work, is the present President of Lincoln Institute. Since he took charge in June, of 1918, President Richardson has taken a firm hold of the situation at the school, and is trying to re-shape its policies to fit the needs and wants of the people of Missouri. For the first time in the history of the school the farm is in the control of the school authorities for educational purposes. Prior to President Richardson's administration, the farm was under a white man, and only a small part of the land was given the school for the teaching of gardening. For the first time in seventeen years the College department is once more open. It is the purpose of the present President to build up a strong college course leading to the A. B. Degree.

Isaac Fisher

T HE University Editor at Fisk University, Mr. Isaac Fisher, holds a rather unique position in the list of persons who have attracted public attention because of unusual services rendered the public.

In the first place, although not a college graduate, he holds one of the most responsible positions in Fisk University, that of Editor of the school's official organ—"Fisk University News," and of all the publications of the University. The way Mr. Fisher came to be called to such a position is the story of his public services for his race.

He was graduated from the Tuskegee Institute, Alabama, in 1898, after having won the admiration of the late Dr. Booker T. Washington for his persistence in working to pay his education, and for his great ability as a speaker. As soon as Mr. Fisher received his diploma, Dr. Washington sent him to the Schofield School in Aiken, South Carolina, to teach in the class-room and to organize conferences of farmers in that State; called him from this position to present the cause of the Tuskegee Institute in New England; transferred him from the East, upon Mr. Fisher's request, to organize farmers' conferences for Tuskegee, in Alabama; and, to meet an emergency call for an able disciplinarian, sent him to fill out an unexpired term of principal of Swayne High School, in Montgomery, Alabama. Mr. Fisher was re-elected to this position at the close of the short term for which he had been elected, only to find that Dr. Washington, asked to name a man to go to Arkansas to become President of the State Agricultural and Mechanical College for Negroes, at Pine Bluff —"A man who is without fear and thoroughly progressive," had recommended him for the place. Although but twenty-five years of age, Mr. Fisher accepted the call.

He held this position for nine years—from 1902 to 1911—giving the school new dignity and standard; but he resigned in 1911. It was while he was at the head of this school that the country discovered that he was an essayist of the first rank. In a series of essay contests open to the entire nation, Mr. Fisher began taking the highest prize in each case. The subject made no difference—he generally succeeded in writing the best essay on the subject given. For example, when Missouri

wished to have drafted the "Ten Best Reasons Why Persons Should Go to Missouri" Mr. Fisher gave the best reasons although he had never even passed through the State. When Everybody's Magazine wanted to have the last word about the liquor question, Mr. Fisher gave that last word, although he has always been a total abstainer from alchoholic drinks.

Thirty or more times he won in these nation-wide contests and the colored people of the country began to see that he was in his quiet way demonstrating the possibilities of the Negro mind to all the people of the earth.

In 1914, the Tuskegee Institute called him back again to become the first editor of "The Negro Farmer;" and he had made this journal take a commanding position in its field when the newly-elected President of Fisk University, Dr. Fayette Avery McKenzie, who had been watching Mr. Fisher's literary career for several years, called him to become University Editor at Fisk. It was a bold step to take; but Dr. Washington had been willing to say over his signature in Everybody's Magazine, that if a position required tact, ability, fearlessness and devotion, he never hesitated to recommend Mr. Fisher for it, knowing that if he were not the equal of some others, when he accepted the work, within a short time he would fully qualify for the tasks given him. And, so, Dr. McKenzie took the risk of calling this young writer-educator to his present work.

In his position at Fisk University, Mr. Fisher has justified Dr. Washington's estimate and Dr. McKenzie's judgment, for his editorials in the Fisk University News attracted national attention from the first, and that magazine is recognized as one of the constructive forces of journalism because of the national outlook which its editor takes; and as a professor at Mt. Holyoke College remarks, "It is the one college journal which is of interest to persons outside of college circles." In addition to his other duties at Fisk, Mr. Fisher gives instruction in argumentation, and under his direction, Fisk's debating teams have developed astonishing strength in intercollegiate debating contests.

Mr. Fisher was married in 1901, to Miss Sallie A. McCann, of Birmingham, Alabama ,and has one daughter, Constance. At forty, he is one of the quiet and effective workers of his day.

Fisk---Past, Present and Future

FISK—PAST

At a time when all Americans were not agreed that the colored people in the United States had sufficient mental capacity to profit by any formal education above the most elementary grades, the American Missionary Association founded in the City of Nashville, Tennessee, a school for Freedmen, under the exalted name of Fisk University a school which was to become "in time a first class college"—a great university that should adequately provide for the newly emancipated people and their descendants forever the advantages of Christian education, to whatever extent the capacity and energy of the race should in the future demand

On January 9, 1866, this University of "faith" was formally opened in an old Government hospital building—a frame shanty

When the complete story of Fisk University is told, the facts following will not be forgotten

The University was founded by a religious organization, which has distinguished itself for the brave Fight it has made for the highest interests of the colored race, one of the two men who were sent in 1865 to select a site for the new school-- Rev E M Cravath—was a Soldier, the University was opened in hospital buildings and on land which had been used by Soldiers Fisk was named for a Soldier Gen Clinton B Fisk then chief of the Freedmen's Bureau for Tennessee and through whose efforts and interest the buildings and the ground on which they stood were turned over to the A M A for the school, and, finally, the first President and the great outstanding figure in the history of Fisk University, Dr Erastus Milo Cravath, was a Soldier

If these facts possess no significance out of the ordinary, it remains true, nevertheless, that Fisk from the first, Has Fought---Is Fighting Still for the very highest standards of scholarship and character, in the face of persistent efforts, sometimes open and oft-times concealed to reduce these standards for colored people below those demanded by and for the white race

JUBILEE SINGERS At one time of darkness and doubt it was decided to close the "University," but a few brave souls thought otherwise Head of this small number was Professor George L. White, teacher of Music who conceived the plan of training a body of students to sing the slave songs of their fathers before such bodies as would hear them, in the hope that friends might thereby be raised up for the school It was a daring project, no precedent being known for

such a course, and it was only because Professor White could not be made to see the obstacles in the way nor to give weight to the objections of his friends that the tour was finally begun With practically no funds against heavy odds and in the face of prophecies of failure, Professor White, with his unmovable faith in the future of the colored people and the providence of God, left the University in 1871, carrying with him the little group of students whom he had trained in song

Thus was begun the work of the famous "Jubilee Singers," who first brought the folk songs of the colored people to the attention of the world Touring New England and Great Britian, they earned enough money to purchase the present site of the University and to erect its first building, Jubilee Hall

PRESIDENTS From its beginning until 1875, the School and University were under the charge of Prof John Ogden (1866-1870) and Prof A K Spence (1870-1875) Under Prof Spence began the real development of the college work of the University

In 1875, Dr E M Cravath was elected President of the University Simple justice demands the statement that he stamped Fisk with its present high ideals, and under his guidance was builded the visible university as well as the one "not made with hands" Of the eleven buildings comprising the school, eight were erected during his administration He was a soldier and statesman with the type of courage needed to build and defend a school of highest standards for an unpopular race at a time when a member of the white race who was identified with such a work paid a bitter, bitter price

President Cravath fell asleep in 1900 He was succeeded by President James G Merrill, in 1901 Gentle, loving, and lovable, he took up the work of his great predecessor and prosecuted it with the same faith as had moved the founders Three new buildings were added during his Presidency He resigned his work in 1908, and was succeeded in 1909 by Dr Geo A Gates On account of ill health this splendid scholar and executive remained but a short time with the University—from 1909 to 1912 Fisk's present executive, Fayette Avery Mc-Kenzie, Ph D, LL D, was elected in 1915 Dr McKenzie is a close student of social questions and a man thoroughly saturated with the ideals which have made Fisk University synonymous with culture—with the higher education of the colored people in the United States

BIRD'S-EYE VIEW OF FISK CAMPUS—FISK UNIVERSITY

FISK—PRESENT

WHAT FISK IS. "Fisk University," to quote President McKenzie, "is the symbol, the corporate realization of education and culture for the Negro race in the South." The United States Commissioner of Education, Dr. Philander P. Claxton, said, recently, that Fisk "is a great national institution," and that the ten millions of colored people in the United States "look to Fisk University very largely for the leadership that will enable them to develop in all of their lines."

Stated in more concrete terms, Fisk is the second largest arts college for colored people in the world. Its faculty, taken from the best schools of the United States, numbers 40; and it has upward of 560 students in all departments. The school owns thirty-five acres of land, fourteen buildings, including Jubilee Hall for Women; Livingstone and Bennett Halls for men; Chase Hall for Science; Fisk Memorial Chapel; Daniel Hand Training School; Carnegie Library; a Gymnasium and Workshop; and Magnolia Cottage for the Music Department.

In the past the College has offered four courses of study, all leading to the degree of BACHELOR OF ARTS, i. e., classical, scientific, education, and home economics. But the requirements have now been so liberalized that those who desire may specialize along with the fixed requirements essential to general culture, in practically any subject they may choose.

In the Graduate Department courses are offered leading to the degree of MASTER OF ARTS. Many of the best northern colleges accept Fisk students, class for class, on a parity with their own.

Fisk's major work has been the training of teachers, but she has sent a host of graduates into practically all of the learned professions.

The Department of Music at Fisk has been and still remains of such a character that the University has come to be recognized as the leading conservatory of music for colored people in the whole country. A large number of the most successful musical artists of the race received their training in this department.

FISK—FUTURE

President McKenzie thus defines the ideals for the future: "We are working every year to reach the best standards of scholarship. But we are not content with mere book learning. Character is still the first object of the University. Honesty, truthfulness, morality, and economy are constantly urged upon the students. As of old, so now it is and in the future it will be that 'Fisk Stands for Mind, for Life, for Divinity, and for Eternity.'"

RECENT DEVELOPMENTS AT FISK

Under the brief administration of the present President, Dr. McKenzie, there has been maintained the best traditions of the past, and new steps of considerable importance have been taken. The plant, by reason of lack of funds, had for many years remained without adequate repairs. Through the generosity of the General Education Board and the Carnegie Corporation, and a number of other friends, the sum of one hundred and fifty thousand

BIRD'S-EYE VIEW OF FISK CAMPUS FISK UNIVERSITY

dollars was made available in the summer of 1917. This money made possible the installation of a modern and efficient central heating plant, located upon a spur of the railroad, thus providing coal without the cost of hauling by wagon. The buildings were wired for electricity, which replaced the old kerosene lamps in lighting the dormitories. Practically all the floors of the main buildings were relaid in hard wood, and the walls and ceilings were repaired and repainted in beautiful tan shades. Student toilet and bathing facilities of the most modern approved type were installed on every floor of all the dormitories. With these improvements the University plant was put into unusually splendid condition.

During the same period of time the University has taken over the house known as the Waterman house, has purchased four acres of land upon which there stood three buildings, once the property of the Nashville Institute and has bought a little house and some adjoining land, in order to provide a right of way for the pipe lines connecting the campus with the power plant on the railroad track. One of the three buildings purchased from the Nashville Institute has been turned into a teachers' dormitory, where a very considerable number of our teachers are given very comfortable quarters. Not only are there dormitory rooms, but there are one or more general assembly rooms, a dining room, a kitchen, and a small laundry. Another of the houses has been turned into a two-apartment house. The third has been converted into a modern laundry, equipped with electrically run machinery, and supplied with hot water from the central heating

plant. The removal of the boilers and laundry from Jubilee Hall has made that building far safer and has opened up new spaces for additional activities in that building. The girls have a splendid little laundry for themselves, the music department has at least seven additional music rooms in the basement, and a large recreation-study hall has been provided for the girls. In the kitchen there has been placed five new ranges; a dishwashing machine, and a number of other modern conveniences. The kitchen and diningroom are thoroughly clean, and every precaution is taken to protect the health of the students.

New offices have been provided for the President, and for the registrar, and thus the administrative details of the University have been made much easier to handle.

All these changes have been, in a way and to a large degree, merely the background and foundation for the more important work of the University. Once the physical foundation has been thoroughly provided, the attention of the administration was turned to developments of a more immediate educational character. Already a number of very important changes have been made. The work of physical education has been very greatly changed and enlarged. The University believes that health is a prerequisite for good mental effort, and also believes that regular, systematic exercise in the gymnasium and on the campus will not be an encroachment upon the time for study, but a means of increasing the efficiency and enlarging the product of mental effort. It is hoped to place all the physical and athletic activities upon the highest standards which modern thought can suggest The standards of the best institutions of the world are the standards which Fisk aims to establish and maintain Nothing less than the best is satisfactory to the University

One of the most important changes of the recent years has been the new emphasis placed upon the monthly publication of the University The Fisk News, under the editorship of Mr Isaac Fisher, has made a splendid national reputation for itself and for the University

Increased variety of subjects for study has also marked the policy of President McKenzie New courses have been added in Greek, in history, in modern languages, in social science, in physics, in chemistry, in agriculture, in manual training in music and in various other lines In order to get the most benefit out of such a wide range of electives the University has adopted a scheme of majors, by which each student is allowed and required to concentrate to the extent of one-fourth, or possibly to even one-third, of his full four years, upon one subject or specially related group of subjects In addition he is required to take a certain range of subjects which will assure him a liberal point of view Every effort is being made to standardize the methods of marking among the various teachers, so that full credit—and uniform credit—shall be given to the work of all students in every department

In the crisis years of the war, Fisk has not failed to play its part among the institutions of the country Early after the declaration of war with Germany telegrams went from the University offering the services of the students Since that time more than one hundred alumni, former students and students of the present year, have volunteered or been drafted into the army of the republic Many of them are already in France, some of them may already have taken part on the battle line Among them there is one major, in the medical service, several captains, many first lieutenants, and still more in other official positions In fact, there are very few who have been at Fisk who remain privates very long after entering military service The training which they have secured in the University has prepared them for larger service even in the army.

In contributions of money to the Army Y M C A, to the Red Cross, to Armenian Relief, Fisk has not failed to show its loyalty in large degree Thrift stamps have been purchased in large numbers and the faculty, and some students, have purchased liberally of Liberty Bonds The girls and women have not forgotten that even knitting can be made a patriotic service

The University has not forgotten that it can serve by sacrifice of its own working force It has sent into the army and into the various war work activities, a considerable proportion of its teaching force Mr Dexter Lutz is in the Aviation Corps, Dr L E Weiker in the Medical Corps in France, Professor A F Shaw is a Y M C A Secretary with the Portugese, Professor J W Chambers a Y M C A Secretary with the Irish in Ireland, Professors J N Haskell and G D Yonkum in Y M C A work in France, Professor Messenger and Professor Belsinger are among the drafted men in camp Dr George E Haynes has been lent to the government for the period of the war, as Director of Negro Economics and Advisor to the Secretary of Labor, on the question of Negro Labor and Negro migration, thus providing one of the most important national services any one of the Negro race could possibly render The Jubilee Singers, who are travelling on the road, have given without price, of their time and services that the soldiers of the various camps scattered over the country might enjoy their singing for an evening

The last service which the government has asked —and one which the University was glad to render —was to open the campus as a receiving, or concentration camp for six hundred soldiers for the period of mobilization This plan has meant the giving over to the army of practically three of the buildings of the University, it has meant the feeding of six hundred soldiers in the dining room where formerly less than three hundred students were ordinarily fed, it has meant the putting of all our male students in one building where formerly they occupied two, it has meant crowding to a very unusual degree, it has meant the limitation of activities of the University life in many respects It has all been done gladly, that the University might serve with her fellow institutions in whatever way would contribute to the success of the great struggle which the allied nations are now waging for the liberty of the world

All these things suggest clearly the fact that Fisk University, which started at the close of the great Civil War, which was in some senses the outcome of that War, has labored in season and out of season for half a century so that she might be prepared to render a new service—a large one —to the nation and to the world in a new war of larger significance to the liberties of mankind Fisk hopes to continue to fight for liberty ,not long upon the battlefields of military force, but forever in the arena where the struggle is made for the liberty of the mind Fisk will always struggle for that "truth which shall make men free," and which shall make not only men free but races free and nations, and which shall establish peace on earth as it is also in Heaven

Written for year 1917-1918

362

CHARLES VICTOR ROMAN. A. M., M. D., PH. D., LL. D.

HOEVER has heard the resonant voice of C. V. Roman, A. M., M. D., LL. D., sound from pulpit or platform, dropping now a classical allusion, now bits of history, now logic, would never set him down as the great eye, ear, nose and throat specialist of the Meharry Medical College. It would be thought that he had given days and nights to the study of the poets and philosophers rather than to the ailments of the delicate organs of the human body.

Born in Williamsport, Pennsylvania, July 4, 1864, Dr. Roman migrated to Ontario, Canada when but eight years of age. His mother, a Canadian, was the daughter of a fugitive slave. His father also anticipated Lincoln's proclamation by more than a score of years.

Dr. Roman attended the Ontario public schools, graduating from the Hamilton Collegiate Institute, of Hamilton, Ontario. Then he returned to the United States to make his way in the world. He planned to enter the medical profession, but means were lacking to pursue his course. He turned aside and taught school in Kentucky and Tennessee, in both of which states he taught on his first grade licenses. He then enrolled as a student of medicine in Meharry Medical College receiving the degree of M. D. in 1890.

The same year he opened office in Clarksville, Tennessee, where he remained three years and was successful from the outset. He removed to Texas, where he continued his practice for eleven years. In 1904 he was called to Meharry to accept the chair of instruction in eye, ear, nose and throat diseases. Here as a professor and specialist in his subject he has remained, teaching, practicing and delivering popular lectures, working in the church and joining energetically in uplift work of every kind for the race.

He is one of the strongest laymen in the A. M. E. Church, and wherever members of the African Methodist Episcopal Church are assembled in large numbers, there will you find Dr. Roman, making addresses and joining in counsel. He is a member of the Southern Sociological Congress and has addressed that body on nearly every occasion of its gathering.

To satisfy a youthful ambition, he studied at Fisk University and gained the degree of Master of Arts, in philosophy and history. He took post graduate courses in Chicago, in Philadelphia and in London, England. On his accepting the chair at Meharry Medical College in 1904, Paul Quin College honored him with the degree of Ph. D., and seven years later, in 1911, Wilberforce University conferred the degree of LL. D.

He has been, three times, a delegate to the General Conference of his church. He was delegate to the Ecumenical Conference of Methodism which met in Toronto, Canada, in 1911, and was widely credited as making the ablest address of the occasion. In 1903 he was elected president of the National Medical Association and in 1909 was one of the founders of the National Medical Journal, of which he is still editor-in-chief. He has been honored as the guest of the medical societies of Philadelphia, New York, Chicago, New Orleans and Dallas, Tex.; and the invited guest of the State Associations of New Jersey, Alabama, Mississippi, South Carolina, Georgia and Texas. He is the author of "American Civilization and the Negro," the most comprehensive work of the kind written by a Negro. He is a prominent Odd Fellow and Knight of Pythias and a man much traveled in America and in Europe.

He is one of the advisors and associate editors of these pages, one whose advice and good judgment are highly prized on all social and racial questions.

Dr. Roman was married to Miss Margaret Lee Voorhees of Columbia, Tennessee, in 1891. The family lives in Nashville, surrounded by a host of friends and admirers.

Intellectual pursuits and altruistic efforts engage his mind so completely that he has but little room for the consideration of material things. He is, however, a good provider though he has accumulated but little of the world's goods. Having no children, and with a mind centered upon the welfare of others the incentive to save was not strong in him.

Dr. Roman has been one of the strongest personalities in America so far as influencing the religious life of young Negro professional men, by thousands of whom in every part of the new World he is sincerely loved.

WILLIAMS HAYNES, B. TH., D. D.

PEAKING of the good deeds of Dr. William Haynes on the occasion of his election as corresponding secretary of the Sunday-school Publishing Board of the National Baptist Convention, Dr. Sutton E. Griggs says—"As a worker, the Rev. Mr. Haynes has been a success in his personal and public undertakings. He has massed some amount of property for himself and he did this in a thoroughly open and honest way by unceasing labor and strict economy.

On the east bank of the Cumberland river, just North of the city of Nashville, situated on a high ground, you will see some of the finest brick buildings to be found anywhere in the South. Here stands Roger Williams University. Some years ago, this school located elsewhere, was burned. Its rise from the ashes and its journey to the present location and stage of development, are to be attributed in a large measure, to the firmness, energy and integrity of Rev. William Haynes, another founder of Roger Williams University. This is high praise for any one man and such praise stands as a substantial monument to so hard a worker as Rev. Haynes. The beauty of his service to Roger Williams was that he was doing all this for his Alma Mater, discharging a moral debt, which all men feel toward the school which gave them a

grip on things. Dr. Haynes graduated from the Normal Department of Roger Williams University in 1889, and the Theological Department in 1899. He did not wait until his graduation to begin preaching the Gospel, but started preaching as early as 1881. Unlike many ministers, Rev. Haynes has been a sticker.

He has been in Nashville for more than 20 years. He has spent most of his time pastoring two or three churches. Two of the churches he really built and for that purpose, he raised a total amount of $15,000, and he stood by each of these churches until they were freed of debt. While engaged in church work, his heart was also in Roger Williams. He is the chairman of the Trustee Board of Roger Williams University, and when he was Educational Secretary, he paid $10,000.00 for the new site of that institution. This Dr. Haynes considers as the principal episode in his life.

As Secretary of the Sunday School Publishing Board, Dr. Haynes is doing a good work in trying to hold together the Baptists of the country. He also served as pastor of the old celebrated Spruce Street Baptist Church, and is now serving as pastor of the Sylvan Street Baptist Church.

In 1890, Dr. Haynes was married to Miss Anna R. Wilson, of Davidson County, Tenn. Dr. and Mrs. Haynes have a large family of happy sons and they all show the early training received in a good Christian home. One of his sons, Rev. J. C. Haynes, is a teacher as well as a minister. Another son, W. H. Haynes, is a professor in Morehouse College, Atlanta, Ga. The younger sons are students.

In conclusion, Dr. Haynes is a man who has done a great deal of traveling over the country as Educational Secretary of Roger Williams, and his name will never die. He leaves too great a monument behind him and especially will he be remembered by Roger Williams University.

THE TRUSTEES OF ROGER WILLIAMS UNIVERSITY

On the thirteenth day of February, 1883, the Nashville Normal and Theological Institute was incorporated under the laws of the State of Tennessee, as Roger Williams University. The following are the trustees in 1918 and 1919, Wm. Haynes, B. Th., D. D., who is at this writing the chairman of the Board and was efficient in re-establishing New Roger Williams University after the burning of "Old Roger," and made the first payment of ten thousand dollars ($10,000.00) for the site. Dr. G. H. Bandy is the Secretary of the Trustee Board and one of the most proficient practitioners in medical profession. He is also an alumnus of Roger Williams University, who has given much of his valuable time to the University. A. B. Hill,

INMAN E. PAGE, A. M., A. B., LL. D.

Esq., (white), has been of great help to the University, as he is one of the leading business men of the city of Nashville. Dr. J. B. Singleton, now President of the Peoples Savings Bank and Trust Co., and one of the leading dentists in the City of Nashville, has deep interest in the University, and he has shown a willingness to be on hand at all of the meetings to advise as his experience would allow him. Rev. A. D. Hurt, D. D., is Superintendent of Missions in Tennessee, and is doing much to make the University a success. Dr. A. M. Townsend, A. B., is the Ex-President of the University. He, having resigned last year, was among the most proficient presidents that the University has ever had. He is now pastor of the Metropolitan Baptist Church, in Memphis, Tenn. As an educator, he is splendid; as a pastor he is kind, as a Gospel preacher, he is effective. He did much to bring Roger Williams University upon a level with other schools of its kind.

E. M. Lawrence, B. Th., D. D., is an alumnus of Roger Williams University, and is among the oldest trustees of the University. He, having been elected long before "old Roger" burned, was instrumental in creating enthusiasm among the constituents of the Baptist denomination. After the burning of the University, as he was superintendent of Missions at that time, he gave Rev. Haynes who was President of the Missionary and Educational Baptist Convention at that time, substantial help. Rev. A. O. Kenney, B. Th., D. D., is also an alumnus of the University who has been about the University for thirty odd years as a teacher. He has been a great asset to the success of the school. Dr. Chas. A. McMurry, A. M., Ph. D., (white), is a teacher at Peabody who came to us recently and is intensely interested in the education of the Negro. Rev. Peter Vetrees, D. D., is one of the oldest teachers of Sumner County. He taught thirty odd years in Gallatin, Tenn., the county seat of the above named county. Rev. Rufus W. Weaver, Th. D., D. D., resigned. Dr. H. M. Green, Ph. D., of Knoxville, Tenn., is one of the leading physicians of that city, and a staunch friend to "Roger Williams University." B. J. Carr, Esq., of Nashville, Tenn., is a farmer of enormous capacity, having owned two or three farms and success has attended him as such. He has the courage of his conviction, contending what he believes to be right. He is loyal to Roger Williams University, and believes in the rights of the Trustee Board.

A STATEMENT CONCERNING THE LIFE AND WORK OF PROF. JOHNSON BY MRS. ANNA R. HAYNES.

Prof. J. W. Johnson, first president of new Roger Williams University, was born in Columbia, Tenn., June 23, 1863. After receiving his public school education in Columbia, he entered Roger Williams University, in September, 1882, under Dr. Daniel Phillips, first President of Roger Williams University.

He graduated from the Classical Department in May, 1889, receiving an A. B. degree. He was an energetic young man and taught in the rural schools during his vacation and in that way, helped himself through school. After he had completed his graduation, he taught two years in Hopkinsville, Ky. While there without any solicitation on his part, he was elected as a Professor in Roger Williams University, which place he held with credit to himself for eight years. During his vacation, he spent a deal of his time in county institutes helping to prepare teachers for their work.

From 1900 to 1907, he was principal of the public school, at Martin, Tenn., and while there he organized the Educational Congress of West Tennessee. This great work gave him prestige with the teachers of the State of Tennessee, and especially the alumni of Roger Williams University, which caused him to be elected as the first President of the new Roger Williams University, in 1905. He willingly came on the scene under very discouraging features and made a great success out of what many of his friends thought an impossibility. But

365

BIRD'S-EYE VIEW OF ROGER WILLIAMS UNIVERSITY

he had won the hearts of the alumni of Roger Williams University, and many of the best friends, both white and colored, and especially Dr. Morehouse, who was at that time corresponding secretary of the American Baptist Home Mission Society. With the unfaltering confidence in these friends, he and four other teachers entered Roger Williams University. As they labored, the school grew in number from four teachers and thirty-eight students in 1907, to twelve teachers and one hundred eighty students in 1913.

The property of the school at that time was valued at $10,000.00, and rose to $65,000.00. The girls' building was completed and is now called Phillips Hall. Many other improvements were added during the presidency of Prof. Johnson.

DR. INMAN EDWARD PAGE

In August 1918, the Board of Trustees of Roger Williams University elected as President of that Institution, Dr. Inman Edward Page, then President of Western College, Macon, Mo. This election was the result of the resignation of Rev. A. M. Townsend, who had been at the head of the institution the past five years, and who had resigned to accept the pastorate of the Metropolitan Baptist Church, of Memphis, Tenn.

The Board of Trustees was fortunate indeed to secure the services of a man so able as Dr. Page, a man of a broad and ripe experience bringing to the University an experience of forty years in educational work. Dr. Page is not only a man of education, but is an educator, a fact well attested by his Alma Mater, Brown University, in conferring upon him in May, 1918, the honorary degree of Master of Arts, in recognition of his services in his chosen field of labor. Dr. Page had long since received in cursu this degree from his Alma Mater. But this last act of honor was given in true recognition of his long and imminent service as an educator, and at a time when honorary degrees were conferred upon Senator Henry Cabet Lodge, President William A. Neilson and many other distinguished men.

At the time this honor was conferred upon him, The Evening Bulletin, Providence, R. I., had this to say: "Inman Edward Page was graduated from Brown University, with the class of 1877, receiving the degree of A. B., and A. M., upon completing his course. At Commencement he was chosen by his class to be class orator.

In the Fall of 1877, he became a teacher at Natchez Seminary, Natchez, Miss. Soon after he was called to become Vice President of Lincoln Institute, Jefferson City, Mo. At the end of two years in that position, he was made President and was at the head of the institution which is the State institution of Missouri, for the collegiate, normal and industrial education of the Negro for 18 years. In 1898, Mr. Page became President of the Agricultural and Normal University, at Langston, Okla. He was there for seventeen years, resigning to become head of the Western College, at Macon, Mo.

Dr. Page had been previously honored twice, the degree of Doctor of Law having been conferred upon him by Howard University and Wilberforce University. Thus it will be seen that Roger Williams has before it a bright future, having at its head an upright and Christian gentleman, and a man of broad experience in matters in general, but particularly in matters educational.

DR. A. M. TOWNSEND—AS PRESIDENT OF ROGER WILLIAMS UNIVERSITY

It is said in speaking of Jesus, John 21:25: "And there are also many other things which Jesus did, the which, if they should be written every one, I suppose that even the world itself could not contain the books that should be written." I hope we do not border upon sacrilege by our comparison here, but those who have taken note of Dr. Townsend's work and labor of love, as the efficient president of Roger Williams University, will agree that it would require, at least, many books to contain the deeds of daring, love and sacrifice during his incumbency as President of Roger Williams University.

Dr. Townsend was first a student of that institution, and then an alumnus, and then a trustee, and on he went, becoming President of that institution in 1913.

After five years of arduous toil as President, he retired from the scene, leaving a splendid faculty, student body, president's mansion, and other adequate facilities, coupled with the love and esteem of the Baptists of Tennessee.

MATHEW W. DOGAN, A. B., D. D.

OR the last quarter of a century Mathew W. Dogan, President of Wiley University, has been a conspicuous figure in Negro education, and in the work of the Methodist Episcopal Church. He has kept up a close relationship with all educational movements, both in the church and in the secular world, has been instrumental in bringing men and women together from many various organizations, and has, to keep himself fresh in school matters, slipped away to attend summer schools whenever he could spare the time.

Dr. Dogan was born in Pontotoc, Mississippi, December 21st., 1863 His early years were spent in want, so much so that any sort of education seemed for a long time absolutely beyond his reach. Such meagre educational advantages as his home town offered he embraced, when he could spare the time from the task of earning his bread. During those days of hardship he worked at whatever task he could find. For a time he was a boot-black in his father's shop. The few pennies he gathered here were put to a very practical use, not squandered as spending change. He had heard of Rust University, at Holly Springs, and was determined to complete a course there. Thus the boot black money was used to pay his way in this school.

He was not of those to be satisfied with a little education, however. He wanted a college, as well as preparatory course. Thus the finishing of the one only gave thirst for the other. To stem the tide of want he at one time engaged in the grocery business. But the gods of merchandise would not yield him the coveted crown of wealth and prosperity, may be they knew he was marked for another career. When all seemed fair to succeed the flames came and swept all away, his dreams of wealth as well as his world's goods. With all his struggling and economy he was not able to stem the tide of circumstances in college. And so for two years he bade his alma mater adieu. In the interim he turned his undertakings to school teaching, at which he so well succeeded that he was able to return to college and complete his course without further interruption.

Clearly the President of Wiley was no mean pupil; for in spite of money worry, in spite of interruptions, he was graduated in the class of 1886, from the full college course and what is more to the point, at the head of his class. Was he better or worse for the hardships, for the interruptions, for the concern over the money to defray his expenses?

It is one thing to win distinction as a scholar; it is quite another thing to win a place as a man worthy to conduct classes and to take a hand in the management of a college. Dr. Dogan had won both of these distinctions in graduating from Rust University. In the fall term following his graduation from Rust he was elected to a place on the Rust University faculty, a place which he held for the next five years. In 1891, he was elected as a teacher of mathematics in the Central Tennessee College, at Nashville. This institution is now Walden. Five years later he was chosen President of Wiley University, the position which he still holds.

Under Dr. Dogan's Administration many changes for the better have taken place in Wiley University. While this is, of course a church school, and while it is true that church leaders and classical scholars are expected to come out of this and other schools of a like character, yet Wiley, like many other institutions, has so shaped its courses under Dr. Dogan's presidency that it can meet the demands of modern times, as well as supply courses for those who wish to pursue the more formal studies for church and school. It has added science, and those industrial phases which fit students for a practical and immediately useful life. It has put new life into its whole student body by lending all possible encouragement to the various kinds of

MAIN BUILDING—WILEY UNIVERSITY

athletics and sports; teaching that these features are also very essential elements in modern life. For all these more modern phases of adaption, Wiley is very largely indebted to her President, Dr. Dogan.

As a member of the Methodist Episcopal Church, Dr. Dogan is almost as active as he is in the school. He belongs to the General and is a member of the Board of Education of his church. This post he has held for twelve years. In secret orders he is a member of the Knights of Pythias. He has been Prsident of the Texas State Teachers' Association, and President of the National Association for Teachers in Colored Schools. He is still active in both of these bodies, being on the Executive committee of the latter and a frequent attendant at the meetings of the former. He has traveled very extensively, having been into most of the States of the Union, on pleasure and on educational tours.

Dr. Dogan was married to Miss Fannie F. Falkner, of Memphis, Tenn., in 1888. Dr. and Mrs. Dogan have five children—four girls and one boy. The oldest daughter attended Oberlin, but had to drop out in her Junior year because of poor health. The second daughter finished college at Wiley this year. The other children are in the preparatory course, at Wiley.

With all his handicaps at the outset, Dr. Dogan has managed to accumulate a goodly share of the world's goods. He now pays taxes on $7,000 worth of property.

Of all the States of the South and Southwest, Texas has the fairest record in good schools and high educational standards for the Negro. Galveston, Houston, Dallas, Beaumont, and many other of the big cities of the State boast of the High Schools; schools with the best equipment and the ablest teachers that can be found. Flanking these all about the State are the colleges and normal schools. The colleges are for the most part fostered by denominational boards. The oldest of these, oldest not only of Texas, but west of the Mississippi, is Wiley University.

Wiley was founded by the Freedmen's Aid Society, of the Methodist Church, in the year 1872. It received its charter nine years later, in 1882. As has been stated it is the oldest institution of college grade open to Negroes west of the Mississippi River. From its beginning it has carried a good record for scholarship, sound business principles and clean religious teachings. During its history of nearly fifty years it has graduated more than five hundred students and has taught and influenced and directed the lives of thousands of undergraduates. Some years ago the question as to the standing and the rating of various Negro colleges was widely discussed. Many of the so-called colleges received the black eye. Not so with Wiley University. Many experts from the North gave it a high rating, and four state boards of education, among which is Texas, placed her on the roll of first class colleges.

CARNEGIE LIBRARY—WILEY UNIVERISTY

While the institution was begun as a University, yet it has so adjusted its courses to the needs of the people and the times that a student may receive a complete course for almost any career he wishes to follow. Due to the early needs of the people, Wiley opened, and continues to maintain, a grammar school department and a college preparatory department. Thus one can enter at the bottom of the intellectual ladder, and ascend all the way through his college course.

In the college department are a classical course, a course in Education, in Music and in Commerce. Along with these Wiley maintains an industrial course for girls. This course covers the various forms of housekeeping, needle work, and many of the handicrafts. These are all furnished by the King Industrial Home, which is just across the street from the University, and is under the direction of the Woman's Home Missionary Society of the Methodist Episcopal Church.

As her course has grown to meet the demands of the times so have her buildings. Wiley University Plant consists of a Main Building, of the President's Home, a Carnegie Library, two Recitation Halls, a Science Hall, a Laundry, Coe Hall, which is a dormitory, and four cottages, which are frame structures. It carries a full nine months session, has recitation periods of fifty minutes, and maintains all the clubs, athletic teams, and debating activities common to the college of the first rank. Three new buildings are to grace her campus next year.

Having a faculty of moderate size, Wiley numbers among her teachers men and women from many of the leading institutions of the country.

Its staff numbers twenty-four teachers. It has an income of $56,932 dollars. This sum comes largely from the Freedmen's Aid Society, which, in addition to paying salaries and providing money for current expenses, keeps a field Secretary on the road looking after the interest of Wiley, and other institutions under its charge. Deserving young men and women, who demonstrate that they are really in earnest, and who are willing to work seldom, if ever, have to leave school on account of lack of funds. Employment about the campus, in the dormitories, in the dining room, and in the office of the school, as well as work in the town provide ways for industrious students to earn a good deal of their expenses through school.

The President of Wiley University is Dr. M. W. Dogan, D. D., who is a graduate of Walden University in Nashville, Tenn., and a former Professor in that institution. Dr. Dogan is responsible for many of the changes in the University during the twenty-two years he has been at the head. Of these the adjustment of courses and the increase of buildings and courses have been the most important

Some time ago several experts in school matters visited Wiley and examined her work. Here is their verdict:

"Wiley is an example of the best work done by the Methodist Episcopal Church for the Negro."

Mr. W. T. B. Williams, Agent for the Jeanes and Slater Funds, said: "Wiley is one of the three schools of the Freedmen's Aid Society that should do full college work."

Of like character was the testimony of President Holgate, of North Western University, and of President Plantz, of Lawrence College.

PRESIDENT'S HOME, WILEY UNIVERSITY

KENT HOME—BENNETT COLLEGE—GREENSBORO, N. C.

ENNETT College was founded in 1873, by the Freedmen's Aid Society. Located at Greensboro, North Carolina, which is situated in Guilford County, it has a very large colored population to draw on. In Guilford County alone, there are more than fifteen thousand colored people, a large percent of them being illiterate. In fact considering the condition of the colored people in that section, the founders of Bennett College could not have chosen a more appropriate place in which to build a school. Although Bennett carries a College department and a Normal department, its greatest number of pupils is enrolled in the primary department.

Bennett College owns thirty-seven acres of land within the city limits of Greensboro. Of this amount about twenty are under cultivation. This furnishes not only a source from which to get fresh vegetables, but also a place where a practical education in Agriculture may be had. The rest of the land is used for a campus. On this campus there are several buildings. Central Building is four stories high and is used for office, Library, classrooms, dining room and girls' dormitory. The President's house is a new building and suited to its use. Carolina Hall contains the chapel and the boy's dormitory. Besides the three main buildings there are two frame structures that are in use for industrial work and laundry. The valuation of the buildings is $30,000. The value of the land is $35,000, and movable equipment $5,000.

The attendance at Greensboro is between 300 and 350. More than half of these are in the elementary grades due in part to lack of room in the public school. The greater portion of the pupils are from Greensboro, but the entire State of North Carolina is fairly well represented.

In addition to the regular subjects taught in the course of study there are offered sewing and cooking for girls and gardening has been recently added. The girls have in connection with the school Kent Home. This home is owned and supported by the Woman's Missionary Society, of the Methodist Episcopal Church. The finances of the Kent Home are entirely separate from those of the College, but the home is a vital part of the school and the training received by the young women who are enrolled in the Home is very thorough and is what is needed by the young women of the race. The teachers in charge of the Home are three white women who see to it that the girls take good care of their rooms, and personal surroundings and that they are well trained in all the domestic virtues

The teachers at Bennett College are twelve in number. All of them are colored. They are equally divided as to sex and they enter into the work of the school and in the training of the young with enthusiasm. The President of the school is Mr. Frank Trigg, A. M. President Trigg has had charge of the school since 1916 and is developing the school along progressive lines.

Most of the funds for the maintenance of Bennett are derived from the Freedmen's aid Society, $3,800 being the sum that is given by this body for the support of the institution. The next largest income is from the tuition and fees. This amounts to over $1500 annually. Money derived from other sources amounts to very little. Non-educational receipts were received from the boarding department and amounted to $3,720.

Bennett College is placed where it can be a mighty force for good in the up-lift of the Negro race. That the work of the institution has been hampered to some extent in the past is true. But Bennett has in spite of all this accomplished a lot for our people.

REVEREND D. J. JENKINS

HE founder of the Jenkins Orphanage and Reformatory was born near Bamberg, South Carolina, in April, 1865. He was reared by a careful, prayerful mother, aided by Mrs. Dickerson, in whose home he was placed. He got such education from the public schools as he could in those days.

He was married in 1881 to Miss Lena James of Barnwell County. Eight years later he entered Benedict College to study theology and at the same time was assistant pastor of the Fourth Baptist Church.

One cold winter morning on passing the railroad track he saw some half dozen naked children huddled together in a freight car where they had taken refuge for the night. He reasoned that these were but a remnant of what were cast about in cellars, and alleys and corners—yes, and in jail. Thus on December 16, 1891, he opened his orphanage in an old shed at 666 King Street, Charleston, with three boys and one girl. In a few months the number had increased to 96. The next year, 1892, the orphanage moved to Franklin Street and increased its number of waifs to 360. In the same year it became regularly incorporated, and by 1898 it had enrolled 536 pupils, with very little funds, food or clothing to make the children comfortable.

To meet all their needs Rev. Jenkins had but one combined recourse—prayer and toil. By persistent struggle he caught the ear of the white people and the colored people of his State, and here and there gained a friend in the North. The former gave him 130 acres of land with the equipment of a blacksmith shop, saw mill and farm. Deacon Wild, of Brooklyn, N. Y. added one hundred acres to this, making 230 acres available for training the children.

The names of all donors with the amount given is published in the "Charleston Messenger," a weekly published by the Jenkins Orphanage with Rev. Jenkins as Editor. The City Council has granted the orphanage a sum of money each year for the last fifteen years. Beginning with a grant of $200 in 1897, it increased the amount year by year until in 1904 it gave $1,000, in 1914 it gave $2,500, which sum it has continued to grant.

There is also in addition to the orphanage a Jenkins Reformatory which is located at Ladson, South Carolina. Here children are kept free or at a small cost, educated in books and manners and taught one or more trades. In all cases, in the Orphanage and in the Reformatory, Agriculture is made a specialty.

The school is supported mainly by donations. Securing these, falls wholly upon the shoulders of the founder and such friends as he may draw to him, North and South. He travels much, writes many letters and has many workers in the field. One of his most popular means of making known the needs and merits of his school is with the Jenkins' Band. With this he has traveled much, both in America and in Europe. The Little Musicians are a crowning and shining light of the kind of pupils that are taken in and an indisputable instance of what one consecrated man can do in the hands of his Maker.

Five years ago he resigned the pastorate of the Fourth Tabernacle Baptist Church in order to give his entire life to the cause of the Orphanage. But the church would not accept and passed a resolution unanimously electing him for life and doubling his salary accordingly.

His first wife was a mother of eleven children, of whom nine are dead, only two survivors, namely: Edward T. Jenkins, who won his scholarship in the Royal Academy, London, England in every contest that he entered, and is now 20 years of age. Little Mildred, the baby daughter, is the only girl living. Dr. S. H. Jenkins, his oldest son, came out at the head of his class in Pennsylvania Dental College. His oldest daughter, Lena, came out head in her class in Howard University, Washington, D. C.

The most regretted part—his older children after attaining years of usefulness and help to his work, departed this life.

SCENE OF ROYAL UNDERTAKING COMPANY—SAVANNAH, GA.

R. L. M. Pollard is one of those big
enterprising Negro business men,
of Savannah. Like Messrs Scott
and Sherman, men whom he
works with, and like many other
men of large vision in Savannah,
Mr. Pollard believes in and practices co-operative business. With
him, opportunities for the Negro business are too
numerous, the race too young, and modern competition far too keen in the business world today.

Mr. Pollard is among the comparatively few
men anywhere to see opportunity near at hand.
This is true of his life in Savannah. All his energies have been spent here; all his successes attained here.

He was born in Savannah, December 12, 1867.
He was educated here, having attended the public
schools and Beach Institute, which is also in Savannah. On finishing his school career, Mr. Pollard turned his attention to civil service; for here
an uneducated colored man found employment that
compared most nearly with his training, with a
faint hope of advancement. And this, by the way,
explains the presence of so large a number of educated colored men in government service. It explains also why Negroes often pass the Civil Service Examinations when white people fail. White
people with an equal grade of training have larger
opportunities open to them, while the educated colored man was and is limited largely to teaching in
six months schools, on a pittance for a salary, or
preaching in four country churches per month for
sustenance. Happily the growing love of the old
black man for his son is rapidly opening the door
of business for the educated Negro.

Mr. Pollard entered the civil service in 1890. For
twelve years he was a letter carrier for Savannah.
By this time he had put by a few dollars and felt
himself ready to venture forth in business. In
1912, he, with his partners began the Royal Under-

taking Company. Mr. Pollard became general
manager.

In the life of Savannah and in the organization
of the State Mr. Pollard is also a useful and leading member. He is a member of the Episcopal
Church of his city. In his church he takes an active part in the Church and in the Sunday School.
In the latter he is especially interested, being particularly fond of working with children and with
those who have the children in charge. He is Senior Warden in the Saint Stephens Episcopal church
and director of the Primary school and kindergarten.

The experience with the Royal Undertaking
Company opened Mr. Pollard's eyes to the many
business chances that lay right at his door. Therefore as capital increased rapidly he joined in opening other business houses of one kind or another.
In a little while the Savannah Savings and Realty
Corporation swung open the doors for business.
Mr. Pollard was one of the charter members and is
today one of the directors of the bank. Then
came the Guaranty Mutual Life Insurance Company. Mr. Pollard was made treasurer and is still
treasurer of this organization, one of the safest
companies of its kind in Georgia.

Mr. Pollard is a Mason, a Knight of Pythias, an
Odd Fellow. Indeed, he is an active member of all
local lodges.

Mr. Pollard was married in Savannah, on November 28, 1901. Mrs. Pollard was Miss Nellie
Scott, of Savannah. Two children, Miss Eleanor
Scott and Miss Susan, have been reared by Mr.
and Mrs. Pollard. They have been educated in
their home and in the South, and are now pursuing courses in New York City.

WALTER SANFORD SCOTT

Mr. Walter Sanford Scott, banker and prime
mover of a long list of Negro enterprises in Savannah, Georgia, is an apostle of the doctrine, "Cast
down your bucket where you are." To be sure,

there is something peculiarly apt in his adopting this principle, for he not only sat at the feet of the man who made this doctrine famous, but was graduated from Tuskegee in 1895, the year that Dr Washington made this address at Atlanta Exposition

Mr Scott was born in Savannah, July 26th, 1877 After spending the years of his youth in Savannah, he went to Tuskegee where he was graduated from the Academic Department and from the trade of Printing, in 1895 Mr Scott then lost no time in putting into application the theory of Dr Washington He returned to Savannah and for several years worked at his trade

Seven years after his graduation from Tuskegee Institute Mr Scott made his appearance as one of the business men to be reckoned with in Savannah In 1902 he became the Secretary and Treasurer of the Wage Earners Loan and Investment Company The next year he opened an ice cream parlor and a dry goods store The year following, the leading thinkers of Savannah felt the need of a health benefit insurance This company was organized under the name of Life and Health Insurance Company Mr Scott, who by this time had become known as a sort of genius in Secretary-Treasurer posts was made Secretary and Treasurer of this company Savannah by the way is now perhaps the leading city of the world for successful Negro Insurance Companies

Organizing and promoting business enterprises now became with Mr Scott a habit In 1906 the Royal Undertaking Company a firm that has long since become established is one of the big Negro businesses of Savannah Mr Scott was made treasurer of the firm With this he appears to have graduated from Secretary-Treasurerships and to have gone to higher honors In 1913 he was elected President of the Mutual Health Insurance Company, a post which he still holds The next year 1914 he was elevated to the Presidency of the Royal Undertaking Company This post he still holds also Mr Scott organized the Savannah Savings and Real Estate Corporation Of this he was made President in 1915

Thus very literally he has cast down his bucket in his native city, and then too, when it came up it has had clear, cool fresh—gold and satisfaction of doing a constructive service for his neighbors and for his race Mr Scott owns his home, a beautiful residence on East Taylor Street in Savannah He has under way plans and specifications for a country home He is a good active church member being a member of the Episcopal Church He is a Mason Odd Fellow and Knight of Pythias

Mr Scott's reputation for handling and organizing business long ago became both State wide and National His talent was soon sought everywhere, by those who needed business methods He is Vice-President of National Negro Bankers' Association A member of the Executive Committee of the Standard Life Insurance Company, of Atlanta, Georgia, Associate member of the State Council of Georgia, a council which has for its purpose the production and conservation of food He has been appointed by the Governor of Georgia as the director of the Y M C A Former Governor Harris appointed him during his administration and now Governor Dorsey has reappointed him

Mr Scott was married on December 26th, 1910 to Miss Laura McDowell of Savannah Mr and Mrs Scott have three children Laura Gertrude and Walter S All are little folk in school Mr Scott is still young still vigorously active in pioneering in business

EDWARD WINIFRED SHERMAN

Somebody has written a lecture on the heroism of a private life Herein the quieter constructive virtues were extolled The hero was lorded not for the peaks he scaled or for the armed foes he vanquished, but for living his opinions, rearing his family and for being a law-abiding loving citizen and a good neighbor

Such have been the virtues of Edward W Sherman, of Savannah, Georgia Mr Sherman was born in Washington County, Georgia, March 17, 1868 He attended the public schools, gaining what training he could from these and worked at home until he was ready to advance training elsewhere Mr Sherman then went to Atlanta University, completed his education and settled down immediately to his life work

On leaving Atlanta he secured employment with the Government and has been in its employ ever since, never having sought any other employment However, he has quietly lent his influence interest and means to many phases of Negro advancement He has always been interested in education of Negro children, and both from the child's side and from the view point of the school has been a ready and eager helper In like manner he has seen a big future for the black man in business To this end, once more he has been a ready helper with money and time and influence He has, therefore, been a sort of charter member or prime mover in many of the business endeavors of Savannah—in Savannah where Negro Grocery stores, dry goods houses insurance offices and banks are common Mr Sherman is himself a member of several of these concerns He is a stockholder in the Guaranty Mutual Insurance Company, in the Savings Bank, and is one of the Real Estate Corporations He has also several pieces of valuable real estate in very desirable locations of Savannah In this last however, he takes no special delight, that is, none compared with the satisfaction of having seen Negro business grow from nothing to such gigantic proportions as it has done, in Savannah, and to know that he himself has given some little impetus to it

Mr Sherman belongs to several organizations of uplift In these he gives his quiet but sure and substantial support He is a Congregationalist being a member of the First Congregationalist Church of Savannah He is also a Knight of Pythias, and is a member of the Endowment Board of this body He holds membership in and gives support to the N A C P, National Association for the Advancement of Colored People This organization he believes in and has great hopes for He is also a member of the Negro Protective Association

Mr Sherman was married to Miss Mary Elizabeth Harne of Hawkinsville Georgia Their children are deceased The eldest, Miss Alberta Winifred, died during her first year as a student at Atlanta University

THOMAS ALEXANDER CARR

O win distinction, it is not necessary for a man to live in the limelight. Many a man who has pursued his course in a quiet and unostentatious manner has left his mark upon the world for its good. Thomas Alexander Carr belongs to this class.

Mr. Carr was born October 26th, 1868, in Orange County, in the State of Texas. He attended the common school until he was twelve years of age. After that date he gained such additional information as he could absorb from reading at nights and at odd times during the day.

There are two ways of learning—one from study and the other from observation. Mr. Carr, while denied the former strictly adhered to the latter, and was not slow to imitate the strong points he saw in others.

At an early age he entered the employment of the Morgan Line of Steamships, then plying their trade, along all of the Southern ports. While this work took him away from home, it gave him an opportunity to see many interesting places and to enjoy a rich and varied experience.

During his cruises he visited Galveston, Texas, Vera Cruz, Mexico, Havana, and Morgan City.

After five years service with the Morgan steamship Line, he located in New Orleans and took up steamboating. From steamboating he went to work in a boarding house at a salary which never exceeded twenty dollars per month. He finally landed the job of janitor for the Southern Athletic Club, of New Orleans, which he held for fifteen years. Here he made a record for punctuality of which he is very proud. During his entire term of service he never missed but sixteen days from his work, and that was due to sickness.

It has been his privilege to serve all the first-class Prize Fighters, like Corbett, Killrain, and others of that day. He also served the first Foot Ball team of the S. A. C., and went with their Battalion to Chicago during the World's fair.

Mr. Carr had long desired to enter the arena of business, and first thought of entering the dry goods business, but his sympathetic and loyal disposition frequently called him to the bed side of the sick, and to the house of mourning. This service brought him into constant touch with undertakers, one of whom, Jas. H. Taylor, formed a strong friendship for him, which resulted in his becoming connected with the Boyne & Taylor Co., Ltd., and finally its sole owner upon the death of Mr. Taylor. In 1918, he dissolved the Company, and formed a co-partnership with R. J. LLopis, under the firm name of Carr and LLopis, which is now doing a good business.

Mr. Carr is emphatically a man of peace and honesty. He never gets in broils and has steered away from Courts. He cannot ever recall having been before the court even as a witness.

Mr. Carr is a strong advocate of athletics but he believes it is not inconsistent with the life of a Christian, so he found his place in the church. He is a member of the First Street Methodist Episcopal Church, of New Orleans.

He is also a member of a number of Negro Societies, such as Cresent City Lodge, Knights of Pythias, Past Superior of Pilgrim Tabernacle, G. G. A. A. B. and S. of L. and C., and now Chairman of the Order's Burial Board; a member of Cresent Lodge, G. N. O. O. Fellows; a member of Grand Council M. O. H., of La., Past Grand Treasurer of Supreme Council of the State of Louisiana, A. O. Order Scottish Rite of Free Masonry, and various other benevolent orders and clubs.

He married Marst 31st, 1885, Miss Octavia Carter, and the only cloud upon an unusual happy married life was the death of their only child, Octavia Caroline Carr, who died in 1892.

MAIN BUILDING—CENTRAL ALABAMA INSTITUTE

ENTRAL Alabama Institute is located in Birmingham, Alabama. It was founded in 1872, at Huntsville Alabama. In 1904, it was moved to Birmingham. Here in Birmingham it has a larger number from which to draw students. The school is owned by the Freedmen's Aid Society, but the Central Alabama Conference of the Methodist Episcopal Church co-operates with the Freedmen's Aid Society in the support and supervision of the work.

Central Alabama Institute offers elementary courses, college, preparatory, and normal courses. Although the school is small, it fills a place much in need, in that it trains teachers for the rural districts. The pupils who attend the elementary department could be in the public schools of the city, but in this Model school they are being trained to teach.

The courses followed in the preparatory and Normal courses are outlined by the Freedmen's Aid Society. In this particular the school co-operates with all the other institutions directly under the supervision of this society. It has, however, the opportunity to do individual work as far as doing the work thoroughly is concerned. This, the President, Mr. J. B. F. Shaw and his corp of workers, endeavor to do.

Provision is made for sixty boarding pupils. Here in the school, the pupils who make it their home are taught, not only the books prescribed by the Freedmen's Aid Society, but they are given lessons in "How to Live." They are required to care for the buildings in which they live and for the grounds around. In this way the boys and the girls get valuable lessons in home making. The girls are taught plain sewing by one of the matrons. All the pupils, whether they have money or not, are required to give one hour each day in work. In this way the interest of each student is kept up in the general appearance of the buildings and grounds. This hour of work is aside from caring for their own personal rooms.

The school owns forty acres of valuable land in Mason City, a few miles from Birmingham. There are six buildings on the grounds. Two of these are large brick structures. The buildings are new and are in good repair. They are worth $25,000. The value of the entire plant is about $42,500.00. The Freedmen's Aid Society gives to the school $29,000 yearly, but this is not enough to run the plant. From other sources they receive about $1500.00. With this and the tuition money, they manage to keep the school in good shape.

The faculty consists of eleven teachers. Three of these do the grade work and three do the Academic work. There is a strong music department.

That the entire plant is doing good work is seen from the work of those who go out from the school. In the report of the Commission of specialists who made an exhaustive study of all Negro schools, they recommend "That the training of teachers for rural districts be made the main object of the school.

MINOR FRANCIS McCLEARY, M. D.

FTEN it happens that an incident, frequently in early life, determines a man's life work. He catches an inspiration from it which grips his soul and moulds his after career. It was so with Dr. McCleary. When a boy, only ten years of age, he witnessed the amputation of a man's leg. He watched the physicians as they skillfully removed the injured member and was so impressed with it that then and there he decided to enter the medical profession. He adhered to the decision thus early formed, and in due course of time had the satisfaction of having M. D. written after his name.

There was a long stretch from the formation of his purpose and its accomplishment and the way was hard for it called for years of study and preparation which he obtained mainly through his own efforts.

Dr. McCleary was born January 22nd., 1876, in Fernandina, Florida. Here in the land of sunshine and flowers, where Jaun Ponce de Leon sought "the fountain of perpetual youth," he spent his early days and to this state he returned to spend his remaining days in the service of his people.

He began his educational development in the Public Schools of his native City, and after completing his course he entered the Central Tennessee College. Finishing his course here, he went to Meharry Medical College, to perfect himself for his life work. His boyhood dream was now about to be realized, and he applied himself while at this college with a zeal born of an intense desire to succeed in a profession which he had chosen in his youth.

He had to rely upon his own exertions to raise the money to pay his tuition, but this was a slight obstacle to a man who had purposed in his heart that he would be a physician. The difficulties added greater zest to his efforts. After finishing at Meharry he took a Post-graduate course at the Rush Medical College.

He began his practice in 1901, in Kansas City, Missouri, and for one year worked in the Medical College. For five years he was the assistant to the Marine Physician at Key West, Florida, and in 1907, he moved to Jacksonville, Florida, where he hung out his shingle and soon established himself in his profession. While he does a general practice surgery is his specialty, and he takes great pride and pleasure in his work. No doubt he often recalls the incident of his boyhood, when dressed in the surgeon's garb, and holding the keen blade knife ready to operate upon some unfortunate patient. Aside from the opportunity to serve which his profession has brought him, it has enabled him to accumulate quite a handsome property. The value of his realty holdings is estimated to be thirty thousand dollars. This is evidence that Dr. McCleary has a turn for business, as well as medicine, and speaks well for his business sagacity, and thrift.

Dr. McCarty's family consists of a wife and two children. He was married September 16th, 1908, to Miss Margaret Anna Daunt, of Washington, Penn. There was born to them two children— Margurite Grace, and Minor Francis, Jr.

He is ambitious that these children shall find their places in life in some honorable and useful occupation.

In religious belief, Dr. McCleary is a Romanist, and in respect to the policy of his church has refrained from joining secret societies.

While the Doctor has not crossed the briny deep he is nevertheless something of a traveler. He has traveled in Cuba, Canada, and the greater part of the United States. He has followed the plan to see America first, and as he is yet a young man, he will no doubt visit Europe, and the battlefields of the great war.

MRS. MARY McLEOD BETHUNE

HE Daytona Normal and Industrial Institute for Negro Girls stands as a monument to Mrs. Mary McLeod Bethune. Mrs. Bethune is a woman of faith and of works. The institution of which she is still principal is evidence of that.

Mrs. Bethune was born in South Carolina. Here she received her early training. She not only got all that she could from the public school system, but attended and was graduated from the Scotia Seminary, Concord, North Carolina. Her work in Scotia but whetted her appetite for more learning. She entered the Moody Bible School, of Chicago, Illinois, and once more applied herself to acquiring knowledge. Here in the Moody School she had her religious life deepened, and all through her teaching, the influence of this institution is felt.

Having completed the work at Chicago, Mrs. Bethune began teaching. For a number of years she taught in the missionary schools and in the public school system. But there was a greater

work for this Christian woman, and in 1904 she made the first step in its development. In October of that year Mrs. Bethune started the Daytona Normal and Industrial Institute for Negro Girls, in a rented cabin. She had as her first class, five little girls. She had as assets $1.50, firm faith in God and determination to make a success of the effort. How well the school has succeeded is told in the history of the school. This history is in a large measure the personal history of the founder. The two cannot be very well separated.

In the interest of her school, Mrs. Bethune has traveled over the greater part of this country. In her travels she has made many friends for herself and for the school. Because of the school, Mrs. Bethune had to develop her powers as a speaker. She has made many notable addresses. On a number of occasions she has appeared before large audiences of prominent speakers when she was the only colored speaker. Among these may be mentioned an address in Waldorf-Astoria, before the Colony Club, in the Belasco Theatre, Washington, D. C. Her ability along this line has won for her a number of honorary positions. She was a Red Cross Lecturer of the Potomac Division. She was also an Officer of the Circle of Negro War Relief of New York City. Indeed Mrs. Bethune was one of the founders of this last named organization. Another position which Mrs. Bethune has held and still holds is that of President of the Florida Federation of Colored Women's Clubs. Through this organization she has been able to reach most of the women of the State in which she has located her school.

At the dedication of one of her buildings, Mrs. Bethune was able to assemble a very noted crowd of speakers. Among them were Vice-president Marshall, Governor Catts and his staff, and the Mayor of Daytona. This gathering of very busy men goes to show with what esteem and with what interest the work of Mrs. Bethune is held.

Mrs. Bethune is a member of the A. M. E. Church. In this church she is an active worker. But her endeavor along Christian lines can be more readily seen through her students than through her church. Mrs. Bethune is the wife of Mr. Albert Bethune. There is one son who is a student in the Army Training Corps. Morehouse Camp, Morehouse College, Atlanta, Ga.

The good that Mrs. Bethune has done can never be estimated. She could not have chosen a more needy spot in which to plant her school. Through faith and prayer she has been enabled to develop this institution from its small beginning to the place where it is a real factor in the advancement of the colored people of Florida.

DAYTONA NORMAL AND INDUSTRIAL INSTITUTE

N October, 1904, Mrs. Mary Mc-Leod Bethune, a native of South Carolina, established in a little rented cabin the Daytona Normal and Industrial Institute. She had five little girls for pupils, $1.50 for cash and a firm faith in God and a great deal of grit as resources. Since that time the school has grown in size and in usefulness till today it is one of the widely known schools for Negro girls in the South. By means of concerts, festivals and the like Mrs. Bethune was enabled to purchase the land on which the school now is located.

In all the school now owns twenty acres of land. In 1907 a four story frame structure was "Prayed up, sung up and talked up." The name of this building is Faith Hall. Back of this was placed a two story frame building which is used for kitchen, etc. In 1918 the new $40,000.00 auditorium was completed and dedicated. Mrs. Bethune was able to assemble many people of note for this service. The vice-President Marshall of the United States, the governor of Florida, the Mayor of Daytona and many other White men of prominence. Emmett J. Scott, Special Assistant to the Secretary of War and Dr. J. W. E. Bowen of Gammon Theological Seminary were both on the programme. Such an assembly of prominent men and women show in a measure the esteem in which Mrs. Bethune is held and the regard that is given her work.

The school stands for broad, thorough, practical training. Its purpose is to train its students to become strong, useful, Christian women, to afford them an opportunity to learn a vocation, so that when they leave the school they may be self supporting, and by precept and example, in a very definite way help to improve the communities in which they live. A sound body, a trained mind, hand and heart, is Mrs. Bethune's idea of a complete education.

For the training of the mind the courses offered are from the primary through high school and then special studies for teacher training. This work is done in a thorough manner. For the hand there are offered sewing, dressmaking, domestic science, gardening, poultry raising, raffia work, rug weaving, chair caning, broom making and nurse training. For the training of the heart, the Bible is studied throughout the school and twice a day a short time is set aside for "quiet hour." This time is devoted to personal devotion. Then there is the musical department and the business course, both of which train the head and the hand. Throughout all that section of Florida there is no other school that compares with the Daytona Normal and Industrial Institute in the training that is given to the Negro girls.

The work of the Institute is made so practical that when the pupils go out they fit into the life of the community. They do not have to go through

A FIELD OF EARLY PEAS ON THE INDUSTRIAL SCHOOL FARM

the period of once again adjusting their lives to the rural life. Mrs. Bethune never lets the young people who came under her care get too far away from practical life. This in spite of the fact that the book training is thoroughly done.

One of the ways in which the school becomes a very definite part of the community of Daytona is through its hospital and nurses. In the hospital a three years' course is offered. After three months probation and then one year of training, the nurses in the McLeod Hospital are permitted to take cases in the city. In this way the school becomes an asset in the health of the community. The hospital sends out a community nurse, who helps in the care of the sick children and of the old people and of young mothers. To give some idea of the amount of work done the report of the hospital for 1917-1918 follows:

Number of patients cared for _____230
Number of Dispensary patients _____518
Number of Operations _____ 38
Number of free patients _____ 84

Another extension work that is carried on from the Daytona Institute is the Public Building for men and boys. There is no adequate educational system for the boys and men of that section. Mrs. Bethune seeing this need has in a way tried to help the young men. A building has been obtained some distance from the campus. This has been fitted up for the boys and men. Much good has come from this. They have improved in manners and have learned to enjoy reading good books. The spirit of saving and investing money has gotten abroad.

Although there is no extensive training for the men and boys the use of this building has improved the manhood of Daytona.

This school stands as a monument to the founder. Faith is indeed the chief corner stone of this institution of learning. Beginning with $1.50 fifteen years ago the work has developed to this extent. The needs of the school are still many, but with the Faith of Mrs. Bethune and of her Christian workers they have gone forward and developed the school to the point where it can offer to the colored girls of that section a training that compares favorably with that offered by similar schools anywhere. The girls who have already gone forth justify all that has been done for this institution.

TEACHING DOMESTIC SCIENCE

JAMES SETH HILLS, M. D.

MONG the professions it seems that medicine appeals most to the colored man, and a number of them have taken a high stand in this profession. Among this number and one who stands at the very head of the profession is Dr. James Seth Hills. Fired by ambition, a thirst for knowledge and a determined spirit, causes such men to reach their goal. Dr. Hills is of that class.

Dr. Hills, now a resident of Jacksonville, Florida, was born in Gainesville, this State, May 19th, 1872. His early environments and the influences at work upon him had a tendency to turn his mind to a business rather than a professional career, but a good Providence was at work upon him too, and he was finally led into a profession that has given him an unbounded field for usefulness.

When a boy, only eleven years of age, he entered a cigar factory and learned the cigar maker's trade. This he followed for seven years, earning money to pursue his studies. He attended the Public School of his native city, but before and after school hours he worked at the factory.

During the vacation months he helped his father. His father was a builder and had built up a large business, which he no doubt hoped to lead his son into, but his son had ideas of his own, and it was not in the contracting line. However, he worked with his father and learned both the carpenters and and plasterers trade. It is needless to say that he did his work well and was dependable in this as in all of his occupations. By means of his work he was enabled to send himself to school, paying all of his expenses except his course in the Long Island College Hospital.

While acting as Secretary to the head waiter of a Long Island Hotel, his affable manner made him many friends among the guests. One of them, a lady guest, brought him to the attention of Mr. S. V. White, of New York, a prominent Wall Street business man.

Mr. White took a great liking to him, and was so impressed with his keen and active mind that he interested himself in his education. He gave expression to his interest in the young man by directing that all of the expenses of young Hills' tuition as well as his personal expenses he sent to him for payment. As stated the foundation of his education was laid at the Public School of his native city, and here he made the most of his opportunity and paved the way for further advance in other institutions.

From the Public School he entered the Cookman Institute, a school under the supervision of the Freedmen's Aid Society of the Methodist Episcopal Church. Finishing his course in the Cookman Institute he entered the Walden College, located at Nashville, Tennessee. From here he entered the Long Island College Hospital, and took the medical course. Not satisfied with even the fine training he received here, his next move was to take a Post-Graduate Course in several of the European countries. He took these courses in England, Ireland, France and Germany. Returning to this country, he was for several years intern at the Freedmen's Hospital, Washington, D. C.

In 1896 he moved to Jacksonville, Florida, and began his practice of special and general surgery. For thirteen years he was surgeon for the Clyde Steamship Line, and for eleven years surgeon for the Jacksonville Traction Company.

He has practiced in Jacksonville for twenty years and is recognized as a surgeon of marked ability.

Dr. Hills is a member of the Episcopal Church, and is Secretary to the Board of Vestrymen.

He is a member of the City, State and National Medical Associations. He has traveled extensively, and has seen much of this country and Europe.

Although a single man, Dr. Hills owns and occupies a very handsome residence in Jacksonville. His possessions mark him as a success in business as well as in his chosen profession.

JOSEPH NEWMAN CLINTON

OSEPH N. Clinton, of Tampa, Florida has spent about his whole life in the services of the United States Government. Change of administrations, war and locality have not affected appariently his hold upon his position.

Mr. Clinton was born in Pittsburgh, Pennsylvania in 1854. He is the oldest son of Bishop Clinton, of the A. M. E. Church, one of the pioneer Bishops who established and planted this church. He was educated in the public schools of his native city, and in Lincoln University. Graduating from Lincoln in 1873, he taught school, and finally entered the service of his government.

As a school teacher, he used his spare moments and midnight oil to prepare himself for a better place. Strange enough to read like fiction, Mr. Clinton believed his opportunity lay in the South, and he determined to emigrate to the land of flowers and sunshine. To this end he secured a position as teacher in the schools of Florida. As it turned out this was but the mildest of a series of shocks Mr. Clinton was to administer to his friends. Progressive and Aggressive to a marked degree,

he soon secured a position as clerk in the land office at Gainesville, Florida. When Mr. Clinton's Pittsburgh friends heard this, they were thunder struck. Already amazed at the success of the young pedagogue, they thought it the height of foolhardiness, for him to tempt a kind providence further by accepting a Federal position in the untamed South. But Mr. Clinton had learned better. He saw that while his path was no bed of roses, as long as a Negro was law-abiding and self respecting he was as safe from physical violence in Florida as he was in Pennsylvania. He held this clerkship at Gainesvil'e through two Presidential administrations, Benjamin Harrison and James A. Garfield. He was then promoted and transferred, though he remained in the State of Florida. He was sent to Pensacola, where he was made inspector of customs. This post he held under President Harrison, which was nothing more than his friends back home expected at this time from his past remarkable record. However, they received their final shock when Mr. Clinton was reappointed by Democratic President Grover Cleveland.

This successful record of a Northern Negro in the South stamps Joseph M. Clinton as one of the most remarkable characters in public life. He afterwards worked fifteen years for the treasury department of the Government as Revenue Collector of the Tampa District, in Tampa, Florida. This position he held until after the inauguration of President Wilson.

During his many years of public service, Mr. Clinton conducted himself in a manner that reflected credit on himself and on his people. Always remembering that not only he himself, but through him the Negroes as a race were on trial before the most critical jury in the world, his every action bespoke the studied consideration of a highly trained public servant, towards the public he was appointed to serve. He was just as considerate of those serving under him and they felt a distinct sense of loss upon his retirement from public life.

Mr. Clinton has erected for himself and his wife, formerly Miss Agnes Stewart, of Atlantic City, to whom he was married in 1882, an elegant bungalow in Tampa, Florida. Mr. Clinton has accumulated a fine property consisting of some nine rent houses in Tampa, and holdings in two other counties. The Clintons are members of the A. M. E. Church, and take an active part in all religious and civic work.

They were not only liberal contributors to the Red Cross, Y. M. C. A., Salvation Army, and all War Camp Community service, but bought liberally of Liberty Bonds and Thrift Stamps during the World War. Mr. Clinton also gave freely his services.

JOHN T. T. WARREN

R. Warren, born in Hot Springs, Arkansas, and starting life under the greatest handicap possible, the loss of both parents before he was a week old, Mr. Warren lived to reach a pinnacle of commercial success and Fraternal popularity, attained by few and surpassed by none.

The death of his mother when he was two days old and of his father, a captain in the U. S. Army two days later, left him in the care of his grandmother, who died when he was nine years old. For a while he lived with an aunt, whose only interest in him was to get all the work out of him possible.

Even at this early age he displayed that spirit of independence and grit, that was in later years to make him famous. He had been delivering baskets of clothes to his aunt's patrons and becoming tired of this servitude, he set the basket in the street and struck out for himself.

Although he missed many a meal, and had only the sky for a canopy night after night, he never faltered in his determination to make good.

Accepting odd jobs as porter and errand boy he finally landed as a waiter in the Waverly Hotel. This was the turning point in his career. By careful study of the wishes of those he served, he rose

in a short time to the position of Head Waiter. From there he went to the Park Hotel as a bath house attendant, and soon saved enough to start in the Undertaking business. While he always devoted a great deal of his time to this business, and conducted it in a manner that made him many friends, he also developed into a realty operator of no mean ability. At the time of his death he owned besides his undertaking establishment and an elegant home, twenty-eight rent houses in Hot Springs, two farms near there, and property located in Pine Bluff, Ark., Chicago, Ill., Parigona, Okla., and Phoenix, Arizona.

In spite of his many financial interests, and the numberless calls on his time, he was never too busy to respond to requests for assistance in forwarding the interests of his fellow citizens. He was not only a member of every fraternity that a Negro could join in the State of Arkansas, (eighteen in number) and of the Chicago Elks, but an active participant in their work and a liberal contributor to all of their charities. He went through every elective station in each lodge of which he was a member and at the time of his death was Grand Worthy Councillor of the Court of Calanthe of the State of Arkansas, and Dictator of the Knights of Honor of Arkansas.

He was made manager of the K. of P.'s bath house at Hot Springs, Arkansas, and conducted that resort in a manner that gave it a national reputation.

An astute politician, he was made chairman of the Republican State Executive Committee. Enjoying the confidence and esteem of the white citizenship, he was appointed a deputy sheriff. This gives evidence of his executive ability and no less evidence of his personal magnetism and popularity. Large as were his commercial interests and strong as his fraternal ties, he always put his religion and his home first. He married Miss Mamie Hancock, who dying, left him one son Lance Warren, the idol of his eye, who died April 17, 1918. Mr. Warren married Miss Laura J. Curtis of Hot Springs, Jan. 22nd, 1919, only a few months before his death. He was a trustee and a consistent member of Tanner Chapel A. M. E. Church.

Mr. Warren died in the month of June, 1919, and his funeral, which was held from Visitor's Chapel, A. M. E. Church June 29th, was said to be the greatest tribute ever paid a citizen of Hot Springs. Not only did his associates come from all parts of the country to pay their last respects, but the white citizens, headed by the Hon. Walter M. Ebel of the Business Men's League, joined in honoring a man that was a credit to his country and to his people.

HON. ROBERT L. SMITH

ONORABLE R. L. Smith, as he is commonly known, is one of the few genuine leaders of business and uplift enterprises among Negro farmers. Thoroughly trained to what is often termed as the higher things, such as school teaching, business, politics, he has preferred to put all these behind him and to cast in his lot working among men of the soil.

Mr. Smith was born in Charleston, South Carolina, January eighth, 1861. He was educated in the city schools of Charleston, at Avery Institute, and at Atlanta University. Finishing his education he decided to enter the profession of school teaching. Texas at that time offered the fairest field for the aspirant for distinction in the schoolroom; and so in 1885 he went to the "Lone Star" state and began his career.

Before leaving for Texas he had gone back to Charleston from school and had after the collapse of the Reconstruction Government run a Republican paper. His journal went down with the final defeat of the government it supported. It was then he bade adieu to his state and moved to Texas. However, having been nominated in his absence

much to his astonishment, he ran for the Texas Legislature in 1895. Supported by a large number of white voters he won his seat, served his first term and was re-elected by an increased majority for a second term.

His election to the legislature did not, however, divert him from his real chosen profession in Texas. He had begun to work among farmers a system of personal improvement, which looked to independence and to the accumulation of property and wealth.

When Mr. Smith landed in Oakland and began teaching in Freedmanstown, which was the colored section of Oakland. He found the farmer's land mortgaged and they heavily in debt. This condition of affairs caused him no little worry and he determined to correct it. He put his mind to work and developed a plan which he put into successful operation and which has brought about changes beyond his most hopeful expectation and to the lasting benefit of his people. And so Mr. Smith organized the Farmers' Improvement Society. The organization saved money for its members by purchasing all kinds of products in large quantities and distributing them pro rata, but its chief features were its fight against the mortgage system, its improvement of methods of farming and the establishing of business enterprises on the principle of co-operation. To this Mr. Smith added a plan of a general improvement of the homes of its members. To accomplish this he made the organization fraternal and gave degrees on the following basis. The first degree was conferred upon him who kept out of debt for three months; the second, to him who kept out of debt for nine months; and so on through the year. Other degrees required a surplusage of money, or land or some possessions in addition to keeping clear of debt. To this Mr. Smith has added a bank, which is located in Waco, and a school, which is known as the F. I. S. Agricultural College located in North Texas, near Ladonia. The members of the order in addition to adhering to the first principles of the order, keeping out of debt, own some 80,000 acres of farm land, which is estimated at one and a half million dollars, and live stock valued at $300,000.

He is an active member of the Negro Business League, the Farmers' Conference and a member of the Anna T. Jeans Board. He is president of the Farmers' Improvement Bank at Waco, the head of an Overall factory and president of the Board of Trustees of the Agricultural School. He successfully inaugurated the Agricultural Extension Work.

Mr. Smith was married in 1890 at Oakland, Texas, to Miss Isabella Isaacs. There are two children. Mr. Roscoe Conkling Smith, the son, is cashier of the Farmers' Improvement Bank at Waco. Miss Olive Bell is a teacher in the Farmers' Improvement Agricultural College.

JACOB AUGUSTUS WHITE, M. D.

R. Jacob A. White, of Tampa, Fla., loves the soil of his nativity. He is one of those who see opportunities near at hand instead of far away. Not many miles from where he now labors, he was born and to some extent educated. Had there been a good Negro school of medicine near at hand it is doubtful if he would have gone beyond the confines of the land of flowers to complete his training.

Dr. White was born in Marianna, September 19, 1876. His youth was spent in and about his native city, where he attended the public schools and worked at odd times. His public school career ended, he went to Florida State College. Completing his work at the Florida State College he entered Howard University, in Washington, D. C. Having long before decided to study medicine, he took the Howard Medical course, and graduated in 1903.

Going back to Florida and passing the State examination, he opened office first in Apalachicola. Here he practiced for thirteen years, then moved to the city of Tampa, where his reputation as a physician is being made.

Long before he returned to his native state, Dr. White had thoroughly diagnosed Florida. He knew her needs for a physician or physicians; he knew her need for competent sane leadership; and he knew what opportunities lay everywhere for a hardworking, competent man. In Tampa, therefore, he began not only to practice medicine, but enter the lives of the people and to take interest in their affairs, to establish such organizations as would promote the general good. In 1917, he established in Tampa a sanitarium which served not only for the ailing and tired out people of Tampa, but for colored people everywhere. This sanitarium sent abroad not only its presence as a benefactor but the reputation of Dr. White, as a surgeon. Foreseeing the grave crisis that was coming upon the people because of the shortage of food, Dr. White began to preach Agriculture along with health. All through South Florida, indeed wherever he went he made Agriculture his theme, stimulating the people to raise more, preserve more food. In 1917, he was President of South Florida Fair, which brought to a very happy climax, all the good things he had been preaching.

Much of his influence is due to the fact he has allied himself with most of the worth while bodies in Florida. He is a member of the A. M. E. Church in his community, and gives as much time as his busy life will permit, to his church work. He is a Mason, an Odd Fellow, a Knight of Pythias, an American Woodman, a member of the Household of Ruth, and of the Court of Calanthe. Holding active membership in all these bodies, he does not find it difficult to secure cooperation for any uplift undertaking which one may set apart.

Working hard for the public weal, Dr. White has realized returns in many ways. His financial returns have been moderate; his returns in gratitude of the people and in the satisfaction of seeing needed service rendered and the results gained have been large; and his returns in honors bestowed and in confidence entrusted are perhaps his dearest rewards. The Household of Ruth has entrusted to him the examination of all candidates and members, he being the Medical Director for that body throughout the State of Florida. He is interested in the movement for the betterment and defense of colored people. He has been made President of the Tampa branch of the National Association for the Advancement of Colored People. Founder of the South Florida Fair, he was chosen President of that organization. He is also President of the Gasparilla Carnival, and banker for the American Woodmen. This, his life in his native state, grows each day richer in service, in opportunity, in satisfaction at seeing things accomplished.

Dr. White was married in Tampa, in 1915, to Miss Sarah Stanley, of Sanford. They have one son, Jacob Augustus, Jr.

CAMPUS SCENE—SCHOFIELD NORMAL AND INDUSTRIAL SCHOOL.

CHOFIELD Normal and Industrial School of Aiken, South Carolina, is one of those score or more institutions to spring up immediately after the Civil War. Inspired with zeal to give all black men training in skilled labor, Miss Martha Schofield of Pennsylvania went to South Carolina in 1865 and began to teach among the freedmen. For three years Miss Schofield taught on the coast. In 1868 she made her way into Aiken, and there began to assemble the colored people, for a school.

Like Hampton, like Fisk, Atlanta University and many other institutions of this period, the school had little trouble with enrolling enough students to insure a school. Like most of the institutions referred to, Schofield was dependent largely upon voluntary contributions. Its staunchest friends were, and are, the Society of Friends. Backed by these and by public donations, Miss Schofield added now an acre or two of land, now a building or two, now a teacher or a trade. Today it has three large and substantial brick buildings, and several frame structures, four hundred acres of farm land, one hundred and twenty-five acres of which are under cultivation. It has a faculty of twenty members and is teaching six trades. It carries a registration of 600 students and has an endowment of $106,000. The value of the property is $50,000. It is free from debt.

Much of the history of the school has been destroyed or lost, especially pertaining to the early offices of the school. However the school enjoys an unusual distinction in having at its head a lady, who is a Bachelor of Arts and a minister of long and varied experiences. The Reverend Miss L. Louise Haight is the Superintendent of Schofield. The Rev. Miss Haight was educated at Alma College, Saint Thomas County, North Carolina, at Swathmore College, Swathmore, Pennsylvania, and at the Meadville Theological School, Meadville, Pennsylvania. Miss Haight preached for twelve years. After this she left the pulpit and engaged in educational and social work in Chicago and Philadelphia. It was from this work that she was called to the head of the Schofield Normal and Industrial School.

Schofield points with pride to many milestones in her career. She rejoices that, thanks to her influence, Aiken is one of the most peaceful spots on earth for anybody, especially the Negro. She is rather proud that on her farm, in the gardens and shops many students who would remain in darkness are given a chance to earn their way through school. Finally, she is exceedingly gratified by the records made by her seven hundred or more graduates. She numbers principals and founders of schools, business men, clergymen, physicians, among whom is a woman physician and surgeon, successful farmers, missionaries to Africa, on the list of her alumni. This is her ideal:

"The first and constant aim of the school, is to give such moral, mental and industrial training as will fit them to take their respective places in the world as intelligent, self-supporting, self-respecting citizens, to prepare young men and young women to be better husbands, wives, farmers, artisans, skilled, conscientious in their duties and obligations,

ST. LUKE PENNY SAVINGS BANK—MISS MAGGIE L. WALKER AND OTHER OFFICERS.

THAT a prophet is without honor in his own country is a saying that does not hold good in the case of Mrs. Maggie L. Walker. She was born, educated and worked her way to prominence in the same town. She must be the exception that proves the rule.

Mrs. Walker was born in Richmond, Virginia. Here she attended the public school, the High School and the Normal School, finishing each in turn. After she had completed her course of study she took up the work of teaching. She taught in the Public Schools of Richmond till her marriage in 1890, when she gave up the work in the public school system and began teaching in a private school. The life of Mrs. Walker has been a very active one. While still teaching she became the agent for the Woman's Union. This is an insurance company that looks solely after the interest of women. Then in 1900 she accepted the very important post of Secretary-Treasurer of the Independent Order of St. Luke. This is a fraternal organization that operates in several states and has at present many thousand members. When Mrs. Walker took up the work it was given up by a man because of the condition of affairs in the order. These are the reasons why he declined to serve the order further: the order was at its lowest ebb; there was no money in the treasury; the order was not spreading as it should; there was a lack of co-operation between the Grand Officers and the Officers and members of the Subordinate Councils and the salary paid for the work ($300.00) per year was not justifiable.

To take up any work after the person leaving it has given it such a reputation shows courage of the highest order. This courage Maggie L. Walker had and she assumed the responsibilities of the office and the steadiness of its growth is a monument to her ability as an organizer and as an executive. In the Building of the Independent Order of St. Luke the experiences of Mrs. Walker have been such as all pioneer workers encounter. The organization numbered less than one thousand when she took up the work. Today it has a list of fifty thousand financial members.

The organization had no assets whatever. Today it has assets to the amount of $150,750.00. All this marvelous growth is due directly to the untiring efforts of Mrs. Walker and to her great ability and charming personality. She has been able to reach the people, as they had not been reached before, by the appeals of other secretaries. When a bank was opened in connection with the order Mrs. Walker was the one chosen to serve in the capacity of President.

Mrs. Walker has taken an active part in every organization in the city of Richmond that is managed be persons of color. Among these are the Eastern Star. Household of Ruth. Court of Calantha, Richmond Benefit Insurance Company, and the American. Mrs. Walker is deeply religious in her make up. She has been a member of the Old Historic First African Baptist Church from early childhood.

Throughout the State of Virginia, Mrs. Walker is honored in the various organizations among colored women. She is president of the Council of Colored Women, Auditor of the Virginia State Federation, Trustee of Girls' Home School, Peake, Virginia, Grand Matron of the Juvenile Depart-

ST. LUKE PENNY SAVINGS BANK

ment of the Independent Order of St. Luke, Vice-President of the Richmond Branch of the National Association for the Advancement of Colored People, Vice-President of the Negro Organization Society of Virginia, and one of the Advisory Committee of the National Training School, Lincoln Heights, D. C.

September 14, 1899 she was united in marriage to Mr. Armstead Walker, Jr., of Richmond. There are two sons in the family. The older, Russell E. T. Walker, is in the work of the Independent Order of St. Luke, serving the organization in the capacity of auditor. The second son, Melvin DeWitt Walker, is a student in the College Department of Shaw University, at Raleigh, North Carolina.

The Independent Order of St. Luke has recently passed its fifth anniversary. At this time they held quite a gathering in honor of the occasion. And the occasion was one worthy of honor, for the amount of good done by and through this organization cannot be estimated. The Order was first started in the City of Baltimore, Maryland, by Miss Prout, in 1867. Looking about her and seeing the suffering among the sick and aged of our race, and seeing the distress in some of the families for lack of means with which to bury their dead, this sainted, Christian woman conceived the idea of a fraternal Order. The first thought was for women only as members, but as the work grew, men were admitted. She carried the work from Baltimore into Norfolk, Portsmouth, Petersburg, and Richmond, Virginia, accepting as members of the council some of the best men and women of the Methodist Episcopal Faith.

As the Order was started in Maryland it was the Grand United Order of St. Luke. Mr. Richard Forrester led in a movement to pull the Virginia Councils out of the Grand body. This was done and it became known as the Independent Order of St. Luke. He proved his worth to the order by revising and compiling the Ritual of the Order. Those who know the merit of the work say of it: "It was declared perfect, and will live to honor his name after we all have passed away. This Grand piece of work proved his worth to the Order and to the community at large." Mr. W. T. Forrester was the active Secretary for thirty-five years.

But in 1899 he refused to serve longer because, as is stated elsewhere in these pages, the work had ceased to develop under his leadership. The order was turned over to Mrs. Maggie L. Walker, with fifty-seven benefited Councils, 1,080 financial members, $31.61, turned over from the Grand Treasurer J. J. Carter, and bills amounting to $400.

One year after the Order was turned over to Mrs. Walker, it had doubled itself. Mrs. Walker gathered around herself advisors of good sound judgment and they took steps that were for the betterment of the whole organization. The order spread. It was taken into New York and the District of Columbia. By careful handling of the funds they accumulated money enough to invest 500 dollars in the St. Luke Association in 1902, and at the same time they made a first payment of $5.00 on the printing press, from each of the two branches of the order. With the press purchased they started the St. Luke Herald, which was the mouthpiece of the Order.

The next year the amount paid into the St. Luke Association was $2000.00. The Grand Secretary reported 4,101 new members added during the year and a total financial membership of 10,200 adults. While the Grand Chief changed from time to time, Mrs. Maggie L. Walker continued to hold the position of Grand Secretary of the Order. And under her direction it grew from year to year. The growth was rapid. Space forbids that we recount all the steps in the progress of this upward growth. In 1907 the report included the statement that the Order had in the Penny Savings Bank over on Broad Street, the sum of $7200.00. This was under the head of Emergency Fund, and was held to await the orders of the Subordinate Councils. It was in this year that the laws of various States in which the Order was being operated made it imperative for them to have a large reserve fund. Had these laws been passed the year that the Order changed Secretaries it would of necessity have gone under. But under the new order of things they were prepared for the emergencies that confronted them. This was done by building up an order that was able to weather all financial storms.

April 1, 1911, they began using a new system of Book-keeping, which had been installed at a cost of $1000. With the new system the whole business end of the Order was put on an up-to-date footing. With the use of this system it was an easy matter to keep track of all the money paid in and of each individual member.

To estimate the good of this organization is beyond us. They have provided work for a large number. They have looked after the interest of many bereaved persons. They have developed the business ability of the people who came to work for them. They have acquired property—they own a large building in which they have their offices, meetings, etc., and a building in which they operate the Penny Savings Bank. Through the administration of their affairs, they have compelled the respect of the best people of both races. They are never afraid to open their books to the inspection of others, for they keep their affairs in perfect order. This is the record of the I. O. of St. Luke.

REV. JOHN O. WILLIAMS, A. B., B. D.,
AND TRINITY CHURCH

EVEREND Mr. Joshua O. Williams, of Marshall, Texas, is one of those ministers who set education above riches and placed learning as the only true foundation of genuine achievements. To him no hardships were too severe, no privation too sharp, if only he could make his way into the schools to drink from the fount of knowledge.

Mr. Williams is in bone and fibre a Texan. He was born at Montgomery, Montgomery County, Texas. He appeared for advanced work in the public schools of his native county and town. From the public schools of Montgomery County he went to the State Normal School, to Prairie Normal and Industrial Institute, at Prairie View. From Prairie View he went to Wiley University, at Marshall. Here he received his Bachelor of Arts degree, and completed in a fair measure all of the courses Texas could give him for his particular purpose in life.

He had long before made up his mind to enter the ministry. He had been converted and had joined the Methodist Episcopal Church. Leaving Marshall he entered Gammon Theological Seminary, at Atlanta, Georgia, where he received the degree of Bachelor of Divinity. He spent sometime as a school teacher both in Georgia and in his native State.

However, his great work has been done in his chosen calling, the ministry. This too, like the most of his schooling, has been done in Texas. He has held some of the largest appointments in the Texas Methodist Episcopal Conference. Among these are numbered Ebenezer, at Marshall, Texas; Mount Vernon, at Houston, Texas; Tabernacle, at Galveston, Texas; Trinity, at Houston, Texas, and the District Superintendent of Paris, Texas.

Recognized as a leader and an unselfish worker, he has been placed at the head of many organizations in his state. He has been president of the Preachers' Aid Society, of the Texas Conference; president of the Board of Trustees of his alma mater, Wiley University; president, and this in the business world, of the Boley Light and Power Company of Boley, Oklahoma. Boley it will be remembered, is a Negro town. He was a member of the last General Conference, which met at Saratoga Springs, New York, in 1916. He has traveled from the Atlantic to the Pacific, from the Lakes to the Gulf, and into Canada. He is a Knight of Pythias, a member of the Mosiac Templars and of the Court of Calanthe. In these bodies, as in the church and in business organizations, he is regarded by his fellows as a man of universal power and leadership.

Rev. Williams has twice been married. The first Mrs. Williams was Miss Katie Kendall, of Atlanta, Georgia. They were married in 1894. To them three children—one son and two daughters were born. But only two are living. The mother herself soon passed away.

Rev. Williams was married the second time to Miss Lenora B. Green, of Galveston, Texas. They were married in 1900. There are two children in the Williams home, a young lady and a young man. Through these the father is establishing a family tradition, as it were, by sending them along the paths which he trod, both in education and in vocation. Miss Lillian Katy Williams, the daughter, is a student at Wiley University, like her father years ago, she is a candidate for the degree of Bachelor of Arts. Robert M. Williams, the son, has already run the early gauntlet in preparing for a career. Like his father back there in the eighties, he is now a student at Gammon Theological Seminary, and is a candidate for the degree of Bachelor of Divinity.

Rev. Williams own a handsome residence in Marshall, Texas, has valuable property in Houston, and owns an apple farm in the State of Washington.

State Agricultural and Mechanical College

THE State Colored Normal Industrial, Agricultural and Mechanical College, at Orangeburg, South Carolina, was founded in 1896, by the State of South Carolina. It is supported partly by the State and partly by the Federal government. The Federal money drawn is from the funds set aside for agricultural and mechanical training. The board of trustees that governs the affairs of the institution is elected by the Legislature. Of this Board the Governor of the State is ex-officio chairman.

The courses of study offered by the State Colored Normal, Industrial, Agricultural and Mechanical College are elementary, preparatory and Normal. Doing this work there are fourteen teachers in Academic work. The other teachers on the faculty, thirteen in number, devote their time to teaching the trades and agriculture.

The attendance at this college is very good. There are about 700 pupils in all of the courses. Of this number the greater portion is enrolled in the Elementary Course. In the Secondary Courses there are enrolled only 197. The school does good work with the equipment they have. But the teaching force is small for so large a number of pupils.

The Industrial work is in charge of teachers well prepared in the lines they teach. An interest in the work is shown by all the students. The system used in the State Colored Normal, Industrial, Agricultural and Mechanical College in combining the industrial work with that of the academic department is the part time system. The classes are required to devote one day each week to the trade work.

The shop in which this trade work is taught is well fitted up for teaching. Carpentry, bricklaying, tailoring, plumbing, blacksmithing, wheelwrighting, painting, and harness making are the mechanical trades offered to the young men.

The young women of the school are offered two trades, sewing and cooking. The work is in charge of two well prepared teachers. The girls are taught these subjects not from the standpoint of using them as trades, but every girl in the school is required to take up the two trades because they should be a part of a normal woman's knowledge.

The agricultural department has a farm of eighty-five acres, an agricultural building, dairy and stables. The work is in charge of four teachers. Aside from the actual work done on the farm there is some class room work in the subject of agriculture. The work on the farm is done largely by the students under the direct supervision of the teachers in charge. The course in agriculture begins in the senior preparatory class. In this class they have to do two hours each week in market gardening. The Normal classes have two courses in agriculture besides one in rural sociology and one in agricultural economics.

The State College at Orangeburg is, besides being a State College, a Land Grant School. From the Land Grant Fund, it draws the greater portion of its support. The amount from this source is $30,754.00. The State appropriations are $12,614.00. Then the fees paid by the students and money from farm and shops raised the amount more than two thousand dollars.

The school owns 130 acres of land. Of this number only eighty-five acres are under cultivation. The entire tract of land is valued at $50,000.00. The buildings on the place are valued at $227,000.00 The two larger buildings are Morrill Hall, boy's dormitory, and Bradham Hall, the girl's dormitory. The latter is a large two story brick structure with rooms to accommodate 400 girls and the administrative offices. The dining hall is a one-story building which accomodates 750. Industrial Hall is a large two-story brick building. It contains all the shops and is well equipped throughout. There are smaller buildings—the President's home, six teacher's houses, agricultural building, the dairy, two barns and a heating and electrical building.

The man at the head of this State College is President R. S. Wilkinson. Mr. Wilkinson belongs to that type of instructors whose success has been won by their combining a splendid education, and a natural talent for educational leadership, with a gift of diplomacy that enables them to not only successfully manage the affairs of their colleges, but to obtain the maximum allowances from the State at large for the support and extension of Negro educational enterprises. Mr. Wilkinson has made a record at the head of State A. & M. College that has not only gained the commendation of his fellow citizens, but established for him a reputation as an educator and constructive leader throughout the country. Mr. Wilkinson is not only a leader along educational lines, but takes a prominent part in all civic and religious movements. He proved himself a power for good in the world war, and placed his services unreservedly at the disposal of his country.

PICKFORD HALL—LECTURE HALL—VIRGINIA UNION UNIVERSITY

MONG the first schools organized for the training of freedmen by the Christian people of the North were those which were later united into Virginia Union University. Both the American Baptist Home Mission Society and the National Baptist Institute and University began work in Washington and Richmond, immediately after the close of the war.

In 1865, Maryland Seminary was opened as well as the National Theological Institute in Washington. After a few years the latter was merged with the former, and under Dr. G. M. P. King, the new Maryland Seminary became a prosperous and strong Normal School and Academy, at which hundreds of young men and women prepared for useful and honored service especially in teaching and preaching. Dr. King was President from 1867 to 1897, and gave untiring zeal and unstinted devotion to his work.

In 1865, a theological school was opened in Richmond, Va., known successively as Colver Institute, Richmond Institute, and Richmond Theological Seminary. Among its earliest teachers were Dr. J. C. Binney, Dr. Nathaniel Colver, the famous abolitionist and preacher, Dr. Robert Ryland, for many years President of Richmond College, and Dr. C. H. Corey, President from 1868 to 1898. After 1886 this school limited its work strictly to those preparing for the Christian ministry, and trained many of its leading colored preachers.

Virginia Union University, combining these two schools was opened in the Fall of 1899 in new granite buildings on the outskirts of Richmond, as an Academy, College and Theological Seminary for young men.

The campus and farm comprises about 50 acres of land on a gentle elevation in the Northwestern part of the city. Here 250 years ago was Nathaniel Bacon's quarters, and here 60 years ago Confederate soldiers encamped and defended the capitol of the Confederacy at Battery number 9.

The buildings include ten substantial and beautiful granite structures and four frame residences. Most of the buildings were erected with money secured by the American Baptist Home Mission Society. Their cost was about $300,000. The main group consists of Library and Chapel, Lecture Hall, two Dormitories, and Dining Hall. A subordinate group includes Industrial Hall, Power House and Barn.

The University is controlled by a Board of Trustees composed of Northern and Southern White and Colored men in about equal numbers. The American Baptist Home Mission Society of New York which at present contributes three fourths of the cost of the school outside the boarding depart-

COBURN HALL CHAPEL AND LIBRARY

HUNTLEY HALL—DORMITORY—VIRGINIA UNION UNIVERSITY

ment has large influence in determining the policy of the University.

Three purposes are prominent in the establishment and management of the school. (1) To train Christian leaders—especially preachers and teachers, with the emphasis on Christian. (2) To give to colored young men of ability the opportunity to secure in the South a higher education equal to that open to white young men. (3) To secure the cooperation of both races and all parts of the country in giving the highest education to colored men.

The faculty consists of seventeen professors and teachers, graduates from the best Normal schools and colleges North and South. The Library contains 13,000 bound volumes, and is open for consultation twelve hours each day. The science laboratories are well equipped for the work given. The Industrial Hall is fitted out with anvils, forges, carpenters benches, turning lathes, tools, and a twenty horse power gasoline engine. The buildings are heated by steam and lighted by electricity. The dormitories accommodate about two hundred-fifty young men, in rooms provided with the necessary heavy furniture. The Dining Hall seats about two hundred and seventy-five. A farm of about twenty acres, cultivated largely by students, furnishes a large part of the vegetables and the milk for the table. A fenced athletic field gives space for sports and recreation.

The University comprises a standard four year College Course, requiring fifteen units of secondary work for entrance, with school year of thirty-six weeks, and an enrollment (1916-17) of sixty-five students; a standard three year theological course with college graduation as entrance requirements for the degree of B. D., and fifteen secondary un-

its as entrance requirement for regular students, and an enrollment of thirty. In addition to these, eighty five in other departments are preparing to preach; and a four year high school academy course with manual training, and an enrollment of 234. The total enrollment for the school year was 350.

A summer Normal under the State Board of Education, is held for six weeks. Last year the enrollment was 208 teachers.

In fifty years this school, with its predecessors, Maryland Seminary in Washington, and Richmond Theological Seminary, has trained about 4000 colored students of all grades, about 1500 preachers about 1000 teachers; 12 foreign missionaries, many physicians and hundreds of leaders of the race in other professions and occupations. The full graduates from the different departments number nearly 1000. They are to be found in positions of prominence and leadership in the ministry, in education, in medicine, in editorship, and in social service. Whatever the profession they naturally take a leading part in temperance and health and moral movements for the betterment of the people.

MARTIN L. GRAY HALL DINING HALL.

WESLEY WARREN JEFFERSON, D. S.

MONG the professions which have come into very great prominence lately, because of the number of young men who have entered them, and because of the good being accomplished, Dentistry ranks high. For years, colored people everywhere suffered from all the ills directly traceable to bad teeth, without having Dentists of their own race to teach them proper tooth care, or to remedy the ill from this lack of care. But of recent years, such great stress has been laid on this particular branch of work, that many of our young men have taken up the profession. Among these is Wesley Warren Jefferson.

Dr. Jefferson was born in Florence, South Carolina, on July 25, 1879. As lad he attended the public schools of Florence. Mr. Jefferson, like many another lad, was ambitious enough to overcome the obstacle of no cash; and so he pressed on to his goal of a thorough education by earning with his hands, during vacations and before and after schools hours, money enough to support himself. When he finished the public school course in Florence he was ambitious to be a thorough tradesman, and so he entered Tuskegee Institute. Tus-

kegee was just coming into prominence at that time, and the young man went with the crowds that were beginning to throng its halls. Dr. Jefferson was graduated from Tuskegee Institute in 1899. Throughout his after life, Dr. Jefferson found that the general training at working, which he received while in Tuskegee, as well as the rigidly taught habits came to his aid many times.

On leaving Tuskegee Institute, Dr. Jefferson went to the West Indies, and taught school there for two years. He then returned to the United States. He had tried teaching and did not like it well enough to make it his life work. So when he returned to this counry he matriculated at Howard University, as a student in Dentistry. Dr. Jefferson needed to earn his way through school and so he took the Civil Service examination and secured a position with the government, and earned enough to pay his way through college.

He was graduated from the Howard course of Dentistry with the degree of D. S., in 1904. After graduation, Dr. Jefferson, realizing that all professional men go through the "starvation period" if they have no money for the start, decided to continue in his government work for a period. For three years Dr. Jefferson therefore worked in Washington, and thus eliminated the period of pinched circumstances suffered by most professional men while the public gets used to the sign.

In 1910, Dr. Jefferson opened his office in Norfolk, Virginia. In the same year he was married to Miss Geraldine Merriam Muldraw, of Florence, South Carolina. The young couple made their home in Norfolk and began to make friends. They joined the Baptist Church of Norfolk, and began to take part in all the activities of the people. It was not long before the new dentist and his wife had many friends and the former a very large practice. For seven years, Dr. Jefferson has practiced in Norfolk, and during that time he has made for himself a great reputation and he stands out as a leader of his people and as a worker. Dr. Jefferson has also the respect and good will of the white people.

Dr. Jefferson has traveled extensively. While still a student, he began his travels, having to go about at times in connection with his work. He has traveled over the United States, both North and South, and in the West Indes.

By hard work and very careful economy, Dr. Jefferson has been able to live comfortably, to equip and keep up-to-date his large office, and at the same time accumulate a goodly number of property holdings. He owns his own home, which is a very attractive residence on Queen Street. He owns two rent houses, and several vacant lots. Thus Dr. Jefferson is numbered not only among the leading professional Negroes of Norfolk, but among the most substantial business men.

Dr. and Mrs. Jefferson have no children of their own, nevertheless their home is a happy one, and is presided over very charmingly by Mrs. Jefferson.

Robert Horace Brooks, M. D.

HILE much has been written derogatory to the State of Georgia, in the treatment of Negroes, a study of the colored citizens that are making good will convince the most skeptical, that while conditions are by no means ideal, there is no state in the union where there is greater opportunity for the self-respecting and law-abiding citizen to make good. A splendid example of this is shown by the success of Dr. Brooks, in Rome, Ga. The citizens of this beautiful and aristrocratic old Southern town point with genuine pleasure and pride to the success of Dr. Brooks. His reputation as a successful practioner, is only equalled by his record as a business man, and his credit rating the equal of almost any merchant in the city.

In spite of all that has been said and written, the Georgia Negro has made giants strides, especially in the cities. You will go far and look wth argus eyes to find a state with so much Negro business enterprise, refinement, talent and education. Take Atlanta for an example. It flourishes with handsome Negro homes. It is the home of the famous Odd Fellows Building, the still more famous Standard Insurance Company, writing its policies like the best of the old line companies, sending forth its agents and establishing branch houses in the leading cities over the land. Education is in the keenest competition here. Morehouse College stands on one hill; Atlanta University on another; Clark University and Morris Brown University in other parts of the city; Spelman Seminary, the largest school in the world for the education of Negro girls is here sending out all over the South and into foreign lands, especially into Africa, her well-rounded students. Atlanta is not in a class to herself. Close to her come Savannah, Athens, Brunswick and other cities in which we find many refined Negroes—all this goes to show that where determination abounds, success does also abound.

It is here that one of the most scholarly of the Negroes lives and follows his calling in all safety day by day. This man is Dr. Robert Horace Brooks who is known as the Scholarly Physician." Regardless of race or creed he wears and defends this title. On questions of History, of literature, of Geography, of War and Peace, and of education, as well as of the medical profession, he is very often referred to as the final arbiter, because his judgment is sound and his reading and study wide and thorough.

Unlike many of his brother practioneers, he had the advantage of a splendid early education. Born in Trinidad British West Indies, his parents from the first inbued him with the spirit of thoroughness, typical of the British subject wherever he is found.

Education under the British Flag is by no means so general, certainly higher education is not so popular, but the training in the literary branches is most exhaustive, so much so that your lad of fifteen is already a scholar in his habit of mind and as thoroughly a Britisher as your decendant of Plantagenet—wiry, confident, unpeturbed.

Having gone to and finished the public schools of Trinidad he entered Queens College. Finishing here he came to America, in 1900, and enrolled in the medical department of Howard University, Washington, D. C. His course was broken into on account of the serious illness and death of his mother which called him home. In 1902, he returned to America to take up again his duties in medicine. Instead of returning to the Howard University he entered as a student of medicine Shaw University, Raleigh, N. C. Dr. Brooks was graduated from the Shaw Medical College in 1906. After graduating at Shaw Medical College he took a Post Graduate course at Jefferson College and from there went to Tuskegee and served as an intern in the hospital at Tuskegee Institute, gaining experience of people of this country, as well as practice in medicine. His year of internship ended, Dr. Brooks began practice in Madison, Ga. Here he remained for five years. In 1912, he moved to Rome, Georgie, where he is now practicing and where he is held in such high esteem as a doctor and a scholar. While he is an able practitioner and well versed in medical science, his natural aptitude and inclination leads him to surgery, in which branch he is an expert. Dr. Brooks is known not only in Rome and surrounding country, but pretty generally through the State of Georgia. He is a Roman Catholic in Faith. He is a member of the Masonic Lodge and of the Pythians. He is medical examiner of his town for the Standard Life Insurance Company, of Atlanta, for the Columbia Life and for the Mutual Life Insurance Companies.

Dr. Brooks is much traveled, having in addition to spending time in North Carolina and in Alabama as a student, traveled through the Eastern states, through the South and on many of the Islands.

Dr. Brooks was married in 1907, to Miss Anita Rochon, of New Orleans, Louisiana. There are two sons born to Mr. and Mrs. Brooks, Robert Horace, Jr., and Frederick.

UNDERTAKING ESTABLISHMENT OF
W. I. JOHNSON & SONS

R. William Isaac Johnson was born of slave parents in 1852, in Charlotte County, Virginia. At the close of the Civil War he attended the free schools that had been started for the freedom of the South, in the city of Richmond. He finished the Richmond Normal School course and taught for two years. His next work was that of letter carrier, in which work he was engaged for twelve years. But Mr. Johnson, like a great number of our men, saw no future for himself in the work of letter carrier. So, with no previous training in business, he gave up his steady income and launched out into business for himself. With undaunted courage and energy, he has forged ahead until to-day he is one of the leading undertakers of his race in this country.

The firm first opened in 1886, at 23 West Broad Street, where for five years they did a prosperous business. Outgrowing this establishment, Mr. Johnson bought property at 207 N. Foushee St., where he conducted the business for twenty years. In 1911 once more Mr. Johnson considered his quarters unsuitable, and so he sold the property on Foushee Street for the sum of $25,000.00, and bought and built his present commodious establishment at 10 West Leigh Street, and two residences adjoining. The building is a three-story brick and is well equipped. On the first floor are the offices, show room, stock room, ware room and the morgue. The second floor is taken up by an auditorium which is used as a chapel and for various other public functions. The third floor is divided into four beautiful lodge rooms which are used by various fraternal societies throughout the city. The entire building is heated by steam and lighted by electricity.

In addition to the Undertaking business and entirely separate from it is the Garage, owned and managed by this firm. The Garage, formerly the stable, is a two-story brick structure, that extends from one street to the other. It was formerly equipped with a full line of horse-drawn vehicles for the conduct of their business. Most of these have been recently disposed of and replaced by auto vehicles, a black and grey motor hearse, four seven passenger limousines, three seven passenger touring cars, one Ford sedan, two Ford touring cars, and two motor delivery wagons. Their equipment is sought by the leading funeral directors of the city.

In building up this business for himself, Mr. Johnson has made a place for his sons. In 1911, he took the two sons into the business with him. One of them serves as his father's principal assistant. The other is now in he Army, and has for the time given up his active work with the firm. The business methods of the firm are of the highest order, their equipment up-to-date, and they enjoy the confidence and the highest respect of all classes of citizens, both in their own locality and in the undertaking profession at large.

Mr. Johnson has taken time from his business to serve in other concerns. He is a member of the Henrico Lodge of Ancient, Free and Accepted Masons. He is director of the St. Luke Penny Saving Bank, of Richmond, and a Director of the Crown Savings Bank, of Newport News. To these organizations he brings his great business ability and helps to hold the confidence of the public. Many honors have been shown to Mr. Johnson because of the great work he has done and is doing in the colored business world. Among these might be mentioned—he was President of the Negro exhibit of the Jamestown exposition and he is a trustee of the Negro Reformatory of Virginia.

Mr. Johnson is a member of the National Negro Business Men's League. He has been present at most of their gatherings. Most of the traveling that Mr. Johnson has taken the time to do has been in going from one section of the country to another while in attendance upon the National League.

In May, of 1889, Mr. Johnson was married to Miss Maria Cooley, of Richmond, Virginia. To them have been born three children. Mrs. Tarquinia A. Middleton is a daughter who now resides in Chicago. W. I. Johnson, Jr., is his father's mainstay in the undertaking and livery business, and the other son, Jas. A. C. Johnson, is a Sergeant in the United States Army. Mr. and Mrs. Johnson live in one of the new residences which they have recently built and the sons, with their wives, live in the other. It is a far cry from the poverty-stricken boyhood of this man to the place he now occupies in the world of business and in the social world. He has shown what one who has made up his mind to succeed, can really do in thirty-two years.

Reverend John Franklin Drane

WHEN you think of Kentucky, your mind is likely to go out to the Cobbs, the Watersons, Breckenbridges and others of that noble strain which makes the blue grass state so universally popular and lovable. When you add to this her fame for beautiful ladies you might well wonder why everybody doesn't pull up and go down there to live. Perhaps this would be so were it not that men are so devoid of the spirit of adventure and of romance, both being wholly eclipsed by the everlasting tugging after sordid gains.

The Negroes of the state are no less famed among their brothers than are the whites among theirs. Kentucky has a high scale of general education, good taste and refinement. Perhaps in no other Southern state or semi-Southern state does one hear so little of that modern epedemic, race friction. This is without doubt due to the high standards of both the races, for almost without exception, when misunder-standings come they are started by the lower element of one race or the other.

Kentucky is a sort of Baptist strong-hold. Indeed the Baptists feel, and not without considerable warrant in this case, that they lead the race. They have more schools, better schools and handsomer churches than do the others. They have keener competition for places of leadership in the schools, in the churches, in the clubs and civic bodies than do most of the other sects. Their papers and their journals are more numerous and are longer lived.

Therefore, to be pastor of one of the largest and most costly churches in one's state is no distinction to be passed over lightly. Such is the good fortune of Rev. John F. Drane, of Bowling Green, Ky. The church of which he is pastor is known as the State First Baptist Church. It has a seating capacity of eleven hundred and cost twenty thousand dollars.

Rev. Drane's ascent to his post has been steady and unwavering, though born in a state where the Baptists are legion and where the Baptist preachers are among the giants in the pulpit. He was born shortly after the war, in 1866, to be explicit,

when the school house doors nor the theological school doors did not swing so easily on the hinge as they do now. Rev. Drane was born in Washington County. He spent some time in the country schools and then went to Louisville, where he attended the Central High School for eight years. For a long time he worked and studied. It was not for him to go away to take formal courses in theology and in the doctrines. He had to fight the battle for daily sustenance where he was and study his theology when and where he could.

To educate himself for the ministry, which he was resolved to enter, he made various shifts. For a good while he had a private tutor, J. T. Sullivan. Then he applied himself much alone; then he studied by correspondence, taking courses in the McKinley Extension University of Oak Park, Ill. Finally when thirty years of age, feeling that he was in a measure prepared to do the work to which he aspired, he entered the ministry. He began at Louisville, Ky., in 1898, with the church of the Good Shepherd. In a few years he was in Covington, where he purchased the Ninth Street Baptist church. From Covington he went to May's Lick, where he inaugurated the Building Fund for a church there. On January 1st, 1915, he was called to take charge of the big church at Bowling Green. Thus in fifteen years, Rev. Drane has climbed to the highest round of the ladder as a pastor in his native State.

As a pastor and as a citizen he has carried his full quota of extra duties outside of the church. In Lodge affiliations he is a Mason, an Odd Fellow and a Good Samaritan. In religious bodies he is a member of the Baptist Foreign Mission Board of the National Convention and chairman of the Union District Association and Sunday School Convention. He is editor of the "Blaze," a weekly paper of Bowling Green, and past Grand Chaplain of the F. and A. M.

Rev. Drane has traveled much, having toured the whole country on business or pleasure trips. He was married in 1910, to Miss Mary F. Jordan, of May's Lick, Ky. They have one son, Joseph Franklin Drane, who will soon be a pupil in the public school.

JOHN B. KEY.

HE life of John B. Key, should be an inspiration to any boy who has for his ambition the acquiring of a good share of this world's goods; for in this story we have a lad who earned his way in the common schools by shining shoes —advanced to the position of owner of Real Estate and Oil Lease Business, and worth in his own right over one million dollars.

John B. Key is a southerner by birth. He was born in Florence Alabama, June 10, 1867. Here he lived with his parents till he was nine years of age. Up to that time he was a little farm lad, attending school during the short sessions held in the rural districts. At the age of nine he was sent to his first cousin in Memphis, Tennessee, Mr. Randall Clay, who was a finished mechanic in the James and Graham Wagon Factory. Here his opportunities for getting an education were greater. He entered the Clay Street Public School. Here he remained, applying himself to the work in hand till he completed the English branches. In order to remain in school for this length of time he had to work at something that would take only out of school time. For this purpose he chose shoe-shining. After leaving school he tried working successively in Foundry, Hotel and Wagon Factory.

While still a young man, Mr. Key worked his way from the position of porter to that of clerk in one of the best white hotels of that period, and operated the United States Barber Shop, at Hot Springs, Arkansas. Later he moved to Port Arthur, Canada, and clerked in the Northern Hotel. But Mr. Key was not altogether satisfied with the life of a hotel clerk. He felt that there were bigger things and better opportunities in store for him. So once more we find him moving. This time he moved out to the territory of Oklahoma, in 1891. Here he got a farm for himself and set for himself the task of learning to run it. This was a farm of 160 acres of land. Mr. Key has never since given up his interest in farms and farming. At present he own 2800 acres of farm land. Later he engaged in the Mercantile business. In this business he continued till 1917, when he opened up a real estate and oil lease business. In this business he is still engaged and it is growing rapidly under his direction. He organized a company with a capital stock of $100,000 under the corporate name of J. B. Key Oil & Gas Company, which has secured some of the best oil leases in the Peoner Oil Fields, and is now drilling in the famous Willcox Pool, in the heart of production. In addition to this lease the company owns leases on several thousand acres.

It is the purpose of this company to erect a refinery and conduct a banking business in addition to boring for oil and gas. In addition to the land owned by Mr. Key he has several blocks of improved real estate and considerable interests in valuable oil production, to the amount of over one million dollars. He has just finished two more blocks of fine three-story brick buildings containing 128 rooms and 6 stores, 25 by 100 feet.

Mr. Key is a member of the A. M. E. Church, being a Trustee and Steward of the Church of which he is a member. But in religious matters, Mr. Key is broad and liberal. He visits all the Churches of the colored people of Okmulgee and contributes liberally to the support of them all. In this manner, Mr. Key shows that he is broader than any creed. In fraternal matters, Mr. Key is a member of the Knights of Pythias, of the Mosiac Templars of America and of the United Brothers of Friedship. In the order of the Knights of Pythias he serves as Grand Master of EXQ.

Mr. Key is the President of Flipper-Key-Davis University, he is also a member of the board of Trustees. This school is maintained by the A. M. E. Church in the State of Oklahoma. The school has his name as a part of its own. He is not only President and Trustee but a very liberal supporter of this institution of learning.

As recorded in the first part of this sketch, Mr. Key went with his work from place to place. And so in travels he has gone over the whole of the United States, over part of Canada, and has traveled extensively in Mexico.

Mr. Key was married to Miss Annie B. Collins on the 22nd day of February, 1888. She has been a true helpmate to him. In all his business undertakings he has asked for and gotten her advice and very frequently it was the joint plans, rather than the plans of one that have made the successful business deals.

There are no children in the family, but the Key's have made up for this by loving and rearing the children of relatives.

Thomas F. Parks

M R. Parks was born in Albany, Ga., in 1864. When a child his parents moved to Greensboro, Ga., where he received his first school training. This was very meagre and when he moved to Louisville, Ky., he brought with him the determination to succeed. Unable to go to school in the day time as he was compelled to earn his living, he entered a night school where in a remarkably short time he became proficient in all branches necessary to business success. Quick to see and grasp an opportunity, Mr. Parks was impressed with the fact that there was a splendid field for the development of an insurance agency that catered exclusively to the Negroes. He became identified with the Insurance Business in 1899, and is today special agent for the National Benefit Association of Washington, D. C., and one of the leading producers for that company. In settling the death claims incident to this business, he saw the need of a cemetery where his peoples last resting place would be a beautiful tribute of the love and affection of those left behind. It was with this idea in view that he organized a stock company and purchased the site for beautiful Greenwood Cemetery. A park located right in the city, and one that could hardly be purchased to-day.

To quote the Company's circular: "About twelve years ago the Greenwood Cemetery was opened; since that time more than three thousand of our relatives and friends have been buried there," a statement that shows what the cemetery has meant to the colored people of Louisville.

Quite different were the impulses which prompted Mr. Parks to enter the real estate business. He was paying rent. He figured that if he could only get the first house he could make one building pay for the other.

To accomplish this he joined a building and loan association, paying $50.00 per month for membership fee, then he borrowed $800.00 from the company and $200.00 from a bank and put up for himself a two and a half story brick house. Then he began to put up other houses until today he owns and collects rents from eight houses, this in addition to his two and half story residence.

Mr. Parks once started a dairy business, but about the time he was beginning this, he was advocating that the city appoint a truant officer to look after absent colored children who stay from school. As he had been chief advocate, he was appointed. Thus, he had to sell his dairy outfit. In working as truant officer he found that the children were not only out of school, but were sadly ignorant, they and their parents of the opportunities for an education.

Thoroughly engrossed in business and uplift work, Mr. Parks has given but little time to other organizations. He is a Mason, an Odd Fellow and a Knight of Pythias. He once served for nine years as Vice-President of the Board of Guardians for Children.

Beyond membership in these bodies and his business, Mr. Parks devotes most of his time to his family. He was married in 1887, to Miss Iola May Lewis, of Louisville. Two boys and a Girl compose the family circle in the splendid Parks brick home on Chestnut Street. They are Lewis Parks, who was formerly a student at Ohio State University, but had to cease studying on account of ill health; Miss Margaret, who was graduated from the Louisville High School, and from Fisk University, carrying off at Fisk the highest honors, and Albert Paul, who is associated with the father in business.

Mr. Parks realizes keenly that this is the day of the highly developed specialist and of the thoroughly trained business man and is determined to hold what he has so successfully fought to gain. With this end in view he has taken his son, Albert Paul, into business with him and is giving him the advantage of his practical experience. Many boys are given the advantage of a thorough education, and many are given the advantage of a practical training, but fortunate is the boy that has the benefit of both under the care of a loving father.

Desirous of securing a first hand estimate of Mr. Parks as a public servant from the officers of the city of Louisville, the authors interviewed several, which resulted in convincing them that Mr. Parks record had given the officials a very high regard for him both as an officer and a man.

GEORGE CLAYTON SHAW, D. D.

HE Mary Potter Memorial School, founded in 1910, by the present principal, Rev. G. C. Shaw. Rev. Shaw is a graduate of Lincoln University, (Pa.), class of 1886, and of Auburn Theological Seminary, Auburn, N. Y., in 1890. He also studied one year at Princeton, Theological Seminary, N. J. He was born at Louisburgh, N. C., in 1863, being next to the youngest of six children. His parents were slaves but his mother was given a fairly good edu-cation by her mistress. Also his two oldest sisters who were eight and six years old, respectively, at the close of the war, were taught to read and write and were among the first colored teachers of North Carolina, having begun to teach in 1872. Each of the six children began to teach as soon as they were old enough and there has not been a year since 1872 that some of them have not been teaching in North Carolina.

Rev. Shaw married, in 1890, Miss Mary E. Lewis, of Penn Valley, Pa., a highly educated woman. She has been a faithful worker with her husband in establishing and developing Mary Potter School.

While a student at Auburn, Rev. Shaw attracted the attention of Mrs. Mary Potter of Schenectady who became very much interested in him. Through her influence he went to Oxford, N. C. In addition to establishing the school which bears the name of his friend Mrs. Mary Potter, he organized a Pres-byterian Church. He is still pastor of the church and has organized in the county two other Presbyter-ian churches and one in the adjoining county (Vance). Mrs. Potter died soon after the work was started. Through her friends and the Freed-men's Board of the Presbyterian Church, Rev. Shaw has been able to develop the work to its pres-ent proportions. It has 485 students.

The school is conducted by Rev. Shaw along carefully conceived lines that not only equip the students for business and home, but impress upon them the beauties of a Christian life. A born ped-agogue, and a forceful speaker, Rev. Shaw is at all times the kindly gentle leader and instructor of youth. His sound judgment and wise policies have made him a capable leader of the older element in his community, and Dr. Shaw has the respect and esteem of both races. No man of any people could wish for a higher eulogy than was paid him by a prominent white citizen of Oxford, N. C., who said, "Dr. G. C. Shaw is a citizen that any town would be proud to claim."

MARY POTTER MEMORIAL SCHOOL.

Reverend Mansfield Temple Cooper

REVEREND Mansfield Temple Cooper is a native of Mississippi. He was born in Hinds County, Mississippi, in the year 1866. His father lived in the country, and the early life of Mansfield was spent on the farm. While he did his share of the farm work and was being trained in handling the hoe and plow the training of his mind was being neglected for want of the proper facilities for educational development. He early evinced a desire to learn and to the credit of his father, this desire was enlarged rather than held back. To give him the proper mental training meant the loss of a worker on the farm, but this wise father saw the possibilities of a greater life for his son, if he was trained for service, and he cheerfully made the sacrifice in the interest of his son's education. When about twelve years of age, his father sent him to town where he could obtain better educational facilities than the country afforded.

Leaving the farm, he went to the town of Edwards, where he entered the public school. He applied himself diligently to his books and proved a good student. By hard work he passed through the public schools ending with his course in the high school. After finishing at Edwards he went to Jackson, Mississippi, the capital of the state, and entered the High School there. He finished his course at the Jackson High School when he reached the age of nineteen, and then entered college. He first attended the Granada and Zion College, then entered Princeton University and Tougaloo College. At all of these institutions he applied himself diligently, paying his way by hard work.

While his father helped him to secure an education he did not depend upon him altogether, but worked to help himself. During the progress of his education and for some years after his graduation he followed the profession of teacher and at one time it seemed that this would be his life work, but God had other work for him, and laid its call upon his heart and conscience and finally led him to the ministry. He began to teach when he was sixteen years of age, and before he had finished his High School Course. He left school when he was about twenty-two years old and first took up the occupation of teaching. His first appointment was that of principal of the public school at Charleston, Mississippi, which he served for four years. He next served the school at Harrison Station, Mississippi, as principal for three years. This station is now known as Enid. His work at these schools was of the best and the schools flourished under his management.

From Harrison Station he went to Memphis, Tennessee. There he continued teaching for a short while, but gave it up to engage in manual labor. He continued at hard labor for sometime when he recognized the call to preach and then gave it up to prepare for the ministry.

He entered the ministry in the year 1895 and since that date has been actively engaged in church work. When he gave himself to the work of the ministry he made a complete surrender of all personal ambition and sought only to serve God and humanity. He went where duty called and regarded not the field from the standpoint of self. He was satisfied it he could serve and the larger the service the greater joy he experienced. In the course of his labors he has served some of the humblest mission stations and some of the leading churches in the State of Tennessee.

Thirteen years out of the twenty-one years he has spent in Tennessee, he has lived at Memphis. There he was pastor of Providence three years and accomplished a good work for his charge. He paid off a mortgage on the church property of over $2,000. During his pastorate at Tyler Chapel, he built a church edifice at a cost of $1500. He was pastor at St. Andrews for five years, and when he retired from that pastorate he had raised $5,000 with which to erect a new building.

In 1917 he returned to Providence church and is today the pastor of that people.

It is not often that a pastor can return to a church that he formerly served and do his best work, but Rev. Cooper is an exception. He not only keeps up the interest of his flock in many lines of church work, but has reduced the debt on the church property from $4,000 to $1500. In 1916 he was a delegate to the General Conference which met in Philadelphia.

He has served on the board of trustees of Wilberforce University, and is now a trustee of Turner College, and has held the position for ten years. He was the Statistical Secretary of the West Tennessee Conference for seven years and could have continued, but resigned in favor of another.

In 1892, he married Miss Clara Key, of Robersonville, Mississippi. They have one child, Mansfield Temple Cooper, Jr. Rev. Cooper's travels have been confined to the South and East. His extensive labors in connection with his church life have not prevented him from taking an active interest in a number of fraternal organizations.

He is a member of the Masons, Knights of Pythias, Odd Fellows and the Knights of Tabor. For several years he was the Chancellor Commander of the Knights of Pythias.

HARRY C. SMITH

ON. Harry C. Smith, the subject of this sketch, a native of West Virginia, has lived for half a century in Ohio, at Cleveland, where he secured his education in the public schools of that city. It was in August, 1883, that Mr. Smith and three other members of the race started The Cleveland (Ohio) Gazette, which he has edited and managed from the beginning and owned for more than twenty-five years. It is the one race weekly newspaper in this country that has been issued every week on time since its birth twenty-six years ago—and has done such good, consistent and constant work for the colored people that it is known to Afro-American readers throughout the country as one of their truest and best race newspapers and advocates, and its editor as one of their most aggressive and successful race leaders.

When Senator Joseph Benson Foraker was Governor of Ohio, many years ago, he caused Harry C. Smith to be appointed a Deputy State Oil Inspector, the first time in their history the colored race had been so honored in this country.

This position he held for four years. In 1893 Mr. Smith was elected a member of the Ohio Legislature; in 1895 and 1899 he was re-elected to a second and third term ,serving six years in all. His most conspicious work as a Legislator in the interest of his people was the passage of Ohio's Civil Rights' Law, in 1884, and Ohio's Anti-Lynching Law in 1896. New York State's "Malby Civil Rights Law" and Illinois' Anti-Lynching Law are largely copies of Ohio's. Illinois and Ohio are the only States in the Union that have affective laws against mob violence and both were introduced by Afro-American Legislators.

Editor Smith, though a member of the Legislature and a very busy one, too, continued his newspaper work. In recent years thrice Mr. Smith has successfully called upon the State Railroad Commission of Ohio to stop Southern railroads from running coaches bearing "Jim Crow" car signs into Ohio.

The following tribute was paid to him by W. S. Scarborough, President of Wilberforce University:

"This paper (Mr. Smith's paper—The Gazette) has proven a success and is now by far the best Colored paper published in the State of Ohio, and is one among the best edited by Colored journalists in the United States. It is vigorous in tone, fearless in its defense of right, a strong advocate of equal rights to all men without any distinction, an uncompromising enemy of prejudice in all its forms, and a staunch Republican in politics—with principle rather than expediency as the basis.

Mr. Smith has always wielded an able pen for right and truth. He has fought squarely in behalf of his race, demanding for it recognition wherever denied. No other proof of this is needed than The Gazette itself."

Hon. Frederick Douglas pays him this tribute a few years prior to his death:

"In the midst of hurried preparations for a long tour in Europe I snatched my pen and spend a few moments to tell you how completely I sympathize with your political attitude." Then again he adds: 'I do exhort your readers to stand by you in your efforts to lead the Colored citizens of Ohio to wise and successful political action."

Tributes such as the above are well worth striving for, and when deserved, speak volumes as to the character and ability of the one to whom they are paid. Mr. Smith is eminently deserving of the tribute.

Charles Banks

THE fact that he engineered the tour of the Tuskegee "Wizard" through Mississippi is sufficient proof that Mr. Banks stands far above the ordinary man. Booker T. Washington made mistakes, as who does not, but in some things he was exceedingly sure. It is doubtful if the Founder of Tuskegee ever made a bad speech or made a bad selection of a man to do a particular job. Banks is certainly a demonstration of Dr. Washington's ability to select men who could combine action with thought. He was Dr. Washington's special choice because the Tuskegean discerned that Charles Banks could stem the tide of prejudice of the white Mississippian, the tide of superstition of the black Mississippian, the tide of competition of the Negro banker and the tide of jealousy of the politician.

Another reason Dr. Washington clung to Charles Banks was that the latter was an instance of one of Dr. Washington's theories. Not a pure blooded Negro himself, he nevertheless believed in the ability of men of genuine African blood, so that he could point to these and no one could say, "Ah well it's the white blood that's in him that accounts for his success." Thus it was he was fond of having ever ready men like Dr. Moton, Bishop Clinton, and Charles Banks to prove beyond a doubt that the Negro race, regardless of individual complexion was capable of the highest degree of civilization and refinement.

There is as great a variety of business men as there are differences in men generally. Some men have only one idea and bend all of their energies to working it out; some men can only see beyond their nose, and are too timid to venture out of their sight—some men have visions of large ventures, but lack the ability to work them out; others have the visions and the skill to execute and become the founders of great enterprises. Of this latter class belongs Charles Banks, the subject of this sketch.

Mr. Banks was born at Clarksdale, Mississippi, March 25, 1873, and has spent his life in his native State. He is the son of Daniel A. and Sallie Ann Banks. He received his education in the public schools and at Rust College, Holly Springs, Mississippi.

In 1893, he married Miss Tremna O. Booze, of Natchez, Mississippi. She has contributed largely to the wonderful success of her husband's career. She is a woman of high character and culture and deservedly takes a position of leadership among the women of her race in Mississippi. From 1889

to 1903, Mr. Banks was engaged in a mercantile business in Clarksdale, under the firm name of Banks & Bro.; they did a general merchandise business.

In 1903, he made his home in Mound Bayou, and organized the Bank of Mound Bayou, which is capitalized for $100,000. He served the bank as Cashier for eleven years. In 1907, he organized the Mound Bayou Oil Mill and Manufacturing Company, a corporation of $100,000 capital. It is the only manufactory of such proportion owned by the colored race in America. He is general manager of the company.

He also organized the Mound Bayou Land and Investment Company, with a capital of $50,000, which has for its aim the keeping of the farm lands in and around Mound Bayou in the ownership of the Negro.

He is a director of the Union Guaranty Company of Jackson, Miss., and of the Mississippi Beneficial Insurance Company, of Indianola. In a word he stands in the front rank of the progressive and influential citizens of the Negro town of Mound Bayou.

In 1901 he was elected third Vice-President of the National Negro Business League, and in 1907 was elected first Vice-President.

He is a trustee of Wilberforce University, and of Campbell College.

Mr. Banks is a Republican and has taken an active part in politics. In 1904 and again in 1908, he was a delegate to the Republican National Convention, and in 1912 he was a delegate at-large. He was the original Taft supporter in Mississippi, and at the Chicago Convention was the choice of the Negroes to second the nomination of Mr. Taft. He had charge of the tour of the late Dr. Booker T. Washington, through Mississippi, which was considered by many to be the most elaborate demonstration ever given the distinguished educator.

Mr. Banks is a member of the African Methodist Episcopal Church, and is active in its work and support. Mr. Banks owns the controlling interest in the Mound Bayou Bank and is a large owner of town property and of the surrounding farm lands.

He is connected with the leading fraternal organizations among the Negroes. He is a Mason, member of Odd Fellows, and of Knights of Pythias.

Mr. Banks is not only a business man of high character, and remarkable executive ability, but he is a public speaker of unusual talent.

WILLIAM A. CREDITT, A. B., A. M., S. T. B.,
D. D., LL. D.

ILLIAM A. Creditt was born in
the city of Baltimore, July 14th,
1864. His parents, Bushrod Creditt and Mary L. Creditt, were
considered people of means and
they were also free born. Mr.
Creditt had all the advantages of
the public schools of the city of
Baltimore. He was very studious, and at the age
of seventeen he had finished the public school
course. He then matriculated at Lincoln University. From this institution he was graduated with
honor before he reached his twenty-first birthday.
All through his college course he was an honor student and he had the honor of the philosophical Oration.

Dr. Creditt looked forward to the Gospel Ministry from his earliest childhood. After finishing
his college course he entered the post graduate
course of the same institution, and upon the completion of this course entered the old Newton Theological Institution of Newton Center, Massachusetts. This is the oldest and most renowned Theological Institution among the White Baptists of
America. From this institution he was graduated
in 1899, with the honor of delivering the Class Oration to the Boston Social Union, at Tremont Temple.

Dr. Creditt then entered upon a long life of use-

fulness. He was President of the Normal Department and University Preacher for a year. He
served as pastor for the Corinthian Baptist Church,
Frankfort, Kentucky, during the same year. He
next took examination for professorship at the
State Normal Institution in 1890. He retained the
pastorate at Frankfort and at the same time served
as Professor at the State Institution. In 1892 he
accepted the pastorate of the Berean Baptist
Church, at Washington, D. C., and held this position for five years. One of the things in which
Dr. Creditt takes pride is that while pastoring in
Washington he frequently had in his audience at
the same time, Hon. Frederick Douglass, Hon.
John R. Lynch, Senator B. K. Bruce, and men of
kindred significance While in Washington he did
not confine his efforts to his church. He was in
charge of the University Extension Course of
Wayland Institution and lectured frequently at
Howard University. He organized an Evening
Bible Class. Upon leaving Washington he turned
this class over to Howard University. Out of this
class has grown the present evening class, at Howard, for the training of young ministers.

In 1897 he became pastor of the old Cherry
Street Baptist Church, of Philadelphia. Under his
leadership the church grew and purchased new
property on 16th and Christian Streets. This was
a step in the development of the church and a
step in the advancement of the colored people of
Philadelphia as well, for this purchase opened up
to them one of the finest residential sections. Dr.
Creditt kept the charge of this church till 1915,
when he gave it up to devote more of his time to
the Downingtown School. During his pastorate he
added to the membership of the church an average
of 100 members per year.

One of the characteristics of this church and
school worker is that of an organizer. He organized the Reliable Mutual Aid Society of Philadelphia, one of the strongest Industrial Insurance
companies of the country. He was also one of the
founders of the Cherry Building and Loan Association. Through these organizations he influenced
a great number of people to buy their own homes.
Not satisfied with working with the older people,
Dr. Creditt with Mr. John S. Trower, his faithful
friend, decided to found an Industrial School for
the training of Colored Youths of the North, along
industrial lines. Elsewhere in these pages the
story of his school is told. It stands as a monument to this man, who has never once lost courage
during the years of the development of this school.

Many honors have been showered upon Dr.
Creditt because of his long years of usefulness. He
has the degrees A. B., A. M., S. T. B., D. D., and in
the year 1909 Lincoln University, his Alma Mater,
conferred upon him the degree LL. D. Dr. Creditt
was the fifth man in the institution to receive this
degree. The National Baptist Convention invited
him to deliver the Booker T. Washington Oration
before that body in 1917. He is noted for his sermons and orations and is much in demand as a lecturer and preacher. He has potential influence
with the white citizens of this country and especially the people of Pennsylvania, and is one with
marked influence among his own people.

DOWNINGTOWN INDUSTRIAL AND AGRICULTURAL SCHOOL

OWNINGTOWN Industrial and
Agricultural School grew out of
the recognized need of training in
these subjects for the colored
Northern Youth. In the year
1905, John S. Trower and William
A. Creditt of Philadelphia, called together a number
of leading colored men of various religious denominations from every section of the state of Pennsylvania, and laid before them this great need. After consideration those present decided that the
school be established. The charter of the Downingtown Industrial and Agricultural School was
granted the same year and Dr. Creditt was prevailed upon to accept the presidency.

The property now owned by this school was
paid for by Mr. J. S. Trower, and his heirs still hold
mortgages on the property. The property of the
school consists of 110 acres of land valued at $8,250
—one hundred acres of this land is cultivated as a
school farm and ten acres are used as a campus.
There are two large stone buildings used for dormitories, administration, and class rooms; two
small stone buildings; a stone barn and two frame
buildings. The total value of the buildings amounts
to $44,850.00. In addition to this property there
is movable property owned by the school which is
valued at $9,000.00.

The institution receives some aid from the State,
which therefore has supervision of the financial affairs of the school. The State of Pennsylvania donates to the upkeep of the school the sum of
$10,000.00. This amount, with the general dona-
tions received and the money received from the va-

rious departments of the institution form the bulk
of the income for this plant.

The motto of the institution is "Self Help
Through Self Work." To further the aims of the
school the courses are planned to give to the individual student the studies that will best fit him
for what he plans for his life work. In this way
the student who has for his object the work in
trade is given more time in trade work and the
minimum of work in the literary subjects. The
reverse is true when the student is striving toward
a vocation in the professional world. In this case
the maximum of literary work is given and the
minimum of trade work.

The Downington Industrial and Agricultural
School fills a unique place in the State in which it
is located. All the opportunity necessary for a certain kind of education was already provided by the
State. But this institution has its place in the
training of the Northern youth, along industrial
lines. That the school is on the hearts of the colored people of Pennsylvania is shown by the number of colored churches and organizations of one
kind or another that help the school. The Auxiliary that gives the greatest amount of help is the
Fanny Coppin Association. This is a body of two
hundred women. They have rallied to the needs
of the institution and have been instrumental in
getting a great deal of aid for it.

There are a number of influential people who are
personally interested in the success of this venture
to give industrial training to the colored youth of
the North.

REVEREND CALVIN SCOTT BROWN

EV. Calvin Scott Brown was born in Salisbury, N. C., March 23, 1857. His early days were spent amid the trying scenes which followed the Civil War, a period often referred to as "Reconstruction days," and which was fraught with grave problems for white and black to solve. His father died when he was a mere lad, leaving his mother dependent upon her son for a support. To assume such a responsibility at such a time was a man's work, but young Brown went to his task with a brave heart and a strong affection for his widowed mother.

When the soldiers were relieved of the care of the Federal Cemetery at Salisbury, this young boy was employed to look after it, which he did, among his duties being that of keeping the record of those buried there. The placing of such a task upon such young shoulders speaks highly of his ability no less than his reliability.

The first school he attended was one opened by the Friends Association of Philadelphia, at Salisbury. Here he made remarkable progress and in the end of his course he received a first grade teacher's certificate. This was in the year 1878, when he had reached his twenty-third birth-day.

In 1879 he entered Shaw University and graduated from both the college and theological departments in 1886. When he entered Shaw University he had only $5.00 in his pocket, but he made a start with this small sum and a brave heart and worked his way through. He took part in a debate which held out a scholarship as the prize and came out victor. This helped him through college.

His diligent and commendable demeanor won for him the close friendship of President Tupper, who made him his private Secretary.

He started upon his career as a school teacher and in 1886 he founded and became President of the Waters Normal School, a rural school of elementary grade. He is still the head of this Institution. Rev. Brown is a Baptist, and for twenty-two years he has held the office of President of the Lott Carey Foreign Mission Convention and for thirty-four years he has held the position of Corresponding Secretary of the North Carolina Baptist State Convention. He is pastor of four large country churches and moderator of the Baptist Association of which his churches are members.

His work in connection with the Lott Carey Convention has caused him to become a great traveler.

He made an inspection trip to Hayti in an effort to organize the Baptist interest there; he visited Liberia to bring about the centralization of the Baptist missions in that country; he attended the World's Baptist Congress, which met in London, and made an address in Albert Hall. He made two tours of Europe and has visited the principal countries and cities of Northern Africa; he has visited Hayti, Santo Domingo and Porto Rico. He has served as Grand Secretary of the Good Templars; Grand Chief and Supreme Grand Secretary of the Good Samaritans; and is now officially connected with the Masons, Odd Fellows and Knights of Pythias. He was for several years a member of the County Board of Education.

Rev. Brown was married in December, 1886 to Amaza J. Drummond, of Lexington, Virginia. She has borne him eight children, four of which are boys and four girls; William D; Flora B. Joyner; Julia A. Delaney; Calvin S. Jr.; Marie E.; Purcell T.; Enice H.; and Schley Brown. Those (that are grown) are filling useful places in life. No greater joy can come to parents than to see their children walking uprightly and working industriously Rev. Brown owns his own home, situated in Winton, North Carolina, and worth $3500; also two farms, one valued at $6000, and one at $1500; in addition to these he owns other buildings of less value.

PARTIAL VIEW OF CAMPUS—INDUSTRIAL AND EDUCATIONAL INSTITUTE.

N 1895 two colored workers seeing the need of some training for the very young colored children in and around Topeka founded a kindergarten and sewing school. The work was one that was needed. The children continued to come and still needed the training after they had passed the kindergarten age. In 1900 the work was placed under a board of trustees. Seven years later the State Agricultural and Industrial Department was created and appropriations made for the erection of buildings. The schools were then taken over by the State and put under a board of regents appointed by the Governor. There is still an independent board of trustees, but they act in an advisory capacity only.

For a number of years Prof. Wm. R. Carter was at the head of this institution. But in 1918 he resigned, and Prof. G. R. Bridgeforth was given the presidency. Mr. Bridgeforth's training for the position has been a very thorough one.

His early training was received in the A. M. A. Schools of Alabama, the last of which was Talladega College. From Talladega he went to the Amherst Agricultural College, in Massachusetts. After graduating from Amherst, Prof. Bridgeforth went to Tuskegee Institute, Alabama. Here for a number of years he served as the head of the Agricultural Department. In this work at Tuskegee he got all the training that is necessary for him to make a success of his new field. He had under him a number of teachers and had all the duties that devolve upon the head of such a large department. Leaving Tuskegee in 1918, Mr. Bridgeforth assumed the duties of the President of Topeka Industrial and Educational Institute.

The enrollment of the Kansas Industrial and Educational Institute ranges from 128, to 175 with 20 teachers. Of this number about half are from Kansas, and the rest from other states. In this school only a few students below the seventh grade are admitted. There has been constantly an effort to keep the elementary work confined to the seventh and eighth grades. In the secondary work there are four years.

In the Industrial courses, Laundrying, cooking, and sewing are provided, for the girls; and tailoring, woodworking, printing, blacksmithing and auto repairing for the boys. In the Agricultural department a genuine effort is made to give thorough instruction in Agriculture. All the pupils below the Senior class are required to pursue the full course in market gardening and poultry raising.

The School was made a State Institution by the Kansas Legislature of 1919. The State made an appropriation of $90,700 for two years support. The value of the plant is estimated at $225,000. The sources of income are State appropriations, $90,700 for two years; tuition and fees, $1,359; donations, $1,351; special receipts $408; miscellaneous $712. This money is spent wisely for the various needs of the school, and the accounts turned over to the board of regents.

The school owns 105 acres of land, some two miles out of Topeka. Of this 80 acres are under cultivation, 15 acres are in pasture, and 10 acres in the campus.

This land is valued at $21,000. The school has its own water system, and the whole plant is in a well kept condition. The buildings are well constructed and very attractive. They are all made from stone, which was quarried on the place. There are five buildings, three cottages and a stone barn. The cottages are used as homes for the teachers. The other buildings are Boys' dormitory, Girls' dormitory, Boys' Industrial Building, Administration and Class room building, and Girls trade building. The first three named are three-story buildings, and the last two are only two-stories high. The plant is attractive, well kept, and used to good advantage.

BENJAMIN BRAWLEY

HE subject of this sketch is classed by Dr. John Hope, President of Morehouse College, as the best posted English scholar of the Race. Not many young men with the great advantages of birth and education, enjoyed by Benjamin Brawley, have made the most of them in the thorough manner that he has. It was his good fortune to have for his father, Dr. E. M. Brawley, who was at that time, and still is, one of the greatest teachers the race has produced.

Although his training was not confined to the home, this added to his public school instruction, accounts for the early age at which Mr. Brawley finished his college work.

Born in Columbia, S. C., April 22, 1882, Mr. Brawley's parents moved with him to Nashville, Tenn., then to Petersburg, Va., when he was a mere lad, and in both places he was sent to the public schools. Mr. Brawley proved such an apt pupil, that he soon entered Morehouse College, where he graduated with the degree of A. B., in 1901. Although he had not reached his 20th birthday the work done by him in the class room was so exceptional, the president of the college asked him to return to the school as instructor in English. This offer was accepted by Mr. Brawley and this position held by him for five years.

Mr. Brawley then took a literary course in Chicago University. On receiving his degree of A. B., in 1906, he returned to Morehouse as professor of English, which position he held until 1910. Mr. Brawley then accepted a position as professorship of English at Howard University, Washington, D. C., and at the same time served as head of the department of English for two years. The President of Morehouse, however, had no idea of losing this brilliant young instructor, so persuaded him to return to his Alma Mater in 1912, as Dean, which position Mr. Brawley still holds.

In 1907, 1908, Mr. Brawley studied a year at Harvard University, where he won his Masters Degree. Since that time he has spent a year of study in Chicago University. While serving as Dean of Morehouse, Mr. Brawley has spent the summers of 1912, 1914, 1915 as an instructor in the summer school at Hampton Institute.

He is a lecturer of note and a man interested in all the problems pertaining to college work and college life. At present he is serving as President of the Association of Colleges of Negro Youth. In this capacity he has the opportunity to influence for good the work of all the institutions for the higher training of young people of the colored race.

Not only is Mr. Brawley known to all educated Negroes as a good teacher and an authority on questions of English, but he is widely known as an author. His "History of the American Negro is being used as a text book in some of the schools where the wish is to have Negro children know all about the lives and the works of their people. Among the works published by Mr. Brawley, are:

"A Short History of the American Negro," MacMillan, 1913-revised 1919; "History of Morehouse College," 1917; "The Negro in Literature and Art", Duffield & Co., 1918; "Our Negro Neighbor," MacMillan, 1918; "Africa and the War," Duffield, 1918; "New Era Declamations," Sewanee University Press, 1918; "Women of Achievement," W. A. B. H. M. Society, Chicago, 1919. This is a notable list of work from the pen of one so young as Mr. Brawley. He has given himself unreservedly to the work of a man of close studious habits.

In July, of 1912, Mr. Brawley married in Washington, D. C., Miss Hilda Demaris Prowd, of Kingston, Jamaica, B. W. I. Mrs. Brawley is a woman of great personal charm and one who takes pride in the literary attainment of her husband, giving to him the moral support that has helped him in his achievements in recent years.

TINGLEY MEMORIAL HALL—CLAFLIN UNIVERSITY

AT the close of the war between the States the Methodist Episcopal Church was foremost in establishing missions and schools both among the Freedmen and the rural white people. As a result the Methodist Episcopal Church now has one or more Conferences in each of the Southern States and more than forty schools.

Claflin University, founded in 1869 by the Claflin family of Boston, is one of this system of schools. Courses of study have been provided with wise reference to the needs of the many in the most useful subjects.

Teacher training, manual training and Christian training have been especially emphasized. A full College course, however, has been maintained for the few who desired to enter professional life.

Claflin University being under the control and supported very largely by the Methodist Episcopal Church has stressed the training of its youth for efficient service in the Church as well as in the world. Its motto has been, "Training for Character". This is in accordance with the teaching of the Book of Books. "Seek ye first the Kingdom of God and his righteousness and all these things shall be added unto you." Learning, wealth or prominence are of little value unless they are re-inforced by enlightened and sturdy character.

The Claflin University plant consists of 220 acres of land, seven brick and five frame school buildings all valued at about $300,000.

The Institution employs 25 teachers and enrolls about 600 students annually.

On account of the lack of rural schools for colored youth, the Institution, like most others of its kind, is obliged to maintain Grades for the majority of its students. These are followed by two parallel courses, Teacher Training and College preparatory. Then follows a four years College course leading to the degrees A. B. and B. S.

The Institution also maintains a large Industrial plant, a business course, and cultivates a well equipped farm.

RESOURCES

Claflin University is supported in part by Annual appropriations from the Freedman's Aid Society of the Methodist Episcopal Church, by the John F. Slater fund, by the S. C. Annual Conference of the Methodist Episcopal Church and by special donations from friends North.

The Institution now has a productive endowment of $60,000, and has on hand a lively campaign for an additional forty thousand. It is probable that no school in the South has a stronger local backing. The friends of higher Christian education in South Carolina are determined to place the Institution not only in class A, but among the very best of its kind. L. M. Dunton has been its President for thirty-four years.

G. W. FRANKLIN

few years ago a colored undertaker, of Chattanooga. Tenn., sold a piece of city property for fourteen odd thousand dollars. He took some of the payments in cash, the others in notes. As the notes fell due the undertaker cashed them at the bank. "What, you mean to say, you are holding those notes and cashing them when they fall due?

They had been used to having colored business people cash their notes at a discount, not to hold them for time and interest. The owner of these notes was G. W. Franklin of Chattanooga, Tennessee, undertaker, business man, farm-owner and President of the Negro National Undertakers' Association.

Mr. Franklin began his career as a poor farm lad in Georgia. His education was meagre. Singularly enough his system of training was like that now in vogue in Tuskegee Institute. Mr. Franklin's father was a blacksmith. He was ambitious to educate his two sons, and at the same time to train them in some useful occupation. Thus he employed them on alternate weeks paying the one who worked 50c per week.

Having learned his trade, Mr. Franklin came to Chattanooga, and began the struggle for himself. While following the blacksmith trade, he took up the study of undertaking. In a little while he was starting his business on a small scale. Now he added a horse, now a vehicle, most of the vehicles however he made himself, as they were too expensive for his very small purse—small at that time.

Though he made most of the vehicles, Mr. Franklin found with buying lumber the process was very expensive. Thus instead of purchasing lumber, he turned his attention to farms. He searched out a farm with plenty of timber on it, bought the tools for his shop and began the task of making hearses and carriages, indeed practically every kind of woodwork used in his business.

"Yes sir," said Mr. Franklin, "I lie on my bed at night and work out all my designs. I rent my farms and use the timber as lumber for my vehicles."

Mr. Franklin keeps a stable of 40 odd horses, with plenty of carriages and hearses to match. He has educated his son and so taught him the business that the son can manage almost as well as the father. A New York paper places Mr. Franklin's worth at $52,000, which is very conservative.

But G. W. Franklin is a good deal more than a maker of money. He is a most useful citizen. Every Sunday finds him in the choir of the Chattanooga M. E. Church, where he faithfully plays the cornet for religious services. He has been President of the Negro Undertakers' Association for many years. More than this he is a good speaker.

"Dr Washington swung me off," he says, "I was timid, afraid, but Dr. Washington told me to just get up and tell what I did. I followed his advice and I have been speaking to all kinds of audiences ever since.

Mr. Franklin has continually improved on his education by travel and contact until he is not only one of our best business men, but a man of education and refinement.

Working up from a boyhood of poverty and want to a manhood where command of thousands of dollars is his, to a manhood where the respect and the esteem of the people of his community are given unreservedly, this is the life of Mr. Franklin in a nut-shell. A man with the determined character of G. W. Franklin would make good in any line he cared to undertake for his life work. One of the things that has contributed largely to the success of this man in his line of business is his careful attention to detail.

BYRD PRILLERMAN, B. S., M. A., LITT. D.

YRD Pillerman was born in Franklin County, Virginia, October 19, 1859. He now lives at Institute, West Virginia. He was born a slave, being the youngest of the seventeen children of Franklin and Charlotte Prillerman. He takes his surname from his maternal grandfather, Jacob Prillerman, who was the owner as well as the father of his mother.

The Prillermans came from Holland about 1760, and settled in Franklin County, Virginia.

In 1868, young Prillerman, then eight years of age, walked with his parents and other members of the family from Franklin County, Virginia, to Kanawha County, West Virginia, and settled on a farm near Charleston. The distance walked was 250 miles. The journey was taken in March.

Byrd first attended school in Charleston, in 1872, after the death of his father. He then attended school at his home, Sissonsville, West Virginia, until he was twenty-years of age, when he became a teacher of the same school November 10, 1879. After teaching three or four terms he entered Knoxville College, Knoxville, Tennessee, September 3, 1883. He graduated from this institution with the degree of Bachelor of Science in May, 1889. He returned to his home in West Virginia, and became a teacher in the public schools of Charleston, West Virginia. He was largely instrumental in the building up of the West Virginia Collegiate Institute and became the first assistant teacher in this institution in 1892. He has been connected with this institution as teacher and president since that date. On the death of President J. McHenry Jones, September 22, 1909, he was the next day made President of the State Board of Regents, in which capacity he has served with a marked degree of success. Under his administration the course of study has been so improved that graduates from the secondary course of the institution enter the best colleges and universities of the West without examination. The name of the school has been changed from the West Virginia Colored Institute to the West Virginia Collegiate Institute, and was raised to college rank by an act of the Legislature in 1915.

He owns a farm near Sissonsville, where he was reared, a house and lot in Charleston, a small farm at Institute, and several vacant lots. He is a lay member of the Baptist Church. He has served as moderator and clerk of the Mount Olivet Baptist Association, of which Booker T. Washington was clerk from 1872 to 1875. Mr. Prillerman has the distinction of being the only lay-man in West Virginia to serve as moderator of an association. He is now President of the West Virginia Sunday School Convention. Mr. Prillerman became a member of the Executive Committee of the West Virginia Sunday School Association in 1918. In the same year, he was made a member of the Executive Committee of the International Sunday School Association and attended the session in Toronto, Canada, February, 1919.

He is a Republican and was an alternate Delegate to the Republican National Convention in Chicago, which nominated Theodore Roosevelt for President. He has served as a Notary Public since March 17, 1897.

He has taught some in each year since 1879. He was largely instrumental in organizing the West Virginia Teachers' Association, which he served as President for nine years. He is a trustee of the National Training School for Women and Girls at Washington, D. C. In 1895, Westminster College New Wilmington, Pa., conferred upon him the degree of M. A. In 1916 Selma University (Alabama) conferred upon him the degree of Litt. D. He has been an active member of the National Education Association since 1891.

Mr. Prillerman's travels have been principally connected with the work of education. He has visited most of the schools in this country for the education of Negro youth and has been a regular attendant upon the National Education Association and the Association of Agricultural Colleges for a number of years. He attended the reception of President McKinley, in the White House in 1898, and of President Woodrow Wilson in 1914, where he was introduced to the President by President W. O. Thompson, of the Ohio State University. He was an honorary pall-bearer at the funeral of Dr. Booker T. Washington, with whom he was very intimately associated.

Mr. Prillerman married Miss Mattie E. Brown, a graduate of Wayland Seminary, July 24, 1893. They have two boys, Delbert McCullouch and Henry Laurence, and two girls, Ednora Mae and Myrtle Elizabeth.

JAMES C. NAPIER

AMES C. Napier, was born in Tennessee, near Nashville, June 9, 1848. He received his early education in the public schools and in 1859 went to Wilberforce University, Ohio, and thence to Oberlin College, Oberlin, Ohio, where he remained until near the completion of his junior college year, when he left school to accept a position in the government service war department, in Washington.

While in Washington he took a course in the law department of Howard University, and graduated from that Institution in 1873. His residence in Washington also gave him an opportunity to study the methods of the world's greatest debaters and to note the different styles of oratory. It would be difficult to conceive what influence they had upon his future career.

While still in the government service he passed a civil service examination and became a clerk in the bureau of the sixth auditor, the first of his race in that branch of the government service.

After one promotion he was appointed revenue agent for Kentucky, Alabama, Tennessee, and Louisiana, and later returned to Nashville to become an internal revenue department gauger.

When Grover Cleveland was elected President of the United States, the change in administration, brought about his retirement from office.

Immediately after his retirement he began the practice of law in Nashville, and has been engaged therein ever since. He has taken a conspicuous part in the municipal affairs of Nashville, and was four times elected a member of the City Council. While a member of the Council he succeeded in securing the appointment of Negro teachers in the Negro public schools, and the erection of new and additional school buildings, and the increase of the educational and financial condition of the colored people.

Mr. Napier reached the height of his government service when he was appointed Register of the Treasury at Washington, D. C., which position he held for a long period.

Mr. Napier is not only a lawyer of high standing and ability, but a business man of judgment and fine executive turn. He is cashier of the Penny Savings Bank, of which Rev. Dr. R. H. Boyd is President, and he has been for several years chairman of the Executive Committee of the National Negro Business League.

He is a large property owner in Nashville, and is regarded as one of the most substantial colored citizens of Tennessee.

In 1878 he married a daughter of Hon. John M. Langston, then United States minister to Hayti. Mr. Napier is active in political affairs. He has been a member of the Republican State Executive Committee nearly twenty years, and has four times been a delegate to the Republican National Convention, an unusual honor. Mr. Napier is not only interested in the business movements of his race, but is keenly alive to every movement which has for its object their uplift and betterment.

Though pushing his three score alotment of years, J. C. Napier is still exceedingly active in all his work. He runs his bank, keeps up his business, church and social relations, and still carries heavy cares of the race. Along with all his daily routine, which is tedious even for a young man, Mr. Napier took over the Presidency of the National Negro Business Men's League, the largest organization of its kind among colored people in the world. Booker T. Washington, the founder and till his death the president of this organization, has let this part of his mantle fall upon the shoulders of his life long friend. And he upon whom even the hem of the mantle of Booker T. Washington falls, needs to be a patient and stalwart worker. Mr. Napier is this. As president of this organization he has been able to keep the organization in all of its units thoroughly alive and active and this too in the turmoil of war times when counter interests shut the door of so many men's shops.

Miss Nannie H. Burroughs

NOW is the age when woman is coming into her own, and the world is fast recognizing her capacity for labor in all departments of life, religious, mental and physical. In that department of life which requires physical strength and endurance man has the advantage but in religious and mental endeavor she is his equal. Because of long training man may appear to excell woman in these departments but in reality he does not, and he is being brought face to face with that fact.

Miss Nannie H. Burroughs is a striking illustration of woman's capacity for labor in these new fields. She is Corresponding Secretary of the Women's Convention, Auxiliary of the National Baptist Convention and President of the National Training School for Women and Girls at Washington, D. C., the only vocational training school for colored women in the world and is a writer and lecturer of rare powers, and a leader of unusual gifts and influence among the colored Baptists, who number nearly two thirds of the membership of the Negro churches in the land.

Miss Burroughs was born in Orange, Va., May 2, 1878. Her parents had been slaves, and her grandfather was known as "Lizah, the Slave Carpenter."

At the age of seven she was stricken with typhoid fever, and remained out of school four years. On her return, for several years she made two grades a year, graduating from the high school and from the academic course in the Washington High School, making a good record in deportment and scholarship in both departments.

On account of her remarkable oratorical powers and executive ability, she was soon after head of a Girls' Literary Society, and participated in all public debates. She took an active part in the church and Sunday School work.

Leaving Washington, she became associate editor of the Christian Banner, of Philadelphia. Returning to her home, she took a position as bookkeeper for a manufacturing house.

Her interest in the work of the Church brought her in contact with the officers of the National Baptist Convention. She was for several years private Secretary for Dr. L. G. Jordan, Secretary of the Foreign Mission Board, and when the Women's Convention Auxiliary was organized, Miss Burroughs was selected to take part in the work. She lectured in various parts of the country, and wrote very much for denominational papers. New life came into the churches, and Missionary work was stimulated as never before. In the ten years since the Auxiliary was organized much good has been done, and in 1908, the colored women gave more than $13,000 for missionary and educational work. Many girls and boys have been brought from Africa to be educated by the National Baptist Convention and have returned home to work among their own people. Miss Burroughs says: "We do this because it strengthens our sympathy and makes us more convinced of our duty to our brothers who are bone of our bone and flesh of our flesh."

The work that perhaps will reflect the greatest credit upon this young woman as leader and organizer, able to bring things to pass, is the establishment of the National Training School for Women and Girl's, at Washington, D. C. This school was opened October 19, 1909. It is national in scope, and opened to women and girls of all denominations. Miss Burroughs is President, and directs the affairs of this school. She says the prospects are very bright for its success.

"Two thirds of the colored women must work with their hands for a living, and it is indeed an oversight not to prepare this army of breadwinners to do their work well.

In July, 1905, Miss Burroughs attended the World's Baptist Congress, in London. She gave an address at the Congress on "Woman's Part in the World's Work," which caused favorable comment from delegates from all parts of the world. The London Mirror said: "She was one of the most notable personages at the meeting. She addressed thousands at a great mass meeting in Hyde Park, London."

A friend writing of Miss Burroughs, says: "She lives a simple life, and is free from vanity and affection. She has a head full of common sense, and that head is well pinned on. Success does not turn it. Women in all walks of life admire her. She is not affected by praise. Here is a story of a young woman who is just beyond thirty and has come from the bottom of the round to the position of President of the only school of national character over which a Negro woman presides."

Miss Burroughs is part owner of the Douglass Building, Walnut Street, Louisville, a fine office building, headquarters of the Women's Auxiliary, the Foreign Mission Board, and other work of the National Baptist Convention. She is the originator and successful promoter of the "Negro Picture Calendar," which, with its pictures of homes and incidents in the lives of colored people, has met with large success.

BISHOP GEORGE WYLIE CLINTON

NE of the self made men of our race, is Bishop George Wylie Clinton. He was born of poor parentage, slave parents as a matter of fact, and his father died when he was but two years of age. This put the matter of his education squarely up to the young fellow. But attend school he did and for a number of years.

During his early life he lived on a farm doing the chores of a farm lad and taking advantage of the country schools that were near him, both public and private. Part of the time he walked to the nearest school, a distance of seven miles. This distance seems great, but when you remember that he was a farm lad and that he had to milk the cows, three in number, before he could start on the journey it seems a little harder. But Bishop Clinton was even then a man of determination. In order to get a chance to study he had to gather pine knots that he might have light to read. Part of the time he attended night school. This work went on till the young man was fifteen years of age.

Under the tutorage of J. H. Stewart, Bishop Clinton was prepared for college. In October of 1874 he entered South Carolina University, where he took up the classical college course, going as far as the Junior Class. He also studied at Brainard Institute, at Chester, South Carolina, and for two years in Theological Department, in Livingstone College, Salisbury, N. C. Because of lack of funds Bishop Clinton through all these years had to work and work hard. He worked before and after school, he taught school during the summer vacations, he studied hard and entered the competitive examinations of scholarship in the State school at the age of fifteen. This he won and so his education was assured.

At the age of sixteen years Bishop Clinton taught his first school. At the age of eighteen years he began the study of law under a white firm. This he gave up, however, when he felt that he was called to be a minister of the gospel. He then took up the study of the ministry and at the age of nineteen was preaching. For thirteen years Bishop Clinton served as a pastor, for six years he served as an editor and for twenty-three years he has served as a Bishop in the African Methodist Episcopal Zion Church.

Bishop Clinton for the past twenty-five years has taken an active part in every movement for the betterment of the Negro race. He is widely known as a lecturer. He has for years lectured at Tuskegee Institute, Alabama, he worked in the Campaign for War Funds, he has served in Educational Campaigns conducted by his church, he has served three times in the Ecumenical Conference, he has served as President of Atkinson College, Madisonville, Kentucky. Everywhere he has gone and at all times he has worked for the betterment of the race.

Bishop Clinton has been twice married. There is one son in the family, Geo. William Clinton, who is now a student in the Dental College of Philadelphia. Bishop Clinton has traveled extensively, both in this country and abroad. He toured five states with Dr. B. T. Washington, has traveled in Canada, and while in Europe he visited Belgium, France, England, Ireland, Wales and Holland.

It is estimated that the property holdings of Bishop Clinton amount to between $18,000.00 and $25,000.00. The home is valued at $10,000.00.

Bishop Clinton has interested himself in all the lines of work taken up by the Colored people. He has also interested himself in the organizations that are conducted by them. He is a member of the Odd Fellows, and of the Masons. He is a man full of energy that he puts to work for his people and for his church.

George C. Hall, M. D.

TARTING out in his public life with "A man can be whatever he chooses to be if he is willing to pay the price," for a motto, Dr. George C. Hall has made the statement come true. The thing that he chose to make of himself was a great surgeon, a surgeon that would be known for his good work regardless of color. He was willing to pay the price, the price of constant attention to duty, the price of never ceasing to study, the price of taking great care in the smallest detail, the price of serving all who came—he was willing to pay this price and he is today one of the most eminent surgeons in the country. So far has his fame spread as a great surgeon that in every part of the country there are persons who bare the mark of his knife on their bodies, and because of these scars they enjoy good health.

Not only has Dr. Hall developed himself along the line of the surgeon, but he is a great teacher of surgery as well. To so many of the young men of the colored race who are aspiring to the medical profession, he is an inspiration. It is an inspiratoin to them to watch this great surgeon at his task. He has the patience to show and to teach them just how each step is taken in the work. Dr. Hall even goes one step farther—he can write in detail just how he has accomplished an end. This gives him a place among the few great surgeons in the country, for from three standpoints he can see and perform his work—for himself alone, the swift, clean, sure work; for the student standing by and watching him—each step distinct and yet not slow; for the medical journals—where older doctors may see just how he has done the work and come back to him with criticisms and suggestions.

Dr. Hall was born in Ypsilamti, Michigan, in 1864. His father was a minister of the gospel in the Baptist Church. When the subject of this sketch was but five years old his father moved to the city of Chicago. Here he had advantages of good educational systems that gave him habits of close studiousness. From the Chicago High School he went to Lincoln University in Pennsylvania. From this school he was graduated with honors in the year 1886. The young student had his mind already made up as to the calling he wished to follow and so he lost no time when he returned to Chicago, in matriculating at the Bennett Medical College. He was not from a family that had wealth enough to support him through school for this great number of years, and so we find him working his way through college. For half the day he

worked, the other half he devoted to study. So well did he apply himself to the tasks that were set for him that at the end of the course he was at the head of his class. This rank made him best out of a class of fifty-four young men who were about to begin the practice of medicine.

After completing the course of study, Dr. Hall spent a great deal of time in the practice of his profession before he decided to specialize in surgery. For this work he studied under Dr. Byron Robinson and later under Dr. T. J. Watkins. He has operated in Chicago and out of the city. He has been before a number of the state Medical Associations where he has held surgical clinics, thus bringing to a great many of the doctors in the South, opportunities, here-to-fore denied them. Among these states are Alabama, Tennessee, Kentucky, Virginia, Georgia, and Missouri. Wherever Dr. Hall has gone his work has been eagerly received.

Since the founding of Provident Hospital, Dr. Hall has been one of its main supporters. While still a physician he took his patients to the hospital and then helped plan for places for them. He has been an active member of the board of trustees since 1897, he was twice elected president of the medical staff and later he was chosen a member of the surgical staff. The hospital is dear to the heart of Dr. Hall and he gives to it some of his very best work.

Not only is Dr. Hall interested in the Negro and his welfare from the standpoint of his health, but wherever there are movements for the improvement of the colored man, Dr. Hall is ready and willing to take a part. He is a director and treasurer of Frederick Douglass Center; a member of the Western Economic Society; chairman of the committee in charge of the erection of the Y. M. C. A. Building; a member of the Chicago Association of Commerce; one of the organizers of the Local Medical Association and for a number of years a willing worker in the National Medical Association of Colored men. One of the pieces of work for which he deserves great credit is the organization of the Civic League of Illinois. Through this organization he has been enabled to bring about many improvements in the housing conditions of the colored people of Chicago.

Dr. Hall has managed to save and invest some of the money he has earned in the practice of his profession, and he is considered one of the substantial Colored citizens of the city of Chicago. Working with the advancement of his people ever in his mind and the development of his own skill as a surgeon ever before him, Dr. Hall has made a place for himself that is enviable. "A man can be whatever he chooses if he is willing to pay the price," was in the case of Dr. Hall, an excellent motto.

REV. R. H. BOYD

HE work of Rev. R. H. Boyd, for the development of his people is one of the most remarkable achievements in the history of the Race. Although past 74 years of age he is still active in all the affairs of the National Baptist Publishing House, which is the outgrowth of his well laid plans. This mammoth institution, owned and controlled and operated by Negroes stands as a monument to this ex-slave.

Rev. Boyd does not like to talk about himself so a great deal of the personal history of the man is not to be had. He was born a slave. He stood by and watched the dying groans of his master. He had left the home in Texas and gone with the master into the army. Here he saw some of the struggle between the North and the South that was the battle for his freedom. When his master died, he took the body and returned to Texas with it. He then took upon himself the man's tasks of disposing of the farm produce and making the necessary purchases for the family of his dead master. It is this slave, this property of a Confederate soldier, this man unlearned in books without the knowledge of the textbook itself, but true to every principle of the Southern home; this slave who stood by his master till his death and then went to the assistance of the widow; it is this slave who had the sterling qualities needed to es-

tablish such a wonderful organization as the National Publishing House.

Rev. Boyd was married to Miss Harriet Moore, of Texas, in 1868. Mrs. Boyd has been to him in every sense of the word a helper. Through her very strict economy the education which Rev. Boyd had the privilege of securing late in life was made possible. She even surpassed most of her sisters in this respect and was one with her husband in all his efforts. From this union there came six children: Mrs. Annie Boyd-Hall, Galveston, Texas, wife of undertaker and embalmer; Mrs. Mattie Boyd-Bennefield, Nashville, Tenn.; Rev. Henry Allen Boyd, Nashville, Tenn., Secretary Sunday School Congress, Assistant Secretary National Baptist Publishing Board, Manager Nashville Globe, Secretary National Negro Press Association; Mrs. Lula Boyd-Landers, Nashville, Tenn. Mr. J. Garfield Blaine Boyd, Nashville, Tenn., general foreman National Baptist Publishing Board's plant; Mr. Theophilus Bartholomew Boyd, Nashville, Tenn., Linotype operator and machinist at the National Baptist Board's plant.

The plant itself fills a niche in the commercial life of Nashville, that is a credit to the city, the State and the nation. All who know Dr. R. H. Boyd, regardless of race, regard him as a conscientious, honest, well-thinking, well meaning, industrious citizen who knows how and who really does make the conditions between the races more tolerable, for he spends no time in attempting to solve the race problem. He abhors any inference at social equality, believes implicitly in the fact that the Negro should work out his own salvation and become a worthy citizen in his own city, in his own community and in his own State, and that he should uphold the flag of the nation and march under the principles of their respective denominations.

It is interesting to note the achievements of the institution of which this ex-slave is the founder. It is inspiring to see his devotion, even to the cause that his old master fought so nobly for. Without any show of demonstration, he has fought the business fights that must be fought by large concerns, succeeding without any philanthropic effort, without a donation of as much as one dollar from the treasury of the National Baptist Convention for the maintenance and operation of the plant or the purchase of property and machinery, he has in some way and somehow managed to keep this institution going and to make steady and constant improvements from time to time and from year to year. The past quarter the institution broke all former records in the receipt of mail and the dispatch of the output of the product of the institution. For instance, from Monday morning, March 20, up to Saturday afternoon, March 25, the letter carrier on that route delivered to the National Bap-

PLANT OF NATIONAL BAPTIST PUBLISHING HOUSE

tist Publishing Board, of which Rev. R. H. Boyd is Secretary, 7,657 letters. On one of the days, Wednesday, March 22, 2,221 of these letters were delivered. This is a record unequaled during the years that the concern has been in operation.

There are many interesting facts about the plant managed by Dr. Boyd which make it one of the plants of interest for the sight-seer and visitor to this city. The secretary and the employes are intensely religious in their work and in their everyday life, but the most interesting feature about the work of the National Baptist Publishing House is the steady and persistent advancement that it has made as a substantial institution, measuring up to similar concerns operated in this, the capital city of the Volunteer State. It is interesting to read of the National Baptist Publishing Board's success. To know what has been accomplished by an ex-slave for the Negro Baptists of the United States within a decade, and an inside glimpse of the life of a constructive genius and his contribution to race development; to see what he has been able to do for the Baptist Churches and Sunday Schools, at the same time soliciting their patronage to an institution where members of his race have made good as skilled artisans, and then to see the gigantic scores of members of the race who send out millions of copies of religious literature annually, is inspiring to the Negro youth. The success that the Rev. R. H. Boyd has achieved is nothing less than marvelous.

Tall and commanding of stature, very intelligent in conversation, he makes friends and holds them. In a recent publication there appeared the following concerning the institution:

Were some one to put the National Baptist Publishing Board's plant in this city on a moving picture film, showing the wonderful achievements and the accomplishments of the gigantic institution that has been built up for the Negro Baptists of the United States, and for their posterity, it would take a film hundreds of yards long, which would entertain thousands of people. The National Baptist Publishing House has come into existence within the past twenty-one years, and today towers magnificently over anything which has been accomplished by the race, whether it be in the religious, educational or in the business world.

"It has furnished and is furnishing employment to scores of Negro boys and girls that hitherto were shut out of what is commonly known as the art preservative among printers and publishers. It has given a rating in the commercial world to the race and denomination that has no parallel. It has put the Negro Baptists on an equal footing with the denominations of other races because of the creative genius displayed in operating and maintaining the institution. It has forged a link in racial pride that has brought together more support for one institution than has ever been attempted before. It has outstripped Jack's bean stalk story in its growth and development. It has served as an opener of the "door of hope" to the ambitions and deserving members of the race that has been closed to them by labor unions, which refuse to allow members of the race to acquire certain knowledge in printing and book binding. It has put the race on the map in the theological world as producers of a religious literature distinctively their own. It has installed and is operating printing machinery of the most complicated and intricate designing and this, too, with amateur help that has been found in the race. It has helped to make intellectual lights out of what has been regarded as a race of hewers of wood and drawers of water.

"This institution was founded by an ex-slave, the Rev. R. H. Boyd, who still lives, and who is secretary and manager. Many say that Rev. Dr. Boyd saw the invisible in his early pioneer days, and that after operating on a very small scale in his Texas home he succeeded in convincing the Negroes to see the wisdom of supporting a plant on a national scope. It was the latter part of 1896, when he began his pilgrimage to Nashville, Tenn., after having looked all over the United States for a location that would be suitable for his work. It has been said that he was directed by God from his Texas home, like Abraham, of the Chaldeans, when God said to him: "Get thee out of thy country and from thy kindred, and from thy father's house, unto a land that I will shew thee." Whatever way it was, it is a known fact that the Negro Baptists had no publishing plant and were preparing and sending out no Sunday school literature; they were giving no employment to the Negro boys and girls, doing nothing tangible until Dr. Boyd came upon the scene.

"His book, 'The Story of the Publishing Board,' which has just been issued and is now in great demand has proven one of the most interesting narratives that has come from the lips of any man. Stranger than fiction, and yet as real as the gospel itself, the story is told and then the thousands of wheels that revolve at the plant and the millions of copies of books and publications that are sent out each quarter, together with the magnificent institution, standing like the pyramids of Egypt, attest the substantial part of the story. The founder of the institution has often been referred to as a giant oak in a forest among the Negro Baptists of the United States. His far-sighted

REVEREND HENRY ALLEN BOYD

business tact in building up the institution has attracted the attention of the entire business world as well as the entire race to which his denomination belongs, and who feel indebted to him and are standing loyally by the institution which has been built up for them, and which will stand for ages to come by the support that is being given from every quarter of the globe. At the close of the last fiscal year, Dr. Boyd showed in his report the work of the institution for the past eighteen years. The figures themselves are staggering. In this number of years the institution has written and circulated 136,794,339 copies of religious literature, which does not include the thousands of volumes of books which have been made up and distributed throughout the civilized world. They have written and received 3,684,149 letters, and it is said that sometimes as high as 2,000 letters are received in a single day."

"It developed that the National Baptist Publishing Board furnishes employment to more Negro men and women, boys and girls, than any other institution of a commercial nature operated by the race. Very little is said to be known of Dr. Boyd, who has refused all along to allow anything to be written about his life. He knows that he was born a slave and he was 40 years old before he went to school, and that his mother, who died only a few months ago, was over 95 years of age.

"The publishing house, his life's work, is looked upon as a monument that he has built as an humble worker in his denomination and as his contribution to the race as a constructive genius. Nashville, Ten., the home of the institution, is now as well known as a religious publishing center as it is an educational center, having been made possible by the millions of pages of religious tracts and literature that have been issued from this gigantic religious and commercial business institution."

Upon investigation it has been found that one of the great achievements of Dr. Boyd was the bringing out and setting to music the Negro plantation melodies, the songs that were sung in the days of slavery by his parents and their ancestors. In the preparation of this work, Dr. Boyd says that he has given a rich heritage to unborn generations. Thus National Jubilee Melody Song Book, as it is called, has met a popular demand.

Other publications turned out by the institution include a full line of literature, a complete line of church helps for Baptist Sunday Schools and churches, among which are to be found Boyd's Pastors' Guide, Boyd's Church Record, Theological Kernels, a National Baptist Sunday School Lesson Commentary, Boyd's Record and Roll Book, An Outline of Negro Baptist History, and twenty-three different song books. In fact, the plant is able to print anything from a calling card to an encyclopedia, or from a postal card to a Bible.

The plant is estimated to be worth over a quarter of a million dollars. The operating expenses are estimated at $400.00 per day. Dr. Boyd declared that the prayer service held each morning at 9:30 o'clock in their own chapel, where each employe is required to be present, and which costs $17.50 per day, is his collection to the Lord. This "hour of prayer," as they call it, has proven of great benefit to the employees. At these meetings Dr. Boyd often delivers an address, the Bible is always read, and good singing is indulged in.

As a religious publishing plant their printing department is complete in every particular.

WILLIAM TAYLOR BURWELL WILLIAMS, A. B.

ILLIAM Taylor Burwell Williams, was born at Stonebridge, Clarke County, Virginia. He attended the public school at Millwood, in this county, and at seventeen, became a teacher in one of its public schools. Later he spent two years at Hampton Institute, Hampton, Va., graduating in the class of 1888. He then taught a year in the Whittier School, the elementary department of this institution. His next step was to enter Phillips Academy, Andover, Mass., from which he was graduated in the class of 1893. From Phillips Academy he went to Harvard University, where he took his A. B. degree with the class of 1897.

Upon the completion of his college course, Mr. Williams was appointed principal of School No. 24, subsequently named the McCoy School, Indianapolis, Indiana. Here he served with conspicious merit for five years, when he resigned to accept work at his Alma Mater, Hampton Institute, as field agent for the school and for the Southern Education Board. His first duty was to make a study of educational conditions in Virginia, and in the other Southern States, and to help relate Hampton Institute effectively with its field.

He soon became the field agent also of the General Education Board, the John F. Slater Fund, and finally of the Negro Rural School Fund, popularly known as the Jeanes Fund. Since all of these foundations are either primarily for Negro education or are greatly interested in promoting education among colored people, Mr. Williams' work has brought him constantly for years into direct contact with every phase of Negro education in the South. And he has played a helpful constructive part in the education of Negro youth. He has been especially active in promoting industrial training in the private schools and colleges, in directing the work of the Jeanes Industrial teachers, and in building up the recently created County Training Schools in all the Southern States.

Mr. Williams' work has also brought him into direct, sympathetic contact with such noted white educators as Dr. Wallace Buttrick of the General Education Board, Dr. H. B. Frissell, of Hampton Institute, and Dr. James H. Dillard, President of the Jeanes and Slater Funds as well as with the leading Negro schoolmen of the country.

Mr. Williams has been one of the most active and serviceable members of the National Association of Teachers in Colored Schools. He served this organization as President for two terms and is a member of its executive committee. He is also a member of the National Education Association. And he is a leader in the work of the Virginia State Teachers' Association. He was one of the organizers of the Negro Organization Society, of Virginia. He served this body as Secretary, and is now its treasurer. And in addition to his regular duties as field agent for Hampton Institute, director of the Jeanes and Slater Funds, Mr. Williams has, during the fall of 1918, acted as Assistant supervisor of vocational training in colored schools for the Committee on Education and Special Training of the War Department, and aided in the work of establishing vocational units of the Students Army Training Corps.

Mr. Williams is thoroughly a school man. It is safe to say that he is the best informed man there is on the subject of Negro education. Mr. Williams has gotten this information at first hand. He has for a number of years traveled all over the United States in the interest of Negro education. He has visited all the schools, has met and known personally the teachers in the schools and colleges. Wherever men are gathered together in the interest of Negro Education there Mr. Williams is sure to be giving freely of his advice and store of information when he is asked, but never trying to show that he is superior in knowledge of facts on the subject. He is an Associate Editor of the Cyclopedia of the Colored Race.

HUBBARD HOSPITAL—MEHARRY MEDICAL COLLEGE

THE Meharry Medical College was organized as the medical department of Central Tennessee College, in 1876, with two teachers and eleven students. It was the first institution in the South to open its doors for the education of Negro physicians.

It was named for the five Meharry Brothers who contributed largely to its establishment and support.

The Dental Department was opened in 1886, and the Department of Pharmacy in 1889.

The Medical Faculty consists of 26 members, Dental 10, and Pharmacy 4, making a total of 40.

During the 40 years of its existence there has been 1450 graduates in medicine, 325 in dentistry, 233 in pharmacy and 55 in nurse training, making 2063 in all. These graduates constitute about one-half of the regular colored members in these professions in the Southern States. They have been well received by the white professional brethren, and they have met with good success both professionally and financially. A large proportion have comfortable, and many elegant homes, and they have been potent factors in establishing kindly feeling between the two races.

A unique feature of Meharry is the perfect record kept of all the alumni after they leave school. One can get a complete professional record of the success of nearly every man and woman that holds a diploma from this school.

The courses are well planned, and the addition of the Anderson anatomical laboratory makes the equipment as complete as is possible with the funds available.

Medical: The medical department requires for admission graduation from an approved high school and one year of college work in physics, chemistry, and biology. The regular course for the degree of M. D. covers a period of four years of 32 weeks each.

Dental: The dental department requires for admission graduation from an accredited high school. The degree of D. D. S. is granted upon the satisfactory completion of the course, which covers four years of 28 weeks each.

Pharmacy: The pharmacy department requires for admission two years of high school work, including one year of Latin and physics. Three years of 28 weeks each are required for graduation from this course. Those who comply with the requirements receive the degree of pharmaceutical chemist (Ph. C.)

Nurse Training: A good nurse-training course is provided at Hubbard Hospital. The requirement for admission is graduation from a four-year high school. The course covers three years of eight months each.

Every one of these departments furnished their quota of graduates in the world's war.

MEHARRY MEDICAL COLLEGE

The buildings, 5 in number, consist of the Meharry Medical College, the Meharry Dental and Pharmaceutical Hall, the Auditorium, the Dormitory and the George W. Hubbard Hospital. The Geo. W. Hubbard Hospital is of sufficient size to accommodate from 75 to 100 patients.

The Anderson Anatomical Hall, the gift of Dr. J. W. Anderson and wife of Dallas, Texas, was completed in time for use for the session of 1917-1918. This gift is of especial interest because it was given by one of Meharry's own sons, and because it is among the few buildings of the kind to be given by any colored person. The value of the buildings and grounds is about $140,000.00. The Library, furniture and apparatus $10,000.00.

Meharry Medical College is a member of the Association of American Medical Colleges, of the National Association of Dental Faculties and of the American Conference of Pharmaceutical Faculties.

GEORGE WHIPPLE HUBBARD

George Whipple Hubbard, the President of Meharry, was born in North Charleston, N. H., August 11th, 1841. Was educated in the public schools of New Hampshire, New Hampshire Conference Seminary, and New London Literary and Scientific Institute.

He was delegate of the Christian Commission in the Army of the Potomac, and also in the Army of the Cumberland in 1864. Taught a regiment School in the 110th U. S. C. L. in 1865-6, Principal of the Belle View public School of Nashville, 1867 to 1874.

Graduated from the Medical Department of Nashville University, 1876, and from Vanderbilt University 1879.

MEHARRY AUDITORIUM

In 1876 he was appointed by the Freedmen's Aid Society of the Methodist Episcopal Church, to organize a Medical Department at Central Tennessee College, Nashville, Tenn. This school was opened in October, 1876, and was the first school established in the South for the education of colored physicians. More than one-half of the regularly educated Negro physicians of the South are graduates of this school. He served as Dean for 40 years.

Dr. Hubbard was Professor of Natural Science at Central Tennessee College, from 1876 to 1891, and from 1889 to 1894 was acting Dean and Professor of Hygiene and Toxicology in the Medical Department of New Orleans University.

In 1916 a Separate Charter for Meharry Medical College was procured and in October, 1916, he was inaugurated as its President.

MEHARRY MEDICAL & PHARMACEUTICAL HALL

NATHAN B. YOUNG

ATHAN B. Young, President of the State School for Negroes, at Tallahassee, Florida, like many other of our prominent men had a poor start in life. He was born in Newbern, Alabama, in 1862. Here on a farm he worked in the fields and with the stock, and enjoyed at the same time the simple pleasures of country life. When there was nothing urgent to be done on the farm he was permitted to attend school, provided there was a school in session within walking distance. Even though he attended school but irregularly he got a taste for knowledge and when the chance came for him to attend better schools he had the desire within him.

In Tuscaloosa, Alabama, he attended a private school, getting all he could from the course of study offered there. Later he matriculated at Talladega College, Talladega, Alabama. Here in Talladega, he obtained a real thorough training in the branches he chose. Later he entered Oberlin College, Ohio. As Mr. Young went through these schools he gathered not only a knowledge of books and things, but a knowledge of men. Because of this in his life as a teacher, he has been able to gather around him some of the best teachers

that the race affords and he has been able to so organize them that the work goes on in such a manner as to be a pleasure to all, both teachers and pupils. In speaking of the difficulties that confronted him in obtaining his education, Mr. Young said "I had no special difficulty to speak of—I worked a bit, paid in cash a bit, borrowed the rest."

Practically all of the life of Mr. Young has been spent in the school room. First as a student, then as a teacher. While making up his mind as to his life work between his work at Talladega and his work at Oberlin, Mr. Young taught in Mississippi. Since his graduation he has worked in Alabama, Georgia, and now he is located in Florida. Wherever he was working there he was a leader among the school people. He was at one time President of the Alabama State Teachers Association, and later of the Florida State Teachers' Association. So high was Mr. Young held in the educational circles of our people that the National Association of Teachers in Colored Schools also had him as its President.

In church affiliation, Mr. Young is a Congregationalist. He was educated in the schools supported by that denomination and has at all times been a faithful worker in the churches. He is now serving as the acting President of the Congregational Workers. Through his work in the church and through his work in the schools, Mr. Young comes in direct contact with thousands of people during the course of several years—but through his leadership in the national organizations his influence is greatly enlarged and widened. In the cause of education and for pleasure he has traveled over the greater part of the United States.

Mr. Young has been twice married. His first wife was Miss Emma M. Garrette, of Selma, Alabama. They were married in 1892. In 1905, Mr. Young was married to Miss Margaret Bulkly, at Charleston, S. C. There are five children in the Young family. Nathan B. Young, Jr., is a lawyer in Birmingham, Alabama. Frank Deforest, William Henry, Emma Garrette, and Julia Bulkly are in school in Tallahassee. The young people make the home a happy and an interesting one.

Through the Presidency of the Florida Agricultural and Mechanical College for Negroes, Mr. Young has done his greatest work. He has the work thoroughly organized and his knowledge of men and women has enabled him to choose a good faculty and to get them to work with him for one end. Through the school he is awakening an interest, not only in the study of books, but the problems that will confront the students when they go out from the school. Mr. Young might be taken for an example of a good organizer, and thorough school man.

John Mitchell, Jr.

JOHN Mitchell, Jr., is one of the Negroes who should be known to all our young people. One of the reasons that his life should be known to them is his fearlessness. Another is his manner of using one step to go on up to a higher plane. Born of slave parents, he has steadily made his way to the front till, today, he is a man of affairs, both in the financial world and in the world of journalism.

John Mitchell, Jr., was born in Henrico County, Virginia, in 1863. He received his early education in the public schools of the State, graduating from the High and Normal School at Richmond, in 1881. Like most men who received training, he went through the period of teaching. This period with Mr. Mitchell lasted but three years. At the end of that time he gave up the work to connect himself with the Planet. The Planet is a weekly journal that is published in the interest of the Colored Race. After working on the staff of the Planet for some time, Mr. Mitchell became the owner of the sheet. Through this means some of the best things in the life of Mr. Mitchell have come and through it some of the hardships.

At one time when a lynching had taken place, Mr. Mitchell condemned the act in no uncertain terms, through the columns of his paper. This offended the persons most concerned in the lynching. One result was a threat to Mr. Mitchell. An unsigned letter containing a piece of hemp and a drawing of a skull and cross bones was sent to him. This in no way kept Mr. Mitchell from doing his duty. He visited the place where the lynching had occured, in this way showing that he did not regard the threat on his life. Mr. Mitchell was for a number of years President of the National Afro-American Press Association. All through the South Mr. Mitchell is known to the reading public through his paper, and one of the things that stamp him a man is the fearless manner in which he speaks out where the interest of the colored man is at stake.

The interest, next to the Planet that marks Mr. Mitchell a man of action is the Mechanic's Savings Bank. This bank was organized by Mr. Mitchell in 1901. The need of the bank was felt by him. This in itself was reason enough for its establishment. The bank owns property valued as high as six figures, and the aggregate deposits of this bank when written run into seven figures. The building in which this business is housed is owned by the institution and is one that is a credit to the race and an ornament to the city in which it is placed. Just as Mr. Mitchell was a leader among newspaper men, in just the same manner is he a leader in the banking world of the colored people. At one time he attended the banking association in New York City. He was asked to make an address. This was favorably received and was commented upon all over the country. He is the only colored man who has had the honor of occupying a seat in the body.

In church affiliation, Mr. Mitchell is a Baptist. He brings to the church that same enthusiasm that has characterized his efforts in the financial world and in the world of journalism. Mr. Mitchell is a large property holder and through his life and works he has won the esteem and the good will of all the people who know him, be they white or black. Some one in writing about Mr. Mitchell says of him that his success is due to three things— his application to business, his strict integrity and to his always keeping his word and his engagements with others. Any one who can have these three things truthfully said concerning him, is indeed a person who is worthy of emulation.

Mr. Mitchell, born of slave parents has this long line of accomplishments to his credit: President of the Mechanic's Savings Bank, proprietor of the Richmond Planet, former President of the National Afro-American Press Association, member of the Common Council for two years, member of the Board of Aldermen for eight years, worker in the interest of the colored man, man of means, a man of great fearlessness and a man of his word.

PANORAMIC VIEW AGRICULTURAL AND INDUSTRIAL STATE NORMAL SCHOOL

THE State Normal Schools — one each in East, Middle and West Tennessee, and the Agricultural and Industrial State Normal School for Negroes—were authorized by Chapter 26 of the Acts of 1909, popularly known as the "General Education Bill." This bill set aside twenty-five per cent of the gross-revenue of the State for public Educational purposes, and was amended by Chapter 23 of the Acts of 1913, by the increase of this appropriation to thirty-three and one-third per cent.

PURPOSE: It is the purpose of the Agricultural and Industrial State Normal School to practically train its students that they may better grasp their great economic opportunity in becoming community leaders, farmers and teachers.

The school recognizes the fact that scientific farming and other industries pursued on a scientific basis is the hope of the South, and it is endeavoring to fulfill its place in furnishing better farmers and mechanics as well as teachers who are able to instruct the children of our different communities in both literary and industrial pursuits.

The Academic Department will take those who have finished the grammar grades in the county or city schools and prepare them for the Normal or Professional courses. In the Normal or Professional Department the prescribed literary course is taken with the choice of electives. The electives are Teaching, Agriculture, Domestic Science, Domestic Art, Manual Arts, Trades and Business. Industrial training is given all students. Instruction in domestic science and domestic art is given according to the latest scientific methods with special reference to their practical application in the home.

The buildings of the Agricultural and Industrial State Normal School are ideally located on a bluff overlooking the Cumberland River. The campus proper, consisting of 35 acres is within the corporate limits of the city of Nashville, "the Athens of the South," and is furnished with water and electric lights.

The farm is located just outside the city limits at the foot of the bluff on which the buildings are situated and slopes gradually to the Cumberland River. The farm consists of 135 acres adjoining the campus. Students taking Agriculture do not have to waste an hour or more of time in going to a farm a mile or two away, as is the case in a great many agricultural schools, but can change clothing and go immediately from the class room where the theory is taught, to the farm where they learn also the practical side.

The control of the Colored Normal as in the case of all Tennessee's State Normal Schools, is vested in the State Board of Education and it is due to their wisdom and liberal spirit that this school is so well located and its material equipment is so thoroughly modern and well appointed that the general health of the student body is well conserved.

BUILDINGS AND EQUIPMENT: The buildings include a main or Academic Building, two dormitories for women and men, the trades building with heating plant, residence for the President, two cottages, three barns and several farm houses. The main building is a modern brick and stone structure three stories in height. In it are the offices, laboratories, recitation rooms, Library, reading room, auditorium, dining hall, kitchen, laundry and women's rest room—in all forty rooms.

The Auditorium, with gallery will accommodate

PANORAMIC VIEW—AGRICULTURAL AND INDUSTRIAL STATE NORMAL SCHOOL

nine hundred persons. The class rooms are furnished with modern desks and recitation seats and the laboratories are fully equipped with all needed apparatus and supplies. The Industrial Training Department occupies commodious quarters. The Manual Training rooms are fitted up with the most modern initial equipment, and the students in this department are taught to make additional equipment as it is needed. The Trades building is fitted out with its necessary machinery which is run by two big electric motors. A large dairy barn with modern equipment was built by students during the school term of 1915, and a dairy herd has been purchased. The school is well fitted to teach scientific methods in dairying.

The school has more than 2000 books listed in its library. These books have been selected to meet the peculiar needs of instruction and to suit the conditions of the rural communities from which the students are selected. Over seventy-five leading magazines and periodicals are on file for the use of the students. A spacious, excellently lighted and ventilated reading room is accessible to all who use the library and a competent librarian has been placed in charge. The young men and women are exceptionally fortunate in having modern and comfortable quarters. The dormitory buildings are three-story brick with steam heat, electric lights, bathrooms, with hot and cold water, large, bright and well ventilated outside bed rooms.

All the work in the building is done by the students under the supervision of two excellent matrons, who rotate the work so as to give complete round of housekeeping and nurse training experience to each student, and at the same time hold before them a high standard of living.

The laundry, which is under an experienced matron, has been fitted with machinery, steam washer extracter, mangle, and electric irons. The machinery is operated by the students.

Special attention is given the girls in order to train them in matters pertaining to dress, health, physical development and the simple rules of good manners. They are under the constant care of the preceptress and other female teachers who give them kind and helpful instruction as needed.

The men's dormitory is also in charge of an experienced preceptress who sees that the rights of the young men are carefully guarded and their needs faithfully met. A school physician may be called whenever necessary.

It has an "Aesthetic Club" to promote correct standards of life.

Societies: It has four Literary Societies; an Athletic Association; society of Agricultural and Mechanical Students; and numerous clubs organized for mutual welfare and enjoyment of the students.

The school gives special attention to the religious training and life of the students. Every third Sunday services are held at the school and Sunday school is held every Sunday. A Bible Training Class is maintained in connection with the Sunday school.

W. J. HALE, the President of the Institution, has the honor of being the first president of the First State Normal School for Negroes in the State of Tennessee. He was elected again last year for another term, which was a year before the expiration of his previous election. President Hale stands high not only as an educator, but as a man of sterling worth, a genuine friend of his race, and a wise and safe leader.

HARRY T. BURLEIGH, A. M.

ELF made men in this country are not so rare in the business world, but in the world of music the self made man is an object of wonder. Harry T. Burleigh has the distinction of being a self made musician. He was born in Erie, Pennsylvania, where he attended the high school of the city. Here in Erie Mr. Burleigh was fired with the ambition that has never died within him, the ambition that has spurred him on and on to higher endeavor in his line till today, he is not only a great singer, but a great composer as well. The opportunity to hear real music came to him through service. His mother worked in the family of a lady who was fond of music and who often entertained the great musicians when they visited that city. He heard them at times and realized that music was in his soul and that he wanted to hear and to produce good music. On one occasion when a great artist was coming to town, young Burleigh stood out under the drawing room windows in order that he might hear the concert at any cost. The snow was deep —up to his knees. As a result of this exposure for the love of music he became ill. When questioned, his mother found out what he had done. After that she obtained for him the permission to help serve the guests in order that he might hear the music.

Through serving in this home there came to Harry Burleigh a few years later the great chance for his advancement in the musical world. Hearing that there were to be scholarships in the National Conservatory of Music, he went up to try for one. After trying out his voice, he went away to await the decision of the judges. He went back the next day for the decision. He had fallen a little below the mark required. The registrar was a lady whom he had served at one of the musical festivals back in his home town of Erie. He recognized her, told her who he was and she was not only interested and sympathetic, but she went to work and secured for him the scholarship that he so much wanted, the scholarship that gave him his chance to become the great musician that we now know.

Although his tuition was free, his living expenses caused him much concern, and it was through hard work that he was enabled to continue his studies. In 1894, competing with sixty applicants, he won the position of baritone soloist at St. George's Church in New York—a position which he has held for twenty-five years. Speaking of his work on the completion of his twenty-fifth year, the Bulletin of the church said of him—"Through all these years, with their inevitable changes, he has been a faithful and devoted helper, friend and worker in the varied activities of this church."

Although Mr. Burleigh says of himself that he is a singer, not a composer, he is known to more people as a writer of music than as a singer of songs. Thousands of people who have never heard him sing, who do not even know that he is a man of color, sing his compositions and enjoy them. One of these in particular has won for him great popularity—"Deep River." It is one of the most popular of the concert pieces. Many of the songs from his pen are popular. Among these are "The Grey Wolf," "Ethiopia Saluting the Colors," "The Young Warrior," "The Soldier" and "Jean." These are only a few of the songs that have been arranged by Mr. Burleigh. In choosing his texts he is always careful to choose poems with big meanings. He says "The text determines the character of the song." Mr. Burleigh has remembered this himself in his own musical compositions.

February 1898, Mr. Harry T. Burlegh was married to Miss Louise Alston in Washington, D. C. There is one son in the family, Alston Waters Burleigh who is a student in Howard University.

Mr. Burleigh has traveled in England, in 1908 and 1909. In 1917 he was awarded the Springarn prize. Another honor that has come to him is the Master of Arts Degree from Atlanta University.

Austin M. Curtis, A. B., A. M., M. D.

DR. A. M. Curtis is a man who while he has won distinction in the profession of his choice has also had time to engage in other duties that make for the uplift of the whole people. Thus while a man whose time has many calls upon it for its skilled work, we still see him with time to go to the various churches and deliver lectures to the masses on "Sanitation and Hygiene." In this manner he has done much to bring about better health conditions in all the communities in which he has lived. Another phase of work that has taken much of his time is the Y. M. C. A. In Washington, District of Columbia, when funds were needed to complete the $100,000.00 building that they had under way, it was Dr. Curtis who was made chairman of the campaign committee, because of his ability to organize men and get them to respond to his plans.

Dr. Austin M. Curtis was born in Raleigh, North Carolina, in 1868. He was one in a family of ten. The schools of Raleigh were pretty good and in them Dr. Curtis proved himself to be a pupil so apt and so willing to apply himself that through the kindness of a Northern lady teaching in the schools of Raleigh, he obtained a scholarship in Lincoln University, Pennsylvania. Although this scholarship made life a little easier for the ambitious young man, he still had to work, and work hard to keep himself in funds during the winter month. Thus we find him during the summer months engaged in some sort of lucrative work.

After four years of college work in Lincoln University, Dr. Curtis was graduated with the well earned degree of A. B. Later, because of the good work that he had done after leaving school the University conferred upon him the degree of A. M. But on leaving Lincoln, Dr. Curtis was still unsatisfied with his training. He wanted to be a professional man. Once more he matriculated, this time in Northwestern University Medical School, Chicago. From this institution he was graduated in 1891 with honors.

For seven years after his graduation he practiced his profession in Chicago.

During this time he served as attending surgeon to Provident Hospital and for one year he served on the staff of the Cook County Hospital of that city. Dr. Curtis was the first physician of the Negro race to hold the position on the Cook County Hospital Staff. In 1898, Dr. Curtis was appointed Surgeon-in-Chief of Freedmen's Hospital, Washington, District of Columbia. He gave up the work in Provident Hospital in Chicago and took the work in Freedmen's, the most noted of all the hospitals in the country. Here at Freedmen's Dr. Curtis made a national reputation as a surgeon, many of his cases receiving mention in surgical literature. After four years Dr. Curtis gave up the work to take up a private practice. He still serves Freedmen's in the capacity of attending Surgeon, however, and at the same time is consulting surgeon at the Provident Hospital, Baltimore, Maryland, and of Richmond Hospital, Richmond, Virginia. In addition to these duties, Dr. Curtis makes frequent trips into the South to perform operations in various cities.

Dr. Curtis also serves as a teacher of his science. He is Associate Professor of surgery, Howard Medical School, and clinical professor of surgery in the Post Graduate School of Howard University. In this manner, Dr. Curtis has hopes of passing on some of the knowlege that he has gained from his extensive practice. And those who see the work of the young men who go out from under his instruction realize that he has had his hopes come true.

At the Jamestown exposition, Dr. Curtis had charge of the medical exhibit of the Negroes. He installed a model hospital and had it in good working order. Here he was able to show the progress of the medical science among his people and to show the best methods of management of the hospital.

Dr. Curtis has an interesting family. The sons in the family are following in the footsteps of their father and are one by one taking up the practice of medicine as a profession. To the father this is most gratifying for it shows that to his own family he has been their ideal of a man. No greater honor can be done any man than to have his own children take him for a model.

Dr. Curtis is a man who has traveled extensively and the contact that he has gotten from this travel shows in his bearing, he is thoroughly at home in any emergency, is a good friend and is always ready to help those who need him.

MAJOR ROBERT R. JACKSON

AJOR Robert R. Jackson was born in Malta, Illinois, September 1st., 1870. At an early age he entered the public schools of Chicago, and remained in them till he completed the High School Course. While still in school, Major Jackson served as a newsboy. From this work he gained a business training that has served him in all his after life. After leaving school, Major Jackson took the Civil Service Examination and was appointed to a clerkship in the Chicago Postoffice. In this capacity he served for twenty-one years. For twelve years he served as Assistant Superintendent of the Armour Station Post Office. This is the highest position ever held by any member of the Colored Race, in the Post Office System of Chicago.

During his life as a public man Major Jackson has served in a number of capacities. He has worked in the Civil Service, he has served as a soldier and he has done good work as a politician. As a soldier he has made a splendid record. He served in the Spanish-American War in 1898, and on the Mexican border in 1916. In all he served his country as a soldier for twenty-five years. He was given his honorable discharge in 1917. Major Jackson did his part to bring fame to the Illinois National Guard, Eighth Regiment. Of this regiment he was a charter member and with it he worked for the twenty-five years that he put in the service.

In the political life of the city of his adoption he has for a number of years been very prominent. He was elected to the forty-eighth General Assembly and was seated just a short time before the Legislature adjourned sine die. He was re-elected to the forty-ninth General Assembly and once more to the Fiftieth General Assembly. He had the opportunity to get in some good work for the colored people while serving these three terms. For one thing, the fiftieth anniversary of the emancipation of the slaves claimed his attention and he supported a bill appropriating $25,000.00 for that purpose. After his re-election he passed a bill for an additional $25,000.00 for the Half Century Exposition. It was through his tireless endeavor that the famous Jackson law was passed which put the Birth of a Nation out of business. In 1918, Major Jackson was elected Alderman from the Second Ward to the City Council of Chicago. This election was for two years.

In church affiliation Major Jackson is an African Methodist Episcopal. His membership is in the Quinn Chapel, of Chicago. He is a Knight of Pythias, a Mason, An Odd Fellow, an Elk and a member of the United Brothers of Friendship. In the first named of these secret orders he holds high rank, being the Major General Uniform Rank of Knight of Pythias. This position he has held for the past twenty years.

Major Jackson owns a Fraternal Press, Printing and Publishing, which is conservatively valued at $55,000.00. This is one of the largest printing establishments of Chicago. Through his press he is able to reach many people.

In May 1888, he was married to Miss Annie Green, of Chicago, Illinois. To them two children have been born. George Jackson is a clerk in the City of Chicago, and the daughter, Naomi, is now married and busy making a home of her own.

In the interest of his work, and a soldier, Major Jackson has traveled all over the United States. To him came the chance to train during his twenty-five years of service, forty thousand men for military service. This work he did willingly and well. In summing up what he had tried to do in his long life of usefulness Major Jackson says that the principal episodes of his life have come in "Fighting for the Race and for the Flag of our Country."

William A. Warfield, M. D.

DR. Warfield is a good example of the man who has stayed in one place and steadily worked his way up from the ground floor to the top. That he has done this has been due to perseverance and to real merit. Dr. Warfield was born at Hyattstown, Maryland, in 1866. In the public schools of his county he received his early training, and then he entered Morgan College, Baltimore, Maryland. From Morgan he was graduated in 1890 and ever since that time he has done honor to the school that gave him his grasp on things. And Morgan is justly proud of this son of hers that has won so much distinction in the profession that he made his life work. After completing the course at Morgan Dr. Warfield entered the Howard School of Medicine and was graduated with the degree M. D., in 1894. Since that time Freedmen's Hospital, the hospital connected with the medical school of Howard University has been the scene of Dr. Warfield's labors.

He first entered the hospital as an intern. In this capacity he served in 1894 and 1895. His next step in the ascent was to that of school assistant surgeon. At this post he served from 1895 to 1896, when he was once more promoted, this time to the work of First Assistant Surgeon. As first assistant surgeon he served from 1897 to 1901. At this time he was appointed surgeon-in-chief, which position he still holds. When Dr. Warfield was serving his internship at Freedmen's he was under Dr. Dan Williams, of Chicago, who was at that time surgeon-in-chief of Freedmen's Hospital. He could not have chosen a better man to work under if he had had the power of choice, for Dr. Williams has given to the medical science some points that will make him a name forever in the medical and surgical world.

Since 1901, Dr. Warfield has been at the head of Freedmen's. During that time the work of the institution has grown, the plant has been enlarged, and the work strengthened. Much of the credit for this is due Dr. Warfield. With untiring effort he has wisely administered the affairs of the Hospital and has brought it up to the point where it serves a large number of persons, not only persons from the District of Columbia but people from all over the United States, who go there to take advantage of the skill of the staff employed in the work there.

Dr. Warfield is Professor of abdominal surgery at Howard Medical School. Indeed Dr. Warfield is inclined to make a specialty of this line of work and has won rank among the most noted of our clever operators in this work. The interest of Dr. Warfield is in all lines of work of his profession as is easily shown by the organizations with which he has affiliated himself. He is a member of the American Hospital Association, he is a member of the National Medical Association and he is a member of the Medico-Chururgical Society of the District of Columbia.

Dr. Warfield has found time to serve in other capacities that are not strictly in his profession. He is a member of the Board of Childrens' Guardians in the District of Columbia and he is a member of the Masonic order. In church connection, Dr. Warfield is a Methodist and in political belief he is a Republican. During the crisis through which our country has just passed, Dr. Warfield gave freely of his time and energies and ripe wisdom to the service of his country. Early and late, even when he was needed to see after the affairs of the Hospital he was off to serve on the Exemption Board, or to help with a drive or in some way to help keep the work of the war under way.

In Baltimore, Maryland, Dr. Warfield was married to Miss Violet B. Thompson, in 1891. From this union two children have been born to help the parents enjoy life and to make the life worth living for them. These two young people, William and Violet are being given opportunity to take advantage of all the educational facilities that are afforded in such an abundance in the Capitol City.

Dr. Warfield still remains in the place where he begun the practice of his profession. He started at the bottom, as an intern. Step by step, and through years of self development and self application he has continued up, till now he is at the head of Freedmen's and since Freedmen's is the largest and best institution of her type, we might say that Dr. Warfield stands in the medical profession today without a peer.

C. H. JAMES

register held a facination for him, so he determined to become a mercant.

There being no money to back him and no stores in which he could get an apprenticeship, he bought such articles as he could afford from his teacher's wage, packed them in a sack and started forth a peddler. The thing was a novelty, goods were scarce; and so the business prospered. It grew too large to carry on his back. Profits increased until the young peddler felt able to pay rent and to buy a fairly large assortment of goods. Thus was begun on a small scale the well known firm of C. H. James and Sons, wholesale commission merchants.

The business has been continuous in its growth and while he has kept a stock adequate to meet the greater demands of his business, he has been enabled to use a good per cent of his profits in enjoying the comforts of life and in making good real estate investments. He owns his residence, which is a handsome structure and has invested largely in other real estate. His possessions embrace improved and unimproved lots valued at $130.00.

Mr. James is every inch a business man and he has made such a great success of his business by giving it his strict and constant attention, so much so, that he has resisted the temptation of outside attractions. In early years there was no partner, no one to share the responsibilities, hence he must needs be on hand by day and by night. In later years his son has come in to share the burdens as well as the earnings of the firm. He is a good and loyal Baptist, a Knight of Pythias and a Mason. Here and there he has had a few hours to devote to political interests. Of course he is a Republican. In 1912 he was a delegate to the convention at Chicago, to nominate Colonel Theodore Roosevelt on the Progressive Ticket. This was one of the big events of his career, not only in politics, but in being away so long and care-free from his business.

In civic life, however, he never permits political prejudice to influence him in the least and always stands for the right regardless of party affiliation. There is no public movement started in Charleston without his being consulted.

Mr. James was married to Miss Roxie A. Clark, of Meigs County, Ohio, September 24, 1884. Three children have been born to and reared by Mr. and Mrs. James. Mr. Edward L. James is the partner in the firm of C. H. James and Sons. Miss Estella A. is a teacher in the public schools of Charleston. Miss Carrie B. is now Mrs. B. A. Crichlow, being the wife of Dr. B. A. Crichlow of the Crichlow Hospital. Mrs. Crichlow was formerly of the C. H. James and Sons, having served as the bookkeeper for this firm for several years.

ISTORY centers around the name of C. H. James of Charleston, West Virginia. His father was a soldier in the Union Army. Honorably discharged in West Virginia in 1865 the father set to work to make a career for himself and for his family. Before entering the war he had made up his mind to preach. He now began his chosen work. He was the first colored ordained minister in West Virginia; and he and his sister Lucy were the first public school teachers of West Virginia. Thus does the son, C. H. James come into an envious heritage.

Mr. C. H. James was born in Gallia County, Ohio. The father having gone to the war, the son lived with and was reared by his grandfather.

He remained with his grandfather until he reached the age of eighteen, when he, with other members of the family, joined the father in West Virginia. When he reached his new home he thought to follow the steps of his father and so entered upon a career of teaching but the school room was not to his liking, his taste and inclantion leading in another direction. The game of buying and selling appealed to him and the counter and cash

RICHARD H. BOWLING, D. D., LL. D., AND FIRST
BAPTIST CHURCH—NORFOLK, VA.

EV. Richard Hausber Bowling, D.
D., LL. D., church builder, preacher and religious leader, was born
Sept. 4, 1864, in a rude cabin between Old Point and Hampton,
Va. The first fifteen years of his
life were spent in farm work, fishing and helping
out in his father's little store. It was then his
good fortune also as a student to come under the
influence of the noted General Armstrong, founder and principal of the Hampton Normal School.

When about fifteen years old in December 1879
"Fighting Dick," as he was then called, ran away
from his home in Hampton. From Norfolk he got a
chance to work his way on a boat to Boston, Mass.
After a year in Boston he went West for some
eighteen months. The next year he spent in New
York working as butler and attending school. During the next three years he worked in the Summer
as a waiter on Shelton's Island and in the Winter
as a farm hand in Connecticut. That he did not
relax in his efforts for an education, however, is
evident in the story he used to tell of himself, of
how he fell asleep one night while studying and
awoke to find that his candle had burned low and
set fire to his little soap-box bookcase and all its
precious contents.

It was during these last few years that he recog-

nized the call to the ministry and announced his
purpose to enter the sacred office. He joined the
then famous Mt. Olivet Baptist Church, pastored
by Dr. Daniel W. Wisher, who took note of the
young man and gave him frequent opportunities
for the exercise of his gifts. It was apparent from
the start that he was endowed with unusual gifts
as an orator and he was encouraged to go forward
in his chosen profession. Although a young man
his reputation began to spread and it was not long
before he received a call to a church. Returning
home when about twenty-one or two years old the
young Mr. Bowling received his first call to a
church from the little Baptist church in Waynesboro, Virginia, at a salary of but $15 per month.
Then followed in quick succession brief pastorates
in Harrisonburg, Va., where he drew great crowds
of both races to hear his eloquent preaching, and in
Steelton, Pa., where he built a comfortable church
house.

While on a visit to his old home in Hampton in
December 1889, he heard of the efforts then being
made by the historic old First Church of Norfolk,
Va., to secure a pastor. His engagement with
them was filled so acceptably that on Jan. 1st, 1890
he received a unanimous call. The twenty-three
years that followed the acceptance of this call until his death in July 1913 were busy and filled with
successful labors. During his Norfolk pastorate he
conducted a number of unprecedented revivals,
added large numbers to the church, encouraged his
people by precept and example to buy homes, educate their children and live soberly, served as
President of the Y. M. C. A., helped organize a colored insurance company, and gave himself unselfishly to every civic and philanthropic movement.

In October, 1890, he married Miss Haynes
whom he had met some years before. Being a
graduate of Fisk and also a young woman naturally endowed with a sweet disposition and the
power of convincing speech she proved to him a
helpmate indeed. To them were born seven children, four of whom are still living. His first wife
having died in February 1905, he was married again
in 1907 to Miss Grace P. Melton of Winton, N. C.
To them were born three chidren.

For fourteen years he was the president of the
Virginia Baptist State Convention, which under
him paid for and operated successfully the Virginia
Theological Seminary and College at Lynchburg,
Va. As an orator and preacher he was well and
favorably known all through the South and in the
larger cities of the East.

The crowning achievement of his life perhaps
was the building and paying for in the last seven
years of his life of the beautiful stone church, now
pastored by his son, Richard Hausber Bowling, Jr.,
at a total cost of a little over $72,000.

He was a hard worker and a close student. He
strove for a better feeling between the races and
thereby won the love and respect of them both.
Above all he was honest, dependable and of a spot-
less character.

HEMAN E. PERRY

EMAN E. Perry, born in Houston, Texas, March 5, 1873, his early experience was not unlike many of the colored men who have risen from the huts of poverty and traversed the roads of hardships to the high positions they have filled in the affairs of men. He did not enjoy a finished education, his schooling carrying him only through the seventh grade of the public school, but what he lacked in this particular he more than made up in a natural adaptibility for business, and in gifts along this line he seems to have received a double portion. Coupled with his keen, active business mentality, he possessed an indomitable will, which would not yield to the most discouraging conditions. His business career started when quite young as a clerk in his father's grocery store, where he remained for two years. His father gave up the grocery business and went to the farm, taking his son with him.

Here he engaged in general farm work and in the harvest season peddled the farm products from door to door.

He was twelve years of age when he went to the farm, and he continued there for about two years, when he returned to the city and spent the next ten years working for a cotton firm, during which time he became an expert cotton sampler and clas-

ser. Having learned the business he decided to shift for himself, so he gave up the position he had filled for so long a period, and offered his services to the trade as an expert in the lines above mentioned.

His ability as a sampler and classer was generally recognized and he had no trouble in securing contracts from the large and well known firms, such as George H. McFadden and Hooper & Co.

He eventually gave up the cotton business and sought a wider field in which to develop his talent.

He commenced as a life insurance solicitor and worked for the Equitable, Manhattan Life, Fidelity Mutual and the Mutual Reserve. He spent about twelve years as a solicitor and the experience he gained in the field was of great help to him when he organized the company which has established his reputation as an insurance man. To gain further knowledge of the business he went to New York and obtained employment in the home offices of several of the companies he had worked for in the field. While thus employed he formed the acquaintance of actuaries of national reputation.

When he worked he dreamed, and he saw in his minds eye an insurance institution owned and operated by Negroes. After a while his dream began to take concrete form, and he left New York and came to Atlanta, Georgia, to launch his enterprise.

STANDARD LIFE INSURANCE COMPANY

The organization of this company did not have easy sailing, in fact the first attempt met with failure, and had another hand been at the helm instead of that of Mr. Perry, it would no doubt have sunk to rise no more.

In 1908 he gathered together a group of business men in the Young Men's Christian Association hall at Atlanta, and unfolded to them his purpose and plan to organize a Life Insurance Company among the Negroes and to start with a capital of One Hundred Thousand Dollars. Some of those who were present sat up and gasped, and others thought that the young man was crazy. Some of them did not hesitate to say so. They could hardly believe their ears when he told them in a frank, straight forward way, that the least amount with which they could begin business would be $100,000 paid in capital which must be invested in bonds and deposited with the State Treasurer for the protection of the policy holders of the company.

These men who had been in business and in the professions in Atlanta for many years, a number of whom had grown wealthy through real estate investments, and who had been accustomed to see things done on a large scale by the white citizens of Atlanta, were not prepared to see a Negro with an idea as big as this. They plied him with questions and thought they must have misunderstood his proposition, that he meant $10,000, and not $100,000 and then they did not know the meaning of some of the technical insurance terms he used, which he had to explain. He finally convinced them that he was in sober, serious earnestness, and while he succeeded in enthusing them a little with the enterprise, they left the hall without committing themselves, and went home to think it over.

While it burned with but a faint glow at first the fire kindled at that meeting never went out. Little by little the idea grew and men and women in every walk of life became interested in what this stranger was trying to do He opened a subscription list, which provided that not one penny of the money paid in should be used for the expenses of the organization that if the Company was not launched every dollar received, with 4 per cent interest should be returned to the subscriber

A charter of incorporation was secured in January 1909 Then began the real struggle for the charter was granted with the provision that the company should begin business within two years from the date of issuance or the money received for subscriptions be refunded to subscribers and the charter revoked January 28 1911, was the last day on which the Standard Life Insurance Company could begin to do business under the charter

After two years of the hardest kind of work and the greatest of sacrifices in the closing days of 1910 there was little more than $60 000 in hand and it needed $40 000 more before anything could be done Mr Perry was a man of faith as well as determination and energy and by herculean efforts within the next thirty days he raised another $10 000 but when the 11th of January dawned it became apparent to him that the remaining $30 000 necessary could not be raised from subscribers so he made an effort to borrow the amount While those to whom he applied recognized his absolute integrity and honesty of purpose and sympathized with his intense earnestness he only found encouragement from one banker and as he required time to consult his lawyer and board his enterprise was placed in great jeopardy, for the 28th of the month was rapidly approaching when either business must begin or the charter surrendered The fatal day finally arrived and he had not accomplished his purpose and with a keen disappointment, but a brave heart he gave up his charter and paid the subscribers back their money with 4% interest as promised He had borne the burden of the fight, defrayed his own expenses, and hired others to help him using up his own resources and going in debt to others for means necessary to carry on the work

It would seem that the end of the Standard Life Insurance Company had come It would have been the end to an ordinary man It would have crushed a weak man But the man who had worked for two years making untold sacrifices was made of sterner stuff

After the sting of the crushing defeat had lost its pain he set about the task of doing it all over again, and this time he succeeded

Long before the time limit of his charter had expired, he had sold the 1000 shares of stock at $125 to $150 per share, collected over $50,000 in cash and had taken notes for the balance of $80 000 and with the cooperation of his associates in the organization had borrowed on the notes of the stockholders $50,000 more, and purchased and deposited with the treasurer of the State of Georgia $100,000 in bonds The company was born, but it was only in its swaddling clothes, only a beginning —much work still remained to be done and it had to be developed The man who founded the enterprise was equal to the task of developing it It has succeeded marvelously The policy of the com

pany from the beginning was to give full publicity to its affairs, so that both the public and those financially interested might have complete confidence and security It has been examined by a number of expert accountants and actuaries and their reports given wide publicity

The death claims paid in 1918 amounted to $79 733 47, and the total amount of beneficiaries paid since organization is $145 353 78

In 1913 the insurance in force was $381 500 and the premium income $10 293 68 in 1918 the insurance in force amounted to $8 208 720 and the Premium income to $339 327 77 It bears the distinction of being the only Old Line Negro Life Insurance Company

OFFICERS

Heman E Perry President, Harry H Pace Secretary-Treasurer, J A Robinson, Auditor, C C Cater, M D Medical Director Wm H King Director of Agencies D P Cater Cashier C A Shaw, Director of Inspection J S Blocker Supt Policy Division Geo Dyre Eldridge (Boston, Mass) Actuary, Candler, Thomson and Hirsch Counsel

DIRECTORS

Henry A Boyd, Nashville, E C Brown Philadelphia Walter S Buchanan, Normal, B J Davis Augusta J F Dugas Augusta, A D Hamilton Atlanta, Thos H Hayes, Memphis J W Huguley Americus, R L Isaacs Prairie View, Sol C Johnson Savannah R F Jones New Orleans, A L Lewis Jacksonville, Harry H Pace Atlanta J O Ross Atlanta, Emmett J Scott Washington Walter S Scott Savannah; N B Young Tallahassee

In addition to the officers mentioned the Company has an advisory board composed of the leading financiers, educators and religious teachers of the Negro race, who live in different sections of the country, where they are easily accessible for information and advice

The organization of the Standard Life Insurance Company is not the only achievement of Mr Perry

He organized the Citizens Trust Company, with a capital stock of $250 000, and a surplus of $250,-000 This Company is located in Atlanta Georgia The company bears the distinction of being the only one passing the Capitol Issues Committee, Sixth Federal Reserve District and in Washington

He also organized "The Service Company," with a capital stock of $100,000 The purpose of this organization is to equip and operate a chain of laundries and dry cleaning plants in different cities It now has two plants in successful operation one in Atlanta another in Augusta, Ga

Mr Perry organized the hospital association which purchased the Old Bishop Turner home for fifteen thousand dollars and obtained the promise of $150 000 from Eastern Philanthropists contingent on a certain sum being raised by the association for the erection of a hospital in Atlanta Ga

He has recently purchased the Old Calico House Atlanta at present occupied by the Wesley Memorial Hospital and the two adjoining lots and will construct here a handsome office building for colored tenants This project will involve several hundred thousand dollars

REVEREND FREDERICK LEE LIGHTS

IKE many who have risen from the ranks of the colored race to occupy places of distinction, Dr. Lights was reared in the lap of poverty and passed through a stage of trial and tribulation before he reached his goal. He was born in the State of Louisiana, where his boyhood struggles began. His parents were poor, his father being a Baptist minister, whose labors extended back to 1859, who appreciated the value of an education but was unable to give his son Frederick the benefit of one. Young Fredrick had the ambition and desire to learn and the grit and energy to seek an education which he finally secured by the labor of his hands.

At the age of twelve, he left his native State and moved with his parents to Bayou, Texas. Here he enrolled in the public schools and was permitted to attend them for a while without undue anxiety and care. His respite from struggle was of short duration for in a little while his father died and placed upon his shoulders the care and responsibility, not of himself alone, but in a large measure the entire family. He met the burden with fortitude and strength and at once addressed himself to the problems thus thrust upon him. To meet the situation he found it necessary to devote his days to labor but he robbed work of its fatigue and night of its repose and spent many of the hours which should have been devoted to sleep in hard study. He finished his course in the public schools and then entered the Hearne Academy. He was among the first to enter this institution of learning, remaining there until he had completed his course.

While at Bayou he was converted and joined the Baptist Church, being the church his father organized.

The deep religious impressions made upon him in his youth continued to grow until they finally decided him upon his life work. When he completed his work at the Hearne Academy he went to Edge, Texas, and was there ordained as a minister. This was in 1882, and immediately after his ordination he began his ministerial work. Among the churches he served as Pastor was the Baptist church, at Hearne, the church at Bayou, his old home; the church at Franklin, at Dremond, at Cannon, at Rockdale, at Hamstead, at Hannon Colony, at Allen Farm, and at Wellsburn. At three of these—Edge, Franklin and Cannon, he built houses of worship.

From the beginning of his ministerial career he has grown in wisdom and popularity and has been enabled to accomplish a large work. His record shows that he has received into the church more than five thousand members and has united in marriage more than one thousand couples.

His labors have not been confined to the local church but have also been of an international character.

In 1905 he was a messenger to the World's Baptist Congress, which met in England.

He took advantage of the opportunity while in Europe to make a tour of England, Ireland, Scotland and France. Again in 1910 he visited Europe as a delegate to the World's Mission Congress, which met in Edinburgh. This time he visited Germany, Belgium and Wales, and revisited France.

He also took an active part in the National meetings of his denomination and was instrumental in a large measure, for the National Baptist Convention, being held in Houston Texas, in 1912.

Dr. Light was married in 1895, to Miss Pearl Augusta Reed, of Houston, Texas. At the time of their marriage she was a teacher in the Public Schools of Houston. Six children have been born to them, five of whom are living. Freddie Lee, Ada Estelle, Emerson Augusta, Roger Williams, Pearl Emma Eduara, and Louise Venara, deceased.

S. W. Bacote, B. D., M. A., D. D., and Second Baptist Church

 HOEVER visits Kansas City, Missouri, for any length of time will, if he wishes to know anything at all about the religious life of the people, come very soon to the Second Baptist Church and its pastor, Rev. S. W. Bacote. The Second Baptist Church building is one that will make a stranger enquire about it, the pastor of the second Baptist Church is one who will make the stranger feel at home within his city.

Rev. Bacote was born at Society Hill, South Carolina. Here in the public schools he received his earliest training for his life work. He next entered Benedict College, where he remained for five years. Benedict is one of those schools supported by the Baptists of the North in which such thorough training is offered to our young people. Rev. Bacote next entered Shaw University, Raleigh, North Carolina. Here he remained for one year and then entered Richmond Theological Seminary, from which he received the degree of B. D., in 1891, he received his master's degree in 1900 and the degree of D. D. in 1904. Thus, Rev. Bacote went from one school to another, from one degree of training to another till he was fitted for the work he had in his heart and in his mind to do.

In 1902 Rev. Bacote married Miss Lucy Jeanette Bledsoe, of Topeka, Kansas. Mrs. Bacote is as much of a help to her husband as his very thorough training. She is active in every line of work that is taken up by the church, knows just how to make the people feel at home in the church and stands in all matters right with Rev. Bacote, ready to help him wherever a woman's help is needed. To the Bacote home four children have come: Samuel and Geraldine (deceased); and Clarence and Lucille.

Rev. Bacote is a man who has chosen to work in a few places and who has done his work so well in those places that he is wanted there permanently. His first pastorate was in Alabama, where he pastored the Second Baptist Church, at Marion, and at the same time served as President of the Marion Baptist College. He left this work to enter the field at Kansas City, Mo. Here he is pastor of the Second Baptist Church. The history of this church is in a way the history of the work of Rev. Bacote.

When he took charge of the work of that church in 1895 the basement of the new church was built and had been built for some time, but there it stood, doing good to no one, depreciating in value with the passing of time, yet the people of the church, without the proper leader, had not the will to carry the structure to completion. Rev. Bacote, like the good business man that he is, said to his people——"We will pay as we go." So they set to work to raise the funds for the church. When they had funds they were spent carefully, so that all might see the work go up another step. So with each rally of the people the building went up. Not till they came to the roof did they seek aid from borrowed money. But when they reached this point, the money necessary to hurry it through was borrowed and the congregation moved in. But they did not wait to get the money together to pay off this bill. That was one thing that Rev. Bacote abhored and it was one of the things that he tried to teach his people to look upon with disfavor. So the sum that was necessary to cover the Second Baptist Church was soon paid back.

The edifice stands as a monument to the tireless endeavor of this man and his faithful workers. It is well planned, well built, and is kept in the best of order. The church is worth $100,000.00.

Rev. Bacote does not spend all of his energies in the work of the people of Kansas City. He has also a national interest in the affairs of the Baptists. He was elected statistician of the National Baptist Convention in 1902. In this work he continued for a number of years organizing it so thoroughly that all the facts could be seen at a glance. Among the things that have been written by Rev. Bacote are "Who's Who Among the Colored Baptists of the United States," and The National Baptist Year Book. The interests of Rev. Bacote are in the work. He has the work in his heart as can be seen from his talks, his work in his church and his work in the national organizations and in his writings. Rev. Bacote is the type of minister to whom we can point with pride and say: "There is a man, thoroughly trained, with the interest of the work and the people upon his heart. Let us take him for an example."

EDWARD RANDOLPH CARTER, D. D.

ROM the shoemaker's bench there has gone forth many illustrious men who have made themselves felt in the world's progress. Since the days of William Carey, men have turned from their work upon the soles of shoes to labor for the salvation of the souls of men.

Rev. Edward Randolph Carter, D. D., was once a cobbler, but like Carey, he cobbled for a living while his real work was the carrying on the work of his Lord. Dr. Carter was born in Athens, Georgia, about the year 1867, being the son of Thomas and Sibble Carter.

After the foundation of his education was laid in the public schools, he attended Morehouse College. The degree of D. D. was conferred upon him by this college and the Gaudeloup College, Texas.

He took a course in Hebrew at the Chicago University. While securing his education he followed the shoemakers trade and gave some time to teaching. Atlanta, Georgia, has been the seat of his ministerial work and in fact the center of his active life.

Since 1882 he has been the pastor of the Friendship Baptist Church, Atlanta, and while serving this church as pastor he has been actively identified with a number of denominational institutions and enterprises. He is a trustee and secretary of the Board of Trustees of Morehouse College; for a number of years he has been President of the Baptist Educational Convention of Georgia; was President of the Baptist State Convention, of Georgia a number of years; is editor of Reflections of National Baptist Convention Teacher.

Through his efforts a home for the old folks was established in Atlanta, and he is now building a home for boys and girls.

For nine years he was Vice-President of the International Baptist Association.

He was a pioneer in the prohibition campaign in the South among the Negroes. He made speaking tours in all of the counties of Georgia, Tennessee, the Carolinas and Virginia. He is a member of the National Baptist Publication Board, and of the founder's committee of this board.

He is a member of the Southern Sociological Congress. He was a delegate to the World's Missionary Congress, which met in Edinburgh Scotland in 1910. He is Lecturer of West side Baptist Ministers' Union, Atlanta, Georgia.

Dr. Carter has been a great traveler and has seen more of the world than is the privilege of but few men. He has visited the countries of Europe, Palestine, Syria, Asia, Asia Minor, Africa and Egypt.

In 1876 Dr. Carter married Miss Obeie Ceicil Brown, at Athens, Georgia. She has borne him five children: Edward Randolph, Jr., M. D.; Capt. Raymond H., M. D.; Earnest Mays, Ph. D.; James B. Electrician; and Madam Iola Rogers.

Dr. Carter's manifold duties have occupied so much of his time that he has had but little opportunity to devote to his secular interests though he has accumulated property to the value of $5000.

A recent honor conferred upon Dr. Carter and one which speaks highly of his ability and worth, was being selected by the personal war council to go to France to lecture to the colored soldiers.

The offices held by Dr. Carter are not mere positions of honorary distinction, but call for much labor, and the fact that he fills them so acceptably goes to show that he is a man of work.

To be elected to an office and then neglect the duties connected therewith, is to strip the position of its honor, for the honor lies in duty well performed.

Taking this view of place, Dr. Carter is entitled to all the honors attaching to the positions he holds. Dr. Carter is yet in his prime and hopes to accomplish much for his people before he encounters the feebleness of old age.

JOSEPH HAYGOOD BLODGETT

HAT a man of energy and talent should rise above his obscure surroundings and become a factor in the world's progress and make a name for himself, is no argument against education but is an encouragement to those who are denied the great benefits of an education.

Joseph Haygood Blodgett was denied the advantages of a mental training, such as is supplied by the common schools and colleges and yet he has made a success of his life.

He spent his early years upon the farm where the strength of his youth was employed in tilling the soil.

He was born in Augusta, Georgia, February 8th, 1858, and remained on the farm until young manhood when he moved to Summerville, South Carolina. Here he began as a common laborer but soon branched out for himself. His first venture was a hauling contractor for delivering phosphates from the mines and then for four years he furnished cross-ties and wood to the South Carolina Railroad Company. After this he engaged in farming upon an extensive scale and succeeded in sinking all the money he had saved.

The loss disappointed him, but did not discourage him—it only served to stimulate his energies for another effort. Leaving Summerville, he went to Jacksonville, Florida, and arrived there with only one dollar and ten cents in his pocket. For six months he worked for the Railroad Company at one dollar and five cents per day after which he again ventured for himself. He went into the drayage business and started with one team. He added to this a wood yard and ran a farm. He also operated a restaurant. From this he went into building contracting, which he began in 1898. The great fire of 1901 swept away his buildings and left him only vacant lots.

The State Bank of Florida, came to his rescue and loaned him five thousand dollars to improve his vacant lots, payable in five years. With this assistance he went to work and was soon doing a large business in improving vacant lots and selling them. He has built two hundred and fifty-eight houses, one hundred of which he now owns.

To J. H. Blodgett is due the credit for the beautiful residence section of elegant homes for Jacksonville's colored population—a section that is unsurpassed for beauty.

His home, "Blodgett Villa," is one of the show places of Florida. It is a fine two story brick residence, beautifully finished inside and out and is elegantly furnished in the best of taste. His home is one of the finest owned by colored people anywhere. In it he has entertained the late Booker T. Washington, and many other notables. It is his ruling passion, and since his retirement from active business, he spends most of his time with his garden and flowers. Although ill health keeps him at home, of recent years, he is still a power in the business world of Jacksonville, and his advice is eagerly sought on nearly all matters of business. He is a great lover of the State of his adoption, and is fond of recounting his conversations with John Wannamaker and that merchant prince's astonishment at a southern Negro being able to accumulate a fortune in the South. Without capital and without education. It is a remarkable fact that there are very few men of any race in Jacksonville today who could borrow more from the banks on an unendorsed note, than J. H. Blodgett. In fact he has so conducted himself and his business that his credit is almost without limit.

Mr. Blodgett's business engagements do not consume so much of his time that he cannot give attention to religious matters. He is a member of the Methodist Episcopal Church and contributes to its support, both in time and money.

In 1894, he married Miss Sallie O. Barnes, of Bamburg, South Carolina, who has been a potent factor in Mr. Blodgett's success.

ROBERT C. WOODS, A. M.

VIRGINIA Theological Seminary and College, located at Lynchburg, Virginia, was founded in 1887, as Virginia Seminary. In a session of the Virginia Baptist State Convention, convened in Alexandria, Va., May 1887, the plans for the establishment of the Institution were perfected, the Trustee Board elected and immediate work started. It was incorporated February 24, 1888, by the act of the General Assembly. July, 1887, the corner stone of the Main Building was laid. The class room work began in 1890 and the first class was graduated in 1894. In 1899 the charter was revised and college and theological departments were added. The name was then changed to Virginia Theological Seminary and College.

COURSES: The courses offered are Normal-Industrial, Academic, College and Theological. The Normal-Industrial Course is especially adapted to the work of teacher training, the course being the uniform course recommended by a committee, under the supervision of the State Board of Public Instruction. The Academic Course is four years in length, modern in its appointments and prepares for College and Professional schools. The College Course is a standard Bachelor of Art Course, (A. B.), covering a period of four years, doing special work in the Social, Moral and Physical Sciences, Languages, with other standard college outlines. The Theological Course embraces three years, leading to the degree of Bachelor of Theology (B. Th.) and Bachelor of Divinity (B. D).

The Bachelor of Divinity Degree is awarded only to those who offer as entrance units a minimum of two years college work and upon completion of the full outline course. The Bachelor of Theology degree is awarded to those that have not the college credits and who do not cover the language courses in the department.

Among some of the comments of educators on the class of work done at this institution is one submitted from Junior Dean G. W. Fiske of the Graduate School of Oberlin College.

"Allow me to say that I held Mr. * * * * 's application in abeyance for about ten weeks, during the summer, while I investigated the standing of the institution at Lynchburg (Virginia Theological Seminary and College.) Having satisfied myself the course which Mr. * * * * completed was of college grade. His scholarship is fully equal to that of graduates from Fiske University and Lincoln University."

The work of the Institution receives full credits from the leading universities of the country. Students go from here to such universities as Oberlin, Syracuse, University of Michigan, Bucknell and others, to do professional and graduate work and receive the very best rating.

FACULTY: Beginning with the Academic year of 1917-18, the faculty numbers twenty-one active professors and instructors, fifteen male and six female, who come from the leading American institutions. Among the institutions represented in the faculty at present are, Yale, Oberlin, University of Pittsburgh, Hillsdale College, and other leading institutions. All members of the faculty are Christians, being well trained and with years of experience.

GROUNDS AND BUILDINGS: The Institution owns on the City limits an immediate campus of six acres —in addition it has other properties consisting of houses and lots in this city and in other cities, left from estates to the Institution. The buildings on the grounds, which are all brick, consist first of the Main Building, four story which includes recitation hall, with fine spacious class rooms, library and reception rooms, with two additional stories for dormitories used for young men. To this main building is attached an annexed three-story which includes laboratory for Physical and Biological Sciences, Domestic Science Department, the other

MAIN BUILDING—VIRGINIA THEOLOGICAL SEMINARY AND COLLEGE.

story used as a dormitory for men. Fox Hall is three-story building above basement, which includes Chapel, offices and dormitory for young women. The Board authorized for immediate erection, in its past session, of dining hall and hospital. These buildings which were completed during the year 1917-18, are each two-story brick, with such facilities as are needed. The President's home is a large frame structure. All these buildings are modernly equipped with steam heat, electric light, hot and cold water. Many members of the faculty live adjacent to the Institution on property owned by themselves.

The Board authorizes the buying of a farm, where the Institution will begin upon a new field of endeavor, such as farming and dairying, etc.

The valuation of the property at present is $175,000.00 (One hundred seventy-five thousand dollars) free of all indebtedness. The additional buildings added $25,000.00 (Twenty-five thousand dollars) to the property valuation.

STUDENTS AND GRADUATES: The institution had an attendance in the 1916-17 session, three hundred ten students, one hundred sixty young men and one hundred fifty young women. These were distributed in all departments, with twenty-seven in College and sixty-seven in Theological departments. These students represent twenty-two states and four foreign countries. There are four hundred graduates. Of this number 118 are actively engaged in the ministry, pastoring leading

churches in every city in Virginia and leading cities of the United States, including many of the Southern cities in the far South. Eight are missionaries of foreign fields, twenty doctors of medicine, ten pharmacists, ten dentists, ten lawyers, thirty academy and college professors, two college presidents, two principals of academies, eighteen civil service workers, four trained nurses. Of the two hundred eight remaining, they chiefly fill positions as teachers in the public school system in the cities and rural districts.

The graduates hold prominent places as officials in leagues, conventions, and take active part in civic and religious life of the people.

The first president was Phillip F. Morris, D. D., from 1888 to 1891, the second president was Gregory W. Hayes, A. M., from 1891 to 1906, from 1906 to 1908, there was an acting president, Mrs. G. W. Hayes, the third president was Jas. R. L. Diggs, A. M., 1908 to 1911, the fourth and present president is Robert C. Woods, A. M., from 1911.

SOURCES OF SUPPORT: The Institution is supported by the Virginia Baptist State Convention of Virginia, the Baptist State organizatons from Virginia to Maine and personal donations. The annual subscription for the present year will amount to twenty five thousand dollars. There is a small endowment and small income from properties. The Institution is denominational, but is open alike to students of all denominations.

There are more than two thousand former students.

PRESIDENT L. E. WILLIAMS IN PRIVATE OFFICE—WAGE EARNERS SAVINGS BANK

AGE Earners Savings Bank, of Savannah, Georgia, reputed to be the leading Negro Savings Bank in America, has truly served as a mighty stimulating agency. For the thoughtful Negroes were only waiting for the formation of such an institution to be promoted and led on by such men of their race as heads the Wage Earners Savings Bank today.

Miraculously as it may seem, about ten or a dozen ambitious Negroes met in the home of one of their number in the year 1900 for the purpose of organizing a bank, and the magnificent sum of One Hundred and Two Dollars was all they could raise. But it was a bank that these Negroes wanted for themselves and their race, and today, a bank they have, domiciled in their own building, which is said to be the finest banking building owned by Negroes in the United States.

Through the careful management of the officers of this Negro Bank, it has been able to declare a dividend of 12 per cent per annum for a number of years. Deposits payable on demand earn 5 per cent, per annum, compounded quarterly. Deposits of One Hundred Dollars or over, when left for a year earn 6 per cent. The slogan of the Wage Earners Savings Bank to the Negroes everywhere

is "Own Your Own Home," and since this bank started in business they have built or otherwise aided the people of its race in Savannah to obtain more than 1000 homes. Its officers and directors are: L. E. Williams, President; Sol. C. Johnson, Vice-President; R. A. Harper, Cashier; E. C. Blackshear, Asst.-Cashier; Mrs. R. L. Barnes, G. H. Bowen, E. Seabrook, J. M. Ferreebee, Thos. M. Holly, Dr. J. W. Jamerson, Jno. F. Jones, J. C. Lindsay, Nathan Roberts, A. B. Singfield, W. J. Williams, H. B. Wright.

Through well directed plans and efforts, and down-right rugged honesty, the Wage Earners Savings Bank has grown from $102.00 in 1900 to a volume of business, as shown by the files of the State Bank Examiner of Georgia, of the condition of the Bank at the close of business November 21st, 1917, as follows:

RESOURCES

Loans and discounts	$233,333.82
Stocks, Bonds and Investments	37,828.08
Banking House and Fixtures	72,554.20
Cash on hand & due from Banks	33,016.66
	$376,732.76

LIABILITIES

Capital stock paid in	$ 50,000.00
Surplus & undivided profits	25,066.33
Unpaid dividends	271.20
Deposits	271,395.23
Bills Payable	30,000.00
	$376,732.76

Simmeon L. Carson, M. D.

 R. Simmeon L. Carson was born at Marion, North Carolina. His parents had been slaves and had been denied the advantages of education and the very fact that they had been deprived of the blessings and opportunities which come to the educated man, made them more determined that their children should have the proper chance to rise to a higher plane of usefulness and honor in the battle of life.

After giving the matter mature thought they decided that they could best secure an education for their children in the State of Michigan, so they left their home in North Carolina and went to the State of Michigan and located in the City of Ann Arbor.

It was here in Ann Arbor that Dr. Carson began that preparation which fitted him for his life work; it was here that he discovered the possibilities that were wrapped within himself and it was here that he gave himself up to hard work and earnest study to fan into a flame the embers of genius which lay dormant in his soul. His entire educational training was received in this city and that it was thoroughly done his after life has fully demonstrated. He was at first a student in the public schools, completing all the courses they had to offer and later entered the medical college of that place and graduated with honors.

His ability as a physician was early recognized by those who were close to him and when the opportunity offered he was not slow in convincing others of that fact.

In 1904, Dr. Carson was appointed government physician to Lower Brule, Indian Reservation, at Lower Brule, South Dakota. He received this appointment as a result of a competitive examination. For four years Dr. Carson remained on this reservation doing the medical work that was required of him and gaining much knowledge along his line. When he was appointed to this position his services in the main were devoted to medicine and relieving the sick of the ordinary ailments, but the time came when his ability as a surgeon was put to the test and he came out of the ordeal with flying colors and his surgical skill was generally admitted. His success as a surgeon has continued to grow until today he enjoys a national reputation. His first operation was the removal of an incipient cancer from the face of a woman on the reservation. Having performed this operation successfully and receiving praise from the State Board of Health for removing the cancer while it was in that stage made Dr. Carson ambitious for other work

along surgical lines. He made a close study of many books written about the science and thereby obtained a great knowledge of the theory of surgery to which he added the practical knowledge secured by experience. At first his operations were performed more from the standpoint of professional pride than of remuneration, the fee being a secondary consideration, and it is no doubt due to this spirit that he has taken such high rank in the profession.

In 1908 he once more entered a competitive examination. This time it was for the position of Assistant Surgeon in the Freedmen's Hospital, at Washington, D. C. Once more he was successful, and in October of that year he received his appointment to the position. Here for the past ten years Dr. Carson has labored, gaining experience every day and growing more skillful all the time.

Today Dr. Carson stands as one of the best surgeons in the country. He does not restrict his work to any one portion of the body, but pays special attention to neck, stomach and intestinal surgery. He is frank with his patients and treats them in such a manner that they have the utmost confidence in him. And through the trying period of convalescence, Dr. Carson still puts thought into the work he has done and by his general atmosphere of good cheer and good will helps his patients on to a thorough recovery. At no place in the United States could a colored Surgeon get a greater amount of practice than he can get in Freedmen's Hospital.

Dr. Carson is just opening up for himself in the city of Washington, D. C., a sanitarium. To this work he brings a rich experience. With this experience he brings also to this endeavor of his own, one of the most perfectly controlled nervous systems possible for man. He can go into an operation without a quaver and without stimulant of any kind. This great steadiness of nerve he attributes to the clean, simple life that he has led.

In June of 1905, Dr. Carson was married to Miss Carol Clark, of Detroit, Michigan. Mrs. Carson is a woman of great charm and pleasing personality. To the Carsons have been born twins, a boy and a girl, Carol Carson and Clark Carson. These two little folks are now twelve years of age and they are a great source of joy to their parents.

In speaking of Dr. Carson, Dr. Kenney, in his book, "The Negro in Medicine" says: "He is among the best of the race in this field, and while he has already made his mark, we feel sure that great things are in store for him."

GRAND LODGE OFFICERS OF SOUTH CAROLINA PYTHIANS

Thomas H. Henry and South Carolina Pythians

THOMAS H. Henry, Grand Chancellor of the Knights of Pythias of South Carolina is pointed to by his fellow Knights as well as by his neighbors as the man who created and multiplied the Knights of Pythias as an organization in South Carolina, giving it confidence, popularity, and strength. This, however, was an instance of achieved distinction in this direction, as nothing was farther from his thought at the beginning of his career, than a Grand Chancellorship of the Knights of Pythias or of any other organization.

Mr. Henry was born in Dallas, Gaston County, North Carolina, August 19, 1871. His education was acquired here and there as the opportunity presented itself he having been compelled to go to work at an early age.

When he was twenty-six years of age, in 1899, he entered the service of the United States Government, as a mail weigher. This position he gained in Wheeling, West Va., running from Wheeling to Kenova.

In 1901, changing his position and place of residence, he moved into South Carolina as a locomotive fireman on the Southern Railroad. The next year found him a letter carrier in Columbia, having made the highest grade of thirty-five who took the examination. It was at Columbia, and as a letter carrier, that he began his active career as a Knight of Pythias.

In 1902 he was appointed Deputy Supreme Chancellor by Supreme Chancellor S. W. Starks. In this position, he went into Greenwood, South Carolina, and organized the first lodge there, with thirty members. This one act established him immediately as an organizer. In a few years, being given free rein because of his aptness in organizing, he had organized 216 lodges, with a membership of 8,000. No wonder his fellow Pythians elected him Grand Chancellor in 1906, and still honor him with this post, for who is so fit to hold an organization together as he who made it?

Mr. Henry was married in 1894, to Miss Rosa A. Davis, of Carlisle, South Carolina. Loys Ernestine, Mildred Anita, and Thomas Houston are their three children. The two younger are still in school. The oldest, Loys E., is a teacher in the public schools of Columbia.

HISTORY OF THE PYTHIAN ORDER IN SOUTH CAROLINA.

The first Negro Pythian Lodge in South Carolina was Ionic No. 1, at Charleston, organized by Prof. S. H. Blocker, of Augusta, Ga., June, 1888. This Lodge and Vashti No. 2, located at Charleston also, had among its membership some of the leading colored men of the race. A roster of the membership of these Lodges show that Dr. W. D. Crum, Mr. F. P. Crum, Col. W. H. Robertson, Colonel Commanding a Regiment of State Militia, Rev. J. H. M. Pollard, an Episcopal clergyman were prominent advocates of the principles of Pythianism.

The Order soon after its advent in the State became one of the most popular in South Carolina, and in a short while nearly every town of any size boasted of a Pythian Castle. In the year 1891 there arose a controversy about the conduct of the Endowment Department by the Supreme Lodge, the membership in this State was not satisfied with some features of the Endowment Law, this caused an upheaval in the State and resulted in the withdrawal of all the subordinate Lodges from the parent body. Under the leadership of Rev. J. H. M. Pollard, the seceding Lodges affiliated with an organization known as the Knights of Pythias of the Eastern & Western Hemisphere, this name being assumed to distinguish the organization from the parent body the "Knights of Pythias of North America, South America," etc.

For a number of years the E. & W. H. Order flourished and became a power in the coast counties invaded middle and Piedmont Carolina, established a Grand Lodge and numerically ranked with the Odd Fellows.

The parent body was apparently dead and there was not a single advocate in the State until T. H. Henry, of Columbia, holding a deputy's commission from Supreme Chancellor S. W. Starks, organized Greenwood Banner Lodge No. 1, at Greenwood, November 4, 1902. This date marks the renaissance of Pythianism in South Carolina.

Soon after the institution of Greenwood Banner Lodge No. 1, fifteen others were organized. The E. & W. H. Order began to decline and it was not long before the entire membership of this branch of Pythianism consolidated with the parent body. A Grand Lodge was organized in Charleston, Nov. 4, 1904, by Supreme Chancellor S. W. Starks, assisted by Grand Chancellor Chas. D. Creswell, of Georgia, and the following Deputy Supreme Chancellors: F. M. Cohen; John Bollen, of Ga.; and T. H. Henry, with the following officers: Julius A. Brown, Grand Chancellor, Robt. P. Scott, Grand Vice Chancellor, Wm. H. Houston, Grand K. R. & S.

Mr. Brown served two terms as Grand Chancellor; T. H. Henry, was elected Grand Chancellor in 1906, and still holds this post.

The growth of the Order since the organization of Greenwood Banner Lodge No. 1, has been phenominal. On the first day of October, 1907, the Grand Lodge assumed control of the Endowment Rank of Insurance without a penny and with a number of death claims due, determined to win its way into the hearts of the people by living up to the principles of the Order, has demonstrated its ability to redeem every promise by raising $203,543.26 for the mortuary department, and have paid to the widows and orphans of its deceased members $131,431.48.

There is connected with the Order a branch known as the Uniformed Rank, comprising twenty two companies and two cadet organizations and at their annual military display prizes are given.

Another healthy branch is the Woman's Auxiliary known as the Court of Calanthe, with a membership of thirty-five hundred. It has collected $30,000, since organization and has an Endowment Fund of $10,000.00 to its credit.

HOTEL DALE—CAPE MAY, N. J.

 HE Colored people have long felt the discomforts of traveling accommodations and adequate arrangements for their needs when visiting cities and pleasure resorts. The demand for better quarters has been met in at least one instance in the establishment of Hotel Dale, at Cape May, an ideal all the year recreation resort.

About seven years ago the management of the Hotel Dale undertook the gigantic responsibility to submit to the traveling public the opportunity to choose as a place of abode, during their vacation in the summer season, a first-class hotel, to supplant the old custom of being crowded into small lodging and boarding houses, where the sanitary conditions, as a rule, were not conducive to good health. In so doing the management was confronted with a number of problems to solve to insure the confidence of the public in general, that success might be attained. The Hotel Dale is not a pictorial structure on paper, but, in reality, an architectural building—a work of art, a monument to good taste.

Every known device which makes for safety and comfort has been introduced to make this as complete a living place as possible, for the accommodation of the colored race, where they can enjoy the pleasure of life, with pleasant surroundings and the demands of all classes met. The interior of the hotel, conceived in perfect taste, even in seemingly insignificant details, cannot be surpassed. The rooms are light, airy and luxuriously furnished and contain every modern convenience, suites with bath. The dining room is operated on the European system, and its cuisine rivals that of the finest hotels of record. It is a place where those who appreciate simple elegance of service and all that makes for ease of living may have their desires satisfied without extravagance.

The Abyssinian Orchestra renders afternoon and evening concerts daily during the season. The op-en-air amusements are numerous, with lawn tennis courts on the premises.

The moral status of the hotel is above reproach, and reflects credit on the management, who have passed the crucial period and stood the test of the most profound critics, and today it is the most popular hostelry of color in the country.

Until one has seen for himself the charming rooms in this palatial building, it is not possible to conceive the grace and elegance of the decorations—lighting and furnishing of the room floors. The dining room, halls and public parlors are handsomely decorated and adorned with works of art. In the decoration of these rooms, an air of elegance has been maintained, that never has been attempted at the shore. Another important feature of Hotel Dale is the large and spacious reception room, well furnished and a model of beauty and comfort. The hotel has fifty sleeping chambers and ten baths. The furniture of these rooms is of the best and they are equipped with hot and cold water and with telephones. Recreation features are provided for both in and out door pleasures.

The success of his hotel enterprise has been very gratifying to Mr. Dale, and he realizes that he made no mistake in the opening of this gem of seashore resorts. The hotel is personally managed by Mr. Dale, with a corps of attendants, who are thoroughly experienced in every department, and their efficiency of service enables them to give satisfaction to the guests without friction.

Cape May is an ideal all-the-year recreation resort. It is at the extreme southern point of New Jersey; with the waters of the Atlantic Ocean on the South and East, and the Delaware bay on the west. Its proximity to the Gulf stream tempers the severity of the northern winter. The location of Hotel Dale is superb, on the highest point in Cape May, and directly opposite the Cape May Golf Club links, which are unsurpassed in the country. The golf games can be viewed from the hotel veranda.

BED ROOM HOTEL DALE

Kelly Miller, A. B.

A man who is outspoken when the interest of the Negro is in question, a man who can speak upon any given subject with all the ease and grace of an accomplished orator a man, who in the class room and in all college activities is an inspiration to the young, a man who is thoroughly at home with all people, this is Professor Kelly Miller.

Kelly Miller was born in South Carolina, in 1867. His early training in schools was like that of most of our people who made their homes in the country. The schools lasted but a short time, three or four months a year, but for that time Kelly Miller was a studious person and used his mind. From his early childhood he showed a fondness for arithmetic and his mind developed unusual clearness from following his inclination in this direction. When school was not in session, Kelly Miller had to do the usual work of the farm boy. Here on the farm he learned to love the animals, the cows, the horses and the dogs. He was even as a child a good example of the kind of workman a really clear minded person can make. He did not leave his wits behind him in the school room but took them with him to his daily tasks. Through this application to the task in hand he earned the distinction of being the fastest cotton picker among the boys of his neighborhood.

When Kelly Miller was thirteen years of age he left the country school that he had attended and went to the Fairfield Institute. Every morning and every afternoon he walked the distance of two miles in order that he might learn. From Fairfield he went to Howard University. In this justly famous school he was one of the banner pupils. He was graduated from Howard in 1886, with the degree of A. B. Still seeking knowledge he went to John Hopkins University, Baltimore, after completing his course in Howard. Here he spent two years. We cannot say that his school days really ended here. Kelly Miller has never left the school room. And although his position now is that of teacher, he is himself a deep student of books, of men and of conditions.

In 1889 Professor Miller was appointed teacher of mathematics in the Washington High School. Here he served only one year for the next year he was asked to return to his Alma Mater. Here he was given the Chair of Mathematics. This position he still holds. In addition to this work in the mathematical courses of Howard University, Professor Miller has served as Dean of the College of Arts and Sciences since 1906.

But the activities of Kelly Miller have not been confined to the work of Howard University. He is a man of great activity and a tireless worker. Because of this he has found time to take a deep interest in the affairs of the race at large. He has taken up his pen in the behalf of our people and has written some things that will live on and on. One of these is an open letter to Thomas Dixon, Jr., written in 1905, "As to The Leopard's Spots." This is considered the greatest single contribution that has been made to the literature of the race problem. Through this work and through other similar works, through his many addresses in various parts of the country, Kelly Miller has made his influence felt in all sections of the country. As a matter of fact he is called upon to travel all over the country, both North and South to fill engagements on the lecture platform. His contributions to the leading magazines and periodicals are accepted and read. This broadens his influence. One of his writings, "Race adjustment," which is a book published in 1908 is referred to as an "authority to all serious students of the problems growing out of the contact and attrition of the races."

Kelly Miller was born in the South, but has lived in Washington, D. C., longer than in any other section of the country. He has had the oportunity to study the facts concerning the relation of the races at first hand. He has had the clear brain developed by years of study along general lines and special training in mathematics, to see these facts in their right relationship. He has the literary skill to give these facts in a pleasing and logical manner. All that he has written in the interest of the race has been right to the point, and all that he has written has been for the uplift of the Negro and to help him bear his burden.

The influence of Kelly Miller is far reaching. Hundreds of young people come under his direct instruction during the year and hundreds of others hear him talk and see him in every day life, thousands of people go to hear him lecture and others, by the thousands read his articles in the magazines and read his books. Surely he has done what he could to help in the uplift of the Negro race.

THIRKIELD SCIENCE HALL—HOWARD UNIVERSITY.

 N 1865 General W. T. Sherman wrote Major General O. O. Howard assuring him of sympathy with his projects for the spiritual and intellectual redemption of the four million Negroes of America, and expressing confidence in his sincerity and ability. "But," said General Sherman, "you have a Hercules' task." In the light of this sincere but very discouraging letter, it is interesting to reflect that within less than two years from the date on which he received it, General Howard was instrumental in establishing a University which on March 2, 1917, celebrated its Fiftieth Anniversary, a monument to the faith, the wisdom and the courage of its founders.

The Institution was incorporated under an act of the United States Congress.

Without one cent in the treasury, the normal and preparatory departments opened on May 1, 1867, in a rented frame building, with five students, and the authorities arranged for the purchase of 150 acres of land at $100 per acre.

Like many similar institutions, the first ten years of its life, were of feverish growth. Its first structures were the main building of the University, a woman's dormitory, and dining-room, a men's dormitory, the Medical Building, and the Professors' homes. The departments too, multiplied rapidly, so that by 1872, the original Theological Seminary, which existed on paper only in 1866, had expanded into Normal, Preparatory, Military, Musical, Industrial, Commercial, Collegiate, Law, and Medical Departments, with a Library and a Museum. The money which later sustained the first decade of the work came by accident—through the refusal of another school to accept it.

$500,000 received from the Freedmen's Bureau, together with the income from the sale of much of the 150 acres of land at four times its cost, cleared the University of debt and started an endowment fund. Thus was faith justified.

The panic of '73 gave the University a severe set-back, but it soon recovered. Its first twenty-seven years was a period of consolidation; the last twelve a period of material expansion. This first period was inaugurated by Dr. Patton, the first President to give his undivided attention to the University.

It was during his presidency that the United States Congress began to make annual appropriations to assist the University.

President Thirkfield pursued a policy of material expansion. During his term of office, he secured from Congress $675,700. With this income a Science Hall, an Industrial Building, and a central heating and lighting plant were added.

THE ANDREW RANKIN MEMORIAL CHAPEL
HOWARD UNIVERSITY.

444

BIRD'S-EYE VIEW OF HOWARD UNIVERSITY—WASHINGTON, D. C.

In conformity with the spirit of the charter of the University, the Medical School, including the Medical, Dental and Pharmaceutical colleges, is open to all persons, without regard to sex or race, who are qualified by good moral character, proper age and suitable preliminary education.

In addition to individual instruction in vocal and instrumental music, there are various classes in which careful training is given. A vested choir of about fifty voices is maintained. There are also Young Men's and Young Women's Glee Clubs thoroughly drilled by instructors of the University. The University Chorus has given Mendelssohn's "Elijah," "Handel's "Messiah," and Coleridge-Taylor's "Hiawatha."

The charter contains no religious test or limitation. The University, however, is distinctly Christian in its spirit and work. It is not denominational, and its students are drawn from all churches, including the Roman Catholic.

Washington has been called a university in itself. To live in such an atmosphere is a liberal education to an eager, receptive mind. Students of all departments have unusual opportunities for general culture and the larger outlook upon life gained through lectures, concerts and entertainments of an elevating character. On the floors of the Senate and House of Representatives, leaders in national thought and statesmanship may be heard on vital questions. Many lectures of fine order are given in the city, and not a few of them are free.

The University buildings are all located on the main campus with the exception of the Law School building, which is on Judiciary Square. They are heated with steam and lighted by electricity. They are in charge of a superintendent of buildings and grounds and a competent engineer. Pains are taken to keep the buildings always in a sanitary condition, and the healthfulness of the campus and surroundings is well known.

On the square adjacent to that on which the Medical College Building stands have been erected, hospital buildings at a cost of $600,000.

The hospital has the advantage of being designed primarily for teaching purposes, as practically all the patients admitted are utilized freely for instruction.

Each student is obliged to attend 80 per cent of the exercises in every course of study for which he seeks credit. Students must obtain a passing grade in each study in order to receive credit for the same. A student whose work, for any reason is not satisfactory, will be notified, and if no improvement is noted, he will be asked to terminate his connection with the school. The advantages stated and the strict rules governing the institution have made Howard one of the best Medical schools in the land. Its lecture courses embrace many subjects and lists speakers and lecturers of national reputation.

Howard University took a most active part in the establishment of an officer's training camp for colored men during the war at Fort Des Moines, Iowa, and made a large contribution of men who entered the training. Approximately 200 Howard men joined the camp. Of the 659, who were commissioned from this camp ninety-five were sons of Howard.

It has sent forth nearly four thousand graduates to every state in the Union, to the Islands of the Sea and to Africa, Asia, Europe, and South America.

FREEDMEN'S HOSPITAL, HOWARD UNIVERSITY WASHINGTON, D. C.

Judge Robert H. Terrell and Mary Church Terrell

ROBERT H. Terrell, Washington, District of Columbia, has a long line of achievements in the literary world to his credit. He was born in 1857, in Virginia. His early training was received in the public schools of Washington, District of Columbia. He went to Massachusetts for his academic work and received his bachelor of arts degree from Harvard in 1884. In 1889 he received the degree of LL. B., from Howard University, LL. M., in 1893., A. M., in 1900, and LL. D., from Livingstone College, Salisbury, North Carolina, in 1913.

Robert H. Terrell is one of the Negroes to whom the rest of the colored people point with great pride. He is municipal judge and has held this position since 1909. Under Roosevelt, Taft and Wilson, he has received this same appointment. All the life of Judge Terrell is one of action. He began his career as a teacher and was soon made principal of the Colored High School of Washington. His next work was that of Chief of the Division of the Treasury. This position he held from 1889 to 1893. At this time he was admitted to the Bar of the District. For five years he was in business with John M. Lynch.

From 1902 to 1909 he served as Civil Magistrate and at that time he was appointed Judge in Municipal Court. In this manner has the time of Judge Terrell been spent since completing his studies. One thing that might be pointed out as contributing to the success of Judge Terrell is this—his very thorough preparation before he entered any line of work. This was an uncommon thing in the day in which Judge Terrell began his work, and it is still rare for our people. But where the time and the means are to be had this should be encouraged and the success which has attended all the efforts of Judge Terrell could be pointed to as an example of the type of work that can be done by the thoroughly prepared man.

In church work Judge Terrell is a Congregationalist. He is a member of the Sigma Pi Phi. He is a member of the Odd Fellows and of the Masons. Of the last named organization he has served as Grand Master of his lodge for four terms.

In 1891 Judge Terrell was married to Miss Mary Church, of Memphis, Tennessee.

Mrs. Mary Church Terrell was born of well-to-do parents and had therefore as her birthright many of the things denied most of our young women. She was educated in Oberlin College, receiving both the Bachelor and the Master of Arts Degree. After leaving schools, Mrs. Terrell was appointed teacher of languages in the Colored High School, of Washington. Here she worked for a short time and then went abroad to further prepare herself for the school work. She spent two years abroad spending the time in France, Switzerland, Germany and Italy. In 1890 she returned to the work in the High School of Washington. The next year she was offered the position of Registrar of Oberlin. She was the first Colored woman to whom this work had been offered. She had to decline the position, however, because of her approaching marriage.

Mrs. Terrell has never given up her work for the public good. She was for three terms president of the National Association of Colored Women's Clubs and after that time she was made Honorary President of the organization. She has traveled all over the country as a lecturer and her speeches are listened to with great interest. She is the only woman who ever held the position of President of the Bethel Literary and Historical Association of Washington, D. C., and this position she filled with such marked ability that it helped her in other work later.

When it was decided to appoint two women on the board of Education for the District of Columbia, Mrs. Terrell was one of the women appointed. On this Board she served for five years doing credit to her own training and to the race in general.

Mrs. Terrell is a woman in public affairs, but she has a home and a home life that is ideal. She is also a mother. The daughter is named for Phillis Wheatley. In this name, Mrs. Terrell shows honor to the Negro poetess who helped make an opening for the black women of America. Mrs. Terrell has done much for the advancement of her sisters. Through her many honors have come to the race that would not have come to us, but for her great tact and great ability. One thing that was said of her in the press when she was lecturing before the Chautauqua of Danville, Illinois, was "She should be paid to travel as a model of good English and good manners." Mrs. Terrell is a woman of high ideals, thorough education, and action, when that action means the advancement of her sisters of her race.

Charles William Anderson

HARLES William Anderson is a native of Ohio, and was reared under conditions quite different from those which faced many of the colored race living in the South. He had better educational advantages and his surroundings were different. He was born at Oxford, Ohio, April 28, 1866, where he spent his early life, passing through the public schools. From Oxford he went to Middleton, Ohio, and took a course in the High School. He took a course in Cleveland Spencerian Business College. He also attended the Berlitz School of Language, located at Worcester, Massachusetts.

In 1890 he was appointed United States guager, for the Second District of the State of New York, which office he held for three years. For two years from 1893 to 5, he was the private secretary to the state treasurer of New York. From 1895 to 8, he was the chief clerk in the State Treasury. He was the supervisor of accounts for the New York Racing Commission during the years of 1898-1905. In 1905, he was made collector of Internal Revenue in the Second District of New York, and continued in this office until 1915.

New York World pays him this glowing tribute:

"Charles W. Anderson goes out of office today after holding for ten years this responsible post under the Treasury. Many millions of dollars have passed through his hands. His dealings have been practically all with white men of the keenest intellect and of substantial business standing. Capacity and courtesy have been the qualities most remarked in his conduct of an office maintained always in the highest efficiency. In Collector Anderson's time, three complicated and important new revenue measures, in income tax, the corporation tax and the war revenue tax, have made this office the most difficult, as it is the most important ever held by a colored man under the Government. He has stood the test. No race is fairly judged by holding up as types for reprobation its most degraded specimens. Every race has the right to be judged by its patient, toiling, useful average, and its best."

He was President of the New York Commission to the Tennessee Centennial Exposition, at Nashville, in 1897, appointed by Governor Morton.

When the Columbia Post, G. A. R. tendered a banquet to President William McKinley, at Buffalo, N. Y., Aug. 4, 1897, he was selected as one of the speakers.

He was also a member of the citizens committee of the Hudson Fulton Celebration Committee to welcome Admiral George Dewey and the fleet on its return from the Phillipine Islands, and a member of the citizens committee to welcome Admiral William T. Sampson and Winfield S. Schley when the fleet returned from Cuba.

He was a member of a committee appointed to welcome Theodore Roosevelt on his return from Africa. He was an honorary pall bearer at the funeral of Mayor William J. Gaynor, of New York. At the Peace Banquet of Citizens representing fifty foreign nations at Hotel Astor, New York. Jan. 4, 1914, he was one of the speakers.

He was a member of the citizens committee appointed to receive the bodies of the United States Marines killed at Vera Cruz, Mexico, in 1914. He is a permanent member of the New York City Independence Day Commission; Director of the Colored Advisory Committee of The National Republican Committee, 1916; member of the Mayor's Committee to entertain the Right Honorable Arthur J. Balfour and the English High Commission at official banquet at the Waldorf-Astoria, in 1917; member of Mayor's Committee to entertain Marshal Joffe, Mons. Viviani and the French Commission, at official banquet at Waldorf-Astoria, 1917; member of Mayor's Committee to entertain His Royal Highness, Prince Ferdinand, of Savoy, Signor Marconi, Prime Minister Francesco Nitti, and the Italian Royal Commission, at official Banquet at Waldorf-Astoria, 1917; member of Mayors' Committee to entertain Viscount Ishii, and the Imperial Japanese Commission at official Banquet at The Waldorf-Astoria, 1917; member of Mayors' Committee to entertain the Russian High Commission at official Banquet at the Ritz-Carlton Hotel, 1917; member of the Catskill Aqueduct Celebration Committee, 1917; Chairman of Local Board (Draft) No. 139, from the beginning to the end of the draft; Honorary Colonel of the 367 Infantry, (The Buffaloes); now serving as Supervisory Agent of the Department of Farms and Markets of the State of New York.

He served on the Republican State Committee sixteen years. He is a member of the National Geographical Society, the Metropolitan Museum of Art, Institute of Art and Sciences of Columbia University, Academy of Political Science, New York Peace Society, Japanese Franchise League.

Appointed by Mayor Hylan, a member of "Mayor's Committee on Receptions to Distinguished Guests." Among those expected are: His Royal Highness, The Prince of Wales; His Majesty, King Albert of Belgium, Marshal Foch; General Pershing, and His Majesty, the Shah of Persia.

He married Miss Emma Lee Bonaparte, of Hampton, Va.

JOSEPH ALBERT BOOKER, A. B., A. M., D. D.

 OSEPH Albert Booker, was born at Portland, Ashby County, Arkansas, before the Civil War. He was early left an orphan, his mother dying while he was in his second year and his father followed his mother to the grave when he was only four years of age. After the death of his parents he went to live with his grand-mother (Amy Fisher,) who had the care of him until he reached his sixteenth year. She reared him with the tenderest care and consideration and used he best endeavor to prepare him for life.

She taught him the alphabet and spelling, which was as far, as she could carry him, which the children of her former owner supplemented by teaching him the elements of Geography, Arithmetic and Grammar. His high school training was received at the Branch Normal College, Pine Bluff, Arkansas, and his college and theological training was secured at the Roger Williams University, at Nashville, Tennessee.

While those who taught him in his boyhood days were willing and did the best they could to instruct him he was greatly handicapped for want of books, etc., he frequently used charcoal instead of pencils for writing and in working his sums in arithmetic. When he entered college he again encountered difficulties for lack of funds and found it necessary to pay his way by manual labor. He washed the dishes, chopped the wood and made the fires at the college and in this manner he worked his way through.

During his early years and in fact, until he was 19 years of age, his life was spent on the farm. Here he learned to till the soil, look after the stock and perform other farm duties, but during this period his mind was active and was employed in the interest of his people.

When only ten years old he taught a night school—giving the daylight hours to farm work. At the age of sixteen he was a teacher in the public school.

After graduation he was ordained a minister of the Missionary Baptist Church, and for a while was pastor of a church, but Providence pointed to another sphere of work which has proved his life calling.

For thirty two years he has been the President of the Arkansas Baptist College, and as he expressed it himself, he has been so enthused with his work that he has had but little time to bestow upon his worldly affairs. For thirty years he has edited a paper known as the "Baptist Vanguard."

Dr. Booker has figured conspicuously in the councils of his denomination and is a frequent attendant of its conventions, both state and National. He was a messenger to the Baptist European Congress in 1913. He has traveled extensively over the United States and North Western Europe.

June 28, 1887, he married Mary J. Cover, in Helena, Ark., who has borne him eight children, four boys and four girls.

While his time and talents have been devoted almost exclusively to the development of the Arkansas Baptist College, Dr. Booker has acquired some property. He owns a few houses and lots in Little Rock, Ark., and a small farm. He has also identified himself with a number of the secret orders of his race. He is a member of the Masons, Knights of Pythias, Mosiac Templars and others. Dr. Booker has been brought face to face with death on three occasions, and he attributes his deliverance to an over-ruling Providence. When a boy he was in bathing with his companions when he got beyond his depth and was going under for the last time when rescued; again he was in a burning building where a number were injured before being delivered; and on his way home from Europe, the train on which he was traveling, when nearing Malmo, Sweden, was wrecked, and about twenty around him were killed and he escaped with but a slight hurt. He felt that the Lord had a use for him and preserved his life.

REVEREND RICHARD CARROLL.

EV. Richard Carroll was born in Barnwell County, South Carolina, just when the slave regime was making place for the freedom which came to the black race after the war. His mother was a trusted house-servant in the home of a prominent South Carolina family and as was often the case an attachment grew up between the servant and the family she so faithfully served. The interest in the mother extended to the son and no doubt accounts, in a measure, for the influence he exerted in later life in bringing about a better understanding between the two races.

Richard Carroll grew up on the plantation and was afterwards educated at Benedict College, South Carolina. He developed early unusual gifts of eloquence in public speech. When he came to manhood, he distinguished himself by his interest in all that contributes to the welfare of his race and in bringing about a better and more helpful understanding between the whites and the blacks.

He became a Baptist minister and developed at Columbia, South Carolina, a home for Negro orphans and youthful delinquents. In order to do this he resigned his commission as chaplain in the army during the Spanish-American War, which influential white leaders desired him to hold. He took up the scheme of the orphanage without a dollar in sight with which to build it. He proposed to build it on faith and through prayer to God. He did build it on this foundation, and accomplished through it a great amount of good, confirming the good opinion which both white people and black people were forming of him in his native State.

During this period, it was my privilege to help in opening the way for the subject of this sketch to appear before the white Baptist District Association in South Carolina and present his Institution and also make an appeal for better race relations. This campaign strengthened and confirmed his hold among white people and he became one of the most influential Negro leaders in South Carolina or the South. He made frequent trips to the North for funds to aid his uplift enterprises, but he always seemed to prize most the good will and encouragement of Southern white people. He had learned that they were the friends of his people and that they really had their interest at heart and were willing to aid him in his efforts to help them.

It was about 1908 when Mr. Carroll instituted a race conference in South Carolina which has since met annually. The propaganda which eventuated in this conference was conducted in the paper the "Plowman," which he edited for a number of years. This Annual Conference is still conducted and is accomplishing most helpful results.

In 1913 Brother Carroll accepted a position as Evangelist to Negroes of the South under the pay of the white Baptist Home Mission Board of Atlanta. He is holding this position still and has added to his reputation as a wonderful organizer of men and as a trusted Negro leader. His outstanding popular gift is that of oratory and there are surely few public speakers in the South more gifted. It is a difficult thing for a Negro leader to tell white people the truth about certain significant things in the relation of the two races without giving offense. Dr. Carroll has done this repeatedly and with such wonderful tact that his white audiences always want to hear him again. Mr. Victor I. Masters, Supt. of Publicity, of the white Baptist Home Mission Board of Atlanta, Ga., prepared this sketch by special request, as a token of the esteem in which the subject is held.

WILLIAM HENRY HOLTZCLAW

T is no mean distinction to be called a "Second Booker T. Washington," for it argues great poise of mind and intellectual ability and carries with it the idea that the man who has this distinction, like the illustrious head of the Tuskegee Institute, has devoted his life to the uplift of his race. William Henry Holtzclaw is so designated. Having come into personal touch with Booker Washington he no doubt caught his spirit and went forth from the Tuskegee Institute to follow his example.

Professor Holtzclaw was born in Roanoke, Alabama, but the date of his birth is unknown. His father and mother could not write and for this reason a record of his birth was not kept.

He received his education in the main from the Tuskegee Institute and Harvard College. While at the Tuskegee Institute he was greatly impressed with the work being done for the colored race by that institution and the spirit of it remained to influence his life work. After completing his education or rather graduating, for he is still a learner, he set about the establishing of an educational institute somewhat after the pattern of his almamater.

He established his school, the Utica Normal and Industrial Institute, in 1903, and has been its principal since its organization. It is an elementary school with a few pupils in secondary subjects. It is located in a rural community and has done much good work in the county. It has an attendance of 376; male 154, and female 222. Of these 241 are boarders. It has twenty-seven teachers and workers, all colored. Of these, ten are male and seventeen are female. The school owns about two hundred and ten acres of land, ten of which are in the campus and two hundred in the school farm. In addition the school owns 1390 acres of land which was given as an endowment. The land holdings of the school are estimated to be worth $48,800. The estimated value of the buildings is $77,230. All the buildings except one are frame structures. The exception is a three story concrete structure. Of the frame buildings three are used for dormitories, and one each for trades, offices, hospitals, and agriculture. There are also two barns and a number of small cottages and houses. The equipment, including furniture, shop equipment, farm equipment, electric plant, saw mill, etc., is valued at $28,000.

This school is the largest Industrial School in the State of Mississippi and is a monument to the energy, wisdom and patient and persevering efforts of Professor Holtzclaw. Professor Holtzclaw is an orator of considerable force and the forceful speech he made in 1908 in the interest of his school at Bar Harbor Maine secured a collection for his school of $5000, while Booker Washington who presented the claims of his institution only got $3000. This incident caused Booker Washington to remark: "It will not require a prophet to tell of the future of young Holtzclaw."

Professor Holtzclaw is a member of the Baptist Church, and takes an interest in religious work, but is not connected with any of the secret orders. His time is so much taken up in the work of his school and organizations related to education that he has so far refrained from joining the secret orders of the race. He is a member of American Academy of Political and Social Science, Black Belt Improvement Society, Geographic Society, etc.

He has traleved extensively in this country and in Canada. His property holdings amount to some few thousand dollars.

Mr. Holtzclaw was married in 1901, to Miss Mary Ella Patterson. They have five children.

BIRD'S-EYE VIEW OF UTICA INSTITUTE UTICA INSTITUTE, MISS

Daniel Hale Williams, M. D.

NO record of the achievements of the Negro along lines of medical science would be complete without mention of the life of our pioneer Negro surgeon, Dr. Daniel Hale Williams, of Chicago, neither would a record of the works of Negroes in all lines of endeavor be complete without his personal history.

Dr. Williams is a native of Pennsylvania, but at an early age moved to the Northwest, where he received his early training. Even when in the secondary schools, Dr. Williams showed a fondness for science and things pertaining thereto. Finishing his academic work he entered Northwestern University and graduated from this institution in 1883. The institution from which he was graduated saw in him a young man of great promise and gave to him the position of demonstrator of anatomy. In this place he served for six years doing credit to the position and gaining a richer, broader foundation for his work in the world.

It was during the early years of his practice that Dr. Dan Williams made for himself the name of a great surgeon. That place he has kept and has improved in his work with each passing year, till today he is recognized among the leaders of the profession without regard to color. From 1884 to 1891 Dr. Williams was so placed that he received an abundance of practice in the line he wished to perfect. He was surgeon at the Chicago South Side Dispensary. At the same time he was surgeon and physician in the Chicago Protestant Orphan Asylum. In these two places he laid the foundation for his very great skill along surgical lines.

Seeing the need of better hospital facilities for colored people, Dr. Williams, with prominent colored citizens organized the Provident Hospital, of Chicago. The hospital has grown along with the surgeon who helped found it and who never lost interest in it, even during the five years he spent as surgeon-in-chief of Freedmen's Hospital, in Washington, District of Columbia.

During the five years that Dr. Williams spent in Washington, he was able to better organize the plant at the Freedmen's Hospital. It was he who installed the first corps of colored interns in this institution and it was he who organized the first training school for colored nurses in connection with the hospital.

Dr. Williams is a member of the American Medical Association, the Chicago Medical Society and the Illinois Medical Society. For three years he served on the Illinois State Board of Health and he has served as attending physician at the St. Luke's Hospital of Chicago, and as a member of the International Medical Congress. As a matter of fact, Dr. Williams has his profession very much on his heart and wherever he can either give inspiration or knowledge or receive either of these there you may find him busily engaged. He is professor of clinical surgery at Meharry Medical College, and each year holds a surgical clinic at this school that benefits a great number, both patients and young doctors.

But the thing that will claim for Dr. Dan Williams the lasting gratitude of all surgeons all over the world is his creation of a method by which the heart can be sutured. Everywhere he is looked upon as a wonder because of this discovery. Still one other thing will keep him ever alive in the minds of men of his profession. He invented "a peculiarly arranged knot, by which the delicate tissues of the spleen can be ligated to prevent hemorrhage of that organ." While this last named invention is one of great importance, it has not won for Dr. Williams the distinction that the other did. As a matter of fact, when you say Dr. Dan Williams, even to a layman, he immediately says "The heart specialist."

While Dr. Williams has spent a great deal of time on this organ and while he has the honor of being the first to operate upon this most delicate and most important organ of the whole system, he still works upon other portions of the body and is a well rounded surgeon that would be a credit to any people, to any city, to any country.

Not only does Dr. Williams operate, both privately and for the benefit of young doctors, but he writes out the things of importance that he finds, thus giving to a larger number of doctors the benefit of his ripe wisdom. All men in the profession look up to him. He is a man who has honor not only in his profession, but in the social world as well. Mrs. Williams, formerly Miss Alice Johnson, of Washington, D. C., is in all these matters his helper. They live in their beautiful home in Chicago, where she is a charming hostess.

Dr. Williams is to all Negro Doctors, old as well as young, a source of inspiration.

EDWARD C. BROWN

HILE the Negro has proved himself to be enterprising in many fields of endeavor, there are still some that only few have entered. In nearly every kind of business the black man has been able to succeed in a one-man concern. He has run his tailor shop, his restaurant, or hotel, his dry goods store, his shoe shop, as the case may be, but rare indeed is the Negro who in any sense has become a "Kress," a "Woolworth," a "Fred Harvey," or any of these leading men who have been able through far sighted planning to establish a chain of business stretching throughout the United States.

When Edward C. Brown, who was born in Philadelphia, in 1877, and educated in the public schools and Spencerian Business College of that city, started in to emulated these mighty captains of industry, with a chain of banks, a business requiring the highest type of business skill, the colored business world was amazed.

Mr. Brown first came into public notice through the Philadelphia banking firm of Brown and Stevens, of which he is President and founder. Always a firm believer in co-operation, and knowing that in Union there is strength, Mr. Brown has

dreamed and worked always with plans that were nation wide in their scope. While others have been busy organizing and successfully launching local enterprises, he has been working and laying the foundation of a financial organization sufficiently strong to furnish backing for national holding companies that could take over local business throughout the country, susceptible of being organized and conducted in a manner that would not only increase their earnings, but put sufficient capital behind them to insure their being developed to their highest degree of efficiency. Mr. Brown in 1909, organized the Brown Savings Bank, of Norfolk, Va., of which he is President. This bank has grown under his direction to a position of financial strength and state-wide influence. It has a paid in capital stock of $50,000, and the last statement to the state comptroller shows $341,000 assets, which are growing at a rate that will put them over the half million mark in the near future. Mr. Brown is also President of the Beneficial Insurance Co., of Norfolk, and of a bank in Newport News, Va. His main interests and work for some time, however, lay in Philadelphia, where he, with his associate, Andrew F. Stevens, conduct a banking and realty business. Mr. Brown's outside investments in Virginia seem to have been "Feelers," and were so successful, that his reputation as a financier was firmly established.

On the death of Philip A. Payton, of New York, which occurred Aug. 29th, 1917, Mr. Brown was the main figure in forming the Payton Apartments Corporation in order to perpetuate the work started by that noted realty dealer. The following clipping from the New York Times gives some idea of the magnitude of this undertaking: "The Payton Apartments Corporation, formed at Albany, a few days ago, with a capital of $250,000 has identified with it Edward C. and W. H. C. Brown, and Andrew F. Stevens, bankers, of Philadelphia and Washington; Emmett J. Scott, Secretary of the Tuskegee, Normal and Indusrial Institute of Tuskegee, Ala., and Heman E. Perry, President of the Standard Life Insurance Company of Atlanta, Ga. Its purpose is to take over the six story modern elevator apartments at Nos. 117 to 143 W. 141 St., and Nos. 130 to 148 W. 142nd St., which were bought last year by the late Phillip A. Payton from the New York Title and Mortgage Company. The houses were valued at $1,000,000 in that deal."

The most recent and by far the greatest of Mr. Brown's undertakings is the organization of a theatrical syndicate for the leasing and operating of a chain of colored theatres and picture houses in every city in the United States having a large Negro population.

Brown Savings Bank, Norfolf, Va.

HE Brown Savings and Banking Co., incorporated, of Norfolk, Va., was organized April 10, 1909. It was the second link in a chain of banks being established by that financial genius E. C. Brown, of Philadelphia and New York. Mr. Brown was elected president and had associated with him one of the most prominent physicians in the country, Dr. Andrew J. Strong, who has shown marked ability as a financier. The entrance of Negroes into the banking world, being at that time in its infancy, the officers were unable to secure a cashier with practical banking experience, so President Brown with his usual sagacity fell back on an institution with world wide reputation for turning out graduates, that not only "made good" but were invariably recognized as leaders in their chosen professions. Crossing Hampton Roads to the Alma Mater of Dr. Booker T. Washington and Major R. R. Moton, Mr. Brown was fortunate in securing the services of William M. Rich. Trained in the unexcelled Commercial Department of Hampton Institute, Mr. Rich combined a keen business sagacity with a pleasant personality, that enables him not only to attract patrons to the bank, but to hold them by successfully managing the banks affairs in such manner as to enable it to fill a long needed place in financing worthy colored business enterprises. Following the footsteps of his illustrious fellow graduate Major Moton, he is devoting his talents to aid in establishing for the Negroes successful enterprises of their own. In this connection it might be stated he even followed the Major in choosing a wife from the same family, although there is room for argument as to whether he was following the Major, or it "just happened." The bank has been so successfully conducted, that two years ago the directors were compelled to grant Mr. Rich an assistant cashier, and it speaks volumes for Mr. Rich and his Alma Mater that they elected Edward H. Vaughn, another Hampton graduate to the position. The bank has not only grown to a position of financial power in Norfolk, but did yeomans service during the world war in handling Liberty Bonds and Thrift Stamps. The bank as an institution, and its personnel as individuals, were always to the forefront in all war work, and liberally contributed to all Red Cross, Y. M. C. A., Salvation Army and Camp Community Service Drives. The bank is establishing a pride of race and a spirit of thrift in the Negroes of Norfolk, that makes it a distinct gain to the community, and there is a carefully nourished spirit of fellowship between the depositors and officers that causes these depositors to come to the bank with all of their financial troubles for advice, and in this way the laboring class as well as the merchants are being taught that thrift means independence and independence means self respect. This institution and its work has also gained the respect, and increased the co-operation between the white and Negro business elements of Norfolk, and is bringing about a friendlier spirit which is enabling the Negroes to secure better schools and other civic improvements. Nothing will show more clearly the very remarkable growth of the bank in the last two years than an advertisement which appeared in "The Journal Guide."

"BROWN SAVINGS AND BANKING COMPANY INCREASES ITS CAPITAL STOCK

Capital Paid In	$ 50,000
Surplus	20,900
Resources	341,047.53

Beginning ten years ago with a paid in capital of $10,000, by faithful application of sound business methods, Brown Savings and Banking Company has enjoyed phenominal growth and attained resources that are today over a quarter of a million dollars.

ENLARGED FACILITIES.

To handle our increasing volume of business and to render our patrons and the community at large the best possible service our directors at a recent session authorized an increase of the bank's capital to $50,000. This remarkable growth is an evidence of the hearty co-operation which we have received from the public, and in return we have endeavored, and will continue to render the best service consistent with sound business principles."

(Signed),

BROWN SAVINGS & BANKING CO., INC.,

NORFOLK, VA.

E. C. BROWN, Pres.
A. J. STRONG, Vice-Pres.
Wm. M. RICH, Cashier.
E. H. VAUGHN,
Asst. Cashier.

The increase of $234,000 in the bank's resources in three years as shown by the bank's statement speaks for itself.

"Efficiency" and "courtesy" is the bank's motto, and embraces every department. Misses Reddick and Tolson insure sympathetic assistance to any ladies having business dealings with this institution. The stockholders are to be congratulated on the first ten years growth which bids fair to put the resources of the bank over the half million mark in the near future.

LACY KIRK WILLIAMS, A. B., D. D.

EV. Lacey Kirk Williams was born in a one-room cabin in Eufaula, Alabama, where he spent his babyhood days and in a two room cabin later until he was six years of age, when he moved with his father to Texas.

When 12 years of age he was converted and baptized into the Thankful Baptist Church, by its pastor, Rev. A. Rivers.

In securing an education he passed through the public schools of Texas, and then attended respectively, Hearne College, Hearne, Texas; Bishop College, Marshall Texas, where he finished the Theological and Academic courses, and then the Arkansas Baptist College, where his A. B. course was finished.

In 1914 the Selma University conferred upon him the degree of D. D.

In 1894, he organized his first church, which started with four members. It was located at College Station, Brazos County, Texas.

He built church edifices at Lyons Station, Cameron, Macedonia, Dallas, Mt. Gilead and Ft. Worth, Texas. The church at Ft. Worth cost $95,000, and is a most beautiful structure.

He is now pastor of Olivet Baptist Church, Chicago, Illinois. This church has a membership of 8600; it collected and spent in 1918, $64,000. To accommodate its large membership requires three places of worship, and every Sunday it is necessary to hold three to four overflow services.

He has held many honorary positions: Chairman of the State Prohibition Association of Texas; President LaGrange District Baptist Sunday School Convention; President for 12 years of the Baptist Missionary and Educational Convention of Texas; President of the I. & M. College, Fort Worth, a Dean of Theology of the same school prior to being elected President; Editor Western Star, official organ of the Colored Baptists of Texas; and now President of the Baptist State Convention of Illinois.

Mr .Williams was the only minister appointed by Governor Lawuden to serve on a mixed board of prominent citizens to study and report on interracial relations in Chicago.

August 16, 1894, he married Miss Georgia Lewis, of Pitt Bridge, Texas. They have one child, a boy 13 years old.

Many regard Dr. Williams as the foremost speaker and leader of the Negro Baptists since the death of the lamented Booker T. Washington.

CABIN IN WHICH DR. WILLIAMS WAS BORN

W. CURTIS REID

OLIVET BAPTIST CHURCH, CHICAGO, ILL.

PETER JAMES BRYANT, D. D.

ETER James Bryant, is what is often termed a precocious youth, but in reality, with him, it was the early unfolding of a strong and active brain. He was born in Sylvania, Screven County, Georgia, April 13, 1872. At the early age of four he gave evidence of that characteristic which finally led to his life work. While yet on the borderland of babyhood he would call the children about him and preach to them. His gift was so pronounced that the older people had him preach to them and listened attentively to his messages.

His parents, though poor, had an ambition to educate their children, numbering nine, and made great sacrifices to send them to school.

At the age of six years Peter was sent to the Public Schools at Guyton, Georgia, and after finishing at the lower school he entered the Pilgrim High School, of the same town. He was an apt student and led his classes. After finishing at the Pilgrim High School, he went to Atlanta, Georgia, and entered Morehouse College. Here again he applied himself diligently, and advanced rapidly. While in Atlanta, he also took a course in the American Normal Correspondence School, of Danville, New York. When ten years of age, he was converted and joined the Macedonia Baptist Church of Guyton, Ga., and he developed such an aptitude for religious work, that at the age of twelve years, he was made superintendent of the Sunday School.

When fourteen years of age he took up the work of teaching, and was placed in charge of a rural school. From the rural school he advanced to teacher in the public school of Madison, Georgia, and of Jonesboro, Georgia.

He began his ministerial work among the country churches, which he served faithfully, but a man of his ability was needed in the larger fields and it was only a few years before he had charge of the Wheat Street Baptist Church of Atlanta. Under his able leadership the congregation has grown until it ranks among the largest in the United States. The church was burned in the big fire that swept Atlanta in 1918. Dr. Bryant, nothing daunted is raising the funds with which to build a greater and grander edifice; one that will in every way measure up to the high religious ideals of the congregation and minister. Needless to say the work will succeed, for this noted divine doesn't know the meaning of the word failure.

His ability as a pulpit orator is only second to his ability as a successful pastor, and many members of other congregations frequent his church.

He is deeply interested in the Baptist Young People's Union, and served as President of the Georgia State Convention of this Union and also President of the National Baptist Young People's Union. He served as Corresponding Secretary of the Young People's Christian and Educational Congress of America, representing forty denominations, at Guyton, Georgia, and at Atlanta. He is a member of the Commission of Church and Country Life of American Federation of Churches; Chairman of Colored Department of Associated Churches, Atlanta, Georgia; and a member of the Executive Committee both of the Georgia and National Baptist Conventions. He has traveled over America, England, Scotland, Wales, Ireland, France, Italy, Switzerland, Greece, Egypt, Palestine, and Syria.

October 26, 1892, he was married to Miss Sylvia Cecil Jenkins, of Savannah, Georgia. They have no children. He owns his residence and several lots valued at $6000. He is a Mason, member of Knights of Pythias, and of the Supreme Circle.

He rendered patriotic service during the war and was one of the four minute speakers. He also took part in the War Workers Campaign and raised $60,000 in ten days.

During his ministerial work he has baptised more than 8000 converts.

W. H. Harris, M. D.

DR. W. H. Harris, Grand Secretary of the Improved Order of Samaritans is a man who has helped his people from three different angles—doing all of the work well. His first endeavor along the line of public uplift was made as a teacher, his next as a doctor and his present as a lodge man where he helps to look out for the fatherless and the widows.

In all of these endeavors he has taken front rank and has made his influence felt in the lives of those he has touched, and has already made a record which will keep him in fond remembrance and of which any man could well be proud, though his work is still in its active stage.

Dr. Harris was born in Augusta, Georgia, immediately after the days of slavery, when the South was in the throes of reconstruction, and when the transition from slavery to freedom was attended with many trials and great hardships. He was one of fourteen children and his father found it difficult to provide them with bread and was in no postion to have him educated. He early felt the cravings for an education and notwithstanding his environment which seemed an impassable barrier to his ambition, he determined to secure one.

He studied alone and with such help as he could get for a time. He then entered Clark University, Atlanta, Georgia, in 1886. Here he remained till 1890. His next studying was done in Meharry Medical College from which institution he received a degree in 1893. Since that time he has done post graduate work in both Harvard and New York Clinical School and so prepared himself thoroughly for the profession of his choice.

Before taking up the study of medicine, still a young man in his teens, Dr. Harris taught school for a number of years. He taught in a number of places in the Northern part of Georgia. After he finished his medical course he settled down to the practice of medicine in the city of Athens. Here for twenty-five years he followed this profession of his choice. Like most conscientious Doctors, his was the opportunity to learn of the inside lives of his patients, his was the chance to send them on a higher endeavor after relieving their bodily suffering, his was the duty to show nobler ways of living. During the twenty-five years that Dr. Harris spent in this work, he did great good along all these lines. He also served as the first President of the Georgia State Medical Association of Colored Doctors.

His duties as Grand Secretary and Chief Medical Examiner of the Improved Order of Samaritans claimed so much of his attention, as to finally cause him to give up his active practice of medicine, and to this order he is giving his time and talent.

Under his wise and conservative management the order is making great progress and gaining much strength. Through his untiring efforts and leadership the order has built a magnificent temple, costing $50,000, which is a modern structure in all of its appointments.

Dr. Harris is well prepared for this work. As a teacher he became well acquainted with the working of the mind, as a Doctor he became well acquainted with the functioning of the parts of the body, and also with the ideals and aspirations of our people. To the widows and the orphans he is one who understands and one who can advise. Through the organization, Dr. Harris has been able to continue the uplift work that he began while still in his teens—that of helping others.

In line with his other work, he organized the E. D. Harris Drug Company, of which he is president, which conducts one of the largest and best equipped drug stores for the colored people in the whole country.

In church connections he is an African Methodist Episcopal, being a member of the Pierce Chapel of the faith in Athens, Georgia. Besides being a member of the Good Samaritans, Dr. Harris is an Odd Fellow, a Mason, a Knight of Pythias, and an Elk. Through these organizations he has come in contact with many of the problems that confront colored people everywhere. Not all of his time and interest have gone into the school, the church, the practice of medicine and the lodges. Dr. Harris has also been interested in the National affairs. He is chairman of the Ninth Republican Congressional District and he has been elected delegate to the Republican National Convention four times. His old interest in schools stills holds as is seen from the fact that he now serves as trustee of Morris Brown University.

In the Harris family there are five children, Hattie, Marie, Roderick, Percival, and Taliaferro Harris. The oldest son is General Manager in Fraternal Insurance work and the oldest daughter is chief book-keeper. Another of the sons is a pharmacist. Mrs. Harris was Miss Mary Jane Badger. They make an interesting family and have served to keep Dr. Harris with a keen interest in the lives of young people.

Dr. Harris has succeeded in saving a competence for the care of his family and to meet the demands of old age. He is estimated to be worth $50,000.

JUDGE SCIPIO A. JONES

Judge Scipio A. Jones

TWENTY, even ten years age, to speak of illiteracy or of a backward country, was to conjure up a picture of the Arkansas made famous by Opie Read. A country that from the Mississippi delta to the Ozarks, was supposed to be people by a semi-civilized people, the height of whose ambition was to gather at some out of the way community store and talk politics. Such a type could be found in Arkansas, and can still be found there as they can in every other state in the Union, but they are not types of the state's citizens, but of a small minority, too remotely located from schools, to receive any educational advantages. There is another type in Arkansas, that is representative of the majority of her citizens. It is this type that is draining the immensely fertile Mississippi delta lands that comprise a big part of the Eastern half of the state, and putting them in a state of productivity that is bringing untold riches to her farmers and merchants. It is this class of men that have changed the picturesque Ozark Mountains from a vast wilderness to the greatest apple producing country in the world. It is this type of citizens that have made such modern cities as Little Rock, Hot Springs, Ft. Smith, Pine Bluff, and Helena possible, and it is all these as a whole that are fast putting Arkansas in the forefront of progressive states. It has been truthfully said that a chain is as strong as its weakest link. Therefore in judging the progress of a state or community, any one at all qualified for the task, would at once seek to find the results, being obtained, not by those with the greatest opportunities, but those who were overcoming the greatest difficulties. The splendid record of the Arkansas Negroes in the professional, commercial, rural and religious life of the State has contributed wonderfully to the State's development. There are quite a number of colored citizens, whose records are a source of pride to the communities in which they reside and to the State at large, irrespective of race. Prominent among these is Judge Scipio A. Jones, of Little Rock.

Admitted to the Pulaski Circuit Court, June 15th, 1889, Attorney Jones began the practice of law at a time when conditions necessarily made a great part of his work pure charity, his only reward being the knowledge that he was, in a measure, protecting his people and aiding them in getting justice.

His ability became so marked that he attracted the attention of J. E. Bush, of Little Rock, President and founder of the Mosiac Templars. Mr. Bush, who has been likened to Andrew Carnegie in his ability to find and develop talented heads of departments for his interests, in or about 1895, appointed Judge Jones, National Attorney General for the Mosiac Templars. It is sufficient to state that for the last twenty years Judge Jones has guided this remarkably successful organization through the shoals of legal entanglements, in a manner that stamps him as a corporate attorney of exceptional ability. Many members of the bar are ever on the alert for personal publicity and rush their clients into court on the slightest provocation. It has always been the Judges' principle to appeal to the courts only as a last resort. He has unbounded confidence in the integrity of his fellow man and goes on the principle that calm reasoning, and common sense save court costs. Judge Jones' position with the Mosaic Templars requires only part of his time, and he has builded a private practice in Arkansas, second to none. His offices are located at Little Rock, where his work necessitates him having a large corps of highly trained assistants. Judge Jones was admitted to the Supreme Court of Arkansas, Nov. 26th, 1900. To the U. S. District Court for the Western Division of the Eastern District of Arkansas, and the U. S. Circuit Court for Arkansas October 30, 1901. To the U. S. Supreme Court, May 29th, 1905, and to the U. S. Court of Appeals, Dec. 10, 1914.

The Judge's personal popularity in his home town was shown by his election as Special Judge in the Municipal Court of Little Rock, April 8th, 1915, which position he filled with credit to himself and to his people.

The Judge is not only National Attorney for the Mosaic Templars, but an active member of all of the strongest fraternities with lodges in Little Rock, and attends the State and National Conventions whenever possible.

No greater tribute can be paid to the Judge's patriotism than to quote from his speech to the National Grand Lodge of the Mosaic Templars at the outbreak of the world's war.

"These are perilous times. Among those who will march under the flag of the United States will be true and tried Mosaics. These Mosaics will leave their families and go to fight and die for you and for me. Your Executive Committee bought thirty thousand dollars ($30,000.00) worth of Liberty Loan Bonds, but we ought to go further, as the "end is not yet." If you can't fight with your musket you can fight with your dollars! There are no cowards among us, no slackers on our rolls."

State Normal School, Normal, Ala.

 HE oft-quoted saying of Emerson, that an "institution is the lengthened shadow of one man," is especially applicable in the case of the State Agricultural and Mechanical College, at Normal, Alabama. Normal, as the institution is commonly designated, is the lengthened shadow of the late William Hooper Council, ex-slave, legislator, educator and author.

Dr. Council was born in Fayetteville, North Carolina, in 1848. Sold through the famous "Richmond Slave Pen," he was shipped into Alabama in 1857, when a lad of but nine years. Young though he was, he was put to work in the cotton fields, where he toiled till the Emancipation Proclamation severed his bondman's shackles. His freedom gained, he looked about for a place to improve his mind. It chanced that missionaries from the North had come down to Stevenson, Alabama, in 1865 to open a school. Dr. Council was one of the first pupils to enter. He remained at Stevenson three years, which though a short time within itself, gave the young ex-slave habits of study and of thought and aided him much in mapping out a future career.

Leaving school but still studying hard, Dr. Council taught, preached, and indeed threw the weight of his strong personality into many channels of service for the benighted colored people of his state. His rise in the public activities of Alabama was rapid, yet secure; for the footing which he gained in those early days of Reconstruction, he held and expanded to the day of his death.

Four years after leaving the school at Stevenson saw him a prominent figure in the state. He was Enrolling Clerk in the Alabama Legislature from 1872 to 1874. In 1875 he was appointed, by President Grant, as Receiver of the Land Office for the Northern District of Alabama. Two years later he founded the "Huntsville Herald," which he edited for seven years and through which he did much to educate his people and to shape their thoughts properly on public matters.

Though he gave much time to public service, Dr. Council never neglected to improve himself. Continuing his studies under private instruction, he developed a rare proficiency, regardless of race and previous limited advantages, in the modern languages, in the sciences, in higher mathematics, in the classics, and in history. He was an authority on race history and conditions as is well attested by his "Lamp of Wisdom," a splendid compendium of Negro history, published in 1898. He studied

law and was admitted to the Supreme Court of Alabama, in 1883. For his rare scholarship he was honored by Morris Brown College, with the degree of Doctor of Philosophy. He was an orator much in demand and widely known; so well known indeed that when he traveled in Europe he was most cordially received by Hon. William E. Gladstone, and by King Leopold of Belgium. He spoke, wrote and labored incessantly for industrial education, for African Missions, and for better trained teachers and workers. He was a strong advocate of temperance, and contributed many helpful race articles to magazines and newspapers. Among his published works are two books: "The Lamp of Wisdom," mentioned before, and "The Negro Laborer-A Word to Him." He left in manuscript form three books: "The History of My Life," "The Teacher's Manual," and "The Silver Lining." He ranked high as a churchman and was an important factor in our fraternal organizations.

However, through all his activities, he remained what he began, a school teacher, an educator. Normal was founded by him in 1875, the same year that he was made Receiver of the Land Office in North Alabama. The school through his powerful influence secured substantial financial backing from the beginning, receiving from the state an annual appropriation of $1000. It opened in May, 1875, with sixty-one pupils and two teachers, and in rented quarters. The large property now owned by the College had its origin in the self-sacrificing labors of Dr. Council, assisted by a devoted faculty that taught with him in the first few years of the institution's existence. Under his inspirational influence, the teachers signed with him a contract donating a certain percentage of their salaries to be used in the purchase of a school site. The site was purchased in Huntsville, Alabama, and deeded to the state for the exclusive use of furthering the education of the Negro youth. This was the first property owned by the College and it formed the nucleus and the incentive for all that followed. In 1878, the annual state appropriation was raised to two thousand dollars.

Self-made, knowing the struggles, needs and yearnings of his people, Dr. Council sought to shape the policies of the institution to help as many classes of people as possible. In 1885 the State increased the grant from two thousand to four thousand dollars per year, to which was added later help from the Slater and Peabody Funds, and from private donors who gave at the solicitation of Dr. Council.

In 1891 the Legislature of Alabama made this

RESERVE OFFICERS' TRAINING CAMP.

VARSITY BASEBALL TEAM 1919.

REPAIRING A BIG GASOLINE ENGINE.

A GROUP IN TAILORING.

THE PRINTERY.

A CLASS IN FANCY SEWING.

A CLASS IN COOKING.

NURSES.

DEPARTMENT VIEWS—STATE NORMAL SCHOOL—NORMAL, ALA.

school the beneficiary of the fund granted by Act of Congress, approved on August 30. 1890, "for the more complete endowment and the support of the colleges for the benefit of agriculture and mechanic arts."

Thus supported, Normal was not long in becoming an important educational factor in the state of Alabama. One by one brick buildings went up, students increased and courses were added until the school was numbered with the larger Negro institutions of the nation.

Happily Dr. Council lived to a ripe old age and was able to see the institution thoroughly established in equipment in courses and in practical usefulness in the state. For more than a third of a century he served as its head, and died in office, April 14, 1909.

His successor Mr. Walter S. Buchanan, is carrying out and re-enforcing all the policies laid down by the founder. Mr. Buchanan is thoroughly trained for the office to which he succeeds. He was born and reared in Troy, Alabama. Having attended the public schools of Troy he entered Tuskegee Institute where he was graduated in 1899.

From Tuskegee President Buchanan went to Aiken. S. C. where he taught for two years in the Schofield School before going to Boston, Massachusetts, where he enrolled in the Sloyd Training School from which he was graduated in 1902. After preparing with the help of private tutors and the Y. M. C. A. night school of Boston he entered Harvard University in 1904 and was graduated with the degree, B. A. S, in 1907. On graduating from Harvard, Mr. Buchanan served two months as Southern Agent for Tuskegee Institute. He was called from Tuskegee to accept the principalship of the Corona Industrial Institute Corona Alabama. Here he remained for two years, becoming President of Normal in 1909. It was during this year that he married Miss Ida Council the daughter of the founder. Three children have blessed the union.

Under him Normal is now realizing to the full the meaning of the dreams of its founder. It has added many new buildings the most important of which is perhaps the new hospital which serves as a health center not only for the student body, but for the whole community. In all the institution

has twenty-one buildings, and a total property valuation of $185,000. It has one hundred eighty-two acres of land, ninety of which are under cultivation for educational purposes and to aid in running the school. It has twenty-nine instructors, twenty four students taking the college course and three hundred seventy-nine taking other courses, most of which are practical in their training.

It is in offering courses of study that Normal has shown itself the most useful and adaptable. Seeking as it did under its founder to fit the young for all pursuits, Normal in addition to its college courses, has departments giving Mechanical Agricultural Domestic Commercial and Nurse Training Courses in all their various detail. Thus in the Agricultural Department are taught Truck Farming Dairying and the like, in the Department of Mechanical Industries Steam and Electrical Engineering Carpentry Wheelwrighting and Blacksmithing Shoe-making Printing Tailoring etc. in Domestic Arts Cooking Sewing, Dress-making Millinery and Handicrafts. The Department of Commercial Arts gives instruction in Typewriting Shorthand and Bookkeeping. Normal is one of the few Negro Colleges that offers a thorough business course.

But the school realized years ago that it must go outside of the class room to give the full measure of service. Hence for years, Normal has been the North Alabama center for farmers' institutes and Conferences, rural club meetings for farmers' wives and for rural children. When the Corn Club, Pig Club and Tomato Club idea struck the South, Normal was one of the first institutions to put an agent in the field, to establish such clubs among Negroes. Under the Smith-Lever Bill it has been able to extend its services as well as prolong them among the Negro boys and girls of North Alabama. To perpetuate and improve these endeavors among rural folk the college is training students in all the phases of rural extension work. In summer and in winter it keeps open its doors to instruct both students and teachers to teach others. This holds not only in giving special instruction from texts and in trades, but also in showing the student how to organize and lead communities and to touch their lives for good in material progress and in clean living.

CHARLES HARRY ANDERSON

HE subject of this sketch who to-day ranks as one of the foremost Negro financiers of the Country, inherits his ability from his mother, Charlotte (Lewis) Anderson. This remarkable woman was left heavily in debt and with seven little children to support. By taking in washing and working almost day and night she managed to not only support the children but pay the indebtedness left by her husband. As the children grew older, she started a little store and a truck garden, in this way they not only aided in making a living, but were given the practical training that was to serve them so well in later years.

Charles Harry Anderson, her mainstay, was born in Jacksonville, Fla., July 25, 1879. He was educated at the Florida Baptist Academy of that place, and took a business course in a Philadelphia Business College.

His first independent business venture was in 1902, buying fish by the barrel and peddling them from a street corner. So well did he succeed that it was only a short time before he rented a store and opened a fish and oyster business. By close attention to detail, and carefully studying the wants and needs of his customers, he has built up the present splendid business of the Anderson Fish and Oyster Co., of which he is proprietor. This establishment is located on Broad Street, and here is installed the most modern cold storage and sanitary equipment throughout.

Mr. Anderson makes it a rule to employ only clerks, whose unfailing courtesy make them an asset to his business and he has made the motto of the Anderson Fish & Oyster Co., "sell goods that won't come back, to customers that will."

From his very first business venture, he saw the need of a banking institution that would serve a two fold purpose in teaching his people to have and to aid them in starting businesses of their own. It was here that the early training he received from his mother stood him in good stead, as the experience of his own family had demonstrated to him that by application to business and square dealing, Negroes could succeed in business for themselves, and all they needed was encouragement and a little help in starting. It was the knowledge of this need and the confidence he had in the ability of his people to succeed that caused him in 1914, to start a private banking institution under the name of Anderson Tucker & Co.

One year later, Mr. Tucker's interest was bought by Mr. Anderson's Brother, Richard, and the firm name changed to Anderson and Co. This banking institution is located on the main corner, ground floor of the magnificent Masonic Temple Building on Broad Street. It is here that more than a quarter of a million dollars belonging to the Negroes of Jacksonville is handled with an efficiency that is attracting the attention of the business interest of the whole State of Florida and the Bank bids fair to develop into a state wide institution for the promotion of Negro business enterprises.

With a paid in Capital of $15,000.00, the esteem in which these bankers are held by the Negroes of Jacksonville is best shown by the fact that, although the bank has still to be nationalized, the last statement to the comptroller of the State of Florida, made June 30, 1919, shows Deposits of $217,029.82, with additional deposits in the Xmas Savings Club, of $16,932.14. No greater endorsement could be given any men by their people. Hundreds of depositors in this bank are laborers who cannot reach the bank during regular banking hours and the officers, in keeping with their policy of accommodating their clients first, keep the doors open for deposits until six P. M. daily and 9 P. M. Saturday.

Mr. Chas. H. Anderson was married to Margaret H. Myatt, of Jacksonville, Fla., Sept 18, 1907. They have four children: Hodge, Seattle, Chas. H. Jr., and Joseph M. The Andersons occupy their own home, an elegant residence on 8th and Centre Streets. An atmosphere of quiet refinement pervades the home, and serves as an inspiration to those fortunate enough to be guests of the family.

Mr. Anderson is an active member of the A. M. E. Church, and is also an active member of the K. f P's, and Odd Fellows.

MASONIC TEMPLE BUILDING—JACKSONVILLE, FLA.

Union Grand Lodge of Masons, Florida Jurisdiction

THE present Union Grand Lodge of Masons in the State of Florida was formed in 1879, by consolidating the then Union Grand Lodge and the Sovereign Grand Lodge. The committee designated to draw up terms of union between the two Grand Lodges was composed of Charles H. Pearce, Tillman Valentine, and Edward A. Brown, from the Union Grand Lodge; and Richard L. Jones, Jasper N. Tully, Alonzo R. Jones and James A. Meadows from the Sovereign Grand Lodge. The report rendered by the committee was the basis of union of the two grand bodies, thus making the beginning of the career of the present Most Worshipful Union Grand Lodge whose former grand masters have been: Most Worshipful John R. Scott, Most Worshipful Tillman Valentine, Most Worshipful S. H. Coleman, Most Worshipful R. S. Mitchell, Most Worshipful John H. Dickerson, and the Most Worshipful D. D. Powell, the present incumbent.

The organization and successful operation of the Masonic Benefit Association, the more perfect working of the large corps of deputies whose duties cover a jurisdiction now comprising a membership of nearly twelve thousand Master Masons, not including the hundreds who hold membership in the Royal Arch, Knights-Templar, and Mystic Shriners division. The affiliated branches of the Order of the Eastern Star, and the Heroines of Jericho are also reckoned in the growth of the craft in this jurisdiction in the past decade.

The Masonic Temple at the corner of Duval and Broad Sts., Jacksonville, Fla., is one of the best edifices of its kind owned by colored people in this country. All classes of our citizens irrespective of their affiliation, point with pride to the Masonic Temple. It is the one thing in Jacksonville which stands ahead of all others, demonstrating what our people can do when we marshal our resources, combine our forces and work unitedly for one end. In the erection of this splendid building, of which Rev. John H. Dickerson, ex-Grand Master of the Most Worshipful Union Grand Lodge of Florida, was the projector, it was not only necessary to overcome the incredulity which is peculiar to our people, but with the elements of character which ex-Grand Master Dickerson possessed to a marked degree to push forward and overcome obstacles which were in his pathway. This he did, which resulted in the completion of the building in the fall of 1913.

The temple is located in the heart of the city and is a six story massive structure of reinforced concrete and steel, and is finished with fine pressed brick and marble. The corridors are twelve feet wide, with tiled floors. There are forty-six office rooms, which are used for business purposes by some of the leading colored men of Jacksonville, whose offices are splendidly furnished and well equipped for their different lines of business, and which are heated by steam in winter and lighted by electricity. The ground floor has six commodious store rooms, all of which are occupied. The offices and reception room of the Grand

Master are located on the fifth floor, and are elegantly furnished. It is from these apartments with the aid of his private secretary, stenographers and clerks that he directs the Masonic forces of the State, and makes plans to advance the interests of the craft. The director's room adjoins the apartment of the grand master and is splendidly furnished in keeping with the dignity of the order. On the sixth floor is the beautiful Eastern Star Chamber and the lodge room of the Mystic Shriners and Sublime Princess of the Royal Secret. Above all this is an elaborate roof garden, where in summer evenings 300 guests may enjoy the cool atmosphere that wafts with the breeze that is always to be felt at a high attitude.

The basement of this magnificent building is splendidly furnished, and it is here that the members of the Masonic Clubs meet and "jolly" each other concerning their last experience in "riding the goat." Set basins are in every office in the building, two elevators are operated to carry persons to different floors janitor service is furnished to keep the offices and apartments clean, and every modern convenience which goes to make a first class business is to be found in this splendid edifice. The furnishings, equipments and paraphernalia used in the lodge rooms and departmental quarters are also first class and up-to-date and "goat riding," which is still hazardous, is conducted with just a bit more dignity, pomp and splendor than it used to be by the brethren of the craft in the task of inducting "raw recruits" into the sublime mysteries of the degree of the fraternity.

A sketch of Florida Masonry, however, brief, would not be complete without special mention of the present most Worshipful Grand Master, D. D. Powell, and Rt. Worshipful Grand Secretary, William A. Glover.

Grand Master Powell first came into the limelight when he organized Solomon Lodge 166 and was elected first Worshipful Master. He quickly attracted the attention of the State officers by his ability as an organizer, and was elected District Deputy Grand Master. He was elected Junior Grand Warden in 1909, Deputy Grand Master in 1910, and Grand Master in 1916. Mr. Powell still occupies this position with a brilliancy that is adding luster to the Masonic body of Florida. He is a 33rd degree Mason, Royal Arch Mason, Knight Templar, Shriner and member of the Eastern Star. He is also a member of the K. of P's and Odd Fellows and a Deacon in the Spring Hill Baptist Church.

William A. Glover, Grand Secretary, is also a 33rd degree Mason, Royal Arch Mason, Knight Templar, Shriner, Member of Eastern Star, and Master of Finance of M. C. B. Mason Lodge No. 97 K. of P's. Secretary Glover enjoys the distinction of being the oldest officer in the Masonic body of Florida. He joined the Masons in 1894, and has served continuously since. He organized Myrtle Lodge 136, organized the Masonic Benefit Association and served as its first Secretary. Served as Grand Chancellor K. of P's, of Florida from 1896 to 1903, and is now serving fourth term as Grand Secretary of the Masons.

LAWTON LEROY PRATT

 AWTON Leroy Pratt, proprietor of the L. L. Pratt Undertaking Co. was born in Lake City, Florida, Dec. 23, 1885. Mr. Pratt came to Jacksonville when a mere lad, and got his first business experience selling papers on the street corners.

Mr. Pratt always ambitious to rise saved and skimped to pay his way through Cookman Institute. After finishing here he continued to sell papers until he had saved sufficient funds to take a course in Parks School of Embalming at Cincinnati, Ohio. On receiving his diploma he returned to Jacksonville where he started in the Undertaking business for himself with a capital of $60.00.

Mr. Pratt's personality from the very start made him many friends. Always courteous and unassuming, being ever alert to protect the feelings and sensibilities of bereaved relatives in the hours of deepest sorrow, he soon drew to himself a patronage that taxed his establishment to the utmost to handle.

Thoroughly trained himself in the most modern schools, he is a firm believer in modern methods and modern equipment. While occupying the building at 416 Broad Street, he conceived the idea of building an establishment that would be not only the most complete undertaking and embalming plant owned and operated by Negroes, in connection with splendid stables for his horse drawn vehicles and garage for his magnificent hearses, but to have the upper floors fitted up with every modern home convenience so that he might, at all hours of the day and night, be in close personal touch with his business. In this he was aided by the advice of his talented wife, who was Mrs. Mamie L. Anderson, of New York City. Mrs. Pratt is a graduate of Barnes School of Anatomy, Sanitary Science and Embalming, having received her diploma in 1909.

Immediately after their marriage in 1913 they began the study of the plants and methods of the finest undertakers in both the South and East. They determined that the best was none too good for Jacksonville, and that the Pratts were going to furnish that best. They even made special trips East in order to study the equipment and arrangement of the newest plants. When fully satisfied, plans were drawn for the present modern building on West Beaver Street. The main building is of pressed brick two stories in height. On the first floor are the offices and private reception rooms. Just back of these are the casket rooms. On the side of the building leading back to the garage and stables, is a broad concrete drive. The stables and garage are kept as scrupulously clean as the rest of the place. There are three horse drawn hearses, that five years ago would have been sufficient for the most up-to-date establishment, but the Pratts have so educated their clientile up to expecting the latest that they have been compelled to buy three auto hearses. On the second floor is located the living apartments of the Pratts, and it is here that many noted Northerners and Easterners are guests in the tourist season, and are entertained in a manner that sends them home with pleasant memories of Southern hospitality. The real record of the Pratts success is best given in Mr. Pratts own words: "Years ago, in my school days, I learned the motto, 'Aim at a definite end.'" This motto made a special impression on me. Whatever success I have achieved in my profession has been through observing this motto, and aiming at a definite end—giving the best possible service to our patrons. I realized that to succeed we must do things different from others, and better than others. When I think of the small way in which we started eleven years ago, in an obscure room, I believe that our efforts have really met with success, for our present establishment provides facilities not found in this part of the country.

In our Chapel there is nothing to remind one that it is a funeral home. The utmost care is shown

UNDERTAKING ESTABLISHMENT OF L. L. PRATT

to remove from grief stricken people any reminder of this nature. The same care is taken to secure the utmost privacy so that the remains of loved ones shall not be open to the inspection of the merely curious. In our embalming room where preparations are made for burial including embalming by the most scientific methods special attention is given to the Sanitary features. Refined and tender natures only should ever attempt this delicate service. In view of this fact, only men of experience and ability, and who are qualified to perform in a proper and respectful manner the sacred duties of this profession, have been selected.

Some thought at first that the motor funeral was introduced as a matter of style. But this is not the case. The motor funeral is not for style, speed or fashion, but is simply the result of the era of the automobile. The motor car has succeeded the family carriage everywhere. Practically no one rides in carriages any more. Liverymen have been selling out for years as a result of lack of business. When all pleasure vehicles and most business vehicles are motor driven, the time is certainly here for us to offer our patrons at least the choice of horse-driven or automobile service. The automobile funeral has several distinct advantages —it is the most comfortable, and owing to absence of noise it is also the most dignified. The charge for motor equipment is just the same as for horse-

drawn equipment, and it often actually saves expense by enabling the family and friends who have cars to use them. It is the most simple and natural. Persons are accustomed nowadays to ride in motor cars, they feel more at ease under such conditions. The motor funeral does not hurry and on the other hand it does not waste time, or needlessly prolong the strain to which friends and relatives are subjected. We have no desire to urge our patrons to use motor equipment against their wish. Our experience leads us to suggest, however, that it will be found more satisfactory. One rule we insist upon, service must be all horse drawn or all automobile. It cannot satisfactorily be part one and part the other. We know that the life of loved ones does not end. It simply goes on. Its work is done here only to take up its work in "the other room," and our work is modeled with this knowledge always to the fore."

With such sentiments, it is small wonder that from a mere pittance Mr. Pratt's holdings have grown until he is ranked with the foremost of Jacksonville's business men. He is a member of all the leading Fraternal orders of Jacksonville, a member of the National Negro Business League, and a consistent churchman. He is a liberal contributor to every movement having for its object the betterment of his country or his people. As a citizen he is a credit to his home and country.

W. W. ANDREWS

NOW, which melts on ridges, peaks and sides of mountains on account of its consequent slope runs down the mountain side. This little stream, while wending its way downward, meets a number of other little streams. A confluence takes place. A larger stream is formed, which continues its course, meeting other streams, it joins them, which is ladened with greetings and contributions from contiguous mountain sides. Then a mighty stream is formed, which, with many meanderings, wends its way to the sea, where it contributes some matter in solution, others in solidity, but at the same time bearing upon the bosom of its waters numerous craft loaded with products of commerce to be distributed into the diversified channels of trade.

The coming of Columbus to an unknown world; the discovery of the Land of Flowers by Ponce de Leon in search of a Fountain of Youth, the confluence of those mountain streams, of which mention has been made in the preceding paragraph, to form the rivulet, and the rivulets to form the sluggish or impetuous river, are of no greater value or import to the populace of Florida than the visit to our Fair Florida of Sir S. W. Green, the present Supreme Chancellor of New Orleans, La., and Sir Bell, of Mississippi, in the Spring of 1886. These two Pythian Knights came to Jacksonville with, I am told, a complete set of Lodge Paraphernalia to be given as a premium to the first person who formed a Knights of Pythias Lodge. A few gentlemen were initiated into the work in Jacksonville among whom was D. M. Pappy, of St. Augustine. Upon returning to his home city, the said D. M. Pappy proceeded to organize a Pythian Lodge. In a short time, during the month of June, the Pythian banner was unfurled to the breeze in the State of Florida; San Marco Lodge No. 1 was organized with the following officers: Alfonso Pappy. C. C.; William Pappy, V. C.; D. M. Pappy, M. of W.; John Williams, K. of R. and S.; Lee Saunders, M. of F.; James Mongum, M. of Ex.; S. Martin, I. G.; Pierce Reddick, O. G.; Frank Johnson, M. of O. Having been created a P. C., along with a Brother McGinniss, of Jacksonville, to whom the information was imparted by Sir Green, that the paraphernalia which he had brought into the state was to be given to the first Past Chancellor who organized a lodge, Mr. Pappy returned to Jacksonville, received the paraphernalia and delivered the same to San Marco Lodge No. 1. This paraphernalia was used by San Marco Lodge No. 1 for many years.

With the melting of the snow in the organization of San Marco Lodge, followed by a sufficient number of Subordinate Lodges to form the Grand Lodge, the Order of Knights of Pythias in this State started as a little stream down the mountain side. In due course of time other little streams were met. and with the election of J. C. Jordan in Pensacola three years after the organization of the Grand Lodge there were ten votes in the Grand Lodge. D. M. Pappy was again elected in Ocala, then the little streams began to form a little rivulet. The little rivulets began to form a little larger rivulet when W. A. Glover was elected for the first time in Fernandina. Then Col. H. James, who is now the Supreme Outer Guard, took hold of affairs, convoked the Grand Lodge at St. Augustine, where Col. D. G. Adger, the present Past Grand Chancellor, was elected. Then the little rivulets began to form larger rivulets, the rivulets began to unite to form a river, the Order began to take on flesh, took her place among leading secret organizations of the State, caused men and women to recognize it and see that it had to be reckoned with. With the election of W. W. Andrews, the present Grand Chancellor at the Apalachicola session, a new era dawned upon the Pythian horizon. The streams, rivulets and rivers began to form into one mighty and powerful river, and with velocity safe, certain

HOME OFFICE OF FLORIDA PYTHIANS AND RESIDENCE OF GRAND CHANCELLOR.

and sure, noiselessly but steadily made its way into the great sea of progress, took its place at the head of all secret organizations in this State, causing persons who formerly looked upon the order as a pigmy to now recognize it as a giant and bow as suppliant minions before its shrine.

K. OF P.'S FLORIDA.

Any one who studies the records of Colored Fraternalism, will be impressed with the fact that the K. of P.'s have been remarkably fortunate in the selection of their officers. A splendid example of this is shown in the elevation of W. W. Andrews to the post of Grand Chancellor of the Jurisdiction of Florida.

Born in Sparta, Ga., Feb. 4, 1874, Mr. Andrews worked in the cotton fields to earn the money to pay for his early education. As soon as he was old enough, he secured a position in the barber ship of Angelo Harden & James F. Reeves. It was only a short while before he had mastered the trade and saved enough to move to Apalachicola, and open his own shop. It was here in 1901 that he joined the order, the upbuilding of which in future years was to become his life's work. The order who's membership, always quick to recognize exceptional executive ability, has promoted him through successive steps to the highest office in the gift of the State Jurisdiction.

Mr. Andrews was elected State Grand Lecturer of the K. of P's in 1905, State Grand Keeper of Records & Seals in 1907, and State Grand Chancellor in 1910. The Florida Jurisdiction has grown under his chancellorship until today it embraces 220 lodges with a membership of thirteen thousand. The endowment bureau has paid since 1912, $200,000.00, to widows and orphans and has assets of $160,000.00 fifty thousand of which are in Liberty Bonds and seven thousand in Thrift Stamps.

Mr. Andrews has served in the Uniform Rank from private to brigadier general. He is also a 32nd degree Mason, having joined the order in 1899, and is a consistent member and trustee of the C. M. E. Church. Mr. Andrews was married to Miss Henrietta G. Smith of Apalachicola, Fla., Sept. 15, 1900, and has two sons, Cyril B. and W. W., Jr., both school boys. Although Mr. Andrews has a home in Apalachicola, a plantation near Jacksonville and a handsome two story mansion in Jacksonville, he spends most of his time on the road in the interest of the order so dear to his heart and leaves his efficient wife in charge of the Home office, the results of whose work speaks for itself. Mrs. Andrews, a highly trained and efficient business woman, is to the Grand Chancellor what Emmett Scott was to the late Booker T. Washington.

A. L. LEWIS, PRESIDENT
AFRO-AMERICAN INSURANCE CO.

HE editor once heard the President of one of the South's largest Banking Institutions, state that Negro insurance companies were doing more in building the communities in which they were located than all other colored businesses combined. He stated that ten years ago there were millions of dollars annually collected by insurance companies centered in the east, that left the country never to return, while now, the vast bulk of this business was underwritten by local companies, and invested in local securities, and he believed these companies should have the hearty co-operation of both the white and Negro business organizations whereever they were located.

It is the work being done by such institutions as the Afro-American Industrial Insurance Co., of Jacksonville, Florida, that called forth this comment. This company was founded in March, 1901, by Messrs. E. J. Gregg, D. D., A. W. Price, Dr. A. W. Smith, J. E Spearing. W. H. Hampton, Geo. W. Branning. J. Milton Waldron, D. D., A. L. Lewis, Tillman Valentine, E. W. Latson, L. H. Myers and Dr. Thos. E. Butler. These citizens determined to organize an industrial insurance company that would give the Negroes of the state the greatest protection possible, for their money. Rev. E. J. Gregg, was elected first President, Rev. J. Milton, Secretary. and Dr. A. W. Smith, Medical Director.

Offices were opened at number 14 Ocean St., April 1st, 1901. These offices were destroyed by the great fire in May of the same year, and the company moved to the residence of A. L. Lewis, at 621 Florida Ave. In two years time the company had outgrown these quarters, and moved to 609 Main Street. They remained here about four years. In the mean time, their success had been so phenominal the company paid $10,000.00 for the property at 722 Main St. The soundness of this investment was demonstrated when they later sold it for $40,000.00.

They erected the present building at 105 East Union Street, in 1908 This property, besides giving ample office room for the company brings sufficient rentals to pay good interest on the investment. The company itself has grown from a one-room office to an organization owning its own office buildings in Jacksonville, Tampa and Miama, having 81 branch offices throughout the state and giving employment to 178 people, all colored. The capital stock of $20,000.00 is fully paid in and the company bought and owns $10,000.00 in Liberty Bonds. The present President, Mr. A. L. Lewis, born in 1864, and now just in the prime of life, deserves a big share of the credit for making the Afro-American what it is today. Mr. Lewis married Mary F. Samis, of Jacksonville, Fla., and has one son, James H. Lewis, 33 years of age, and an able assistant in his fathers' office.

Mr. Lewis along with a group of progressive, constructive citizens, has set an example in home building for Negroes that is at once the admiration and envy of every other city in the country. They have done more to open the eyes of the Northern tourist to the real ability of the colored people to make good, than all the publicity from other sources combined. Northern tourists are anxious to see for themselves how Southern Negroes live, and homes of the Lewis type are a revelation to them. Mr. Lewis is not only a man of splendid executive ability, but possesses a pleasing personality that is worth many dollars to any organization fortunate enough to have his services as an officer. In fact, the company has been exceptionally fortunate in the selection of its officers. Mr. Lewis has in Messrs. J. E. Spearing, Vice-Pres., L. D. Ervin. Gen. Mgr., T. W. Bryan, State Supt., and Wash Hampton, Secretary, a quartette hard to equal and gives the company a well rounded force and a combination of brains and capital that are bound to succeed.

W. S. SUMTER

MRS. HENRIETTA E. SUMTER

ECORDS of the Union Mutual and William Seymour Sumter, its founder and first president are so blended, and interwoven, that it is impossible to write a historical sketch of one without the other. Incorporated under the State laws of Florida, in 1904, this company under the able leadership of President Sumter, began business in February of that year and has enjoyed continuously great prosperity during this period of time and has found its way into thousands of homes of the good people of this fair State.

When first organized the company employed about ten persons, from the President to the Solicitors. This has grown until the company has more than 40 agencies throughout the state employing about one hundred and twenty-five people. The Sumters from the President down have a record truly remarkable for the combined co-operation of the family in both their home and business life. Mr. Sumter married Henrietta Albertina Ewart, a graduate of Cookman Institute. He was strongly opposed to his wife's participation in the worries of business life, and made a studied effort at all times to keep their home life free from care. A devoted father, he gave his children the benefit of the best education obtainable. A true son, he placed his father in the position of sick claim adjuster for the company.

When Mr. Sumter died Aug 27, 1918, he left be-

sides his widow, four daughters, Aline, who at the age of 22 is head clerk, Irene at 19 cashier of the company which he founded. The other two girls, Wilhelmina and Julia, age 16 and 11, respectively, are still school girls, although Wilhelmina has inherited her parents' business ability to such a marked degree that she was able to take her sister's place as cashier during the summer vacation. Although Mrs. Sumter had been carefully guarded from the cares of the business during the life of her husband, after six months deliberation and careful consideration, the Board of Directors voted unanimously to elect her to succeed him as President of the company. Mrs. Sumter, public spirited to a marked degree, and with an undying pride in the work her husband had so painstakingly builded, agreed to accept the responsibility and to perpetuate his memory by continuing the company along lines that made it a public benefaction.

The Sumters in their work have been ably assisted by an exceptionally strong directorate, composed of the President, F. J. Thorington, Vice-President; M. S. Adams, Secretary; W. W. Parker, Gen-Mgr.; and J. M. Sumter sick claim adjuster. When seen at the home office 411 Broad Street, Jacksonville, Florida. The President, H. E. Sumter, on being asked to give a brief statement of the aims of the company, said: "It is our aim to build an institution that will enable the educated colored youth to find employment that gives him an opportunity to take advantage of his training."

471

REVEREND JOHN ELIJAH FORD, D. D.,
PRESIDENT LELAND UNIVERSITY

ELAND University was located on St. Charles Ave., New Orleans, La. until 1916. It was founded in 1869, by Holbrook Chamberlain, a philanthropist of Brooklyn, N. Y., who purchased the land and erected the buildings. It was incorporated in 1870.

Title to the property is invested in an independent, self-perpetuating board of trustees. The act of incorporation provides that: The trustees shall not have the power to encumber by mortgage, the whole, or any part of the property or to use the principal of any endowment funds for the current expenses of its work." The last scholastic year, there was a total attendance of 300 pupils. There were fourteen teachers, six men and eight women. The sources of income at that time were: Endowment fund $8,000, tuition and fees $2,240. Alumni and Baptist Associations $362.00. The non-educational receipts were from the boarding department, and amounted to $5,700.00. The school was closed in 1916, and the plant sold, as the trustees had decided to move to Alexandria, La., where they could obtain sufficient land to build and operate an Industrial College in keeping with the need and training of present conditions of this section of the country. To this end, 258 acres of land has been bought and paid for; $75,000.00 added to the endowment fund. A plant which will be a model in every respect is in course of construction. The trustees have taken a long step forward in electing Rev. John E. Ford, D. D., of Jacksonville, President and assuring him their support in the selection of an able faculty. He is splendidly endowed, both by education and native ability to fill the chair of President of the new and finer Leland University. Born in Owensboro, Ky., his parents moved to Chicago, while he was yet a child. He obtained his early education in the public schools of Chicago, under the most adverse and trying circumstances. His parents were twice burned out, once in the great fires of 1871, and again in 1874. Nothing daunted, young John not only continued his duties but working out of school hours, aided his parents in rebuilding their home and in educating his younger brothers and sisters. Determined to have a thorough training at all cost, he worked his way, with the aid of one white friend, successively through Fisk University, Nashville, Tenn., Beloit College, Wisconsin, and the University of Chicago. Not satisfied with this he took a post graduate course at the University of Denver. Most of his college courses were paid for by money earned while working as a stenographer in Chicago. After graduating from Chicago University Divinity School, Dr. Ford Pastored the Bethesda Church, Chicago, Tabernacle Church, Los Angeles, Cal., Zion Church, Denver, Col., and is at present pastor of Bethel Institutional Church, Jacksonville, Fla. He served one year, 1906, as President of State University of Kentucky. Was delegate in 1907 to the World's Sunday School Convention, at Rome, Italy. While there he visited England, France, Spain and Switzerland. Dr. Ford has also visited Cuba and South America. He is president of the Progressive Baptist State Convention of Florida, and Chairman of the Board of Trustees of Florida Baptist College. Dr. Ford is also a member of the American Geographical Society of Applied Science. By this it will be seen that, to one of the finest academic educations obtainable, Dr. Ford has added a wonderful course of practical experience in the schools of travel and human nature. In him is found a combination of the highly educated, aggressively constructive Yankee, and the whole-souled sympathetic Southerner. He has the knack of spurring his co-workers on to a pitch of enthusiastic energy that makes him peculiarly fitted for the task of presiding over a southern college. Dr. Ford was married to Miss Elizabeth Walker Wilson, of Raleigh, N. C., in 1918.

CLASS ROOM—WALKER BUSINESS COLLEGE

THIS institution enjoys the unique distinction of being one of the youngest and the largest exclusive Negro business colleges in the United States. Prof. R. Wendell Walker, President, is a graduate of the High School and Fairmont College at Wichita, Kansas, and the Topeka Business College, at Topeka, Kansas. He has also taken post graduate courses in several other colleges in Michigan and Ohio (all white schools and colleges). He served five years as a stenographer in the United States Department Service, and has therefore had the necessary practical experience to qualify him to be a successful teacher and a practical business man. He established the Walker Business College in Jacksonville a little more than four years ago—beginning in one rented room with five pupils, and himself as the only teacher. Today the college owns its own building valued at $50,000.00; a faculty of eight competent teachers and over 1,000 students enrolled.

The remarkable success of the college is attributed by those who know, to the thorough training of the President combined with an abundance of "Pep," and enthusiasm so necessary to success in these days of specialization and keen competition. He is thoroughly modern in his methods and beliefs

and keeps consistenly and continuously driving to get hold of raw material, and turn out a finished product that will prove an endless chain of success and an ever-growing practical testimonial to the thoroughness of the college work. Even now, with only four short years elapsed since the foundation, graduates are filling responsible positions all over the country, and the demands on the school so great that lucrative positions are always waiting graduates.

The Walker College is filling a long felt want in establishing a summer course, as it enables grammar students to save time and money by getting a business training even before finishing their regular school work.

As the college grew, President Walker found many Negroes wished to take a business course, but were unable to attend day school as they were compelled to make their own living. To enable these men and women to take advantage of the college. Prof. Walker established night classes, where a full course in all branches of the day courses are taught.

The rapidly developing business interests of the Negroes requiring trained help, make the Walker Business College a welcome addition to the educational institutions of the country.

James W. Ames, M. D.

THE lives of men differ in many ways and their paths are devious, yet in many respects they have the same experience. This is particularly so regarding the Negro race. Most of them are born in poverty and are reared amidst great hardships. Looking at them in early life the imagination can hardly picture them as men who would win distinction in the various departments of life. Yet this book is full of sketches of boys who have risen above the discouraging environments which surrounded their youth and have made for themselves names which will live in the history of their race.

James W. Ames is one of the boys. His early life was not marked with many thrills and yet his path was far from being strewn with flowers. He fought his way through the ordinary vicissitudes incident to the Negro youth and forged ahead step by step until he reached his goal.

A double demand was made upon his energies and strength, for while he was securing an education he had to work hard to meet his physical demands. He had to eat and sleep and obtain clothing decent to appear at school, besides the cost of education, and to provide for these required incessant labor.

His first schooling was in the public schools of New Orleans, Louisiana. While attending these schools he worked at the Cooper's trade. When he finished the public school he entered Straight College, an institution founded by the American Missionary Association of the Congregational Church, from which he graduated, in the Literary Department, with the class of 1888. He also took a year's course in the law school and a year's course in the Theological School of the same Institution. Here, too, it was work and study, for his tuition must be paid and he had no other way to raise the money but by his own exertions.

During the summer months, he taught a rural school which enabled him to continue at college during the winter months.

After finishing his course in Straight College, he went to Washington, and entered the Medical Department of the Howard University. His experience here to advance his education differed only in the character of work he engaged in, for here as elsewhere he paid his own way.

From 1890 to 1894, he worked as clerk in the War Department, serving in the Record and Pension Division. From his salary he saved sufficient money to enable him to attend the Medical School of the Institution during the spring months.

By close application to his studies he completed his course in 1894, and June 5th, of that year he went to Detroit, Michigan, and entered upon his career as a physician. His rapid rise in the profession attest how well he had applied himself during the days of his preparation. He was appointed physician to the United States prisoners and served the Government in this capacity for one year. He was recognized as an expert diagnostician, and for sixteen years he served on the Detroit Board of Health as such.

While holding these public positions he has continued his private practice, and has won a large clientile and built up a lucrative business. Without apparent effort he has ingratiated himself into the good graces of the citizens and commands the respect and confidence of all classes.

In September, 1898, he married Miss Florence P. Cole, who died after bearing him four children: Chester C., who is a medical student; William E., who is studying electrical engineering; Marion C., a music and pedagogic student, and Florence F., who is a student of Domestic Science. Thus it will be seen that he has ambition for his children to occupy useful places in life.

In 1908 he again married and this time to Miss Norma Alembro.

He is the secretary of the Cole Realty Company, a family corporation capitalized at $95,000, which represents the family real estate interests.

Dr. Ames is a member of the Presbyterian church and while interested in religious work he is not officially identified with the church. He is also a member of the Masonic body, Knights of Pythias and Elks. He has held official positions in several orders of which he is connected; he is Past Grand Secretary of I. B. P. O. C.; Past Grand Secretary of the Knights of Pythias, of the State of Michigan; alternate delegate to the National Republican Convention since 1908; and a member of the Michigan State Legislature 1901-1902.

Honorable James Thomas Peterson

WHEN in the course of human events an individual, born under circumstances the most unfavorable, and struggling against difficulties too numerous to be mentioned, by force of character and a dogged determination to rise in spite of environments and oppositions, lifts himself from the poverty in which he was born to a commanding position in the affairs of the nation, that individual's life should be held up before the adolescent youth as a worthy example, and his career may be studied with profit by all ambitious young people who are struggling against odds to prepare for a life of efficient service, for the Poet Longfellow very tritely said in his "Psalm of Life", "lives of great men but remind us, we can make our lives sublime; and departing, leave behind us, footprints on the sand of time."

Such is example we have in Hon. James Thomas Peterson, who was born near Calhoun Station, Lowndes County, Alabama, June 22, 1867.

Patsy Peterson, his mother, prayed, as did Hagar in the wilderness, for God's blessing upon her and her child, who though not daring to tell it, had the blood of royalty coursing through his veins.

She, with her boy, moved to Greenville, in order that he might have a chance for an education and for several years he attended the public school there.

When James was about fifteen years of age, his mother moved with him to Pensacola, Florida, where he entered the Black Public School, which he attended for two years, when, with her, he came to Mobile, where he found it necessary to begin life for himself. He secured a position as buss boy at the Point Clear Hotel at a salary of $2.50 per week and his board. Here he attracted the attention of Mr. George C. Bennett, who at an increase of wage, employed him as a porter in the club rooms then conducted by him at No. 6 North Royal Street.

The energy and enthusiasm of James attracted the attention of General James E. Slaughter, Post Master of Mobile, who felt that so intelligent a boy should be given a chance, and employed him as a substitute letter carrier. He served in this capacity for eighteen months, when, not receiving the promotion which he felt was him due, to be appointed as a letter carrier, he left the service, and then went to St. Louis, Missouri, and engaged as a Pullman porter over the Iron Mountain Route, which gave him a splendid opportunity for enlarging his knowledge by travel through various parts of Texas and intervening places. In 1892, he returned to Mobile and again served as a letter carrier under Colonel P. D. Barker, who had become postmaster.

Under Postmaster Barker, Mr. Peterson, by dint of hard, earnest, consecrated devotion to duty worked himself into the body of the office, then later to a clerkship, thence to the General Delivery Clerk, then Foreman of the carriers, and lastly to the Superintendent of the Post Office.

Shortly after his appointment as a letter carrier,

Mr. Peterson had the good fortune to become acquainted with Hon. Allen Alexander, at that time the most influential Negro politician in Southern Alabama. It was through the efforts of Hon. Alexander that Mr. Peterson was elected as alternate delegate to the National Republican Convention, which met in Minneapolis, Minnesota. Mr. Peterson displayed such rare political ability at the 1896 Convention that in 1900 he was elected a delegate to the National Convention which met in Philadelphia. At this Convention he taught the world to know him by his uncompromising stand for the nomination of Messrs. William McKinley and Theodore Roosevelt for President and Vice-President respectively.

He was elected without opposition to the National Republican Convention, which met in 1904, and was one of the most aggressive of the supporters of Mr. Roosevelt for President. In 1908, he was again elected to the National Convention, which met in Chicago, and was a conspicuous character among those whose efforts resulted in the nomination of Mr. William Howard Taft. His aggressiveness made him such a necessary factor in the National political affairs of the Republican Party that he was constrained to drop out of the post office and serve as a member of the Republican National Executive Council which met in the tower of the Metropolitan Building on the tenth floor.

In 1912 Civil Service Rules inaugurated prevented Mr. Peterson from leaving his positions in the Post Office to attend the National Convention and he nominated Hon. C. W. Allen, who was elected as his choice.

In 1915, he again severed his relations with the Post Office of Mobile and engaged actively in real estate, a business which had always appealed to him because of the many successful transactions which he had made from time to time.

In 1918 he purchased a complete job and newspaper office outfit and organized a company which does a very thriving job printing business and besides, publishes a weekly newspaper, "The Forum," which is the largest Negro Paper in the South.

Mr. Peterson has never been married, but is very fond of children, whom he delights to assist and make happy.

He is very active in all public affairs for the upbuilding of the race, and during the world war he was a member of the Four Minute Organization, a member of the Advisory Committee to the Draft Board, and is now an active member of the War Camp Community Service Executive Committee. He is a member of the St. Louis St. Baptist Church, P. N. F., of Thompkin Lodge No. 1521 G. U. O. of O. F. P. M., of St. John No. 2 Free & Accepted Masons, is Chairman of the War Council Reconstruction Work Committee of Mobile, President of the Union Mutual Aid Insurance Co., and President of the Forum Publishing Co.

He is said to pay tax on more real estate than any Negro in Southern Alabama, and his wealth is variously estimated at from two to three hundred thousand dollars.

Edward Thomas Belsaw, D. S.

DR. Belsaw is the son of Rev. J. T. and Mary Chambers Belsaw. His father was an African Methodist Episcopal minister, which caused Belsaw to live in a number of different localities. He was born in Madison, Georgia and when eight years of age he had the misfortune to lose his mother. His father being engaged in his ministerial duties, Edward was to a large extent left to shift for himself. His school life and working hours became so correlated that he was soon enabled to support himself. He was educated in the Public Schools of Atlanta, Georgia, and after his course there he entered Dickerson Institute, however, he did not enter Dickerson Institute immediately, but during the interval he was not idle with his books. He studied under many private tutors, notably among them being Professor G. E. Masterson, of Morris Brown College, who trained him for quite a while in Higher Mathematics and Languages. He also took a course in dentistry in the Meharry Dental College where he applied himself with such diligence as to win distinction among his fellow students and paved the way to the honors bestowed upon by the dental organizations after he established himself in business.

Instead of spending his vacation in rest and the pursuit of recreational diversions, as so many of his companions were privileged to do, he had to center his mind and his time in making provision for the next session, so his vacations instead of being given over to pleasure, were spent in various occupations to earn the money to pay his way through school. In the accomplishment of this end he did not confine himself to any one line of work. Like many successful Negroes who have worked their way to distinction and left their mark upon the world, he served a time in the Pullman Car Service, working in the Dining Car Department. Here he was uniformly courteous and attentive to the passengers and made many friends.

Then he spent a time in the school room and stood at the school master's desk and taught in the State of Georgia; and then he entered the arena of business and hung out his shingle as a Real Estate dealer in the city of Birmingham.

During all this time he kept his mind centered upon the career he had decided upon and let all of these occupations contribute a mite to the desired end.

In 1908 he went to Mobile, Alabama, and opened an office in that city for the practice of dentistry and is now there, where he has built up a good and lucrative business.

As an evidence of his prosperity he has purchased a home in Mobile, and is the owner of other property. On the 25th of August, 1901, he was married to Miss Marie V. Lowell.

He is a member of the State Street African Methodist Episcopal Zion Church, Mobile, Ala.

Dr. Belsaw is a man of social instincts and likes to mingle with his fellow men. He is a member of many benevolent societies and social organizations, both local and national in character, membership, in which he takes an active interest. He is a Mason and is now Past Master of that order. He is also a Past Chancellor of the Knights of Pythias, and a prominent member of the Mosiac Templars. Dr. Belsaw has held many honorary positions, among which might be mentioned, that he was a member of the Republican National Convention, in 1916; President of the Alabama Medical, Dental and Pharmaceutical Association in 1915; Executive Secretary National Medical Association since 1912; Member Inter-State Dental Association; Member Missouri Pan-Medical Association; member United States Navy League; and a member of the National Geographic Society.

Dr. Belsaw has traveled extensively, both in this country and in foreign lands, which has enlarged his vision of human family and has added to his equipment for service.

Dr. Belsaw has held the honorary positions mentioned above, not through favor, but because of his personal ability and character, which is generally recognized and appreciated. He is loyal to his party and friends and conscientious in the performance of duty. He has the interest of his people at heart and never tires in working for their betterment. The same honest and capable service rendered in his dental parlor, which has won him such large patronage, is shown in his relation to the different orders and associations of which he is a member and which makes him so popular among his fellows. He is a man of good physique and pleasing address and with a dignity of bearing which commands respect, while at the same time he has a cordiality of manner which makes it easy to approach him.

He is a man who makes friends and having made them holds them. The man is fortunate who possesses this gift. It is a gift which many covet but few possess.

Walter Thomas Woods

IT often happens that a man's talent as a financier is brought to light through other agencies than through the marts of trade. It was so with Walter Thomas Wood. He came into light as a financial genius by reason of his connections, in the main, with a number of fraternal organizations. Mr. Wood was born in Mobile, Alabama, February 14, 1872, which city is still his place of residence. He was educated in the public schools of Mobile, but his way to learning was marked with many hardships and intense labor.

At the age of twelve he was forced to give up school and go to work, and during the period that he attended school his morning and afternoon hours, before the opening and closing exercises, he devoted to manual labor.

In May, 1908, he was married to Miss Louise Harney, a teacher in the public school. From this union was born two sons and a daughter: W. T. Woods, Jr., James Harney Wood, and Claribelle Emma Woods.

He is a member of the African Methodist Episcopal Church, of Mobile.

We now come to consider the distinguishing feature of his career, which, as has been suggested, grew out of his connection with fraternal organizations, especially that of the Masonic order. In 1892, when he was twenty years old, he became a Mason. His first official position in the lodge was that of Senior Deacon.

In 1894, he was admitted to the St. John Lodge No. 2, in which he was soon elected Senior Warden, an office he held for one year and was then elected to the office of Worshipful Master—which position he filled for seven years.

He declined to serve longer in this office for the reason that the law of the Grand Lodge would not permit him to continue as Worshipful Master and at the same time hold an office in the Grand Lodge. When he was first elected Worshipful Master of the lodge the lodge did not have a penny in the treasury and was in debt. Under his wise and skillful administration of seven years service, when he voluntarily surrendered the gavel, the lodge was free of debt and had to its credit in bank one thousand dollars. In addition to this the membership of the lodge had been increased by twenty members. In token of its appreciation of his valuable services the lodge presented him with a beautiful Masonic apron.

In 1905, at Selma, Alabama, he was elected Grand Junior Warden of the Grand Lodge and was re-elected to the same position in 1906.

In 1907, he was elected Grand Senior Warden, and was continuously re-elected to this office until the Lodge met at Tuskegee Institute in 1911, when he was chosen Deputy Grand Master.

When the Mobile Masons decided to erect a temple, a building committee was formed consisting of one member from each lodge. Mr. Wood represented his lodge upon this committee. Under the guidance of this committee the temple was built at a cost of $24,000.

In 1916 he was elected a delegate to the International Conference of Grand Masters which met in Chicago. He was elected First Vice-President of the Conference, a position he still holds.

When he was elected Grand Master of the Grand Lodge of Alabama Masons, the lodge was one hundred thousand dollars in debt, which debt he has removed. He wears with a great deal of pleasure and pride a beautiful 32nd degree watch charm presented to him by St. Johns Lodge upon his election as Grand Master. Mr. Wood is also a member of the Odd Fellows. For four years he was Deputy Grand Master of the Odd Fellows. He represented this lodge at the eleventh B. M. C., 1904, at Columbus, Ohio; at the twelfth B. M. C., Richmond, Va., in 1906; and at the thirteenth B. M. C., 1908 at Atlantic City, New Jersey.

While the fraternal orders no doubt awakened his financial and executive ability his services in this line did not end with them.

From 1899 to 1906 he served as President of Protector Fire Company No. 11. When he took charge of the company it was in debt but under his management the debt has been paid, their hall remodeled, the sidewalk paved; with a balance in the treasury of $2400.

When he resigned the company presented him with a beautiful watch and chain, valued at $150, in recognition of his services and as a mark of high appreciation.

In 1898 he stood and passed the Civil service examination and was appointed a mail carrier in the Mobile Post Office, a position he still holds. Mr. Wood takes deep interest in matters looking to the improvement and development of the colored race and encourages his people in their efforts to establish business enterprises.

He is a stockholder and director of Mobile's only shoe store owned and operated by Negroes, and Chairman of Board of Directors of Mobile Forum, a colored newspaper.

H. Roger Williams, M. D.

IN the balmy, gulf-cooled atmosphere where flows the "Bayou La Teche," made famous by Longfellow in his "Evangeline," just as the sugar-laden stalks of cane were ripening into liquid sweetness, and the multitudinous crops from the fertile soil of Southern Louisiana were being gathered, on the fourth day of September, 1869, was born, in a dirt-floored two roomed plantation cabin, Henry Roger Williams, whose name was destined to be a household word and whose life was to be inspiration for multitudes of struggling Negro children.

His babyhood was not unlike that of thousands of other plantation Negro children. He was the eighth of the thirteen children born to his parents, both of whom were sold into Louisiana as slaves—his father from Tennessee and his mother from Virginia. In 1876 his parents moved to Baldwin, five miles West of their home, and invested their savings in a ten acre farm. Here the children were sent to a school taught by Northern White teachers, who had come South as missionaries to the Negroes.

In 1880, Henry, with thirteen other children of the school were taken North as a band of singers, in the interest of the institution, by Dr. W. D. Godman and his family. Their tour through the New England States was so successful, and the impression they made was so favorable, that Mr. W. L. Gilbert, of Winsted, Connecticut gave to the school his check for $10,000, in honor of which the name of the institution was changed to Gilbert Academy.

In the spring of 1881 these same children were taken North and placed in homes of culture and refinement to test the value of environment in their development. Henry had the good fortune to be placed in the home of the Godman family in Michigan, and attended the public schools at Dexter and Lansing.

In the summer of 1885, he was sent by the Godman's to Connecticut and finished a course in printing at New Haven. In 1888 he was called to his home town and taught his trade in the same institution which he, by his vocal talent had helped to create. While teaching, he continued his studies preparing for college.

In 1890, his mother died, and he resigned his position at Baldwin, and entered the Walden University (then known as Central Tennessee College,) Nashville, Tenn. While here he pursued the study of sacred theology in connection with his college work.

In 1897 he entered the Meharry Medical Department of the same school and graduated a Doctor of Medicine with the class of 1900.

His travels in connection with entertainment troupes during the summer enabled him to visit practically every city of note in the United States.

After graduating at Meharry he went to Mobile and opened an office in the year 1900. In September of the same year he married Miss Fannie Brandon, of Huntsville, Alabama, a graduate of the A. & M. College there, and who at the time was a teacher in the public school of her home town. They have two children, Hirschell and Ariel, whom they look upon as jewels beyond the value of money. They inherit their father's musical talent. Hirschell is a master of the violin and Ariel is a pianist of considerable gifts.

In connection with his practice as a physician, Dr. Williams owns a large, well stocked drug store. His drug store is located on one of Mobile's principle thoroughfares and his home is situated across the street from it.

He has a large, growing practice and has made a success of his drug business. He takes great pride in his library which is worth exceeding $2,000. His library is not for show but is a collection of rare volumes which afford him great delight and recreation. He also possesses property in value about $20,000. Dr. Williams is a clear thinker, a forceful speaker, a sound advisor and a thoughtful and talented writer. His best known published works are "The Blighted Life of Methuselah," "Isaac and His Two Sons of Different Nationalities," "Fifty Years of Freedom," and "The American Negro."

He is an active member of the Warren St. M. E. Church, for which he secured an organ by setting aside $300 a year from his income. He represented the Alabama Churches as a lay delegate to the General Conference which met in Los Angeles, California. He is a Mason and member of Knights of Pythias.

Seventeen times his local church recommended him for deacon's order, but he declined the honor, preferring to work in the humble sphere of a layman.

He is President of the Mobile Medical Society, President of the Mobile Negro Business League, General Chairman of the Mobile Emancipation Association, and Chairman of the Executive Committee of the War Camp Community Service. He was regarded as one of the most active Negroes taking a conspicious part in all the various drives, and was the organizer of the Red Cross Society among the Colored women of the city.

He was a member of the Advisory Committee of the draft Board and chairman of the Four Minute Men.

Thomas H. Hayes

M R. Hayes was born in the suburbs of Richmond, Virginia, Aug. 15th, 1868. When only three years old, his parents moved to the western part of Tennessee and located on a plantation near LaGrange. Like so many other great men, he spent his childhood days on the farm. He continued on the farm until he was sixteen years of age, but as he thirsted for knowledge and there was no means of obtaining it where he was, he moved to Memphis, Tenn. Like so many country boys, Mr. Hayes thought that all he had to do to acquire knowledge was to move to the city. His first position was with the Millburn Iron Works Co. Here he saved a bit of money and returned to the farm but only for a short while. On his return to Memphis, he worked as a porter on Front Street for ten years. His first business venture was a grocery on Gholston Street, which proved a failure. He next opened a grocery on Beal Ave. which also failed. His third attempt was on South Second Street and went the way of its predecessors.

Believing he had as much native ability as any of the men who were succeeding where he failed, Mr. Hayes began to hunt for cause of his lack of success. He was convinced a lack of education was one reason, and entered Howe University, where he was assigned to the lowest classes. From the beginning his success was remarkable, and he was promoted so rapidly that he reached the eighth grade in two years. In order to complete his education, Mr. Hayes bought an outfit and opened a barber shop, although he had never worked as a barber. This shop was located on Poplar Street and was a success from the first. There is something inspiring in the superb confidence, of this comparatively uneducated boy in his ability to succeed in business for himself. Failure served only to strengthen his determination. On leaving school he sold clocks and Bibles for the Red Star Supply Company, of Memphis, Tenn. While on the road for this firm, Mr. Hayes developed his ability as a salesman until he felt competent to succeed in the business that had previously proved his "Jonah." He organized the Central Grocery Company, which soon not only swept away his savings, but left him heavily in debt. Thoroughly honorable, his next step was the liquidation of this indebtedness, which

he accomplished by returning to hard work on Front Street. As soon as he was free from debt, Mr. Hayes started his fifth grocery. However, he this time had gained the knowledge he heretofore lacked, that is, if you want a thing well done, do it yourself.

He started this venture on a capital of thirty-five dollars, but with a line of credit that enabled him to stock his store, Mr. Hayes successfully conducted this store, until by a mere accident, he entered the undertaking business. On account of the death of a local undertaker, leaving a vacancy in that field, and knowing Mr. Hayes had a large barn that could be quickly utilized, a friend persuaded him to form a partnership, which was the real foundation on which Mr. Hayes fortune has been built. He was at that time as ignorant of the undertaking business, as he was of the grocery business when he started his first store, but he was now thoroughly aware of the value of knowledge of ones business and immediately began to study his new venture. Today, Mr. Hayes is one of the best posted undertakers in the business. Beginning in 1902, with a capital of $1400.00, his undertaking company is pronounced today by impartial commercial travellers as one of the most substantial and best equipped plants in the country. It has a commodious chapel, and the morgue, embalming rooms, stables and garages are modern in every detail.

From 1902, Mr. Hayes' financial success has been nothing short of marvelous. He is today a stockholder of the Mississippi Beneficial Life Insurance Co., and officer and heavy stockholder in the Solvent Savings Bank & Trust Co., of Memphis, Tenn., and a stockholder in the Standard Life Insurance Co., of Atlanta, Ga.

In addition to his handsome residence he has valuable rental property all over the city and suburbs. Mr. Hayes is an active member of all leading colored fraternities represented in his home town, and a substantial and consistent member of St. Johns Baptist Church. He was married to Miss Florence Taylor, of Covington, Tenn., March 31, 1898, and several children have blessed this union. Mrs. Hayes has proven a wise counsellor for her husband in his business undertakings, whose advice receives careful consideration.

Willie Lee Hamblin, D. D.

REV. Hamblin, born near Camden in Madison County, Miss., May 19th, 1878. He received his first educational training from Liberty Chapel Public School to which he was sent until ten years of age. He is said to have shown marked ability as a scholar from the time he entered school, and was considered an infant prodigy. His teachers were compelled to advance him time and again, in the middle of school periods, beause he would master his lessons so far ahead of his classes. His parents moved to Canton, Miss., and he entered Lincoln High School. Mr. Hamblin proved such an apt pupil he was appointed an assistant teacher four months before he graduated. It is the good fortune of some men to succeed in everything they undertake. Nature seems to have given them a greater scope of vision and foresight than she has bestowed on the generality of men, and this in a great measure accounts for their uniform success. After all, the ability to succeed lies in a mans character. Real success comes from within the individual, and must be attained by the individual himself. The life story of Dr. Hamblin is the story of a successful man and one who is proud to be identified with the Negro race. It is the story of a man whose success is not the result of a patrimony or of any other external cause, but of his own strong mind and indomitable energy of action.

Dr. Hamblin entered the ministry in 1895, when he was licensed to preach by Bishop J. B. Small, at Durant. Bishop Small passed on twelve applicants at this time, and stated that Dr. Hamblin stood by far the best examination of them all. At this time he was still nothing but a boy. He was ordained an elder at Meridian, Miss., about 1898, just as he was rounding out his majority. Dr. Hamblin's first charge was at Harpersville, in Scott County, Miss. From there he moved to Kosciusko, Miss., where he was principal and teacher of Theology in Hazley Institute, a graded school. He was transferred from the South Mississippi to the West Alabama Conference and sent to Citronelle, Ala. At that time, it was a thriving winter resort for Northern people, with plenty of life and wealth. When Dr. Hamblin arrived there were many who wanted to know why the powers that be, had sent a "kid" to pastor a charge where he had to meet the critical approval of a highly educated and intelligent class of Northerners, who were not only frequent attendants and supporters of this church, but exerted a strong influence over its members.

On his first Sunday the church was crowded, many coming out of curiosity to see what that "kid" would have to say. It can be said to his everlasting credit that the "kid" met this trying ordeal in a manner that won the friendship and approval of the most skeptical. From Citronelle, Dr. Hamblin was sent to Meridian, where he pastored two years. But Alabama was not to be denied, and he was called to Clinton Chapel, of Selma, Ala., where he remained three years. After his Selma charge, Dr. Hamblin pastored Hunter's Chapel of Tuscaloosa, Ala., for three and a half years. From this place he was moved to the Historical Old Ship Church of Montgomery, Ala., where he was kept until made a Presiding Elder five years later. In the interval between charges, he completed a course in Livingston College, where he graduated with honors in 1909. In about 1917, Dr. Hamblin was made presiding elder of the Mobile District, under Bishop Caldwell, which important position he now holds.

During the World War, Dr. Hamblin used every ounce of his intellect and ability as an orator, in guiding his people in the path that would immortalize them in the years to come.

Dr. Hamblin married Miss Minnie M. Bennett, June 28th, 1899. This estimable couple have three girls, all of whom inherit their parents brilliant intellect to a marked degree. Dr. Hamblin is giving these talented young ladies every educational advantage possible. Gladys, although only 19 is a graduate of and has finished the sewing, nursing, and Literary courses at State Normal, of Montgomery, Ala. The other two, Fostina and Bernice, aged 16 and 11, respectively are still students: one at State Normal and the other in the graded schools. During the world war, Dr. Hamblin wielded the influence and power his position gave him, in a manner that aided in no small way, his county and his people.

It is, no doubt, only a question of time as to when the Bishop's mantle will be bestowed on this Eminent Divine and Christian Citizen.

480

E. W. D. Isaac, D. D.

THE subject of this sketch is highly endowed with the three talents most essential in a man of his calling. Fortunate indeed is the possessor of a combination such as Dr. Isaac is endowed with. His gift of making friends and holding them, enables him to fill the churches when he occupies the pulpit. His gift of explaining the teachings of Christ, enables him to use his gift of oratory in a manner that is at once instructive and inspiring to his hearers. His gift of music enables him to build choirs that are glorious. Not only a wonderful speaker, he is doubly gifted in being able to write as well as he speaks and thereby thousands are reached that would never have the opportunity to hear him.

Dr. Isaac has been for ten years corresponding Secretary of the National Baptist Young People's Union Board of the National Baptist Convention, and editor of the National Baptist Union, the organ of the denomination.

He was born in Marshall, Texas, January 2, 1863. His early home was fifteen miles from the county seat on the banks of the Sabine River, where his father, a pioneer Baptist preacher, lived and was permitted to conduct religious services among his people, enjoying the privilege of a gospel minister, during the days of slavery.

He first attended school at Marshall Academy, and then went to Wiley University, a Methodist school at Marshall, and Bishop College, one of the schools of the American Baptist Home Mission Society. After his graduation from Bishop College, he served as Missionary of the Louisiana and Texas Associations, and was then called to the pastorate of the First Baptist Church, Tyler, Texas, where he served six years in one of the largest and most progressive Baptist Churches in Western Texas. During his residence at Tyler, he taught music in the public schools and served as a member of the Board of Commissioners for the colored teachers in Smith County.

At the close of his Sunday-School pastorate, he was elected State Sunday-School Missionary and served the Texas Baptist State Sunday-School Association in co-operation with the American Baptist Publication Society for several years.

He served ten years as pastor of the New Hope Baptist Church, Dallas, Texas, the largest Negro church in the State. During his pastorate the membership was increased from 900 to 2,000. The first pipe organ that was installed in a Negro church in Texas, was put in the New Hope Church. He served three years in the Missionary and Educational Convention of Texas, as editor of the denominational paper, the Baptist Star. For the past ten years, he has been connected with the successful work of the Young People's Union Board of the National Baptist Convention.

So much for the record of Dr. Isaac. He was doubly fortunate in having a Christian father and mother and in being born near such a noted seat of learning as Marshall, Texas. Something in the atmosphere of the Grand old State of Texas seems to imbue her native sons with the fighting spirit so necessary to the success of leaders in any line in these days of turmoil and strife. Like M. M. Rogers, of Dallas, Texas, Emmett J. Scott, of Tuskegee Institute, Ben J. Davis, of Atlanta, Ga., and other noted Texans by birth, Dr. Isaac is always selected as a leader of any movement he becomes identified with. Like them in another respect, he never confines his sphere of action to local issues. During all his pastorates, he was continually working and planning for the success of the National Baptist Convention. His election as corresponding secretary of the National Baptist Young People's Union Board and editor of the Baptist Union gave him the opportunity he had so long desired, and his ability as a writer of national reputation was soon established. Dr. Isaac played a prominent part in helping his country support "the men behind the guns." And his influence and advice set a splendid example for his people in the trying times of German Propaganda.

Personally, Dr. Isaac is one of the most magnetic men in public life. Wielding a virile pen, he is no less a forceful speaker and talented musician. He is a powerful and uncompromising fighter for any cause that he believes is right and just, yet he is always ready and willing to lend a sympathetic ear to any one in trouble and distress. The State of Tennessee is fortunate in the acquisition of this gifted son of Texas.

NATHAN W. COLLIER, A. B., A. M., Litt. D.

ATHAN W. Collier, A. B. A. M., Litt. D., is a native of Augusta, Georgia, and came from one of the best known and most highly esteemed families of that city. In his early boyhood days and through most of his public school career he worked under his father who followed the brick mason's trade. Under the direction of his father he became quite proficient as a brick mason. He did not choose, however, to follow this trade for his inclinations led in other directions.

After graduating at Ware High School, a public institution of his native city, he became an apprentice at the Georgia Baptist Printing Office, one of the oldest and most reliable printing establishments among colored people in the South. He applied himself diligently to his new trade and developed into a first class printer.

In 1890, Mr. Collier entered the Atlanta University, Atlanta, Georgia, and remained in that institution until he had completed his college course, and graduated with high honor. He received the degree of A. B., in the class of 1894. Mr. Collier, while at the University, became noted as an orator and as a scholar. On two occasions he won the Boston Quizz Club prize for oratory and stood among the best in his class for scholarship.

In 1894 he was called to Florida as assistant principal of the Florida Baptist Academy at Jacksonville. In 1896, he was unanimously elected President of the same Institution, which position he has held for twenty-four consecutive years, and is now its President, honored and beloved by thousands of young people whose lives he has touched, and who are now settled all over this country.

Mr. Collier has traveled extensively over this country and Canada, speaking before large audiences, presenting his work and pressing the claims and interests of his people. In Florida, where he has done most of his life's work in building up one of the leading secondary schools in this Southland and from which many of the leading men of Florida have gone forth into larger institutions, the business world, and the professions Mr. Collier's name is a household word. He is known everywhere as a polished Christian gentleman. He numbers his friends by the hundreds among both races.

One of the most notable addresses delivered by Mr. Collier, was the one before the World's International Sunday School Convention held in Atlanta, some years ago. He sat on the platform with Governor Chandler of the State of Georgia, and representatives from this country, Canada, England and other foreign countries. He represented the colored people of America. Of this address, Mr. W. S. Witham, a millionaire representative of the International Association, said, "Your speech is the best I have ever heard in my life and I have heard thousands."

Mr. Collier received the degree of Doctor of Literature from Selma University, Selma, Alabama, in May, 1916.

June 5, 1918, one of the greatest audiences ever assembled in Jacksonville was to present an Honor Flag to the colored citizens of that city in recognition of the splendid work they had done in the sale of Third Liberty Loan Bonds, raising the magnificent sum of $298,000. The hall was packed with both white and colored citizens, and it fell to the honor of this scholarly man, Nathan W. Collier, to make the speech of acceptance. This is the first

honor flag ever presented to the Negro race in the United States.

Mr. Collier feels that he can best serve his race by helping the youth of his people to acquire an education and does not consider an education complete that does not deal with the moral and spiritual, and so he is devoting his life through the institution over which he presides in educating the whole man. That he is succeeding in his undertaking is attested by the noble band of young men and women that are going out from this school to fill places of trust and usefulness.

Not alone does his denomination serve and honor him but he is held in high esteem by all members of the Negro race and maintains the respect and confidence of the white race.

FLORIDA BAPTIST ACADEMY

The Florida Baptist Academy was founded in 1892, by the Florida Negro Baptist Convention. It is owned and controlled by a Board of nine trustees, of whom four are white. The American Baptist Home Mission Society gives it aid and supervision. It is a secondary school with large elementary enrollment. Training in gardening and simple industrial work is provided. The management is very effective. It has a large enrollment of between four and five hundred students, who come from a number of states other than Florida. The teaching force, numbering eighteen, is all colored; four are male and fourteen female. The elementary work is done in eight grades by five regular teachers. Two of the academy teachers give part time to the grades. The Secondary work

outlined in the catalogue is divided into "college preparatory" and "normal" courses. In practice the majority of the pupils combine the essential studies of the two courses.

Manual training in wood and iron is provided for boys; cooking, sewing, dressmaking, millinery, and house cleaning for girls. The Industrial teachers are well trained.

While the Institution had a splendid plant at Jacksonville, valued at $75,000, it was thought best for the school to change its location. October 1, 1918, this was done, when the institution found a new home at St. Augustine, Florida. Here it has acquired a thousand acres of land and has started on a new career, with promise of becoming one of the greatest schools for colored people in all the Southland.

The encouragement and support received by the school and the hearty endorsement given the trustees in their efforts to build a bigger and better school were so spontaneous and unanimous that a drive is now being conducted for funds with which to complete the plant on a scale that will be in keeping with the high type of institutions for which the state of Florida is noted; the splendid faculty has been secured, and the many students who have expressed a desire to enroll for a course in this noted seat of learning.

The success of Dr. Collier at the start, gives promise of putting "Florida Baptist" over the top in a manner that will be a splendid Institute to all concerned.

PARTIAL VIEW OF THE NEW HOME OF FLORIDA BAPTIST ACADEMY

J. R. E. Lee

PROBABLY no Negro in America, certainly in modern times, has been flattered with as many offers for presidencies of schools as has J. R. E. Lee. These offers have come as the result not of wire-pulling or because Professor Lee has in any way gone aside to make special friends, rather they have come because for nearly a half century Professor Lee has made himself indispensable, as nearly so as the average man does in the whole field of education.

Born, reared and educated in Texas, Mr. Lee was fortunate enough to fall heir to the training given by the early graduates of the Mission schools, that is, graduates of Fisk and other such Institutions. Inspired by the personality as well as the teaching of the Missionaries from the North who went into the South to teach these graduates carried with them not merely a good store of book learning, but the zeal for service. It is to these that J. R. E. Lee owes much of his zeal for school work and for social work.

Graduating from Bishop College, Marshall, Texas, Mr. Lee spent several years teaching in his native state. From Texas he went over into the south, taking the professorship of mathematics at Tuskegee Insttiute.

Literally by dint of hard work Mr. Lee outgrew the position as the head of the division of mathematics at Tuskegee Institute. From Tuskegee Institute he went to Benedict College, South Carolina. From Benedict he went to Corona, Ala. In both of these he was the booster of education in all its forms as he afterwards became nationally. From Corona Professor Lee was recalled to Tuskegee Institute to become head of the Academic Department of that Institution. It was during his half score or more years here, that Mr. Lee rendered yeoman service not only to Tuskegee Institute as an educator but to the whole South. In the Institution Professor Lee developed to its highest pitch the Tuskegee Educational Scheme of Correlation; that is, the teachers under him so managed their Geography, English and Mathematics as to give them a particular naming in every-day life. The mathematics for example dealt with actual measurements and weights; the English, with the daily occurrences both local and national.

While pushing this scheme at Tuskegee Mr. Lee at various intervals travelled over the whole south boosting the cause of education. He was instrumental if not pioneer in establishing and putting on its feet the State Teachers Association of Alabama. He was organizer and promoter of the National Association for Teachers in colored schools. He was chief organizer and booster under Dr. Washington for the National Negro Business Mens' League. Of the first two bodies he was president and secretary for a number of years. As president of the National Association, he travelled from state to state even paying his own expenses, to inspire various state organizations to fall in line with the National Organizations. In the same way he assumed the personal responsibility for publishing minutes and various kinds of data for both the State Teachers Association, and the National Body. He corresponded at his own expense and at the expense of Tuskegee Institute with all the leading teachers of the country to get them in line with the current thoughts in education. It will be a long time before the South appreciates fully the service rendered to education by J. R. E. Lee.

From Tuskegee Institute Professor Lee went to Kansas City, Mo., where he became principal of the Lincoln High School. It is difficult at this time of writing to determine whether Professor Lee has excelled the more by putting the school on a higher educational plane, or at social service work in Kansas City. In the latter he has organized Mothers' Clubs, hospital clubs, savings clubs, indeed an almost innumerable list of social service bodies to promote better living in the City. At the same time he is a big Church worker in Kansas City, and is very active on the hospital board of the Phyllis Wheatley Hospital. Though Mr. Lee has left the South, the States and schools have not forgotten him. Each summer during his vacation time he has been called back to work either for the schools, or for the summer schools in the states. One summer the state of Arkansas engaged him to intruct its teachers in public schools. Another summer the State of Louisiana engaged his services; a third, he was called back to Alabama to lecture at Tuskegee Institute, at Miles Memorial College and at Normal, Ala.

With all the experience coming from contact and from service Professor Lee has nevertheless kept the student's mind. Travelling here and there and working endlessly he has nevertheless found time to go to school. He has attended Summer school at Chicago University, at the University of Michigan, and at other places even after making his trips south and lecturing and teaching for the various states and Institutions.

Professor Lee has reared and educated a large family. He had four sons enlisted in the recent war. His eldest son, Edwin, is a practicing physician in Kansas City, having graduated from Tuskegee Institute, from Columbia University, where he was an honor man, and from the Medical College of Howard University. The second oldest son, George, was graduated from Tuskegee Institute and from the School of Pharmacy at Howard University. Robert E. is a student at Virginia Union University in Richmond, Va. Maurice is a student in Morehouse College, Atlanta, Ga. Ralph, the youngest son, is in public school in Kansas City, Mo. There are also two daughters, Mrs. Birdie Lee Jones and Miss Beatrice Lee. Mrs. Birdie Lee Jones is at Tuskegee Institute and Miss Beatrice is a teacher of music at Lincoln Institute. Both were graduates of Tuskegee and Spellman.

Professor Lee was recently offered the presidency of the State School in WestVirginia and was also offered the post to go to France to do educational work there. Both of these he declined, preferring to develop the many schemes he has set afoot in Kansas City.

LANE COLLEGE—JACKSON, TENNESSEE

T Lane College the literary and religious ideas of education are emphasized and harmoniously blended. Founded in 1882 by the Colored Methodist Church, it was the first to be made a connectional school of that denomination and is one of the most representative of its denomination in enterprise.

Bishop Isaac Lane, in whose honor the institution is named, at one time a slave, was denied the advantages of education. Largely through his own efforts he learned to read and write and acquired a good education that placed him in the front ranks among his brothers. After his election as bishop he was impressed with the idea of establishing an institution for the training of the youth of his race. His untiring efforts, splendid leadership, and self-sacrifice brought the results within a few years that stand to his credit today,—for it is to him that the institution owes its success and usefulness. The school began in November, 1882, under Miss Jennie E. Lane, who continued it until January. Prof. J. H. Harper finished the unexpired term.

Lane College is located in a railroad and manufacturing town in western Tennessee, where the colored population is greatest and where there is a lack of higher institutions of learning. The college has seven buildings, located on a campus of about seven acres. These serve as administration hall, reading room, chapel, lecture hall, class rooms, laboratories, and teachers' cottage and dormitories. The school owns a farm of about forty-two

acres, about half a mile from the institution. It is well cultivated, well watered, and is a large profit to the college. In addition to the regular college, normal, teacher-training, college, preparatory, normal preparatory, English, and music courses, the theological course of four years is maintained. Better-prepared ministry is one of the great demands today, and Lane College is doing everything possible to prepare the young men for this work, as well as fit others to be more useful in churches, the Sunday-school, the Epworth League, and other departments of religious work.

The college seeks to qualify these students to become leaders in thought. It is strictly religious in its work, and everything else is made subsidiary to this one idea. Graduates of Lane College are to be found in all ranks,—in the ministry, in the school room, as president, principal, and teachers, in the office, and in the other lines of professions and business; on the farm, in the shop, and in stores of their own. As a rule they strive to cultivate peace.

November 4, 1904, fire destroyed the girls' dormitory building and the main hall, a beautiful three-story brick structure. By reason of much self-sacrifice among the people, contributions have been secured, so that the buildings destroyed by fire have been replaced by commodious ones at a cost of about $42,000. One of these and a steam heating plant, was installed at a cost of $7,200. A strong asset of the college is a complete commercial course.

The Negroes have given hundreds of thousands of dollars to this institution.

Robert Elijah Jones A. B., A. M., B. D., LL. D.

 MIDST the commercial, industrial and literary progress of the South, there has also come up a younger crop of men who while while grasping the hand of their sires nevertheless are squinting their eyes into the future. This generation of younger men has retained a great deal of the old sentiment for the South, of the politeness if not the humility of their sires.

At the same time it has not hesitated to go forward in all those ideals which make a finer grade of American citizenship. They have recognized the value of money, the value of religion, the value of education, the value of social contact, the value of a decent environment. Appreciating these in their highest, they have come out and asked for them with a positiveness that almost belies their modesty under more ordinary circumstances.

Robert Elijah Jones, Clergyman and Editor, stands in the vanguard of this generation. With headquarters in New Orleans, La., where men still revel in many of the older theories, Dr. Jones has been outspoken on all the leading questions that bear upon the interest of the Negro.

R. E. Jones was born at Greensboro, North Carolina, on the 19th of February, 1872. He is the son of Sidney Dallas and Mary Holly Jones. North Carolina is far from being one of the backward states of the South. Greensboro is one of the more liberal cities of this fairly liberal southern state. Here in Greensboro, Dr. Jones received a good elementary education. Later he attended Bennett College in his native city, receiving the degree of Bachelor of Arts in 1895. Three years later he received from the same institution the degree of Master of Arts. Working and studying in turns Dr. Jones later attended Gammon Theological Seminary where he received the degree of Bachelor of Divinity. Howard University made him L.L.D. in 1911.

Dr. Jones began his career as a local preacher at Leeksburg, N. C., in 1891. He was ordained in the M. E. Ministry in 1892 and was made Elder in 1896. From the Leeksburg ordination, Dr. Jones pastored successfully a number of churches. These were in Lexington, in Thomasville, and in Reidsville of his native state.

Beginning with 1897, Dr. Jones entered upon new fields of religious work. For a time he was assistant manager of the South Western Christian Advocate in New Orleans, La. Later he served as field Secretary, of the Board of Sunday Schools of the M. E. Church. This work he did between the years of 1901-04. In 1904 he was made editor of the South Western Christian Advocate.

For the past 15 years he has edited this now celebrated periodical. This paper's reputation for clean, straight-forward Christianity, is in itself a splendid monument to Dr. Jones.

As editor of the Advocate Dr. Jones has traveled much over the country attending conventions, not only of the church, but of all bodies which mean the development of the Negro race. In the same way he has served in whatever capacity he could to improve the religious and social life of the black man. He has been President of the Negro Y. M. C. A. in New Orleans, Vice-President and Trustee of New Orleans University, Vice President of the Board of Trustees of Bennett College. He is a trustee of Gammon Theological Seminary, and President of the colored Travellers Protection Association. He is first Vice-President of the National Negro Press Association and Chairman of the Executive Committee of the National Negro Business League.

His efforts are not confined to service of this kind or to religious work. He is a platform speaker much in demand. One of his addresses "A Few Remarks on Making Good in Life" is illustrated in the Masterpieces of Negro eloquence.

Dr. Jones was married January 2nd, 1901, to Miss Valena T. MacArthur, of Bay St. Louis, Mississippi. He is the father of a happy family living on Constant St. in New Orleans, Louisiana. There are few men in the church, be the denomination what it may, who do more of the kind of service which usually falls under the head of secular; there are fewer men classed as secular, who throw themselves into the church with the abandon of Robert E. Jones.

The following excerpt from the Southeastern Christian Advocate, shows clearly Dr. Jones' broad mindedness and level headedness:

"There is grave danger in the position that some of our race leaders are taking in charging that the white race as a whole is an enemy to the Negro race, and therefore such race leaders are seeking to array race against race and to meet prejudice with prejudice, hatred with hatred, and bitterness with bitterness. This position is wrong. In the first place, it is wrong as a matter of policy. We will get nowhere in our effort to secure justice and equity if we array ourselves as a race against a race that has superior numbers, intelligence and wealth, and social and political advantage. It would be far better to seek to show the white people themselves and the world the fairness of our appeal.

ARNETT HALL—WILBERFORCE UNIVERSITY—GALLOWAY HALL

HE institution traces its history to 1847, when the Ohio Conference of the African Methodist Episcopal Church opened Union Seminary, twelve miles west of Columbus, Ohio.

The present site of Wilberforce University was purchased in 1856 by the Ohio Conference of the Methodist Episcopal Church.

The conferences of the Methodist Episcopal and the African Methodist Episcopal churches then formed a corporation and appointed a board of trustees for the new institution. Both schools were closed by the war. In 1863 Bishop Payne, of the African Methodist Episcopal Church, purchased the Wilberforce property; the Union Seminary property was sold and the two schools combined. In 1870 an appropriation of $26,000 was made to the institution by the United States Congress and legacies were bequeathed by Chief Justice Chase and the Avery estate.

The institution is managed by a board of trustees elected by the church conference.

In 1889 the Ohio legislature passed a law establishing the "combined Normal and Industrial Department."

This department is practically a separate institution. Payne Theological Seminary was founded in 1891 with a separate board of directors.

The pupils of the preparatory and collegiate department of the university are not required to take industrial courses in the "C. N. and I." department, and those electing such courses receive no credit for these electives toward graduation in the university proper. Classes in elementary subjects are provided for the few pupils not prepared for secondary classes.

The secondary course covers four years. The following subjects are taken by all: English, Latin, Elementary Sciences, Mathematics, Chemistry and Physics. The college subjects are Mathematics, English, Latin, Greek, German, French, Spanish, Biology, Chemistry, Physics, History and Philosophy.

The languages and mathematics receive greater emphasis than the other courses.

While the theological seminary has a separate board of directors, it is supported by the African Methodist Episcopal Church and its management is closely related to that of the university. It offers two three-year courses in theological subjects.

Its sources of income are from Church conferences, tuition and fees, state appropriations, general donations and from other sources.

Wilberforce University stands for the united education of head, heart and hand, and is located to do this work to a decided advantage. It is contiguous to a territory of three states, each having a large Negro population. It draws from these and the entire belt of southern states, together with the immediate large Negro belt in Ohio. It presents to its patrons an exceptional race environment, where high ideals and practices obtain, where race social life is on a high plane, where evil surroundings are few, where country air and influences do their healthful work, where race friction is quite unknown, where is found on every hand for youth the greatest possible inspiration to right living, right thinking, industry, sobriety, and success in life.

It has illustrated to the world what the race can do for itself. For over fifty years the work has continued and President Scarborough is now reaching out in a broad endeavor to expand its usefulness.

With its continuous growth, its needs have kept pace, so to-day the school faces pressing necessities. It needs $100,000 added to its small endowment. It cannot accommodate the numbers applying for admission, and more room must be provided.

Wilberforce University is doing a noble work for both sexes. The number of students who have received instruction in this institution go into the thousands, and some of the ablest preachers in the denomination are proud of Wilberforce as their Alma Mater.

487

MISS EVA D. BOWLES

ISS Bowles' record as a war secretary for the Young Women's
Christian Association not only in
the selection of well trained
women to take charge of hostess
houses that were provided at various camps and cantonments,
but in keeping alive the fires of
patriotism among the colored women of the country, entitles her to rank with the greatest war heroes the country produced. Working day and
night, going from place to place, lecturing and
otherwise working for the betterment of social
conditions in army camps, she brought order out of
chaos, and set a standard of patriotic effort that
hardly has a parallel in the history of colored
women.

Miss Bowles brought to the place an experience
gained by many years work in associated charities
and Y. W. C. A.s' and this experience was gladly
welcomed by a board that had offers of service
from many volunteers but very few of them were
experienced workers. Miss Bowles is a native of
Columbus, Ohio, where for four years she was district visitor of associated charities. Her early education was obtained from the public schools of Columbus. After finishing high school, she entered
and completed the literary course in Ohio State
University. After graduating, Miss Bowles taught
for ten years in the schools of the South. She is

a member of St. Philips Episcopal Church, Columbus, Ohio, and an ardent church worker. It was
her love of religious life that led her to become affiliated with the active work of the Colored Young
Women's Christian Association. Her ability as an
organizer and lecturer is so marked that she was
appointed to the position of General Secretary,
Colored Women's Branch, Young Women's Christian Association of New York City and Executive
Secretary of Colored Work in cities, under National Board of Y. W. C. A. When war was declared she was proffered the position of Executive
Secretary for colored work, under the War Work
Council of the National Board of the Young Wom-
en's Christian Association. It was in the last named place that she became nationally famous. Miss
Bowles is a profound scholar of human nature, a
tireless worker and magnetic speaker.

Since her election to the Young Women's Christian Association Secretaryship in 1913, there has
been a steady increase in the number of city associations, and they are rapidly being affiliated with
the National organization. Miss Bowles has the
happy faculty of gaining and holding the best
wishes of the white people as easily as she does the
colored. She has long since realized the benefits
which always accrue by cultivating the good will
and friendship of all that she comes in contact with,
irrespective of race or creed, with the result that
she is in position to be and is of inestimable service to her people.

Miss Bowles had associated with her in the War
Work Council as heads of departments a splendid
galaxy of patriotic workers. The heads of the departments assisting her were Miss Mary E. Jackson, Special Industrial Worker among the Colored
Women for the War Work Council; Miss Crystal
Bird, Girls' Worker; Mrs. Vivian W. Stokes, who
at one time was associated with the National Urban League and assisted in making a survey of
New York City in connection with the Urban
League of New York; Mrs. Lucy B. Richmond,
special worker for town and country; Miss Mabel
S. Brady, recruiting secretary in the Personnel Bureau; Miss Juliette Dericotte, special student
worker; Mrs. Cordelia A. Winn, formerly a teacher in the public schools of Columbus, Ohio; Mrs.
Ethel J. Kindle, special office worker. Miss Josephine V. Pinyon was appointed a special war worker in August, 1917. She is a graduate of Cornell
University, a former teacher, and a student Y. W.
C. A. Secretary from 1912 to 1916. She is a tireless worker and her services were invaluable.

The field workers were Mrs. Adele Ruffin, South
Atlantic Field, appointed in October, 1917. Mrs.
Ruffin was a teacher for some years at Kittrell
College, and then secretary of the Y. W. C. A.
branch at Richmond, Virginia. Miss May Belcher
had charge of the South Central field and Miss
Maria L. Wielder of the Southwestern field. Miss
Elizabeth Carter was loaned to the Association
work by the Board of Education of New Bedford,
Massachusetts, where she is the only colored
teacher in the city. She is chairman of the Northeastern Federation of Colored Women's Clubs, and
former President of the National Association of
Colored Women's Clubs. She was placed in charge
of the center in Washington, D. C.

Mrs. Alice Dunbar Nelson

T is not often that famous men wed famous wives; that is, women who are able to maintain a social and intellectual position in the world without the borrowed light of their husbands. Among the few who have been able to do this is Mrs. Alice Dunbar Nelson.

Mrs. Nelson was formerly Mrs. Paul Laurence Dunbar. However, long before she met the poet, she had a popularity and a standing all her own, having achieved an enviable record in her school life and made for herself a more enviable career afterwards as school teacher, writer and social worker.

Mrs. Nelson, who was Miss Alice Ruth Moore, was born in New Orleans, La., July 19th, 1875. She attended the public schools of her native city and afterwards Straight University. She was graduated from Straight University in 1892. Upon graduation she taught for a number of years in the public schools of her native city. She belonged to that class of progressive teachers who strive eagerly to improve themselves, and who work to increase their efficiency in some one chosen subject.

In 1896, Mrs. Nelson went to Boston and then to New York to study Manual Training. In New York she pursued her course at Teachers College in Columbia University. The East quickly learned to appreciate the services of this daughter of the fair South. In 1897, she became teacher in the public schools in Brooklyn, N. Y. She had met the poet laureate of his race, Paul Laurence Dunbar, in the year following in March, 1897. As has already been said, Mrs. Nelson had made for herself a career. While she was teaching in Brooklyn, she took active part in many forms of real life. She was then as she is now a worker in Missions and in social settlements. On the east side in New York she taught manual training classes and classes in kindergarten work in the evenings and after school hours also. Born Missionary that she was, she did this and many other kinds of work without pay save the consolation of rendering needed services.

But Mission work and teaching were not the only fields in which Mrs. Nelson excelled. Though she could not sing as could her poet husband, she could wield her pen with great ease and she could picture life and make plots. Thus while the poet sang and loved because God gave him "The gift of Song," the wife was weaving her plots and making for herself a name and place in the magazines as a writer of short stories. While still in New York, she contributed many stories to the newspapers and magazines. Among the latter are numbered such publications as the McClure's Magazines, Smart Set, Ladies' Home Journal and Leslie's Weekly.

Upon her marriage with the poet, Mrs. Nelson moved to Washington, where she continued her work as story writer, article writer, helper, inspirer and secretary to the great Negro poet. However, she has several books to her credit. In 1895 appeared her first effort entitled, "Violets and other Tales." Her second publication was the Goddess of St. Roque," which appeared in 1899. Both of these publications were most kindly received by the public.

Soon after the death of the poet, Mrs. Nelson again entered upon more active public life. She compiled an authentic volume of Dunbar's poems along with his Biography and some stories. She has also put together the most serviceable of the master pieces of Negro Eloquence. Mrs. Nelson was thus engaged in writing and publishing when the great war in Europe broke out.

Widely known as a social worker she became indispensable in leading and directing the war work campaign among the colored women. In the newspapers and in the reports of the Red Cross, Y. W. C. A. and other such organizations, Mrs. Nelson's name frequently appears; indeed, in the East, and especially in and around New York she is regarded as the bone and sinew of the social and religious work for the Negro soldiers. Her chapter in a recent book by Emmett J. Scott on the American Negro in the World War, is one of the most enlightening and instructive on the Negro Women's share in that great upheaval.

Mrs. Nelson writes with a grasp not only upon the specific work in which she and her sisters are engaged, but with an intimate touch upon peoples and movements everywhere. Though her specific work was that of mobilizing colored women for the United States war work under the auspices of the Council of National Defence, yet her pen appears only to have to be prompted in order to recite all the names and actions of the colored women in every section of the country and in every line of endeavor.

Mrs. Nelson is easily reckoned as one of the race's greatest and noblest women.

Solomon Porter Hood A. M., D. D.

LERGYMAN. teacher, writer, Dr. Hood ranks high in all these callings, and has a splendid record in the diplomatic service of his country, in addition to his other laurels. He is the son of Lewis P. and Matilda Hood and was born at Lancaster, Pa., July, 1853. Although there were eight children in the family his parents managed to give them an education. He entered the public schools when he was eight years of age. He graduated from Lincoln University with the degree of A. M. and Livingstone College with degree of D. D. He studied at both Princeton and Columbia University. Took an extension course at the University of Pennsylvania. He was a teacher in the public schools of Middleton, Pa., from 1873 to 1877, in the preparatory department of Lincoln University, from 1877 to 1880. Was principal of Beanfort (S. C.) Normal and Industrial Academy from 1883 to 1887.

He was converted and joined the Presbyteian Church in 1869; was licensed to preach in 1880 at Lincoln University by the Presbytery of Chester and ordained deacon at the same time. He joined the annual conference of the A. M .E. Church in 1887 at Georgetown, S. C., under Bishop Arnett; has received the following appointments in the A. M. E. Church; Port au Prince, Haiti, 1889; Morris Brown, Phila., 1893; Lamott, Pa., 1895; Reading, Pa., 1896; Frankfort, Pa., 1900; Harrisburg, Pa., 1904; Orange, N. J., 1907; Trenton, N. J., since 1911. He remodeled church and built parsonage at Reading at a cost of $5,000 in 1897 and 1898; remodeled the church at Frankfort at a cost of $3,000 in 1901 and 1902; has taken about 400 people into the church. He has been delegate to one general conference in 1904. He was a member of the educational board from 1904 to 1908.

The political experience of the Doctor and the consequent national renown he gained therefrom, was when he was acting as under secretary in the American Legation at Haiti in 1890. He carried the message of peace under the United States flag. out of Port au Prince from Legitime to Hypolyte. He was the chief organizer and Director General of the Emancipation Exposition of New Jersey in 1913 under the auspices of the State Legislature. These in brief are, the cold facts of Dr. Hood's career as a teacher, mini-ter, writer and public official. As a teacher he began his career in the public schools of Middletown, Pa., in 1873. He taught here for four years until 1877, when he resigned to accept a position with the noted Lincoln University, Pa. Dr. Hood taught here for three years. The rest of his time as an educator was given to the Beaufort Normal and Industrial Academy which he founded at Beaufort, South Carolina, and which he remained principal of until 1887. Doctor Hood's career as a clergyman includes the assistant pastorate of Shiloh Presbyterian Church, New York City, under Rev. Henry Highland Garnet and the organization of the Bereau Presbyterian Church at Beanfort, S. C.

He then joined the African Methodist Episcopal Conference in 1887 and was sent as a missionary to Haiti. In 1889 he returned to this country and has since confined his labors to Pennsylvania and New Jersey. Among his most prominent works as an author are Sanctfred Dollars, published in 1910, and What Every African Methodist Should Know, published in 1913.

His writings are chaste, scholarly, instructive and entertaining. They flow from a heart full of tenderness and love toward mankind and show a simple faith in Christ, which is touching and tender. He longs for a higher spirituality himself, and seeks to impress the same earnestness of soul into the minds of others.

There is much that is potential in one's personality, for an agreeable personality is one of the most valuable assets in the character of any one. There is something wholesome and refreshing in the personality of this man. The hearty handshake, the wreathing smile demonstrate the fact that nature was in her best humor when she produced him. He is one of the most popular as we. as one of the most capable ministers of the race.

Dr. Hood has been for some time literary editor of the African Methodist Episcopal Sunday School Teachers' Quarterly, and is a valued contributor to other church magazines and periodicals. He was made a Presiding Elder of the A. M. E. Church in 1916.

He married Miss Mary A. Davis of New York City, in 1880. They have one adopted daughter. His present home is Trenton, N. J.

JOHN WESLEY E. BOWEN, A. B., A. M., B. D.,
Ph. D., D. D., LL. D., S. T. D.

HIS noted theologian, the son of Edward and Rose Bowen, was born at New Orleans, La., Dec. 3rd, 1855. He received the degree of A. B., from New Orleans University in 1878 and the degree of A. M. in 1882. From New Orleans he went to Boston, Mass., where he entered Boston University. He received the degree of B. D. in 1885 and Ph. D. in 1887. He afterwards entered the Theological Department of Gammon where he earned his D. D. in 1893.

Thus equipped, Dr. Bowen began the career of minister, orator, theologian scholar, author and publicist that was to bring him world-wide fame.

Doctor Bowen has served in the pastorates of churches in Boston, Newark, N. J., Baltimore, Maryland, Washington, D. C.

In his professional work, Doctor Bowen served as follows: In Walden University, Nashville, Tennessee, four years professor of Ancient Languages and Literature; Morgan College, Baltimore, Md., professor of Systematic Theology and Historical Theology; Howard University, Washington, D. C., Professor of Hebrew; Gammon Theological Seminary, Atlanta, Ga., twenty-six years. Professor of Historical Theology and religious education, four of these years he was President of the Seminary and is now its Vice-President, occupying his same chair. He is a contributor to religious and social periodicals of the day, and one of the contributing editors of the National Cyclopedia of the Colored Race.

He has been a delegate to the General Conference of his church in 1896; 1900, 1904, 1908; 1916. He was also a delegate to represent his church to the Ecumenical Conference of Methodism in Washington, D. C., 1891; and London, 1901.

He is author of the following books:

(1) National Sermons; (2) Africa and the American Negro; (3) The United Negro; (4) Appeal to the Kind; (5) Appeal for Negro Bishops; (6) Psychological Process of History; (7) The Negro A Missionary Investment; (8) The Theodocial and Philosophy of the Negro Plantation Melodies, In preparation; Pastoral Theology "The Psychology of Personality Teaching." Dr. Bowen has lectured and is still lecturing before chautauqua Assembles and literary gatherings in all parts of the country. Mr. Cyrus C. Adams, one of the editors of the New York Sun speaking of Doctor Bowen in an article to the Sun says: "It is doubtful if there is another man of his race in this country who combines in a higher degree than Doctor Bowen ripe scholarship, intellectual vigor and the gift of eloquence." The editor of the Valley Tribune in Washington, writes in his paper this estimate: "It was thought by many that the representations of his oratorical powers were exaggerated. Now that he has come and gone, we have to say that those representations were not extravagant and that they might very well have been supplemented by the assurance that he was not only a man of extraordinary gifts in public speech, but a scholar, a trained intellect, a man of wide culture, familiar with the best thought of our day and especially profoundly versed in political philosophy of the times in which we live. He is an orator equal to the best this country has produced, an orator after the style of that grand galaxy of orators of the ante-bellum fame with Brother Beecher in the lead. He has the strong rich mellow voice that the great Brooklyn divine is said to have possessed; he has the same flow of invective when that is needed in the uninterrupted flow of chaste exuberant English. He is an orator, scholar and statesman combined.

He had the honorary degre of LL. D., conferred on him by Wilberforce in 1917 and the S. T. D. by Lincoln University, Penn., in 1918. He has been a member of the Board of Control, secretary of the committee on Episcopacy, and secretary of the Stewart Missionary foundation for Africa, (all of the M. E. Church), for eight years. He is a member of the Masons, The American Negro Academy, American Academy of Political Science, and the Burbank Scientific Association. He was a member of the speakers division in the late world war, and was elected to go to France to conduct institutes among the Negro soldiers.

Dr. Bowens first wife, Miss Ariel S. Hodegs, of Baltimore, Md., died in 1904. She was a woman of refinement, and a talented musician. This union was blessed with four children: Irene Theodosia, John E. E., Jaunita and Portai Edmonia. The last name died in 1900.

Dr. Bowens present wife, who was Miss Irene Smallwood, was a prominent leader in the social and club life of Atlanta.

Main Building, Offices, Dormitories and Lecture Rooms — Gammon Theological Seminary

Dining Hall Gammon Theological Seminary

Library of Gammon Theological Seminary

GROUP OF BUILDINGS OF GAMMON THEOLOGICAL SEMINARY, ATLANTA, GA.

THE Rev. Bishop Gilbert Haven, D. D., LL. D., the resident Bishop of the Methodist Episcopal Church, residing in Atlanta, at the time, sat under a famous Oak, at the East End of Christman Hall, and saw with the vision of a seer, a great University and Theological Seminary rising up upon these hills and amid the wooded forests of South Atlanta, for the Education of the Negro race and its leaders. That Oak is called by Bishop Walden—"The Gilbert Haven Oak."

The Freedmen's Aid Society took up the thought of Bishop Haven and saw his vision also and cooperating with the Bishop, purchased 500 acres of this land and in 1881 ,with Bishop D. W. Clark, then resident in Atlanta, moved Clark University from its cramped quarters in Atlanta to this new site, The Rev. Richard S. Rust, D. D., LL. D., was the Corresponding Secretary of the Board at the time and contributed heartily in all these plans of his rich store of knowledge and wisdom.

In the early Spring of 1882, the Rev. Bishop Henry W. Warren, D. D., LL. D., the resident Bishop in Atlanta at the time, presented the case of the necessity for a trained Ministry for the Negro people's to the Rev. Elijah H. Gammon, of Batvaria,

Illinois, a retired minister of the Rock River Conference, and set forth this large opportunity for him in the use of his consecrated wealth. After deliberation and prayer and in consultation with Mrs. Gammon, who with her usual womanly sagacity had sensed the Bishop's errand 'ere he had spoken and who saw the path of divine opportunity with the swiftness of characteristic instinct, Mr. Gammon gave $20,000.00 to endow a Chair of Theology in Clark University, and a pledge of $5,000.00 towards a new hall with only two conditions, viz: the professor should be a young man, and that Bishop Warren should raise $20,000.00 more to complete the New Hall of Theology.

Bishop Warren went to his task with faith, fervor and untiring effort and more than met Mr. Gammon's requirement.

The Corner Stone of Gammon Hall was laid May 12, 1883, and the Rev. Wilbur P. Thirkield, A. M., B. D., was elected Dean of the Gammon School of Theology in June, 1883, and began his work with the school Oct. 3, 1883.

Allied by marriage with the cultured daughter of Bishop Haven, and by natural instinct, sympathy and broad vision with the colored people. Dean Thirkeld took up the work of his life for the training of the Negro ministry, and has made Gammon Theological Seminary the chief corner stone of the splendid arch of his valuable service to the church, and mankind

The building was formally dedicated Dec 18, 1883 and named Gammon Hall, to the surprise of Mr Gammon but to the delight of the vast concourse of interested friends

THEOLOGICAL SEMINARY FOR THE WHOLE SOUTH

Early in 1887, at the request of Mr Gammon, the Society purchased about seven acres additional to give a suitable frontage for the campus on McDonough road Mr Gammon had been for a great many years a trustee of Garrett Biblical Institute which was entirely separate from the adjoining literary institution the Northwestern University About this time he proposed to set aside property conservatively valued at $200,000 as the endowment It was to be held in trust by the trustees of the Methodist Episcopal Church and its income paid to the Freedmen's Aid Society, which was to administer it in maintaining the school During Mr Gammon's lifetime he was himself to administer the income for the purpose of further accumulation and for additional buildings and equipment During the same time the Freedmen's Aid Society was to pay the salaries of the professors except the one provided for by Mr Gammon's first gift The only condition was that the school should be purely theological and entirely separate He desired it to sustain the same relation to all the schools of the Freedmen's Aid Society The charter was granted March 24 1888 In drawing it the Hon Grant Goodrich of Chicago, who had drawn the charter of Garrett Biblical Institute and had been one of its trustees from its founding, was consulted The charter provides for a Board of Trustees of nine, of which the President and Corresponding Secretary of the Freedmen's Aid Society and the President of the Seminary are ex-officio members The board of trustees acts conjointly with the board of managers of the Freedmen's Aid Society But in most matters the former alone has the initiative

In April, 1887, the official connection of the school with Clark University dissolved, and it was placed upon an independent basis with its own Charter and Board of Trustees and the "Dean" was elected President under the new Charter This Charter was printed March, 1888

On April 3, 1891, Mr Gammon passed to his reward He had made the Seminary a legatee to one half of the residuary portion of his estate This was in addition to what he had given during his life-time Next to Mr Gammon's death the greatest loss the Seminary ever suffered was in the sudden death of Mrs Gammon December 22, 1892 During all the years she had heartily co-operated with Mr Gammon in his gifts and plans for the Seminary

The following comprise the building of the Seminary Aside from the main hall Mr Gammon gave funds for the erection of four modern well-equipped residences for the professors 1886 President Thirkield's residence, 1887-1888, Doctor's Murray's and Parks' residences, in 1888, the Library building and in 1888-1889 Doctor Crawford's residence In March, 1915, the new and artistic Gammon Refectory was erected under Bishop F D Leete and President P M Watters, D D

STEWART MISSIONARY FOUNDATION FOR AFRICA

This Foundation is in the interest, especially among American Negroes, of missionary work for Africa It has been established by Rev W F Stewart, A M, of the Rock River Conference of the Methodist Episcopal Church It is the outgrowth of many years of thought in the consecration of a large portion of his property

THE ADMINISTRATIONS OF THE SEMINARY MAY BE SUMARIZED AS FOLLOWS

1883-1887—Rev Wilbur P Thirkield, D D dean of "Gammon School of Theology," a department of Clark University

1887-January, 1900—The Rev Wilbur P Thirkield, D D, president of Gammon Theological Seminary

January, 1900-May, 1901—The seminary administered by the remaining members of the Faculty, each member serving a portion of the time as "Chairman of the Faculty"

May, 1901—January 19 1906—The Rev L G Adkinson, O O, president

January, 1906-October, 1906—The seminary administered by the remaining members of the Faculty, Doctor Bowen, the office and treasury, Doctor Trever, general correspondence, Doctor Yates students, buildings, and grounds

October, 1906-August 16 1910—The Rev J W E Bowen, Ph D, D D, president

August, 1910-March, 1914—The Rev Silas E Idleman, D D, president

March 1914—The Rev Phillip M Watters, D D, president

This Seminary has had upon its records from its beginning nearly 3,000 students and has graduated over 500 men and through the work of the Department of Missions, has sent into the home field and foreign field nearly 50 men and women

These men and women are found doing yeoman service for mankind in the Methodist Episcopal Church, the African Methodist Episcopal Church, the Zion African Methodist Episcopal Church, the Colored Methodist Episcopal Church, the Baptist Congregational, Episcopal, Presbyterian Churches

Remove Gammon Theological Seminary from the life of the Negro race and you cripple and impoverish the moral forces at work for the stability of our democratic institutions in the South, and you stunt or handicap the Negro race in its steady March towards the best things in the Kingdom of God For this institution perhaps more than any other in the South, represents the pulsating sonscience of Christianity upon the ethics of the Bible

Faculty Rev Philip Melancthon Watters, D D, President and Professor of Apologetics and Christian Ethics

Rev J W E Bowen, Ph D, S T D, L L D—Vice-President and Professor of Church History and Religious Education

Rev Geo H Trever Ph D, D D—Professor of New Testament and Christian Doctrine

Rev Chas H Haines, D D—Professor of Public Speaking and Sacred Rhetoric

Rev Dempster D Martin, D D—Professor of Christian Missions

Rev Willis J King S T B, D D Professor of Old Testament and Christian Sociology

493

ROBERT ROBINSON TAYLOR, B. S.

OBERT Robinson Taylor was born in Wilmington, North Carolina. His father was a building contractor and from his earliest years he was brought in contact with building matters. He attended Gregory Institute, a school maintained by the American Missionary Association in Wilmington, graduating from that school at the head of the class.

With the necessary preparation he went to Boston and entered the Massachusetts Institute of Technology, graduating from that Institution in the year 1892, with the degree of B. S., being the first colored graduate from this school.

After working in some architectural offices he yielded to the persuasion of Dr. Booker T. Washington, and accepted a position at the Tuskegee Normal & Industrial Institute as instructor of Architectural and Mechanical drawing and architect for the Institution. After remaining at the Institution for a number of years during which he designed and superintended the construction of all of its buildings, he resigned and went to Cleveland, Ohio, where he remained four years, working in an architects' office and later engaging in private work.

He was asked to return to Tuskegee as Head of the Mechanical Industries and accepted this position which he has since held. Mr. Taylor has designed and superintended the construction of most of the buildings at the Tuskegee Institute and has had charge of the other mechanical trades which have been largely developed under his direction.

In addition to his work at the Tuskegee Institute he has done a large amount of private architectural work in many states including school houses, churches, libraries, residences, etc. His work has been most favorably spoken of by great numbers of persons who have seen it and for whom he has executed work.

Mr. Taylor is a member of the Society of Arts of Boston, Mass., of the American Economic Society, of the Masonic Fraternity, the Local Business League of Tuskegee, the Educational Association of Teachers and of other educational, business and technical associations.

He was invited and delivered an address at the fiftieth Anniversary of the founding of the Massachusetts Institute of Technology, in Boston, and has appeared before educational societies, schools and organizations of various kinds.

Mr. Taylor has been asked to take responsible positions in other places, among these the Presidency of a College, but preferred to remain at Tuskegee believing that he could be of more service to the race in helping to develop this Institution in its industrial side than in other places and has held to this belief in spite of more lucrative offers.

Tuskegee Institute was selected as one of the schools to train soldiers in vocational work during the great war. As Head of the Mechanical Industries, Mr. Taylor was in charge of this work with the soldiers and it was so well organized and conducted as to draw forth most complimentary comments from the inspecting officers. He is chairman of the Executive Committee of the Local Red Cross Society. This chapter of which he is chairman is the only distinctive colored chapter in the United States.

He was also very active in the drives for Liberty Loans, being asked to assume chairmanship of the local committee for one of these drives among colored people.

His home life is particularly happy. His wife is most helpful and there is a family of five children consisting of three boys and two girls. The oldest son and daughter have finished school at Tuskegee and are now attending college.

Mr. Taylor has served on many occasions as Acting Principal of the Tuskegee Institute, in the absence of the Principal, and Vice-Principal which positions he regularly fills when the two are away from the school.

494

BALLARD INDUSTRIAL BUILDING—LIVINGSTONE COLLEGE

EADING educational institution of the African Methodist Episcopal Zion Denomination, "The finishing school" of the church. It was incorporated in 1879, and the first session was held in one room of a colored minister's parsonage, the late Bishop C. R. Harris, in Concord, N. C., in 1880, but was more definitely organized in 1882, and moved to the present premises the first Wednesday in October of that year. The new site consisted of one building and forty acres of land in Salisbury, N. C. The school opened with three teachers, three pupils and a matron. It was chartered as a college in 1885. The idea of an educational institution for the training of colored youths was the result of a conference of colored ministers for the promotion of self-reliant education among the colored people.

Livingstone College has gradually increased from year to year in numbers, efficiency and the list of substantial friends. During the thirty-seven years it has had in attendance students from nearly every State in the Union, Canada, Central America, the West Indies, and Africa.

It has now five large buildings on the campus, a small one and an auditorium. Huntington Hall was totally destroyed by fire December 31, 1819.

Hood Theological Seminary was regularly opened with competent instructors in 1911. Quite a number of young men have entered and are in training for the ministry. Advantages are offered also for persons to be trained for Home and Foreign Missions. The first floor has four large recitation rooms, a practice chapel and offices for the President and Dean of the Theological Department. The second floor affords dormitory accommodation for persons in direct training for the ministry.

The new Girls' Dormitory, Goler Hall, a magnificent and imposing structure recently completed, is named in honor of ex-President W. H. Goler. It is a three-story and basement brick structure with 102 dormitory rooms, music rooms, reception rooms, a large and commodious as well as light and airy dining hall, steam heated, lighted by electricity, and with all modern conveniences attached. Each room is an outside room.

The teaching force now numbers about twenty-four persons and the pupils more than five hundred annually.

Starting with forty acres and property valued at $4,600, the plant at this time consists of 310 acres of land and nine buildings valued at $250,000.

D. C. Suggs, Ph. D., succeeded Dr. W. H. Goler as President of the college in 1917. He is assisted by an exceptionally strong faculty, that has been carefully selected for the qualifications necessary to success in their respective departments.

LIBRARY LIVINGSTONE COLLEGE

DODGE HALL, LIVINGSTONE COLLEGE

ADMINISTRATION BUILDING.

DINING HALL.

DORMITORY.

GROUP OF BUILDINGS OF ST. JOSEPH COLLEGE, MONTGOMERY, ALA.

T. Joseph's College is a Boarding School for Catholic colored boys. It is located five miles from Montgomery, Ala., on Mt. Meigs Road. The premises include a farm of two hundred and sixteen acres, and a healthier or prettier site for an Institution could hardly be found.

The Institute is owned and controlled by a Society of Missionary priests, with Headquarters in Baltimore, Md. This Society works exclusively among the Negroes. It has churches and schools in Delaware, Maryland, Virginia, N. Carolina, Florida, Tennessee, Arkansas, Alabama, Mississippi, Louisiana and Texas. Of the six colored priests listed in the American Catholic Eclesiastical Directory, three owe their promotion to this Society.

St. Joseph's College was founded in 1901, and incorporated in 1911. Rev. Thomas B. Donovan, a native of Kentucky, pioneered the undertaking, followed in succession by Fathers Kellogg, Tobin, Butsch, and McNamara. The present incumbent is Rev. J. St. Laurent, who took charge in 1909. The Institution consists of several frame buildings, put up tentatively, with a view to permanent rebuilding when circumstances permit the expansion.

The accompanying cut shows some of the buildings and the style of construction.

The Institute is neither a Trade, nor Divinity School. Its aim is to prepare bright boys, from good homes, for entrance into professional schools, by forming, along with the Christian character, the student type, and laying the foundation required by post graduate studies. The discipline, while severe, is paternal, and no corporal punishment is allowed. A certain amount of manual labor is required of all students, both for its moral effect and for economic reasons. No charges are made for tuition, but a fee of five dollars a month is asked for bed and board. This requirement is more a matter of principle than of income, as may readily be inferred from a knowledge of the heavy expenses to which a boarding school is put. For its maintenance the Institution chiefly depends on the voluntary contributions of its friends and the assistance given by the Catholic Mission Boards.

The Institution carries about fifty students, hailing from seven Southern States. The Administration is hopeful of success, and while busy with matters of fundamental import, is accumulating the funds that will enable it to take care of three hundred students.

C. First Johnson

AS the years succeeding the emancipation of the Negro have drifted into the dim mists of the past, and the race has gained in experience and knowledge of the world, it has been able to pause in its career and take an inventory of its stock in the material world. When it is considered that four million ex-slaves, wholly unprepared for citizenship, were literally turned loose in all of their ignorance and poverty on the cold charity of the master classes and the philanthrophy of the world at large, the Negro has made marvelous progress. Not only has the percent of illiteracy been decreased many fold, but all of the evils that follow in the wake of illiteracy and ignorance have decreased in like ration. The great increase in intelligence on the part of the Negro is reflected in the business life of the race, for it is in the domain of business life that all knowledge is most effective and serviceable.

The commercial life of every race is a matter of evolution and comes only with increased knowledge of the world, and confidence in the members of the race in their relationship with each other. The progress of the Negro in business life in the past few years has been indeed highly gratifying, and there seems to be at hand a regular tidal wave of business prosperity unprecedented in the history of the race. If the signs of the times look auspicious for the business life of the Negro it is due to the indefatigable efforts of the premier business men of the race, who have labored unceasingly to promote the business interests of their people.

High up among these men ranks C. First Johnson of Mobile, Ala. Born in Hayneville, Ala., of former slave parents, he received his first education from the "blue back speller down on the farm." His first view of Montgomery was from the top of a bale of cotton, on which he ate and slept as his father drove in from the far-away country home. At the age of fourteen he entered the State Normal School at Montgomery from which he graduated. He left school and entered politics. He became secretary of the Republican Executive Committee of the State; was at one time employed at the Mobile Custom House, and received minor appointments, among them a chance to run the Custom House elevator. He gave up politics to enter business.

The successful launching of a great insurance company is not only a matter of unremitting labor for a period of many years, but it entails great expense. Mr. Johnson organized the Union Mutual Aid Association and in this work as its first and only general manager he has demonstrated his executive and financial ability. The company under his management blazed the pathway through doubt and prejudice, demonstrated the administrative ability of the Negro, inspired confidence in the company's stability by being faithful to every promise, and establishing its operation upon such a high plane as to merit the confidence and patronage of the best citizens of the State of Alabama.

In the truest sense of the word is Dr. Johnson a race man. There is no Negro in the South that has done more, according to his means, towards getting young men and women started on successful careers. His company gives employment to hundreds of clerks and solicitors. Many successful teachers, physicians, and others have graduated from their ranks. He exhibits a keen sight into the psychology of business, and all of his letters bear a purpose, carry a message of straightforward business dealing.

Trite and bromide are many of his expressions in the weekly letters he sends all of his men, and that appear in some of the books he has written.

For example:

"God never made a man for failure. In this land of opportunity it is a disgrace for a man to live in poverty."

"Men who exercise initiative are builders of empires. All others are merely tenants, janitors and followers."

These epigrams are a part of the man. A part of his daily work, of his daily life. He is and always has been a leader in the religious and civic life of the community. He stands high in the councils of the Baptist Church of which he is a deacon. He is a Past District Grand Master of the Grand United Order of the Odd Fellows, and is one of the best fixed Negroes financially in the country. Some time ago he purchased as a home for his parents, who are still living, a part of the old plantation of their former master.

Verily, C. First Johnson is a man with a message for his people. He delivers that message in season and out of season. Surely in the life of the people of the South there is a place for many more such men. Men who are getting their larger satisfaction in the knowledge of duty well done. Not only does Mr. Johnson rank with the foremost among the colored people, but stands high in the respect and esteem of the business leaders of his state, and his war work ranks him a patriot of the purest type.

It might be of interest to add that the association founded by Mr. Johnson was recently made a stock company under the name of the Union Mutual Insurance Co., with a paid in capital of $25,-000,00.

"BIG ZION," A. M. E. ZION CHURCH, MOBILE, ALA.

Reverend Green W. Johnson

HEN a great preacher becomes the pastor of a great and historical church, and the leader of a large and influential congregation, nothing but great results are looked for. "Big Zion" A. M. E. Zion Church of Mobile, Alabama, is just what its name implies: Big in every sense of the word. Founded in the days of slavery, it has grown in power and influence, until today, it ranks with the strongest churches in the state, financially, numerically, and in moral influence. Therefore in calling a leader, a man had to be sought that was thoroughly trained and mentally equipped to administer not only to the moral welfare of his charges, but to manage the finances of an organization that requires the raising and expenditures of thousands of dollars annually. The present pastor, Rev. Green W. Johnson, not only has the requisite qualifications to a marked degree, but is a leader in all civil movements in Mobile, having for their object the betterment of his country, his town, and his people. He is a splendid example of the highly educated religious leader that has done so much for the advancement of the Negro in the last fifty years. Rev. Johnson is a native of South Carolina, where he first saw the light of day about sixty years ago. When quite a youth he moved to Charlotte, North Carolina. While living here he attended Biddle University where he received the foundation of his mental training that was to serve him so well in later years. He later did active work as a minister but was not satisfied until he had taken a course in the "Finishing School" of his church. While preaching, he attended Livingstone College until he was thoroughly equipped for the ministsry. About twenty-three years ago, he became pastor of a church at Citronelle, a winter resort for Northern tourists, located a few miles north of Mobile. His reputation as a leader spread and he went to Pittsburg, Pa. From there he went to Boston, Mass., and afterward to Brooklyn, N. Y. However, the call of the South was too strong to be denied and he returned to Mobile as the pastor of the A. M. E. Zion congregation whose splendid house of worship is pictured on the opposite page.

Rev. Johnson is a forcible, eloquent speaker, and always brings something to his audience that is worth listening to. In his sermons there is a happy mixture of scholarship and spiritual fervor. He has never forgotten the fact that the primary object of all preaching is the conversion of souls to Christ, and that is the great ambition of his life. He is a profound theologian, but he does not put this power in as much evidence as he does that spiritual power which for years has made him one of the most effective preachers in his church. He is a great preacher, and to be a gifted preacher of the gospel is to rank not subordinate even to a bishop.

Wherever Rev. Johnson goes he preaches and lectures on the necessity of education, morality and religion for the race. His discourses are thoughtful, his advice timely, and his counsel wise. He has all the equipment of the forceful public speaker. He is entertaining, witty, eloquent and profound at will. He is not an extremist along any line that would provoke fierce antagonism either in the ranks of the race or outside. He is temperamentally sound on all questions affecting the welfare of his people, and is thus fitted by nature for leadership.

His lectures throughout the country are always noted for his vigorous treatment of the social evils of the times. He is constantly exhorting his people to make themselves decent, industrious, respectable ,law-abiding citizens, so that they may be worthy of the respect of all classes of people white and black alike. He exhorts them to buy lands, build homes and live lives of industry and sobriety. He wants the race to wake up from its Rip Van Winkle sleep and take hold of the inheritance that every man has left to them, the opportunity to work and make a living by the sweat of their own brows, to be honest men and women and respect themselves in the laws of common sense and common decency.

Rev. Johnson's course during the World War gained for him an added love and admiration from his own people and the respect and friendship of the white people of Mobile.

Sunday School Union of A. M. E. Church

SUNDAY School Union of A. M. E. Church was organized August 11, 1882, at Cape May, N. J., by Bishops Daniel A. Payne, Alexander W. Wayman, Jabez P. Campbell, John M. Brown, Thomas M. D. Ward, William F. Dickerson, Richard H. Cain and Rev. Chas. S. Smith. Bishop Payne was the first president and Rev. C. S. Smith was its first corresponding secretary and prepared its constitution. Its purpose was the organization and development of Sunday Schools. It was first located at Bloomington, Ill., and here the first publication—"Our Sunday School Review"—was published in January, 1883. In January, 1886, it was moved to Nashville, Tenn., and in April the Teachers' and Scholars' Quarterlies were published. The publication of these was followed by the Juvenile and Gem Lesson Papers in July of the same year. February 28, 1886, Rev. C. S. Smith purchased at 206 Public Square, Nashville, for $9,000, a brick and stone building, five stories high, including the basement. The Sunday School Union was then incorporated, the incorporators being Chas. S. Smith, Henry M. Turner, Evans Tyree, Green L. Jackson and Louis Winter. An outlay of printing material was bought in February, 1889, over $5,000 being expended for this purpose. In order that the work might be fostered, there was set aside a special day, known as "Children's Day," first observed in October, 1882, and thereafter the second Sunday in every June, when the whole connection rallied to the support of the Sunday School Union. From 1884 to 1900 Rev. C. S. Smith served as secretary-treasurer, pushing the work forward for the good of the Sunday Schools throughout the Church. In 1900 he was elected to the bishopric and Rev. Wm. D. Chappelle of South Carolina, was elected to succeed him and served from 1900 to 1908. In the meantime, the Children's Day collections were increased and the work kept alive by the rallies ,every June, of the army of loyal Allenites throughout the Connection. The Sunday-School Union had now been running as an organization (1882-1908) for twenty-six years, and as an incorporated institution nearly twenty years. The subsidy known as Children's Day money had been sent to the Union for all these years and the time was ripe when there was to be demonstrated the truth that an institution running for a quarter of a century should now be self-supporting.

In 1908 the general conference elected Mr. Bryant as secretary-treasurer, without Children's Day funds or financial assistance. His first task was to organize a competent working force. Then came the task of building the foundation of a publishing plant which would be able to print anything needed by the Church or race. And so, as the proceeds increased, the result of Mr. Bryant's tact and economy, modern machinery was installed. A complete typesetting and typemaking department was put in at a cost of thousands of dollars. Presses, folders, binders, feeders, stitchers and trimmers were purchased and the building at 206 Public Square became too small to meet the needs of the department. Over $50,000 worth of machinery has been purchased, and paid for from the proceeds from the work done by the plant. The literature issued compares favorably with this class of matter published by any other publishing house in the country. The Richard Allen Monthly, a magazine for teachers, is the latest addition. At the Young People's Congress, at Atlanta, Ga., in July, 1914, hundreds of preachers and laymen saw the Sunday School Department in another light.

All the helps and printed matter, vari-colored and illustrated, from cradle roll to home department, such as any Sunday school might need, were on exhibition, and represented advancement along this line made by the Sunday School Union. The biggest achievement of Mr. Bryant has been the purchase and building in 1914 of the most commodious and well-designed publishing plant owned by colored people. This building is valued at more than $50,000 and contains an automatic fire sprinkler system, valued at $5,000. The entrance to the building brings to view the main office where the clerical force receive orders upon top of orders daily, and after recording them pass them on to the well-arranged mailing room just to the rear. Here tons of mail of all description are sent down the chute to the auto trucks waiting in the subway to transfer it to the main post office. In this part of the building are located; on the second floor the editorial rooms, offices of the Allen C. E. League, evangelical bureau and Secretary Bryant. The reception room, the display room and the beautiful "Bishops' Room"—an assembly room where services or meetings may be held—are also located on this floor. The rest room is adjacent, and is fitted up with swings, improvised tables and kitchen, all used for entertainment and refreshment. The third floor is a large hall in which, if need be, large gatherings may be had. But the department which most interests the visitors, is the mechanical division, all situated in well-lighted and freely ventilated apartments. From the street one views the mammoth cylinder presses, turning out the large contracts ,the job presses, trimmers and folders, all working with clocklike regularity. To the rear is the wonderful monotype plant where the young ladies may be seen operating the typesetting keyboards, with skill and dexterity, while the casting machines are noisily transfering molden lead into type, ready for the printer's use. The bindery is another beehive. Here a big force of girls is continually folding, stitching, binding, pasting and trimming books and periodicals of all sizes and folios.—From Encyclopaedia of African Methodism, by R. R. Wright, Jr.

TWO OF THE SIXTEEN BUILDINGS OF ST. AUGUSTINE SCHOOL.

HE school was founded in 1867 by Dr. J. B. Smith. It is owned by an independent board of trustees and is supported and supervised by the Board of Missions and the American Church Institute of the Protestant Episcopal Church.

The school is located at Raleigh, North Carolina, and the principal is A. B. Hunter.

It is a school of elementary and secondary grade with provision for industrial training, and its influence on the character of the pupils is very effective. The Institution is accomplishing a good work and is commended by the United States Department of the Interior who recommends that it receive encouragement.

The attendance is about 264 divided among the elementary and secondary grades and boarders. Of the elementary pupils about 30 were in the "evening school." Of the secondary and night-school pupils about 39 were male and 55 were female.

The teaching force is divided between white and black, being ten male and eighteen female teachers.

Nine of the teachers are white and nineteen colored. They embrace teachers in all departments of the school, grades, academic, industries, music, drill, bookkeeping and nurse training.

Good elementary work is done in the eight grades of the day school. The evening school has three classes corresponding roughly to the fourth, fifth and sixth grades. The pupils work during most of the day and go to school from 4 to 6:10 p. m.

Secondary work is done in the "normal" course and covers a period of three years. The collegiate course includes Latin, French, Greek, Mathematics, English, Elementary Science, History, Economics, Bible and Psychology.

A few pupils take a half year of history, sociology, and geometry.

Considerable provision is made for industrial training. The required courses are cooking, sewing, printing, woodworking or bricklaying.

There are also classes in basketry, chair caning, and weaving. The time given to this work varies from seven to nine periods per week.

The work in cooking and sewing for girls is well planned and effective.

A two-year course is given in a well-equipped hospital under the direction of competent instructors.

The resident staff consists of a physician and a head nurse.

The school property consists of $163,000 in the plant and $37,000 in endowment.

The value of the land is estimated at $22,000. The land comprises one hundred and ten acres, of which seventy-five are used for the farm. The school has a beautiful campus of over twenty acres.

The buildings are estimated to be worth $123,000. There are sixteen buildings, including the hospital, chapel and library.

Eight of the buildings are of stone or brick; the others are of frame construction. Three are four stories high and five are of three stories. The buildings are in good condition and the rooms are well kept.

A large part of the equipment is in hospital, industrial, and farm equipment and is valued at $18,000.

An excellent system of accounting has been installed and the books are audited annually.

It receives its income from the Episcopal Board of Missions, American Church Institute, general donations, special donations and scholarships, endowments, special funds, Slater Fund and rent of house.

The income from the St. Agnes Hospital amounted to approximately $12,000 practically all of which was used for maintenance.

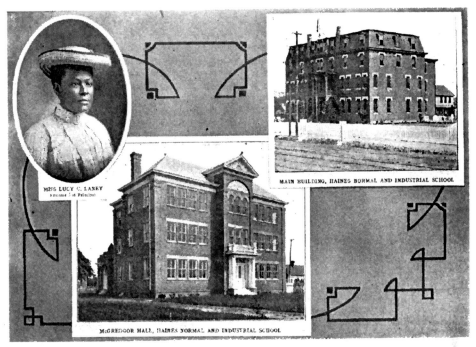

MISS LUCY C. LANEY
Founder and Principal

MAIN BUILDING, HAINES NORMAL AND INDUSTRIAL SCHOOL

McGREGGOR HALL, HAINES NORMAL AND INDUSTRIAL SCHOOL

HAINES NORMAL SCHOOL AND MISS LUCY LANEY, FOUNDER.

NE of the schools in Georgia that has done such effective work as to win the confidence of the people, all the people, regardless of race, color or creed is the Haines Normal and Industrial Institute, located in Augusta, Georgia. The school was founded by Miss Lucy Laney, the present principal, in 1886. It is affiliated with the Presbyterian Board of Missions for Freedmen; in fact the property is vested in the Presbyterian Board. But the school is not run by this organization. It has a separate board of trustees. Haines School has an attendance that runs near 900 pupils. By far the larger number are registered in the elementary work, though the secondary grade work has about 150 pupils registered for subjects in that department. Some of these students are boarders and a great number who attend the school live in the City of Augusta. The courses are well planned and the teachers are well prepared and the teaching thorough. Because of all these conditions the reputation of the school is very high.

Most of the pupils are girls. Indeed, one of the aims in the mind of Miss Laney in founding this school was the betterment of the Negro womanhood. That she has accomplished this in so many cases is due to the very conscientious work that is being done by all members of the faculty. There are twenty-two teachers. All colored, and most of them women. These teachers were chosen because of their preparation for work of this kind.

Along with the work in the academic department there is carried on an industrial department. For the girls instruction in cooking and in sewing is provided. For the boys, manual training and gardening. The funds for the support of the industrial courses in Haines Normal and Industrial School are inadequate. But as far as they allow, the training is thorough. The school proper is on a tract of land comprising a city block. On this are two large-brick structures and several smaller ones, arranged in such a manner as to give the maximum light and ventilation. In these buildings are class rooms, a model kitchen and a well equipped sewing department, where the girls are not only taught to be self-supporting but are given instructions in many of the finer crafts that go to make the model housewife. Here also are located the carpenters shop for the boys. A model garden is run in connection with the school for the benefit of both boys and girls. Across the street are located the cottages of the teachers, which were arranged with the view of making Haines School a real home for them. Miss Laney, the founder and principal of the school is a graduate of Atlanta

502

University On completion of her studies, she taught in several different schools in the State Like many others of her people Miss Laney felt keenly the need of more institutions for training of girls and boys to become useful men and women She realized the terrible handicap of illiteracy had to be met and overcome before her people could advance very far, and with an impulsive generosity that is characteristic of her every act, she determined to devote her life to the establishment of an institution that would equip boys and girls for life's battles and teach them to lead the lives of Christian men and women

In 1886, she gave up her position as teacher, and on her own volition, without backing of any sort, went to Augusta, Ga with the fixed determination of starting the work she had so long dreamed of It has been truthfully said that no cause involving the welfare and uplift of humanity can well succeed without the efforts of a woman In all ages of the world women have worked, played and made every possible human sacrifice for the cause of human progress and none are more potential today in the affairs of the world than that noble band of pioneers in the development of Negro schools Consecrating her life to the betterment of her people is the noblest contribution one can make to human society The very earnestness of Miss Laney made her many friends from the very start, and gained their support in getting the school started A devoted Christian she interested the members of the Presbyterian Church, of which she was a member in aiding her to secure the support of the Presbyterian Board of Missions for Freedmen Gradually building the school, step by step Raising the money by every honorable means, by lecture tours, by entertainments, by soliciting private contributions, Miss Laney can look today upon a work that represents a money value of around fifty thousand dollars, with an income running into the thousands But who can estimate the value of the good accomplished for the race and for humanity? Only those that have been lifted from depths of poverty and illiteracy, and given an opportunity to become part of a better and brighter world, can even remotely estimate this One need not, however, rely on the eulogies of the students and alumni of Haines College All one needs to be convinced of the high character of the work being accomplished by Miss Laney, is to ask any citizen of Augusta irrespective of race, or pay a visit to the school, where the work speaks for itself

Hon William H Taft, shortly before his inauguration as President of the United States, visited Haines School and speaking of Miss Laney, who is considered one of the most brilliant daughters of the colored race said to the friend with him

"That a colored woman could have constructed this great institution of learning and brought it to its present state of usefulness speaks volumes for her capacity Therefore, I shall go out of this meeting, despite the distinguished presence here, carrying in my memory only the figure of that woman who has been able to create all this?"

The faculty and pupils of Haines College, from the Principal down took a prominent part in all world war work, always, oversubscribing their quota of Bonds and Thrift Stamps, as well as being liberal contributors to the Red Cross Y M C A Salvation Army, and all War Community Services Haines always answered 'Ready" when our country called

Vol 2 of Negro Education, published by the government makes the following statement of Haines Normal and Industrial School

A secondary school with a large elementary enrollment Two-thirds of the pupils are girls The management is effective The wise administration of the principal has won for the school the confidence of both white and colored people

It is affiliated with the Presbyterian Board of Missions for Freedmen, but has an independent board of trustees Title to the property is vested in the Presbyterian Board

Attendance—Total, 860, elementary 711, secondary 149, male 289, female 571 Of the pupils above the eighth grade 84 were boarders Of those reporting home address 65 were from Augusta, 47 from other places in Georgia, and 35 from other states 17 were from farm homes and 132 from city homes

Teachers—Total 22, all colored, male 4, female 18, academic 19 industrial 2, music 1 The teachers are well prepared and doing thorough work

Organization—Elementary There are eight grades and kindergarten

Secondary The secondary course requires English, 4 years, Mathematics 4, and History 3 Elective subjects included Latin, taken by 91 pupils, French, taken by 31, German 26, Greek, 17, psychology, 21 physics, 16, physiology, 14, chemistry, 9, history and civics, 19, sociology, 6

Financial—The accounts of the school are honestly kept

Sources of income Presbyterian Board, $4,595, tuition and fees, $1,680, general donations, $1,561, entertainment, $989 The non-educational receipts were from the boarding department and amounted to $3,751

Items of Expenditure Supplies for boarding and other departments, $6751, salaries, $4,554 fuel light, and water, $976, equipment $596, labor, $480, repairs, $86

Thomas T. Pollard

THOMAS T. POLLARD, a Texan by birth, rearing and occupation, is one of the men who made the "Lone Star State" famous in education. Mr. Pollard was born in Danville, Montgomery County, Texas, February 22nd., 1866. Having spent sufficient time in the public schools of his native county, spending his spare hours on the farm, he matriculated at the Prairie View Normal and Industrial Institute. Graduating on the twenty-sixth of June, 1888, he immediately entered the profession of school teaching. Mr. Pollard was fortunate enough to be elected to a principalship at the outset. He became the head of one of the ward schools of Beaumont, and has remained in his post these thirty years. He has grown with educational ideas, introducing into his school new methods as the time demanded such.

Further finding that the school teacher should take the lead not only in the progress of educational ideas, but in all that pertains to the life of a community, he has several times ventured into business, and into plans for the improvement of his community.

In 1900 he organized the People's Drug Company of Beaumont, having seen a crying need for a congenial place where his people could buy drugs and sodas unmolested. The business was a success from the day it opened its doors. Foreseeing that everyone must live more and more out of his own garden, Professor Pollard introduced Home Gardening into his school. From here, he took it into the city homes. This he has been making a speciality, thereby training the people to cope with the stringency of the times.

Few school men allow more real life to come into their routine than does this principal at Beaumont. He is classed among the most daring and yet the safest bear and deer hunters in East Texas. He had at one time a hand to hand encounter, so to speak—no—not with a bear—but with a 140 pound buck, which had been wounded. His rifle being inaccessible, he had to despatch the beast with his hunter's knife.

He is like many a Texan, a live politician. In 1896, he was a delegate from the fourteenth Congressional district to the Republican National Convention, in Saint Louis, which gave the country William McKinley, for President.

Active in politics and in sports, he takes also a leading part in church and secret orders. He is a Missionary Baptist, a Free and Accepted Mason, a Knight of Pythias, and an American Woodman. He is not an extensive traveler having covered only a few of the Southern and Western states, but like the Uncle in Snow Bound, he knows the brooks and shrubs, the nooks and by patches, in the woods and in the vast fields of his section of Texas.

Professor Pollard was married June 30th, 1892, at Beaumont, to Miss Francis Ventun Charlton. Mr. Pollard owns personal property, valued at $10,000.

He is one of the veteran educators of his state, and seems to have dedicated the best and most conscientious energies of his life to the profession of teaching. He is an affable, congenial and unassuming man, and enjoys universal appreciation and confidence. Success has crowned his efforts in the past and the future will but the more emphatically bestow upon him the rewards and glories which an honorable, upright and useful life will always merit. With him the profession of teaching is a labor of love. The almighty dollar influences him not, for in continuing to teach school he is really making a sacrifice instead of a gain of dollars; but it is his love for the work and his earnest desire to do good for the race that cause him to continue to pull in pedagogical harness. Prof. Pollard is not of a grasping, avaricious nature, nor does he consider the dollar as the sum total of human existence. He realizes that there is a serious responsibility devolving upon the educated colored man of the South, and that it is the bounden duty of the educated colored man to do his part in the great work of uplifting his benighted people. Personally he is in practically independent circumstances, but it has ever been his earnest desire to lift others up with him while he was climbing. He considers the educational advantages that he has received as a dispensation from Providence to enable him to help his struggling and benighted people, and for this reason he has found the attraction of service and hard work in the school room to be greater than any other attraction in life.

Rev. William Thomas Silvey

EV. William Thomas Silvey has studded ris whole crown of life with church buildings. He cares not for the size of the church, the grade of the congregation, the large salary, the brilliant choir; that is these things are not the main ideal with him. His ambition throughout his career has been to see the people housed, to watch the building rise from the ground. All the struggle at campaigning for funds, the holding of suppers, giving concerts, using collection cards and the thousand other devices resorted to for the raising of funds have been to him so many thrilling detail by-plays of the game.

Rev. Silvey began life in Ohio. He was born in Greene County in 1853, when slavery held his brothers in bondage in the South and when Ohio was doing yeomen service as a haven of refuge and a way station for the run-a-away slave. For several years he attended the common schools of the county, making his way slowly as the boy of his race had to do in those trying days.

However, he could not remain in school very long; neither did the way appear whereby he could study and work. Thus he soon bade farewell to the school room and sought employment on the farm. Forty-five years ago saw him a farm laborer earning his bread, with only hopes and ambition to lead him to a higher position of service to himself and to others. In 1877 he left the farm, having studied and thought as best he could, and entered the Baptist ministry. For all he had not been able to specialize to any great degree, he nevertheless had a great advantage of the mass of his brethren of the cloth, many of whom had had but little schooling of any kind and that under the most trying circumstances.

His first charge was given him at Eddyville, Ky. Immediately he saw the crying need for the Negro churches. Moving now and then, but working fervently, he has built during his forty years in the ministry, fourteen churches in the State of Kentucky. The last was indeed worthy of his crowning effort. It was the handsome modern brick building, the First Baptist Church of Frankfort, Ky. Over this church, though he is well into his sixties, he still presides, in many ways as vigorous and as ambitious as in the early days of his career.

Notwithstanding the fact that Rev. Silvey is a minister of the gospel and an eloquent divine, yet his very life, humble in origin, filled with struggles and hardships in its early days, and now beautified and glorified with unbound success, is the most eloquent sermon that he has ever preached in the course of his brilliant career. By reading his life and comparing his humble origin with his present position of influence, dignity and power, every ambitious youth of the race may be encouraged, stimulated and inspired to persevere until he reaches the goal of his ambition. From an untutored, hard-working boy on a farm to the leadership of one of the great churches of the race is a sublime height to climb, and this great honor is a fitting monument to his patience, perseverance and determination to make himself serviceable to his race, to the cause of humanity and to the Creator of mankind. The Rev. Silvey is really a beacon light of inspiration that lights up the pathway of hope for the youth of the whole race, and no son or daughter of Africa should be discouraged in the ambition to aspire to the best and the greatest in American life. Whether as plowboy on the farm, or hard laborer in the ditch, or student in the school room, or teacher in the small churches, or an inspired minister of the gospel, the life of Rev. Silvey is worthy of emulation by the aspiring youth of the race, and should be treasured by them as one of their most precious legacies.

The leadership of a race is something that can not be assumed by any man, for it is an attribute that results from the mental attitude of those whose prerogative it is to accord or withdraw. Rev. Silvey has every requisite and every equipment for the ideal leader of the race that he is. He is one of the best prepared men in the galaxy of the race's greatness, and his many years of consecrated effort for the advancement and uplift of the race is worthy of the race's greatest appreciation. He is one of the pillars of his branch of the Baptist Church, and his clarion notes have been heard in a majority of the churches of Kentucky, exhorting the race to take a stand against vice, corruption and iniquity, and to show to the world that it stands for education, morality, religion and everything that will help the world to move ever upward, onward and heavenward

Rev. Silvey owns his residence and one other, which he rents. These are valued at $5,000. He was married in Lime County in 1878, one year after entering the ministry, to Miss Ida Holland. There have been eight children born into Rev. Silvey's family. One of these, Miss Virginia, is deceased. Two others, Marion and Ed, are coal miners. Miss Gertrude and Bessie are married. Miss Catherine is a seamstress and Miss Lutitia and Willie are engaged in school teaching.

TYPE OF GRADUATES OF PHILANDER
SMITH COLLEGE

HILANDER Smith College, a school offering elementary and secondary grade as well as college courses is located in Little Rock, Arkansas. The school is owned and controlled by the Freedmen's Aid Society of the Methodist Episcopal Church. The school owes its existence chiefly to the generosity of the family of Philander Smith of Oak Park, Illinois. He gave the first ten thousand dollars toward the present main building. This gift was made in the early part of 1883. The school was at this time six years old.

In connection with the Philander Smith College the Adeline Smith Home for Girls is maintained. The Home is the property of the Woman's Home Missionary Society of the Methodist Episcopal Church and was dedicated in 1884. In this home for girls the true principles that underlie strong, honest womanhood, are taught, and daily practiced. The Home is strictly religious, giving much time to the teaching of the Bible and requiring each girl to get a good portion of it in her memory. In the Home the courses offered are cooking, organization of home, sewing, fancy work. In all these branches of Domestic Art the teaching is thorough and is so taught as to make it a real part of the lives of the students.

In the government, appeal is made direct to the students' sense of right. In so far as possible self-government is practiced. But the rules and regulations of the institution are rigid and all must obey. All the work and activities of the Adeline Smith Home is a part of the educational activities of Philander Smith College. Although the work of the two plants is separate in some things, the real school work is together.

The land owned by the Philander Smith College is valued at $15,000. It is in two separate lots. The main building is located on a lot which comprises about half a city block. The Girls' Home is on a large city lot some distance from the Main Building. The Main Building is a four-story brick structure that is used for offices, classrooms and boys' dormitory. The girls' dormitory is a three-story brick building and is a new, well constructed one. There are in addition to these, two frame buildings used for classes in grade work and for shops.

The course of study is based largely on the Freedmen's Aid Society course. Strong emphasis is placed on the classical languages. The courses include the Elementary, with industrial work for the girls in the Adeline Smith Home; College Preparatory and Normal courses; and a College course. In industries the work is limited to the Domestic Art work in the Home for the Girls.

In offering a thorough Teachers' Normal Course the school fills a great need of the state. Like most of the Southern States the teachers in the rural districts are lacking in thorough training. In establishing this course the authorities of Philander Smith had in mind the preparation of well-trained and efficient teachers for public and rural schools. The course of study was so arranged as to meet the needs of the Normal Training High Schools of the State. Along with the regular studies required in this course there are several literary and social activities that are compulsory upon students taking this course. These are the Literary Society, Y. M. C. A., Y. W. C. A. and the lecture course. Although in most schools these organizations exist they are not compulsory. Realizing the needs of all teachers of well rounded lives, this school has made the attendance upon these organizations compulsory.

The man at the head of this school is Mr. J. M. Cox. Through his efforts he has brought the school up to a good standard. Mrs. H. M. Masmyth, a white woman, is superintendent of the Girls' Home that is connected with this college.

George L. Knox and W. A. Attaway M. D.

GEORGE L. KNOX

HE veteran editor and publisher of the Indianapolis Freeman first saw the light of day in Wilson County, Tenn., during the days of slavery. For many years while a slave he worked as a plantation laborer. He was afterwards transferred by his master as an apprentice in the shoe makers business. He served in the Union Army for one year and after the war took up the barber's trade. From the barber shop he entered the journalistic field and became publisher of the Indianapolis Freeman. This paper under Mr. Knox has grown to be a power to be reckoned with.

Mr. Knox is a self-made man in every sense of the word; he educated himself and at the same time supported his family. He is a staunch member of the M. E. Church.

Mr. Knox married Miss Aurrila Harvey of Indianapolis, Indiana in 1866. This couple have five children, four boys and one girl. The only surviving boy, Edward C., is the business manager of the Freeman.

Dr. Attaway, has been a factor in the professional and financial life of the State of Mississippi for a number of years, yet he is still a man, in the very prime of life. He has been tried in the crucible of business responsibility, and has demonstated to the world his ability to make good. His success as a business promoter in the State of Mississippi has been phenomenal and few other members of the race have been endowed with the same degree of confidence to bring to a successful conclusion such undertakings, when confronted with the same difficulties.

The subject of this sketch is the President of the Mississippi Beneficial Life Insurance Company, a company that is chartered under the laws of Mississippi, and is now operating in all sections of the state. The insurance company in question is the result of the brain, finance and confidence of Dr. W. A. Attaway, who was willing to blaze out the path to success in this novel business venture and, if necessary, sacrifice his career as an exceptionally successful physician trying to promote the business welfare of the race.

It is one of the few insurance companies operated by Negroes that is now writing all kinds of old line insurance policies.

It is the history of business institutions that they are monuments to the brain and brawn of some one man, who not only has every requisite for intelligent and successful leadership, in the business ventures with which he is connected but is endowed with a sixth sense that enables them to select assistants of a type that can be welded into an organization that is the acme of efficiency.

Dr. Attaway is a big man in every department of human excellence. He is one of the leading physicians of the Southland; he is a successful business promoter and business man; he is among the foremost insurance magnates of the country; he is broad in his conceptions for the welfare of the Negro. He has made good as have few men in the ranks of the state's leading men.

The subject of this sketch is not only a splendid physician, but a business man of first magnitude, and his mere word stands for as much as that of any other in the State of Mississippi. He is the central figure in one of the largest combinations of capital that has ever been gotten together in the state, and this combination of capital is but a faint testimonial of the appreciation in which his remarkable business talents are held by his admirers and friends.

He stands high in the respect and esteem of both races in his home town of Greenville, Miss.

A. F. Henderson and A. D. Price

MR. Herndon is one of the wealthiest Negroes in Atlanta, Georgia. He is said to be worth well up in six figures. His rise in the scale of prosperity was marked by many hardships which required an indomitable will and true courage to overcome. He was born a slave in Walton County, Georgia, June 26, 1858.

After emancipation his mother went out into the world with two children, a corded bed, and a few quilts. Hiring out by the day, she received in pay potatoes, molasses and peas, to maintain the family. She found shelter in a one room log cabin also occupied by four other families.

The space allotted to his mother was only sufficient for her bedstead, under which she stored her daily earnings.

Alonzo Franklin (the boy's name), began to work at the early age of about seven years and worked for his grandfather until he was thirteen years old for his board and keep, at which time he was pulling a cross-cut saw with full-grown men.

His old master then hired him for three years, paying his mother $25 for the first year, $30 for the second and $40 for the third.

At the age of twenty, with his meager savings of $11.00 he stole away in the darkness of night, with his little hand-trunk on his shoulder, and walked fourteen miles to Covington, Georgia.

He had received twelve months schooling in the common school before he was twenty, receiving five weeks a year.

When he reached Atlanta he hired himself to a barber for $6 per month. He soon learned the trade and passed from one stage to another in it, finally establishing a shop of his own which has grown until now he owns three shops, all modern, and one noted as the largest sanitary barber shop in the world. The pictures in this shop cost twelve thousand dollars and it is one of the show places of Atlanta. It has twenty-five chairs and requires the services of forty men.

Mr. Herndon founded the Atlanta Mutual Insurance Association, which absorbed eight other companies. It is one of the largest insurance companies in America owned by Negroes and doing purely industrial insurance business with colored people.

He is President of Atlanta Loan & Trust Company, Secretary Southview Cemetery Association; Director Atlanta State Savings Bank, Gate City Drug Store, Inc., Trustee Leonard Street Orphan Home.

He is a member of the Congregational Church, Member Odd Fellows, and in politics a Republican.

His first wife was Adriene McNeal, who died leaving him one child.

May 30, 1912, he married Jessie Gilespie, of Chicago, Ill.

Mr. Herndon is a great believer in real estate as an investment and is showing his faith by his works. He owns about one hundred rental houses.

His magnificent home situated on a high hill, overlooks Atlanta near Atlanta University.

One of the remarkable signs of development of the colored race is the large number of men who are engaged in large business enterprises. There was a time when the activities of the colored man were cast in a small mold, but that time is past and a new day has dawned for them.

He has rightly reasoned that if others could accomplish great things so could he if he would prepare himself for his work and apply himself diligently to his task. Realizing that a man must be informed who desires to do big things he has set himself earnestly to secure an education, for he knows that the educated man has an advantage over the ignorant one.

Such a man is A. D. Price of Richmond, Virginia. He was born in Hanover County, Virginia, August 9, 1860, and has risen to his high standing as a business man in his native state.

Commencing in a small way, step by step, he has advanced to a position which commands the respect of both the white and black citizens of Richmond.

He attended the first public school established for colored children after the Civil War.

After leaving school he began his business career as a clerk, which he followed for several years. Standing behind the counter was not to his taste so he gave it up and learned a trade. He took up blacksmithing and after working with others until he had mastered the science, in 1881, he opened a shop of his own. Here he began to recognize his powers of business management. His blacksmith and wheelwright establishment grew to such an extent that it required the services of twelve men and boys. In his employment were both white and colored laborers. In 1886 he began to branch out. He established an undertaking and livery business, but it failed to meet with the success anticipated so he gave it up. However, he never gave up his purpose to establish such a business, and in 1893 he again entered it. His next effort was crowned with great success and he now has the satisfaction of being the proprietor of one of the best arranged and conducted undertaking establishments in the South.

It requires twenty-five persons to carry on the business.

Mr. Price is the President of the Southern Aid Society of Virginia. This institution is doing a world of good in the State of Virginia ,where it reaches hundreds of homes with its benefits.

He has learned that real estate is the true foundation of wealth and when wisely purchased is sure to prove a fine investment. The value of his real estate holdings is estimated at six figures.

He owns a business block in which are located halls used for lodge rooms and for other public purposes. He owns some of the most modern tenement buildings in the City of Richmond for colored tenants. His residence is one of the finest owned by one of his race in the South.

Mr. Price is interested in other business institutions. He is a director of the Mechanic's Savings Bank, the Capital Shoe and Supply Co., and the American Beneficiary Insurance Company.

Nathan K. McGill and Robert R. Church, Jr.

NATHAN K. McGILL

ORN of a slave mother Nathan K. McGill of Jacksonville, Fla., knows the day, month and place of his birth but not the year. But he also knows that as a pickaninny he was hungry for an education. Student in Cookman Institute, Jacksonville, Fla., whose principal secured for him a chance to run a barber shop at Monument Beach, Mass., during the summer vacation.

It was at this seaside resort that he met the noted Boston Philanthropist, Rufus B. Tobey, who agreed to assume all expense of completing his education on condition that when properly trained, he would return to Jacksonville and devote his life to assisting his people, a promise he has faithfully kept.

Graduate Boston University Law School in June, 1912. Qualified to practice before the Court of every state in the Union as well as before the U. S. Supreme Court. Mr. McGill is a member of Ebenezer M. E. Church.

He married Idalee P. Thornton, August 1st, 1917. They have one boy, Nathan K. Jr.

Robert Reid Church, Jr., is among the comparatively few American Negroes to have a big name to defend and uphold.

Mr. Church was born at Memphis, Tenn., October 26, 1885. He is the son of Robert R. Church and Annie Wright Church, and a brother of Mrs. Mary Church Terrell of Washington, D. C., the noted writer and wife of Judge R. R. Terrell. Robert R. Church was a well known man. He was looked upon as one of the biggest and wealthiest citizens of Memphis, Tenn., regardless of color. Indeed some of his acts led the Memphis citizens to regard him not only as a leader, but as a benefactor. When Memphis was in a bankrupt condition the elder Church was the first citizen to come forward and aid.

He purchased No. 1 of the city bonds at $2000. This act was looked upon by the leading citizens of Memphis as one of great importance. When in 1894 the big daily Memphis Schimitar, issued its 50th anniversary edition, Robert Church was the only Negro recognized in its pages. The paper gave him a full page article with a portrait of family and engraving of his home.

Robert Church, Jr., was educated in the Protestant Episcopal Parochial School at Memphis, Tenn., and completed his course at Oberlin College, Ohio. From the first the younger Church looked forward to assuming the responsibility of carrying forward his father's business. On finishing at Oberlin, he plunged immediately into business. He began his career as cashier of the Solvent Savings Bank and Trust Company in Memphis, Tenn., in 1905. Three years later, that is in 1908, he became its President.

Conducting the business of the Solvent Savings Bank and Trust Co. with success brought Mr. Church unlimited prestige in the Negro business world.

Also Mr. Church like his father, took active interest in the public affairs of the city and in the affairs of the nation. In both of these arenas, he soon became an effective worker. When the Standard Life Insurance Company of Atlanta, Ga., was established Mr. Church was chosen one of the directors.

He is a staunch Republican and was the only colored delegate from Tennessee to the National Republican Convention in 1912.

Mr. Church is a Mason and is a member of the famous "Frogs" in New York City. He was married July 26th, 1911, to Miss Johnson of Washington, D. C. Mr. and Mrs. Church have one daughter, Sarah Roberta, who lives with them at their beautiful home on South Lauderdale Street in Memphis.

Enos L. Scruggs and Mrs. Anna R. Fisher

ENOS L. SCRUGGS, B. D., A. M., D. D.

R. Enos L. Scruggs was born in Cole County, near Jefferson City, Mo., Feb. 23rd, 1858. He was left an orphan when a boy. He graduated from Lincoln Institute, Jefferson City, Mo., in 1885. Union Theological Seminary. (now the Divinity School of the University of Chicago), with the degree of B. D. in 1890. Dr. Scruggs' first pastorate was the Second Baptist Church of Ann Arbor and while there he attended a course of lectures at the University of Michigan. Accepted the presidency of Western College, Macon, Mo., in 1892. Became pastor of Calvary Baptist Church, Monmouth, Ill., in 1906; took charge of Mt. Emory Church, Jacksonville, Ill., in 1915. From Jacksonville, he went to his present pastorate in Jefferson City, Mo., Oct. 1st, 1918.

In recognition of his services as an educator, Western College and Lincoln Institute conferred the degree of Master of Arts upon him, and the Arkansas Baptist College, Little Rock, honored him with the degree of Doctor of Divinity.

When visiting in Missouri, in almost any part, if you talk about men and women who have gone out with nothing for a start and made good, very soon some one will mention the name of Mrs. Anna R. Fisher.

Mrs. Fisher was one of a large family of children and since her parents were poor, she had little opportunity to attend school. She did attend the district school nearest her when she could be spared from the work at the house and in the fields, but this was not for a long time.

But the little foundation gained by Mrs. Fisher at this time has proved sufficient for her to amass quite a fortune for a colored woman. She is a caterer. She is just naturally one. She started out with little and added to her stock and undertook larger affairs till now she owns silver, china and linen enough to set a table for one thousand. Aside from using this silver for her own banquets and dinners, she rents it out, at her own figure, to others who want to serve large numbers.

Mrs. Fisher owns a beautiful home. She bought the stone, the brick, the lumber, herself; lived in a tent on the place, hired all the workmen and bossed the job. Asked what her home cost her she said: "Well, I've never told anybody yet." Asked again, "Do you know what it cost you?" she replied, "Yes Madam, to the fraction of a cent." Mrs. Fisher makes beaten biscuit which she ships to all points in and out of the State. Catering is her trade, but on the side she runs a farm. Here she raises all the hams that she uses in her dinners and banquets as well as a great many other things.

Besides her catering business she sells about five hundred dollars worth of meat a year from her farm; her rental property brings her twelve hundred a year more.

RESIDENCE OF MRS. ANNA R. FISHER

510

Isaiah J. Whitley

HE life of Isaiah J. Whitley differed much in his youth from the majority of the Negro boys who came up out of poverty and great tribulation to occupy their stations in life.

He was born in Franklin, Washington County, Alabama, of honest, industrious and respected parents. His father was a prominent farmer of the county in which they lived and was the leading Baptist of his day. Isaiah was reared on the farm and because his father was in good financial condition he never experienced the life of a servant.

After receiving an elementary education he entered the Selma University and graduated with honor, being valedictorian of his class. While at Selma University he was President of the College Y. M. C. A. and served as assistant bookkeeper to the institution.

He also took courses at both the Tuskegee Institute and the Hampton Institute, studying the trade at both institutions.

He chose teaching as his profession and has served a number of schools. He taught school at Fairford, Alabama, and five years in the common schools of Alabama; three years in the State of Mississippi; served one year as principal of the Aldrich Grammar Schools, Aldrich, Alabama; and for the past eight years has been principal of Mobile County Training School. Under his management the school has grown from 80 pupils and two teachers to 441 pupils and nine teachers.

Mr. Whitley is broad minded and progressive. He is a prime mover in every educational and uplift work in the community. He is a member of the National Association of Teachers in Colored Schools, is secretary of the Alabama State Teachers' Association, and president of the National Rural Teachers' Association. He is the founder of the Plateau Farmers and Truckers' Conference, and his work in this connection cannot be too highly praised. He not only stands high in the esteem of the Negroes, but is so well thought of by the white citizens of his home county, that he was made a member of the Draft Board, and Colored County Food Administrator during the World War and was highly commended for his work in both places.

He married Miss Cornelia Leon Carrington, Sept. 8, 1910. They have two boys and one girl. He is a member of the Baptist Church, a Mason, and K. of P., and the owner of a comfortable home.

Unlike a great many members of the Negro race the career of Dr. Leath has been smooth and pleasant. The secret of his tranquil life is no doubt due to his loving and sympathetic disposition and his intense spirit of loyalty. He was an affectionate and loyal son and brother, and always rendered to his parents that honor and consideration due from a child to its father and mother. His father died in 1900 and his mother in 1912 and it is a source of great satisfaction to him that he can let his mind dwell upon them with only thoughts of sweet and pleasant memories.

He was one of thirteen children, and frequently did his part in helping his mother clean house and cook. In the course of his life he has worked on the farm, stood behind the barber's chair, solicited insurance, filled the office of teacher and now stands in the pulpit and on the rostrum. In securing an education he attended the public schools of Columbia, Alabama, afterwards teaching in these same schools, then went to the Tuskegee Normal and Industrial Institute, graduating in 1897; then to Payne University; graduating from the scientific course in 1901; he took a correspondence course in Howard University, studying Greek under German scholars. Having received the necessary preparation for his work he entered the ministry of the African Methodist Episcopal Church, and in the course of his ministry, has served some of the best colored churches in the South. He is now Presiding Elder of the Mobile, Alabama, district.

He is the Secretary of the Board of Trustees of Payne University. His ministerial career has been one of continued success and he has made friends in every field where he has labored. He was especially fond of children and because of his intense love and sympathy for them he won many of them to himself and to the cause of his Savior. Dr. Leath is an able man from every standpoint. He is an able orator, a great educator and a splendid preacher and pastor. He is an untiring worker and gave his services unstintingly in behalf of his country during the Worlds War. He is a member of the Masons and has held high office in that body.

Dr. Leath has prospered from the material standpoint and owns a 100 acre farm, and a house and lot at Greensboro, Ala.

The position he has obtained in the district he presides over has made it possible for him to be of great service to other members of his race.

He married Miss Pinkie C. Reece of Autaugaville in 1901, who has been a great help to him in his work.

C. W. Allen

IT is said a prophet is without honor in his own country, but this declaration is far from being a fact in the case of the serviceable and popular subject of this sketch, whose life story forms the burden of this narrative, for no other man of the race in the city of Mobile, Ala., be he native born or otherwise, has been more highly honored or shown himself to be more deserving of trust, confidence and honor.

Mr. Allen is a native of the city of Mobile, and was born October 17, 1872. Unlike the majority of men that have risen to place and prominence in the domain of church or state, he can not claim the pride of birth on a farm; nor can he claim an experience with any of the hardships that are incident to farming life. In his case, at least, it has been demonstrated that it is not necessary to be born on a farm and inured to its hardships in order to attain to the highest degree of service and usefulness to one's fellow citizens and country.

The fact that he is one of the worthy native sons of Mobile, possibly accounts for the high esteem in which he is held by the citizens of Mobile.

The parents of Mr. Allen were in most humble circumstances; and thus could not give to their son the educational advantages that they would have been glad to do if they had been able. His education was gained largely by his own earnest efforts and hard work. He was educated in the public schools of Mobile, Ala., and at Emerson Institute of the same city. Emerson Institute is one of the pioneer educational institutions of the race in the city of Mobile, and has done much to improve the intellectual and moral life of that community. This school was long ago established by the American Missionary Association, and has been the only Alma Mater of many of the worthiest and most successful men and women of the city of Mobile. Mr. Allen has not the honor of a diploma from this worthy institution, but he gained in its hallowed halls an inspiration to accomplish something worthy in life.

He started out in life early to make an honest living. At the age of fifteen years he took up the responsibilities of a wage-earner. Beginning at the humblest stage of menial service, he gradually worked his way up to employment in the government service in the position of carrier in the Mobile postoffice. He served as a carrier for ten years, and made a record for high efficiency. While serving in postoffice he had the honor of representing the Mobile Letter Carriers' Association three different times at the National Conventions of Letter Carriers at its sessions in Denver, Col., Chicago, Ills., and New York City.

Mr. Allen is a veteran dealer in real estate, and in co-partnership with Mr. James T. Peterson, he successfully engaged in the realty business for several years. The firm operated under the name of Peterson & Allen, and it was one of the leading real estate firms in the State of Alabama.

On the 10th of November, 1904, Mr. Allen, in partnership with Mr. Harney, purchased the undertaking firm of A. N. Johnson, which at that time was one of the most complete and one of the costliest funeral establishments in the South. Since purchasing this well established business they have added to their equipment, modernized it and developed it along progressive and up-to-date lines, until now it is second to few, if any, in this whole country.

The Company has modern and up-to-date equipment and facilities and it can satisfy the wishes of the greatest dignitary in the State. "A maximum of service for a minimum cost" is the business maxim of this premier funeral establishment of the race, and it is the concensus of opinion on the part of the people of Mobile that the company carries out its business maxim to the letter.

On the 6th of June, 1893, Mr. Allen married Miss Josephine Blackledge, of Mobile, Alabama. She is a graduate of the Mobile Colored High School, and was also a student of Emerson Institute of the same city. A woman of great intelligence and influence in her community, she is one of the useful and serviceable women of the race, and has done much for their welfare and uplift.

Mrs. Allen was an honored teacher in the Mobile Colored High Schools for three years. In the year of 1898 she organized the widely known Josephine Allen Private School. The growth of this school has been phenomenal in every respect from its very beginning.

Mr. Allen is an organizer and a man of splendid executive ability. As a financier he has few superiors, if any, and his administration of affairs, both fraternal and personal has demonstrated the fact that he is an extraordinary business man.

Ralph W. Tyler

NE of the later fields for the Negro to enter was that of journalism. While the Negro journalist soon learned to do well on papers of his own he found it difficult to enter the arena with the reporters of the big daily and metropolitan papers. Here as elsewhere he found an almost impassable barrier. First of all he had no background, his only hope of commendation would have to be based upon experience and excellence in the calling. The only way of getting these was upon these very dailies for which he aspired to work, thus the thing ran in a circle, shutting door after door to him.

In the South, it is customary to have at least one Negro reporter on all the dailies, but as yet few of the northern papers have adopted this policy.

Among the few upon whom the goddess of Tolerance smiled in the Editorium Sanctum, was Ralph W. Tyler of Columbus, Ohio. Fortunately Mr. Tyler gained an entrance in his native town. Born and reared here at Columbus, he did not have the awful task of getting used to the Editors of his town, or having them to get used to him.

On finishing High School at Columbus, Ohio, Mr. Tyler began his journalistic apprenticeship. He gained his experience on the staff of the Columbus Evening Despatch, where he began work in 1884. The satisfaction which he gave the editors of this paper both as an apprentice and as a seasoned worker must have been the best for he remained on the Evening Despatch for 17 years. Working for the Despatch he rose from reporter to assistant to the Manager and confidential secretary to the publisher.

Leaving the Evening Despatch, Mr. Tyler accepted work with the Ohio State Journal. Here he remained for three years. Throughout this score of years on the Evening Despatch and the Ohio Journal Mr. Tyler was the only Negro regularly employed on a white daily paper in the State of Ohio.

In 1905 because of his effective work as a journalist, Mr. Tyler was called to a position of prominence in the United States Government. In this year he was appointed by President Theodore Roosevelt as auditor to the Navy. He was reappointed by President Taft, thus he served in this post for eight years.

During the interim between 1913 and 1916, Mr. Tyler was contributor to both the white and colored newspapers. When Emmett J. Scott became special assistant to the Secretary of War, Mr. Tyler took work in Mr. Scott's office as publicity agent. In this capacity he had one of the most trying positions in public life to fill. He was compelled to see that the magnificent part being played by the Negro in the world was brought before the public and kept there. It was his duty to see that conditions needing correction, were brought before the public in a way that would bring the desired result without gaining the antagonism of that class of the press that is always ready and willing, on the slightest provocation to flaunt the red flag. That he met the issue with honor to himself and to his people is shown by the fact that he was the one Negro war correspondent sent abroad by the United States Government to tell the story of our troops in France.

Mr. Tyler is a descriptive writer of rare ability. He not only ranks as the foremost Negro Journalist and special correspondent, but ranks high among that galaxy of stars irrespective of race, that were selected by their countries to send the news back home of the every movement of the armies that contained the flower of their young manhood. His writings are of such character that he will be remembered not as a great Negro Journalist, but as a great American Journalist and war correspondent.

Who has not read the wonderful word pictures drawn by this brilliant young journalist?

Who has not been thrilled by his stories of the exploits of the Famous 92nd Division?

There is something inspiring in the human interest stories that he sent back from the battle scarred fields of Europe, and it is certain that many of his articles will be handed down to future generations as classics.

For more than thirty years Mr. Tyler has been engaged in newspaper and publicity work. He has served on the staff of some of the most famous dailies in the United States, and has made a reputation that is nation wide for his fearlessness in defending the interests of the Negroes. His efforts in behalf of the race cannot ever be approximated.

VIRGINIA HALL—SUNG UP BY THE HAMPTON SINGERS, 1872-73.

AMPTON Institute, the pioneer industrial school for the training of colored and Indian youth, which is situated on the Lower Peninsula of Virginia, is now preparing for intelligent public service and at the expense of generous citizens who represent many sections and classes, some 900 earnest Negroes and a small group of Indians in its Boarding Department.

Between four and five hundred colored boys and girls attend the Community graded school, known as "The Whittier School," which "offers excellent opportunities for the training of teachers under natural conditions."

The Hampton boys and girls are making a brave struggle to become leaders in community improvement work and efficient homemakers.

Over one hundred and fifty Hampton men are already in the United States Army and Navy doing their bit—intelligently and cheerfully to make the world safe for democracy.

Founded in 1868 by Gen. Samuel C. Armstrong, for over fifty years, through the co-operation and support of many of the best people of America, Hampton Institute has been training young people for unselfish and reliable service to their respective races and to their white neighbors.

The training of an army of over 2000 graduates and nearly 8000 former students—"soldiers of the common good"—represents a vast sum of money and effort which the American public has invested in carefully selected, ambitious colored and Indian youth.

Increased returns from farm lands, the multiplication and improvement of public schools, the building of good churches, the establishment of clean, pure homes—these are some of the fruits of the "Hampton Spirit."

The late Dr. Hollis B. Frissell, principal of Hampton from 1893 to 1917, said in his last report to the trustee:

"We hear much, in these days of preparedness for service, of how young people can be trained so as to be of the greatest possible use to their community and their country. This is the keynote of Hampton. He said shortly before his death: "Tell the American people that Hampton is a war measure."

The Robert C. Ogden Auditorium, designed by Ludlow & Peabody, of New York, is now completed. It accommodates some 2500 persons and has cost over $200,000. The money was raised by popular subscription. Gifts have come from white, colored, and Indian friends.

The General Education Board of New York has donated $25,000. The interest from this fund will be used for the maintenance of the Ogden Auditorium.

Students of the Hampton Institute Trade School recently completed their work on the new Administration Building.

They have also placed a new water tank on the tower of "Stone Building," which is one of the larger dormitories for boys. This tank will be used in connection with the sprinkler system for fire protection which is to be installed in the auditorium.

James Hall, the building of which was made possible through the gift of the late Mrs. Willis D. James, of New York, is a modern, fireproof dormitory which accommodates about 175 boys. It was built by Hampton Institute students.

Mrs. John S. Kennedy, of New York, through a

OGDEN HALL—IN MEMORY OF ROBERT C. OGDEN

similar gift, will make possible the building of new dormitories for the Hampton girls.

Clarke Hall, a two-story brick building, which is another Hampton Trade School product, was the first Negro student Y. M. C. A. building in this country.

Some 250 acres adjacent to "Shellbanks," the Hampton Institute farm, which is some six miles out from Hampton, have been acquired to give more Hampton students practical training in farming.

Hampton Institute also has a modern cold-storage equipment, as well as facilities for making steam, ice, and electricity.

Hampton Institute is, in short, an industrial village, and "an educational demonstration center where three races work out daily, with a minimum of friction, the problems of everyday life."

General Armstrong described the aim of Hampton in these striking words: "To train selected youth who shall go out and teach and lead their people, first by example by getting lands and homes —to teach respect for labor; to replace stupid drudgery with skilled hands; and to these ends to build up an industrial system, for the sake not only of self-support and intelligent labor, but also for the sake of character."

This aim was not changed by Dr. Frissell. It was developed, however, with rare skill and wisdom through his remarkable principalship of nearly twenty-five years.

Hampton has always emphasized the importance of self-sacrifice and service. Dr. Booker T. Washington, who founded Tuskegee Institute, and Dr. Robert R. Moton, who has succeeded Dr. Washington as principal of Tuskegee, were both trained at Hampton under General Armstrong and Doctor Frissell.

Hampton students have been fitted for life. They have also been trained to live for others. Throughout the South and West especially, there are many communities which have been literally reconstructed through the patient, thoughtful, and persistent work of Hampton graduates and former students.

Since Hampton Institute aims to train young people to earn an honest living and help improve the economic and social conditions of their races, the courses of study combine industrial training with academic work.

The regular courses are four years in length, and include Academic-Normal, Agricultural, Business, and Trade courses in any one of the following thirteen trades: Blacksmithing, Bricklaying and Plastering; Cabinet making; Carpentry; Machine Work; Painting; Printing; Shoemaking; Steamfitting and Plumbing; Tailoring; Tinsmithing; Upholstery; and Wheelwrighting. A two-year, advanced course in Teacher-training is also offered. Through the Hampton courses young men and women are trained to earn an honest living by practicing a useful vocation.

Colored and Indian girls at Hampton receive thorough training in cooking, sewing, laundering gardening, and methods of teaching.

In the Domestic Science Work Class, for example, "the girls work daily for twelve months in the laundry and in the boarding departments under the supervision of experienced teachers, and carry on their academic studies in the evening the same as the boys in the Work Class.

"The mental and moral training that the year of combined work and study gives makes it one of the most valuable years of the course. The working day for the girl is shorter than for the boy; but a girl can earn from $15 to $18 a month. This

CLASS IN DOMESTIC SCIENCE
HOME ECONOMIC DEPARTMENT

enables her to be entirely self-supporting during her first year in school, and to accumulate a balance toward defraying the expenses of the second year.

"In the Academic-Normal course girls receive training in Agriculture, Art, Bible, Business Transactions, English, Georgraphy, History, Home Economics, Physical Training, Sociology, and training in Teaching." The object of all Hampton's work is to fit leaders for service to their communities.

Some interesting tributes have been paid to Hampton and its constructive work.

President Wilson has said: "The people who are aiding Hampton Institute are doing a really great work for their country."

Former President Taft, who is the President of

RUG WEAVING
HOME ECONOMIC DEPARTMENT

the Hampton board of trustees, says: "Hampton is small compared with many great universities, but it is not the size, it is the type, it is the method, it is the result in the individual, that gives it today the right to be considered the most important single institution of learning in the country."

Through General Armstrong and Doctor Frissell, as well as a large company of devoted workers and friends Hampton Institute has rendered a significant service to the nation (1) by training thousands of colored and Indian youth to believe in themselves and in their races; (2) by teaching hundreds of thousands of white people to believe in members of the red and black races; and (3) by helping to reshape public opinion, not only in matters of racial goodwill, but also in matters of sound educational policy.

Dr. Frissell's stirring words will live on and on: "Out from Hampton there are going every years young people who carry the thought of service to others—the thought which Christ brought into the world when He said, 'Whosoever will save his life

PRESS ROOM OF PRINTING DEPARTMENT
HAMPTON TRADE SCHOOL

shall lose it; and whosoever will lose his life for My sake shall find it."

Dr. James E. Gregg, formerly a Congregational minister of Pittsfield, Mass., is the present principal of Hampton Institute. William Howard Taft, former President of the United States, who is the chairman of Hampton's board of trustees, refers to Dr. George as "straight-forward, effective, earnest, religious, broad, and feeling the joy of service and full of the greatness of the task he has assumed."

George Foster Peabody, Hampton's senior trustee, introduced Dr. Gregg to the great Hampton family of friends, alumni, workers, and students in these words:

"The new principal, Doctor Gregg, brings to his task the moral courage which made General Armstrong daring and the spiritual serenity which made Doctor Frissell wise. The friends of the school look with renewed confidence and hope to the beginning of Hampton's half-century of national service under the leadership of a man so well equipped as Doctor Gregg."

Sidney Dillon Redmond, A. M., M. D.

MOST striking and one of the most sensational examples of professional and financial success in the great State of Mississippi, or in the whole of the United States, for that matter, is in the case of Dr. Sidney Dillon Redmond, of the capital city of the State of Mississippi. It is true that in fortunate mining investments and in lucky speculative ventures fabulous fortunes have been the reward of the efforts of a few years or a few months; but in the ordinary channels of legitimate business and professional skill there are indeed few men in the State or Nation, regardless of race, that have as much in a material way to show for their labors as has the successful physician and sterling business man whose name not only graces this sketch, but is a source of inspiration to thousands of the race, who are ambitious to give a better account of themselves in the material walks of life.

Dr. Redmond was born at Ebenezer, in Holmes County, Miss., Oct. 12, 1872. His father having died when he was twelve years of age, his mother moved to Holly Springs, Miss., for the purpose of providing for her children the advantage of a good education. After completing the graded school courses, Dr. Redmond entered Rust University, from which he graduated in 1894. As an evidence of the esteem in which his scholarship was held, by the powers of Rust University, he was called to fill the chair of mathematics in that institution, which position he held one year. At the expiration of that time, he was promoted to the principalship of Meridian Academy, Meridian, Miss., which school is one of the preparatory centers for Rust University. He left here to enter the Illinois Medical College, in 1894, and graduated with honors in 1897.

Many times during his course at Illinois he was hard pressed for funds, but he knew that his people were suffering in many cases from poorly trained physicians and surgeons and he determined that he would obtain a training that would enable him to give his patients the benefit of every amount of skill and knowledge it was possible for him to obtain.

After his graduation in 1897, he decided to return to his native State to practice his profession. Carrying this resolution into effect, he arrived in the city of Jackson, Miss., November 15, 1897.

The only asset of the doctor at this time was a splendid education. He passed with flying colors the rigid examination of the medical board of examiners of the State of Mississippi, and it is said that the Board of Examiners gave him the honor of having passed the best examination of the two hundred and fifty (250) applicants that were present at that time, and one of the best in the history of the State, irrespective of race. After practicing his profession in the city of his choice for a season, he went to Boston, Mass., and pursued a post-graduate course in medicine at Harvard Medical College. He is one of the best prepared physicians in the medical profession, and his opinions have the weight of authority among his fellow practitioners. He is a specialist in surgery, with a State-wide reputation.

That the doctor is a capital business man is evident from the various business enterprises with which he is connected. He owns stock in the Capital Light and Power Company and in a number of the banks of Jackson, Miss.

It is believed by many people who are in position to know, that Dr. Sidney Dillon Redmond is the owner of more city property than any other colored man in the State of Mississippi. However, doubtful this statement may be, the writer is certain of the fact that the doctor is the owner of more than one hundred houses in the city of Jackson, among which are some of the most substantial and most pretentious buildings in the city. He owns business blocks in the center of the city's business section. In addition to his residence property, he owns a number of stores, several three and four story office buildings and a theater and roof garden in the heart of the city. The doctor is the owner of two of the largest drug stores in the city of Jackson, one of them being located on the main part of the principal street in the city.

In 1894, the doctor married Miss Ida Alcorn Revels, of Holly Springs, Miss., the talented daughter of ex-United States Senator H. S. Revels of the State of Mississippi. Mrs. Redmond is a graduate of the Academic Department of Rust University; and taught for a year as assistant to her husband when he was at the head of Meridian Academy. Two children have been born to the doctor and his estimable wife—Esther and Sidney Dillon, Jr.

Hon. Perry W. Howard, A. B., A. M., LL. B.

FOR some reason thousands of the foremost men of the nation have taken great pride in calling to the attention of the world the fact that they have rejoiced because their infant mouths missed the proverbial golden spoon that, figuratively speaking, plays such a prominent part in the lives of those who are born to the purple; but there is one distinguished man in the State of Mississippi that brings to his rescue no plea of poverty by birth, but who, on the contrary, is proud of the fact that the circumstances of his parents were such as enabled them to look well to the interest of their children from every standpoint involving their welfare. This exceptional man is none other than Honorable Perry W. Howard, the able and eminent barrister of Jackson, Miss.

Like his fellow citizens, that eminent physician, surgeon and financier, S. D. Redmond, Mr. Howard was born at Ebenezer, Holmes County, Miss. He first saw the light of day June 14, 1878. His father was a successful blacksmith in comfortable circumstances, who believed in using his means for the education of his children. After completing his preliminary studies in the public schools of Holmes County, Mr. Howard entered Alcorn A. & M., in 1891. In 1893, he transferred his allegiance to Rust University, of Holly Springs, Miss., from which place he graduated with the degree of Bachelor of Arts, in 1899.

Immediately after his graduation from Rust University he was elected to the presidency of Campbell College, of Jackson, Miss., one of the leading colleges of Central Mississippi, and he served at the head of this institution until the conclusion of the school session in the year of 1900. In the same year, while serving as President of Campbell College, it was the pleasure of the trustees of that well-known Institution of learning to confer upon the distinguished subject of this sketch the honorary degree of Master of Arts, as an humble testimonial to his ability. From the Presidency of Campbell College he was elected to fill the chair of mathematics in Alcorn A. & M. College, and he served in that capacity for five years, or until the year of 1905. While occupying the chair of mathematics in Alcorn University he diligently applied himself to the study of law. Three months of each year were spent at the Illinois College of Law, Chicago, Ill. He graduated from this law school in the year of 1905, with the degree of LL. B. He resigned the chair of mathematics in Alcorn College, began the practice of law in Jackson, Miss. He demonstrated his fitness for the practice of his profession by running the gauntlet of examination by the members of the Supreme Court of Mississippi.

In abandoning the profession of teaching for that of law, he was merely carrying out the plan of life, adopted by him when he first entered college, and adhered to throughout.

He was a teacher of the highest qualification and that breadth and depth of mind that enabled him to take such a high rank in the teachers' profession have enabled him to take a rank of even greater magnitude in the legal profession. He is one of the leading political orators of the State, and an effective man on the hustlings in any capacity. He did Yeoman's service for his country in this respect during the world's war.

Mr. Howard is as successful in business as he is in the practice of law. He is a large stock holder in many of the commercial enterprises of the city of Jackson.

He married Miss Wilhelmina Lucas, of Macon, Miss., in 1907. Her mother, who was a Miss Robinson, was the first female graduate of Fisk University, Nashville, Tennessee, and a member of the original Fisk Jubilee Singers for five years. Mrs. Howard is a graduate of Fisk University, and had much experience in the teachers' profession. She was once a teacher in the literary department of Tuskegee Normal Institute, and at another time she was a teacher in the music department of Alcorn A. & M. College.

Lawyer Howard is peculiarly adapted by temperament for success in the practice of his profession. He has had the literary training; he has had the legal training, and he has undying confidence in his ability to look well after the interests of his client, and confidence under such conditions is nine points in his favor. His gentlemanly bearing and unfailing courtesy have won for him the friendship and respect of both the white and colored members of the State bar of Mississippi.

Louis K. Atwood, A. B.

 OME score of years ago, somebody asked if it was Booker T. Washington who discovered Mississippi. Since the wizard of Tuskegee is blamed and credited with so many feats it would not be altogether inappropriate to credit him with the Right discovery of Mississippi. To be sure everybody knew that the land of Private John Allen and Jefferson Davis was there, but the real resourceful Mississippi and especially Negro Mississippi was not known until recent years. Then it was found on the farms, in the delta lands, in the villages, in the small towns and in a few large towns there were Negroes of considerable wealth.

To be a peer with a financier of Mississippi is no mean post. Such is the good fortune of L. K. Atwood of Jackson, Mississippi. Mr. Atwood was born in Alabama. He completed the work in elementary education in his native state. He then went to Lincoln University in Pennsylvania, whence he was graduated in 1874 with the honors of his class. For some years after graduation he taught school in Hinds County, Mississippi.

Showing greater freedom and aspiring to manage larger finances, Mr. Atwood engaged in the mercantile business. In the mean time he also read law and in 1879 was admitted to the bar in Mississippi. In this year and in 1883 he was a member of the Mississippi Legislature. In both years Mr. Atwood goes down in history as the candidate who won the best vote ever polled for a representative in Hinds County. His most distinctive work in the Mississippi Legislature was that of securing liberal appropriation for Alcorn College. In 1899 Mr. Atwood was made Deputy United States Collector of Internal Revenue for the States of Mississippi and Louisiana. In business and in a number of the secret organizations Mr. Atwood is a man of great power and far-reaching influence.

Probably no one Negro in the State of Mississippi can state with greater pride his regard for benevolent society work than Mr. Atwood. In the year 1884 he joined the Order of Jacobs. Under his leadership, for he was master of the order, this body has paid out more than $410,000 in benefits to the Negroes in the State of Mississippi.

This powerful fraternity is one of the most beneficent organizations soliciting the patronage of the public. It has come before the people of Mississippi for recognition and support solely on its merits. It is founded on Gibraltar like business principles. While its ritualistic work is sublime, the fact must not be overlooked that this fraternity is first of all, a high class business organization. While the primary object of any fraternal organization is the promoting of the moral, physical, intellectual and material welfare of its members, Mr. Atwood knows this can be done only by combining correct business principals with proper mental and moral training and this accounts for his success with the Jacobs.

Mr. Atwood is Editor of the Jacobs Watchman as well as master of the order. Through this paper he reaches and knows many people both in and out of the State of Mississippi. Finding a success in the order and in politics, Mr. Atwood turned his attention to banking. In the year 1904 he organized at Jackson, the American Trust and Savings Bank. Its first dividend paid 27 per cent. Two years later he resigned his place with the American Trust and Savings Bank and organized the Southern Bank, of which he is president.

There is not a man in the State of Mississippi that is more widely and more favorably known than Mr. Atwood. He conducts all of his business on a safe and sane basis and his pronounced success in this particular should be an inspiration to others. In his relation to his many employes he accords them every courtesy. He has not resorted to domineering methods to get the required work out of the men in his employment, but has ever been just and considerate and gets the maximum of service and loyalty from his employes. As measured by his achievements, he is a highly successful man. He is an organizer and a worker and has the power of initiative so essential for the success of any leader. He has the ability to carry on to a successful conclusion, a great many different enterprises at one time. He is a convincing conversationalist and a forceful orator. He is well poised and never loses his dignity.

He is widely known both in Mississippi and in Negro business circles as a successful banker, astute lawyer, and able financier.

IRVINE GARLAND PENN, A. M., LITT. D

RVINE Garland Penn was born at New Glasgow, Virginia, October 7, 1867, and is 52 years of age. His present place of residence is Cincinnati, Ohio. His parents. Isham and Maria Penn, moved to Lynchburg, Virginia, when he was five years of age to give their children the advantage of city educational facilities. He graduated from the elementary and High School of Lynchburg and received his college training under private tutorage and was given the degree of Master of Arts from Rust College. Later the honorary degree of Doctor of Literature was conferred upon him by Wiley College.

He is the oldest of five children. He had therefore to get an early training in life that he might help his parents educate his brothers and sisters. His father never earned more than $30.00 per month and for years received only $25.00 as his wage.

He began therefore to teach in the public schools of Virginia at 18, was editor of a newspaper at 19 and principal of the public schools in Lynchburg, Virginia, at 20, continuing until he resigned in 1895 to accept the National Commissionership of Negro Exhibits at the Cotton States and International Exposition.

He has been a general officer in the Methodist Episcopal Church for 23 years. He has also been a member of the General Conference of the Methodist Episcopal Church which is the highest law making body of the church, for 28 years in continuous service. He has held four important salaried positions in 34 years of public life, always resigning the one to accept another, namely, principal in the public schools in Virginia, for 10 years, National Commissioner Negro Exhibits Cotton States and International Exposition, Atlanta, Georgia, one year 1895, General Secretary for colored people of the Epworth League of the Methodist Episcopal Church residing in Atlanta, Georgia, 16 years and Corresponding Secretary of the Freedmen's Aid Society of the Methodist Episcopal Church residing in Cincinnati 7 years.

He has traveled extensively for 23 years throughout the United States as a general officer in the Methodist Episcopal Church.

He married December 26, 1889, in Lynchburg, Virginia, Miss Anna Belle Rhodes, a teacher in the city schools of Lynchburg and a classical graduate of Shaw University, Raleigh, N. C. He has been married 30 years and has seven children and three grandchildren. The names of these children are Mrs. Wilhelmina Franklin, Cincinnati; Rev. I. Garland Penn, Jr., Maysville, Kentucky; Mrs. Georgia S. Williams, Little Rock, and Misses Elizabeth, Louise, Marie and Anna B. Penn.

When at Atlanta, Georgia, as National Commissioner of the Cotton States and International Exposition in 1895, he received a gold medal of first award for the excellence of the Negro Exhibit. He is credited with having given Dr. Booker T. Washington and Tuskegee its new impetus because he selected Dr. Washington to make the famous address which was conceded to be the turning point in the life of that great man.

His career in literary life has been that of the author of the Afro-American Press, a book of 600 pages and the only authoritative history of Negro journalism and its relationship to the abolition of slavery. He is also co-author with Dr. Northrup in the preparation and publication of The College of Life or Self Educator and with Dr. J. W. E. Bowen in the publication of the United Negro. He was the originator of the Congress of Christian Workers and Educators known as the Young Peoples' Christian and Educational Congress, which met in Atlanta in 1902 and in Washington in 1906. These meetings have been since duplicated in various churches throughout the United States and furnished greater stimulus to religious and educational work among Negro people than any other meetings ever held. The meeting at Atlanta was attended by 10,000 of the most representative people of the Negro race and has the record of being the largest attended meeting ever held before the since of the Negro race.

Secretary Penn participated in the Centenary of the Methodist Episcopal Church as the Freedmen's Aid representative by appointment of his Board. He helped in the raising of the 112 millions for education and missions. This Centenary is to benent the Freedmen's Aid Society in contributing to the endowment and building program of the schools.

SAMUEL N. VASS, D. D.

R. Vass, son of Major W. W. and
Annie Victoria (Mitchell) Vass,
was born in Raleigh, N. C., May
22, 1866, and educated in St. Augustine School and Shaw University, located in his native city. At
fourteen years of age, being poor, he began teaching school in the country during vacation and also
for two months during the school session, but he
kept up with his studies. Graduating from St.
Augustine School at seventeen, he was elected
Vice-Principal of one of the public schools in Raleigh, was called to teach at Shaw University. He
began at the bottom, but was promoted gradually
until he was the Dean of the college department.
He resigned at Shaw in 1893, to become Sunday
School Missionary of the American Baptist Publication Society for Virginia, Maryland, and the District of Columbia. After serving as Missionary for
about three years, he was made the District Secretary for the Southern States, with headquarters
at Atlanta, Ga.

About this time many leaders of the colored
race inclined to a policy of entire separation from
their white friends in all denominational work, and

the great National Baptist Convention itself lent
its influence for a while in this direction, and great
race bitterness was developed, and bitter dissen-
sions among the Negro Baptist leaders. Dr. Vass
was the central figure in this controversy, which
lasted a decade, his position being that the time had
not arrived for Negroes to part with their white
friends in denominational work, and he advocated
cooperation as the proper policy of the race and
denomination.

Today, co-operation is the watchword of the entire Negro Baptist family. Negro Baptist constitute so large a percentage of the Negro race that
the policy of the Baptists largely dominated the
policy of the race, with the result that Dr. Vass began to assume national importance and is today
one of the most prominent men of the race.

During the sixteen years he has been continuously in the service of the Publication Society, he has
been twice offered the presidency of one institution
of learning, and was recently elected to take charge
of another school, at Augusta, Ga. He has also
been urged to assume the pastorate, but he has
preferred the field work on account of the great
possibilities of reaching the largest number for
good.

The Publication Society has promoted Dr. Vass
to become its Superintendent for Colored Work for
the entire United States. He supervises the field
work of colored missionaries and suggests to them
the best methods of doing the field work, and from
time to time calls them all together into a school of
methods.

Dr. Vass has made a specialty of normal work,
and he restricts his normal work to its application to Bible study and teaching. He illustrates
his method of actually imparting Bible knowledge
at the same time he teaches method. In fact, he
pays as much attention to teaching the Bible as he
does to imparting method, and he often gathers
ministers and other workers in conference at strategic points for the special study of the Bible. A
recent conference at Shreveport, La., had an attendance of more than a hundred preachers.

He is often invited to do this normal Bible work
before state conventions. There is very close co-
operation between the work of Dr. Vass and that
of the National Baptist Convention, and he holds
joint meetings with National Convention workers
on the field and occupies an important and influential place among the leaders of that body today.
Dr. Vass enjoys the highest confidence of the great
society under which he works.

He has a national reputation as an author and his
works are widely read.

Dr. Vass' married Mary Eliza Haywood, of Raleigh, N. C., June 1885. They have two children,
M. and Lillian. (Mrs. N. F. Bass), and Dr. R. S. Vass,

Richard Robert Wright, Jr., A. B., A. M., B. D., Ph. D.

RICHARD Robert Wright, Jr., is the son of Major R. R. and Mrs. Lydia Elizabeth Howard) Wright. His father has been for twenty-five years the president of the Georgia State Industrial College, Savannah, Ga., and was major and paymaster of the United States Volunteers in the Spanish-American war. He was born April 16, 1878, at Cuthbert, Ga. He is a member of a family of nine children. Entered school at the age of six years, and attended school about eighteen years in all, attending the graded schools of Augusta, Ga.; Haines Institute, Augusta, Ga.; Georgia State College, University of Chicago and University of Pennsylvania. Graduated from the normal department of the Georgia State College in 1895, receiving gold medal for scholarship. He received A. B. degree from Georgia State College, 1898; A. M., Georgia State College, 1901; B. D., from the University of Chicago, 1901; A. M., from the University of Chicago, 1904; Ph. D., from the University of Pennsylvania, 1911. He was Research Fellow in Sociology, 1905-6, and Special University Fellow in Sociology at University of Pennsylvania, 1906-8. During 1903-1904 he studied in the University of Berlin, Germany; in 1904 he was a student at the University of Liepzig, Germany. He refused to accept the honorary degree of D. D. from Wilberforce University, in 1914, because of the conviction that no man under forty years of age should receive an honorary degree. He was converted February, 1891, and joined Bethel A. M. E. Church, Augusta, Ga. He has been an exhorter, local preacher, Sunday school teacher, secretary and assistant superintendent of Sunday schools, and president of Allen Christian Endeavor. Licensed to exhort by Rev. S. D. Roseborough, in 1898, and licensed to preach in 1899 at St. Phillip's, Savannah, Ga., by Rev. T. N. M Smith; joined the Iowa Annual Conference under Bishop Arnett, September, 1899, at Bethel Church, Chicago, Rev. R. C. Ransom, pastor; ordained deacon, September, 1900, at Minneapolis, Minn., by Bishop Grant; ordained elder September, 1901, at St. Stephen's, Chicago, by Bishop Grant. Dr. Wright has held the following appointments: Assistant pastor of the Institutional Church, Chicago, 1900-01; instructor of Hebrew and New Testament Greek in Payne Theological Seminary, 1901-1903; on leave of absence to study in Germany, 1903-1904; Elgin, Ill., 1904; Trinity, Chicago, 1904-1905; in University of Pennsylvania, 1905-1908; Conshohocken, Penn., 1908; editor Christian Recorder since 1909. He was a member of the general conference of 1912, and business manager of the Book Concern, as well as editor from February, 1909 to 1912, succeeding I. H. T. Johnson editor and Dr. J. H. Collett, manager, both deceased. He was a delegate to the Ecumenical Conference, Toronto, Canada, 1911; was elected editor of Christian Recorder in 1912 and re-elected without opposition in 1916. Married Miss Charlotte Crogman, daughter of Dr. W. H. Crogman, then president of Clark University, at Atlanta, Ga., in 1909. They have three children—Ruth, 5 years; Richard R., III, 3 years; Alberta, 1 year. In July, 1911, when the Book Concern was to be sold by the sheriff for a $5000 judgment, Dr. Wright prevented the sale by purchasing the judgment for $1900 of his own funds. In 1916 he purchased a permanent church home for St. John's Mission, Philadelphia, for more than $2000 cash.

Dr. Wright was elected instructor of sociology in Howard University, at $1500 per year, but declined. He is the founder and president of Eighth Ward Settlement Building and Loan Association, member of board of managers of Association for Protection of Colored Women, Spring Street Social Settlement, member board of direction of Work for Colored Churches, of Federal Council of Churches of Christ in America, Abolition Society, Mercy Hospital, member American Academy of Political and Social Science, Sigma Pi Phi, Alpha Boule, American Negro Academy. Author of "Negro in Pennsylvania," "Teaching of Jesus," "The Negro Problem," and numerous pamphlets, magazine articles. His sociological studies have been published by United States Bureau of Labor, Pennsylvania Bureau of Industrial Statistics, Pittsburgh Survey, Annals of American Academy of Political and Social Science, Southern Workman, Star Center, Inter-Municipal Review, publications of the Southern Sociological Society. He has lectured at Howard University, Wilberforce, Georgia State College, Morris Brown University, Allen University, Campbell College, A. and M. College (Mississippi), Lincoln Institute (Missouri), A. and T. College (Greensboro, N. C.), the University of Pennsylvania, Institute for Colored youths, and numerous educational institutions.

The above sketch reproduced from the "Encyclopedia of African Methodism" gives some idea of the preparation of the guiding spirit in that tremendous undertaking and accounts for the high character of the contents. The Encyclopedia of African Methodism was compiled by Dr. Wright in 1916, assisted by John R. Hawkins.

Toussaint L'Overture

TOUSSAINT L'Overture is regarded by historians and the thinking world as one of the best instances of what a pure blooded Negro can make of himself even under trying conditions. He was born a slave near Cape Francais in the Island of Hayti, in 1743. His father and mother were African slaves. His particular work on the farm was that of coachman, and afterwards assistant to the overseer on his master's sugar plantation. In contact with the overseer and his master in these two capacities, he gained some education which as all the world knows he used to great advantage for his fellow countrymen. As is well known, the French Revolution broke out in 1789. The islands of Hayti and Santo Domingo being among the chief if not the chief possessions of the French Government quickly imbibed the spirit of Revolution. Negroes had been imported upon these islands from every section of the world. So numerous had they become that they out-numbered the whites about 17 to 1. The population of Hayti in 1700 numbered about 500,000. Of these 38,800 were Europeans, 23,370 were free mulattoes. Caught in the whirl of the Revolutionary spirit, the Negroes started a revolution.

The European Governments saw to it that even the mulattoes had little freedom, though the latter were wealthy and intelligent as a class. In May, 1791, the French General Assembly gave to the free Negro rights of citizenship. These rights, however, the Colonial planters were inclined to suppress. In August of the same year the slaves began their insurrection. The mulattoes and whites dropped their quarrels and turned their attention to the Revolution. The mulattoes joined forces with the slaves. It was in this uprising that Toussaint L'Overture won distinction.

In the second battle in 1792, Toussaint joined with the Spaniards and succeeded in routing the French. The next year the French Commissioners proclaimed universal freedom. This won the Negro to the colours of the French Republic. At this time the English were besieging Port Au Prince. Toussaint rushed to the aid of the French and succeeded in repelling the English. The French General who was defending Port Au Prince was named Laveaux. It is from Laveaux, so history records, that Toussaint gained his surname L'Overture.

Laveaux is said to have exclaimed: "Mais set homme fait ouverture patout." After this L'Overture was made a general of the division and fought bravely against the Spaniards.

In 1796 he was made Commander-in-chief of the French forces on the Island. The next year he caused the surrender of the English who were at that time invading Hayti. In a quarrel with the French Commissioner Hedoville, Toussaint sent him home. By 1801, he had put down all foes and had the island under complete subjection.

From now on he was the dictator on the island, however he ruled with moderation and justice towards all classes. Under his dictatorship, both Hayti and Santo Domingo reached great heights of prosperity. It is probable also that in no periods of these has there been such uniform peace.

In his private life, he was said to have been kind, reasonable and modest. In public he assumed a good bit of pomp in order to inspire his followers. His title was "Life President."

At last, however, the French Commander Leclerc promised the whole island absolute freedom. He thus won to him the Negro chieftain. Toussaint was treacherously seized and sent to France to die in a dungeon.

The climax of Wendell Phillips' speech in comparing Toussaint L'Overture with other great generals of the world should be known by every Negro. Phillips says: "Hayti from the ruins of her colonial dependence, is become a civilized State, the seventh Nation in the catalogue of commerce with this country, inferior in morals and education to none of the West Indian Isles. Foreign merchants trust her goods as willingly as they do our own. Thus far she has foiled the ambition of Spain, the greed of England and the malicious statesmanship of Leclerc. Toussaint made her what she is. In this work there have been grouped around him a score of men mostly of pure Negro blood who ably seconded his efforts. They were able in war and skilful in civil affairs, but not like him remarkable for that rare mingling of high qualties which alone makes true greatness and ensues a man leadership among those otherwise almost his equals. Toussaint was indisputably their chief. Courage, purpose, endurance—these are the tests. He did plant a state so deep that all the world has not been able to root it up.

I would call him Napoleon, but Napoleon made his way to empire over broken oaths and through a sea of blood. This man never broke his word; "No retaliation," was his great motto and the rule of his life; and the last words uttered to his son in France were these: "My boy, you will some day go back to Santo Domingo; forget that France murdered your father."

Hon. Edward Wilmont Blyden, LL. D.

WITHOUT doubt, the Hon. E. W. Blyden was the most learned man of the race, especially in the languages, and as such, was acknowledged a man of a most gigantic intellect and acquisitive powers. He was born in St. Thomas, one of the Danish West Indies, August 3, 1832, but lived in the United States for some time during his youth. From this country, accompanied by his brother, he went to Liberia, landing January 26, 1851. At this time he was about nineteen years old. He was educated at Alexander High School, of which he became principal. This school was situated up the river St. Paul, about twenty miles from Monrovia. He has held many positions of honor and trust under the Liberian Government. He has been twice the Secretary of State of Liberia, and secretary of the interior once. For eight years he was minister plenipotentiary and envoy extraordinary to the Court of St. James. He was candidate and nominee of the Liberia Republican Party, for the Presidency, in 1884, but was defeated by H. R. W. Johnson, who was for years President of Liberia.

Dr. Blyden was a distinguished linguist and oriental scholar, and a prolific magazine writer, and had a wonderful knowledge of the Arabic language, having been professor of this language at one time. The following notice appeared in the London Official Gazette and is here quoted by way of information:

"The Liberian Minister To The Court of St. James."

"Osborne, August 3.—This day had audience of Her Majesty, Edward Wilmont Blyden, esq., Minister Plenipotentiary from the Republic of Liberia, to deliver new credentials, to which audience he was introduced by the Marquis of Salisbury, K. G., Her Majesty's principal Secretary of State for Foreign affairs.

Dr. Blyden has the honor of being the first Negro Plenipotentiary of the First Christian Negro State in Africa ever received at a court in Europe. In 1866, he visited Palestine and Egypt, and afterwards published an account of his travels in a volume, entitled "From West Africa to Palestine." In 1871, he resigned his professorship in the college and traveled in England. On his return to Africa he accepted the appointment from Governor Kennedy of Sierra Leone, of envoy to the pagan King of the Soolima Country. His report on that expedition was printed by the government and published in the proceedings of the Royal Geographical Society.

In 1873, he was sent by Governor J. Pope Hennessy on another mission to a Mohammedan chief, three hundred miles northeast of Sierra Leone. In 1874, he was authorized to re-open the Alexander High School, on the St. Paul River, which is now in charge of an assistant. In 1877, he was appointed by President Payne, minister to England, and President Gardner has continued the appointment.

Dr. Blyden has contributed several articles to the Methodist Quarterly Review in New York, and Fraser's Magazine in England. His local paper on "Africa and the Africans" has appeared in Fraser for August, 1878.

Dr. Blyden has been chosen an honorary member of the Atheneum Club, one of the most aristocratic and exclusive clubs of London. On the committee who elected him are such men as Sir John Lubbock, Lord Carnarvon, Herbert Spencer, Viscount Caldwell and Dean Church. The Marquis of Salisbury, the foreign secretary, is a member of the club. Dr. Blyden is probably the first Nergo who has been so honored."

It is said that he was acquainted with more than forty languages and speaks all of them fluently. He has been a believer in the Christian religion, but it is now currently reported and pretty satisfactorily understood that he became an advocate of the Mohammedan faith. He wrote a series of articles upon that topic to the A. M. E. Review, in which it is apparent he seeks to commend the fine points concerning the doctrines of that faith. Being brought in contact with many of the Arabic professors, he had an abundant opportunity of inquiring into the faith more practically than any one else of his color, because he gathered his information from the actual professors of that faith.

Mr. Blyden returned to Africa and spent the balance of his days there. He was formerly a Presbyterian minister, but abandoned the pulpit. This man's ability, scholarship and talent was a wonderful example of the native ability of the Negro. His intellect towers above that of ordinary men as the church steeple above the brick chimney of the ordinary house.

Thomas Green Bethune, "Blind Tom"

THOMAS Green Bethune, better known as "Blind Tom," was born May 25, 1849, in Columbus, Georgia. Thomas was born blind and as the beauties of nature could only be revealed to him through the sense of hearing, and retained by the power of memory and imitation, these faculties were cultivated to a remarkable degree, making him a marvel to the age in which he lived.

He was the embodiment of music, and in this art his powers were unlimited.

He first had access to a piano when he was four years of age, and his joy could not be imagined when he could perform on the instrument the thoughts of his youthful brain.

After exhausting his store of lessons he began to improvise for himself, playing what he said "the wind said," or the trees or birds.

His "Rain Storm," composed during a thunder storm when Tom was but five years old, is so perfect that the hearer instinctively looked for the lightning flash. His soul was the master of music, and so great a master that musicians declined to instruct him. Said one musician: "I can't teach him anything; he knows more of music than we know or can know. We can learn all that great genius can reduce to rule and put in tangible form; he knows more than that. I do not even know what it is; but I feel it is something beyond my comprehension. All that can be done for him will be to let him hear fine playing; he will work it all out by himself after awhile."

When a babe Thomas seemed totally blind and it was because of this that he received the cognomen, "Blind Tom." As he grew he was enabled in time to enjoy to a limited extent the blessing of sight.

When a young child, often he might be seen with head upturned, gazing intently upon the sun, and he would thrust his fingers into his eyes with such force that they would bleed.

This he continued until he became able to distinguish any very bright object.

Mr. Trotter says of him: "Considering that in early life he learned nothing, and later but little from sight, that he is possessed by an overmastering passion which so pervades his whole nature as to leave little room for interest in anything else, and the gratification of which has been indulged to the largest extent, it is not surprising that to the outside world he should exhibit but few manifestations of intellect as applicable to any of the ordinary affairs of life, or that those who see him under its influence should conclude that he is idiotic."

He had a most extraordinary memory of names, dates and events, a wonderful power of imitation and an elegance of taste and power in his performances.

He adhered strictly to what he believed was right, was uniformly polite and exhibited a nice sense of propriety.

Eminent musicians both in America and Europe bear testimony to his musical genius.

Among his classical selections was Andante by Mendelssohn and Sonata "Pathetique" by Beethoven. His marches include "Delta Kappa Epsilon," Pease; "Grand March de Concert," Wallace; "General Ripley's March," Amazon March, Masonic Grand March.

His powers of imitation were so perfect as often to deceive the hearer. They were imitations of the Music Box, Dutch Woman and Hand Organ, Harp, Scotch Bagpipes, Scotch Fidler, Church Organ, Guitar, Banjo, Douglass' Speech, Uncle Charlie, The Cascade, Rain Storm and Battle of Manassas. The two latter were his own composition, representing his descriptive music.

His fame is world wide. He has visited all the large cities of America and Europe and has entertained thousands, who have listened to his performances with wonder and accorded him enthusiastic applause.

Doubtless more persons have flocked to see and hear him than any other living wonder.

After playing, he generally sprang up and applauded himself vociferously.

For a while he disappeared from the stage, but reappeared in New York in 1904-05 and finally ended his career in Hoboken, N. J., in 1908, where he died.

An article of this length can merely touch upon his most wonderful career.

Samuel Coleridge Taylor

OMMON are the names of the Negro poet, the orator, the business man, indeed the names of black folk in nearly every achievement. But somehow when you call for the Negro composer the names are not so familiar. It appears that only in very recent years has the Negro himself begun to appreciate either music or the musician in our midst, and especially the genuine composer.

Coleridge Taylor, or to give him his full name, Samuel Coleridge Taylor, is worthy of the name he carries. The poet, after whom no doubt his name has been chosen, though differently placed, was in everything a mystic. The critics say that ever in his composition the musician is true in this mysticism to the spirit of the past. Coleridge Taylor comes almost fresh from the land of mystery and weird songs and lurid lights. His father was a native of Sierra Leone; his mother a British woman.

For a while after their marriage the parents lived happily together in England. Then the father returned to Africa. The lad remained in England with his mother. Young Taylor was a prodigy from the first. His aptness inspired his mother to direct even at a very early age, his attention specifically to music, thus saving time and energy and perhaps saving to the world a splendid musician; for had she tried to send him through regular curriculum who knows what might have happened to the musical prodigy.

Born in London, in 1875, young Taylor entered the Royal Academy of Music at the age of fifteen. Before entering he had had some training with the violin and the piano. At the Royal Academy the young man soon took his place as the most brilliant in the school, for he distinguished himself by winning the prize for musical composition in 1893, during his third year there. He continued his studies here, putting himself under the famous Villivers-Stanford until 1896.

In 1903, he landed his first endeavor in organization. Fortunately he hit upon the task in which he was to excel at the very first. At Craydon, in the year mentioned he organized and brought to a very successful conclusion a series of orchestral concerts.

This marked the beginning of musical fame, both as a composer and as a musical director. From that time on the world knew him for his weird and melancholy music. From this time for a score of years later he held sway first in the British music halls and then in American.

Phileas, it is said got all of his images of the Greek Gods from the poet Homer. The sculptor took the blind poets words and made them live in stone. Such was the genius of Coleridge Taylor. He took the words of the poet and gave them a new meaning with note and bar. Who does not know his Hiawatha, which he rendered himself with a chorus, more than once in this country. His music but puts new meaning into the words of Longfellow. So with the poems of Dunbar and with the works of others, he gave to them the touch which only music can offer as the finish to verse.

No real music shelf is now complete without one or two pieces of his work. Indeed, few entertainments, and none among Negroes are given without at least one selection from his hand. In addition to Hiawatha and the poems of Dunbar already mentioned, Coleridge Taylor has the following famous pieces: "The Blind Girl of Castle;" "Guille," "The Atonement," "Dream Towers," which is an operetta. He has also piano music, and anthems as well.

Whatever may be his fate abroad and in his native land, Coleridge Taylor is pretty sure of immortality among the American Negroes. He will probably never be popular but among those who strive for perfection and for the highest in musical composition he will always be famous. During his life time and immediately after his death, the devotees of the art sought to make his election to popular fancy sure by naming many choral clubs after him. No doubt this will hold his name before the public a little longer, but before it binds itself around the public heart, the worshippers at his shrine must raise the standard so high that the rag-time and the jog will not so easily drown out the voice of the master. Until they can accomplish this let the few continue to worship at his shrine and the whole race rejoice that at least one Negro commands the best artists, wherever good music is loved and played.

LT. COLONEL CHARLES YOUNG

MIDST the sharp, even harsh, competition for rank, it is a rare and glorious honor to be distinguished in any one of the wars of America. How happy must the soldier be therefore who receives laurels from any battle fields and from periods of history, and who amidst it all is a candidate for new fields and battles and a rival for the highest military honors his nation has to give.

Such is the good fortune of Lieutenant Colonel Charles Young, who received the rank of Lieutenant Colonel in 1916 during the world war. The subject of this sketch had by his skill, intelligence, courage and hard work been in the ascendency for the last score of years. Indeed Colonel Young is one of the picked men. The rank he now holds is the highest ever attained by a Negro in the regular army. He is one of the three Negroes to be graduated from West Point, having completed the course there in 1889.

Colonel Young is a native of the State of Kentucky. On completing his course at West Point he was commissioned to the Tenth Cavalry. It was not long before his distinguished services won for him the rank of Major. It was during the Spanish-American War that Colonel Young and his horse began to win fame. It was the famous Tenth who, following their tactics which they had learned in fighting the Indians, succeeded in rescuing the Rough Riders and their Colonel, Roosevelt, from sure defeat. From now on Colonel Young and his men are famous whether they are camping, doing a practice drill or actual service.

Following the Spanish-American War Colonel Young was assigned to the Island of Philippines. Once more thorough workmanship, coolness under fire, geniality and diplomacy characterized his life here. At another period of his life he was Commandant of cadets at Wilberforce University in the State of Ohio. Another time he was sent to the Republic of Liberia to give instruction in Military science, a post which he filled with credit to himself, his race and his country as well.

When Mexico under Villa, began to attack America on the southern border Colonel Young was sent to Texas with his men to protect his country. As in all other battles he and his famous Tenth came off with the glory. During the war in Europe some question arose as to the health of Colonel Young. It was alleged that his heart was too weak to stand the strain of European service. Specialists examined him, but found his heart sound. However, he was for a time retired and sent back to Wilberforce. To demonstrate the soundness of the whole man, Colonel Young rode horse back all the way from the West to the Nation's Capitol. He was re-instated during the latter part of the war.

Not only is Colonel Young a soldier, he is a military scholar and a man of exceptional diplomacy, and while in the army so conducted himself as to gain the respect and esteem of every officer he came in contact with. Colonel Young is an authority on cavalry. He has written a most learned treatise on cavalry service. Much of his time since the war Colonel Young has spent in appearing in public, inspiring the Negro to patience and hope under the new conditions brought by the war in Europe.

Personally, Colonel Young is modest and unassuming, and no one would ever judge by his conversation that he was one of the most noted cavalry leaders this country has produced.

He set an example of military discipline and respect for superior officers that would make a splendid standard for any country to adopt.

He is absolutely fearless and inspired his men in a manner that made them absolutely fearless.

Colonel Young deserves to be classed with the really Great Negroes, and it is regrettable that he did not see active service in Europe.

Hon. Pinckney Benton Stewart Pinchback

THE subject of this sketch was born May 10, 1837, while his mother was in transit from Virginia to Mississippi. His father was a prominent planter in Holmes County, Mississippi. His mother, Eliza Stewart, was of mixed blood and known as a mulatto, though she claimed to have Indian blood in her veins.

Though freed, she returned with the father of her children to Virginia. Pinckney was born free.

In 1846, in company with his brother Napoleon, who was seven years his senior, Pinckney was sent by his father to Cincinnati to attend Gilmores High School.

In 1848 they returned home. The same year his father died, and his mother with five children, were sent to Cincinnati by the administrator of his father's estate. His brother Napoleon, the mainstay of the family, lost his mind in Cincinnati, which compelled Pinckney at the tender age of twelve to start out into the world on his own responsibility.

He secured work as a cabin boy at eight dollars a month on a canal boat on the Miami canal, running from Cincinnati to Toledo, Ohio.

Several years were spent in canal boating on the Miami, and also the Ft. Wayne and Toledo canals.

From 1854 to 1861 he followed steamboating on the Red, Missouri and the Mississippi rivers and had reached the position of steward, when the war interrupted that business.

May 10, 1862, in Yazoo City, Mississippi, he abandoned the steamer Alonzo Childs, of which he was steward, ran the Confederate blockade and arrived in New Orleans two days after.

May 16, 1882, he had a serious difficulty with his brother-in-law, John Keppard, who was wounded in the encounter. The civil authorities arrested him, but he gave bail. While awaiting trial, the military authorities re-arrested, speedily tried and convicted him for assault with attempt to murder and sentenced him to two years in the work house.

May 25, 1862, he was committed and August 18, 1862, released to enlist in the First Louisiana Volunteer infantry. A few days after enlistment he was detailed to assist in recruiting the Second Louisiana infantry.

October 12, 1862, the second regiment, Louisiana Native Guards, with Captain Pinchback in command of Company A was mustered into the service of the United States.

The Federal soldiery, rank and file, in the main were as hostile as the bitterest Confederates.

In his efforts to maintain the manhood and equality of rights of the colored soldiery, Captain Pinchback was often placed in great peril.

His boldness always excited admiration, and many have wondered that he did not lose his life.

Passing over further notice of his military career we come now to consider his advent into politics.

April 9, 1867, he made his first move in the political field, upon which he afterward won such distinction, by organizing the Fourth Ward Republican Club of New Orleans, Louisiana.

From that time on he filled a large place and many important positions. Almost continuously he was a member of the Louisiana Republican State Committee.

The first civil appointment for which he held a warrant was Inspector of Customs, made by the Hon. William P. Kellogg, May 22, 1867, who at that time was collector of the port of New Orleans. However, the position was declined.

He was an influential member of the Convention called for the purpose of establishing a constitution and civil government for the State of Louisiana.

At the election to ratify the Constitution, April 17 and 18, 1868, he was elected a State Senator. The same year he was elected a delegate at large to the Republican National Convention held at Chicago, May 20, 1868.

In 1869 he was appointed registrar of the land office at New Orleans, but declined the office.

December 25, 1870, he started the publication of the New Orleans Louisianian, which he ran for eleven years with great credit to himself and advantage to his race. From March 18, 1871, to March, 1877, he served as Educational School Director of the City of New Orleans.

He was nominated by the Republican State Convention for Governor of Louisiana, but in order to bring together two factions of the party, a compromise was made and he was elected to the United States Congress. In 1873 he was elected United States Senator.

To recount all the honors heaped upon Mr. Pinchback and the incidents of his active career, would require more space than that given to this article. He has made his place in history and his name will live, although he has passed into the other world.

He was a prudent, economical financier, and accumulated a very handsome fortune. His income from stocks and bonds amounted annually to about $10,000.

Hon. John Mercer Langston, A. B., A. M., LL. D.

THE subject of this sketch is not only one of the greatest Negroes of America, but is on the list of America's great men irrespective of color. He was born in Louisa County, Virginia, December 14, 1829, and the blood of three races ran through his veins: Indian, Negro and Anglo-Saxon. He has the fortitude of the first, the pride of the second and the progressiveness of the third.

He was born in slavery, his father being his owner, so he took the name of his mother's family, which was Indian and Negro mainly, and was closely related to the family of Pocahontas.

By will his father emancipated him when a mere child, and he was sent to the State of Ohio, where he grew to manhood, and was educated and pursued a professional and official life to the year 1867.

In 1884 he entered Oberlin College, located at Oberlin, Ohio, and graduated after five years regular collegiate study in 1849. He then sought admission to a law school, conducted by Mr. J. W. Fowler, at Ballston Spa, New York, but was refused admission on account of his color.

He was also refused admission to a law school in Cincinnati, Ohio, for the same reason.

His next step to secure a legal education was to seek a situation as a student in some lawyer's office. He made but poor success in this direction. Only the Hon. Sherlock J. Andrews, of Cleveland, Ohio, would consent to furnish him books, with an occasional opportunity for explanation of law doctrines and principles, so that no interference was made in ordinary office business. He accomplished but little in this way and the attendant embarrassment so discouraged him, that he abandoned the study for a while, and entered the Theological Department of Oberlin College, from which he graduated in 1853.

He finally entered upon the study of law under the tuition of Hon. Philemon Bliss, of Elyria, Ohio, at the time one of the first lawyers of the Ohio Bar. About one year later, Mr. Langston appeared by order of the court for examination, with reference to his admission to the bar, before a special committee appointed by the court, composed of two Democrats and one Whig.

The matter of admitting colored men to the bar was novel. No one of this class up to that time had the temerity to offer himself as a candidate for such an honor.

The question of legality of admitting a colored man to the Ohio Bar arose and was decided against such admission. The question of Langston's color was inquired into and it was decided that he had more white than Negro blood, so he was ordered to be sworn by the court as a lawyer, October 24, 1854.

Owing to ill health, and upon the advice of his physician, immediately after being admitted to the bar, he went upon a farm in Brownhelm, Lorain County, Ohio. He was the only colored person residing in that section of Ohio, but he received a cordial welcome and given opportunity for the employment of all the ability, legal and otherwise, which he possessed.

In the fall of 1854, one of the leading lawyers associated with him in an important case involving landed interest. The court, the witnesses, the lawyers, except Langston, were all white. Such was the success of the colored lawyer in connection with the case that he found himself at once surrounded by numerous clients with fat retainers. From that time he grew in business and influence rapidly.

In 1855, he was elected to the clerkship of one of the most advanced townships of the state by a white vote.

He moved to Oberlin in 1856 and was at once elected clerk of the township of Russia; next year he was elected a member of the City Council of Oberlin, a position he held for two years, and for eleven years was a member of the Board of Education.

In the fall of 1860, he was engaged in looking after the school interests of the colored youth of Ohio, organizing schools among them and supplying teachers thereof.

In 1867 he was appointed to act as general inspector of the schools of the freed people of the country, and in July of that year he made his first trip Southward on the errand indicated.

In 1867, he was admitted to practice in the Supreme Court of the United States.

In 1869 he was called to a professorship in the Law Department of Howard University. He at once became Dean of that department, organizing it, and for seven years he was at the head of what was recognized as one of the finest law schools in the country.

In 1877 he was appointed by President Hayes, United States minister resident and consul-general to Hayti. As a diplomat he was an entire success, and won the respect and approval of all with whom he had to deal.

In 1885 he was elected by the Board of Education of Virginia, President of the Virginia Normal and Collegiate Institute.

Richard Theodore Greener, A. B., LL. B., LL. D.

THERE are some men whose lives or opportunities in life, you envy. It is not that they have necessarily done anything startling or lasting. Indeed this question is not considered. But somehow certain men manage to be on hand at the right moment and this, too, through no ingenuity or forethought of their own.

Such was the good fortune in many ways of Richard T. Greener, of Washington, D. C. In the first place, Mr. Greener escaped many of the hardships of slavery and the vexations of the days of reconstruction. Shortly after the Civil War the Boston daily papers carried two news stories. In the one they told of a young Southerner, a former Rebel soldier, who was entering Harvard College. In the other they related that a Negro was also matriculating here. Thus came together under the shade of the old Elms the three forces of the great struggle of '63, the Yankee, the Southerner and the Negro.

Mr. Richard T. Greener was this Negro. Happy the man to be at Harvard at any time. Thrice happy to be there is those days! There was Charles Sumner, and Wendell Phillips and William Loyd Garrison and Holmes and Longfellow and Emerson and Lowell—Alas! one almost chokes with both envy and despair at the luxury of being even in or around Cambridge in those days. Why there was Mr. Greener right in the wake of the making of those essays, poems and orations, not to mention Hawthorn's and Poe's influence, that have made American literature. One could no doubt almost feel on the breeze from Back Bay the impulses from "Self-Reliance," from the "American scholar," from the "Chambered Nautilus," and the "Village Blacksmith," so pregnant was the air with the inspiration from the rich harvest of geniuses.

Mr. Greener lived in this atmosphere, caught much of the inspiration and turned it to account. Mr. Greener prosecuted his studies, won scholarships, and came forth the first Negro to receive a degree from Harvard University and he lives today, the oldest Negro graduate from the halls of the crimson.

Leaving his Alma Mater, Mr. Greener like most educated Negroes of that time felt called to the school room. For many years he taught and managed in the schools of South Carolina. Having completed his law studies he became after a time Dean of the Law Department of Howard University. Here, as afterward, all that culture which he gained from living in that refined and intellectual atmosphere at Cambridge stood him in good stead. He was able to give by his very life a culture that few Negroes at that time could impart.

Mr. Greener also took part in the affairs of state. Under the McKinley and Roosevelt administrations he was both a national and an international figure. His most signal service was that rendered as Consul in Russia, especially at Vladivostok. He spent seven and a half years in Russia, seeing few Americans and fewer Negroes. Both his diplomacy and his general conduct were during this time above reproach.

On returning to America, Mr. Greener took to the lecture platform and to his pen. He is optimistic in his messages to the black American. His experience and long life give him a perspective denied to many. Nothing better illustrates this than a paragraph from one of his addresses:

"I am old enough to remember when John Brown fired the shot at Harper's Ferry heard 'round the world—the shot which made a rebellion possible and precipitated a conflict which, had it not come then would, perhaps, have left us in a condition of slavery today. I remember, too, at the beginning of the war when Negro slaves were not allowed to help preserve the Union—when the Negro was simply known as a "contraband of war." When I recall the condition of the colored people at that time throughout the United States I venture to think that those who are unduly alarmed at the sporadic instances of race persecution, of which we hear so much at times—do not value the extent of the opportunities we have for substantial progress, nor do they measure adequately the force and effect of the real American civilization of today."

Mr. Greener represented officially Japanese and British interest during the Russian-Japanese War. For service to Chinese Boxer War in 1900 and for aid to Shansi famine sufferers, he was decorated with the order of Double Dragon by Chinese Government, 1902; the only colored man so honored.

Major John R. Lynch

 R. Lynch, was born in Concordia Parish, Louisiana, September 10, 1847. The bonds of slavery fastened themselves upon his young life and held him from the benefits of freedom, culture, and from developing into a full grown man, such as the peculiarity of our institutions can bring forth. Destitute of the means by which a youth is inspired to greatness, he came forth after the war naturally lacking those qualities which would make a competent statesman and a capable leader. It is astonishing, indeed, how great have been the achievements of most of the despised race when we remember that without any previous training they were called to the most important stations in American affairs; and the wonder is that they made no more mistakes than they did.

Few have succeeded in coming out of the turmoil, strife, and political contest of the past with a reputation so untarnished as that of Mr. Lynch. He remained in slavery until Abraham Lincoln, with a stroke of his pen, cut the Gordian knot and gave liberty to the bondmen.

He had no early education, but began to apply himself as soon as he was permitted to do so. A purchaser of his mother had carried her with her children to Natchez, where, when the Union troops took possession he attended evening school for a few months. He has given diligent attention to private instructors to the acquirement of a first class English education, and has read with considerable attention the best works published of ancient and modern literature.

He engaged in the business of photography at Natchez, until 1869, when Governor Ames appointed him a Justice of the Peace for Adams County, Natchez, Mississippi. He held that position until the fall of the same year, when he was elected to the State Legislature from that county for the term of two years. He was re-elected in 1871, and served during the latter term as speaker of the House of Representatives. He was elected a representative from Mississippi in the Forty-third Congress as a member of the lower house, receiving fifteen thousand three hundred and ninety-one votes against eight thousand four hundred and thirty for H. Cassidy, Sr., (Democrat), and was re-elected to the Forty-fourth Congress as a Republican, defeating Roderick Seals (Democrat). He was also re-elected to the Forty-seventh Congress, but was not allowed to take his seat. It

will be remembered that the contest was between Lynch and Chalmers, in what was known as the "Shoestring" district of Mississippi.

In the National Republican Convention at Chicago, in 1884, he was elected temporary chairman over Bowell Clayton, by a majority of thirty votes. Clayton was the nominee of the representatives of the Blaine interests; Mr. Lynch was nominated and supported by the different elements that were opposed to Mr. Blaine, but he also received the vote of the minority of the Blaine men. He is the first and only colored man who has ever presided over any National Convention of the Republican Party, and in this respect it shows very plainly that he is a man of large influence and of high standing in party councils—one who has so conducted himself as to be chosen from all the vast number of colored men who have from time to time attended these conventions, to preside over the deliberations of a convention which was fraught with so much interest and pregnant with such vast results.

Mr. Lynch, like Langston and Bruce, worked his way into the political world against the keenest competition possible. He was a representative from Mississippi in the Forty-third, Forty-fourth, and Forty-seventh Congress. Thus he spent six years in Washington and conducted himself coolly and courteously under trying circumstances. He has been an inspiration and a source of pride to the Negro both young and old, since his day.

Major Lynch served his country faithfully during the Civil War. Following the War as has been pointed out, he served both his country and race. When he could no longer be a soldier or representative statesman, Major Lynch was appointed auditor in the treasury for the Navy Department, Washington, D. C., from 1889 to 1893. He then began the practice of law in Washington, under the firm name of Lynch and Terrell, and followed this profession until 1898. He was paymaster in the United States Army from 1898 to 1911 when he was retired with the rank of Major. This last named position was made famous by the way in which it was handled by him.

Major Lynch is a member of the Episcopal Church. A Mason and honorary member of the Appomatox Club. He is author of: "The Facts of Reconstruction," which is considered a master essay on that turbulent period. Major Lynch married Mrs. Cora E. Williamson, of Chicago, Ill., August 12, 1911.

Henry Ossawa Tanner

EVER since Colonial days the American Negro has steadily progressed in the field of Art. The acme of progress has been made in this direction by Henry O. Tanner, of Philadelphia, Penn., who makes his home in France. Mr. Tanner is the son of Bishop Benjamin T. Tanner, of the A. M. E. Church.

The artist, Henry O., was born at Pittsburg, Penn., in 1859. He prosecuted his studies in the Academy of fine arts under Thomas Eakins. Later he opened a photographic gallery in Atlanta, Ga., where he also undertook to teach art. This venture failing he taught for a time the subject of Freehand drawing in Clark University in the same town.

However his general ambition was to study in Paris. With the assistance of friends, Mr. Tanner being poor, he finally made his way to France. Here he studied under Jean Paul Laurens, and Benjamin Coustad.

His first real success was in 1900. In this year he won the Lippincott prize at Philadelphia, and the Medal at the Paris Exposition.

Growing up in religious environments the artist chose almost invariably his themes from the Bible. These he has been able to surround with a mysticism that reflects Bible times and Bible spirits upon canvas without parallel.

His "Raising of Lazarus" hangs in the Luxembourg gallery, his "Christ and Nicodemus," and "The Denunciation" are both in Philadelphia. The former is in the academy of fine arts, the latter in Memorial Hall at Fairmont Park.

Nothing gives better appreciation of Mr. Tanner and his art than the article published some years ago in the New York Herald. The art critic in the Herald says of Mr. Tanner and his work:

"Works of Mr. Henry Tanner, a distinguished American Artist, long resident in Paris, who has been honored abroad, are shown in a comprehensive exhibition for the first time at the American Art Galleries. All are religious paintings, and veal, as in flights of poetic fancy, the story of "The Prince of Peace." The thirty-three canvasses form a veritable epic, and unfold the life of Christ from the Nativity to Golgotha, and then picture events that followed the Resurrection."

Mr. Tanner is the son of a bishop and from his earliest years the inspiring traditions of the Old Testament and the New have been to him realities. With the development of his genius came the wish to show his conception of the ideals which to him had been realities from a child. Yet his point of view is not that of a religionist, but that of a true artist. He has sensed events, removed by the lapse of nineteen centuries, and has depicted them with such sincerity and feeling that the personages seem to live and breathe. Such qualities as these enabled him to make a deep impression in Paris, and two of his canvasses were purchased by the French Government for the Luxembourg.

The largest painting in the present exhibition was received with the warmest praise and occupied a prominent place in the last Paris Salon. It is entitled "Behold the Bridegroom Cometh," and its theme is the familiar parable of the wise and foolish virgins. This with its numerous figures of life size, occupies an entire panel of one of the galleries. The Master of Ceremonies is in the act of giving his summons and the maidens are forming themselves into the procession which is to go forth and meet the Lord. The masterly composition, the oriental richness yet softness of the colouring, the instinctive command of detail have drawn the various elements together into a convincing picture.

Among notable canvasses are several which, on account of the ideality of their conception and beauty of their tone, will at once draw to them the notice of the observer. They are: "Christ at the home of Mary and Martha," "Christ and Nicodemus," "The Return of the Holy Women," "On the Road to Emmanaus," and "He vanished out of their sight."

To Henry O. Tanner all true lovers of art point with pride. He is an American recognized everywhere as one of the best. To Henry O. Tanner the Negro points not only in pride, but in hope.

He is a man that commands the respect of the white race to the same extent that he does the people of his own race. He is a man among men irrespective of race, and his friends who are legion, treasure his friendship as one of their most priceless possessions. His place is made with the "Immortals."

Crispus Attucks

FROM the Boston Gazette, of October 2, 1750, the only copy in existence, now carefully preserved in the great antiquarian library of Worcester, Mass. Advertisement of that slave is as follows: "Ran away from his master William Brown, of Framington, on the 30th of September last, a mulatto fellow about twenty-seven years of age, named Crispus, six feet two inches high," etc., describing his dress and warning ship captains not to hire him. "Ten pounds reward, old tenor, will be paid for his return." Crispus Attucks was not returned but served as a sailor up and down the coast and worked on the wharves of Boston. He became known as a powerful turbulent fellow, leader of the street gang and Deacon Wm. Brown didn't try further to get him back.

When British troops occupied Boston, and that port was under embargo, there were no vessel-loading or unloading and hence no work for wharf men. This made the street mob angry at their jobs and Attucks, now forty-seven years old was their fearless leader.

On that famous evening of March 8, 1770, in Boston, about eleven o'clock, the young fellows on the street near the Old State House were making noise when out came the British Captain Preston with a file of soldiers and ordered them to disperse. Attucks encouraged them to refuse, shouted: "These soldiers don't dare fire," stepped up to the line, seized one of the men, threw him down and took his musket away from him. Then to show his contempt he tossed the man's musket away from him and turned away with a laugh. The angry soldier springing up seized his gun and without orders shot Attucks dead. Captain Preston then ordered his men to fire and as the dead patriot's companions rushed forward over his body four more of them were killed. The whole five fell within a circle of about ten feet diameter, which is now marked by the paving bricks being there laid in concentric circles to distinguish that sacred spot from the rest of the street pavement. It was near midnight. There was newly fallen snow on the ground and, in the starlight, the red blood of these martyrs poured out on it made a vivid contrast.

On Boston Common near the Tremont Hall stands a granite monument, twenty feet high, bearing on it's base a bronze tablet picturing that Boston Massacre. In the upper shaft are carved the names of these five martyrs of the Revolution with Crispus Attucks at the top. The old Granary burying ground is on Tremont Street, just off the Common. At the extreme right hand corner near the front iron fence is the granite boulder which marks the grave of that Revolutionary champion of American liberty, Governor Sam Adams. And next to that is a long mound which then bore five little flag staffs and flags. At the head of this stood and still stands, a polished slab of dark stone bearing this inscription, "here are buried the remains of five victims of the Boston Massacre of March 8, 1770." Then follows the names, the third of which is Crispus Attucks. Immediately after his death the following lines appeared:

"Long as in freedom's cause the wise contend,
Dear to your country shall your fame extend;
While to the world the lettered stone shall tell,
Where Caldwell, Attucks, Gray and Maverick fell.'

Daniel Webster said, speaking of the assault, "From that Moment we may date the severance of the British Empire."

For all his heroism, Attucks, like Toussaint L'Overture, like Phyllis Wheatley, like Booker T. Washington, was born a slave. History places his birth about 1720. He was a half breed Indian or mulatto. His birth place is Framingham, Massachusetts. Little is known of his boyhood and youth, it is evident however that he was a restless temperament, and that he did not take peacefully the change of freedom even in New England. Some say he was a mere loafer and lounger, others say he was a seaman and that on the action of the massacre he had just returned from a voyage.

Be he slave or vagabond, be he full Negro or Indian or half-breed, he still holds the title of being the first to give his life for the cause of American freedom. From him date the American Negro Soldier, and the American Negro patriot. Both the white people and the Negroes in America are coming more and more to do him honour as the years go by. Thus can the Negro point to an unbroken line of service, from the revolution to the world's war.

Senator Blanch K. Bruce

LANCH K. Bruce, the famous Mississippian of Reconstruction days, falls into that class of the enviable first and only. He was the first Negro to put his signature to the money of the United States Government. In 1881, on the twenty-third of May he was made Registrar of the treasury by James A. Garfield. He had won this honor by his distinguished services in the State of Mississippi.

Like his contemporary John M. Langston, Blanch K. Bruce was born in the State of Virginia. Like Langston also Bruce was born a slave. He was a native of Prince Edward County, where he was born in 1841. In his early training Bruce was exceptionally fortunate. In other cases, even where the Negro child was akin to the master, the line between the two was closely and persistantly drawn. In Bruce's case, however, this was not done. Thus the Negro lad gained his early training with his master's son.

Receiving his freedom, Bruce went into the State of Missouri, where for several years he taught school. For a time he studied at Oberlin College, in Ohio. Wearying of school teaching, Mr. Bruce went south, and in 1869 became a planter in the rich bottoms of Boliver County in Mississippi. Here in the home of his adoption he became a big man and he continued to be a man of affairs and a large cotton planter. Even in recent years his widow still handled many hundreds of bales of cotton from their plantation. As a man of affairs, Bruce was at one time sheriff of the county and at another superintendent of public schools. As is well known he was Senator from Mississippi from 1875 to 1881. Here again, Bruce blazed the way, as he had done in Mississippi. He had been the first Negro sheriff of his section, he had also been the first Negro county Superintendent of schools in Mississippi. He was the second Negro to hold a seat in the United States Senate. It was at the conclusion of his career as Republican Senator from Mississippi that Bruce was made Registrar of the Treasury, in 1881. Just prior to this appointment he had refused offers as Minister to Brazil and 3rd Assistant Postmaster General. This post he held for four years, going out of office in 1885.

However, Bruce was no slacker either with his purse, his brain or his endeavors. He continued to do yeoman labor for the Republican Party, so that when William McKinley came to office he once more appointed Bruce in 1897. However, he had done his work. With the armor of the good soldier on, he died in 1898.

B. K. Bruce exerted a wonderful influence over the Negro youth of America. His had been a different experience in his early childhood from that of most of the other celebrated Negroes. These had been tardy in their educational advantages. They had not known culture and contact, without which true education is incomplete, as had Bruce. Thus the Senator from Mississippi fell heir naturally to many things those giants like Douglass and Washington had to struggle for. This the black youth of the country saw and still sees, and by it was, and is, inspired to seek refinement from every possible source.

Again Bruce became a man of wealth. He made no noise about it, because once more wealth was to him a natural heritage. Even though he had not been used to owning it he had been accustomed to contact with it. Handling bales of cotton by the hundred, handling plantation hands, mules, implements, were all education that had come to him by contact. This served him greatly when he was in the presence of those who thought and spoke and dealt with things on a big scale. He married Miss Josephine B. Wilson, of Cleveland, Ohio, June 24, 1878, and made a bridal tour of the principal countries of Europe, where marked attention was shown the young couple by European statesmen and members of the American embassies. They were highly entertained by Minister Welch in London, and Minister Noyes at Paris.

All this has gone into the life of the Negro youth of America who honor and appreciate him more than even the youths themselves know or proclaim.

Senator Bruce was a splendid orator, and devoted much of his time in his later years to the lecture platform. He never became so engrossed in his work that he would not, on short notice, deliver one of his forceful speeches if he thought it was for the good of his people.

Brief History of the Negro Race

THE NEGRO IN HISTORY

Only a brief sketch of the part that the Negro has played in the world and in civilization can be given here. Wherever races have played a part the Negro from the dawn of history has come in for his share of responsibility and for his share of the glory.

First let us decide what a Negro is. As a general rule the term Negro is applied to black people of unmixed blood and also to persons of any race whatsoever who have some Negro blood in their veins.

The states where the Negro question is most acute have undertaken to define definitely the term Negro. Kentucky, Maryland, North Carolina, Tennessee and Texas state that "a person of color is one who is descended from a Negro to the third generation inclusive, though one ancestor in each generation may have been white. In Alabama one is a Negro who has had any Negro blood in his ancestry in five generations. In Michigan, Nebraska, and Oregon one is not legally a person of color who has less than one fourth Negro blood, while in Florida, Georgia, Indiana and Missouri and South Carolina one eighth Negro blood makes a Negro of a man. But in general practice the term Negro is applied to any person having any Negro blood whatever.

Because of this definition of the race, the colored race includes persons of all colors, many of whom are fairer than some members of the white race. It is of this race with its many mixtures that we are trying to give a brief history. The black people are natives of Africa, Asia and the Pacific Islands. From his native home he has been brought by traders to this country and to other countries. The first Negroes brought to America were with the the explorers. As early as 1501 Negroes were brought to Hispaniola and as early as 1516 Negroes were helping in the affairs of America. It was in that year that Balboa with the assistance of thirty Negroes built the first ship that was ever constructed on the Pacific Coast of America. After that the Negro was in most of the expeditions. They were with Cortez in his conquest of Mexico; they were with Vasques de Ayllon in his attempt to establish a settlement in what is now North and South Carolina; they were with the expeditions of Panfilo de Narvaez to conquer Florida; and in many of the other expeditions. The second settler in the State of Alabama (1540) was a Negro who was a member of the De Soto expedition.

In this manner the Negroes first came to this country. Afterward they were brought over as servants and as slaves later. The history of slavery in the United States is outlined more fully elsewhere. But in bringing over the Negro men and women for slave purposes there were brought over more than one class of Africans. The Negro who was a slave in his own country and was sold to traders for a small sum represented by bright bits of colored beads and bright colored cloth was brought over. With him came Negroes from other tribes that had been taken in war between the tribes. This second class were of a higher type. But the highest type of Negroes brought direct from Africa was taken from the ruling class. Some of these were gotten by being fooled aboard ships and other underhand methods used by the unscrupulous traders who first got the interest and the confidence of the Negro and then took advantage of it. Among those who are represented in this class we have an ancestor of Robert R. Moton, Principal of Tuskegee Institute. The story of the coming to this country of this Negro of royal blood is interesting and is told as follows: The young prince with a drove of slaves to sell to the trader went down to the ship. The commander of the vessel after settling for the slaves he had purchased asked the young prince if he would not like to look over the vessel. Replying in the affirmative he went aboard and was shown around with a great deal of ceremony. When he came back from his tour of inspection the ship was miles out at sea. While speaking of this case it might be added that R. R. Moton, recognized as one of the leaders of the race is of pure blooded African descent. This goes to prove that the theory, that all the achievement of the Negro in this country is due to the white blood that is now mixed in the race, is false.

Another case will show that the Negroes of royal blood from Africa were held in respect by the others. There was brought to Massachusetts a young girl of the ruling class. Two men from her tribe were in the same place. The owner of the men tried to make one of them marry the girl or at least mate with her but remembering that she had royal blood in her veins even in this country where they were held in bondage he refused to so insult the daughter of his king.

Not only were the Negroes brought over of different classes, but there were brought over persons who were sold as Negroes who were not in the strictest sense of the word Negroes but were of the other darker nations that occupy the continent. This in a measure accounts for the different types we have at present where mixed blood cannot be offered as the solution.

Thus from the beginning of the history of the Negro in this country there was more then one class, and with the education and development and the mixing of the races there has been developed a race of men far superior to the general conception when the term Negro is used. Since coming to the United States the Negro has played an important part in the affairs of the country, directly and indirectly for indirectly the Negro is responsible for the great wealth that has come to this country through the cotton industry.

HISTORY OF SLAVERY IN AMERICA

African Slave trade was begun by Portugal in 1442. Spain, took a part in it in 1517. England France, Holland, Denmark and the American colonies one by one took part in this trade. The American Colonies afforded a good place for the trading of these slaves. Thus to our country came the institution of slavery.

In the year 1619 the first African immigrants were landed in Virginia. According to Monroe N Work, in the "Year Book" these twenty Negroes were not necessarily sold into slavery but into service. He says "It was not uncommon practice in this period for ship masters to sell white servants to planters, hence an inference that these twenty Negroes were slaves, drawn from the fact that they were sold to the colony or planters would be unjustified." The first record of a "Negro servant for life" or a slave in the state of Virginia was in the year 1640. In that year also the first record of discriminating against Negroes in the state of Virginia is recorded. Both came out in the same account. Three servants ran away, one a Dutchman one a Scotchman and one a Negro. They were caught. Each was given thirty lashes. The Dutchman and the Scotchman were condemned to serve four years beyond their indenture. The Negro John Punch was condemned to servitude for life. In the year 1662 slavery was declared hereditary in the State of Virginia. This was done by

decreeing that the issue of slave mothers should follow in the condition of servitude. Thus by the end of the year 1662 slavery was fully established in Virginia, the oldest of the colonies.

New York (1628), New Jersey (1628) Massachusetts (1630) Connecticut (1631-1636), Delaware (1636) Rhode Island (1647), South Carolina (1665) North Carolina (1669) one by one saw the traffic in slaves fully established within their borders. New Hampshire was founded in 1679 with slavery in all probability already established. Pennsylvania was ceded to William Penn in 1681 with slavery probably already established. Georgia was founded in 1733, but slavery was forbidden within the borders till 1749. The reason for the change of attitude toward the institution was the lack of progress being made by the State. The surrounding states were in a very prosperous condition, due to the labor of the slaves. Seeing this Georgia changed her laws in order that some of the wealth derived from Negro labor might come her way.

Slavery in the Colonies did not develop without opposition. As early as 1688 the first step was taken to check the sale of Negroes. Virginia, the state that led in the establishing of slavery also tried to lead in the prohibition of the importation of slaves but the mother country England did not allow any of these acts to become law.

In the far South the Negroes soon outnumbered the whites and this caused the whites to live in constant fear of an uprising. For this reason they placed very heavy duties on the importation of slaves. None of these measures however, were able to check the rapid growth of the institution once it had a good start.

There are those among colored people today who claim that their people were never slaves. This is especially true of people coming from Virginia and the Carolinas. There is some ground for the claim. Back in the days of the colonies there were many free Negroes. The Negro gained his freedom in several ways. Some were allowed to hire their time to other people. All that was earned above the $100 the master required for their time became the possession of that particular slave. After years of toil some had money enough to purchase their own freedom. Sometimes a master at death gave a number of his slaves their freedom. Slaves were sometimes given their freedom because of some act for the good of the community. But by far the larger number of free Negroes during the days of the colonists "inherited" their freedom. There was a law making free the children of indentured white mothers and Negro fathers after a period of thirty or thirty-one years of service. From these various ways the number of free Negroes increased. But the lives of these free Negroes were hedged about with difficulties and hardships. He could not associate with the Negro slaves without being held under suspicion. His one great advantage came in his being able to purchase land and purchase the liberty of his family if they were enslaved.

SLAVERY IN THE STATES

The Negro played a part in the war which gave to the States their freedom from the English yoke. Sentiment had been aroused against slave trade in England. When the war broke out, the governor of Virginia promised freedom to all Negroes who would join the English army and fight against their masters. Thousands did this. Alarmed, the colonists changed their attitude and began to enlist the Negroes in the American Army. It is estimated that three thousand Negroes served in the American army, many of whom were given their freedom at the close of the war.

From the first the question of the slave and the rights of the free Negro became an issue in the newly formed republic. Vermont was the first state to prohibit and abolish slavery.

This measure was adopted by Vermont in 1777, but she was not admitted to the Union till 1791. Several of the states passed laws for the gradual abolition of slavery. By this method the children of slave parents remained in service till the boys and girls were twenty-eight and twenty-five respectively. While this method took some time it gave freedom to the slaves at a much earlier date than other states. New York, New Jersey, Connecticut, Rhode Island and Pennsylvania were states with the gradual abolition system. Massachusetts, New Hampshire, Vermont and Ohio took very definite stand against the institution and prohibited the barter of human beings.

Georgia ceded to the Union the land which afterward became Alabama and Mississippi. This was done on the condition that slavery should not be prohibited within this territory. An effort was made to keep the number of free and slave states about the same. In this manner there was hope that no harm would result to the central government. But there were forces at work for the freeing of this slave people. For years there was sentiment against the enslaving of the colored people in most of the northern states. And in some of the southern states there were persons who took the stand that slavery was wrong.

Of all the forces that were at work for the freedom of the slaves the book, Uncle Tom's Cabin by Harriet Beecher Stowe did most to bring it about. Based on facts, it pictured the life of the slave in its best and in its worst forms. This book was published in 1852. Next to the influence of this book, Henry Ward Beecher, pastor of Plymouth Church, Brooklyn, Charles Sumner of the United States Senate along with many others talked openly against the institution of slavery. John Brown, with his enthusiastic attack on the arsenal at Harpers' Ferry, Virginia, in 1859 really supplied the spark that set the whole country in flames on the subject of Negro Slavery in the States.

The question of slaves was discussed in all portions of the country. In some places the slaves were declared free as for instance, in Georgia, only to have the proclamation rescinded by President Lincoln. But the question could not go on unsettled. On September 22nd 1862, President Lincoln issued the preliminary proclamation of emancipation. January first 1863 the Emancipation Proclamation was issued. This proclamation was supported by the Civil War and by the amendments to the constitution which followed. One by one the States in which slavery had been abolished by voluntary acts, took up the matter and declared the non-existence of slaves within their borders.

THE UNDERGROUND RAILROAD

The Underground Railway had none of the features of the modern railway, except the carrying of passengers, and these were limited in kind and in the direction of the travel. No one could obtain passage on this road, unless he or she were a slave, and wanted to be free. The trains ran in but one direction, and that was Northward. There were no "Jim Crow" cars, no sleepers, and no smokers, and all passengers were carried free of charge. It was a railroad without stockholders, but it had innumerable directors. No dividends were paid except to passengers, and such dividends were in the form of certificates of freedom from bondage.

To be more explicit the Underground Railway was a system of clandestine travel, extending from the borders of "Mason and Dixon's Line" through the North and West to Canada.

It required large sums of money to keep this Underground Railway system in motion. The runaways must be fed, clothed, and their passage paid across the lake to Canada. Mr. Douglass was in the lecture-field most of the time to raise money to do his part. The Female Anti-Slavery Society, with its branches throughout the North, solicited funds and clothing and as these unfortunate fugitives were invariably destitute, means had to be supplied them until they could secure employment under the British flag.

The majority of the escapes were made in Winter, when the oversight on the plantation was less rigid than in the working season and many who were given passes during the Christmas holidays to visit neighboring towns or plantations, seized that opportunity for a longer journey.

The western and southwestern branch of the Underground Railway was operated from Cincinnati, Ohio, and through Michigan to Canada. Fugitive slaves from Kentucky, Tennessee, Mississippi, Arkansas and Louisiana took this route. The whole number of slaves who successfully made their escape through the system has never been ascertained.

The manner of Douglass's flight—riding out of Baltimore, Maryland, in daylight and in sight of those who knew that he was a slave—is a good illustration of the boldness and ingenuity of some of the escapes. Among the hundreds of interesting cases cited by Mr. Still is that of William Crafts, who gained his liberty by acting the part of a valet or body-servant of his wife. She was of light brown complexion, and for this adventure wore men's clothing. Another case is that of a slave-woman who hitched up her master's horse and carriage, and taking her family of five children and several others, drove off to liberty. Box Brown was the name of a slave, who permitted himself to be nailed up in a box and sent by express to Baltimore. Two colored women dressed in deep mourning and rode Northward to freedom in the same coach as their masters who did not know them. In some cases slaves secreted themselves for several months and, when search for them had ceased, crept off unsuspected. In hundreds of instances, the parts were as cleverly played as if the fugitives had had special training in the drama of running away from their masters. In nearly all cases these black men and women took desperate chances. The conductors of the Underground Railway were everywhere, and at all times on the alert. They knew every path, the byways and highways in which slaves might hide or on which they might travel to reach freedom. The stations were always open and ready to receive them. It was never too late, or too early, or too difficult, or too perilous to be on the lookout to welcome, to protect, and pass on fugitives to the next place of safety. Clothing, food, shoes, carriages, wagons, horses, and mules were always at hand. No secret society has ever veiled its proceedings in deeper mystery than this widely separated army of determined conspirators and emancipators. The secret-service men of the government tried to locate the stations and the station agents, but the more they searched the less they found. It is a curious fact that the United States secret service men seem to have had just as little success in uncovering the systematic plans for aiding slaves to escape to the Northern states as in preventing the smuggling of slaves from Africa into the Southern states. The traffic of the Underground Railroad continued to increase in volume and the slave once off United States soil was beyond reach of recall.

Whereas on the 22nd day of September in the year of our Lord one thousand eight hundred and sixty-two, a proclamation was issued by the President of the United States, containing, among other things, the following, to-wit:

That on the first day of January, in the year of our Lord one thousand eight hundred and sixty-three, all persons held as slaves within any State or designated part of a State, the people whereof shall then be in rebellion against the United States shall be then, thenceforward and forever free, and the Executive Government of the United States, including the military and naval authority thereof, will recognize and maintain the freedom of such persons, and will do no act or acts to repress such persons, or any of them, in any efforts they may make for their actual freedom.

That the Executive will on the first day of January, aforesaid, by proclamation, designate the States and parts of States, if any, in which the people therof respectively shall then be in rebellion against the United States, and the fact that any State, or the people thereof shall on that day be in good faith represented in the Congress of the United States by members chosen thereto at elections wherein a majority of the qualified voters of such State shall have participated shall in the absence of strong countervailing testimony, be deemed conclusive evidence that such State and the people thereof are not then in rebellion against the United States.

Now, therefore, I ABRAHAM LINCOLN, President of the United States, by virtue of the power in me vested as Commander-in-Chief of the Army and Navy of the United States in time of actual armed rebellion against the authority and Government of the United States and as a fit and necessary war measure for suppressing said rebellion do, on this first day of January, in the year of our Lord one thousand eight hundred and sixty-three and in accordance with my purpose so to do publicly proclaimed for the full period of one hundred days from the day first above mentioned, order and designate as the States and parts of States, wherein the people thereof respectfully are this day in rebellion against the United States, the following, to-wit:

"Arkansas, Texas Louisiana (except the parishes of St. Bernard Plaquemine Jefferson, St. John St. Charles, St. James, Ascension, Assumption, Terre Bonne, LaFourche St. Mary, St. Martin, and Orleans, including the city of New Orleans). Mississippi Alabama Florida, Georgia South Carolina, North Carolina and Virginia (except the forty-eight counties designated as West Virginia, and also the counties of Berkley, Accomac Northampton, Elizabeth City, York Princess Anne, and Norfolk, including the cities of Norfolk and Portsmouth) and which excepted parts are for the present, left precisely as if this proclamation was not issued

"And by virtue of the power and for the purpose aforesaid, I do order and declare that all persons held as slaves within said designated States and parts of States are and henceforward shall be free, and that the Executive Government of the United States, including the military and naval authorities thereof will recognize and maintain the freedom of said persons

"And I hereby enjoin upon the people so declared to be free to abstain from all violence, unless in necessary self-defense, and I recommend to them that in all cases when allowed they labor faithfully for reasonable wages

"And I further declare and make known that such persons, of suitable conditions will be received into the armed service of the United States to garrison forts positions stations, and other places, and to man vessels of all sorts in said service

"And upon this act, sincerely believed to be an act of justice, warranted by the Constitution upon military necessity, I invoke the considerate judgment of mankind, and the gracious favor of Almighty God

"In testimony whereof, I have hereunto set my name and caused the seal of the United States to be affixed

"Done at the City of Washington, this 1st day of January, in the year of our Lord 1863 and of the independence of the United States the eighty-seventh

ABRAHAM LINCOLN

By the President
   William H Seward,
      Secretary of State.

NEGRO IN BUSINESS

Perhaps the two greatest agents to foster and promote Negro business in this country have been the Negro banks and the Negro secret organizations. The secret orders have undoubtedly been the prime movers because they have not only been built by Negro capital in large sums, but the buildings themselves are of such a sort that any one would be proud to conduct a business within them. Such buildings as the Mosaic Temple in Little Rock Arkansas Odd Fellows Building in Atlanta Georgia Pythian Temple in New Orleans Pythian Building in Louisville, Kentucky Mosaic Temple in Jacksonville Fla , Pythian Building in Dal

las Texas furnish inspiring centers for the colored people to have their businesses in

The factory that was established by Madam Walker and in which she gave employment to hundreds of Negro women and girls is another type of building that has been erected by the colored race and that has done so much good for the uplift of the race This work of Madam Walker is described in full elsewhere in this volume Similar to the establishment of Madam Walker in the point of the articles manufactured is the Poro Building

Under the name of Poro College, there is operated in St Louis Missouri, the largest manufacturing plant of its kind in the world It is owned controlled and operated wholly by colored people Through this plant 40 000 girls and women are enabled to earn a livlihood 150 of this number work in the plant It was founded in 1900 by Mrs Annie M Pope-Turnbo Malone, who had made a specialty of the study of chemistry and put her knowledge into these compounds which together with the Poro System have revolutionized Hair Culture

The new Poro Building which was completed in 1918, cost upward of $250 000 00 The building is three stories, has basement, mezzanine floor and roof garden It is indeed an inspiration to any one to visit this wonderful plant It is so planned that all the needs of the visitor can be satisfied within the plant There are 95 dormitories, there is a public dining room is an auditorium with a seating capacity of 800, is a refrigerating plant that furnishes ice water for the entire building and Lamson pneumatic tube carriers In the section that is reserved for beauty hair and scalp treatment there are thirty-one booths The kitchen is most modern and is thoroughly equipped the halls reserved for receptions are very beautiful and spacious there is in the rear a room set apart for the care of small children where they may receive kindergarten training Everything about this plant is wonderful The order, the spirit of cheer the most wonderful art of all working toward one end—all are to be felt when paying a visit to this establishment

The two people who are responsible for this wonderful piece of business among the Negroes are Mr and Mrs A E Malone Mrs Malone spent her early life in Metropolis and Peoria Illinois Mr Malone for a number of years was a teacher in Illinois, serving as principal of some of the large schools Both of these people who are still young are genii in the business world and it is through their wise administration of their affairs that the phenomenal success of Poro has come Mr and Mrs Malone are philanthropists In the St Louis Y M C A they gave $75,000, the largest sum given by colored people to any one institution A

RES. OF W. G. PEARSON,
DURHAM, N. C.

RES. OF F. W. BRUNER,
OKLAHOMA CITY, OKLA.

RES. OF MRS. BARNES,
SAVANNAH, GA.

RES. OF ALEX. HUGHES,
SPRINGFIELD, MASS.

RES. OF J. H. BLODGETT, JACKSONVILLE, FLA.

REPRESENTATIVE HOMES OF NEGROES IN DIFFERENT SECTIONS OF THE COUNTRY

RES. OF L. H. STEWART — EVANSVILLE, IND.

RES. OF J. J. EVANS, — SHREVEPORT, LA.

RES. OF PRESTON TAYLOR-GREENWOOD PARK, NASHVILLE, TENN.

RES. OF JOS. L. JONES, CINCINNATI, OHIO.

RES. OF DR. S. H. GEORGE, — PADUCAH, KY.

RES. OF DR. W. T. FULLER, — SUFFOLK, VA.

RES. OF J. N. CLINTON, — TAMPA, FLA.

Res. of W. Curtis Reich, Muskogee, Okla.

RES. OF DR. S. W. HARRISON, — FT. SMITH, ARK.

REPRESENTATIVE HOMES OF NEGROES IN DIFFERENT SECTIONS OF THE COUNTRY

few months ago to Tuskegee Institute they gave $1200, and to Wilberforce they gave $1000.00 They support the St Louis Orphans Home and contribute largely to many institutions without letting the public know anything about it

With Poro College as a manufacturing plant and hotel for our people, Mr and Mrs Malone deserve great credit for producing a business of this size that is perfectly planned perfectly executed and wholly an asset to the race

Another business of great importance to the Race is that in Durham North Carolina known as the North Carolina Mutual and Provident Association This was founded by John Merrick This work is described in full elsewhere in this volume

The Standard Life Insurance Company of Atlanta Ga, the only Old Line Insurance Company owned and controlled by Negroes

E C Brown's Theatrical Syndicate details of which are found elsewhere in this volume

The Baptist Publishing House at Nashville Tennessee is another example of a large business owned and operated by members of the colored race This work is told in full elsewhere A M E Sunday School Union Publishing House In nearly every town and city where Negroes are at all in prevailing numbers are found various Negro stores, some of them run in as orderly a fashion as those run by members of the other race There are in all about 43,000 places of business being run by colored people This does not include barber shops shoe shops, and blacksmith shops The National Negro Business League is responsible for stimulating and increasing Negro Business enterprises It was for this purpose that Dr Washington in his wisdom organized this League and through it and its branches in the various cities of the country the colored man has been shown just what can be done through organized effort

NEGRO HOMES

Nothing has been a greater source of pride to the colored man in America than the progress he has made in the improvement of his home and home life Beginning at Boston Massachusetts, running the whole length of the coast to the Gulf and going across the continent to San Francisco to Denver to Portland one finds dotted here and there Negro residences comparing favorably with any Many of these homes cost from $10,000 to $20,000 and there are a few that cost a great deal more than that notably among these last is the home of Madam C J Walker on the Hudson which cost $300,000.00 These homes are kept with the same skill and neatness as those of any people in similar circumstances There are hundreds and thousands of homes that are not so pretentious but are models in the manner in which they are

kept It is for the purpose of training the young girls and women of the race in matters pertaining to home making that the courses in Home Economics and Domestic Science are maintained in all of the schools that are provided by the church and the state This training is now even being offered in the courses of the rural schools of the Southland There is still a large class of people who remain unreached, but the beginning is made and it is a great and good beginning

Some of the cities are more noted for the beautiful residences owned by the colored people than are others In Washington New York Baltimore, Richmond Raleigh Durham Atlanta Birmingham Jacksonville St Louis and Chicago there are homes that are second to none owned by the average well-to-do citizen In these various centers are sometimes whole streets owned by Negroes One instance of this is the Beautiful West Belle, in St Louis This was once an exclusive residential district for white people Gradually it has changed hands and is now the best residential section for Negroes These property holders have made an effort to keep up the standard of the street and it is beautiful to visit

Home life among Negroes has developed during the past fifty years as has everything else that belongs to them But even in the days of slavery when many lived under the worst circumstances there were examples of beautiful home life beautiful from the standpoint of the regard in which the members of the family held each other and the character that the mothers tried to build up in their children From these families have sprung some of the best and most noted of the colored people who are prominent today Take for an example Booker T Washington He lived in a hut with his mother and brother and sister yet this mother managed to surround them with the spirit of home the spirit that made her provide food for them at regular intervals the spirit that made her gather them together and teach them to pray and to fear God and live right It was the spirit that made the home. Many are the humble examples of this type of home today in which are trained some of the best people

But the same spirit may be had in the great and rich homes as well as in the humble ones Take the home life of Booker T Washington after he was able to have the comforts and some of the luxuries of life The same spirit of keeping the children together that his mother had shown in her humble home was apparent in his home If he came home and missed one of the boys immediately that child was asked for and if necessary sent for Although he was much away from home he always tried to get back to his family for the holidays in order that he might be with his wife and children

42

The spirit of love, of tenderness, of protection in which he held his children was beautiful to see This side of this wonderful man is one that is not often referred to, but is one of the things that helped make him the great man that he was

There are many other examples that might be cited of the beautiful home life within the beautiful home of beautiful home life within the well kept modest home In fact it has been in a large measure the home life that has made for the wonderful advancement of the Negro during the past fifty odd years

NEGRO IN PUBLIC LIFE

Ever since Crispus Attucks fell in Boston, the Negro of America has had some claim to public office Regardless of politics he has managed, somehow to hold office under nearly every administration Among these a few of the noteworthy examples may be mentioned—Blanche K Bruce born in the State of Virginia, a slave, was sent to the United States Senate in 1895, from the State of Mississippi

Another Senator from the State of Mississippi was a colored man This was Hiram R Revels, a native of North Carolina, and a free man He was educated during the days of slavery at Knox College, from which he was graduated in 1847 He became the first of all the colored United States Senators Judge Robert H Terrell of Washington, D C Congressman John M Langston of Virginia John R Lynch of Mississippi, George W Murray of South Carolina Charles W Anderson of New York City Hon John W Green of Cleveland, William H Lewis of Boston, J C Napier, and Henry W Furniss, most of whom are told about in full elsewhere are examples of colored office holders who during the terms of office received from two to ten thousand dollars per year for their services

Of another type of public man was Frederick Douglass who became such a help in the cause of freedom through his lectures

A bright example of the man in public life as a public speaker of this day we have Roscoe C Simmons who is a native of Mississippi and still a man in his early thirties This young man is gifted as a speaker and is employed in a number of public issues as a speaker He has the ability to thrill his audience and paint pictures as very few men can do Regardless of color Simmons is a great orator and uses his gift in the interest of his people

NEGRO FARMER

Of all the operations in which the Negro won distinction perhaps farming is the most marked In every section of the country the Negro farmer

has won his spurs and the encouraging feature of the whole matter is that though many young people leave the farms yet when the total is taken the number of Negro farmers as well as the number of Negro farms has increased year by year Today the Negro owns farm property to the extent of five hundred million dollars in value Nor has he restricted his work to any one branch, dairymen, stock-breeders poultry-men cotton growers, grain growers potato growers, indeed, there is not a branch of agriculture in which the Negro is not classed One might name such men as the potato king, Junius G Groves of Kansas the famous horsebreeder, Bass, of Mexico Missouri the cotton grower, Deal Jackson of Georgia as instances of Negroes who excel in the various branches of agriculture

In the South Negro farming has been greatly improved during the last decade by the constructive work of the State government and of the Federal government Both of these have co-operated in employing agents to teach practical agriculture Women trained in housekeeping in cooking gardening and poultry raising have gone into the homes of the Negro farmer and taught the wives the details of scientific methods of good housekeeping Men trained in agriculture have taught the Negro farmer more scientific methods of plowing, harvesting, selecting seed, and given most valuable instruction on the selection and treatment of stock These teachers going from farm to farm have increased farming values in the South

Coming under this head something of the life of Groves mentioned above will without doubt prove an inspiration to boys who may read this Junius Groves was born a slave in Kentucky In 1879 he moved to Kansas where he hired out as a farm laborer at forty cents a day From the first his ambition was to have a farm of his own, the second year he rented a small plot of ground and after taking out all expenses he found that he had cleared $125 He continued to add to the number of acres that he tilled and to add to his savings till in 1884 he had $2 200 in the bank to his credit Then Mr Groves began to purchase land for himself and on this land he specialized in raising the white potato Today as a result of this careful hoarding of his means and a careful planning of his crops Mr Groves is worth $80,000 He has earned the title of "Potato King " by producing in a single year 100 000 bushels of potatoes Mr Groves is not only classed as a farmer, but as a business man He has made a business of his farming

NEGRO'S CONTRIBUTION TO EDUCATION

For a long time it appears that the Negro did not feel that education of his children depended at all upon contributions from the black man's coffers Reared as a dependent and sent forth as such he for a long time, looked to those who had been his master to educate the black children However as he gained self-confidence and refinement he began to invest his money in the education of his own, and today in almost every section of the South, the Negro in addition to paying his regular tax as assessed by the county and State is taxing himself to build better schools for his children to buy better equipment, extend the school term and to secure better school teachers

Also with his religion the Negro carried the conviction that his children should be educated thus through the church, the denominational schools of the South and of the West receive staunch support from the colored people The Year-book estimates that the Negro through the churches and other means raised about a million five hundred thousand dollars The school property being valued at two million five hundred thousand dollars In some instances the schools are run by Negroes alone, that is, the Negro has purchased the ground, selected the field elected their own trustees and own teachers Such schools as Morris Brown, Atlanta, Ga Selma University in Selma, Ala and Western College in Macon Missouri, gain their sustenance almost wholly from Negro effort

Perhaps in no one field of labor has the Negro achieved so much as he has in that of the school The Negro as a school founder organizer and school teacher is probably taken for all and all, the best product that the black man of America can show for his sixty years of freedom The Negro school man sacrificing his insight, his almost super-human struggles and his willingness to turn his efforts back into the education of his own people for a mere pittance brings him forward as the most sublime of his race One needs only to think of the labors of Booker T Washington and the men and women who surrounded him and of the efforts of Negro school teachers in every school of the country today To justify this claim made for the Negro school man, add to this the fact that he in part can never be an out and out teacher and you have even a sublimer situation For every Negro man, even to this day, who interprets his task in the light of modern education must be father, mother, in a word he must be "Black Mark Hopkins on the other end of the log"

NEGRO ARTIST

Under the Negro artists let us include the painter and the sculptor They like the literatee named above have been in some instances thought to interpret their own people, but not so strictly More often their subjects have been universal in selection and treatment rather than specific Among the Negro painters perhaps Henry O Tanner, a modern artist, is the most celebrated and famous An American by birth and rearing he pursued his studies abroad The greater part of his work has been done in France where his pictures hang among those of many of the French and Italian immortals in the great art gallaries in Paris and in the Louvre

Among his most famous paintings are the Holy Family Moses and Elisha and Christ Walking on the Sea "Hiding of Moses," "Christ at the Home of Lazarus " A full sketch of his life appears elsewhere in this volume

The first in point of time to achieve distinction as a Negro painter was E M Bannister His paintings seem to live, though perhaps he is best remembered by his organization of art clubs and by his promotion of the study of art than by any parcular work

A young artist of great promise is William Edward Scott, of Indianapolis, Indiana He, like Henry O Tanner has studied abroad but he has done most of his actual work in America

The leading Negro sculptor is a woman, Edmonia Lewis who resides in Italy Her most celebrated productions are the "Freed Woman " "Marriage of Hiawatha " " Death of Cleopatra "

Mrs Meta Vaux Warrick Fuller, of Pennsylvania rearing, but now residing in Massachusetts is accepted as the leading sculptor of today She too spent much time abroad studying art in Paris "The Dancing Girl " "The Wrestler " and "Carrying the Dead Body" are among her best known subjects

NEGRO SCHOLAR

Perhaps one of the earliest ambitions to throb in the Negroes breast was that to achieve distinction in scholarship Perhaps one of the first and most fascinating points in the White man's civilization to attract him was that of the Caucasian's mastering and using things found in books Thus we find ex-slaves men who in some cases would have been regarded as having passed the plastic stage of learning, achieving quite wonderful things in scholarship attainment However, they got no particular credit in the annals of scholarship The Negro scholar as understood in popular circles, is he who has had the persistence and intellect to go forth and win the highest college degrees attainable in some of the best universities of the country At present there are at least four thousand Negro college graduates and about twenty Negroes to gain the degree of Dr of Philosophy from the leading Universities of the country, such as Harvard, Yale University of Pennsylvania Columbia University, and the like Further, the Negro has won his spurs in every phase of scholarship Some of these degrees have been given in History, some

544

in Sociology some in Mathematics and some in Science. The Negro has proved himself a ready scholar and has numbers of students to become members of the Phi Beta Kappa in these leading Universities of the North competing with the sons of those who were scholars generations ago. There are some fifty of these in this country.

NEGRO AUTHORS

The Negro in the field of letters began to arrive in some respects somewhat late. This was inevitable for several reasons. First of all there had, of course to be education and the ability to interpret, in the second place, the Negro had to learn that there was material for literature in the emotions of his people. in the third place he had to learn to love his people in order to grasp their feelings and interpret them to a somewhat indifferent public. This, of course, is a general statement and refers to the conspicuous authors of later date.

As a matter of history the Negro author was among the first, foremost and most lasting authors in America. As has been pointed out elsewhere, Phillis Wheatley was one of the first and foremost women poets of America and still remains the leading colored poet of America.

She was not only the first Negro woman poet, but was one of the first and foremost of American poets.

Benjamin Bannaker as a later writer and advocate of justice for his people was another conspicuous literary light of the early Colonial days. His rare scholarship was equalled by few Americans of any race in that day.

The authors whose works will undoubtedly defy the savages of time, as Shakespeare would put it are Paul Lawrence Dunbar, W. E. B. DuBois Booker T Washington, Charles W Chestnut, Kelly Miller James W Johnson Benjamin G Brawley Dr C V Roman these have already established their claim to immortality and others by the score are clamoring for a place, but the test of time has not been fully applied.

Abroad Alexander Dumas of France, and Alexander Puskin known as "Father of Russian poetry" transcend all boundaries of time, or place, of race or nation. They belong to the world. Each of these authors both American and foreign have received attention elsewhere in this volume.

NEGRO MUSIC

That the Negro is naturally musical is admitted by all even his enemies. Back in the days of slavery there were among the free, educated Negroes many who wrote music. Among these may be mentioned Dede Snael, and Bates Basil. Where the Negro could not write music he made up the words and sang them to tunes that fitted perfect-

ly. These songs are now classed as the Real American Music. Some of our best Musicians of this day have made exhaustive study of these Negro Melodies.

Samuel Coleridge Taylor of London England 1875-1912 was one of the most distinguished of colored writers as well as one of the best known modern composers regardless of race. The work that is best known from this famous musician is Hiawatha. This composition won for its writer fame on both sides of the Atlantic.

Other musicians of note are Will Marion Cook, James Reese Europe J Rosamond Johnson Scott Joplin N Clark Smith and Harry T Burleigh— these men and a number of others have endeavored to produce music that represents the feeling of the race, in such a manner that the compositions will live forever.

Will Henry Bennett Vodery is the leading composer of popular music. Mr Vodery's ability as a composer and arranger is recognized by the big Broadway producers. His services are constantly in demand by Klaw and Erlanger, Schubert, Ziegfield and others.

The race has also produced a number of noted singers. Among these Madame Sisseretta Jones of Providence, Rhode Island, is very popular. She has sung in all the principal cities of Europe with marked success. For the past twenty years she has been at the head of her own company. With this company she has appeared in all the leading cities of the United States, the West Indies and Central America.

Other singers of note are Mrs Azalia Hackley, Mrs Martha Broadus Anderson Madam Anita Patti Brown, Harry T Burleigh the most famous baritone singer of the race, and Roland W Hayes who is regarded as one of the most remarkable tenors in America.

Joseph Douglass, of Washington, and Clarence C White, of Boston, and Kemper Harold of Atlanta are violinists of distinction. Maud Cuney Hare, Carl Diton and L H Caldwell are pianists of great note.

The Negro race has also produced Thomas Greene Bethune better known as Blind Tom, 1849-1908, who for years traveled in concert all over America and Europe. John William Boone "Blind Boone" is another musical prodigy of the Negro race. A native of Missouri he has traveled regularly over the Western States and Canada in concert since 1880.

There are a number of organizations that have acquired national fame. Williams Famous Singers a concert company that is fully described elsewhere in the Cyclopedia, are known wherever there is a lover of fine music. Who has not heard of Fisk

Jubilee Singrs, with a record dating back for generations.

A splendid work is being done by the Clef Club of New York City and the Thomas L. Shoop Musical Organization of Detroit Michigan organizations that train and furnish singers, quartettes, instrumentalists, and dancers for private entertainments, cabarets, etc. The wealthiest class of society people are their chief patrons.

THE NEGRO AS A SOLDIER

Very early however, though he was confined to the work of the fields, the Negro began to develop the qualities of a soldier. The Negroes were with Lewis and Clark. In Colonial warfare, Negroes wherever called upon showed themselves equal to any race in endurance, in discipline and in marksmanship.

During the Revolution Negroes in the South were drafted into service and served in many capacities sometimes fighting for their masters and sometimes by the side of their masters. In Massachusetts during the Revolutionary War Negroes wrote their names on the pages of history there to remain. Crispus Attucks Peter Salem Salem Poors with many others won distinction against the British. The famous Negro regiment that allowed itself to be cut down almost to a man to save its commander, Colonel Nathaniel Green at the battle of Redbank New Jersey, will always be remembered in the pages of American history. A large number of Negroes as is well known won their freedom by fighting in the Revolutionary War. In the war of 1812 the black soldiers came even further to the front, so well did they fight at the battle of New Orleans that they won from so stern a commander as "Old Hickory," one of the finest compliments paid to American soldiers anywhere. In an address to them Andrew Jackson said at the conclusion of the battle, "To men of color soldiers from the shores of Mobile, I called you to arms, I invited you to defend the glory of your white countrymen I expected much from you, for I was not uninformed of those qualities which must render you so formidable a foe I knew you could endure hunger and thirst and all the hardships of war. I knew that you loved the land of your nativity and that like ourselves you had to defend all that is most dear to man but you surpassed my hopes I have found in you united to these qualities that noble enthusiasm which impels great deeds." "Just as he behaved on land so he behaved on sea." Commander Perry said of the black soldier In this war they seemed to be absolutely insensible to danger.

In the Civil War they were almost 200,000 strong There were 160 regiments, of which 140 were infantry, 7 cavalry 12 heavy artillery and 1 light

The first Negro regiment is said to have come from South Carolina. Probably the most famous in the Civil War was the 54th Massachusetts, which organized on February 9th 1863. The Negroes were in practically every battle of any importance in the Civil War. They were conspicuous for their bravery and endurance at Milliken's Bend at Port Hudson at Fort Wagner, at Charleston and Petersburgh From the time of the Civil War nobody has questioned the Negro's ability as a soldier There has been some doubt as to the rank he could hold, but nobody has questioned his ability to fight and to endure.

In the Spanish-American War, in 1898 one needs only to mention Theodore Roosevelt the Rough Riders and San Jaun Hill to bring to mind the valiant deeds of the 9th and 10th Cavalry and the 25th Infantry. At the outbreak of the great world war when American forces joined with those of the Allies the Negroes once more came to the front as soldiers. Once more also the famous 9th and 10th won distinction on the field of honor. At Carranzal in Mexico Negro soldiers walked to their death singing. Their deeds here marked the one conspicuous fight and noble sacrifice in that rather desperate skirmish between the United States and Mexico. In France as far is known, the Negro fought in the front with other nations.

NEGRO CHURCH

Of all the agencies to foster Negro education and advancement the church has played the most conspicuous part. The Negro was early taught in his church, he has for half a century featured the talent of his people in his church. With the exception of the schools that have sprung up and with the exception of a few places and a few people Negro talent can find vent only in the Negro church.

The early Negro churches were not buildings but simply places to assemble to sing and pray. Among the early church buildings is the Baptist church at Williamsburgh Virginia which is said to have been erected in 1785. The M. E. Church of Pennsylvania, founded by Richard Allen in 1757. The St Thomas Episcopal Church in Philadelphia in 1791. The A M E Zion Church, founded in New York in 1796. The Abyssinian Baptist Church in 1800. The Presbyterian Church of Philadelphia in 1857. The Negro church spread rapidly over the whole country and was often the one good place where colored people were allowed. Today they extend from Boston to Key West. In every large city where Negroes are in considerable numbers the Negro Church stands out as one conspicuous building for them. Negro churches in Boston New York, Philadelphia Baltimore Richmond Birmingham, Jacksonville Lexington, Louisville St Louis, and Kansas City, and other cities stand out as conspicuously for architecture and grandeur as do churches of any people in these cities and in many instances they have added educational and social features such as night schools, industrial schools playgrounds, rest-rooms etc indeed all means of improvement for their members and for the Colored people generally Several Negro denominations own their own publishing houses notably among these are the Boyd Publishing House and the A M E Publishing House of Nashville, Tennessee In fifty odd years church property alone is worth some seventy-five millions of dollars, a fact which indicates not only spiritual progress but great material wealth

THE NEGRO INVENTOR

For a long time, owing to the rulings of the Government the Negro inventor got no recognition for his patents, but the Negro inventor, like the Negro soldier, early took his place in American history

BENJAMIN BANNEKER as is pretty well known was not only an early Negro writer of the United States, but was among the foremost American inventors Be it said by the way also that his efforts were not confined to inventions alone but he was a leading thinker, writer and worker of the period as well as an inventor He was a noted astronomer Born free November 9th 1731 in Baltimore County, Maryland Received some education in a pay school Early showed an inclination for mechanics He constructed the first clock made in America

JAMES FORTEN

Of Philadelphia who died in 1842 invented an apparatus for managing sails

ROBERT BENJAMIN LEWIS

Born in Gardiner Maine in 1802 invented a machine for picking oakum This machine in all its essential particulars is said to still be used by the ship-building interests of Maine

WILLIAM B PURVIS

Of Philadelphia, began in 1912 to invent machines for making paper bags and his improvements in this line of machinery are covered by a dozen patents He was also granted patents on electric railways, a fountain pen a magnetic car-balancing device and for a cutter for roll holders His inventions covered a variety of subjects

JOSEPH HUNTER DICKINSON

Of New Jersey, has invented devices for automatically playing the piano His various inventions in piano-player mechanism are adopted in the construction of some of the finest player pianos on the market He has more than a dozen patents to his credit already and is still devoting his energies to that line of invention He is at present in the employ of a large piano factory

GEORGE W MURRAY

Of South Carolina, former member of Congress, from that State has received eight patents for his inventions in agricultural implements including mostly such different attachments as readily adapt a single implement to a variety of uses

HENRY CREAMER

Of New York has patents covering seven different inventions in steam traps

ANDREW J BEARD

Of Alabama has a number of inventions to his credit in car-coupling devices

WILLIAM DOUGLASS

Of Arkansas has received patents for various inventions for harvesting machines

JAMES DOYLE

Of Pittsburgh, has patented an automatic serving system This device is a scheme for dispensing with the use of waiters in dining rooms, restaurants and at railroad lunch counters

SHELBY J DAVIDSON

Of Kentucky a clerk in the office of the Auditor for the Post Office Department operated a machine for tabulating and totalizing the quarterly accounts which were regularly submitted by the postmasters of the country Mr Davidson's attention was first directed to the loss in time through the necessary periodically stopping to manually dispose of the paper coming from the machine He invented a rewind device which served as an attachment for automatically taking up the paper as it issued from the machines, and adapted it for use again on the reverse side thus effecting a very considerable economy of time and material He also invented an attachment for adding machines which was designed to automatically include the government fee as well as the amount sent when totalizing the money orders in the reports submitted by postmasters

ROBERT PELHAM

Of Detroit employed in the Census Office Bureau devised a machine used as an adjunct in tabulating the statistics from the manufacturer's schedules in a way that displaced a dozen men in a given quantity of work doing the work economically speedily and with faultless precision The United States Government has leased his patents, paying him a royalty for their use in addition to his salary for operating them

GRANVILLE T WOODS

Of New York, assisted by his brother Lyates bears the distinction of having taken out more patents than any other Negro His patents number more than fifty His principal inventions relate to electrical subjects such as telegraph and telephone instruments electric railways and general systems of electrical control

ELIJAH McCOY

Of Detroit stands next to Woods as an inventor, in point of number of inventions. His first patent was secured July, 1872, and since that period he has about forty patents to his credit. His patents cover a wide range of subjects but relate particularly to the lubricating machinery. He was pioneer in the art of steadily supplying oil to machinery in intermittent drops from a cup so as to avoid the necessity for stopping the machine to oil it

JOHN ERNEST MATZELIGER

Born in Dutch Guiana 1852 died in Lynn, Mass., 1889. He is the inventor of the first machine that performed automatically all operations involved in attaching soles to shoes. This was the only machine invented up to that time that would discharge the completely soled shoe from the machine, everything being done automatically and requiring less than a minute to complete a single shoe

Matzeliger attempted to capitalize his patents by organizing a company but failing health frustrated his plans. After his death the patent and much of the stock of the company organized by Matzeliger was bought up. The purchase laid the foundation for the organization of the United Shoe Machinery Company, the largest and richest corporation of the kind in the world

The list of inventors among the Negroes is almost endless from inventing farm implements and manufacturing implements to the designing and running of airplanes and machinery devices for submarines

NEGRO Y M C A.

The first colored Young Men's Christian Association was organized in Washington, D C, in December, 1853. Anthony Brown colored, was the first president. He worked in the Patent Office. The second to be organized was in Charleston, South Carolina in April, 1866 and the third in New York City, February, 1867, E B C Cato, President. The first colored student association was organized at Howard University in 1869. E B Cato who attended the Montreal Convention in 1867 was the first colored delegate to attend an international Y M C A Convention. William A Hunton was the first colored man to enter the secretaryship of the Young Men's Christian Association work. In January, 1888 he was appointed the General Secretary of the Colored Association in Norfolk Virginia. In 1890 he succeeded Mr Brown as an International Secretary

The Y M C A work has been established in a number of places in connection with large corporate industries in which numbers of Negroes are employed. The company usually puts up the building and pays the secretary. The running expenses are paid out of annual and monthly dues. The first rural Young Men's Christian Association for Negroes was organized in 1913 in Brunswick County Virginia. It is under the supervision of the St Paul Normal and Industrial Institute which is located in this county

However, until the famous philanthropist, Julius Rosenwald, of Chicago, offered to give $25,000 to any city whose Negroes would raise $75,000, the Negro Y M C A stood for little. It was an out-of-the-way house whose rooms were dingy, whose equipment was dilapidated and whose secretaries, existing on small pay, worked but a short time. True, the organization began as early as 1853, but the Rosenwald fund enabled the colored people to put up such brick buildings as those for example in Indianapolis, Indiana, Chicago Illinois, Kansas City, Missouri, St Louis Missouri, Atlanta, Ga, and to establish the Negro Y M C A, as a lasting organization in America

In the recent War the "Y' work, as it was called rendered valuable service to the Negro boys on the front. Be this also added that the Negro men who volunteered to serve the Y M C A were among the best that the race could produce, and thus far, the war having terminated at this writing, no Negro "Y' worker has been convicted of any adroit dealings in office. Today there is scarcely a state or a city where Negro population abounds but has a respectable Y M C A

NEGRO Y W C A

In 1893, students associations had been organized in a number of Negro schools. Associations at Claflin, Straight, and Tougaloo Universities Spelman Seminary and the Alabama A and M College became affiliated, in the early 90's with what was then the National Association of Young Women's Christian Association. In 1906 the National Board of Young Women's Christian Associations of the United States of America was formed. Its program included plans for the supervision and extension of the association movement among colored women

The Y W C A is an organization much like the Y M C A. The Y W C A is now doing effective work, both in the schools and among the general public for colored young women. The Y W C A is scarcely more than a quarter of a century old. Certainly its active work does not date back much further than this. Such colored women as Mrs Wm A Hunton wife of Y M C A Worker W A Hunton Mrs Elizabeth Ross Haines, Mrs Eva D Bowles, Mrs Josephine Penyon, are among the early sponsors for the work of the Y W association. Mrs William A Hunton was the first colored secretary. She spent the winter of 1907-08 investigating the colored field and interesting

Y.M.C.A. Building,
Nashville, Tenn.

Y.M.C.A. Building, Columbus, Ga.

Y.M.C.A. Building, Ashville, N.C.

Y.M.C.A. Building,
Louisville, Ky.

Y.M.C.A. Building, Chicago, Ill.

Y.M.C.A Building, Washington, D.C.

TYPES OF MODERN NEGRO Y. M.C. A. BUILDINGS

the colored women in the work She founded fourteen student Associations and four City Associations New York, Brooklyn, Baltimore, and Washington In 1908, Miss Elizabeth Ross was appointed to be the special worker for the National Board among colored students Miss Ross was succeeded in 1910 by Miss Cecelia Holloway, and Miss Holloway, by Miss Josephine Pinyon

In 1910, Mrs Elizabeth Ross Haynes and Mrs Hunton undertook a systematic and intensive development of city association work among colored women and the placing of trained secretaries in local associations In 1913, Miss Eva D Bowles was appointed by the National Board to have special supervision of the city work In order that prospective secretaries may gain a definite knowledge of association methods and principles and their practical application, training centers are provided in addition to the regular training school courses Special summer courses have also been provided for those desiring to prepare for the secretaryship

In recent years the association has broadened the equipment of its corps of workers, going far and wide throughout the nation Not only have many buildings been put up in the cities, but some very careful and effective work has been done in saving and educating girls of various large cities In the recent war the Y W, like the "Y" rendered most helpful service Perhaps one of the greatest services was the establishment of lodgings for young women who travel In this way the Y W saves many a girl who travels from possible ruin

COLORED EXPLORERS

Two men must be mentioned among the colored explorers The first is Estenvanillo or Estevanico, sometimes referred to as "Steve" He was with the ill fated expedition of DeNarvaez This expedition set out from Spain in 1627 Only four men survived Of this number Estevanico was one He with a companion set out to investigate for himself He was one of the first persons to cross the continent of America For eight years he wandered over the plains of Texas, and discovered Arizona and New Mexico To him also belongs the credit of the discovery of the Zuni Indians

The other explorer of prominence in the Negro race is Matthew A Henson Henson was born in 1866 in Maryland He had the honor of accompanying Commander Robert E Peary on all his expeditions in search for the North Pole, with the exception of the first one He was with Commander Peary when the final dash was made in 1909 In fact he was the only civilized person with the commander at that time Of Henson's part in the discovery of the North Pole Commander Peary said

"On that bitter brilliant day in April ,1909, when the stars and stripes floated at the North Pole, Caucasian, Ethiopian, and Mongolian stood side by side at the Apex of the earth in the harmonious companionship resulting from hard work, exposure, danger, and a common object

"Mathew A Henson, my Negro assistant, has been with me in one capacity or another since my second trip to Nicaragua in 1887 I have taken him on each and all of my expeditions, except the first, and also without exception on each of my fartherest sledge trips This position I have given him primarily because of his adaptability and fitness for the work and secondly, on account of his loyalty He is a better dog driver than any man living except some of the best Esquimo hunters themselves "

Negro Education

ANY forces have been working together for the education of the
Negro in the South. The Northern born Negro is no problem.
While he has not always availed
himself of fine chances for good
education, still the choice is left largely with the
individual.

This is not so in the South. The Public school
system all over the Southland is inadequate. The
terms in the rural districts are too short, the buildings and the equipment too poor. The city schools
are too few in number to afford training for the
vast number of children of color who have to attend them. As I said, at the first, many forces
have been at work for the education of the Negro.
In the Rural District the Jeans' Fund Workers are
making a marked change in the class-room work.
The Rosenwald Fund is making a vast change in
the physical surroundings of the schools. Through
these two funds as they are used in the rural districts in the South, much good has been derived
for the betterment of the educational facilities of
the rural Negro.

The larger cities have come, some of them lately
and some of them a long time ago to realize the
need for High Schools. In Washington, D. C., there
is the Dunbar High School, and the Manual Training School, which is of High School grade. There
is an excellent High School in both St. Louis and
in Kansas City, Missouri. A newly established
High School in Sedalia is also clamoring for recognition as a first class High School. Savannah,
Georgia, Birmingham, Alabama, Little Rock, Arkansas; Muscogee, Oklahoma, Louisville, Kentucky,
and all the larger cities of Texas are able to boast
of their High School for Colored Children. There
are some other cities that are doing part High
school work, but the number is far too small for
the number of children that need the training.

COUNTY TRAINING SCHOOLS

Arising to fill a long felt need in the training of
colored youth the County Training Schools in the
South have come forward to a place of prominence.
In most of the rural communities of the South the
time spent, equipment and the ability of the teach-
er of the rural school have held the children back.
To quote from Dr. James H. Dillard, of the Slater
Fund:

"The movement for the establishment of County
Training Schools for Negroes came from the county superintendents. In an address delivered in 1913
at the Southern Sociological Congress Mr. B. C.
Caldwell said: "Three years ago a parish superin-

tendent in Louisiana applied to the Slater Fund for
assistance in establishing a county high school for
Negro children. Almost at the same time a county
superintendent in Arkansas, one in Virginia, and
one in Mississippi proposed substantially the same
thing. It was the purpose in each case to train
teachers for the schools of the county.

Every county in the South has felt the need of
fairly well trained teachers in its rural schools. But
so far as we know this is the first time that superintendents have deliberately planned to get them
by training them at home." This correspondence
led to discussion of plans and investigation of conditions, to which Messrs. Caldwell, Davis, and W.
T. B. Williams devoted careful attention. The result was that for the session 1911-12 the Slater
Fund contributed $500 in each of four counties with
the understanding that the schools should be public schools supported by the public funds.

"Our purpose in these four instances is to aid in
establishing a county industrial training school for
Negroes as a part of the public school system.

"One great need, as I have previously stated to
the Board, is to provide means for some sort of
preparation for the rural teachers, hardly any of
whom have been able to attend any institution outside of their own county or some adjoining county."

Many of these County Training Schools were
crude in their beginnings, but the superintendents
and supervisors and all concerned have struggled
to develop them to a point where they will serve
the purpose for which they were established. To
get a good teacher in the rural districts was almost impossible. The well trained teachers preferred to work in the town, cities and private
schools. The County Training schools were established to prepare teachers in the county for the
work of the county. That the plan has succeeded
is shown by the steady increase in the number of
County Training Schools.

The minimum requirement of the Slater Board
which has furnished assistance for these schools
follows:

MINIMUM REQUIREMENTS OF THE SLATER BOARD

"To aid in the establishment of these schools, the
Trustees of the John F. Slater Fund have voted
an appropriation of $500 to each for maintenance
subject to the following conditions:

1. The school property shall belong to the state,
county, or district, and the school shall be a part
of the public school system.

II. There shall be an appropriation for main-

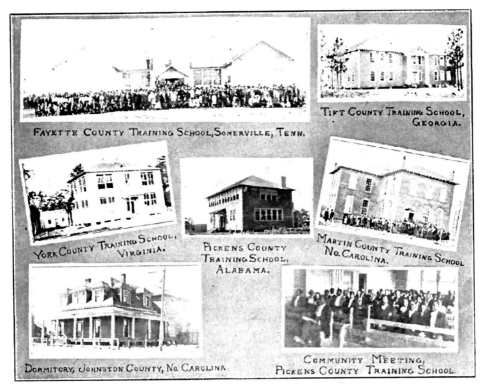

FAYETTE COUNTY TRAINING SCHOOL, SOMERVILLE, TENN.

TIFT COUNTY TRAINING SCHOOL, GEORGIA.

YORK COUNTY TRAINING SCHOOL, VIRGINIA.

PICKENS COUNTY TRAINING SCHOOL, ALABAMA.

MARTIN COUNTY TRAINING SCHOOL, No. CAROLINA.

DORMITORY, JOHNSTON COUNTY, No. CAROLINA.

COMMUNITY MEETING, PICKENS COUNTY TRAINING SCHOOL.

ILLUSTRATIONS OF MODERN TRAINING SCHOOLS.

tenance of not less than $750 from public funds raised by the state, county, or district taxation.

III. The teaching shall extend through the eighth year, with the intention of adding at least two years as soon as it shall be possible to make such extension."

These County Training Schools become the centres of learning for the county in which they are located and for the neighboring counties. Better teachers may be had for them because of the better pay and because of the emphasis that is being placed upon them.

The good that is being accomplished in this new development in the Public School system of the South is great. The larger institutions of learning in the South can furnish teachers enough for these educational centers. The pay and the life offered are sufficiently enticing to make the new teachers happy. These teachers carry to the rural districts all the ideas that they have gained through years of association with real educators. The pupils in the County Training schools will in turn go out into the remote places of the country and establish better and bigger schools and in this way the people on the farms will learn to live a broader,

more wholesome life. Too much cannot be said in praise for these New County Training Schools.

In addition to the work that is done through the public school system and through the various funds helping out the public school system there have been a number of organizations that will have to be studied separately in order to get some idea of the scope of the work that has been done by them.

AMERICAN BAPTIST HOME MISSION SOCIETY.

The work of the American Baptist Home Mission Society in the South was begun in 1862. The following resolution marked the beginning of their endeavor for the colored people, "Resolved, That we recommend the society to take immediate steps to supply with Christian instruction by means of missionaries and teachers, the emancipated slaves. From that day the organization has worked steadily for the education of the Negro youth. While at the start the teachers nd officers employed by this Society to manage the schools it was founding were of necessity white, the schools have gradually added to the list of teachers per-

PARTIAL BIRD-EYE VIEW OF BENEDICT COLLEGE

sons of color till today there are a greater number of colored than white teachers working in these schools. Several of the larger schools have been given over entirely into the hands of the colored people. So well have these institutions been managed that they have gone forward and have steadily increased in efficiency.

Among the schools established by the American Baptist Home Mission Society may be mentioned Morehouse College, established in 1867, Spelman Seminary, Atlanta, Ga., established in 1881. These two schools are told of in full elsewhere in this volume and represent the type of work being done by all the schools owned and controlled by this body. Benedict College, in South Carolina, was established in 1871. Bishop College, in Texas, was established in 1881, Hartshorn Memorial College, in Virginia, was established in 1883, Shaw University in North Carolina is one of the oldest of the schools established by this Society. This institution dates

from 1865. Another of the earliest institutions is the Virginia Union University, established in 1865.

The number of Baptists among colored people of the South outnumbers any other denomination. For this reason the Baptist boards working for the colored people have had a large field. Many have been the problems that have arisen because of the division of the work in this denomination. In several of the states the colored Baptists have divided. One branch of colored Baptists supports the schools organized and owned by the American Baptist Home Mission Society. The other branch supports the schools that they have organized and run in opposition to American Baptist Home Mission Schools. This has been but an outcome of the Negroes' ambition to apply the lessons of self help that have been implanted in his breast while attending these institutions of learning. The colored man is yet too poor to finance properly his own schools for higher education. Where the at-

SHAW UNIVERSITY RALEIGH, N. C

Bishop Hall
(Girls Dormitory)

The Mansion
(President's Residence)
and The Pool

Bishop College Campus Entrance

Rockefeller Hall
(Girls' Dormitory)

Marston Hall and The Pool
(Boys' Dormitory)

GROUP OF VIEWS OF BISHOP COLLEGE, MARSHALL, TEXAS.

HARTSHORN MEMORIAL COLLEGE, RICHMOND, VA

tempt has been made they have suffered from insufficient funds.

Another division of the Baptists in the work for the colored people is the Northern and the Southern whites. The Northern whites have done most for the Negro, but Southern Baptists have also felt the responsibility for the training of the Colored youth. In 1916 the Southern Baptists pledged fifty thousand dollars for a Theological School for Negroes.

The work that is done by the American Baptist Home Mission Board is strongly supported by the Woman's American Baptist Home Mission Board. In fact the schools that are helped by the Woman's branch are also helped by the regular board. Together these two boards own and control twenty-four institutions that are classed as "larger and more important" in the U. S. Bulletin Number 38. The total valuation of these twenty-four schools is $3,870,744. This represents a great investment for the development of the Colored Baptists of the South. Not only has the Northern White man given of his money, to the development of this cause, but he has sent his sons and daughters into the field to labor as well. Then when there were colored men sufficiently trained to share the responsibility the work was divided with him. John Hope, President of Morehouse College, Atlanta, Ga., is the type of colored man that this Society has placed at the head of its institutions. Z. T. Hubert, President of Jackson College, Jackson, Mississippi, is another young colored man who, having been given the responsibility of the management of one of the larger schools supported by Northern Baptists, has made good.

The good of these two organizations cannot be estimated. Never in the history of any race has the progress upward been so rapid as that of the Negro race. When we consider the untiring efforts of these unselfish people and others equally zealous for our uplift, we can in a small way begin to realize the great force that was back of this rapid rise. Never will the Negro of the South forget the efforts of the Northern white man in behalf of his educational uplift.

AMERICAN MISSIONARY ASSOCIATION

The American Missionary Association was organized September 3, 1846. From the first the organization held high ideals and it was run by men of broad educational training. These men were strong men, men of power and vision. The organization was not formed to furnish relief for the black men, but at the outbreak of the War, it was in a very good position to do so. For fifteen years it had carried on work in the South hoping to arouse the Southern Whites to a realization of the evils of slavery. The Association in 1858 founded Berea College, Kentucky. This school was not founded for Negroes alone, but for all who needed training. In 1868 this College had an attendance of 200 pupils, and two-thirds of these were Negroes.

From the first efforts of this Association were strong for the education of the Negro. In 1866 Fisk University was established. The story of the progress of this institution and of its becoming independent is told elsewhere in this volume. In 1867 Talladega College was established. This school is one of the strongest supported by the Association. It is situated at Talladega, Alabama, and stands for the thorough preparation of colored men and women in all lines of endeavor. The work of

555

CHORUS IN THE CHAPEL, TOUGALOO, UNIVERSITY, TOUGALOO, MISS.

the college department is of such grade that two years in Harvard or Yale wins for Talladega men their degree.

In 1868, Hampton Institute was founded. It was of course not then what it is today, but out of the school planted in that year has grown our great Hampton of today. Hampton, like Fisk, is now an independent school. Hampton stands for the training of both the head and the hand. There are 900 boarding pupils, 400 day pupils in the elementary school, and about 400 teachers attending summer school. The work took its shape under General Armstrong, the first principal and Dr. Frissell carried out the ideas that were started by him. The work is now under Dr. Gregg.

In 1869, both Atlanta University at Atlanta, Ga., and Straight University, at New Orleans, were established. Both these schools now have the reputation of doing very thorough classical work. Atlanta University is one of the best known institutions for the training of the Negro youth of the South. It is also one of the schools in which the most thorough work is being done. They carry an enrollment of about 500 pupils, a great number of these come from the city of Atlanta. It is one of the best equipped of the schools doing work for the colored people.

Straight, like Talladega College, is still under the control of the American Missionary Association. It has a strong faculty and is religious in its training. Straight is one of the first class institutions for the higher education of the Negroes of the South. Although chartered as Straight University in 1915, the name was changed to Straight College as that more nearly represented the scope of the work that could be done by this school.

In the same year as the two above mentioned schools were established. Tougaloo College was founded in the State of Mississippi. This school is still under the control of the A. M. A. It is one of the oldest and strongest of the schools still supported by this organization. Tougaloo is especially strong in its musical course. If the good of an institution is to be counted by the work done by the graduates that go from its doors, then Tougaloo is one of the best of our Southern schools.

STRAIGHT COLLEGE, NEW ORLEANS, LA.

GROUP OF BUILDINGS OF TALLADEGA COLLEGE, TALLADEGA. ALA.

The work of the American Missionary Association can be estimated by the work of the Universities and colleges established and maintained by it.

The good that has been done through establishment of smaller schools in all parts of the South has also to be taken into account. These schools were invariably put in the care of good earnest Christian workers. At first most of these workers were white men and women, but as soon as there were colored workers sufficiently trained for the positions they were added to the list of workers in these secondary schools. Among these schools might be mentioned Lincoln School, at Meridian, Mississippi, for a number of years under the leadership of Mrs. H. I. Miller, of Topeka, Kansas. The Emerson School in Mobile, Le Moyne Institute, in Memphis, Cotton Valley, which is out in a country district of Alabama. In fact the number of these schools is too great for them all to be mentioned. But the good training they have given to the Ne-

gro girls and boys, and the inspiration that has come through them for better living has made them a great factor in the development of the Negro in the South.

The schools of the American Missionary Association, both the small schools and the colleges have been a great factor in making the progress of the Colored man so rapid.

FEDERAL SCHOOLS, LAND GRANT SCHOOLS, AND STATES SCHOOLS FOR THE NEGRO

That the educated Negro is far more of an asset in the state than an uneducated one has gradually become an established and known fact among the white people of the South. At first the white man was not over sympathetic with the education of the Negro. But the Religious bodies of the North continued to work for his education and uplift, till even the Southern white man saw that an educated Negro was an improvement on the uneducated one.

CARNEGIE LIBRARY, STATE A. & M. COLLEGE, TALLAHASSEE, FLA., MECHANICTS ART BUILDING

GIRLS, DORMITORY, PRAIRIE VIEW, N. & S. INSTITUTE, ADMINISTRATION BLDG. AND FOSTER HALL.

When this fact dawned upon the Southern law-maker, they began to establish state schools for the training of the colored boys and girls.

The Land-Grant schools are the greatest in number. The Morrill Fund under which these schools receive Government money was established in 1862. The Negroes at first came into only a small share of this money. In Virginia, Hampton Institute received $12,000 from this fund as early as 1870. In South Carolina, Claflin University received a portion of the fund for the development of an industrial course. In Mississippi, however, Alcorn College was opened to both white and colored for training. In 1876 Alcorn was practically wholly colored. But the school did not take a definite place in the education of the colored youth till much later. It was still much later that the State school and Land Grant School for the Negro became a real factor in the development of the colored boy and girl in Southern States.

Of the Land Grant Schools there are now sixteen. All of the Southern States have taken advantage of the liberal appropriation of the Government for the school training of the young. The amount of money invested in the plants of these sixteen schools is more than two million, five hundred thousand dollars. Some of these schools are taken up in full in other parts of this book—The Alabama Agricultural and Mechanical College for Negroes at Normal; Princess Anne Academy of Maryland; and the Lincoln Institute of Missouri. But there are others that are doing equally as good work and some of the others are larger. For example the Florida Agricultural and Mechanical College for Negroes, at Tallahassee, has played a great part in the training of the youth of that state. Mr. N. B. Young, who has been at the head of this institution for years has developed the work along all the lines that make for the full development of strong character. This is probably the best organized of all the Land Grant Schools.

This is the complete list of the Land Grant Schools—Alabama Agricultural and Mechanical

College, Normal, Alabama. Walter Buchanan, Pres.; Branch Normal, Pine Bluff, Arkansas, J. G. Ish, President; Delaware State College for Colored Youth, Dover, Del., W. C. Jason, President.;Florida Agricultural and Mechanical College, Tallassee, N. B. Young, President; Georgia State Industrial College, Savannah, R. R. Wright, President; Kentucky Normal and Industrial Institute for Colored, Frankfort, G. P. Rusell, President; Southern University, Baton Rouge, Louisiana, J. S. Clark, President; Princess Anne Academy, Princess Anne, Thomas H. Kiah, President; Alcorn Agricultural and Mechanical College, Alcorn, Mississippi, L. J. Rowan, President; Lincoln Institute, Jefferson City, Missouri; Clement Richardson, President; Colored Agricultural and Technical College, Greensboro, N. C., James B. Dudley, President; Colored Agricultural and Normal University, Langston, Oklahoma, J. M. Marquess, President; Colored Normal, Industrial and Mechanical College, Orangeburg, S. C., R. S. Wilkinson, President; Agricultural and Industrial State School, Nashville, Tenn.; W. J. Hoyle, President; Prairie View State Normal and Industrial College, Prairie View, Texas, I. M. Terrell, President; West Virginia Collegiate Institute, Institute, W. Va., Byrd Prillerman, President.

Hampton Institute might be mentioned as a Land Grant School, for it received part of its support fund from this source. These schools represent an annual investment of more than one million, one hundred eighty-five thousand dollars in the training of the colored youth of the South.

The State schools of the South are supported entirely by the state receiving no funds from the Federal Government. There are eleven of these schools. Alabama has one, Kansas two, Maryland one, New Jersey one, North Carolina three, Ohio one, and Virginia and West Virginia one each.

The Federal school is Howard University located at Washington, D. C. Howard represents an investment of one million seven hundred fifty odd thousand dollars.

FREEDMEN'S AID SOCIETY

The Freedmen's Aid Society of the Methodist Episcopal Church was organized in Cincinnati, Ohio in 1866, and at once sent school teachers into the South to gather the scattered and ignorant people together in any sort of shack or building, or even in open air to teach them responsibilities of manhood and womanhood and citizenship. Gradually the Church responded to calls of the Society for money necessary to put up buildings and pay teachers, until after fifty years of earnest and faithful service on the part of teachers and liberal giving by the Church, there are at the present time under the control of the Freedmen's Aid Society eighteen institutions of learning, located in strategic centers throughout the Southern States, with 334 teachers and 5,702 students sending out their streams of intellectual, industrial, and moral influence into the masses of the Negro race now grown to be twelve million. During the half century of their work over 200,000 boys and girls have attended the schools. Large numbers of them have graduated and are now the leading factors in the ministry and membership not only of the Methodist Episcopal Church but of all the colored churches in the South. From nothing the property of the Society has grown until today it is valued at $2,008,750, and the annual income from collections in the churches, bequests gifts, and legacies with payments from students themselves amounts to a round half million of dollars and the permanent endowment is now one million dollars and daily growing.

The 350,000 colored members of the Methodist Episcopal Church, with their 3,375 churches, 215,206 Sunday-school scholars (and a church property valued at $8,091,929), would have been impossible were it not for the trained and converted leaders who have gone out from the schools. The work could not have been carried on in these churches and Sunday schools were it not for the young life constantly pouring out of the schools into their ministry and membership. Ten millions of dollars make up the total cost for fifty years. Just about the price of one battleship or less than the money wasted in the European war in half a day.

WHAT GOD HATH WROUGHT FOR THE NEGRO RACE IN AMERICA IN FIFTY YEARS

Half a century ago the Negro was a chattel without education property, or opportunity of any sort. Four millions of him then, twelve millions now, but what a wonderful contrast between the condition of the twelve millions of today and the four millions of fifty years ago. Read both sides of this parallel and see what has been accomplished through fifty years of Christian training.

THE NEGRO FIFTY YEARS AGO

Population census 1860 Slaves 3,953,750 Free, 487,970, total	441,730
Illiteracy	90%
Value of property estimated at	$1,200,000
Number of colleges and universities	1
Number of college graduates, estimated at	30
Number of practicing physicians and pharmacists	0
Number of lawyers	0
Number of banks operated by Negroes	0
Number of Negro towns	0
Number of newspapers	1
Number of churches owned estimated at	400
Value of church property	$500,000
Membership of Negro churches estimated at	40,000
Number of children in schools, estimated at	25,000

HALF A CENTURY OF NEGRO PROGRESS

Total Negro population (United States), 1910	9,828,294
Homes owned by Negroes	500,000
Churches owned by Negroes	31,393
Church Membership	3,207,305
Sunday schools	24,380
Sunday-school scholars	1,448,570
Illiteracy, census 1910	30.5%
Value of property, estimated at	$1,000,000,000
Number of farms owner	250,000
Value of church property	$65,000,000
Number of college and university graduates	8,000
Professional men	75,000
Number of practicing physicians estimated at	3,500
Number of practicing lawyers	1,500
Number of business men, estimated at	50,000
Number of children in schools	2,000,000
Number of Negro towns	50
Number of Negro teachers	30,000
Land owned by Negroes acres or 31,000 square miles	20,000,000
Drug stores	300
General stores and other industrial enterprises	20,000
Newspapers and periodicals	398
Hospital and Nurse training schools	61
Banks owned by Negroes	72
Insurance companies	100
66.2 per cent of all Negroes in the United States, ten years of age or over, are engaged in gainful occupations	
Property owned by Negro secret societies	$8,000,000

Capital stock Negro banks........... $2,000,000
Annual business done by Negro banks $20,000,000

The Freedmen's Aid Society has contributed a large share of this magnificent result through its eighteen schools. During that time it has sent out more than 200,000 young people who received the broader and higher outlook from its Christian teachers.

The work of these young people is the largest factor among the Negro people in making the world safe for democracy.

SOCIETY'S NEW OUTLOOK

The Methodist Episcopal Church has just completed a drive in which ONE HUNDRED AND TWELVE MILLION DOLLARS was raised for missions and education home and foreign. THE THREE HUNDRED AND FIFTY THOUSAND NEGRO membership of that church subscribed FOUR MILLION DOLLARS. The entire one hundred and twelve millions covers a period of five years so the Negroes will have eight hundred thousand dollars per year to raise. While but two months of the first year have passed since the close of the drive the Negro membership has paid in approximately two hundred thousand in cash.

The colored people gave but four million on the basis of the five year period but eight million will be expended in building churches and employing church workers in the North and the South and in education.

The Freedmen's Aid Society which directs the educational institutions of the Methodist Episcopal Church for the education of Negroes is the agency to push the new program of education.

That Society will have available in the five year period two million dollars over its regular income to be applied to endowment, new buildings and equipment. At a recent meeting the Board of Managers advanced the current appropriations to the schools for the year 1919-1920 from $95,985.61 to $118,000. The appropriation for Morgan College and branches which are operated by a self-perpetuating Board of Trustees amounts to $15,410 making a total appropriation $133,410.00. Nor is this all of direct appropriations, because each institution gets the amount raised in the patronizing colored conferences. All of the above is extra from the regular income of the school in fees, board and tuition.

ANNUITIES AND SPECIAL GIFTS

In addition to the offerings from the churches the Society receives many gifts of large amounts during each year. For those who wish to contribute to the work of these schools and who need the income from their money while they live, the Society pays a liberal annuity during the lifetime of the donor. This makes sure that such gifts shall go on fulfilling a great commission, in the name of these donors for all time to come.

The schools operated by the Freedmen's Aid Society are Gammon Theological Seminary Atlanta Ga., Meharry Medical College, Nashville Tenn., Flint-Goodridge Hospital New Orleans La., Clark University So. Atlanta Ga., Morristown Normal College Morristown, Tenn., Morgan College and Princess Anne Academy, Baltimore, Md., New Orleans College, and Gilbert Academy, New Orleans La., Rust College, Holly Springs Miss., Philander Smith College Little Rock, Ark., Sam Huston College Austin, Texas, Bennett College, Greensboro N. Carolina George R. Smith College Sedalia Mo., Haven Institute Meridian Miss., Central Alabama Institute Birmingham Ala., Cookman Institute, Jacksonville Fla., Claflin College Orangeburg So. Carolina, Wiley College Marshall Texas.

The officers of the Freedmen's Aid Society are as follows:

BOARD OF MANAGERS—Bishops W. F. Anderson, F. J. McConnell, F. D. Leete, W. P. Thirkfield, W. A. Quayle and F. M. Bristol. Ministers J. C. Hartzell, H. C. Jennings, A. J. Nast, D. L. Aultman, Herbert Scott, John H. Race, C. E. Schenk, V. F. Brown, W. B. Slutz, E. R. Overley, W. H. Wohrly and E. C. Wareing. Laymen R. B. McRary, F. R. Graham, L. N. Gatch, L. C. Harley, C. F. Coffin, C. L. Swain, H. H. Garrison, Harlan C. West, George D. Webb, and Charles Hommeyer.

OFFICERS OF THE BOARD—Bishop W. F. Anderson President, Bishop F. D. Leete, First Vice-President, Bishop W. P. Thirkfield, Second Vice-President, Rev. C. E. Schenk Third Vice-President, Rev. W. H. Wohrly, Fourth Vice-President, C. L. Swain, Fifth Vice-President, Rev. John H. Race Treasurer, Rev. D. Lee Aultman, Recording Secretary, Rev. P. J. Maveety and I. Garland Penn Corresponding Secretaries. Assistant Recording Secretary, Miss May Getzendanner, Assistant Treasurer, E. R. Graham.

PROMINENT MEN WHO ARE FREEDMEN'S AID GRADUATES

Half of all the colored physicians in the United States are graduates of Meharry Medical College one of the Freedmen's Schools. Such outstanding and prominent men as Dr. Emmett J. Scott, Secretary-Treasurer of Howard University Washington D. C., Dr. R. F. Jones, Editor South Western Christian Advocate, New Orleans, La., Dr. Warfield Surgeon-in-Chief Freedmen's Hospital Washington, D. C., Lawyer W. Ashbie Hawkins Baltimore Md., Dr. J. W. E. Bowen Professor Historical Theology Atlanta Ga., Dr. Ernest Lyon former Minister to Liberia and a host of others are graduates of these schools.

GRLS' DORMITORY, PAUL QUINN COLLEGE, WACO, TEXAS.

OTHER PROMINENT INSTITUTIONS SUPPORTED BY THE METHODIST CHURCH

The Methodist Church has the honor of taking the first definite steps for the education of the colored youth. This step was taken in Ohio in the year 1844. At that time the Ohio Conference of the A. M. E. Church appointed a committee to select a site for the Seminary of learning. It was three years later when the school was opened. The same state took the next step for the education of the colored man. This was when they established Wilberforce University. The object of Wilberforce was the higher order of education of colored people generally and the site for it was purchased in 1856.

From the first the broad principle that there should be no race discrimination was established Wilberforce changed hands in 1863, when Bishop Payne of the A. M. E. Church purchased the institution from the M. E. Church. The school has been in the hands of strong race leaders. They have builded well for the distinctive University that is now Wilberforce. The present President is Dr. W. S. Scarborough, who was for a number of years prior to this Professor of Latin and Greek in this University.

While Wilberforce is by far the best known and the largest of these schools, Kittrell College, Kittrell, North Carolina, with President G. A. Edwards at its head is well known and is doing a good work. Ranking along with Kittrell we have Paul Quinn in Texas and Morris Brown in Atlanta, Georgia. These schools all receive their support from the church, and in turn send out trained young people to work in the interest of the denomination.

LINCOLN UNIVERSITY

The first step for Negro education was taken in Ohio, in 1844. Ten years later, 1854, Pennsylvania took the next step when Lincoln University was first founded. The first charter was granted under the name of Ashmun Institute. When the name was changed in 1866, the plan was to have training in the various professions; theology, medicine, law—in adition to the regular preparatory department and college course. The courses were one by one discontinued, however, till in 1893, there remained the College and the Theological Seminary as departments of the University.

OTHER CHURCH SCHOOLS

Besides the schools that fall into the groups that have already been considered there are the Presbyterian Schools, the Catholic Schools, Christian Schools, The Schools owned by the Societies of Friends, the schools of the Lutheran Board, the Episcopal Boards, the United Presbyterion Board and then there are Negro Church Boards maintaining schools.

The work done for the Negro through these various boards shows the genuine interest of the churches in the social uplift of the colored man. The Baptist Board with its large investment in Negro education has a large Negro membership in its denomination. While they do not limit the students in anyway to persons of their own faith, they have a very large number of young men and women of their own faith to draw on. The same is true of the Methodists. While not so numerous as the Baptists they are present in vast number. This is not true of the other boards that are struggling to help the Negro in his upward strides. They

561

are working for the Negro through their love of humanity. This fact will be more and more recognized.

Less than 4 percent of the Negro population of the United States are connected with churches other than Baptist and Methodist. The other religious bodies however, including the Congregationalists have invested more than seven million dollars in the education of the Colored people. This is a sum that equals the combined investment of the two leading denominations. This shows the interest of these broad-people in education in its broadest sense. The good thus done for the Negro has meant much in his rapid progress during the past fifty years. The schools established and controlled by these organizations are for the most part well supervised and amply supported.

CONGREGATIONALISM AND THE NEGRO

Congregationalism is apostolic in origin. In its modern meaning, it dates as far back as the close of the Sixteenth Century when Puritanism arose in the days of "Good Queen Bess." Under James I one group began to meet by themselves, and to worship in an unorthodox way. These were days when religious toleration was not known, hence they were "harried out of the land," and found refuge first in Holland, and after twelve years, found a home in the wilds of the new world, at Plymouth, in 1620.

Then splendid heroism is a matter of history. How they toiled and suffered and died in laying the foundations of a church without a Bishop, and of a State without a King is known by every school boy.

Their ministers, from Robinson down were men of letters. Education was fostered along with religion as a matter of course. Harvard, Yale, Andover, Dartsmouth, Princeton, and scores of other colleges and schools of high rank bear eloquent witness to their intellectual zeal.

They were, however, pre-eminently a spiritual-minded folk and felt themselves divinely led in all matters of both church and state.

The church in the wilderness grew and flourished, sometimes "with toil and persecution." Their ears caught the macedonian cry from lands afar, and in 1810 they organized the American Board of Commissioners for Foreign Missions, the first organization of the kind in the new world and mother of an illustrious progeny in all the churches. In 1846 the American Missionary Association was organized. Five other Societies followed these in rapid succession but we shall dwell mainly on the work of the American Missionary Association because of its relation to the Negro. For quite three quarters of a century this organization has stood in the very van of the agencies that have been at work for the uplift and enlargement of the Negro in America and in Africa.

It was at Hampton, shortly after Gen Butler had declared the Negroes within the federal lines "contraband of war," that the work of education began. That beginning has through the passing years culminated in the organization of more than 250 Negro churches and in the establishing of half dozen colleges and universities such as Fisk, Atlanta Talladega, Tougaloo besides more than fifty primary and Secondary schools in strategic centers extending from Virginia to Texas.

These schools have administered to the threefold need of the Negro in his struggle for a place in the ranks of the nineteenth and twentieth century progress. First of all was seen the need of educated trained leadership. No race can advance to its promised land without its Moses and Aaron and Joshua and Samson, and Samuel and the rest.

The dawn of freedom discovered the Negro leaderless, save for a group of Negro preachers whom nature in a mysterious way, had provided. They did their best under the handicap of illiteracy and the unwrought traditions of two hundred and fifty years of servitude. In many, if not in most instances this leadership was in blind obedience to the instinct of worship and reverence, and on the other hand reverence and obedience to priestly and prophetic authority. It was a concrete case of the "blind leading the blind."

And yet in this very thing was contained the seed of promise and of hope. The soul of the race was crying aloud for light and for enlightenment and through the A.M.A the Congregational Church answered that cry by founding and sustaining the schools and churches already mentioned. Thousands of graduates and undergraduates have gone out to service from these schools. There is now in attendance eight or ten thousand Negro youths in these schools. Here, leaders have been trained for the task of guiding the race along the safe and sure way of racial respectability and racial eminence and freedom. For the past half century yeoman service has been done in church and school and community. Remarkable wisdom, and tact and patience have revealed themselves in the delicate task of raising a backward people up to the standards and ideals of a progressive people among and with whom they lived and by whom they were measured. Honesty, efficiency thrift, industry and Christian good will have been the burthen of their teaching. This has added tremendously to the economic progress of the entire South and has kept down clashes of a racial nature.

The leadership of the Negro is still in the hands of the minister, and it is here that emphasis has been stressed. Intellectual and industrial leaders have not been undervalued But the descendants of the Pilgrims are true to their traditions and are still insisting on the supreme place of the spiritual The educated minister has always been put to the front At Talladega College, alone the venerable and beloved Dr G W Andrews has taught and sent out more than two hundred Negro preachers to the various branches of the Negro church The Baptists and the various branches of the Methodist Churches with rare exceptions, gladly acknowledge their debt to congregationalism for some of their foremost leaders

The Congregational Churches among Negroes serve mainly as models and stimulants to the other churches They are not a separate body from the general Congregational brotherhood Just as there are Italian groups Slav groups and other racial groups, so is there this Negro group having the fullest fellowship and amplest privilege in all the general affairs of the great Congregational Church For the past several years Negroes have held the office of vice-president of the National Council of Congregational Churches and have presided with dignity and acceptably over that august body There are five Negro Superintendents of church work now in the field, there are a number of Negroes on various boards of trustees of our Colleges and numbers of Negro deans, professors and teachers laboring side by side in utmost harmony with the white co-laborers in the work of church and school All the benevolences go through the common channel of our national administrative boards

Our churches are necessarily small for they came South late due to their attitude toward slavery They have a definite purpose and a definite mission that is, to train the abundant emotionalism of the race into submission to reason and restraint and to present to the great church catholic an element of worship that must greatly enrich and enhance the religion of Jesus Christ of Nazareth Thus, shall Ethiopia stretch forth her hands unto God offering her princely gift to bless all mankind

L E SCOTT,
Montgomery Ala

July 3 1919

NATIONAL WOMAN'S CHRISTIAN TEMPERANCE UNION WORK AMONG COLORED PEOPLE

National Superintendent, Mrs Eliza E Peterson Texarkana Texas

Associates Mrs J W Sexton, Mobile, Ala , Mrs Phoebe Allen Cincinnati, Ohio

Advisory Committee on College Work President Miss Mary A Lynch Livingston College, Salisbury N C Secretary Mrs Elizabeth Ross Haynes, Fisk University Nashville Tenn

Work among colored people became a separate Department in 1881, with Mrs Jane M Kenney of Michigan, as Superintendent Mrs Frances E Harper of Pennsylvania, became superintendent in 1883 and continued to fill the position until 1890 In 1891, Mrs J E Ray, of North Carolina was a committee on "Home and Foreign Missionary Work for Colored People In 1895 Mrs Lucy Thurman, of Michigan, became superintendent of the colored work She continued in this position until 1908 when she was succeeded by the present superintendent Mrs Eliza E Peterson

The W C T U work among colored people is carried on in Alabama Arkansas, California, Colorado Delaware, District of Columbia Georgia, Illinois Indiana Iowa New York Kansas Kentucky Louisiana Maryland Michigan Minnesota Mississippi, New Jersey, North Carolina, Ohio, Pennsylvania, South Carolina, Tennessee Texas and West Virginia The colored women are organized into local unions and in the District of Columbia Louisiana, North Carolina South Carolina Tennessee, Texas and West Virginia they have separate State organizations with their own State officers Many colored women belong to mixed unions Altogether the colored membership in the W C T U is about 6 000

Texas has the largest paid W C T U membership among colored women of the United States The city with the largest paid membership is Nashville Tenn Prairie View State Normal and Industrial College, Prairie View Texas has the largest young people's branch among colored women in the United States The branch has 150 young women who are paid-up members

WORK OF THE AMERICAN BAPTIST PUBLICATION SOCIETY AMONG NEGROES

This society has carried on such work since emancipation

During the past year the Society maintained six Sunday School workers among colored people in Alabama, North Carolina, South Carolina, Texas and Virginia These workers held Sunday School Conventions Bible Institutes and delivered addresses to Sunday Schools and Churches They visited the past year over 800 Sunday Schools and Churches The names of these workers and their fields are as follows

S N Vass D D , Box 430, Raleigh N C General Superintendent of Negro Work of the Society throughout the United States

D A Scott, D D Austin, Texas State Sunday School Missionary for Texas

L W Calloway D D Selma, Ala State Sunday School Missionary for Alabama

E R Roberts, D D , Florence, S C State Sunday School Missionary for South Carolina

Rev. T. C. Walker, Gloucester, Va., State Sunday School Missionary for Virginia.

Rev. M. A. Talley, Raleigh, N. C., State Sunday School Missionary for North Carolina.

THE SALVATION ARMY AND THE NEGRO

The Salvation Army is making an attempt to reach the Negro mainly through Negroes who are being trained in the Salvation Army Workers' School, in New York City. Only a few Negroes thus far have gone through this school. As they finish, they are sent in to the South. At present work is being conducted exclusively among Negroes in Washington, D. C., Richmond, Va., and Charleston, S. C.

WORK AMONG NEGROES BY THE INTERNATIONAL SUNDAY SCHOOL ASSOCIATION

Believing that the colleges and the normal schools should be the source of supply for efficient Sunday School teachers in the local churches, the committee on Work Among Negroes of the International Sunday School Association, appointed by Dr. H. C. Lyman, 78 East Mitchell Street, Atlanta, Georgia, to introduce in these schools a special course for the training of Sunday School teachers. "Beginning in 1911 with the five colleges in Atlanta the interest has gradually grown until Sunday School teacher training has been presented in practically all of the 263 Boarding Schools that carry six or more teachers. Recognition of the need for better teachers in the local Sunday Schools was instant. The fine body of students in the colleges is the logical source of supply. They are the natural leaders. Enlistment in a specific work for the practical betterment of the home church appeals to them. Community betterment may be realized by working for the younger generation through the Sunday School. There is no better guarantee that these college students will become permanent factors in the local churches. The results have more

than justified the efforts. Two hundred teachers training classes have been organized. The enrollment in these classes for 1915-1916 was 3060. In forty-seven schools this work is required and regular credit given for it.

In addition to the work done in the colleges a Training School for the leaders of these teacher training classes was held at Knoxville, Tennessee, with an enrollment of forty-seven, representing nineteen institutions. Co-operation between the white Sunday School workers and the colored has been established at Birmingham, Ala., Louisville, Ky., Atlanta, Ga., and Greensboro, N. C. Six other cities have given encouragement that it will be done. Whenever the white people have a special School of Methods they give the same work by the same speakers to the colored Sunday School workers of the community. Rev. R. A. Scott, Rev. E. C. Page, and Prof. K. D. Reddick, have been appointed Associate State Secretaries in Mississippi, West Virginia and Georgia respectively. These are efficient and trained men. Their work is closely supervised by the General Secretaries of the State Sunday School Associations and their reports are passed upon by the State executive committees. Their salaries are largely paid by the white state associations. Kentucky, North Carolina and Virginia State associations have signified a purpose to inaugurate a similar cooperative work as soon as efficient men are found for the positions. Summer schools at State institutions have been visited in North Carolina, Virginia and West Virginia. In this way about four hundred rural school teachers have been reached each year and enlisted in more aggressive and efficient Sunday School methods. Because of the work done in the colleges four of the denominations have stressed the Sunday School teacher training work. The Baptists, the African Methodists and the African Methodist Zions have regularly appointed Superintendents for this work. The Colored Methodists and the African Methodist

VIEW OF CAMPUS, KNOXVILLE COLLEGE, KNOXVILLE, TENN.

Zions have formally approved of the teacher training as a regular part of their Sunday School program

THE WORK OF THE AMERICAN SUNDAY SCHOOL UNION AMONG NEGROES

This society has had some general work among the Negroes of Virginia for several years Recently it inaugurated the policy of placing a missionary in connection with an industrial school in which he teaches the Bible and Sunday School normal class work on two days of each week and spends the remaining part of the week in pastoral visitation and in organizing the work in the adjacent territory

These new schools organized by the missionary are placed under the care of officers and teachers for the most part taken from the ranks of the student body who have been under his instruction Work of this kind is carried on at Fort Valley High and Industrial School Fort Valley, Georgia Prentiss Normal and Industrial Institute at Prentiss, Mississippi, Bettis Academy Trenton, S C , Voorhees Industrial School, Denmark, S C , and Utica Normal and Industrial Institute, Utica Mississippi The American Sunday School Union is deeply interested in the religious welfare of the Negroes of the South and is seeking to cooperate with every agency looking toward their moral and religious betterment The headquarters of the American Sunday School Union are 1816 Chestnut Street, Philadelphia, Pennsylvania The officers are Martin L Finckel President, William H Hirst, Recording Secretary, John F Stevenson Treasurer, George P Williams D D Secretary of Missions and in charge of the work among Negroes, Edwin W Rice D D , Editor of Publications, James McConaughty, Managing Editor

THE CATHOLIC CHURCH AND COLORED WORK

By Rev J D Bustin, Asst Director General and Field Secretary of The Catholic Board for Mission Work Among the Colored People

The Catholic Church has been interested in Christianizing and educating the colored people from the earliest days of their appearance in this country Her sphere of influence has been until recent years, confined to those territories where the population was largely Catholic, the Western shore of the Chesapeake bay in Maryland and that strip, fifty miles in width lying along the Gulf of Mexico, from Pensacola, Florida to Corpus Christi, Texas, including also most of State of Louisiana In these territories the Church dealt with the Negro as with any other unit of the population through the Parish system The Church did not nor does not look upon the Negro as a distinct race to be segregated but rather a part of the whole population and as such, to be handled by the group leader the Parish Priest, in the system devised for all the people living in the fixed territory lying within easy reach of the Parish Church and school This system of necessity varied greatly In the large and wealthy centres the churches were equipped with a large number of priests and teachers, schools of importance, hospitals and all those influences that make for the betterment of old and young, in new and sparsely settled districts however the parish working machinery often consisted of a log church, a single priest, and a pair of saddle bags The results of the system differed as widely as the equipment Some places education flourished in others illiteracy, one priest, with instincts of a great leader fired his parish with ambition and religion of lofty type, another let them drift along at any gait

Under this varied influence was the Negro as a part of the parish, the weakest part also,—the slave for the most part Although there was a considerable number of free Negroes in the Gulf district, some of whom possessed wealth and education These like the rest of the population shared in the parish life

When anti-slavery agitation came under the leadership of William Lloyd Garrison about 1824 a new phase of the agitated question began to show Heretofore there had been, as inherent to slavery injustice, brutal treatment and exploitation but no general race antipathy showed itself against the Negro as such Now the color and African origin began to be the test and sufficient reason for love or hate, for reward of punishment Unjust as this may be it has continued to be the underlying principle of law and literature from Garrison's day to ours

It was to overcome this new difficulty to Negro education and betterment that the Oblates of Providence were founded in 1829 at Baltimore Four young colored women Elizabeth Lange Rosa Boegis, Magdalen Balas and Teresa Duchemin under the guidance of Father Joubert, organized this society to conduct schools for colored girls to provide for orphans and to seek the erring The Oblates have been pursuing their lofty purpose for nearly a century and today have about 200 women in the society and are conducting houses of study in Baltimore, Washington, St Louis Leavenworth, Charleston Havanna and other places on the West India Islands

The Congregation of the Sisters of the Holy Family was founded at New Orleans in 1842 by Harriet Delisle Juliette Gaudin, Josephine Charles and Miss Alcot "free women of color" who devoted their wealth and lives to instruct and care for those of the colored people whom they could reach These Sisters now conduct Houses for aged Colored men and women The community now numbers nearly 200 women

After the Emancipation when race prejudice first showed itself in absolute segregation of the colored people, the Catholic Church was forced against her will to take up with the new system Many foreigners were coming into the country in the seventies and eighties of the last century who demanded churches and schools of their own language respectively Slowly the authorities yielded to the demand and from that date began to be seen German Churches, Polish Churches French Churches and Italian Churches and so on

When it became evident that this insane race prejudice was here to last for many years the Catholic authorities had to modify the parish system or lose their influence on both races

So when Monsignor Bourne afterward Cardinal Bourne the founder of the Missionary Society whose members are commonly known as Josephites visited this country in 1871 and was afterwards allowed to send four priests of his community to devote their entire attention to Negro religious work, the interest of the Catholics began to be directed to the work as never before

At the council of Baltimore in 1884 the prelates in attendance took especial care to awaken enthusiasm by decreeing that a regular collection should be taken up in all the Catholic Churches of the United States on the first Sunday of Lent, part of which should be devoted to Negro Missionary work

In 1907 a Board was established to which were appointed seven Arch-bishops and Bishops who should have general charge of this branch of Catholic Missionary activity Incorporated under the laws of Tennessee it is known as "The Catholic Board of Mission Work among the Colored People" The Arch-bishops selected as their personal representative Rev John E Burke, who for twenty-four years had been pastor of the Colored Church of St Benedict the Moor, in New York City, and since then this clergyman has been Director-General of the Board Beyond the supervision of Missions in the South the Director-General solicits funds in Northern churches in which labor he is assisted by other priests assigned to the work At the present time Rev D J Bustin, Rev Jas J Mulholland, both of Scranton, and Rev Chas A Edwards of Providence Rhode Island, are the colleagues of Father Burke In recognition of his zeal in this field Father Burke was elevated to prelatial dignity by the Pope and as a member of the Papal household he has the title of Monsignor

Since the establishment of this Board sixty new mission centers have been started Over 10,000 new pupils have been added to the list of children

who attend parochial schools, making the entire enrollment over 20,000 children The Board pays the salary of 140 teachers, besides paying the whole, or greater part of the salary of 21 priests engaged exclusivevly in the Colored Missionary Work

Priests having charge of Missions for Colored People—Josephites Fathers, 71, Diocesan 33 Fathers of the Divine Word, 10, Lyons Mission Fathers, 10, Holy Ghost Fathers, 24, Congregation of the Missions. 5, Jesuit Fathers 4 Franciscans, 1

There are 554 teachers in Catholic Schools to Colored Children, mostly Sisters and there are 15 Brothers in Industrial School Work

The Catholic Mission Work among the Colored People during 1918 cost approximately $350,000

PRESBYTERIAN WORK AMONG THE NEGROES

There are seven different branches of the Presbyterian denomination in the United States, viz The Presbyterian Church in the United States of America, The Presbyterian Church in the United States, The United Presbyterian Church, The Reform Presbyterian Church of the United States The Reform Pisebyterian Church of America The Associate Presbyterian Church, and The Cumberland Presbyterian Church The two first named are more commonly known as the Northern Presbyterian and Southern Presbyterian respectively All of these branches maintain organizations for mission and school work among the Negroes A good illustration of the type of schools being operated by the Presbyterian Boards, is Biddle University found elsewhere in this volume Scotia Seminary at Concord, N C is one of the leading female colleges of the Presbyterians

The Presbyterian Church in the United States the chief work of this church for colored people is embraced in the Snedecor Memorial Synod, consisting of 4 Presbyteries with 35 ministers, serving 62 churches and missions and 2700 communicants, with mission schools at Louisville Ky, Atlanta Ga, Richmond Va Abbeville, S C, and other places There were added to our colored churches last year 155 persons upon profession of faith Stillman Institute with three white teachers is maintained for the education of the colored ministry The annual meeting of the Colored Synod is held at Tuscaloosa in May, in connection with the commencement at Stillman Institute The Executive Committee conducts a helpful Institute and Bible Conference for the colored ministers in connection with the Synod and also aids the commissioners in the matter of expenses Our colored churches are greatly encouraged in their work by this Conference, and are being stimulated to self help in having their own organization Rev W A Young, our colored evangelist, is doing a splendid work among the churches of the Synod

WORK AMONG NEGROES OF THE PRESBYTERIAN BOARD OF PUBLICATION AND SABBATH SCHOOL WORK

The Presbyterian Church in the United States of America began its mission Sunday School work among Negroes in the South in 1890 Since that time more than 3000 schools have been organized Out of them several hundred churches have grown

The aim is two-fold Missionary and Educational It is the duty of the missionary to visit the homes in which the children are not attending church or Sunday School and distribute religious literature while at the same time he ministers to the religious life of that home If it is possible, he organizes a Sunday School provides it with necessary literature, and subsequently fosters the growth and development of this school

At the same time, this missionary is ministering to the educational life and development not only of the mission Sabbath School under his care, but of all the Negro Presbyterian Sabbath Schools within the territory assigned to him

DISCIPLES OF CHRIST

By J B Lehman, Supt Educational and Evangelistic Work for Negroes under the Christian Woman's Board of Missions

The Disciples of Christ expended last year $90000 00 for the work among the Negroes The money was expended for Educational Institutions, organizing in the Sunday Schools and Missionary Societies, Evangelistic and Church help at strategic points and General Supervision

It will perhaps be necessary to give a few words on the origin of the Disciples of Christ in order to be able to make clear the nature of the work In 1809 Thomas Campbell, a Seceder Presbyterian Minister recently come from Scotland protested against sectarian divisions in the church This protest drew upon him much antagonism which resulted in forcing him and his followers into a separate people which now numbers over one and a quarter million communicants, with about six hundred churches among the Negroes This people was not a great missionary people from the beginning because taking upon themselves the task of righting a serious defect in the church life itself they were naturally a little slow in finding the Missionary task Their membership was nearly as strong in the South as in the North and there was never any organic division between Negro and White Churches Consequently, when they undertook to do missionary work among the Negroes they could move no faster than they could carry

with them the three somewhat discordant elements But while this way was slow in the beginning it was building on a sure basis, and the delay is amply compensated for in the results Now our Southern and Northern and Negro Churches are cooperating in perfect harmony and the enthusiasm for the work in the Southern Churches is not one whit behind that in the Northern Churches

The schools consist of the following

1 The Southern Christian Institute at Edwards Mississippi, with 1265 acres of land and a plant worth $175,000 00 Its President is J B Lehman and the entire faculty is white The average attendance is about 225 During the last few years students matriculated from every Southern State, from the West Indies and from Africa A faculty of twenty-four teachers and workers is maintained The courses of instruction consist of College, Academic Ministerial and the Primary and Preparatory Grades The Industrial work consists in large part in building up and maintaining the school

2 Jarvis Christian Institute Hawkins, Texas, with 800 acres and a plant worth about $50,000 The average attendance has been about 100 It is a new plant which was started in 1912 and has had a remarkable growth in this time It draws its students largely from Texas Oklahoma, and Arkansas Its President is J N Ervin and its faculty numbering about eighteen is colored The same courses of instruction are maintained as described above

3 Piedmont Christian Institute, Martinsville, Virginia This school, up to the present has been a town high school since Martinsville maintained no high school for the colored people But we have now purchased a tract of land and very soon buildings will be erected and the school will take its place as an academy or college This school is presided over by James H Thomas, and has a faculty of seven members

4 The Alabama Christian Institute, Lum, Alabama This school has sixty acres and is attempting to do a rural work in a plantation section where conditions are very primitive The work is presided over by I C Franklin and has a force of seven workers

5 Plans are now on foot to build a new school of college grade to be known as Central Christian Institute and to be located somewhere in Kentucky or Tennessee In a very short time the location and plans will be determined upon

The Sunday school work is under the direction of P H Moss who has made himself an expert of note Since 1916 he has been at work to bring out the efficiency of the Sunday schools of our six-hundred churches and the work has developed to the extent that plans are now on foot to divide it into districts and send some four others into the field to help in it

Miss Rosa V Brown is in charge of the work of organizing the women into Missionary Societies About one-hundred and twenty-five societies have been organized and are in a very fair working order

State Evangelists are maintained in Texas Oklahoma, Missouri, Arkansas, Tennessee, Mississippi Louisiana, Georgia, Florida and South Carolina Churches are aided in Oklahoma, Texas Ohio, Tennessee, Kentucky and Virginia

Plans are now under way for greatly enlarged enterprises along all lines The Negroes themselves raised a Jubilee Fund of $20,000, to commemorate the fiftieth anniversary of freedom and will now take their full and equitable share of all the new work

SOCIETY OF FRIENDS

The object of this article is not to go into the history of the Society of Friends nor to exploit their faith, but merely draw attention to some of the schools established by them for the education of the Negro race The Friends have been consistent in their opposition to slavery and have shown great sympathy and made every effort to free the Negroes, and now that they are free they are doing their part to free them of the shackels of ignorance They have established a number of schools for Negroes but space allotted to this article will not permit the mentioning of more than a few

The High Point Normal and Industrial School is located at High Point, North Carolina

It was founded in 1893 by the annual yearly meeting of the Society of Friends

The institution is equipped with model buildings and grounds It has one of the largest school libraries in North Carolina

In addition to the usual courses, it offers several industrial courses without extra charge Its effort is to give superior instruction in all courses It is the purpose of the institution to give young men and women a practical academic education, a thorough industrial training and to prepare teachers for the public schools

The school is thoroughly Christian and every religious influence is thrown around the students

The value of the property is $40 000 and its annual expense is $8,500

Southland College and Normal Institute, Southland, Arkansas, was founded in 1864 by the Indiana Society of Friends

The college is located on a farm of over 300 acres, which lies to the northwest of Helena about nine miles Besides four large buildings, there is, on the campus a dwelling for laborers a large laundry, kitchen commissary store power house and necessary out houses

It has a fine library with valuable works of antiquity, ancient and modern history biography science and general literature, to which the students have access This institution, too, is surrounded with a religious atmosphere, and the students are encouraged to live the higher life

The property is valued at $50 000 and the annual expense is $10 000

The aim of the work done is to make the students useful and law-abiding citizens of the commonwealth a blessing to their race and a benefit to the state

Institute for Colored Youth, located at Cheney Pennsylvania This school was founded by the Friends in 1837 It gives a course of instruction both academic and industrial, and prepares its students to go forth as agents to uplift the colored race and to live useful and upright lives It is well serving the race in the accomplishment of these ends There is a complete description of Schofield Normal and Industrial Institute elsewhere in this volume

Many of the schools mentioned in the educational section are fully described elsewhere in this work

NEW ASSOCIATIONS

The most recently organized associations that are taking up work in connection with the Negro are Inter-Racial Co-operation Commission of the South, composed of representative white men from each of the Southern States The organization was formed in May 1919, at Atlanta, Ga

Mr J J Eagan a noted capitalist of Atlanta, was elected first president and R H King of Atlanta, secretary The object of the commission is to study ways and means of bringing about a better understanding and a closer co-operation among the white and colored people of the South

The Federal Council of the Churches of Christ in America Dr George S McFarland of Philadelphia, secretary The council is composed of all churches in the United States and its object is the study of all religions There is a special department for the study of colored religions

Co-Operative School Building

BY CLINTON J. CALLOWAY
Director of the Extension Department of Tuskegee
Institute.

AGENTS ROSENWALD RURAL SCHOOLS.

 N June, 1914, Mr. Julius Rosenwald of Chicago, authorized Tuskegee Institute, of which he is a trustee, to launch a campaign in the South for better rural schoolhouses for colored people. Eight months previous to this time, Mr. Rosenwald had permitted the Extension Department of Tuskegee Institute to try out six near-by communities in Alabama, to see if they would give a worth-while response. Two communities in Macon County, one in Lee County, and three in Montgomery County were selected. Plans for a one-teacher schoolhouse, to cost about $600, were drawn in the Architectural Division of Tuskegee Institute. When these were presented to the communities they were readily accepted. Mr. Rosenwald offered one dollar for every dollar furnished by each of the communities, up to the amount of $300.

The county superintendent of education of each of the counties, the Jeanes Fund supervisors, pastors of churches located in the communities and the county agricultural agents were asked to give their co-operation in helping to rally the people to raise their share of the funds necessary to com-

plete the buildings. After many visits by representatives of Tuskegee's Extension Department, the six schools were finished at a cost of about $700 each. They were furnished with home-made desks and the necessary chairs and tables. The people were so happy and grateful that they wrote many letters to their good friend, Mr. Rosenwald, about their beautiful buildings.

The coming of the Rosenwald schools marked the period of educational awakening; the time when the people ceased to think of the city as the only place for decent schoolhouses; the time when patrons began to realize the possibility of organized effort. There were other evidences of community improvement. The white people seemed to recognize the aspirations of their Negro neighbors to higher and better things and contributed towards the new schoolhouses. The school terms were lengthened from four to seven months. The attendance of the children improved. The teachers were able to do better work by reason of the conveniences in the classrooms, the increased comfort of the buildings, and the general awakening in the community.

Mr. Rosenwald continued to encourage commu-

TEACHERS ROSENWALD RURAL SCHOOLS

nities by offering his aid in blocks of 100 schools at a time until the number reached 300 in November, 1917, at which time he offered to aid in the building of 300 more schoolhouses; and on account of the increased cost of building material, he raised, in 1918, the maximum amount of each schoolhouse to $400 for a one-teacher school and $500 for a school built for two or more teachers.

Possibly the most interesting part of the campaign work is the manner in which the Negro responds to the call to raise money in his little community, composed of twenty-five or thirty families, to meet the conditions of Mr. Rosenwald's offer. This is usually made in a meeting where nearly every family is present. Pledges are made in cash, labor, or material. In many cases farmers can do hauling. In some instances the material is donated by the patron from saw-milling timber on his land. In such cases the patrons meet in the woods, cut the saw stock, carry it to the mill, and have the lumber sawed on shares.

In one of these meetings where pledges were made, a widow of ninety years subscribed one dollar toward the building. The next day she was seen about the community selling ginger cakes which she had baked. In this way she succeeded in raising the amount of her pledge. In many communities the children are organized into little clubs

STATES	No. of School Houses Projected	AMOUNTS CONTRIBUTED BY				
		STATES	White People	People Colored	Mr. Rosenwald	TOTAL
Alabama	184	$ 45,576.00	$ 8,465.00	$ 93,514.93	$ 57,350.00	$204,905.93
Arkansas	31	15,839.00	1,735.00	18,034.00	13,800.00	49,408.00
Georgia	31	5,625.00	10,552.00	26,507.77	11,300.00	53,984.77
Kentucky	20	17,895.00	2,500.00	7,741.50	7,700.00	35,836.50
Louisiana	61	14,600.00	3,750.00	41,410.57	13,000.00	72,760.50
Maryland	6	7,700.00	600.00	2,575.00	2,250.00	12,125.00
Mississippi	33	3,613.50	14,249.95	21,623.27	14,275.00	55,761.72
North Carolina	111	44,706.00	4,129.25	50,633.75	35,565.00	135,034.00
South Carolina	10	3,900.00	8,428.00	6,644.00	4,400.00	23,372.00
Tennessee	76	80,755.00	4,275.00	48,796.00	46,775.00	180,601.00
Virginia	46	32,405.00	750.00	25,444.80	22,000.00	80,599.80
	649	$272,614.50	$59,434.20	$342,925.59	$228,415.00	$904,389.22

PUPILS AND PATRONS OF A ROSENWALD SCHOOL

other agencies are actively at work trying to get communities to qualify for his help.

The writer, in company with Mr. George D. Godard, state agent for rural schools in Georgia, visited a school community in that state and on the day of the visit found the county superintendent of education leading a volunteer group of colored farmers in the construction of the new schoolhouse. The superintendent was enthusiastic over the work. He was not a carpenter, but, with his bruised and bleeding hands, he was a real inspiration to the others at work.

The significance of this work in co-operative school building is shown in the table on the previous page, which covers the "Rosenwald School Improvement Campaign" up to March 1, 1919.

for the purpose of raising money to meet Mr. Rosenwald's offer.

Many communities must get rid of petty prejudices and old ideals if they are to succeed in obtaining a modern schoolhouse. Now and then friendly progressive leaders must wait until some old influential opposer dies and is respectfully put out of the way. A common viewpoint for Baptist and Methodist must be found. It sometimes becomes necessary to convince the white landowner that no harm, but rather substantial returns, will come by encouraging the building of a comfortable Negro schoolhouse near his land. Perhaps the greatest difficulty is the absence of strong community leadership.

It is Mr. Rosenwald's desire to help only in those states where state officers of public school funds, and others who, in any way, control the public schools, wish this help. No community will be granted aid by Mr. Rosenwald toward the erection of schoolhouses whose school term does not run at least five months. Neither will Mr. Rosenwald aid in the building of schoolhouses unless the money raised by the community, county, and state, added to what he gives, is sufficient to complete and furnish the schoolhouse. In the eleven states where Mr. Rosenwald is extending his aid, state officers and

It was found at the very beginning that school patrons, as well as others, need information first hand from agents who might attend the meetings to explain the necessity of better school buildings and the importance of sticking to certain modern lines of procedure in the erection. For the purpose of helping in this way Mr. Rosenwald has contributed each year additional funds to pay one-half the salary and traveling expenses of agents to assist the state agents for rural schools. In North Carolina, Arkansas, Kentucky, Mississippi,

A HOME MAKERS' CLUB.

Louisiana, and Alabama, agents have been employed by the state especially to look after this kind of work. In all these states except one, one-half the expenses of agents' assistants have been paid by local funds. Some of these assistants have raised as much as $5000 in one month toward the erection of schoolhouses. The General Education Board and the Jeanes Fund have heartily co-operated in the work.

Although much better teaching is being done in these new buildings, though the terms have been lengthened, and the attendance has been much better, there is still room for improvement in

ROSENWALD SCHOOL REPLACING THE OLD ONE BESIDE IT

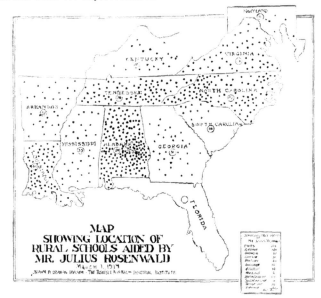

MAP
SHOWING LOCATION OF
RURAL SCHOOLS AIDED BY
MR. JULIUS ROSENWALD

many cases. To encourage the movement and make these schools meet the needs of the community Mr. Rosenwald has recently offered to help in extending school terms where the community, county, and state are willing to furnish a like amount. The hope is that all who can possibly do so will join the forces already at work and improve the chances for country boys and girls by helping to place one of these modern schoolhouses in needy communities.

The Church Among Negroes

THE following information is published through the courtesy of the Negro Year Book, edition 1916-17, published annually at Tuskegee Institute, and edited by Monroe N. Work in charge of Division of Records and Research.

DATE OF THE ORGANIZATION OF THE COLORED DENOMINATIONS

1865. Colored Asbury Methodist Episcopal Church.
1813. Union Church of Africans.
1816. African Methodist Episcopal Church.
1821. African Methodist Episcopal Zion Church.
1836. Providence Baptist Association of Ohio.
1838. Wood River Baptist Association of Illinois.
1853. Western Colored Baptist Convention.
1864. Northwestern and Southern Baptist Convention.
1867. Consolidated American Baptist Convention.
1850. African Union Church.
1850. Union American Methodist Episcopal Church.
1860. First Colored Methodist Protestant Church.
1865. Colored Primitive Baptist Church.
1866. African Union First Colored Methodist Protestant Church.
1869. Colored Cumberland Presbyterian Church.
1870. Colored Methodist Episcopal Church.
1880. National Baptist Convention.
1882. Reformed Zion Apostolic Church.
1896. Reformed Methodist Union Episcopal Church.
1896. Church of God and Saints of Christ.
1899. Church of the Living God (Christian workers for friendship.)
1899. Church of the Living God (Apostolic.)
1899. Church of Christ in God.
1900. Voluntary Missionary Society in America (Colored.)
1901. United American Free-Will Baptist.
1905. Free Christian Zion Church in Christ.

Note: There are approximately five hundred thousand Negroes in the United States who are members of white churches.

DATE OF THE ORGANIZATION OF THE COLORED CHURCHES

1785. Colored Baptist Church, Williamsburg, Va.
1787. Independent Methodist Church, Philadelphia, Pa.
1788. First African Baptist Church, of Savannah.
1790. African Baptist Church, Lexington, Ky.
1791. St. Thomas Episcopal Church, Philadelphia.
1793. Springfield Baptist Church, Augusta, Ga.
1796. African Methodist Episcopal Zion Church, New York City.
1800. Abyssinia Baptist Church, New York City.
1802. Second Baptist Church, Savannah, Ga.
1805. African Meeting House, Boston, Mass.
1809. First African Church, Philadelphia, Pa.
1807. First African Presbyterian Church, Philadelphia, Pa.

1812. Colored Peoples Church, Clinton, N. J.
1805. Asbury Methodist Episcopal Church, Wilmington, Del.
1818. St. Phillips Protestant Episcopal Church, New York City.
1824. St. James First African Church, Baltimore.
1838. First Bethel Baptist Church, Jacksonville.
1867. Plymouth Congregational Church, Charleston, S. C.
1878. First Lutheran Colored Church, Little Rock.

NOTED NEGRO PREACHERS.

George Leile, born 1750. Freed by master and became famous preaching to the slaves of Savannah, Ga., during Revolutionary War.

Andrew Bryan, born 1788. Founded the first African Baptist Church of Savannah, Ga.

Lemuel Haynes, born 1753, at West Hartford, Conn. Revolutionary Soldier and first Congregational Minister.

Richard Allen, born at Philadelphia, in 1760. Was first A. M. E. Bishop.

Joseph Willis, born in 1762, organized the first Baptist Church west of the Mississippi.

Daniel A. Payne, born 1811. Bishop A. M. E. Church, and one of the founders of Wilberforce University.

John Jasper, born in 1812. Famous Richmond, Va., preacher. He became a national character by trying to prove by the Bible that "The Sun Do Move."

Alexander Crummell, eminent Episcopal minister, born at New York City in 1818. Died 1898.

Caeser Blackwell, born in Lowndes County, Ala., in 1828. Bought by the Baptist Association of that state and set free to preach to slaves.

Dock Phillips, born at Cotton Valley, Macon County, Ala., in 1828. The Alabama Baptist Association tried to buy him of his master? John Phillips, but he refused to be sold. Was universally respected by whites and blacks.

Harry Hosier, born in 1810. First American Negro preacher in the Methodist Church.

John Chavis commissioned by the Presbyterian General Assembly as a missionary to the Negroes. He was the first Negro in the Presbyterian Church to be prepared for Christian leadership. Chavis is said to have been born in Granville County, North Carolina in 1801.

It was not as a preacher, but as a teacher of white boys and apparently white girls also, that Chavis is best remembered in North Carolina. The greater part of the time after he was silenced as a preacher and probably for a large part of the time from his return to North Carolina until his death in 1838, he conducted a private school in Wake County, and also probably in Chatham, Orange and Granville counties. Some of his pupils later became distinguished. Among these were Charles Manly, Governor of North Carolina and Priestly H. Mangum, brother of Senator Mangum and himself a lawyer of distinction.

BETHEL BAPTIST
INSTITUTIONAL CHURCH.

MT. ZION A.M.E. CHURCH AND PARSONAGE, JACKSONVILLE, FLA.

SIXTH AVE BAPTIST
CHURCH

SIXTH AVE. BAPTIST CHURCH,
BIRMINGHAM, ALA.

EBENEZER METHODIST
EPISCOPAL CHURCH,
JACKSONVILLE, FLA.

FIRST CONGREGATIONAL
CHURCH,
ATLANTA,
GA.

BROADWAY TEMPLE A.M.E. ZION CHURCH,
LOUISVILLE, KY.

SIXTEENTH STREET BAPTIST CHURCH,
BIRMINGHAM, ALA.

A GROUP OF REPRESENTATIVE NEGRO CHURCHES.

THE NATIONAL BAPTIST CONVENTION
By E C Morris, D D

The National Baptist Convention the largest organization among Negro Christians in the world now has a membership of 3,018 341 according to the latest religious census

The first National Organization among Negro Baptist was the Foreign Mission Convention of the United States, which organization was effected at Montgomery Ala , in 1880 The first president of the Convention was the Rev W H McAlpine, of Alabama

The preliminary work of getting the Baptists together was done by the Rev W W Colley of Richmond Va who had spent three years in Africa as a Missionary under appointment from the Foreign Mission Board of the Southern Baptist Convention

Nothing was done the first three years of the organization, except to gather means and arouse an interest in the denomination for the establishment of a Mission station on the West Coast of Africa The first Missionaries were sent out to Africa in 1883

Up to 1883 there had not been a religious census taken of the Negro organizations, and but little was known of their numerical strength hence in 1886 the Rev Wm J Simmons, D D of Louisville Ky organized at St Louis, Mo The American National Baptist Convention and was elected its first president The object given was, "To gather statistics, and study the moral conditions of the race"

In 1893, the Negro Baptists organized the National Educational Convention, the object being to study and promote the educational interests of the denomination The Rev W Bishop Johnson, of Washington, D C , was the founder, and Rev M Vann, of Tennessee was the first president The Convention began at once the publication of the National Baptist Magazine, which was suspended in 1895

The three above named organizations met annually in the same city each occupying two days, but under different management until 1895 When the three were merged into, one, under the name "The National Baptist Convention," the consolidating of the three Conventions took place at Atlanta Georgia, in 1895 and Rev E C Morris, was elected President, which position he has held continuously for twenty-three years

Immediately upon the consolidation of the three conventions three Boards were chosen by the Convention to represent the interest of the three former Conventions, and the work has been prosecuted by these Boards under the direction of the Convention since that time In 1896 a Home Mission

Board was created by the Convention, and was charged with the duty of publishing Sunday School literature for the denomination, and conducting the mission work on the Home field In 1888 the Home Mission Board by authority of the National Baptist Convention, organized the National Baptist Publishing Board, and the work of Home Missions and publications were practically under the same management until 1914, though an order had been given as far back as 1904 for the separation of the Home Mission and Publishing Boards

In 1899 the National B Y P U Board was organized at Nashville, Tennessee, and its headquarters located at that place Rev E W D Isaac, D D , was chosen as Corresponding Secretary of the Board This Board has organized hundreds of thousands of Baptist Young People into local Societies, for training in religious work

In 1900 the Woman's Auxiliary Convention was organized at Richmond Va and Mrs S W Layton was chosen President and Miss N H Burroughs was chosen Corresponding Secretary This organization meets at the same time and place of the National Baptist Convention and reports annually to the parent body The Woman's Auxiliary Convention supports a Woman's and Girl's Training School at Washington D C

THE MINISTERS' RELIEF BOARD

The Ministers Relief Board was organized in 1903, the first chairman was Rev C B Brown of Marianna, Ark , and the Rev W A Holmes was the first Corresponding Secretary This Board seeks to gather means with which to give relief to old worn out ministers, who are not able to earn a support in their declining years

The youngest of the Board of the National Baptist Convention, is the Church Extension Board, located at Memphis, Tenn The Chairman of this Board is the Rev J B Roberts, the Corresponding Secretary is the Rev B J Perkins Already this Board which is less than two years old has afforded relief to several struggling churches and has built some churches where the people were not able to build for themselves

The principal object before the National Educational Board at this time is the building of a Theological Seminary for the training of ministers The Southern Baptist Convention (White) has voted to put 150 000 into the project and the hope is held out that the Northern (White) Baptists will give a like amount

The Home Mission Board of the National Baptist Convention co-operates with the Home Board of the Southern Baptist Convention in Missionary work in the Southern Field The Home Mission Board of the National Baptist Convention is at present being directed by Dr Jos A Booker, of

Little Rock Ark About twenty Missionaries are being regularly employed by this Board

The Foreign Mission work is under the superintendency of Rev L G Jordan, and is at present confining its labors to Africa, which has been greatly disturbed by the war, but the Missionaries have not left the field and are being supported by the Foreign Mission Board

The Headquarters of the Foreign Mission Board is 701 S 18th St, Philadelphia, Pa

The Sunday School Board is located at 418 N 4th Ave, Nashville, Tenn, the present Corresponding Secretary is the Rev Wm Haynes This Board publishes the Sunday School literature used in a majority of the Negro Baptist Sunday Schools in this country

There are three strong District organizations viz, The New England Convention, the Lot Carey Convention and the General Convention of the Western States and Territories, all of which are in cooperation with the National Baptist Convention

The officers of the National Baptist Convention for 1918, are F C Morris, D D, President, Rev W G Parks, D D Vice President at large Prof R B Hudson A M Secretary, Rev T O Fuller, D D D E A Wilson D D, E H McDonald, D D, and J H Nesbit, A B Assistant Secretaries Rev A J Stokes, D D Treasurer Prof M M Rogers Auditor There is elected from each State one Vice-President, at every annual meeting who together with the officers of the Convention constitute an Executive Committee

AFRICAN METHODIST EPISCOPAL CHURCH
By Bishop C H Phillips

Resenting what they considered bad treatment upon the part of their white brethren and imbued with the spirit of independence then in the American atmosphere, being led by Richard Allen a colored local preacher in the Methodist Episcopal Church in Philadelphia a number of persons of African descent, withdrew from St George's Methodist Episcopal Church in Philadelphia and established a society of their own This was in 1787 from which date the history of this church began

After withdrawing from the white church they took immediate steps to secure a building of their own which was not accomplished until they had overcome many trials and difficulties Their building was finally completed and at their request Frances Asbury then Bishop of the Methodist Episcopal Church opened the house for divine worship It was named "Bethel Church"

Soon Negroes of other Pennsylvania localities and of New York, New Jersey Delaware and Maryland followed the example of the Philadelphians, and formed distinctively African congregations—often with the encouragement of the whites

In 1816 representatives, sixteen in all, from Bethel African Church in Philadelphia and African churches in Baltimore, Md, Wilmington, Del, Attleboro, Penn, and Salem, New Jersey met in Philadelphia and formed a church organization or connection under the title of 'The African Methodist Episcopal Church'

They adopted the policy and doctrine of the Methodist Episcopal Church with some slight changes and elected one of their number, Richard Allen as their Bishop Bishop Allen died in 1831 He was their first Bishop but the denomination has had a succession of able superintendents, some of whom have been remarkable for administrative talent and pulpit eloquence

During the first fifty years, the church was confined almost entirely to the Northern States and its growth was comparatively slow but after emancipation its development became rapid In 1816 it had only 7 churches and 400 members, in 1836 it had 86 churches and 7,594 members in 1866 it had 286 churches and 73 000 members, in 1896 it had 4,850 churches and 518,000 members and in 1916 it had 7,500 churches and 650 000 members It started with one Bishop in 1816 and had 16 Bishops in 1916 The number of conferences in 1816 was 2 and in 1916 they had grown to 81 It had no schools until 1866 and then only one but in 1916 it had 24 schools The value of its property in 1816 was $25,000, and in 1918 it was -12 500 000

Plans for the first school were laid in 1844—a manual labor school—near Columbus Ohio and in 1863 it secured Wilberforce University, now one of the largest Negro institutions of higher learning in America Since then an institution of learning has been established in most Southern States

In 1848 the Missionary Department was originated and in 1864 put into actual operation, although a missionary had been sent to Haiti in 1824

In 1916 more than a hundred missionaries and native workers are in foreign lands

In 1852 "The Christian Recorder," a weekly newspaper was established as the official organ and has been maintained ever since

In 1882, the Sunday School Department was organized By it all of the literature of the A M E Sunday Schools is edited and published

The A M E Church has successfully solved the problems of Negro organization from the religious side

AFRICAN METHODIST EPISCOPAL ZION CHURCH

The African Methodist Episcopal Zion Church was organized June 21, 1821 in New York City It grew out of the decision of the Colored Methodists to declare for independence It differed in organization somewhat from the other Methodist churches It was governed by Bishops quadrennially elected but not set apart by the usual forms of ordination

They got their name of Zionists from the name of the local church called Zion church which started the movement that eventuated in the establishment of the denomination

James Varick became the first Bishop of the church The denomination has had a marvelous growth and has churches throughout the land

It now has twelve Bishops three thousand one hundred and eighty churches with five hundred and sixty eight thousand six hundred and eight communicants It has three thousand and one hundred Sunday Schools and one hundred and seven thousand six hundred and ninety two scholars Its church property is valued at $4 833 207 It has a publishing house located at Charlotte, N C Its foreign mission work was organized in 1892 It has in its foreign mission fields three stations five outstations and eleven organized churches There are five ordained ministers and thirteen native workers and other helpers In 1878 the church did not own a single school building nor any school property worth mentioning There were no pupils in schools controlled by the church Thirty years later, at the General Conference Philadelphia June 1908 Rev S G Atkins A M Ph D, of Wiston-Salem, N C, Corresponding Secretary of the Board of Education reported 10 colleges institutes and academies, with an enrollment of 1 842 pupils, and controlling property valued at $276 500

Two of the schools of the denomination are located in Alabama three in North Carolina two in South Carolina, and one each in Kentucky, Tennessee and Virginia One of its schools, Livingstone College located at Salisbury is an institution of real college rank

The aim of the denomination is to develop two more of its schools to such a rank and to advance the Livingstone College into the field of University work

Secretary Atkins writing under date of April 6 1909, said

"We think we have the foundation for a significant and comprehensive work in connection with the uplift of the Negro people of the country With our schools graded and co-ordinated, and all brought into harmony with the latest requirements of the science of education we shall hope to have a system that will take rank with the best educational forces of the world especially as the enlightenment and Christianizing of nearly a million people will soon be on our hands "

THE COLORED METHODIST EPISCOPAL CHURCH
By Bishop C H Phillips, D D

Before the Civil War colored people were very largely Methodists, Baptists Presbyterians, Episcopalians and what not according to the religious beliefs of their owners

But they had no church organization separate from the white people, for the laws of the South did not allow them to hold meetings among themselves

At the beginning of the war in 1861 the Methodist Episcopal Church South had in the slave-holding States a colored membership of 207 766 But after emancipation the African Methodist the African Methodist Episcopal and the African Methodist Episcopal Zion Churches, which already had organizations across Mason and Dixon's Line began to establish their churches in the South with great rapidity and marvelous success

The fortunes of war had wrought such changes between the master-class and the slave and the declaration of freedom had made such an impression on the minds and hearts of the colored people that any association with white people in religious affairs was, not only looked upon with disfavor and suspicion, but was regarded an act of disloyalty to the race on the one hand and base ingratitude for the new birth of freedom on the other

Under these conditions propagandists for churches which had existence at the North entirely distinct from white people, found a most responsive and fruitful field for operations in the South

For, when the war closed out of 207,766 only 78 000 remained in the M E Church South There had been an exodus of the colored members of this Church into the A M E A M E Zion and M E Churches To save this remnant was the supreme thought of the leaders of the Church South This remnant desired to be organized into a Church organization of their own and the M E Church South acceded to that request by appointing at its General Conference in May 1870 Bishop Paine, and Doctors A L P Green Samuel Watson, Thomas Taylor and James A Heard to assist in the organization

In December of this year in Jackson, Tennessee the Church was formally organized and named the "Colored Methodist Episcopal Church in America" William H Miles of Kentucky, and Richard H Vanderhorst of South Carolina were elected and consecrated the first bishops of the new organization

With two Bishops, eight annual conferences about seventy eight thousand members legal and constitutional in organization, legitimately descended from the very Father of Methodist, firm in its doctrines and principles, the Colored Methodist Episcopal Church started upon its career, "clear as the sun, bright as the moon, and terrible as an army with banners."

At its beginning it had no schools, colleges, publishing house, or churches at the North. Today it has church organizations from the Atlantic to the Pacific, a Publishing House located at Jackson Tennessee which, in the near future will be removed to Nashville 10 schools and colleges, 7 living Bishops, 34 Annual Conferences, 3285 churches 3402 preachers and 267,361 members This church publishes three papers which voice its sentiments advocates its enterprises and performs such other functions as are peculiar to denominational organs

The Missionary Church Extension Epworth League, Educational, and Superannuated Preachers, Widows and Orphans Departments are helpful adjuncts to our Church Machinery and are powerful exponents of everything that is necessary to push the Kingdom of Jesus Christ among men Some of her leaders have had a measure of success in the field of literature. "Auto-Biography and Addresses" by Bishop L H Holsey, "Auto-Biography," by Bishop Isaac Lane. "Sermons and Addresses" by Bishop R S Williams, "History of the C M E Church" by Bishop C H Phillips "Morning Meditations" by Bishop R A Carter "Auto-Biography" by Bishop M F Jamison, and "Doctrines of Christ and His Church. by Dr R J Brown, deserve special mention

The Church is making preparations to celebrate the centenary of the establishment of the first Missionary Society in this country and the Semi-Centennial of our Church organizations in 1920 It proposes to raise $1,000,000 for Church-extension missionary, educational and other purposes

The Colored Methodist Episcopal Church has had a phenomenal growth and development It is fortunate in its inheritance, rich in its possibilities, and Evangelical and truthful in all its operations

It preserves all the traditions and spiritual fervor of Methodism, and as a part of the invisible Church of Jesus Christ it essays to do its portion in bringing on the era of peace and good will among men

COLORED CUMBERLAND PRESBYTERIAN CHURCH

Prior to the Civil War the colored members of the Cumberland Presbyterian Church belonged to the same congregations as the white people and sat under the same pastor though they had preachers of their own race and often held separate meetings They were estimated to number at that time about 20,000

After the close of the War conditions changed and the Colored members thought it best to form themselves into a separate organization and made application to the white congregations to be set apart to themselves Their request was granted, and they were legally set apart by the General Assembly of the Cumberland Presbyterian Church at Murfreesboro, Tennessee, in May 1869

The first synod organized was the Tennessee Synod in 1871 at Fayetteville and the first General Assembly was organized in 1874 at Nashville

The Educational work of the church includes three schools one each in Tennessee Alabama and Kentucky with eleven teachers 350 pupils and property valued at $6750

The church has also a publishing plant, valued at $1500 In 1906 the church had 196 church edifices, 18,066 communicants 92 Sunday Schools with 6952 scholars and property valued at $203,778

COLORED PRIMITIVE BAPTISTS

During the years of slavery the Colored Primitive Baptists worshipped with the white churches They were provided seats in the gallery, but had no voice in the management of the churches After emancipation they withdrew from the white churches

In 1865, Elder Thomas Williamson at Columbia, Tennessee organized the White Springs Primitive Baptist Church

The first association, the Big Harpeth Primitive Baptist Association, was organized in 1866 in the State of Tennessee, and soon thereafter other churches began to spring up in the Southern States

In 1867 the first church was formed in West Florida

The churches of America number 797 with a membership of 35,076, they have 166 Sunday Schools and 6,224 scholars The value of the church property is $296,539.00

UNITED AMERICAN FREEWILL BAPTISTS

The lines between the white and colored Freewill Baptist churches in the Southern States for some years after the Civil War seem not to have been drawn very sharply

The increase of the colored churches and the enlargement of their activities finally led to their separation from the white churches In 1901 they were organized as separate denomination

The church has two large schools—one Kinston College, North Carolina the other at Dawson Ga There is also a printing establishment at Kinston N C which issues a weekly paper

There are 251 churches, 14,489 communicants, 100 Sunday Schools, 3,307 scholars and church property valued at $79,278.00

National and Fraternal Organizations

THE NATIONAL ASSOCIATION FOR THE ADVANCEMENT OF COLORED PEOPLE.

THE National Association for the Advancement of Colored People is an indirect result of race riots, in Springfield, Ohio, the home of Abraham Lincoln, in the summer of 1908.

It was decided to inaugurate a campaign on Lincoln's birthday, February 12, 1909. On that day a call was published signed by Jane Addams, of Chicago; Harriet Stanton Blatch; Prof. John Dewey; Hamilton Holt; Charles Edward Russell; Oswald Garrison Villard; Rabbi Stephen S. Wise, and Horace White, of New York; Judge Wendell Stafford, of Washington; Lincoln Steffens, of Boston, and many other public spirited people.

On May 30, 1909, a Conference was held in New York City, at which a Committee of forty was formed and a Secretary employed. Four mass meetings were held and thousands of pamphlets distributed. It was followed by a second Conference in 1910, at which the National Association for the Advancement of Colored People was organized. The officers were: National President, Moorfield Storey, Boston; Chairman of the Executive Committee, William English Walling; Treasurer, John E. Milholland; Disbursing Treasurer, Oswald Garrison Villard; Executive Secretary, Frances Blascoer; Director of Publicity and Research, Dr. W. E. B. DuBois. Through Dr. DuBois the Association was brought closely in touch with a group of Colored people known as the Niagara Movement, which had attempted a work of legal redress similar to that of the Association.

In the same year, 1910, was published the first number of "The Crisis," a monthly magazine, edited by Dr. Dubois, which early in 1919 had attained a circulation of 105,000.

Concurrent with a constant effort to organize Negroes for the maintenance and defense of their rights as United States citizens throughout the country, the Association devoted itself to a number of activities which may be classified as: The fight against lynching; Fighting the color line; Educational and publicity work; Legislative work and investigations; and during the world war Welfare and defense of the colored soldier.

In the fight against lynching trained investigators were employed to ascertain the facts underlying outbreaks of mob brutality against Negroes, and the facts were then published in periodicals and made available for publication in the press. One consequence of this work was the publication in 1919 of the booklet entitled "Thirty Years of Lynching in the United States," containing all available statistics.

In the closing years of the world war the Association made its greatest membership gains. From a membership of 9,282 comprising 80 branches in December, 1917, the Association grew to 165 branches and 43,994 members in December 1918. At the conclusion of the tenth anniversary meeting of the Association, held in Cleveland, Ohio, in June, 1919, the Association had increased to 237 branches and 68,031 members. The information from which this article was prepared was furnished by James W. Johnson, Field Secretary of the National Association for the Advancement of Colored People.

NATIONAL URBAN LEAGUE.

George Edmund Haynes founded the league about 1912 in the city of New York. It first was local in its work and scope but like many institutions looking to the betterment of the race it soon overleaped the bounds of locality and developed into a National movement.

When the National League on Urban Conditions was formed it began to study the problems of the Negro in cities upon the basis that it was a question which called for the co-operation of the best men and women, white and colored. The program of work which was adopted was elastic and well adapted to the new situation created in many cities by recent events.

During the Fall of 1916, concentrated efforts were made to organize movements in local communities where the problems were in danger of becoming acute. The result of this effort has brought about the organization of branches in more than thirty cities.

The first year of the organization its annual budget amounted to $2,500.00 and now it is over $100,000.00. Until several years ago the work of the National League and the New York branch were conducted in the same office, but the growth of the work has made it necessary to separate the two organizations.

The League advocates the forming of organizations for the purpose of fostering good feeling between the two races; to study the health, school and work needs of the Negro population; to develop agencies and stimulate activities to meet those needs; by training and health protection to increase the industrial efficiency of Negroes and to encourage a fairer attitude toward Negro labor especially in regard to hours, conditions and regularity of work and standard of wages; and to increase the respect for law and the orderly administration of justice.

The rapid development of the League and the valuable work it has already accomplished is clear evidence that it has a mission in the world and the carrying out of that mission is sure to work well in the uplift of the Negro race.

Its labors should continue until every city in the Union has a branch established in it.

This effort of the Negro race to ameliorate the condition of its members is meeting with a hearty response by their white friends, who not only sympathize with it but give its substantial support.

This was illustrated when the great conflagration swept Atlanta and destroyed many Negro homes. There the white and colored co-operated in good spirit to care for the unfortunate.

The work relief for the colored families was under the general supervision of the Urban League.

THE NATIONAL NEGRO BUSINESS MENS' LEAGUE.

The trend of the modern Negro as he grasps the scheme of things, is towards organization. Once he rushed into this, but disappointed, yes shocked by trickery of his brothers of both races he for a long time stood aloof with distrust. Education has re-adjusted his faith, as it has reformed the plans of those who lead. The Negro therefore organizes now for protection, for ideas, for strength, and for inspiration.

Among the many bodies that leaped to the fore for the welfare of the black man, the National Negro Business Men's League stands foremost. It is comprehensive in its membership and most benevolent in its platform. Beginning with a few members in Boston twenty years ago, it has grown in importance and in its composite scope until it has absorbed at least a goodly part of every Negro organization of importance in the land. Under its general head come the National Negro Insurance

Association, National Negro Retail Merchants Association, National Negro Farmers' Association, National Negro Undertakers Association, National Negro Bar Association, National Negro Medical Association.

The League was founded by Booker T. Washington, and had its first meeting in Boston. Booker T. Washington was there chosen president and Emmett J. Scott secretary. Officials in other capacities went and came, but Dr. Washington and Emmett J. Scott continued to serve; the former to his death and the latter to this day.

Immediately upon its incorporation, the Negro Business men of all sections rallied to its colors. Drawing no very distinct lines, Dr. Washington enlisted the educated and the uneducated so long as the candidate stood for some progress in his community. Thus he had meet in one body and appear on the same platform an illiterate, but successful farmer, a leading teacher, a bishop of the church, a banker, a merchant, a hair dresser, a boot black, a dentist, an undertaker.

The League members all had a story to tell, a tale of success, brief, succinct, full of hardship, prejudice, and frequently, humor. The press was enlisted at the League's annual gatherings, and year by year the public was, and still is, told those tales America loves so well, of the steady plod from poverty to wealth. Some men at these meetings grew discontented with themselves because they had done so little. Others took courage and ventured to walk where once they had scarcely dared to crawl.

Beginning thus with encouragement in simple business undertakings, the League soon became the center from which radiated many plans of organized effort for the welfare of the Negro throughout the country. When it seemed best for the Negro to celebrate the fiftieth anniversary of his freedom, the League took up the matter and through its press association and through the assistance of the

GROUP NATIONAL NEGRO BUSINESS MENS' LEAGUE DURING DR. WASHINGTON'S LIFE TIME.

Associated Press let the world know that there were in America persons of color known as the American Negro, that this same American Negro had once been enslaved, but now he was free, and that the same freeman, so far from lack of appreciation, so thoroughly rejoiced over his freedom that he had built churches, bought farms, erected schools, cut down illiteracy against all sorts of encroaching odds, accumulated millions of dollars and gathered from his contact with his white neighbors, taste, culture, refinement, business acumen, tact and diplomacy. All this he wished the world to know about and the National Negro Business Men's League saw to it that the public was informed.

Thus it was with every notion of uplift or enterprise. It aids and encourages the banker, the undertaker, the journalist. When the idea of a clean up time became current, the League seized upon it and gave it impetus, until it reached the black man in every section of the country. When pig clubs and canning clubs attracted the economists of the Nation, the League saw to it that the Negro in the school, in the church, on the farm, played their part in aiding the government to conserve food and to perpetuate the idea of economy and thrift. It sent out appeals for better homes, better schools, cleaner living and a more cordial relationship between the two races everywhere.

Though the members of the League are all colored men it has managed to enlist the good will and

co-operation of Governors of States, ministers, jurists, philanthropists and public men in all walks of life. Theodore Roosevelt kept in the closest touch with its activities, as did many of his cabinet members. Andrew Carnegie was one of its personal friends, aiding it financially for a number of years. George Foster Peabody, of New York, John E. White, of Atlanta, Georgia; Colonel Henry Waterson, of Louisville, Colonel Parker, of Louisiana, have all been in close touch with it at one time or another.

For years it supported, largely through the help of Andrew Carnegie, an organizer, who went from State to State and from city to city, to organize or to rejuvenate smaller leagues. This was kept up until every state and every city where there is a large number of Negroes could boast of a local league. Delegates from these make up the great cosmopolitan, the National League. First, foremost, and always, whether the business League survives or perishes, it will always be one of the monuments to Booker T. Washington, to his foresight, to his genius for service and organization.

The officers of the League at this writing are: Mr. John C. Napier, banker, of Nashville, Tennessee, is the President; Chas. Banks, First Vice-President, Mound Bayou, Mississippi; C. H. Brooks, Second Vice-President, Philadelphia, Penn.; John M. Wright, Third Vice-President, Topeka, Kansas; Fred R. Moore, Fourth Vice-President, New York; Robert R. Church, Fifth Vice-President, Memphis.

WAGE EARNERS SAVINGS BANK, SAVANNAH, GA.

Tennessee, Emmett J Scott Washington, D C Secretary, Albert L Hosley, Assistant Secretary. Tuskegee Institutee, Alabama, Charles H Anderson, Treasurer, Jacksonville, Florida, F H Gilbert, Brooklyn, N Y, Registrar, R E Clay, Asst Registrar, Briston Tennnessee, William H Davis, Official Stenographer, Rosecraft, Maryland, Ernest T Attwell, Transportation Agent Tuskegee Institute, Alabama

MEDICAL DENTAL AND PHARMACEUTICAL ASSOCIATION

From the hoodooism of African jungles and the "root docterm" of the benighted Southern slave plantations to the modern treatment of typhoid fever, the administration of salvarsan and the abdominal section, has been a long stride for the Negro physician But this stride he has taken—sometimes by plodding, sometimes by leaps and bounds till he now occupies a position in the medical world that is recognized and respected

While a few educated physicians and apothecaries, some of them slave-born, were practising among their people as early as the end of the eighteenth century, yet the majority of the Negro 'doctors" consisted till far into the nineteenth century of "herb doctors" who healed by spells and by practising superstition After the Civil War, however, a number of Negroes took up the scientific study of medicine and medical colleges in the United States alone have graduated many thousand such students

In general these colored physicians, surgeons and pharmacists have the esteem of their white colleagues and contribute notably to the improvement of the hygiene of their race which still leaves much to be desired It is indubitable that these colored physicians have made the greatest progress of any members of their race, and together with the teachers, have been of the greatest service to it, as is clearly shown by the slowly decreasing mortality of the Negroes The colored physician like his white colleague in North America is often the proprietor of a pharmacy Patent medicines are as much beloved by the Negroes as by the people of North America in general

Another element in the work of improving the health of the Negroes, is the rise of the Negro hospitals These hospitals and sanitariums are well patronized and have not only done much to prevent the sufferings of the colored people, but have proven financially successful

Along with the establishment of Negro hospitals have arisen the nurses' training schools Most of the hospitals mentioned above have connected with them such schools, which are sending out from year to year a large number of colored women, who are not only getting ready employ

ment among the white people but are taking their share of the burden of spreading the gospel of good health and right living among Negroes

The National Medical Association is composed of Negro physicians dentists and pharmacists, and was organized in Atlanta Georgia, in 1895 during the Cotton States and International Exposition The object of the Association is to organize for mutual benefit and helpfulness the Negro physicians, dentists and pharmacists and to insure progressiveness in the profession It is also the object of the Association to help improve living conditions among the Negro people by teaching them the simple rule of health

NATIONAL NEGRO PRESS ASSOCIATION

By Henry Allen Boyd, Corresponding Secretary

The National Negro Press Association is an organization of newspaper men, publishers and correspondents organized for the highest development of Negro journalism The Association came into existence more than thirty-five years ago The plan is the result of matured thought on the part of some of the race's foremost journalists It had its existence back in times and days during the reconstruction period following close on the heels of the civil war For a number of years it simply marked time, but within the past ten years it has been very active, having succeeded in blending together one hundred and twenty-six publications and their representatives with a combined weekly circulation of 2,300,000 journals, or in other words more than 20% of the population are furnished publications each week through the efforts of the National Negro Press Association and its members

Among the things accomplished in the recent years by the Association was the standardization of advertising, the inaugurating of reciprocal news service the promotion of inter-telegraph circles among the larger publications, the dividing of membership into zones, the formation of a code service committee that is preparing a special code to be used by the members belonging to the Association, the placing of a permanent exhibit of bound volumes of the publications to be sent to various fairs and expositions, to work for the mutual uplift of the smaller journals to see that only wholesome literature is sent in the rural districts the co-operating of all agencies in helping the government in solving perplexing problems the assisting in stamping out crime in the race and the reducing of illiteracy by the dissemination of purer literature and the working for an untrammeled Democracy among the people of the United States, the making of America safe for Americans The officers for 1919 aer as follows

582

MEETING OF PROMINENT COLORED EDITORS IN WASHINGTON, D. C., DURING WORLD WAR.

C. J. Perry, Philadelphia, Pa., President; W. E. King, Dallas, Texas, Vice-President; J. H. Anderson, Charlotte, N. C., Second Vice-President; Henry Allen Boyd, Nashville, Tenn., Corresponding Secretary; J. A. Hamlett, Jackson, Tenn., Recording Secretary; Miss Blanche Johnson, Newport News, Va., Assistant Recording Secretary; B. J. Davis, Atlanta, Ga., Treasurer; E. A. Williams, Cincinnati, Ohio, Auditor; Jos. L. Jones, Cincinnati, Ohio, Chairman, Executive Committee.

NATIONAL ASSOCIATIONS, WHEN ORGANIZED.

American Negro Academy, 1897.

American Negro Historical Society, 1897.

National Association of Teachers in Colored Schools, 1904.

Negro National Educational Congress, 1910.

Negro Society for Historical Research, 1911.

The Alpha Phi Alpha Fraternity, at Cornell University, 1906.

Kappa Alpha Psi Fraternity, at Indiana University, 1911.

National Negro Business League, 1900.

National Negro Insurance Association.

National Negro Bankers' Association, 1906.

National Railway Employees' Protective Ass'n.

National Association of Funeral Directors.

National Marine Cooks', Stewards', Head and Side Waiters' Association.

National Negro Retail Merchants Association.

National Alliance of Postal Employees, 1913.

National Medical Association, 1895.

National Association of Colored Graduate Nurses, 1908.

National Negro Bar Association, 1909.

National Negro Press Association, 1909.

Western Negro Press Association.

National Association of Colored Musical and Art Clubs, 1908.

National Equal Rights League, 1910.

National Colored Democratic League.

National Association of Colored Women, 1895.

Southern Negro Anti-Saloon Federation.

The National Association for the Advancement of the Colored People, 1909.

NEGRO MASONRY.

Extracts from "Prince Hall and His Followers" by Geo. W. Crawford.

"The test of the legitimacy of a Masonic body is this: Is the authority by which it assumes to practice and exemplify Masonic principles derived from the proper source and did the manner of the derivation of such authority conform to the accepted Masonic usage for the time being? Tried by this test, the Negro Masonry of the United States, which is in direct line of succession from Prince Hall Grand Lodge, can make out as good a case for the legitimacy of its existence as any Masonry in the Western hemisphere."

The clean cut and orderly work of Prince Hall, Provincial Grand Master and the father of Negro Masonry in America, is well established.

Concerning the constitution of African Lodge No 459, F and A M (subsequently No 370) and the establishment of all that is in Masonic sequence thereto there is not the slightest difficulty in determining what was done and upon what authority

In 1775, in an Army Lodge holding a warrant under the Grand Lodge of England, and attached to one of the Regiments at Bunker Hill Prince Hall and fourteen other men of African descent were duly initiated passed and raised Nine years later almost to a day these fifteen Negro Masons applied to the Grand Lodge of England to be set apart as a regular lodge Their application was granted and a warrant issued to them September 29 1784 authorizing them to be constituted into a regular lodge under the designation as African Lodge No 459

This warrant, which follows, was delivered to them three years later, i e May 2 1787 and the lodge was duly organized four days after that date, with Prince Hall as its Master

WARRANT OF AFRICAN LODGE, NO 459
WARRANT OF CONSTITUTION A G M
To All And Every

"Our Right Worshipful and Loving Brethren — We, Thomas Howard, Earl of Effingham, Lord Howard, etc, Acting Grand Master, under the authority of his Royal Highness, Henry Frederick, Duke of Cumberland, etc, Grand Master of the Most Ancient and Honorable Society of Free and Accepted Masons, send greeting

"Know ye that we at the humble petition of our Right Trust and well beloved brethren, Prince Hall, Boston Smith, Thomas Sanderson, and several other brethren residing in Boston, New England in North America, do hereby constitute the said brethren into a regular Lodge of Free and Accepted Masons under the title or denomination of the African Lodge, to be opened in Boston, aforesaid and do further, at their said petition and of the great trust and confidence reposed in every one of the said above-named brethren, hereby appoint the said Prince Hall to be Master, Boston Smith, Senior Warden and Thomas Sanderson, Junior Warden, for opening the said Lodge, and for such further time only as shall be thought by the brethren thereof, it being our will that this our appointment of the above officers, shall in no wise affect any future election of officers of said Lodge, but that such election shall be regulated agreeable to such By-Laws of the said Lodge as shall be consistent with the Grand Laws of the society, contained in the Book of Constitutions, and we hereby will and require of you the said Prince Hall, to take special care that all and every, the said brethren are to have been regularly made Masons

and that they do observe, perform and keep all the rules and orders contained in the Book of Constitutions, and, further that you do from time to time cause to be entered in a book kept for that purpose an account of your proceedings in the Lodge together with all such Rules, Orders and Regulations as shall be made for the good government of the same, that in no wise you omit once in every year to send to us, or our successors Grand Masters or Rowland Holt Esq our Deputy Grand Master, for the time being an account of your said proceedings and copies of all such Rules, Orders and Regulations as shall be made as aforesaid together with the list of the members of the Lodge and such sum of money as may suit the circumstances of the Lodge, and reasonably be expected toward the Grand Charity "Moreover, we will and require of you, the said Prince Hall as soon as conveniently may be to send an account in writing of what may be done by virtue of these presents

"Given at London, under our hand and seal of Masonry, this 29th day of September A L 5784 A D 1784, by the Grand Master's command.

R Holt, Deputy Grand Master
Attest William White Grand Secretary "

In the same year African Lodge was formerly entered upon the English Registry along with other colonial Masonic bodies

This lodge continued as a subordinate lodge, exercising all the prerogatives of a regular Masonic body, until June 24 1791, when it was superceded by African Grand Lodge which was organized in Boston, Massachusetts on that date

At no time during the 18th century was there any accepted form of constituting a Grand Lodge Especially was this true of early American Grand bodies Scarcely any two of these were formed in the same way Some were organized by Provincial Grand Masters acting under deputations from England, others by self assumption of Grand Lodge powers, still others by union of lodges in her localities

It was some years after the achievement of American independence before these provincial bodies were totally emancipated by the English Grand Lodge, they were all carried upon the English registry until 1813 when the "Ancients' and "Moderns" agreed upon terms of peace and became united

The African Grand Lodge was formed at Boston, Massachusetts, on St John's (The Baptist) Day 1791 The meeting was presided over by Provincial Grand Master Prince Hall and participated in by many of the members of the craft who had been made in African Lodge No 459

The badge of recognition alone would be a complete answer to the critics of African Grand Lodge

tor in countless ways the treatment accorded African Grand Lodge and Prince Hall Grand Lodge in England shows conclusively that they were considered by the Mother Grand Lodge to be higher than subordinate bodies in dignity

African Grand Lodge does not have to rely upon English recognition however, for no matter which of the three procedures outlined above was followed there are numerous and weighty precedents in favor of its regularity To impeach the regularity of African Grand Lodge it is manifest that there must be shown a violation of some vital principle of Freemasonry universally recognized

Masonry is entirely different from all other fraternal organizations In other fraternal bodies, if one element of its membership is offended because of the presence of another element the disgruntled ones usually settle the difficulty by withdrawing and setting up for themselves an "Independent" or "Improved" branch of the same order In Masonry such things cannot be done Masonry knows no caste The badge of a Mason to its worthy possessor is an honor which is equal to any which he could ever receive from Kings or Potentates To a true Mason an admission of his inferiority to any man is a disavowal of his Masonry

THE KNIGHTS OF PYTHIAS OF NORTH AMERICA SOUTH AMERICA EUROPE ASIA AFRICA AND AUSTRALIA

By John L Jones Supreme Vice-Chancellor

This well known and aggressive Order is one of the strongest and best governed institutions among colored fraternities It is non-sectarian and non political Its mottoes are Friendship, Charity and Benevolence

It was patterned after the Order instituted by J H Rathbone and others just after the Civil War Several attempts were made by colored men to join the Order instituted by Mr Rathbone, but in each case the applicants were met by refusal

Finally the degrees were unwittingly conferred upon several colored men, led by Dr Geo A Place of Macon, Miss, Dr Thos W Stringer of Vicksburg, Miss, and Mr A E Lightfoot, of Lauderdale, Miss

Dr Stringer, regarded as the founder of the Order lost no time in launching the work among his race The first lodge organized was Lightfoot Lodge No 1 at Vicksburg, Miss, March 26th, 1880

The female department of the order known as the Order of Calanthe was authorized at a Supreme Lodge meeting at Vicksburg, May 14th, 1883 and the first Subordinate Court of Calanthe was instituted at Whitehall La, during the same year

The Military Department of the Order, known as the Uniform Rank, Knights of Pythias, and re-

cognized as the best governed military organization of the race, was also authorized in May, 1883

There is also a Military Cadet Department attached to the U R K P for boys and a Juvenile Department for girls and boys attached to the Calanthe Department

The growth of this order has been phenomenal and lack of space here forbids the mention this Order deserves For the benefit of those desiring further information, we refer them to that very complete History of the Colored Knights of Pythias sold by the Central Regalia Co, of Cincinnatti Ohio

GROWTH AND RESOURCES OF THE ORDER
RECAPITUATION

The following statement from the official reports show the growth and financial resources of the Order

Number of Lodges July 1, 1915 ----------- 3,185
Number of Lodges July 1 1917 ---------- 3,113
Decrease for the term ---------------- -- 72
Number of Members July 1 1915 ---------105,140
Number of Members July 1 1917---------118 210
Increase for the term -------------------- 13,070
Total amount of Endowment paid out for term ending July 1, 1915--$1,182,574 39 Total amount of Endowment paid out for term ending July 1 1917—$935,153 4 Amount of Endowment in treasuries July 1, 1915—$338,838 6 Amount of Endowment in treasuries July 1 1917—$463 688 08 Increase over last term—$124 850 02 Amount of Grand Lodge Fund on hand July 1, 1917—$42,356 62 Amount of Supreme Lodge Fund on hand July 1st 1917—$16,936.32 Value of property owned by Grand Lodges—$702 848 90 Value of property owned by Supreme Lodge—$70 000 00 Value of Property owned by Subordinate Lodges — $474 619 83

FINANCIAL RESOURCES OF THE ORDER

Endowment in treasuries ------------$463 688 08
Grand Lodge Funds on hand -------- 42,356 62
Supreme Lodge Funds on hand -------- 16 936 32
Property owned by Grand Lodges ----- 702,848 90
Property owned by Supreme Lodge --- 70,000 00
Property owned by Subordinate Lodges 474,619 83

Total Resources -------------------$1,770 449 75

There are about eighty thousand women members of the Order of Calanthe and about twenty-five thousand members of the Military Department The very efficient executive officers of the several Departments of the Order are Smith W Green, of New Orleans La, Supreme Chancellor of Lodge Dept Jos L Jones, of Cincinnatti Ohio Supreme Worthy Counsellor of the Order of Calanthe R R Jackson of Chicago, Ill Maj General of the Uniform Rank, J L V Washing-

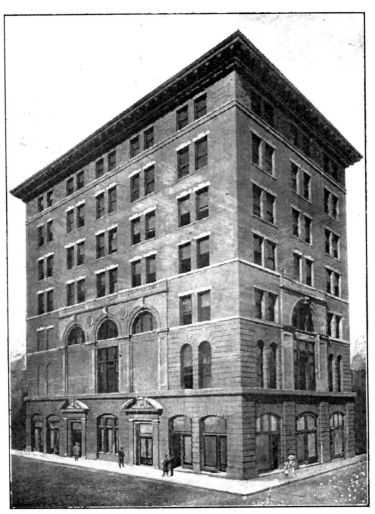

COLORED PYTHIAN TEMPLE, NEW ORLEANS, LA.

ton of Louisville, Ky Royal Potentate of the Dramatic Order of Knights of Omar

There are twenty-eight Grand Lodge or State Organizations of men and twenty-five Grand Courts of State Organizations of women The Military Department of this Order holds encampments biennially at the place where the Supreme Lodge and Supreme Court meets The affairs of this Department are modeled after the United States Army, and their encampments of five thousand Sir Knights or more every two years receive high commendation from the daily press

This Order owns Pythian Temples in many States The Supreme Lodge owns and operates at Hot Springs Ark the Pythian Sanitarium and Bath House—and in Chicago it owns two valuable pieces of property

INDEPENDENT ORDER OF ODD FELLOWS

An international secret fraternal beneficiary society The history of its English Odd Fellows Society projenitors runs back to about 1745 The early English order appeared about twenty-five years after the modern revival of Free Masonry in 1717 at London Fragmentary historic records and conjectures intimate that the first English Odd Fellows were an outgrowth of rivalry to the Masons, who had acquired prominence in the early half of the 18th century, particularly among the so-called upper classes, in the army navy, diplomatic service and among the nobility The distinctive feature of the order not only the early English branches but also those resulting from consolidations and from schism as well as the now Independent American child of English Odd Fellowship is found in their being based on definitely expressed obligations to care systematically, financially and otherwise, for sick distressed, and dependent members of their family

That Odd Fellowship in England was the fount from which flowed the stream of non-secret friendly societies there is no doubt, and it was the activities of the latter that suggested the flood of American secret assessment, life insurance and beneficiary societies of the last fifty years

The earliest recorded English Odd Fellows Lodge is that of Aristarchus No 9 which in 1748 met at the Globe Tavern, London

Almost all secret society meetings, in the United Kingdom, except those of the Masons, were proscribed by the British Government late in the 18th century and the Odd Fellows, Orangemen and friendly societies of that time suffered accordingly There was a revival of activity early in the 19th century and a Grand Lodge of Odd Fellows for England was formed at London in 1803 In 1809 one of the subordinate lodges at Manches-

ter declared itself independent and started as a grand lodge to form a new order of Odd Fellows

By 1813 the Independent Order of Odd Fellows Manchester Unity, had become fully established and constitutes the largest English branch of the order today The Manchester Unity was responsible for the introduction of the order into the United States in 1819

In 1843 the Grand United Order of Odd Fellows of England established a lodge in the United States petitioners for the same being Negroes

The American Independent Order of Odd Fellows had previously refused such a petition, on the ground of racial incompatibility The English Grand United Order found fertile soil among Negroes in the United States and has continued to establish lodges upon application from them since

It thus has a white membership in England and black in the United States This explains the apparent anomaly of the existence of Colored Odd Fellows in the United States, side by side but not connected, with an order having a similar, but not the same name

Peter Ogden was the founder of the Order of Odd Fellows among Negroes in the United States He had joined the Grand United Order of Odd Fellows of England and secured a charter for the first Negro lodge, Philomethean, No 646, of New York, which was set up March 1, 1843 Negro Odd Fellows in America are under the jurisdiction of England and are regularly represented in the general meetings of the Order

KNIGHTS AND DAUGHTERS OF LABOR

The Order of Twelve of Knights and Daughters of Tabor, was not organized under a sudden impulse, but rather the growth of an inspiration born of a desire to break the shackles of slavery, which came to Rev Mose Dickson, of Ohio who interested with him eleven companies who in August 1846, formulated a plan which they put into immediate execution The plan was one fraught with great danger both to originators and those who should follow their lead For this reason the organizers were careful to pick the men that were courageous, patient temperate and possessed of sound common sense The oath that bound them together was so binding that it could not be broken One feature of it was "I can die, but I cannot reveal the name of any member until the slaves are free" This oath never was broken

The first organization that was created, under the distinct name of the Order of Twelve, was organized in the city of Galena Ill by Mr Dickson at the residence of Alfred H Richardson, in August 1856 The secret work of the Knights of Liberty was not imparted to this Society At the close of the war so far as is known seven men of that great number returned from the battlefield

In 1871, Mr Dickson organized an order to perpetuate the the memory of the TWELVE that organized the Knights of Liberty He organized a Temple and Tabernacle in Independence, Mo , a Tabernacle in Kansas City, Mo a Temple and Tabernacle in Lexington, Mo With these five organizations a Convention was called to meet in Independence Mo , the second Tuesday in August 1872

This Convention organized the National Grand Temple and Tabernacle of the Order of Twelve, of Knights and Daughters of Tabor The Child of Destiny was born, and named The Order was of rapid growth and spread from State to State, gathering strength in its onward march Within forty-seven years this Order has taken its place and rank with the greatest organizations of the world It is united by the strongest ties of friendship, and bound together by solemn obligations and established on a firm basis, for the purpose of making a united and effective effort in aiding each member in sickness or distress to protect and defend each other, to aid and help the widows and orphans of members that died in good standing, to inculcate true morality to build up and spread the Christian religion

The Order is non-sectarian—all members being free to make a choice of any Evangelical Church

The members are encouraged to use every honorable method to advance the cause of education, to avoid intemperance, to cultivate true manhood, and to eschew immoral and degraded people They are encouraged to acquire real estate It seeks to help and elevate the colored race

THE ROYAL KNIGHTS OF KING DAVID
By W G Pearson, Supreme Grand Scribe

The Royal Knights of King David, an organization carrying endowment, was organized in the city of Durham, N C , the 24th of Sept, 1883

This organization is composed of departments of men and women and children

It has a governing department known as The Supreme Grand Lodge, with headquarters in the city of Durham It is a purely Negro organization, organized for the protection and advancement of the Negro race The Initiation fee is small, which with monthly dues of only twenty-five cents each entitles a member in case of death to ONE HUNDRED dollars The local Lodge, in addition to this, pays twenty-five dollars burial expenses It also gives weekly indemnity when sick, and further, it furnishes physicians and free medicine to its sick members This organization has had a

phenominal growth and has a membership of 100,000 It has paid to widows and orphans and male beneficiaries since its organization $750 000 in sick and death benefits

It has bought and paid for $25,000 worth of State bonds, and $11,000 worth of government bonds and has much holdings in other securities

In the Actuary's report of 1918 among other things he said that "The Royal Knights of King David is a substantial institution, and is one of few among the many, regardless of color who has a reserve in compliance with the Laws of the State in which they operate' He said further "If The Royal Knights of King David initiated NO MORE, and every one who is now a member remain in the Lodge till his death that the Order would be able to pay off each and every assessment and then have a BALANCE of $70,586 82 "

The Supreme Grand Lodge—with headquarters in Durham employs NINE regular commercially educated clerks Its system of book-keeping is very far in advance of anything seen of its kind in this country Too much cannot be said of the work this organization is doing throughout this country

It is operated and managed by the Supreme Grand Scribe—Prof W G Pearson of Durham N C

FRATERNAL ORGANIZATIONS

Secret societies among the Negroes may be roughly divided into two classes the old line societies, such as the Masons, Odd Fellows and the Knights of Pythias , and the benevolent secret societies such as the Mosaic Templars Royal Knights of King David United Order of Good Shepherds Independent Order of St Luke Royal Circle of Friends of the World, the Knights and Daughters of Tabor all of which have been treated in full elsewhere in this volume Other societies of note are

Improved Benevolent and Protective Order of Elks organized 1899 National Ideal Benefit Society United Order of True Reformers Grand United Order of Galilean Fishermen organized in 1856 United Brothers of Friendship and Sisters of the Mysterious Ten organized in 1854 Grand United Order of Wise Men, organized in 1901, The United Brothers of Friendship Grand United Order of Tents of the J R Giddings and Jollifec Union organized in 1866 Independent Benevolent Order, Independent Order of Brothers and Sisters, Sons and Daughters of Moses, organized in 1868, Grand United Order Sons and Daughters of Peace organizer in 1900 Grand United Order of Brothers and Sisters of Love and Charity

Example of Successful Negro Towns

RESIDENCE OF CHARLES BANKS, BOOKER T
WASHINGTON DAY.

STREET SCENE—MOUND BAYOU.

MOUND BAYOU—THE BLACK MAN'S PRIDE

A bank, a post office, an ice factory, a school, a Carnegie Library, a cotton seed oil mill, shops, stores, farms, laws, all in the hands of colored people, administered by a Negro town council, a Negro Mayor and a Negro marshall—who does not feel pride and hope surging in the breast? Here all the "Jim Crow" laws and customs are reversed; the black man's waiting room is in the front; the black man is in the ticket office, the black man maintains law and order.

Prior to 1887, this fair little town of black folk was a wilderness, dense with trees and foliage, being in Bolivar County, a very rich delta section. In the fall of 1887, Isaiah T. Montgomery, a former slave, landed here with a few followers to clear this forest and to establish a colony of colored people. For nearly a year they worked away with ax and saw, living in shanties and eating what food they could find. In 1888 the settlers returned home and brought their families and the town began.

At the time there was no land sufficiently cleared to cultivate. But the railroads needed cross ties, hence the men sawed and hewed, and thus earned their bread while they were clearing land for tillage. Three years then passed rapidly by. When they looked around they had cleared 4078 acres of land and had made ready some 1250 acres for cultivation. The sum of $8,780 had been earned from timber, 370 bales of cotton had been raised and 3045 bushels of corn. The squatter settlement now became the mecca for black folk, not only in Mississippi, but in nearly every state in the South. The town soon grew from three or four families to scores, then to hundreds. Today it numbers a thousand families, making a population of 5000. The people own 40,000 acres of land, and produce cotton in abundance, cultivating about 65% of the 40,000 acres. It produces one-twentieth of the cotton crop of Bolivar County, and Bolivar is one of the leading cotton producing counties of the world.

So much for the historical side of the town. He who has not seen Mound Bayou has missed one of the blessings of the age. Whether one approves of racial isolation or not, he is inspired by the sturdy independence, the genial atmosphere, the stride of progress and the spirit of cooperation of its inhabitants. There is about the town the old time communal spirit. Everyone knows his neighbor, speaks of him as he does of his own family. The formality of knocking at the door, or of ringing door bells appears never to have entered the town; you walk right in, put down your grip and say whether or not you are hungry, how long you are staying and the like. Stores, banks, offices, are all open, no sign or secrecy, no jealous guarding for fear of stealing goods, money or ideas.

The people in the town and about the country do most of their buying in a cooperate store, which is in charge of**********Booze, son-in-law of the founder. They bottle their own soft drinks, having voted liquor out of the town long before the state joined the ranks of prohibition. They manufacture their own ice; they ship lumber, they have all the agencies for modern improvement.

The bank of Mound Bayou, over which Charles Banks, the financial genius of the place presides, has taught the proper use of checks, how to deposit and draw out money; indeed, given them instruction in business.

Thus does Mound Bayou flourish, demonstrating that the Negro can organize, obey and live together in peace and good will.

MOUND BAYOU OIL MILL.

Negro Progress in the South and in the North

COLORED ATLANTA

By J. W. Davidson, Managing Editor of the
Atlanta Independent, Atlanta, Ga.

OF Atlanta's two hundred twenty-five thousand people, its colored citizens number seventy-five thousand. The city itself radiates from a common center like the spokes radiating from the hub of a wheel, and the colored people live in all parts of the city except in places where the extraordinary price of land preclude people of ordinary means.

The relationship of the races is most cordial. However different the past may have been, the present is certainly harmonious.

Colored Atlanta is as progressive as white Atlanta, and the progressiveness characteristic of both combined, constitutes what the world knows as "the Atlanta spirit."

For this brief review, we shall group colored Atlanta as follows:

1. RELIGIOUS, denominational:

A. BAPTIST. Comprise four-tenths; its principal churches are Friendship, Rev. E. R. Carter, pastor; Wheat Street, Rev. P. James Bryant, pastor; Liberty, Rev. Ernest Hall, pastor; Mt. Olive, Rev. T. L. Ballou, pastor; these being chiefest among a hundred others.

B. METHODIST. All branches constitute about three-tenths sub-divided as follows:

(a) A. M. E.—composing fully two-thirds of Methodism; Main churches, Big Bethel, Rev. R. H. Singleton, pastor; Allen Temple, Rev. J. A. Lindsey, pastor; St. Paul, Rev. Wm. McLendon, pastor; Cosmopolitan, Rev. W. J. Williams, pastor; and a score of others. Big Bethel is a general refuge for all colored Atlanta. Its distinguished exponents, resident, the late Bishops Turner and Gaines, and J. S. Flipper, presiding Bishop of the diocese.

(b) M. E.—composing about one-sixth of colored Methodism; chief churches, Central Avenue, Rev. L. H. King, pastor; Warren Chapel, Rev. E. H. Oliver, pastor; South Atlanta, Rev. James Demory, pastor; and a few others.

(c) C. M. E.—about one-twelfth of colored Methodism; largest churches Butler Street, Rev. H. W. Evans, pastor; Holsey Temple, Rev. Willie Williams, pastor; West Mitchell Street C. M. E. Church; and a few others. The distinguished exponents of the church, resident, being Bishops L. H. Holsey and R. A. Carter.

(d). All other branches of Methodism about one-twelfth of colored Atlanta, the leading of the remaining branches being the A. M. E. Z. Church, represented by the A. M. E. Z. Boulevard Church, Rev. W. Q. Welch, pastor.

ODD FELLOWS BLOCK—SHOWING AUDITORIUM AND OFFICE BUILDING.

All other denominations combined make up about three-tenths of colored Atlanta, the more important being

C Congregational Rev H H Proctor, pastor, Rush Memorial Rev Geo F Thomas pastor

D Presbyterian principal church(Radcliffe Memorial, Rev E C Haines pastor

E Episcopal, principal church St Paul, Father L Q Rogers, rector

F Catholic Boulevard Mission and a large variety of minor churches

2 EDUCATION

City and state provision includes common schools thru the seventh grade, there being no higher educational provisions All high school and collegiate training is provided for by colored Atlanta itself and by Northern philanthropy as follows

A ATLANTA UNIVERSITY, Edward T Ware President, strictly collegiate, founded under the auspices of the American Missionary Association in 1867 It has graduated more prominent colored leaders and educators than any institution for colored people in America Its presidents and officers include such distinguished men as Edmund Asa Ware founder, Dr Horance Bumstead, Prof J N Chase, Rev Cyrus W Francis Mrs Lucy F Case and Dr W E B Dubois all very dear to the hearts of colored Atlanta

B CLARK UNIVERSITY, Harry Andrews King, president founded in 1870 by the Freedmen's Aid Society under the patronage of the M E Church, provides normal academic and classical training

C SPELMAN SEMINARY, Miss Lucy Hale Tapley principal the largest female institution in America for colored girls, founded under Baptist auspices under its distinguished first principal Miss Packard, and her associate, Miss Hattie E Giles provides for training in normal, nurse training and domestic science courses, patronized by the Rockefellers

C MORRIS BROWN UNIVERSITY, founded officered and maintained by the A M E Church in Georgia exclusively Wm Alfred Fountain president Bishop J S Flipper Chancellor, provides preparatory, normal commercial, classical and theological training

D MOREHOUSE COLLEGE, founded in the sixties by the Baptist Home Mission Board at Augusta Georgia, under the lamented Dr Roberts, president, later removed to Atlanta under the late Dr Graves, as president, rehabilitated and renamed under its present president John Hope, provides normal, academic classical and theological courses

E GAMMON THEOLOGICAL SEMINARY, organized under the auspices of the M E Church, largely endowed located on the campus of Clark University, provides higher theological training Dr J M Waters, president Dr J W E Bowen, vice president

These colleges dot the hills surrounding Atlanta and are generally erected upon the breastworks thrown up for the defense of the city in the war between the states They constitute an educational center for that section of the United States where colored people live in largest numbers and make Atlanta an educational center greatly accounting for the marvelous progress of the colored people of the Gate City of the South

3 FRATERNITIES—Colored Atlanta easily leads all other cities in America from a fraternal standpoint, and the Grand United Order of Odd Fellows leads all others here

A ODD FELLOWS—District Grand Lodge No 18 G U O O F of America Jurisdiction of Georgia has assets in money stocks, bonds and real estate aggregating a million dollars with no mortgage encumbrance upon it whatsoever It has disbursed among its members thru the local lodges and its Atlanta headquarters over three million dollars under the capable direction of B J Davis, its guiding spirit Its headquarters in Atlanta, covering a city block and valued at over a half million dollars, is easily the largest property of its kind owned by colored people in the United States and has been the principal factor in inspiring the race with the spirit of cooperation race pride and race consciousness Out of its successful operation has grown the remarkable strides that colored Atlanta has taken in economic and business lines In its office building there is housed Negro corporations of upwards of over a half million dollars in authorized capital stock, and its membership in the state approximates forty thousand

B MASONS

(a) Ancient Free and Accepted Masons generally spoken of as state rite Masons easily predominate in the state among Masons with their headquarters in the Odd Fellows Building, where their Grand Master Dr H R Butler and the secretary of their endowment bureau Mr W C Thomas have their offices Their growth has been steady and conservative as characteristic of the fraternity, with a large membership embracing some of the brightest and best citizens of the race

(b) Ancient Free and Accepted York rite Masons, having a considerable membership in the state have their principal office in Atlanta, this being the home of their Grand Secretary Mr J H Dent, capable and efficient

( ) B O A large and flourishing fraternity,

has its headquarters in Atlanta, owning and occupying a three-story brick building on Bell Street near the Odd Fellows Building The officer in charge of its Headquarters is W S Cannon, active energetic and progressive

D KNIGHTS OF PYTHIAS—has a large membership both in its straight fraternity and its uniform ranks here, but none of its general officers are domiciled here

F GOOD SAMARITANS—has a considerable following in the state and Atlanta is the home of its Grand Secretary, W H Whittaker

I KNIGHTS AND DAUGHTERS OF TABOR —has a considerable following in the State and one of its principal officers, T W Holmes, the Grand Secretary is domiciled in the Odd Fellows Building There are scores of minor secret societies in the city

4 BUSINESS

A STANDARD LIFE INSURANCE COMPANY—straight old line life insurance capital stock paid up $125,000, assets $295,000, income, $382,000, total insurance outstanding, $8,200,000, total paid beneficiaries since its organization in 1913, $145,350 Heman E Perry, president, Harry H Pace secretary Its officers and directors comprise some of the most prominent and successful business men in the race throughout the country It occupies fully an entire floor and one-half in the Odd Fellows Building to transact its business

B GATE CITY DRUG STORE—capitalized at $20,000 00, the pioneer colored drug store of Georgia and the South Moses Amos manager and founder Its store, in the Odd Fellows Building, is one of the finest in the entire south irrespective of race There are also in the city the Walton Drug Store Auburn Avenue South Atlanta Drug Store and some two or three others

C ATLANTA STATE SAVINGS BANK—capital stock authorized $100,000, has grown steadily since its organization having the entire confidence of the people J O Ross president C C Cater cashier, are retired merchants bringing to the banking business the experience gained from successfully conducted commercial enterprises for a number of years occupies one-fourth of the ground floor of the Odd Fellows Building

D THE SERVICE COMPANY—capital stock $100,000, business headquarters in the Odd Fellows Building, H E Perry president, conducts an up-to-date laundry in a four-story brick building on Auburn Avenue and an equally large establishment in Augusta Ga

E ATLANTA MUTUAL INSURANCE COMPANY—the largest industrial insurance company in the State with headquarters in the Odd Fellows Building, A F Herndon president

F FIRESIDE INSURANCE COMPANY—F K Gibson Manager, is officered and promoted by the wealthiest colored men in Atlanta

Other insurance companies with headquarters elsewhere conduct large businesses here, viz The Pilgrim Health and Life Insurance Company, S W Walker, Manager, Guaranty Mutual Life Insurance Company, Thomas Taylor, Manager, Georgia Mutual Insurance Company J D Whitlow Manager, and the North Carolina Mutual J L Wheeler Manager, a North Carolina Company doing business here both industrial and straight life insurance with capital stock and other resources of over fully $500,000

G GROCERY BUSINESS—Men engaged in the retail grocery business are many there being upwards of fifty-three well stocked and prosperous grocery concerns in the different parts of the city

H PRINTING HOUSES—There are three printing establishments owned and operated by colored men, the principal of which is the Union Publishing Company under the capable management of C A Bullard There is one large printing establishment owned by the Odd Fellows

I REAL ESTATE—The real estate business is well represented in agents and corporations that are prosperous There are the Standard Loan and Realty Company W J Shaw secretary the Auburn Loan and Savings Corporation, B H Townsley manager both located in the Odd Fellows Building There are S Cunningham Broad Street H D McGhee, Broad Street, A Graves, Wall Street and scores of others

J AMUSEMENTS—There is but one place for theatrical amusement the Auditorium Theatre, a moving picture concern located in the Odd Fellows Building under the capable management of R Black

K UNDERTAKERS—David T Howard and Son under the management of David T Howard one of the wealthiest of Atlanta s Colored men and most charitable and public spirited of its citizens Cox Brothers, C S Cox, manager, Atlanta Undertaking Company, Sam Ware, manager, A B Cummings Dunn Brothers Ivery Brothers H H and P E Williams and J M Robinson complete the list of prosperous undertakers the latter J M Robinson in addition conducting on a large scale one of the largest sale feed and livery stables

L CAFES—We have upwards of 115 well regulated cafes, the most up-to-date of which are Robt J Harper's cafe in the Odd Fellows Building, Elijah Best, Cafe de Luxe and Mrs Scott Sutton's

M NEWSPAPERS—The Atlanta Independent leads Its circulation is the largest, its mechanical make-up perfect, and its editorial page the most straightforward comprehensive and courageous of any weekly publication in America B J Davis editor, J W Davidson, managing editor, its offices in the Odd Fellows Building

5 PROFESSIONS

A PHYSICIANS—There are forty-four regular licensed and practicing physicians in the city graduates of all the leading medical colleges in the country

B DENTISTS—There are eight dentists in the city alumni of the most representatives of American colleges

C LAWYERS—There are four colored lawyers in the city, some of whom rank among the best Henry Lincoln Johnson is the Dean

D MISCELLANEOUS—There are four chiropodists on occulist, six pharmacists, seventeen automobile mechanics, one surveyor and engineer, and one architect

E BARBERS—Atlanta boasts of the finest, most elaborate and comprehensive barber shops in the country and of these A F Herndon's shop on Peachtree Street operated for white customers, and J F Griffin's shop in the Odd Fellows Building operated for colored customers, are each the last word in art, sanitation arrangement and equipment

F CONTRACTORS—A D Hamilton & Sons, J G Harris Geo L Goosly R E Pharrow, and a few others are contractors on a large scale

G CHARITIES—Carrie State Orphans' Home Leonard Street Orphans Home Carter s Old Folks Home and Meadow Brook Old Folks Home, supported by public charity

H CEMETERIES—South View Cemetery

J HOSPITALS—St Luke's Hospital, made from enlargement of the home of the late Bishop Turner

J MISCELLANEOUS INDUSTRIAL—Brickmasons organized under American Federation of Labor are fully a half of this branch of skilled labor as are also the lathers and plasterers, tailors and pressers, carpenters and joiners, numerous painters harness and shoe-makers and repairers, stone-masons tinners in fair numbers, blacksmiths and dressmakers, chauffeurs coachmen railroad and electric wire laborers abound, few plumbers bakers confection makers numerous, wagoners exclusively, porters, janitors char-women maids cooks butlers in abundance

6 Colored Atlanta as regards it home manifests the high ideals inculcated by its educational environment, they stand easily at the head of the list in architecture and design They are Southern in taste but Yankee in keeping Very nearly each home is well filled with choice literature the Bible generally taking the chief place in the library, music of all kinds—classic and modern Not one graduate of all the colleges has ever been convicted of crime or even charged with heinous offense

THE WEALTHIEST NEGRO COLONY IN THE WORLD—HARLEM—NEW YORK CITY

In uptown New York flourishes the wealthiest Negro Colony in the world There are those among them who count their possessions in six figures This Colony is usually spoken of as Harlem It extends roughly from 131st street to 144th Street and from Seventh Avenue to the Harlem River But this boundary is constantly changing for the Colony is constantly growing

Within this area is to be found every thing that is needed for the comfort, convenience and pleasure of an intelligent people There are apartment houses churches institutions shops restaurants, clubs theatres and dance halls The homes are varied Some are modest and well appointed some apartments rent from $20 to $60 a month and some of the people live in their own handsome residences Several of the apartment houses are luxurious There are rich rugs marble statuary valuable paintings in the corridors Liveried servants sometimes foreign born whites are to be seen in some of the more pretentious homes

In some of the restaurants the food served compares with the best served on Broadway In fact all the necessary things for comfortable living are to be had right in the community There are all sorts of business enterprises that are flourishing Many of these are incorporated and well capitalized The professions are also well represented there being many physicians dentists, lawyers and publishers Three newspapers are supported also in this Colony

Social life in the Colony finds expression in Church festivals and clubs Among the principal clubs are the New York Colored Men's Association the United Civic League and the Pullman Porter's Club Here in this section the Colored people of New York have built for themselves a little world where they can develop along all lines They have their own moving picture shows theatres, places of amusements of all kinds Their churches are up-to-date and form social centers, giving to their members all kinds of recreations They run their own businesses They own automobiles and all sorts of luxuries

The famous fifteenth regiment was the first in the State of New York to receive its full quota They are all justly proud of this fact Indeed they are very proud of the record of the regiment and of its leader—Major Tandy With this justly famous regiment is the European Band This band is winning distinction for its music in France It was two men from this regiment—Robinson and Johnson—who were decorated for bringing in a number of German prisoners Harlem should, with all colored America be proud of her soldiers

The Republic of Liberia

LIBERIA COURT OF ARMS

IBERIA is situated on the west coast of Africa between Sierra Leone and the Ivory Coast. The Republic has a coast line stretching along the Atlantic for about 350 miles Northwest to Southeast.

Three promonitories, Cape Mount, Cape Mesurado and Bafu Point are the only actual interruptions of a monotonous coast line. There are no good harbors. Ships regularly anchor at a considerable distance from the shore and load and unload by means of small boats sent from the towns.

Its area is approximately 43,000 square miles—a little larger than the State of Idaho. Only the coast strip with an average width of seven miles is under development and a strip of not over 40 miles is under administration and this line is constantly being contended by hostile natives. Be it said to the credit of the D. E. Howard administration's positive dealings with these hostile .tribes in 1917, persons might walk from Monrovia to Cape Palmas without being attacked for the first time since the foundation of the Republic. Five sixths of the total area of the Republic is covered with dense tropical forests. The highest lands are found in the eastern half of the country. With the exception of the coast lands all the interior is

elevated and rolling, in some places there are large plateau regions covered with tall grass and few trees.

Liberia is exceptionally well watered. Some thirty-five rivers furrow its bosom supplying moisture for plant life, and furnishing fish and means of travel. Few of them are navigable to any distance. The St. Paul can be ascended only to a distance of 25 miles; the Dukvia only 30 miles and the Cavalla only 80 miles.

Brilliantly plumed birds flit through the tropical forests and flowers in rich profusion bloom everywhere.

Mahogany, ebony and other valuable trees are found in large quantities and rubber producing trees and plants abound. Fruit trees which bear almost perennially bend beneath the weight of luscious tropical fruit.

CLIMATE

Throughout Liberia the climate is salubrions. There are two rainy seasons—one in June and July, the other in October and November. There is a marked difference between the climate of the forest region and that of the Mandingo Plateau. In the forest region, the dry season is short, it is the hottest period of the year and includes the months of December and January. The temperature ranges from 55 degrees at night to 100 degrees in the shade at mid-day. During the wet season the constant temperature stands at about 75 degrees. The coolest month of the year is August with a day temperature of 69 degrees and a night temperature of 65 degrees. On the Mandingo Plateau the dry season extends from November to May. The hottest time of the year is at the beginning and end of the rainy season when the thermometer may mark more than one hundred degrees at mid-day.

HISTORICAL

The Republic of Liberia owes its origin to the efforts of the National Colonization Society of America, organized in 1816 for the purpose of colonizing in Africa the free colored people of the United States. Several attempts were made at colonization but nothing was permanent until 1821 when a treaty was concluded by Lieut. Stockton with certain native princes by which a tract of land suitable for the purpose was acquired about Cape Montserrado. Liberia existed as a colony till July 26, 1847, when the Declaration of Independence was signed.

THE FLAG, ETC.

The flag consists of eleven stripes alternately red and white; the field, blue bears a single star

POLITICAL

The Constitution of Liberia is framed after that of the United States. Executive authority is vested in a President and Vice-President elected for four years and a council of six members. Legislative power rests with a Congress of two houses known as the Senate consisting of eight members and the House of Representatives with fourteen members. Voters must be of Negro blood and own Real Estate. Natives have not yet availed themselves generally of the suffrage. No foreigner can own real estate without the consent of the government.

The President, Vice-President and Congressmen are elected, all other officers of state are appointed by the President subject to the approval of the Senate.

There are also Quarterly Probate and Justice courts for each of the countries and territories. Monrovia recently abolished the Justices of the Peace and established a Municipal Court with a special judge whose tenure of office is during good behavior.

The actual Military forces consist of militia volunteers and police. All able-bodied men between the ages of 16 and 50 are liable for military service.

POPULATION AND SETTLEMENT

Liberia has a population of two and one-half millions and more than two millions are aborigines. The rest are Americo-Liberians. The truly native population consists of many different tribes each with its own language, territory, government and life. Most of the native tribes are pagan. In the western half of Liberia, however Mohammedanism has taken hold of the great tribes of Mandingo and Vai. Among all these natives tribal organization and government remain in full force although most of them recognize the sovereignty of the Republic native dress art and industries remain, among the pagan tribes poligamy is common domestic slavery still exists witchcraft is recognized and the ancient ordeals are practiced. Most of the Americo-Liberian settlements are on the coast although there are a number along the St Paul River and a few along other rivers. The Republic is divided into four counties viz Montserrado Grand Bassa Sinoe and Maryland. There are four cities in the Republic, with Mayor and common council viz Monrovia, Grand Bassa Edina and Harper. These cities, with Marina, Nifu Sarstown and Fishtown are the only ports open to foreign trade.

Monrovia the capital city is the best representative of the development. It is a city consisting of about 7000 inhabitants. It is sharply divided into two divisions a civilized quarter upon the summit of a ridge some 200 feet in height here live the Americo-Liberians and the European residents.

While nearly all around the city are the village and native towns composed of members of various tribes from all parts of the republic. To illustrate this I have found the name of Jesus given in 14 dialects in a group of about 200 persons.

The Liberians are a sociable people. They love to gather on almost any occasion. There are practically no places of public amusement. In 1831 there was a public library with 1200 volumes in the city of Monrovia, today there is no public library or reading room in the capital city. The number of secret organizations is very large. Literary societies and lyceums are from time to time organized. There is one at Cape Palmas which has had a continued existence for many years. A respectable Bar Association has been in existence for several years has annual meetings and prints its proceedings.

A considerable number of men write remarkably well. The public documents of the Republic have always been well worded and forceful.

The message of successive presidents to the legislature have shown extraordinary ability. In deliberation they show judgment and in diplomatic procedure extraordinary skill.

RESOURCES

Liberia is rich in material resources. Perhaps in all the world there can not be found a more fertile soil and a more productive country. Cotton grows plentifully and sugar cane flourishes also rice coffee edible roots, and oil palms may be found in the clearings. Bananas and plantains grow in rich profusion. Salt is common in some places and 'salt sticks' form a desirable article of trade. For the present and for sometime to come the country must necessarily depend upon its trade in raw products. Wealth must come from palm nuts and oil passava rubber and the like. In such products the Republic has enormous wealth none of which has been developed save to a very limited extent.

RELIGION

The Liberians are said to be very religious. The Bible is read in many homes with a devotion which people in better favored lands might emulate. Sunday is a day of rest and religious duty and woe to him who desecrates it. Most of the leading denominations are found there either as an independent church or as Missions.

EDUCATION

Education is not neglected in Liberia although it has always been difficult to raise money to conduct Schools. The Superintendent of Public Instruction is a Cabinet Officer. In 1912 there were ninety-one Schools under his direction.

Liberia College is fifty years old and many men prominent in Liberian affairs received their education here. There are many Mission schools also which are doing high grade, useful work.

Colored Theatricals

By Lester A. Walton, of the New York Age,
New York City.

OLORED theatricals are on the boom. When announcement was made by the daily and colored press in June of this year (1919) that a circuit of first class colored theatres had been formed and the merger was generally regarded as the most far reaching step ever taken in the history of the stage in which Negroes prominently figured, both colored and white people evinced more than ordinary concern in this piece of information.

Since the publication of the first statement about the colored circuit white publications have vied with colored papers and magazines in telling of the big project in which thousands of dollars are involved—of the systematic movement launched by colored promoters to create a more agreeable condition throughout the United States for the colored theatregoer and also open up opportunities for the colored performer.

The first significant move to establish a chain of colored houses taking in the principal cities of the North and South, was made in the early part of June, when a syndicate headed by E. C. Brown, the colored banker, of Philadelphia and Norfolk, took over the lease of the Lafayette Theater, at 131st Street and Seventh Avenue, New York, and assumed all outstanding contracts which the Quality Amusement Company had with the Lafayette Players. The Lafayette Theatre is the best known colored theatre in America, and the Lafayette Players is the best known dramatic organization among colored people in the country.

The next important house is the Dunbar Theatre of Philadelphia, just completed, which has a seating capacity of 1600 and is situated at Broad and Lombard Streets, only two blocks from the Shubert Theatre. This large and modern structure was built by a company headed by E. C. Brown, president; Lester A. Walton, vice president; Andrew F. Stevens, secretary and treasurer. The ground, building and equipment cost $375,000.

The Howard Theatre, Washington, D. C., the Avenue Theatre, Chicago, and the Lyceum Theatre, Cincinnati, were the other houses originally included in the chain, but the numerical strength of the circuit has been greatly increased since June. The Pershing Theatre, controlled and managed by Negroes, has been taken in, as well as theatres in Richmond, Norfolk, Savannah and New Orleans. Before the year it is expected that St. Louis, Louisville, Detroit, Cleveland, Baltimore, Memphis, Birmingham and Nashville, will be represented.

In organizing a chain of first class theatres the promoters had in mind the bettering of conditions for colored amusement-lovers, especially in the South. The existence of what are known as "colored" theatres in such cities as New York, Philadelphia, Chicago and Detroit are due to the presence of thousands of Negroes residing in a district and such houses are the natural product of a community as a Jewish theatre in a Jewish community or a German theatre in a German community. Colored people in these cities also attend houses under white management.

The reason for opening colored theatres in the Southland is vastly different. In this section of the country there are many cities where the Negro is not wanted at all as a patron, and when he is admitted it usually is in the gallery and then he is set off to himself. There are thousands of self-respecting colored people who do not take kindly to this policy and, therefore, religiously remain away from the white theatres. They also refuse to patronize colored theatres where the performer is permitted to say and do what he pleases and the management is lax and general conditions extremely objectionable.

With theatres built in the South for colored people where an effort will be made to afford clean, wholesome entertainment, and race standards will be put on a higher plane, the colored person with high ideals will be given an opportunity to secure up-to-date amusements and at the same time support meritorious race enterprises.

The theatres on the circuit will be provided with attractions by the Quality Amusement Corporation of New York, of which E. C. Brown and Andrew F. Stevens are controlling factors, and Lester A. Walton is general manager. A school of dramatic art has been opened for young colored men and women who give indication of possessing histrionic ability, and they will be brought to New York from all sections.

Various companies—dramatic and musical—are being organized by Quality Amusement Company and the dramatic directors employed are the best that can be secured in New York.

With the enforced withdrawal from the scene of action of the William & Walker, Cole & Johnson and Ernest Hogan companies some ten years ago, colored theatricals have been at a low ebb. These companies played in cities throughout the North and West, appearing in theatres owned and controlled by white managers. The advent of the movies, which turned many of such theatres into moving picture houses, was largely responsible for the disappearance of the big colored musical show on the road.

Colored theatricals are now being revived along practical and sane lines. Instead of depending on others, the Negro is taking the initiative and exploiting among his own people a field hitherto untouched, one pregnant with wonderful possibilities. He is, therefore, making opportunities for himself and race—which is one of the most constructive pieces of work the colored American has undertaken during this great era of rehabilitation.

Reminiscences of Slavery Days

By J. W. Beverly, Principal State Normal School,
Montgomery Ala

Slavery was introduced into English colonies by way of the colony of Virginia in 1619. However, the first landing of slaves in what is now the United States was in Florida in 1565.

As early as 1637 some Pequod Indians were exchanged for Negroes from the Bermudas. It is worth while to note that the Indians were exchanged because they would not obey their masters.

Note—the Negro, as a class, had always been obedient to authority. Of course there have been and will always be cases of disloyalty, but the Negro as a class is loyal even when he is mistreated. A mere declaration of this sort would amount to but little, but all history will bear out this statement.

In some cases in the New England colonies, there is record of the fact that when slaves were no longer serviceable to their masters by reason of having spent their energies, they manumitted them to live on charity or do otherwise. But in 1702 in Connecticut, a law was soon passed compelling the former owners to care for these manumitted and worn out slaves.

Washington and Jefferson were both opposed to buying or selling Negroes off the plantations to which they belonged. Washington manumitted his slaves in his last will. Thomas Jefferson never favored slavery, and Benjamin Franklin was opposed to the traffice in human beings.

Patrick Henry said of the overseer of his time, "They are the most abject, and unprincipled race." The above statement is quoted to show that most of the oppression and cruelty practiced against Negroes came not from the hand of the master, but from that of the overseer.

Sometimes, yes often times, cruel and oppressive Negroes were used as slave drivers. These Negro drivers were most crude in many instances.

History fails to produce a parallel case to that of the fidelity of the Negro towards his master in the time of the Civil War.

While the best blood of the South was at the front fighting to retain slavery, the Negro, the bone of contention was at home and was tilling the fields and caring for the family left behind.

The leading white men and the public press have ever since that day declared that this act of fidelity on the part of the Negro is deserving to be celebrated in song, and to be recorded on the pages of history. They have declared that the Negro fidelity in these trying times has endeared the race to the entire white South.

Almost any other race on the face of the globe with conditions so favorable for revolt and destruction, would have used the opportunity.

Many colored men went to the war to act as body guards to their masters and when the master was cut down the Negro body guard with loving hands would remove the body and accompany it home to be laid away in the home cemetery. And well does the writer know of instances, where the faithful Negro slave would turn over the body of his dead master and search it for valuable belongings such as a gold watch a fine ring and would report these things to the white folks at home. And many a time the family would say to the faithful slave "you may have the watch or what not."

In this world, and as we colored people are wont to stay "in this cold and unfriendly world" there is no abiding place, no continuing city unless it be in the loving remembrance of good deeds done which will enshrine us in the heart and affection of mankind.

The late Booker T. Washington used to say that, every Negro had his white man that he could go to in times of need and that every white man had his Negro friend that he could trust in the dark house of this unfriendly world.

And there is much in this—inter-dependence the white needing the Negroes, and the Negroes needing the whites. What do the Scriptures say about this? The members of the body can not say the one to the other 'I have no need of thee. Can the eye say to the hand I have no need of thee?"

That many masters were cruel to their slaves no one will deny but the main source of cruelty was not the master, but usually the overseer, or Negro driver. He had no interest in the slave, and so had no care for him.

There were many free Negroes even in the slave states. The free Negro in a slave state had to be under the protection of some white man, who represented him in some legal phases. Some masters manumitted their slaves. George Washington the father of his country it is said manumitted his slaves. Many masters allowed certain skilled mechanics of their slaves to hire themselves out for a certain wage by the year a portion of the wage to go to the slave and a portion to the master in the way of purchase of the slave by his own labor.

The writer's own great grandfather a good doctor purchased himself from his master.

Thousands of the best blood of the South will forever bless the memory of the Negro race for the many kind and nice attentions given by the "Black Mammy" and the attachment between the white children and the "Black Mammy" have come down from the days of slavery with endearing sentiment to many distinguished white men of the South.

Many a "Black Mammy" has been cared for while living, and peacefully laid away after death by the loving hands of white men whose parents used to own them.

And these "Mammies" in the days of slavery were the real rulers of the household. What they demanded for the children of the family usually was granted even in opposition to the mistress' wishes. The "Mammy" had her way in most matters that concerned the whims or welfare of the children, and to her would the children look for refuge even to the restraining of the rod corrections in conduct.

TOP VIEW—Raw recruits arriving at cantonment, Copyright Underwood and Underwood.
CENTER VIEW—325th Field Signal Battalion co'ored troops, boarding boat for Camp Merritt. Copyright Western Newspaper Union.
BOTTOM VIEW—Temporary resting place between Pont a Maisson and Metz, of Heroes of the 92nd division who made the "Supreme Sacrifice." U. S. Official.

The Negro in the World War

By EMMETT J. SCOTT, Secretary-Treasurer of Howard University, Washington, D. C.

Prepared for this publication in October, 1918—thirty days before signing of Armistice

EMMETT J. SCOTT, Special Assistant to the Secretary of War, who prepared the article which follows, is by virtue of his commanding position and closeness of view to the incidents and circumstances which are shown herein, most happily situated to give authentic testimony concerning "THE NEGRO'S PART IN WINNING THE WAR."

The office of Special Assistant to the Secretary of War was created because of the recognized importance and weight of the Negro in the National equation, and because of the broad-minded opinion of the Hon. Newton D. Baker, Secretary of War, that the problems growing out of the relations of the 12,000,000 colored people of the country in a period of war, with new conditions and new demands to be met and adjusted, were of sufficient importance to justify the establishment of a special bureau to deal exclusively with their affairs. Seeking the best fitted man of the race in America to handle the delicate and far-reaching questions that must necessarily arise in a crisis that touches the fundamental principles of Government, Secretary Baker placed at his right hand to advise him with reference to the Negro millions, a man, who needed no introduction to the American people of any race and whose selection was at once acclaimed by all as the very best that could have been made.

For eighteen years Mr. Scott was the Secretary and confidential advisor of the late Booker T. Washington, and he has had intimate contact with the most influential forces of the nation, white and black. The wide experience thus gained and valuable acquaintanceships formed, coupled with native zeal, wisdom and industry render him an ideal man for this post of exacting responsibility.

That the office, with its increasing volume of intricate questions and broadening scope of activities, is giving excellent service, is convincingly attested by the laudatory comments at the hands of the United press of the country, and the warm personal congratulations received by Mr. Scott by telegram, letter and "word of mouth" every day in the year, as well as by the grateful acknowledgments of hundreds of persons in all sections of the land, who have been faithfully and efficiently served through the official channels covered by this Bureau. It is a veritable "clearing house" for Negro problems military and civil, emphasized by reason of the war and it is universally admitted that the condition of the race has been improved beyond measure since the establishment of this direct point of contact between the Negro and the high officials of the War Department. Mr. Scott has justly earned the commendation of the entire nation by his comprehensive grasp of the vital issues of the day and wrought out concrete results through his courageous mastery of them in conference, on the platform, and through the public prints.

Secretary Baker is a true friend of the Negro people—not as Negroes per se, but as human beings and citizens of the Republic. He is a genuine 100 per cent American and a democrat—in the strictest interpretation of those lofty terms—and has indicated in a thousand forceful ways that race prejudice has no place in his personal make-up, and he has made it plain that he would brook no color discrimination or the practice of narrow-gauged methods in the administration of his official duties. His high regard for the welfare of the 12,000,000 colored Americans has been demonstrated in a most practical fashion by his organization of the Bureau for the consideration of affairs directly affecting this loyal and productive group of citizens which, under the sympathetic and painstaking supervision of Mr. Scott, has proven its worth to the nation and to all concerned.—(Editor.)

The NEGRO in the present war for LIBERTY AND WORLD-WIDE DEMOCRACY is proving to be a notable and inspiring figure. The Colored American in common with his brother in White realizes more and more that this is THE PEOPLE'S WAR, and it is his determination to remain in the fight to the finish. He is cheerfully laying upon the altar of his country's honor every ounce of his manhood strength, his individual influence and the limit of his means to bring VICTORY to the only flag he claims as his own. The Negro is 100 per cent American and rightly regards it as his FIRST DUTY to utilize every resource at his command to aid the nation to win its battle for civilization and justice in this hour of humanity's peril.

THE NEGRO'S "MAN-POWER" IN THE PRESENT CONFLICT

The Negro now (October, 1918) has in the military establishment of the nation nearly 400,000 men. He entered the war with four regiments to his credit—the 9th and 10th Cavalry and the 24th and 25th Infantry of the Regular U. S. Army—these regiments embracing about 10,000 men. In the National Guard as it was formerly known—

TOP VIEW—Negro soldiers arriving at a typical French village.
UPPER CENTER VIEW—Colored Soldiers advancing along a camouflaged road in France.
LOWER CENTER VIEW—Gas mask drill in France.
BOTTOM VIEW—Narrow gauged railroad used in trench warfare on French battlefields.
U. S. Official.

made up of units from several states, such as the 8th Illinois, the 15th New York, the First Separate Battalion of the District of Columbia, the First Separate Company of Maryland, a company from Massachusetts and one from Connecticut, the 9th Ohio, etc., the race also had about 10,000 men. A large number of these forces came through voluntary enlistments and their work on the field and in camp has been of the highest possible order.

To this call to the colors the Negro responded with a cheerfulness that made the world stare in wonderment. It is worthy of note that in the first draft in June, 1917, there were 737,628 colored registrants, or nearly 8 per cent of the total registration of the country which was 9,586,508. Of the first group of 208,953 colored registrants examined under call of November 12, 1917, 36.23 per cent of them were accepted for service. Out of 2,873,996 white men examined at approximately the same time, 24.75 per cent of them were accepted. In groups representing nearly an identical proportion it will be noted that in relative military fitness the Negro race outranked other races by about 12 per cent. It is also a matter of pride with the Negro to note that the percentage of colored men claiming exemption from military service is much lower than that of other groups. Many thousands of colored men are on duty overseas.

NEGRO REPRESENTED IN NEARLY EVERY BRANCH OF SERVICE

The Negro is represented in practically every branch of the military service—including Infantry, Cavalry, Engineers, Field and Coast Artillery Signal Corps (radio, or wireless, telegraphers, etc.), Medical Corps, Hospital and Ambulance Corps, Aviation Corps, (ground section) Veterinary Corps and in the noncombatant forces which embrace, among other organizations, the Stevedore Regiments, Service of Labor Battalions, Depot Brigades. These latter render valuable service behind the lines and are indispensable to the well-being of the troops on the firing lines. Many Negroes are employed as chemists, draftsmen surveyors etc. A premium is placed on men who are skilled in the technical and mechanical pursuits, such as electricians, auto-repairers, wheelwrights, blacksmiths carpenters etc.

The colored combat troops overseas are now comprised in the 92nd and 93rd divisions, commanded respectively, at the time of their assignment, by Major-General C. C. Ballou and Brigadier-General Roy C. Hoffman.

MORE THAN 1,000 NEGRO OFFICERS NOW UNDER COMMISSION

The Negro now has passed far beyond the 1,000 mark in the matter of commissioned officers, the number being now fully 1,200. There were few

in the original Regular Army. The highest in rank was Charles Young, of Ohio who, prior to his retirement from active service, had risen to the rank of Colonel in the 10th Cavalry, and had served with distinction in the Indian fights on the American border, in the Spanish-American War, in the Philippines and Mexico, and had won honors as the formative genius in the Government Constabulary and as United States Military Attache in Haiti. He is a graduate of West Point Military Academy. The highest active officer of the race now in the Army is Lieut-Col Benjamin Oliver Davis, of the 9th Cavalry, a native of Washington, a product of her public school system, who entered the service at the outbreak of the Spanish-American War as a private in a volunteer regiment. He rose to his present station by merit. He has been military instructor at Wilberforce University United States Military Attache and head of the Constabulary in Liberia and is now stationed with his regiment in the Philippines. Walter H. Loving, also a Washingtonian developed the famous Philippine Constabulary Band and is now a Major on the retired list, but engaged in a special work for the Government in the present conflict.

In the National Guard, several colored men well versed in military tactics and with fine capacity for organization have held ranks as Colonels, Majors, and officers of subordinate grade and have given an excellent account of themselves in preserving order in their respective States and have assisted the Federal Government in instances of national emergency.

CAPABLE YOUNG OFFICERS FROM THE NEW TRAINING CAMPS

The present war has brought to the front a splendid array of talented and capable young men who have won commissions as officers in the new training camps that have been formed for the purpose of supplying leaders for the new United States Army. Out of the Reserve Officers' Training Camp at Fort Des Moines, came 639 colored officers, commissioned as captains and first and second Lieutenants, after a course of intensive training covering four months, concluding in October, 1917. Many of these commanders were college men, hailing from such standard institutions of learning as Harvard, Yale, Columbia, University of Pennsylvania, Amhurst, University of Chicago, Howard, Fisk, Wilberforce and Lincoln University. In the field service these officers, for the most part, have "made good," and are in command of troops of the race at a number of camps on this side and across the sea. They have stood up bravely through their "baptism of fire," and in cases now almost numerous, they have won the French Croix De Guerre and were conspicuous in the terrific en-

TOP VIEW—The men and officers of the 369th Infantry were decorated at the Stadium of City College by General Collerdet of the French Army and Colonel Hayward of the 369th Infantry who is in command of the unit. The view shows the officers at attention during the playing of the Marsellaise. Copyright Underwood & Underwood. N. Y.

BOTTOM VIEW—Decks of the "France" loaded with New York's Colored Troops. The "France" brought back New York's famous colored regiment the 389th Infantry, better known as the old 15th. These men covered themselves with glory, were the first American soldiers to reach the Rhine, never had one of their men captured by the Hun and received the Croix De Guerre for their bravery in action. Copyright Western Newspaper Union.

gagement which led to a whole regiment of Negroes being cited for valorous conduct, and the report of the same to the War Department at home by General Pershing, the intrepid and square-dealing Commander-in-Chief of the American Expeditionary Forces in France

Speaking of the Colored troops in general, a military expert has said "They are notably steady under fire patient to endure hardships and cheerful and good-natured at all times—and 'THEY CAN FIGHT'" In addition to the officers already mentioned shortly after the Fort Des Moines group there were graduated at training camps 114 officers in Infantry 11 in Cavalry and 35 in Field Artillery At the close of the series ended August 31 33 colored men were commissioned as Lieutenants of Field Artillery at Camp Taylor Louisville Ky and 107 were graduated and commissioned as Lieutenants of Infantry at Camp Pike Little Rock Ark They will be given desirable assignments with troops of the race With the output of Fort Des Moines this brings the total of officers from the training camps alone up to 941 Those commissioned in the Medical Reserve Corps number about 250 about 100 of these are still on the inactive list The hope is expressed that as the numbers of colored men brought into the army through the selective draft are increased many colored officers of the Medical and Dental Reserve Corps will be needed and will therefore be given their place in active service

Three regiments of Field Artillery were formed, made up of colored troops and the doors were thrown open for colored officers A goodly number of colored officers qualified for the work and at Camp Meade and other points where instructions was given it is said by competent judges that the young men detailed for this training showed marked adaptability for the intricate problems involved and their college equipment stood them in timely stead The Field Artillery Regiments referred to are the 349th 350th, and 351st, and they were stationed in the East, prior to their departure for France The reports from the Officers' Training Schools at Camp Taylor and Camp Pike are of a flattering character and the personal conduct of the young men was highly praised by the commandant in charge and the people of the adjacent cities welcomed their visits when they were on furlough

At the Field Artillery School at Camp Taylor Louisville Ky which closed August 31, 1918, there was a total enrollment of 2,500 candidates In the list of graduates, thirty-three were colored The official report shows that out of the first fifteen graduates five (or one-third) were colored whose respective ratings ran from fourth, with a percentage of 82 44, to fifteenth with a rating of 81 11

merely a difference of one and one-third per cent between the standing of the candidate who stood fourth and the one who stood fifteenth

FORTY-SEVEN COLORED CHAPLAINS IN THE ARMY

There are now forty-seven colored Chaplains in the several branches of the Army They are without exception a fine body of men—"sturdy, upstanding, red-blooded men"—such as the regulations call for, and they have been specially selected because of their knowledge of the weakness and the strength of mankind and are thus particularly well-fitted for the work of giving wise counsel under trying circumstances and getting the best out of the thousand-and-one types that are necessarily thrown together in army life Before they are designated for the training school for Chaplains for the five-weeks' course prescribed, candidates are passed upon by the General War-Time Commission on Churches, the Federal Council of Churches and by the chief officials of their own denomination and they are compelled as has been intimated to meet the requirements of a most rigid educational physical and moral standard An effort is made to select Chaplains as far as possible, who represent the faiths to which the soldiers belong in the largest numbers with a fair division among the several denominations

Chaplains are appointed after the five-weeks' training for war work and are commissioned as First Lieutenants receiving $2 000 per annum in this country and $2,200 abroad and they are promoted by seniority to the highest grade attainable before retirement for age

SPECIAL TRAINING IN TECHNICAL AND MECHANICAL BRANCHES

A very recent achievement and one to which the race points with pardonable satisfaction is the provision by the Government for special training of the young colored men in technical and mechanical work which will add to their efficiency as a factor in the Army, enlarging their opportunities for usefulness and for preferment, and rendering them more capable of earning a livelihood for themselves at the close of the war Since May, 1918 fifteen of the leading educational institutions of the land have been carrying on this training and not less than 3 000 Colored men have finished courses in such essential subjects as electricity radio (or wireless telegraphy) bench wood-working, chauffeur, auto-mechanics, concrete working, blacksmithing wheelwrighting, army truck driving, carpentry, cobbling horse-shoeing pipe-fitting and general mechanics

Of the total graduating up to September 15 1 140 came out of Tuskegee Institute 600 from Howard University 250 from Hampton 270 from

TOP VIEW (Left to Right)—Capt. Stewart Alexander, Lieut. Frank Robinson of New York's colored regiment who won the Croix De Guerre for conspicuous bravery. This regiment has the honor of being the first American Unit to reach the Rhine. Copyright Western Newspaper Union.

CENTER VIEW—Heroes of old 15th Infantry, New York City all received the Croix De Guerre from the French Government. Front (left to right) Privates "Eagle Eye" Ed. Williams, "Lamplight," Herbert Taylor, Leon Traitor, "Kid Hawk," Ralph Hawkins (back row) Private H. D. Prunes, Sgt. D. Stormes, Private "Kid" Woney, Joe Williams, Arthur Menly, Corporal Taylor. Copyright western Newspaper Union.

BOTTOM VIEW The men of a colored unit receiving the D. S. C. at Finistere, France. Major General Eli Helmick is decorating the men. Admiral Moreau of the French Navy just behind the general. Copyright Underwood & Underwood, N. Y.

the Greensboro, (N C) Agricultural and Technical College and varying numbers from all the rest of the fifteen So successful was the experiment, that the War Department Committee on Education and Special Training which is in control of this phase of the work, has decided to continue the work and training in technical and mechanical branches will be given in fourteen of the principle colored schools where Vocational Training Detachments are being formed under the instruction and command of carefully selected army officers

During the month of August and into September at Howard University, a special school for student-instructors was carried on under the direction of Lieut Russell Smith formerly of the 10th Cavalry a graduate of the Fort Des Moines Officers' Reserve Training Camp and a disciplinarian and military tactician of the First rank This school comprised 450 students and members of faculties sent from the various schools and colleges of the race who, after receiving the prescribed forty-seven days of intensive training in military science and tactics at Howard have returned to their respective institutions to instruct others in the courses which they have just finished From this school 320 went out September 15th 1918 fully equipped for the work of instructing the units of the Student's Army Training Corps established in their several institutions

Provision has been made by the Special Committee on Education and Special Training for the instruction of this year and the next, of fully 20 000 colored men in technical and mechanical branches in conjunction with their military training The effect of this training and discipline undoubtedly holds untold benefits for the race for all the future

The executive Secretary of the Committee on Education and Special Training is Dr R B Perry of Harvard University, one of the ablest, broadest-visioned and most resourceful educators in this country He is not only concerned about doing that which will enable the American Negro to lend himself most effectively toward winning the war but he is desirous at the same time to do for this struggling race, a service that will best aid the Negro to win a better position in life for himself

THE STUDENT'S ARMY TRAINING CORPS

Following closely upon the heels of the Special Vocational Training Detachments for the fourteen technical and mechanical schools, comes a provision by which young colored men of eighteen and over, who desire to secure a college education, may carry on a thorough course in military science and tactics while engaged in their academic studies at any college on the list of institutions with which the Government has entered into a contract The

young men of college standard who have registered with their local boards and who wish to be inducted into the military service after matriculating subject to the regulations of the college chosen, constitute a new division of the constructive work planned by the Committee on Education and Special Training, and this is styled "The Students' Army Training Corps,' designed to fit young men for the Army while permitting them to continue their higher education And all this is at the expense of the Government, which obligates itself to pay for the subsistence housing uniform tuition and equipment and allow the student-soldier $30.00 per month besides Graded by proficiency indicated the student may later be assigned to military duty, either by transfer to an officers' training camp or to a non-commissioned officers' training school or to a vocational training school, or he may be transferred to a cantonment for duty as a private Or if it is deemed best he may be directed to continue his scientific studies in the school where he is enrolled Under this admirable Student Army Training Corps system these young men will have the advantage of a skillful preparation in war work before entering upon their duties in the field, and will not be losing precious moments from their mental advancement

Eleven schools forming nine units, have been selected for the Collegiate Section of the Student Army Training Corps, as follows

Howard University Washington, D C
Lincoln University Chester County Penn
Fisk University, Nashville, Tenn
Meharry Medical School Nashville, Tenn
Atlanta University and Morehouse College, (combined) Atlanta, Ga
Wiley University and Bishop College (combined) Marshall, Texas
Talladega College Talladega, Alabama
Virginia Union University, Richmond Virginia
Wilberforce University Wilberforce Ohio

SCHOOLS IN WHICH VOCATIONAL DETACHMENTS HAVE BEEN ESTABLISHED

The institutions in which the Vocational Training Detachments of the S A T C have been established are

Tuskegee Institute, Tuskegee Institute, Alabama
Hampton Institute, Hampton Va
Howard University, Washington, D C
Atlanta University Atlanta, Ga
Georgia State A and M College, Savannah, Ga
North Carolina A and F College, Greensboro.
South Carolina A and M College Orangeburg
Prairie View N and I College, Prairie View, Texas
Lincoln University, Chester County, Penn

TOP VIEW (Left)—Lieut. Thos. A. Painter, of the 370th (Chicago) Infantry, decorated for conspicuous bravery in action, who arrived with his regiment on the transport "France," February 10th, 1919. Copyright Underwood & Underwood, N. Y.

TOP VIEW (Right)—Lieut. Robert Campbell, of Company I, 368th U. S. Infantry, hero of the battle of Argonne Forest. The first man in the 92nd Division to receive the Distinguished Service Cross for bravery. Copyright Western Newspaper Union.

BOTTOM VIEW—Famous Jazz Band Leader back with colored 15th. Lieut. Europe, (deceased) who for years has been N. Y. society's favorite orchestra (dance) leader, and who was formerly with Mr. Vernon Castle, returned Feb. 12th with his regiment, the 369th, (Colored 15th). He is above shown with his band. Copyright Underwood and Underwood, N. Y.

West Virginia Collegiate Institute, Institute W
Va

Wilberforce University, Wilberforce, Ohio
Alabama A and M College Normal Ala
Tennessee A and M College, Nashville, Tenn
Louisiana A and M College Baton Rouge, La

WAR WORK OF THE COLORED Y M C A

Vigorously supplementing the religious labors of
the forty-one Chaplains in the United States Army
fully 200 earnest colored men are engaged in Y M
C A work in the various camps and cantonments
where colored men are stationed Some of them
are also in France with the troops under General
Pershing carrying the cheering message of the
"Red Triangle" These helpful agents of the Master not only assist in lifting up the moral nature of
the men with whom they are brought into daily
contact but they are working out systems of instruction whereby the deplorable illiteracy so prevalent in certain quarters may be reduced to a minimum and the mental attitude of indifferent soldiers
changed to one of enthusiasm and aspiration The
Y M C A "huts" are serving as the social centers
of the camps where conveniences for writing and
reading and conversation are made available and a
home atmosphere is generated "Hostess Houses"
in a constantly increasing number are being established at the camps with high-purposed women in
charge and additions to the present list will be
made as rapidly as funds and competent workers
can be provided for the same These "Hostess
Houses" throw around female visitors a chaperon-
age that is essential to the well-being of the camp
and remedy many evils long complained of There
is an insistent and very proper call from every
Camp for Hostess or Community Houses to improve social conditions Back of the movement
will be the Y M C A Secretary, who is not infre-
quently the real "drive-wheel" of the camp when
any ingredients for comfort are to be secured for
the "boys" On the staff of Dr J E Moorland
International Secretary of the Y M C A in
charge of war work of the "Y" among colored
people are forty-seven executive secretaries embracing some of the race's foremost men and they
are getting results They with their army of assistants cover a wide range of territory serving
not only in the army camps but have extensions
ramifying into the government training schools
into centers where colored men are employed in
large numbers on industrial work, shipyards munitions plants, nitrate works, lumber sections and
the like The scope of the Y M C A's labors is
growing day by day, and its sweetening influence
is manifesting itself perceptibly in every direction
If some service is wanted by a visitor at a camp
the first man to whom he should turn is the Y M
C A Secretary

WORK OF COMMISSION ON TRAINING CAMP ACTIVITIES

To make a soldier "fit to fight," is is the belief
of the War Department that his mind should be
freed from "dull care" and during the time he is
released from the routine duties of the day Men
and women consecrated to the upbuilding of the
morale of the nation's valiant defenders, are engaged in the service of providing amusement and
recreation for the men in the various camps This
branch of work is under the control of the War Department Commission on Training Camp Activities, of which Dr Raymond B Fosdick is Director
It co-ordinates the work for the soldier planned by
all of the welfare institutions like the Y M C A,
the Y W C A the Knights of Columbus the
Jewish Welfare League, etc . organizes the singing
units of the camps directs the operations of the
theaters and furnishes the talent for the vaudeville, athletic, dramatic and other amusements and
recreations At many of the camps there has been
established a "Liberty Theater" as a center of recreational diversions and where the men assemble
to enjoy the various dramatic musical and athletic
programs and view educational moving pictures
Lester A Walton of the New York Age New
York City, is the colored representative on the
Commission having in charge these theatrical attractions Camp songs, plantation melodies, folk-
songs and "spirituals" have proven popular and the
men are receiving instruction in this type of singing by skilled directors, of whom Mr J E Blanton
is one of the best-known Some keen-witted observer has said "You cannot defeat a singing nation" and he had made the War Department believe it—and the colored boys are "some singers"

An important and far-reaching phase of the
work of the Commission on Training Camp Activities is the educational propaganda to combat the
spread of venereal diseases among the colored men
handling this campaign in conjunction with the office of the Surgeon-General of the Army under
the immediate supervision of Capt Arthur B
Springarn who is manifesting in many practical
ways his deep interest in the moral and physical
well-being of the colored wing of the service Moving pictures of the type of "Fit to Fight" are being shown to emphasize the dangers that come
through the "social evil" and a course of instructive lectures has been arranged with that eminent
specialist Dr C V Roman, of Nashville Tenn
as a major campaigner, assisted by a group of experienced physicians who understand the psychology and the pathology of this menace to our men
in the camps and cities

The War Camp Community Service is another
wing of army auxiliaries that is doing much to
make the soldiers' lot a happy one Clubs for the

General view of parade of famous 369th Infantry on Fifth Avenue, N. Y. C. New York welcomed its colored heroes of Colonel "Bill" Hayward's famous "Hell Fighters" of the 369th Infantry in a parade on Fifth Avenue. Photo shows immense crowds at the New York Public Library 42nd Street and Fifth Avenue as the Dusky heroes marched by. Copyright Western Newspaper Union.

accommodation and entertainment of soldiers and sailors have been established under War Camp Community Service auspices at many points, and comfortable and well-appointed recreation centers may be found in New York City Washington (2), Louisville Ky Battle Creek, Mich, Des Moines Iowa Rockford Ill Petersburg, Va, Chillicothe, Ohio Newport News, Va and Baltimore, Md Plans are under way for additional clubs at Greenville S C, Atlanta and Macon, Ga In fact, it is the intention to have clubs in every community near the camps where colored troops are stationed as the good resulting from such centers fully justifies the expense incurred through their maintenance A very pleasing circumstance is the appointment of Prof John M Gandy President of the Virginia Normal and Collegiate Institute, Petersburg Va, as special assistant to the War Camp Community Service in the South on colored work Capable assistants are being named to aid the work at all points and the organization is approaching a most satisfactory stage Hostess houses are also being established at many camps and others are in contemplation.

WAR WORK OF COLORED WOMEN

The colored women of the country are nobly doing their share of the work that must win the war In the Red Cross Society they are particularly active and enthusiastic They are represented in nearly every community through either the Red Cross or the Young Women's Christian Association or in some form of voluntary service organization to assure the casting of the soldiers' lines in pleasant places, over here and over there They are vieing with their brothers, fathers and sons in the high quality of their patriotism and in the practical methods of manifesting the same

Mrs Alice Dunbar Nelson of the faculty of the Wilmington (Del) High School, an educator, author, social worker and organizer of tried capacity, has been appointed as a field agent by the War Department and the Woman's Committee of Council of National Defense, to mobilize the colored women of the country and to indicate to them how they may best aid the nation to win the war She has just concluded a broad survey of the Southern States and has formed many new patriotic organizations in support of the War aims of the government and revived and stimulated many others that have been allowed to elapse in their activities Mrs Dunbar's report is highly encouraging and is an earnest of the loyal labor that may be expected of the Negro womanhood of the country

CONCRETE EVIDENCES OF THE NEGROE'S LOYALTY

Concrete evidences of the Negro's loyalty to his country's flag have been abundant in all the struggles and combats of the Republic from its inception to the present day The colored American has never been a laggard or "slacker" He is all-American He knows no hyphen in his citizenship and can have no divided allegiance His only ensign is the Stars and Stripes For the defense and maintenance of his country's ideals he is ready to lay down his own life and to offer his beloved sons upon her altars He gives liberally of his means and substance to uphold the lofty principles of manhood and civic opportunity that the flag so proudly represents Be it remembered that a Negro, Crispus Attucks, was the first man killed in the Revolutionary War A Negro was the first to lose his life in the Spanish-American War—Elijah McCoy, a sailor, being drowned in line of duty in the harbor of Havana A Negro company, the First Separate Battalion of the District of Columbia was the first to be called out to defend the National honor in the present European conflict, having been summoned at the outbreak of war under command of the gallant Major James E Walker, to guard the public buildings, the bridges power plants, reservoirs, etc or the nation's Capital From Bunker Hill to Carrizal in Mexico, as well as with Pershing in the St Mihiel sector, the Negro has given indisputable evidence of his loyalty and of his quality as a fighting unit for "Old Glory"

The story of the dashing exploits of Needham Roberts and Harry Johnson is still fresh in the memory of all, and the huzzahs from press and public white and black, extended in such gracious and instituted measure, has unquestionably strenghtened the morale of the race and stimulated to an incalculable degree the endeavors of the Negro people in those lines of endeavor that call for patriotic service and self-sacrifice

In one instance an entire regiment of colored fighting troops was cited for extraordinarily heroic conduct and were accorded the Croix de Guerre In another case, a stevedore regiment of Negroes won honorable mention in the dispatches for breaking the world's record by unloading and coaling the monster steamship "Leviathan" at a French port—56 hours In the trenches, in the officer's habitat and in the cities of France, the colored troops are welcomed, highly respected and treated with exceptional courtesy by soldiers and by the populace

COLORED NURSES ACCEPTED FOR SERVICE IN THE ARMY

There was general rejoicing when the announcement was made in July, 1918 that colored nurses who had registered with the Red Cross Society to the number of about 2,000 would be accepted for service in the army Plans were worked out for the assignment of colored nurses at six of the base hospitals at camps where nearly 40,000 colored

TOP VIEW (Reading Left to Right)—Col. Frank Denison; Col. Thos. A. Roberts; Lt. Col. Otis B. Duncan
CENTER VIEW—Another group of officers of the 370th (Old 8th Illinois) on the deck of the La France
before landing. Reading left to right 2nd Lt. Lawson Price; 2nd Lt. L. W. Stearls; 2nd Lt. Ed White; 2nd Lt.
Eli F. E. Williams; st Lt. Oasola Browning; Capt. Louis B. Johnson; 1st Lt. Frank Bates; 1st Lt. Binga Desmond.
BOTTOM VIEW—Chicago homecoming of the 370th Regiment (Old 8th Illinois) passing in parade at 113th
Street and Michigan Avenue.

troops were stationed The camps named for this service were Camps Funston, Grant, Dodge, Taylor, Sherman and Dix Comfortable buildings are now being erected at several camps for the accommodation of these nurses General Pershing is considering the use of Colored nurses in the base hospitals in France

In addition to this the Woman's Committee of the Council of National Defense launched a movement to secure 25,000 nurses for army service, and organized a Student Nurses Training Corps, and threw open its doors to young colored women who wished to prepare for army work As a result, many responded and at an early date it is expected that they will be assigned for instruction to various colored hospitals in their respective localities preparatory to being enlisted ultimately in the work of caring for the sick and wounded soldiers in this country and among the American Expeditionary Forces abroad

CAMPAIGN OF "GINGER" BY THE Y W C A

The statement has been made that the War Council of the Y W C A is to devote $400,000 of its $5,000,000 war budget to its work among Negro women The money is being used, and more will be forthcoming, for the maintenance of Hostess Houses, housing for the families of colored troops and recreational work among colored girls in war industrial centers Workers are being furnished for places where there is no Y W C A, and to do all that is possible to protect colored girls for the period of the war, and to help the female relatives of the men in the service to take advantage of the present unprecedented opportunities in the industrial world Large recreational centers are planned for Washington, where a $200,000 plant is to be established at an early date and in New York, Brooklyn Philadelphia, and other cities, some of which in a limited way are already in operation Col Theodore Roosevelt has just given $4,000 from the Nobel Peace Fund for the furtherance of this work A number of colored women have been sent abroad to develop this phase of work among our men on the western front in France, Mrs Helen Curtis and Mrs A W Hunton being among this group The colored secretary of the National Board of the Y W C A, Miss Eva D Bowles, 600 Lexington Avenue, New York City, is in charge of this excellent movement Although much has been done to speed up and put "pep" into the labor of increasing the technical skill of Negro men and women and reducing the illiteracy found in many quarters, much remains to be done It is asserted by the Y W C A authorities that the demand for qualified workers and college-trained individuals has far exceeded the supply When a specific thing is to be done, they say they find it exce-

ly hard to find the person who can render the service at a 100 per cent mark of efficiency

The women of the race have displayed their spirit of self-sacrifice and patriotism by their readiness to enter the arena of industry, as well as in the more refined branches of war service, many are found in the mills, factories in stores and offices, on wagons and auto trucks running elevators, caring for live stock and even in the field doing farm work of the most exhausting character—and all this, too, without complaint

It is not doubted that there are in the army thousands of Roberts and Johnsons' in embryo eager to repeat their courageous deed

SALE OF LIBERTY BONDS WAR SAVINGS STAMPS AND KINDRED AIDS

In the purchase of Liberty Bonds, War Savings Stamps and kindred aids the Negro has done, and is still doing his full duty Few Negroes are wealthy, but the masses are thrifty, and out of their moderate incomes they have bought generously of all three issues of the Liberty Loan Bonds, and of the War Savings and Thrift Stamps, besides contributing heavily to the Red Cross, the War Chest, and many other war relief institutions, and lending themselves without limit to the support of the Y M C A and the Y W C A ministrations They show no signs of weariness in well-doing

A few notable instances of the financial aspect of the Negro's patriotism may be cited by way of illustration The North Carolina Mutual and Provident Association a Negro corporation of Durham, N C, has taken a total of $125,000 worth of Liberty Bonds The Mosaic Templars of America, with headquarters at Little Rock, Ark, subscribed for $110,000 worth of Liberty Bonds, with provision for an additional $40,000 in February, next, and purchased outright $1,000 worth of War Savings Stamps The Atlanta Mutual Insurance Company and the Standard Life Insurance Company, both of Atlanta, Ga, bought $50,000 each of Liberty Bonds The Grand United Order of Odd Fellows took $50,000 worth, and the Improved Benevolent and Protective Order of Elks of the World followed with the purchase of $30,000 worth The Knights of Pythias of Florida bought $25,000 worth Various churches in many states a policy of investing the surplus fund treasury in Liberty Bonds as did fraternities and social clubs Th tist Church of Pittsburgh, is $10,000 purchase One Tusk ham V Chambliss, individua worth

The colored citizens of Charles H A

[lower right text obscured/overlapping:] ch-worth popular as-morale of the ulpit are sounding or and intelligence OF COLORED EDITORS DERS was held in Washington, J Scott, representing the and the Committee on Public Information, an important conference of colored ed-

TOP VIEW (Round broken for Base Unit to Assist in care of colored soldiers. Different organizations
CENTER VIEW—e breaking of the ground for the McDonough Memorial Hospital at West 133rd Street,
before landing. Reading l:The plant can be completed and equipped and furnished for $100,000. It will be a
Eli F. E. Williams; st Lt. Oasotta Hospital Building. The Institution is named in honor of Dr. David Kearney
BOTTOM VIEW—Chicago homecomel New York City. Copyright Underwood & Underwood, N. Y.
Street and Michigan-Avenue.   ne who have been wounded or gassed back on the "Giuseape
                                          nyright Western Newspaper Union

Liberty Bonds of the third issue. At the close of the campaign they had subscribed for bonds to the amount of $250,000, and won an honor flag. At Suffolk, Va., the colored committee, led by Robert Williams, won honors in each of the Liberty Bond "drives" and subscribed over $15,000 in the Red Cross rally of last May. Many Negroes purchased their bonds at banks where they do business, independent of other purchases as members of organizations, and no record was kept as to the color of the investor. Robert L. Smith, a colored banker of Waco, Texas, contributed a full-page advertisement to a daily paper of his town in promotion of a Liberty Bond campaign, and a similar gift was made by the colored citizens of Louisville, Ky., through the Louisville News, a colored paper. J. E. Taylor, a public spirited colored man of Wilmington, N. C., disposed of over $2,000 worth of Bonds in a single day, and in a "drive" in Philadelphia, Pa., Amos Scott sold $80,000 worth among his people. The colored people of Washington, D. C., in a War Savings Stamp "drive," captained by Dr. William A. Warfield, and Rev D. E. Wiseman, sold $52,000 worth to colored people from February to May, and the colored school children in the same period averaged $200 per week, and this total does not include the purchase by individuals in the Federal departments or independent of the campaign committee. These are tangible evidences that the fires of patriotism are burning brightly in the breast of the American Negro, North and South, East and West, alike. Totals for the country at large are not available by races but with these scattering notations as a basis for calculation it can be seen that the Negro is "doing his bit" in the matter of putting forward his MONEY POWER, just as it has herein been shown that he is not a derelict in responding to the call for MAN-POWER. Secretary of the Treasury McAdoo has made a public acknowledgment of his gratitude over the ready, prompt and generous response of the Colored Americans everywhere to the nation's appeal for financial aid. It is certain that in the Fourth Liberty Loan campaign, just concluded, the Negro will maintain the high average he has made in the past.

THE NEGRO LENDS A HAND IN INDUSTRIES AND PRODUCTION

To the demand of the Food Administration for increased production in the food essentials and in the conservation of Food already in hand the colored man has responded with equal cheerfulness and fidelity.

In the field of agriculture, in the mines, in the munitions and nitrate plants, building trades, on the railroads and in the general industrial arena, as well as in the business and professional world,

the Negro is laboring with all his might, and playing his part with no less fervor than is true of his brother of lighter hue. Wherever and whenever a patriotic duty is to be done, the Colored American is quick to step forward and exclaim: "Here I am, Uncle Sam, take me!" If the Negro has any one complaint above another, it is that Uncle Sam has not found tasks enough for his willing hands to perform.

THE SPEAKERS' COMMITTEE OF ONE HUNDRED

Through the office of the Special Assistant to the Secretary of War, in conjunction with the Committee on Public Information, a Speakers' Bureau has been placed in operation and one hundred specially-equipped men of the race are in the field taking part in an intensive campaign of education, presenting the war aims of the Government in a plain and straight fashion and their logical statement of the issues involved in the present world-wide conflict in going far toward inspiring a livelier patriotism among all classes of colored people and encouraging them to engage more heartily in the activities designed to help America to win the war. These speakers are all known quantities, accepted leaders in their respective spheres of influence and represent every group and section with which the colored people are identified. Their services are made more effective by their close co-operation with the State Councils of Defense in the North, East, South and West.

PRESS AND PULPIT SOUNDING THE "TOCSIN"

In connection with this campaign of education due credit must be given to the press and the pulpit, which are doing their full duty in the circulation of information that tends to enlighten the masses and therefore strengthen them in the cause that lies nearest to all American hearts. The colored editors, with a unanimity that cannot be other than gratifying, are giving columns of their valuable space weekly, to propaganda matter, without charge to the Government, and at a positive sacrifice of time and money, while the ministers are delivering powerful sermons on the divinity of service and the bounden duty of a Christian people to fight for the establishment of justice throughout the world, and are allowing the use of their churches rent-free for patriotic meetings and popular assemblies devoted to improving the morale of the race. Both the press and the pulpit are sounding the tocsin of liberty with vigor and intelligence.

A FRUITFUL CONFERENCE OF COLORED EDITORS AND LEADERS

In June, 1918, there was held in Washington, under call of Emmett J. Scott, representing the War Department and the Committee on Public Information, an important conference of colored editors and a selected group of leaders of thought and action. To the number of about fifty they gathered at the nation's capital, and after three days of free, frank and full discussion of all the issues relating to the Negro in the War and in civil life, the conference agreed unanimously upon an address for submission to the President of the United States, the Secretary of War and the Committee on Public Information, which set forth in a most illuminating fashion the grievances and desires of the colored people, together with suggestions looking to a correction of inequalities complained of and making specific requests for certain benefits, under the head of "A Bill of Particulars." The well-tempered and wholly patriotic attitude of this editorial conference so impressed the Federal authorities, who thus sought the confidence of the Negro people through their accredited spokesmen, that in the few weeks that have followed this significant exchange of views, the response to the conference's "Bill of Particulars" has come in the form of

(a) A message from the President in denunciation of the practice of mob violence

(b) The enrollment of colored Red Cross nurses for service in the camps and cantonments of the army.

(c) The continuance of the training camps for colored officers and the increase in their number and enlargement of their scope of training

(d) Betterment of the general conditions in the camps where Negroes are stationed in large numbers, and positive steps taken to reduce race friction to a minimum everywhere soldiers are brought into contact

(e) The extension to young colored men of opportunity for special training in technical mechanical and military science in the various schools and colleges of the country

(f) An increase of the number of colored Chaplains for army service

(g) The establishment of a woman's branch under the Council of National Defense with a colored field agent, to organize the colored women of the country for systematic war work

(h) Steps taken to recall Colonel Charles Young to active service in the United States Army

(i) The appointment of the first colored, regularly-commissioned war correspondent, to report military operations on the western front in France

(j) The granting of a loan of $5,000,000 for the relief of the Republic of Liberia

TRADITIONAL LOYALTY OF OTHER DAYS ADHERED TO BY NEGRO

From this somewhat rambling recital of the activities, aspirations and achievements of the Negro American of these times, it will be seen that he is more than living up to his traditional loyalty of other days. As has been stated, the Negro has taken part in all the wars of the Republic, and from Boston Common to France's bleeding western front he has never failed to give a creditable account of himself. He is an inseparable factor in the history that this nation has made.

In war he has been brave, in peace, he has been faithful and true. There can be no doubt that the "sacred jewel of liberty" is safe in his hands. Whenever called upon to choose an alliance, he invariably stands shoulder to shoulder with the substantial forces of social and political fabric, and is never identified with the reactionary or revolutionary elements that menace the tranquility and civic order of our land. In the present conflict the Negro is participating in more and larger ways than ever before and from the superb showing he has thus far made there is reason to believe that in the future he will be, in a still larger and more effective way, a DISTINCT AND VALUABLE ASSET TO THE NATION

The Negro is not forgetful of his RIGHTS in all this strife and turmoil, but he chooses in this crisis, to place the deeper emphasis on his DUTIES. He is expecting that when the FRUITS OF VICTORY shall come to be distributed that he shall be awarded the share he has justly won by his patriotism, and through his efficient service in battle and in the not less essential work behind the lines

Other Prominent Individuals and Institutions

ALLEN, DAVID B, merchant, born at Danville, Va, Jan 2, 1855, moved to Newport, Va, 1880, where he still resides. Started as cook and eventually established largest restaurant in Virginia, sold out in 1916 and started bakery and delicatessen in his own building. Married Charlotte Allen in 1892. Member A M E Church, Mason, Odd Fellow, Independent Order of St Luke's National Negro Business League, and a charter member Newport Board of Trade

ALLISON, CHARLES WILLIAM, preacher, born on his father's farm near Nashville, Tenn. Graduate Meigs High School, Nashville and Central City College. Member A M E Church and began preaching in 1911. Held many important charges in church and its organizations. Member of U B F 's. Married Miss Elizabeth Cecil Harlan of Mitchellsburg, Ky. Now pastoring at Stanford, Ky.

ANDERSON, JOSEPH CLINTON, minister, born March 1, 1862, in Fluvanna County, Va. Graduate Taylor University. McCormick Theological Seminary. Converted at age of 23, ordained a minister in the A M E Church, trustees of Wilberforce University, fraternal delegate to the M E General Conference which met at Saratoga Springs, New York in 1916, member Odd Fellows, Mason, International Order of Twelve, Knights of Tabor. Married Miss Musadora Donley of Rockford, Ill. Now pastor prominent Chicago church

ANDERSON, MAJOR JACKSON born at Jefferson County, Florida, Oct 23, 1863. Graduate Florida Baptist Institute (now Florida Memorial College), at Live Oak. Florida State College at Tallahassee. Graduated Meharry Medical College, February, 1897. He is now a prominent physician of Tampa, Florida. The Doctor has been twice married, and has two daughters, Mirian J and Rebar

THE ARLINGTON LITERARY & INDUSTRIAL SCHOOL. One of five schools for Negroes in Wilcox County Ala, founded and fostered by the United Presbyterian Church, with headquarters in Pittsburg, Penn. The plant is situated on the highlands near Arlington station on the Southern Railway and consists of 510 acres of land, school buildings, dormitories, saw mill, brick yard, carpenter shop, blacksmith shop, dairy and piggery. The principal of the school, Prof John T Arter, has made a splendid record for his school

BALDWIN, MISS MARIA, noted educator. Has made a national reputation as principal of the Agassey School, Cambridge Mass. This school is considered one of the best in New England and a majority of the pupils are white. It is under the shadow of that noted seat of learning, Harvard University, where thorough intellectual training is taken as a matter of course, which makes Miss Baldwin's record all the more noteworthy

BARNES ROBERT C, attorney born Sept 22, 1856, in Mercer County, Ohio. Educated, public schools, Liber College, Ada Normal Institution, Wilberforce University. Admitted to the Ohio and to the Michigan Bar in 1889. Began practice in Detroit the same year. For the past twenty-three years he has associated in practice with Walter H Stowers. Married Miss Mabel Brown Dec 25 1877 in Putnam County, Ohio

CONWAY HIRAM, minister, born in Northumber County, Va 1851. Graduate Richmond Institute now Virginia University 1886. Mason, a Gallilean Fisherman and President Bay State Missionary Society of Massachusetts. Married in 1892 Miss Josephine Montgomery of Columbia S C. Now pastoring prominent church of Worcester, Mass

DEBERRY PERFECT R, minister First Congregational Church, Raleigh N C. Like most of the Congregational ministers, Rev DeBerry is highly educated. Is a man of fine principles and is doing splendid work. He is well thought of by the citizens of Raleigh, irrespective of race

DINKENS, EDWARD J, merchant New Port, R I. A splendid example of what the Negro can accomplish even in the face of keen New England competition. Mr Dinkens chose to match wits with the sharpest merchants of the country and his success speaks volumes for the native ability of the colored man

DUMAS A W, physician and surgeon, Natchez, Miss, was born at Houma, Louisiana, Sept 9, 1876. Educated at Houma Academy, and at the age of 19 years completed the scientific course. Took up the study of medicine at the Illinois Medical College Department of Medicine of Loyola University Chicago, Ill, graduated 1899. Came to Mississippi, in 1899, began practice at Natchez. He has been eminently successful as a physician, and financially, having accumulated considerable valuable real estate. In connection with the practice of medicine, he operates a first-class drug store, and a modern private infirmary for the care of the sick, where many difficult medical and surgical cases have been treated. He is held in high esteem by both white and black citizens

FAUCETT, I J. Leading colored physician of Lynchburg, Va. He is well recognized by the white physicians as well as other citizens. He believes heartily in everything that tends to develop and uplift the Negro race. Has done many deeds of charity and always contributes liberally of time and money to whatever he believes is beneficial to humanity. Has a splendid practice and is financially successful

FORTE ORMAND ADOLPHUS scholar, publisher, born in Bridgetown, Barbados, W I, Dec 17 1887. Educated St Mary's Public School, Combermere Collegiate School, Harrison College, Barbados, W I Matriculated Student University of Cambridge Eng, 1907 Asst Master St Mary's School French Correspondent Mackay & Co, and Special Asst Office of Official Assignee at Barbados W I (British Civil Service) In 1914 founded the Cleveland Advocate, now editor and proprietor Director National Colored Soldiers Comfort Committee Member of St Andrew's Episcopal Church Cleveland Ohio Married Ida Grant, at Cleveland, Ohio, July 27 1910

HAMILTON RICHARD THEODORE, M D, born at Montgomery, Ala, March 31 1869 Ed Alabama State Normal School Graduated Howard University, 1901 Interne in Freedmen's Hospital Took special course in Organic Chemistry, Bacteriology and Pathology Opened office in Dallas Tex, in 1901 In 1906 appointed medical inspector of the Dallas Colored Schools Medical examiner Endowment Department G U O of O F, and Household of Ruth

HARRIS, J SILAS Mr Harris is a native of the State of Missouri He has for years been a leading worker in State and Educational matters

HARRISON, COLUMBUS WILLIAM, physician, born at Tarboro, N C, educated in New England, and graduated from Tuft's College in 1906 Practicing physician, official examiner for the Odd Fellows of Boston, Pocahontas Lodge of Elks, Lodge of Knights of Pythias, and the auxiliary women's lodges of these organizations Treasurer Columbus Day Activities for the colored citizens of Boston Owns beautiful summer home at Plymouth, Mass, and residence in Boston

HARTFIELD, ISHAM, a product of Tuskegee Institute and a business man of Vicksburg, Miss, was born in Issequannah County, Miss, Jan 4th 1884 He is the owner of a good home, trustee and class leader in the Bethel A M E Church and a Mason Mr Hartfield married in 1904 Miss Bonnie Lou Collins of Vicksburg

HICKS, LUCIUS SUMNER born at Plymouth, N C His father died when he was very young and his mother moved with her two sons to Boston Mass, in 1894 Graduated Boston Law School 1908 Admitted to the Suffolk Bar in 1909 and immediately began to practice in Boston Republican, Episcopalian Mason Served as Assistant Registrar of Voters, Assistant Corporation Counsel of Boston

HILL, LESLIE P Mr Leslie P Hill is a graduate of Harvard University He was for a good many years, in charge of the Department of Education at Tuskegee Institute From Tuskegee he went to Manassas where he was principal for several years Manassas owes its development very largely to Mr Hill Mr Hill is at present principal of Cheney Institute Cheney, Pa

HOLMES D A physician residing at 711 New Jersey Ave, Kansas City, Mo One of the leading physicians of Missouri and has many admirers both of his professional skill and personal affability Has an extensive and growing practice and is ranked as an eminently successful practitioner

JACKSON, GEORGE W, born at Smith Station, Lee County, Ala Graduated from Fisk University, Nashville, Tenn 1887 Has taught in schools of Texas 34 years At present principal, Douglass High School, Corsicana, Tex Supervising Principal Negro Public Schools and church worker in many capacities Author Married Miss Jessie A Blythe (deceased), in 1887 Miss M L Morris, Helena, Ark, in 1903

JONES, WILLIAM B, dentist, born in Warren County, N C, March 16, 1881 Graduate Shaw University, Raleigh, N C, and Dental Department University of Pennsylvania, Philadelphia Opened dental office at Springfield, Mass, in 1908 Gets splendid practice from both races Member Baptist Church, President Men's Community Club Married Miss Cathrine Hill of Windsor, Conn, in 1910

KNOX L AMASA, lawyer, born in Greenville County, Va, Jan 6, 1869 Educated at Virginia N & I Institute, Petersburg, and LL D from Howard University, Washington, D C Member firm of Knox and Henderson, Kansas City, Mo Baptist, Past Master Mason, Odd Fellow, K of P For the two last named he is Grand Attorney Member Board Federated Charities, Board of Management of the Pasco Y M C A, Treasurer Wheatley-Provident Hospital, member Draft Board Division 11 Married at Washington, D C June 26 1901, Miss Clara Tarquinia Chase

LLOYD, AARON W, born at Little Springs, 1885 In April, 1863, he came to St Louis, Mo He became a member of the Knights of Pythias in June, 1885 was elected Grand Chancellor of Missouri in 1900, which office he has successfully filled for 19 years When Mr Lloyd was complimented on the manner in which the affairs of the Knights of Pythias of Missouri were found, he replied "That's my specialty I know that work and don't try to do any other" This one fact alone shows the reason why the work has developed so under his leadership

LUSHINGTON, AUGUSTINE NATHANIEL doctor, born and received his early education in the British West Indies Came to America and graduated Cornell University Principal Trinidad Public Schools Returned to America and graduated from Department of Veterinary Science, University of Pennsylvania, and opened office in Philadelphia, taught in St Emma Agricultural College in Rock-castle, Va Moved to Lynchburg, Va, where he built large practice Member I O St Lukes Reporter to the United States Department of Agriculture probation office of the Juvenile Court of Lynchburg Married Miss Elizabeth N Govino of Antigua, B W I in 1890, three daughters

THE MODEL TRAINING SCHOOL—The work of Mrs Julia C Jackson Harris, an earnest Christian worker who has gone into the rural district near Athens, is one that deserves mention The work done in this school is exceptional Mrs Harris' plan is to uplift the entire community This is done through the class room, the church, the home and various clubs Four weeks of the ten months school year are devoted to the training of the teachers in the county schools In such high esteem is the work of this school held that the board of education has made it compulsory upon the county teachers to attend the Model Training School during the session for the teachers

One of the unique features of the work of Mrs Harris is her method of getting the people into better homes They were formed into clubs and the club purchased property When it was paid for it was divided and each member had a site for a home

MONEY, THOMAS JEFFERSON, born at Clayton, Arkansas Educated Tuskegee Institute as a bookkeeper, overseer on plantation, solicitor Union Grocery Company, opened grocery store there for himself, in Vicksburg, where he is still doing a successful business He financed himself playing baseball Episcopalian, a member of his church's financial board Married in 1916 Miss Rosia E Koeher of Vicksburg

MUTUAL BENEFIT SOCIETY of Baltimore, incorporated 1903 in the State of Maryland Operates only in Maryland Number of financial policy holders, December 31st, 1917 28,369 Amount of insurance in force $1,799,080 00 Legal Reserve Life Insurance Company providing reserves for life on the basis of American Experience and three and one-half per cent a sick benefit reserve and an emergency reserve, Harry O Wilson, Gen Mgr

McCURDY, THEODORE E A, physician born in British Guiana, South America, April 27, 1877 Graduate Leonard Medical College, Raleigh, N C, in 1901 While in college he won prizes in obstetrics and in surgery After graduating he opened an office in Boston, Mass Member National Medical Association, Bay State Medical and Dental Association, and the Massachusetts Medical Society Member of the Baptist Church Mason, Odd Fellow and K of P

NICHOLS, HENRY WASHINGTON, physician, born in Carroll County, Miss, in 1875 Educated Tougaloo College Graduated from Meharry Medical College in 1901, immediately thereafter opened an office in Clarendon, Ark, where he remained one year and then moved to Clarksdale, Miss, where he is now practicing Member A M E Church and K of P 's Married Miss Georgia Roberts, of Pickens, Miss, in 1902

PHILLIPS, HENRY C, preacher, born at Jamaica, British West Indies, March 11, 1847 Graduate Philadelphia Divinity School of the Protestant Episcopal Church 1875 ordained the same year, served a year as Rector of St Thomas' Protestant Episcopal Church in Philadelphia, from 1876 to 1912 served the church of the Crucifixion In 1912 appointed Archdeacon of colored work in the Diocese of Pennsylvania, which position he now holds President and trustee of several charitable institutions K of P and Odd Fellow Married Miss Sarah Elizabeth Cole of Philadelphia, Dec 2, 1875

POTTER, M D clergyman, editor born at Dawson, Ga, educated public schools of Dawson, Howard Normal School Cuthbert, Ga Taught in Georgia public schools three years and thirteen years in Florida Entered ministry in 1903 Built fine church and parsonage in Florida Editor, manager and owner of the Tampa Bulletin, and Publishing Co Member A M E Church, Sons and Daughters of Jacob, Odd Fellows, trustee Edward Waters College, Jacksonville, Fla president Ministerial Alliance of Tampa, Fla

ROBINSON, WILLIAM PATRICK, born in Cheraw, S C, July 23, 1878 Benedict College Started undertaking business in 1909 and is one of the most successful in the state Mason, K of P and Odd Fellow Secretary local lodge Odd Fellows and of Clinton Chapel A M E Z Church, of Charlotte, N C, his home town Married Miss Sarah I Wilson in 1905

SHAFFER CORNELIUS THADDEUS, Bishop A M E Church Born Troy, O, Jan 3 1847 Ed Berea College, Ky Private tutors, M D Jefferson Medical College, Phila Honorary D D Allen U Columbia, S C Honorary D D and LL D from Wilberforce Veteran Civil War, Author Takes prominent part in upbuilding of Wilberforce U Married Miss Annie Maria Taylor of Lexington, Ky, in 1870 Resides in Chicago

STEWART, R T, New Port News, Va, has been engaged in the grocery business for the past 20 years His business has increased to such an extent that he employs three or four clerks in his store and a number of trucks on the outside for the purpose of delivery Ex-Cashier Crown Savings Bank Member Baptist Church, Mason Odd Fellow a Pythian and a Good Samaritan

STOWERS, WALTER HASLIP, attorney, born on February 7th 1859, at Owensboro, Ky, educated High Schools of Detroit, Mich, Mayhew's Business University, Detroit College of Law Admitted to the bar in 1895, and for the past twenty-three years has associated in the practice of law with Robert C Barnes at Detroit They are one of the leading firms of attorneys of the country Married Miss Susie F Wallace, February 23rd 1886, Oberlin, Ohio

WILLIAMS JAMES STEVE, born in Franklin Parish, La, April 21 1871 Educated there and in New Orleans University In 1900 he entered the undertaking business In this and in the business of real estate he is still engaged in the city of Shreveport, La He is a member of the Christ Temple Church president of the Louisiana Negro Business League and vice-president of the Undertaker's Association of the U S Married Miss Carrie Bell Thomas, of Shreveport, in 1900

INGE, HUTCHINS Mr Inge is a prominent lawyer and leading citizen of St Louis, Missouri He is a graduate of Hampton and an old schoolmate of Booker T Washington

Statistical Review

PART OF BUSINESS SECTION COLORED JACKSONVILLE.

Within fifty-six years American Negroes have acquired over $700,000,000 worth of property.

There are about fifty thousand Negro business enterprises covering practically every line of endeavor and doing an approximate business of one and a quarter billion dollars annually.

They have shown a correspondingly keen interest in education and have reduced their illiteracy from nearly 100 per cent to less than 30 per cent.

Annual expenditures for public schools by Southern States are eleven million dollars.

Total number of schools for Negroes of certain religious boards 300. Number of teachers 2,028. Annual expenditures (1914-15) of boards, permanent funds and contributions $3,856,996.

It is estimated there were about 35 Negroes in each regiment in the Revolutionary War. There was altogether about 3,000 Negro soldiers employed by the Americans.

In the War of 1812, there were two regiments of Negroes, a total of 2,000. In the Civil War there were 141 infantry, 7 cavalry, 12 heavy artillery and 1 light artillery regiments of Negroes with a total strength of 178,975.

There were several regiments of free Negroes in the Confederate Army, notably one of 1,400 men

reviewed in New Orleans, La., February 9, 1862.

July 28, 1866, Congress passed a law that Negro regiments should be a part of the regular army. Under this act the Ninth and Tenth Cavalry and the Thirty-eighth, Thirty-ninth, Fortieth and Forty-first Regiments of Infantry were organized.

In the Spanish-American War there were in addition to the regulars, ten regiments of volunteers.

In the World War there were nearly 400,000 Negro soldiers in the U. S. Army and Navy, of these, 10,000 regulars and 10,000 trained volunteers were ready when war was declared.

There were 106 captains, 329 first lieutenants and 204 second lieutenants, commissioned from the training school at Ft. DesMoines, Iwoa.

COLORED OFFICERS IN THE REGULARS WHEN WAR WAS DECLARED.

Lt. Col. Allen Allensworth (retired) Chaplain, Twenty-fourth Infantry.

Major William T. Anderson (retired) Chaplain, Ninth Cavalry.

Major John R .Lynch (retired) Paymaster.

Major Richard R. Wright, Paymaster, 1898, Spanish-American War.

Major Charles Young, Tenth Cavalry.

Captain George W Prioleau, Chaplin, Twenty-fifth Infantry

Captain Theophilus G Steward (retired) Chaplain Twenty-fifth Infantry

First Lieutenant Benjamin O Davis, Tenth Cavalry

First Lieutenant John E Green Twenty-fifth Infantry

First Lieutenant W W F Gladden, Chaplain, Twenty-fourth Infantry

First Lieutenant Oscar J W Scott, Chaplain, Tenth Cavalry

First Lieutenant Louis A Carter, Chaplain, Ninth Cavalry

NEGROES AT WEST POINT

Three Negroes have graduated from the United States Military Academy at West Point New York Henry O Flipper, 1877 John Alexander, 1887 Charles Young, 1889

NEGROES TO WHOM THE CARNEGIE HERO FUND HAS MADE AWARDS

John B Hill, 1905, George A Grant, 1906, Theodore H Homer, 1908 Albert K Sweet 1909, Geo E McCune, 1908, Martha Generals. 1906, Harley Tomlinson, 1909, Frank Forest, James L Smith, 1909, Boyce Lindsay, 1910, John G Walker, 1909, Charles A Smith, 1910, Mack Stallworth, 1910, James Pruitt, 1911, James Hunter, 1911, Nathan Duncan, 1907, Nathan Record, 1908, Lucy G Edwards, 1912, Elbert Gray, Nolden Townsell, 1912, Arthur Lockett 1912, Beecher Roberts, 1912 Robert Kenney, 1913, Henry West, 1913, Lumis Little, 1913 James Williams, 1912, William R Dyke 1913, Woodson Graham, 1913 James W Brice Sr, 1914, Abner Sullivan, 1914, Walter Roberson 1914, John E. Rufus, 1913, Henry H Rogers, 1914, William Pratt, 1914

There are twenty-eight white persons to whom the Carnegie Hero Fund has made awards for saving Negroes

HAITI

The area of the Republic, which embraces the western portion of the Island of Haiti is estimated at 10,204 square miles The population estimated to be 2,029,700 is mainly Negroes There are also large numbers of mulatto Haitians, the descendants of the former French settlers There are some 5,000 foreigners, of whom about 10 per cent are white The population of the principal cities are Port-au- Prince, the capital, 100,000, Cape Haiti, 30,0000, Les Cayes, 12,000, Gonaives, 13,000 Port de Paix 10,000 The language of the country is French Most of the common people speak a dialect known as Creole French

FIFTY YEARS ECONOMIC PROGRESS

	1866	1916	Gain in Fifty Years
Homes Owned	12,000	600,000	588,000
Farms Operated	20,000	981,000	961,000
Businesses Conducted	2,100	45,000	42,900
Wealth Accumulated	$20,000,000	$1,000 000,000	$980,000,000
Educational Progress—			
Per Cent Literate	10	75	65
Colleges and Normal Schools	15	500	485
Students in Public Schools	100,000	1,736,000	1,636,000
Teachers in all Schools	600	36,900	36,300
Property for Higher Education	$60,000	$21,500 000	$21,440,000
Expenditures for Education	700 000	14,600 000	13,900,000
Raised by Negroes	80,000	1,600 000	1,520,000
Religious Progress—			
Number of Churches	700	42,000	41,300
Number of Communicants	600,000	4,570,000	3,970,000
Number of Sunday Schools	1,000	43,000	42 000
Sunday School Pupils	50,000	2,400,000	2,350,000
Value of Church Property	$1 500 000	$76,000 000	$74,500,000

Reference Negro Year Book

	1860	1910		1860	1910
Number of college graduates	30	8 000	Drug Stores	0	300
Number of professional men	450	75 000	General stores and other industrial enterprises	--	20,000
Number of practicing physicians and pharmacists	0	3,500	Hospitals and nurse training schools	0	61
Number of Lawyers	0	1 500	Insurance companies	0	100
Number of Banks	0	72	Property owned by secret societies	--	$8,000 000
Number of Negro Towns	0	50	Capital stock Negro banks	0	$2,000,000
Number of Newspapers and Periodicals	1	398	Number of Negroes in U S Government employment civil	0	22,087
Number of business men, estimated	600	50,000			Census 1910

INDEX

CPSIA information can be obtained at www.ICGtesting.com
Printed in the USA
BVOW040322090212

282454BV00004B/16/P